Scale 1:208,000
or 3.28 miles to 1 inch
(2.08 km to 1 cm)

1st edition March 2005

Published by AA Publishing (a trading name of Automobile Association Developments Limited, whose registered office is Southwood East, Apollo Rise, Farnborough, Hampshire GU14 0JW, UK. Registration number 1878835).

Mapping produced by the Cartography Department of The Automobile Association.
This atlas has been compiled and produced from the Automaps database utilising electronic and computer technology (A02147).

ISBN–10 0 7495 4268 3
ISBN–13 978 07495 4268 9

A CIP Catalogue record for this book is available from the British Library.

Printed in China by Everbest.

The contents of this atlas are believed to be correct at the time of the latest revision. However, the publishers cannot be held responsible for loss occasioned to any person acting or refraining from action as a result of any material in this atlas, nor for any errors, omissions or changes in such material. This does not affect your statutory rights. The publishers would welcome information to correct any errors or omissions and to keep this atlas up to date. Please write to the Cartographic Editor, Publishing Division, The Automobile Association, Fanum House, Basing View, Basingstoke, Hampshire RG21 4EA, UK.

Information on National Parks in England provided by The Countryside Agency.

Information on National Nature Reserves in England provided by English Nature.

Information on National Parks, National Scenic Areas and National Nature Reserves in Scotland provided by Scottish Natural Heritage.

Information on National Parks and National Nature Reserves in Wales provided by The Countryside Council for Wales.

AA

Great Britain Atlas

Atlas contents

Map pages	**II-VII**
Mileage chart	**VIII**
Road map symbols	**1**
Road maps 1:208,000 scale	**2-237**
Western Isles 1:583,000 scale	232-233
Orkney Islands 1:530,000 scale	234
Shetland Islands 1:530,000 scale	235
Channel Islands 1:125,000 scale	236
Isle of Man 1:264,000 scale	237
Index to place names	**238-320**
County, administrative area map	238-239

Information on Forest Parks provided by the Forestry Commission.

The RSPB sites shown are a selection chosen by the Royal Society for the Protection of Birds.

National Trust properties shown are a selection of those open to the public as indicated in the handbooks of the National Trust and the National Trust for Scotland.

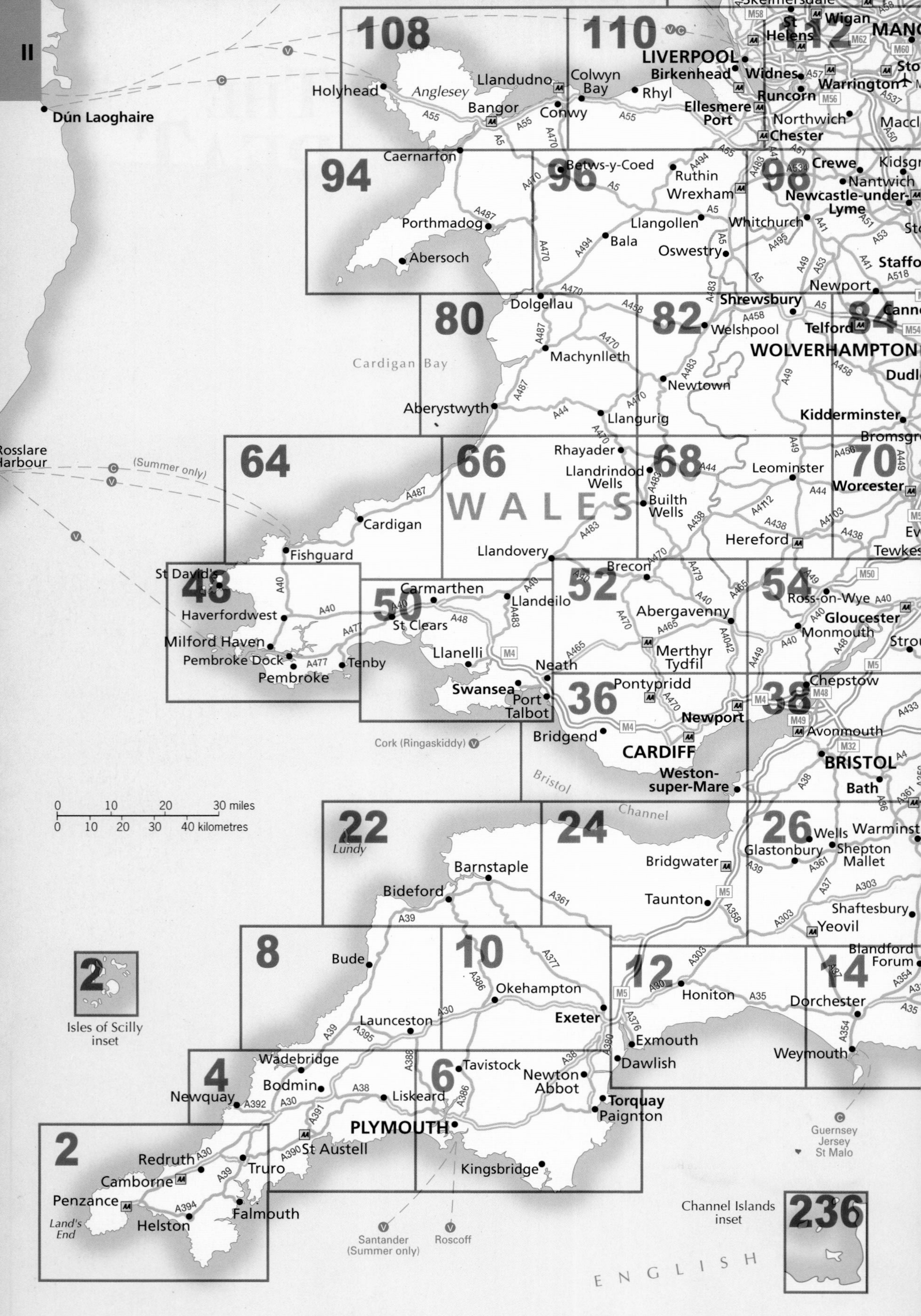
108
110
112
94
96
98
80
82
84
64
66
68
70
48
50
52
54
36
38
22
24
26
8
10
12
14
4
6
2
236
Skelmersdale
Bolton
Wigan
St Helens
MANC
LIVERPOOL
Birkenhead
Widnes
Warrington
Runcorn
Ellesmere Port
Northwich
Chester
Holyhead
Anglesey
Llandudno
Colwyn Bay
Rhyl
Bangor
Conwy
Dún Laoghaire
Caernarfon
Betws-y-Coed
Ruthin
Wrexham
Crewe
Nantwich
Newcastle-under-Lyme
Porthmadog
Llangollen
Whitchurch
Bala
Oswestry
Abersoch
Stafford
Newport
Dolgellau
Shrewsbury
Welshpool
Telford
WOLVERHAMPTON
Machynlleth
Cardigan Bay
Newtown
Aberystwyth
Llangurig
Kidderminster
Bromsgrove
Rosslare Harbour
(Summer only)
Rhayader
Llandrindod Wells
Leominster
Worcester
WALES
Builth Wells
Cardigan
Hereford
Tewkesbury
Fishguard
Llandovery
St David's
Brecon
Carmarthen
Llandeilo
Ross-on-Wye
Haverfordwest
Abergavenny
Gloucester
St Clears
Monmouth
Milford Haven
Llanelli
Merthyr Tydfil
Pembroke Dock
Tenby
Neath
Pembroke
Chepstow
Swansea
Pontypridd
Port Talbot
Newport
Avonmouth
Cork (Ringaskiddy)
Bridgend
CARDIFF
BRISTOL
Bristol Channel
Weston-super-Mare
Bath
0 10 20 30 miles
0 10 20 30 40 kilometres
Lundy
Wells
Warminster
Glastonbury
Shepton Mallet
Barnstaple
Bridgwater
Bideford
Taunton
Shaftesbury
Yeovil
Blandford Forum
Bude
Okehampton
Honiton
Dorchester
Isles of Scilly inset
Launceston
Exeter
Exmouth
Weymouth
Wadebridge
Tavistock
Dawlish
Bodmin
Newton Abbot
Newquay
Liskeard
Torquay
Paignton
PLYMOUTH
Guernsey
Jersey
St Malo
Redruth
Truro
St Austell
Camborne
Kingsbridge
Penzance
Land's End
Helston
Falmouth
Channel Islands inset
Santander (Summer only)
Roscoff
ENGLISH

Map pages

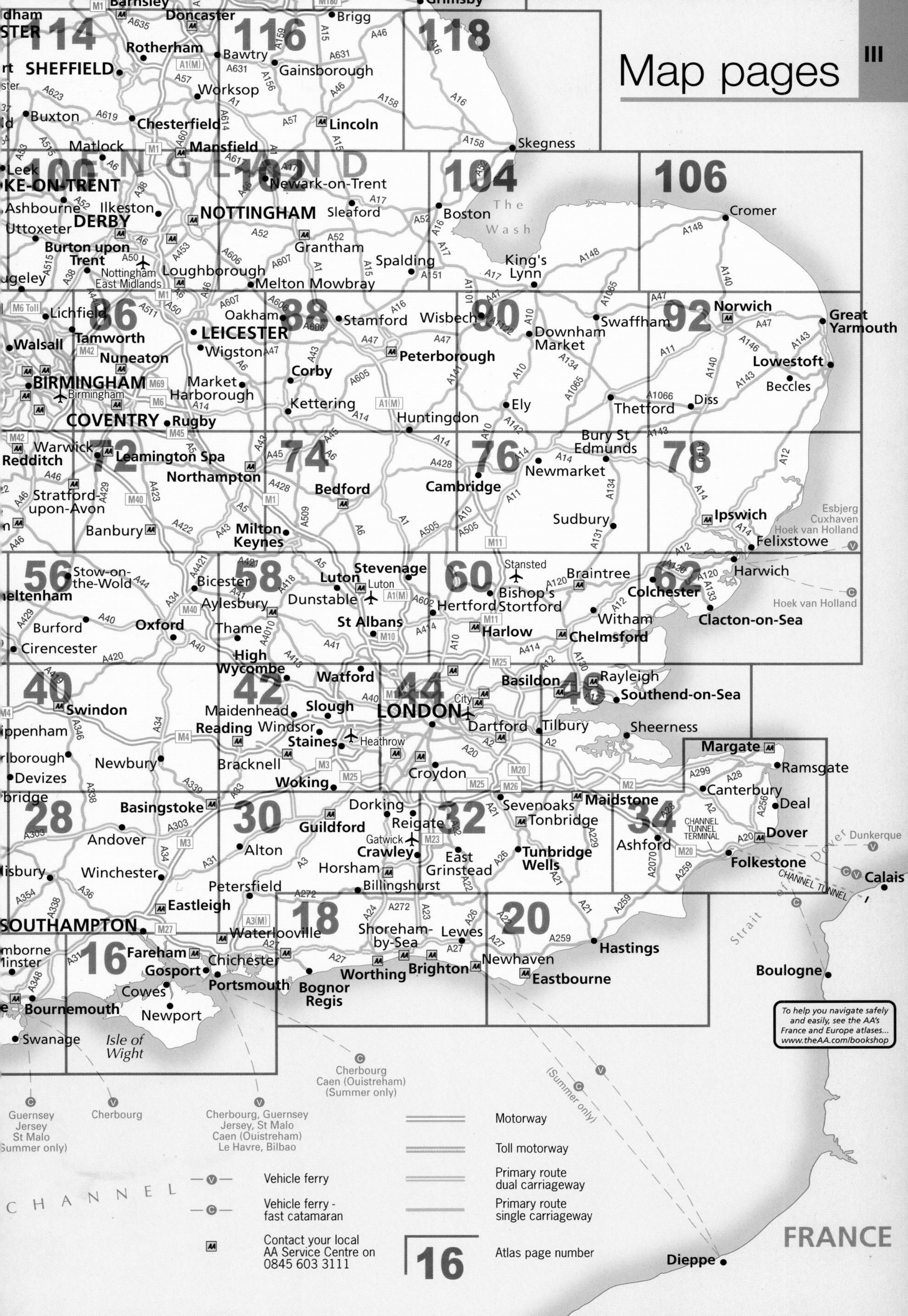

Huddersfield
Barnsley
Grimsby
Doncaster
Brigg
114
116
118
Rotherham
Bawtry
SHEFFIELD
Gainsborough
Worksop
Buxton
Chesterfield
Lincoln
Matlock
Mansfield
Skegness
E N G L A N D
Leek
100
102
104
106
Newark-on-Trent
KE-ON-TRENT
Ashbourne
Ilkeston
NOTTINGHAM
Sleaford
Boston
The Wash
Cromer
DERBY
Uttoxeter
Grantham
Burton upon Trent
Nottingham East Midlands
Loughborough
Spalding
King's Lynn
Melton Mowbray
86
88
90
92
Lichfield
Oakham
Stamford
Wisbech
Swaffham
Norwich
Great Yarmouth
Tamworth
LEICESTER
Downham Market
Walsall
Nuneaton
Wigston
Peterborough
Lowestoft
Corby
BIRMINGHAM
Birmingham
Market Harborough
Beccles
Kettering
Ely
Thetford
Diss
COVENTRY
Rugby
Huntingdon
Bury St Edmunds
72
74
76
78
Warwick
Leamington Spa
Redditch
Northampton
Newmarket
Cambridge
Bedford
Stratford-upon-Avon
Ipswich
Sudbury
Esbjerg
Cuxhaven
Hoek van Holland
Felixstowe
Banbury
Milton Keynes
56
58
60
62
Stow-on-the-Wold
Bicester
Luton
Stevenage
Stansted
Braintree
Harwich
Cheltenham
Aylesbury
Dunstable
Bishop's Stortford
Colchester
Hertford
Hoek van Holland
Witham
Burford
Oxford
Thame
St Albans
Harlow
Clacton-on-Sea
Chelmsford
Cirencester
High Wycombe
40
42
44
46
Watford
Basildon
Rayleigh
Swindon
Slough
City
Southend-on-Sea
Maidenhead
LONDON
Chippenham
Reading
Windsor
Dartford
Tilbury
Sheerness
Staines
Heathrow
Margate
Marlborough
Newbury
Bracknell
Ramsgate
Croydon
Devizes
Woking
Canterbury
Trowbridge
28
30
32
34
Basingstoke
Dorking
Sevenoaks
Maidstone
Deal
Reigate
Tonbridge
CHANNEL TUNNEL TERMINAL
Guildford
Gatwick
Dover
Andover
Alton
Crawley
East Grinstead
Tunbridge Wells
Ashford
Dunkerque
Horsham
Folkestone
Salisbury
Winchester
Petersfield
Billingshurst
Calais
CHANNEL TUNNEL
Eastleigh
18
20
SOUTHAMPTON
Waterlooville
Shoreham-by-Sea
Lewes
Strait of Dover
16
Hastings
Wimborne Minster
Fareham
Chichester
Newhaven
Gosport
Worthing
Brighton
Boulogne
Portsmouth
Cowes
Bognor Regis
Eastbourne
Bournemouth
Newport
Swanage
Isle of Wight
To help you navigate safely and easily, see the AA's France and Europe atlases... www.theAA.com/bookshop
Cherbourg
Caen (Ouistreham)
(Summer only)
(Summer only)
Guernsey
Jersey
St Malo
(Summer only)
Cherbourg
Cherbourg, Guernsey
Jersey, St Malo
Caen (Ouistreham)
Le Havre, Bilbao
CHANNEL
FRANCE
Dieppe
Motorway
Toll motorway
Primary route dual carriageway
Primary route single carriageway
Vehicle ferry
Vehicle ferry - fast catamaran
Contact your local AA Service Centre on 0845 603 3111
16
Atlas page number

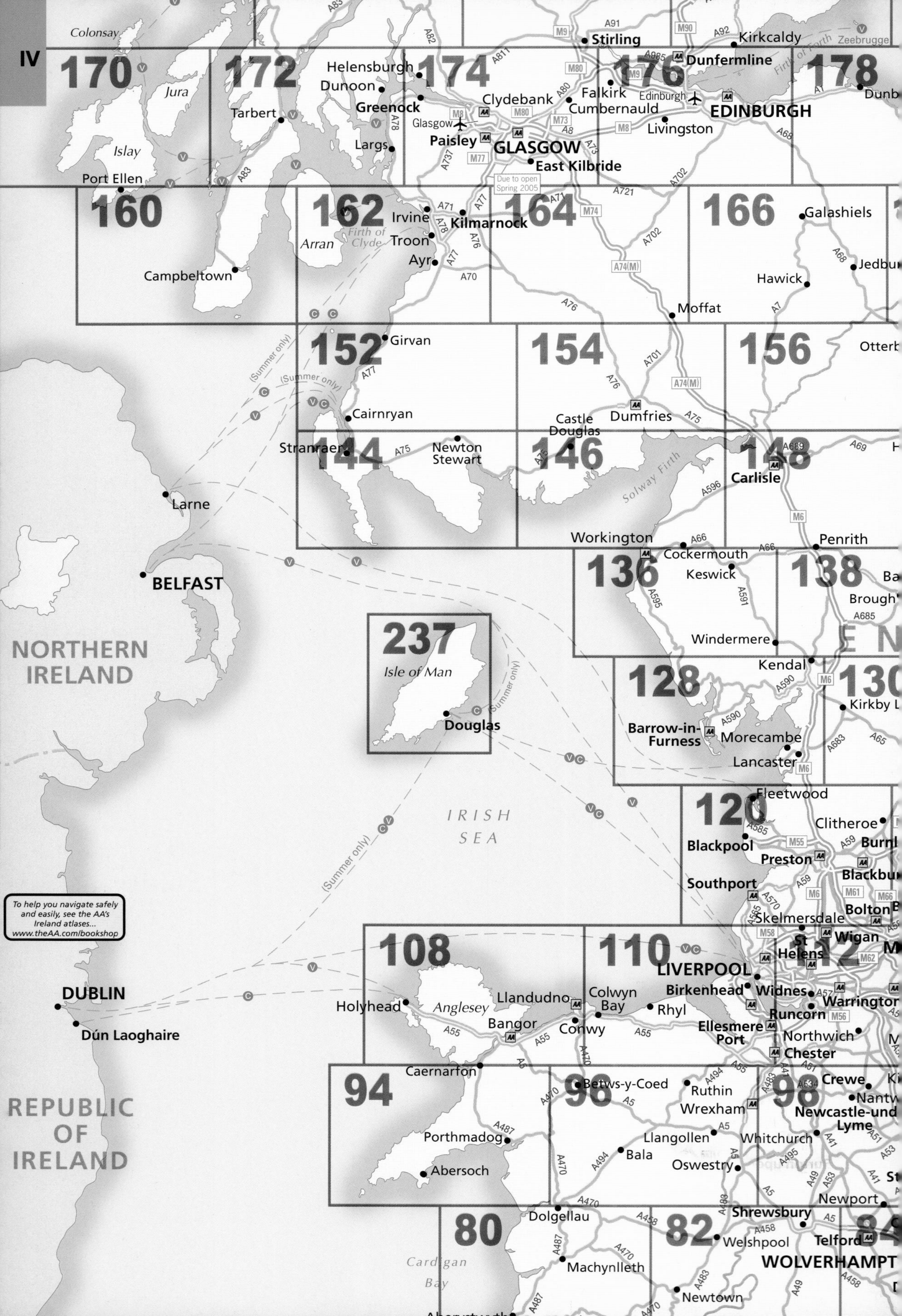

IV
170
172
174
176
178
160
162
164
166
152
154
156
144
146
148
136
138
237
128
120
108
110
94
80
82
Colonsay
Jura
Islay
Port Ellen
Tarbert
Helensburgh
Dunoon
Greenock
Largs
Glasgow
Paisley
GLASGOW
Clydebank
East Kilbride
Due to open Spring 2005
Stirling
Kirkcaldy
Zeebrugge
Dunfermline
Falkirk
Cumbernauld
Edinburgh
EDINBURGH
Livingston
Firth of Forth
Arran
Firth of Clyde
Irvine
Kilmarnock
Troon
Ayr
Campbeltown
Galashiels
Hawick
Moffat
Girvan
Cairnryan
Stranraer
Newton Stewart
Castle Douglas
Dumfries
Solway Firth
Carlisle
Larne
BELFAST
Workington
Cockermouth
Keswick
Penrith
Windermere
Kendal
NORTHERN IRELAND
Isle of Man
Douglas
Barrow-in-Furness
Morecambe
Lancaster
Fleetwood
Clitheroe
Blackpool
Preston
Southport
Skelmersdale
Wigan
St Helens
IRISH SEA
(Summer only)
To help you navigate safely and easily, see the AA's Ireland atlases... www.theAA.com/bookshop
LIVERPOOL
Birkenhead
Widnes
Warrington
Runcorn
Ellesmere Port
Northwich
Chester
DUBLIN
Dún Laoghaire
Holyhead
Anglesey
Llandudno
Colwyn Bay
Rhyl
Bangor
Conwy
Caernarfon
Betws-y-Coed
Ruthin
Wrexham
Crewe
Newcastle-under-Lyme
REPUBLIC OF IRELAND
Porthmadog
Llangollen
Whitchurch
Bala
Oswestry
Abersoch
Newport
Dolgellau
Shrewsbury
Welshpool
Telford
Machynlleth
Cardigan Bay
Newtown
Aberystwyth
M9
M90
M80
M8
M73
M74
M77
A74(M)
M6
M55
M61
M66
M58
M62
M56
A1
A7
A8
A68
A70
A71
A75
A76
A77
A78
A82
A83
A91
A92
A596
A595
A591
A66
A69
A685
A590
A683
A65
A585
A59
A570
A565
A57
A55
A5
A470
A487
A494
A458
A483
A495
A49
A53
A41
A51
A534

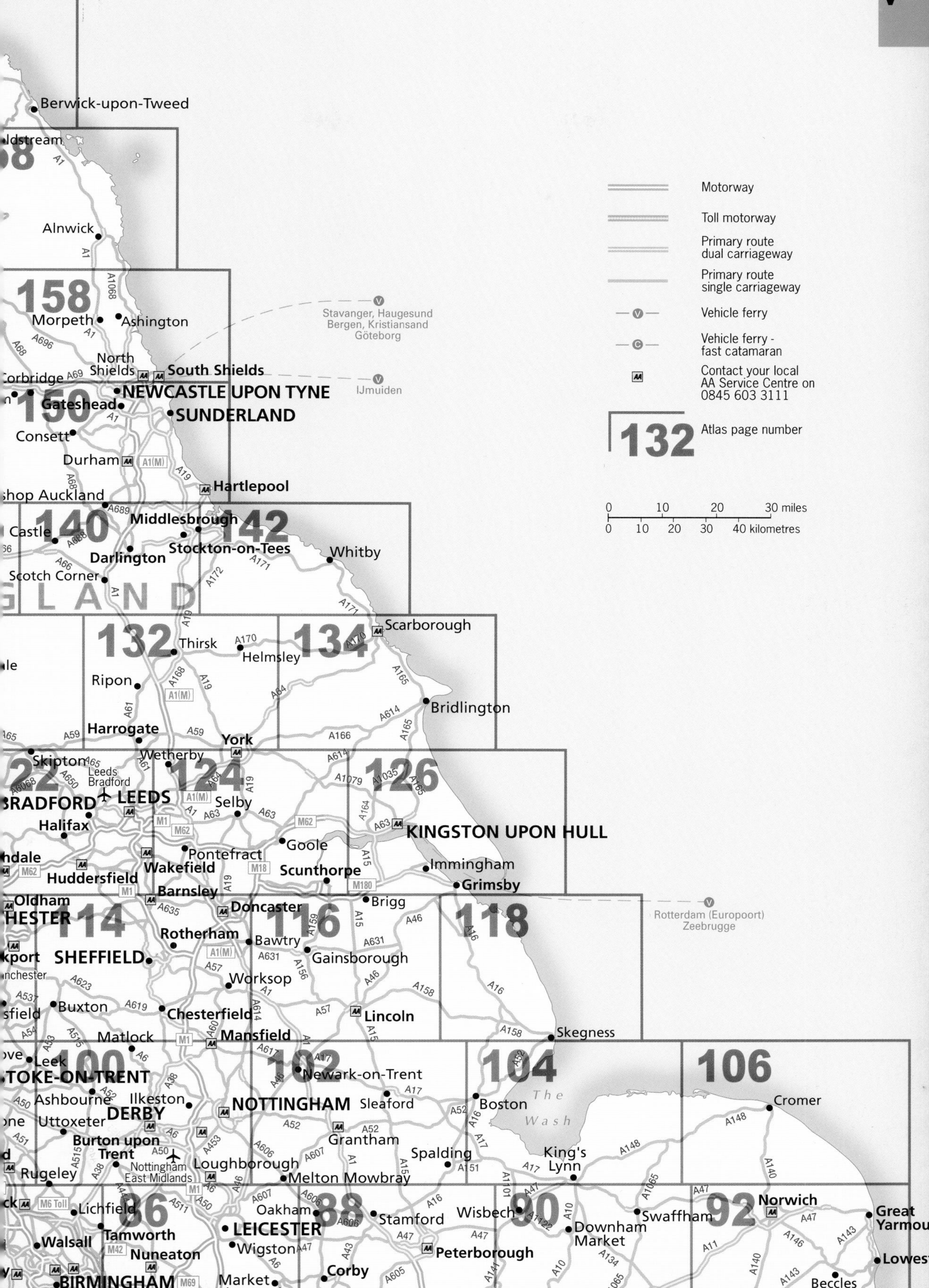
Motorway
Toll motorway
Primary route dual carriageway
Primary route single carriageway
Vehicle ferry
Vehicle ferry - fast catamaran
Contact your local AA Service Centre on 0845 603 3111
132 Atlas page number
0 10 20 30 miles
0 10 20 30 40 kilometres
Berwick-upon-Tweed
Alnwick
158
Morpeth
Ashington
North Shields
South Shields
Stavanger, Haugesund Bergen, Kristiansand Göteborg
IJmuiden
Corbridge
150
NEWCASTLE UPON TYNE
Gateshead
SUNDERLAND
Consett
Durham
Hartlepool
140
142
Middlesbrough
Darlington
Stockton-on-Tees
Whitby
Scotch Corner
132
134
Thirsk
Helmsley
Scarborough
Ripon
Bridlington
Harrogate
York
Skipton
Wetherby
124
126
Leeds Bradford
BRADFORD
LEEDS
Selby
Halifax
KINGSTON UPON HULL
Goole
Pontefract
Wakefield
Immingham
Huddersfield
Scunthorpe
Grimsby
Barnsley
Oldham
Brigg
Doncaster
Rotterdam (Europoort) Zeebrugge
114
116
118
Rotherham
Bawtry
SHEFFIELD
Gainsborough
Worksop
Buxton
Chesterfield
Lincoln
Matlock
Mansfield
Skegness
100
102
104
106
Leek
Newark-on-Trent
Ashbourne
Ilkeston
NOTTINGHAM
Sleaford
Boston
Cromer
Uttoxeter
DERBY
The Wash
Grantham
Burton upon Trent
Nottingham East Midlands
Loughborough
Spalding
King's Lynn
Rugeley
Melton Mowbray
86
88
90
92
Lichfield
Oakham
Stamford
Wisbech
Swaffham
Norwich
Great Yarmouth
Tamworth
LEICESTER
Downham Market
Walsall
Nuneaton
Wigston
Peterborough
Corby
BIRMINGHAM
Birmingham
Market Harborough
Kettering
Ely
Thetford
Diss
Beccles

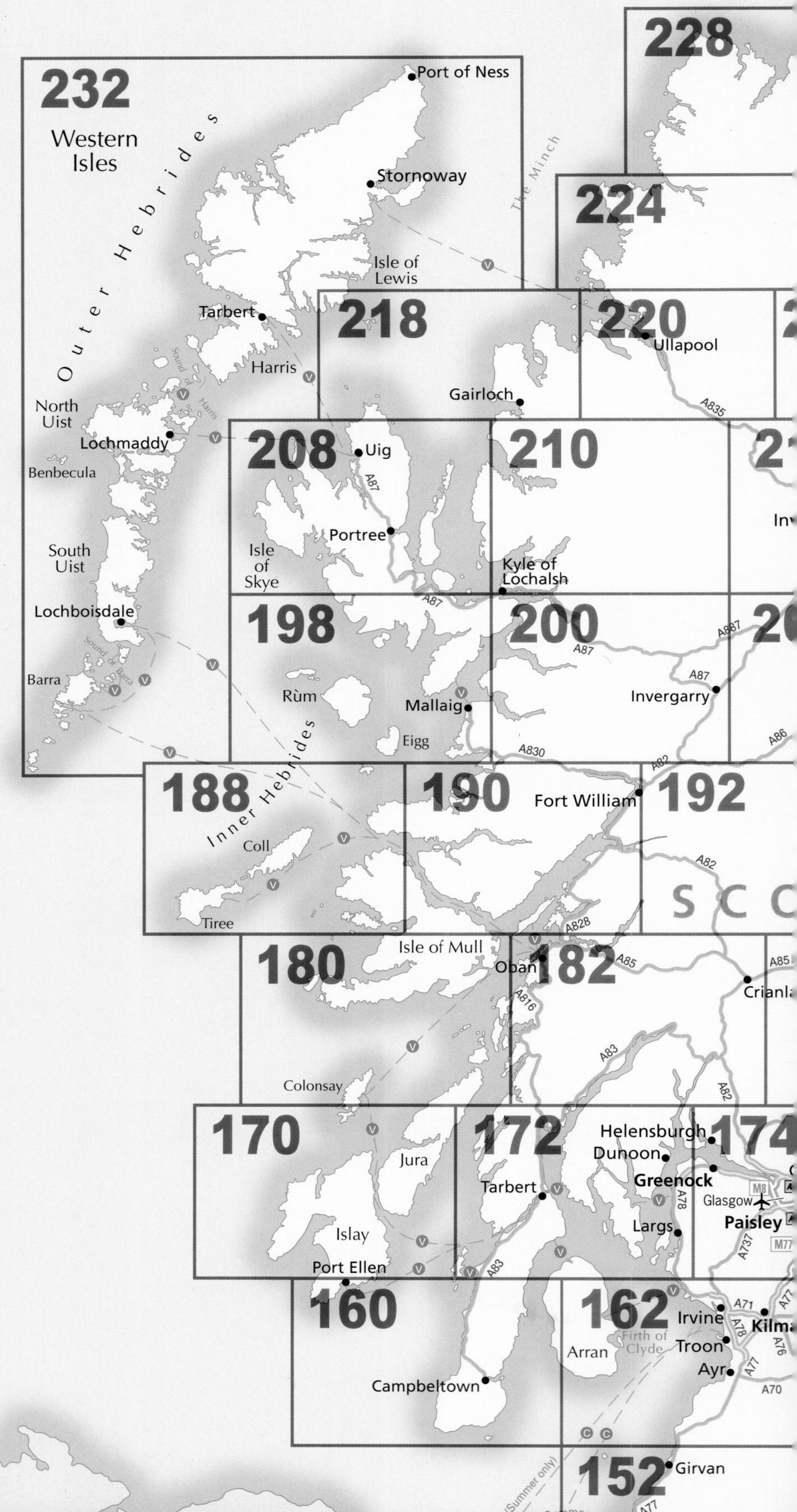

232
Western Isles
Outer Hebrides
Port of Ness
Stornoway
The Minch
Isle of Lewis
Tarbert
Sound of Harris
Harris
North Uist
Lochmaddy
Benbecula
South Uist
Lochboisdale
Sound of Barra
Barra
228
224
218
220
Ullapool
A835
Gairloch
208
Uig
A87
Portree
Isle of Skye
210
Kyle of Lochalsh
198
Rùm
Mallaig
Eigg
Inner Hebrides
200
A87
A887
A87
Invergarry
A830
A82
A86
188
Coll
Tiree
190
Fort William
192
A82
S C O
Isle of Mull
A828
180
Oban
182
A85
A85
A816
A83
A82
Colonsay
170
Jura
Islay
Port Ellen
172
Tarbert
A83
Helensburgh
Dunoon
174
Greenock
A78
M8
Glasgow
Paisley
A737
M77
Largs
160
Campbeltown
162
Arran
Firth of Clyde
Irvine
A71
A77
A78
Troon
A76
Ayr
A77
A70
152
Girvan
A77
(Summer only)
(Summer only)

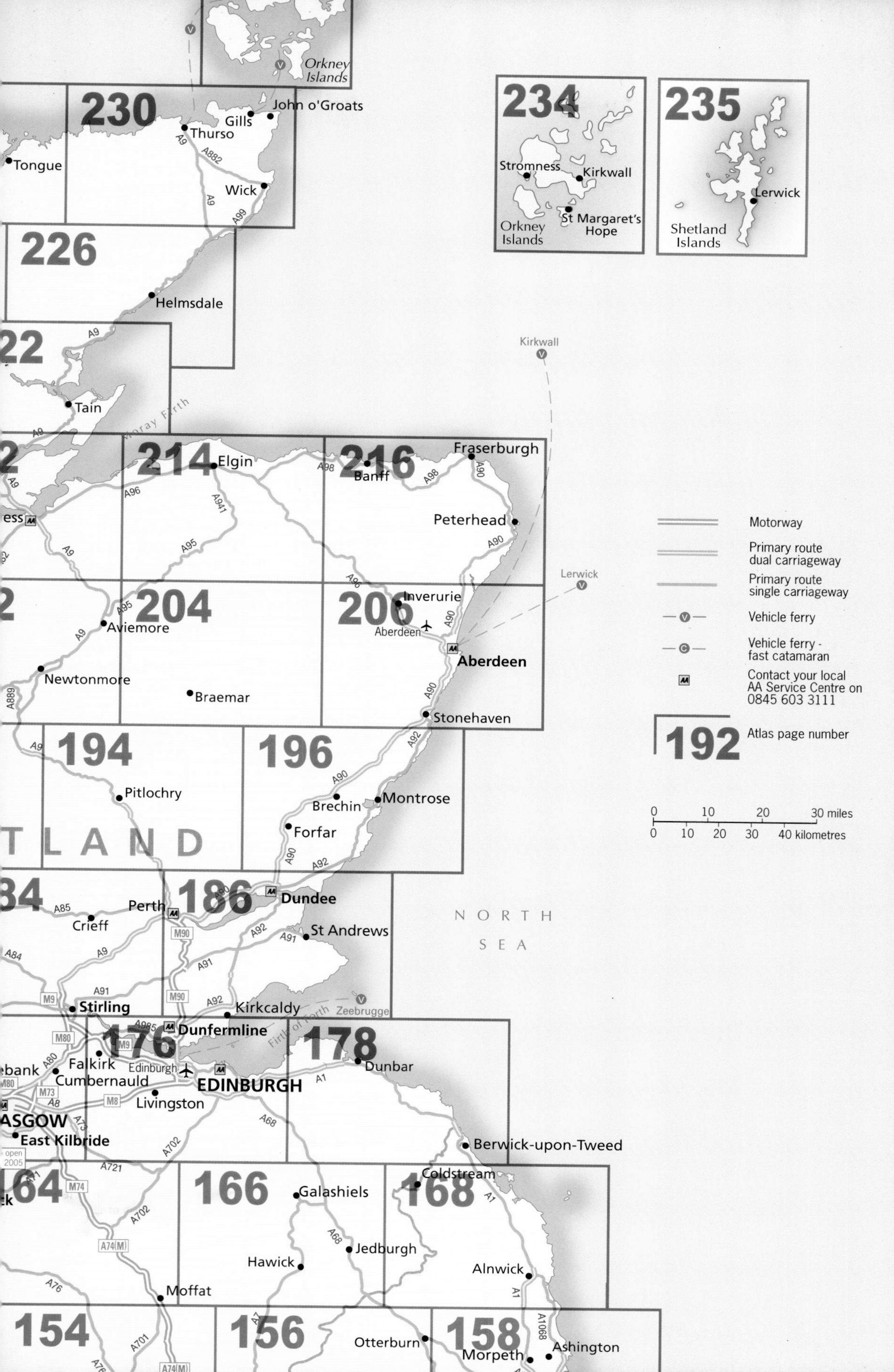
Orkney Islands
230
John o'Groats
Gills
Thurso
A9
A882
Tongue
Wick
A99
226
Helmsdale
22
A9
Tain
Moray Firth
234
Stromness
Kirkwall
Orkney Islands
St Margaret's Hope
235
Lerwick
Shetland Islands
Kirkwall
214
Elgin
216
Fraserburgh
Banff
A98
A90
A96
A941
A95
Peterhead
A90
A9
204
A95
Aviemore
206
Inverurie
Aberdeen
A90
Lerwick
Aberdeen
Newtonmore
Braemar
A889
A90
Stonehaven
194
196
A92
Pitlochry
A90
Brechin
Montrose
Forfar
TLAND
A90
A92
186
Dundee
A85
Perth
Crieff
M90
A92
A91
St Andrews
A84
A9
A91
NORTH SEA
M9
A91
Stirling
M90
A92
Kirkcaldy
Firth of Forth
Zeebrugge
A985
Dunfermline
178
M80
176
M9
Falkirk
Edinburgh
A80
Cumbernauld
EDINBURGH
Dunbar
A1
M73
A8
M8
Livingston
A73
A68
East Kilbride
A702
Berwick-upon-Tweed
A721
M74
166
Galashiels
Coldstream
168
A1
A702
A68
Jedburgh
A74(M)
Hawick
Alnwick
A76
Moffat
A1
154
156
158
A1068
A701
Otterburn
Ashington
Morpeth
A76
A74(M)
Motorway
Primary route dual carriageway
Primary route single carriageway
Vehicle ferry
Vehicle ferry - fast catamaran
Contact your local AA Service Centre on 0845 603 3111
192
Atlas page number
0 10 20 30 miles
0 10 20 30 40 kilometres

Mileage chart

The mileage chart shows distances in miles between two towns along AA-recommended routes. Using motorways and other main roads this is normally the fastest route, though not necessarily the shortest.

The journey times, shown in hours and minutes, are average off-peak driving times along AA-recommended routes. These times should be used as a guide only and do not allow for unforeseen traffic delays, rest breaks or fuel stops.

For example, the 378 miles (608 km) journey between Glasgow and Norwich should take approximately 7 hours 28 minutes.

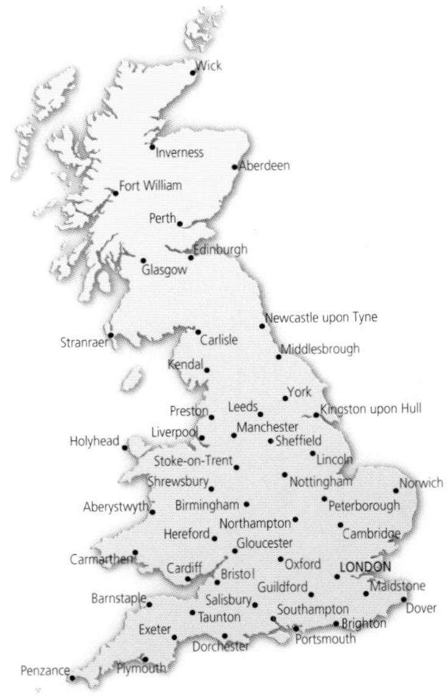

journey times

	Aberystwyth	Barnstaple	Birmingham	Brighton	Bristol	Cambridge	Cardiff	Carlisle	Carmarthen	Dorchester	Dover	Edinburgh	Exeter	Fort William	Glasgow	Gloucester	Guildford	Hereford	Holyhead	Hull	Inverness	Kendal	Leeds	Lincoln	Liverpool	Maidstone	Manchester	Middlesbrough	Newcastle	Northampton	Norwich	Nottingham	Oxford	Penzance	Perth	Peterborough	Plymouth	Portsmouth	Preston	Salisbury	Sheffield	Shrewsbury	Southampton	Stoke-on-Trent	Stranraer	Taunton	Wick	York	LONDON
Aberdeen	906	1052	750	1051	913	907	936	426	1020	1047	1108	236	1027	357	301	836	1007	850	843	735	240	517	655	753	636	1029	632	545	510	840	1007	757	907	1246	151	837	1114	1039	558	1009	721	747	1024	703	505	950	513	643	955
Aberystwyth		436	249	538	301	431	229	444	115	432	612	647	412	901	624	251	443	158	234	436	959	359	345	430	244	533	304	456	527	340	554	339	354	631	720	419	459	455	317	412	350	154	439	252	713	335	1231	410	455
Barnstaple			326	423	200	501	234	629	335	206	513	832	115	1047	810	227	339	303	636	547	1144	544	529	507	456	434	448	628	700	409	624	422	319	233	906	452	145	324	503	232	500	403	307	400	858	109	1417	543	403
Birmingham				310	147	154	210	327	311	321	334	530	301	745	507	110	226	125	334	233	842	242	216	157	153	255	146	315	346	102	316	108	126	520	604	142	348	258	200	243	146	101	243	058	556	224	1115	229	217
Brighton					301	213	336	628	436	232	154	831	351	1045	808	301	102	348	635	451	1143	543	436	353	454	116	447	535	606	223	320	329	200	610	905	248	438	109	501	151	406	402	127	359	857	319	1416	449	128
Bristol						315	059	451	159	144	337	654	134	908	631	048	206	124	457	408	1005	405	351	328	317	258	310	450	521	224	439	243	134	353	727	313	221	217	324	128	321	224	202	221	720	057	1238	404	218
Cambridge							347	448	448	345	210	637	438	906	628	247	200	302	516	248	1003	422	242	149	336	131	319	335	407	112	135	144	201	657	721	044	525	252	342	254	221	243	244	240	717	401	1236	250	129
Cardiff								514	116	230	413	717	210	931	654	117	241	117	455	431	1029	429	414	351	340	334	333	513	544	257	511	307	210	429	751	337	257	253	347	210	345	239	237	245	743	133	1302	428	254
Carlisle									558	625	649	207	605	422	145	414	545	429	421	316	519	056	237	334	214	610	210	200	125	418	549	338	445	824	241	418	652	618	136	547	300	326	602	241	233	528	752	225	533
Carmarthen										330	513	756	310	1011	734	217	341	200	349	531	1108	508	454	451	359	434	414	605	637	357	611	407	310	529	830	436	357	353	427	310	444	249	337	344	822	233	1341	520	354
Dorchester											345	828	123	1042	805	222	208	258	631	542	1139	539	525	454	451	306	444	624	655	315	503	417	222	342	901	356	210	135	458	102	455	358	118	355	854	104	1412	538	242
Dover												838	445	1106	829	337	145	424	656	449	1204	604	442	350	515	046	508	536	607	241	318	345	236	704	922	245	532	238	522	254	422	423	244	420	918	411	1436	450	145
Edinburgh													807	311	057	616	747	630	623	505	332	257	426	523	416	759	412	315	240	620	738	527	647	1026	049	607	854	819	338	749	455	527	804	442	301	730	605	414	735
Exeter														1022	745	202	311	238	611	522	1119	519	504	442	431	406	423	603	635	344	559	357	254	225	841	427	057	254	438	203	435	338	237	335	833	044	1352	518	338
Fort William															242	831	1002	845	838	733	140	512	653	751	631	1027	627	615	541	835	1005	754	902	1241	234	835	1109	1034	552	1004	716	742	1019	657	441	945	413	641	950
Glasgow																554	725	609	601	456	353	235	417	514	354	750	350	340	305	558	728	518	625	1004	115	558	832	757	316	727	440	506	742	421	207	708	625	404	713
Gloucester																	208	053	420	331	928	328	314	251	240	258	232	413	444	155	410	206	110	421	650	236	249	219	247	147	244	147	204	144	643	125	1201	327	217
Guildford																		254	551	410	1059	459	352	314	410	106	403	451	523	139	310	245	116	530	821	210	358	058	418	120	323	318	106	315	813	238	1332	406	052
Hereford																			353	345	943	343	328	305	254	345	247	427	458	211	425	221	156	457	704	251	325	306	301	233	258	122	250	159	657	201	1215	341	303
Holyhead																				412	935	335	321	426	221	617	241	432	503	424	638	351	451	830	657	457	658	623	254	553	327	239	608	247	649	534	1208	347	539
Hull																					831	249	109	105	217	410	148	200	234	239	332	143	326	740	549	219	608	458	209	447	115	312	443	229	545	444	1103	058	349
Inverness																						609	751	848	728	1124	724	642	607	932	1102	852	959	1338	243	932	1206	1131	650	1101	814	840	1116	755	556	1042	237	738	1047
Kendal																							158	308	129	526	125	149	205	333	522	300	400	739	332	352	607	532	050	502	214	240	517	155	324	443	843	209	448
Leeds																								129	124	405	054	124	155	223	343	127	310	722	510	213	550	442	116	431	048	224	427	139	506	426	1024	040	338
Lincoln																									236	311	205	221	253	151	227	057	238	701	607	117	529	407	228	359	108	242	355	200	603	405	1122	136	250
Liverpool																										437	046	237	308	244	450	211	311	650	450	317	518	444	047	413	142	137	428	107	443	354	1001	152	359
Maidstone																											429	457	528	201	239	306	157	625	843	206	453	159	443	215	343	343	205	341	839	332	1357	411	106
Manchester																												208	239	236	419	146	304	642	446	249	510	436	045	405	106	144	420	059	439	346	957	122	352
Middlesbrough																													048	321	436	225	408	822	359	306	650	540	226	529	153	338	525	253	429	526	914	109	436
Newcastle																														351	506	256	438	853	324	336	721	611	244	559	223	408	555	323	354	557	839	142	506
Northampton																															234	114	058	604	653	100	432	231	250	219	152	150	215	147	646	308	1204	235	123
Norwich																																253	324	820	823	154	648	400	444	413	324	406	403	355	820	524	1338	352	245
Nottingham																																	201	615	611	115	443	333	218	322	056	151	318	108	607	319	1125	139	229
Oxford																																		514	721	152	342	136	318	125	238	218	120	215	714	217	1232	321	115
Penzance																																			1100	646	148	514	657	423	654	557	457	554	1053	303	1611	737	558
Perth																																				652	928	853	412	823	535	601	838	517	318	804	516	458	809
Peterborough																																					514	303	313	306	152	232	255	214	648	350	1206	221	146
Plymouth																																						341	525	250	522	425	324	422	920	131	1439	605	425
Portsmouth																																							450	054	410	350	030	347	846	222	1404	453	145
Preston																																								420	134	159	435	114	405	401	923	144	406
Salisbury																																									359	320	037	317	816	130	1334	442	150
Sheffield																																										224	356	124	529	357	1047	107	307
Shrewsbury																																											335	102	554	301	1112	251	306
Southampton																																												332	830	205	1349	437	140
Stoke-on-Trent																																													509	258	1028	206	302
Stranraer																																														757	829	453	802
Taunton																																															1315	441	301
Wick																																																1011	1320
York																																																	352

distances in miles (one mile equals 1.6093 km)

	Aberdeen	Aberystwyth	Barnstaple	Birmingham	Brighton	Bristol	Cambridge	Cardiff	Carlisle	Carmarthen	Dorchester	Dover	Edinburgh	Exeter	Fort William	Glasgow	Gloucester	Guildford	Hereford	Holyhead	Hull	Inverness	Kendal	Leeds	Lincoln	Liverpool	Maidstone	Manchester	Middlesbrough	Newcastle	Northampton	Norwich	Nottingham	Oxford	Penzance	Perth	Peterborough	Plymouth	Portsmouth	Preston	Salisbury	Sheffield	Shrewsbury	Southampton	Stoke-on-Trent	Stranraer	Taunton	Wick	York
Aberystwyth	472
Barnstaple	608	214
Birmingham	436	124	180
Brighton	613	288	210	171
Bristol	518	130	100	90	169
Cambridge	463	215	267	97	120	170
Cardiff	537	111	128	109	202	44	203
Carlisle	236	236	371	199	376	281	256	300
Carmarthen	520	48	190	172	264	107	266	68	284
Dorchester	600	206	94	172	119	62	184	120	364	182
Dover	587	326	272	208	82	205	124	239	381	301	200
Edinburgh	126	336	471	299	476	381	333	400	100	386	463	458
Exeter	593	198	44	165	178	84	259	113	356	175	57	248	455
Fort William	156	435	570	398	576	480	456	499	199	485	562	580	137	554
Glasgow	150	332	467	295	472	377	353	396	96	382	459	477	47	451	102
Gloucester	484	113	126	56	155	36	150	63	248	125	118	192	346	110	445	343
Guildford	571	224	175	128	44	106	96	139	335	201	97	97	433	150	532	430	99
Hereford	487	79	144	59	189	54	153	59	250	85	136	225	349	129	448	346	34	133
Holyhead	464	102	339	167	345	249	259	202	228	150	331	369	326	323	425	323	215	302	156
Hull	376	227	320	139	258	230	138	250	170	311	312	262	247	304	367	266	196	239	198	218
Inverness	106	496	631	459	637	541	517	561	260	546	623	641	157	616	66	176	507	595	510	488	430
Kendal	283	189	324	153	330	234	251	254	47	240	316	354	145	309	245	143	200	288	203	181	164	307
Leeds	329	173	301	120	262	211	146	230	123	224	293	271	200	285	321	219	177	220	179	165	59	383	110
Lincoln	388	199	275	98	216	185	95	205	182	267	246	220	258	260	379	277	151	173	154	204	44	441	176	74
Liverpool	362	110	272	101	278	182	193	202	126	158	264	302	224	257	324	222	148	236	151	102	128	386	79	74	139
Maidstone	545	284	234	166	50	167	82	200	339	262	161	41	416	209	537	435	153	58	186	327	220	599	313	231	178	261
Manchester	357	134	261	89	266	171	160	190	120	184	253	290	219	245	318	216	136	224	139	125	97	380	74	44	85	34	248
Middlesbrough	276	244	357	176	318	267	197	286	95	294	349	322	146	341	283	190	232	276	235	235	89	308	84	64	122	145	280	114
Newcastle	235	275	388	207	349	298	229	317	60	325	380	353	106	372	242	153	264	307	266	266	142	267	102	95	154	176	311	145	39
Northampton	486	174	212	56	133	115	56	162	249	224	159	155	348	196	447	345	79	90	111	217	152	509	203	136	94	151	113	139	189	220
Norwich	488	278	329	160	168	233	63	266	282	328	241	172	359	313	480	378	212	160	215	321	147	542	276	174	103	240	130	185	223	254	118
Nottingham	395	162	232	51	193	142	86	161	189	223	224	210	266	216	387	285	107	151	110	178	93	449	164	77	39	112	168	71	130	161	64	119
Oxford	510	160	170	68	109	73	82	107	274	169	115	146	373	154	472	370	48	67	81	242	190	534	228	174	132	176	107	164	227	258	44	146	102
Penzance	702	308	108	274	287	193	368	222	466	284	167	357	564	109	663	562	220	259	238	434	415	726	419	403	370	367	318	356	451	482	326	433	326	265
Perth	86	388	523	351	529	433	378	453	152	438	515	503	42	507	102	64	399	486	401	379	291	114	199	245	303	278	461	275	192	150	400	404	310	426	617
Peterborough	435	204	263	86	158	173	37	193	229	255	204	162	306	248	427	325	139	115	142	225	110	489	223	121	51	159	120	132	170	201	45	78	58	86	357	351
Plymouth	633	239	62	205	218	124	299	153	397	215	98	288	495	44	594	493	151	190	169	365	346	657	350	334	301	298	249	287	382	413	257	364	257	196	78	544	288
Portsmouth	596	244	162	154	53	125	137	158	360	220	73	141	458	132	558	456	118	45	152	328	276	620	314	260	215	262	102	250	313	344	130	204	188	85	241	508	157	172
Preston	326	146	281	110	287	191	209	211	89	197	273	311	188	266	287	185	157	245	160	138	122	349	43	69	134	36	269	35	103	139	159	235	121	184	375	237	180	306	270
Salisbury	549	184	118	121	90	52	145	98	313	160	39	160	411	93	511	409	72	62	105	281	261	573	267	244	202	215	121	203	298	329	115	212	173	70	203	461	165	134	44	223
Sheffield	397	166	272	91	233	182	122	201	161	263	264	247	236	256	359	257	148	191	150	157	66	421	115	38	47	79	205	39	100	131	104	148	45	142	366	309	93	297	228	73	212
Shrewsbury	417	75	220	48	226	130	140	111	181	110	212	250	279	205	379	277	96	184	52	105	162	441	135	119	124	65	208	71	190	221	98	203	87	123	314	329	129	245	209	92	161	88
Southampton	578	225	142	135	66	106	136	140	342	201	53	152	440	111	539	437	100	49	133	309	258	601	295	241	199	243	113	232	294	325	111	204	169	67	221	489	157	152	20	252	23	209	191
Stoke-on-Trent	392	112	220	48	226	130	140	150	156	211	212	250	254	205	353	251	96	184	99	123	129	415	109	93	91	57	208	46	164	195	98	172	54	123	314	303	99	245	209	66	161	50	38	191
Stranraer	235	342	477	305	482	387	363	406	106	392	469	487	132	461	181	86	352	440	355	333	276	261	153	229	288	232	445	229	201	163	354	388	295	380	571	149	333	502	466	195	418	267	287	447	261
Taunton	560	165	50	132	160	51	226	80	323	142	45	224	422	34	521	419	77	126	96	291	272	583	277	261	228	225	185	213	309	340	183	291	184	123	144	471	215	75	114	234	70	224	172	94	172	429
Wick	207	597	732	560	738	642	618	662	361	647	724	742	258	716	166	277	608	695	610	588	531	104	408	484	543	487	700	484	409	367	609	644	550	635	826	215	589	757	721	451	673	523	542	702	516	362	684
York	323	201	314	133	275	224	154	243	116	251	306	279	193	298	314	212	189	233	192	192	38	376	91	24	79	102	237	71	51	89	146	180	87	184	408	239	125	339	269	96	254	57	146	251	120	223	265	477
LONDON	550	239	216	121	54	120	59	153	314	215	125	78	413	200	512	410	102	31	136	282	186	574	268	201	143	216	39	204	254	285	68	118	129	56	310	462	86	241	75	225	85	169	163	77	161	420	167	675	211

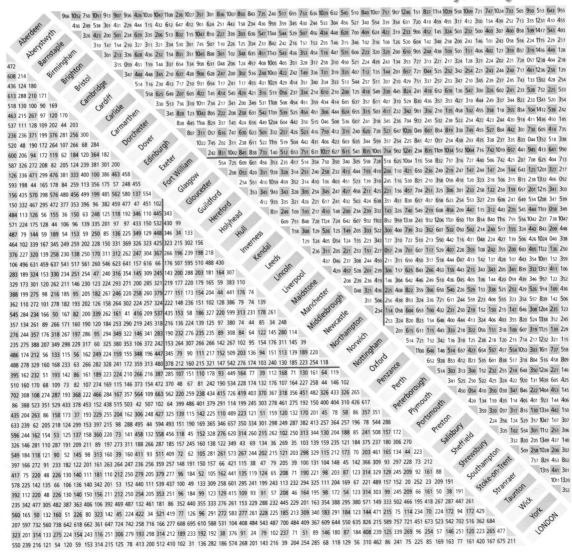

Atlas symbols

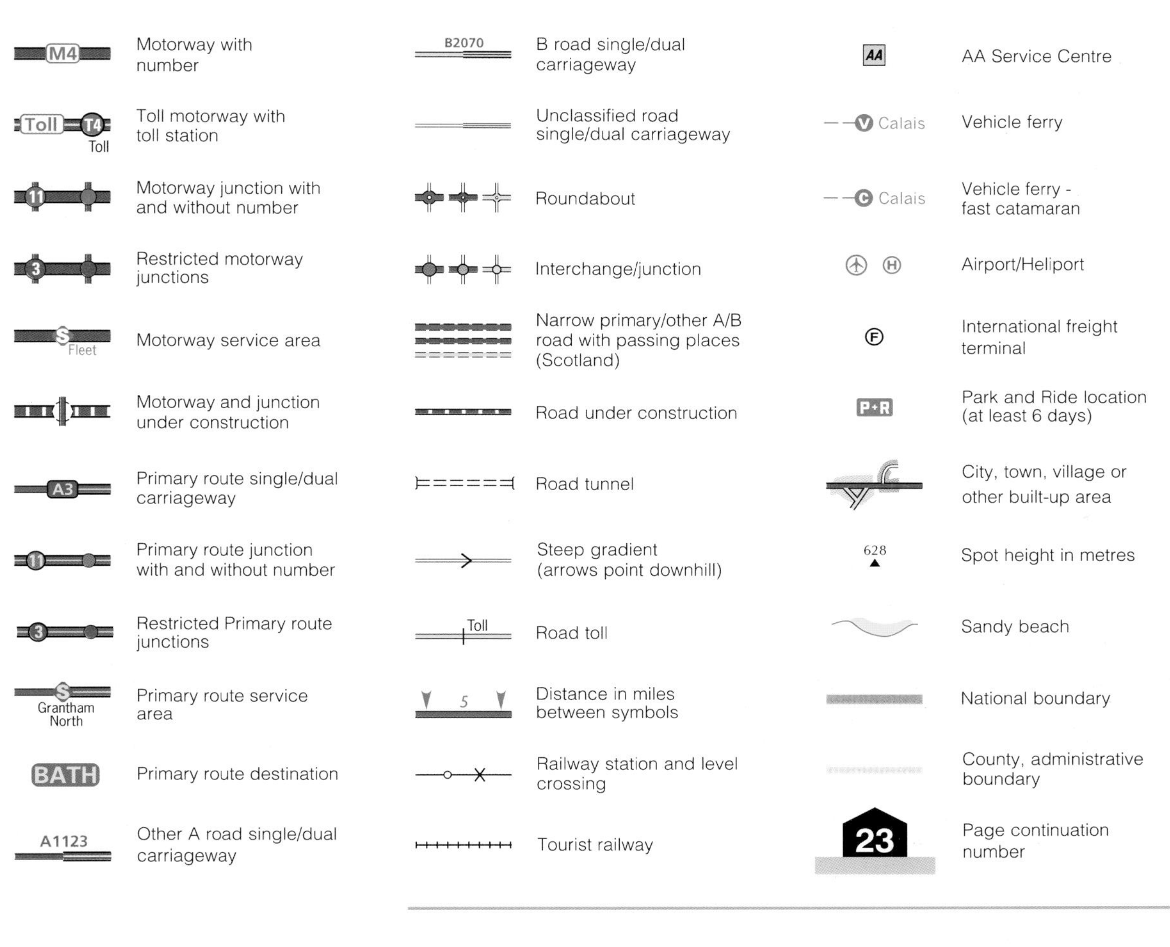

Tourist Information Centre (all year/seasonal)	Country park	Viewpoint	Rugby Union national stadium
Visitor or heritage centre	Agricultural showground	Picnic site	International athletics stadium
Abbey, cathedral or priory	Theme park	Hill-fort	Horse racing/Show jumping
Ruined abbey, cathedral or priory	Farm or animal centre	Roman antiquity	Motor-racing circuit
Castle	Zoological or wildlife collection	Prehistoric monument	Air show venue
Historic house or building	Bird collection	1066 Battle site with year	Ski slope (natural/artificial)
Museum or art gallery	Aquarium	Steam centre (railway)	NT NTS National Trust property (England & Wales/ Scotland)
Industrial interest	RSPB RSPB site	Cave	Other place of interest
Aqueduct or viaduct	National Nature Reserve (England, Scotland, Wales)	Windmill	Attraction within urban area
Garden	Local nature reserve	Monument	Forest Park
Arboretum	Forest drive	Golf course	National Park and National Scenic Areas
Vineyard	National trail	County cricket ground	Heritage coast

2
Isles of Scilly
White Island
ST MARTIN'S
St Martin's Head
King Charles's
BRYHER
Old Grimsby
Cromwell's
Old Blockhouse
Higher Town
Isles of Scilly Heritage Coast
New Grimsby
Lizard Point
Great Ganilly
Tresco
Tresco Abbey
Crow Bar
TRESCO
Innisidgen Tomb
Great Arthur
Samson
Crow Sound
Bant's Carn Burial
ST MARY'S
North West Channel
Harry's Walls
Longstone
Deep Point
Hugh Town
Porth Hellick Downs Tombs
Garrison Walls
Isles of Scilly (St Mary's)
Old Town
Annet
St Mary's Sound
Peninnis Head
Broad Sound
Gugh
Middle Town
ST AGNES
Horse Point
Smith Sound
Western Rocks
3 miles
5 kilometres
Carn Naun Point
The Island or St Ives Head
St Ives Bay
Zennor Head
St Ives
Gurnards Head
Carbis Bay
South West Coast Path
Zennor
B3306
Halsetown
Towednack
Lelant
Pendeen Watch
Carn Galver NT
Men-An-Tol
Mulfra Quoit
Penwith Heritage Coast
Morvah
Chysauster
Canonstown
A30
Geevor Tin Mines
New Mill
St Erth
Pendeen
Levant Steam Engine NT
Great Bosullow
Lanyon Quoit
Crowlas
B3318
Ludgvan
Botallack
Trengwainton Garden NT
Penzance
Gulval
Cape Cornwall
St Just
A3071
Madron
Longrock
St Hilary
Newbridge
Heamoor
Chyandour
Marazion
Ballowall Barrow
Goldsith
Perranuthnoe
Penzance
Kelynack
Sancreed
St Michael's Mount NT
Carn Euny
Drift
Newlyn
Whitesand Bay
Land's End
Kerris
Paul
Crows-an-Wra
Cudden Point
Sennen Cove
Mousehole
St Buryan
MOUNT'S BAY
LAND'S END
Sennen
B3283
The Merry Maidens
Trevescan
B3315
Lamorna
Trethewey
Lamorna Cove
Porthcurno
Treen
Submarine Telegraphy
Merthen Point
Porthgwarra
St Levan
Minack Open Air Theatre
Cribba Head
Gwennap Head
4 miles
5 kilometres

Land's End & the Lizard
3
G
H
J
K
L
M
1
2
3
4
5
6
7
8
4
Ligger or Perran Bay
Crantock
Lane
Quintrell Downs
A392
St Columb Road
Newlyn East
Lappa Valley
St Enoder
A30
Summercourt
Fiddlers Green
Mitchell
Scarcewater
A3058
A3076
A3075
Perranporth
Cligga Point
Bolingey
Rose
Goonhavern
World in Miniature
B3285
St Agnes Heritage Coast
Trevellas Downs
ST AGNES HEAD
St Agnes
Perranzabuloe
Penhallow
Mithian
Callestick
Barkla Shop
Marazanvose
St Allen
A39
Trispen
New Mills
Ladock
Wheal Coates
Goonvrea
Goonbell
St Erme
B3275
Probus
B3277
Porthtowan
Mount Hawke
B3284
Shortlanesend
Idless
Tresillian
South West Coast Path
Godrevy-Portreath Heritage Coast
Portreath
B3300
Cambrose
Mawla
Blackwater
R. Kenwyn
Kenwyn
A390
Truro
Navax Point
Bridge
Illogan
Chacewater
A30
Higher Town
Merther
Tehidy
Scorrier
Mount Ambrose
P+R
Kea
St Clement
Malpas
St Michael Penkevil
Ruan Lanihorne
B3301
Cornish Engines NT
St Day
Reskadinnick
Redruth
Twelveheads
Old Kea
Lamorran
Tuckingmill
Pool
A3047
Carn Brea
Carharrack
B3298
Bissoe
Carnon Downs
Kehelland
Carn Brea
Camborne
Carnkie
Gwennap
Trelissick Garden NT
Philleigh
Perranwell
Devoran
Connor Downs
Penponds
B3297
Lanner
A393
Perranarworthal
Angarrack
Barripper
Four Lanes
Penhalvean
Feock
B3289
Trewithian
Gwinear
Carnhell Green
B3303
Troon
Ponsanooth
Gerrans Bay
Erth Praze
Stithians
Mylor Bridge
St Just-in-Roseland
Praze-an-Beeble
B3280
Portscatho
Carrick Roads
Mylor
Gerrans
Carnkie
Longdowns
Leedstown
Crowan
Porkellis
Rame
Mabe Burnthouse
Penryn
Flushing
Greeb Point
B3302
Townshend
Drym
Argal & College Water Park
Treverva
Pendennis
St Mawes
Godolphin Cross
Trenear
Poldark Mine
Bohortha
Budock Water
Falmouth
Pendennis Point
South West Coast Path
Prospidnick
Wendron
A394
Seworgan
ZONE POINT
Crowntown
Carleen
Trevarno
Penjerrick
Falmouth Bay
Coverack Bridges
Brill
Ashton
Sithney
Breage
Constantine
Mawnan Smith
A394
Helston
Trebah
Carwinion
ROSEMULLION HEAD
Porth Navas
Glendurgan NT
Rinsey Head
Gweek
Helford Passage
Durgan
Mawnan
Toll Point
Trewavas Head
Flambards
Seal Sanctuary
Helford River
B3304
Porthleven
A3083
Helford
St Anthony
Mawgan
Manaccan
Nare Point
Halliggye Fogou
Garras
Tregidden
Gunwalloe
Porthallow
White Cross
B3293
Porthoustock
Manacle Point
Cury
Goonhilly Satellite Earth Station
St Keverne
GOONHILLY DOWNS
Poldhu Point
Marconi Memorial
B3294
Lowland Point
Mullion
B3296
Mullion Cove
Mullion Island
Mullion Cove
Coverack
Ruan Major
Kuggar
Predannack Head
Black Head
Ruan Minor
Vellan Head
Cadgwith
The Lizard Heritage Coast
South West Coast Path
Devil's Frying Pan
Lizard Head
Kynance Cove
Church Cove
Lizard
LIZARD POINT
Bass Point

A
B
C
8
D
E
F
1
2
3
4
5
6
7
8
Rumps Point
Port Quin Bay
Kelland Head
Varley Head
Port Isaac Bay
Pentire Point
Padstow Bay
Port Quin
Port Isaac
Hayle Bay
Stepper Point
Polzeath
Trelights
B3314
St Endellion
Trebetherick
St Minver
Trevose Head Heritage Coast
Gunver Head
TREVOSE HEAD
Mother Ivey's Bay
Harlyn Bay
Dinas Head
Constantine Bay
Prideaux Place
Trevone
Rock
Harlyn
Padstow
Chapel Amble
Windmill
Constantine Bay
St Merryn
A389
B3276
St Issey
Wadebridge
Porthcothan
Little Petherick
St Breock
Royal Cornwall
Penrose
Trenance
Park Head
St Ervan
Rumford
Burlawn
Trelow
Bedruthan Steps
Crealy Great Adventure Park
St Breock Downs Monolith
Trenance
B3274
Nine Maidens
A39
Berryls Point
Mawgan Porth
Ruthernbridge
Griffins Point
Trevarrian
B3276
Vale of Mawgan
St Mawgan
Talskiddy
Rosenannon
St Wenn
Withiel
Watergate Bay
Newquay
Gluvian
Towan Head
Newquay Bay
St Columb Minor
A3059
St Columb Major
Tregonetha
Newquay
Porth
B3274
Victoria
Fistral Bay
A3058
High Town
West Pentire
Colan
Bosoughan
Ruthvoes
Kelsey Head
Pentire
Mountjoy
Holywell Bay
Crantock
Lane
Quintrell Downs
A392
Roche
Penhale Point
Tresean
St Columb Road
Bugle
Holywell
Treveal
Kestle Mill
Fraddon
Indian Queens
B3279
Ligger Point
Trerice NT
Dairyland
A3058
Whitemoor
Cubert
St Dennis
B3274
Newlyn East
St Enoder
Stenalees
Ligger or Perran Bay
Lappa Valley
A30
Nanpean
Carthew
Summercourt
Treviscoe
Wheal Martyn Heritage Centre
Fiddlers Green
A3076
Foxhole
A3075
Perranporth
Rose
Scarcewater
Mitchell
Automobilia
Cligga Point
Goonhavern
High Street
World in Miniature
A3058
St Austell
Bolingey
St Stephen
Trewoon
St Agnes Heritage Coast
Trevellas Downs
B3285
St Mewan
ST AGNES HEAD
Perranzabuloe
New Mills
Penhallow
A39
St Stephen's Coombe
St Agnes
Polgooth
Mithian
Callestick
St Allen
Trispen
Ladock
Wheal Coates
Barkla Shop
Marazanvose
Grampound Road
Sticker
Goonvrea
Goonbell
St Erme
B3275
Hewas Water
B3273
Porthtowan
B3277
Probus
A390
B3284
Grampound
Mount Hawke
Shortlanesend
Idless
Creed
Pengrugla
The Lost Gardens of Heligan
Tresillian
B3287
St Ewe
Cambrose
Mawla
Blackwater
R Kenwyn
Kenwyn
River Fal
A390
Truro
Polmassick
Kestle
B3300
Chacewater
Tregony
Illogan
A30
Higher Town
Merther
Portmellon
Scorrier
St Clement
Mount Ambrose
Kea
Malpas
St Michael Penkevil
Ruan Lanihorne
St Michael Caerhays
Rescassa
Gorran
Cornish Engines NT
St Day
3
Redruth
Twelveheads
Lamorran
A3078
Pool
A3047
Carharrack
Old Kea
Boswinger
Carn Brea
Bissoe
Carnon Downs
B3298
Trelissick Garden NT
Camborne
Carnkie
Gwennap
Philleigh
Veryan Bay
B3297
Lanner
A393
Perranwell
Devoran
Perranarworthal
A39
Veryan
Portloe
Four Lanes
DODMAN POINT
Penhalvean
Feock
B3289
Trewithian
The Roseland Heritage Coast
Ponsanooth
Gerrans Bay
Stithians
Mylor Bridge
St Just-in-Roseland
Nare Head
B3280
B3297
Portscatho
Carnkie
Longdowns
Mylor
Carrick Roads
Gerrans
Mabe Burnthouse
Penryn
St Mawes
Flushing
Greeb Point
Porkellis
Rame
A39
Pendennis
Bohortha
Budock Water
Falmouth
Pendennis Point
Seworgan
Penjerrick
South West Coast Path
ZONE POINT
0 1 2 3 4 miles
0 1 2 3 4 5 kilometres

Mid-Cornwall
5
8
6
BODMIN MOOR
Camelford
Lanteglos
Trewalder
Helstone
Watergate
St Teath
Treveighan
Michaelstow
Trelill
Churchtown
St Breward
Trequite
St Kew Highway
St Tudy
Lank
De Lank River
BROWN WILLY
419
346
347
Treween
Altarnun
Wesley's Cottage
Trewint
Polyphant
Fivelanes
Trebullett
Trewarlett
Lezant
Illand
Congdon's Shop
Jamaica Inn
Bolventor
North Hill
Coad's Green
Middlewood
SMALLACOMBE DOWNS
Bathpool
Treburley
Bray Shop
Stoke Climsland
Linkinhorne
South Hill
Rilla Mill
Upton
Henwood
Upton Cross
The Hurlers Stone Circle
Sterts Open-Air Theatre
Minions
Downgate
Pensilva
Golberdon
Callington
Frogwell
Common Moor
Darite
Trethevy Quoit
Tremar
St Cleer
Golitha
St Ive
Merrymeet
Cadson Bury
Newton Ferrers
Quethiock
Pillaton
St Mabyn
Blisland
Colliford Lake
Colliford Lake Park
Temple
BROWNGELLY DOWNS
Pencarrow
Washaway
Helland
Warleggan
Cardinham
Mount
St Neot
Carnglaze Caverns
Dobwalls Family Adventure Park
Dobwalls
Lanivet
Bodmin
Bodmin & Wenford Railway
West Taphouse
Moorswater
Liskeard
Trevelmond
East Taphouse
St Pinnock
Menheniot
Lanhydrock NT
Sweetshouse
Restormel
Lockengate
Bodwen
Lostwithiel
Porfell Animal Land
Herodsfoot
St Keyne
Paul Corrin Music
Lanlivery
Luxulyan
Duloe
Widegates
Tideford
Budge's Shop
St Erney
Trerulefoot
Penwithick
Trethurgy
Eden Project
St Blazey
Tywardreath
Par
Lerryn
Lanreath
Muchlarnick
Sandplace
Morval
Hessenford
Polbathic
Golant
St Veep
Penpoll
Pelynt
St Martin
Monkey Sanctuary
Sheviock
Crafthole
Bodigga Cliff NT
Seaton
Downderry
Portwrinkle
Looe
Looe Bay
Lanteglos Highway
Bodinnick
Crumplehorn
Model Village
Porthallow
Looe Island
Polkerris
Fowey
Lansallos
Polperro
Talland Bay
Polruan
Lantic Bay
Pencarrow Head
Lantivet Bay
South West Coast Path
Gribbin Head - Polperro Heritage Coast
St Austell Bay
GRIBBIN HEAD
Porthpean
Black Head
Mevagissey Bay
Chapel Point
Whitsand
A30
A38
A39
A390
A391
A388
A387
A3082
B3257
B3266
B3268
B3269
B3254
B3252
B3251
B3253
B3247
B3359
G
H
J
K
L
M
1
2
3
4
5
6
7
8

6
9
10
5
DARTMOOR
FOREST
Marystow
Lawhitton
Meadwell
Chillaton
Kelly
Quither
North
Brentor
Hilltown
Hexworthy
Bradstone
Milton
Abbot
Lezant
Horndo
Mary Tavy
Cudliptown
Trekenner
Dunterton
Chaddlehanger
COCKS
HILL
Rezare
Bealsmill
Treburley
Lamerton
Peter
Tavy
539
GREAT
MIS TOR
442
COXTOR
Kingston
Sydenham
Damerel
Ottery
Bray
Shop
Horsebridge
Tavistock
Stone Rows & Circle
Stoke
Climsland
Oldmill
Luckett
Latchley
Sampford
Spiney
Princetown
406
ROYAL HILL
South
Hill
Downgate
Chilsworthy
Gulworthy
Whitchurch
347
Kit
Hill
St Ann's
Chapel
Gunnislake
Golberdon
Harrowbarrow
Dupath
Well House
Albaston
Morwellham Quay
Horrabridge
Walkhampton
Callington
Metherell
St
Dominick
Cotehele
NT
The Garden
House
Burrator
Reservoir
Dousland
Frogwell
Calstock
Calstock
Viaduct
Buckland
Monachorum
Yelverton
Sheepstor
Buckland
Abbey NT
Meavy
Cadson
Bury
St
Mellion
Bere
Alston
Milton
Combe
Upper Plym
Valley
Newton
Ferrers
Cotts
Sowton
Clearbrook
Quethiock
Pillaton
Weir
Quay
Maristow
471
SHELL
TOP
Dewerstone NT
Cargreen
Bere
Ferrers
Shaugh Prior
Hatt
Bickleigh
Landulph
Tamerton
Foliot
Roborough
Botusfleming
Notter
Plymouth
Carkeel
Boringdon
Tideford
Landrake
Saltash
Dartmoor
Wildlife Park
Lutton
Harford
Crownhill
Cornwood
St Erney
Trematon
PLYMOUTH
Hemerdon
Sparkwell
Trerulefoot
South
Pill
Toll
St
Budeaux
Eggbuckland
Venton
Ivybridge
Trehan
St
Stephens
St Germans
Plympton
Woodland
Polbathic
Antony NT
Lee Mill
Saltram
NT
Sheviock
Crafthole
Antony
Torpoint
Devonport
St
John
St John's
Lake
Stonehouse
Plymouth Dome
Elburton
Westlake
Plymstock
Portwrinkle
Cremyll
Mount Edgcumbe
Hooe
Brixton
Worston
Spriddlestone
Dunstone
Yealmpton
The
Sound
Freathy
Millbrook
South West
Coast Path
Flete
Staddiscombe
Whitsand Bay
Kingsand
Cawsand
Cawsand
Bay
Down Thomas
Holbeton
West
Wembury
Rame
Heybrook
Bay
Wembury
Newton
Ferrers
The Old
Mill NT
Penlee Point
Bridgend
RAME HEAD
Wembury
Bay
Noss Mayo
Mothecombe
Kingston
Rame Head
Heritage Coast
Gara
Point
Ringmore
Erme
Mouth
Stoke
Point
Beacon
Point
(Summer Only)
Bigbury-on-Sea
Burgh Island
Santander
Roscoff
Bigbury Bay
SITTAFORD TOR
517
501
480
River Tamar
River Tavy
R Meavy
R Plym
River Yealm
River Erme
R Erme
Blackbrook R
A388
A38
A390
A386
A374
A379
B3357
B3362
B3257
B3212
B3267
B3247
B3249
B3378
B3432
B3417
B3214
B3186
0 1 2 3 4 miles
0 1 2 3 4 5 kilometres
A
B
C
D
E
F
1
2
3
4
5
6
7
8

South Devon
7
11
12
G
H
J
K
L
M
1
2
3
4
5
6
7
8
Dartmoor National Park
Grimspound
Hameldown Tor
Lustleigh
Bovey
Manaton
Lustleigh
Canonteign Falls & Country Park
Trusham
Harcombe
Exeter
Kenton
A La Ronde NT
Hulham
Water
Becky Falls
Southcott
Hennock
Chudleigh
Hound Tor Medieval Village
Bovey Tracey
Chudleigh Knighton
Ugbrooke Park
Ashcombe
Cockwood
The Model Railway
Dawlish Warren
Widecombe in the Moor
Haytor 454
Haytor Vale
Church House NT
Dunstone
Ilsington
Rippon Tor
Brimley
Ideford
Luton
Dawlish
Liverton
Coldeast
Stover
Sandygate
Preston
Horridge
Halford
Corndon Tor
Ponsworthy
Buckland in the Moor
Lower Town
Teigngrace
Kingsteignton
Bishopsteignton
Coombe
Holcombe
Teignmouth
Poundsgate
Bickington
Highweek
Newton Abbot
Coombe Cellars
Ringmore
Shaldon
Netherton
Combeinteignhead
Stokeinteignhead
West Ogwell
Middle Rocombe
Lower Gabwell
Higher Gabwell
Holne
River Dart
Ashburton
Woodland
East Ogwell
Denbury
Hedgehog Hospital
Abbotskerswell
Hembury Castle
Coffinswell
Maidencombe
Daccombe
Kingskerswell
Buckfast
Barton
Coombe Pafford
Model Village
Babbacombe Bay
Forder Green
Torbryan
Buckfastleigh
Landscove
Ipplepen
St Marychurch
Babbacombe
Babbacombe Pottery
Butterfly Farm
Woolston Green
Broadhempston
Shiphay
Ellacombe
Torquay
Dean
Staverton
Combe Fishacre
Compton
Deancombe
South Devon Railway
Cockington
Marldon
Dean Prior
Dartington
R Dart
Littlehempston
Rockend
Hopes Nose
Harbourneford
Hollicombe
Preston
Berry Pomeroy
Westerland
Lutton
Rattery
Cott
Berry Pomeroy
Aish
South Brent
Tigley
Blagdon
Paignton
Tor Bay
Totnes
Longcombe
Collaton St Mary
Belsford
Harberton
Aish
Yalberton
Goodrington
West Leigh
East Leigh
Avonwick
Diptford
Great Englebourne
Luscombe
Ashprington
Stoke Gabriel
Waddeton
Galmpton
Brixham
Berry Head
North Huish
Tuckenhay
Cornworthy
Harbertonford
Greenway NT
Ugborough
Washbourne
Dittisham
Churston Ferrers
St Mary Bay
Curtisknowle
East Cornworthy
Higher Brixham
Sharkham Point
Lupridge
Allaleigh
Capton
Paignton & Dartmouth Railway
Halwell
Moreleigh
Dartmouth
Boohay
Coleton Fishacre NT
Scabbacombe Head
Woodlands Leisure Park
Lixton
Blackawton
Bayard's Cove Fort
Kingswear
Dartmouth
Warfleet
Loddiswell
Woodleigh
Stoke Fleming
East Allington
Aveton Gifford
Blackpool
Churchstow
Goveton
Strete
Buckland-Tout-Saints
Harleston
South Devon Heritage Coast
Slapton
Kingsbridge
Sherford
Frittiscombe
Upton
East Charleton
Chillington
Start Bay
South Milton
West Alvington
Stokenham
West Charleton
Frogmore
Torcross
Sutton
Kingsbridge Estuary
North Pool
Beeson
Beesands
Malborough
Ford
South Pool
Kellaton
Bolberry
Collaton
Salcombe
Chivelstone
East Portlemouth
Hallsands
South Allington
South West Coast Path
Overbecks NT
Rickham
Lighthouse
Start Point
East Prawle
Bolt Head
Prawle Point
A38
A380
A381
A383
A384
A385
A3022
A379
A3122
B3387
B3344
B3193
B3192
B3195
B3196
B3205

A
B
C
D
E
F
1
2
3
4
5
6
7
8
Higher Sha
Lower Sha
Dizzard Point
St Gennys
Coxfor
Crackington Haven
Cambeak
Sweets
B3263
Witchcraft
Pentire Point - Widemouth Heritage Coast
Boscastle
Tresparrett
Marsh
Lesnewth
Trevalga
Tintagel
TINTAGEL HEAD
Trethevey
Tintagel
Bossiney
B3266
B3262
Old Post Office NT
Davidstow
Penhallic Point
Trewarmett
Treknow
British Cycling
Tremail
Trebarwith
B3314
Gaia Energy Centre
Trefrew
South West Coast Path
Delabole
Pengelly
Crowdy Reservo
Westdowns
Camelford
Port Isaac Bay
Lanteglos
Rumps Point
Kelland Head
Varley Head
Trewalder
Helstone
Port Quin Bay
Watergate
Pentire Point
Port Quin
Port Isaac
Port Gaverne
B3314
St Teath
Padstow Bay
Long Cross
B3267
419
BROWN WILLY
Hayle Bay
Trelights
Pendoggett
Treveighan
Stepper Point
Polzeath
Michaelstow
4
B3314
St Endellion
A39
St Minver
Churchtown
Trevose Head
De Lank River
Jamaica
TREVO
Trequite
St Breward
0 1 2 3 4 miles
0 1 2 3 4 5 kilometres
Rock
St Kew
St Kew Highway
St Tudy
Lank
Head
Trevone
Constantine
Padstow
Chapel

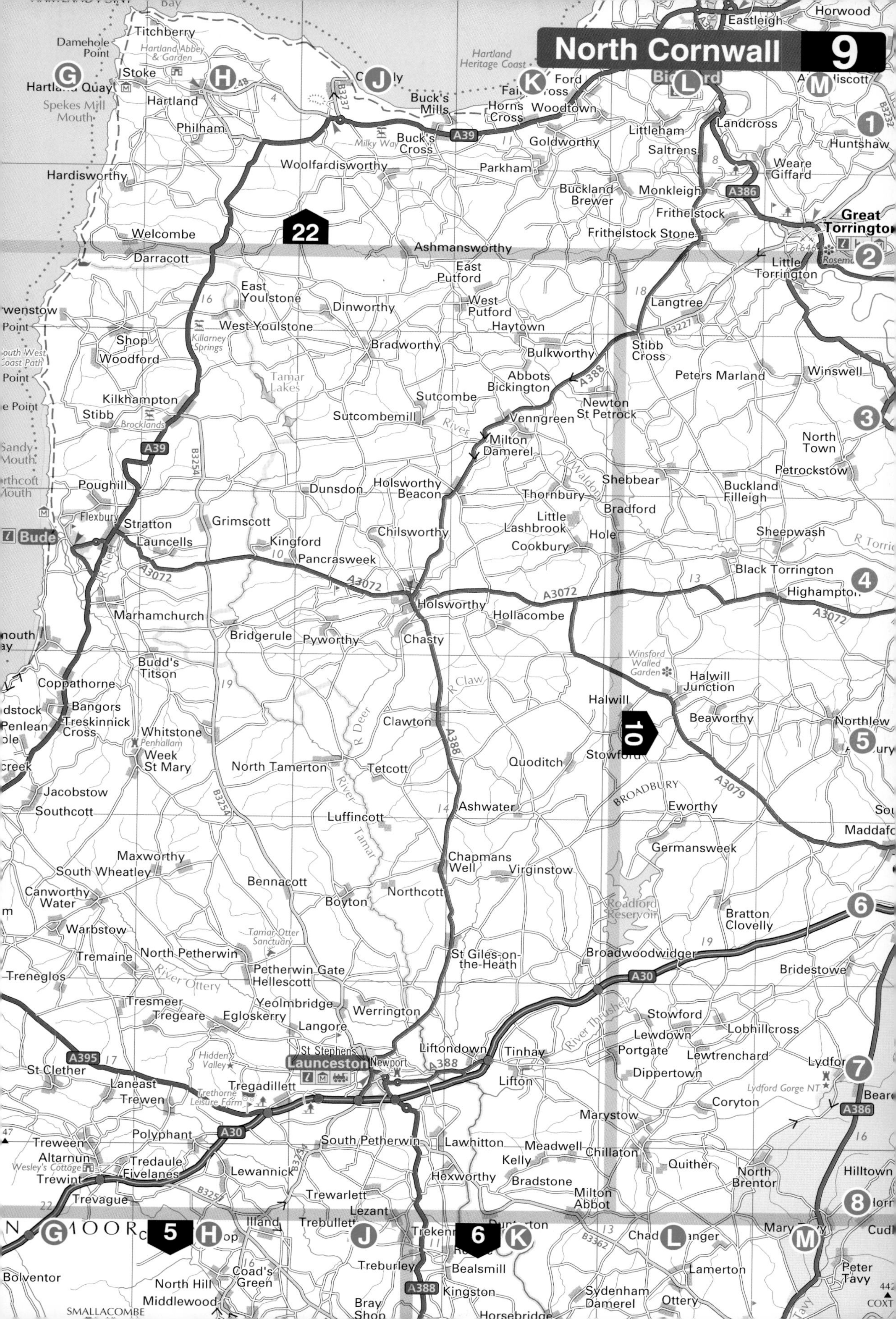
Titchberry
Dameholе Point
Hartland Abbey & Garden
Stoke
Hartland Quay
Spekes Mill Mouth
Hartland
Philham
Hartland Heritage Coast
Buck's Mills
Horns Cross
Woodtown
Buck's Cross
Milky Way
Goldworthy
Littleham
Landcross
Huntshaw
Saltrens
Weare Giffard
Eastleigh
Horwood
Woolfardisworthy
Parkham
Hardisworthy
Buckland Brewer
Monkleigh
Frithelstock
Great Torrington
Frithelstock Stone
Welcombe
Ashmansworthy
Darracott
East Putford
Little Torrington
East Youlstone
West Putford
Langtree
Dinworthy
West Youlstone
Haytown
Killarney Springs
Shop
Woodford
Bradworthy
Stibb Cross
Bulkworthy
Peters Marland
Winswell
Tamar Lakes
Abbots Bickington
Newton St Petrock
Kilkhampton
Sutcombe
Stibb
Brockiands
Sutcombemill
Venngreen
North Town
Sandy Mouth
Milton Damerel
Petrockstow
Poughill
Dunsdon
Holsworthy Beacon
Shebbear
Buckland Filleigh
Thornbury
Flexbury
Bradford
Bude
Stratton
Grimscott
Little Lashbrook
Launcells
Kingford
Chilsworthy
Hole
Sheepwash
Pancrasweek
Cookbury
Black Torrington
Holsworthy
Hollacombe
Highampton
Marhamchurch
Bridgerule
Pyworthy
Chasty
Winsford Walled Garden
Halwill Junction
Budd's Titson
Coppathorne
Halwill
Bangors
Treskinnick Cross
Clawton
Beaworthy
Northlew
Penlean
Whitstone
Penhallam
Week St Mary
North Tamerton
Tetcott
Quoditch
Stowford
Broadbury
Jacobstow
Southcott
Ashwater
Eworthy
Luffincott
Maddaford
Maxworthy
Germansweek
South Wheatley
Chapmans Well
Virginstow
Bennacott
Canworthy Water
Boyton
Northcott
Roadford Reservoir
Bratton Clovelly
Warbstow
Tamar Otter Sanctuary
St Giles-on-the-Heath
Tremaine
North Petherwin
Broadwoodwidger
Bridestowe
Treneglos
Petherwin Gate
Hellescott
River Ottery
Tresmeer
Yeolmbridge
Tregeare
Egloskerry
Werrington
Stowford
Langore
Lewdown
Lobhillcross
Portgate
Lewtrenchard
St Stephens
Liftondown
Tinhay
Hidden Valley
Launceston
Newport
St Clether
Laneast
Trewen
Tregadillett
Lifton
Dippertown
Lydford
Trethorne Leisure Farm
Lydford Gorge NT
Coryton
Marystow
Treween
Polyphant
South Petherwin
Lawhitton
Meadwell
Chillaton
Altarnun
Tredaule
Kelly
Quither
North Brentor
Hilltown
Wesley's Cottage
Fivelanes
Lewannick
Hexworthy
Bradstone
Trewint
Milton Abbot
Trevague
Trewarlett
Lezant
Illand
Trebullett
Trekenner
Chadd
Mary Tavy
Bolventor
Coad's Green
Treburley
Bealsmill
Lamerton
Peter Tavy
North Hill
Kingston
Sydenham Damerel
Middlewood
Bray Shop
Ottery
Horsebridge
Smallacombe
A39
A386
A388
A3072
A3079
A30
A395
B3237
B3232
B3227
B3254
B3257
B3362
River Waldon
River Tamar
R Deer
R Claw
R Neet
River Thrushel
R Torridge
South West Coast Path
22
10
5
6

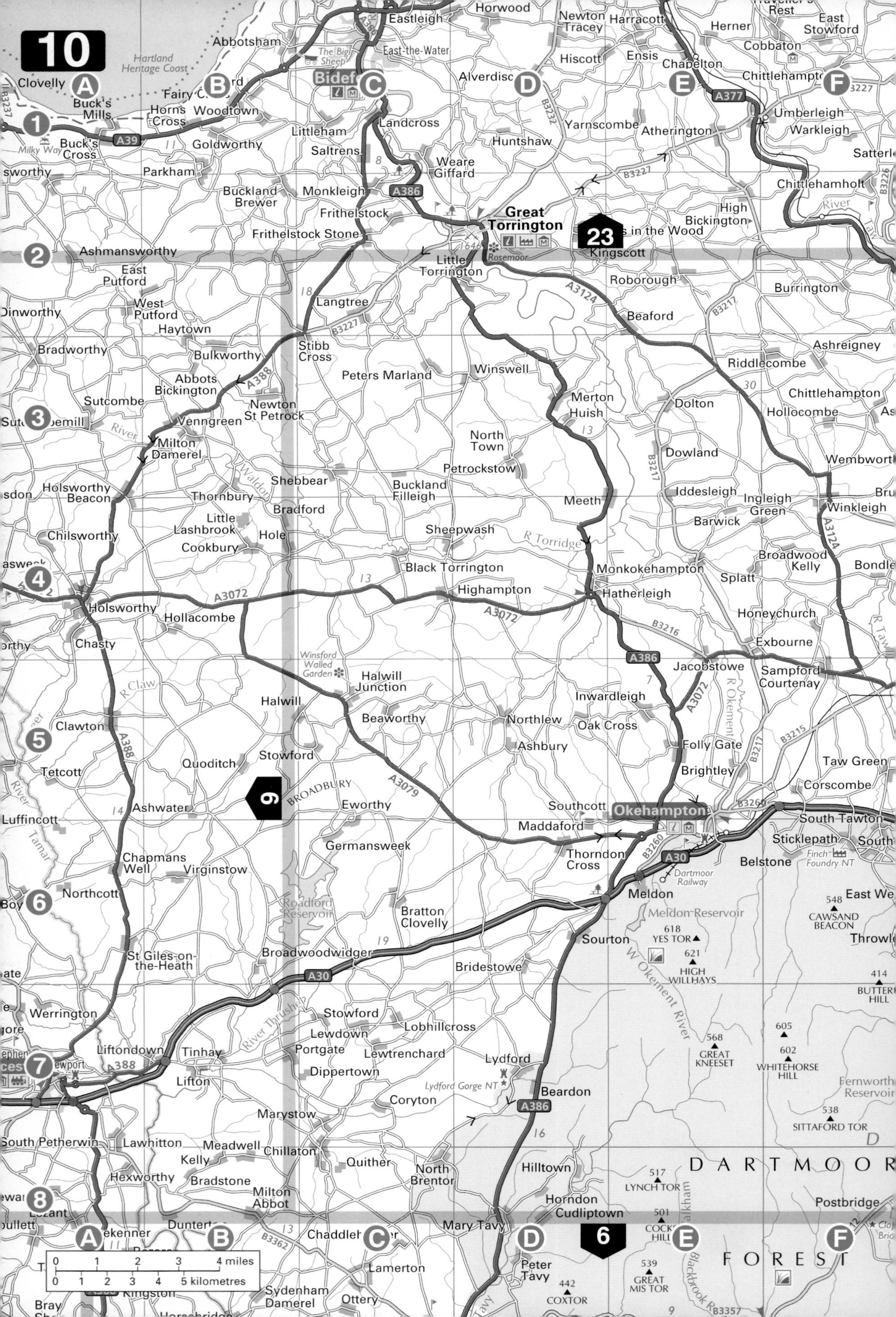

10
Clovelly
Abbotsham
Hartland Heritage Coast
Buck's Mills
Horns Cross
Woodtown
Bideford
Eastleigh
East-the-Water
The Big Sheep
Horwood
Newton Tracey
Harracott
Hiscott
Ensis
Chapelton
Herner
Cobbaton
East Stowford
Chittlehampton
Umberleigh
Warkleigh
Alverdiscott
Landcross
Littleham
Saltrens
Goldworthy
Buck's Cross
Parkham
Monkleigh
Buckland Brewer
Frithelstock
Frithelstock Stone
Weare Giffard
Huntshaw
Yarnscombe
Atherington
Great Torrington
Little Torrington
Rosemoor
St Giles in the Wood
Kingscott
High Bickington
Chittlehamholt
23
Ashmansworthy
East Putford
West Putford
Haytown
Bradworthy
Bulkworthy
Abbots Bickington
Sutcombe
Venngreen
Milton Damerel
Holsworthy Beacon
Chilsworthy
Holsworthy
Hollacombe
Chasty
Langtree
Stibb Cross
Peters Marland
Newton St Petrock
Shebbear
Thornbury
Little Lashbrook
Cookbury
Bradford
Hole
Winswell
Merton
Huish
North Town
Petrockstow
Buckland Filleigh
Sheepwash
Black Torrington
Highampton
Meeth
Roborough
Beaford
Burrington
Ashreigney
Riddlecombe
Dolton
Chittlehampton
Hollocombe
Dowland
Iddesleigh
Ingleigh Green
Barwick
Wembworthy
Winkleigh
Broadwood Kelly
Splatt
Monkokehampton
Hatherleigh
Honeychurch
Exbourne
Jacobstowe
Sampford Courtenay
Bondleigh
Winsford Walled Garden
Halwill Junction
Halwill
Beaworthy
Northlew
Inwardleigh
Oak Cross
Ashbury
Folly Gate
Brightley
Clawton
Tetcott
Quoditch
Stowford
Broadbury
Ashwater
Luffincott
Eworthy
Southcott
Okehampton
Maddaford
Thorndon Cross
9
Germansweek
Chapmans Well
Virginstow
Northcott
Roadford Reservoir
Bratton Clovelly
Meldon
Meldon Reservoir
Dartmoor Railway
Belstone
Finch Foundry NT
South Tawton
Sticklepath
Taw Green
Corscombe
Sourton
618 YES TOR
621 HIGH WILLHAYS
548 CAWSAND BEACON
St Giles-on-the-Heath
Broadwoodwidger
Bridestowe
W Okement River
414 BUTTER HILL
Werrington
Stowford
Lewdown
Lobhillcross
Portgate
Lewtrenchard
Liftondown
Tinhay
Lifton
Dippertown
Lydford
Lydford Gorge NT
Beardon
568 GREAT KNEESET
605
602 WHITEHORSE HILL
Fernworthy Reservoir
538 SITTAFORD TOR
Launceston
Newport
Coryton
Marystow
South Petherwin
Lawhitton
Meadwell
Kelly
Chillaton
Quither
North Brentor
Hilltown
Hexworthy
Bradstone
Milton Abbot
Horndon
Cudliptown
Mary Tavy
517 LYNCH TOR
501 COCKS HILL
DARTMOOR
Postbridge
FOREST
6
Dunterton
Chaddlehanger
Peter Tavy
442 COXTOR
539 GREAT MIS TOR
Lamerton
Sydenham Damerel
Ottery
Kingston
Bray Shop
0 1 2 3 4 miles
0 1 2 3 4 5 kilometres
A39
A386
A377
B3227
B3232
A3124
B3217
A388
A3072
B3216
A3079
B3215
B3260
A30
B3362
B3357
River Torridge
River Taw
River Waldon
R Claw
River Tamar
R Okement
River Thrushel
Walkham
Blackbrook R

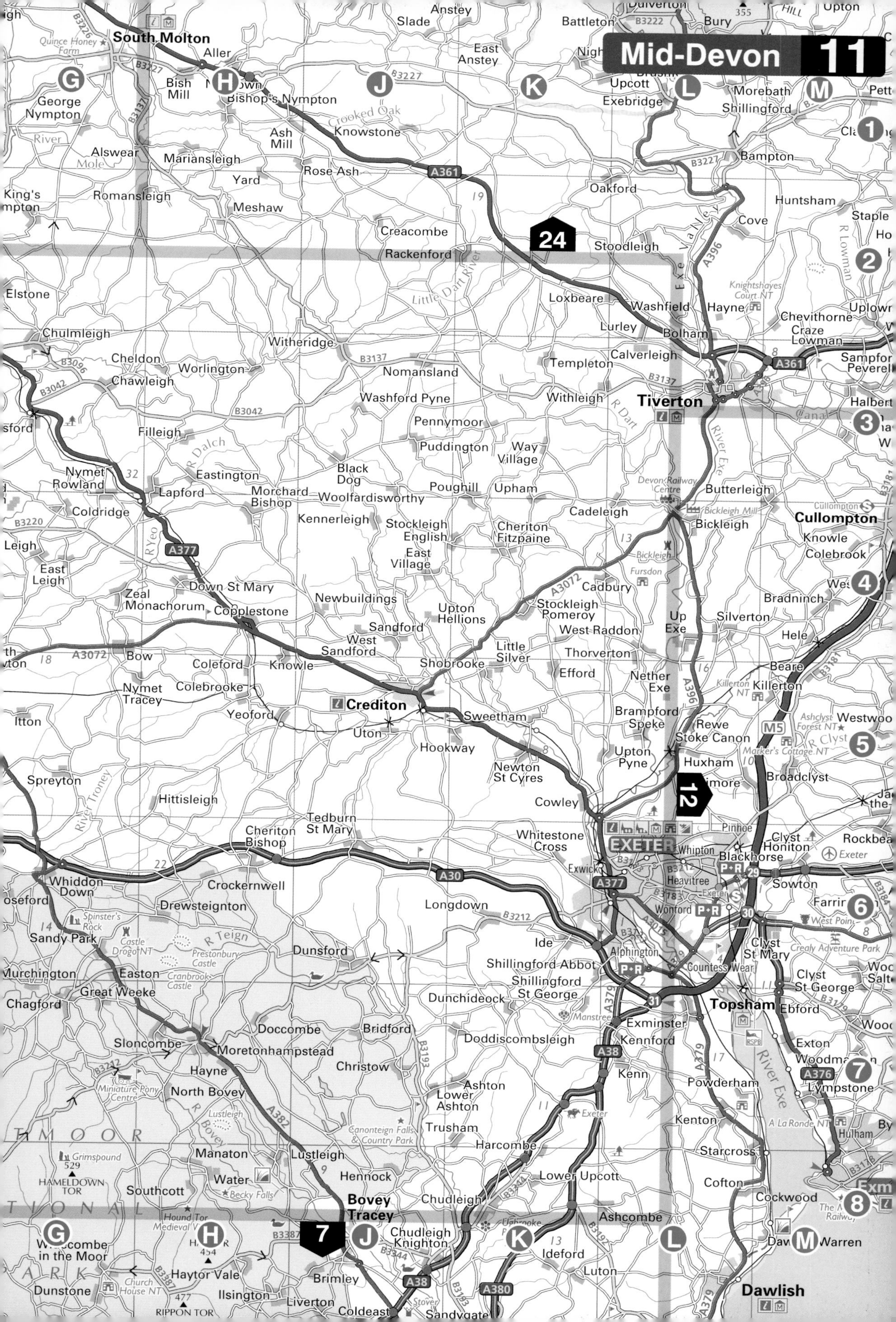

Mid-Devon
11
South Molton
Quince Honey Farm
Aller
Bish Mill
Bishop's Nympton
Anstey
Slade
East Anstey
Battleton
Bury
Upton
Upcott
Exebridge
Morebath
Shillingford
Bampton
George Nympton
River Mole
Alswear
Marriansleigh
Ash Mill
Knowstone
Crooked Oak
Rose Ash
Yard
Meshaw
Romansleigh
King's Nympton
Creacombe
Rackenford
Oakford
Huntsham
Cove
Staple
Stoodleigh
Little Dart River
Knightshayes Court NT
Elstone
Loxbeare
Washfield
Hayne
Chevithorne
Craze Lowman
Uplowman
Chulmleigh
Lurley
Bolham
Witheridge
Cheldon
Chawleigh
Worlington
Nomansland
Templeton
Calverleigh
Sampford Peverell
Withleigh
Tiverton
Halberton
Washford Pyne
Pennymoor
Filleigh
R Dalch
Puddington
Way Village
Nymet Rowland
Eastington
Black Dog
Poughill
Upham
Devon Railway Centre
Butterleigh
Lapford
Morchard Bishop
Woolfardisworthy
Cadeleigh
Bickleigh Mill
Bickleigh
Cullompton
Coldridge
Kennerleigh
Stockleigh English
Cheriton Fitzpaine
Knowle
Colebrook
Leigh
East Leigh
East Village
Fursdon
Down St Mary
Cadbury
Zeal Monachorum
Copplestone
Newbuildings
Upton Hellions
Stockleigh Pomeroy
Up Exe
Bradninch
Silverton
Sandford
West Raddon
West Sandford
Little Silver
Thorverton
Hele
Bow
Coleford
Knowle
Shobrooke
Efford
Nether Exe
Beare
Nymet Tracey
Colebrooke
Killerton NT
Killerton
Crediton
Brampford Speke
Ashclyst Forest NT
Westwood
Itton
Yeoford
Uton
Sweetham
Rewe
Stoke Canon
Hookway
Upton Pyne
Huxham
Marker's Cottage NT
Broadclyst
Spreyton
Newton St Cyres
River Troney
Hittisleigh
Cowley
Tedburn St Mary
Cheriton Bishop
Whitestone Cross
Pinhoe
EXETER
Whipton
Clyst Honiton
Blackhorse
Rockbeare
Exeter
Exwick
Heavitree
Whiddon Down
Crockernwell
Sowton
Drewsteignton
Longdown
Wonford
Farringdon
Spinster's Rock
Castle Drogo NT
R Teign
Prestonbury Castle
West Point
Sandy Park
Ide
Dunsford
Alphington
Clyst St Mary
Crealy Adventure Park
Easton
Cranbrook Castle
Shillingford Abbot
Countess Wear
Clyst St George
Murchington
Shillingford St George
Great Weeke
Chagford
Dunchideock
Topsham
Ebford
Manstree
Exminster
Doccombe
Bridford
Moretonhampstead
Doddiscombsleigh
Kennford
Exton
Sloncombe
RSPB
Christow
Kenn
Woodmanton
Hayne
Powderham
Miniature Pony Centre
North Bovey
Ashton
Lower Ashton
Lympstone
R Bovey
Lustleigh
Exeter
River Exe
Kenton
A La Ronde NT
Canonteign Falls & Country Park
Trusham
Hulham
DARTMOOR NATIONAL PARK
Harcombe
Grimspound
529
Manaton
Lustleigh
Starcross
Hameldown Tor
Water
Hennock
Lower Upcott
Southcott
Becky Falls
Cofton
Bovey Tracey
Chudleigh
Cockwood
Hound Tor Medieval Village
Ugbrooke
Ashcombe
The Railway
Widecombe in the Moor
Haytor
454
Chudleigh Knighton
Ideford
Dawlish Warren
Haytor Vale
Luton
Church House NT
Dunstone
477
Rippon Tor
Ilsington
Brimley
Liverton
Coldeast
Stover
Sandygate
Dawlish
A361
A396
A377
A3072
A30
A38
A379
A380
A382
A376
A3015
M5
B3227
B3137
B3042
B3096
B3220
B3212
B3193
B3344
B3387
B3192
B3181
B3179
B3178
24
12
7

12
Templeton
Withleigh
Lurley
Bolham
Calverleigh
Tiverton
Chevithorne
Craze Lowman
Sampford Peverell
Halberton
Ash Thomas
Willand
Whitnage
Ayshford
Appledore
Woodgate
Prescott
Culmstock
Craddock
Coldharbour Mill
Ashill
Davy
Rosemary Lane
Clayhidon
Hemyock
Stapley
Bolham Water
Churchinford
Bolham R
25
A
B
C
D
E
F
1
2
3
4
5
6
7
8
A361
A396
A3072
A377
A379
A38
A380
A381
A376
A3052
A3015
A375
A373
A30
M5
B3181
B3191
B3212
B3183
B3174
B3179
B3180
B3178
B3176
B3177
B3184
B3192
B3344
B3193
Way Village
Upham
Cadeleigh
Cheriton Fitzpaine
Devon Railway Centre
Bickleigh Mill
Bickleigh
Butterleigh
River Exe
R Dart
Fursdon
Cadbury
Stockleigh Pomeroy
West Raddon
Up Exe
Silverton
Little Silver
Thorverton
Efford
Nether Exe
Brampford Speke
Upton Pyne
Newton St Cyres
Cowley
Whitestone Cross
Exwick
EXETER
Whipton
Heavitree
Wonford
P+R
Ide
Alphington
Countess Wear
Shillingford Abbot
Shillingford St George
Dunchideock
Manstree
Exminster
Kennford
Kenn
Powderham
Kenton
Starcross
Cofton
Cockwood
Dawlish Warren
Dawlish
Holcombe
Teignmouth
Shaldon
Ringmore
R Teign
Bishopsteignton
Luton
Ideford
Ashcombe
Lower Upcott
Harcombe
Ugbrooke Park
Exeter
Ashton
Lower Ashton
Combe Cellars
Netherton
Combeinteignhead
Stokeinteignhead
Middle Rocombe
Lower Gabwell
Higher Gabwell
Maidencombe
Coffinswell
Daccombe
Abbotskerswell
Kingskerswell
Barton
Coombe Pafford
St Marychurch
Babbacombe Bay
Babbacombe Pottery
TORQUAY
Hopes Nose
Marldon
Rockend
Cullompton
Knowle
Colebrook
Westcott
Bradninch
Hele
Beare
Killerton NT
Killerton
Rewe
Stoke Canon
Huxham
Poltimore
Broadclyst
Ashclyst Forest NT
Westwood
Marker's Cottage NT
R Clyst
Pinhoe
Clyst Honiton
Blackhorse
Sowton
Rockbeare
Exeter
Farringdon
West Point
Crealy Adventure Park
Clyst St Mary
Clyst St George
Topsham
Ebford
Exton
Woodmanton
Lympstone
A La Ronde NT
Hulham
Exmouth
The Model Railway
World of Country Life
Littleham
Woodbury
Woodbury Salterton
Yettington
East Budleigh
Bicton Park
Dalditch
Bystock
Knowle
Budleigh Salterton
Kersbrook
Otterton
Otterton Mill
River Otter
Ladram Bay
East Devon Heritage Coast
Diggerland
Bradfield
Kentisbeare
Blackborough
Sheldon
Dunkeswell
Dulford
Kerswell
Wolford Chapel
Broadhembury
Hembury
Norman's Green
Colliton
Langford
Plymtree
Upton
Luton
Payhembury
Clyst Hydon
Clyst St Lawrence
Talaton
Newtown
Escot
Fenny Bridges
Whimple
Fairmile
Taleford
Hand and Pen
Cadhay
Jack-in-the-Green
Allercombe
Ottery St Mary
Aylesbeare
Marsh Green
West Hill
Fluxton
Wiggaton
Tipton St John
Coombe
Perkins Village
Venn Ottery
Southerton
Harpford
Bowd
Newton Poppleford
Colaton Raleigh
Pinn
Sidmouth
Sidford
Sidbury
Woolbrook
Salcombe Regis
The Donkey Sanctuary
Street
Weston
South West Coast Path
Harcombe
Southleigh
Blackbury Castle
Farway
Street
Church Green
Gittisham
Alfington
Feniton
Buckerell
Awliscombe
Weston
Honiton
Offwell
Combe Raleigh
Smeatharpe
Madford River
Upottery
Luppitt
Rawridge
Beacon
0 1 2 3 4 miles
0 1 2 3 4 5 kilometres

Broadway
Whitelackington
Seavington
Over Stratton
Little Norton
Buckland St Mary
Birch Wood
Horton
Donyatt
Ilminster
Kingstone
25
26
G
H
J
K
L
M
Combe St Nicholas
Beetham
Knowle St Giles
Wake
Ludney
St George
Merriott
Hardington Mandeville
East Coker
Northay
Wadeford
Chardleigh Green
Cudworth
Chillington
Higher Chillington
Haselbury Plucknett
Pendomer
Whitestaunton
Chaffcombe
Crewkerne
North Perrott
Hardington Marsh
Howley
Higher Wambrook
Purtington
Roundham
A303
A30
A358
A356
A3066
Cricket St Thomas
Hewish
Chard
Woolminstone
Misterton
South Perrott
BIRTS HILL
182
Yarcombe
Wambrook
Forton
Wayford
Clapton
Burridge
Whatley
Winsham
Seaborough
Mosterton
East Chelborough
Tatworth
Netherhay
Corscombe
STOCKLAND HILL
Stockland
Forde Abbey
Drimpton
River Axe
Chedington
Furley
Chard Junction
Laymore
B3162
Chardstock
Membury
Hewood
Blackdown
Benville
Alston
Tytherleigh
Thorncombe
Burstock
Broadwindsor
Cotleigh
Ham
Churchill
Holditch
B3164
B3163
Toller Whelme
Pilsdon Pen
Dalwood
Loughwood Meeting House NT
Birdsmoorgate
Stoke Abbott
Beaminster
Wilmington
Smallridge
Hawkchurch
B3165
Bettiscombe
Parnham
Mapperton
Hooke
A35
Axminster
Weycroft
Marshwood
Pilsdon
Netherbury
Melplash
North Poorton
Shute
Kilmington
Shute Barton NT
Monkton Wyld
Wootton Fitzpaine
Marshwood Vale
Broadoak
Whitchurch Canonicorum
Oxbridge
Waytown
Salwayash
West Milton
South Poorton
Powerstock
Nettlecombe
Whitford
Musbury
Maidenhayne
Harcombe Bottom
Catherston Leweston
Ryall
North Chideock
Bradpole
Loders
Uploders
Colyton
R Coly
Pymore
Symondsbury
Morcombelake
14
Uplyme
Charmouth
Allington
St Andrews Well
Colyford
Chideock
Walditch
Bothenhampton
Seaton
Axmouth
A3052
Lyme Regis
GOLDEN CAP
189
Seatown
Eype
Bridport
Watton
Rousdon
Seaton Tramway
B3174
Shipton Gorge
Chilcombe
Litton Cheney
West Dorset Heritage Coast
West Bay
Beer
Pecorama
Burton Bradstock
R Bride
B3157
Swyre
Heritage Coast
West Bexington
LYME BAY
Coast Path
1
2
3
4
5
6
7
8

14
Plucknett
Brympton
Barwick
A30
Sherborne
North Wootton
Allweston
Stourton Caundle
Bishop's Caundle
Lydlinch
St Mary
Sturminster Newton
Bagber
Manston
Hammoon
Fontmell Parva
Bradford Abbas
26
Folke
Caundle Marsh
A3030
A357
R. Stour
Hardington Moor
East Coker
Stoford
Thornford
Yetminster
Longburton
Holwell
Fifehead Neville
Sturminster Common
Fiddleford
Child Okeford
A
B
C
D
E
F
1
Hardington Marsh
Pendomer
Beer Hackett
Ryme Intrinseca
Knighton
Crouch Hill
King's Stag
Okeford Fitzpaine
Shillingstone
R. Lydden
A352
Closworth
Hamlet
Holnest
East Pulham
West Pulham
Kingston
Fifehead St Quintin
Belchalwell
A357
182
BIRTS HILL
Halstock
A37
Leigh
Glanvilles Wootton
B3146
Pulham
Droop
Belchalwell Street
Durweston
Melbury Osmond
Chetnole
Middlemarsh
Hazelbury Bryan
Ibberton
Turnworth
East Chelborough
Stockwood
Hermitage
Duntish
B3143
Stoke Wake
Woolland
Blandford
Corscombe
2
Melbury Bubb
Lyon's Gate
Bulbarrow Hill
Hilfield
Mappowder
Winterborne Houghton
Buckland Newton
Evershot
Minterne Magna
Henley
Higher Ansty
Winterborne Stickland
Holywell
Batcombe
Lower Ansty
Hilton
Winterborne Clenston
Benville
Uphall
Up Cerne
Alton Pancras
Melcombe Bingham
B3163
Rampisham
Frome St Quintin
The Giant
Milton
Toller Whelme
Lower Wraxhall
Up Sydling
Cerne Abbas
Plush
Bingham's Melcombe
Milton Abbas
Beaminster
Higher Wraxhall
Hooke
Mapperton
Rare Breeds Centre
3
Cattistock
Sydling St Nicholas
Piddletrenthide
Cheselbourne
North Poorton
Chilfrome
White Lackington
PUDDLETOWN DOWN
Dewlish
A354
Toller Porcorum
A356
Maiden Newton
Nether Cerne
Godmanstone
R. Cerne
Piddlehinton
Milborne St Andrew
13
South Poorton
Toller Fratrum
Hog Cliff
Milton
Powerstock
Nettlecombe
West Compton Abbas
Wynford Eagle
Frampton
Higher Waterston
Athelhampton
Tolpuddle
A35
Bere Regis
EGGARDON HILL
Loders
Uploders
Southover
Grimstone
Stratton
B3142
Puddletown
Compton Valence
Burleston
Affpuddle
Turners Puddle
Spyway
Askerswell
4
Bradford Peverell
Charminster
YELLOWHAM HILL
Athelhampton
Briantspuddle
Chideock
Kingston Russell
Hardy's Cottage NT
Tincleton
Higher Bockhampton
Pallington
Winterbourne Abbas
Dorchester
Stinsford
Woodsford
B3390
Chilcombe
15
Kingston Maurward
West Stafford
Clouds Hill NT
Litton Cheney
Long Bredy
Nine Stones
B3150
B3159
River Frome
R. Bride
Winterbourne Steepleton
Martinstown
Winterborne Came
Whitcombe
Moreton
Burton Bradstock
B3157
Littlebredy
Maiden Castle
Swyre
Puncknowle
Kingston Russell
West Knighton
Crossways
Tank
Abbotsbury Castle
Hardy Monument NT
Winterborne Monkton
A354
West Bexington
WHITE HILL
Portesham
Broadmayne
Warmwell
Owermoigne
Galton
Wool
5
Abbotsbury
South West Coast Path
20
A352
Bincombe
Watercombe
East Knighton
Chapel
Swannery
Rodden
White Horse
Poxwell
Osmington
Winfrith Newburgh
B3071
West Dorset Heritage Coast
Langton Herring
Preston
Upton
West Chaldon
East Chaldon (Chaldon Herring)
Lulworth Castle
Buckland Ripers
Overcombe
A353
Osmington Mills
CHALDON DOWN
RSPB
Weymouth Bay
Ringstead Bay
West Lulworth
B3070
BINDON HILL
B3157
Chickerell
Lulworth Cove
Chesil Beach
The Fleet
Fleet
Durdle Door
6
Water Gardens
Weymouth
Chesil Bank & The Fleet
Westham
Deep Sea Adventure
Nothe Fort
Lulworth Cove
Wyke Regis
Portland Harbour
A354
Portland
Fortuneswell
7
West Bay
Easton
PORTLAND
Portland Museum & Shipwreck Centre
Guernsey
Jersey
St Malo
Portland Bill Lighthouse
PORTLAND BILL
8
A
B
C
D
E
F
0 1 2 3 4 miles
0 1 2 3 4 5 kilometres

Dorset Coast
15
27
28
16
G
H
J
K
L
M
1
2
3
4
5
6
7
8
Waldron
New Town
Farnham
Gussage St Andrew
Chettle
Boveridge
Damerham
Burgate
Cranborne
Iwerne Minster
Gussage St Michael
Tarrant Hinton
Edmondsham
Alderholt
North Gorley
South Gorley
Ibsley
Dorset Heavy Horse Centre
Stourpaine
Pimperne
Tarrant Launceston
Tarrant Monkton
Long Crichel
Gussage All Saints
Moor Crichel
Romford
Verwood
Royal Signals
Woodlands
Horton
Manswood
Tarrant Rawston
Witchampton
Forum
Mannington
Three Legged Cross
Ringwood
Poulner
Charlton Marshall
Tarrant Rushton
Hinton Martell
Moors Valley
Charlton on the Hill
Tarrant Keyneston
St Leonards
Tarrant Crawford
Badbury Rings
Holt
West Moors
Kingston Great Common
Avon Heath
Spetisbury
Kingston Lacy NT
Shapwick
Abbott Street
Hillbutts
Colehill
Ferndown
FOXBURY HILL
Sandford
Bisterne
Sturminster Marshall
Pamphill
Wimborne Minster
Leigh Park
Hampreston
Knoll
Winterborne Zelston
Canford Magna
Longham
Dudsbury
West Parley
Bournemouth
Avon
Ripley
Bransgore
Hurn
Sopley
West Morden
Morden
Corfe Mullen
Bearwood
West Howe
Kinson
Cudnell
Ensbury
Red Hill
Alice in Wonderland
Throop
East Morden
Lytchett Matravers
Broadstone
East Howe
Moordown
Burton
Canford Heath
Wallisdown
Winton
Upton
Newtown
Branksome
Iford
Somerford
Christchurch
Organford
Lytchett Minster
Pokesdown
Tuckton
Wick
Mudeford
Hamworthy
Lake
Parkstone
Westbourne
Boscombe
Southbourne
Christchurch Bay
HENGISTBURY
Lower Hamworthy
Lilliput
Branksome Park
BOURNEMOUTH
POOLE
Sandford
Poole Harbour
Canford Cliffs
Arne
Northport
Binnegar
Wareham
Brownsea Island
Sandbanks
POOLE BAY
East Stoke
Stoborough
Ridge
Toll
Stoborough Heath
West Holme
East Holme
Purbeck Heritage Coast
Hartland Moor
Studland Bay
ISLE OF PURBECK
East Creech
East Lulworth
Purbeck Hills
Corfe Castle
Studland
THE FORELAND
(Summer Only)
Corfe Castle NT
Church Knowle
Swanage Railway
Harman's Cross
Ulwell
Ballard Point
Tyneham Village
Swanage Bay
Kingston
Kimmeridge
Swanage
Kimmeridge Bay
South West Coast Path
Langton Matravers
Durlston
Guernsey
Jersey
St Malo
Cherbourg
DURLSTON HEAD
Chapman's Pool
Worth Matravers
Anvil Point
Purbeck Heritage Coast
ST ALDHELM'S OR ST ALBAN'S HEAD
A350
A354
A31
A35
A351
A349
A341
A348
A347
A338
A3049
A3060
A3040
B3078
B3081
B3072
B3082
B3075
B3074
B3068
B3061
B3073
B3347
B3369
B3065
B3070
B3351
B3069

28
15
Bramshaw
Newbridge
Copythorne
Brook Hill
Fritham
Brook
Cadnam
Winsor
Calmore
Testwood
M271
Shirley
Portswood
West End
Bitterne
M27
Millbrook
Rufus Stone
Bartley
Netley Marsh
Totton
Eling
Northam
Sholing
North Gorley
South Gorley
Ibsley Common NT
Furzey
Woodlands
Minstead
Ashurst
SOUTHAMPTON
Longdown Dairy Farm
Woolston
Isle of Wight Ferry Terminal
Marchwood
Bursledon
Rockford Common NT
Emery Down
Lyndhurst
Otter & Owl Centre
Dibden
Netley
Southampton Water
Royal Victoria
Bank
Beaulieu River
Langdown
Dibden Purlieu
Hythe
Hamble-le-Rice
Warsash
A31
A35
A337
A336
NEW FOREST NATIONAL PARK
(Proposed Area)
Burley Street
B3056
A326
Hardley
Holbury
Fawley
B3054
Kingston Great Common
National Motor Museum
Blackfield
B3053
MARKWAY HILL
Burley
Brockenhurst
B3055
Beaulieu
Calshot
Sandford
Bisterne
Bucklers Hard
Langley
Stanswood Bay
Thorney Hill
East Boldre
Exbury
Ripley
Sway
Boldre
Bransgore
B3058
Pilley
Norleywood
Spinners
Needs Ore Point
South Baddesley
Cowes
East End
Gurnard Bay
Gurnard
New Milton
Ashley
Hordle
Lymington
Burton
Walkford
Everton
Braxton
Rew Street
Thorness Bay
Somerford
Highcliffe
Highcliffe Castle
Barton-on-Sea
Downton
Hamstead Heritage Coast
Northwood
Christchurch
Newtown Bay
Mudeford
Wick
Christchurch Bay
Keyhaven
Porchfield
Newtown
Milford on Sea
Old Town Hall NT
A3020
HENGISTBURY HEAD
Sconce Point
Yarmouth
Hurst
A3054
Ningwood
Shalfleet
Carisbrooke
Colwell Bay
Thorley Street
B3401
Totland
Norton Green
Newbridge
Totland Bay
Wellow
Freshwater
Watermill
ISLE
Afton
Afton Down NT & Compton Down NT
Chessell Pottery
Calbourne
Bowcombe
Alum Bay
Dimbola Lodge
B3399
BRIGHSTONE DOWN
Blackwater
B3322
BROOK DOWN NT
B3323
Gatcombe
THE NEEDLES
Needles Old Battery NT
Compton Bay
Brook
Hulverstone
Chillerton
Hanover Point
Mottistone
Limerstone
Shorwell
Tennyson Heritage Coast
Brighstone
Chilton Chine
Kingston
Brighstone Bay
A3055
Chale Green
Atherfield Point
St Catherine's Oratory
Whale Chine
Chale
Blackgang Chine
Rocken End
ST CATHERINE'S POINT
Cherbourg
0 1 2 3 4 miles
0 1 2 3 4 5 kilometres

Durley
Waltham Chase
Shirrell Heath
Soberton Heath
Hambledon
Catherington
Chalton
Curdridge
Shedfield
Newtown
Blendworth
Wickham
Forestside
Curbridge
Worlds End
Soake
Stoughton
Burridge
North Boarhunt
Cowplain
Rowland's Castle
Bow Hill
WATERLOOVILLE
Walderton
Swanwick
Southwick
Westbourne
Funtington
Woodend
West Stoke
Boarhunt
Ports Down
Purbrook
Stakes
HAVANT
Woodmancote
Mid Lavant
Royal Armouries
West Ashling
East Ashling
Wallington
Bedhampton
Hambrook
Catisfield
Cosham
Drayton
Southbourne
Broadbridge
Titchfield
FAREHAM
Portchester
Farlington
Brockhampton
Langstone
Emsworth
Nutbourne
Walton
Fishbourne
Castle
Portsmouth Harbour
Northney
Chidham
Bosham
Stubbington
Hilsea
THORNEY ISLAND
Dell Quay
Bridgemary
Whale Island
North End
North Hayling
Hill Head
Elson
Continental Ferry Terminal
Langstone Harbour
Stoke
HAYLING ISLAND
West Thorney
Donnington
Fort Brockhurst
Rowner
Hardway
GOSPORT
Portsea
Fratton
West Itchenor
Birdham
Lee-on-the-Solent
South Hayling
Chichester Harbour
Spinnaker Tower
Isle of Wight Ferry Terminal
Southsea
West Town
Shipton Green
Stokes Bay
Alverstoke
Eastney
Somerley
PORTSMOUTH
Hayling Bay
West Wittering
East Wittering
Gilkicker Point
Spitbank Fort
Earnley
Osborne
East Cowes
Osborne House
Bay
SPITHEAD
Bracklesham Bay
Whippingham
Fishbourne
Ryde
Wootton Bridge
Binstead
Puckpool Point
Flamingo Park
Nettlestone Point
Seaview
Brickfields Horse Country
Rosemary
Havenstreet
Nettlestone
(Summer Only)
Isle of Wight Steam Railway
Little Whitefield
St Helens
The Duver NT
Robin Hill
East Ashey
Bembridge
Bembridge Windmill NT
Life Boat Station
FORELAND
Newport
Nunwell
Brading
Cherbourg
Guernsey
Jersey
St Malo
Caen (Ouistreham)
Le Havre
Bilbao
Cherbourg
Caen (Ouistreham)
Arreton
Haseley Manor
Newchurch
Alverstone
Bembridge Down NT
Whitecliff Bay
Dinosaur Isle
Merstone
Queen's Bower
Yaverland
Culver Cliff
Rookley
Winford
Sandown
Branstone
Lake
Sandown Bay
Apse Heath
Sandford
Whiteley Bank
Shanklin
Old Smithy & Gardens
Shanklin Chine
Luccombe Village
Luccombe Chine
Appuldurcombe
Wroxall
Ventnor Down NT
DUNNOSE
Whitwell
Ventnor
IOW Glass
Botanic Garden
Rare Breeds and Waterfowl Park
St Lawrence
The Undercliffe
Binnel Bay
M27
M275
A3(M)
A27
A32
A3
A259
A2030
A3023
A286
A3054
A3055
A3056
A3020
A3021
B3333
B3334
B3385
B3330
B3395
B3327
B2177
B2150
B2149
B2148
B2147
B2146
B2178
B2179
B2198
B2145
29
30
18
G
H
J
K
L
M
1
2
3
4
5
6
7
8

18
Liphook
Linchmere
Kingsley Green
Hollycombe Steam
Fernhurst
Milland
Woodmansgreen
Redford
Henley
Black Down NT
280
BLACKDOWN HILL
Lurgashall
Lickfold
Northchapel
Ebernoe Common
Plaistow
Loxwood
Toyhorse Int Stud Farm
Slinfold
Broadbridge Heath
Five Oaks
Barns Green
Kirdford
Fishers
Billingshurst
Balls Cross
Wisborough Green
Coneyhurst Common
Fyning
SOUTH DOWNS
Chithurst
Iping
Woolbeding
Lodsworth
River
Upperton
Petworth House NT
Petworth
Byworth
Adversane
Broadford Bridge
Coolham
R Rother
Trotton
Stedham
Easebourne
Midhurst
Tillington
Nyewood
Harting
NATIONAL PARK
30
Minsted
Selham
Little Bognor
Codmore Hill
River Arun
Elsted
Cocking Causeway
West Lavington
South Ambersham
Fittleworth
Stopham
Nutbourne
Dial Post
Didling
(Proposed Area)
Pulborough
Marehill
Holly Gate Cactus Garden
Treyford
249
Bepton
LINCH DOWN
Cocking
Upper Norwood
Duncton
Coates
Hardham
West Chiltington
Thakeham
Heyshott
Graffham
Coldwaltham
RSPB
Ashington
North Marden
South Downs Way
Duncton Hill
Barlavington
Greatham
East Lavington
Roman Villa
Watersfield
Chilgrove
LEVIN DOWN
170
255
DUNCTON HILL
Sutton
Parham
Storrington
Singleton
Bignor
225
BIGNOR HILL
Rackham
Marden
West Dean
Upwaltham
Amberley
212
KITHURST HILL
Washington
Charlton
East Dean
Bury
Houghton
Amberley Museum
Weald & Downland
Goodwood
The Trundle
206
THE TRUNDLE
Halnaker Hill
North Stoke
Bow Hill
Kingley Vale
144
NORE HILL
South Stoke
Burpham
167
HARROW HILL
Eartham
West Stoke
East Lavant
Offham
Wepham
Findon
Mid Lavant
Waterbeach
Slindon
Wildfowl & Wetlands Trust
Cissbury Ring
Goodwood
Strettington
Fontwell Park
Halnaker
Fontwell
Arundel
Warningcamp
Clapham
East Ashling
Summersdale
Boxgrove
Binsted
Poling Corner
Patching
High Salvington
Broadbridge
Tangmere
Norton
Nyton
Denmans Garden
Walberton
Westhampnett
Aldingbourne
Eastergate
Poling
HIGHDOWN HILL
Durrington
Salvington
Walton
Palace
Westergate
Fishbourne
Chichester
Oving
Woodgate
North End
Lyminster
Wick
Angmering
West Tarring
Broadwater
Bosham
Apuldram
Merston
Barnham
Yapton
Ford
Dell Quay
Colworth
Climping
Rustington
East Preston
Ferring
Goring-by-Sea
West Worthing
Donnington
Runcton
Shripney
Bilsham
Littlehampton
Hunston
North Mundham
North Bersted
Birdham
South Mundham
South Bersted
Flansham
Street End
Sidlesham
Rose Green
Felpham
Middleton-on-Sea
Aldwick
Highleigh
Nyetimber
BOGNOR REGIS
17
Pagham Harbour
Pagham
Earnley
Church Norton
Wittering Bay
Selsey
SELSEY BILL
A
B
C
D
E
F
1
2
3
4
5
6
7
8
0 1 2 3 4 miles
0 1 2 3 4 5 kilometres
A272
A286
A283
A29
A264
A285
A27
A284
A24
A280
A259
A2032
B2131
B2070
B2133
B2138
B2139
B2141
B2146
B2178
B2201
B2166
B2145
B2179
B2198
B2233
B2132
B2187
B2140
B2132

Horsham
St Leonards Forest
West Hoathly
Balcombe
Handcross
Wakehurst Place NT
South of England
Highbrook
Ardingly Reservoir
Staplefield
Ardingly
Horsted Keynes
Bluebell Railway
Ouse Valley
Manning's Heath
Lower Beeding
Slaugham
Monk's Gate
Southwater
Warninglid
Leonardslee
Nuthurst
Crabtree
Copsale
Maplehurst
Cuckfield
Lindfield
Danehill
Nutley
Fairwarp
Haywards Heath
Maresfield
Five Ash Down
Buxted
Sheffield Park/NT
Splayne's Green
Fletching
Scayne's Hill
Ansty
Bolney
West Grinstead
Cowfold
Piltdown
Newick
Uckfield
Wineham
Hickstead
Worlds End
Wivelsfield
North Chailey
Partridge Green
Twineham
Burgess Hill
Wivelsfield Green
Chailey
New Town
Ridgewood
East Sussex National
Lavender Line
Sayers Common
South Chailey
Town Littleworth
Little Horsted
Isfield
Henfield
Blackstone
Hurstpierpoint
Plumpton Green
Halland
Keymer
Albourne
East Chiltington
Barcombe Cross
Bentley Wildfowl & Motor Museum
Hassocks
Ditchling
Woodmancote
Street
Barcombe
Upper Wellingham
Clayton
Westmeston
Plumpton
Laughton
Woods Mill
Pyecombe
Hamsey
Small Dole
Ditchling Beacon
South Downs National Park (Proposed Area)
Mount Harry
Offham
Ringmer
Edburton
Poynings
Upper Beeding
Truleigh Hill
Fulking
Devil's Dyke
Pangdean
Saddlescombe
South Malling
Bramber
Lewes
Wallands Park
Stanmer
Mount Caburn
Glynde
Botolphs
Patcham
Coldean
Kingston
Coombes
Withdean
Hollingbury
Falmer
Beddingham
West Firle
Lancing College Chapel
Mile Oak
Hangleton
Moulsecoomb
South Downs Way
Iford
Rodmell
Charleston Farmhouse
West Blatchington
Portslade
Old Shoreham
Preston
Newmarket Hill
Breaky Bottom
Monk's House NT
Firle Place
Firle Beacon
Shoreham
Southwick
Woodingdean
Southease
Tarring Neville
Lancing
Shoreham-by-Sea
Portslade-by-Sea
Hove
Brighton
Kemp Town
Ovingdean
Telscombe
Worthing
Rottingdean
Saltdean
Piddinghoe
Paradise Park
Denton
Newhaven
Norton
Bishopstone
East Blatchington
Peacehaven
Fort
Seaford Bay
Sutton
Seaford
Seaford Head
Dieppe
Dieppe
(Summer Only)
South Downs
20
31
32

20
Mark Cross
Sparrows Green
Wadhurst
Three Leg Cross
Flimwell
Hawkhurst
Tidebrook
Rotherfield
Ticehurst
The Moor
Pashley Manor
River Limden
Stonegate
Sweethaws
Fairwarp
Witherenden Hill
Hurst Green
Kent Ditch
Etchingham
Mayfield
River Rother
Bodiam
Bodiam Castle NT
High Hurstwood
Five Ash Down
Pound Green
32
Five Ashes
33
Burwash
Salehurst
Buxted
Hadlow Down
Bateman's NT
Robertsbridge
Staple Cross
Broad Oak
Burwash Common
Burwash Weald
Cross in Hand
Heathfield
Cade St
R Dudwell
Uckfield
Blackboys
Framfield
Brightling
Punnett's Town
Mountfield
New Town
Three Cups Corner
Wood's Corner
Ridgewood
Little London
Waldron
Maynard's Green
Dallington
Netherfield
Whatlington
Rushlake Green
Little Horsted
Warbleton
Netherfield Road
Battle
Vines Cross
Horam
Ponts Green
Halland
East Hoathly
1066
Bodle Street Green
Hale Green
Gun Hill
Cowbeech
Shortgate
Chiddingly
Catsfield
Whitesmith
Laughton
Muddles Green
Crowhurst
Herstmonceux
Windmill Hill
Ninfield
Henley's Down
Hellingly
The Truggery
Lower Dicker
Horsebridge
Magham Down
Boreham Street
Lunsford's Cross
Ripe
Upper Dicker
Knockhatch
Leap Cross
Hailsham
Herstmonceux Castle & Observatory
Hooe
St Leonards
Mount Caburn
Chalvington
Michelham Priory
Wartling
Little Common
Sidley
Pevensey Levels
Cooden
West Firle
Selmeston
Arlington
Firle Place
Charleston Farmhouse
Bexhill
219
FIRLE BEACON
Alciston
Cuckmere R
Polegate
Berwick
Drusillas
Westham
Pevensey
Wilmington
Wannock
Folkington
Lower Willingdon
Alfriston
The Long Man of Wilmington
Willingdon
Hampden Park
Langney
Clergy House NT
Pevensey Bay
Norton
Litlington
Ratton Village
St Anthony's Hill
Bishopstone
Jevington
Roselands
East Blatchington
South Downs Way
Langney Point
Westdean
Sutton
Old Town
Friston
Seaford
EASTBOURNE
Seven Sisters
East Dean
South Downs Way
Seaford Head
Beachy Head Countryside Centre
Sussex Heritage Coast
BEACHY HEAD
Dieppe
Summer Only
A26
A21
A267
A265
A272
A22
A2100
A271
A269
A27
A259
A295
A2270
A2280
A2021
A2036
B2100
B2101
B2102
B2192
B2124
B2096
B2203
B2204
B2095
B2104
B2182
B2103
B2244
B2092
B2159
A
B
C
D
E
F
1
2
3
4
5
6
7
8
0 1 2 3 4 miles
0 1 2 3 4 5 kilometres

Historic Vehicles Collection
Rolvenden
Rolvenden Layne
Tenterden Vineyard Park
Small Hythe
Reading Street
B2080
34
Eastbou
A2070
Snargate
Brenzett
A259
Brookland
Kent & East Sussex Railway
Newenden
Wittersham
ISLE OF OXNEY
Stone
The Stocks
Rother Levels
River Rother
Royal Military Canal
Northiam
B2088
A268
Beckley
Clayhill
B2165
Peasmarsh
Rye Foreign
Iden
Houghton Green
WALLAND MARSH
Playden
Rye
East Guldeford
Broad Oak
R. Tillingham
Cock Marling
B2089
Broadland Row
Udimore
Brede
River Brede
Camber
Winchelsea
Broad Street
Icklesham
A28
Rye Bay
Power Station Visitor Centre
Old Lighthouse
DUNGENESS
Three Oaks
Guestling Thorn
Guestling Green
Pett
Idslow
Cliff End
Ore
Fairlight
HASTINGS
22
A
B
1
2
3
4
5
6
7
8
G
H
J
K
L
M

C
D
E
F
North West Point
Lundy Heritage Coast
LUNDY
142
Marisco
Surf Point
Shutter Point
3
Baggy Point
Croyde B
4
BARNSTAPLE
OR
BIDEFORD BAY
5
Westward
Shipload Bay
HARTLAND POINT
Titchberry
Abbotsham
Damehole Point
Hartland Abbey & Garden
Hartland Heritage Coast
Stoke
Clovelly
Ford
Hartland Quay
B3248
B3237
Fairy Cross
6
Hartland
Buck's Mills
Horns Cross
Woodtown
Spekes Mill Mouth
Philham
A39
Buck's Cross
Goldworthy
Milky Way
Woolfardisworthy
Parkham
Hardisworthy
Buckland Brewer
Frith
Welcombe
Ashmansworthy
7
Darracott
9
East Putford
East Youlstone
West Putford
Morwenstow
Dinworthy
Haytown
Higher Sharpnose Point
West Youlstone
Bradworthy
Shop
Killarney Springs
Bulkworthy
South West Coast Path
Woodford
Tamar Lakes
Abbots Bickington
8
Lower Sharpnose Point
A388
Kilkhampton
Sutcombe
Steeple Point
Brocklands
River
Milton Damerel
A
B
Sandy Mouth
A39
B3254
Northcott Mouth
Poughill
Dunsdon
Holsworthy Beacon
Thornbury
0 1 2 3 4 miles
0 1 2 3 4 5 kilometres

Ilfracombe
Lynton
Lynmouth
Countisbury
Combe Martin
Berrynarbor
Barnstaple
Braunton
Bideford
Northam
Great Torrington
South Molton
Chulmleigh
EXMOOR FOREST
River Taw
Morte Bay
Woolacombe
Mortehoe
Croyde
Saunton
Georgeham
Instow
Appledore
Westleigh
Fremington
Bickington
Newport
Landkey
Swimbridge
Chittlehampton
Umberleigh
Atherington
Yarnscombe
Kingsheanton
Muddiford
Shirwell
Arlington
Parracombe
Kentisbury
Martinhoe
Trentishoe
Barbrook
Challacombe
North Molton
Eggesford
Dolton
Beaford
Burrington
Roborough
Merton
Winkleigh
Lapford
Chawleigh
Cheldon
Romansleigh
King's Nympton
George Nympton
Filleigh
Heasley Mill
Brayford
Stoke Rivers
Goodleigh
Pilton
Chivenor
Wrafton
Knowle
Marwood
West Down
Bittadon
East Down
Trimstone
Lee
Slade
Hele
Rockford
Brendon
Watersmeet House NT
Foreland Point
HOAROAK HILL 474
SPAN HEAD
A39
A361
A399
A3123
A377
A386
A3124
A3125
B3226
B3227
B3230
B3231
B3232
B3233
B3343
B3358
B3042
B3096
B3217
B3137
24
10

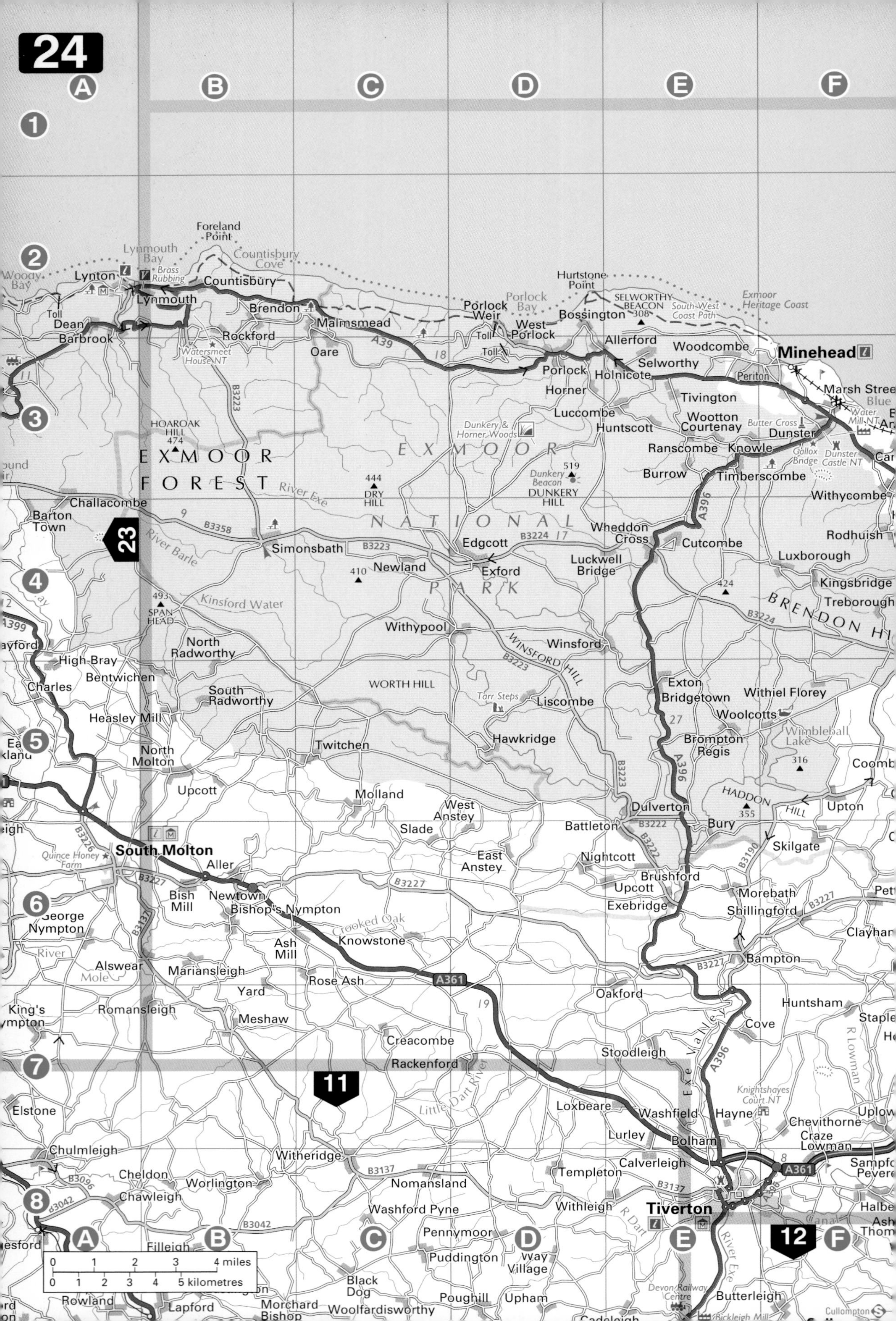

Foreland Point
Lynmouth Bay
Countisbury Cove
Woody Bay
Lynton
Brass Rubbing
Countisbury
Lynmouth
Brendon
Toll
Dean
Barbrook
Rockford
Watersmeet House NT
Malmsmead
Oare
A39
Porlock Weir
Porlock Bay
Hurtstone Point
SELWORTHY BEACON 308
Bossington
South West Coast Path
Exmoor Heritage Coast
West Porlock
Allerford
Woodcombe
Minehead
Porlock
Holnicote
Selworthy
Periton
Horner
Tivington
Marsh Street
Blue Anchor
Luccombe
Wootton Courtenay
Water Mill NT
Huntscott
Butter Cross
Dunster
Dunkery & Horner Woods
B3223
HOAROAK HILL 474
EXMOOR FOREST
EXMOOR NATIONAL PARK
Ranscombe
Knowle
Gallox Bridge
Dunster Castle NT
Carhampton
Burrow
Timberscombe
Withycombe
Dunkery Beacon 519
DUNKERY HILL
444 DRY HILL
River Exe
Challacombe
Barton Town
B3358
River Barle
Wheddon Cross
Rodhuish
Cutcombe
Luxborough
Simonsbath
B3223
Edgcott
B3224
Exford
Newland
410
Luckwell Bridge
424
Kingsbridge
Treborough
BRENDON HILLS
B3224
493 SPAN HEAD
Kinsford Water
A399
Withypool
North Radworthy
Winsford
WINSFORD HILL
High Bray
Bentwichen
Charles
WORTH HILL
Exton
Bridgetown
Withiel Florey
South Radworthy
Tarr Steps
Liscombe
Woolcotts
Heasley Mill
A396
Wimbleball Lake
Brompton Regis
Hawkridge
Twitchen
North Molton
316
Coombe
Upcott
Molland
West Anstey
Dulverton
HADDON HILL 355
Upton
Slade
Battleton
B3222
Bury
B3226
South Molton
Quince Honey Farm
Aller
East Anstey
Nightcott
B3190
Skilgate
Brushford
B3227
Bish Mill
Newtown
Bishop's Nympton
Upcott
Exebridge
Morebath
Shillingford
George Nympton
B3137
Crooked Oak
Knowstone
Clayhanger
River Mole
Alswear
Mariansleigh
Ash Mill
Bampton
Rose Ash
A361
Yard
Oakford
Huntsham
King's Nympton
Romansleigh
Meshaw
Cove
Staple
R Lowman
Creacombe
Stoodleigh
Exe Valley
Rackenford
Little Dart River
Elstone
Loxbeare
Washfield
Knightshayes Court NT
Hayne
Uplowman
Chevithorne
Lurley
Craze Lowman
Chulmleigh
Bolham
Witheridge
B3137
Calverleigh
Sampford Peverell
Cheldon
Templeton
B3096
Worlington
Chawleigh
Nomansland
B3042
Washford Pyne
Withleigh
R Dart
Tiverton
Halberton
Ash Thomas
Canal
Pennymoor
Filleigh
Puddington
Way Village
River Exe
0 1 2 3 4 miles
0 1 2 3 4 5 kilometres
Black Dog
Devon Railway Centre
Rowland
Lapford
Morchard Bishop
Woolfardisworthy
Poughill
Upham
Butterleigh
Bickleigh Mill
Cadeleigh
Cullompton

Exmoor & Taunton
25
Steep Holm
WESTON-SUPER-MARE
A371
37
26
12
13
G
H
J
K
L
M
1
2
3
4
5
6
7
8
Oldmixon
Bleadon
Brean
Loxton
A370
Lympsham
Edingworth
Biddisham
Sedgemoor
East Brent
Berrow
B3140
Brent Knoll
Edithmead
Burnham-on-Sea
Highbridge
BRIDGWATER
BAY
Hinkley Point Visitor Centre
Stolford
Steart
Huntspill
Secret World
Bason Bridge
East Huntspill
West Huntspill
Stretcholt
M5
A38
B3141
Combwich
Pawlett
Puriton
Woolavington
Dunball
Chilton Trinity
Cossington
Chilton Polden
Horsey
Bawdrip
POLDEN
Cannington
Wembdon
Bridgwater
Chedzoy
Durleigh
Lexworthy
Bussex
Huntworth
Westonzoyland
Middlezoy
North Petherton
Shearston
North Newton
St Michael Church
Burrow Bridge
Burrow Mump
A361
Lyng
Hedging
Durston
Athelney
Willow Craft
West Lyng
Woodhill
Stoke St Gregory
Creech Heathfield
Meare Green
Charlton
Creech St Michael
Knapp
Huntham
Heale
North Curry
Ham
Ruishton
Henlade
Thornfalcon
Greenway
RSPB
A378
Wrantage
Curry Mallet
Fivehead
Isle Brewers
Abbotts
Meare Green
Stoke St Mary
A358
West Hatch
Hatch Beauchamp
Beercrocombe
Westport
Stewley
Ashill
Ilton
Puckington
Ilford
Kenny
Windmill Hill
Curland
A303
Whitelackington
Blackwater
Broadway
Horton
Donyatt
Ilminster
Kingstone
Knowle St Giles
Combe St Nicholas
Chardleigh Green
Cudworth
Chaffcombe
Cricket St Thomas
Wadeford
Whitestaunton
Higher Wambrook
Howley
A30
Newtown
Beetham
Buckland St Mary
Birch Wood
Bishopswood
Churchinford
Churchstanton
STAPLE HILL
Blackwater
Lilstock
Knighton
Stockland Bristol
Burton
Shurton
Otterhampton
Stogursey
Stringston
Kilve
East Quantoxhead
St Audries Bay
West Somerset Railway
Watchet
B3191
Doniford
Old Cleeve
Tropiquaria
Washford
Cleeve
Williton
West Quantoxhead
Staple
Weacombe
Woolston
Sampford Brett
Holford
Dodington
Coleridge Cottage NT
Nether Stowey
Woodlands
Fiddington
A39
Over Stowey
Aley
QUANTOCK HILLS
Bicknoller
Newton
Kingswood
Halsway
Charlinch
Adscombe
Spaxton
Four Forks
Enmore
Crowcombe
Lower Roadwater
Roadwater
B3188
Monksilver
Stogumber
Preston
Lawford
A358
Combe Sydenham
Elworthy
B3190
B3224
Triscombe
Aisholt
Lower Aisholt
Lower Merridge
Flaxpool
Lower Vexford
Willett
Courtway
Goathurst
Huntstile
Clatworthy Reservoir
Brompton Ralph
Rooks Nest
Coleford Water
Seven Ash
Tolland
Lydeard St Lawrence
West Bagborough
Combe Florey
East Combe
Fyne Court NT
Broomfield
Toulton
Clatworthy
Gaulden Manor
Pyleigh
Bishops Lydeard
Ash Priors
Kingston St Mary
Thurloxton
West Newton
Whitefield
Tarr
West Leigh
Langley Marsh
Chapel Leigh
Ford
Northway
Pickney
Fulford
Adsborough
Hestercombe
Gotton
Maundown
Langley
Fitzhead
Halse
Nailsbourne
Wiveliscombe
B3227
Vale of Taunton Deane
Preston Bowyer
Heathfield
Cheddon Fitzpaine
Staplegrove
West Monkton
Monkton Heathfield
Langaller
Bathpool
B3187
Milverton
Hillcommon
Norton Fitzwarren
A3027
Hele
Bishops Hull
R Tone
Waterrow
Oake
Hillfarrance
Taunton
Bradford-on-Tone
Langford Budville
Bathealton
Kittisford
Cider Farm
Trull
Stawley
Runnington
Dipford
West Buckland
Staplehay
Shoreditch
Orchard Portman
Thurlbear
Taunton
Thorne St Margaret
Appley
Tonedale
Holywell Lake
Wellington
Greenham
Duddlestone
Heale
Corfe
Taunton Deane
Slough Green
Pitminster
Staple Fitzpaine
Blagdon
A38
White Ball
Sampford Arundel
Ford Street
Lowton
M5
Sampford Moor
Wrangway
Wellington Monument
Red Ball
Westleigh
Holcombe Rogus
BLACKDOWN HILLS
Blagdon Hill
B3170
Burlescombe
Nicholashayne
Simons Burrow
Ayshford
Culm Davy
Appledore
Woodgate
Rosemary Lane
Clayhidon
Burnworthy
B3391
Prescott
Culmstock
Hemyock
Stapley
Uffculme
Bolham Water
Craddock
Coldharbour Mill
Bolham R
Ashill
Smeatharpe
Blackborough
Diggerland
Bradfield
Kentisbeare
Sheldon
Madford River
R Otter

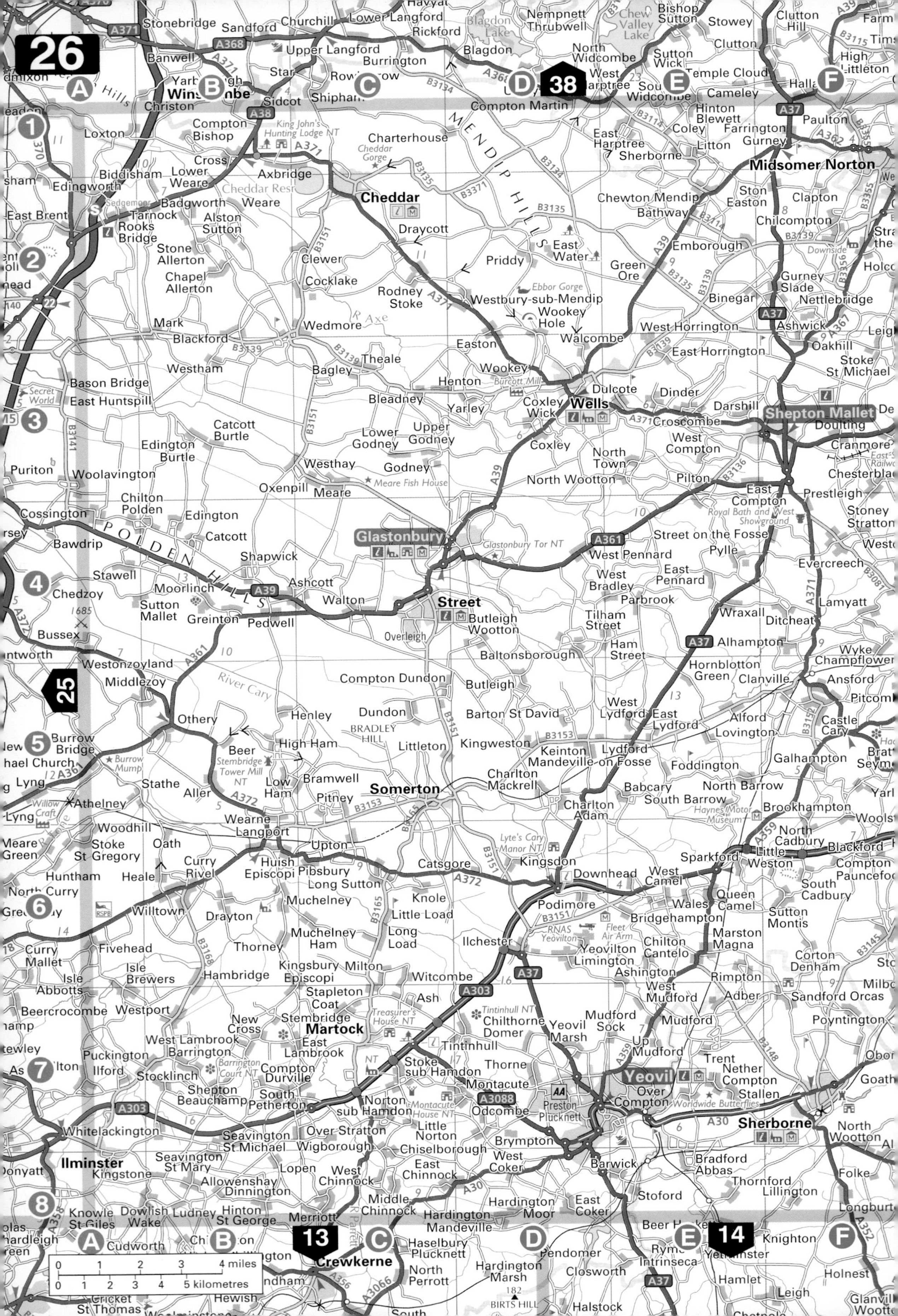

26
Stonebridge
Sandford
Churchill
Lower Langford
Rickford
Blagdon Lake
Nempnett Thrubwell
Chew Valley Lake
Bishop Sutton
Stowey
Clutton Hill
Clutton
Banwell
Upper Langford
Burrington
Blagdon
North Widcombe
Sutton Wick
Temple Cloud
High Littleton
Yarborough
Winscombe
Star
Rowberrow
West Harptree
South Widcombe
Cameley
Hallatrow
Christon
Sidcot
Shipham
Compton Martin
Hinton Blewett
Paulton
Loxton
Compton Bishop
King John's Hunting Lodge NT
Charterhouse
MENDIP HILLS
East Harptree
Coley
Farrington Gurney
Litton
Sherborne
Cross
Cheddar Gorge
Midsomer Norton
Biddisham
Lower Weare
Axbridge
Edingworth
Cheddar Resr
Cheddar
Chewton Mendip
Ston Easton
Clapton
Sedgemoor
Badgworth
Weare
East Brent
Tarnock
Alston Sutton
Bathway
Chilcompton
Rooks Bridge
Draycott
Emborough
Downside
Stone Allerton
East Water
Clewer
Priddy
Green Ore
Gurney Slade
Chapel Allerton
Cocklake
Ebbor Gorge
Binegar
Rodney Stoke
Westbury-sub-Mendip
Nettlebridge
Wookey Hole
Mark
Wedmore
R Axe
Ashwick
Blackford
West Horrington
Walcombe
Oakhill
Easton
Theale
East Horrington
Stoke St Michael
Westham
Bagley
Wookey
Bason Bridge
Henton
Burcott Mill
Dulcote
Dinder
Secret World
East Huntspill
Bleadney
Yarley
Coxley Wick
Wells
Darshill
Shepton Mallet
Croscombe
Doulting
Catcott Burtle
Upper Godney
Lower Godney
Coxley
West Compton
Cranmore
Edington Burtle
East Somerset Railway
Puriton
Woolavington
Westhay
Godney
North Town
Chesterblade
Oxenpill
Meare
Meare Fish House
North Wootton
Pilton
Prestleigh
Chilton Polden
East Compton
Cossington
Edington
Royal Bath and West Showground
Stoney Stratton
Catcott
Glastonbury
Street on the Fosse
Bawdrip
POLDEN HILLS
Shapwick
Glastonbury Tor NT
West Pennard
Pylle
Stawell
Ashcott
West Bradley
East Pennard
Evercreech
Chedzoy
Moorlinch
Walton
Street
Parbrook
Lamyatt
Sutton Mallet
Greinton
Pedwell
Butleigh Wootton
Tilham Street
Wraxall
Ditcheat
Bussex
Overleigh
Ham Street
Alhampton
Westonzoyland
Baltonsborough
Wyke Champflower
Middlezoy
River Cary
Compton Dundon
Hornblotton Green
Clanville
Ansford
Butleigh
Othery
Henley
Dundon
Barton St David
West Lydford
East Lydford
Castle Cary
Alford
Lovington
BRADLEY HILL
Burrow Bridge
High Ham
Littleton
Kingweston
Keinton Mandeville
Lydford-on-Fosse
Galhampton
Burrow Mump
Beer
Stembridge Tower Mill NT
Foddington
Low Ham
Bramwell
Charlton Mackrell
Lyng
Stathe
Aller
Somerton
Babcary
North Barrow
South Barrow
Athelney
Willow Craft
Pitney
Charlton Adam
Brookhampton
Haynes Motor Museum
Woodhill
Wearne
Langport
North Cadbury
Oath
Upton
Lyte's Cary Manor NT
Sparkford
Little Weston
Blackford
Stoke St Gregory
Huish Episcopi
Curry Rivel
Pibsbury
Catsgore
Kingsdon
Downhead
West Camel
Compton Pauncefoot
Huntham
Heale
Long Sutton
Queen Camel
South Cadbury
North Curry
Muchelney
Knole
Podimore
Wales
Willtown
Drayton
Little Load
Bridgehampton
Sutton Montis
Fleet Air Arm
RNAS Yeovilton
Muchelney Ham
Long Load
Marston Magna
Curry Mallet
Fivehead
Thorney
Ilchester
Yeovilton
Chilton Cantelo
Corton Denham
Limington
Isle Brewers
Hambridge
Kingsbury Episcopi
Milton
Ashington
Isle Abbotts
Witcombe
Rimpton
Stapleton
West Mudford
Adber
Sandford Orcas
Beercrocombe
Westport
Coat
Ash
Treasurer's House NT
Tintinhull NT
Mudford Sock
New Cross
Stembridge
Martock
Chilthorne Domer
Yeovil Marsh
Mudford
Poyntington
West Lambrook
East Lambrook
Tintinhull
Barrington
Up Mudford
Trent
Puckington
Barrington Court NT
Compton Durville
Stoke sub Hamdon
Thorne
Nether Compton
Ilford
Stocklinch
Montacute
Yeovil
Over Compton
Stallen
Shepton Beauchamp
South Petherton
Norton sub Hamdon
Montacute House NT
Preston Plucknett
Worldwide Butterflies
Whitelackington
Odcombe
Sherborne
North Wootton
Seavington St Michael
Over Stratton
Little Norton
Brympton
Ilminster
Seavington St Mary
Wigborough
Chiselborough
West Coker
Barwick
Bradford Abbas
Kingstone
Lopen
West Chinnock
East Chinnock
Folke
Allowenshay
Dinnington
Thornford
Lillington
Middle Chinnock
Hardington Moor
East Coker
Stoford
Knowle St Giles
Dowlish Wake
Ludney
Hinton St George
Merriott
Hardington Mandeville
Longburton
Cudworth
Haselbury Plucknett
Pendomer
Knighton
Crewkerne
Ryme Intrinseca
Yetminster
Hardington Marsh
North Perrott
Closworth
Hamlet
Holnest
Hewish
Cricket St Thomas
BIRTS HILL
Halstock
Leigh
Glanvilles Wootton
38
25
13
14
0 1 2 3 4 miles
0 1 2 3 4 5 kilometres

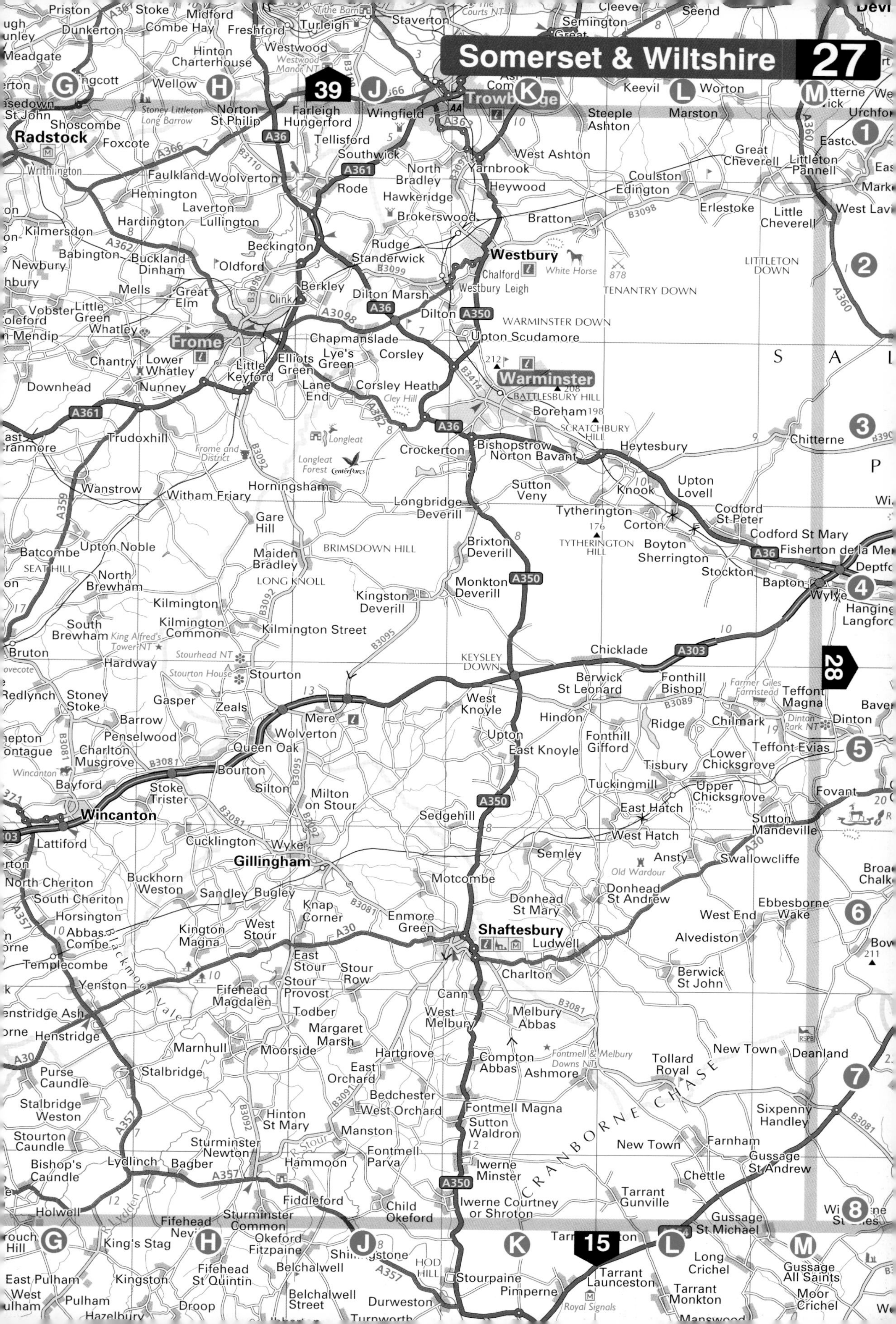

Somerset & Wiltshire
27
39
28
15
Priston
Stoke
Midford
Tithe Barn
Staverton
Courts NT
Cleeve
Seend
Semington
Dunkerton
Combe Hay
Freshford
Turleigh
Meadgate
Hinton Charterhouse
Westwood
Westwood Manor NT
Wellow
Farleigh Hungerford
Wingfield
Trowbridge
Keevil
Worton
Steeple Ashton
Marston
Urchfont
Stoney Littleton Long Barrow
Norton St Philip
Shoscombe
Radstock
Foxcote
Tellisford
Southwick
West Ashton
Great Cheverell
Littleton Pannell
Writhlington
Faulkland
Woolverton
Rode
North Bradley
Yarnbrook
Heywood
Coulston
Edington
Hemington
Laverton
Hawkeridge
Erlestoke
Little Cheverell
West Lavington
Hardington
Lullington
Brokerswood
Bratton
Kilmersdon
Babington
Buckland Dinham
Beckington
Rudge
Standerwick
Westbury
Newbury
Oldford
Chalford
White Horse
LITTLETON DOWN
Mells
Great Elm
Berkley
Clink
Dilton Marsh
Westbury Leigh
TENANTRY DOWN
Vobster
Little Green
Whatley
Dilton
WARMINSTER DOWN
Mendip
Frome
Chapmanslade
Upton Scudamore
Chantry
Lower Whatley
Little Keyford
Elliots Green
Lye's Green
Corsley
Warminster
S A L
Downhead
Nunney
Lane End
Corsley Heath
Cley Hill
BATTLESBURY HILL
Boreham
SCRATCHBURY HILL
Trudoxhill
Longleat
Crockerton
Bishopstrow
Norton Bavant
Heytesbury
Chitterne
Cranmore
Frome and District
Longleat Forest
Center Parcs
Knook
Upton Lovell
Wanstrow
Witham Friary
Horningsham
Sutton Veny
Longbridge Deverill
Tytherington
Corton
Codford St Peter
Gare Hill
Brixton Deverill
TYTHERINGTON HILL
Boyton
Sherrington
Codford St Mary
Batcombe
Upton Noble
Maiden Bradley
BRIMSDOWN HILL
Fisherton de la Mere
SEAT HILL
North Brewham
LONG KNOLL
Stockton
Bapton
Deptford
Wylye
Kilmington
Kingston Deverill
Monkton Deverill
Hanging Langford
South Brewham
Kilmington Common
Kilmington Street
King Alfred's Tower NT
Bruton
Stourhead NT
Chicklade
Hardway
KEYSLEY DOWN
Stourton House
Stourton
Berwick St Leonard
Fonthill Bishop
Farmer Giles Farmstead
Teffont Magna
Redlynch
Stoney Stoke
Gasper
Zeals
West Knoyle
Hindon
Ridge
Chilmark
Dinton
Dinton Park NT
Mere
Barrow
Penselwood
Wolverton
Upton
Fonthill Gifford
Teffont Evias
Charlton Musgrove
Queen Oak
East Knoyle
Tisbury
Lower Chicksgrove
Wincanton
Bourton
Tuckingmill
Upper Chicksgrove
Fovant
Bayford
Stoke Trister
Silton
Milton on Stour
Sedgehill
East Hatch
Sutton Mandeville
Lattiford
Cucklington
Wyke
West Hatch
Gillingham
Semley
Ansty
Swallowcliffe
North Cheriton
Buckhorn Weston
Old Wardour
Motcombe
Broad Chalke
South Cheriton
Sandley
Bugley
Donhead St Mary
Donhead St Andrew
Horsington
Knap Corner
Enmore Green
Ebbesborne Wake
Abbas Combe
Kington Magna
West Stour
Shaftesbury
West End
Ludwell
Alvediston
Templecombe
East Stour
Stour Row
Charlton
Berwick St John
Yenston
Fifehead Magdalen
Stour Provost
Cann
Henstridge Ash
Blackmore Vale
Todber
West Melbury
Melbury Abbas
Henstridge
Margaret Marsh
Marnhull
Moorside
Hartgrove
Compton Abbas
Fontmell & Melbury Downs NT
Ashmore
Tollard Royal
New Town
Deanland
Purse Caundle
Stalbridge
East Orchard
CRANBORNE CHASE
Stalbridge Weston
Bedchester
West Orchard
Fontmell Magna
Hinton St Mary
Sutton Waldron
Sixpenny Handley
Stourton Caundle
Sturminster Newton
Manston
Farnham
R. Stour
Bishop's Caundle
Lydlinch
Bagber
Hammoon
Fontmell Parva
Iwerne Minster
New Town
Gussage St Andrew
Chettle
Holwell
Fiddleford
Child Okeford
Iwerne Courtney or Shroton
Tarrant Gunville
Fifehead Neville
Sturminster Common
Gussage St Michael
Crouch Hill
King's Stag
Okeford Fitzpaine
Shillingstone
Long Crichel
Gussage All Saints
East Pulham
Kingston
Fifehead St Quintin
Belchalwell
HOD HILL
Stourpaine
Pimperne
Tarrant Launceston
Tarrant Monkton
Moor Crichel
West Pulham
Pulham
Droop
Belchalwell Street
Durweston
Royal Signals
Hazelbury
A36
A361
A362
A366
A350
A3098
A303
A30
A357
A359
A360
A371
B3098
B3099
B3110
B3090
B3092
B3095
B3081
B3089
B3091
B3414

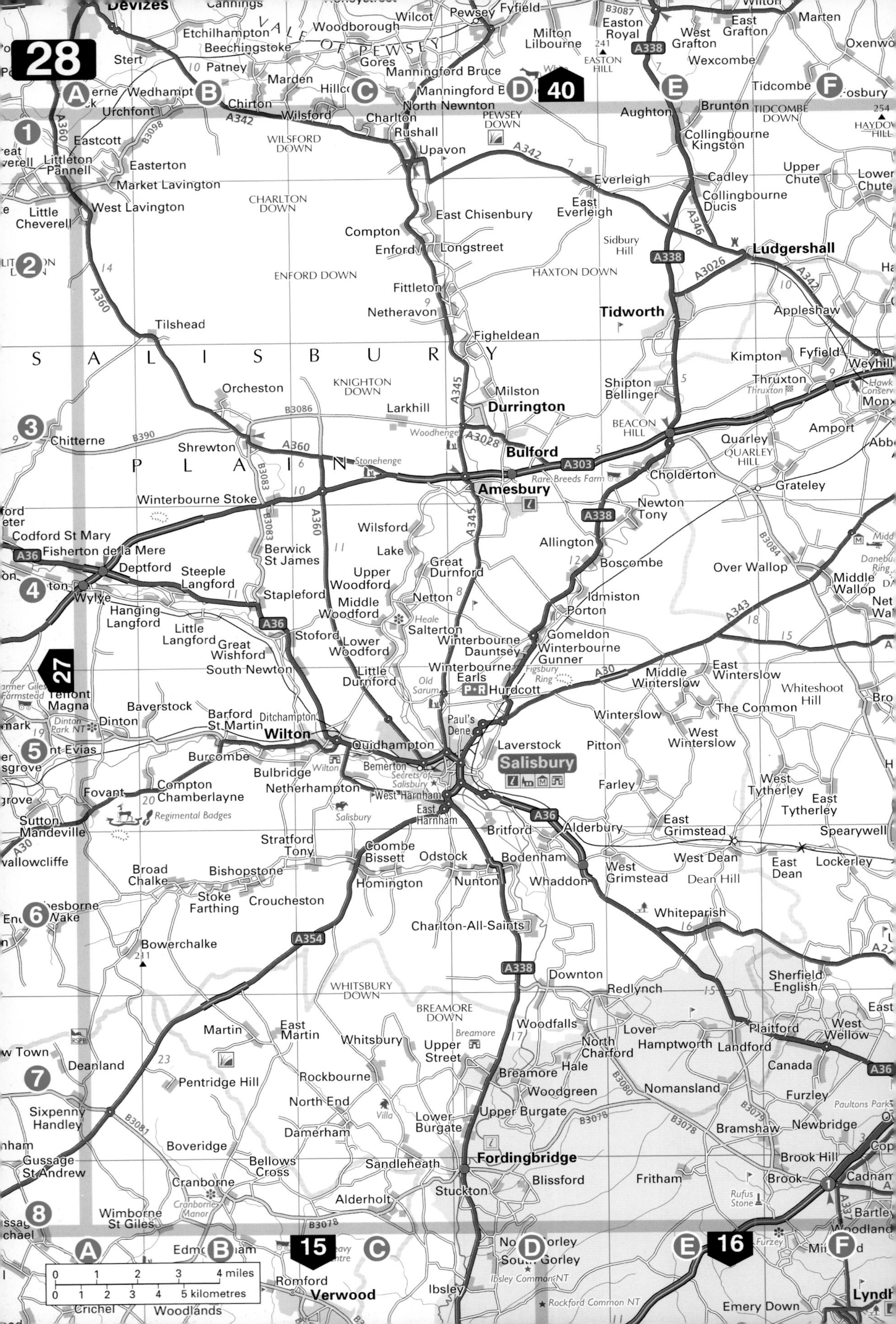
28
Devizes
Etchilhampton
Beechingstoke
VALE OF PEWSEY
Woodborough
Wilcot
Pewsey
Fyfield
Milton Lilbourne
Easton Royal
EASTON HILL
West Grafton
East Grafton
Marten
Wexcombe
Stert
Patney
Marden
Gores
Manningford Bruce
Manningford B
Hillc
40
Wedhampt
Urchfont
Chirton
A342
Wilsford
Charlton
North Newnton
Rushall
PEWSEY DOWN
Upavon
Aughton
Brunton
TIDCOMBE DOWN
Tidcombe
Collingbourne Kingston
Eastcott
WILSFORD DOWN
Littleton Pannell
Easterton
Market Lavington
West Lavington
Little Cheverell
CHARLTON DOWN
East Chisenbury
Everleigh
East Everleigh
Cadley
Upper Chute
Lower Chute
Collingbourne Ducis
A346
A338
Compton
Enford
Longstreet
Sidbury Hill
Ludgershall
A3026
A342
ENFORD DOWN
HAXTON DOWN
Fittleton
Netheravon
Tidworth
Appleshaw
A360
Tilshead
Figheldean
Kimpton
Fyfield
Weyhill
S A L I S B U R Y
KNIGHTON DOWN
Orcheston
Milston
Shipton Bellinger
Thruxton
A345
B3086
Larkhill
Durrington
Amport
Chitterne
B390
Woodhenge
A3028
BEACON HILL
Quarley
QUARLEY HILL
Shrewton
Bulford
A303
P L A I N
Stonehenge
Rare Breeds Farm
Cholderton
Grateley
B3083
Winterbourne Stoke
Amesbury
Newton Tony
Codford St Mary
A36
Fisherton de la Mere
Deptford
Wilsford
Lake
Allington
Berwick St James
Boscombe
Over Wallop
Middle Wallop
B3084
Steeple Langford
Upper Woodford
Great Durnford
Wylye
Stapleford
Middle Woodford
Netton
Idmiston
Porton
A343
Hanging Langford
Little Langford
Heale
Salterton
Stoford
Gomeldon
Great Wishford
Lower Woodford
Winterbourne Dauntsey
Winterbourne Gunner
South Newton
27
Little Durnford
Winterbourne Earls
Figsbury Ring
Middle Winterslow
East Winterslow
Whiteshoot Hill
A30
Old Sarum
P+R
Hurdcott
Teffont Magna
Farmer Giles Farmstead
Baverstock
Barford St Martin
Ditchampton
Winterslow
The Common
Dinton Park NT
Dinton
Wilton
Paul's Dene
West Winterslow
Quidhampton
Laverstock
Pitton
Burcombe
Bemerton
Salisbury
Bulbridge
Secrets of Salisbury
Compton Chamberlayne
Netherhampton
Farley
West Tytherley
East Tytherley
Fovant
West Harnham
Regimental Badges
East Harnham
Alderbury
East Grimstead
Sutton Mandeville
Britford
Spearywell
Stratford Tony
Coombe Bissett
Odstock
Bodenham
West Dean
East Dean
Lockerley
West Grimstead
Dean Hill
Broad Chalke
Bishopstone
Homington
Nunton
Whaddon
Stoke Farthing
Croucheston
Whiteparish
Charlton-All-Saints
A354
Bowerchalke
A338
Downton
Sherfield English
Redlynch
WHITSBURY DOWN
BREAMORE DOWN
Woodfalls
Martin
East Martin
Breamore
Lover
Plaitford
West Wellow
Whitsbury
Upper Street
North Charford
Hamptworth
Landford
Deanland
Hale
Canada
Pentridge Hill
Rockbourne
Breamore
B3080
Nomansland
Woodgreen
Furzley
North End
Villa
Sixpenny Handley
Lower Burgate
Upper Burgate
B3078
B3079
Paultons Park
B3081
Damerham
Bramshaw
Newbridge
Boveridge
Gussage St Andrew
Bellows Cross
Sandleheath
Fordingbridge
Brook Hill
Cranborne
Blissford
Fritham
Brook
Cadnam
Stuckton
Alderholt
Rufus Stone
Cranborne Manor
A337
Bartley
Woodlands
Wimborne St Giles
B3078
15
16
Furzey
Edmondsham
North Gorley
South Gorley
Ibsley Common NT
Romford
Verwood
Ibsley
Rockford Common NT
Emery Down
Lyndhurst
Crichel
Woodlands
0 1 2 3 4 miles
0 1 2 3 4 5 kilometres

Combe
East Woodhay
East End
Pilot Hill
Highclere
Highclere Castle
Sandham Memorial Chapel NT
Ecchinswell
Browninghill
Baughurst
Pamber Green
Bramley Green
Linkenholt
41
Faccombe
G
H
J
Sydmonton
K
L
M
Pamber End
Ramsdell
Crux Easton
Beacon Hill
Ladle Hill
Ladle Hill (unfinished hill fort)
Cottington's Hill
A339
Hannington
Monk Sherborne
Sherborne St John
The Vyne NT
Chineham
Upton
Dean
A34
Ibthorpe
Ibworth
Binley
Hurstbourne Tarrant
Litchfield
Wootton St Lawrence
BASINGSTOKE
Basing House (Ruins)
Old Basing
A340
A339
A343
B3048
Stoke
B3051
Deane
Wooldings
Southington
Ashe
Oakley
Little London
St Mary Bourne
Freefolk
Overton
Kempshott
M3
Cliddesden
Enham-Alamein
Smannell
B3400
Laverstoke
Whitchurch
Tunworth
Winslade
Steventon
Weston Corbett
Hurstbourne Priors
Tufton
Silk Mill
Finkley Down
A3093
A30
B3046
North Waltham
Farleigh Wallop
Herriard
Andover
B3400
Longparish
Dummer
Ellisfield
Bagmore
B3042
A303
Middleton
Upper Clatford
Bury Hill
Forton
Micheldever Station
Woodmancott
Axford
A339
Lasham
B3420
Bransbury
B3048
Preston Candover
Bradley
Wherwell
Newton Stacey
Barton Stacey
Bullington
Chilton Candover
Lower Wield
Bentworth
A3057
Hunton
Weston Colley
Northbrook
East Stratton
Fullerton
Chilbolton
Sutton Scotney
Wonston
Stoke Charity
Micheldever
Brown Candover
Upper Wield
Wivelrod
B3420
Longstock
Leckford
Northington
Medstead
A33
Crawley Down
M3
Swarraton
B3046
A30
A272
The Grange
Winchester
Crawley
Four
Bighton
Soldridge
30
Houghton Lodge
B3049
Old Alresford
Little Somborne
Littleton
Kings Worthy
Abbots Worthy
Martyr Worthy
Itchen Abbas
New Alresford
Gundleton
Houghton
Up Somborne
B3420
B3047
B3047
Easton
Itchen Stoke
Avington
Harestock
Headbourne Worthy
Bishop's Sutton
Ropley Dean
Ropley
Ashley
Sparsholt
Dean
Weeke
Fulflood
Ovington
Tichborne
B3046
King's Somborne
Farley Mount
Winnall
Monkwood
West Tisted
Winchester
B3404
A31
A31
Stanmore
B3040
P+R
A272
1644
Bramdean
Cheriton
Chilcomb
St Catherines Hill
Hinton Ampner NT
Hinton Ampner
A3090
B3335
Oliver's Battery
Mottisfont
Mottisfont Abbey NT
Michelmersh
Standon
Shorley
Beauworth
Braishfield
Compton
Morestead
Kilmeston
Hursley
Shawford
Timsbury
Hillier
A3090
Twyford
West Meon
Owslebury
Ripplington
Otterbourne
Ampfield
Colden Common
Baybridge
Warnford
B3335
East Meon
M3
Old Winchester Hill (Archaeology Trail)
Romsey
Fryern Hill
Hensting
Marwell
A32
Coombe
North Baddesley
A27
Allbrook
Fisher's Pond
Upham
Exton
Corhampton
Old Winchester Hill
Salt Hill
B3043
B3354
Broadlands
R Test
Chandler's Ford
Bishopstoke
Lower Upham
Dean
Meonstoke
Chilworth
B3037
Fair Oak
B3035
B2177
Rownhams
M27
Durley Street
Bishop's Waltham
Droxford
Brockbridge
A335
EASTLEIGH
Southampton
Bishop's Palace
Meon Valley
Upton
Rownhams
Nursling
Bassett
Swaythling
Itchen Valley
B3035
B2177
Swanmore
B2150
Soberton
M27
Hillstreet
Durley
M271
A35
A33
A3057
Shirley
Portswood
Waltham Chase
M27
B3038
Shirrell Heath
Vineyard & Winepress
Hambledon
Calmore
Testwood
West End
Curdridge
Soberton Heath
Catherington
A336
Millbrook
A3057
Bitterne
A27
Botley
Shedfield
Newtown
A33
A334
Wickham
A334
Totton
Eling
Northam
Thornhill
Hedge End
Wickham
Denmead
A3024
A32
SOUTHAMPTON
Woolston
Isle of Wight Ferry Terminal
Sholing
Manor Farm
A3051
Curdridge
17
B2177
Worlds End
Soake
Dairy Farm
Marchwood
A3025
Lower Swanwick
Burridge
North Boarhunt
WATERLOOVILLE
B2150
Otter & Owl Centre
Bursledon
Swanwick
Southwick
Dibden
Netley
Sarisbury
Boarhunt
Purbrook
Beaulieu
Park Gate
M27
Pyts Down

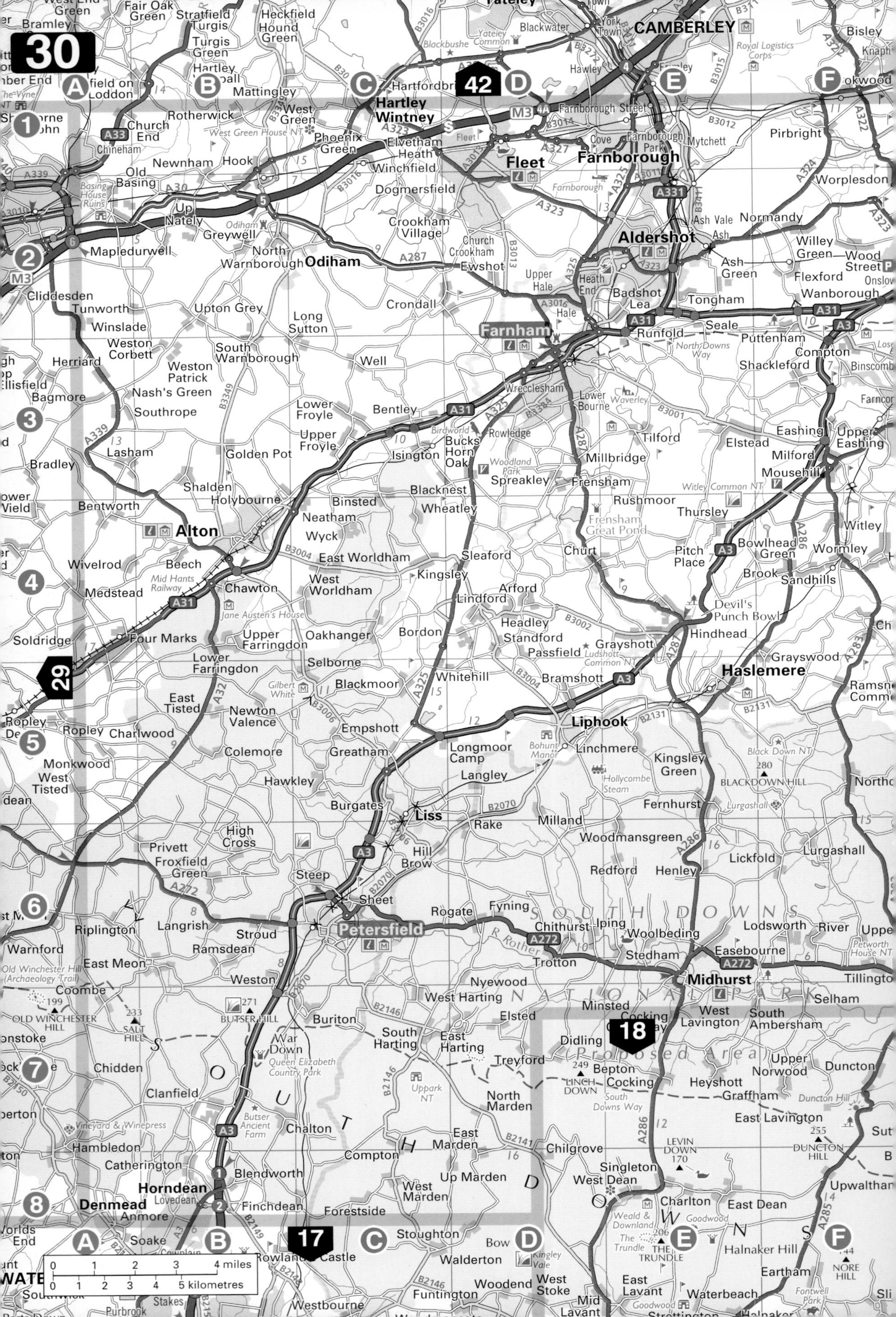
30
Yateley
CAMBERLEY
Bramley
Fair Oak Green
Stratfield Turgis
Turgis Green
Heckfield
Hound Green
Blackwater
York Town
Blackbushe
Yateley Common
Bisley
Knaphill
Royal Logistics Corps
Hartley Wespall
Mattingley
Hartfordbridge
42
Hawley
Frimley
Hartley Wintney
West Green
Rotherwick
Farnborough Street
Pirbright
Church End
West Green House NT
Phoenix Green
Elvetham Heath
Winchfield
Fleet
Cove
Farnborough
Farnborough Park
Mytchett
Chineham
Newnham
Hook
Old Basing
Basing House (Ruins)
Up Nately
Greywell
Odiham
North Warnborough
Dogmersfield
Crookham Village
Church Crookham
Ewshot
Worplesdon
Ash Vale
Normandy
Ash
Aldershot
Willey Green
Ash Green
Wood Street
Flexford
Onslow
Mapledurwell
Cliddesden
Tunworth
Winslade
Upton Grey
Long Sutton
Crondall
Upper Hale
Heath End
Badshot Lea
Hale
Tongham
Wanborough
Farnham
Runfold
Seale
Puttenham
North Downs Way
Compton
Shackleford
Binscombe
Weston Corbett
South Warnborough
Herriard
Weston Patrick
Ellisfield
Nash's Green
Bagmore
Southrope
Well
Wrecclesham
Lower Bourne
Waverley
Farncombe
Lower Froyle
Bentley
Upper Froyle
Isington
Birdworld
Bucks Horn Oak
Rowledge
Tilford
Elstead
Eashing
Upper Eashing
Lasham
Golden Pot
Woodland Park
Spreakley
Millbridge
Milford
Mousehill
Bradley
Frensham
Witley Common NT
Shalden
Holybourne
Binsted
Blacknest
Rushmoor
Thursley
Lower Wield
Bentworth
Neatham
Wheatley
Alton
Wyck
Frensham Great Pond
Witley
Bowlhead Green
Churt
Pitch Place
Wormley
Wivelrod
Beech
East Worldham
Sleaford
Mid Hants Railway
Chawton
West Worldham
Kingsley
Brook
Sandhills
Medstead
Arford
Lindford
Devil's Punch Bowl
Jane Austen's House
Headley
Hindhead
Soldridge
Four Marks
Upper Farringdon
Oakhanger
Bordon
Standford
Grayshott
Passfield
Ludshott Common NT
Lower Farringdon
Selborne
Grayswood
Whitehill
Bramshott
Haslemere
29
Gilbert White
Blackmoor
Ramsnest Common
East Tisted
Newton Valence
Ropley
Ropley Dean
Charlwood
Empshott
Liphook
Longmoor Camp
Bohunt Manor
Linchmere
Kingsley Green
Black Down NT
Monkwood
Colemore
Greatham
280
BLACKDOWN HILL
West Tisted
Hawkley
Langley
Hollycombe Steam
Northchapel
Burgates
Liss
Rake
Fernhurst
Lurgashall
Milland
High Cross
Woodmansgreen
Privett
Froxfield Green
Hill Brow
Lickfold
Lurgashall
Redford
Henley
Steep
Sheet
Rogate
Fyning
SOUTH DOWNS
Riplington
Langrish
Stroud
Petersfield
Chithurst
Iping
Woolbeding
Lodsworth
River
Warnford
Ramsdean
R Rother
Trotton
Stedham
Easebourne
Petworth House NT
East Meon
Old Winchester Hill (Archaeology Trail)
Weston
Nyewood
Midhurst
Tillington
Coombe
199
OLD WINCHESTER HILL
233
SALT HILL
271
BUTSER HILL
West Harting
NATIONAL PARK
Selham
Elsted
Minsted
Cocking Causeway
West Lavington
South Ambersham
Buriton
South Harting
East Harting
18
War Down
Queen Elizabeth Country Park
Didling
(Proposed Area)
Upper Norwood
Duncton
Chidden
Treyford
249
LINCH DOWN
Bepton
Cocking
Heyshott
Graffham
Clanfield
Uppark NT
North Marden
South Downs Way
Duncton Hill
East Lavington
Butser Ancient Farm
Vineyard & Winepress
Chalton
East Marden
Hambledon
255
DUNCTON HILL
Catherington
Compton
Chilgrove
LEVIN DOWN
170
Blendworth
Up Marden
Singleton
West Dean
Horndean
West Marden
Upwaltham
Lovedean
Denmead
Anmore
Finchdean
Forestside
Charlton
East Dean
Weald & Downland
Goodwood
Worlds End
Soake
17
Stoughton
Bow Hill
206
THE TRUNDLE
The Trundle
Halnaker Hill
144
NORE HILL
Rowland's Castle
Walderton
Kingley Vale
Eartham
West Stoke
Woodend
East Lavant
Waterbeach
Stakes
Funtington
Mid Lavant
Westbourne
Fontwell Park
Purbrook
0 1 2 3 4 miles
0 1 2 3 4 5 kilometres
A B C D E F
1 2 3 4 5 6 7 8
M3 A33 A339 A30 A323 A287 A31 A325 A331 A3 A32 A272 A286 A283 A285 B3349 B3004 B3006 B2070 B2146 B2141 B2149 B3384 B3001 B3002 B2131 B3013 B3016 B3012 A322 A324

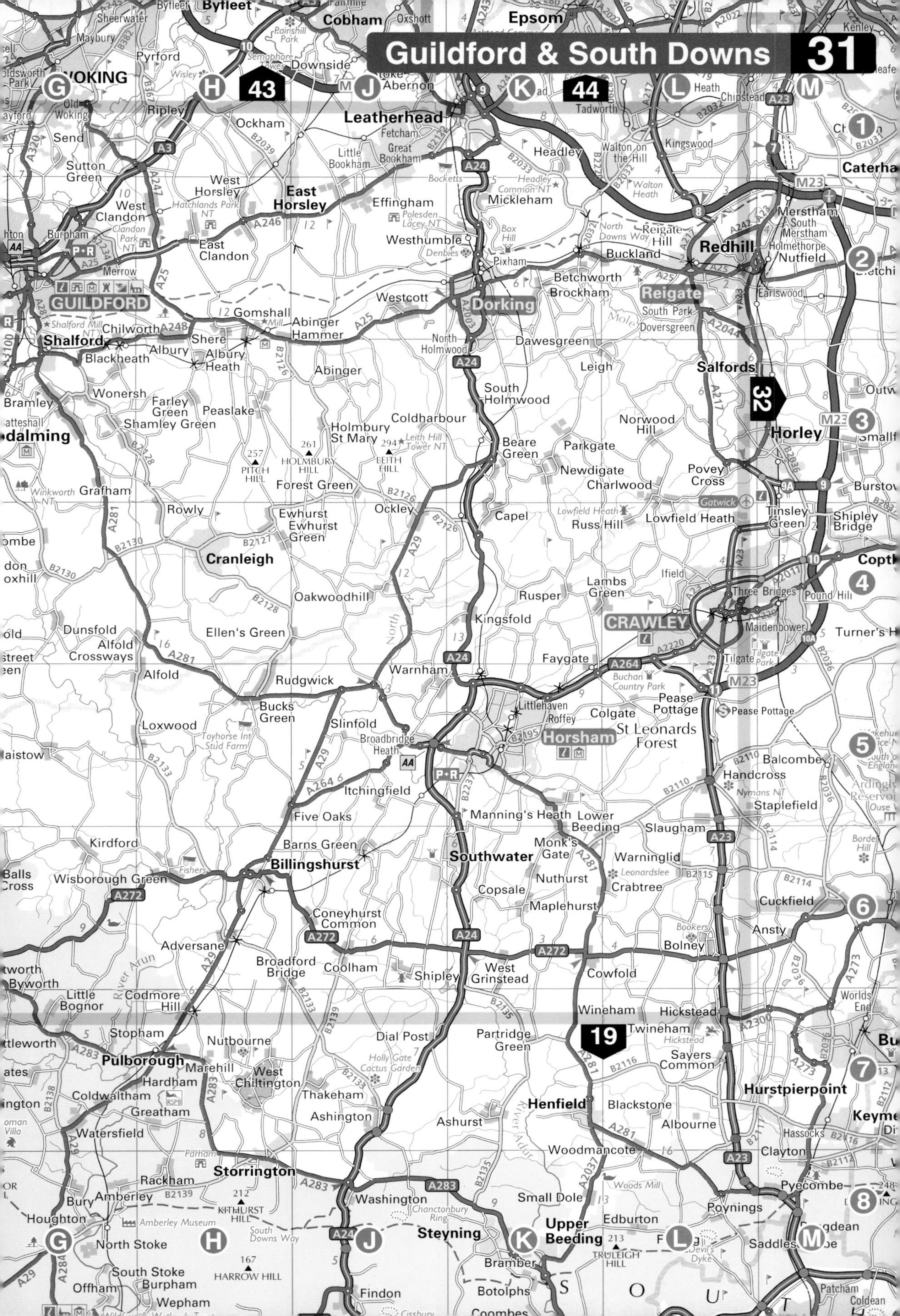
Byfleet
Sheerwater
Cobham
Oxshott
Epsom
Painshill Park
Maybury
Pyrford
WOKING
Wisley
Semaphore Tower
Downside
Stoke d'Abernon
Old Woking
Ripley
Ockham
Leatherhead
Fetcham
Tadworth
Heath
Chipstead
Send
Sutton Green
West Horsley
Little Bookham
Great Bookham
Headley
Walton on the Hill
Kingswood
Caterham
Bocketts
Headley Common NT
Walton Heath
Hatchlands Park NT
East Horsley
Effingham
Mickleham
West Clandon
Polesden Lacey NT
Burpham
Clandon Park NT
East Clandon
Westhumble
Box Hill
North Downs Way
Reigate Hill
Redhill
Mersham
South Mersham
Holmethorpe
Nutfield
Denbies
Pixham
Buckland
Merrow
GUILDFORD
Betchworth
Brockham
Reigate
Earlswood
Westcott
Dorking
South Park
Gomshall
Shalford Mill NT
Chilworth
Abinger Hammer
Mill
Mole
Doversgreen
Shere
Shalford
Albury
Blackheath
Albury Heath
North Holmwood
Dawesgreen
Leigh
Salfords
Abinger
South Holmwood
Wonersh
Bramley
Farley Green
Peaslake
Shamley Green
Coldharbour
Norwood Hill
Holmbury St Mary
Leith Hill Tower NT
Beare Green
Parkgate
Horley
Godalming
HOLMBURY HILL
LEITH HILL
PITCH HILL
Newdigate
Povey Cross
Charlwood
Winkworth NT
Grafham
Forest Green
Gatwick
Burstow
Lowfield Heath
Rowly
Ewhurst
Ewhurst Green
Ockley
Capel
Russ Hill
Lowfield Heath
Tinsley Green
Shipley Bridge
Cranleigh
Ifield
Copthorne
Lambs Green
Oakwoodhill
Rusper
Three Bridges
Pound Hill
North
Kingsfold
CRAWLEY
Maidenbower
Dunsfold
Alfold Crossways
Ellen's Green
Turner's Hill
Faygate
Tilgate
Tilgate Park
Alfold
Warnham
Rudgwick
Buchan Country Park
Pease Pottage
Bucks Green
Littlehaven
Roffey
Colgate
St Leonards Forest
Loxwood
Slinfold
Broadbridge Heath
Horsham
Toyhorse Int Stud Farm
Balcombe
Handcross
Itchingfield
Nymans NT
Staplefield
Five Oaks
Manning's Heath
Lower Beeding
Slaugham
Kirdford
Barns Green
Monk's Gate
Southwater
Warninglid
Leonardslee
Billingshurst
Fishers
Balls Cross
Wisborough Green
Nuthurst
Crabtree
Copsale
Cuckfield
Maplehurst
Coneyhurst Common
Ansty
Bookers
Bolney
Adversane
West Grinstead
Broadford Bridge
Coolham
Cowfold
Shipley
River Arun
Byworth
Little Bognor
Codmore Hill
Wineham
Hickstead
Worlds End
Stopham
Nutbourne
Dial Post
Partridge Green
Twineham
Pulborough
Holly Gate Cactus Garden
Marehill
West Chiltington
Sayers Common
Hardham
Coldwaltham
RSPB
Greatham
Thakeham
Henfield
Blackstone
Hurstpierpoint
Ashington
Ashurst
Albourne
Keymer
Watersfield
River Adur
Hassocks
Parham
Woodmancote
Clayton
Storrington
Rackham
Pyecombe
Amberley
Woods Mill
Bury
KITHURST HILL
Washington
Small Dole
Poynings
Houghton
Amberley Museum
Chanctonbury Ring
Edburton
South Downs Way
Steyning
Upper Beeding
North Stoke
TRULEIGH HILL
Devil's Dyke
Saddlescombe
HARROW HILL
South Stoke
Bramber
Offham
Burpham
Wepham
Findon
Botolphs
Patcham
Coldean
Coombes
Cissbury

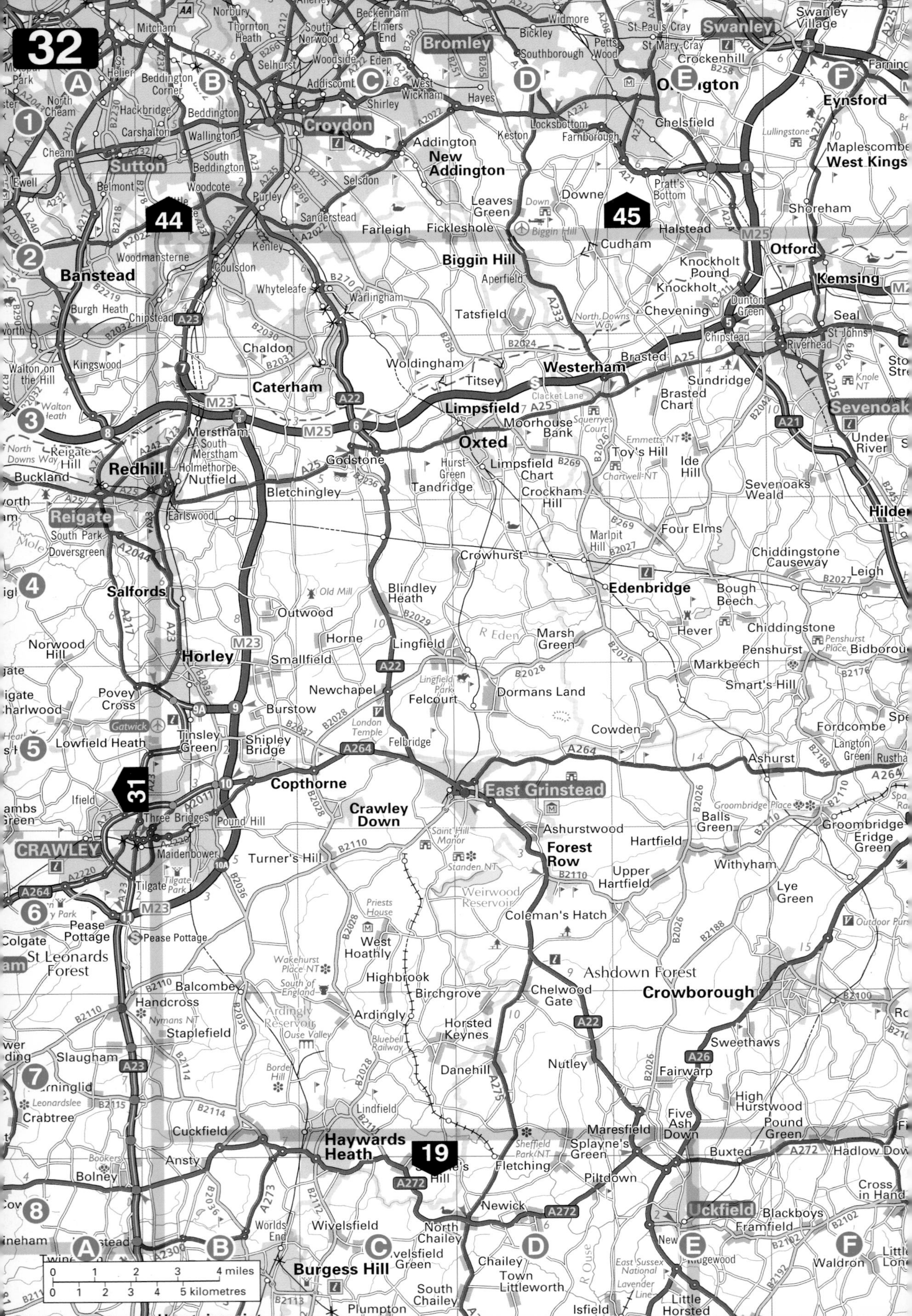

Longfield
New Barn
Cobham
Strood
ROCHESTER
CHATHAM
Sole Street
Fawkham Green
Hartley
Meopham
Luddesdown
Borstal
North Downs Way
Rainham
Wigmore
Newington
Bobbing
Milton Regis
New Ash Green
Ash
Wouldham
Halling
Walderslade
Hartlip
Chalkwell
Hodsall Street
Harvel
Culverstone Green
Paddlesworth
Medway
M2
Hill Green
Borden
Tunstall
Stansted
Fairseat
Vigo
Snodland
Burham
Lords Wood
Bredhurst
Oad St
Stockbury
46
Trosley
Birling
Ryarsh
Trottiscliffe
Eccles
Wildlife Trust
Tyland Barn
South Green
Highsted
Bredgar
Wrotham
Heaverham
Addington
Lunsford
Aylesford
Kent County
A249
Bicknor
Milstead
Leybourne
Larkfield
M20
Boxley
Detling
Hucking
Borough Green
West Malling
Tower
Ditton
Thurnham
Wormshill
Ightham
Platt
Offham
British Legion Village
East Malling
Broad Street
Frinsted
Kings Hill
Herne Pound
MAIDSTONE
P+R
Bearsted
Hollingbourne
Old Soar Manor NT
Ivy Hatch
Mereworth
Wateringbury
Teston
East Barming
Tovil
Willington
Eyhorne Street
Plaxtol
Ightham Mote NT
Dunk's Green
West Farleigh
East Farleigh
Shepway
Otham
Leeds
Harrietsham
West Peckham
Nettlestead
Nettlestead Green
Loose
Boughton Green
Langley
Broomfield
Lenham
Hadlow
Sandway
Yalding
Coxheath
Linton
Boughton Monchelsea
Chart Sutton
East Peckham
Parkers Green
Hale Street
Hunton
Benover
Chainhurst
Grafty Green
Boughton Malherbe
Hilden Park
Golden Green
Laddingford
Sutton Valence
Ulcombe
River Beult
Barnes Street
Hop Farm
Mockbeggar
Tonbridge
Medway
Whetsted
Fowlhall
Five Oak
Tudeley Green
Rhoden Grn
Collier Street
Cross-at-Hand
34
The Forstal
Queen Street
Wanshurst Green
Headcorn
Capel
Colt's Hill
Paddock Wood
Claygate
Marden
RSPB
Southborough
Marden Thorn
Staplehurst
Iden Croft Herbs
Smarden Bell
Smarden
Maltman's Hill
Matfield
High Brooms
Lower Green
Pembury
Brenchley
Horsmonden
River Teise
Winchet Hill
Frittenden
Kipping's Cross
Curtisden Green
Knox Bridge
Standen
TUNBRIDGE WELLS
Marle Place
Three Chimneys
Sissinghurst NT
Biddenden
Owl House
Goudhurst
Iden Green
Sissinghurst
High Halden
Bayham
Lamberhurst
Finchcocks
Union Mill
Scotney Castle NT
Kilndown
Cranbrook
East End
Biddenden
Bells Yew Green
Hook Green
Lamberhurst Down
St Michaels
Cousley Wood
Wood's Green
Goddard's Green
Hartley
National Pinetum & Garden
Tenterden
Bewl Water
Stonecrouch
Benenden
Mark Cross
Sparrows Green
Wadhurst
Three Leg Cross
Flimwell
Iden Green
Historic Vehicles Collection
Rolvenden
Hawkhurst
Tidebrook
Tenterden Vineyard Park
Small Hythe
The Moor
Four Throws
Ticehurst
Rolvenden Layne
Smallhythe Place NT
River Limden
Pashley Manor
Sandhurst
Kent & East Sussex Railway
Stonegate
Kent Ditch
Newenden
Wittersham
ISLE OF
Witherenden Hill
Hurst Green
Great Dixter
21
Mayfield
Etchingham
River Rother
Bodiam
Bodiam Castle NT
Burwash
Salehurst
Ewhurst Green
Northiam
20
Bateman's NT
Beckley
Rye Foreign
Broad Oak
Burwash Common
Burwash Weald
Robertsbridge
Staple Cross
Millcorner
Clayhill
Peasmarsh
Heathfield
Cade St
R Dudwell
Brightling
Punnett's Town
Three Cups Corner
Wood's Corner
Mountfield
Oak
R Tillingham
Cock Marling
Maynard's Green
Dallington
Netherfield
Whatlington
Broadland Row
Udimore
Rushlake Green
Warbleton
Vines Cross
Netherfield Road
Battle
Sedlescombe
Brede
River Brede
Winchelsea

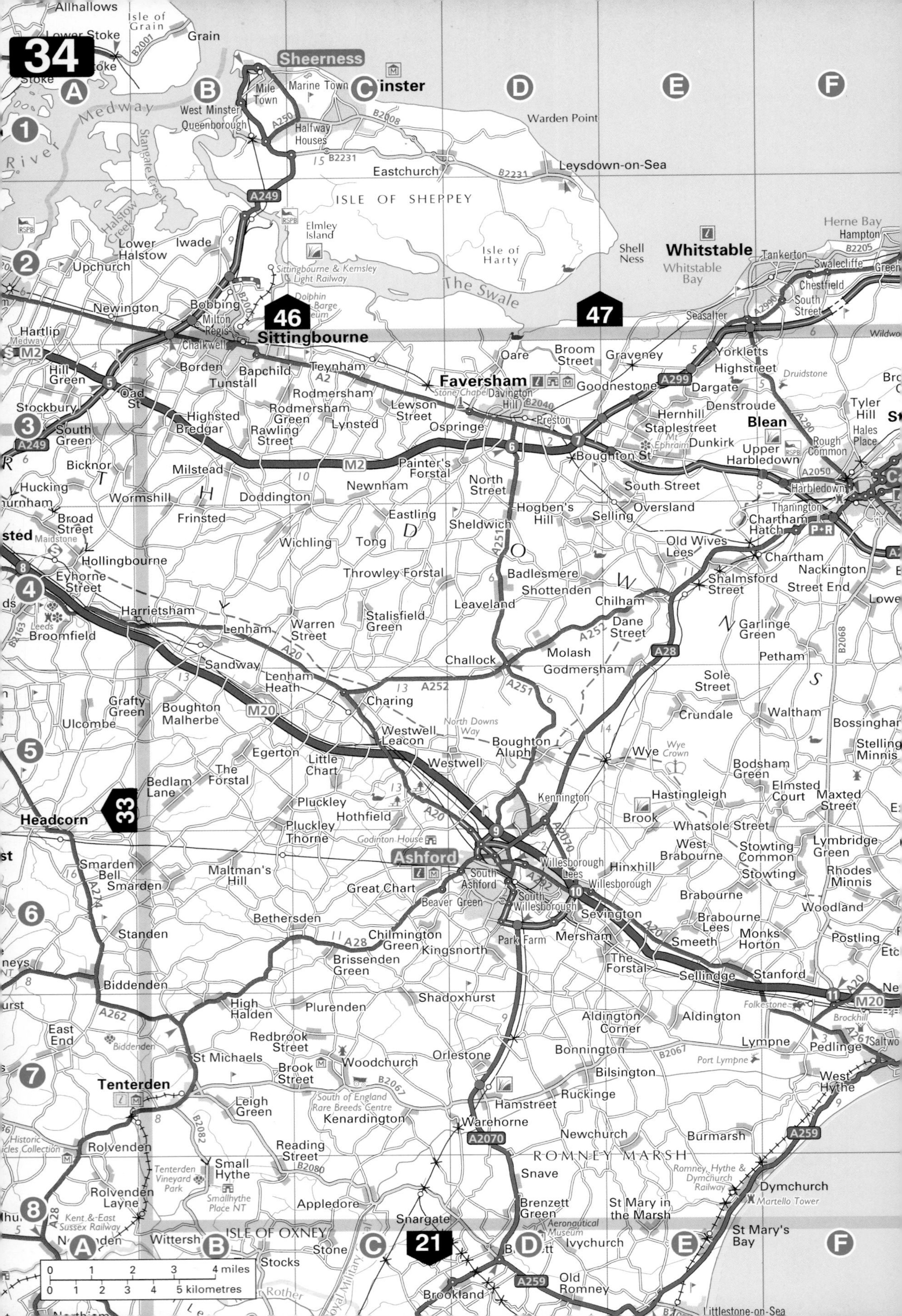

MARGATE
Foreness Point
Westgate on-Sea
Westbrook
Cliftonville
Kingsgate
Northdown
NORTH FORELAND
Minnis Bay
Garlinge
Reading Street
Lighthouse
Herne Bay
Birchington
Salmestone Grange
St Peter's
Bishopstone
Reculver
Lydden
Broadstairs
Beltinge
ISLE OF THANET
Westwood
Broomfield
St Nicholas at Wade
Acol
Dumpton
Herne
Boyden Gate
Manston
Hereson
Sarre
Monkton
St Lawrence
Ramsgate
Chislet
Durlock
Hoath
Minster
St Augustine's Cross
Viking Ship 'Hugin'
Pegwell
Upstreet
West Stourmouth
R Stour
Hersden
East Stourmouth
Pegwell Bay
Westmarsh
Westbere
Richborough
Stodmarsh
Preston
Elmstone
Cop Street
Prince's
Sandwich Bay
Old Town Hall
Hoaden
Wickhambreaux
Littlebourne
Seaton
Ash
Sandwich
Ickham
Durlock
Royal St George's
Wingham
Marshborough
Stone Cross
Howletts
Toll
Bramling
Staple
Woodnesborough
Worth
Bekesbourne
Goodnestone
Eastry
Statenborough
Patrixbourne
Ham
Hacklinge
Adisham
Ratling
Chillenden
Finglesham
Higham Park
The Downs
Aylesham
Nonington
Sholden
North Downs Way
Betteshanger
Northbourne
Deal
Womenswold
Tilmanstone
Great Mongeham
Upper Deal
Elham Valley
Elvington
Barham
Lower Eythorne
Ripple
Walmer
Barfrestone
Eythorne
Sutton
Woolage Green
East Kent Railway
East Studdal
Ringwould
Shepherdswell
Ashley
Sutton Downs
Kingsdown
North Downs Way
West Langdon
Denton
Lydden
Coldred
Martin
Wootton
Geddinge
Rural Heritage Centre
Whitfield
East Langdon
Selsted
Lydden
Guston
St Margaret's at Cliffe
Temple Ewell
St Margaret's Bay
North Elham
Ewell Minnis
Kearsney
West Cliffe
Pines
SOUTH FORELAND
River
Swingfield Minnis
Swingfield Street
Lighthouse
NT
Butterfly Centre
Buckland
South Foreland Heritage Coast
Langdon Cliffs NT
Alkham
St Radigund's
Densole
South Alkham
Maxton
Upper Standen
Drellingore
West Hougham
DOVER
Calais
Dunkerque
Hawkinge
Lower Standen
Channel Tunnel Terminal
Battle of Britain
Capel le-Ferne
Boulogne
Samphire Hoe
Dover - Folkestone Heritage Coast
Cheriton
Morehall
East Wear Bay
Channel Tunnel
FOLKESTONE
Calais
Sandgate
STRAIT OF DOVER
A299
A28
A253
A291
A257
A256
A258
A255
A254
A2
A20
A260
A259
B2051
B2052
B2048
B2190
B2046
B2011

Rhydyfro
Cilmaengwyn
Fynydd
Craig Llangiwg
Cilybebyll
Gellinudd
Crynant
Mynydd March Hywel
Alltwen
River Dulais
Vale of Neath
River Neath
A465
B4242
Blaengwrach
Resolven
383 RESOLVEN MOUNTAIN
600 CRAIG-Y-LLYN
Rhigos
Hirwaun
Penywaun
Cwmdare
Trecynon
Aberdare
Llwydcoed
Mynydd Ystradffernol
Aberaman
Cwmaman
Abercwm
A4059
A4061
A4233
Glais
Bryn-côch
Cilfrew
Cadoxton Juxta-Neath
Aberdulais Falls NT
Aberdulais
Clyne
B4434
493 MOEL-YR HYRDDAD
A4067
B4291
A474
Birchgrove
Llansamlet
Tonna
Cefn Mawr
Glyncorrwg
Cefn Marfydd
Afan Forest Park
Treherbert
Maerdy
Neath
Skewen
A465
Winshwen
Cimla
B4287
Abercregan
Duffryn
Cymer
A4107
Blaengwynfi
Abergwynfi
Cwmparc
Treorchy
Pentre
Ferndale
Ystrad
Rhondda Valley
478
Tylo
Efail-fach
Briton Ferry
FOEL MYNYDDAU
371
Cynonville
Pont-rhyd-y-fen
Afan Argoed
371 MOEL TRAWSNANT
Caerau
Croeserw
556 MYNYDD CAERAU
571 WERFA
Nant-y-moel
A4061
Clydach Vale
B4221
Llwynypia
Trealaw
Tonypandy
Penygraig
B4290
B4286
A483
Pwll-y-glaw
P+R
Baglan
Cwmafan
Bryn
B4282
Blaengarw
Mynydd Llangeinwyr
Pontycymer
Glanllynfi
Maesteg
A4064
Ogmore Vale
Gilfach Goch
B4564
B4278
A48
A4241
Aberavon
Port Talbot
Swansea Bay
Taibach
Margam
Mynydd Margam
Cwmfelin
Llangynwyd
Llangeinor
A4093
Betws
321 MOEL TON-MAWR
Margam Park
A4063
Coytrahen
Bryngarw
Brynmenyn
Blackmill
Mynydd Maendy
Tondu
Heol-y-Cyw
B4283
M4
Afon Kenfig
Cefn Cribwr
Aberkenfig
Sarn Park
Pant-ffrwyth
Brynna
Llanharan
B4281
Pyle
Mawdlam
North Cornelly
Kenfig
Bridgend
Coity
Pencoed
B4280
A473
Llanilid
Llanharry
Brynsadler
South Cornelly
Laleston
A4061
B4181
Coychurch
A4229
NEWTON DOWN
A4106
Tythegston
Rest Bay
Nottage
Merthyr Mawr
Ewenny
Treoes
Llangan
Porthcawl
Newton
Ogmore R.
Corntown
Ogmore
Penllyn
Maendy
Porthcawl Point
St Bride's Major
B4265
Colwinston
Pentre Meyrick
B4268
Ogmore-by-Sea
B4524
Llysworney
Cowbridge
Southerndown
Llandow
B4270
Llanblethian
Llandough
St Hilary
Wick
Sigingstone
Llandow
St Mary Church
Broughton
B4270
Flemingston
Monknash
Marcross
B4265
Llanmaes
St Donats
Llantwit Major
St Athan
Nash Point
Gileston
Glamorgan Heritage Coast
Lambert Bay
51
52
A B C D E F
1 2 3 4 5 6 7 8
0 1 2 3 4 miles
0 1 2 3 4 5 kilometres

Abertillery
Pontypool
Bargoed
Oakdale
Crumlin
Newbridge
Treharris
Pengam
Penmaen
Blackwood
Pontllanfraith
Gelligaer
Abercynon
Ynysybwl
Abercarn
Cwmbran
Crosskeys
Risca
Caerleon
Pontypridd
Llanbradach
Bedwas
Caerphilly
Rogerstone
NEWPORT
Church Village
Beddau
Llantrisant
Tongwynlais
Radyr
CARDIFF
Penarth
Barry
WESTON-SUPER-MARE
MOUTH OF THE SEVERN
Flat Holm
Steep Holm
Sully Island
Lavernock Point
Tredegar
Llanhilleth
Merthyr Vale
Aberfan
Nelson
Ystrad Mynach
Senghenydd
Machen
Rhiwbina
Llanishen
Whitchurch
Llandaff
Fairwater
Canton
Roath
Splottlands
Llandough
Dinas Powys
Sully
Lavernock
Rhoose
Porthkerry
Cold Knap Point
Barry Island
Kewstoke
Milton
Ashcombe
Uphill
Oldmixon
Bleadon
Locking
Hutton
Lympsham
Edingworth
Wick St Lawrence
Sand Bay
Woodspring Bay
Sand Point
Brean Down
Tropical Bird Garden
Marshfield
Castleton
St Brides Wentlooge
Peterstone Wentlooge
Nash
Goldcliff
Michaelstone-y-Fedw
Lisvane
Llanedeyrn
St Mellons
Llanrumney
Rumney
St Fagans
St Brides super-Ely
Peterston-super-Ely
St George's
St Nicholas
Bonvilston
St Lythans
Wenvoe
Michaelston-le-Pit
St Andrew's Major
Cadoxton
Moulton
Penmark
Llantrithyd
Pendoylan
Miskin
Groes-faen
Creigiau
Pentyrch
Taff's Well
Efail Isaf
Tyn-y-nant
Llantwit Fardre
Pen-y-coedcae
Trefforest
Trehafod
Cilfynydd
Ynysboeth
Abertridwr
Groes-Wen
Cwmfelinfach
Ynysddu
Wattsville
Pontywaun
Cwmcarn
Maesycwmmer
Hengoed
Trelewis
Bedlinog
Troedyrhiw
Pentrebach
Abercanaid
Brithdir
Markham
Bedwellty
Argoed
Manmoel
Cwmtillery
Monkswood
Griffithstown
New Inn
Llanbadoc
Coed-y-paen
Llangybi
Llandegveth
Tredunhock
Llanfrechfa
Ponthir
Llantarnam
Croesyceiliog
Pontnewydd
Henllys
Malpas
Maindee
Bettws
Christchurch
Liswerry
Llanwern
Bassaleg
Rhiwderyn
Draethen
Rudry
Lower Machen
Lower Penarth
Cogan
Penarth Head
Cosmeston Lakes & Medieval Village
A470
A48(M)
A4232
M4
A4042
A48
A469
A4119
A4226
A370
A371
53
25
38
G
H
J
K
L
M
1
2
3
4
5
6
7
8

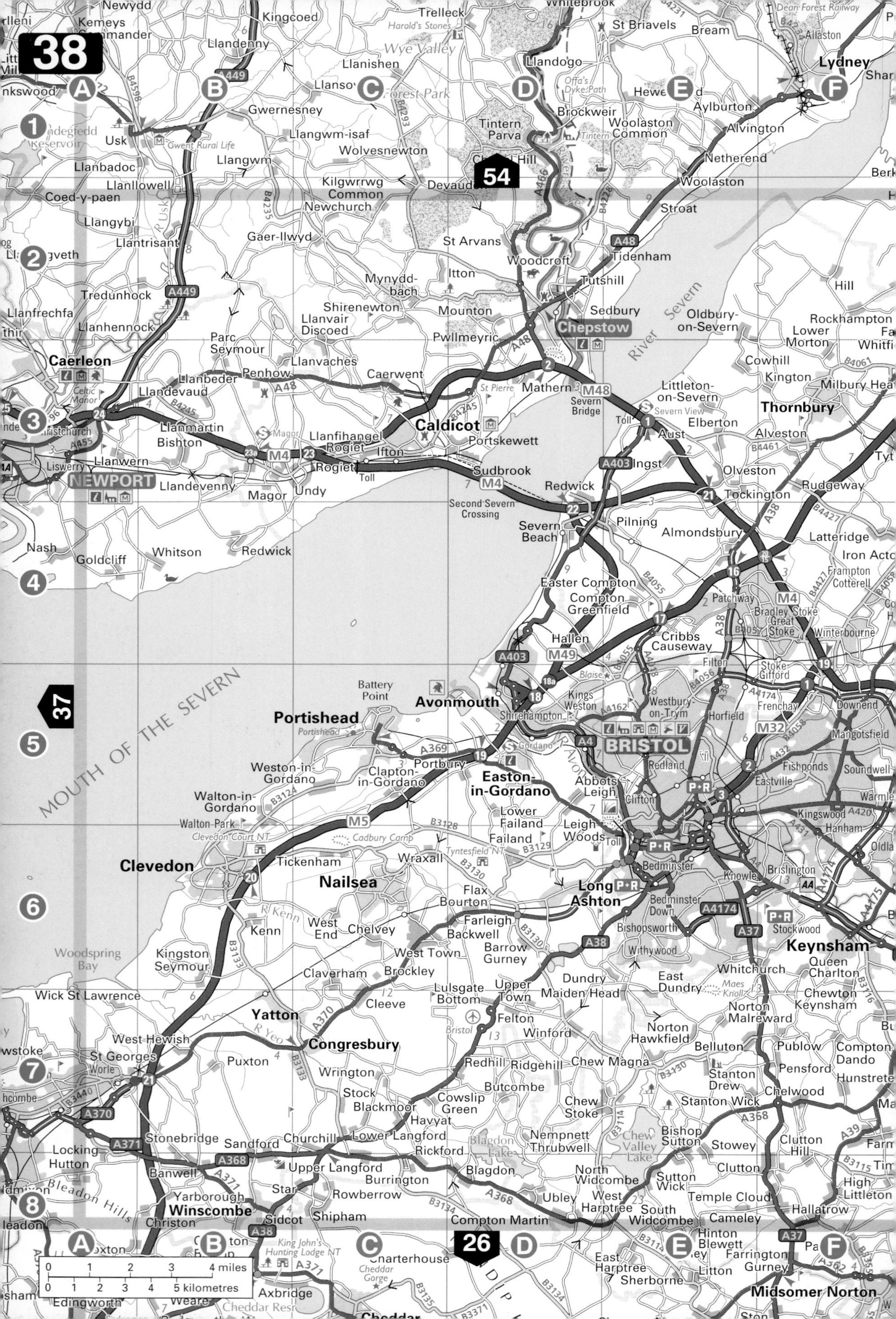
38
Newydd
Kemeys Commander
Kingcoed
Trelleck
Harold's Stones
Whitebrook
St Briavels
Bream
Dean Forest Railway
Allaston
Lydney
Llandenny
Wye Valley
Llandogo
Llanishen
Llansoy
Forest Park
Offa's Dyke Path
Hewelsfield
Aylburton
Usk
Gwernesney
Brockweir
Woolaston Common
Alvington
Llandegfedd Reservoir
Gwent Rural Life
Llangwm-isaf
Tintern Parva
Tintern
Wolvesnewton
Chapel Hill
Netherend
Llanbadoc
Llangwm
Llanllowell
Kilgwrrwg Common
Devauden
54
Woolaston
Coed-y-paen
Newchurch
Stroat
Llangybi
Llantrisant
Gaer-llwyd
St Arvans
Tidenham
Llangwm
Woodcroft
Tutshill
Mynydd-bach
Itton
Hill
Tredunhock
Shirenewton
Mounton
Sedbury
Oldbury-on-Severn
Rockhampton
Llanfrechfa
Llanvair Discoed
Chepstow
River Severn
Lower Morton
Llanhennock
Pwllmeyric
Parc Seymour
Llanvaches
Cowhill
Caerleon
Caerwent
Kington
Penhow
Mathern
Littleton-on-Severn
Milbury Heath
Llanbeder
St Pierre
Celtic Manor
Llandevaud
Thornbury
Severn Bridge
Severn View
Elberton
Christchurch
Llanmartin
Caldicot
Aust
Alveston
Bishton
Magor
Llanfihangel Rogiet
Portskewett
Llanwern
Ifton
Ingst
Olveston
Liswerry
Rogiet
Sudbrook
Rudgeway
NEWPORT
Llandevenny
Toll
Redwick
Magor
Undy
Tockington
Second Severn Crossing
Pilning
Severn Beach
Almondsbury
Latteridge
Nash
Whitson
Redwick
Goldcliff
Iron Acton
Easter Compton
Frampton Cotterell
Patchway
Compton Greenfield
Bradley Stoke
Great Stoke
Winterbourne
Hallen
Cribbs Causeway
Filton
Stoke Gifford
Blaise
Battery Point
Avonmouth
Kings Weston
Westbury-on-Trym
Horfield
Frenchay
Downend
37
Portishead
Shirehampton
Mangotsfield
MOUTH OF THE SEVERN
Portbury
Gordano
BRISTOL
Redland
Fishponds
Soundwell
Weston-in-Gordano
Clapton-in-Gordano
Easton-in-Gordano
Abbots Leigh
Eastville
Walton-in-Gordano
Clifton
Warmley
Lower Failand
Kingswood
Walton Park
Leigh Woods
Hanham
Clevedon Court NT
Cadbury Camp
Failand
Tyntesfield NT
Clevedon
Tickenham
Wraxall
Bedminster
Brislington
Nailsea
Flax Bourton
Long Ashton
Knowle
Kenn
West End
Chelvey
Farleigh
Backwell
Bedminster Down
Bishopsworth
Stockwood
Woodspring Bay
Kingston Seymour
West Town
Barrow Gurney
Withywood
Keynsham
Claverham
Brockley
Dundry
Whitchurch
Queen Charlton
Wick St Lawrence
Lulsgate Bottom
Upper Town
Maiden Head
East Dundry
Maes Knoll
Chewton Keynsham
Yatton
Cleeve
Felton
Norton Malreward
Bristol
West Hewish
Winford
Norton Hawkfield
Congresbury
Belluton
Publow
Compton Dando
St Georges
Worle
Puxton
Redhill
Ridgehill
Chew Magna
Pensford
Wrington
Stanton Drew
Hunstrete
Butcombe
Stock
Blackmoor
Cowslip Green
Chew Stoke
Stanton Wick
Chelwood
Havyat
Locking
Stonebridge
Sandford
Churchill
Lower Langford
Blagdon Lake
Nempnett Thrubwell
Chew Valley Lake
Bishop Sutton
Stowey
Clutton Hill
Hutton
Rickford
Banwell
Upper Langford
Blagdon
North Widcombe
Clutton
Bleadon Hills
Burrington
Sutton Wick
High Littleton
Yarborough
Star
Rowberrow
West Harptree
Ubley
Temple Cloud
Winscombe
Christon
Sidcot
Shipham
Compton Martin
South Widcombe
Cameley
Hallatrow
Bleadon
Loxton
Hinton Blewett
26
King John's Hunting Lodge NT
Charterhouse
Cheddar Gorge
East Harptree
Farrington Gurney
Litton
Sherborne
Axbridge
Midsomer Norton
Edingworth
Weare
Cheddar Reservoir
Cheddar
Ston Easton
0 1 2 3 4 miles
0 1 2 3 4 5 kilometres
A B C D E F
1 2 3 4 5 6 7 8
M4 M5 M48 M49 M32 A48 A449 A466 A403 A4 A38 A369 A370 A371 A368 A37 A4174 A39 A420 A432 A4162 A4018 A4174

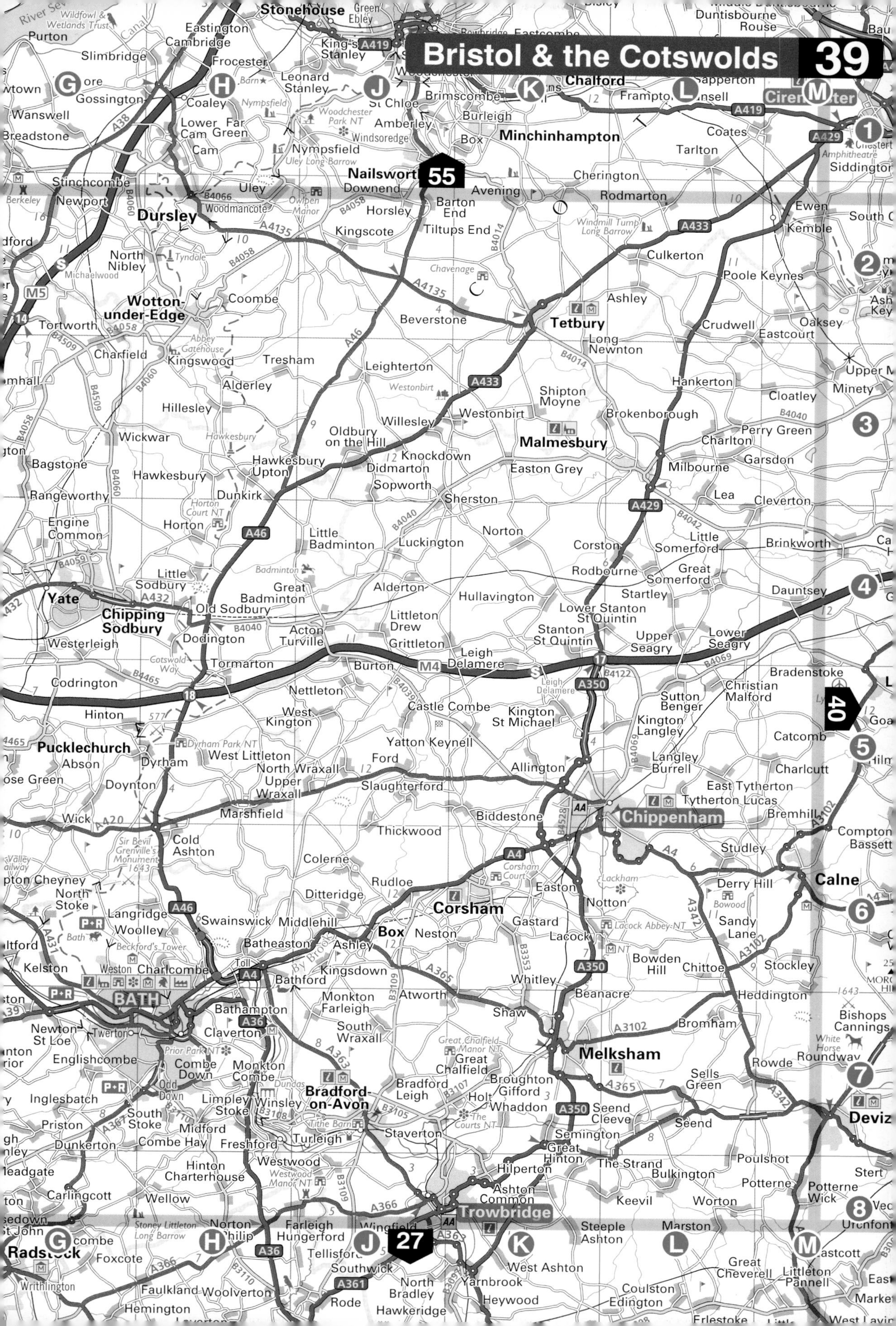
Stonehouse
Eastington
Cambridge
Purton
Slimbridge
Frocester
Leonard Stanley
King's Stanley
Chalford
Frampton
Cirencester
Gossington
Coaley
Nympsfield
Woodchester Park NT
Brimscombe
Burleigh
Minchinhampton
Coates
Tarlton
Amberley
Windsoredge
Box
Lower Cam
Far Green
Cam
Nympsfield
Uley Long Barrow
Nailsworth
55
Cherington
Siddington
Stinchcombe
Newport
Berkeley
Uley
Downend
Owlpen Manor
Avening
Rodmarton
Ewen
South Cerney
Dursley
Woodmancote
Horsley
Barton End
Kingscote
Tiltups End
Windmill Tump Long Barrow
Kemble
North Nibley
Tyndale
Michaelwood
Chavenage
Culkerton
Poole Keynes
Wotton-under-Edge
Coombe
Beverstone
Tetbury
Ashley
Ashton Keynes
Tortworth
Abbey Gatehouse
Kingswood
Charfield
Tresham
Long Newnton
Crudwell
Eastcourt
Oaksey
Upper Minety
Leighterton
Westonbirt
Alderley
Shipton Moyne
Hankerton
Minety
Cloatley
Hillesley
Willesley
Westonbirt
Brokenborough
Wickwar
Hawkesbury
Oldbury on the Hill
Malmesbury
Perry Green
Charlton
Knockdown
Bagstone
Hawkesbury Upton
Didmarton
Easton Grey
Milbourne
Garsdon
Hawkesbury
Sopworth
Rangeworthy
Dunkirk
Sherston
Lea
Cleverton
Horton Court NT
Engine Common
Horton
Little Badminton
Luckington
Norton
Corston
Little Somerford
Brinkworth
Badminton
Rodbourne
Great Somerford
Little Sodbury
Yate
Great Badminton
Alderton
Hullavington
Startley
Dauntsey
Chipping Sodbury
Old Sodbury
Littleton Drew
Lower Stanton St Quintin
Westerleigh
Dodington
Acton Turville
Stanton St Quintin
Upper Seagry
Lower Seagry
Grittleton
Leigh Delamere
Cotswold Way
Tormarton
Burton
Bradenstoke
Codrington
Leigh Delamere
Christian Malford
Nettleton
Hinton
West Kington
Castle Combe
Kington St Michael
Sutton Benger
Kington Langley
Catcomb
Pucklechurch
Dyrham Park NT
Yatton Keynell
Abson
Dyrham
West Littleton
Ford
Langley Burrell
Charlcutt
North Wraxall
Upper Wraxall
Allington
Doynton
Slaughterford
East Tytherton
Tytherton Lucas
Wick
Marshfield
Biddestone
Chippenham
Bremhill
Thickwood
Cold Ashton
Sir Bevil Grenville's Monument 1643
Compton Bassett
Colerne
Studley
Upton Cheyney
North Stoke
Rudloe
Corsham Court
Easton
Derry Hill
Calne
Bowood
Ditteridge
Lackham
Langridge
Corsham
Notton
Sandy Lane
Swainswick
Middlehill
Gastard
Woolley
Box
Neston
Lacock Abbey NT
Beckford's Tower
Batheaston
Ashley
Lacock
Kelston
Weston
Charlcombe
Kingsdown
Bowden Hill
Chittoe
Stockley
Bathford
Whitley
BATH
Monkton Farleigh
Atworth
Beanacre
Heddington
Bathampton
Shaw
Bishops Cannings
Newton St Loe
Twerton
Claverton
South Wraxall
Bromham
Prior Park NT
Great Chalfield Manor NT
Melksham
White Horse
Englishcombe
Combe Down
Monkton Combe
Great Chalfield
Roundway
Odd Down
Dundas Aqueduct
Bradford Leigh
Broughton Gifford
Rowde
Sells Green
Inglesbatch
Limpley Stoke
Winsley
Bradford-on-Avon
Holt
Whaddon
Seend Cleeve
Devizes
Priston
South Stoke
The Courts NT
Seend
Midford
Tithe Barn
Staverton
Semington
Dunkerton
Combe Hay
Freshford
Turleigh
Great Hinton
Poulshot
Westwood
Hilperton
The Strand
Bulkington
Hinton Charterhouse
Westwood Manor NT
Potterne
Carlingcott
Wellow
Ashton Common
Keevil
Worton
Potterne Wick
Trowbridge
Stoney Littleton Long Barrow
Norton St Philip
Farleigh Hungerford
Wingfield
27
Steeple Ashton
Marston
Urchfont
Radstock
Foxcote
Tellisford
Southwick
West Ashton
Great Cheverell
Littleton Pannell
Writhlington
Faulkland
Woolverton
North Bradley
Yarnbrook
Coulston
Edington
Hemington
Rode
Hawkeridge
Heywood
Erlestoke
River Severn
Wildfowl & Wetlands Trust
40

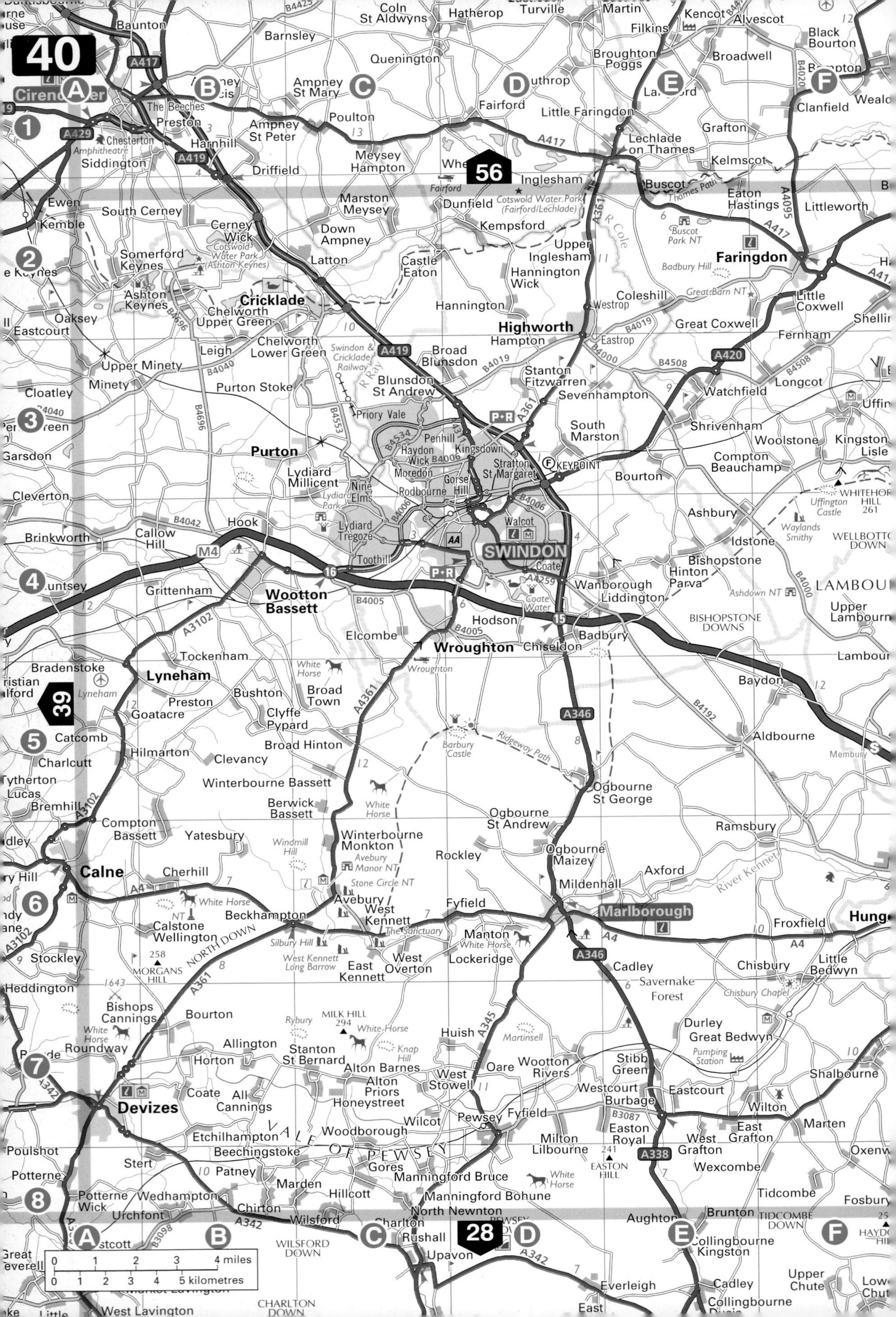

40
Baunton
Barnsley
Coln St Aldwyns
Hatherop
Turville
Martin
Filkins
Kencot
Alvescot
Black Bourton
Quenington
Broughton Poggs
Broadwell
Bampton
Cirencester
Ampney St Mary
Duthrop
Langford
Clanfield
The Beeches
Preston
Ampney St Peter
Poulton
Fairford
Little Faringdon
Chesterton
Amphitheatre
Harnhill
Meysey Hampton
Lechlade on Thames
Grafton
Kelmscot
Siddington
Driffield
56
Inglesham
Buscot
Fairford
Dunfield
Cotswold Water Park (Fairford/Lechlade)
Thames Path
Eaton Hastings
Littleworth
Ewen
Kemble
South Cerney
Cerney Wick
Marston Meysey
Down Ampney
Kempsford
R Cole
Buscot Park NT
Somerford Keynes
Cotswold Water Park (Ashton Keynes)
Latton
Castle Eaton
Upper Inglesham
Hannington Wick
Faringdon
Badbury Hill
Ashton Keynes
Cricklade
Hannington
Coleshill
Westrop
Great Barn NT
Little Coxwell
Oaksey
Chelworth Upper Green
Eastcourt
Highworth
Great Coxwell
Shellingford
Chelworth Lower Green
Swindon & Cricklade Railway
Broad Blunsdon
Hampton
Eastrop
Fernham
Leigh
Upper Minety
Minety
R Ray
Blunsdon St Andrew
Stanton Fitzwarren
Sevenhampton
Watchfield
Longcot
Cloatley
Purton Stoke
Priory Vale
Penhill
South Marston
Shrivenham
Woolstone
Kingston Lisle
Garsdon
Purton
Haydon Wick
Kingsdown
Stratton St Margaret
KEYPOINT
Compton Beauchamp
Lydiard Millicent
Moredon
Gorse Hill
Bourton
Cleverton
Nine Elms
Lydiard Park
Rodbourne
WHITEHORSE HILL
Uffington Castle
Ashbury
Lydiard Tregoze
Walcot
Waylands Smithy
Hook
Brinkworth
Callow Hill
SWINDON
Idstone
WELLBOTTOM DOWN
Toothill
Coate
Bishopstone
Hinton Parva
Grittenham
Wootton Bassett
Coate Water
Wanborough
Liddington
Ashdown NT
LAMBOURN
Upper Lambourn
Lyneham
Hodson
BISHOPSTONE DOWNS
Elcombe
Wroughton
Chiseldon
Badbury
Bradenstoke
Tockenham
White Horse
Lambourn
39
Preston
Bushton
Broad Town
Baydon
Goatacre
Clyffe Pypard
Catcomb
Aldbourne
Charlcutt
Broad Hinton
Barbury Castle
Ridgeway Path
Membury
Hilmarton
Clevancy
Tytherton Lucas
Winterbourne Bassett
Ogbourne St George
Bremhill
Berwick Bassett
White Horse
Compton Bassett
Ogbourne St Andrew
Ramsbury
Yatesbury
Windmill Hill
Winterbourne Monkton
Avebury Manor NT
Rockley
Ogbourne Maizey
Calne
Cherhill
Stone Circle NT
Axford
Mildenhall
River Kennet
White Horse
Avebury
West Kennett
Fyfield
Marlborough
Calstone Wellington
Beckhampton
The Sanctuary
Manton
White Horse
Froxfield
Hungerford
NORTH DOWN
Silbury Hill
West Kennett Long Barrow
Stockley
MORGANS HILL
East Kennett
West Overton
Lockeridge
Cadley
Chisbury
Little Bedwyn
Heddington
Savernake Forest
Chisbury Chapel
Bishops Cannings
Bourton
Rybury
MILK HILL
White Horse
Huish
Martinsell
Durley
Great Bedwyn
White Horse
Roundway
Allington
Stanton St Bernard
Knap Hill
Pumping Station
Horton
Alton Barnes
Oare
Wootton Rivers
Stibb Green
Shalbourne
Alton Priors
West Stowell
Westcourt
Eastcourt
Devizes
Coate
All Cannings
Honeystreet
Burbage
Wilton
Wilcot
Pewsey
Fyfield
Etchilhampton
Woodborough
VALE OF PEWSEY
Milton Lilbourne
Easton Royal
East Grafton
West Grafton
Marten
Poulshot
Beechingstoke
EASTON HILL
Oxenwood
Stert
Gores
Potterne
Patney
Manningford Bruce
White Horse
Wexcombe
Marden
Hillcott
Manningford Bohune
Tidcombe
Potterne Wick
Wedhampton
Fosbury
Urchfont
Chirton
North Newnton
Aughton
Brunton
TIDCOMBE DOWN
Wilsford
Charlton
Rushall
28
Collingbourne Kingston
Upavon
WILSFORD DOWN
Everleigh
Upper Chute
Cadley
Collingbourne Ducis
Great Cheverell
West Lavington
CHARLTON DOWN
0 1 2 3 4 miles
0 1 2 3 4 5 kilometres

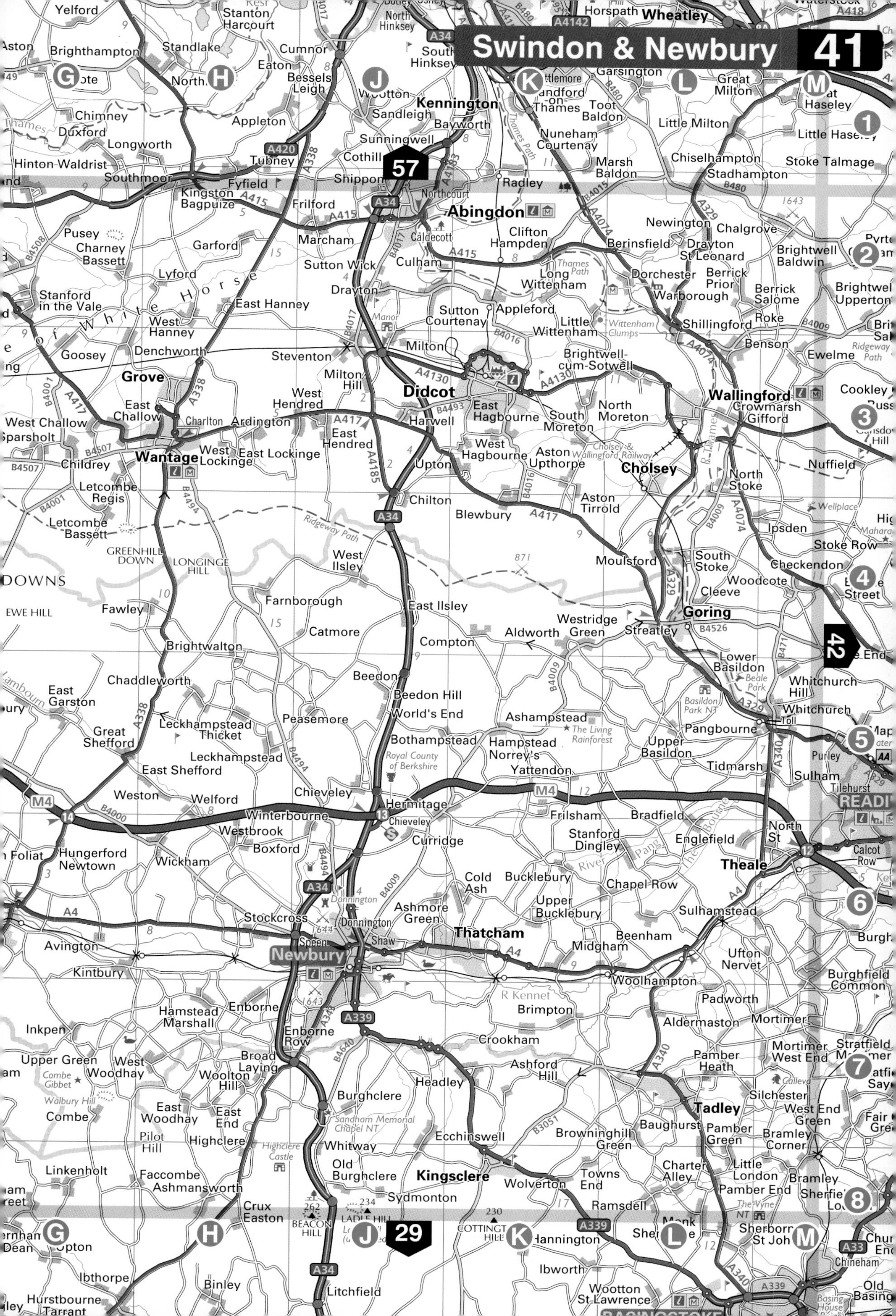
Yelford
Stanton Harcourt
North Hinksey
Horspath
Wheatley
A4142
A418
A34
South Hinksey
Aston
Brighthampton
Standlake
Cumnor
Eaton
G
H
J
K
L
M
North
Bessels Leigh
Wootton
Kennington
Littlemore
Sandford on Thames
Garsington
Toot Baldon
Great Milton
Great Haseley
Thames
Chimney
Duxford
Appleton
Sandleigh
Bayworth
Nuneham Courtenay
Little Milton
1
Little Haseley
Longworth
Sunningwell
Cothill
Thames Path
Hinton Waldrist
A420
Tubney
57
Marsh Baldon
Chiselhampton
Stadhampton
Stoke Talmage
Southmoor
Fyfield
Shippon
Radley
Kingston Bagpuize
A415
Frilford
A34
Northcourt
A4183
B4015
B480
1643
Abingdon
A4074
Newington
Chalgrove
Pusey
Charney Bassett
Garford
Marcham
Caldecott
Clifton Hampden
Berinsfield
Drayton St Leonard
Brightwell Baldwin
2
B4508
A415
Sutton Wick
Culham
Thames Path
Dorchester
Berrick Prior
Berrick Salome
Brightwell Upperton
Lyford
Long Wittenham
Warborough
Stanford in the Vale
Vale of White Horse
East Hanney
Drayton
Sutton Courtenay
Appleford
Little Wittenham
Wittenham Clumps
Shillingford
Roke
B4009
West Hanney
Manor
B4017
B4016
Benson
Ridgeway Path
Ewelme
Goosey
Denchworth
Steventon
Milton
A4074
Grove
Milton Hill
Brightwell-cum-Sotwell
A4130
Didcot
Wallingford
Cookley
East Challow
A338
A417
West Hendred
B4001
A4130
West Challow
Sparsholt
Charlton
Ardington
B4493
East Hagbourne
South Moreton
North Moreton
Crowmarsh Gifford
3
A417
Harwell
East Hendred
Wantage
West Lockinge
East Lockinge
West Hagbourne
Aston Upthorpe
Cholsey & Wallingford Railway
R Thames
B4507
Childrey
A4185
Upton
Cholsey
Nuffield
North Stoke
Letcombe Regis
B4494
Chilton
B4016
Aston Tirrold
B4001
A34
Blewbury
A417
Wellplace
Letcombe Bassett
Ridgeway Path
B4009
A4074
Ipsden
GREENHILL DOWN
LONGINGE HILL
West Ilsley
871
Moulsford
South Stoke
Stoke Row
Checkendon
DOWNS
A329
Woodcote
4
EWE HILL
Fawley
Farnborough
Cleeve
East Ilsley
Westridge Green
Goring
Catmore
Aldworth
Streatley
B4526
Brightwalton
Compton
42
Lower Basildon
B471
Beale Park
Whitchurch Hill
Chaddleworth
Beedon
East Garston
B4009
Basildon Park NT
A329
Beedon Hill
World's End
Whitchurch
Toll
Great Shefford
A338
Leckhampstead Thicket
Peasemore
Ashampstead
The Living Rainforest
Pangbourne
5
Bothampstead
Hampstead Norreys
Upper Basildon
Purley
Royal County of Berkshire
Leckhampstead
A340
B4494
Tidmarsh
East Shefford
Yattendon
Sulham
Tilehurst
M4
Weston
Welford
Chieveley
M4
Hermitage
B4000
Frilsham
Bradfield
14
Winterbourne
13
Chieveley
Westbrook
Stanford Dingley
North St
Calcot Row
Hungerford Newtown
Boxford
Curridge
Englefield
Wickham
River Pang
12
Theale
Cold Ash
Bucklebury
Chapel Row
B4494
B4009
A34
Upper Bucklebury
A4
Donnington
Ashmore Green
Sulhamstead
6
A4
Stockcross
1644
Donnington
Thatcham
Beenham
Speen
Shaw
Avington
Newbury
A4
Midgham
Ufton Nervet
Kintbury
Woolhampton
Burghfield Common
1643
R Kennet
Hamstead Marshall
Enborne
Brimpton
Padworth
A339
Inkpen
Enborne Row
Aldermaston
Mortimer
B4640
Crookham
Upper Green
West Woodhay
Broad Laying
Pamber Heath
Mortimer West End
Stratfield Mortimer
7
Combe Gibbet
Woolton Hill
Headley
Ashford Hill
A340
Calleva
Walbury Hill
Silchester
East Woodhay
East End
Burghclere
Tadley
West End Green
Combe
Sandham Memorial Chapel NT
B3051
Baughurst
Pamber Green
Bramley Corner
Pilot Hill
Highclere
Highclere Castle
Whitway
Ecchinswell
Browninghill Green
Little London
Linkenholt
Old Burghclere
Kingsclere
Wolverton
Towns End
Charter Alley
Bramley
Faccombe
Ashmansworth
Pamber End
Sherfield on Loddon
8
Crux Easton
Sydmonton
Ramsdell
The Vyne NT
262
BEACON HILL
234
LADLE HILL
29
230
COTTINGTON HILL
A339
Monk Sherborne
Hannington
Sherborne St John
Upton
A33
Chineham
Ibthorpe
A34
Ibworth
Binley
Wootton St Lawrence
A339
Old Basing
A340
Hurstbourne Tarrant
Litchfield
Basing House

A B C D E F
1 2 3 4 5 6 7 8
Haseley
Little Haseley
Stoke Talmage
Moreton
Tetsworth
Emmington
Sydenham
Postcombe
Towersey
Ilmer
Longwick
Askett
Pitch Green
Hent
Bledlow
Chinnor & Princes Risborough Railway
Chinnor
Crowell
Kingston Blount
Aston Rowant
Radnage
Lodge Hill
Princes Risborough
Saunderton
Loosley Row
Lacey Green
Great Hampden
Dunsmore
Pulpit Hill
Lee
The Lee Clump
Bellingdon
Asheridge
Chartridge
Ballinger Common
South Heath
Hyde Heath
Prestwood
Great Missenden
Chesham Bois
58
Hughenden Valley
Little Kingshill
Great Kingshill
Little Missenden
Amersham
Cryers Hill
Holmer Green
Penn Street
Coleshill
South Weston
Lewknor
Pyrton
Cuxham
Brightwell Baldwin
Shirburn
Watlington
Stokenchurch
Bledlow Ridge
The City
Bradenham
Naphill
Beacon's Bottom
Hell Fire Club
Hughenden Manor NT
Downley
Widmer End
Hazlemere
Winchmore Hill
Penn
Berrick Salome
Roke
Benson
Brightwell Upperton
Britwell Salome
Ewelme
Ridgeway Path
Ibstone
Cadmore End
Turville
West Wycombe Park NT
High Wycombe
Cressex
Booker
Lane End
Wycombe Marsh
Bekonscot Model Village
Beaconsfield
Fingest
Skirmett
Frieth
Blue Max
Cookley Green
Russell's Water
Park Corner
Pishill
Stonor
Stonor Park
Gangsdown Hill
Nuffield
Nettlebed
Crocker End
Rockwell End
Fawley
Hambleden
Mill End
Marlow Bottom
Marlow
Little Marlow
Flackwell Heath
Wooburn Green
Rare Breeds Centre
Bourne End
Wooburn
Hedgerley
Cookham
Hedsor
Cliveden NT
Burnham Beeches
Highmoor
Maharajah's Well
Highmoor Cross
Bix
Wellplace
Ipsden
Lower Assendon
Aston
Bisham
Medmenham
Hurley
Cookham Dean
Cookham Rise
Maidenhead
Taplow
Burnham
Farnham Royal
Stoke Row
Checkendon
Exlade Street
Greys Court NT
Greys Green
Rotherfield Greys
Remenham
River & Rowing
Remenham Hill
Henley-on-Thames
Cockpole Gn
Warren Row
Burchett's Green
North Town
Cippenham
Rotherfield Peppard
Sonning Common
The Herb Farm
Lower Shiplake
Wargrave
Knowl Hill
Littlewick Green
Braywick
Bray
Dorney
Dorney Court
Eton Wick
Eton
Cane End
Kidmore End
Whitchurch
Beale Park
Tokers Green
Dunsden Green
Binfield Heath
Shiplake
Thames Path
Hare Hatch
Ruscombe
Waltham St Lawrence
White Waltham
Woodlands Park
Holyport
Fifield
Dedworth
Windsor
41
Mapledurham
Watermill
Purley
Sulham
Tilehurst
Caversham
Play Hatch
Sonning
Charvil
Twyford
Paley Street
Legoland
Shurlock Row
Whistley Green
Woodley
Reading
North St
Calcot Row
Kennet & Avon Canal
Whitley
Earley
Winnersh
Dinton Pastures
Hurst
Binfield
Warfield
Newell Green
Winkfield
Winkfield Row
Woodside
Guards Polo Club
Virginia Water
Great
North Ascot
Bullbrook
Ascot
Sindlesham
Shinfield
Wokingham
Three Mile Cross
Burghfield
Arborfield
Easthampstead
Bracknell
Sunninghill
Sunningdale
Burghfield Common
Spencers Wood
Arborfield Cross
REME
Barkham
Gardeners Green
Tower Hill
Swallowfield
Farley Hill
California
Look Out Discovery Centre
Wellingtonia Avenue
Windlesham
Mortimer
Mortimer West End
Stratfield Mortimer
Beech Hill
Riseley
Wellington
Blackwater R
Finchampstead
Crowthorne
Bagshot
Chobham Common
Lightwater
Calleva
Silchester
Stratfield Saye
R Loddon
Eversley
Eversley Cross
Owlsmoor
Sandhurst
College Town
West End
West End Green
Fair Oak Green
Stratfield Turgis
Heckfield
Hound Green
Yateley
Blackwater
York Town
Camberley
Bisley
Bramley Corner
Turgis Green
Blackbushe
Yateley Common
Royal Logistics Corps
Little London
Bramley
Sherfield on Loddon
Hartley Wespall
Hartfordbridge
Hawley
Frimley
Brookwood
The Vyne NT
Mattingley
Hartley Wintney
Farnborough Street
Sherborne St John
Church End
West Green
West Green House NT
30
Fleet
Farnborough Park
Mytchett
Pirbright
Phoenix Green
Elvetham Heath
Winchfield
Cove
Farnborough
Basing
Basing House Ruins
Dogmersfield
Worplesdon
0 1 2 3 4 miles
0 1 2 3 4 5 kilometres
M40
M4
M3
A40
A329
A4010
A404
A4155
A4130
A404(M)
A4
A329(M)
A33
A327
A30
A322
A331
A355
A413
A416
A3095
A308
A321
A325

Ashley Green
Whelpley Hill
Potters Crouch
Colney Heath
Newgate
Bovingdon
Bedmond
Kings Langley
Abbots Langley
Chipperfield
Ley Hill
Flaunden
Belsize
Sarratt
Latimer
Garston
Radlett
Shenley
South Mimms
Ridge
Potters Bar
Botany Bay
Goff's Oak
59
Chenies
Chandler's Cross
WATFORD
Aldenham
Letchmore Heath
Green Street
Hadley Wood
Monken Hadley
Little Chalfont
Chorleywood
Chorleywood West
Croxley Green
Rickmansworth
Bushey
Borehamwood
Elstree
Barnet
Arkley
Cockfosters
New Barnet
East Barnet
Totteridge
Winchmore Hill
Southgate
Oxhey
Merry Hill
Bushey Heath
Batchworth
Eastbury
London Gateway
Highwood Hill
Mill Hill
Friern Barnet
Chalfont Common
Chalfont St Peter
Harefield
Northwood
Hatch End
Stanmore
Harrow Weald
Edgware
Church End
Finchley
Wood Green
Muswell Hill
Denham Green
Gerrards Cross
Ruislip Woods
Pinner Green
Pinner
Eastcote
Wealdstone
Harrow
Kenton
Kingsbury
Hendon
Hornsey
Crouch End
Denham
Ruislip
Harrow on the Hill
Brent Resr
Golders Green
Highgate
Kenwood
Fulmer
New Denham
Ickenham
Sudbury
Wembley
Wembley Complex
Neasden
Hampstead
Holloway
Highbury
Uxbridge
Black Park
Iver Heath
North Hillingdon
Northolt
Cricklewood
Fenton NT
Kentish Town
Camden Town
Willesden
Hillingdon
Perivale
Alperton
Harlesden
Kilburn
St John's Wood
Lords
Cowley
Hayes End
Yeading
Greenford
Park Royal
Marylebone
Holborn
George Green
Iver
Yiewsley
Wood End
Hayes
Ealing
Acton
Paddington
City
Shepherd's Bush
Kensington Palace
Kensington
Westminster
Southall
Norwood Green
West Drayton
Hammersmith
Olympia
44
Langley
Harlington
Heston
Osterley Park NT
Brentford
Chiswick
Earls Court
Chelsea
Lambeth
Oval
Colnbrook
Poyle
Cranford
Osterley
Kew
Chiswick House
Syon
Kew Palace
Mortlake
Barnes
The Wetland Centre
Carlyle's House NT
Battersea
Fulham
Horton
Heathrow
Hounslow
Isleworth
Twickenham
East Sheen
Putney
Clapham
Brixton
Old Windsor
Stanwell
West Bedfont
Hatton
Richmond
Roehampton
Wandsworth
Major roadworks Jct 12-15, due for completion early 2006
Wraysbury
Hythe End
East Bedfont
Petersham
Richmond Park
Balham
Tulse Hill
Ham House NT
Feltham
Ham
Earlsfield
Tooting Bec
Streatham
West Norwood
Egham
Ashford
Lower Feltham
Teddington
Tooting
Thorpe Lea
Felthamhill
Hanworth
Kingston upon Thames
Wimbledon
Merton
STAINES
Queen Mary Resr
Kempton Park
Hampton
Hampton Wick
Norbury
Thornton Heath
Thorpe
Virginia Water
Thorpe Park
Littleton
Sunbury
Upper Halliford
West Molesey
East Molesey
Hampton Court Palace
Norbiton
New Malden
Raynes Park
Morden
Mitcham
Selhurst
Lower Halliford
Thames Ditton
Surbiton
Motspur Park
St Helier
Beddington Corner
Chertsey
Shepperton
Walton-on-Thames
Long Ditton
Tolworth
Malden
Worcester Park
North Cheam
Hackbridge
Beddington
Lyne
Thames Path
Sandown Park
Hinchley Wood
Carshalton
Wallington
Addlestone
Oatlands Park
Weybridge
Hersham
Esher
Hook
Ottershaw
Claygate
Chessington
Cheam
Sutton
South Beddington
New Haw
Claremont NT
Ewell
Belmont
Woodcote
Woodham
Chessington World of Adventures
Little Woodcote
Purley
West Byfleet
Byfleet
Fairmile
Cobham
Oxshott
Epsom
Sheerwater
Ashtead Common
Kenley
Maybury
Rainshill Park
Woodmansterne
Coulsdon
Pyrford
Semaphore Tower
Downside
Stoke D'Abernon
Epsom Downs
Banstead
Wisley
Epsom
WOKING
Ashtead
Burgh Heath
Whyteleafe
Old Woking
Ripley
Leatherhead
Tadworth
Chipstead
Ockham
31
Fetcham
Kingswood
Chaldon
Little Bookham
Great Bookham
Headley
Walton on the Hill
Sutton Green
West Horsley
East Horsley
Bocketts
Effingham
Headley Common NT
Mickleham
Walton Heath
Caterham

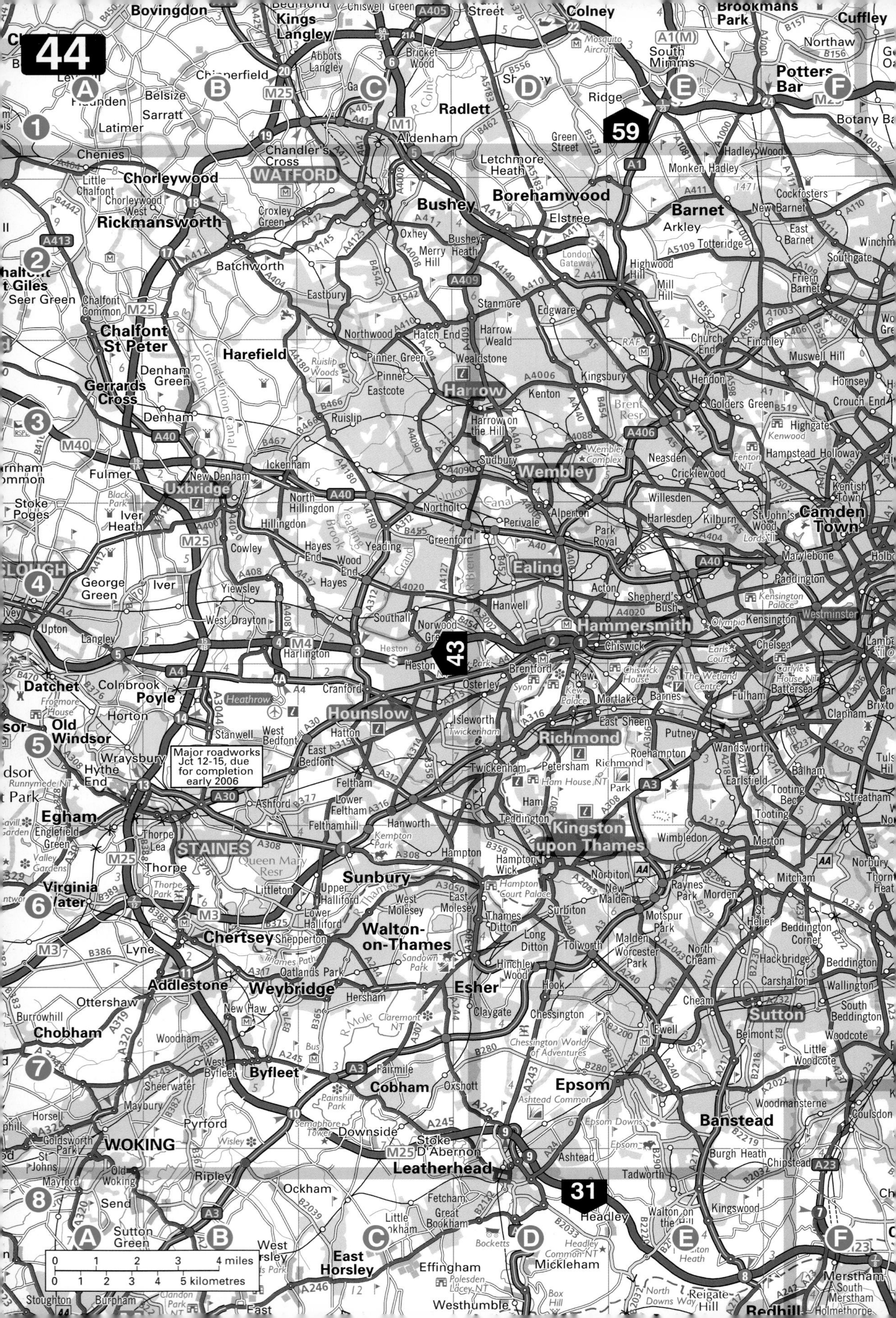
Bovingdon
Kings Langley
Abbots Langley
Colney
Brookmans Park
Cuffley
Northaw
South Mimms
Potters Bar
Chipperfield
Belsize
Sarratt
Latimer
Radlett
Ridge
Aldenham
Chandler's Cross
WATFORD
Chenies
Chorleywood
Little Chalfont
Rickmansworth
Croxley Green
Bushey
Borehamwood
Letchmore Heath
Elstree
Barnet
Arkley
Totteridge
Hadley Wood
Monken Hadley
Cockfosters
New Barnet
East Barnet
Southgate
Batchworth
Oxhey
Merry Hill
Bushey Heath
Highwood Hill
Mill Hill
Friern Barnet
Seer Green
Chalfont Common
Chalfont St Peter
Harefield
Eastbury
Northwood
Hatch End
Stanmore
Edgware
Harrow Weald
Church End
Finchley
Muswell Hill
Gerrards Cross
Denham Green
Denham
Ruislip
Pinner Green
Pinner
Eastcote
Wealdstone
Harrow
Harrow on the Hill
Kenton
Kingsbury
Hendon
Golders Green
Hornsey
Crouch End
Highgate
Kenwood
Hampstead
Holloway
Fulmer
New Denham
Uxbridge
Ickenham
North Hillingdon
Hillingdon
Sudbury
Wembley
Neasden
Cricklewood
Willesden
Harlesden
Kilburn
St John's Wood
Camden Town
Stoke Poges
Iver Heath
Cowley
Hayes End
Yeading
Northolt
Greenford
Perivale
Alperton
Park Royal
Marylebone
Paddington
SLOUGH
George Green
Iver
Yiewsley
Wood End
Hayes
Southall
Ealing
Hanwell
Acton
Shepherd's Bush
Kensington
Westminster
West Drayton
Upton
Langley
Harlington
Norwood Green
Heston
Hammersmith
Chiswick
Chelsea
Datchet
Colnbrook
Poyle
Cranford
Osterley
Brentford
Kew
Mortlake
Barnes
Fulham
Battersea
Clapham
Old Windsor
Horton
Heathrow
Hounslow
Isleworth
Twickenham
East Sheen
Richmond
Putney
Roehampton
Wandsworth
Stanwell
West Bedfont
Hatton
East Bedfont
Balham
Wraysbury
Hythe End
Major roadworks Jct 12-15, due for completion early 2006
Feltham
Petersham
Richmond Park
Earlsfield
Tooting Bec
Streatham
Egham
Englefield Green
Ashford
Lower Feltham
Hanworth
Ham
Teddington
Kingston upon Thames
Wimbledon
Tooting
Merton
Thorpe Lea
STAINES
Felthamhill
Hampton
Hampton Wick
Norbiton
Thorpe
Queen Mary Resr
Sunbury
Upper Halliford
Hampton Court Palace
New Malden
Raynes Park
Morden
Mitcham
Norbury
Virginia Water
Littleton
Lower Halliford
West Molesey
East Molesey
Surbiton
Motspur Park
St Helier
Beddington Corner
Chertsey
Shepperton
Walton-on-Thames
Thames Ditton
Long Ditton
Tolworth
Malden
Worcester Park
North Cheam
Hackbridge
Beddington
Lyne
Oatlands Park
Hinchley Wood
Carshalton
Wallington
Addlestone
Weybridge
Hersham
Esher
Hook
Cheam
Sutton
South Beddington
Ottershaw
New Haw
Claygate
Chessington
Ewell
Belmont
Woodcote
Burrowhill
Chobham
Woodham
Chessington World of Adventures
Little Woodcote
West Byfleet
Byfleet
Fairmile
Cobham
Oxshott
Epsom
Sheerwater
Maybury
Woodmansterne
Horsell
Pyrford
Downside
Banstead
Coulsdon
WOKING
Stoke D'Abernon
Ashtead
Burgh Heath
Chipstead
St Johns
Old Woking
Ripley
Leatherhead
Tadworth
Mayford
Ockham
Fetcham
Headley
Walton on the Hill
Kingswood
Send
Little Bookham
Great Bookham
Sutton Green
West Horsley
East Horsley
Effingham
Bocketts
Mickleham
Polesden Lacey NT
Westhumble
Reigate Hill
Merstham
South Merstham
Redhill
Stoughton
Burpham
0 1 2 3 4 miles
0 1 2 3 4 5 kilometres
59
43
31
M25
M1
M4
M3
M40
A1(M)

Cheshunt
Lee Valley Park
Epping Upland
Epping
North Weald Bassett
Coopersale Common
High Ongar
Chipping Ongar
Hylands House & Park
Waltham Abbey
Upshire
Waltham Cross
Stondon Massey
Mill Green
Fryerning
Doddinghurst
Heybridge
Ingatestone
Enfield Wash
Enfield Lock
High Beach
Theydon Bois
Debden
Nuclear Bunker
Kelvedon Hatch
Navestock Side
Navestock
Mountnessing
King George V Resr
Ponders End
Epping Forest
Loughton
Abridge
Lambourne End
Pilgrims Hatch
Coxtie Green
Shenfield
Hutton
Bush Hill Park
Chingford
Buckhurst Hill
Chigwell
Bournebridge
Stapleford Abbotts
South Weald
BRENTWOOD
Edmonton
Woodford Wells
Woodford
Grange Hill
Chigwell Row
Havering-atte-Bower
Havering
Harold Hill
Brook Street
Little Burstead
Highams Park
Hainault
Collier Row
Ingrave
Thorndon N
Tottenham
Higham Hill
Woodford Bridge
Clayhall
Barkingside
Gidea Park
Harold Wood
Great Warley
Thorndon S
Walthamstow
Walthamstow Group Resrs
Snaresbrook
Newbury Park
Romford
West Horndon
Upper Clapton
Wanstead
Seven Kings
Chadwell Heath
Leytonstone
Leyton
Ilford
Goodmayes
Rush Green
Hornchurch
Stoke Newington
Lower Clapton
Forest Gate
Manor Park
Becontree
Eastbrookend
Elm Park
Upminster
Bulphan
Hackney
Stratford
Barking
Dagenham
Corbets Tey
Dalston
West Ham
East Ham
South Hornchurch
Horndon on the Hill
Bethnal Green
Bow
Plaistow
Mar Dyke
Orsett
Stepney
Whitechapel
Poplar
Canning Town
Creekmouth
Beckton
Rainham
Belhus
South Ockendon
Wennington
North Stifford
LONDON
The Dome
Thames Barrier
City
Thamesmead
Aveley
Isle of Dogs
Bermondsey
Woolwich
Abbey Wood
Belvedere
Rainham Marshes
RSPB
Thurrock
Lakeside
Chadwell St Mary
West Tilbury
Greenwich
Deptford
Charlton
Plumstead
R Thames
Erith
Purfleet
West Thurrock
Grays
Little Thurrock
Peckham
New Cross
Blackheath
Kidbrooke
East Wickham
Slade Green
Dartford Crossing
Queen Elizabeth Bridge
Nunhead
Lee
Welling
Bexleyheath
Tilbury
Dulwich
Lewisham
Hither Green
Eltham
The Red House NT
Crayford
Tolls
Greenhithe
Swanscombe
Northfleet
Hall Place
Dartford
Swanscombe Skull
Forest Hill
Catford
Blackfen
Bexley
Bluewater Park
Chalk
GRAVESEND
Grove Park
Mottingham
New Eltham
Sydenham
Sidcup
Joyden's Wood
Wilmington
Green Street Green
Hook Green
Betsham
Southfleet
Singlewell
Crystal Palace
National Sports Centre
Downham
Hextable
Darenth
Istead Rise
Penge
Chislehurst
Sutton at Hone
Beckenham
Elmers End
Widmore
St Pauls Cray
Swanley
Swanley Village
Dean Bottom
Longfield
New Barn
South Norwood
Bickley
St Mary Cray
Horton Kirby
Bromley
Petts Wood
Crockenhill
Woodside
Eden Park
Southborough
Farningham
Hartley
West Wickham
Fawkham Green
Meopham
Addiscombe
Shirley
Hayes
Orpington
Eynsford
Croydon
Locksbottom
Chelsfield
New Ash Green
Brands Hatch
Addington
Keston
Farnborough
Lullingstone
Ash
New Addington
Maplescombe
West Kingsdown
Harvel
Selsdon
Downe
Pratt's Bottom
Hodsall Street
Culverstone Green
Leaves Green
Down House
Stansted
Fairseat
Vigo
Sanderstead
Farleigh
Fickleshole
Biggin Hill
Halstead
Shoreham
Trosley
Ryarsh
Trottiscliffe
Biggin Hill
Otford
Knockholt Pound
Wrotham
Addington
Aperfield
Knockholt
Heaverham
Kemsing
Leybourne
Warlingham
Dunton Green
Borough Green
West Malling
Tatsfield
North Downs Way
Chevening
Seal
Ightham
Platt
Offham
Chipstead
St Johns
Oldbury
Woldingham
Brasted
Riverhead
King Hill
Herne Pound
Titsey
Westerham
Sundridge
Knole NT
Stone Street
Ivy Hatch
Soar NT
Mereworth
Limpsfield
Clacket Lane
Ide Hill
Sevenoaks
Plaxtol
Dunk's Green
Oxted
Moorhouse Bank
Squerryes Court
Emmetts NT
Ightham Mote NT
Under River
Shipbourne
West Peckham
Nettlestead
Nettlestead Green
Godstone
Hurst Green
Limpsfield Chart
Toy's Hill
Ide
A121
A104
A112
A113
A110
A1069
A406
A12
A118
A124
A1083
A1240
A1112
A125
A127
A128
A129
A176
A13
A1306
A1020
A2016
A206
A209
A220
A207
A2
A20
A205
A21
A222
A223
A224
A225
A226
A232
A233
A25
A228
A227
A1089
A1012
A1090
B1036
B187
B1421
B186
B188
B1007
B1335
B260
B255
B259
B262
B258
B251
B265
B2024
B269
B270
B2026
B2042
B2019
B2016
B275
B181
B182
B1393
B172
B175
B174
B173
B170
B179
B177
M11
M25
M20
M26
60
32
33
46

46
61
45
33
Hylands House & Park
Baddow
Howe Green
Galleywood
Margaretting
Margaretting Tye
Rudley Green
New Hall
Mundon Hill
Bicknacre
Cock Clarks
Purleigh
Steeple
Howegreen
East Hanningfield
Latchingdon
Woodham Ferrers
Cold Norton
Stow Maries
Hyde Hall
Althorne
West Hanningfield
Ingatestone
Stock
Hanningfield Reservoir
Coalhill
South Woodham Ferrers
North Fambridge
Bridgemarsh Island
Burnham
South Hanningfield
Marsh Farm
River Crouch
Downham
Ramsden Bellhouse
Hullbridge
South Fambridge
Canewdon
Hutton
Billericay
South Green
Runwell
Battlesbridge
Wallasea Island
Rawreth
Ashingdon
Paglesham
Wickford
Little Burstead
Shotgate
Hockley
Eastend
Great Burstead
Crays Hill
Hawkwell
Great Stambridge
Potton Is
Ingrave
Rayleigh
Rochford
R Roach
North Benfleet
Barling
BASILDON
Southend
Little Wakering
Great Wakering
Laindon
Thundersley
Pitsea
Lee Chapel
Vange
Bowers Gifford
Eastwood
Prittlewell
Bournes Green
Westley Heights
One Tree Hill
Hadleigh
North Shoebury
Shoeburyness
Wat Tyler
Holehaven Creek
South Benfleet
Hadleigh Castle
Leigh-on-Sea
Westcliff-on-Sea
Southchurch
Thorpe Bay
Horndon on the Hill
Fobbing
Corringham
SOUTHEND-ON-SEA
Leigh Beck
Canvey Point
Shoebury Ness
Orsett
Coryton
Canvey Island
Stanford le-Hope
West Tilbury
Little Thurrock
East Tilbury
Tilbury
Tilbury Fort
Cliffe
St Mary's Hoo
Allhallows
Isle of Grain
Cooling
RSPB
Lower Stoke
Grain
High Halstow
Fenn Street
Middle Stoke
Stoke
Sheerness
Church Street
Milton
Mile Town
Marine Town
Cliffe Woods
Hoo St Werburgh
River Medway
West Minster
Queenborough
Chalk
GRAVESEND
Chattenden
Halfway Houses
Shorne
Singlewell
Thong
Higham
Wainscott
Upnor
Southfleet
Shorne Wood
Frindsbury
World Naval Base
Istead Rise
Strood
Diggerland
ISLE OF
Cobham
Fort Amherst
Riverside
Stangate Creek
Halstow Creek
Elmley Island
New Barn
ROCHESTER
Brompton
Grange
Sole Street
GILLINGHAM
Lower Halstow
Iwade
CHATHAM
Luton
Upchurch
Sittingbourne & Kemsley Light Railway
Meopham
Cuxton
Borstal
Luddesdown
North Downs Way
Rainham
Newington
Bobbing
Dolphin Sailing Barge Museum
Milton Regis
Wigmore
Hartlip
Wouldham
Chalkwell
Sittingbourne
Halling
Walderslade
Medway
Teynham
Harvel
Culverstone Green
Paddlesworth
Lords Wood
Bredhurst
Hill Green
Borden
Bapchild
Tunstall
Snodland
Burham
Oad St
Rodmersham
Vigo
Blue Bell Hill
Stockbury
Highsted
Rodmersham Green
Birling
Bredgar
Lynsted
Ryarsh
Eccles
Wildlife Trust Tyland Barn
South Green
Rawling Street
Aylesford
Addington
Lunsford
Kent County
Bicknor
Larkfield
Milstead
Leybourne
Ditton
Boxley
Detling
Hucking
West Malling
Wormshill
Doddington
Newnham
Thurnham
Offham
British Legion Village
Broad Street
Frinsted
East Malling
Bearsted
Kings Hill
Wichling
Tong
Herne Pound
MAIDSTONE
Hollingbourne
Tovil
Eyhorne Street
Throwley
Willington
Wateringbury
East Barming
Bearsted
Leeds
Otham
Harrietsham
Shepway
Leeds Castle
East Farleigh
Loose
Broomfield
Lenham
Warren Street
Peckham
Nettlestead Green
Boughton Green
Langley
0 1 2 3 4 miles
0 1 2 3 4 5 kilometres

Dengie
Holliwell Point
Foulness Point
Courtsend
Churchend
FOULNESS ISLAND
Warden Point
Leysdown-on-Sea
Isle of Harty
The Swale
Shell Ness
Whitstable
Whitstable Bay
Tankerton
Swalecliffe
Chestfield
Seasalter
Herne Bay
Hampton
Greenhill
Herne
Broomfield
Beltinge
Bishopstone
Reculver
Minnis Bay
Birchington
Westgate on Sea
St Nicholas at Wade
Boyden Gate
Sarre
Chislet
Acol
Monkton
Minster
Faversham
Oare
Broom Street
Goodnestone
Yorkletts
Highstreet
Dargate
Denstroude
Hernhill
Staplestreet
Dunkirk
Blean
Ospringe
Boughton St
North Street
Sheldwich
Hogben's Hill
Selling
Oversland
South Street
Upper Harbledown
Rough Common
Tyler Hill
Hales Place
Sturry
Broad Oak
Hersden
Westbere
Stodmarsh
Fordwich
Wickhambreaux
Littlebourne
Canterbury
Harbledown
Thanington
Chartham Hatch
Chartham
Old Wives Lees
Shalmsford Street
Badlesmere
Shottenden
Leaveland
Chilham
Dane Street
Molash
Challock
Garlinge Green
Bridge
Lower Hardres
Bishopsbourne
Kingston
Bekesbourne
Patrixbourne
Adisham
Aylesham
Bramling
Ickham
Seaton
Preston
Elmstone
Cop Street
Hoaden
Ash
Durlock
Wingham
Marshborough
Staple
Goodnestone
Chillenden
Nonington
Eastry
Tilmanstone
Betteshanger
Westmarsh
East Stourmouth
West Stourmouth
Upstreet
Hoath
Wildwood
Druidstone
Howletts
Higham Park
North Downs Way
Womenswold
Petham
A299
A28
A253
A257
A2
A2050
A290
A291
A251
A252
B2205
B2231
B2040
B2046
B2068
B2190
B2048
34
35
62

48
A
B
C
D
E
F
1
2
3
4
5
6
7
8
Pen Brush
Pwllderi
Pembrokeshire Coast Path
Trefasser
Goodwick
Manorowen
St Nicholas
Ynys Daullyn
Granston
Carreg Sampson
Abercastle
64
Llangloffan
Jordanston
Porthgain
Trefin
Mathry
16
A487
B4331
Abereiddy
Llanrhian
Berea
Croes-goch
Letterston
Treglemais
Treleddyd-fawr
ST DAVID'S HEAD
Whitesand Bay
Rhodiad-y-brenin
Caer Farchell
River Solva
B4330
Llandeloy
B4583
Bishops Palace
Whitchurch
Treffgarne Owen
Hayscastle
Hayscastle Cross
RAMSEY ISLAND
Ramsey Sound
RSPB
St David's
Solva
A487
Pen-y-cwn
178
DUDWELL MT
Leweston
St David's Peninsula Heritage Coast
Newgale
16
Roch
Wolfsdale
PEMBROKESHIRE COAST NATIONAL PARK
Simpson Cross
Keeston
Rickets Head
Nolton Haven
Nolton
A487
St Brides Bay
St Brides Bay Heritage Coast
Druidston
Haroldston West
Portfield Gate
B4341
Broad Haven
Broadway
B4327
Dreen Hill
Little Haven
Walton West
Pembrokeshire Coast Path
Talbenny
14
Tiers Cross
Walwyn's Castle
SKOMER ISLAND
Wooltrack Point
Marloes
B4327
St Ishmael's
A477
Broad Sound
Herbrandston
Steynton
Marloes and Dale Heritage Coast
Hubberston
Hakin
Waterston
Dale
Great Castle Head
Llanstadwell
SKOKHOLM ISLAND
Westdale Bay
Dale Point
Milford Haven
Milford Haven
Popton Point
Angle
Angle Bay
St Anns Head
Rhoscrowther
B4320
10
Rosslare Harbour
Castlemartin Brook
B4320
Freshwater West
B4319
Castlemartin
Warren
Merrion
Linney Head
PEMBROKESHIRE COAST NATIONAL PARK
Pembrokeshire Coast Path
0 1 2 3 4 miles
0 1 2 3 4 5 kilometres

Newport Bay
Fishguard Bay
Bryn-Henllan
Dinas
Newport
Nevern
Felindre Farchog
Castell Henllys
Rhoshill
Pen-rhiw
Newcastle
Lower Town
Fishguard
A487
Mynydd Melyn
311 MYNYDD CAREGOG
Pentre Ifan
Crosswell
Blaenffos
Bwlch-y-groes
Star
Llanychaer Bridge
Brynberian
Crymmych
PEMBROKESHIRE COAST
Pontfaen
B4313
B4329
MYNYDD PRESELI
NATIONAL PARK
65
Tegryn
Hermon
265
Trecwn
Foel Eryr
536 FOEL CWM - CERWYM
Mynachlog ddu
368 FOEL DRYCH
Llanfyrnach
Trelech
Little Newcastle
Puncheston
Rosebush
Gors Fawr
Afon Taf
Glandwr
Castlebythe
Tufton
Llandre Isaf
Hebron
Henry's Moat (Castell Hendre)
Maenclochog
Llangolman
Llanglydwen
Blaenwaun
Rinaston
Cefn-y-pant
Cwmbach
Llanwinio
Ambleston
Llys-y-frân Resr
New Moat
Efailwen
A478
B4299
Llanycefn
Spittal
Llys-y-frân
Login
Llanboidy
Gellywen
Walton East
Pen-ffordd
Scolton
Llandissilio
Afon Cynin
Clarbeston
Meidrim
Clarbeston Road
Bletherston
Eastern Cleddau
Llanfallteg
Clynderwen
Afon Gronw
Cwmfelin Boeth
Llangynin
Llanfallteg West
Whitland Abbey
Wiston
Bethesda
Fenton Brook
Commercial
Llawhaden
A40
Haverfordwest
Whitland
Pwll Trap
St Clears
Robeston Wathen
Llanddewi Velfrey
Uzmaston
B4314
Narberth
Crinow
Lampeter Velfrey
50
Llanddowror
River Taf
Afon Cywyn
Picton Castle
Oakwood Adventure & Leisure Park
B4328
A477
Tavernspite
A4066
PEMBROKESHIRE
A4115
B4315
Templeton
Red Roses
Hook
A4075
COAST
Martletwy
Ludchurch
Llanteg
Crunwear
B4314
Llansadurnen
Llangwm
Cwm Deri
NATIONAL PARK
Colby Woodland Garden
Pendine
Llanmiloe
Loveston
Reynalton
Begelly
Stepaside
Amroth
B4586
Museum of Speed
Lawrenny
Cresswell
Jeffreyston
Kilgetty
Burton
Cresselly
Broadmoor
West Williamston
Carew Newton
Wiseman's Bridge
Toll
Redberth
East Williamston
A478
Saundersfoot
Waterloo
Tide Mill
Cross
Carew
Cosheston
Milton
Monkstone Point
B4322
A477
Sageston
Carew Cheriton
B4318
Manor House
Gumfreston
St Florence
Tenby
Palace
Lamphey
Manorbier Newton
CARMARTHEN BAY
B4584
A4139
Penally
Hodgeston
Jameston
B4319
Giltar Point
Lydstep
Manorbier
B4585
Lydstep Point
Cheriton or Stackpole Elidor
Trewent Point
Monastery
CALDEY ISLAND
Stackpole
South Pembrokeshire Heritage Coast
Barafundle Bay NT
Stackpole Head
St Govan's Head
G
H
J
K
L
M
1
2
3
4
5
6
7
8

Llanfyrnach
Glandwr
Hebron
Llanglydwen
Cefn-y-pant
Login
Llanboidy
Cwmfelin Boeth
Whitland Abbey
Llanfallteg West
Whitland
Llanddewi Velfrey
Lampeter Velfrey
Tavernspite
Red Roses
Llanteg
Crunwear
Colby Woodland Garden
Amroth
Wiseman's Bridge
Monkstone Point
CALDEY ISLAND
Trelech
Blaenwaun
Cwmbach
Llanwinio
Gellywen
Meidrim
Llangynin
Bancyfelin
Pwll Trap
St Clears
Llanddowror
Laugharne
Llansadurnen
Pendine
Museum of Speed
Llanmiloe
CARMARTHEN BAY
Cwmduad
Blaen-y-Coed
Talog
Abernant
Llangynog
Llanybri
Llansteffan
Wharley Point
Ginst Point
River Towy
Ferryside
Llansaint
R Gwendraeth
Kidwelly
Pembrey
Llanpumsaint
Cynwyl Elfed
Gwili Railway
Rhydargaeau
Bronwydd
Carmarthen
Johnstown
Abergwili
Llangunnor
Pensarn
Llanllwch
United Counties
Croesyceiliog
Cwmffrwd
Bancycapel
Pontantwn
Llandyfaelog
Four Roads
Pontyates
Llangendeirne
Bancffosfelen
Meinciau
Carway
Trimsaran
Burry Port
Archddu
Burry Inlet
Broughton Bay
Burry Holms
Llangennith
Llanmadoc
Cheriton
Burry Green
Oldwalls
Rhossili Bay
Rhossili Downs
Rhossili
Llanddewi
Reynoldston
Knelston
WORMS HEAD
Middleton
Paviland
Port Einon
Overton
Culver Hole
Port Einon Point
0 1 2 3 4 miles
0 1 2 3 4 5 kilometres

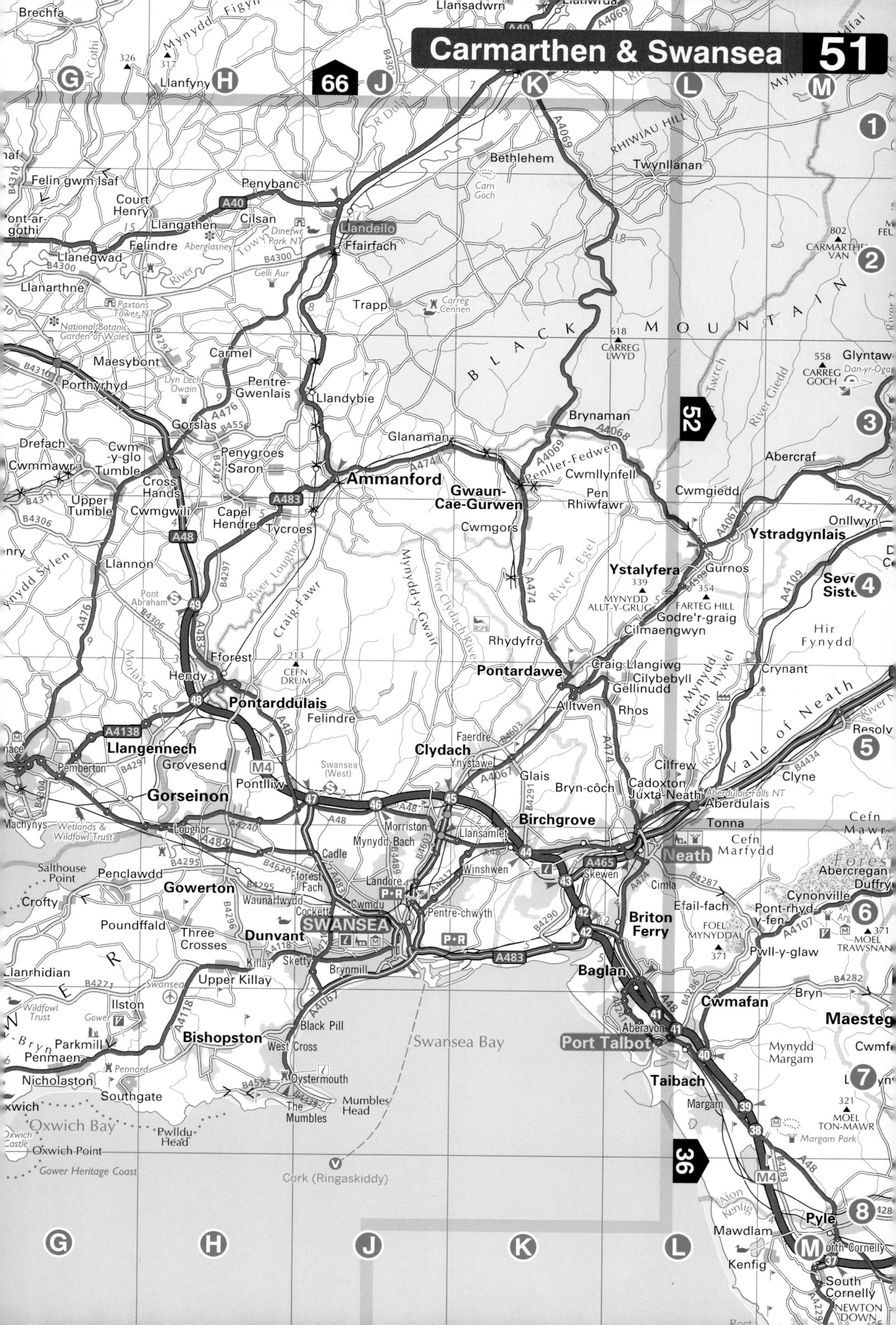
Llandeilo
Ammanford
Gwaun-Cae-Gurwen
Pontardawe
Pontarddulais
Llangennech
Gorseinon
Clydach
Birchgrove
Neath
SWANSEA
Gowerton
Dunvant
Bishopston
Port Talbot
Taibach
Baglan
Briton Ferry
Cwmafan
Maesteg
Pyle
Ystradgynlais
Ystalyfera
BLACK MOUNTAIN
Swansea Bay
Oxwich Bay
The Mumbles
Mumbles Head
Cork (Ringaskiddy)
Gower Heritage Coast
Vale of Neath
66
52
36

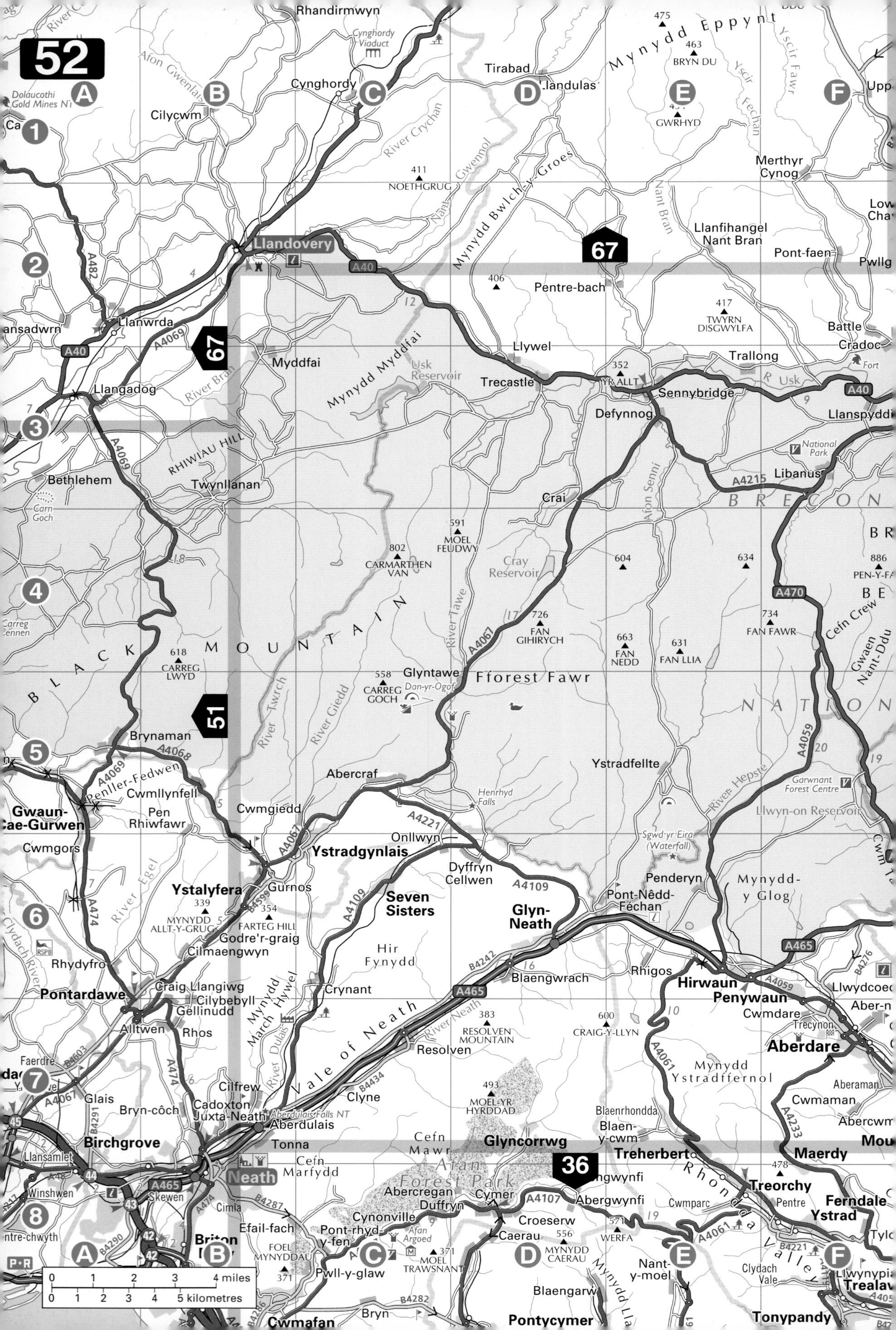
Rhandirmwyn
Cynghordy Viaduct
Cynghordy
Tirabad
Llandulas
475
463
BRYN DU
Mynydd Eppynt
Yscir Fawr
Yscir Fechan
GWRHYD
Dolaucothi Gold Mines NT
Afon Gwenlais
Cilycwm
River Crychan
Nant Gwennol
411
NOETHGRUG
Mynydd Bwlch-y-Groes
Nant Bran
Merthyr Cynog
Llanfihangel Nant Bran
Pont-faen
Llandovery
A40
A482
67
406
Pentre-bach
417
TWYRN DISGWYLFA
Battle
Cradoc
Fort
Llanwrda
ansadwrn
A4069
Myddfai
Mynydd Myddfai
Usk Reservoir
Llywel
Trecastle
352
YR ALLT
Trallong
R Usk
Sennybridge
Defynnog
Llanspyddi
River Bran
Llangadog
RHIWIAU HILL
Twynllanan
Bethlehem
Carn Goch
National Park
A4215
Libanus
Crai
Afon Senni
BRECON
591
MOEL FEUDWY
802
CARMARTHEN VAN
Cray Reservoir
604
634
886
PEN-Y-FA
A470
BLACK MOUNTAIN
River Tawe
A4067
726
FAN GIHIRYCH
663
FAN NEDD
631
FAN LLIA
734
FAN FAWR
Cefn Crew
Gwaen Nant-Ddu
Carreg Cennen
618
CARREG LWYD
558
CARREG GOCH
Glyntawe
Dan-yr-Ogof
Fforest Fawr
NATION
51
River Twrch
River Giedd
Brynaman
A4068
A4069
Penller-Fedwen
Cwmllynfell
Abercraf
Ystradfellte
A4059
River Hepste
Garwnant Forest Centre
Llwyn-on Reservoir
Gwaun-Cae-Gurwen
Pen Rhiwfawr
Cwmgiedd
Henrhyd Falls
Cwmgors
River Egel
A4221
Onllwyn
Ystradgynlais
Dyffryn Cellwen
Sgwd-yr-Eira (Waterfall)
Penderyn
Mynydd-y Glog
A474
Ystalyfera
Gurnos
339
MYNYDD ALLT-Y-GRUG
354
FARTEG HILL
A4109
Seven Sisters
Glyn-Neath
Pont-Nêdd-Fechan
Clydach River
RSPB
Godre'r-graig
Cilmaengwyn
Hir Fynydd
B4242
A465
Blaengwrach
Rhigos
Hirwaun
Penywaun
A4059
Llwydcoed
Aber-n
Rhydyfro
Pontardawe
Craig Llangiwg
Cilybebyll
Gellinudd
Crynant
Mynydd March Hywel
Vale of Neath
River Neath
383
RESOLVEN MOUNTAIN
600
CRAIG-Y-LLYN
Cwmdare
Trecynon
Aberdare
Alltwen
Rhos
Resolven
A4061
Mynydd Ystradffernol
Faerdre
B4603
A4067
Glais
B4291
Bryn-côch
Cilfrew
Cadoxton Juxta-Neath
River Dulais
B4434
Clyne
493
MOEL-YR-HYRDDAD
Blaenrhondda
Aberaman
Cwmaman
Abercwm
A4233
Aberdulais Falls NT
Aberdulais
Birchgrove
Tonna
Cefn Mawr
Glyncorrwg
Blaen-y-cwm
Treherbert
Maerdy
Llansamlet
Winshwen
Skewen
Neath
A465
Cimla
A474
Cefn Marfydd
Afan Forest Park
36
Abergwynfi
Rhondda Valley
478
Treorchy
Cwmparc
Pentre
Ferndale
Ystrad
Abercregan
Cymer
Duffryn
A4107
Croeserw
Caerau
556
MYNYDD CAERAU
571
WERFA
A4061
B4221
B4287
Efail-fach
Cynonville
Pont-rhyd-y-fen
Afan Argoed
FOEL MYNYDDAU
371
MOEL TRAWSNANT
Nant-y-moel
Clydach Vale
Llwynypia
Trealaw
B4290
Briton Ferry
Pwll-y-glaw
Mynydd Llangeinor
Blaengarw
0 1 2 3 4 miles
0 1 2 3 4 5 kilometres
B4282
Bryn
Cwmafan
Pontycymer
Tonypandy
A B C D E F
1 2 3 4 5 6 7 8

Gwenddwr
Erwood
Crickadarn
Clyro
Llowes
Cwmbâch
Boughrood
Glasbury
Llanigon
Llyswen
Aberllynfi
Three Cocks
Tregoyd
Velindre
Bronllys
Talgarth
Llanelieu
Llanfilo
Trefecca
Llandefaelog-Tre'r-Graig
Llanddew
Llanywern
Llangors
Llangors Lake
Llanhamlach
Pennorth
Llanfrynach
Pencelli
Scethrog
Cathedine
Llansantffraed
Cwmdu
Bwlch
Talybont-on-Usk
Tretower
Tretower Court & Castle
Cwm Crawnon
Llangynidr
Crickhowell
Llangattock
Gilwern
Gofilon
Clydach
Llanfoist
Abergavenny
Brynmawr
Beaufort
Nantyglo
Blaenavon
Tredegar
Ebbw Vale
Blaina
Rhymney
Dowlais
Abertillery
Abersychan
Pontypool
Cwmtillery
Llanhilleth
Crumlin
Newbridge
Oakdale
Blackwood
Pontllanfraith
Pengam
Gelligaer
Bargoed
Treharris
Nelson
Hengoed
Ystrad Mynach
Abercynon
Crosskeys
Risca
Cwmbran
Caerleon
Llanthony
Longtown
Oldcastle
Pandy
Llanvihangel Crucorney
Llantilio Pertholey
Mardy
Llanover
Llanellen
Goetre
Penperlleni
Little Mill
Monkswood
Black Mountains
Gader Ridge
Ffawddog Ridge
Black Mountain
Penallt Mawr Range
Hay Bluff
Lord Hereford's Knob
Waun Fach
Pen-y-Gader Fawr
Crug Mawr
Sugar Loaf
Skirrid-Fawr
Talybont Reservoir
Brecon Mountain Railway
Mynydd Llangynidr
Garn Caws
Coity Mountain
Mynydd Garnclochdy
A40
A465
A470
A479
A438
A4042
A472
A467
A469

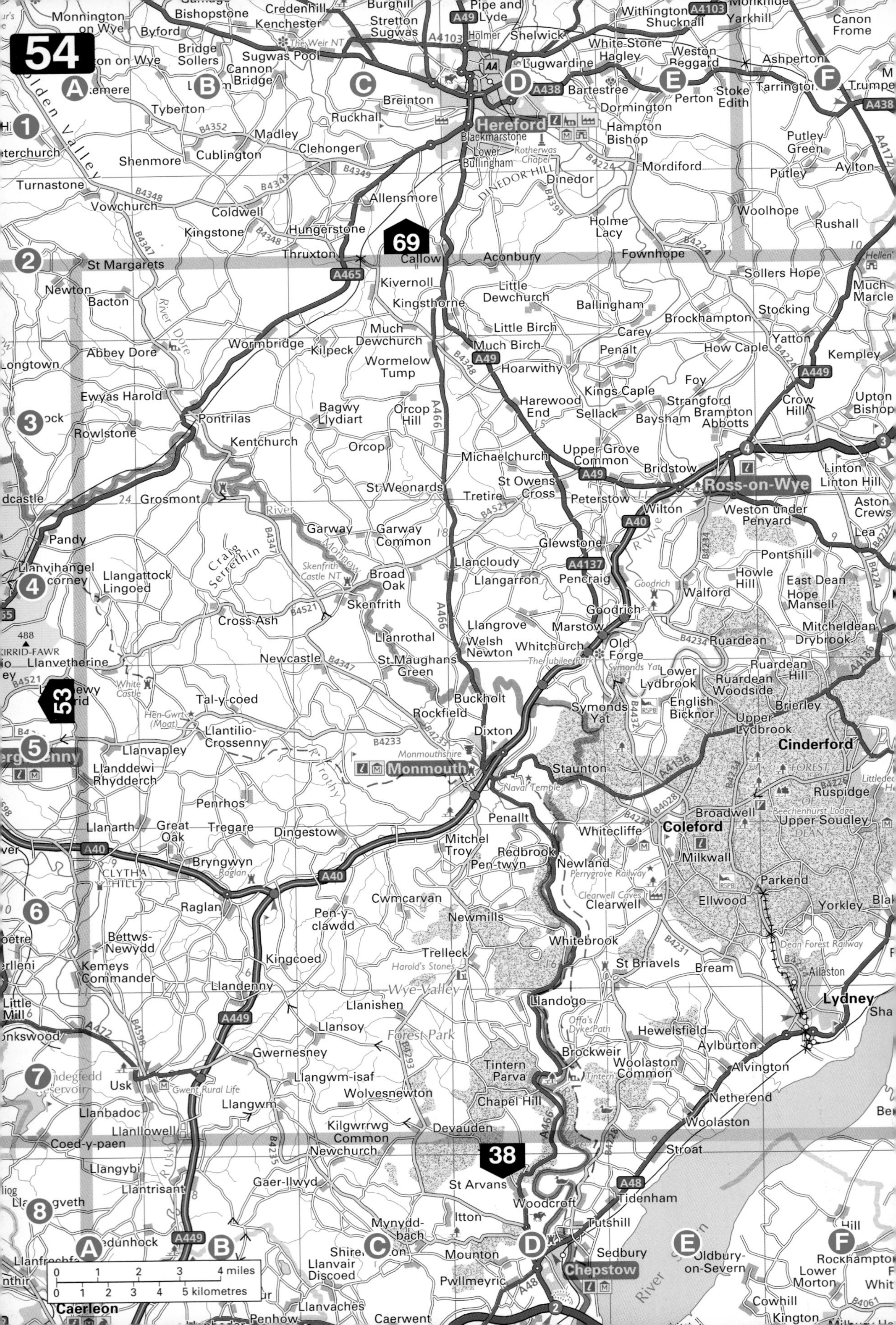

54
69
53
38
Hereford
Ross-on-Wye
Monmouth
Coleford
Cinderford
Lydney
Chepstow
Caerleon
Usk
Raglan
Golden Valley
Wye Valley
Forest Park
River Severn
Craig Serrethin
Dinedor Hill
Kirrid-Fawr
Clytha Hill
Forest of Dean
Skenfrith Castle NT
White Castle
Hen-Gwrt (Moat)
The Weir NT
Rotherwas Chapel
The Jubilee Park
Symonds Yat
Naval Temple
Monmouthshire
Perrygrove Railway
Clearwell Caves
Dean Forest Railway
Beechenhurst Lodge
Harold's Stones
Offa's Dyke Path
Tintern
Gwent Rural Life
Llandegfedd Reservoir
Pontrilas
Grosmont
Kentchurch
Skenfrith
Pandy
Abbey Dore
Ewyas Harold
Kilpeck
Much Dewchurch
Wormelow Tump
Kingsthorne
Much Birch
Hoarwithy
St Weonards
Garway
Broad Oak
Llangarron
Goodrich
Whitchurch
Symonds Yat
English Bicknor
Staunton
Newland
Clearwell
St Briavels
Llandogo
Brockweir
Tintern Parva
Chapel Hill
St Arvans
Tidenham
Tutshill
Sedbury
Woolaston
Alvington
Aylburton
Bream
Parkend
Yorkley
Ruardean
Drybrook
Mitcheldean
Walford
Bridstow
Wilton
Peterstow
Fownhope
Holme Lacy
Mordiford
Dinedor
Aconbury
Callow
Allensmore
Madley
Clehonger
Breinton
Lugwardine
Bartestree
Dormington
Stoke Edith
Ashperton
Tarrington
Woolhope
Much Marcle
Kempley
Llanvetherine
Llantilio-Crossenny
Llanvapley
Dingestow
Mitchel Troy
Trellech
Devauden
Shirenewton
Mynydd-bach
Itton
Mounton
Pwllmeyric
Llanvair Discoed
Penhow
Caerwent
Oldbury-on-Severn
Rockhampton
Kington
Cowhill
0 1 2 3 4 miles
0 1 2 3 4 5 kilometres
A40
A49
A48
A449
A466
A465
A4137
A4136
A438
A4103
A472
B4348
B4349
B4352
B4347
B4521
B4233
B4293
B4235
B4228
B4231
B4234
B4224
B4399
B4028
B4226
B4598
B4061

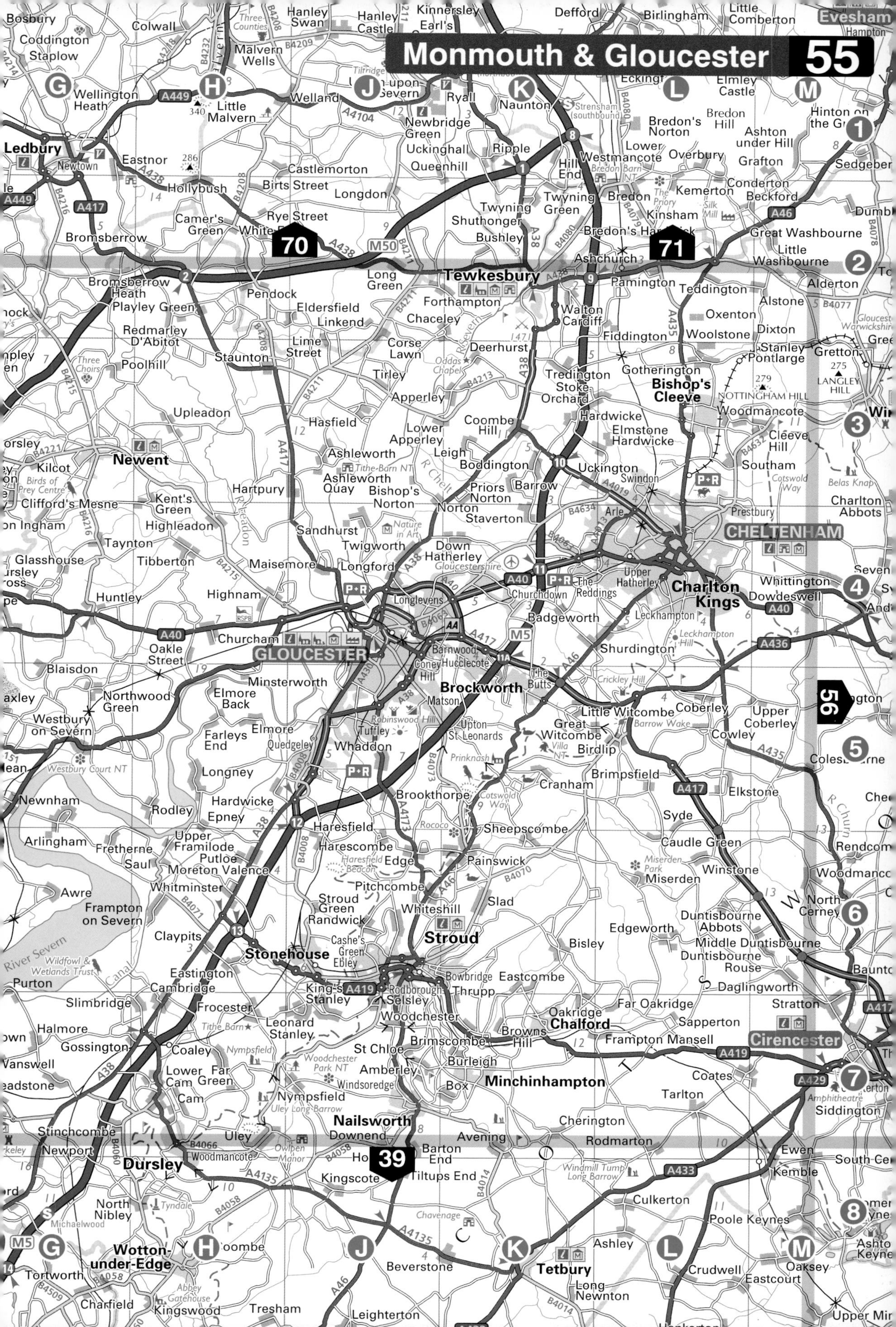

Bosbury
Colwall
Three Counties
Hanley Swan
Hanley Castle
Kinnersley
Earl's
Defford
Birlingham
Little Comberton
Evesham
Hampton
Coddington
Staplow
Malvern Wells
B4209
Tiltridge
Upton-upon-Severn
Ryall
Eckington
Elmley Castle
G
H
J
K
L
M
Wellington Heath
A449
Little Malvern
340
Welland
A4104
Newbridge Green
Naunton
Strensham (southbound)
Bredon's Norton
Bredon Hill
Ashton under Hill
Hinton on the Green
1
Ledbury
Newtown
Eastnor
286
Uckinghall
Queenhill
Ripple
8
Hill End
Lower Westmancote
Bredon Barn NT
Overbury
Grafton
Sedgeberrow
Castlemorton
Hollybush
A438
Birts Street
Longdon
Twyning Green
Bredon
Kemerton
Conderton
Beckford
The Priory
Silk Mill
Kinsham
A449
A417
B4216
Camer's Green
Rye Street
White End
Twyning
Shuthonger
Bushley
A46
Dumbleton
Bromsberrow
70
A438
M50
B4211
A38
B4080
Bredon's Hardwick
71
Great Washbourne
Little Washbourne
B4078
2
Ashchurch
Bromsberrow Heath
Pendock
Long Green
Tewkesbury
9
Pamington
Teddington
Alderton
Playley Green
Eldersfield
Linkend
Forthampton
Chaceley
Walton Cardiff
Alstone
B4077
Oxenton
Redmarley D'Abitot
Staunton
Lime Street
Corse Lawn
Deerhurst
Fiddington
A435
Woolstone
Dixton
Stanley Pontlarge
Gretton
Three Choirs
Poolhill
Tirley
Oddas Chapel
B4213
Gotherington
Tredington
Stoke Orchard
Bishop's Cleeve
275
LANGLEY HILL
279
NOTTINGHAM HILL
Apperley
Upleadon
Hasfield
Coombe Hill
Lower Apperley
Hardwicke
Elmstone Hardwicke
Woodmancote
Cleeve Hill
3
B4221
Newent
Ashleworth
Tithe-Barn NT
Leigh
Boddington
10
Uckington
Swindon
Southam
Kilcot
Birds of Prey Centre
Ashleworth Quay
Bishop's Norton
A417
Hartpury
R Chelt
Priors Norton
Barrow
A4019
P+R
Cotswold Way
Belas Knap
Clifford's Mesne
Kent's Green
Norton
Staverton
B4634
Arle
Prestbury
Charlton Abbots
Highleadon
Sandhurst
Nature in Art
Taynton
Twigworth
B4063
CHELTENHAM
Glasshouse
Tibberton
B4215
Maisemore
Longford
Down Hatherley
Gloucestershire
Seven Springs
11
Upper Hatherley
Charlton Kings
Whittington
Dowdeswell
4
Huntley
Highnam
P+R
Longlevens
A40
The Reddings
Churchdown
A40
RSPB
Badgeworth
Leckhampton
A40
A40
Churcham
GLOUCESTER
Barnwood
A417
M5
Leckhampton Hill
A436
Oakle Street
Hucclecote
11A
Shurdington
Blaisdon
Coney Hill
The Butts
Crickley Hill
Minsterworth
Brockworth
A46
Northwood Green
Elmore Back
A430
Matson
A38
Little Witcombe
Coberley
Upper Coberley
56
Westbury on Severn
Farleys End
Elmore
Robinswood Hill
Tuffley
Upton St Leonards
Great Witcombe
Barrow Wake
Cowley
Quedgeley
Whaddon
Villa NT
Birdlip
5
A435
Colesbourne
Westbury Court NT
Longney
P+R
B4008
Prinknash
B4073
Brimpsfield
Cranham
A417
Elkstone
Newnham
Hardwicke
Epney
Brookthorpe
A4173
Cotswold Way
R Churn
Rodley
12
Haresfield
Rococo
Sheepscombe
Syde
Arlingham
Fretherne
Upper Framilode
Harescombe
Caudle Green
Rendcomb
Saul
Putloe
Haresfield Beacon
Edge
Painswick
Moreton Valence
B4070
Miserden Park
Miserden
Winstone
Woodmancote
Awre
Whitminster
Pitchcombe
Slad
Frampton on Severn
B4071
Stroud Green
Randwick
Whiteshill
North Cerney
6
Duntisbourne Abbots
River Severn
13
Claypits
Stroud
Edgeworth
Middle Duntisbourne
Wildfowl & Wetlands Trust
Stonehouse
Cashe's Green
Ebley
Bisley
Duntisbourne Rouse
Baunton
Purton
Canal
Eastington
Cambridge
Bowbridge
Eastcombe
Daglingworth
King's Stanley
A419
Rodborough
Thrupp
Slimbridge
Frocester
Far Oakridge
Stratton
Leonard Stanley
Woodchester
Oakridge
Chalford
Sapperton
Halmore
Tithe Barn
Brimscombe
Browns Hill
Frampton Mansell
Cirencester
Gossington
Coaley
Nympsfield
St Chloe
A419
Wanswell
Lower Cam
Far Green
Woodchester Park NT
Amberley
Burleigh
Coates
A429
7
Windsoredge
Box
Minchinhampton
Amphitheatre
Siddington
A38
Cam
Nympsfield
Tarlton
Uley Long Barrow
Stinchcombe
Nailsworth
Downend
Cherington
Newport
Uley
B4066
Owlpen Manor
Avening
Rodmarton
Ewen
South Cerney
Dursley
Woodmancote
B4058
39
Barton End
Tiltups End
Windmill Tump Long Barrow
A433
Kemble
Kingscote
A4135
B4060
B4058
B4014
Culkerton
Tyndale
North Nibley
Chavenage
8
Michaelwood
Poole Keynes
M5
A4135
Ashley
Wotton-under-Edge
Beverstone
Tetbury
Crudwell
Oaksey
Tortworth
B4058
Abbey Gatehouse
Eastcourt
B4509
Charfield
Kingswood
Tresham
Long Newnton
B4014
Leighterton
A46
Upper Minety

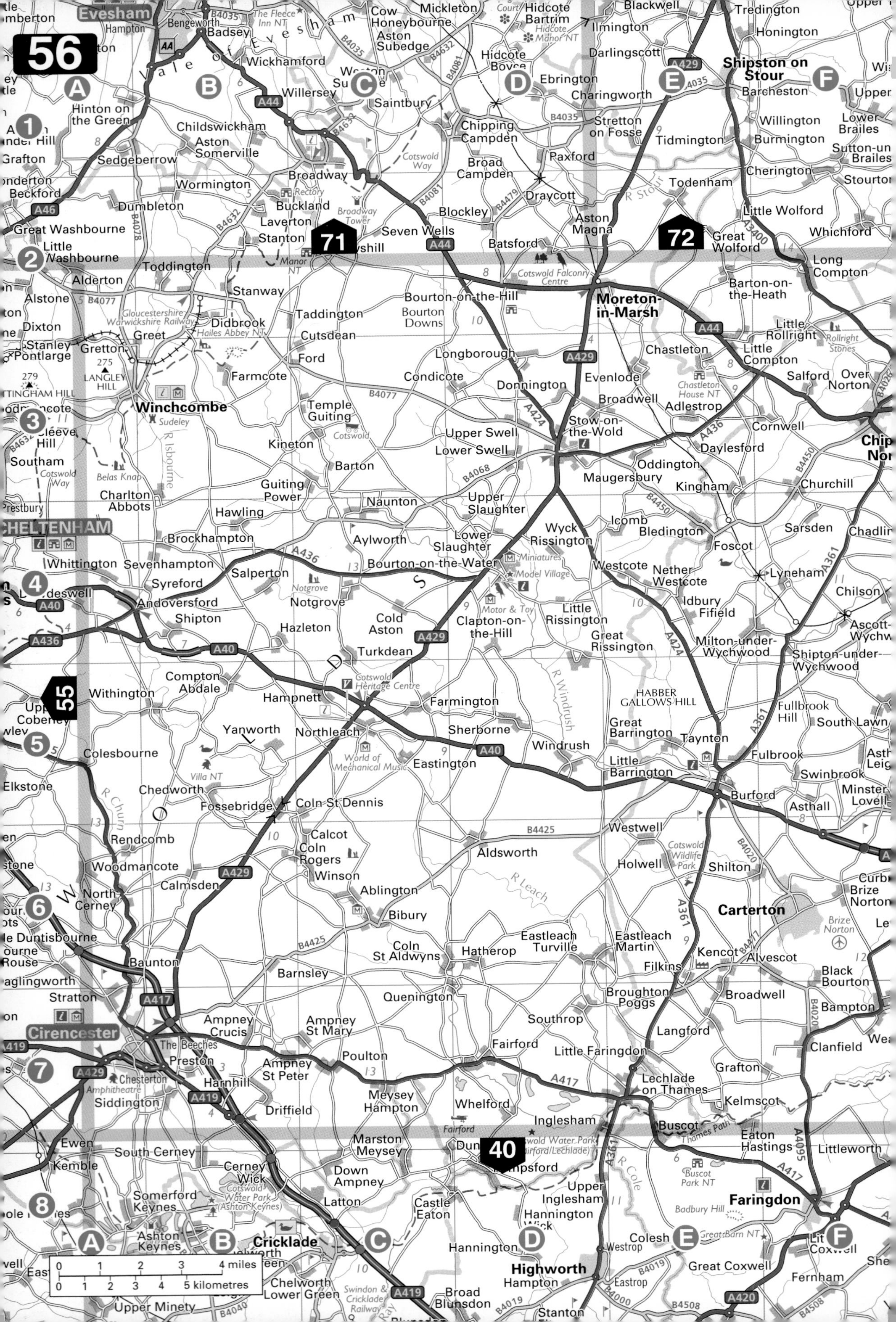
56
Evesham
Hampton
Bengeworth
B4035
The Fleece Inn NT
Badsey
Vale of Evesham
Cow Honeybourne
Aston Subedge
Mickleton
Hidcote Bartrim
Hidcote Manor NT
Ilmington
Blackwell
Tredington
Honington
Darlingscott
Shipston on Stour
Barcheston
A429
B4035
Wickhamford
Weston Subedge
B4632
B4081
Hidcote Boyce
Ebrington
Charingworth
A
B
C
D
E
F
Hinton on the Green
Willersey
Saintbury
A44
Chipping Campden
B4035
Stretton on Fosse
Tidmington
Willington
Burmington
Lower Brailes
Upper
Sutton-under-Brailes
1
Grafton
Childswickham
Aston Somerville
Sedgeberrow
Broadway
Cotswold Way
Broad Campden
Paxford
Cherington
Stourton
Todenham
R Stour
Beckford
A46
Wormington
Dumbleton
B4078
B4632
Buckland
Rectory
Broadway Tower
Draycott
Blockley
B4479
B4081
Aston Magna
Little Wolford
Whichford
Great Washbourne
Laverton
Stanton
71
Snowshill
Seven Wells
A44
Batsford
72
Great Wolford
A3400
Little Washbourne
2
Toddington
Manor NT
Cotswold Falconry Centre
Long Compton
Alderton
Stanway
Bourton-on-the-Hill
Moreton-in-Marsh
Barton-on-the-Heath
Alstone
B4077
Taddington
Bourton Downs
Dixton
Gloucestershire Warwickshire Railway
Didbrook
Hailes Abbey NT
A44
Little Rollright
Rollright Stones
Stanley Pontlarge
Gretton
Greet
Cutsdean
Chastleton
Little Compton
275
LANGLEY HILL
279
CLEEVE HILL
Ford
Longborough
A429
Chastleton House NT
Farmcote
Condicote
Donnington
Evenlode
Salford
Over Norton
Winchcombe
Sudeley
B4077
Temple Guiting
Broadwell
Adlestrop
Woodmancote
3
Cleeve Hill
B4632
Cotswold
A424
Stow-on-the-Wold
Cornwell
Upper Swell
A436
Daylesford
Chipping Norton
Southam
Cotswold Way
Belas Knap
R Isbourne
Kineton
Lower Swell
Barton
B4068
Oddington
Maugersbury
B4450
Prestbury
Charlton Abbots
Guiting Power
Naunton
Upper Slaughter
Kingham
Churchill
B4450
Icomb
Hawling
Wyck Rissington
Bledington
Sarsden
CHELTENHAM
Brockhampton
Aylworth
Lower Slaughter
Foscot
Chadlington
Whittington
Sevenhampton
A436
Salperton
Bourton-on-the-Water
Miniatures
Model Village
Westcote
Nether Westcote
Lyneham
A361
4
Dowdeswell
Syreford
Notgrove
Andoversford
Motor & Toy
Little Rissington
Idbury
Fifield
Chilson
A40
Shipton
Hazleton
Cold Aston
Clapton-on-the-Hill
A429
Great Rissington
Ascott-under-Wychwood
A436
A40
Turkdean
Milton-under-Wychwood
Shipton-under-Wychwood
A424
55
Compton Abdale
Withington
Cotswold Heritage Centre
R Windrush
Upper Coberley
Hampnett
Farmington
HABBER GALLOWS HILL
Fullbrook Hill
Great Barrington
South Lawn
5
Colesbourne
Yanworth
Northleach
Sherborne
Windrush
Taynton
A361
Villa NT
World of Mechanical Music
Eastington
A40
Little Barrington
Fulbrook
Swinbrook
Elkstone
R Churn
Chedworth
Fossebridge
Coln St Dennis
Burford
Minster Lovell
Asthall
Rendcomb
Calcot
B4425
Westwell
Coln Rogers
Aldsworth
Cotswold Wildlife Park
B4020
Woodmancote
Winson
Holwell
Shilton
A429
R Leach
Calmsden
North Cerney
Ablington
A361
Curbridge
Brize Norton
6
Duntisbourne
Bibury
Carterton
Brize Norton
Eastleach Turville
Eastleach Martin
B4425
Coln St Aldwyns
Hatherop
Kencot
B4477
Alvescot
Baunton
Filkins
Barnsley
Black Bourton
Bagendon
Stratton
A417
Quenington
Broughton Poggs
Broadwell
B4020
Bampton
Ampney Crucis
Ampney St Mary
Southrop
Cirencester
Langford
A419
The Beeches
Fairford
Clanfield
Preston
Little Faringdon
Chesterton
Amphitheatre
A429
7
Ampney St Peter
Poulton
Grafton
Harnhill
A417
Lechlade on Thames
A419
Siddington
Driffield
Meysey Hampton
Whelford
Kelmscot
Inglesham
Fairford
Buscot
Thames Path
Eaton Hastings
A4095
Littleworth
Ewen
Marston Meysey
40
Cotswold Water Park (Fairford/Lechlade)
South Cerney
Kemble
Cerney Wick
Down Ampney
Kempsford
A361
R Cole
Buscot Park NT
Upper Inglesham
Somerford Keynes
Cotswold Water Park (Ashton Keynes)
Latton
Castle Eaton
A417
Badbury Hill
Faringdon
8
Poole Keynes
Hannington Wick
Ashton Keynes
Cricklade
Hannington
Westrop
Coleshill
Great Barn NT
Little Coxwell
B4019
Great Coxwell
Highworth
Hampton
Eastrop
Fernham
Chelworth Lower Green
Swindon & Cricklade Railway
A419
Broad Blunsdon
B4019
B4000
B4508
A420
B4508
Upper Minety
B4040
Stanton
0 1 2 3 4 miles
0 1 2 3 4 5 kilometres

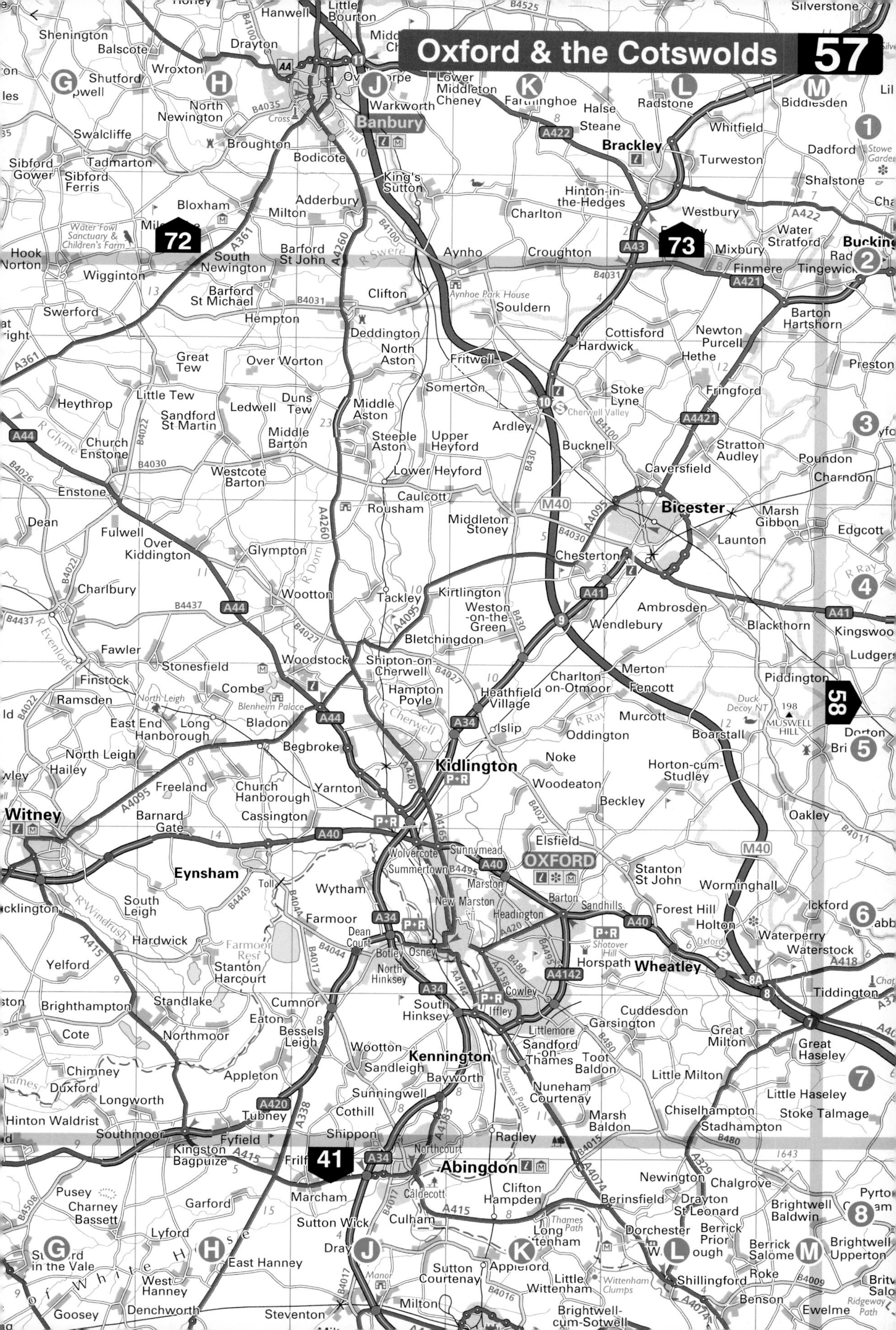
Hanwell
Little Bourton
B4525
Silverstone
Shenington
Balscote
Drayton
Wroxton
Shutford
North Newington
Banbury
Warkworth
Lower Middleton Cheney
Farthinghoe
Halse
Radstone
Biddlesden
Steane
Whitfield
Swalcliffe
Broughton
Bodicote
Brackley
Turweston
Dadford
Stowe Garden
Sibford Gower
Sibford Ferris
Tadmarton
King's Sutton
Hinton-in-the-Hedges
Shalstone
Bloxham
Adderbury
Milton
Charlton
Westbury
Water Stratford
Water Fowl Sanctuary & Children's Farm
72
73
Hook Norton
South Newington
Barford St John
Aynho
Croughton
Mixbury
Finmere
Tingewick
Wigginton
Barford St Michael
Clifton
Aynhoe Park House
Souldern
Swerford
Hempton
Deddington
Cottisford
Hardwick
Newton Purcell
Barton Hartshorn
Great Tew
Over Worton
North Aston
Fritwell
Hethe
Preston
Little Tew
Heythrop
Sandford St Martin
Ledwell
Duns Tew
Middle Aston
Somerton
Stoke Lyne
Fringford
Cherwell Valley
Church Enstone
Middle Barton
Steeple Aston
Upper Heyford
Ardley
Bucknell
Stratton Audley
Poundon
Westcote Barton
Lower Heyford
Caversfield
Charndon
Enstone
Caulcott
Rousham
Bicester
Marsh Gibbon
Dean
Fulwell
Over Kiddington
Middleton Stoney
Launton
Edgcott
Glympton
Chesterton
Charlbury
Wootton
Tackley
Kirtlington
Weston-on-the-Green
Ambrosden
Wendlebury
Blackthorn
Kingswood
Fawler
Stonesfield
Woodstock
Bletchingdon
Shipton-on-Cherwell
Merton
Ludgershall
Finstock
Ramsden
North Leigh
Combe
Blenheim Palace
Hampton Poyle
Heathfield Village
Charlton-on-Otmoor
Fencott
Piddington
East End
Long Hanborough
Bladon
Islip
Oddington
Murcott
Duck Decoy NT
Boarstall
Muswell Hill
58
Dorton
North Leigh
Hailey
Begbroke
Kidlington
Noke
Horton-cum-Studley
Freeland
Church Hanborough
Yarnton
Woodeaton
Beckley
Witney
Barnard Gate
Cassington
Oakley
Eynsham
Elsfield
Wolvercote
Sunnymead
Summertown
OXFORD
Stanton St John
Worminghall
Marston
Wytham
New Marston
Barton
Sandhills
Forest Hill
Ickford
South Leigh
Farmoor
Headington
Holton
Waterperry
Hardwick
Dean Court
Botley
Osney
Shotover Hill
Farmoor Resr
Horspath
Wheatley
Waterstock
Yelford
Stanton Harcourt
North Hinksey
Cowley
Tiddington
Brighthampton
Standlake
Cumnor
South Hinksey
Iffley
Cuddesdon
Garsington
Eaton
Littlemore
Great Milton
Cote
Northmoor
Bessels Leigh
Wootton
Kennington
Sandford-on-Thames
Toot Baldon
Great Haseley
Chimney
Sandleigh
Duxford
Appleton
Bayworth
Nuneham Courtenay
Little Milton
Longworth
Sunningwell
Little Haseley
Hinton Waldrist
Tubney
Cothill
Marsh Baldon
Chiselhampton
Stoke Talmage
Southmoor
Fyfield
Shippon
Radley
Stadhampton
Kingston Bagpuize
41
Northcourt
Abingdon
Newington
Chalgrove
Pusey
Marcham
Caldecott
Clifton Hampden
Berinsfield
Drayton St Leonard
Brightwell Baldwin
Charney Bassett
Garford
Sutton Wick
Culham
Thames Path
Dorchester
Berrick Prior
Lyford
Long Wittenham
Berrick Salome
Brightwell Upperton
Stanford in the Vale
East Hanney
Drayton
Sutton Courtenay
Appleford
Shillingford
Roke
West Hanney
Little Wittenham
Wittenham Clumps
Benson
Goosey
Denchworth
Steventon
Milton
Brightwell-cum-Sotwell
Ewelme
Ridgeway Path

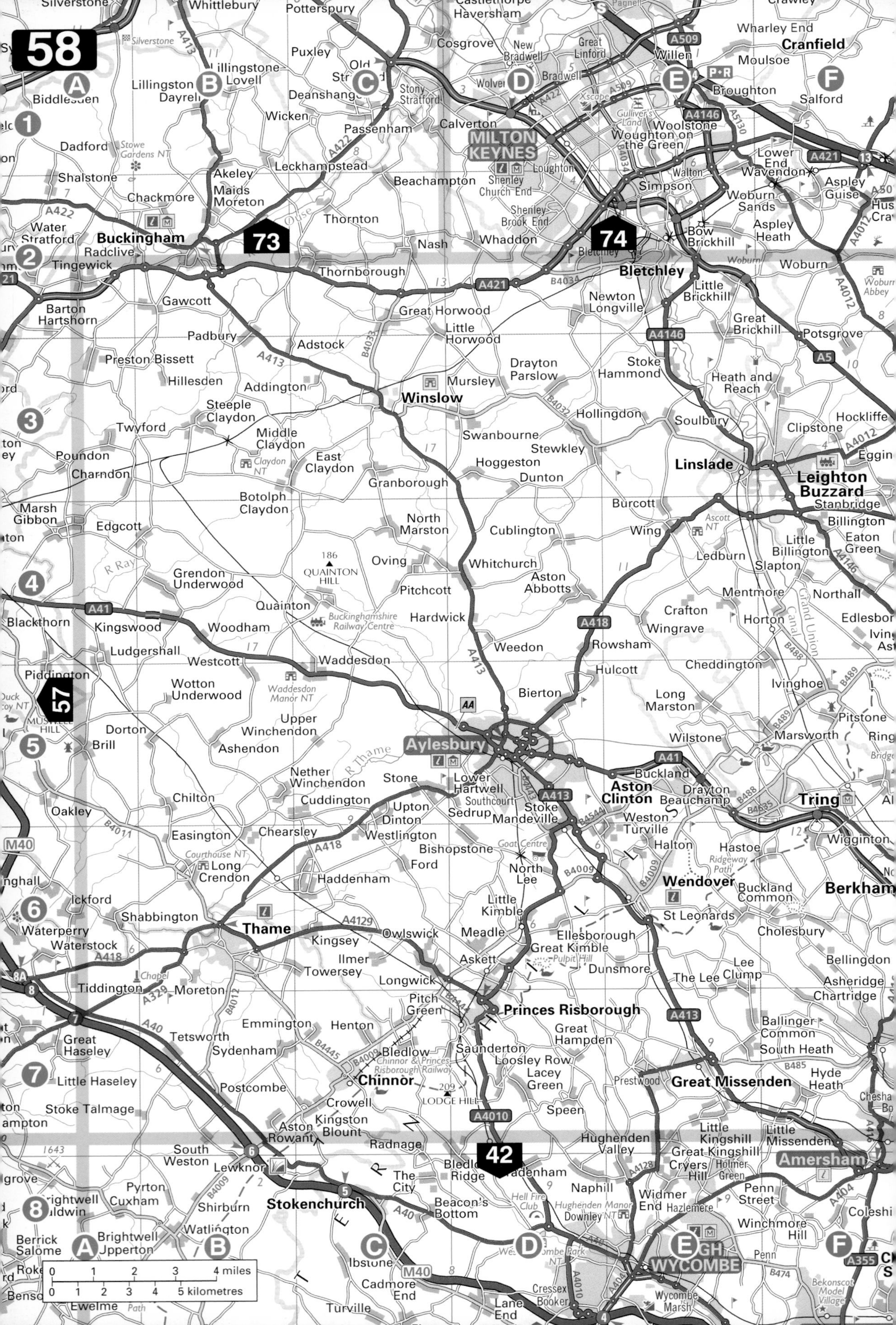
58
73
74
57
42
Buckingham
Milton Keynes
Bletchley
Winslow
Leighton Buzzard
Linslade
Aylesbury
Thame
Princes Risborough
Wendover
Tring
Great Missenden
Chinnor
Stokenchurch
Amersham
High Wycombe
Aston Clinton
Berkhamsted
Cranfield
Woburn
Waddesdon
Haddenham
Long Crendon
Quainton Hill
Lodge Hill
Stowe Gardens NT
Claydon NT
Waddesdon Manor NT
Buckinghamshire Railway Centre
Ascott NT
Courthouse NT
Hughenden Manor NT
Chinnor & Princes Risborough Railway
Grand Union Canal
Ridgeway Path
0 1 2 3 4 miles
0 1 2 3 4 5 kilometres

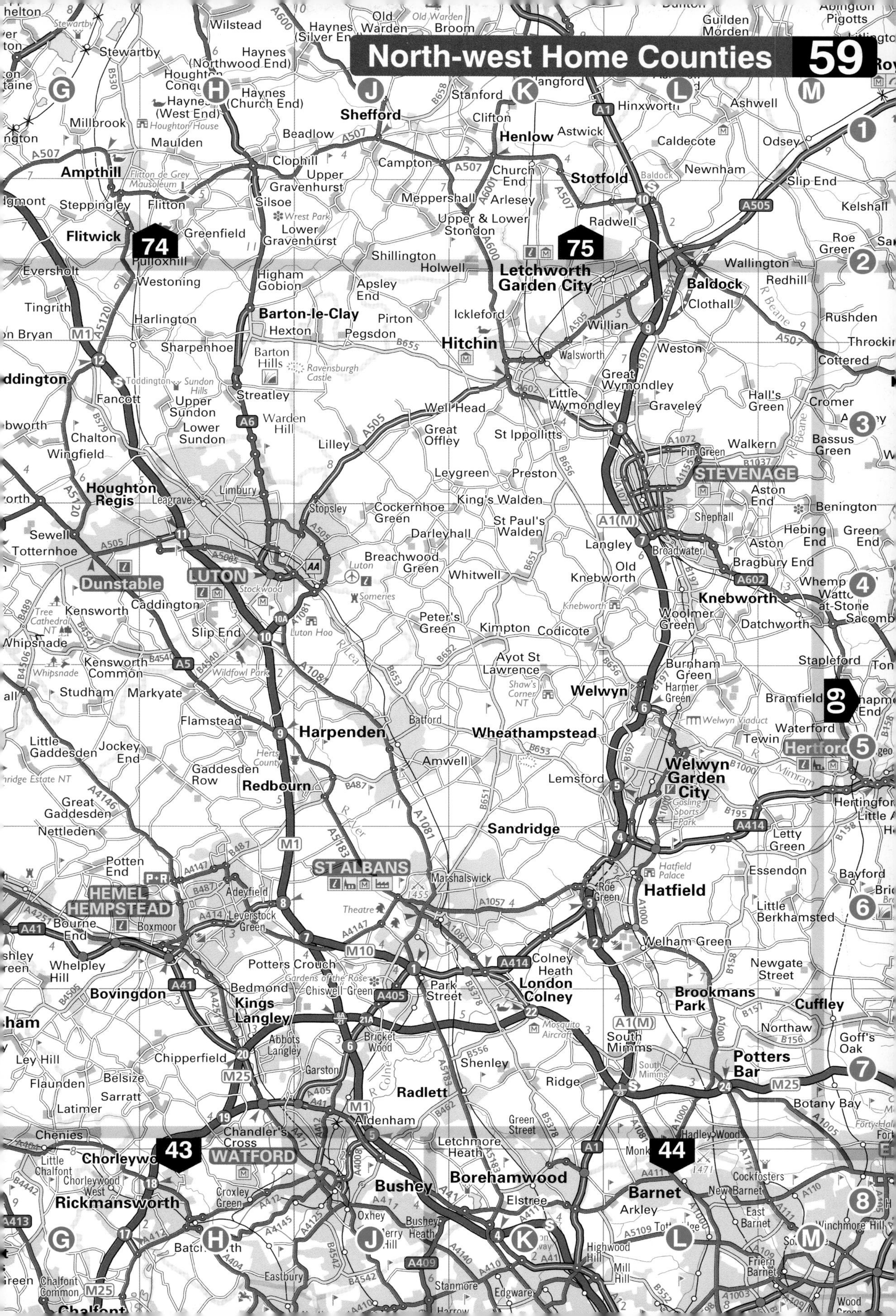

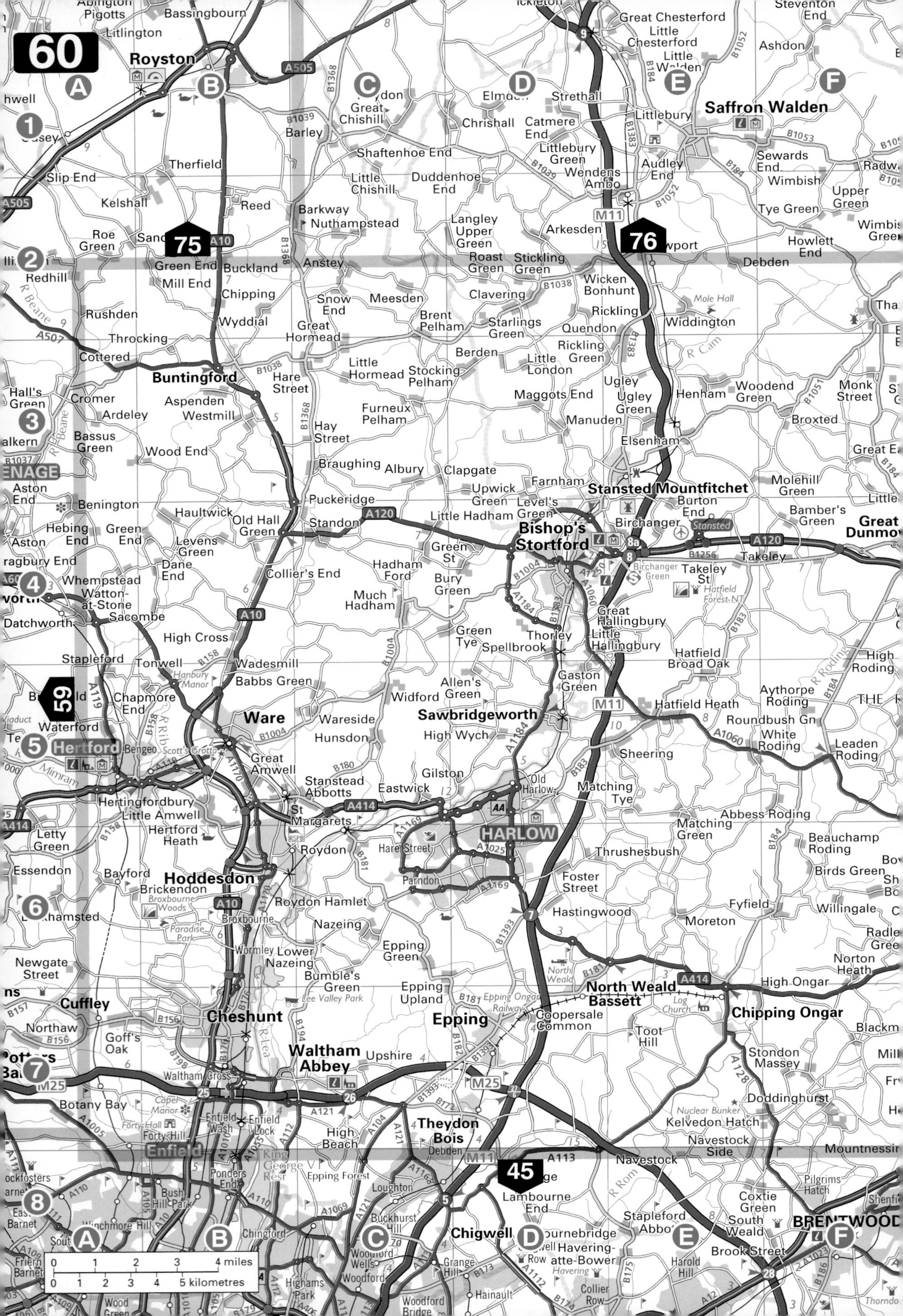

60
Abington Pigotts
Bassingbourn
Litlington
Royston
A505
Therfield
Slip End
Kelshall
Reed
Roe Green
75
A10
Green End
Buckland
Mill End
Redhill
Chipping
Rushden
Wyddial
Throcking
A507
Cottered
Buntingford
Hall's Green
Cromer
Ardeley
Aspenden
Westmill
Bassus Green
Wood End
B1037
Aston End
Benington
Haultwick
Old Hall Green
Hebing End
Green End
Aston
Levens Green
Dane End
Whempstead
Watton-at-Stone
Sacombe
Datchworth
High Cross
Stapleford
Tonwell
B158
Wadesmill
Hanbury Manor
Babbs Green
59
Chapmore End
Waterford
Ware
Hertford
Bengeo
Scott's Grotto
Great Amwell
Hertingfordbury
Little Amwell
Hertford Heath
Letty Green
A414
Essendon
Bayford
Brickendon
Hoddesdon
Broxbourne Woods
A10
Broxbourne
Paradise Park
Wormley
Newgate Street
Cuffley
Northaw
B156
B157
Goff's Oak
Cheshunt
Potters Bar
M25
Waltham Cross
Botany Bay
Capel Manor
Forty Hall
Forty Hill
Enfield
Enfield Wash
Enfield Lock
Ponders End
Cockfosters
Bush Hill Park
Winchmore Hill
East Barnet
Southgate
Friern Barnet
Chingford
Highams Park
Wood Green
Steeple Morden
Barley
Great Chishill
B1039
Heydon
Shaftenhoe End
Little Chishill
Duddenhoe End
Barkway
Nuthampstead
B1368
Anstey
Snow End
Meesden
Great Hormead
Hare Street
Little Hormead
B1038
Hay Street
Braughing
Puckeridge
Standon
A120
Collier's End
Furneux Pelham
Stocking Pelham
Brent Pelham
Albury
Hadham Ford
Much Hadham
Bury Green
Green St
Little Hadham
Clapgate
Upwick Green
Green Tye
B1004
Widford
Wareside
Hunsdon
B180
Stanstead Abbotts
St Margarets
RSPB
Roydon
Roydon Hamlet
Nazeing
Lower Nazeing
Epping Green
Bumble's Green
Lee Valley Park
Epping Upland
Waltham Abbey
Upshire
High Beach
Epping Forest
King George V Resr
Loughton
Buckhurst Hill
Woodford Wells
Woodford
Woodford Bridge
Chigwell
Grange Hill
Hainault
Ickleton
Great Chesterford
Little Chesterford
Little Walden
Elmdon
Strethall
Chrishall
Catmere End
Littlebury
Littlebury Green
Wendens Ambo
Audley End
Saffron Walden
B1053
B184
B1052
B1383
Sewards End
Wimbish
Tye Green
Upper Green
Ashdon
Steventon End
Langley Upper Green
Arkesden
M11
76
Newport
Debden
Howlett End
Roast Green
Stickling Green
Clavering
Wicken Bonhunt
Rickling
Quendon
Rickling Green
Starlings Green
Berden
Little London
Ugley
Ugley Green
Maggots End
Manuden
Mole Hall
Widdington
R Cam
Henham
Woodend Green
Monk Street
Broxted
Elsenham
Farnham
Stansted Mountfitchet
Molehill Green
Great Easton
Level's Green
Burton End
Birchanger
Stansted
Bamber's Green
Bishop's Stortford
Great Dunmow
A120
B1256
Takeley
Takeley St
Birchanger Green
Hatfield Forest NT
Great Hallingbury
Little Hallingbury
Thorley
Spellbrook
Hatfield Broad Oak
High Roding
Allen's Green
Gaston Green
Sawbridgeworth
High Wych
Hatfield Heath
Aythorpe Roding
Roundbush Gn
White Roding
Leaden Roding
A1060
Sheering
Gilston
Eastwick
Old Harlow
Matching Tye
Harlow
Hare Street
Parndon
Matching Green
Abbess Roding
Beauchamp Roding
Thrushesbush
Birds Green
Foster Street
Hastingwood
Fyfield
Moreton
Willingale
North Weald
North Weald Bassett
Norton Heath
High Ongar
Epping Ongar Railway
Coopersale Common
Epping
Log Church
Chipping Ongar
Toot Hill
Stondon Massey
A128
Doddinghurst
Nuclear Bunker
Kelvedon Hatch
Navestock Side
Navestock
Mountnessing
Theydon Bois
Debden
A113
45
Abridge
Lambourne End
Stapleford Abbotts
Coxtie Green
South Weald
Pilgrims Hatch
Brentwood
Passingford Bridge
Havering-atte-Bower
Harold Hill
Brook Street
Collier Row
Navestock
R Rom
0 1 2 3 4 miles
0 1 2 3 4 5 kilometres

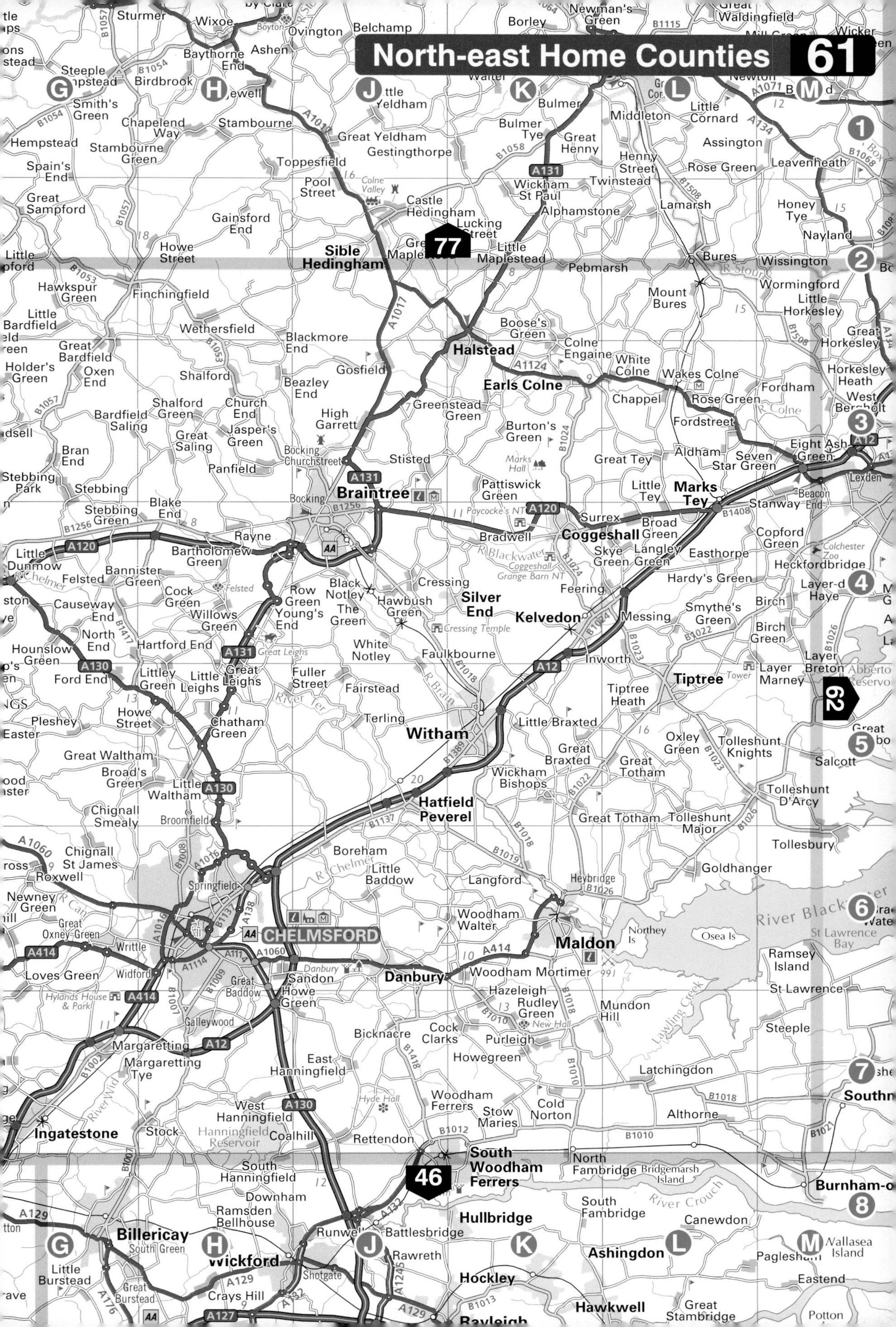
Sturmer
Wixoe
Ovington
Belchamp
Borley
Newman's Green
Great Waldingfield
Steeple Bumpstead
Birdbrook
Baythorne End
Ashen
Smith's Green
Chapelend Way
Stambourne
Little Yeldham
Bulmer
Middleton
Little Cornard
Hempstead
Stambourne Green
Great Yeldham
Gestingthorpe
Bulmer Tye
Great Henny
Assington
Spain's End
Toppesfield
Henny Street
Rose Green
Leavenheath
Great Sampford
Pool Street
Colne Valley
Wickham St Paul
Twinstead
Castle Hedingham
Lamarsh
Honey Tye
Gainsford End
Lucking Street
Alphamstone
Nayland
Howe Street
Sible Hedingham
Little Maplestead
Pebmarsh
Bures
Wissington
Hawkspur Green
Finchingfield
Mount Bures
Wormingford
Little Horkesley
Little Bardfield
Wethersfield
Blackmore End
Boose's Green
Great Horkesley
Great Bardfield
Halstead
Colne Engaine
Holder's Green
Oxen End
Shalford
Gosfield
White Colne
Horkesley Heath
Beazley End
Earls Colne
Wakes Colne
Fordham
Shalford Green
Church End
High Garrett
Greenstead Green
Chappel
Rose Green
West Bergholt
Bardfield Saling
Jasper's Green
Burton's Green
Fordstreet
Great Saling
Aldham
Eight Ash Green
Bran End
Bocking Churchstreet
Stisted
Marks Hall
Great Tey
Seven Star Green
Lexden
Panfield
Stebbing Park
Stebbing
Braintree
Pattiswick Green
Little Tey
Marks Tey
Beacon End
Stebbing Green
Blake End
Bocking
Paycocke's NT
Surrex
Stanway
Broad Green
Rayne
Bradwell
Coggeshall
Copford Green
Little Dunmow
Bartholomew Green
Skye Green
Langley Green
Easthorpe
Colchester Zoo
Bannister Green
R Blackwater
Coggeshall Grange Barn NT
Heckfordbridge
Felsted
Felsted
Cock Green
Row Green
Black Notley
Cressing
Feering
Hardy's Green
Layer-de-la-Haye
Causeway End
Willows Green
Young's End
The Green
Hawbush Green
Silver End
Kelvedon
Messing
Smythe's Green
Birch
North End
Cressing Temple
Birch Green
Hounslow Green
Hartford End
Great Leighs
White Notley
Faulkbourne
Inworth
Layer Breton
Abberton Reservoir
Ford End
Littley Green
Little Leighs
Great Leighs
Fuller Street
Fairstead
R Brain
Tiptree
Tower
Layer Marney
River Ter
Tiptree Heath
Pleshey
Howe Street
Chatham Green
Terling
Little Braxted
Great Wigborough
Witham
Oxley Green
Tolleshunt Knights
Great Waltham
Great Braxted
Great Totham
Salcott
Broad's Green
Wickham Bishops
Little Waltham
Tolleshunt D'Arcy
Chignall Smealy
Hatfield Peverel
Broomfield
Great Totham
Tolleshunt Major
Chignall St James
Boreham
Tollesbury
Roxwell
Little Baddow
R Chelmer
Goldhanger
Langford
Heybridge
Newney Green
Springfield
River Blackwater
Great Oxney Green
Woodham Walter
Northey Is
Osea Is
St Lawrence Bay
CHELMSFORD
Writtle
Maldon
Ramsey Island
Danbury
Woodham Mortimer
Loves Green
Widford
Sandon
Great Baddow
Howe Green
Hazeleigh
Mundon Hill
St Lawrence
Hylands House & Park
Rudley Green
New Hall
Galleywood
Lawling Creek
Margaretting
Bicknacre
Cock Clarks
Purleigh
Steeple
Margaretting Tye
East Hanningfield
Howegreen
Latchingdon
River Wid
Hyde Hall
Woodham Ferrers
Southminster
West Hanningfield
Stow Maries
Cold Norton
Althorne
Ingatestone
Stock
Hanningfield Reservoir
Coalhill
Rettendon
South Woodham Ferrers
North Fambridge
Bridgemarsh Island
South Hanningfield
Burnham-on-Crouch
Downham
River Crouch
South Fambridge
Ramsden Bellhouse
Hullbridge
Canewdon
Billericay
South Green
Runwell
Battlesbridge
Wickford
Ashingdon
Wallasea Island
Little Burstead
Rawreth
Paglesham
Shotgate
Hockley
Eastend
Great Burstead
Crays Hill
Hawkwell
Great Stambridge
Potton
Rayleigh
77
62
46

62
Kersey
Hintlesham
Duke Street
Washbrook
Chantry
P+R
Suffolk
A12
Bucklesham
Hadleigh
Chattisham
Copdock
A1156
Nacton
A14
A1071
A
B
Layham
C
D
Wherstead
E
F
Raydon
Little Wenham
Freston
Levington
Leavenheath
Shelley
Polstead
Great Wenham
Capel St Mary
Tattingstone White Horse
Woolverstone
River Orwell
Trimley
Stoke-by-Nayland
Lower Raydon
Holton St Mary
Bentley
Tattingstone
Holbrook
Chelmondiston
Honey Tye
Thorington Street
Higham
Stratford St Mary
East Bergholt
Alton Water
Stutton
Erwarton
Harkstead
Shotley
Shotley Street
Shotley Gate
77
78
Wissington
Boxted
Carters
Langham
Flatford Mill & Cottage NT
Cattawade
Holbrook Bay
International Ferry Terminal
The Redoubt
Wormingford
Little Horkesley
Boxted Cross
Dedham
Mistley Towers
Mistley
River Stour
Wrabness
Bath Side
Manningtree
New Mistley
RSPB
Dovercourt
Harwich
Boxted Heath
Great Horkesley
Lawford
Bradfield
Upper Dovercourt
Ramsey
Ardleigh Heath
Ardleigh
Little Bromley
Horsleycross Street
Bradfield Heath
A120
Horkesley Heath
Fordham
West Bergholt
A134
A137
Wix
Goose Green
Little Oakley
Great Oakley
Pennyhole Bay
High Woods
Parson's Heath
Great Bromley
Little Bentley
Tendring Heath
Stones Green
Eight Ash Green
A12
COLCHESTER
A120
Tendring Green
B1414
Seven Green
Lexden
Greenstead
Elmstead Market
Hare Green
Goose Green
Beaumont
Horsey Island
Stanway
Beacon End
A133
Frating Green
Beth Chatto
Tendring
Thorpe Green
Thorpe-le-Soken
Kirby le Soken
Walton-on-the-Naze
Copford Green
Colchester Zoo
Wivenhoe
Frating
Great Bentley
Weeley
B1034
Heckfordbridge
Rowhedge
Fingringhoe
Alresford
Weeley Heath
B1033
Kirby Cross
Birch
Layer-de-la-Haye
Malting Green
High Park Corner
Aingers Green
Thorrington
Frinton-on-Sea
Abberton
Cook's Green
Birch Green
Langenhoe
Little Clacton
Great Holland
Layer Breton
Abberton Reservoir
Peldon
R Colne
Brightlingsea
Hurst Green
Great Clacton
Layer Marney
61
B1027
St Osyth
Holland-on-Sea
MERSEA ISLAND
Cudmore Grove
Rush Green
Great Wigborough
East Mersea
CLACTON-ON-SEA
Jaywick
Salcott
West Mersea
Tolleshunt D'Arcy
Colne Point
Shinglehead Point
Tollesbury
Sales Point
River Blackwater
Bradwell Waterside
Bradwell-on-Sea
St Lawrence Bay
Ramsey Island
St Lawrence
Tillingham
Steeple
Dengie
Asheldham
Southminster
B1021
Holliwell Point
Burnham-on-Crouch
47
Foulness Point
Wallasea Island
Courtsend
Paglesham
FOULNESS ISLAND
Potton
1
2
3
4
5
6
7
8
0 1 2 3 4 miles
0 1 2 3 4 5 kilometres

Hollesley
North Weir Point
Hollesley Bay
Hemley
Alderton
Bawdsey
Falkenham
B1083
River Deben
Old Felixstowe
Walton
Felixstowe
79
Landguard Fort
Landguard Point
Hoek van Holland
Hoek van Holland
Cuxhaven
Esbjerg
G
H
J
K
L
M
1
2
3
4
5
6
7
8

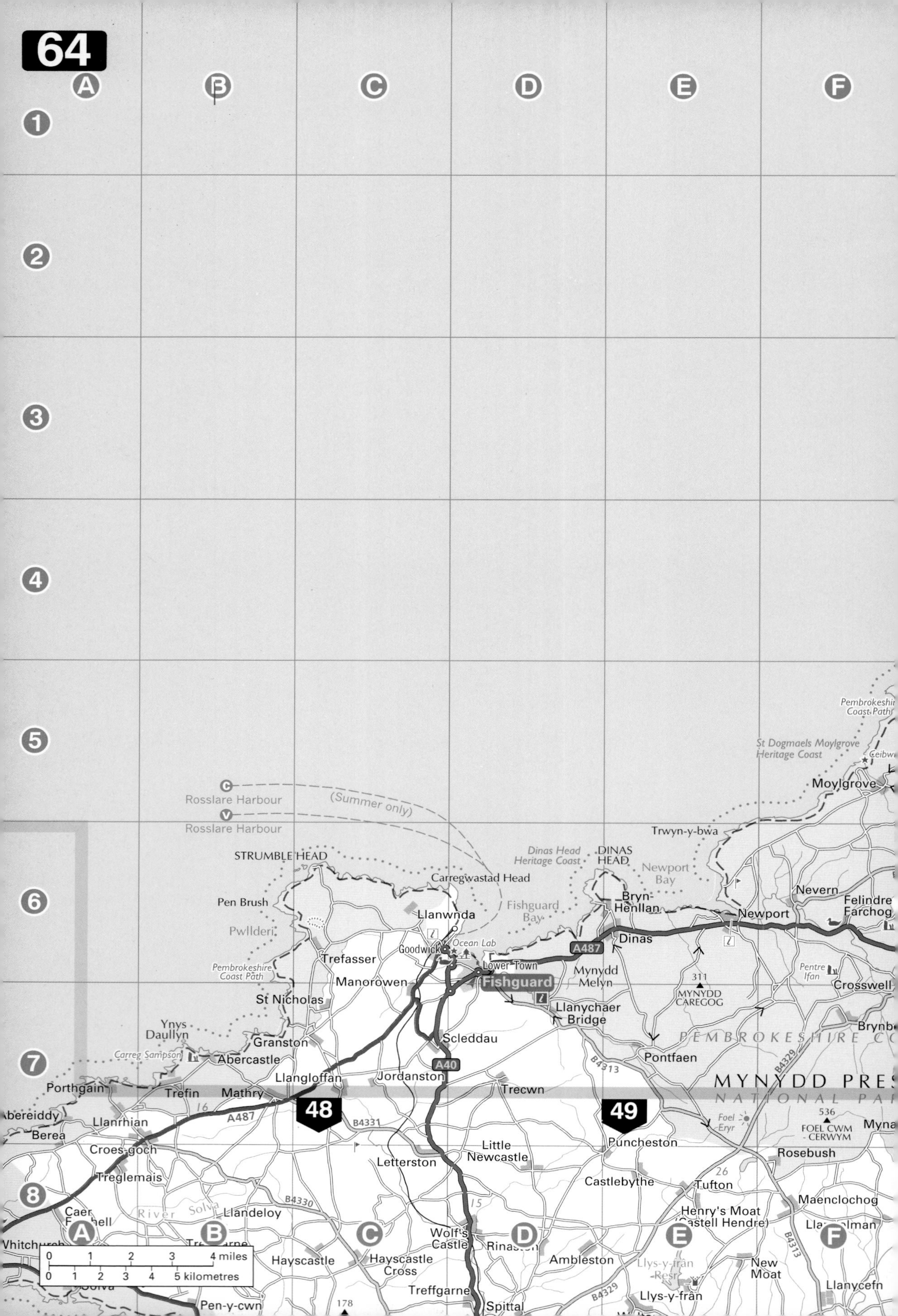

A
B
C
D
E
F
1
2
3
4
5
6
7
8
Pembrokeshire Coast Path
St Dogmaels Moylgrove Heritage Coast
Ceibw
Moylgrove
Rosslare Harbour
(Summer only)
Rosslare Harbour
Trwyn-y-bwa
STRUMBLE HEAD
Dinas Head Heritage Coast
DINAS HEAD
Newport Bay
Carregwastad Head
Pen Brush
Fishguard Bay
Bryn-Henllan
Nevern
Felindre Farchog
Llanwnda
Newport
Pwllderi
Dinas
Goodwick
Ocean Lab
Trefasser
A487
Lower Town
Pembrokeshire Coast Path
Mynydd Melyn
Pentre Ifan
Manorowen
Fishguard
311
MYNYDD CAREGOG
Crosswell
St Nicholas
Llanychaer Bridge
Ynys Daullyn
Scleddau
PEMBROKESHIRE CO
Brynb
Granston
Carreg Sampson
Abercastle
A40
Pontfaen
Llangloffan
B4313
Jordanston
B4329
MYNYDD PRES
Porthgain
Trefin
Mathry
Trecwn
NATIONAL PA
16
48
49
Abereiddy
A487
B4331
Foel Eryr
536
FOEL CWM - CERWYM
Myna
Llanrhian
Berea
Little Newcastle
Puncheston
Croes-goch
Letterston
Rosebush
Treglemais
26
Castlebythe
Tufton
B4330
15
Maenclochog
Caer Farchell
River Solva
Llandeloy
Henry's Moat (Castell Hendre)
B4313
Wolf's Castle
Whitchurch
Rinaston
Ambleston
Llys-y-frân Resr
New Moat
Hayscastle
Hayscastle Cross
Treffgarne
Llanycefn
Solva
178
B4329
Llys-y-frân
Pen-y-cwm
Spittal
0 1 2 3 4 miles
0 1 2 3 4 5 kilometres

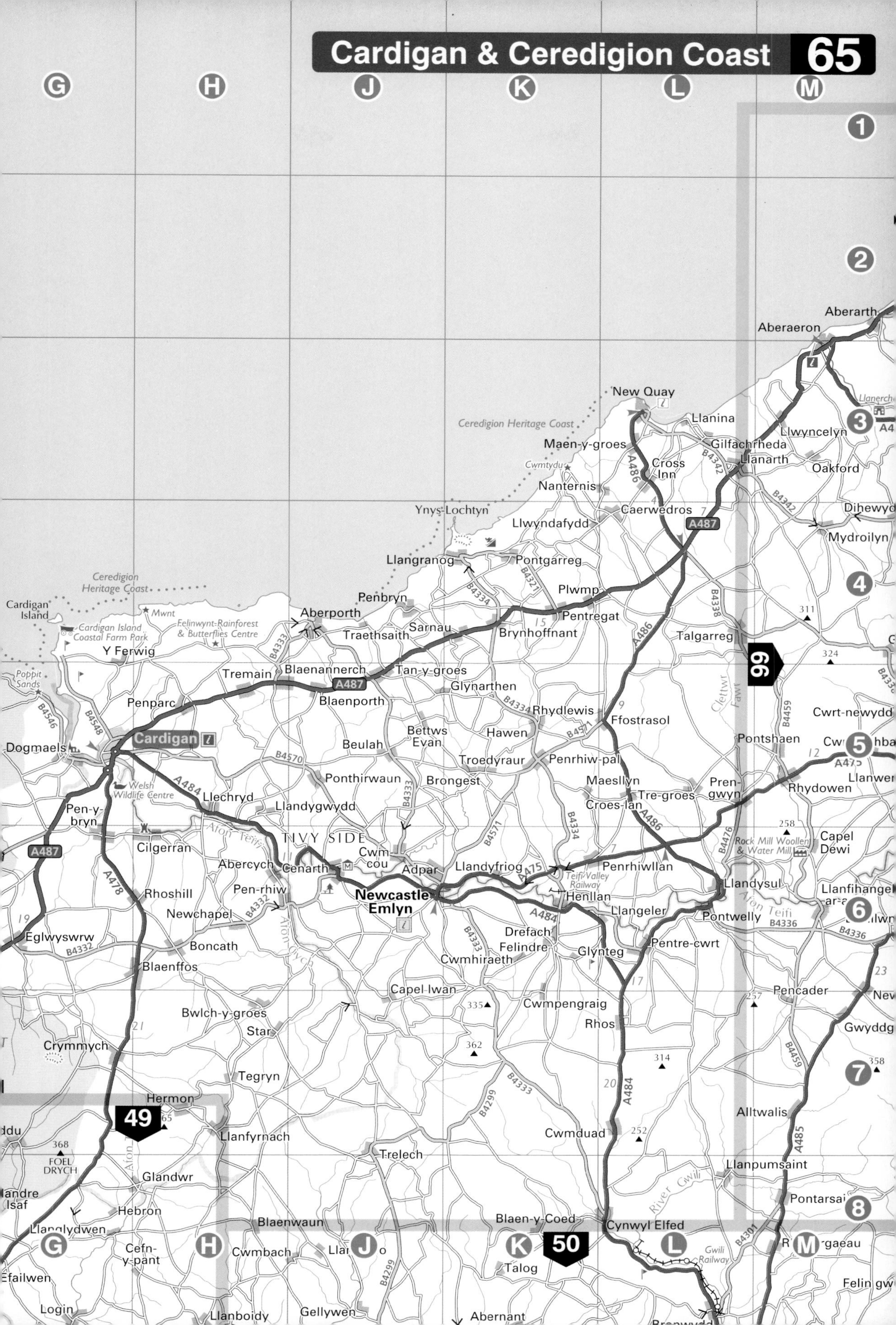

Aberarth
Aberaeron
New Quay
Llanina
Ceredigion Heritage Coast
Maen-y-groes
Gilfachrheda
Llwyncelyn
Llanarth
Cross Inn
Oakford
Cwmtydu
Nanternis
Caerwedros
Dihewyd
Ynys-Lochtyn
Llwyndafydd
Mydroilyn
Llangranog
Pontgarreg
Plwmp
Penbryn
Pentregat
Aberporth
Sarnau
Traethsaith
Brynhoffnant
Talgarreg
Cardigan Island
Ceredigion Heritage Coast
Mwnt
Cardigan Island Coastal Farm Park
Felinwynt Rainforest & Butterflies Centre
Y Ferwig
Poppit Sands
Tremain
Blaenannerch
Tan-y-groes
Glynarthen
Blaenporth
Penparc
Rhydlewis
Ffostrasol
Cwrt-newydd
Cardigan
Bettws Evan
Hawen
Pontshaen
Dogmaels
Beulah
Troedyraur
Penrhiw-pal
Llanwer
Ponthirwaun
Brongest
Maesllyn
Pren-gwyn
Rhydowen
Welsh Wildlife Centre
Llechryd
Tre-groes
Croes-lan
Llandygwydd
Pen-y-bryn
Afon Teifi
TIVY SIDE
Rock Mill Woollen & Water Mill
Capel Dewi
Cilgerran
Cwm-cou
Abercych
Cenarth
Adpar
Llandyfriog
Teifi Valley Railway
Penrhiwllan
Llandysul
Rhoshill
Pen-rhiw
Newcastle Emlyn
Henllan
Llanfihangel
Newchapel
Llangeler
Afon Teifi
Pontwelly
Eglwyswrw
Drefach
Felindre
Pentre-cwrt
Boncath
Glynteg
Blaenffos
Cwmhiraeth
Capel Iwan
Pencader
Bwlch-y-groes
Cwmpengraig
Star
Rhos
Gwyddg
Crymmych
Tegryn
Hermon
Alltwalis
Llanfyrnach
Cwmduad
FOEL DRYCH
Glandwr
Trelech
Llanpumsaint
Hebron
River Gwili
Pontarsais
Llanglydwen
Blaenwaun
Blaen-y-Coed
Cynwyl Elfed
Cefn-y-pant
Cwmbach
Gwili Railway
Talog
Efailwen
Felingwm
Login
Llanboidy
Gellywen
Abernant
A487
A486
A484
A475
A478
A485
B4342
B4334
B4321
B4333
B4570
B4571
B4548
B4546
B4332
B4338
B4459
B4476
B4336
B4299
B4301
311
324
258
335
362
314
257
252
358
368

99
49
50

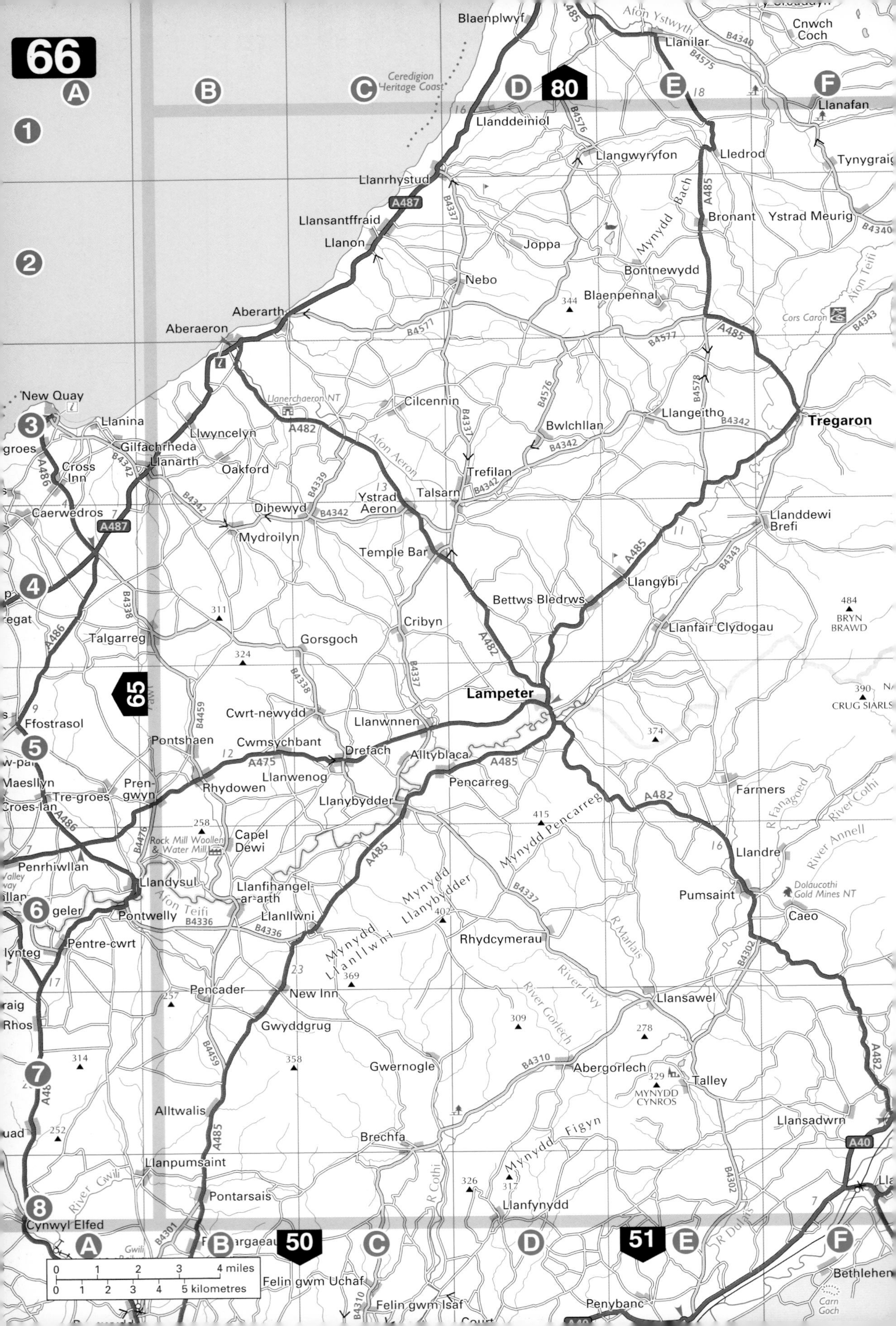

Blaenplwyf
Afon Ystwyth
Cnwch Coch
Llanilar
Ceredigion Heritage Coast
80
Llanddeiniol
Llanafan
Llangwyryfon
Lledrod
Tynygraig
Llanrhystud
Mynydd Bach
Llansantffraid
Bronant
Ystrad Meurig
Llanon
Joppa
Nebo
Bontnewydd
Blaenpennal
Aberarth
Aberaeron
Cors Caron
New Quay
Llanina
Llanerchaeron NT
Cilcennin
Llangeitho
Tregaron
Llwyncelyn
Bwlchllan
Gilfachrheda
Cross Inn
Llanarth
Oakford
Afon Aeron
Trefilan
Talsarn
Caerwedros
Dihewyd
Ystrad Aeron
Llanddewi Brefi
Mydroilyn
Temple Bar
Llangybi
Bettws Bledrws
Cribyn
Talgarreg
Gorsgoch
Llanfair Clydogau
BRYN BRAWD
65
Lampeter
CRUG SIARLS
Ffostrasol
Cwrt-newydd
Llanwnnen
Pontshaen
Cwmsychbant
Drefach
Alltyblaca
Maesllyn
Tre-groes
Pren-gwyn
Llanwenog
Rhydowen
Pencarreg
Croes-lan
Llanybydder
Farmers
Mynydd Pencarreg
Rock Mill Woollen & Water Mill
Capel Dewi
Llandre
Penrhiwllan
River Annell
River Cothi
Llandysul
Mynydd Llanybydder
Llanfihangel-ar-arth
Pumsaint
Dolaucothi Gold Mines NT
Afon Teifi
Pontwelly
Llanllwni
Caeo
Pentre-cwrt
Rhydcymerau
Mynydd Llanllwni
R Marlais
River Livy
River Gorlech
Pencader
New Inn
Llansawel
Rhos
Gwyddgrug
Gwernogle
Abergorlech
Talley
MYNYDD CYNROS
Alltwalis
Llansadwrn
Brechfa
Mynydd Figyn
Llanpumsaint
River Gwili
R Cothi
Pontarsais
Llanfynydd
Cynwyl Elfed
R Dulais
50
51
Bethlehem
Felin gwm Uchaf
Felin gwm Isaf
Penybanc
Carn Goch
0 1 2 3 4 miles
0 1 2 3 4 5 kilometres

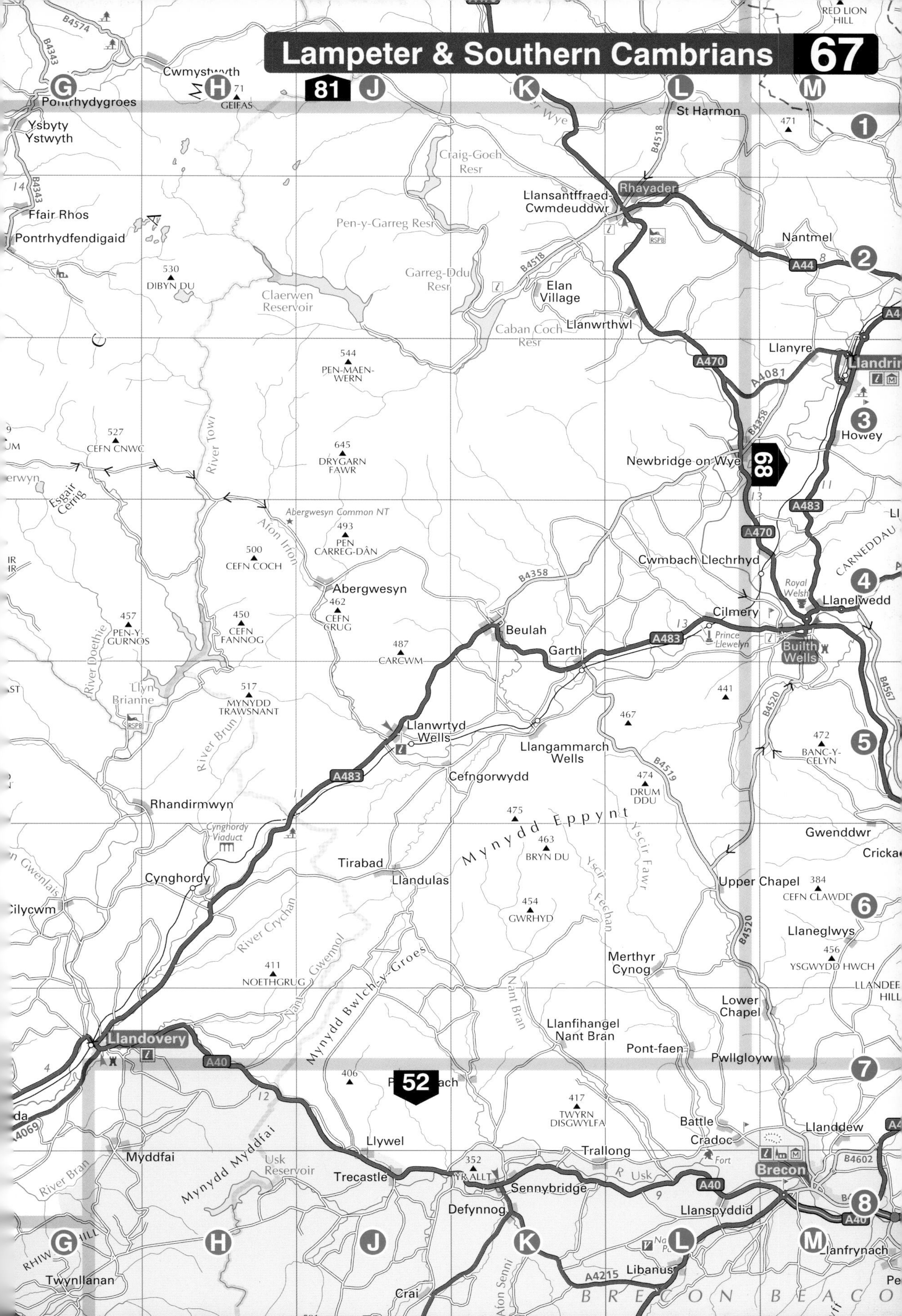
81
52
68
Pontrhydygroes
Ysbyty Ystwyth
Cwmystwyth
Ffair Rhos
Pontrhydfendigaid
St Harmon
Rhayader
Llansantffraed-Cwmdeuddwr
Nantmel
Craig-Goch Resr
Pen-y-Garreg Resr
Garreg-Ddu Resr
Claerwen Reservoir
Elan Village
Caban Coch Resr
Llanwrthwl
Llanyre
Howey
Newbridge on Wye
Cwmbach Llechrhyd
Llanelwedd
Cilmery
Builth Wells
Beulah
Garth
Abergwesyn
Abergwesyn Common NT
Llanwrtyd Wells
Llangammarch Wells
Cefngorwydd
Rhandirmwyn
Cynghordy Viaduct
Cynghordy
Cilycwm
Tirabad
Llandulas
Mynydd Eppynt
Upper Chapel
Gwenddwr
Llaneglwys
Merthyr Cynog
Lower Chapel
Llanfihangel Nant Bran
Pont-faen
Pwllgloyw
Llandovery
Myddfai
Mynydd Myddfai
Usk Reservoir
Llywel
Trecastle
Sennybridge
Defynnog
Trallong
Battle
Cradoc
Llanddew
Brecon
Llanspyddid
Libanus
Twynllanan
Crai
Llyn Brianne
River Towi
Afon Irfon
River Doethie
River Brun
River Crychan
Mynydd Bwlch-y-Groes
Nant Bran
R Usk
BRECON BEACONS
A44
A470
A483
A4081
A40
A4215
A4069
B4358
B4518
B4520
B4519
B4343
B4574
B4567
B4602
530 DIBYN DU
544 PEN-MAEN-WERN
527 CEFN CNWC
645 DRYGARN FAWR
493 PEN CARREG-DÂN
500 CEFN COCH
462 CEFN CRUG
457 PEN-Y-GURNOS
450 CEFN FANNOG
487 CARCWM
517 MYNYDD TRAWSNANT
467
441
472 BANC-Y-CELYN
474 DRUM DDU
475
463 BRYN DU
454 GWRHYD
384 CEFN CLAWDD
456 YSGWYDD HWCH
411 NOETHGRUG
406
417 TWYRN DISGWYLFA
352 YR ALLT
471 GEIFAS
471
591
Royal Welsh
Prince Llewelyn
Fort
RED LION HILL
CARNEDDAU
LLANDEFALLE HILL
Yscir Fawr
Yscir Fechan
Nant Gwennol
Esgair Cerrig
RHIW HILL
River Bran
Llanfrynach

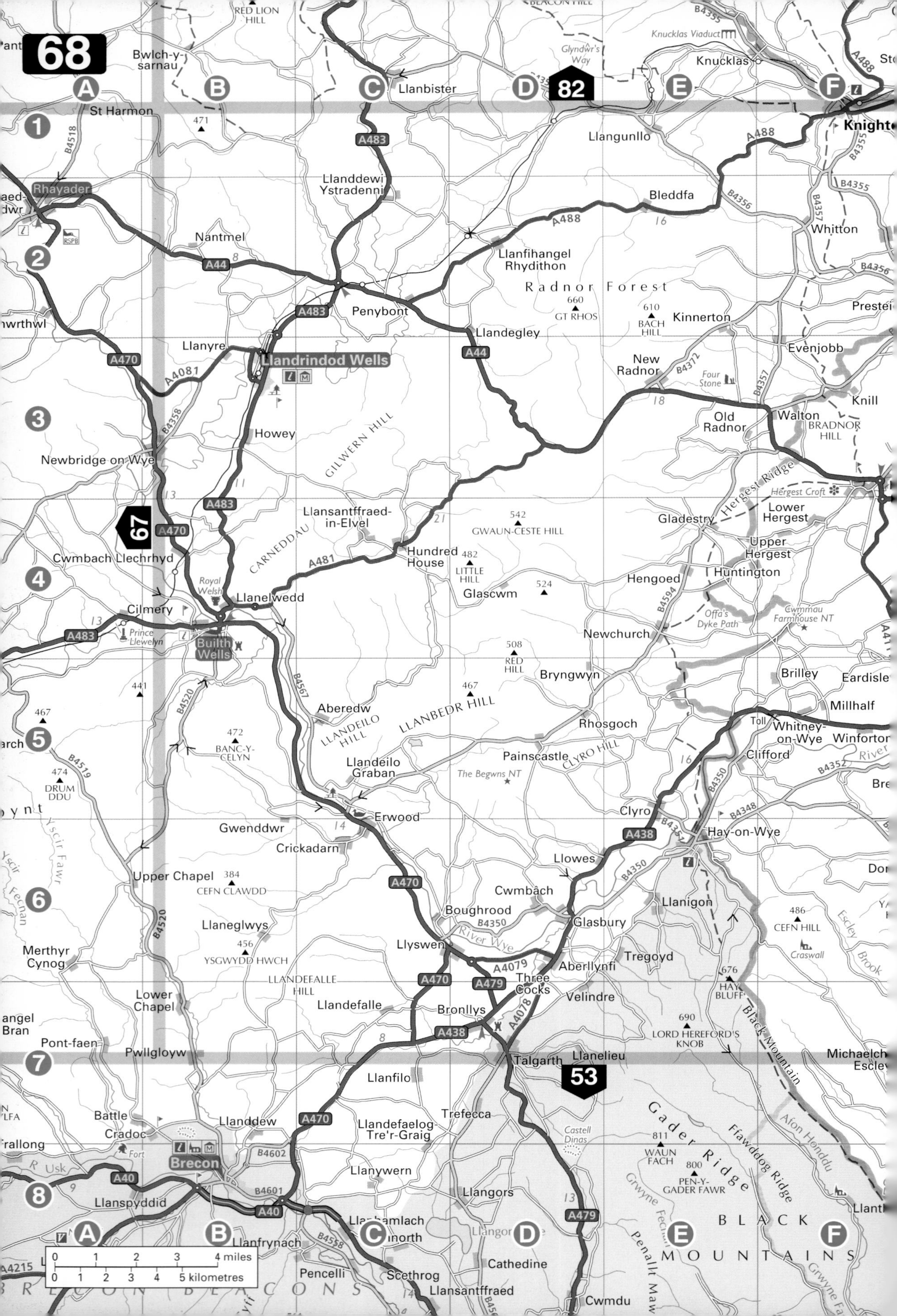
A
B
C
D
E
F
1
2
3
4
5
6
7
8
82
67
53
Bwlch-y-sarnau
Red Lion Hill
Llanbister
Glyndŵr's Way
Knucklas Viaduct
Knucklas
St Harmon
Llangunllo
Knighton
A488
B4355
A483
B4518
Rhayader
RSPB
Llanddewi Ystradenni
Bleddfa
B4356
B4357
Whitton
Nantmel
A44
Llanfihangel Rhydithon
Radnor Forest
660
GT RHOS
610
BACH HILL
Kinnerton
Presteigne
Penybont
Llandegley
Llanyre
Llandrindod Wells
A470
A4081
B4358
Evenjobb
New Radnor
B4372
Four Stone
Knill
Walton
Old Radnor
BRADNOR HILL
Howey
GILWERN HILL
Newbridge on Wye
Hergest Ridge
Hergest Croft
Lower Hergest
Gladestry
Llansantffraed-in-Elvel
542
GWAUN-CESTE HILL
CARNEDDAU
Hundred House
Upper Hergest
Cwmbach Llechrhyd
A481
482
LITTLE HILL
Huntington
Hengoed
Royal Welsh
Llanelwedd
Glascwm
524
Cilmery
Prince Llewelyn
B4594
Offa's Dyke Path
Cwmmau Farmhouse NT
Newchurch
Builth Wells
508
RED HILL
Bryngwyn
Brilley
Eardisley
441
B4520
B4567
467
LLANBEDR HILL
Millhalf
Aberedw
LLANDEILO HILL
Rhosgoch
Toll
Whitney-on-Wye
Winforton
472
BANC-Y-CELYN
CLYRO HILL
Painscastle
Clifford
B4519
474
DRUM DDU
Llandeilo Graban
The Begwns NT
B4352
B4350
B4348
Clyro
Erwood
Gwenddwr
A438
Hay-on-Wye
Crickadarn
Yscir Fawr
Yscir Fechan
Llowes
Upper Chapel
384
CEFN CLAWDD
Cwmbâch
Llanigon
486
CEFN HILL
Boughrood
Escley Brook
Llaneglwys
Glasbury
River Wye
Craswall
Merthyr Cynog
456
YSGWYDD HWCH
Llyswen
Tregoyd
A4079
Aberllynfi
LLANDEFALLE HILL
A479
Three Cocks
676
HAY BLUFF
Lower Chapel
Velindre
Llandefalle
Bronllys
Black Mountain
A4078
690
LORD HEREFORD'S KNOB
Pont-faen
Pwllgloyw
Talgarth
Llanelieu
Michaelchurch Escley
Llanfilo
Gader Ridge
Battle
Trefecca
Cradoc
Llanddew
Llandefaelog-Tre'r-Graig
Castell Dinas
811
WAUN FACH
Ffrawddog Ridge
Afon Honddu
Frallong
Fort
Brecon
B4602
800
PEN-Y-GADER FAWR
R Usk
A40
Llanywern
Grwyne Fechan
Llanspyddid
B4601
Llangors
BLACK MOUNTAINS
Llanfrynach
B4558
Cathedine
Penallt Mawr
Pencelli
Scethrog
Llansantffraed
Cwmdu
BRECON BEACONS
A4215
Grwyne Fawr
0 1 2 3 4 miles
0 1 2 3 4 5 kilometres

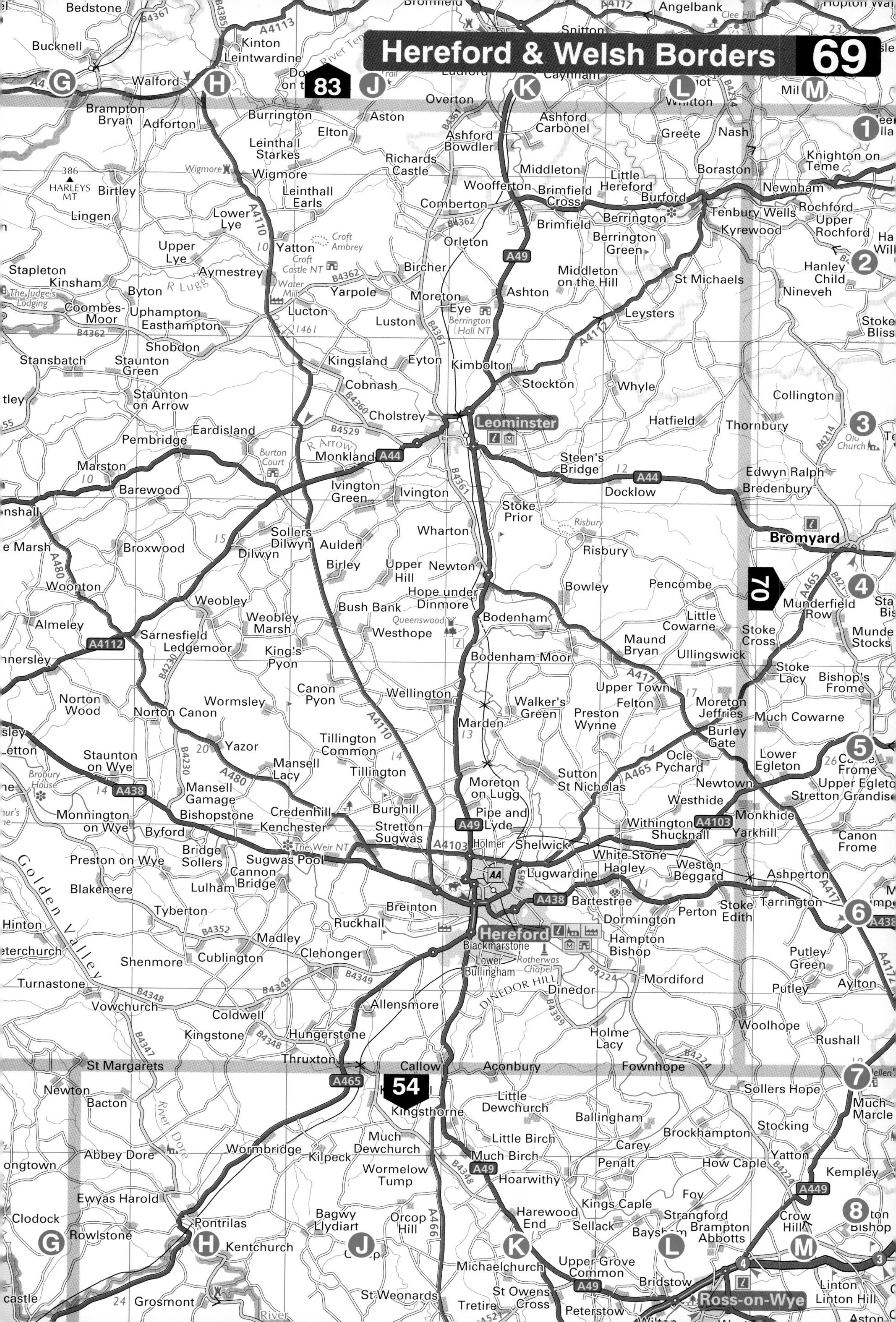
Hereford & Welsh Borders
69
83
70
54
Leominster
Hereford
Bromyard
Ross-on-Wye
Tenbury Wells
Kington
Leintwardine
Bucknell
Walford
Brampton Bryan
Adforton
Burrington
Aston
Elton
Overton
Ashford Carbonel
Ashford Bowdler
Richards Castle
Leinthall Starkes
Wigmore
Leinthall Earls
Birtley
Lingen
Lower Lye
Upper Lye
Yatton
Croft Ambrey
Croft Castle NT
Aymestrey
Stapleton
Kinsham
Byton
Coombes-Moor
Uphampton
Easthampton
Shobdon
Lucton
Yarpole
Luston
Moreton
Eye
Berrington Hall NT
Bircher
Orleton
Comberton
Woofferton
Middleton
Brimfield Cross
Brimfield
Little Hereford
Burford
Berrington
Berrington Green
Middleton on the Hill
St Michaels
Leysters
Ashton
Kimbolton
Stockton
Whyle
Hatfield
Thornbury
Collington
Edwyn Ralph
Bredenbury
Greete
Nash
Boraston
Knighton on Teme
Newnham
Rochford
Upper Rochford
Kyrewood
Hanley Child
Nineveh
Stoke Bliss
Stansbatch
Staunton Green
Staunton on Arrow
Kingsland
Eyton
Cobnash
Cholstrey
Eardisland
Pembridge
Monkland
Burton Court
Marston
Barewood
Ivington Green
Ivington
Stoke Prior
Steen's Bridge
Docklow
Risbury
Wharton
Sollers Dilwyn
Dilwyn
Aulden
Broxwood
Birley
Upper Hill
Newton
Hope under Dinmore
Bush Bank
Queenswood
Westhope
Bodenham
Bowley
Pencombe
Little Cowarne
Maund Bryan
Stoke Cross
Ullingswick
Munderfield Row
Woonton
Weobley
Weobley Marsh
Almeley
Sarnesfield
Ledgemoor
King's Pyon
Canon Pyon
Wellington
Bodenham Moor
Walker's Green
Marden
Preston Wynne
Upper Town
Felton
Moreton Jeffries
Much Cowarne
Stoke Lacy
Bishop's Frome
Norton Wood
Norton Canon
Wormsley
Yazor
Staunton on Wye
Brobury House
Mansell Lacy
Mansell Gamage
Tillington Common
Tillington
Burley Gate
Ocle Pychard
Sutton St Nicholas
Moreton on Lugg
Lower Egleton
Canon Frome
Upper Egleton
Stretton Grandison
Newtown
Westhide
Monkhide
Yarkhill
Withington
Shucknall
Monnington on Wye
Byford
Bishopstone
Credenhill
Kenchester
Burghill
Stretton Sugwas
Pipe and Lyde
Holmer
Shelwick
White Stone
Hagley
Lugwardine
Weston Beggard
Ashperton
Preston on Wye
Bridge Sollers
Sugwas Pool
The Weir NT
Cannon Bridge
Lulham
Blakemere
Breinton
Bartestree
Dormington
Perton
Stoke Edith
Tarrington
Golden Valley
Tyberton
Ruckhall
Madley
Hinton
Cublington
Clehonger
Shenmore
Blackmarstone
Lower Bullingham
Rotherwas Chapel
Dinedor Hill
Dinedor
Hampton Bishop
Mordiford
Putley Green
Putley
Aylton
Turnastone
Vowchurch
Coldwell
Allensmore
Kingstone
Hungerstone
Thruxton
Holme Lacy
Woolhope
Rushall
St Margarets
Callow
Aconbury
Fownhope
Newton
Bacton
Kingsthorne
Little Dewchurch
Ballingham
Sollers Hope
Much Marcle
Stocking
Brockhampton
Much Dewchurch
Little Birch
Carey
Abbey Dore
Wormbridge
Kilpeck
Much Birch
Penalt
How Caple
Yatton
Kempley
Wormelow Tump
Hoarwithy
Ewyas Harold
Bagwy Llydiart
Orcop Hill
Harewood End
Kings Caple
Sellack
Foy
Strangford
Brampton Abbotts
Crow Hill
Clodock
Pontrilas
Rowlstone
Kentchurch
Baysham
Michaelchurch
Upper Grove Common
Bridstow
Linton
Linton Hill
Grosmont
St Weonards
Tretire
St Owens Cross
Peterstow
Angelbank
Clee Hill
Snitton
Whitton
HARLEYS MT
The Judge's Lodging
Water Mill
R Lugg
R Arrow
River Dore
A4113
A4110
A4112
A44
A480
A438
A4103
A49
A465
A417
A466
A4224
A449
B4362
B4361
B4360
B4529
B4230
B4352
B4349
B4348
B4347
B4399
B4224
B4214
B4367
B4385

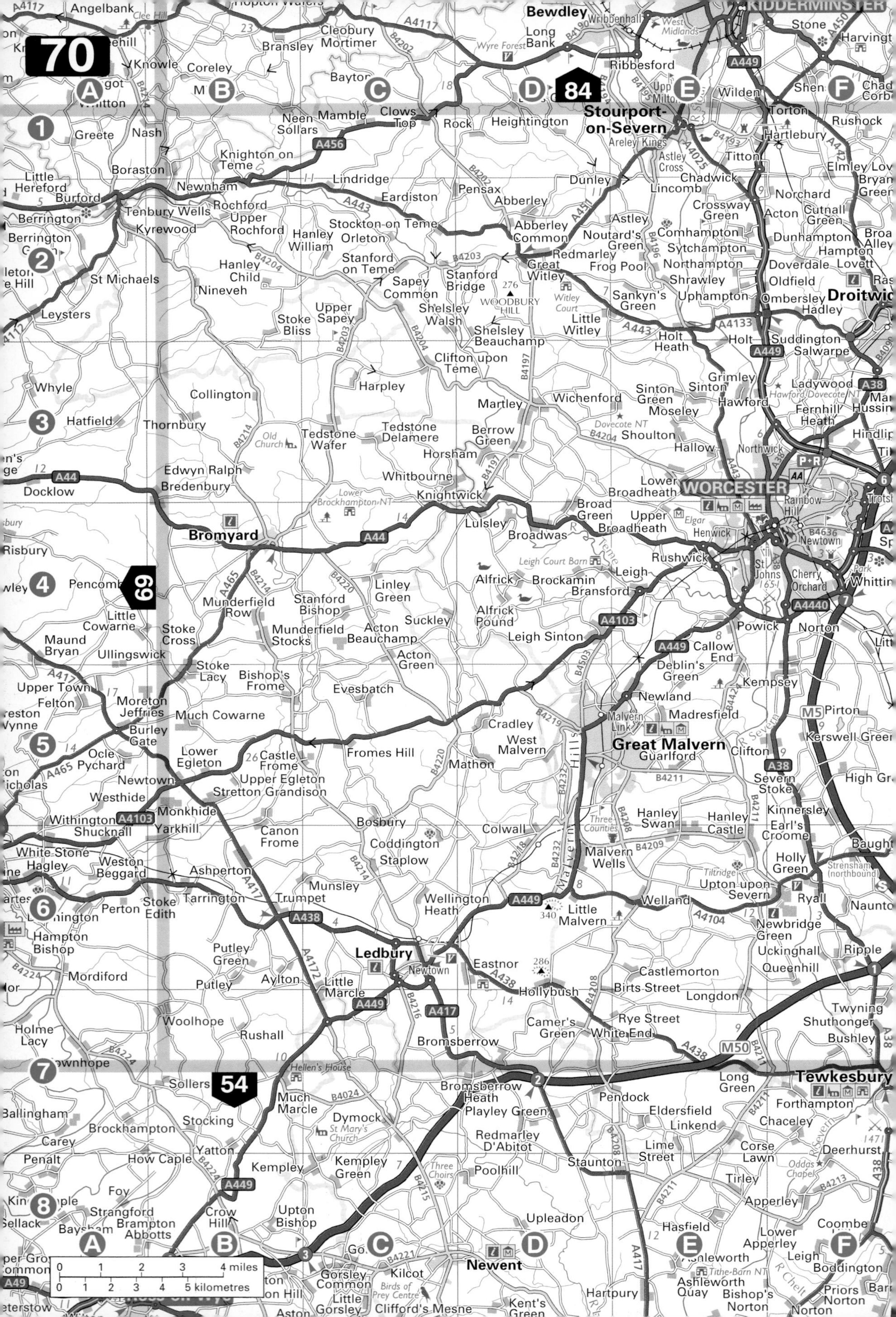
70
84
69
54
A
B
C
D
E
F
1
2
3
4
5
6
7
8
Angelbank
Clee Hill
Knowle
Coreley
Bransley
Cleobury Mortimer
Baytor
Bewdley
Wribbenhall
West Midlands
KIDDERMINSTER
Stone
Harvington
Long Bank
Wyre Forest
Ribbesford
Wilden
Shenstone
Chaddesley Corbett
Whitton
Greete
Nash
Neen Sollars
Mamble
Clows Top
Rock
Heightington
Stourport-on-Severn
Areley Kings
Torton
Rushock
Hartlebury
Titton
Astley Cross
Knighton on Teme
Boraston
Little Hereford
Burford
Newnham
Lindridge
Eardiston
Pensax
Dunley
Lincomb
Chadwick
Elmley Lovett
Bryan's Green
Berrington
Tenbury Wells
Rochford
Upper Rochford
Kyrewood
Stockton-on-Teme
Orleton
Hanley William
Abberley
Abberley Common
Astley
Noutard's Green
Crossway Green
Comhampton
Sytchampton
Norchard
Acton
Cutnall Green
Dunhampton
Hampton Lovett
Broad Alley
Hanley Child
St Michaels
Nineveh
Stanford on Teme
Sapey Common
Stanford Bridge
Great Witley
Redmarley
Frog Pool
Northampton
Shrawley
Uphampton
Doverdale
Oldfield
Ombersley
Hadley
Droitwich
Leysters
Upper Sapey
Stoke Bliss
Shelsley Walsh
Shelsley Beauchamp
Woodbury Hill
Witley Court
Little Witley
Sankyn's Green
Holt Heath
Holt
Suddington
Salwarpe
Clifton upon Teme
Harpley
Whyle
Hatfield
Collington
Thornbury
Martley
Wichenford
Sinton Green
Sinton
Grimley
Moseley
Hawford
Ladywood
Hawford Dovecote NT
Fernhill Heath
Old Church
Tedstone Wafer
Tedstone Delamere
Berrow Green
Horsham
Dovecote NT
Shoulton
Hallow
Northwick
Hindlip
Edwyn Ralph
Bredenbury
Docklow
Whitbourne
Knightwick
Lower Brockhampton NT
Lower Broadheath
WORCESTER
Broad Green
Upper Broadheath
Elgar
Henwick
Rainbow Hill
Bromyard
Lulsley
Broadwas
Newtown
Risbury
Pencombe
Leigh Court Barn
Rushwick
Leigh
St Johns
Cherry Orchard
Whittington
Linley Green
Alfrick
Brockamin
Bransford
Munderfield Row
Stanford Bishop
Little Cowarne
Munderfield Stocks
Acton Beauchamp
Suckley
Alfrick Pound
Leigh Sinton
Powick
Norton
Maund Bryan
Ullingswick
Stoke Cross
Stoke Lacy
Acton Green
Callow End
Deblin's Green
Kempsey
Upper Town
Felton
Bishop's Frome
Evesbatch
Newland
Moreton Jeffries
Much Cowarne
Malvern Link
Madresfield
Pirton
Burley Gate
Cradley
West Malvern
Great Malvern
Guarlford
Clifton
Kerswell Green
Ocle Pychard
Lower Egleton
Castle Frome
Fromes Hill
Mathon
Newtown
Upper Egleton
Stretton Grandison
Severn Stoke
High Green
Westhide
Withington
Shucknall
Monkhide
Yarkhill
Canon Frome
Bosbury
Coddington
Colwall
Three Counties
Hanley Swan
Hanley Castle
Kinnersley
Earl's Croome
White Stone
Hagley
Weston Beggard
Ashperton
Staplow
Malvern Wells
Holly Green
Baughton
Tiltridge
Strensham (northbound)
Munsley
Upton upon Severn
Ryall
Naunton
Stoke Edith
Tarrington
Trumpet
Wellington Heath
Little Malvern
Welland
Perton
Hampton Bishop
Putley Green
Ledbury
Eastnor
Newbridge Green
Uckinghall
Ripple
Mordiford
Putley
Aylton
Little Marcle
Castlemorton
Birts Street
Queenhill
Hollybush
Longdon
Twyning
Shuthonger
Holme Lacy
Woolhope
Rushall
Camer's Green
Rye Street
White End
Bromsberrow
Bushley
Downhope
Hellen's House
Sollers
Much Marcle
Bromsberrow Heath
Playley Green
Pendock
Long Green
Tewkesbury
Ballingham
Brockhampton
Stocking
Dymock
St Mary's Church
Redmarley D'Abitot
Eldersfield
Linkend
Forthampton
Chaceley
Carey
Penalt
How Caple
Yatton
Kempley
Kempley Green
Three Choirs
Poolhill
Staunton
Lime Street
Corse Lawn
Deerhurst
Odda's Chapel
Tirley
Foy
Strangford
Brampton Abbotts
Crow Hill
Upton Bishop
Upleadon
Apperley
Coombe Hill
Sellack
Baysham
Hasfield
Lower Apperley
Newent
Ashleworth
Tithe Barn NT
Leigh
Boddington
Gorsley Common
Kilcot
Birds of Prey Centre
Little Gorsley
Clifford's Mesne
Kent's Green
Hartpury
Ashleworth Quay
Bishop's Norton
Priors Norton
Norton
R Severn
R Teme
R Chelt
Malvern Hills
A4117
A456
A443
A451
A449
A4025
A4133
A38
A44
A465
A417
A4103
A4440
M5
A438
A4172
A4104
M50
A49
B4190
B4202
B4195
B4193
B4204
B4203
B4196
B4197
B4214
B4220
B4219
B4232
B4211
B4208
B4209
B4218
B4216
B4224
B4024
B4215
B4221
B4213
B4636
P+R
AA
0
1
2
3
4 miles
5 kilometres

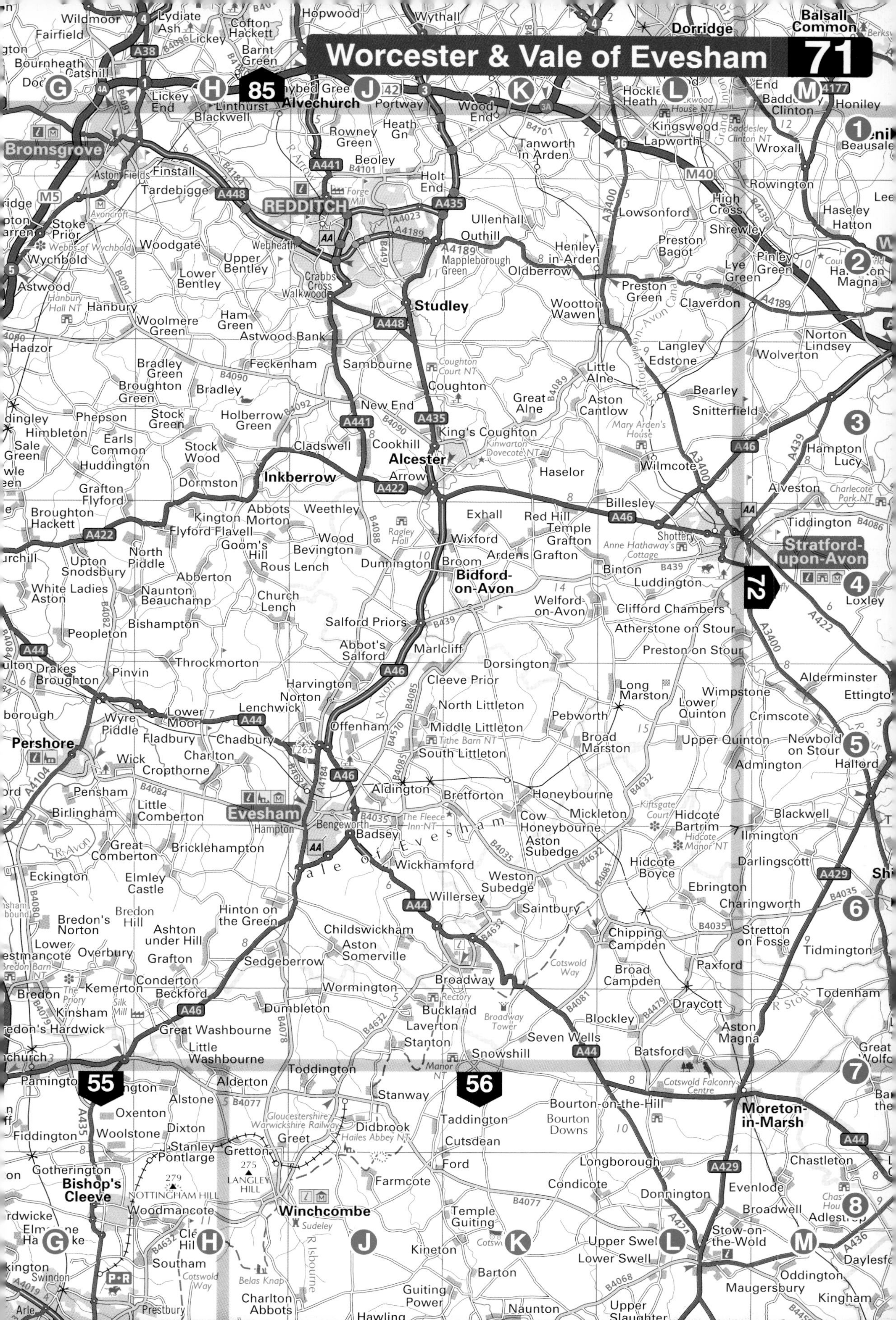
Wildmoor
Fairfield
Lydiate Ash
Cofton Hackett
Lickey
Barnt Green
Hopwood
Wythall
Dorridge
Balsall Common
Bournheath
Catshill
Lickey End
Linthurst
Alvechurch
Portway
Wood End
Hockley Heath
Honiley
85
Blackwell
Rowney Green
Heath Gn
Kingswood
Lapworth
Baddesley Clinton
Baddesley Clinton NT
Tanworth in Arden
Wroxall
Beausale
Bromsgrove
Finstall
Beoley
Holt End
Rowington
Aston Fields
Tardebigge
REDDITCH
Forge Mill
High Cross
Lowsonford
Shrewley
Haseley
Hatton
Avoncroft
Stoke Prior
Webbs of Wychbold
Woodgate
Webheath
Ullenhall
Outhill
Preston Bagot
Henley-in-Arden
Mappleborough Green
Oldberrow
Pinley Green
Lye Green
Hampton Magna
Wychbold
Upper Bentley
Lower Bentley
Crabbs Cross
Walkwood
Preston Green
Claverdon
Astwood
Hanbury Hall NT
Hanbury
Studley
Wootton Wawen
Woolmere Green
Ham Green
Astwood Bank
Norton Lindsey
Hadzor
Langley
Edstone
Wolverton
Bradley Green
Feckenham
Sambourne
Coughton Court NT
Little Alne
Broughton Green
Bradley
Coughton
Great Alne
Aston Cantlow
Bearley
Snitterfield
New End
Phepson
Himbleton
Holberrow Green
Stock Green
King's Coughton
Mary Arden's House
Hampton Lucy
Earls Common
Sale Green
Cladswell
Cookhill
Kinwarton Dovecote NT
Stock Wood
Alcester
Huddington
Arrow
Haselor
Wilmcote
Inkberrow
Dormston
Alveston
Charlecote Park NT
Grafton Flyford
Abbots Morton
Weethley
Exhall
Billesley
Broughton Hackett
Kington
Red Hill
Tiddington
Flyford Flavell
Ragley Hall
Temple Grafton
Shottery
Wixford
Wood Bevington
Anne Hathaway's Cottage
Stratford-upon-Avon
Goom's Hill
North Piddle
Upton Snodsbury
Dunnington
Broom
Ardens Grafton
Binton
Luddington
Rous Lench
Bidford-on-Avon
White Ladies Aston
Abberton
Naunton Beauchamp
Welford-on-Avon
Loxley
Church Lench
72
Clifford Chambers
Bishampton
Salford Priors
Peopleton
Atherstone on Stour
Abbot's Salford
Marlcliff
Preston on Stour
Drakes Broughton
Throckmorton
Dorsington
Pinvin
Harvington
Cleeve Prior
Long Marston
Alderminster
Ettington
Wimpstone
Norton
Lenchwick
North Littleton
Lower Quinton
Crimscote
Wyre Piddle
Lower Moor
Pebworth
Offenham
Middle Littleton
Tithe Barn NT
Broad Marston
Upper Quinton
Newbold on Stour
Pershore
Fladbury
Chadbury
South Littleton
Admington
Halford
Wick
Charlton
Cropthorne
Pensham
Aldington
Bretforton
Honeybourne
Birlingham
Little Comberton
Evesham
Hampton
Bengeworth
The Fleece Inn NT
Cow Honeybourne
Mickleton
Kiftsgate Court
Hidcote Bartrim
Hidcote Manor NT
Blackwell
Badsey
Aston Subedge
Ilmington
Great Comberton
Bricklehampton
Vale of Evesham
Wickhamford
Hidcote Boyce
Darlingscott
Eckington
Elmley Castle
Weston Subedge
Ebrington
Willersey
Charingworth
Bredon Hill
Bredon's Norton
Hinton on the Green
Saintbury
Stretton on Fosse
Ashton under Hill
Childswickham
Chipping Campden
Lower Westmancote
Overbury
Aston Somerville
Tidmington
Bredon Barn NT
Grafton
Sedgeberrow
Cotswold Way
Paxford
Broad Campden
Kemerton
Conderton
Wormington
Broadway
The Priory
Bredon
Beckford
Silk Mill
Todenham
Kinsham
Dumbleton
Rectory
Buckland
Broadway Tower
Draycott
Blockley
Bredon's Hardwick
Great Washbourne
Laverton
Seven Wells
Aston Magna
Little Washbourne
Stanton
Snowshill
Batsford
Great Wolford
Toddington
Manor NT
Alderton
56
55
Pamington
Alstone
Stanway
Cotswold Falconry Centre
Moreton-in-Marsh
Oxenton
Bourton-on-the-Hill
Gloucestershire Warwickshire Railway
Taddington
Bourton Downs
Dixton
Didbrook
Fiddington
Woolstone
Greet
Hailes Abbey NT
Cutsdean
Stanley Pontlarge
Gretton
Gotherington
Longborough
Chastleton
Langley Hill
Nottingham Hill
Bishop's Cleeve
Ford
Farmcote
Condicote
Evenlode
Donnington
Woodmancote
Winchcombe
Temple Guiting
Broadwell
Adlestrop
Sudeley
Cleeve Hill
Kineton
Upper Swell
Stow-on-the-Wold
Lower Swell
Daylesford
Southam
Swindon
Belas Knap
Barton
Oddington
Maugersbury
Guiting Power
Charlton Abbots
Naunton
Kingham
Upper Slaughter
Prestbury
Hawling
Arle

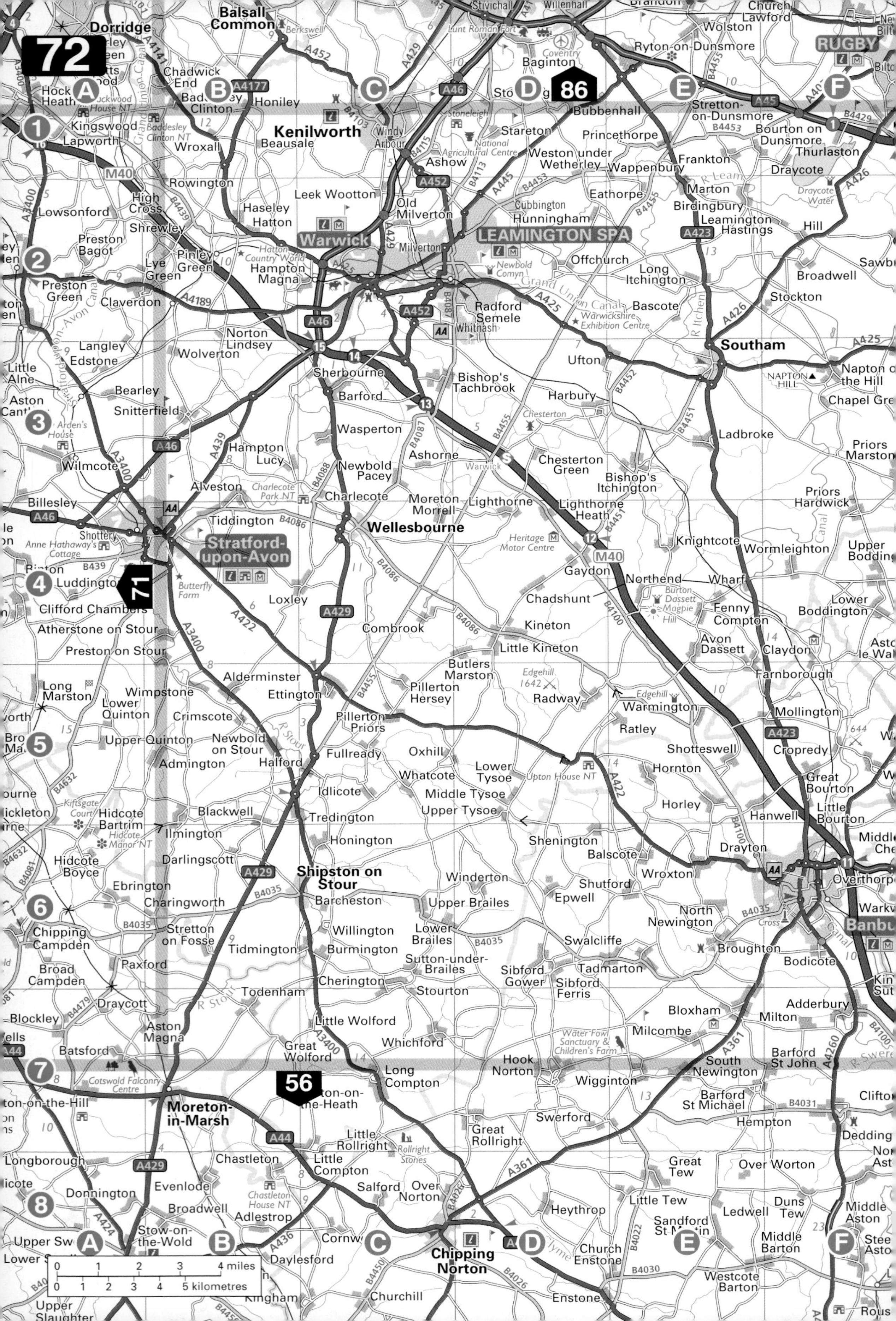
72
86
71
56
Kenilworth
Warwick
LEAMINGTON SPA
Stratford-upon-Avon
Wellesbourne
Southam
Shipston on Stour
Moreton-in-Marsh
Chipping Norton
RUGBY
Banbury
Dorridge
Balsall Common
Lapworth
Kingswood
Lowsonford
Henley-in-Arden
Claverdon
Wootton Wawen
Snitterfield
Wilmcote
Hampton Lucy
Charlecote
Barford
Sherbourne
Bishop's Tachbrook
Whitnash
Radford Semele
Harbury
Ufton
Kineton
Gaydon
Fenny Compton
Farnborough
Cropredy
Mollington
Tysoe
Upton House NT
Edgehill
Alderminster
Ettington
Ilmington
Hidcote Manor NT
Chipping Campden
Blockley
Long Compton
Rollright Stones
Hook Norton
Bloxham
Adderbury
Deddington
Stow-on-the-Wold
Charlbury
0 1 2 3 4 miles
0 1 2 3 4 5 kilometres

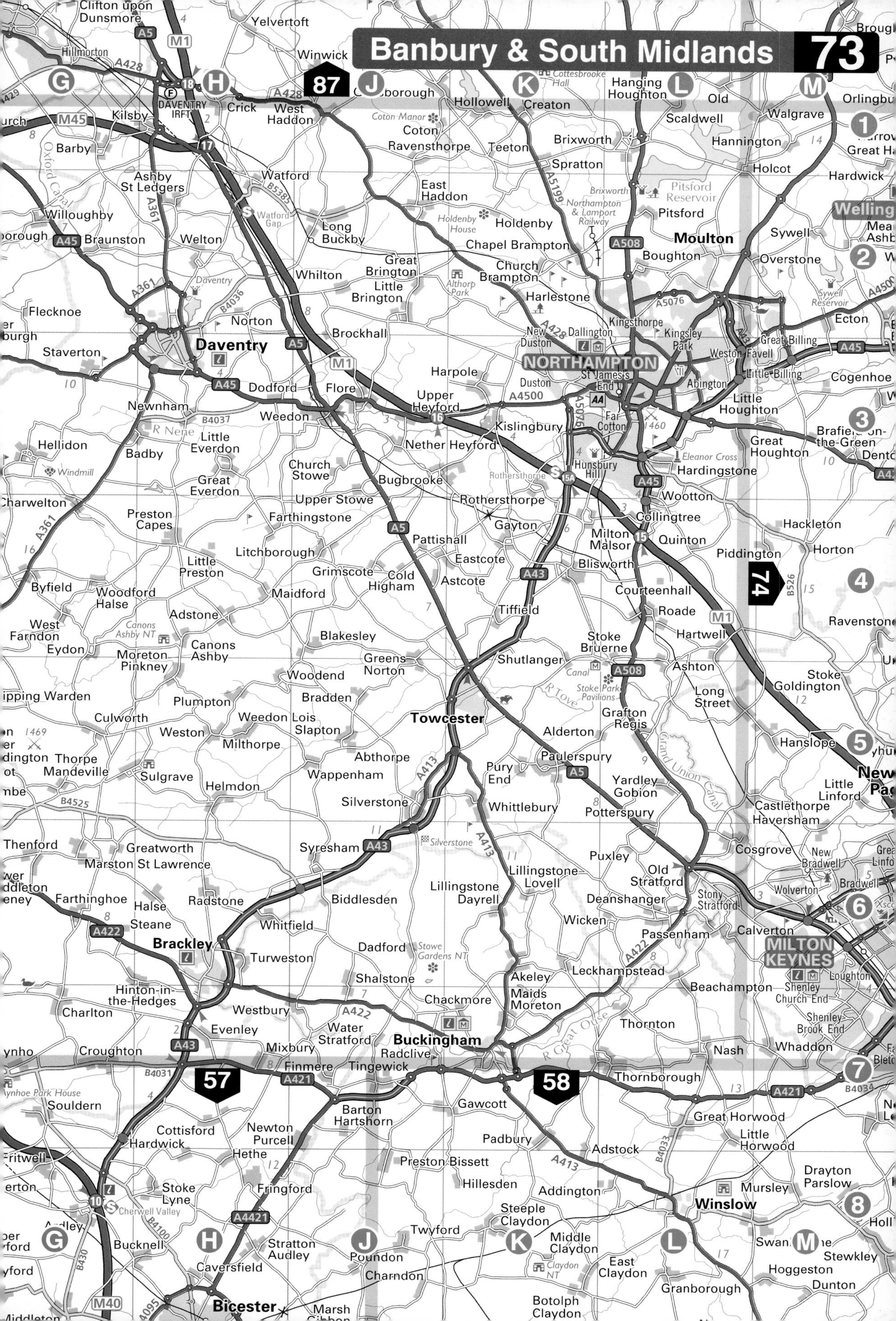

Clifton upon Dunsmore
Yelvertoft
Hillmorton
Winwick
87
Guilsborough
Cottesbrooke Hall
Hanging Houghton
Old
Orlingbury
Daventry IRFT
Crick
West Haddon
Hollowell
Creaton
Scaldwell
Walgrave
Kilsby
Barby
Coton Manor
Coton
Ravensthorpe
Teeton
Brixworth
Hannington
Great Harrowden
Oxford Canal
Ashby St Ledgers
Watford
Spratton
Holcot
Hardwick
East Haddon
Brixworth
Pitsford Reservoir
Northampton & Lamport Railway
Watford Gap
Willoughby
Long Buckby
Holdenby House
Holdenby
Pitsford
Moulton
Sywell
Braunston
Welton
Chapel Brampton
Boughton
Overstone
Great Brington
Whilton
Church Brampton
Little Brington
Althorp Park
Harlestone
Sywell Reservoir
Daventry
Flecknoe
Norton
New Duston
Dallington
Kingsthorpe
Kingsley Park
Ecton
Great Billing
Brockhall
Staverton
Daventry
NORTHAMPTON
Weston Favell
St James's End
Little Billing
Cogenhoe
Harpole
Duston
Abington
Newnham
Dodford
Flore
Upper Heyford
Little Houghton
Weedon
Kislingbury
Far Cotton
R Nene
Little Everdon
Hellidon
Badby
Nether Heyford
Great Houghton
Brafield-on-the-Green
Windmill
Church Stowe
Eleanor Cross
Hunsbury Hill
Hardingstone
Great Everdon
Bugbrooke
Rothersthorpe
Wootton
Charwelton
Upper Stowe
Preston Capes
Farthingstone
Rothersthorpe
Collingtree
Gayton
Hackleton
Pattishall
Milton Malsor
Quinton
Horton
Litchborough
Piddington
Little Preston
Eastcote
Blisworth
74
Byfield
Woodford Halse
Grimscote
Cold Higham
Astcote
Maidford
Courteenhall
Tiffield
Roade
West Farndon
Adstone
Canons Ashby NT
Ravenstone
Eydon
Hartwell
Blakesley
Stoke Bruerne
Canons Ashby
Moreton Pinkney
Greens Norton
Shutlanger
Ashton
Stoke Goldington
Canal
Chipping Warden
Woodend
Stoke Park Pavilions
Long Street
Bradden
R Tove
Plumpton
Towcester
Grafton Regis
Culworth
Weedon Lois
Weston
Slapton
Alderton
Hanslope
Milthorpe
Thorpe Mandeville
Abthorpe
Paulerspury
Sulgrave
Wappenham
Pury End
Yardley Gobion
Little Linford
Helmdon
Silverstone
Whittlebury
Potterspury
Castlethorpe
Haversham
Grand Union Canal
Thenford
Greatworth
Syresham
Silverstone
Puxley
Cosgrove
New Bradwell
Marston St Lawrence
Lillingstone Lovell
Old Stratford
Lillingstone Dayrell
Deanshanger
Stony Stratford
Wolverton
Bradwell
Farthinghoe
Halse
Radstone
Biddlesden
Steane
Whitfield
Wicken
Calverton
Passenham
Brackley
Dadford
Stowe Gardens NT
MILTON KEYNES
Turweston
Leckhampstead
Shalstone
Akeley
Loughton
Beachampton
Shenley Church End
Hinton-in-the-Hedges
Chackmore
Maids Moreton
Charlton
Westbury
Shenley Brook End
Evenley
R Great Ouse
Thornton
Water Stratford
Buckingham
Mixbury
Nash
Whaddon
Croughton
Radclive
Finmere
Tingewick
57
58
Thornborough
Aynhoe Park House
Gawcott
Souldern
Barton Hartshorn
Great Horwood
Cottisford
Newton Purcell
Padbury
Little Horwood
Hardwick
Adstock
Hethe
Preston Bissett
Drayton Parslow
Hillesden
Mursley
Fringford
Addington
Stoke Lyne
Winslow
Cherwell Valley
Steeple Claydon
Twyford
Middle Claydon
Swanbourne
Bucknell
Stratton Audley
Stewkley
Poundon
East Claydon
Hoggeston
Caversfield
Claydon NT
Charndon
Granborough
Dunton
Bicester
Marsh Gibbon
Botolph Claydon

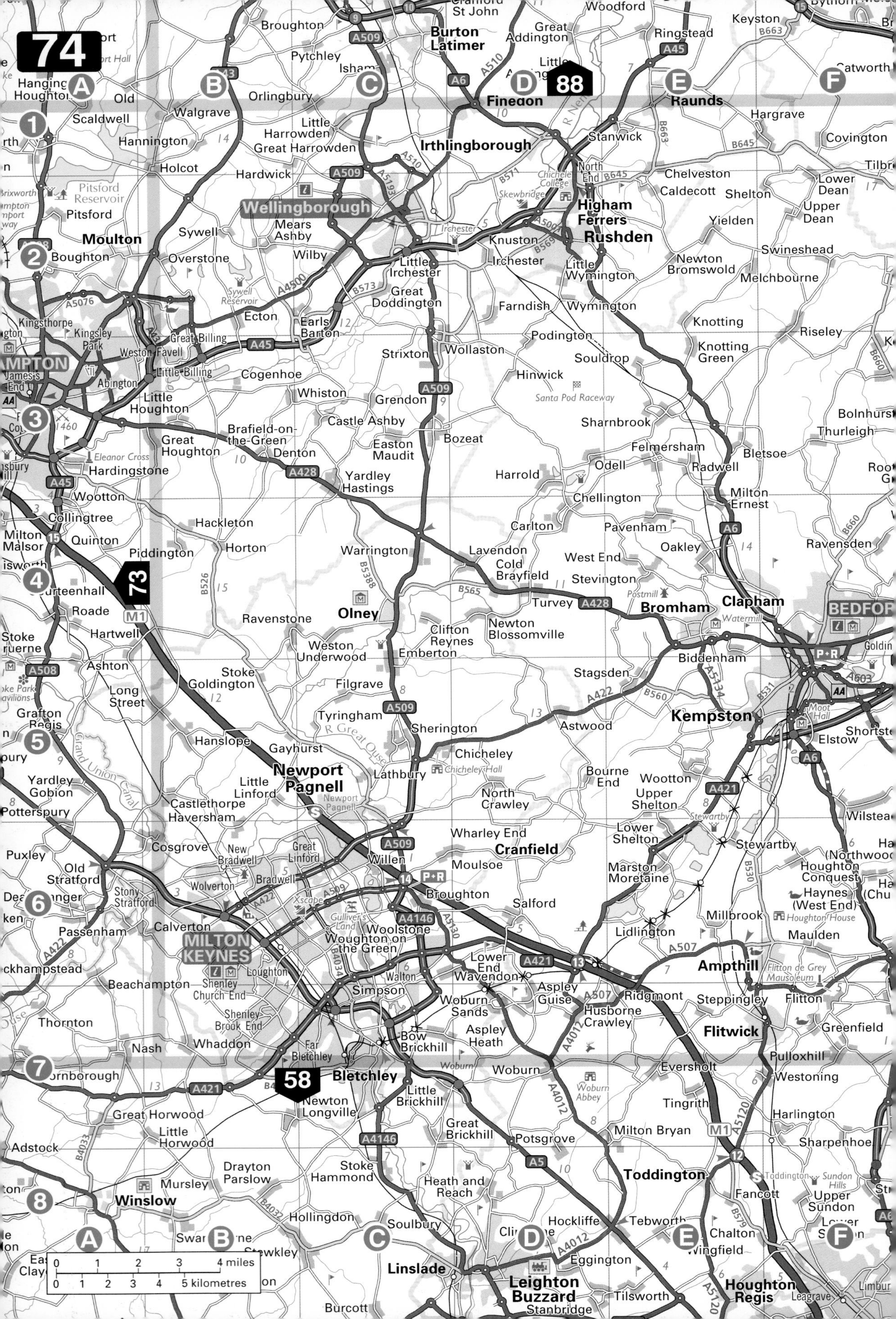
74
88
73
58
Hanging Houghton
Scaldwell
Old
Walgrave
Hannington
Broughton
Pytchley
Isham
Orlingbury
Little Harrowden
Great Harrowden
Burton Latimer
Finedon
Great Addington
Little Addington
Woodford
Ringstead
Keyston
Raunds
Catworth
Hargrave
Covington
Stanwick
Irthlingborough
Chelveston
Caldecott
Shelton
Lower Dean
Upper Dean
Holcot
Hardwick
Pitsford Reservoir
Pitsford
Moulton
Sywell
Wellingborough
Mears Ashby
Wilby
Higham Ferrers
Rushden
Knuston
Irchester
Little Irchester
Chichele College
Skewbridge
Yielden
Swineshead
Newton Bromswold
Melchbourne
Boughton
Overstone
Sywell Reservoir
Ecton
Earls Barton
Great Doddington
Farndish
Little Wymington
Wymington
Knotting
Knotting Green
Riseley
Kingsthorpe
Kingsley Park
Great Billing
Weston Favell
Little Billing
Abington
Cogenhoe
Strixton
Wollaston
Podington
Souldrop
Hinwick
Santa Pod Raceway
Whiston
Grendon
Castle Ashby
Little Houghton
Great Houghton
Brafield-on-the-Green
Denton
Easton Maudit
Bozeat
Sharnbrook
Bolnhurst
Thurleigh
Eleanor Cross
Hardingstone
Yardley Hastings
Harrold
Odell
Felmersham
Radwell
Bletsoe
Wootton
Collingtree
Milton Malsor
Quinton
Hackleton
Horton
Piddington
Chellington
Carlton
Pavenham
Milton Ernest
Oakley
Ravensden
Warrington
Lavendon
Cold Brayfield
West End
Stevington
Courteenhall
Roade
Hartwell
Ravenstone
Olney
Turvey
Postmill
Bromham
Clapham
BEDFORD
Watermill
Stoke Bruerne
Ashton
Weston Underwood
Clifton Reynes
Emberton
Newton Blossomville
Biddenham
Long Street
Stoke Goldington
Filgrave
Stagsden
Kempston
Moot Hall
Elstow
Grafton Regis
Tyringham
Sherington
Astwood
Hanslope
Gayhurst
Chicheley
Chicheley Hall
Bourne End
Wootton
Upper Shelton
Yardley Gobion
Grand Union Canal
Newport Pagnell
Little Linford
Castlethorpe
Haversham
Potterspury
Lathbury
North Crawley
Lower Shelton
Stewartby
Wilstead
Haynes (Northwood)
Puxley
Old Stratford
Cosgrove
New Bradwell
Great Linford
Willen
Wharley End
Cranfield
Marston Moretaine
Houghton Conquest
Haynes (West End)
Deanshanger
Stony Stratford
Wolverton
Bradwell
Xscape
Broughton
Moulsoe
Salford
Millbrook
Houghton House
Passenham
Calverton
MILTON KEYNES
Gulliver's Land
Woolstone
Woughton on the Green
Lidlington
Maulden
Akeley
Leckhampstead
Beachampton
Shenley Church End
Loughton
Walton
Lower End
Wavendon
Aspley Guise
Ridgmont
Ampthill
Flitton de Grey Mausoleum
Steppingley
Flitton
Thornton
Simpson
Woburn Sands
Husborne Crawley
Shenley Brook End
Nash
Whaddon
Far Bletchley
Bow Brickhill
Aspley Heath
Flitwick
Greenfield
Thornborough
Bletchley
Woburn
Eversholt
Pulloxhill
Westoning
Woburn Abbey
Newton Longville
Little Brickhill
Tingrith
Great Horwood
Little Horwood
Great Brickhill
Potsgrove
Milton Bryan
Harlington
Sharpenhoe
Adstock
Drayton Parslow
Stoke Hammond
Heath and Reach
Toddington
Fancott
Upper Sundon
Sundon Hills
Mursley
Winslow
Hollingdon
Soulbury
Hockliffe
Tebworth
Chalton
Wingfield
Lower Sundon
Swanbourne
Stewkley
Clipstone
Eggington
Linslade
Leighton Buzzard
Tilsworth
Houghton Regis
Leagrave
Stanbridge
Burcott
0 1 2 3 4 miles
0 1 2 3 4 5 kilometres

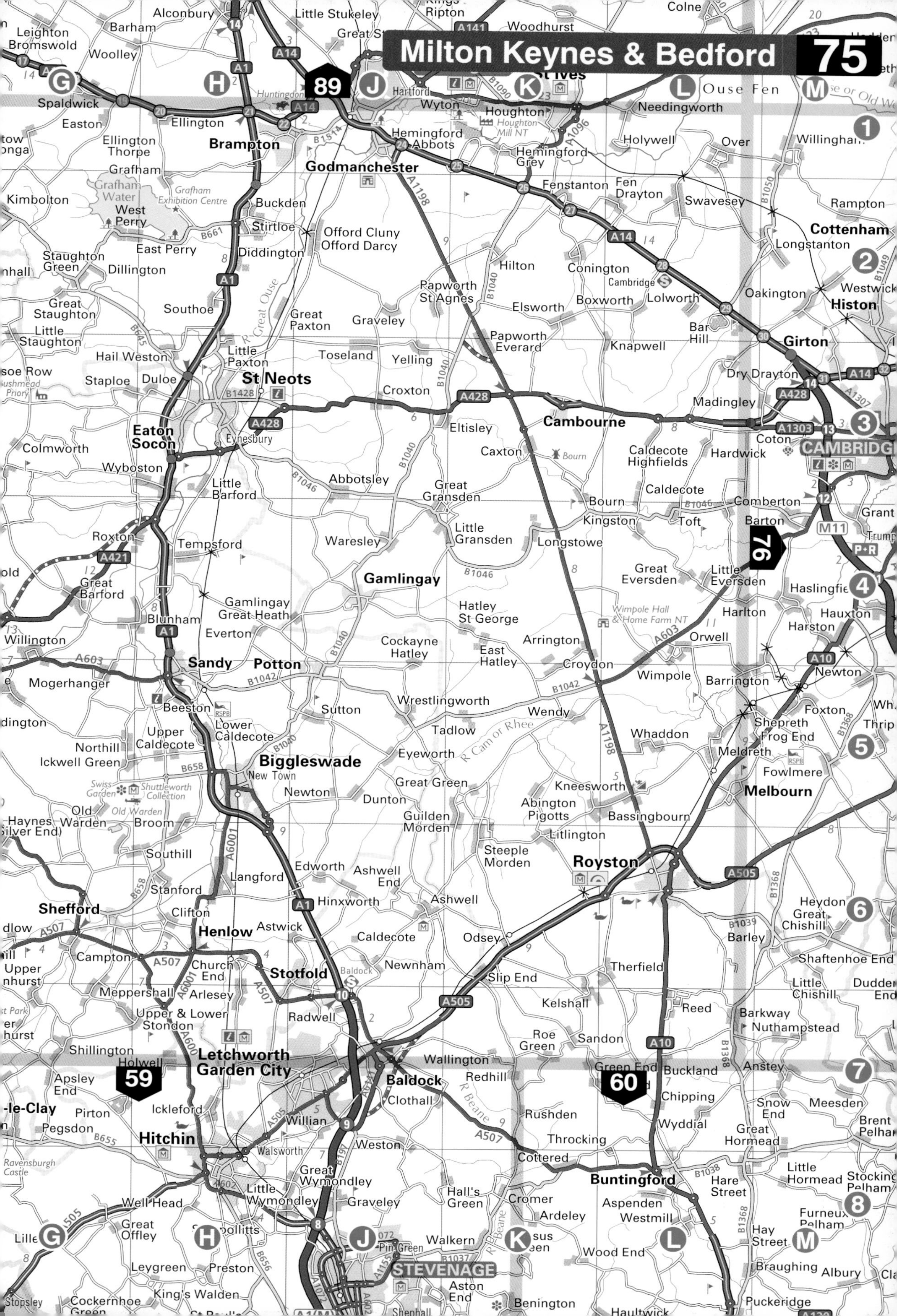
Milton Keynes & Bedford
75
89
76
59
60
Alconbury
Little Stukeley
Great Stukeley
Kings Ripton
Colne
Woodhurst
Leighton Bromswold
Barham
Woolley
Spaldwick
Easton
Ellington
Ellington Thorpe
Brampton
Huntingdon
Hartford
Wyton
St Ives
Houghton
Houghton Mill NT
Ouse Fen
Needingworth
Holywell
Over
Willingham
Hemingford Abbots
Hemingford Grey
Godmanchester
Grafham
Grafham Water
Grafham Exhibition Centre
Kimbolton
West Perry
Buckden
Stirtloe
Offord Cluny
Offord Darcy
Fenstanton
Fen Drayton
Swavesey
Rampton
Cottenham
Longstanton
East Perry
Diddington
Staughton Green
Dillington
Hilton
Conington
Cambridge Services
Lolworth
Boxworth
Oakington
Westwick
Histon
Papworth St Agnes
Elsworth
Great Staughton
Little Staughton
Southoe
Great Paxton
Graveley
Papworth Everard
Knapwell
Bar Hill
Girton
Hail Weston
Little Paxton
Toseland
Yelling
Dry Drayton
Staploe
Duloe
St Neots
Croxton
Madingley
Eaton Socon
Eynesbury
Eltisley
Cambourne
Coton
CAMBRIDGE
Colmworth
Caxton
Bourn
Caldecote Highfields
Hardwick
Wyboston
Little Barford
Abbotsley
Great Gransden
Caldecote
Comberton
Barton
Grantchester
Roxton
Tempsford
Waresley
Little Gransden
Kingston
Toft
Longstowe
Great Barford
Gamlingay
Great Eversden
Little Eversden
Haslingfield
Gamlingay Great Heath
Hatley St George
Wimpole Hall & Home Farm NT
Harlton
Hauxton
Harston
Blunham
Everton
Cockayne Hatley
East Hatley
Arrington
Orwell
Willington
Sandy
Potton
Croydon
Wimpole
Barrington
Newton
Mogerhanger
Beeston
Sutton
Wrestlingworth
Wendy
Foxton
Shepreth
Frog End
Upper Caldecote
Lower Caldecote
Tadlow
Whaddon
Meldreth
Northill
Ickwell Green
Biggleswade
New Town
Eyeworth
R Cam or Rhee
Fowlmere
Swiss Garden
Shuttleworth Collection
Newton
Great Green
Dunton
Kneesworth
Abington Pigotts
Bassingbourn
Melbourn
Old Warden
Haynes
Broom
Guilden Morden
Litlington
Southill
Steeple Morden
Royston
Langford
Edworth
Ashwell End
Stanford
Hinxworth
Ashwell
Heydon
Great Chishill
Shefford
Clifton
Henlow
Astwick
Caldecote
Odsey
Barley
Campton
Church End
Stotfold
Newnham
Therfield
Shaftenhoe End
Upper Gravenhurst
Meppershall
Arlesey
Baldock Services
Slip End
Little Chishill
Duddenhoe End
Upper & Lower Stondon
Radwell
Kelshall
Reed
Barkway
Nuthampstead
Shillington
Holwell
Letchworth Garden City
Wallington
Roe Green
Sandon
Green End
Buckland
Anstey
Apsley End
Baldock
Redhill
Chipping
Pirton
Ickleford
Clothall
Rushden
Snow End
Meesden
Pegsdon
Hitchin
Willian
Wyddial
Brent Pelham
Great Hormead
Walsworth
Weston
Throcking
Cottered
Little Hormead
Stocking Pelham
Ravensburgh Castle
Great Wymondley
Buntingford
Hare Street
Little Wymondley
Graveley
Hall's Green
Cromer
Aspenden
Westmill
Furneux Pelham
Well Head
Great Offley
Ardeley
Hay Street
Walkern
Wood End
Leygreen
Preston
Pin Green
STEVENAGE
Braughing
Albury
King's Walden
Aston End
Benington
Puckeridge
Stopsley
Cockernhoe
Shephall
Haultwick
A1
A14
A141
A428
A1198
A603
A421
A1303
M11
A10
A505
A507
A6001
A600
A602
A1096
A1307
B661
B1040
B1046
B1042
B658
B656
B655
B1039
B1038
B1368
B1050
B1049
B1090
B1514
B1428
B645
B1037
B197
R Great Ouse
R Beane
P+R
Ouse or Old West

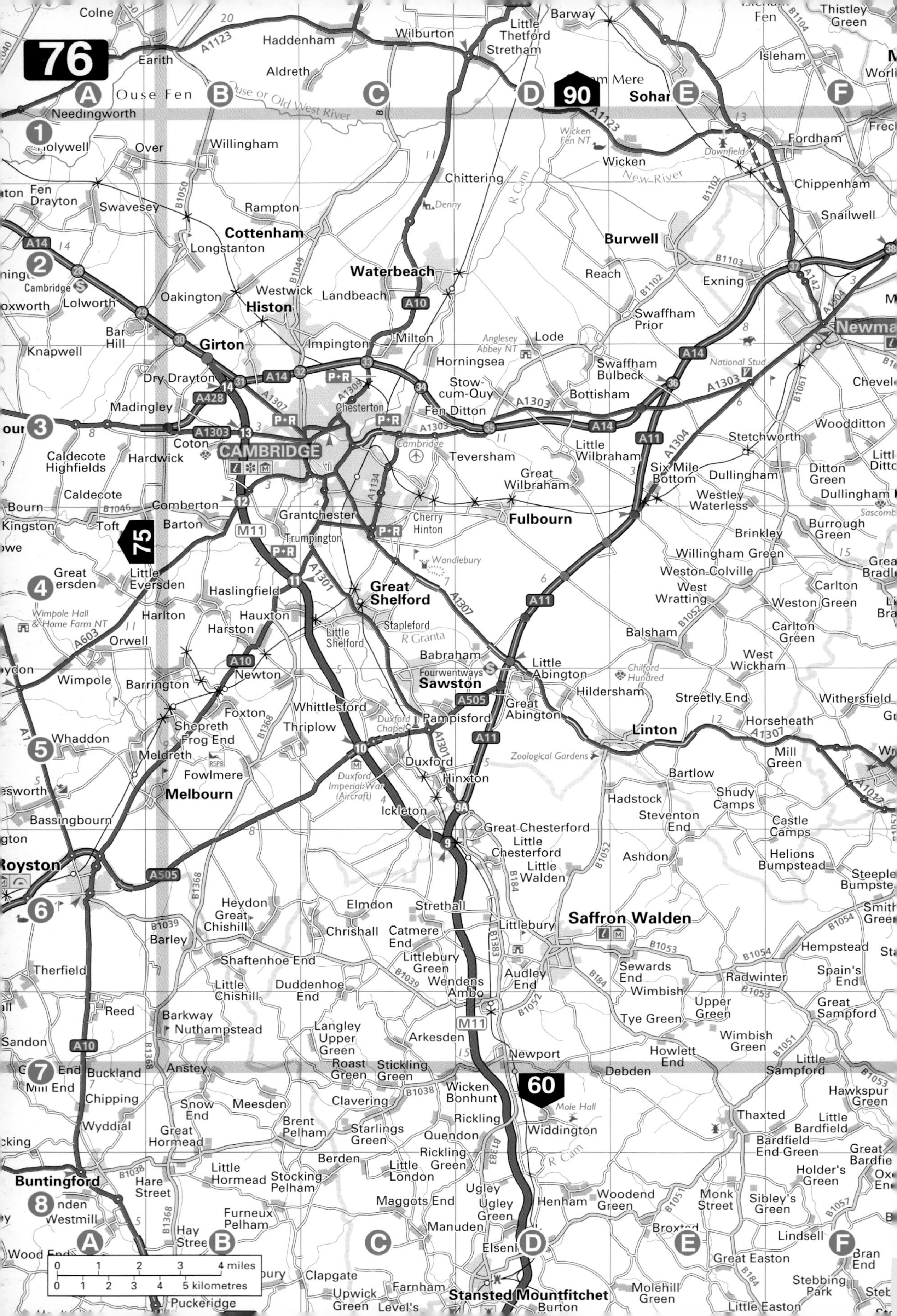
76
Colne
Earith
A1123
Haddenham
Aldreth
Wilburton
Little Thetford
Stretham
Barway
Isleham
Thistley Green
Worli
A
Ouse Fen
B
Ouse or Old West River
C
D
90
Soham
E
F
Needingworth
1
Holywell
Over
Willingham
Wicken Fen NT
Wicken
Downfield
Fordham
Fen Drayton
Swavesey
B1050
Rampton
Chittering
Denny
R Cam
New River
Chippenham
Snailwell
A14
Longstanton
Cottenham
Burwell
2
Cambridge
Lolworth
Oakington
Westwick
Histon
Landbeach
Waterbeach
A10
B1049
Reach
B1102
B1103
Exning
A142
Swaffham Prior
Newmarket
Knapwell
Bar Hill
Girton
Impington
Milton
Anglesey Abbey NT
Lode
Swaffham Bulbeck
National Stud
Dry Drayton
A14
P+R
A1309
Horningsea
Stow-cum-Quy
Bottisham
A1303
A1304
Cheveley
Madingley
A428
A1307
Chesterton
Fen Ditton
3
A1303
Coton
CAMBRIDGE
Teversham
Little Wilbraham
A11
Woodditton
Stetchworth
Caldecote Highfields
Hardwick
Great Wilbraham
Six Mile Bottom
Dullingham
Ditton Green
Dullingham
Caldecote
Bourn
B1046
Comberton
Grantchester
A1134
Cherry Hinton
Fulbourn
Westley Waterless
Kingston
Toft
Barton
M11
75
Trumpington
Brinkley
Burrough Green
Great Eversden
Little Eversden
Wandlebury
Willingham Green
Weston Colville
4
Haslingfield
Great Shelford
A1301
West Wratting
Carlton
Wimpole Hall & Home Farm NT
Harlton
Hauxton
Stapleford
Weston Green
B1052
Orwell
Harston
Little Shelford
R Granta
Balsham
Carlton Green
A603
Babraham
Little Abington
Wimpole
Barrington
Newton
Fourwentways
Sawston
Chilford Hundred
Hildersham
West Wickham
Foxton
Whittlesford
A505
Great Abington
Streetly End
Withersfield
Shepreth
Thriplow
Duxford Chapel
Pampisford
Linton
Horseheath
A1307
Whaddon
5
Frog End
B1368
Meldreth
RSPB
Fowlmere
Duxford
Duxford Imperial War (Aircraft)
Hinxton
Zoological Gardens
Mill Green
Bartlow
Melbourn
Hadstock
Shudy Camps
Bassingbourn
Ickleton
9A
Steventon End
Castle Camps
Great Chesterford
Little Chesterford
Ashdon
Helions Bumpstead
Royston
A505
B1368
Little Walden
B1184
Steeple Bumpstead
6
Heydon
Great Chishill
Elmdon
Strethall
Saffron Walden
Chrishall
Catmere End
Littlebury
B1039
Barley
B1383
B1053
B1054
Hempstead
Therfield
Shaftenhoe End
Littlebury Green
Sewards End
Radwinter
Spain's End
Little Chishill
Duddenhoe End
Wendens Ambo
Audley End
Wimbish
B184
Reed
B1052
Upper Green
Great Sampford
Barkway
Nuthampstead
Langley
Upper Green
Arkesden
M11
Tye Green
Sandon
A10
B1368
Wimbish Green
B1051
Roast Green
Stickling Green
Newport
Howlett End
7
Anstey
Buckland
Debden
Little Sampford
Mill End
60
Wicken Bonhunt
Chipping
Snow End
Meesden
Clavering
B1038
Mole Hall
Hawkspur Green
Brent Pelham
Rickling
Thaxted
Little Bardfield
Wyddial
Great Hormead
Starlings Green
Quendon
Widdington
Bardfield End Green
Rickling Green
R Cam
Berden
Great Bardfield
Little Hormead
Stocking Pelham
Little London
Holder's Green
Buntingford
B1038
Hare Street
Ugley
Henham
Woodend Green
Monk Street
Sibley's Green
8
Westmill
Furneux Pelham
Maggots End
Ugley Green
B1057
B1368
Hay Street
Manuden
Broxted
Lindsell
A
B
C
Elsenham
D
E
F
Bran End
Wood End
Great Easton
0 1 2 3 4 miles
0 1 2 3 4 5 kilometres
Clapgate
Stebbing Park
Upwick Green
Farnham
Stansted Mountfitchet
Molehill Green
Puckeridge
Level's
Burton
Little Easton

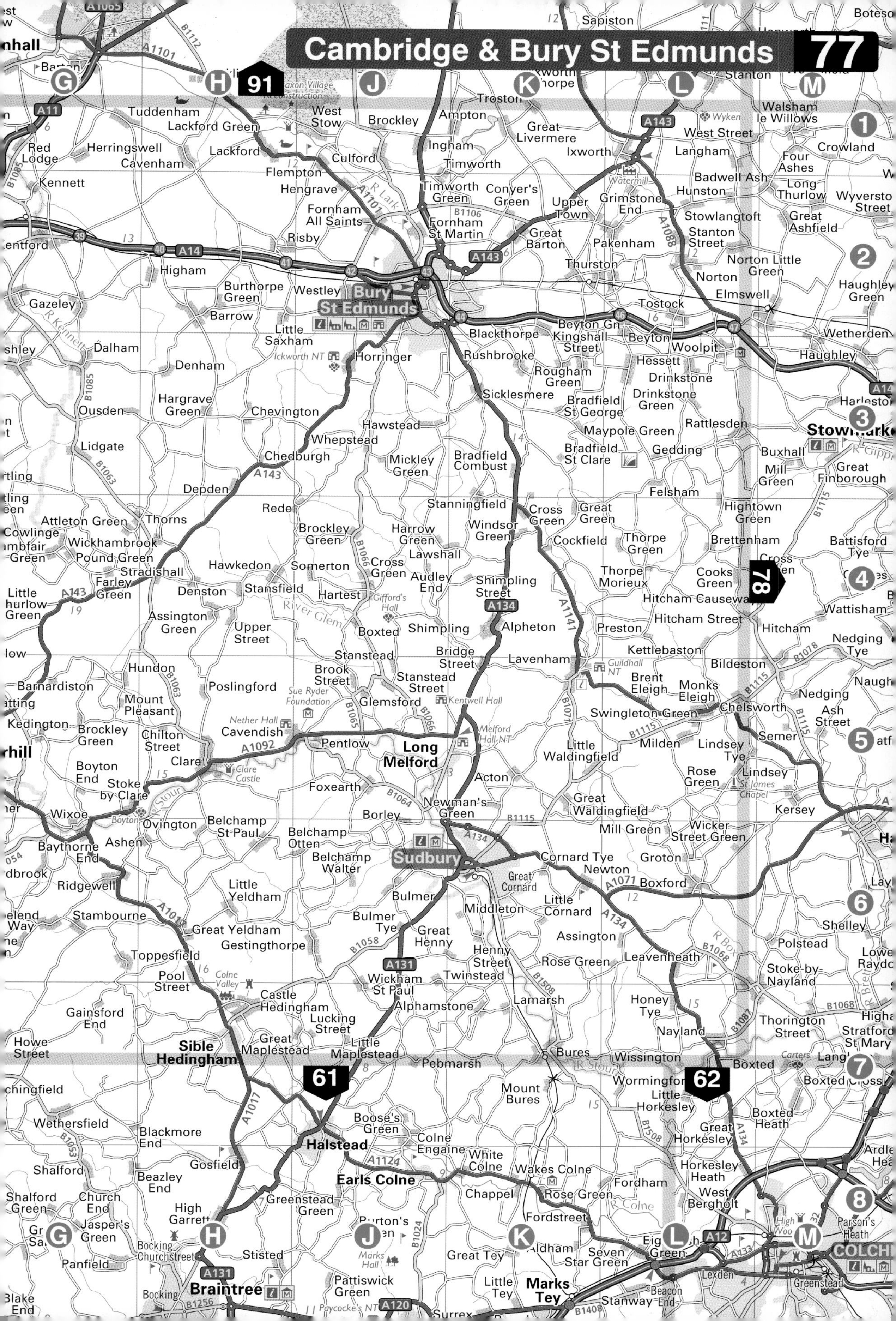

91
78
61
62
Sapiston
Stanton
Troston
Walsham le Willows
Wyken
Brockley
Ampton
Great Livermere
West Street
Crowland
Tuddenham
Lackford Green
West Stow
Ingham
Ixworth
Langham
Four Ashes
Red Lodge
Herringswell
Cavenham
Lackford
Culford
Timworth
Watermill
Badwell Ash
Long Thurlow
Wyverstone Street
Kennett
Flempton
Hengrave
Timworth Green
Conyer's Green
Upper Town
Grimstone End
Hunston
Fornham All Saints
Fornham St Martin
Stowlangtoft
Great Ashfield
Risby
Great Barton
Pakenham
Stanton Street
Higham
Thurston
Norton Little Green
Norton
Haughley Green
Burthorpe Green
Westley
Bury St Edmunds
Elmswell
Gazeley
Barrow
Tostock
Little Saxham
Beyton Gn
Kingshall Street
Beyton
Woolpit
Wetherden
Dalham
Ickworth NT
Horringer
Blackthorpe
Rushbrooke
Hessett
Haughley
Denham
Rougham Green
Drinkstone
Ousden
Hargrave Green
Chevington
Sicklesmere
Bradfield St George
Drinkstone Green
Hawstead
Maypole Green
Rattlesden
Stowmarket
Lidgate
Whepstead
Bradfield St Clare
Gedding
Buxhall
Chedburgh
Mickley Green
Bradfield Combust
Mill Green
Great Finborough
Depden
Felsham
Rede
Stanningfield
Hightown Green
Attleton Green
Thorns
Cross Green
Great Green
Cowlinge
Wickhambrook
Brockley Green
Harrow Green
Windsor Green
Cockfield
Thorpe Green
Brettenham
Battisford Tye
Pound Green
Lawshall
Stradishall
Hawkedon
Somerton
Cross Green
Thorpe Morieux
Cooks Green
Farley Green
Audley End
Little Thurlow Green
Denston
Stansfield
Hartest
Shimpling Street
Hitcham Causeway
Gifford's Hall
River Glem
Hitcham Street
Wattisham
Assington Green
Upper Street
Boxted
Shimpling
Alpheton
Preston
Hitcham
Nedging Tye
Stanstead
Bridge Street
Lavenham
Kettlebaston
Hundon
Brook Street
Guildhall NT
Bildeston
Barnardiston
Stanstead Street
Brent Eleigh
Monks Eleigh
Poslingford
Sue Ryder Foundation
Kentwell Hall
Mount Pleasant
Glemsford
Nedging
Naughton
Swingleton Green
Chelsworth
Ash Street
Nether Hall
Kedington
Brockley Green
Cavendish
Melford Hall NT
Chilton Street
Pentlow
Long Melford
Semer
Milden
Lindsey Tye
Little Waldingfield
Boyton End
Clare
Clare Castle
Stoke by Clare
Foxearth
Acton
Rose Green
Lindsey
St James Chapel
Wixoe
Boyton
Ovington
Belchamp St Paul
Borley
Newman's Green
Great Waldingfield
Kersey
Baythorne End
Ashen
Belchamp Otten
Mill Green
Wicker Street Green
Belchamp Walter
Sudbury
Cornard Tye
Groton
Ridgewell
Little Yeldham
Great Cornard
Newton
Boxford
Bulmer
Little Cornard
Stambourne
Middleton
Great Yeldham
Bulmer Tye
Great Henny
Assington
Shelley
Gestingthorpe
Toppesfield
Henny Street
Rose Green
Leavenheath
Polstead
Twinstead
Stoke-by-Nayland
Pool Street
Colne Valley
Wickham St Paul
Castle Hedingham
Lamarsh
Honey Tye
Alphamstone
Gainsford End
Lucking Street
Nayland
Thorington Street
Stratford St Mary
Howe Street
Great Maplestead
Little Maplestead
Sible Hedingham
Pebmarsh
Bures
Wissington
Carters
Boxted
Boxted Cross
Mount Bures
Wormingford
Little Horkesley
Wethersfield
Blackmore End
Boose's Green
Boxted Heath
Halstead
Colne Engaine
Great Horkesley
Shalford
Gosfield
White Colne
Wakes Colne
Horkesley Heath
Beazley End
Earls Colne
Fordham
Shalford Green
Church End
Chappel
Rose Green
West Bergholt
High Garrett
Greenstead Green
Parson's Heath
Jasper's Green
Burton's Green
Fordstreet
Bocking Churchstreet
Marks Hall
Aldham
Seven Star Green
Eight Ash Green
Colchester
Panfield
Stisted
Great Tey
Lexden
Greenstead
Pattiswick Green
Little Tey
Marks Tey
Braintree
Bocking
Blake End
Paycocke's NT
Stanway
Beacon End
Surrex
A1065
A1101
B1112
A11
A14
A143
A1088
A134
A1141
B1106
B1085
B1063
B1066
B1065
B1071
B1115
B1078
A1092
B1064
A131
A1017
B1058
B1508
A1071
B1068
B1087
A12
A133
A1124
B1024
B1256
B1408
A120
B1053

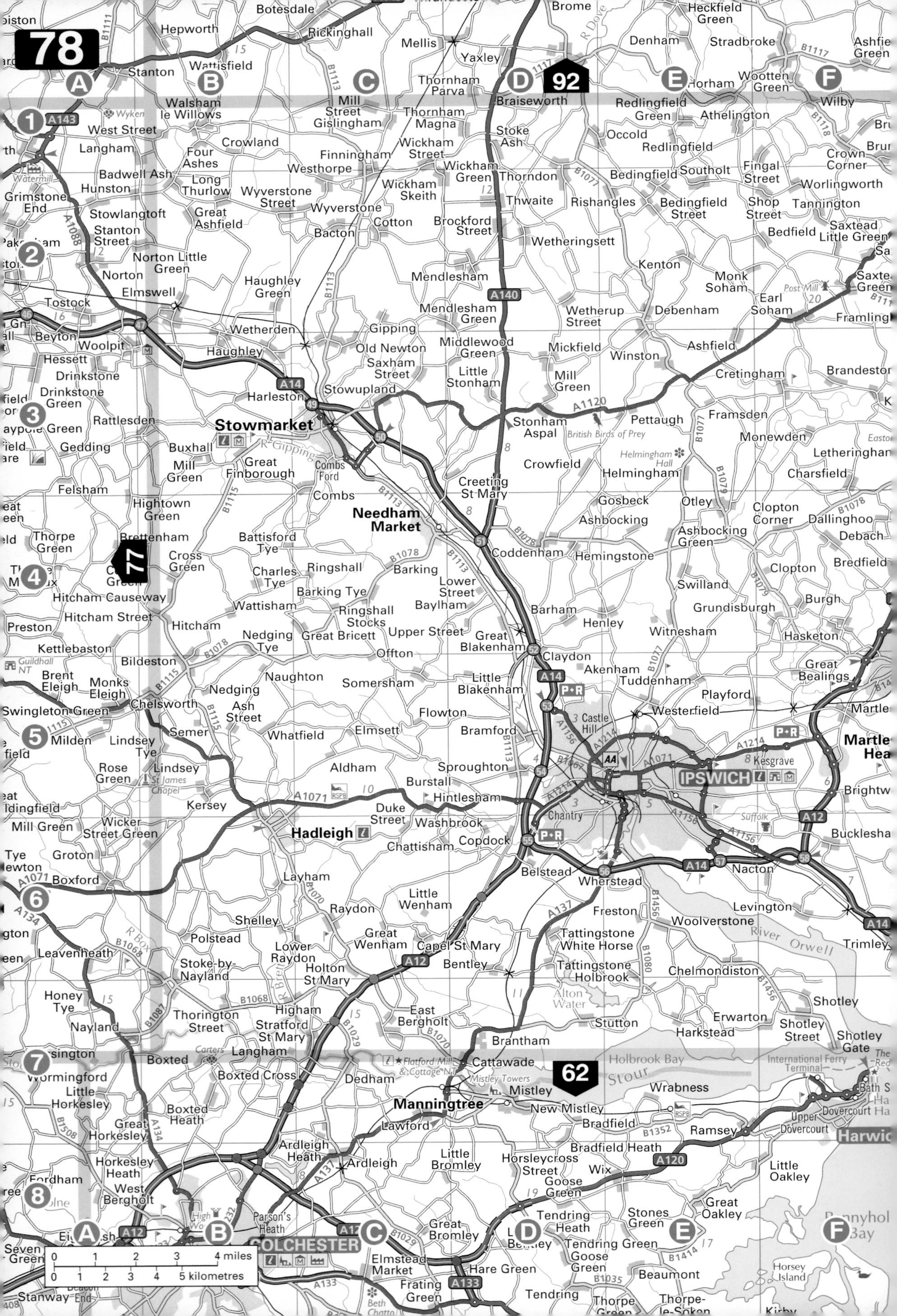
Botesdale
Brome
Heckfield Green
Hepworth
Rickinghall
Mellis
Yaxley
Denham
Stradbroke
Ashfield Green
Stanton
Wattisfield
Thornham Parva
92
Horham
Wootten Green
Wilby
A
B
C
D
E
F
Walsham le Willows
Mill Street
Gislingham
Thornham Magna
Braiseworth
Redlingfield Green
Athelington
1
A143
Wyken
West Street
Stoke Ash
Occold
Redlingfield
Crown Corner
Langham
Crowland
Finningham
Wickham Street
Four Ashes
Westhorpe
Wickham Green
Thorndon
Bedingfield
Southolt
Fingal Street
Worlingworth
Badwell Ash
Long Thurlow
Watermill
Hunston
Wyverstone Street
Wickham Skeith
Thwaite
Rishangles
Bedingfield Street
Shop Street
Tannington
Grimstone End
Wyverstone
Stowlangtoft
Great Ashfield
Cotton
Brockford Street
Bedfield
Saxtead Little Green
Stanton Street
Bacton
Wetheringsett
2
A1088
Norton Little Green
Kenton
Norton
Monk Soham
Haughley Green
Mendlesham
Earl Soham
Post Mill
Saxtead Green
Elmswell
A140
Tostock
Wetherup Street
Debenham
Mendlesham Green
46
47
Gipping
Framlingham
Wetherden
Beyton
Woolpit
Old Newton
Middlewood Green
Mickfield
Ashfield
Hessett
Haughley
Saxham Street
Winston
Drinkstone
Little Stonham
Mill Green
Cretingham
Brandeston
Drinkstone Green
A14
Stowupland
Harleston
49
A1120
3
Rattlesden
Stowmarket
Stonham Aspal
Pettaugh
Framsden
Green
British Birds of Prey
Monewden
Gedding
Buxhall
R Gipping
50
Helmingham Hall
Letheringham
Mill Green
Great Finborough
Combs Ford
Crowfield
Helmingham
Charsfield
Felsham
Combs
Creeting St Mary
Hightown Green
Needham Market
Gosbeck
Otley
Clopton Corner
Ashbocking
Dallinghoo
Thorpe Green
Brettenham
Battisford Tye
Ashbocking Green
Debach
77
Cross Green
51
Coddenham
Hemingstone
Bredfield
4
B1078
Charles Tye
Ringshall
Barking
Clopton
Hitcham Causeway
Lower Street
Swilland
Barking Tye
Burgh
Wattisham
Ringshall Stocks
Baylham
Grundisburgh
Hitcham Street
Barham
Preston
Hitcham
Henley
Nedging Tye
Great Bricett
Upper Street
Great Blakenham
Witnesham
Hasketon
Kettlebaston
Offton
Guildhall NT
Bildeston
52
Claydon
Akenham
Great Bealings
Brent Eleigh
Monks Eleigh
Naughton
Little Blakenham
Tuddenham
Nedging
Somersham
P+R
Playford
Swingleton Green
Chelsworth
Ash Street
Flowton
Westerfield
Martlesham
B1115
53
Castle Hill
5
Milden
Lindsey Tye
Semer
Whatfield
Elmsett
Bramford
A1214
Martlesham Heath
Rose Green
Lindsey
Aldham
Sproughton
AA
A1071
Kesgrave
St James Chapel
54
IPSWICH
Burstall
Brightwell
Kersey
10
RSPB
Hintlesham
Chantry
Mill Green
Wicker Street Green
Duke Street
Washbrook
A1156
Suffolk
A12
Bucklesham
Hadleigh
Copdock
Tye
Groton
Chattisham
55
Newton
A14
Nacton
57
58
A1071
Boxford
Layham
Belstead
Wherstead
56
6
A134
Little Wenham
Levington
Raydon
B1070
Freston
Woolverstone
Shelley
A137
Polstead
Great Wenham
Tattingstone White Horse
River Orwell
Trimley
Leavenheath
B1068
R Box
Lower Raydon
Capel St Mary
Bentley
Tattingstone
Stoke-by-Nayland
Holton St Mary
Holbrook
Chelmondiston
Honey Tye
Alton Water
Shotley
Nayland
Thorington Street
Higham
East Bergholt
Stutton
Erwarton
Shotley Street
B1087
Stratford St Mary
Harkstead
Shotley Gate
B1029
Brantham
7
Boxted
Carters
Langham
Flatford Mill & Cottage NT
Cattawade
62
Holbrook Bay
International Ferry Terminal
Wormingford
Boxted Cross
Mistley Towers
Stour
Little Horkesley
Dedham
Mistley
Wrabness
Bath Side
Manningtree
New Mistley
Dovercourt
Boxted Heath
Great Horkesley
Lawford
Bradfield
Upper Dovercourt
B1508
Ramsey
B1352
Harwich
Ardleigh Heath
Little Bromley
Bradfield Heath
A120
Horkesley Heath
Ardleigh
Horsleycross Street
Wix
Little Oakley
Fordham
Goose Green
8
West Bergholt
Parson's Heath
Great Oakley
Tendring Heath
Stones Green
Great Bromley
Colne
COLCHESTER
B1029
Tendring Green
Goose Green
17
Seven Green
0 1 2 3 4 miles
0 1 2 3 4 5 kilometres
Elmstead Market
Hare Green
B1414
Horsey Island
Frating Green
A133
Beaumont
B1035
Stanway
Tendring
Thorpe Green
Thorpe-le-Soken
Kirby

Southwold
Wenhaston
Blythburgh
Cratfield
Cookley
Blackheath
Huntingfield
Walpole
Walberswick
Thorington
Bramfield
93
Heveningham
Ubbeston Green
Darsham
Dunwich
Sibton
Peasenhall
Yoxford
Westleton
Badingham
Middleton
Minsmere
Middleton Moor
Bruisyard
Bruisyard Street
Theberton
Eastbridge
Cransford
Rendham
Kelsale
Leiston
Shawsgate
Carlton
Sizewell Visitor Centre
Swefling
Saxmundham
North Green
Great Glemham
Benhall Street
Benhall Green
Knodishall
Sternfield
Leiston
Coldfair Green
Aldringham
Thorpe Ness
Parham
Stratford St Andrew
Friday Street
Friston
Thorpeness
Farnham
Hacheston
Snape
Easton
Little Glemham
Snape Street
Marlesford
The Maltings
Aldeburgh
Blaxhall
Iken
Campsea Ash
High Street
Tunstall
Aldeburgh Bay
Ufford
Chillesford
Sudbourne
River Alde
Eyke
Bromeswell
Butley
Orford
Sutton Hoo NT
Orford Ness
Capel St Andrew
Suffolk Heritage Coast
Sutton
Boyton
Orfordness-Havergate
Waldringfield
Shottisham
River Ore
Hollesley
North Weir Point
Hollesley Bay
Hemley
River Deben
Alderton
Bawdsey
Falkenham
Old Felixstowe
Walton
Felixstowe
Landguard Fort
Landguard Point
Hoek van Holland
Hoek van Holland Cuxhaven Esbjerg
A12
A144
A1120
A1094
A1152
B1117
B1123
B1387
B1125
B1122
B1120
B1119
B1121
B1353
B1069
B1078
B1084
B1083
B1116
B1438
G
H
J
K
L
M
1
2
3
4
5
6
7
8

95
A
B
C
D
E
F
1
2
3
4
5
6
7
8
Llanelltyd
Toll
Penmaenpo
Afon Mawddach
A496
A493
Barmouth
Barmouth Bridge
Barmouth Bay
Fairbourne & Barmouth Steam Railway
Fairbourne
CADER
892
621
SNOWDONIA
NATIONAL PARK
Tal-y-llyn
Llwyngwril
Castell y Bere
Afon Dysynni
Llangelynin
Abergynolwyn
667
Rhoslefain
A493
Llanegryn
Tal-y-Llyn Railway
633
TAREN HENDRE
Bryncrug
B4405
Dolgoch Falls
Aber Dysynni
Tywyn
Pennal
Dovey
CARDIGAN
BAY
Aberdyfi
A493
Afon Dyfi (River Dovey)
Gland
RSPB
A487
PEN
B4353
Tre Taliesin
Borth
Tal-y-bont
B4353
Ceredigion Heritage Coast
Llandre
Rhyd-y pennau
Bow Street
Salem
Clarach Bay
Garth Penrhyncoch
Pen-bont Rhydybeddau
A4159
B4572
Capel-Dewi
Waunfawr
Aberystwyth
P+R
Llanbadarn Fawr
Capel Bangor
Goginan
Rheidol Power Station
Aberystwyth and District
Capel Seion
A4120
Llanfarian
Llanfihangel-y-Creuddyn
A485
Blaenplwyf
Afon Ystwyth
Cnwch Coch
Llanilar
B4340
B4575
Ceredigion Heritage Coast
Llanddeiniol
B4576
Llanafan
66
Llangwyryfon
Lledrod
Tynygra
Llanrhystud
A487
A485
Bach
0 1 2 3 4 miles
0 1 2 3 4 5 kilometres

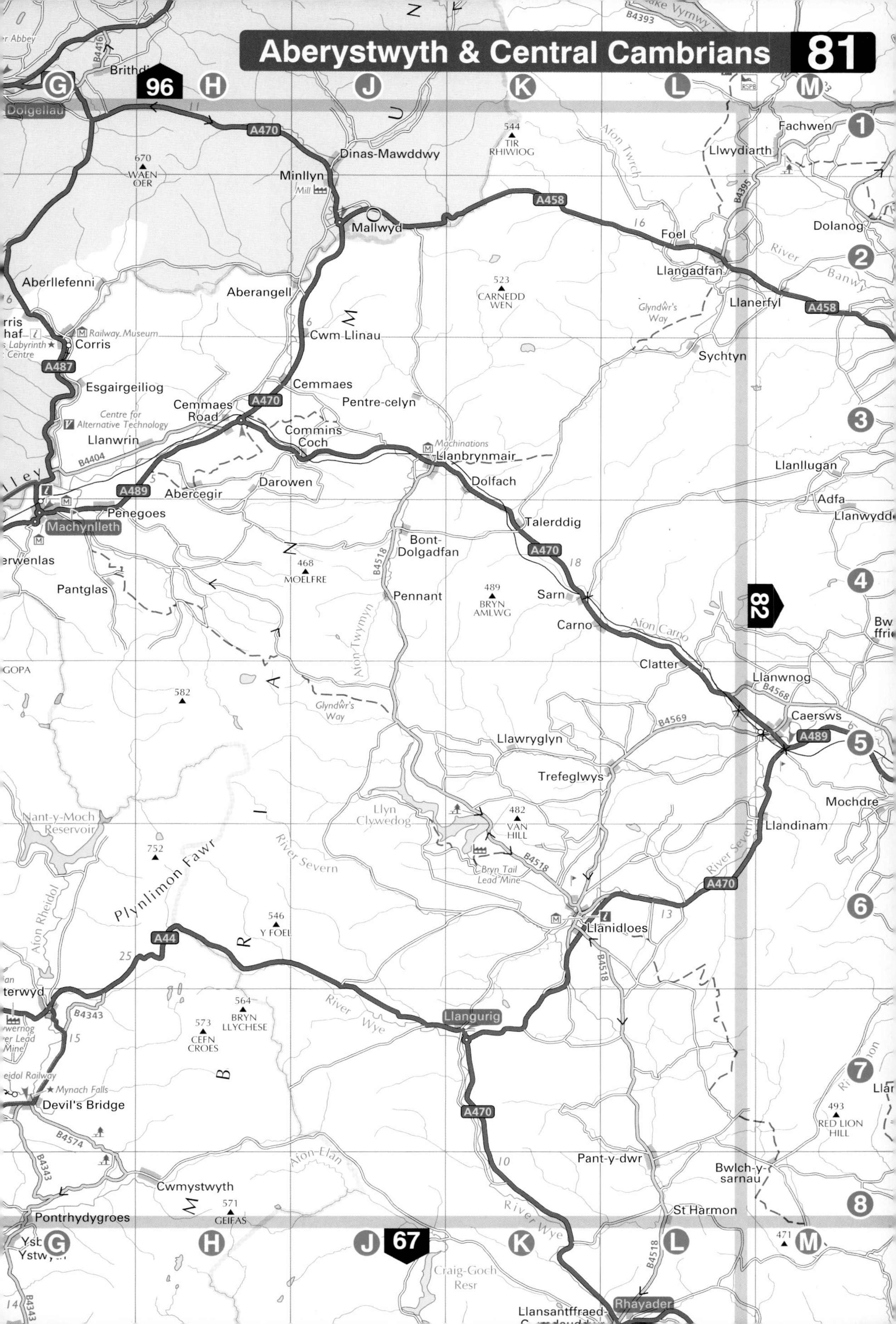
96
82
67
Dolgellau
Brithdir
Dinas-Mawddwy
Minllyn
Mallwyd
Aberllefenni
Aberangell
Cwm-Llinau
Corris
Railway Museum
Esgairgeiliog
Centre for Alternative Technology
Llanwrin
Cemmaes
Cemmaes Road
Pentre-celyn
Commins Coch
Llanbrynmair
Machinations
Dolfach
Darowen
Abercegir
Penegoes
Machynlleth
Talerddig
Bont-Dolgadfan
Pennant
Sarn
Carno
Afon Carno
Clatter
Llanwnog
Caersws
Fachwen
Llwydiarth
Dolanog
Foel
Llangadfan
Llanerfyl
Sychtyn
Glyndŵr's Way
River Banwy
Llanllugan
Adfa
Llanwyddelan
Pantglas
MOELFRE
BRYN AMLWG
TIR RHIWIOG
CARNEDD WEN
WAEN OER
Llawryglyn
Trefeglwys
Llyn Clywedog
VAN HILL
Bryn Tail Lead Mine
Llanidloes
Llandinam
Mochdre
River Severn
Nant-y-Moch Reservoir
Plynlimon Fawr
Afon Rheidol
Y FOEL
BRYN LLYCHESE
CEFN CROES
Llangurig
River Wye
Devil's Bridge
Mynach Falls
Cwmystwyth
Afon Elan
GEIFAS
Pontrhydygroes
Pant-y-dwr
Bwlch-y-sarnau
St Harmon
RED LION HILL
Craig-Goch Resr
Rhayader
Llansantffraed-Cwmdeuddwr
A470
A458
A489
A487
A44
B4518
B4404
B4343
B4574
B4569
B4568
B4395
B4393
B4416
1
2
3
4
5
6
7
8
G
H
J
K
L
M

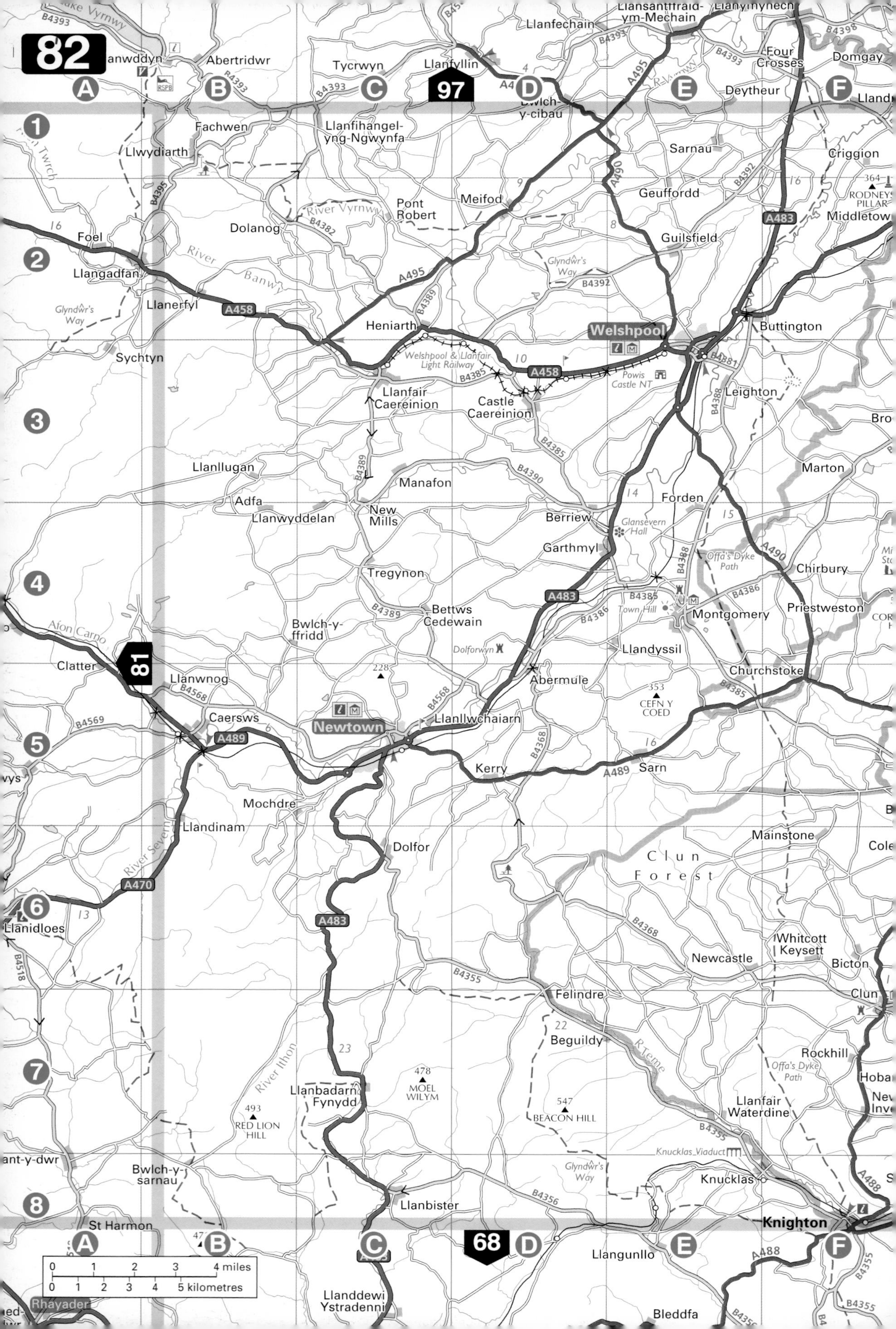

82
97
81
68
Llanfechain
Llansantffraid-ym-Mechain
Llanymynech
Four Crosses
Domgay
Abertridwr
Tycrwyn
Llanfyllin
Deytheur
Bwlch-y-cibau
Fachwen
Llanfihangel-yng-Ngwynfa
Llwydiarth
Sarnau
Criggion
Geufordd
RODNEYS PILLAR
Meifod
Pont Robert
Dolanog
River Vyrnwy
Middletown
Guilsfield
Foel
Llangadfan
River Banwy
Glyndŵr's Way
Llanerfyl
Heniarth
Welshpool
Buttington
Sychtyn
Welshpool & Llanfair Light Railway
Powis Castle NT
Leighton
Llanfair Caereinion
Castle Caereinion
Llanllugan
Marton
Manafon
Adfa
Llanwyddelan
New Mills
Berriew
Forden
Glansevern Hall
Garthmyl
Offa's Dyke Path
Tregynon
Chirbury
Bettws Cedewain
Town Hill
Montgomery
Priestweston
Bwlch-y-ffridd
Afon Carno
Dolforwyn
Llandyssil
Clatter
Churchstoke
Llanwnog
Abermule
CEFN Y COED
Caersws
Newtown
Llanllwchaiarn
Kerry
Sarn
Mochdre
Llandinam
River Severn
Dolfor
Mainstone
Clun Forest
Llanidloes
Whitcott Keysett
Newcastle
Bicton
Clun
Felindre
Beguildy
R.Teme
Rockhill
MOEL WILYM
Llanbadarn Fynydd
River Ithon
RED LION HILL
BEACON HILL
Llanfair Waterdine
Knucklas Viaduct
Bwlch-y-sarnau
Knucklas
Llanbister
Knighton
St Harmon
Llangunllo
Llanddewi Ystradenni
Rhayader
Bleddfa
0 1 2 3 4 miles
0 1 2 3 4 5 kilometres

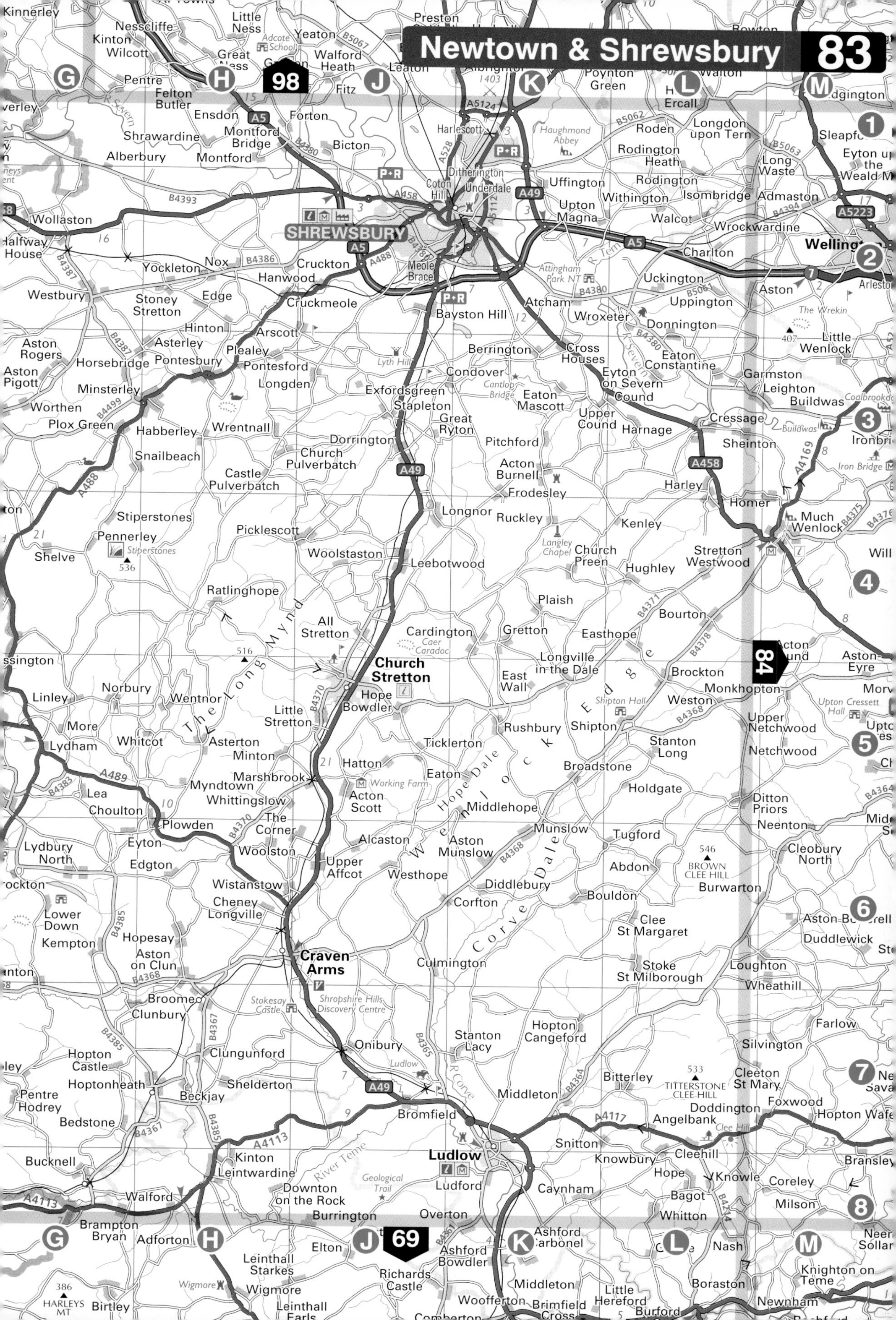
Kinnerley
Nesscliffe
Little Ness
Kinton
Wilcott
Adcote School
Yeaton
Preston
Great Ness
Walford Heath
Leaton
Pentre
Felton Butler
98
Fitz
Poynton Green
Ercall
Walton
Ensdon
Forton
Harlescott
Haughmond Abbey
Roden
Longdon upon Tern
Sleapford
Eyton upon the Weald Moors
Shrawardine
Montford Bridge
Bicton
Rodington Heath
Long Waste
Alberbury
Montford
Ditherington
Rodington
Coton Hill
Underdale
Uffington
Withington
Isombridge
Admaston
Upton Magna
Walcot
Wrockwardine
Wollaston
SHREWSBURY
Charlton
Wellington
Halfway House
Yockleton
Nox
Cruckton
Attingham Park NT
Uckington
Arleston
Hanwood
Meole Brace
Aston
Westbury
Stoney Stretton
Edge
Cruckmeole
Bayston Hill
Atcham
Wroxeter
Uppington
The Wrekin
Hinton
Arscott
Donnington
Little Wenlock
Aston Rogers
Asterley
Berrington
Cross Houses
Eaton Constantine
Horsebridge
Pontesbury
Plealey
Pontesford
Lyth Hill
Condover
Eyton on Severn
Garmston
Aston Pigott
Longden
Cantlop Bridge
Eaton Mascott
Cound
Leighton
Minsterley
Exfordsgreen
Buildwas
Coalbrookdale
Worthen
Stapleton
Upper Cound
Harnage
Cressage
Plox Green
Habberley
Wrentnall
Great Ryton
Sheinton
Ironbridge
Snailbeach
Dorrington
Pitchford
Church Pulverbatch
Acton Burnell
Iron Bridge
Castle Pulverbatch
Harley
Frodesley
Homer
Stiperstones
Longnor
Ruckley
Much Wenlock
Pennerley
Picklescott
Kenley
Shelve
Langley Chapel
Church Preen
Stretton Westwood
Woolstaston
Hughley
Leebotwood
Ratlinghope
Plaish
Bourton
All Stretton
Cardington
Gretton
Easthope
Caer Caradoc
The Long Mynd
Church Stretton
Longville in the Dale
Acton Round
Aston-Eyre
84
East Wall
Brockton
Norbury
Wentnor
Hope Bowdler
Monkhopton
Linley
Little Stretton
Shipton Hall
Weston
Upton Cressett Hall
More
Rushbury
Shipton
Upper Netchwood
Lydham
Whitcot
Asterton
Ticklerton
Stanton Long
Minton
Netchwood
Hatton
Broadstone
Marshbrook
Eaton
Working Farm
Lea
Myndtown
Holdgate
Hope Dale
Choulton
Whittingslow
Acton Scott
Ditton Priors
Middlehope
Wenlock Edge
The Corner
Plowden
Munslow
Neenton
Eyton
Alcaston
Aston Munslow
Tugford
Lydbury North
Woolston
Brown Clee Hill
Cleobury North
Edgton
Upper Affcot
Westhope
Abdon
Wistanstow
Diddlebury
Burwarton
Cheney Longville
Corfton
Bouldon
Lower Down
Clee St Margaret
Aston Botterell
Corve Dale
Hopesay
Duddlewick
Kempton
Aston on Clun
Craven Arms
Culmington
Stoke St Milborough
Loughton
Wheathill
Broome
Clunbury
Stokesay Castle
Shropshire Hills Discovery Centre
Farlow
Stanton Lacy
Hopton Cangeford
Silvington
Hopton Castle
Clungunford
Onibury
Ludlow
Hoptonheath
Shelderton
Bitterley
Titterstone Clee Hill
Cleeton St Mary
Pentre Hodrey
Beckjay
Middleton
Bromfield
Doddington
Foxwood
Bedstone
Angelbank
Hopton Wafers
Clee Hill
Snitton
Kinton
Knowbury
Cleehill
Bucknell
Leintwardine
River Teme
Geological Trail
Hope Bagot
Knowle
Coreley
Bransley
Walford
Downton on the Rock
Ludford
Caynham
Milson
Burrington
Overton
Whitton
Brampton Bryan
Adforton
69
Elton
Ashford Carbonel
Nash
Neen Sollars
Leinthall Starkes
Ashford Bowdler
Knighton on Teme
Wigmore
Richards Castle
Middleton
Little Hereford
Boraston
Harleys Mt
Birtley
Leinthall Earls
Woofferton
Brimfield
Brimfield Cross
Burford
Newnham
A5
A49
A458
A488
A489
A4113
A4117
A4169
A5223
A5112
A5124
A528
B4393
B4386
B4387
B4380
B4499
B4370
B4371
B4378
B4368
B4385
B4367
B4365
B4364
B4361
B5062
B5063
B5061
B4394
B4375
B4376
B4383
B4214

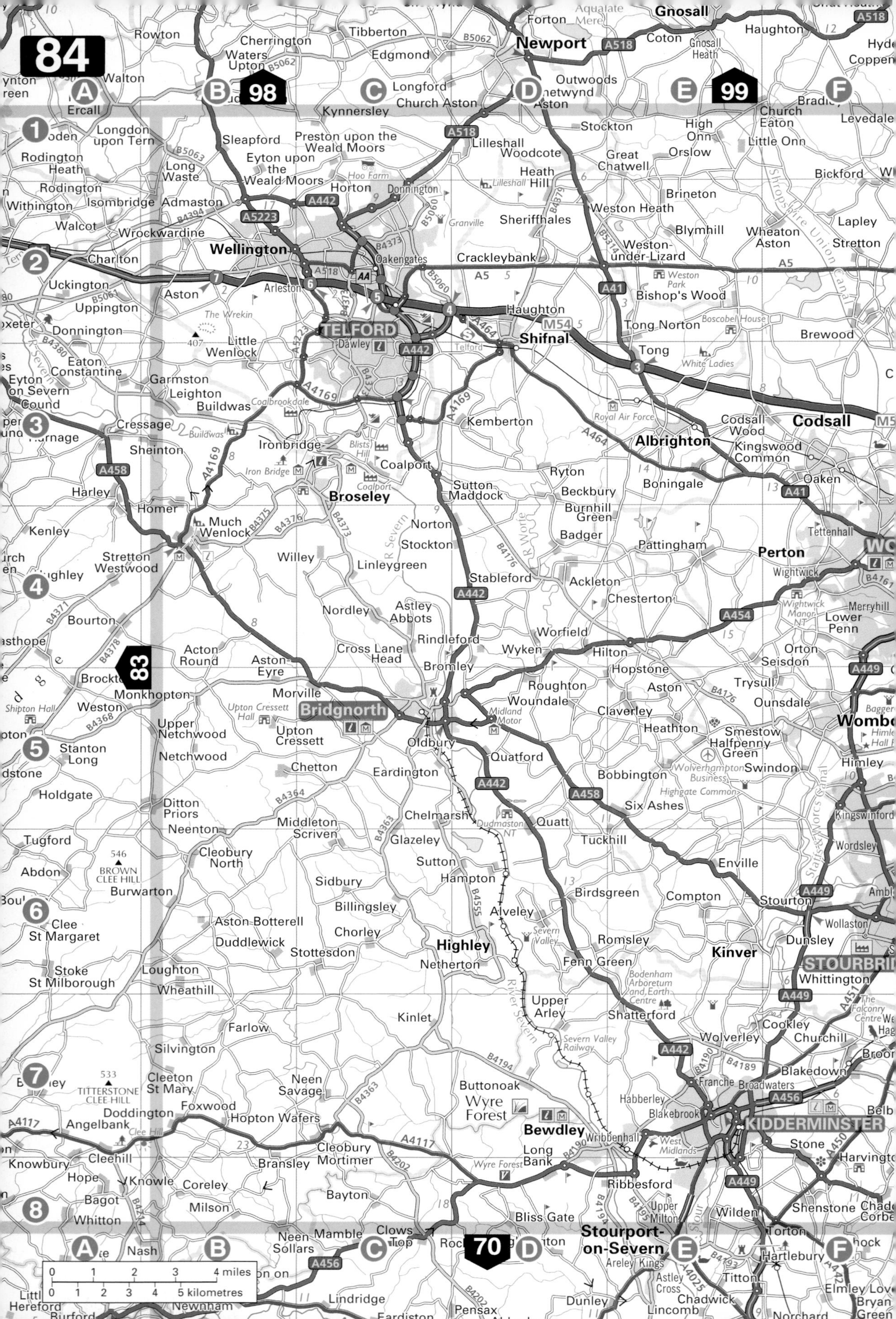

Newport
Gnosall
Wellington
TELFORD
Shifnal
Codsall
Albrighton
Broseley
Ironbridge
Much Wenlock
Bridgnorth
Highley
Kinver
Bewdley
KIDDERMINSTER
Stourport-on-Severn
Cleobury Mortimer
Wombourne
Perton
STOURBRIDGE
Wyre Forest
The Wrekin
BROWN CLEE HILL
TITTERSTONE CLEE HILL
River Severn
Severn Valley Railway
Shropshire Union Canal
Staffs & Worcs Canal
98
99
83
70
0 1 2 3 4 miles
0 1 2 3 4 5 kilometres

Walton-on-the-Hill
Milford
Colwich
Bishton
Colton
Hadley End
Dunstall
Branston
Acton Gnosall
Brocton
CANNOCK CHASE
Wolseley Bridge
Blithbury
Hamstall Ridware
Hill Ridware
Rugeley
Etchinghill
Bednall
Penkridge
Slitting Mill
Mavesyn Ridware
Nethertown
Yoxall
Wychnor
Rosliston
Castle Gresley
King's Bromley
Brereton
Armitage
Birches Valley Forest Centre
Upper Longdon
Longdon
Longdon Green
Alrewas
Fradley
National Memorial
Coton in the Elms
Huntington
Hednesford
Green Heath
Cannock Chase
Castle Ring
Gentleshaw
Farewell
Elmhurst
Lullington
Edingale
Clifton Campville
Hatherton
Heath Hayes & Wimblebury
Lichfield
Streethay
Elford
Harlaston
Haunton
CANNOCK
Bridgtown
Norton Canes
Burntwood
Chase Terrace
Boney Hay
Burntwood Green
Chasetown
Chasewater Railway
Standeford
Cheslyn Hay
Great Wyrley
Hammerwich
Letocetum Baths NT
Whittington
Staffordshire Regiment
Comberford
Thorpe Constantine
Seckington
Wigginton
Shareshill
Featherstone
Hilton Park
Wall
Brownhills
Little Wyrley
Upper Landywood
Shuttington
Amington
Essington
Pelsall
Stonnall
Shenstone
Hopwas
Weeford
TAMWORTH
Hints
Kettlebrook
Glascote
Moseley Old Hall NT
Wood Hayes
Bloxwich
Blakenall Heath
Leighswood
Little Hay
M6 Toll
Drayton Manor
Fazeley
Two Gates
Wednesfield
Harden
Roughwood
Aldridge
Little Aston
Drayton Bassett
Whateley
Baddesley Ensor
WOLVERHAMPTON
Heath Town
Portobello
Willenhall
WALSALL
Middleton
Ash End House
Middleton Hall
Moseley
Monmore Green
Darlaston Green
Caldmore
Palfrey
Barr Beacon
Hurley Common
Ettingshall
Bilston
Darlaston
King's Hill
Allen End
Kingsbury
Hurley
Sutton Park
SUTTON COLDFIELD
Maney
The Belfry
Bradley
Wednesbury
Friar Park
Yew Tree
Kingstanding
Foul End
Coseley
Charlemont
Boldmere
Wylde Green
Walmley
Wishaw
Marston
Nether Whitacre
Churchfield
Curdworth
Whiteacre Heath
Hoggrill's End
Wrens Nest
Tipton
Dudley Port
Birmingham Main Canal
RSPB
Sandwell Valley
Alexander Stadium
Perry Barr
Witton
Erdington
Water Orton
HAMS HALL
WEST BROMWICH
DUDLEY
Handsworth
Castle Bromwich
Shustoke
Over Whitacre
Coleshill
Netherton
Rowley Regis
Oldbury
Smethwick
Maxstoke
Quarry Bank
Bearwood
Ladywood
BIRMINGHAM
Chelmsley Wood
Blackheath
Cradley Heath
Cradley
Small Heath
Yardley
Marston Green
Little Packington
Sheldon
Birmingham
Stonebridge
N.E.C.
Lye
HALESOWEN
Wollescote
Woodgate Valley
Harborne
Edgbaston
Balsall Heath
Acock's Green
Sparkhill
Elmdon
Bickenhill
Meriden
National Motorcycle
Hayley Green
Hasbury
Woodgate
Bartley Green
Illey
Bournbrook
Selly Oak
Moseley
Olton
Hagley Hall
Frankley
Newbrook Farm
Cadbury World
Bournville
King's Heath
Hall Green
Lode Heath
Hampton in Arden
Four Oaks
Lower Clent
Clent Hills
Clent
Romsley
Frankley
Lifford
Sarehole Mill
Yardley Wood
SOLIHULL
Northfield
King's Norton
Eastcote
Berkswell
Bell End
West Heath
Shirley
Barston
Carol Green
Windmill Hill
Rubery
Longbridge
Knowle
Wildmoor
Lydiate Ash
Cofton Hackett
Hopwood
Wythall
Balsall Common
Fairfield
Lickey
Dorridge
Darley Green
Bournheath
Catshill
Barnt Green
Hopwood Park
Tanner's Green
Earlswood
Chessetts Wood
Chadwick End
Dodford
Withybed Green
Hockley Heath
Packwood House NT
Baddesley Clinton
Honiley
Lickey End
Linthurst
Alvechurch
Portway
Wood End
Kenilworth
Bromsgrove
Burcot
Rowney Green
Tanworth in Arden
Lapworth
Kingswood
Baddesley Clinton NT
Wroxall
Grand Union Canal
Beausale
Aston Fields
Finstall
Beoley
Holt End
Rowington
Tardebigge
Forge
High
M6
M5
M42
M40
A38(M)
A34
A449
A460
A5
A513
A51
A515
A38
A5192
A5190
A5148
A461
A452
A453
A454
A4041
A446
A4097
A4040
A41
A45
A456
A458
A491
A441
A435
A452
A4177
A448
100
71
98
Trent & Mersey Canal
Birmingham & Fazeley Canal
R Tame
R Trent
R Arrow

86
100
85
72
A
B
C
D
E
F
1
2
3
4
5
6
7
8
Dunstall
Branston
Barton-under-Needwood
Hartshorne
Swadlincote
Staunton Harold NT
Worthington
Belton
Shepshed
Lount
Smisby
Osgathorpe
Rosliston
Cauldwell
Linton
Ashby-de-la-Zouch
Thringstone
Wychnor
Alrewas
Coton in the Elms
Overseal
Conkers
Moira
Swannington
Whitwick
Charnwood Forest
Mount St Bernard
National Memorial
Snibston Discovery Park
Packington
Donisthorpe
Ravenstone
Coalville
Bardon
Lullington
Netherseal
Oakthorpe
Edingale
Normanton le Heath
Clifton Campville
Chilcote
Measham
Heather
Donington le Heath
Stanton under Bardon
Elford
Harlaston
Haunton
Appleby Magna
Snarestone
Swepstone
Ellistown
Ibstock
Newton Burgoland
No Man's Heath
Appleby Parva
Thorpe Constantine
Seckington
Newton Regis
Norton-Juxta-Twycross
Ashby Canal
Odstone
Bagworth
Thornton
Whittington
Comberford
Staffordshire Regiment
Wigginton
Austrey
Barton in the Beans
Shackerstone
Nailstone
Birmingham & Fazeley Canal
Bilstone
Congerstone
Barlestone
Shuttington
Amington
Alvecote
Twycross
Orton-on-the-Hill
Carlton
Osbaston
Tropical Birdland
Hopwas
TAMWORTH
Warton
Market Bosworth
Newbold Verdon
Desford
Hints
Kettlebrook
Glascote
Polesworth
The Battlefield Line
Cadeby
R Sence
Fazeley
Drayton Manor
Two Gates
Sheepy Magna
Sheepy Parva
Peckleton
Sutton Cheney
Kirkby Mallory
Mallory Park
Dordon
Ratcliffe Culey
Sibson
Drayton Bassett
Whateley
Baddesley Ensor
Grendon
Whittington
Upton
Shenton
Bosworth Battlefield
Stapleton
Middleton
Middleton Hall
Ash End House
Atterton
Earl Shilton
Dadlington
Hurley Common
Atherstone
Witherley
Allen End
Kingsbury
Hurley
Baxterley
Mancetter
Fenny Drayton
Higham on the Hill
Stoke Golding
Barwell
Elmesthorpe
Bentley
Ridge Lane
Hartshill Hayes
Coventry Canal
Foul End
Birchley Heath
Oldbury
Hartshill
Hinckley
Burbage Common & Woods
Stoney Stanton
Wishaw
Lea Marston
Nether Whitacre
Weddington
Curdworth
Whiteacre Heath
Hoggrill's End
Ansley
Stockingford
NUNEATON
Sketchley
Burbage
Aston Flamville
Sapcote
Water Orton
Hams Hall
Attleborough
Burton Hastings
Wigston Parva
Castle Bromwich
Shustoke
Over Whitacre
Arley
Astley
Arbury Hall
Coleshill
Griff
Bramcote
Wolvey
Wolvey Heath
Copston Magna
Maxstoke
Fillongley
Bedworth
Chelmsley Wood
Bulkington
Corley Ash
Marston Green
Ash Green
Corley
Little Packington
Exhall
Shilton
Withybrook
Birmingham
Sheldon
N.E.C.
Stonebridge
Rowley Green
Ansty
Monks Kirby
Little Heath
Foleshill
Elmdon
Bickenhill
Meriden
National Motorcycle
Jaguar Daimler
Keresley
Street Ashton
Pickford
Stretton under Fosse
Pailton
Lode Heath
Hampton in Arden
Allesley
Wyken
Easenhall
Four Oaks
Eastern Green
SOLIHULL
Eastcote
Berkswell
Reeves Green
COVENTRY
Combe
Stoke
Brinklow
Binley
Barston
Tile Hill
Earlsdon
Kings Newnham
Knowle
Carol Green
Canley
Bretford
Long Lawford
Balsall Common
Berkswell
Stivichall
Willenhall
Brandon
Church Lawford
Dorridge
Lunt Roman Fort
Coventry
Wolston
Darley Green
Baginton
Ryton-on-Dunsmore
RUGBY
Chessetts Wood
Chadwick End
Packwood House NT
Baddesley Clinton
Honiley
Stoneleigh
Stretton-on-Dunsmore
Grand Union Canal
Baddesley Clinton NT
Kenilworth
Bubbenhall
Bourton on Dunsmore
Princethorpe
Thurlaston
Beausale
Agricultural Centre
Weston under Wetherley
Frankton
Ashow
Wappenbury
R Leam
Draycote
Draycote Water
Marton
Leek Wootton
Eathorpe
High
0 1 2 3 4 miles
0 1 2 3 4 5 kilometres
M42
M6
M69
A5
A38
A444
A511
A512
A514
A42
A447
A453
A446
A4097
A452
A45
A46
A428
A429
A4177
A4141
A4114
A4600
A4082
A4071
A426
A445
A47
A51
A513
B5003
B5006
B5493
B5404
B5000
B4116
B585
B582
B4668
B4666
B4669
B4114
B4112
B4102
B4098
B4109
B4029
B4065
B4455
B4027
B4104
B4101
B4113
B4453
B4115

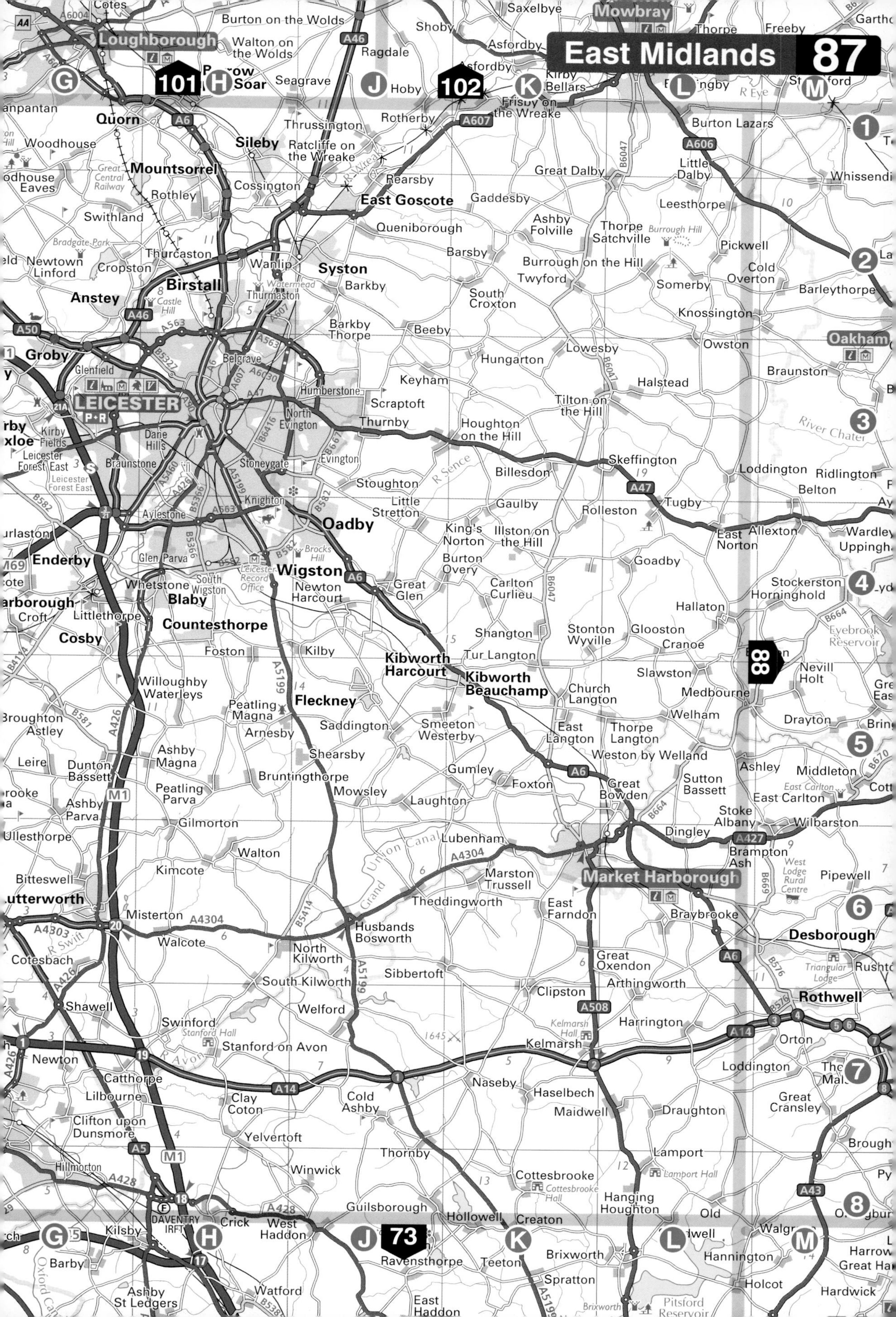
Loughborough
Cotes
Burton on the Wolds
Walton on the Wolds
Quorn
Woodhouse
Mountsorrel
Rothley
Swithland
Sileby
Cossington
Seagrave
Thrussington
Ratcliffe on the Wreake
Rotherby
Hoby
Ragdale
Shoby
Saxelbye
Asfordby
Mowbray
Kirby Bellars
Frisby on the Wreake
Rearsby
East Goscote
Gaddesby
Queniborough
Syston
Barkby
Birstall
Anstey
Thurcaston
Cropston
Newtown Linford
Groby
Glenfield
LEICESTER
Belgrave
Humberstone
Scraptoft
Thurnby
North Evington
Evington
Stoneygate
Knighton
Aylestone
Braunstone
Oadby
Wigston
Stoughton
Little Stretton
Enderby
Whetstone
Blaby
Countesthorpe
Cosby
Croft
Littlethorpe
Glen Parva
South Wigston
Newton Harcourt
Great Glen
Kilby
Foston
Fleckney
Kibworth Harcourt
Kibworth Beauchamp
Tur Langton
Shangton
Carlton Curlieu
Burton Overy
King's Norton
Illston on the Hill
Gaulby
Billesdon
Houghton on the Hill
Keyham
Hungarton
Beeby
Barkby Thorpe
South Croxton
Barsby
Ashby Folville
Twyford
Burrough on the Hill
Thorpe Satchville
Great Dalby
Little Dalby
Burton Lazars
Leesthorpe
Pickwell
Somerby
Cold Overton
Knossington
Owston
Lowesby
Tilton on the Hill
Halstead
Skeffington
Rolleston
Tugby
East Norton
Allexton
Goadby
Loddington
Belton
Ridlington
Braunston
Oakham
Barleythorpe
Whissendine
Stockerston
Horninghold
Hallaton
Glooston
Stonton Wyville
Cranoe
Slawston
Medbourne
Nevill Holt
Welham
Drayton
Church Langton
East Langton
Thorpe Langton
Weston by Welland
Sutton Bassett
Ashley
Middleton
East Carlton
Stoke Albany
Wilbarston
Dingley
Brampton Ash
Great Bowden
Market Harborough
Foxton
Gumley
Smeeton Westerby
Saddington
Laughton
Lubenham
Mowsley
Shearsby
Bruntingthorpe
Arnesby
Peatling Magna
Peatling Parva
Willoughby Waterleys
Ashby Magna
Dunton Bassett
Ashby Parva
Gilmorton
Leire
Broughton Astley
Ullesthorpe
Walton
Kimcote
Bitteswell
Lutterworth
Misterton
Walcote
Cotesbach
Shawell
Swinford
Stanford on Avon
Newton
Catthorpe
Lilbourne
Clifton upon Dunsmore
Clay Coton
Yelvertoft
Husbands Bosworth
North Kilworth
South Kilworth
Welford
Sibbertoft
Theddingworth
Marston Trussell
East Farndon
Great Oxendon
Arthingworth
Clipston
Braybrooke
Desborough
Rothwell
Harrington
Kelmarsh
Orton
Loddington
Naseby
Haselbech
Maidwell
Draughton
Great Cransley
Cold Ashby
Thornby
Winwick
Guilsborough
Hollowell
Creaton
Cottesbrooke
Hanging Houghton
Lamport
Old
Walgrave
Hannington
Brixworth
Teeton
Ravensthorpe
Spratton
Holcot
Pitsford Reservoir
East Haddon
Watford
Ashby St Ledgers
Barby
Kilsby
Crick
West Haddon
Hillmorton
DAVENTRY IRFT
Market Harborough
Pipewell
Triangular Lodge
West Lodge Rural Centre
Eyebrook Reservoir
Kelmarsh Hall
Lamport Hall
Cottesbrooke Hall
Stanford Hall
Great Central Railway
Bradgate Park
Castle Hill
Watermead
Brocks Hill
Leicester Record Office
Burrough Hill
Union Canal
Grand
R Avon
R Swift
R Sence
R Wreake
River Chater
R Eye
A6
A46
A607
A606
A47
A50
A563
A5199
A426
A4304
A5
M1
A14
A428
A508
A427
A43
B6047
B664
B582
B5414
A4303
B581
A6030
101
102
73
88

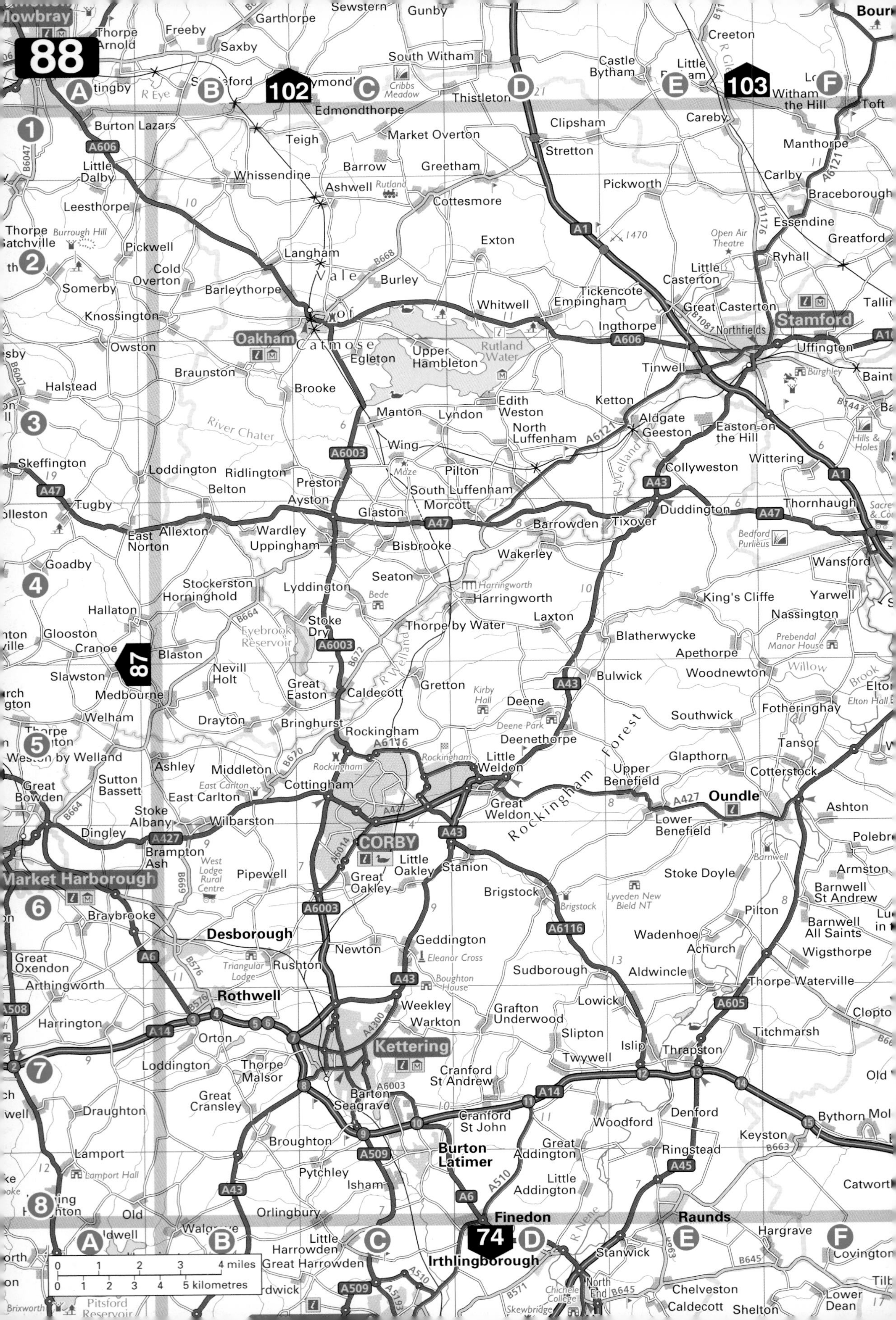

Mowbray
Thorpe Arnold
Freeby
Garthorpe
Sewstern
Gunby
Saxby
South Witham
Creeton
Bourne
Castle Bytham
Little Bytham
102
103
Cribbs Meadow
Edmondthorpe
Thistleton
Witham on the Hill
Toft
Burton Lazars
Teigh
Market Overton
Clipsham
Careby
Stretton
Manthorpe
A606
B6047
Little Dalby
Whissendine
Barrow
Greetham
Carlby
A6121
R Eye
Pickworth
Ashwell
Rutland
Cottesmore
Braceborough
Leesthorpe
Essendine
A1
1470
Exton
Open Air Theatre
Greatford
Thorpe Satchville
Burrough Hill
Pickwell
Langham
B1176
Ryhall
B668
Somerby
Cold Overton
Vale
Burley
Little Casterton
Barleythorpe
Tickencote
Empingham
Whitwell
Knossington
Great Casterton
Stamford
B1081
Northfields
Oakham
Ingthorpe
Owston
of Catmose
Rutland Water
Uffington
Egleton
Upper Hambleton
Baston
Burghley
Braunston
Tinwell
Halstead
Brooke
Edith Weston
Ketton
B1443
B6047
Manton
Lyndon
Aldgate
Geeston
Easton on the Hill
Hills & Holes
River Chater
North Luffenham
A6121
A6003
Wing
Wittering
Skeffington
Loddington
Ridlington
Maze
Pilton
Collyweston
R Welland
A43
Belton
Preston
South Luffenham
A47
Tugby
Ayston
Morcott
Duddington
Thornhaugh
Glaston
Barrowden
Tixover
Sacrewell
Rolleston
East Norton
Allexton
Wardley
Uppingham
Bisbrooke
Wakerley
Bedford Purlieus
Wansford
Goadby
Seaton
Harringworth
Stockerston
Horninghold
Lyddington
Bede
King's Cliffe
Yarwell
Hallaton
B664
Laxton
Nassington
Eyebrook Reservoir
Stoke Dry
Thorpe by Water
Blatherwycke
Glooston
Cranoe
Prebendal Manor House
87
Blaston
B672
Apethorpe
Willow Brook
Slawston
Nevill Holt
Gretton
Bulwick
Woodnewton
Great Easton
Caldecott
Kirby Hall
Deene
Elton
Elton Hall
Medbourne
Welham
Drayton
Bringhurst
Deene Park
Southwick
Fotheringhay
Rockingham
Deenethorpe
Thorpe Langton
A6116
Rockingham Forest
Tansor
Glapthorn
Weston by Welland
Ashley
Middleton
B670
Little Weldon
Upper Benefield
Cotterstock
Sutton Bassett
Rockingham
Great Bowden
East Carlton
Cottingham
Oundle
A427
Stoke Albany
East Carlton
Great Weldon
Lower Benefield
Ashton
B664
Wilbarston
A427
Dingley
CORBY
A6014
Polebrook
Brampton Ash
West Lodge Rural Centre
Little Oakley
Stanion
Barnwell
Armston
Market Harborough
B669
Pipewell
Great Oakley
Brigstock
Lyveden New Bield NT
Stoke Doyle
Barnwell St Andrew
Braybrooke
A6003
Pilton
Barnwell All Saints
A6116
Desborough
Geddington
Wadenhoe
Great Oxenden
Newton
Eleanor Cross
Achurch
Wigsthorpe
A6
Triangular Lodge
Rushton
Sudborough
Aldwincle
Arthingworth
B576
Boughton House
Thorpe Waterville
Rothwell
Lowick
A605
A508
Harrington
A14
Orton
Weekley
Warkton
Grafton Underwood
Clopton
A4300
Slipton
Titchmarsh
Kettering
Islip
Thrapston
Loddington
Thorpe Malsor
Twywell
Cranford St Andrew
Old
Great Cransley
Barton Seagrave
A6003
A14
Draughton
Cranford St John
Woodford
Denford
Bythorn
Molesworth
Broughton
Keyston
Great Addington
Burton Latimer
Ringstead
Lamport
B663
A509
A45
Lamport Hall
Pytchley
Isham
A510
Little Addington
A43
Catworth
Hanging Houghton
A6
R Nene
Old
Orlingbury
Finedon
Raunds
Walgrave
74
Hargrave
Little Harrowden
Great Harrowden
Irthlingborough
Stanwick
Covington
B645
0 1 2 3 4 miles
0 1 2 3 4 5 kilometres
A509
A5193
A510
B571
Chichele College
North End
B645
Chelveston
Caldecott
Shelton
Lower Dean
Brixworth
Pitsford Reservoir
Skewbridge

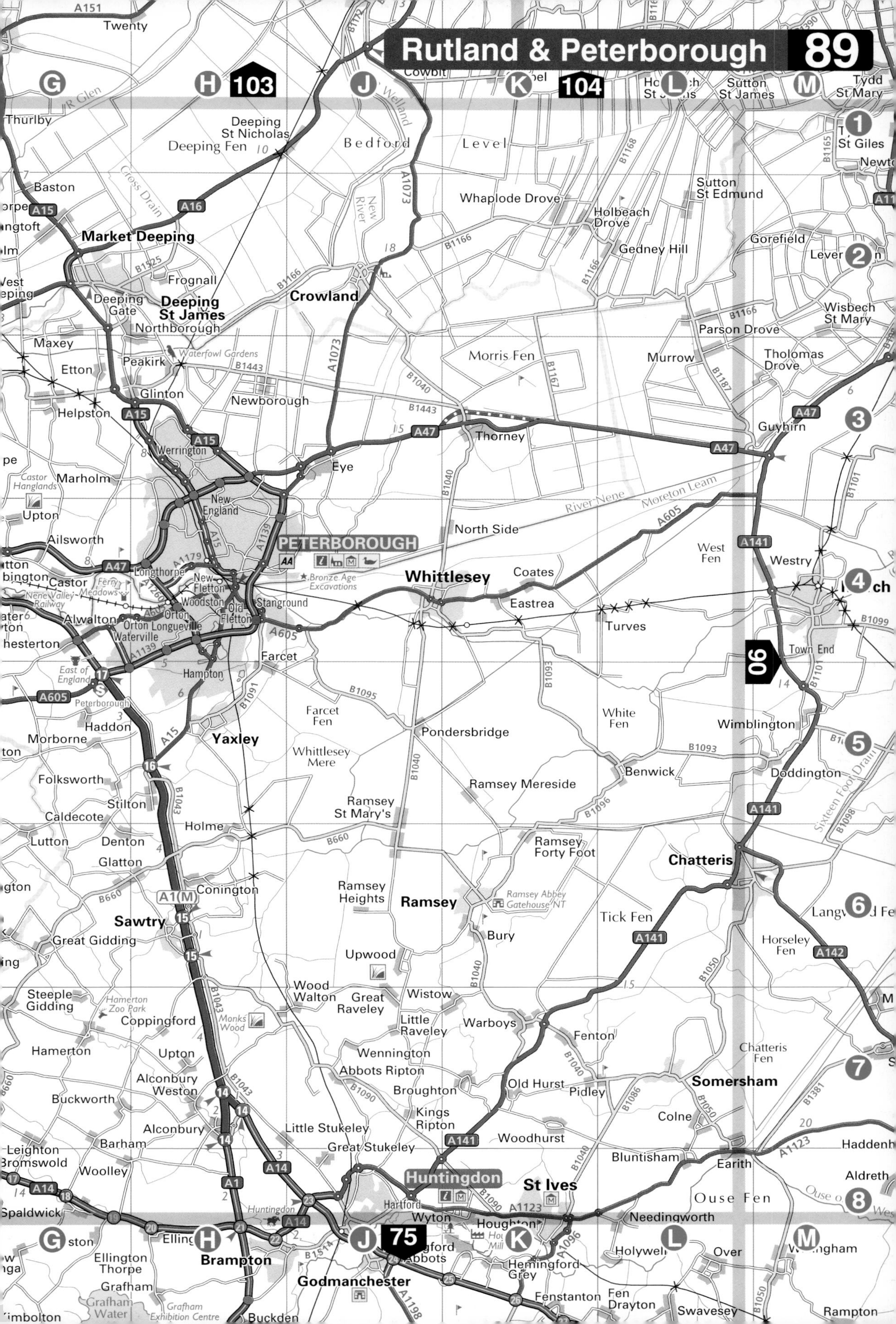
Twenty
Thurlby
Deeping St Nicholas
Deeping Fen
Bedford
Level
Baston
Market Deeping
Whaplode Drove
Holbeach Drove
Sutton St Edmund
Gedney Hill
Gorefield
Frognall
Crowland
Deeping Gate
Deeping St James
Northborough
Parson Drove
Wisbech St Mary
Maxey
Peakirk
Waterfowl Gardens
Morris Fen
Murrow
Tholomas Drove
Etton
Glinton
Newborough
Helpston
Thorney
Guyhirn
Werrington
Eye
Castor Hanglands
Marholm
New England
Upton
Ailsworth
North Side
River Nene
Moreton Leam
PETERBOROUGH
West Fen
Westry
Castor
Longthorpe
Nene Valley Railway
Ferry Meadows
New Fletton
Woodston
Old Fletton
Stanground
Bronze Age Excavations
Whittlesey
Coates
Eastrea
Turves
Alwalton
Orton
Orton Longueville
Orton Waterville
Town End
Farcet
East of England
Peterborough
Hampton
Haddon
Morborne
Yaxley
Farcet Fen
Pondersbridge
White Fen
Wimblington
Whittlesey Mere
Benwick
Doddington
Folksworth
Stilton
Ramsey Mereside
Caldecote
Ramsey St Mary's
Sixteen Foot Drain
Holme
Lutton
Denton
Glatton
Ramsey Forty Foot
Chatteris
Conington
Ramsey Heights
Ramsey
Ramsey Abbey Gatehouse NT
Sawtry
Tick Fen
Great Gidding
Bury
Horseley Fen
Upwood
Steeple Gidding
Hamerton Zoo Park
Wood Walton
Great Raveley
Wistow
Coppingford
Little Raveley
Monks Wood
Warboys
Fenton
Hamerton
Upton
Wennington
Chatteris Fen
Alconbury Weston
Abbots Ripton
Old Hurst
Pidley
Somersham
Buckworth
Broughton
Kings Ripton
Colne
Alconbury
Little Stukeley
Barham
Woodhurst
Leighton Bromswold
Great Stukeley
Bluntisham
Earith
Haddenham
Woolley
Huntingdon
St Ives
Aldreth
Ouse Fen
Spaldwick
Hartford
Wyton
Houghton
Needingworth
Ellington
Brampton
Hemingford Abbots
Hemingford Grey
Holywell
Over
Ellington Thorpe
Godmanchester
Grafham
Grafham Water
Grafham Exhibition Centre
Fenstanton
Fen Drayton
Swavesey
Rampton
Buckden
Kimbolton

103 104 90 75

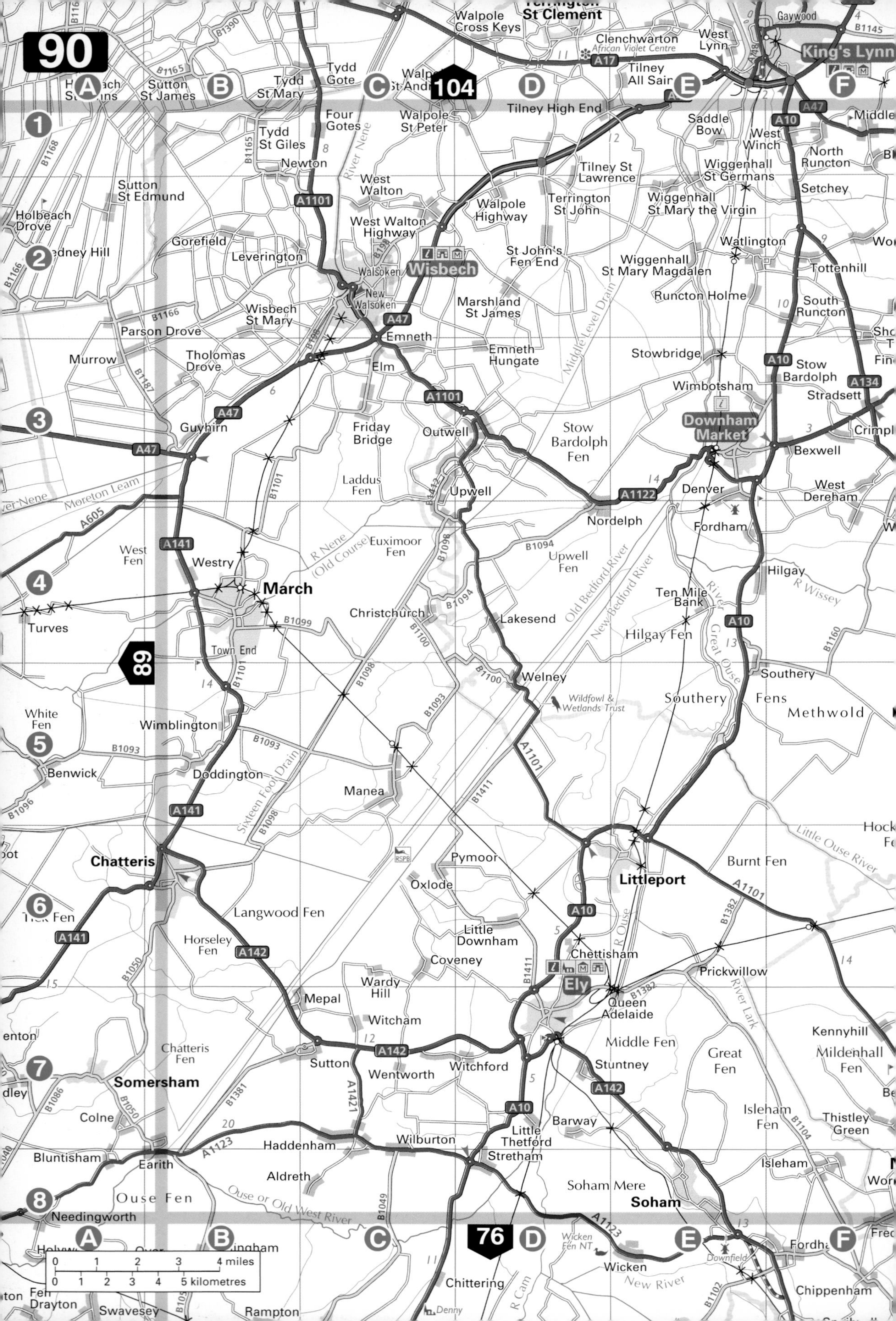
Walpole Cross Keys
St Clement
Clenchwarton
African Violet Centre
West Lynn
Gaywood
King's Lynn
Sutton St James
Tydd St Mary
Tydd Gote
104
Tilney All Saints
Tilney High End
Four Gotes
Tydd St Giles
Walpole St Peter
Saddle Bow
West Winch
Middleton
North Runcton
Newton
Tilney St Lawrence
Wiggenhall St Germans
Sutton St Edmund
West Walton
Walpole Highway
Terrington St John
Wiggenhall St Mary the Virgin
Setchey
Holbeach Drove
West Walton Highway
St John's Fen End
Watlington
Gorefield
Leverington
Wisbech
Walsoken
New Walsoken
Wiggenhall St Mary Magdalen
Tottenhill
Runcton Holme
South Runcton
Wisbech St Mary
Parson Drove
Marshland St James
Murrow
Tholomas Drove
Emneth
Emneth Hungate
Middle Level Drain
Stowbridge
Stow Bardolph
Elm
Wimbotsham
Stradsett
Guyhirn
Friday Bridge
Outwell
Stow Bardolph Fen
Downham Market
Crimplesham
Bexwell
Laddus Fen
Upwell
Denver
West Dereham
Moreton Leam
River Nene
Nordelph
Fordham
West Fen
Westry
R Nene (Old Course)
Euximoor Fen
Upwell Fen
Old Bedford River
New Bedford River
Hilgay
R Wissey
March
Christchurch
Ten Mile Bank
Turves
Lakesend
Hilgay Fen
Town End
89
Welney
Wildfowl & Wetlands Trust
Southery
Southery
Fens
Methwold
White Fen
Wimblington
Benwick
Doddington
Sixteen Foot Drain
Manea
Chatteris
Pymoor
RSPB
Little Ouse River
Burnt Fen
Oxlode
Littleport
Langwood Fen
Little Downham
Chettisham
Horseley Fen
Coveney
Prickwillow
Ely
Wardy Hill
Mepal
Queen Adelaide
River Lark
Witcham
Kennyhill
Chatteris Fen
Middle Fen
Mildenhall Fen
Great Fen
Sutton
Wentworth
Witchford
Stuntney
Somersham
Colne
Barway
Isleham Fen
Thistley Green
Little Thetford
Haddenham
Wilburton
Stretham
Bluntisham
Earith
Isleham
Aldreth
Soham Mere
Ouse Fen
Ouse or Old West River
Soham
Needingworth
76
Wicken Fen NT
Downfield
Fordham
Wicken
New River
Chittering
R Cam
Chippenham
Fen Drayton
Swavesey
Rampton
Denny
0 1 2 3 4 miles
0 1 2 3 4 5 kilometres

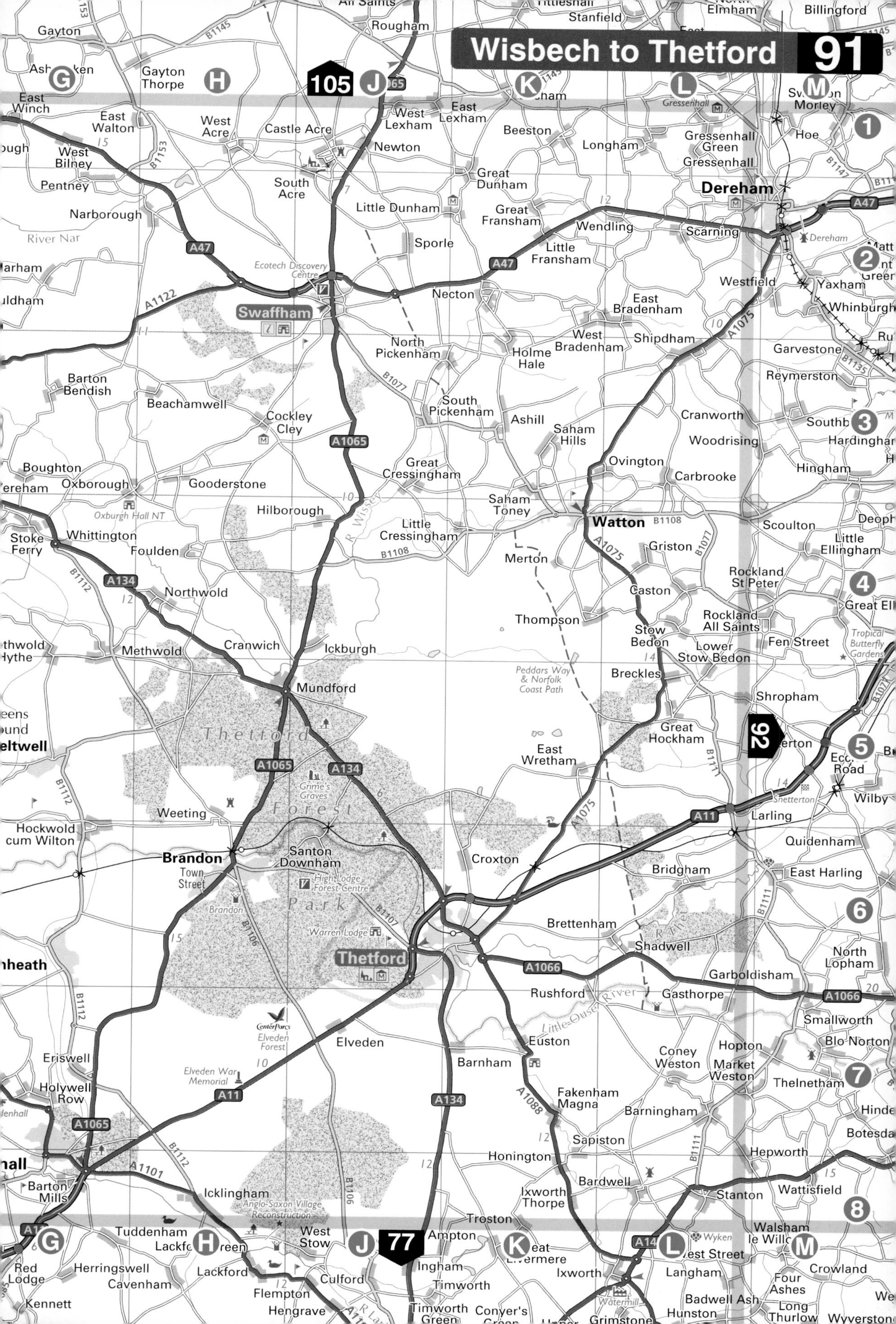
Swaffham
Dereham
Watton
Thetford
Brandon
Mundford
Castle Acre
Thetford Forest Park
Grime's Graves
High Lodge Forest Centre
Oxburgh Hall NT
Ecotech Discovery Centre
Peddars Way & Norfolk Coast Path
Elveden War Memorial
Anglo-Saxon Village Reconstruction
Tropical Butterfly Gardens
Snetterton
Little Ouse River
River Nar
R. Wissey
105
92
77

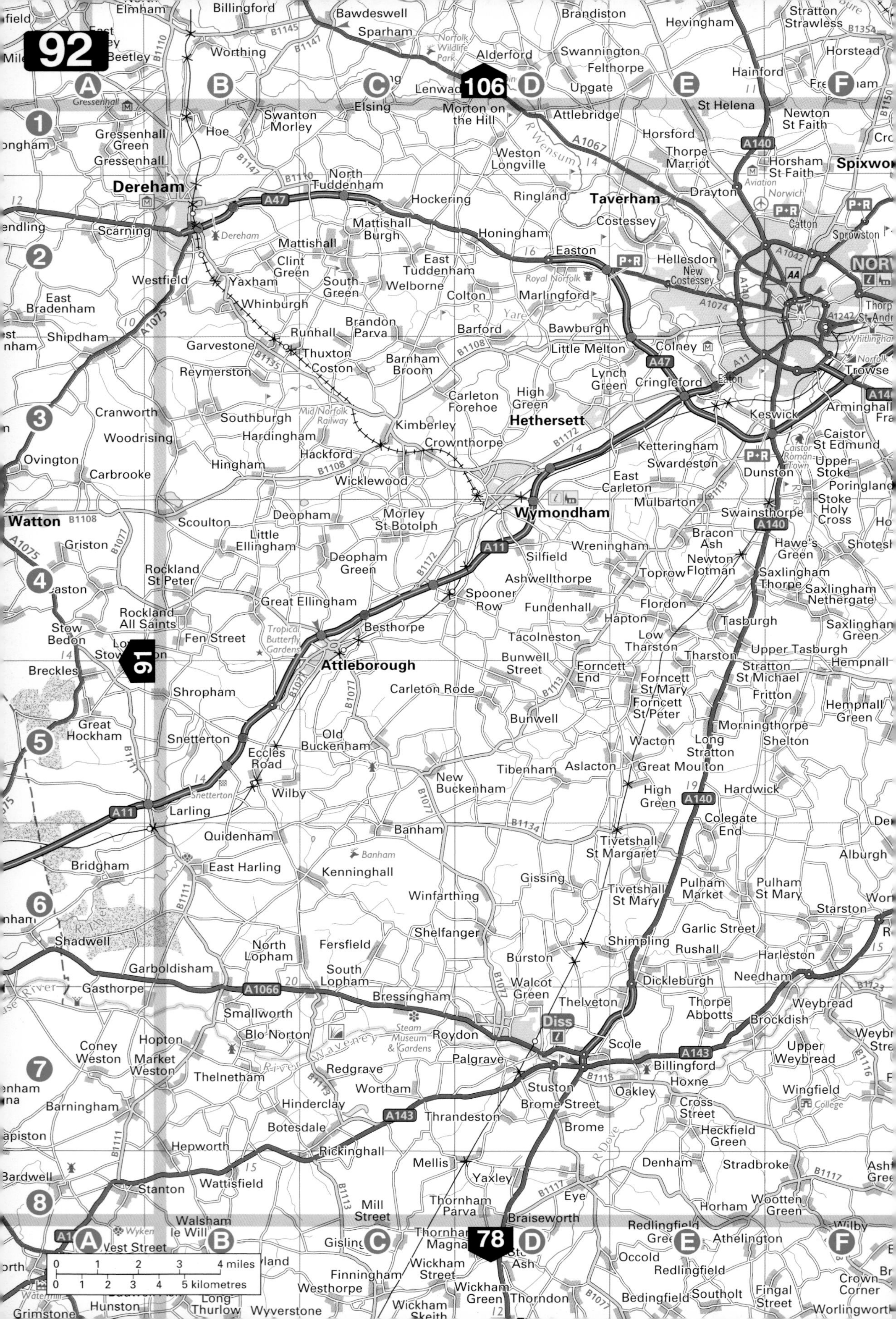

Elmham
Billingford
Bawdeswell
Brandiston
Hevingham
Stratton Strawless
Sparham
B1145
B1147
Norfolk Wildlife Park
Alderford
Swannington
Beetley
Worthing
Felthorpe
B1354
Horstead
B1110
Hainford
A
B
C
D
E
F
106
Lenwade
Upgate
Gressenhall
Elsing
Morton on the Hill
Attlebridge
St Helena
1
Swanton Morley
Newton St Faith
Gressenhall Green
Hoe
Weston Longville
Horsford
A1067
A140
R Wensum
Gressenhall
B1147
Thorpe Marriot
Horsham St Faith
Spixworth
North Tuddenham
Aviation
Dereham
B1110
Drayton
Norwich
12
A47
Hockering
Ringland
Taverham
P+R
Catton
Mattishall Burgh
Costessey
Sprowston
Scarning
Dereham
Honingham
2
Mattishall
Clint Green
East Tuddenham
Easton
Hellesdon
A1042
New Costessey
16
P+R
Westfield
Yaxham
Royal Norfolk
AA
South Green
Welborne
East Bradenham
Colton
Marlingford
A1074
A1140
Whinburgh
R Yare
A1242
St Andrews
Brandon Parva
Shipdham
10
Runhall
Barford
Bawburgh
A1075
Garvestone
B1135
Thuxton
B1108
Colney
Whitlingham
Little Melton
Barnham Broom
A11
Norfolk
Coston
Reymerston
Lynch Green
A47
Cringleford
Eaton
Trowse
Carleton Forehoe
High Green
Cranworth
Mid Norfolk Railway
Southburgh
3
Keswick
Arminghall
Hethersett
Kimberley
Woodrising
Crownthorpe
Hardingham
B1172
Caistor St Edmund
Ketteringham
14
Ovington
Caistor Roman Town
Hackford
Swardeston
Upper Stoke
Carbrooke
Hingham
P+R
Dunston
B1108
East Carleton
Poringland
Wicklewood
Mulbarton
B1113
Stoke Holy Cross
Wymondham
Watton
B1108
Swainsthorpe
Morley St Botolph
Scoulton
Deopham
A140
Bracon Ash
Little Ellingham
Hawe's Green
Griston
Silfield
A1075
Wreningham
B1077
Newton Flotman
Shotesham
A11
Deopham Green
Rockland St Peter
Saxlingham Thorpe
Ashwellthorpe
Toprow
4
Caston
B1172
Saxlingham Nethergate
Spooner Row
Flordon
Great Ellingham
Fundenhall
Rockland All Saints
Hapton
Stow Bedon
Besthorpe
Tasburgh
Saxlingham Green
Tropical Butterfly Gardens
Low Tharston
Tacolneston
Fen Street
Upper Tasburgh
Lower Stow Bedon
91
14
Tharston
Hempnall
Bunwell Street
Forncett End
Stratton St Michael
Attleborough
Breckles
Forncett St Mary
Carleton Rode
Shropham
B1077
Fritton
B1077
Forncett St Peter
B1113
Hempnall Green
Great Hockham
Bunwell
Morningthorpe
Snetterton
Old Buckenham
Wacton
Long Stratton
Shelton
5
Eccles Road
B1111
Great Moulton
Tibenham
Aslacton
New Buckenham
High Green
Hardwick
14
Snetterton
Wilby
A140
19
B1077
Larling
A11
Colegate End
Quidenham
Banham
B1134
Tivetshall St Margaret
Banham
Alburgh
Bridgham
East Harling
Kenninghall
Gissing
Pulham Market
Pulham St Mary
Tivetshall St Mary
6
Winfarthing
B1111
Starston
Shelfanger
Garlic Street
Shadwell
North Lopham
Fersfield
Shimpling
Rushall
Harleston
R Thet
Burston
15
Garboldisham
South Lopham
Dickleburgh
Needham
Gasthorpe
A1066
20
Walcot Green
B1077
Thorpe Abbotts
Weybread
B1123
Bressingham
Thelveton
Little Ouse River
Smallworth
Diss
Brockdish
Steam Museum & Gardens
Blo Norton
Roydon
Coney Weston
Hopton
River Waveney
Scole
Upper Weybread
Market Weston
Palgrave
A143
Billingford
7
Thelnetham
Redgrave
B1118
Hoxne
B1116
Stuston
Wortham
Oakley
B1113
Wingfield
College
Barningham
Hinderclay
Brome Street
Cross Street
A143
Thrandeston
Botesdale
Brome
Heckfield Green
Hepworth
R Dove
Rickinghall
B1111
Denham
Stradbroke
Mellis
Bardwell
Yaxley
B1117
15
B1113
Stanton
Wattisfield
B1117
Eye
8
Thornham Parva
Mill Street
Horham
Wootten Green
Braiseworth
Walsham le Willows
Redlingfield Green
Wilby
Wyken
Thornham Magna
78
Gislingham
Athelington
West Street
Occold
Wickham Street
Redlingfield
Finningham
Westhorpe
Wickham Green
Thorndon
Bedingfield
Southolt
Fingal Street
Crown Corner
Hunston
Long Thurlow
Wyverstone
Wickham Skeith
Worlingworth
Grimstone
12
B1077
0 1 2 3 4 miles
0 1 2 3 4 5 kilometres

Norwich & The Broads
93
107
79
Hemsby
Caister-on-Sea
GREAT YARMOUTH
Belton
Hopton on Sea
Corton
Lowestoft Ness
LOWESTOFT
Kessingland
Benacre Ness
Covehithe
Suffolk Heritage Coast
Sole Bay
Southwold
Walberswick
Dunwich
THE BROADS
Brundall
Bungay
Beccles
Halesworth
Hoveton
Horning
Ludham
Potter Heigham
Acle
Blofield
Loddon
Reedham
Fritton
St Olaves
Herringfleet
Somerleyton
Oulton Broad
Kirkley
Pakefield
Carlton Colville
Gillingham
Worlingham
Wrentham
Wangford
Reydon
Blythburgh
Wenhaston
Yoxford
Darsham
Westleton

Bay
Aberffraw Bay
Heritage Coast
Malltr
Llanddw
CAERNARFON
BAY
Lleyn Heritage Coast
Tre
564
YR EI
Trwyn y Grolech
B4417
Llith
Carreg Ddu
Porth Nefyn
Pistyll
Morfa Nefyn
Nefyn
Edern
Bodfuan
Porth Ysgaden
Llan
Tudweiliog
Llandudwen
A497
Efailn
Dinas
LLEYN
Porth Colman
371
Carn Fadrum
B4415
Rhyd-y-clafdy
Bryn-mawr
Llaniestyn
A499
B4417
Pen-y-graig
Penrhos
Llangwnnadl
Meyllteyrn
Llanbedrog
Sarn
Botwnnog
B4413
B4413
Bryncroes
Trwyn Llanbed
Porthoer
Rhoshirwaun
St Tudwal's Road
Plas-Yn-Rhiw NT
Llangian
B4413
Y Rhiw
Abersoch
Porth Neigwl
Llanengan
Aberdaron
Llanfaelrhys
Porth Ysgo
Bwlchtocyn
St Tudwal's Island East
Aberdaron Bay
St Tudwal's Island West
Bardsey Sound
Porth Geiriad
Lleyn Heritage Coast
St Mary's
BARDSEY ISLAND
0 1 2 3 4 miles
0 1 2 3 4 5 kilometres

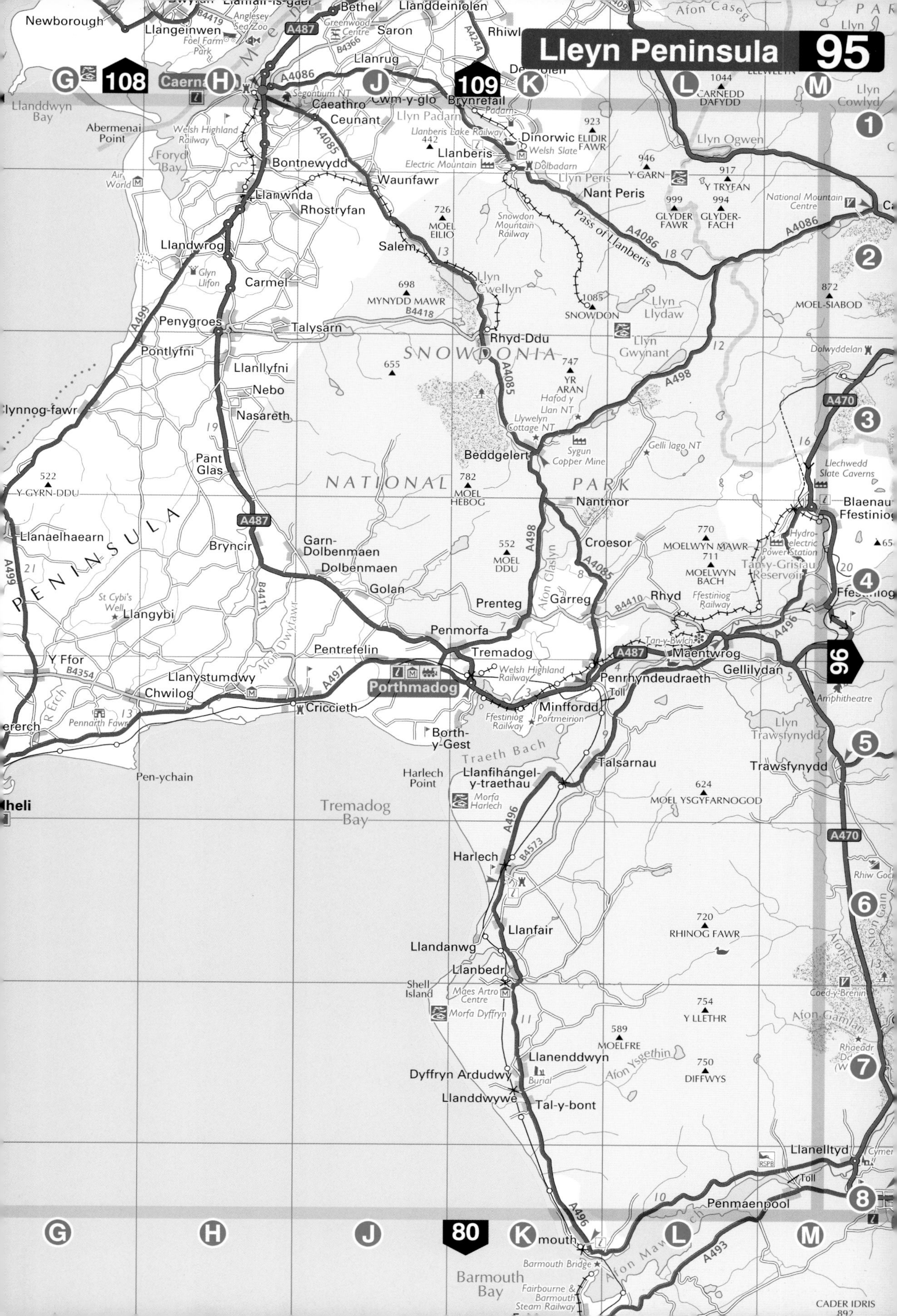
Newborough
Llangeinwen
Bethel
Llanddeiniolen
Saron
Rhiwl
Anglesey Sea Zoo
Foel Farm Park
Greenwood Centre
Llanrug
108
Caernarfon
109
Llanddwyn Bay
Segontium NT
Caeathro
Cwm-y-glo
Brynrefail
Ceunant
Llyn Padarn
Abermenai Point
Welsh Highland Railway
Foryd Bay
Llanberis Lake Railway
442
Dinorwic
Llanberis
Welsh Slate
Electric Mountain
Dolbadarn
Bontnewydd
Waunfawr
Air World
Llanwnda
Rhostryfan
1044
CARNEDD DAFYDD
923
ELIDIR FAWR
Llyn Ogwen
946
Y-GARN
917
Y TRYFAN
Llyn Peris
Nant Peris
999
GLYDER FAWR
994
GLYDER-FACH
National Mountain Centre
Llyn Cowlyd
Afon Caseg
Pass of Llanberis
726
MOEL EILIO
Snowdon Mountain Railway
Llandwrog
Salem
Glyn Llifon
Carmel
698
MYNYDD MAWR
Llyn Cwellyn
1085
SNOWDON
Llyn Llydaw
872
MOEL-SIABOD
Penygroes
Talysarn
Rhyd-Ddu
Llyn Gwynant
Dolwyddelan
Pontlyfni
SNOWDONIA
655
747
YR ARAN
Llanllyfni
Nebo
Clynnog-fawr
Nasareth
Hafod y Llan NT
Llywelyn Cottage NT
Sygun Copper Mine
Gelli Iago NT
Beddgelert
Pant Glas
522
Y-GYRN-DDU
NATIONAL
782
MOEL HEBOG
PARK
Llechwedd Slate Caverns
Nantmor
Blaenau Ffestiniog
PENINSULA
Llanaelhaearn
Bryncir
Garn-Dolbenmaen
Dolbenmaen
552
MOEL DDU
Croesor
770
MOELWYN MAWR
711
MOELWYN BACH
Hydro-electric Power Station
Tan-y-Grisiau Reservoir
Afon Glaslyn
Golan
St Cybi's Well
Llangybi
Afon Dwyfawr
Prenteg
Garreg
Rhyd
Ffestiniog Railway
Ffestiniog
Penmorfa
Tan-y-Bwlch
Pentrefelin
Tremadog
Maentwrog
Gellilydan
96
Y Ffor
Welsh Highland Railway
Penrhyndeudraeth
Toll
Amphitheatre
Llanystumdwy
Chwilog
Porthmadog
Criccieth
Minffordd
Portmeirion
Ffestiniog Railway
Pennarth Fawr
Borth-y-Gest
Llyn Trawsfynydd
Traeth Bach
Talsarnau
Trawsfynydd
Pen-ychain
Harlech Point
Llanfihangel-y-traethau
Morfa Harlech
624
MOEL YSGYFARNOGOD
Tremadog Bay
Harlech
Rhiw Goch
720
RHINOG FAWR
Llanfair
Llandanwg
Llanbedr
Shell Island
Maes Artro Centre
Morfa Dyffryn
Coed-y-Brenin
754
Y LLETHR
Afon Gamlan
589
MOELFRE
Rhaeadr Ddu
Llanenddwyn
Afon Ysgethin
750
DIFFWYS
Dyffryn Ardudwy
Burial
Llanddwywe
Tal-y-bont
Llanelltyd
RSPB
Toll
Penmaenpool
80
Barmouth
Barmouth Bridge
Afon Mawddach
Barmouth Bay
Fairbourne & Barmouth Steam Railway
CADER IDRIS 892
A487
A4086
A4244
A4085
A499
A498
A470
A496
A497
B4418
B4411
B4354
B4410
B4573
A493
G
H
J
K
L
M
1
2
3
4
5
6
7
8

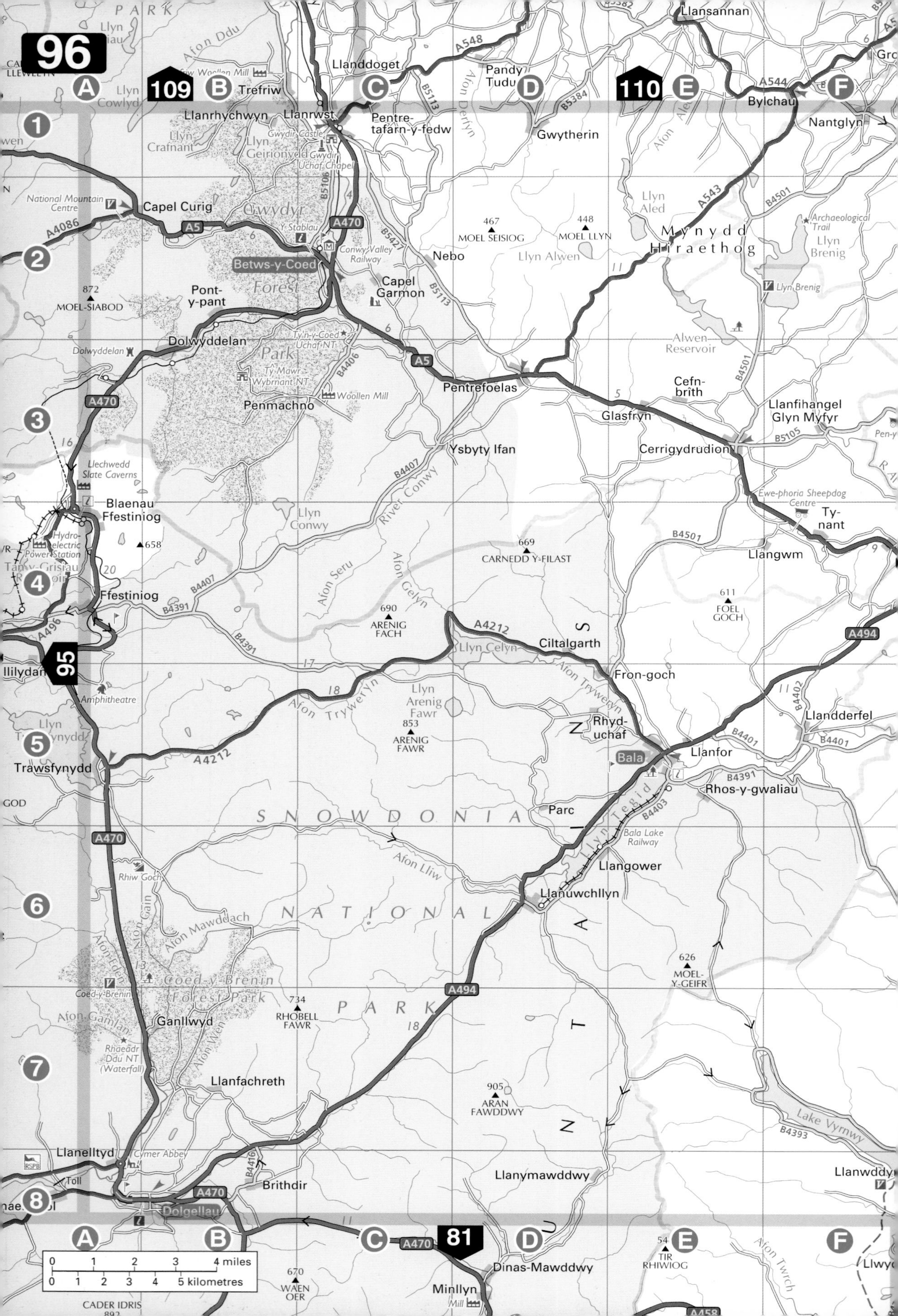
96
109
110
95
81
A
B
C
D
E
F
1
2
3
4
5
6
7
8
Llanrhychwyn
Llanrwst
Trefriw
Llanddoget
Pandy Tudur
Llansannan
Bylchau
Nantglyn
Pentre-tafarn-y-fedw
Gwytherin
Gwydir Castle
Llyn Crafnant
Llyn Geirionydd
Gwydir Uchaf Chapel
National Mountain Centre
Capel Curig
Gwydyr Forest
Y Stablau
Conwy Valley Railway
Betws-y-Coed
Capel Garmon
Nebo
Moel Seisiog
Moel Llyn
Llyn Alwen
Llyn Aled
Mynydd Hiraethog
Archaeological Trail
Llyn Brenig
Moel-Siabod
Pont-y-pant
Dolwyddelan
Ty'n-y-Coed Uchaf NT
Ty Mawr Wybrnant NT
Woollen Mill
Penmachno
Alwen Reservoir
Pentrefoelas
Cefn-brith
Glasfryn
Llanfihangel Glyn Myfyr
Cerrigydrudion
Ysbyty Ifan
Llechwedd Slate Caverns
Blaenau Ffestiniog
Hydro-electric Power Station
Tan-y-Grisiau
Llyn Conwy
River Conwy
Ewe-phoria Sheepdog Centre
Ty-nant
Carnedd y-Filast
Llangwm
Ffestiniog
Afon Seru
Afon Gelyn
Arenig Fach
Foel Goch
Llyn Celyn
Ciltalgarth
Fron-goch
Amphitheatre
Llyn Arenig Fawr
Arenig Fawr
Afon Tryweryn
Llyn Trawsfynydd
Trawsfynydd
Rhyd-uchaf
Llandderfel
Bala
Llanfor
Rhos-y-gwaliau
Parc
Snowdonia National Park
Llyn Tegid
Bala Lake Railway
Llangower
Llanuwchllyn
Afon Lliw
Rhiw Goch
Afon Mawddach
Coed-y-Brenin Forest Park
Rhobell Fawr
Moel-y-Geifr
Ganllwyd
Rhaeadr Ddu NT (Waterfall)
Llanfachreth
Aran Fawddwy
Lake Vyrnwy
Llanelltyd
Cymer Abbey
Brithdir
Llanymawddwy
Llanwddyn
Toll
Dolgellau
Dinas-Mawddwy
Minllyn
Mill
Tir Rhiwiog
Afon Twrch
Waen Oer
Cader Idris
0 1 2 3 4 miles
0 1 2 3 4 5 kilometres
A5
A470
A4086
A543
A544
A548
A4212
A494
A496
B5113
B5106
B5427
B5384
B4406
B4407
B4391
B4501
B5105
B4402
B4401
B4403
B4416
B4393

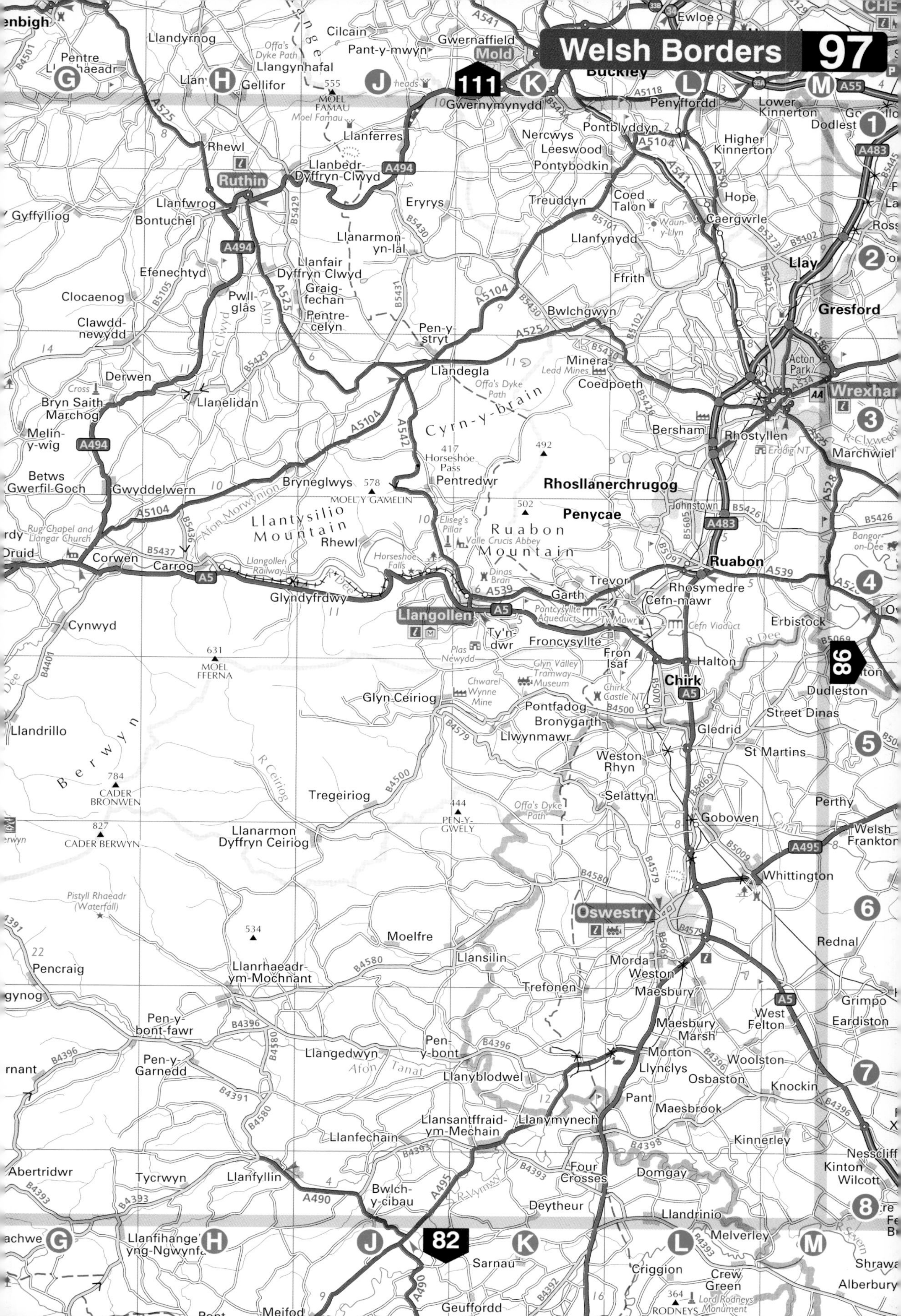

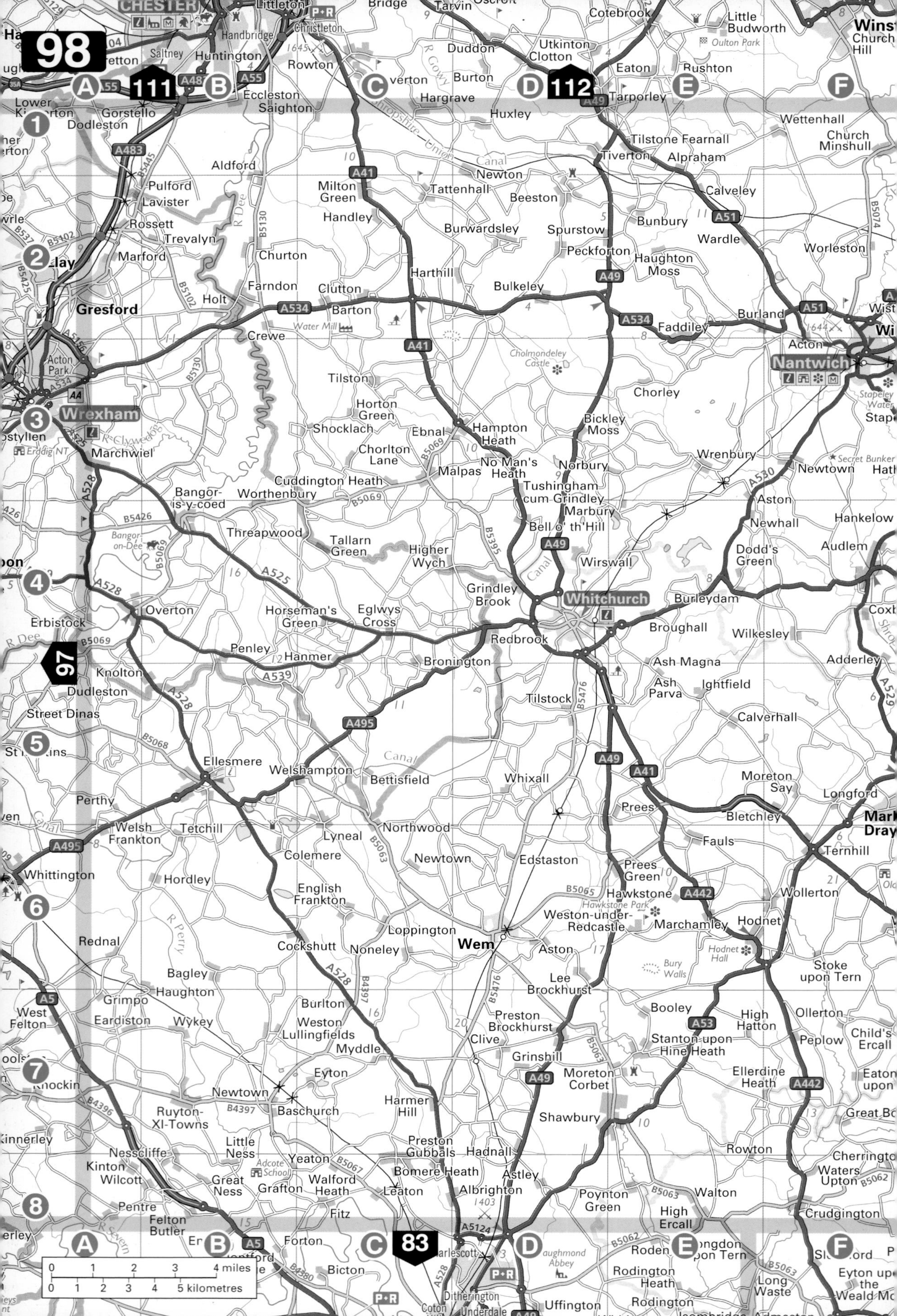

98
Chester
Littleton
P+R
Christleton
Bridge
Tarvin
Cotebrook
Little Budworth
Winsford
Church Hill
Oulton Park
Handbridge
Saltney
Huntington
Rowton
Duddon
Utkinton
Clotton
Eaton
Rushton
A
111
B
C
D
112
E
F
A55
A483
A41
A49
A51
A534
A525
A528
A495
A539
A5
A53
A442
A529
A530
A5124
B5130
B5102
B5069
B5395
B5476
B5063
B5065
B5068
B4397
B4396
B5067
B4380
B5062
B5074
B5445
B5426
B5425
B537
Eccleston
Saighton
Cotton Edmunds
Burton
Hargrave
Huxley
Tarporley
Lower Kinnerton
Gorstello
Dodleston
1
Wettenhall
Church Minshull
Tilstone Fearnall
Tiverton
Alpraham
Aldford
Pulford
Lavister
Milton Green
Newton
Tattenhall
Beeston
Calveley
Rossett
Trevalyn
Handley
Burwardsley
Spurstow
Bunbury
Wardle
Worleston
2
Marford
Churton
Peckforton
Haughton Moss
Harthill
Bulkeley
Holt
Farndon
Clutton
Barton
Gresford
Faddiley
Burland
Acton
Nantwich
Water Mill
Crewe
Cholmondeley Castle
Acton Park
Tilston
Chorley
Stapeley Water
Wrexham
3
Horton Green
Bickley Moss
Shocklach
Ebnal
Hampton Heath
Erddig NT
Marchwiel
Chorlton Lane
Malpas
No Man's Heath
Norbury
Wrenbury
Secret Bunker
Newtown
Cuddington Heath
Worthenbury
Bangor-is-y-coed
Tushingham cum Grindley
Marbury
Aston
Newhall
Hankelow
Threapwood
Bangor-on-Dee
Tallarn Green
Higher Wych
Bell o' th' Hill
Dodd's Green
Audlem
4
Wirswall
Canal
Grindley Brook
Whitchurch
Burleydam
Erbistock
Overton
Horseman's Green
Eglwys Cross
Broughall
Wilkesley
Coxbank
R Dee
97
Penley
Hanmer
Redbrook
Bronington
Ash Magna
Adderley
Knolton
Dudleston
Ash Parva
Ightfield
Street Dinas
Tilstock
Calverhall
5
St Martins
Ellesmere
Welshampton
Bettisfield
Whixall
Moreton Say
Perthy
Prees
Longford
Bletchley
Market Drayton
Welsh Frankton
Tetchill
Lyneal
Northwood
Fauls
Ternhill
Colemere
Newtown
Edstaston
Whittington
Hordley
Prees Green
Hawkstone
Hawkstone Park
Wollerton
6
English Frankton
Weston-under-Redcastle
Marchamley
Hodnet
Rednal
Loppington
Wem
Cockshutt
Noneley
Aston
Hodnet Hall
Bury Walls
Stoke upon Tern
Bagley
Haughton
Lee Brockhurst
Grimpo
West Felton
Eardiston
Wykey
Burlton
Weston Lullingfields
Preston Brockhurst
Booley
High Hatton
Ollerton
Child's Ercall
Peplow
Clive
Stanton upon Hine Heath
Myddle
Grinshill
7
Knockin
Eyton
Moreton Corbet
Ellerdine Heath
Eaton upon Tern
Newtown
Baschurch
Harmer Hill
Shawbury
Ruyton-XI-Towns
Great Bolas
Kinnerley
Little Ness
Preston Gubbals
Hadnall
Rowton
Nesscliffe
Yeaton
Adcote School
Astley
Cherrington
Kinton
Wilcott
Great Ness
Grafton
Walford Heath
Bomere Heath
Leaton
Albrighton
Poynton Green
Walton
Waters Upton
8
Pentre
Felton Butler
Fitz
High Ercall
Crudgington
Forton
83
Roden
Rodington Heath
Rodington
Haughmond Abbey
Bicton
Harlescott
Ditherington
Coton Hill
Underdale
Uffington
Long Waste
Eyton upon the Weald Moors
Sleapford
R Severn
R Perry
R Gowy
Shropshire Union Canal
1645
1644
1403
0 1 2 3 4 miles
0 1 2 3 4 5 kilometres

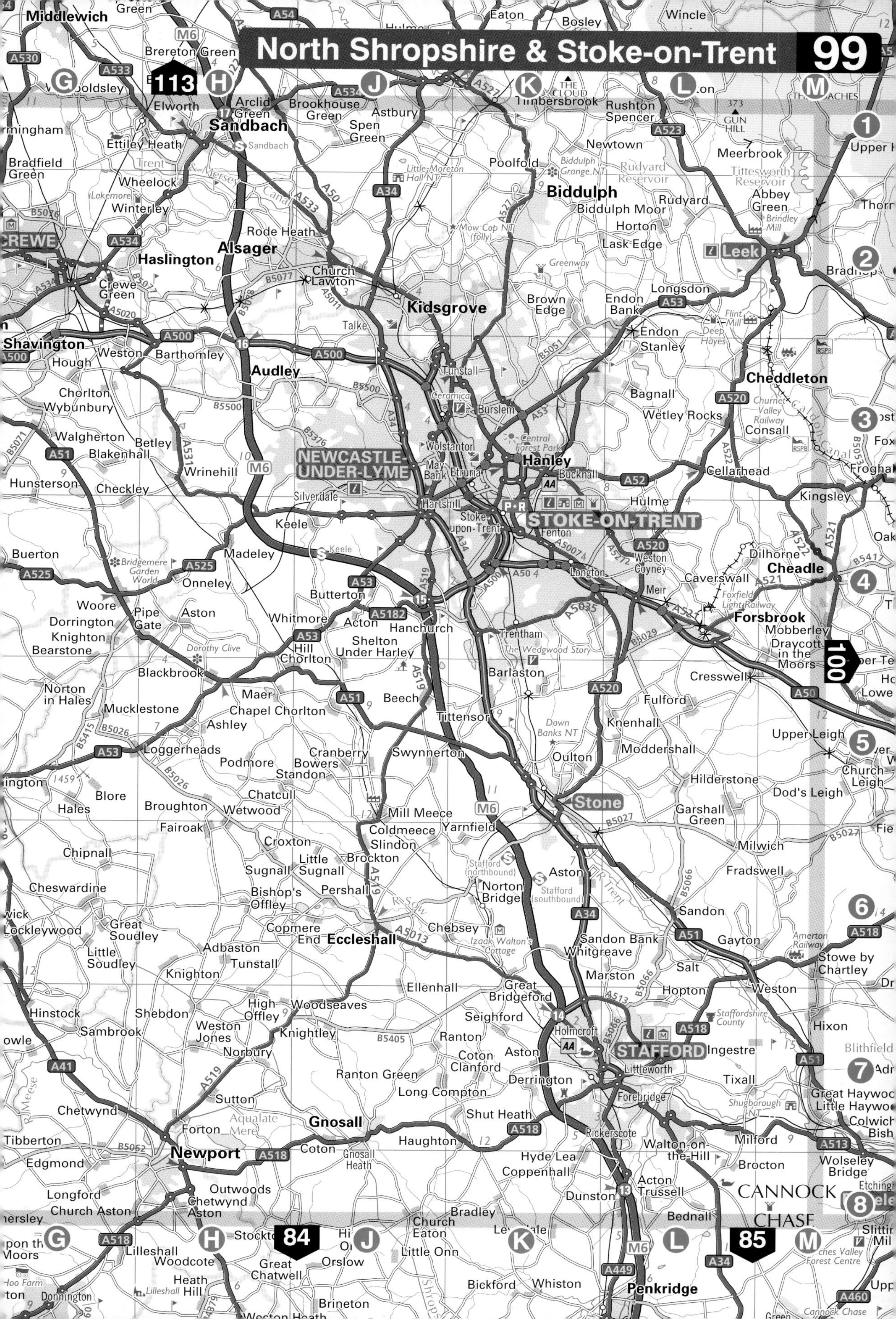
North Shropshire & Stoke-on-Trent
99
Middlewich
Green
A54
Eaton
Bosley
Wincle
M6
Brereton Green
A530
A533
113
G
H
J
K
L
M
Elworth
Arclid Green
Brookhouse Green
Astbury
Spen Green
THE CLOUD
Timbersbrook
Rushton Spencer
373
GUN HILL
Sandbach
Ettiley Heath
Bradfield Green
Wheelock
A534
A50
A34
Little Moreton Hall NT
Poolfold
Biddulph Grange NT
Newtown
Rudyard Reservoir
Meerbrook
Tittesworth Reservoir
Upper H
1
Lakemore
Winterley
B5076
A533
Mow Cop NT (folly)
A527
Biddulph
Biddulph Moor
Rudyard
Abbey Green
Brindley Mill
Thorn
CREWE
Haslington
Alsager
Rode Heath
Horton
Lask Edge
Leek
2
Bradnop
Crewe Green
B5077
Church Lawton
A5011
Kidsgrove
Greenway
Brown Edge
Endon Bank
Longsdon
A53
A5020
Talke
Flint Mill
Deep Hayes
Endon
Stanley
Shavington
A500
Weston
Barthomley
16
A500
B5051
RSPB
Hough
Audley
Tunstall
Cheddleton
Chorlton
Wybunbury
B5500
Ceramica
Burslem
Bagnall
A520
Churnet Valley Railway
Consall
Wetley Rocks
3
B5071
Walgherton
Betley
A531
B5376
Wolstanton
Central Forest Park
Caldon Canal
Blakenhall
A51
NEWCASTLE-UNDER-LYME
May Bank
Etruria
Hanley
Bucknall
A52
Cellarhead
Froghall
Hunsterson
Checkley
Wrinehill
M6
Silverdale
Hartshill
Hulme
Kingsley
AA
P+R
STOKE-ON-TRENT
Keele
Stoke-upon-Trent
Fenton
A5007
A520
Dilhorne
A522
Oak
Buerton
Bridgemere Garden World
A525
Madeley
Keele
A34
A519
A5272
Weston Coyney
Cheadle
A521
A525
Onneley
A53
Longton
Caverswall
4
A500
A50
Meir
Foxfield Light Railway
Butterton
15
A5035
Woore
Pipe Gate
Aston
Whitmore
A5182
Acton
Hanchurch
Forsbrook
Dorrington
Knighton
Bearstone
A53
Hill Chorlton
Shelton Under Harley
Trentham
B5029
Mobberley
Draycott in the Moors
100
Dorothy Clive
The Wedgwood Story
Upper Te
Norton in Hales
Blackbrook
A519
Barlaston
Cresswell
A50
Lower
Maer
A51
Beech
A520
Fulford
Mucklestone
Chapel Chorlton
Tittensor
Ashley
Down Banks NT
Knenhall
B5415
B5026
Upper Leigh
5
A53
Loggerheads
Cranberry
Bowers
Swynnerton
Moddershall
Podmore
Standon
Oulton
Church Leigh
Blore
Chatcull
Hilderstone
Dod's Leigh
B5026
Hales
Broughton
Wetwood
Mill Meece
M6
Stone
Garshall Green
Fairoak
Coldmeece
Yarnfield
B5027
B5027
Croxton
Slindon
Milwich
Chipnall
Little Sugnall
Brockton
Stafford (northbound)
Aston
Sugnall
Fradswell
Cheswardine
Pershall
Norton Bridge
Stafford (southbound)
B5066
Bishop's Offley
R. Sow
R. Trent
Sandon
6
Great Soudley
Lockleywood
Copmere End
Chebsey
A34
A518
Eccleshall
A5013
Sandon Bank
A51
Gayton
Amerton Railway
Little Soudley
Adbaston
Izaak Walton's Cottage
Whitgreave
Stowe by Chartley
Tunstall
Salt
Knighton
Marston
Ellenhall
Great Bridgeford
B5066
A513
Hopton
Weston
Hinstock
Woodseaves
High Offley
Shebdon
Seighford
14
Staffordshire County
Hixon
Sambrook
Weston Jones
Knightley
Holmcroft
A518
Ranton
Blithfield
B5405
Norbury
Aston
STAFFORD
Ingestre
A41
Coton Clanford
A51
7
Ranton Green
Derrington
Littleworth
Tixall
A519
Long Compton
Forebridge
Great Haywood
Little Haywood
Chetwynd
Sutton
Shugborough NT
Aqualate Mere
Shut Heath
Colwich
Gnosall
A518
Rickerscote
R. Meese
Tibberton
Forton
B5062
Haughton
Milford
A513
Walton-on-the-Hill
Edgmond
Newport
A518
Coton
Gnosall Heath
Hyde Lea
Brocton
Wolseley Bridge
Coppenhall
Longford
Outwoods
Acton Trussell
CANNOCK CHASE
Etching
Church Aston
Chetwynd Aston
Dunston
13
8
Bradley
Bednall
Church Eaton
A518
Stockton
84
Levedale
85
M6
A34
Lilleshall
Little Onn
Orslow
Woodcote
Great Chatwell
A449
Heath Hill
Lilleshall
Donnington
Bickford
Whiston
Penkridge
Brineton
Weston Heath
A460
Cannock Chase

100
114
99
85
86
A
B
C
D
E
F
1
2
3
4
5
6
7
8
PEAK DISTRICT
NATIONAL PARK
Hollinsclough
Longnor
Crowdecote
Pilsbury
Arbor Low Stone Circle
Youlgreave
Alport
Haddon Hall
Rowsley
Stanton in Peak
Darley Dale
Middleton
Birchover
Upper Tn
Churchtown
Darley Bridge
Wensley
Oaker Side
Brund
Sheen
Upper Hulme
Upper Elkstone
Hartington
Heathcote
Hulme End
Biggin
River Dove
Elton
Winster
Market House NT
Heights of Abraham
Masson Mills
Bonsall
Matlock Bath
Riber Castle
Abbey Green
Brindley Mill
Thorncliff
R Hamps
Warslow
Grangemill
Aldwark
Ible
Gulliver's Kingdom
Cromford
Cromford Mill
Bradnop
Onecote
Butterton
Alstonefield
Alsop en le Dale
Longcliffe
Middleton
Bolehill
Wetton
Grindon
Hope
Brassington
Ballidon
Wirksworth
Little Bolehill
Whatstandwell
Ford
Milldale
Parwich
R Manifold
Dove Dale
Carsington
Hopton
Alderwasley
Tissington
Bradbourne
Carsington Water
Cheddleton
Winkhill
Waterfall
Ilam
Calton
Hognaston
Kirk Ireton
Beighton Hill
Churnet
Caldon Canal
Waterhouses
Ilam Park NT
Thorpe
Fenny Bentley
Kniveton
Shottle
Ipstones
Cauldon
Blackwall
Idridgehay
Foxt
Blore
Atlow
Biggin
Ireton Wood
Froghall
Swinscoe
Mapleton
Hulland Ward
Hillcliffلane
Shottlegate
Ashbourne
Whiston
Near Cotton
Hulland
Turnditch
Cowers Lane
Kingsley
Stanton
Mayfield
Bradley
Cross o' th' hands
Hazelwood
Ramshorn
Clifton
Oakamoor
Middle Mayfield
Wootton
Osmaston
Dilhorne
Farley
Church Mayfield
Upper Ellastone
Mugginton
Alton Towers
Cheadle
Ellastone
Snelston
Darley Moor
Weston Underwood
Threapwood
Alton
Wyaston
Norbury
Brailsford
Kedleston
Mobberley
Bradley in the Moors
Denstone
Shirley
Kedleston Hall NT
Greatgate
Roston
Upper Tean
Croxden
Croxden
Yeaveley
Rodsley
Hollington
Kirk Langley
Hollington
Rocester
Foston Brk
Great Cubley
Alkmonton
Lower Tean
Marston Montgomery
Thurvaston
Longlane
Checkley
Longford
Little Cubley
Lees Green
Lees
Fole
Mackworth
Upper Leigh
Lower Leigh
Withington
Somersal Herbert
Boylestone
Sutton Brook
Radbourne
Stramshall
Harehill
Trusley
Church Leigh
Upper Nobut
Lane Ends
Dod's Leigh
Doveridge
Mickleover
Uttoxeter
Church Broughton
Sutton on the Hill
Field
Bramshall
Uttoxeter
R Dove
Sudbury Hall NT
Milwich
Foston
Etwall
Burnaston
Birch Cross
Sudbury
Marchington
Scropton
Findern
Hatton
Hilton
Kingstone
Marston on Dove
Gorsty Hill
Egginton
Amerton Railway
Draycott in the Clay
Tutbury
Rolleston
Willington
Stowe by Chartley
Hanbury
Repton
Drointon
Heatley
Stretton
Milton
Weston
Newborough
Anslow
Newton Solney
Hixon
Newton
Abbots Bromley
Anslow Gate
Horninglow
Blithfield Reservoir
BURTON UPON TRENT
Admaston
Winshill
Newchurch
Bretby
Great Haywood
Hoar Cross
Rangemore
Little Haywood
Colwich
Tatenhill
Stapenhill
Bishton
Hartshorne
Milford
Colton
Hadley End
Dunstall
Branston
Swadlincote
Brocton
Wolseley Bridge
Blithbury
Hamstall Ridware
Olive Green
Woodhouses
Barton-under-Needwood
CANNOCK CHASE
Etchinghill
Rugeley
Hill Ridware
Morrey
Yoxall
Walton-on-Trent
Castle Gresley
Trent Valley
Cauldwell
Slitting Mill
Mavesyn Ridware
Nethertown
Wychnor
Rosliston
King's Bromley
Coton in the Elms
Overseal
Armitage
Alrewas
National Memorial Arboretum
Donisthorpe
Longdon
Fradley
Cannock Chase
Lullington
0 1 2 3 4 miles
0 1 2 3 4 5 kilometres
A53
A523
A52
A515
A517
A521
A522
A50
A516
A38
A511
A5121
A518
A51
A513
A444
A514
B5053
B5054
B5056
A5012
B5035
B5023
B5417
B5032
B5030
B5033
B5024
B5020
B5027
B5017
B5013
B5014
B5234
B5016
B5008
B5353
B5004
B5003
R Trent
R Derwent

Peak District & Nottingham
101
115
102
87
G
H
J
K
L
M
1
2
3
4
5
6
7
8
Holmewood
North Wingfield
Stainsby Mill NT
Houghton
New Houghton
Wellow
Alton
Ashover
Clay Cross
Handley
Ogston Resr
Pilsley
Tibshelf
Dunsill
Teversal
Skegby
Clipstone
Sherwood Forest
Eakring
Stretton
Morton
MANSFIELD
Bilsthorpe
Highoredish
Higham
Stonebroom
Newton
Sutton in Ashfield
Huthwaite
Brackenfield
Shirland
Blackwell
Rainworth
White Post Modern Farm Centre
Wessington
Westhouses
Plaistow
South Wingfield
Wingfield Manor
Alfreton
South Normanton
Kirkby in Ashfield
Blidworth
Farnsfield
Edingley
Halam
SHERWOOD FOREST
Pinxton
Ravenshead
Crich
Swanwick
Somercotes
Pye Bridge
Selston
Annesley Woodhouse
Annesley
Blidworth Bottoms
Papplewick Pumping Station
Newstead Abbey
Newstead
Fritchley
Pentrich
Ironville
Midland
Heage
Ripley
Codnor
Papplewick
Linby
Oxton
Halloughton
Underwood
Burntstump
Mount Pleasant
Belper
Loscoe
Denby Potteries
Brinsley
Hucknall
Calverton
Moorgreen
Greasley
Broom Hill
Bestwood Village
Woodborough
Epperstone
Gonalston
Eastwood
Newthorpe
NOTTINGHAM
Lowdham
Kilburn
Denby
Horsley Woodhouse
Heanor
Milford
Holbrook
Makeney
Horsley
Smalley
Shipley
American Adventure
Kimberley
Arnold
Daybrook
Lambley
Burton Joyce
Coxbench
Cotmanhay
Awsworth
Nuthall
Bulwell
Old Basford
Sherwood
Mapperley
Mapperley Park
Gedling
Carlton
Shelford
Ilkeston
Cossall
Bilborough
Whitemoor
Little Eaton
Morley
West Hallam
Kirk Hallam
Little Hallam
Strelley
Trowell
Stoke Bardolph
Breadsall
Stanley
Wollaton
Wollaton Hall
Lenton
Colwick
Adbolton
Holme Pierrepont
National Water Sports
Radcliffe on Trent
Allestree
Darley Abbey
Oakwood
Dale
Stanton by Dale
Stapleford
DERBY
Chaddesden
Spondon
Ockbrook
Risley
Sandiacre
Beeston
Gamston
West Bridgford
Borrowash
Chilwell
Rylands
Toton
Edwalton
Tollerton
Cotgrave
Clipston
Owthorpe
Crewton
Alvaston
Normanton
Breaston
Draycott
Barton in Fabis
Clifton
Elvaston
Allenton
Long Eaton
Ruddington
Plumtree
Normanton on the Wolds
Sinfin
Thulston
Great Central (Nottingham) Railway
Bradmore
Keyworth
Chellaston
Shardlow
Thrumpton
Gotham
Stanton on the Wolds
Aston-upon-Trent
Bunny
Barrow upon Trent
Swarkestone
Weston-upon-Trent
Hemington
Ratcliffe on Soar
Kingston on Soar
Widmerpool
Stanton by Bridge
Castle Donington
Kegworth
West Leake
East Leake
Wysall
Costock
Melbourne
Donington Park
Grand Prix Collection
Nottingham East Midlands
Willoughby-on-the-Wolds
Isley Walton
Diseworth
Long Whatton
Sutton Bonington
Wilson
West Thorpe
Rempstone
Ticknall
Breedon on the Hill
Calke Abbey NT
Calke
Tonge
Zouch
Normanton on Soar
Wymeswold
Hathern
Stanford on Soar
Hoton
Staunton Harold NT
Worthington
Cotes
Belton
Burton on the Wolds
Lount
Shepshed
Loughborough
Walton on the Wolds
Smisby
Osgathorpe
Ragdale
Barrow upon Soar
Seagrave
Thringstone
Nanpantan
Swannington
Charnwood Forest
Mount St Bernard
Beacon Hill
Woodhouse
Thrussington
Sileby
Ratcliffe on the Wreake
Snibston Discovery Park
Whitwick
Packington
Ravenstone
Coalville
Woodhouse Eaves
Great Central Railway
Mountsorrel
Rothley
Cossington
Rearsby
Shoby
Hickling
M1
A61
A617
A614
A60
A38
A6
A610
A611
A608
A609
A6097
A612
A6002
A52
A5111
A514
A50
A453
A6006
A606
A46
A42
A512
A511
A6004
B6014
B6019
B6020
B6386
B684
B5010
B5324
B676
B587

102
A
B
C
D
E
F
116
101
87
88
1
2
3
4
5
6
7
8
Wellow
Moorhouse
Girton
Besthorpe
Carlton-
Scarle
South Scarle
Thorpe on the Hill
North Hykeham
South Hykeham
Low Fields
R Witham
Harmston
Ompton
Ossington
Kneesall
Norwell Woodhouse
Sherwood Forest
A614
Eakring
Maplebeck
A616
Cromwell
Norwell
Caunton
Dolls
Collingham
Swinderby
Haddington
Aubourn
Thurlby
Coleby
Bassingham
Boothby Graffoe
Bilsthorpe
Bathley
Holme
A1133
A46
Brough
Norton Disney
Carlton-le-Moorland
North Muskham
Kirklington
Winkburn
White Post Modern Farm Centre
Winthorpe
Langford
Stapleford
Nottinghamshire Aircraft
R Brant
Welling
Farnsfield
Hockerton
A1
Edingley
A617
Kelham
A6065
1644
Southwell
Normanton
Upton
Averham
Coddington
Beckingham
Brant Broughton
Halam
Newark-on-Trent
A17
Southwell
Rolleston
New Balderton
Balderton
Barnby in the Willows
Stragglethorpe
Leadenham
B6386
Halloughton
Farndon
Fiskerton
Oxton
Morton
A612
East Stoke
Hawton
Fenton
Thorpe
Bleasby
Claypole
Fulbeck
Caythorpe
Thurgarton
Epperstone
R Devon
R Trent
1487
Stubton
Brandon
Elston
Gonalston
Cotham
Dry Doddington
Frieston
A607
Lowdham
Syerston
Hoveringham
Flintham
Hough-on-the-Hill
Normanton
Lambley
A6097
Kneeton
Sibthorpe
Long Bennington
Gelston
Carlton Scroop
Caythorpe
Shelton
Burton Joyce
Gunthorpe
Screveton
Hawksworth
Westborough
Hougham
Sudbrook
Marston
Flawborough
Kilvington
Foston
Honington
East Bridgford
Car Colston
Thoroton
Alverton
Barkston
Shelford
Stoke Bardolph
Newton
Scarrington
Orston
Normanton
Syston
Allington
Saxondale
Aslockton
Bingham
Whatton
Vale of Belvoir
Belton
Belton House NT
Holme Pierrepont
A52
Bottesford
Grantham North
Great Gonerby
Radcliffe on Trent
Elton
Sedgebrook
Londonthorpe
B1174
Cropwell Butler
Sutton
Muston
Tithby
Granby
Barrowby
Grantham
Redmile
New Somerby
B6403
Canal
Barnstone
Cotgrave
Cropwell Bishop
Langar
Barkestone-le-Vale
Belvoir
Woolsthorpe
Clipston
Owthorpe
Plungar
Belvoir Castle
Little Ponton
Normanton on the Wolds
Colston Bassett
Grantham Canal
Denton
Harlaxton
B1176
A606
Harston
Stathern
Knipton
Stroxton
Great Ponton
Kinoulton
Harby
Croxton Kerrial
Branston
Hose
Hickling
Eastwell
Eaton
Bassingthorpe
Long Clawson
Stoke Rochford
R Witham
Easton
Goadby Marwood
Bescaby
Saltby
Skillington
Nether Broughton
Upper Broughton
Waltham on the Wolds
Woolsthorpe Manor NT
Wycomb
Sproxton
Woolsthorpe-by-Colsterworth
Colsterworth
Chadwell
Stonesby
Holwell
Scalford
Old Dalby
Buckminster
Stainby
Ab Kettleby
Wartnaby
North Witham
Grimston
Coston
Melton Mowbray
B676
Saxelbye
Sewstern
Gunby
Garthorpe
Thorpe Arnold
Shoby
Freeby
Asfordby Hill
Saxby
Ragdale
A6006
South Witham
Asfordby
Kirby Bellars
Wymondham
Frisby on the Wreake
Brentingby
Stapleford
Cribbs Meadow
Hoby
R Eye
Edmondthorpe
Thistleton
Burton Lazars
Clipsham
Teigh
Market Overton
Stretton
B6047
Little Dalby
Whissendine
Barrow
Greetham
Ashwell
Rutland
Cottesmore
Gaddesby
Leesthorpe
East Goscote
Rearsby
Thrussington
Ratcliffe on the Wreake
0 1 2 3 4 miles
0 1 2 3 4 5 kilometres

117
118
104
89
G
H
J
K
L
M
1
2
3
4
5
6
7
8
Potterhanworth
Nocton
Sots Hole
Kirkstead
Woodhall Spa
Kirkby on Bain
Enderby
Hareby
East Kirkby
Revesby
Metheringham
Blankney
Martin
Timberland Delph
Mareham le Fen
Tumby
Tattershall Thorpe
Scopwick
Kirkby Green
Timberland
Tattershall
Coningsby
Tumby Woodside
New Bolingbro
Tattershall College
Tattershall Castle NT
Battle of Britain Memorial Flight
Thorpe Tilney
Rowston
Ashby de la Launde
Walcott
Hawthorn Hill
New York
Dogdyke
Scrub Hill
Billinghay
Digby
West Fen
Chapel Hill
Bloxholm
Dorrington
North Kyme
Ruskington
R Witham
Holland Fen
Gipsey Bridge
Frithville
Cranwell
Anwick
Fishtoft Drove
Leasingham
R Slea
South Kyme
Langrick
Evedon
North Rauceby
Holdingham
Ewerby
Anton's Gowt
Kirkby la Thorpe
Howell
Sleaford
South Rauceby
Asgarby
East Heckington
Holland Fen
Boston
Ancaster
Quarrington
Heckington
The Pearoom
Wilsford
Great Hale
Silk Willoughby
Burton Pedwardine
Little Hale
Kelby
Swarby
Helpringham
Culverthorpe
Aswarby
Scredington
Swineshead
Heydour
Oasby
Aisby
Aunsby
Osbournby
Spanby
Bicker
Kirton
Swaton
Dembleby
Newton
Northorpe
Wigtoft
Haceby
Threekingham
Donington
Sutterton
Braceby
Walcot
Horbling
Burtoft
Algarkirk
Billingborough
Sapperton
Pickworth
Folkingham
Humby
South Forty Foot Drain
Quadring
Fosdyke
Laughton
Pointon
Westhorpe
Gosberton
R Welland
Aslackby
Risegate
Lenton
Ingoldsby
Dowsby
Rippingale
Surfleet
Moulton Seas End
Irnham
Kirkby Underwood
Dunsby
Spalding Tropical Forest
Pinchbeck
Corby Glen
Hacconby
Weston
Hanthorpe
Morton
Mill Green
Springfields
Moulton
Elsthorpe
Fulney
Grimsthorpe
Dyke
Spalding
Swinstead
Edenham
Bourne
Twenty
Creeton
R Glen
Little Bytham
Cowbit
Moulton Chapel
Lound
Witham on the Hill
Toft
Thurlby
Manthorpe
Deeping Fen
Bedford
Level
Carlby
Baston
Braceborough
Whaplode Drove
A15
A17
A52
A153
A151
A155
A1121
A16
A152
A6121
A1073
B1178
B1202
B1188
B1189
B1191
B1192
B1183
B1184
B1429
B1209
B1517
B1395
B1391
B1394
B1181
B1397
B1356
B1177
B1176
B1180
B1173
B1172
B1357
B1165
B1135

Hareby
Hundleby
Old Bolingbroke
Bolingbroke
Toynton All Saints
Halton Holegate
Northcote
Monksthorpe
Great Steeping
Bratoft
Burgh le Marsh
A158
Skegness
118
119
A
B
C
D
E
F
East Kirkby
Lincolnshire Aviation
Keal Cotes
Little Steeping
Firsby
B1195
Croft
1
Mareham le Fen
Revesby
Stickford
Fendike Corner
Thorpe St Peter
Wainfleet Haven
Wainfleet All Saints
Tumby Woodside
New Bolingbroke
Stickney
New Leake
Eastville
Gibraltar Point
A52
2
East Fen
Friskney
A16
West Fen
B1183
Northlands
18
Leake Common Side
23
Sibsey Trader
Sibsey
Frithville
B1184
Wrangle
3
Fishtoft Drove
B1183
Old Leake
Hill Dyke
Leverton
Anton's Gowt
Benington
A52
Butterwick
Fen
Boston
A1121
A52
4
Freiston
Fishtoft
Scrane End
Wyberton East
B1391
B1397
103
A16
Frampton
The Haven
RSPB
Kirton
THE WASH
Skeldyke
5
Sutterton
Algarkirk
Fosdyke
A16
R Welland
Holbeach St Matthew
6
Holbeach St Mark's
Holbeach Marsh
Gedney Drove End
B1359
A17
B1357
Saracen's Head
Moulton Seas End
Holbeach Hurn
Penny Hill
Gedney Dyke
Lutton
Fleet Hargate
B1515
The Wash
Weston
A151
Moulton
Whaplode
Holbeach
Fleet
Gedney
7
A17
Butterfly & Falconry Park
Long Sutton
Sutton Bridge
Gedney Broadgate
Great Ouse
B1165
B1168
Terrington St Clement
Walpole Cross Keys
B1390
Clenchwarton
African Violet Centre
West Lynn
B1357
A17
Moulton Chapel
Tydd Gote
Tydd St Mary
Walpole St Andrew
Tilney All Saints
8
Holbeach St Johns
B1165
Sutton St James
Tilney High End
A47
89
90
Four Gotes
Walpole St Peter
Tydd St Giles
B1165
River Nene
Tilney St Lawrence
0 1 2 3 4 miles
0 1 2 3 4 5 kilometres
Newton
West Walton
Sutton St Edmund
A1101
Walpole
Terrington
Wiggenhall
Whaplode Drove

G
H
J
K
L
M
1
2
3
4
5
6
7
8
North Norfolk Heritage Coast
Holkam Bay
Scolt Head Island
Brancaster Bay
Peddars Way & Norfolk Coast Path
Blakeney Point
Holme next the Sea
Old Hunstanton
Hunstanton
Brancaster
Brancaster Staithe
Burnham Norton
Burnham Overy Staithe
Holkham
Wells-next-the-sea
Titchwell
Thornham
Branodunum NT
Burnham Deepdale
Burnham Market
Burnham Overy
Holkham Hall
Warham St Mary
Warham All Saints
Wighton
Ringstead
Burnham Thorpe
New Holkham
Creake
Wells & Walsingham Light Railway
106
Summerfield
North Creake
Heacham
Norfolk Lavender
Peddars Way & Norfolk Coast Path
Docking
Stanhoe
Little Walsingham
Great Walsingham
Sedgeford
South Creake
North Barsham
Houghton St Giles
Fring
Bircham Newton
Snettisham
Park Farm
West Barsham
East Barsham
Great Snoring
Thursford
Ingoldisthorpe
Shernborne
Syderstone
Great Bircham
Bircham Tofts
R Stiffkey
Little Snoring
Dersingham
Sculthorpe
Kettlestone
Anmer
Dunton
Shereford
Tattersett
Coxford
Fakenham
Wolferton
Houghton Hall
Hempton
Sandringham
West Newton
West Rudham
New Houghton
Tatterford
Little Ryburgh
Babingley River
East Rudham
Toftrees
Flitcham
Great Ryburgh
Helhoughton
East Raynham
Colkirk
Harpley
Castle Rising
Hillington
West Raynham
Little Massingham
South Raynham
Gateley
Congham
Horningtoft
Great Massingham
Roydon
Grimston
Weasenham St Peter
Whissonsett
North Wootton
Wellingham
Brisley
Weasenham All Saints
North Elmham
Tittleshall
Stanfield
Gayton
Rougham
East Bilney
King's Lynn
Mileham
Beetley
Ashwicken
Gayton Thorpe
Litcham
Gressenhall
Middleton
East Winch
East Walton
West Lexham
East Lexham
91
West Acre
Newton
Longham
Gressenhall Green
North Runcton
Blackborough End
West Bilney
South Acre
Great Dunham
Setchey
Pentney
Dereham
A149
A148
A1065
A47
A1067
B1155
B1355
B1153
B1454
B1440
B1439
B1145
B1105
B1146
B1110

A
B
C
D
E
F
1
2
3
North Norfolk Heritage Coast
Blakeney Point NT
Blakeney Point
Morston Marshes NT
Wells-next-the-sea
Morston
Blakeney
Cley next the Sea
Muckleburgh Collection
Sheringham
West Runton
East Runton
Cromer
4
Stiffkey
Wiveton
Salthouse
Weybourne
A149
St Mary
Cockthorpe
Kelling
Sheringham Park NT
Upper Sheringham
Beeston Regis
Norfolk Shire Horse Centre
Overstr
Warham All Saints
Langham
Glandford
A1082
Wighton
B1156
Saxlingham
North Norfolk Railway
Bodham
A148
Aylmerton
Sid
105
R Glaven
Felbrigg
A149
Binham
Holt
West Beckham
East Beckham
Northre
Field Dalling
Letheringsett
Felbrigg Hall NT
Crossdale Street
Gresham
Baconsthorpe
B1436
Sharrington
Great Walsingham
Holt Lowes
Metton
Southrepps
Hempstead
Bessingham
Sustead
5
Hindringham
Bale
B1110
Baconsthorpe
Roughton
Houghton St Giles
Thornage
B1436
Brinton
Hanworth
Thursford
Hunworth
Plumstead
Thurgarton
Thorpe Market
Great Snoring
Edgefield Green
A140
East Barsham
Stody
Matlask
Gunthorpe
Briningham
Edgefield
Aldborough
Bradfiel
Thursford
B1354
A149
R Stiffkey
Little Barningham
Antingham
Barney
A148
Melton Constable
Wickmere
Little Snoring
B1354
Erpingham
Suffield
B1149
Croxton
Briston
Calthorpe
Colby
Swanton Novers
Mannington Gardens
Wolterton Park
Kettlestone
Fulmodeston
Saxthorpe
Itteringham
North Wals
6
Pensthorpe Waterfowl Park
R Bure
Banningham
Corpusty
Hindolveston
Ingworth
B1110
Blickling
Blickling Hall NT
Little Ryburgh
Stibbard
Thurning
Oulton
Felmingham
B1146
Tuttington
Wood Norton
Oulton Street
Great Ryburgh
A1067
Heydon
Aylsham
Wood Dalling
B1149
Guestwick
Burgh next Aylsham
R Wensum
Guist
B1145
Foulsham
Salle
Swan Abb
Bure Valley Railway
Gateley
Twyford
Themelthorpe
Oxnead
Cawston
Marsham
Lamas
7
Horningtoft
Reepham
Brampton
B1110
Bintree
Eastgate
Saxon Cathedral
Foxley
Brisley
Whitwell Street
Buxton Heath
Buxton
North Elmham
B1145
R Bure
Billingford
field
Bawdeswell
Brandiston
Stratton Strawless
East Bilney
Hevingham
B1145
Sparham
B1354
B1147
Norfolk Wildlife Park
Mileham
Beetley
Worthing
Alderford
Swannington
Horstead
B1146
Felthorpe
B1110
Hainford
Lyng
Dinosaur
8
Swanton Morley
Lenwade
Upgate
Frettenham
Gressenhall
B1149
Elsing
Morton on the Hill
St Helena
A
B
C
D
92
E
Newton St Faith
F
B1150
Gressenhall
Horst
onghan
Cro
0 1 2 3 4 miles
0 1 2 3 4 5 kilometres
A1067
Vensum
Thorpe Marriot
A140
Weston Longville
Horsham St Faith
Spixwo
B1110
North Tuddenham
Aviation
Dereham
A47
Hockering
Ringland
Taverham
Drayton
Norwich

G
H
J
K
L
M
1
2
3
4
5
6
7
8
Mundesley
Stow Mill
Paston
B1159
Knapton
Bacton
Edingthorpe
Walcott
Edingthorpe Green
Witton
Ridlington
Happisburgh
Whimpwell Green
Meeting House Hill
Happisburgh Common
Honing
Lessingham
Hempstead
Ingham Corner
Sea Palling
Briggate
East Ruston
Worstead
Ingham
Waxham
Stalham
Calthorpe Street
Dilham
A149
Hickling
Smallburgh
Sutton
Hickling Green
Horsey
Barton Turf
Wood Street
Horsey Windpump NT
Tunstead
Barton Broad
Hickling Broad
Neatishead
Catfield
Irstead
R Ant
Potter Heigham
A1151
Winterton-on-Sea
Hoveton
Ludham
Martham
Bastwick
Hemsby
Hemsby Hole
A1062
R Thurne
Upper Street
Horning
Repps
93
Scratby
Woodbastwick
Thurne
Burgh St Margaret
Ormesby St Margaret
Broadland Conservation Centre
California
Clippesby
Ormesby St Michael
Salhouse
Ranworth
Pilson Green
Fairhaven
Cargate
Billockby
Caister-on-Sea
B1140
New

North Anglesey Heritage Coast
The Skerries
Wylfa Head
Cemaes Bay
Porth Wen
Bull Bay
Amlwch
Llaneilian
Cemlyn Bay
Hen Borth
Cemaes
Burwen
CARMEL HEAD
Tregele
A5025
Rhosbeirio
Llanfairynghornwy
Llanfechell
Bodewryd
Penysarn
Holyhead Bay
Church Bay
Llanrhyddlad
Carreglefn
Rhosybol
Dublin
Dun Laoghaire
Llanfaethlu
Llyn Alaw
B5111
Porth Tywynmawr
Llanddeusant
Afon Alaw
Elim
North Stack
Breakwater Quarry
Llanfwrog
Gogarth Bay
Llanerchymedd
Holyhead Mountain Hut Group
B5112
Capel Coch
South Stack
Holyhead
Llanfachraeth
Coedana
Holyhead Mountain Heritage Coast
Penrhos-Feilw
Llyn Llywenan
Kingsland
Llanynghenedl
ANGLESEY
Penrhyn Mawr
Porth Dafarch NT
Trefignath
A5
A55
Valley
B5109
Bodedern
B5111
Trearddur Bay
B4545
Caergeiliog
B5112
Llynfaes
Rhosmeirch
HOLY ISLAND
Four Mile Bridge
Llanfihangel yn Nhowyn
Bryngwran
B5109
Bodffordd
Llanfair-yn-Neubwll
Gwalchmai
Oriel Ynys Mon
Rhoscolyn
Rhoscolyn Head
Plas Cymyran
Anglesey
A5
A5114
A4080
Ty Newydd
Cerrigceinwen
Cymyran Bay
Pencarnisiog
Llangristiolus
Rhosneigr
Llanfaelog
Din Dryfol
A4080
Hen Blas
Pentre Berw
B4422
Capel Mawr
Barclodiad y Gawres
Afon Cefni
Bethel
Porth Trecastell
B4419
Aberffraw
Llangadwaladr
Malltraeth
Bodowyr Burial Chamber
Llangaffo
A4080
B4421
B4419
Aberffraw Bay
Llanfair-y-Cwmwd
Dwyran
Newborough
B4419
Llangeinwen
Aberffraw Bay Heritage Coast
Foel Farm Park
Malltraeth Bay
Caernarfon
Llanddwyn Island
Highland Railway
Foryd Bay
Air World
0 1 2 3 4 miles
0 1 2 3 4 5 kilometres

95

G
H
J
K
L
M
1
2
3
4
5
6
7
8
Dulas Bay
Moelfre
Llanallgo
Benllech
Red Wharf Bay
Red Wharf Bay
Llanddona
Pentraeth
Llangoed
Puffin Island
Penmon Priory
Toll
Black Point
Beaumaris
Gaol & Courthouse
Llansadwrn
Llandegfan
Menai Bridge
Bangor
Anglesey Column
Llanfair P G
Bryn Celli Ddu
Britannia Bridge
Plas Newydd NT
Penrhyn NT
Llandygai
Tal-y-bont
Y Felinheli
Seion
Pentir
Rhyd-y-groes
Glasinfryn
Tregarth
Bethesda
Rachub
Llanllechid
Bethel
Llanddeiniolen
Greenwood Centre
Saron
Rhiwlas
Llanrug
Deiniolen
Segontium NT
Caeathro
Cwm-y-glo
Brynrefail
Llyn Padarn
Llanberis Lake Railway
Llanberis
Electric Mountain
Welsh Slate
Dolbadarn
Waunfawr
Nant Peris
Llyn Peris
Llanfairfechan
Abergwyngregyn
Afon Anafon
Aber Waterfall
580 MOEL WINION
757 Y DROSGL
942 FOEL-FRAS
1062 CARNEDD LLEWELYN
1044 CARNEDD DAFYDD
923 ELIDIR FAWR
946 Y GARN
917 Y TRYFAN
Llyn Ogwen
Afon Caseg
Afon Dulyn
Llyn Eigiau
Afon Ddu
Llyn Cowlyd
Llyn Crafnant
SNOWDONIA NATIONAL PARK
610 TAL-Y-FAN
Penmaenmawr
Dwygyfylchi
Conwy Bay
Conwy
Capelulo
Llansanffraid Glan Conwy
Henryd
Rowen
Ty'n-y-Groes
Llanbedr-y-Cennin
Tal-y-Bont
Dolgarrog
Trefriw Woollen Mill
Trefriw
Llanrwst
Gwydir Castle
Gwydir Uchaf Chapel
Geirionydd
Vale of Conwy
Bodnant NT
Graig
Tal-y-Cafn
Eglwysbach
Llanddoget
Pentre-tafarn-y-fedw
Great Orme Heritage Coast
GREAT ORMES HEAD
Llandudno
Deganwy
Llandudno Junction
Little Ormes Head
Llandrillo-yn-Rhos
National Mountain Centre
A55
A5
A470
A545
A5025
A4087
A5122
A4244
A4086
A4085
A487
A546
B5109
B5110
B5108
B5420
B4547
B4366
B4409
B5106
B5115
B5113
95
96
110

A
B
C
D
E
F
1
2
3
4
5
6
7
8
109
Little Ormes Head
Penrhyn Bay
Rhos-on-Sea
Llandrillo-yn-Rhos
Colwyn Bay
Kinmel Bay
Abergele Roads
Kinmel Bay
Rhyl
Prestatyn
Gronant
Llanasa
Gwaenysgor
Meliden
Trelawnyd
Dyserth
Cwm
Offa's Dyke
Rhuddlan
Towyn
Pensarn
Llanddulas
Llysfaen
Rhyd-y-foel
Abergele
Llandudno Junction
Llanelian-yn-Rhos
Bryn-y-Maen
Llansanffraid Glan Conwy
Dolwen
St George
Bodelwyddan
Rhuallt
St Asaph
Tremeirchion
Caerwys
Betws-yn-Rhos
Dawn
Bodnant NT
Graig
Tal-y-Cafn
Eglwysbach
Vale of Conwy
Llanfair Talhaiarn
River Elwy
Llannefydd
Trefnant
Bodfari
Vale of Clwyd
River Clwyd
Llangernyw
Henllan
Llansannan
Denbigh
Groes
Pentre Llanrhaeadr
Llandyrnog
Llanynys
Llanddoget
Pandy Tudur
Afon Deffyn
Afon Aled
Bylchau
Llanrwst
Pentre-tafarn-y-fedw
Gwythe
Nantglyn
Rhew
Llyn
96
97
A55
A470
A547
A548
A525
A544
A543
A541
A5151
B5115
B5113
B5383
B5381
B5382
B5384
B5428
B5429
B5435
B4501
B5118
B5119
RSPB
0 1 2 3 4 miles
0 1 2 3 4 5 kilometres

LIVERPOOL BAY
Formby
Hoylake
West Kirby
WIRRAL
Heswall
Neston
WALLASEY
BIRKENHEAD
CROSBY
BOOTLE
LIVERPOOL
Maghull
KIRKBY
Knowsley
Halewood
Bebington
ELLESMERE PORT
CHESTER
Connah's Quay
Flint
Holywell
Northop
Hawarden
Buckley
Mold
River Dee
River Mersey
Skelmersdale
Huyton
Speke
Garston
Queensferry

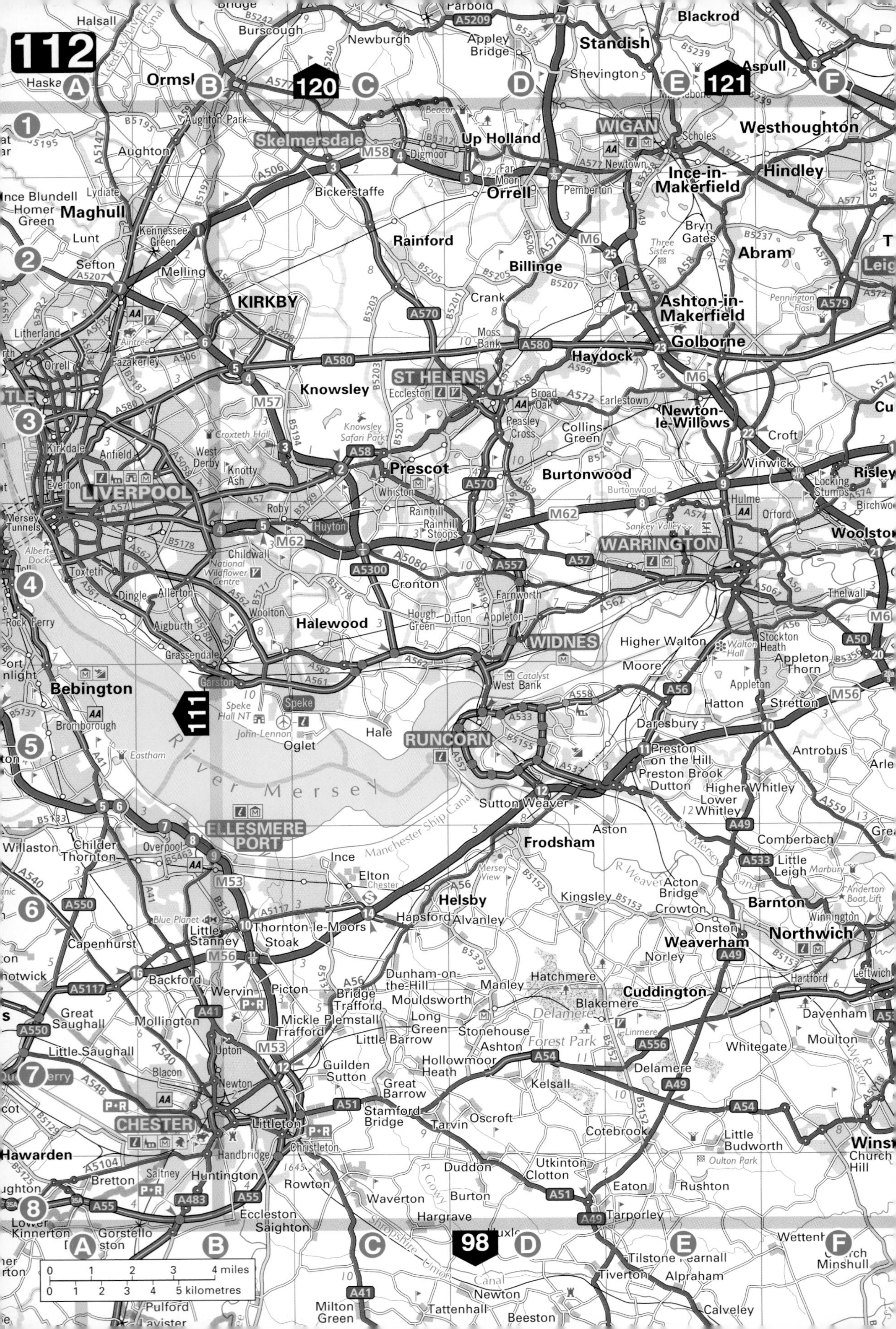

Halsall
Burscough
Parbold
A5209
Blackrod
Newburgh
Appley Bridge
Standish
Aspull
Ormsk
120
Shevington
121
Skelmersdale
Up Holland
WIGAN
Westhoughton
Aughton Park
Aughton
M58
Digmoor
Scholes
Newtown
Ince-in-Makerfield
Hindley
Orrell
Pemberton
Bickerstaffe
Lydiate
Maghull
Homer Green
Lunt
Kennessee Green
Rainford
Bryn Gates
Abram
Three Sisters
Sefton
Melling
Billinge
Leigh
Crank
Ashton-in-Makerfield
Pennington Flash
Litherland
KIRKBY
Aintree
Moss Bank
Golborne
Fazakerley
A580
Haydock
Knowsley
ST HELENS
Eccleston
Broad Oak
Earlestown
Newton-le-Willows
Croxteth Hall
Knowsley Safari Park
Peasley Cross
Collins Green
Croft
Kirkdale
Anfield
West Derby
Knotty Ash
Prescot
Burtonwood
Winwick
Risley
Everton
LIVERPOOL
Whiston
Locking Stumps
Mersey Tunnels
Roby
Huyton
Rainhill
Rainhill Stoops
Hulme
Orford
Birchwood
M62
Sankey Valley
WARRINGTON
Woolston
Albert Dock
Toxteth
Childwall
National Wildflower Centre
Cronton
Dingle
Allerton
Farnworth
Thelwall
Rock Ferry
Woolton
Aigburth
Halewood
Hough Green
Ditton
Appleton
WIDNES
Higher Walton
Walton Hall
Stockton Heath
Appleton Thorn
Port Sunlight
Grassendale
Moore
Catalyst
West Bank
Appleton
Garston
Bebington
111
Speke
Speke Hall NT
John Lennon
Hatton
Stretton
M56
Bromborough
Oglet
Hale
RUNCORN
Daresbury
Eastham
River Mersey
Preston on the Hill
Preston Brook
Dutton
Antrobus
Higher Whitley
Lower Whitley
Sutton Weaver
ELLESMERE PORT
Aston
Childer Thornton
Overpool
Willaston
Frodsham
Comberbach
Manchester Ship Canal
Ince
Elton
Mersey View
Little Leigh
Marbury
Anderton Boat Lift
Helsby
Acton Bridge
Kingsley
Crowton
Barnton
Blue Planet
Little Stanney
Thornton-le-Moors
Stoak
Hapsford
Alvanley
Capenhurst
Weaverham
Northwich
Onston
Norley
Winnington
Shotwick
Backford
Wervin
Picton
Dunham-on-the-Hill
Bridge Trafford
Mouldsworth
Hatchmere
Cuddington
Hartford
Great Saughall
Mollington
Mickle Trafford
Plemstall
Manley
Blakemere
Delamere Forest Park
Davenham
Moulton
Little Saughall
Upton
Little Barrow
Long Green
Stonehouse
Ashton
Linmere
Whitegate
Blacon
Guilden Sutton
Hollowmoor Heath
Delamere
Newton
Great Barrow
Kelsall
CHESTER
Littleton
Stamford Bridge
Tarvin
Oscroft
Cotebrook
Little Budworth
Winsford
Church Hill
Christleton
Hawarden
Handbridge
Oulton Park
Bretton
Saltney
Huntington
Duddon
Utkinton
Clotton
Rowton
Eaton
Rushton
Broughton
Waverton
Burton
Tarporley
Lower Kinnerton
Eccleston
Saighton
Hargrave
Gorstello
Dodleston
Huxley
98
Wettenhall
Church Minshull
Shropshire Union Canal
Tilstone Fearnall
Tiverton
Alpraham
Newton
Pulford
Milton Green
Tattenhall
Beeston
Calveley
Lavister
0 1 2 3 4 miles
0 1 2 3 4 5 kilometres

122
114
99
BOLTON
Farnworth
Little Lever
Radcliffe
Whitefield
Royton
Chadderton
MIDDLETON
OLDHAM
Walkden
Kearsley
Prestwich
Pendlebury
Swinton
Worsley
Failsworth
Mossley
Ashton-under-Lyne
MANCHESTER
Droylsden
Eccles
SALFORD
Audenshaw
Stalybridge
Dukinfield
Urmston
Irlam
Stretford
Denton
Hyde
Partington
Sale
Romiley
STOCKPORT
Altrincham
Gatley
Cheadle
Marple
Hazel Grove
Hale
Bowdon
Bramhall
High Lane
Disley
New Mills
Poynton
Whaley Bridge
Wilmslow
Knutsford
Alderley Edge
Prestbury
Bollington
Macclesfield
Holmes Chapel
Middlewich
Congleton
Biddulph

Marsden
Moor
Meltham
Brockholes
Thurstonland
High Hoyland
A637
Darton
Wilshaw
Scissett
Netherthong
Shepley
Upper Cumberworth
Lower Cumberworth
New Mill
Upperthong
123
Holmfirth
Birds Edge
Denby Dale
Cannon Hall
Cawthorne
A635
A
B
C
D
E
F
Diggle
Hepworth
Upper Denby
1
Dobcross
Holmbridge
Holme
Silkstone
A628
Uppermill
Ingbirchworth
Hoyland Swaine
Saddleworth Moor
A635
17
582
BLACK HILL
Crow Edge
Thurlstone
Silkstone Common
Greenfield
525
Holme Moss
Winscar Reservoir
Millhouse Green
B6106
Penistone
B6175
Townhead
A616
A629
A6024
Mossley
2
Pennine Way
537
FEATHERBED MOSS
A628
A616
Langsett
Oxspring
Thurgoland
450
Woodhead
Midhopestones
Stalybridge
A628
Garden Village
Deepcar
Howden Moors
Stocksbridge
B6105
Hollingworth
Tintwistle
Hadfield
628
BLEAKLOW HILL
546
MARGERY HILL
Bolsterstone
Ewden Village
R Don
Wharncliffe Side
3
A6102
Howden Reservoir
Broadbottom
Glossop
Snake Pass
512
R Alport
Bradfield
Oughtibridge
Werneth Low
Charlesworth
544
FEATHERBED TOP
A57
PEAK DISTRICT NATIONAL PARK
Worrall
A626
Chisworth
ROAD CLOSED SAT/SUN/BH MON
Derwent Reservoir
Low Bradfield
Stacey Bank
HIGH PEAK
Ughill
B6077
Mill Brow
A624
B6076
Rowarth
Brookhouses
THE PEAK
631
Ladybower Reservoir
A57
Stannington
A6101
4
Thornsett
636
14
Hayfield
Redmires Reservoir
Birch Vale
A6015
New Mills
Pennine Way
Edale
476
LOSE HILL
457
HIGH NEB
Fulwood
B6101
569
BROWN KNOLL
Blue John Cavern
R Noe
464
WIN HILL
A6013
Shepherd's Wheel
113
Mam Tor
Treak Cliff Cavern
Hope
Aston
Thornhill
Bamford
Furness Vale
Whaley Bridge
Chinley
Hope
Castleton
Peveril
A6187
Hathersage
B6062
Chestnut Centre
Speedwell Cavern
Peak Cavern
Hathersage Booths
Brick Houses
Dore
5
Tunstead Milton
Sparrowpit
Bradwell
A625
Chapel-en-le-Frith
Abney
Totley
Taxal
Kettleshulme
A623
Cockyard
Eyam Moor
Longshaw Estate NT
B5470
Dunge Valley
Fernilee
Dove Holes
Peak Forest
Little Hucklow
B6049
Great Hucklow
Nether Padley
B6521
A625
B6054
Combs
501
HOB TOR
Wheston
13
Grindlow
Grindleford
Goyt Valley
8
Foolow
Eyam
B6521
Froggatt
Tideswell
6
A6
A5004
Litton
Wardlow
Stoney Middleton
SHINING TOR
559
Fairfield
Tunstead
Calver
Curbar
Buxton
Wormhill
Miller's Dale
Cressbrook
Rowland
A623
A621
B5059
B6049
Great Longstone
B6001
Hassop
515
Poole's Cavern
Blackwell
B6465
Little Longstone
Baslow
B6050
Forest Chapel
A537
Solomon's Temple
Pilsley
551
AXE EDGE
A5270
Taddington
A6
A6020
A619
Chatsworth
Wadshelf
506
SHINING TOR
Chelmorton
Ashford in the Water
A619
Edensor
Hob Hurst's House
7
A54
Flagg
Sheldon
Magpie Mine
Bakewell
Bakewell
B6012
Beeley
Flash
Earl Sterndale
R Dove
Monyash
B5055
Over Haddon
R Wye
Allgreave
A515
Rowsley
Hollinsclough
Haddon Hall
Crowdecote
Alport
Stanton in Peak
R Derwent
Longnor
Arbor Low Stone Circle
Youlgreave
A53
Pilsbury
B5053
B5056
Nine Ladies
Darley Dale
Two Dales
Middleton
505
THE ROACHES
8
PEAK DISTRICT NATIONAL PARK
Stanton Lees
Peak Railway
Birchover
Churchtown
Darley Bridge
Oaker
Side
Brund
Upper
Wensley
100
B5054
Heathcote
Elton
Winster
Market House NT
Hartington
Biggin
Heights of Abraham
Masson Mills
Matlock
Hulme End
Warslow
A5012
B5056
Bonsall
Abbey
0 1 2 3 4 miles
0 1 2 3 4 5 kilometres

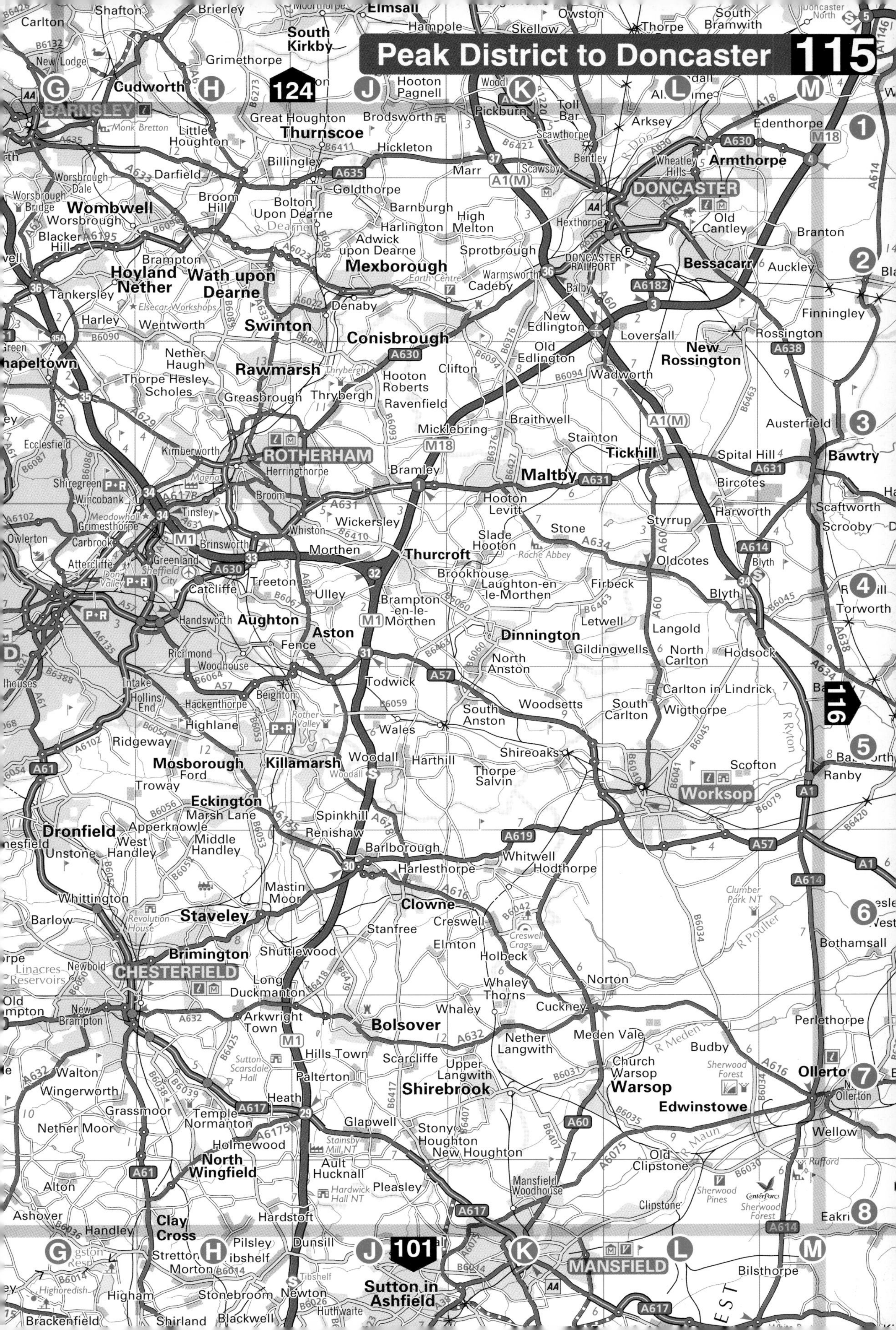
124
101
116
BARNSLEY
DONCASTER
ROTHERHAM
CHESTERFIELD
Worksop
MANSFIELD
Cudworth
Thurnscoe
Wombwell
Hoyland Nether
Wath upon Dearne
Mexborough
Swinton
Conisbrough
Rawmarsh
Armthorpe
Bessacarr
New Rossington
Tickhill
Maltby
Bawtry
Thurcroft
Aughton
Aston
Dinnington
Mosborough
Killamarsh
Eckington
Dronfield
Staveley
Clowne
Bolsover
Shirebrook
Warsop
Edwinstowe
Ollerton
North Wingfield
Clay Cross
Sutton in Ashfield

116
125
115
102
SCUNTHORPE
Burringham
Brumby
Broughton
Althorpe
Ashby
Bottesford
Yaddlethorpe
M180
M181
M18
A18
A1146
B1450
B1207
B1208
Hatfield Woodhouse
Sandtoft
Westgate
Belton
Beltoft
Carrhouse
East Butterwick
West Butterwick
Scawby
Messingham
Sturton
Epworth
Wroot
Old Rectory
Low Burnham
Manton
Scotterthorpe
Susworth
Branton
Auckley
Blaxton
Owston Ferry
Scotter
Gainsthorpe Medieval Village
Westwoodside
Haxey
East Lound
East Ferry
Finningley
B1396
A159
Scotton
Kirton in Lindsey
B1206
B1400
B1398
Rossington
A638
Craiselound
Wildsworth
Laughton
Northorpe
A15
R Idle
Gunthorpe
West Stockwith
Grayingham
Wadding
Misson
Misterton
East Stockwith
Blyton
B1205
Blyborough
Austerfield
Walkerith
Pilham
Aisby
Willoughton
Bawtry
A631
B1403
Walkeringham
R Trent
Morton
Corringham
Harwell
Everton
Chesterfield Canal
Gringley on the Hill
A161
Gainsborough
Hemswell
Scaftworth
Scrooby
Drakeholes
Wiseton
Beckingham
Springthorpe
Harpswell
Hemswell Cliff
A614
Blyth
Mattersey
Heapham
Ranskill
Clayworth
Saundby
Glentworth
B6045
Torworth
Lound
Bole
Lea
Upton
R Till
Fillingham
North Wheatley
B1241
Kexby
Hayton
Knaith
Sutton cum Lound
A634
A620
Willingham by Stow
Barnby Moor
Clarborough
Sturton le Steeple
Coates
Ingham
North Leverton with Habblesthorpe
Fenton
A156
Gate Burton
Cammeringham
Retford
Welham
Littleborough
Marton
Stow
Thorpe in the Fallows
Brattleby
Aisthorpe
Babworth
A1500
Ranby
South Leverton
Grove
Cottam
Brampton
Sturton by Stow
Scampton
A1
Ordsall
B6079
B6420
Treswell
Sundown Adventureland
Torksey
Bransby
Eaton
Nether Headon
Rampton
A57
Stokeham
North Carlton
South Carlton
Headon
Laneham
Gamston
Upton
East Drayton
Laughterton
Kettlethorpe
Saxilby
Fossdyke Navigation
Elkesley
Rockley
Askham
Burton
West Drayton
Dunham
Toll
Markham Moor
Ragnall
Bothamsall
Sibthorpe
Newton on Trent
Burton Waters
Milton
Darlton
North Clifton
Thorney
Skellingthorpe
East Markham
B1190
Bevercotes
West Markham
Fledborough
Walesby
High Marnham
South Clifton
Harby
LINCOLN
Perlethorpe
Tuxford
Wigsley
A46
A6075
Skegby
Spalford
Doddington
B6387
Low Marnham
Hartsholme
Swanpool Garden Suburb
Kirton
Normanton on Trent
Road Transport
Ollerton
Boughton
Egmanton
A1133
Swallow Beck
New Ollerton
Laxton
Weston
B1164
Grassthorpe
Whisby
Eagle
A1434
Sutton on Trent
North Scarle
Wellow
Moorhouse
Girton
North Hykeham
Ompton
Thorpe on the Hill
Rufford
Ossington
Besthorpe
South Scarle
R Witham
Kneesall
Carlton-on-Trent
South Hykeham
Norwell Woodhouse
Eakring
Kersall
Swinderby
Haddington
Harmst
Cromwell
Aubourn
A616
Thurlby
Dolls
Caunton
Bassingham
Coleb
Bathley
Holme
Boothby
Brough
Norton Disney
North Muskham
0 1 2 3 4 miles
0 1 2 3 4 5 kilometres

Ross
Brocklesby
M180
A18
Humberside
Great Limber
Barnetby le Wold
126
Riby
Aylesby
Nunsthorpe
Clee
A46
A16
Brigg
A1084
Bigby
Somerby
Searby
Ownby
Grasby
Clixby
Howsham
Cadney
North Kelsey Beck
North Kelsey
B1434
Caistor
A1173
Swallow
Laceby
Bradley
Irby upon Humber
Waltham
B1203
A1098
B1219
Humber
New Waltham
Holton le Clay
A1031
Barnoldby le Beck
Brigsley
Beelsby
A18
Hatcliffe
Ashby cum Fenby
Waithe
Grainsby
Cabourne
Cuxwold
B1205
Nettleton
Rothwell
South Kelsey
Moortown
A46
East Ravendale
North Thoresby
B1201
Brandy Wharf
Thornton le Moor
Holton le Moor
B1225
Thoresway
Thorganby
Wold Newton
A16
Lincolnshire Wolds Railway
B1205
Snitterby
North Owersby
South Owersby
Normanby le Wold
Claxby
Brookenby
Ludborough
Stainton le Vale
Binbrook
North Ormsby
Kingerby
Usselby
Kirkby
Osgodby
Kirmond le Mire
Walesby
Utterby
Fotherby
Bishop Norton
A1103
A631
Bishopbridge
Glentham
Caenby
West Rasen
Middle Rasen
B1203
Tealby
THE WOLDS
Kelstern
A631
South Elkington
Market Rasen
North Willingham
Ludford
Toft next Newton
A631
A631
A46
Newton by Toft
Owmby
Linwood
Sixhills
Burgh on Bain
Welton le Wold
A157
Hallington
B1202
Legsby
Hainton
118
Raithby
Faldingworth
Spridlington
Cold Hanworth
Friesthorpe
Lissington
South Willingham
Donington on Bain
Withcall
A153
Tathwell
Snarford
Wickenby
East Torrington
West Torrington
Benniworth
R Bain
Holton cum Beckering
Beckering
East Barkwith
Market Stainton
Cadwell Park
Ryland
Snelland
B1399
West Barkwith
Goulceby
Asterby
Maidenwell
Welton
Dunholme
Fulnetby
Rand
A157
Panton
Stainton by Langworth
B1202
Wragby
Sotby
Ranby
Scamblesby
Scothern
Bullington
Oxcombe
A46
Sudbrooke
Langworth
Langton by Wragby
Hatton
Great Sturton
B1225
A153
Belchford
Apley
Barlings
Kingthorpe
Nettleham
A158
Hemingby
Far Thorpe
A158
Baumber
Bardney Limewoods
Fulletby
Reepham
Minting
Cherry Willingham
Fiskerton
B1202
Gautby
Wispington
West Ashby
R Witham
Washingborough
Edlington
Horncastle
B1190
Thimbleby
Greetham
Branston Booths
Canwick
Heighington
Bardney
Bucknall
B1190
Langton
High Toynton
A158
B1188
B1190
Horsington
Thornton
Mareham on the Hill
Branston
B1190
Potterhanworth Booths
B1202
Southrey
Martin
Hamerington
Asgarby
Stixwould
Potterhanworth
B1178
B1183
Hareby
B1202
Sots Hole
Roughton
Moorby
Nocton
Metheringham Delph
Woodhall Spa
Haltham
Miningsby
Dunston
B1191
Wood Enderby
B1188
Kirkstead
Woodhall Spa
Kirkby on Bain
B1178
B1189
103
B1191
Metheringham
A155
B1192
B1202
Blankney
Martin
Timberland Delph
Mareham le Fen
Tattershall Thorpe
Tumby
Kirkby

118
127
117
103
104
A
B
C
D
E
F
1
2
3
4
5
6
7
8
Brocklesby
Keelby
Healing
Great Coates
West Marsh
Cleethorpes
Old Clee
Thrunscoe
SPURN HEAD
Riby
Bylesby
Nunsthorpe
Scartho
Pleasure Island
Humberston
Rotterdam (Europoort)
Zeebrugge
Laceby
Bradley
Irby upon Humber
Waltham
New Waltham
Holton le Clay
Swallow
Barnoldby le Beck
Brigsley
Cabourne
Beelsby
Ashby cum Fenby
Cuxwold
Hatcliffe
Waithe
Tetney
North Cotes
Marsh Chapel
Rothwell
Grainsby
East Ravendale
North Thoresby
Grainthorpe
Thoresway
Thorganby
Wold Newton
Fulstow
North Somercotes
Conisholme
Brookenby
Lincolnshire Wolds Railway
Normanby le Wold
Ludborough
Covenham St Bartholomew
Covenham St Mary
Stainton le Vale
Binbrook
North Ormsby
Yarburgh
Kirmond le Mire
Utterby
Little Grimsby
Walesby
Fotherby
Alvingham
North Cockerington
Tealby
THE WOLDS
Kelstern
South Cockerington
Saltfleet St Peter
Market Rasen
North Willingham
Ludford
South Elkington
Grimoldby
Welton le Wold
Louth
Theddlethorpe All Saints
Sixhills
Burgh on Bain
Manby
Linwood
Hallington
Little Carlton
Great Carlton
Legsby
Raithby
Legbourne
Hainton
Biscathorpe
North Reston
Gayton le Marsh
South Willingham
Great Eau
Lissington
East Torrington
Donington on Bain
Withcall
Little Cawthorpe
South Reston
Tathwell
West Torrington
Benniworth
Withern
East Barkwith
Haugham
Muckton
Beckering
Cadwell Park
Authorpe
Market Stainton
West Barkwith
Maidenwell
Burwell
Panton
Goulceby
Asterby
Belleau
Watermill & Wildfowl Gardens
Wragby
Sotby
Ranby
Scamblesby
Aby
White Pit
Swaby
Oxcombe
South Thoresby
Langton by Wragby
Hatton
Ketsby
Great Sturton
Belchford
South Ormsby
Rigsby
Kingthorpe
Hemingby
Far Thorpe
Tetford
Driby
Baumber
Fulletby
Salmonby
Brinkhill
Well
Bardney Limewoods
Minting
Gautby
Wispington
West Ashby
Somersby
Harrington
Sutterby
Ulceby
Edlington
Horncastle
Ashby Puerorum
Bag Enderby
Langton
Thimbleby
Greetham
Aswardby
Skendleby
High Toynton
Bardney
Bucknall
Langton
Hagworthingham
Sausthorpe
Partney
Horsington
Thornton
Mareham on the Hill
Snipe Dales
R Lymn
Mavis Enderby
Raithby
Hameringham
Asgarby
Ashby by Partney
Southrey
Stixwould
Martin
Spilsby
Hundleby
Hareby
Halton Holegate
Sots Hole
Roughton
Old Bolingbroke
Woodhall Spa
Haltham
Moorby
Toynton All Saints
Northcote
Miningsby
Bolingbroke
Kirkstead
Wood Enderby
East Keal
Little Steeping
Woodhall Spa
Kirkby on Bain
East Kirkby
Lincolnshire Aviation
Revesby
Stickford
Mareham le Fen
Fendike Corner
Tumby
0 1 2 3 4 miles
0 1 2 3 4 5 kilometres
A46
A16
A180
A1098
B1219
B1203
A1031
A1173
A18
B1201
A16
A1031
B1225
B1203
A631
B1200
A157
B1520
A153
B1373
A157
B1202
A158
A1104
A1028
B1190
A158
B1195
B1183
B1191
A155
A153
B1195

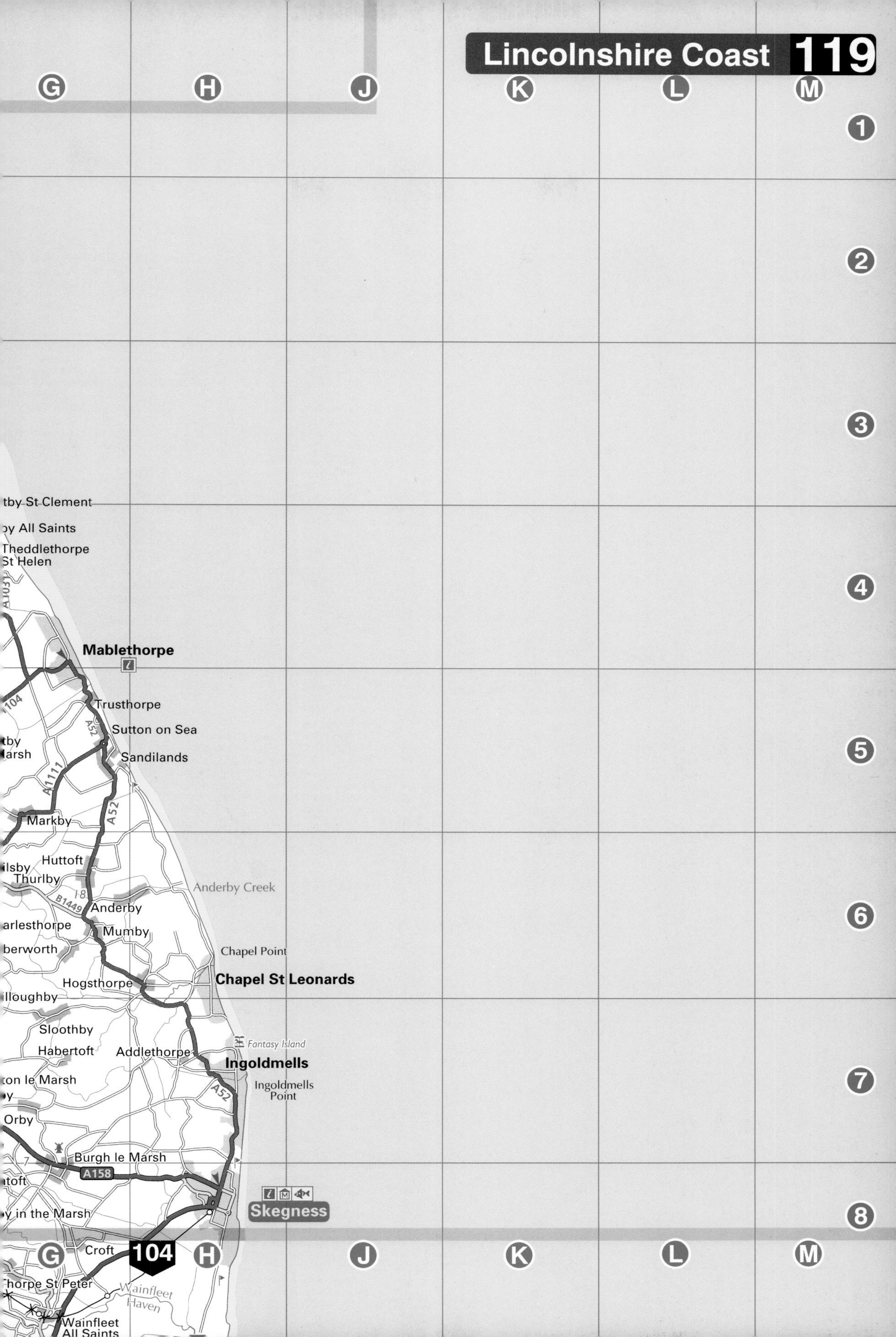
G
H
J
K
L
M
1
2
3
4
5
6
7
8
tby St Clement
by All Saints
Theddlethorpe St Helen
Mablethorpe
Trusthorpe
Sutton on Sea
Sandilands
A52
A1111
Markby
Huttoft
Thurlby
B1449
Anderby
Anderby Creek
Mumby
Chapel Point
Chapel St Leonards
Hogsthorpe
Sloothby
Habertoft
Addlethorpe
Fantasy Island
Ingoldmells
Ingoldmells Point
Orby
Burgh le Marsh
A158
Skegness
Croft
104
Thorpe St Peter
Wainfleet Haven
Wainfleet All Saints

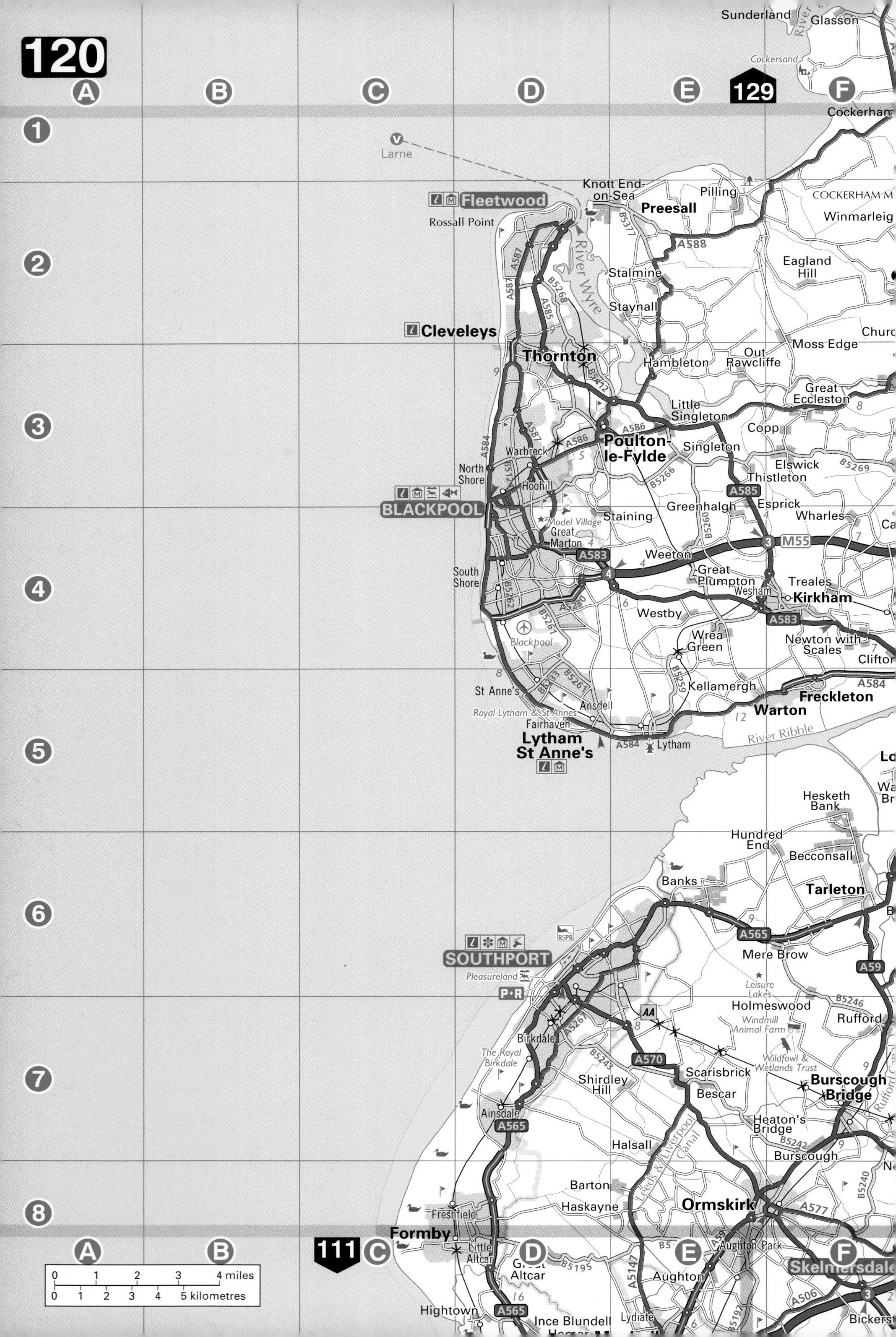

129
Sunderland
Glasson
Cockersand
Cockerham
Larne
Knott End-on-Sea
Fleetwood
Rossall Point
Pilling
Preesall
COCKERHAM M
Winmarleigh
A588
Eagland Hill
Stalmine
River Wyre
Staynall
Cleveleys
Thornton
Hambleton
Out Rawcliffe
Moss Edge
Great Eccleston
Little Singleton
Copp
Poulton-le-Fylde
Singleton
Warbreck
North Shore
Hoohill
Elswick
Thistleton
BLACKPOOL
Greenhalgh
Esprick
Wharles
Staining
Model Village
Great Marton
Weeton
M55
Great Plumpton
Wesham
Treales
Kirkham
South Shore
Westby
Blackpool
Wrea Green
Newton with Scales
St Anne's
Kellamergh
Freckleton
Warton
Ansdell
Royal Lytham & St Annes
Fairhaven
Lytham St Anne's
Lytham
River Ribble
Hesketh Bank
Hundred End
Becconsall
Banks
Tarleton
SOUTHPORT
Pleasureland
P+R
Mere Brow
Leisure Lakes
Holmeswood
Rufford
Windmill Animal Farm
Birkdale
The Royal Birkdale
Wildfowl & Wetlands Trust
Scarisbrick
Shirdley Hill
Burscough Bridge
Bescar
Ainsdale
Heaton's Bridge
Halsall
Burscough
Leeds & Liverpool Canal
Barton
Haskayne
Ormskirk
Freshfield
Formby
Little Altcar
Great Altcar
Aughton Park
Aughton
Skelmersdale
Hightown
Ince Blundell
Lydiate
Bickerstaffe
A565
A570
A59
A577
A584
A583
A585
A586
A587
A5147
A506
111
0 1 2 3 4 miles
0 1 2 3 4 5 kilometres

Bowland
Forest
Abbeystead
Dolphinholme
WHINS BROW
130
Slaidburn
Newton
Dunsop Bridge
Forest Becks
Holden
Bolton by Bowland
HAWTHORNTHWAITE FELL
Calder Fell
TOTRIDGE FELL
BRADFORD FELL
Scorton
Cabus
Oakenclough
Calder Vale
FAIRSNAPE FELL
PARLICK
Bleasdale
Whitewell
Sawley
Grindleton
West Bradford
Rimington
Downham
Bonds
Waddington
Chatburn
Horrocksford
Worston
Chipping
Bashall Eaves
Claughton
Beacon Fell
R Hodder
Clitheroe
PENDLE HILL
White Chapel
Hesketh Lane
Inglewhite
Longridge Fell
Pendleton
Barley
Bilsborrow
Knowle Green
Hurst Green
Great Mitton
Barrow
Barton
Longridge
Wiswell
Sabden
Fence
Newsham
Goosnargh
Frances Green
Whalley
Old Langho
Higham
Broughton
Chingle Hall
Ribchester
Little Town
Read
Simonstone
Padiham
Woodplumpton
Higher Bartle
Grimsargh
Copster Green
Billington
Langho
Gawthorpe Hall NT
Sharoe Green
Cottam
Cadley
Ingol
Balderstone
Great Harwood
Hapton
Fulwood
Ribbleton
Samlesbury Hall
Osbaldeston
Mellor Brook
Mellor
Wilpshire
Clayton-le-Moors
Samlesbury
Rishton
122
PRESTON
Walton-le-Dale
Higher Walton
BLACKBURN
Church
Dial Hall
Accrington
Dunnockshaw
Love Clough
Higher Penwortham
Witton
Pleasington
Oswaldtwistle
Baxenden
Hoghton
Hoghton Tower
Riley Green
Guide
Bamber Bridge
New Longton
Farington
Feniscowles
Rann
Belthorn
Crawshaw
Brindle
Haslingden
Tockholes
Waterside
Higher Wheelton
Blackburn with Darwen
Pickup Bank
Abbey Village
Leyland
Cuerden Valley
Sunnyhurst
Hoddlesden
Helmshore
Textiles Museum
East Lancashire Railway
Whittle-le-Woods
Clayton-le-Woods
Leeds & Liverpool Canal
Brinscall
Darwen
Wheelton
Blacksnape
Euxton
Chatterton
Stubbins
Edenfield
Chorley
R Yarrow
Ramsbottom
Shuttleworth
Eccleston
Cowling
Edgworth
Charnock Richard
Camelot
Turton Tower
Turton Bottoms
Belmont
WINTER HILL
Chapeltown
Jumbles
Egerton
Rivington
Summerseat
Greenmount
Coppull
Grimeford Village
Adlington
Mossy Lea
Horwich
Tottington
Chesham
BURY
Bolton West
Eagley
Smithills Hall
Astley Bridge
Parbold
Blackrod
Halliwell
Breightmet
Appley Bridge
Standish
BOLTON
Aspull
Shevington
Deane
Daubhill
Moses Gate
Marylebone
Radcliffe
Tower
Beacon
112
Up Holland
Scholes
Westhoughton
113
Farnworth
Little Lever
Whitefield
Newtown
Pemberton
Orrell
Far Moor
Ince-in-Makerfield
Hindley
Kearsley
Atherton
Walkden
Prestwich
M6
M65
M61
M60
A59
A666
A680
A671
A677
A675
A674
A56
A6
A49
A5209
A58
A673
B6243
B6478

122
130
131
121
113
A B C D E F
1 2 3 4 5 6 7 8
Skipton
Barnoldswick
Earby
Colne
Nelson
Barrowford
Brierfield
BURNLEY
Padiham
Clitheroe
Whalley
Accrington
Oswaldtwistle
Haslingden
Rawtenstall
Bacup
Todmorden
Hebden Bridge
Haworth
Silsden
KEIGHLEY
Ramsbottom
Whitworth
Littleborough
Milnrow
ROCHDALE
BURY
Heywood
BOLTON
Royton
Shaw
MIDDLETON
OLDHAM
Prestwich
Walkden
Ripponden
Tottington
Radcliffe
Little Lever
Chadderton
Slaidburn
Halton West
Coniston Cold
Gargrave
Paythorne
Gisburn
Bolton by Bowland
Sawley
Rimington
Grindleton
West Bradford
Chatburn
Pendleton
Sabden
Simonstone
Hapton
Clayton-le-Moors
Church
Trawden
Wycoller
Keighley Moor
The Forest of Trawden
Wadsworth Moor
Heptonstall Moor
Forest of Rossendale
Rishworth Moor
Moss Moor
Close Moor
Saddleworth Moor
PENDLE HILL
BOULSWORTH HILL
0 1 2 3 4 miles
0 1 2 3 4 5 kilometres

Blubberhouses
Kettlesing
Fewston Reservoir
Fewston
Swinsty Res
Timble
Bolton Priory
Beamsley
Langbar
Nesfield
Middleton
Denton
Clifton
Askwith
Weston
Farnley
Lindley Green
Braythorn
Stainburn
North Rigton
Huby
Leathley
Ilkley
Ben Rhydding
Rombalds Moor
Burley in Wharfedale
Burley Wood Head
Otley
Newall
Pool
Castley
Weeton
Dunkeswick
Netherby
Harewood
Chapel Hill
Linton
Collingham
Weardley
Arthington
Bramhope
Old Bramhope
Chevin Forest Park
East Carlton
Guiseley
Menston
East Morton
Hawksworth
Yeadon
Leeds Bradford
Rawdon
Eccup Reservoir
Alwoodley
Scarcroft
Thorner
Bramham Park
Sand Hills
East Keswick
Bardsey
Wike
East Rigton
Pannal
Pannal Ash
Rossett Green
Follifoot
Spofforth
Kirkby Overblow
Sicklinghall
Kirk Deighton
North Deighton
Goldsborough
Walshford
High Harrogate
Starbeck
Low Harrogate
Bingley
Baildon
Baildon Green
Charlestown
Saltaire
Thackley
Idle
Shipley
Cross Flatts
Harden
Cottingley
Moorhead
Wilsden
Wrose
Greengates
Eccleshill
Gaisby
Frizinghall
Heaton
Manningham
Undercliffe
Hare Croft
Denholme
Thornton
Allerton
Horsforth
Moortown
Moor Allerton
Weetwood
Meanwood
Chapel Allerton
Roundhay
Gledhow
Harehills
Headingley
Kirkstall
Bramley
Woodhouse
LEEDS
Sheepscar
Scholes
Seacroft
Manston
Cross Gates
Halton
Whitkirk
Colton
Garforth
Osmondthorpe
Cross Green
Temple Newsam
Swillington
Kippax
Great Preston
Bower's Row
Methley
Armley
Farnley
Wortley
Beeston
Hunslet
Thornbury
Laisterdyke
Fartown
Pudsey
BRADFORD
Great Horton
Clayton
Little Horton
Bowling
West Bowling
Tong Street
Tong
Queensbury
Mountain
Ambler Thorn
Shibden Head
Wibsey
Buttershaw
Odsal
Oakenshaw
Birkenshaw
Drighlington
Gildersome
White Rose
Churwell
Middleton Railway
Middleton
Rothwell
Carlton
Ouzlewell Green
Morley
Tingley
Ardsley East
Woodkirk
Carr Gate
Lofthouse
Lofthouse Gate
WAKEFIELD EUROPORT
Normanton
Northowram
Wyke
Hunsworth
Oakwell Hall
Birstall
Cleckheaton
Heckmondwike
Batley
Shibden Hall
Hipperholme
Hartshead Moor
Liversedge
Clifton
Southowram
Brighouse
Rastrick
Hartshead
Roberttown
Dewsbury
Chidswell
Kirkhamgate
Alverthorpe
Flanshaw
WAKEFIELD
Kirkthorpe
Woodhouse
Warmfield
New Sharlston
Sharlston
Nostell Priory
Heath
Belle Vue
Elland
Broad Carr
Clough Head
Netheroyd Hill
Sheepridge
Fartown
Earlsheaton
Savile Town
Mirfield
Ravensthorpe
Ossett
Lupset
Horbury
Sandal Magna
Crofton
Lindley
Edgerton
HUDDERSFIELD
Moldgreen
Upper Heaton
Upper Hopton
Kirkheaton
Thornhill
Whitley Lower
Middlestown
National Coal Mining Museum
Calder Grove
Crigglestone
Walton
New Crofton
Scapegoat Hill
Golcar
Linthwaite
Lower Houses
Greenside
Almondbury
Newsome
Hill Side
Houses Hill
Grange Moor
Overton
Flockton Green
Netherton
Lepton
Flockton
Midgley
West Bretton
Woolley Edge
Hill Top
Newmillerdam
Ryhill
Kinsley
Hemsworth
Netherton
Blackmoorfoot
Highburton
Emley
Yorkshire Sculpture Park
Woolley
Notton
Helme
Honley
Farnley Tyas
Kirkburton
Shelley
Kirklees Light Railway
Skelmanthorpe
Clayton West
Staincross
Royston
Shafton
Meltham
Wilshaw
Brockholes
Thurstonland
High Hoyland
Darton
Carlton
Netherthong
Scissett
Lower Cumberworth
Upper Cumberworth
Shepley
New Mill
Mapplewell
New Lodge
Upperthong
Holmfirth
Scholes
Birds Edge
Denby Dale
Cannon Hall
Cawthorne
Cudworth
BARNSLEY
Upper Denby
Silkstone
Dodworth
Ingbirchworth
Hoyland Swaine
Silkstone Common
Crow Edge
Thurlstone
Millhouse
Worsbrough Dale
Darfield
Little Houghton
Holme Moss
Winscar
Holme
132
114
124

124
132
133
123
115
Harrogate
Starbeck
Goldsborough
Monkton
Overton
Nether Poppleton
Upper Poppleton
New Earswick
Rawcliffe
Kirk Hammerton
Cattal
Hunsingore
Hessay
Clifton
Follifoot
Pannal
North Deighton
Cowthorpe
Tockwith
Knapton
YORK
Osbaldwick
Spofforth
Kirk Deighton
Long Marston
Rufforth
Acomb
Holgate
South Bank
Kirkby Overblow
Bickerton
Hutton Wandesley
Nunthorpe
Sicklinghall
Bilton
Askham Bryan
Dringhouses
Fulford
Angram
Dunkeswick
Walton
Healaugh
Askham Richard
Bishopthorpe
Wetherby
Netherby
Chapel Hill
Linton
Boston Spa
Thorp Arch
R Wharfe
Wighill
Catterton
Bilbrough
Copmanthorpe
Harewood
Collingham
Newton Kyme
Acaster Malbis
Naburn
East Keswick
Clifford
Colton
Bardsey
East Rigton
Tadcaster
Oxton
Appleton Roebuck
Escrick
Eccup Reservoir
Wike
Bramham
Bolton Percy
Bramham Park
Stutton
Kirkby Wharf
Holme Green
Acaster Selby
Scarcroft
Thorner
Sand Hills
Towton
Ulleskelf
Ryther
Stillingfleet
Moor Allerton
Chapel Allerton
Roundhay
Aberford
R Cock
Kelfield
Barwick in Elmet
Cawood
Riccall
Gledhow
Harehills
Scholes
Seacroft
Saxton
Church Fenton
Barkston Ash
Wistow
Lotherton Hall
Manston
LEEDS
Cross Gates
Old Micklefield
Little Fenton
Biggin
Barlby
Sheepscar
Halton
Whitkirk
Garforth
Sherburn in Elmet
Osmondthorpe
Colton
Micklefield
Cross Green
Newthorpe
South Milford
Thorpe Willoughby
Temple Newsam
Swillington
Kippax
Steeton Hall Gatehouse
Hambleton
Brayton
Hunslet
Lumby
Monk Fryston
Great Preston
Ledsham
Middleton Railway
Middleton
Ledston
Hillam
Gateforth
Burn
Rothwell
Carlton
Bower's Row
Allerton Bywater
Fairburn
Burton Salmon
Birkin
Selby Canal
Oulzelwell Green
Methley
Mickletown
Chapel Haddlesey
Ardsley
East Ardsley
Lofthouse
Lofthouse Gate
Castleford
Brotherton
West Haddlesey
Beal
Camblesforth
Temple Hirst
Carr Gate
Sutton
Kellington
Hirst Courtney
Wakefield Europort
Xscape
Knottingley
Normanton
Ferrybridge
Low Eggborough
Hensall
Snaith
Woodhouse
Ackton
Featherstone
Pontefract
Cridling Stubbs
Gowdall
Alverthorpe
WAKEFIELD
Flanshaw
Kirkthorpe
Warmfield
Whitley
Great Heck
Heath
New Sharlston
Darrington
Polling
Belle Vue
Sharlston
Nostell Priory NT
High Ackworth
East Hardwick
Womersley
Balne
Horbury
Sandal Magna
Crofton
Hessle
Low Ackworth
Wentbridge
Little Smeaton
Walden Stubbs
R Went
Aire and Calder Nav
Calder Grove
Crigglestone
Walton
New Crofton
Wragby
Ackworth Moor Top
Kirk Smeaton
Sykehouse
Fenwick
Norton
Hill Top
Newmillerdam
Fitzwilliam
Thorpe Audlin
Ryhill
Kinsley
Badsworth
Woolley Edge
Havercroft
Upton
Campsall
Moss
Askern
Notton
South Hiendley
Woolley
Hemsworth
Kirk Bramwith
Skelbrooke
Haywood
Staincross
Royston
North Elmsall
South Elmsall
Burghwallis
Stainforth
Shafton
Brierley
Moorthorpe
Owston
South Bramwith
Darton
Carlton
Hampole
Skellow
Thorpe in Balne
Barnby Dun
Mapplewell
South Kirkby
Carcroft
New Lodge
Grimethorpe
Adwick Le Street
Kirk Sandall
Cudworth
Clayton
Hooton Pagnell
Woodlands
Toll Bar
Almholme
BARNSLEY
Monk Bretton
Great Houghton
Thurnscoe
Brodsworth
Pickburn
Arksey
Edenthorpe
Little Houghton
Hickleton
Scawthorpe
Bentley
Armthorpe
Billingley
Marr
Scawsby
Wheatley Hills
Darfield
Goldthorpe
DONCASTER
Worsbrough Bridge
Dale
Wombwell
Broom Hill
Bolton
Barnburgh
0 1 2 3 4 miles
0 1 2 3 4 5 kilometres

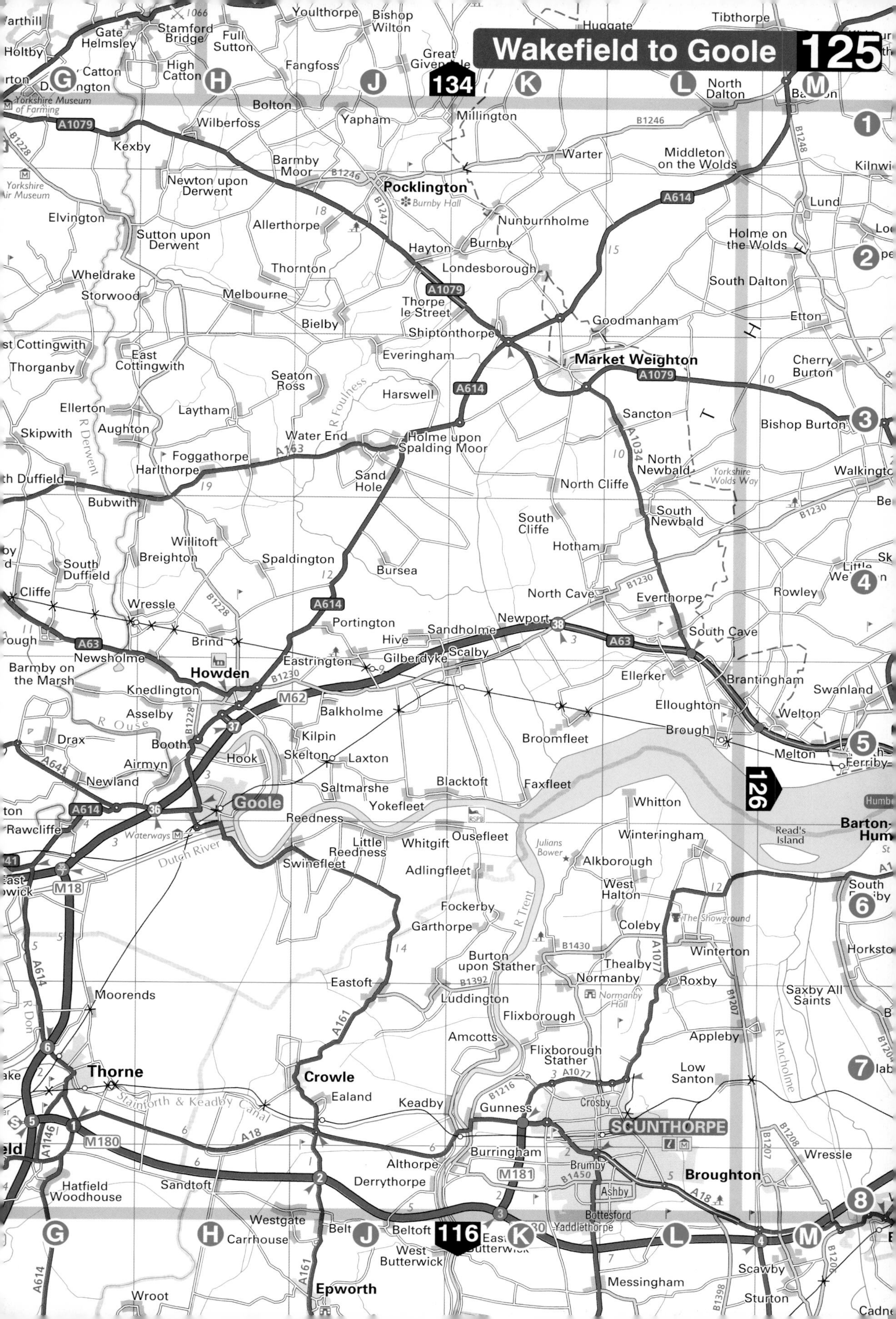

Youlthorpe
Bishop Wilton
Huggate
Tibthorpe
Gate Helmsley
Stamford Bridge
Full Sutton
Holtby
High Catton
Catton
Fangfoss
Great Givendale
134
North Dalton
Yorkshire Museum of Farming
Bolton
Yapham
Millington
Wilberfoss
A1079
Kexby
B1246
Warter
Middleton on the Wolds
Barmby Moor
Pocklington
Burnby Hall
Newton upon Derwent
Yorkshire Air Museum
A614
Lund
Elvington
Sutton upon Derwent
Allerthorpe
Nunburnholme
Holme on the Wolds
Hayton
Burnby
Londesborough
Wheldrake
Thornton
Storwood
Melbourne
South Dalton
Thorpe le Street
Shiptonthorpe
Bielby
Goodmanham
Etton
Everingham
Thorganby
East Cottingwith
Market Weighton
Cherry Burton
Seaton Ross
Harswell
Ellerton
Laytham
Sancton
Bishop Burton
Skipwith
Aughton
Water End
Holme upon Spalding Moor
R Derwent
R Foulness
Foggathorpe
A163
Harlthorpe
North Newbald
Walkington
North Cliffe
Yorkshire Wolds Way
Sand Hole
Bubwith
South Newbald
South Cliffe
B1230
Willitoft
Hotham
Breighton
Spaldington
Bursea
South Duffield
Cliffe
North Cave
Everthorpe
Rowley
Wressle
B1228
Portington
Newport
A63
South Cave
Brind
Hive
Sandholme
Scalby
Newsholme
Eastrington
Gilberdyke
Barmby on the Marsh
Howden
Ellerker
Brantingham
Swanland
Knedlington
M62
Elloughton
Welton
Asselby
Balkholme
R Ouse
Brough
Drax
Booth
Kilpin
Broomfleet
Melton
Ferriby
Hook
Skelton
Laxton
Airmyn
A645
Newland
Saltmarshe
Blacktoft
Faxfleet
Goole
Yokefleet
126
Whitton
Rawcliffe
Reedness
RSPB
Winteringham
Waterways
Dutch River
Little Reedness
Whitgift
Ousefleet
Julians Bower
Read's Island
Alkborough
Swinefleet
Adlingfleet
West Halton
M18
South Ferriby
Fockerby
R Trent
The Showground
Garthorpe
Coleby
Winterton
B1430
A1077
Horkstow
Burton upon Stather
Thealby
Normanby
B1392
Roxby
Eastoft
Normanby Hall
Saxby All Saints
Moorends
Luddington
Flixborough
B1207
R Don
A161
R Ancholme
Amcotts
Appleby
Flixborough Stather
Thorne
Crowle
Low Santon
Ealand
Keadby
Gunness
Crosby
Stainforth & Keadby Canal
SCUNTHORPE
B1216
A18
M180
A1146
Burringham
B1208
Wressle
Althorpe
Brumby
M181
Derrythorpe
B1450
Ashby
Broughton
Hatfield Woodhouse
Sandtoft
Bottesford
Yaddlethorpe
Westgate
Belt
Beltoft
116
Carrhouse
West Butterwick
Scawby
Messingham
A614
Epworth
Wroot
Sturton
B1398

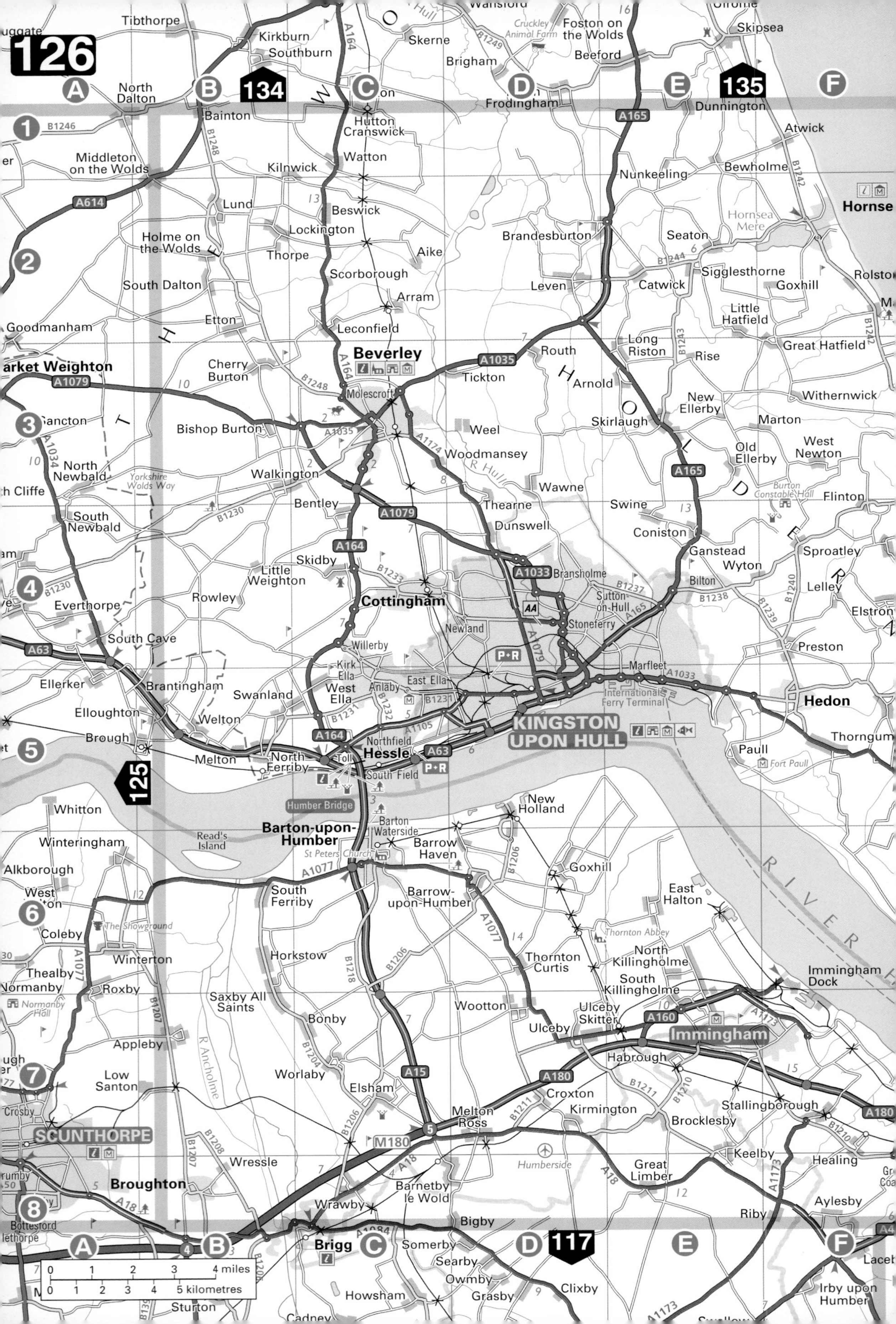
Tibthorpe
Kirkburn
Southburn
Skerne
Foston on the Wolds
Skipsea
Brigham
Beeford
North Dalton
Bainton
Hutton Cranswick
Frodingham
Dunnington
Atwick
Middleton on the Wolds
Watton
Kilnwick
Nunkeeling
Bewholme
Lund
Beswick
Lockington
Hornsea
Hornsea Mere
Holme on the Wolds
Thorpe
Aike
Brandesburton
Seaton
South Dalton
Scorborough
Leven
Catwick
Sigglesthorne
Goxhill
Arram
Goodmanham
Etton
Leconfield
Little Hatfield
Long Riston
Great Hatfield
Market Weighton
Cherry Burton
Beverley
Routh
Rise
Tickton
Arnold
Molescroft
New Ellerby
Withernwick
Sancton
Bishop Burton
Weel
Skirlaugh
Marton
North Newbald
Woodmansey
Old Ellerby
West Newton
Walkington
Wawne
Yorkshire Wolds Way
South Newbald
Bentley
Thearne
Swine
Flinton
Burton Constable Hall
Dunswell
Coniston
Skidby
Ganstead
Wyton
Sproatley
Little Weighton
Bransholme
Bilton
Everthorpe
Rowley
Cottingham
Sutton-on-Hull
Lelley
Stoneferry
Elstronwick
Newland
South Cave
Willerby
Preston
Kirk Ella
Ellerker
Brantingham
Swanland
Marfleet
East Ella
West Ella
Anlaby
International Ferry Terminal
Hedon
Elloughton
Welton
Brough
Kingston upon Hull
Northfield
Thorngumbald
Melton
North Ferriby
Hessle
Paull
Fort Paull
South Field
Humber Bridge
Whitton
New Holland
Barton Waterside
Read's Island
Barton-upon-Humber
Barrow Haven
Winteringham
St Peters Church
Alkborough
Goxhill
West Halton
South Ferriby
Barrow-upon-Humber
East Halton
The Showground
Coleby
Thornton Abbey
Horkstow
North Killingholme
Thornton Curtis
Immingham Dock
Thealby
Winterton
South Killingholme
Normanby
Roxby
Normanby Hall
Saxby All Saints
Bonby
Wootton
Ulceby Skitter
Ulceby
Immingham
Appleby
R Ancholme
Habrough
Low Santon
Worlaby
Elsham
Croxton
Stallingborough
Crosby
Kirmington
Melton Ross
Brocklesby
Scunthorpe
Keelby
Wressle
Humberside
Healing
Great Limber
Broughton
Barnetby le Wold
Aylesby
Wrawby
Bigby
Riby
Bottesford
Brigg
Somerby
Searby
Owmby
Clixby
Laceby
Howsham
Grasby
Irby upon Humber
Sturton
Cadney
River Humber
Wolds
Holderness
A614
A1079
A1034
A63
A164
A1035
A1174
A165
A1033
A1105
A1077
A15
A18
A180
A160
A1173
M180
B1246
B1248
B1249
B1244
B1242
B1243
B1230
B1233
B1237
B1238
B1240
B1239
B1231
B1232
B1206
B1218
B1204
B1207
B1208
B1211
B1210
A1084
134
135
125
117
0 1 2 3 4 miles
0 1 2 3 4 5 kilometres

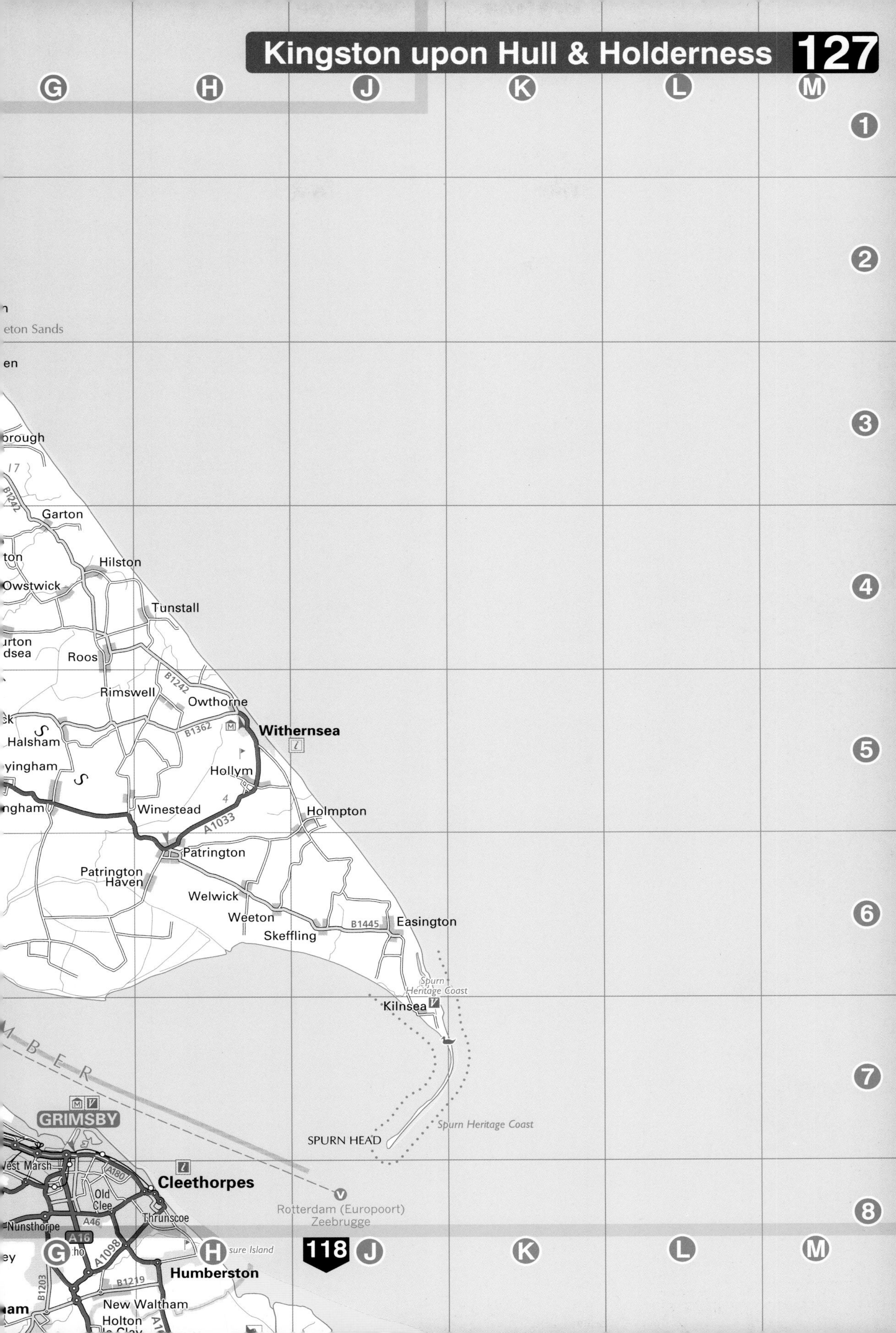

G H J K L M
1 2 3 4 5 6 7 8
eton Sands
brough
B1242
Garton
Hilston
Owstwick
Tunstall
Roos
Rimswell
B1242
Owthorne
B1362
Withernsea
Halsham
Hollym
Winestead
A1033
Holmpton
Patrington
Patrington Haven
Welwick
Weeton
Skeffling
B1445
Easington
Spurn Heritage Coast
Kilnsea
SPURN HEAD
Spurn Heritage Coast
GRIMSBY
West Marsh
A180
Cleethorpes
Old Clee
A46
Thrunscoe
Nunsthorpe
A16
A1098
Humberston
B1219
B1203
New Waltham
Holton
Rotterdam (Europoort)
Zeebrugge
118

Seascale
Hallsenna Moor
Drigg
Holmrook
Eskdale Green
Boot
Eskdale
652
HARTER FELL
Muncaster Mill
Ravenglass and Eskdale Railway
River Esk
Devoke Water
River Duddon
Seathwaite Tarn
Ravenglass
Bath House
Muncaster
A595
Hall Dunnerdale
Seathwaite
136
137
LAKE DISTRICT NATIONAL PARK
Lane End
Waberthwaite
573
WHITFELL
Ulpha
Broughton Mills
A593
Hycemoor
Selker Bay
Bootle
Swinside Stone Circle
Broughton-in-Fu
Lady Hall
Foxfield
600
BLACK COMBE
Whitbeck
The Green
Grize
Gutterby Spa
Whicham
Silecroft
A5093
The Hill
Kirkby-in-F
Beck Si
Soutergate
Kirksanton
Millom
RSPB
Haverigg
Haverigg Point
Ireleth
Askam in Furness
Lindal in Furness
Sandscale Haws
South Lakes Animal Park
North Walney
Dalton-in-Furness
Ursw
Newton
BARROW-IN-FURNESS
Furness Abbey
Bow Bridge
Dendron
Stain with
Vickerstown
Barrow Island
A590
A5087
Lee
ISLE OF WALNEY
Ramps
Sheep Island
Piel
Piel Island
Fou
Piel Bar
Hilpsford Point
A B C D E F
1 2 3 4 5 6 7 8
0 1 2 3 4 miles
0 1 2 3 4 5 kilometres

Hawkshead
Bowness-on-Windermere
Kendal
Grange-over-Sands
Morecambe
Heysham
Lancaster
Carnforth
Bolton le Sands
MORECAMBE
BAY
Cartmel
Arnside
Silverdale
Milnthorpe
Kirkby Lonsdale
Fleetwood
Knott End-on-Sea
Cockerham
Galgate
Ellel
Glasson
Overton
Caton
Hornby
Newby Bridge
Staveley
Levens
Oxenholme
Burneside
Windermere
Coniston Water
137
138
130
120
121

Borrowbridge
Watchgate
Garth Row
Grayrigg
Kendal
Firbank
Sedbergh
Millthrop
Garsdale Head
Garsdale
New Hutton
Killington Lake (Southbound Only)
Oxenholme
Natland
Middleshaw
Killington
Old Hutton
Gawthrop
Dent
Sedgwick
Stainton
Endmoor
Crooklands
Preston Patrick
Old Town
Barbon
Nook
Lupton
Whasset
Farleton
Kearstwick
Casterton
High Casterton
Holme
Holme Park Fell NT
Hutton Roof
High Biggins
Low Biggins
Kirkby Lonsdale
Cowan Bridge
Burton-in-Kendal
Leck
Ireby
Whittington
Overtown
Burrow
Yealand Redmayne
Burton-in-Kendal (Northbound Only)
Priest Hutton
Docker
Tunstall
Cantsfield
Borwick
Arkholme
Wrayton
Melling
Over Kellet
Gressingham
Wennington
Low Bentham
High Bentham
Nether Kellet
Hornby
Wray
Aughton
Claughton
Farleton
Caton Green
Brookhouse
Caton
River Lune Millennium Park
Crossgill
Masongill
Westhouse
Thornton in Lonsdale
Ingleton
Burton in Lonsdale
Newby
Clapham
Austwick
Lawkland
Chapel le Dale
Selside
Horton in Ribblesdale
Wharfe
Stainforth
Stackhouse
Langcliffe
Settle
Giggleswick
Rathmell
Long Preston
Wigglesworth
Tosside
Halton West
Stocks Reservoir
Slaidburn
Bowland
Forest
Abbeystead
Dolphinholme
Newton
Dunsop Bridge
Forest Becks
Holden
Bolton by Bowland
Paythorne
Scorton
Calder Fell
Cautley Spout (Waterfall)
Cross Keys Temperance Inn NT
THE CALF
WILD BOAR FELL
HIGH SEAT
WINDER
National Park Centre
CALF TOP
CRAGHILL
WHERNSIDE
BLEA MOOR
Ribblehead Viaduct
White Scar Caves
INGLEBOROUGH HILL
Ingleborough
GREAT HARLOW
WARD'S STONE
WHINS BROW
TOTRIDGE
BRADFORD FELL
HAWTHORNTHWAITE
PEN-Y-GHENT
DODD FELL
River Rawthey
River Ure
River Ribble
River Lune
R Roeburn
R Wyre
West Gill
East Gill
M6
A6
A683
A684
A685
A65
A687
A590
A591
A6070
B6254
B6257
B6255
B6259
B6479
B6480
B6478
138
139
129
121
122
0 1 2 3 4 miles
0 1 2 3 4 5 kilometres

Keld
R Swale
487
CALVER HILL
Healaugh
Reeth
Fremington
Grinton
Marrick
A6108
B6271
Gunnerside
Muker
Feetham
Low Row
Downholme
Swaledale
The Buttertubs
675
LOVELY SEAT
565
WHITASIDE MOOR
140
B6270
A6136
Scotton
Barden
East Hauxwell
Hunton
Bellerby
Castle Bolton
Whity Gill
Askrigg
Redmire
Preston-under-Scar
Leyburn
Sedbusk
National Park Centre
Bainbridge
Worton
Woodhall
Carperby
Wensleydale
Falls
A684
Constable Burton
Harmby
Finghall
Swinithwaite
Wensley
Gayle
Burtersett
Thornton Rust
Countersett
Aysgarth
Spennithorne
West Witton
Middleham
Thornton Steward
614
WETHER FELL
Semer Water
495
Thoralby
West Burton
546
Agglethorpe
Coverham
Newbiggin
Melmerby
Carlton
Jervaulx
River Ure
East Witton
A6
Sowden Beck
YORKSHIRE DALES
West Scrafton
Ellingstring
643
B6160
Horsehouse
Coverdale
Fearby
Healey
580
BROWN HAW
544
GREAT HAW
Druid's Temple
Leighton Reservoir
Cray
702
BUCKDEN PIKE
605
LITTLE WHERNSIDE
Scar House Reservoir
Roundhill Reservoir
Ilton
NATIONAL
Halton Gill
610
Buckden
617
TOR MERE TOP
Angram Reservoir
River Nidd
Litton
Starbotton
River Wharfe
704
GREAT WHERNSIDE
Middlesmoor
Stean
Lofthouse
132
624
River Skirfare
PARK
Arncliffe
Kettlewell
668
Hawkswick
Nidderdale
Bouthwaite
Ramsgill
575
MEUGHER
Gouthwaite Reservoir
593
538
496
CONISTONE MOOR
532
Kilnsey
Conistone
Kilnsey Park & Trout Farm
Malham Tarn
Wath
Malham Cove
545
B6160
Grimwith Reservoir
Pateley Bridge
Greenhow Hill
Bewerley
Glasshouses
Grassington
Threshfield
B6265
Stump Cross Caverns
B6165
National Park Centre
Malham
Linton
Hebden
359
Dacre Banks
Thorpe
Burnsall
Parcevall Hall
Hanlith
Kirkby Malham
Cracoe
B6160
506
Appletreewick
485
SIMON SEAT
Padside
Darley Head
Airton
Calton
Hetton
Otterburn
Rylstone
Thornthwaite
Winterburn
Barden Tower
Bellifield
R Aire
433
Bell Busk
Flasby
B6451
Forest Moor
A65
Blubberhouses
Coniston Cold
Eastby
Halton East
Bolton Abbey
Bolton Priory
A59
Gargrave
Fewston Reservoir
409
Swinsty Reservoir
Timble
Thorlby
Stirton
Embsay
Draughton
Embsay & Bolton Abbey Steam Railway
Beamsley
Pennine Way
East Marton
Skipton
123
Broughton
B6160
West Marton
Addingham
Nesfield
Middleton
A59
Elslack
A6131
A6034
Denton
Canal
Carleton
Clifton
Bracewell
Low Bradley
Askwith

Hudswell
Marrick
Hipswell
Colburn
Brompton-on-Swale
Easby
Scorton
Bolton-on-Swale
Whitwell
Hutton Bonville
East Harlsey
Catterick Bridge
Catterick
Ellerton
Danby Wiske
Downholme
Tunstall
Great Langton
Yafforth
Brompton
Foxton
Scotton
Kirkby Fleetham
Northallerton
Romanby
Kirby Sigston
Barden
East Hauxwell
Hornby
Hackforth
Fencote
Little Fencote
Thrintoft
Ainderby Steeple
Bellerby
Arrathorne
Hunton
Langthorne
Scruton
Morton-on-Swale
Warlaby
Thornton-le-Beans
Leyburn
Patrick Brompton
Little Crakehall
Constable Burton
Newton-le-Willows
Harmby
Wensley
Finghall
Crakehall
Leeming Bar
Leeming
North Otterington
Thornton-le-Moor
Borrowby
Spennithorne
Wensleydale Railway
Cowling
Bedale
Aiskew
Gatenby
Newby Wiske
Middleham
Thornton Steward
Rookwith
Burrill
Londonderry
Exelby
Firby
South Otterington
Coverham
Jervaulx
River Ure
Thornton Watlass
Thirn
Maunby
Thornton-le-Street
East Witton
Thorp Perrow
Theakston
Burneston
Kirby Wiske
Newsham
Sowden Beck
Snape
Carthorpe
Birds of Prey Centre
Pickhill
South Kilvington
Ellingstring
Low Ellington
High Ellington
Holme
Sandhutton
Thirsk
Well
Sinderby
Fearby
Theakston Brewery
Masham
Kirklington
Ainderby Quernhow
Carlton Miniott
Healey
Nosterfield
Thornborough
Howe
Swinton
Sutton Howgrave
Skipton-on-Swale
Druid's Temple
Warthermaske
West Tanfield
Baldersby
Catton
Leighton Reservoir
Ilton
Marmion Tower
Middleton Quernhow
Baldersby St James
Mickley
Roundhill Reservoir
Wath
Topcliffe
North Stainley
Melmerby
Grewelthorpe
Norton Conyers
Asenby
Rainton
Kirkby Malzeard
Lightwater Valley
Nunwick
Azerley
Middlesmoor
Lofthouse
Laverton
Sutton Grange
Hutton Conyers
Cundall
Galphay
Sharow
Dishforth
Ripon
Winksley
Copt Hewick
Bouthwaite
Studley Royal
Bridge Hewick
Norton-le-Clay
Low Grantley
Ramsgill
Marton-le-Moor
Gouthwaite Reservoir
High Grantley
Studley Roger
Littlethorpe
Kirby Hill
Aldfield
Risplith
Fountains Abbey NT
Skelton
Wath
Sawley
Newby Hall
Langthorpe
Milby
Boroughbridge
Devil's Arrows
Roman Town
Pateley Bridge
Bishop Monkton
Roecliffe
Aldborough
Wilsill
Brimham Rocks (Rock formations)
Markington
Bewerley
Glasshouses
Greenhow Hill
Minskip
Burton Leonard
Bishop Thornton
Wormald Green
Grafton
Stump Cross Caverns
Copgrove
South Stainley
Dacre Banks
Summerbridge
Hartwith
Shaw Mills
Staveley
Marton
Arkendale
Brearton
Bedlam
Dacre
Burnt Yates
Farnham
Ripley
Nidd
Ferrensby
Padside
Darley
Darley Head
Birstwith
Clint
Scotton
Thorpe
Hampsthwaite
Thornthwaite
Killinghall
Scriven
Flaxby
Swincliffe
Allerton Mauleverer
Kettlesing Bottom
Bilton
Knaresborough
Forest Moor
Forest Lane Head
High Harrogate
Starbeck
Low Harrogate
Blubberhouses
Kettlesing
Goldsborough
HARROGATE
Woodlands
Fewston Reservoir
Fewston
Harlow Carr
Great Yorkshire
Swinsty Res
Little Ribston
Walshford
Beckwithshaw
Pannal Ash
Rossett Green
Timble
Bland Hill
Follifoot
Langbar
Pannal
North Deighton
Spofforth
Kirk Deighton
North Rigton
Lindley Green
Braythorn
Stainburn
Kirkby Overblow
Sicklinghall
Clifton
Askwith
140
141
131
123
124
0 1 2 3 4 miles
0 1 2 3 4 5 kilometres

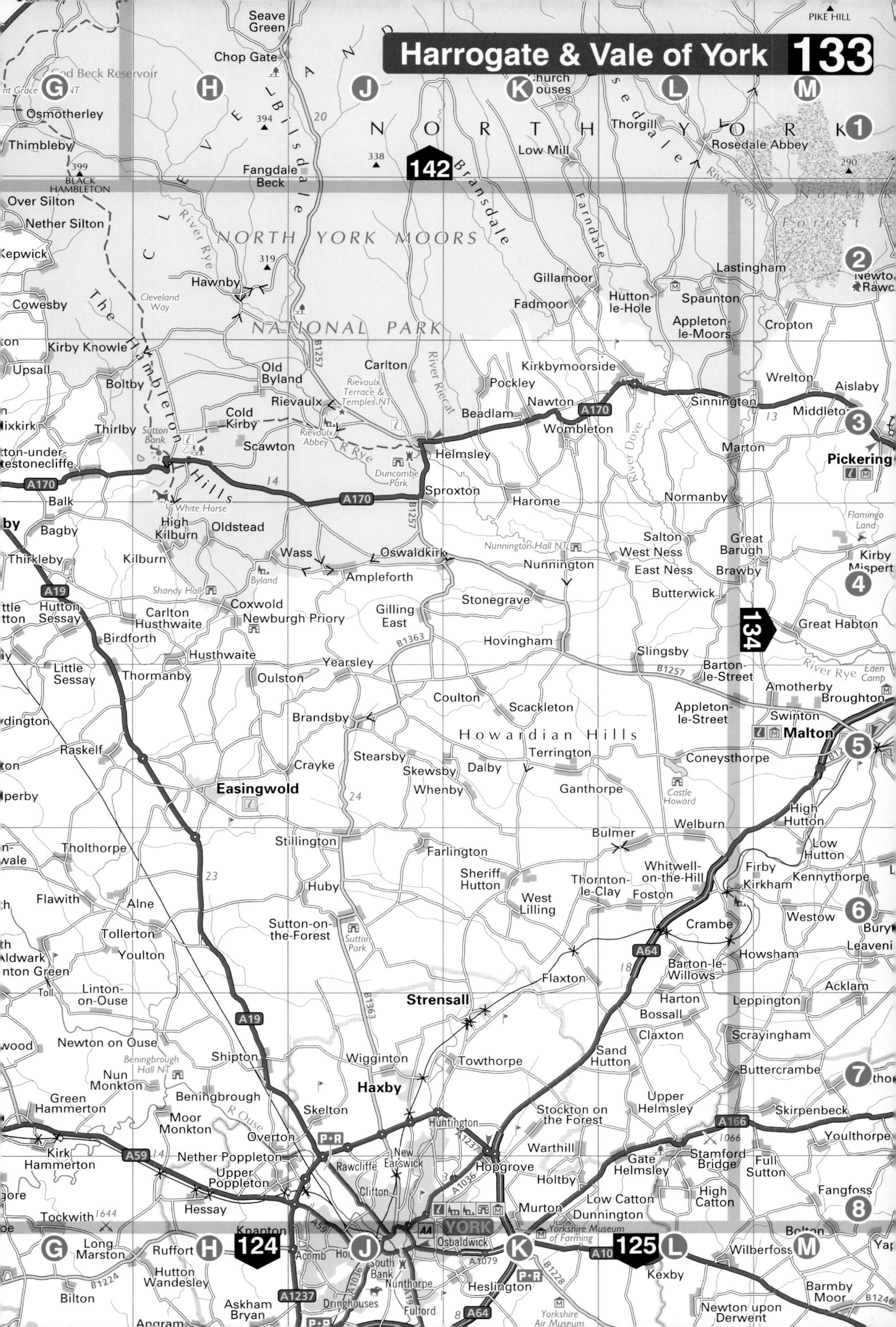
Seave Green
Chop Gate
Cod Beck Reservoir
Osmotherley
Thimbleby
BLACK HAMBLETON
Over Silton
Nether Silton
Kepwick
Cowesby
Kirby Knowle
Upsall
Boltby
Thirlby
Bilsdale
Fangdale Beck
142
Bransdale
NORTH YORK MOORS
NATIONAL PARK
Hawnby
Cleveland Way
River Rye
Old Byland
Rievaulx
Carlton
Cold Kirby
Sutton Bank
Scawton
Rievaulx Terrace & Temples NT
Rievaulx Abbey
Duncombe Park
Helmsley
Sproxton
River Riccal
Hambleton Hills
White Horse
High Kilburn
Oldstead
Balk
Bagby
Thirkleby
Kilburn
Wass
Oswaldkirk
Ampleforth
Byland
Shandy Hall
Coxwold
Newburgh Priory
Carlton Husthwaite
Hutton Sessay
Birdforth
Husthwaite
Little Sessay
Thormanby
Yearsley
Oulston
Gilling East
Stonegrave
Hovingham
Coulton
Brandsby
Scackleton
Howardian Hills
Terrington
Stearsby
Crayke
Skewsby
Dalby
Whenby
Ganthorpe
Easingwold
Raskelf
Tholthorpe
Stillington
Farlington
Sheriff Hutton
Huby
Flawith
Alne
Tollerton
Youlton
Linton-on-Ouse
Sutton-on-the-Forest
Sutton Park
West Lilling
Thornton-le-Clay
Strensall
Flaxton
Newton on Ouse
Beningbrough Hall NT
Nun Monkton
Beningbrough
Shipton
Wigginton
Towthorpe
Haxby
Skelton
Green Hammerton
Moor Monkton
Overton
Kirk Hammerton
Nether Poppleton
Upper Poppleton
Hessay
Tockwith
Long Marston
Ruffort
124
Knapton
Acomb
Rawcliffe
New Earswick
Huntington
Clifton
YORK
Osbaldwick
South Bank
Nunthorpe
Dringhouses
Fulford
Hutton Wandesley
Bilton
Askham Bryan
Hopgrove
Heslington
Murton
Holtby
Warthill
Stockton on the Forest
Yorkshire Museum of Farming
Yorkshire Air Museum
125
Kexby
Low Catton
Dunnington
Gate Helmsley
Stamford Bridge
High Catton
Full Sutton
Upper Helmsley
Sand Hutton
Claxton
Bossall
Harton
Barton-le-Willows
Howsham
Crambe
Foston
Whitwell-on-the-Hill
Kirkham
Firby
Bulmer
Welburn
Castle Howard
Coneysthorpe
High Hutton
Low Hutton
Kennythorpe
Westow
Leppington
Acklam
Scrayingham
Buttercrambe
Skirpenbeck
Youlthorpe
Fangfoss
Wilberfoss
Barmby Moor
Newton upon Derwent
Bolton
Malton
Swinton
Broughton
Amotherby
Appleton-le-Street
Barton-le-Street
Slingsby
Eden Camp
River Rye
Great Habton
134
Butterwick
East Ness
West Ness
Salton
Brawby
Great Barugh
Nunnington
Nunnington Hall NT
Harome
Normanby
Kirby Misperton
Flamingo Land
Pickering
Marton
Middleton
Aislaby
Wrelton
Sinnington
Cropton
Wombleton
Nawton
Beadlam
Pockley
Kirkbymoorside
River Dove
Gillamoor
Fadmoor
Hutton-le-Hole
Spaunton
Appleton-le-Moors
Lastingham
Low Mill
Farndale
Thorgill
Rosedale Abbey
River Seven
Church Houses
NORTH YORK
PIKE HILL
A170
A19
A59
A64
A166
A1036
A1237
A1079
B1257
B1363
B1224
B1228
B1246
1066
1644

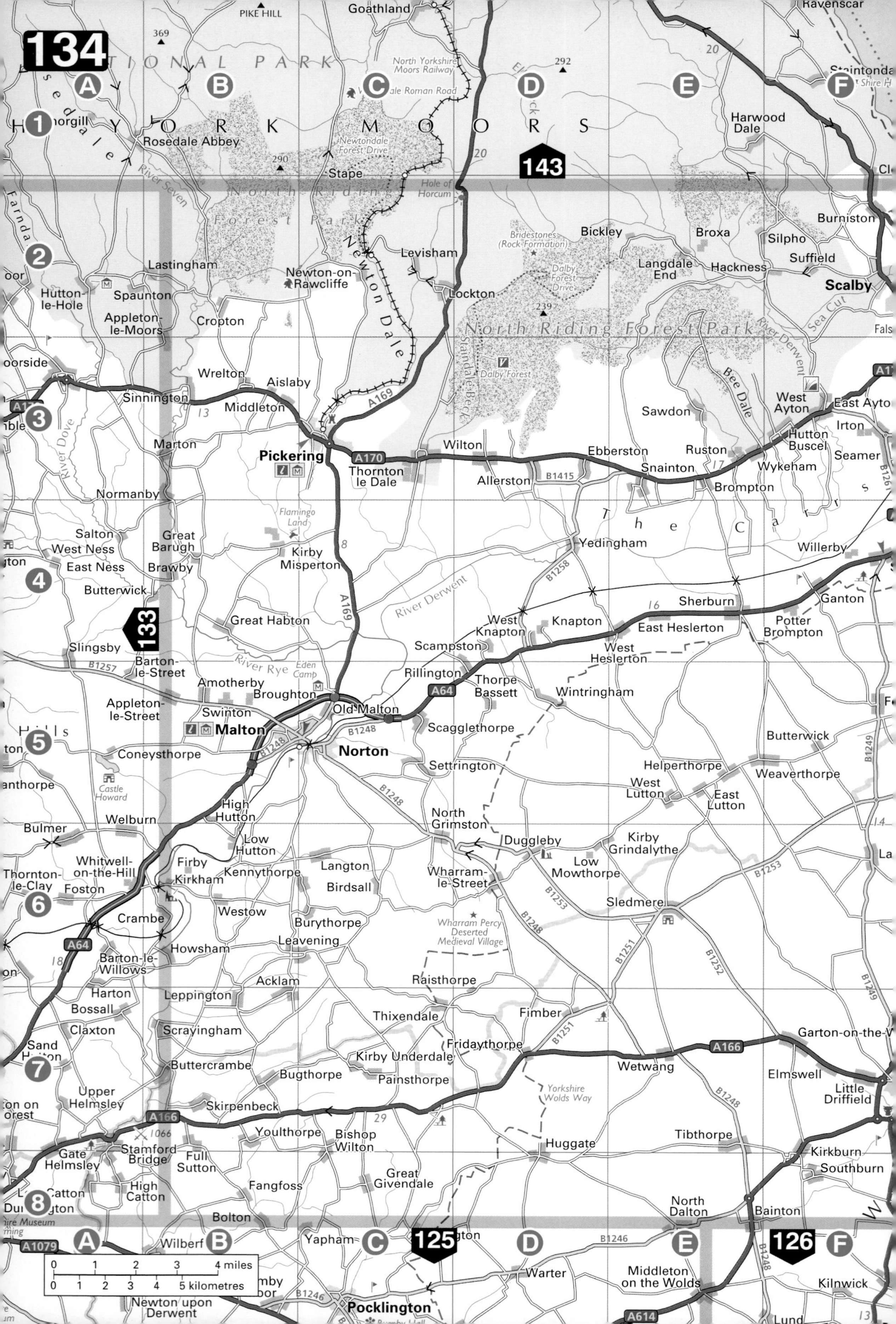
134
PIKE HILL
Goathland
Ravenscar
369
NATIONAL PARK
North Yorkshire Moors Railway
292
20
Staintondale
A
B
C
D
E
F
1
YORK MOORS
Rosedale Abbey
Harwood Dale
Newtondale Forest Drive
143
290
Stape
River Seven
Hole of Horcum
North Riding Forest Park
Farndale
Newton Dale
Bridestones (Rock Formation)
Bickley
Broxa
Burniston
Silpho
2
Levisham
Langdale End
Hackness
Suffield
Lastingham
Newton-on-Rawcliffe
Dalby Forest Drive
Scalby
Hutton-le-Hole
Spaunton
Lockton
239
Sea Cut
Appleton-le-Moors
Cropton
North Riding Forest Park
River Derwent
Staindale Beck
Dalby Forest
Bee Dale
Wrelton
Aislaby
A169
West Ayton
East Ayton
Sinnington
Middleton
Sawdon
3
Irton
River Dove
Marton
13
Wilton
Ebberston
Ruston
Hutton Buscel
Pickering
A170
Seamer
Thornton le Dale
Allerston
B1415
Snainton
17
Wykeham
Brompton
B1261
Normanby
Flamingo Land
The Carrs
Salton
Great Barugh
8
West Ness
Kirby Misperton
Yedingham
Willerby
East Ness
Brawby
B1258
4
Butterwick
A169
River Derwent
Ganton
16
Sherburn
Great Habton
West Knapton
Knapton
Potter Brompton
East Heslerton
133
Slingsby
Scampston
West Heslerton
Barton-le-Street
River Rye
Eden Camp
B1257
Rillington
Thorpe Bassett
Amotherby
Broughton
A64
Wintringham
Appleton-le-Street
Swinton
Old Malton
Malton
B1248
Scagglethorpe
5
Coneysthorpe
Norton
Butterwick
Settrington
Helperthorpe
B1249
West Lutton
Weaverthorpe
Castle Howard
B1248
East Lutton
High Hutton
North Grimston
Bulmer
Welburn
Low Hutton
Duggleby
Kirby Grindalythe
Whitwell-on-the-Hill
Firby
Low Mowthorpe
B1253
Kirkham
Kennythorpe
Langton
Thornton-le-Clay
Foston
Birdsall
Wharram-le-Street
6
Sledmere
B1253
Crambe
Westow
Burythorpe
Wharram Percy Deserted Medieval Village
B1248
A64
Leavening
Howsham
B1251
B1252
Barton-le-Willows
18
B1249
Acklam
Raisthorpe
Harton
Leppington
Bossall
Thixendale
Fimber
Claxton
Scrayingham
Garton-on-the-Wolds
Fridaythorpe
B1251
A166
Sand Hutton
Kirby Underdale
7
Buttercrambe
Wetwang
Elmswell
Bugthorpe
Painsthorpe
Yorkshire Wolds Way
Little Driffield
Upper Helmsley
B1248
A166
Skirpenbeck
29
1066
Youlthorpe
Bishop Wilton
Tibthorpe
Gate Helmsley
Stamford Bridge
Full Sutton
Huggate
Kirkburn
Southburn
High Catton
Great Givendale
Low Catton
Fangfoss
8
North Dalton
Bainton
Bolton
A1079
Wilberfoss
Yapham
125
B1246
126
Warter
Middleton on the Wolds
Kilnwick
0 1 2 3 4 miles
0 1 2 3 4 5 kilometres
Newton upon Derwent
B1246
Pocklington
A614
Lund
B1248
13

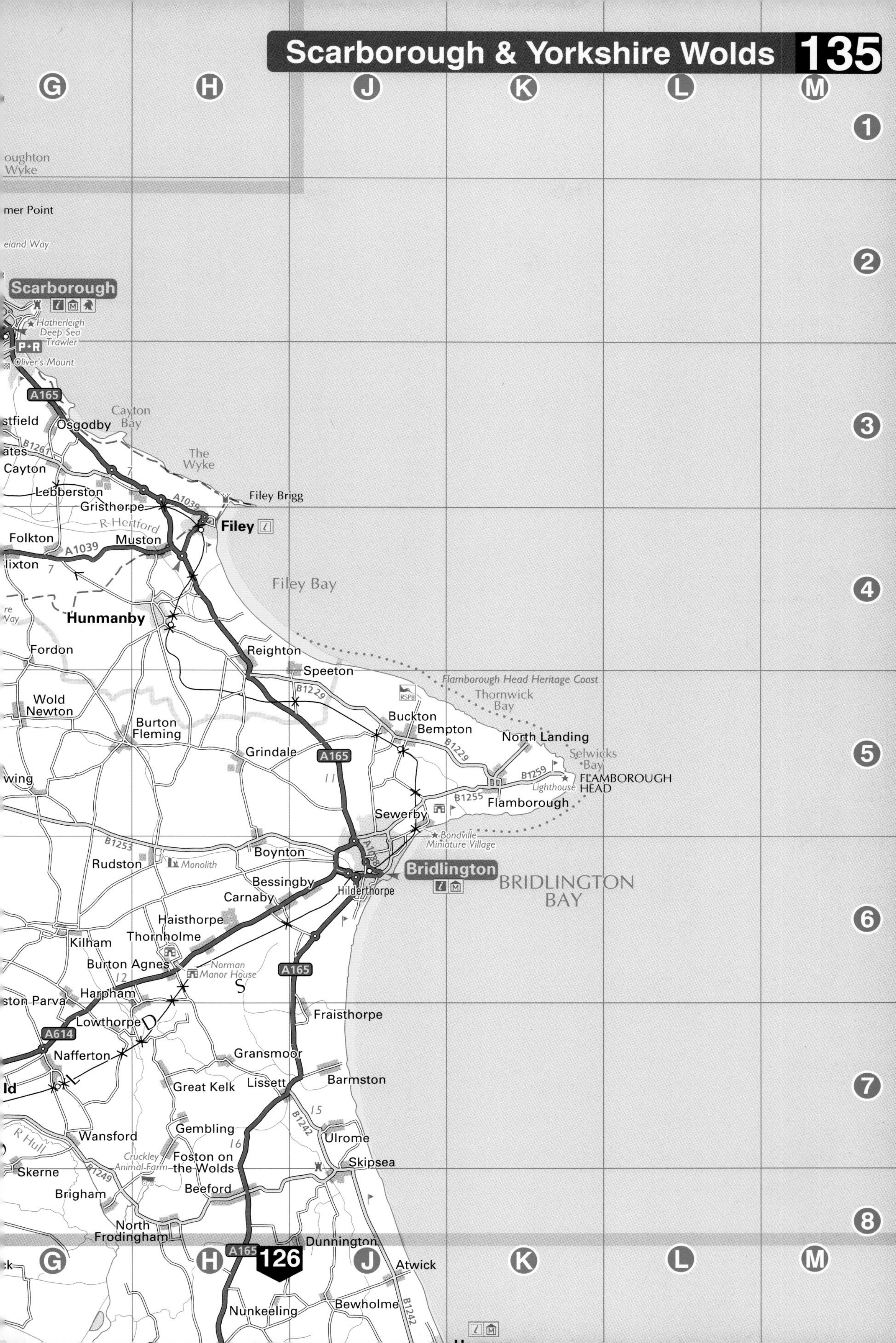
G
H
J
K
L
M
1
2
3
4
5
6
7
8
oughton Wyke
mer Point
eland Way
Scarborough
Hatherleigh Deep Sea Trawler
P+R
Oliver's Mount
A165
Cayton Bay
stfield
Osgodby
B1261
ates
Cayton
The Wyke
Lebberston
Gristhorpe
A1039
Filey Brigg
R Hertford
Filey
Folkton
Muston
A1039
lixton
Filey Bay
Hunmanby
Fordon
Reighton
Speeton
B1229
Flamborough Head Heritage Coast
Thornwick Bay
RSPB
Wold Newton
Burton Fleming
Buckton
Bempton
North Landing
B1229
Grindale
A165
Selwicks Bay
B1259
FLAMBOROUGH HEAD
Lighthouse
wing
B1255
Flamborough
Sewerby
Bondville Miniature Village
B1253
Boynton
A1038
Rudston
Monolith
Bridlington
BRIDLINGTON BAY
Bessingby
Carnaby
Hilderthorpe
Haisthorpe
Thornholme
Kilham
Burton Agnes
Norman Manor House
A165
Harpham
ston Parva
Lowthorpe
Fraisthorpe
A614
Nafferton
Gransmoor
Great Kelk
Lissett
Barmston
ld
B1242
Gembling
Ulrome
Wansford
R Hull
Cruckley Animal Farm
Foston on the Wolds
Skipsea
Skerne
B1249
Beeford
Brigham
North Frodingham
Dunnington
A165
126
Atwick
Nunkeeling
Bewholme
B1242

A
B
C
D
E
F
1
2
3
4
5
6
7
8
147
128
Allerby
Crosscanonby
Crosby
Fort
River Ellen
Maryport
Dearham
Gilc
A594
Tallen
Flimby
Broughton
Moor
Bridekir
Standingstone
Dovenby
A59
Great
Broughton
Papcastle
Camerton
Seaton
Great
Clifton
A66
Brigham
Greysouthen
AA
Stainburn
Little
Clifton
Eaglesfield
Workington
Mossbay
Moss
Bay
Westfield
Salterbeck
A596
A595
Deanscales
Branthwaite
Dean
Harrington
A597
Pardshaw
Ullock
Sosgill
Distington
Mockerkin
Gilgarran
Pica
R Keekle
A5086
Loweswat
Parton
Moresby
Lamplugh
572
A595
Asby
Arlecdon
Kirkland
Rowrah
Whitehaven
Hensingham
Frizington
Saltom
Bay
B5295
B5294
Cleator
Moor
Ennerdale
Bridge
Ennerda
Water
Mirehouse
Sandwith
River Ehen
B5345
Rottington
Cleator
St Bees Head
RSPB
Bigrigg
River Calder
St Bees Head
Heritage Coast
St Bees
Egremont
533
LANK
RIGG
Florence Mine
Worm Gill
Haile
River Bleng
Nethertown
Beckermet
Calder Bridge
Sellafield
Visitor
Centre
R Ehen
Cross
Gosforth
Wellington
B5343
Santo
Seascale
Hallsenna Moor
Drigg
Holmrook
Muncaster
Mill
River E
Ravenglass
Bath
House
Muncaster
A595
Lane
Waberth
Hycemoor
Selker Bay
Bootle
0
1
2
3
4 miles
0
1
2
3
4
5 kilometres

Lake District
137
147
148
138
129
Plumbland
Bothel
Ireby
Hesket Newmarket
High Ireby
Uldale
Aughertree
Sunderland
Blindcrake
BINSEY
Trotters World of Animals
R Derwent
Bassenthwaite
KNOTT
Hutton Roof
Lamonby
Ellonby
Skelton
Little Blencow
Catterlen
Johnby
Great Blencow
Greystoke
Newton Reigny
Mungrisdale
BERRIER HILL
Berrier
Motherby
Newbiggin
Penruddock
Stainton
Dalemain
Dacre
GREAT CALVA
River Caldew
BOWSCALE FELL
SKIDDAW
Mirehouse
Bassenthwaite Lake
SADDLEBACK
Scales
Armaside
LORDS SEAT
Thornthwaite
Whinlatter
High Lorton
Whinlatter Pass
Braithwaite
Great Crosthwaite
LATRIGG
R Greta
Threlkeld
Quarry and Mining
Castlerigg
GREAT MELL FELL
LITTLE MELL FELL
Trout Beck
Pooley Bridge
Longthwaite
Ulcat Row
Watermillock
Thornythwaite
Dockray
Aira Force NT
Ullswater
Portinscale
Keswick
GRISEDALE PIKE
HOBCARTON PIKE
Swinside
Derwent Water
Borrowdale
Mosedale Beck
GRASMOOR
GREAT DODD
STYBARROW DODD
Lodore Falls
HIGH SEAT
LOADPOT HILL
Buttermere
Grange
Thirlspot
Glenridding
PLACE FELL
Patterdale
Bowder Stone
DALE HEAD
Honister Pass
Rosthwaite
Thirlmere
HELVELLYN
HIGH STILE
Seatoller
LAKE DISTRICT NATIONAL PARK
PILLAR
Grisdale Tarn
Brothers Water
HIGH RAISE
Haweswater
Hayes Water
FAIRFIELD
HIGH STREET
KIRK FELL
GREAT GABLE
GLARAMARA
Blea Water
Wasdale Head
HIGH WHITE STONES
CUMBRIAN MOUNTAINS
Kentmere Reservoir
GREAT END
Stickle Tarn
Grasmere
Wordsworth
White Moss Common NT
Kirkstone Pass
TARN CRAG
SCAFELL PIKE
SCAFELL
BOW FELL
Great Langdale
Chapel Stile
Rydal
Rydal Mount
Armitt Museum
Wast Water
Burnmoor Tarn
Rydal Water
Elterwater
Bridge House NT
Ambleside
Kentmere
Green Quarry
PIKE OF BLISCO
R Mite
Hardknott Fort
Hardknott Pass
Wrynose Pass
Little Langdale
Skelwith Bridge
Galava Fort NT
Stagshaw NT
Troutbeck
Townend NT
Boot
Low Wray
The Tarns
National Park Centre
Eskdale
Furness Fells
Outgate
Troutbeck Bridge
HARTER FELL
River Duddon
Levers Water
High Wray
Windermere
River Kent
Devoke Water
Seathwaite Tarn
Far End
Hawkshead Hill
Courthouse NT
Hawkshead
Staveley
THE OLD MAN OF CONISTON
Coniston
Steamboat
Bowness-on-Windermere
Hall Dunnerdale
Seathwaite
Bowmanstead
Steam Yacht 'Gondola' NT
Hill Top NT
Far Sawrey
Esthwaite Water
Brantwood
Near Sawrey
Grizedale
Crook
Torver
Coniston Water
Blackwell
Winster
WHITFELL
Ulpha
Town End
Satterthwaite
Underbarrow
Graythwaite Hall
Crosthwaite
Broughton Mills
High Nibthwaite
Thwaite Head
Crosslands
Stott Park Bobbin Mill
GUMMERS HOW
Row
Stone Circle
Blawith
Rusland
Finsthwaite
Sizergh Castle NT
Broughton-in-Furness
Whitbarrow
Oxen Park
A591
A66
A5091
A592
A593
A5084
A5074
B5299
B5291
B5292
B5289
B5322
B5343
B5285
B5284
B5305
B5320
RSPB

138
A
B
C
D
E
F
1
2
3
4
5
6
7
8
Hutton End
Lazonby
Gamblesby
247
LAZONBY FELL
Glassonby
710
MELMERBY FELL
B6413
Salkeld Dykes
Great Salkeld
Long Meg and her Daughters
Melmerby
740
Lamonby
Plumpton
Little Salkeld
Hunsonby
Ellonby
Skelton
Hutton-in-the-Forest
B5305
B6412
Winskill
Ousby
663
CARROCK FELL
Hutton Roof
Little Blencow
Catterlen
41
148
Langwathby
Skirwith
Johnby
Great Blencow
Edenhall
Blencarn
703
357
BERRIER HILL
Greystoke
Newton Reigny
Penrith
A686
R Eamont
Mungrisdale
B5288
Culgaith
Berrier
Motherby
Brougham
Milburn
40
Newbiggin
Countess Pillar
Acorn Bank NT
Newbiggin
Penruddock
Stainton
Rheged Discovery Centre
Eamont Bridge
Oasis Whinfell Park
Center Parcs
220
Temple Sowerby
Scales
A66
17
Dalemain
Yanwath
Wetheriggs Country Pottery
Kirkby Thore
Tirril
12
Dacre
Clifton
River Eden
A5091
536
GREAT MELL FELL
Trout Beck
B5320
R Lowther
Cilburn Moss
Cliburn
Long Marton
Quarry and Mining
506
LITTLE MELL FELL
Pooley Bridge
Melkinthorpe
13
A66
Mosedale Beck
Longthwaite
Lowther
Hackthorpe
Thornythwaite
Ulcat Row
Watermillock
Askham
Leisure & Wildlife Park
Great Strickland
Morland
Bolton
Dockray
A592
Helton
Newby
Kings Meaburn
856
GREAT DODD
Aira Force NT
Ullswater
11
River Lyvennet
Colby
Little Strickland
840
STYBARROW DODD
671
LOADPOT HILL
Sleagill
Appleby
Burrell
27
Bampton
Bampton Grange
Reagill
Glenridding
657
PLACE FELL
Rosgill
M6
Mauld's Meaburn
Patterdale
950
HELVELLYN
Haweswater
Shap
803
HIGH RAISE
Keld Chapel NT
Crosby Ravensworth
B6260
137
Grisdale Tarn
Brothers Water
Swindale River
873
FAIRFIELD
Hayes Water
817
HIGH STREET
39
316
Shap Summit
Blea Water
RSPB
Great Asby Scar
LAKE DISTRICT
A6
412
Kentmere Reservoir
B6261
485
Kirkstone Pass
15
Orton
Wordsworth
White Moss Common NT
Rydal Mount
663
TARN CRAG
Crookdale Beck
6
Rydal
NATIONAL PARK
Tebay
B6260
B6261
Armitt Museum
Rydal Water
R Lune
A592
Bridge House NT
Ambleside
Kentmere
Green Quarter
Borrow Beck
38
Tebay
12
Skelwith Bridge
Stagshaw NT
Troutbeck
Long Sleddale
Galava Fort NT
Townend NT
Langdale
Low Wray
A591
River Kent
A685
Low Borrowbridge
The Tarns
National Park Centre
Outgate
Troutbeck Bridge
A6
High Wray
Windermere
Courthouse NT
Hawkshead
Staveley
Watchgate
Steamboat
8
B5285
Cautley
677
THE CA
Bowness-on-Windermere
Garth Row
Grayrigg
Hill Top NT
Far Sawrey
Burneside
12
Esthwaite Water
A591
Near Sawrey
B5284
A685
Grizedale
Crook
M6
Grizedale
A5284
Windermere
Blackwell
Winster
129
Kendal
130
WINDER
473
Underbarrow
37
Graythwaite Hall
Crosthwaite
A684
217
New Hutton
A592
Oxenholme
Killington
A6
B6254
Middleshaw
Row
A5074
Natland
A591
A65
Old Hutton
Sizergh Castle NT
Whitbarrow
0
1
2
3
4 miles
5 kilometres

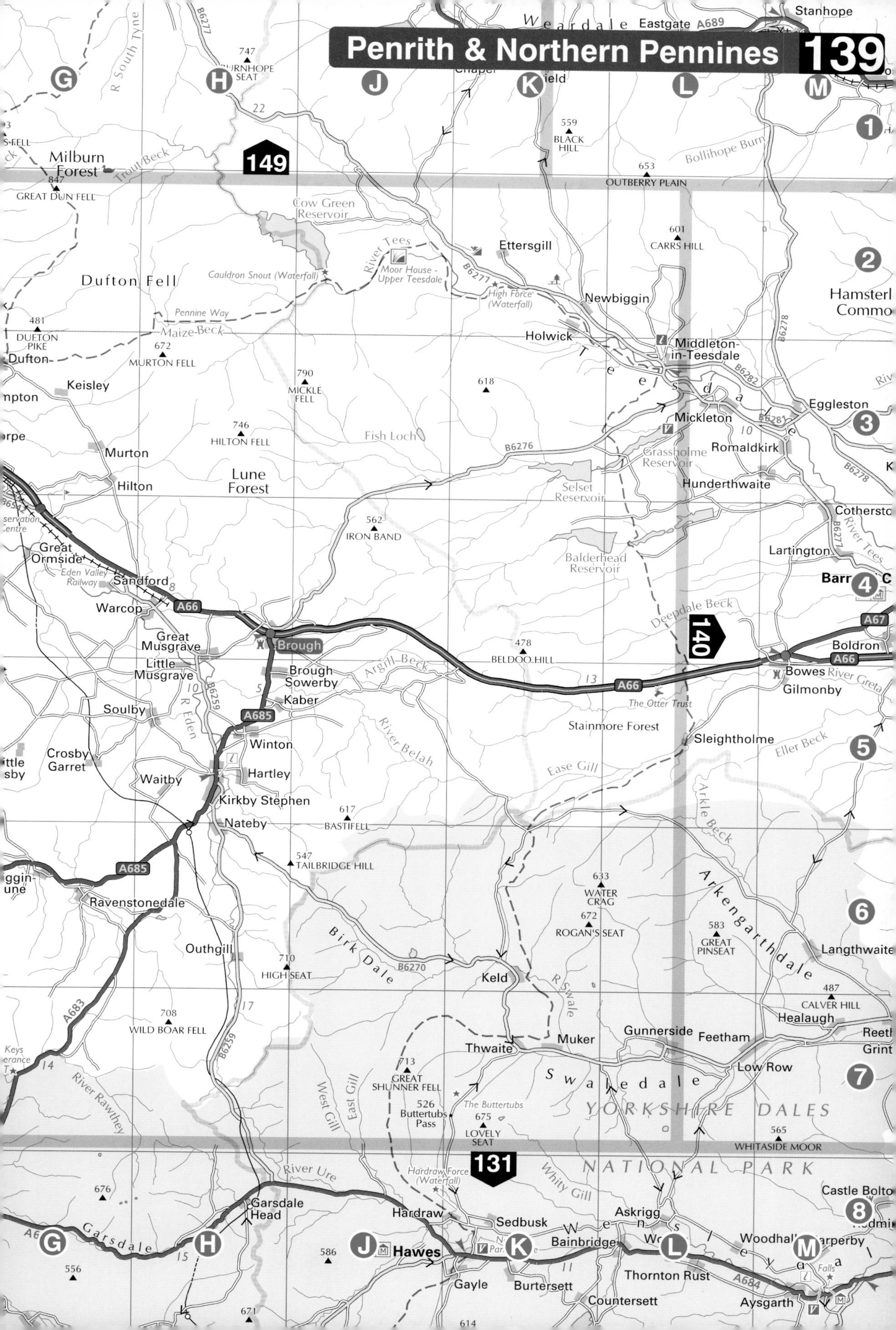
Stanhope
Weardale
Eastgate
A689
Milburn Forest
847
GREAT DUN FELL
Cow Green Reservoir
Cauldron Snout (Waterfall)
Moor House - Upper Teesdale
River Tees
High Force (Waterfall)
Ettersgill
Newbiggin
Holwick
Middleton-in-Teesdale
Dufton Fell
Pennine Way
Maize Beck
481
DUFTON PIKE
Dufton
672
MURTON FELL
790
MICKLE FELL
618
Keisley
Murton
746
HILTON FELL
Hilton
Lune Forest
Fish Loch
Mickleton
Eggleston
Romaldkirk
Grassholme Reservoir
Hunderthwaite
Selset Reservoir
Balderhead Reservoir
Cotherstone
Lartington
562
IRON BAND
Great Ormside
Eden Valley Railway
Sandford
Warcop
A66
Great Musgrave
Brough
Little Musgrave
Brough Sowerby
Kaber
Argill Beck
Deepdale Beck
478
BELDOO HILL
The Otter Trust
Bowes
Gilmonby
Boldron
A67
River Greta
Stainmore Forest
Sleightholme
Eller Beck
Soulby
A685
Winton
Hartley
Crosby Garret
Waitby
Kirkby Stephen
Nateby
River Belah
Ease Gill
617
BASTIFELL
547
TAILBRIDGE HILL
Arkle Beck
633
WATER CRAG
672
ROGAN'S SEAT
583
GREAT PINSEAT
Arkengarthdale
Langthwaite
Ravenstonedale
Outhgill
710
HIGH SEAT
Birk Dale
B6270
Keld
R Swale
487
CALVER HILL
Healaugh
708
WILD BOAR FELL
A683
B6259
Muker
Gunnerside
Feetham
Thwaite
Low Row
713
GREAT SHUNNER FELL
526
Buttertubs Pass
The Buttertubs
675
LOVELY SEAT
Swaledale
YORKSHIRE DALES
565
WHITASIDE MOOR
NATIONAL PARK
River Rawthey
West Gill
East Gill
River Ure
Hardraw Force (Waterfall)
Whity Gill
676
Garsdale Head
Hardraw
Sedbusk
Askrigg
Castle Bolton
Garsdale
Hawes
Bainbridge
Wensleydale
Woodhall
Carperby
556
586
Gayle
Burtersett
Thornton Rust
A684
Aysgarth
Falls
Countersett
671
614
559
BLACK HILL
653
OUTBERRY PLAIN
601
CARRS HILL
Bollihope Burn
Hamsterley Common
747
BURNHOPE SEAT
R South Tyne
Trout Beck
B6277
B6276
B6278
B6282
B6281
149
140
131
G H J K L M
1 2 3 4 5 6 7 8

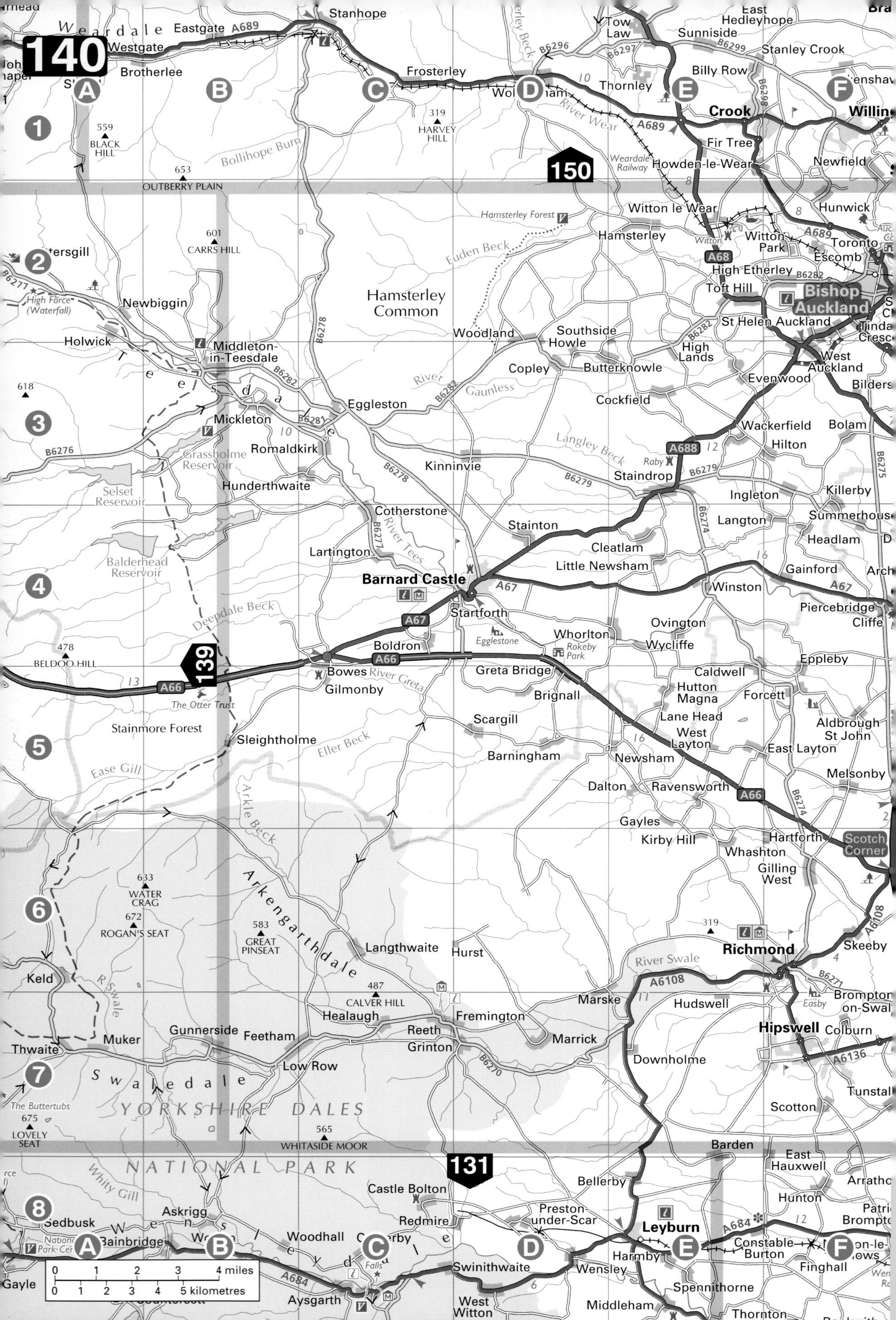
140
150
139
131
Stanhope
Eastgate
Westgate
Weardale
Brotherlee
Frosterley
Wolsingham
Tow Law
Sunniside
East Hedleyhope
Stanley Crook
Billy Row
Thornley
Crook
Fir Tree
Howden-le-Wear
Newfield
Willington
Weardale Railway
River Wear
Black Hill
Harvey Hill
Bollihope Burn
Outberry Plain
Witton le Wear
Hamsterley Forest
Hamsterley
Witton Park
Toronto
Escomb
High Etherley
Toft Hill
Bishop Auckland
St Helen Auckland
West Auckland
Carrs Hill
Euden Beck
Hamsterley Common
High Force (Waterfall)
Newbiggin
Holwick
Middleton-in-Teesdale
Woodland
Southside
Howle
High Lands
Copley
Butterknowle
Evenwood
Cockfield
Eggleston
River Gaunless
Teesdale
Mickleton
Romaldkirk
Grassholme Reservoir
Selset Reservoir
Hunderthwaite
Kinninvie
Langley Beck
Raby
Staindrop
Wackerfield
Bolam
Hilton
Ingleton
Killerby
Cotherstone
River Tees
Stainton
Langton
Summerhouse
Headlam
Cleatlam
Lartington
Balderhead Reservoir
Little Newsham
Gainford
Barnard Castle
Winston
Startforth
Piercebridge
Cliffe
Deepdale Beck
Boldron
Egglestone
Whorlton
Rokeby Park
Ovington
Wycliffe
Beldoo Hill
Bowes
River Greta
Greta Bridge
Caldwell
Eppleby
Gilmonby
Brignall
Hutton Magna
Forcett
The Otter Trust
Stainmore Forest
Scargill
Lane Head
West Layton
Aldbrough St John
Sleightholme
Eller Beck
Barningham
Newsham
East Layton
Ease Gill
Arkle Beck
Dalton
Ravensworth
Melsonby
Gayles
Kirby Hill
Hartforth
Whashton
Scotch Corner
Gilling West
Water Crag
Rogan's Seat
Arkengarthdale
Great Pinseat
Langthwaite
Hurst
Richmond
Skeeby
River Swale
Keld
R Swale
Calver Hill
Marske
Hudswell
Brompton-on-Swale
Easby
Healaugh
Fremington
Reeth
Grinton
Hipswell
Colburn
Thwaite
Muker
Gunnerside
Feetham
Marrick
Downholme
Low Row
Swaledale
Tunstall
The Buttertubs
Lovely Seat
Yorkshire Dales National Park
Whitaside Moor
Scotton
Barden
East Hauxwell
Whity Gill
Castle Bolton
Bellerby
Arrathorne
Hunton
Askrigg
Redmire
Preston-under-Scar
Leyburn
Patrick Brompton
Sedbusk
Wensleydale
Worton
Bainbridge
National Park Centre
Woodhall
Carperby
Constable Burton
Newton-le-Willows
Harmby
Finghall
Falls
Swinithwaite
Wensley
Gayle
Aysgarth
Spennithorne
West Witton
Middleham
Thornton
0 1 2 3 4 miles
0 1 2 3 4 5 kilometres

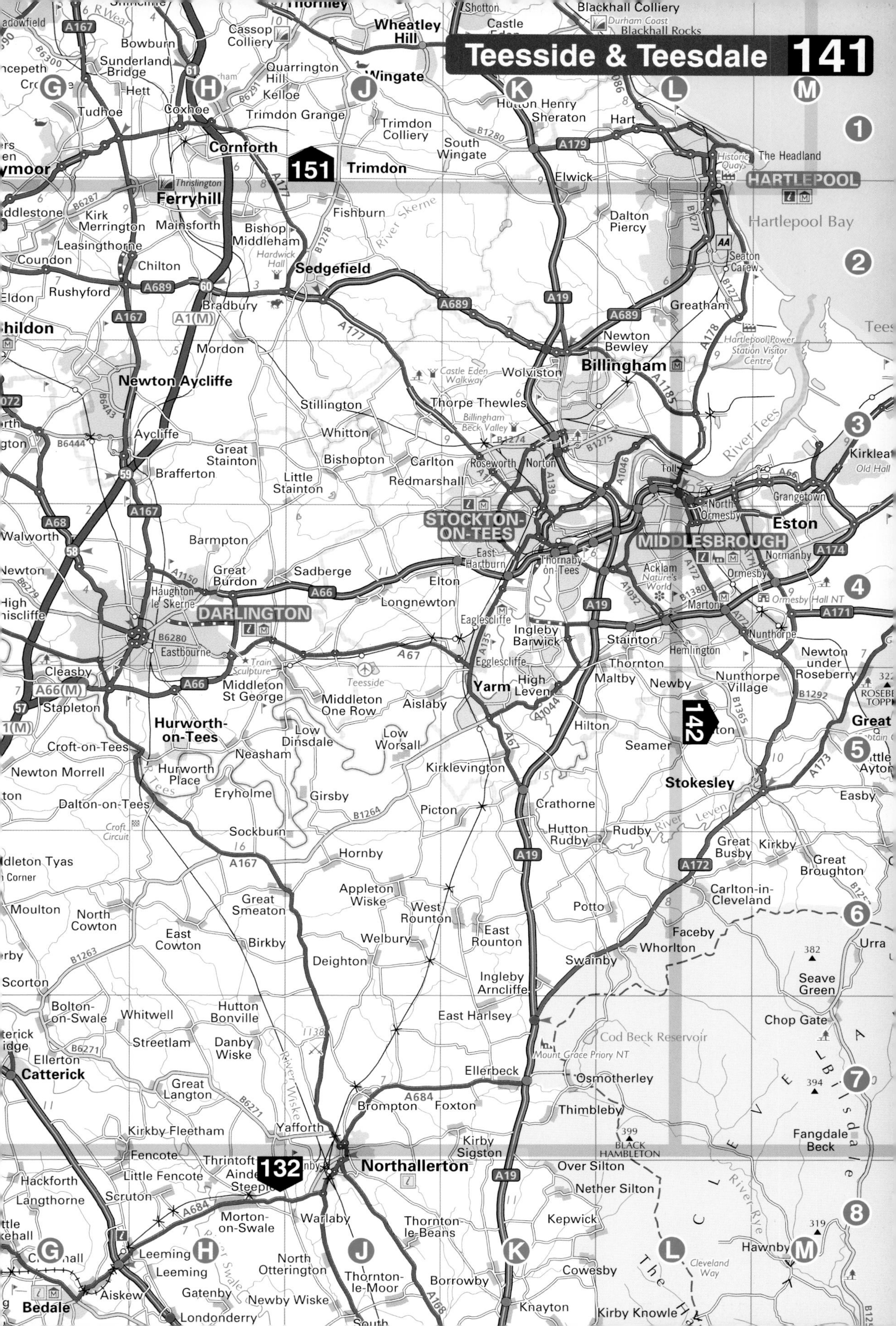
Teesside & Teesdale
141
Wheatley Hill
Wingate
Cassop Colliery
Quarrington Hill
Kelloe
Trimdon Grange
Trimdon Colliery
Trimdon
151
Cornforth
Coxhoe
Bowburn
Sunderland Bridge
Hett
Tudhoe
Ferryhill
Thrislington
Kirk Merrington
Mainsforth
Bishop Middleham
Leasingthorne
Chilton
Coundon
Rushyford
Eldon
Sedgefield
Hardwick Hall
Fishburn
Bradbury
Mordon
Newton Aycliffe
Aycliffe
Great Stainton
Brafferton
Stillington
Whitton
Bishopton
Little Stainton
Carlton
Redmarshall
Barmpton
Great Burdon
Sadberge
Haughton le Skerne
DARLINGTON
Eastbourne
Walworth
Cleasby
Stapleton
Middleton St George
Middleton One Row
Teesside
Hurworth-on-Tees
Croft-on-Tees
Hurworth Place
Neasham
Low Dinsdale
Newton Morrell
Dalton-on-Tees
Eryholme
Girsby
Croft Circuit
Sockburn
Hornby
Great Smeaton
Appleton Wiske
West Rounton
East Rounton
Welbury
Deighton
North Cowton
East Cowton
Birkby
Moulton
Scorton
Bolton-on-Swale
Whitwell
Hutton Bonville
Streetlam
Danby Wiske
Ellerton
Catterick
Great Langton
Kirkby Fleetham
Yafforth
Fencote
Little Fencote
Thrintoft
Ainderby Steeple
132
Northallerton
Hackforth
Langthorne
Scruton
Morton-on-Swale
Warlaby
Leeming
North Otterington
Thornton-le-Moor
Thornton-le-Beans
Newby Wiske
Gatenby
Aiskew
Bedale
Londonderry
Castle Eden
Shotton
Blackhall Colliery
Durham Coast
Blackhall Rocks
Hutton Henry
Sheraton
Hart
South Wingate
Elwick
The Headland
Historic Quay
HARTLEPOOL
Hartlepool Bay
Dalton Piercy
Seaton Carew
Greatham
Newton Bewley
Billingham
Hartlepool Power Station Visitor Centre
Wolviston
Castle Eden Walkway
Thorpe Thewles
Billingham Beck Valley
Roseworth
Norton
STOCKTON-ON-TEES
East Hartburn
Thornaby-on-Tees
Elton
Longnewton
Eaglescliffe
Egglescliffe
Ingleby Barwick
Yarm
High Leven
Aislaby
Low Worsall
Kirklevington
Picton
Crathorne
Hutton Rudby
Rudby
Potto
Ingleby Arncliffe
East Harlsey
Ellerbeck
Osmotherley
Mount Grace Priory NT
Cod Beck Reservoir
Brompton
Foxton
Kirby Sigston
Thimbleby
Over Silton
Nether Silton
Kepwick
Cowesby
Borrowby
Knayton
Kirby Knowle
MIDDLESBROUGH
Acklam Nature's World
Marton
Ormesby
Eston
Grangetown
North Ormesby
Kirkleatham
Old Hall
Normanby
Ormesby Hall NT
Nunthorpe
Stainton
Hemlington
Thornton
Maltby
Newby
Nunthorpe Village
Newton under Roseberry
Hilton
Seamer
142
Stokesley
Great Ayton
Easby
Great Busby
Kirkby
Great Broughton
Carlton-in-Cleveland
Faceby
Whorlton
Swainby
Urra
Seave Green
Chop Gate
Fangdale Beck
Black Hambleton
Hawnby
Cleveland Way
River Tees
River Skerne
River Leven
River Wiske
River Swale
River Rye
Bilsdale
CLEVELAND
A19
A179
A689
A177
A167
A1(M)
A66
A66(M)
A67
A68
A684
A168
A172
A171
A173
A174
A178
A1185
A1032
A1046
A1044
A135
A139
B1274
B1275
B1278
B1280
B1277
B1380
B1365
B1292
B1264
B1263
B6271
B6280
B6444
B6287
B6300
B6291
B6443
Toll
G H J K L M
1 2 3 4 5 6 7 8

142
151
141
133
A
B
C
D
E
F
1
2
3
4
5
6
7
8
Blackhall Colliery
Durham Coast
Blackhall Rocks
Castle Eden
Hutton Henry
Sheraton
Hart
A1086
A179
The Headland
Historic Quay
HARTLEPOOL
Elwick
Dalton Piercy
Hartlepool Bay
B1277
Seaton Carew
A19
A689
Greatham
Tees Bay
Hartlepool Power Station Visitor Centre
Newton Bewley
A178
Billingham
Wolviston
A1185
Thewles
River Tees
Redcar
Marske-by-the-Sea
Saltburn-by-the-Sea
Saltburn Smugglers
Hummersea
B1274
B1275
A1046
A139
Roseworth
Norton
Toll
A66
Kirkleatham
Old Hall
A1042
B1269
A1085
A174
New Marske
Brotton
Skelton
Loftus
Kilton
Easington
Grangetown
North Ormesby
Eston
Wilton
Upleatham
Dunsdale
B1268
A173
STOCKTON-ON-TEES
MIDDLESBROUGH
Normanby
Thornaby-on-Tees
East Hartburn
Acklam Nature's World
A1032
A172
B1380
Ormesby
Marton
Ormesby Hall NT
A171
Boosbeck
Lingdale
Kilton Thorpe
Margrove Park
Liverton
Stanghow
Guisborough
Guisborough Forest
Eaglescliffe
A135
Ingleby Barwick
Stainton
Hemlington
Nunthorpe
Newton under Roseberry
Hutton Lowcross
Cleveland Way
Moorsholm
B1366
Scaling
Gerrick
Egglescliffe
Yarm
High Leven
Thornton
Maltby
Newby
Nunthorpe Village
322
ROSEBERRY TOPPING
B1292
A1044
B1365
Great Ayton
Captain Cook Monument
Commondale
Hilton
Seamer
Tanton
A67
Little Ayton
The Moors Centre
301
Danby
Kildale
Castleton
Ainthorpe
Leaholm
Stokesley
Easby
River Esk
Crathorne
Battersby
River Leven
Hutton Rudby
Rudby
Great Busby
Kirkby
Ingleby Greenhow
Great Broughton
Westerdale
A172
Carlton-in-Cleveland
B1257
Potto
East Rounton
Faceby
NORTH YORK
Whorlton
Urra
454
URRA MOOR
382
Swainby
Seave Green
Ingleby Arncliffe
369
Chop Gate
NATIONAL
Church Houses
Cod Beck Reservoir
Mount Grace Priory NT
Rosedale
Ellerbeck
Osmotherley
394
Bilsdale
NORTH
Thorgill
YORK
Rosedale Abbey
Thimbleby
Low Mill
338
Bransdale
River Seven
399
BLACK HAMBLETON
Fangdale Beck
Kirby Sigston
Farndale
CLEVELAND HILLS
Over Silton
Nether Silton
River Rye
Kepwick
319
Lastingham
Gillamoor
Hawnby
Hutton-le-Hole
Fadmoor
Spaunton
Appleton-le-Moors
Cropton
Kirby Knowle
Kirkbymoorside
Carlton
0 1 2 3 4 miles
0 1 2 3 4 5 kilometres

Staithes
Heritage Centre
Runswick Bay
North Yorkshire and Cleveland Heritage Coast
Runswick
Goldsborough
Overdale Wyke
Ellerby
A174
Lythe
Mickleby
Sandsend
Sandsend Wyke
West Barnby
East Barnby
Whitby
Saltwick Bay
Dunsley
Ugthorpe
Newholm
Ruswarp
Stainsacre
Briggswath
A171
Aislaby
Sneaton
High Hawsker
B1447
Sleights
Ugglebarnby
Egton
Esk Dale
Iburndale
Ness Point or North Cheek
Grosmont
Robin Hood's Bay
A169
Fylingthorpe
Robin Hood's Bay
B1416
Old Peak or South Cheek
A171
Goathland
Ravenscar
North Yorkshire Moors Railway
292
Staintondale
Shire Horse Centre
Wheeldale Roman Road
Eller Beck
Hayburn Wyke
MOORS
Harwood Dale
Newtondale Forest Drive
Cloughton
Cloughton Wyke
Stape
Hole of Horcum
134
Cromer Point
A165
Burniston
Bridestones (Rock Formation)
Bickley
Broxa
Silpho
Cleveland Way
Levisham
Suffield
Langdale End
Hackness
Dalby Forest Drive
Scalby
Scarborough
Lockton
Newton Dale
239
North Riding Forest Park
River Derwent
Sea Cut
A171
Hatherleigh Deep Sea Trawler
Falsgrave
P+R
Oliver's Mount

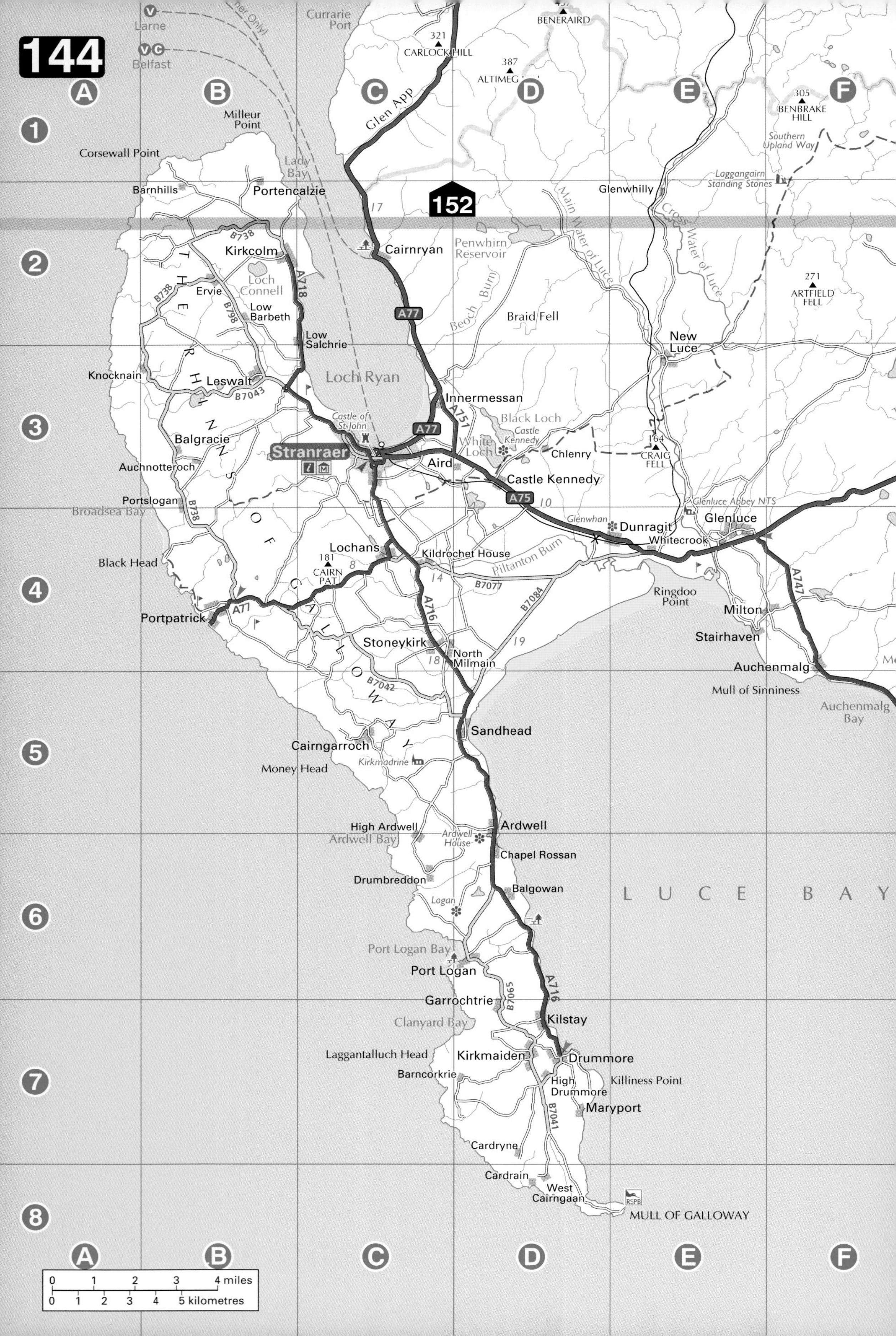

Larne
Belfast
Currarie Port
321 CARLOCK HILL
BENERAIRD
387 ALTIMEG HILL
Glen App
Milleur Point
Corsewall Point
305 BENBRAKE HILL
Southern Upland Way
Lady Bay
Barnhills
Portencalzie
152
Glenwhilly
Laggangairn Standing Stones
Main Water of Luce
Cross Water of Luce
B738
Kirkcolm
Cairnryan
Penwhirn Reservoir
Loch Connell
A718
Ervie
B738
B798
Low Barbeth
A77
Beoch Burn
Braid Fell
271 ARTFIELD FELL
Low Salchrie
New Luce
Knocknain
Leswalt
B7043
Loch Ryan
Innermessan
THE RHINNS OF GALLOWAY
Castle of St John
A77
A751
Black Loch
Castle Kennedy
Balgracie
Stranraer
White Loch
Chlenry
164 CRAIG FELL
Auchnotteroch
Aird
Castle Kennedy
Portslogan
Broadsea Bay
B738
A75
Glenluce Abbey NTS
Glenwhan
Dunragit
Glenluce
Whitecrook
Lochans
Kildrochet House
Piltanton Burn
Black Head
181 CAIRN PAT
A716
B7077
B7084
Ringdoo Point
A747
Portpatrick
A77
Milton
Stoneykirk
North Milmain
Stairhaven
B7042
Auchenmalg
Mull of Sinniness
Auchenmalg Bay
Sandhead
Cairngarroch
Kirkmadrine
Money Head
Ardwell
High Ardwell
Ardwell Bay
Ardwell House
Chapel Rossan
Drumbreddon
Balgowan
LUCE BAY
Logan
Port Logan Bay
Port Logan
B7065
A716
Garrochtrie
Clanyard Bay
Kilstay
Laggantalluch Head
Kirkmaiden
Drummore
Barncorkrie
High Drummore
Killiness Point
Maryport
B7041
Cardryne
Cardrain
West Cairngaan
RSPB
MULL OF GALLOWAY
0 1 2 3 4 miles
0 1 2 3 4 5 kilometres

Creebank
Bargrennan
Glen Trool
Drumlamford
Loch
Minnoch
716
LAMACHAN HILL
675
654
Loch
Bruce's
Black Water of Dee
A712
Loch Ochiltree
Knowe
440
GARLICK HILL
Galloway Deer Range
402
ROUND FELL
471
FELL OF FLEET
153
River Bladnoch
184
URRALL FELL
G A L L O W A Y
Loch Grannoch
Loch Fleet
208
AUCHENCLOY HILL
Skerrow
Carseriggan
Penkill Burn
R Cree
Challoch
Minnigaff
710
CAIRNSMORE OF FLEET
Barfad
Newton Stewart
214
CULVENNAN FELL
Creebridge
Kirroughtree
Big Water of Fleet
Ronald
Shennanton
A714
Palnure
335
WHITE TOP OF CULREACH
A75
Craighlaw
Kirkcowan
Baltersan
Upper Ruscoe
Little Water of Fleet
Causeway End
Gem Rock
B796
R Bladnoch
Creetown
Fleet Valley
146
Clugston
Torhouse Stone Circle
Skyre Burn
Fell Loch
THE
B733
Wigtown
Kirkmabreck
455
CAIRNHARROW
Anwoth
Gatehouse
Cardoness
Bladnoch
Carsluith
Cairnholy Chambered Cairns
Malzie
B7005
MACHARS
Kirwaugh
Water of Malzie
Girthon
Braehead
Ravenshall Point
Mossyard
Fleet Bay
Lennox Plunton
B7005
B7052
B7085
Kirkinner
Orchardton Bay
Culshabbin
Margrie
Barrachan
Whauphill
Chapel Finian (ruin)
B7004
Islands of Fleet
Little Airies
A746
Culscadden
Kirkandrews
A747
Elrig
Druchtag Motte
Sorbie
B7052
Wigtown Bay
Mochrum
Garlieston
Pouton
Borness
Drumtrodden Cup & Ring
Drumtrodden Standing Stones
Drummoddie
Broughton Mains
Cruggleton Bay
Ringdoo Point
Port William
Big Balcraig
B7004
B7063
'Wren's Egg' Standing Stones
B7021
Priory
Barsalloch Fort
Monreith
Barsalloch Point
Whithorn Cradle of Christianity
Rispain Camp
Whithorn
Point of Leg
A747
A746
Portyerrock
Glasserton
St Ninian's Cave
B7004
Isle of Whithorn
Kidsdale
St Ninian's Chapel (ruin)
Cutcloy
BURROW HEAD
G H J K L M
1 2 3 4 5 6 7 8

146
154
145
A
B
C
D
E
F
1
2
3
4
5
6
7
8
Galloway
Balmaclellan
Ironmacannie
281
LARGLEAR HILL
Corsock
Crochmore House
Shawhead
Lochfoot
A712
25
Eastlands
A75
Crocketford
325
CAIRN EDWARD
Knockvennie Smithy
Auchenreoch Loch
Milton Loch
Lochrutton Loch
A713
B794
18
Milton
Mossdale
Airds of Kells
Kirkpatrick Durham
Springholm
Beeswing
208
AUCHENCLOY HILL
Loch Ken
16
Loch Roan
Walbutt
Drumcoltran Tower
14
Loch Skerrow
Slogarie
A762
Old Bridge of Urr
Stonehouse
Kirkgunzeon
334
LOTUS HILL
Woodhall Loch
Crossmichael
Hardgate
Crofts
Clarebrand
B795
Haugh of Urr
Redcastle
A711
Laurieston
B795
Glenlochar
Townhead of Greenlaw
Urr Water
Glaisters Burn
335
WHITE TOP OF CULREACH
19
Hillowton
A745
Threave NTS
Edingham
430
CUIL HILL
Castle Douglas
Loch Whinyeon
Longwood
Threave Garden NTS
Carlingwark Loch
6
Little Knox
Dalbeattie
Kirkconnell
367
BENGRAY
Bridge of Dee
Rhonehouse
A710
B793
8
B796
Fleet Valley
10
Gelston
A711
10
Ringford
Craigley
B736
Barlochan
Palnackie
Caulkert
River Dee
Airieland
Barnbarroch
Fairgirth
Gatehouse of Fleet
B727
Littleton
343
SCREEL HILL
Kippford or Scaur
Drumburn
Sandyhills
Cardoness
15
390
BENGAIRN
Orchardton Tower
Mote of Mark
Twynholm
Tongland
B727
Colvend
East Stewartry Coast
Rockcliffe
Portling
Girthon
A75
Hydros Visitor Centre
Little Sypland
Compstonend
Castlehill Point
Lennox Plunton
8
A755
Wildlife Park
Whinnie Liggate
Kirkchrist
Auchencairn
Auchencairn Bay
Margrie
MacLellan's
Kirkcudbright
Culnaightrie
18
Heston Island
Gledpark
Balcary
Balcary Point
Borgue
B727
Mutehill
Kirkandrews
Dundrennan
Rascarrel
A711
Orroland
Kirkcudbright Bay
Balmangan
Borness
Ringdoo Point
Ross
Balmae
Netherlaw
Little Ross
Abbey Head
0 1 2 3 4 miles
0 1 2 3 4 5 kilometres

Dumfries
Annan
Solway Firth
Silloth
Maryport
Cockermouth
Workington
Wigton
Ecclefechan
Carrutherstown
Mouswald
Collin
Roucan
Lincluden
Maxwell Town
Kingholm Quay
Cargen
Islesteps
Mabie
Kelton
Conheath
Glencaple
Bankend
Clarencefield
Ruthwell
Kirkconnell
New Abbey
Nith Estuary
Shearington
Bowhouse
Ingleston
Blackshaw
Caerlaverock
Wildlife & Wetlands Trust Centre
Cummertrees
Powfoot
Howes
Dornock
Eastriggs
Newbie
Kelhead
Brydekirk
Hoddom Mains
Hoddom Cross
Thomas Carlyle's Birthplace NTS
Kirtlebridge
Bonshaw Tower
Robgill Tower
Eaglesfield
Creca
Warmanbie
Hollee
Dalton
Kettleholm
Waterbeck
Greenlea
Racks
Loch Kindar
CRIFFELL
Carse Bay
Kirkbean
Carsethorn
Borron Point
Arbigland
Mainsriddle
Loaningfoot
Gill Foot Bay
Southerness
Southerness Point
Bowness-on-Solway
Port Carlisle
Glasson
Drumburgh
Easton
Cardurnock
Anthorn
Grune Point
Moricambe Bay
Skinburness
Kirkbride
Whitrigglees
Powhill
Laythes
Newton Arlosh
Calvo
Seaville
Biglands
Abbey Town
Kelsick
Dundraw
Oulton
Lessonhall
Waverbridge
Waverton
Blencogo
Bromfield
Beckfoot
Newtown
Holme St Cuthbert
Mawbray
Mealrigg
Langrigg
Dubmill Point
Westnewton
Bolton Low Houses
Allonby
Allonby Bay
Fletchertown
Hayton
Aspatria
Blennerhasset
Boltongate
Prospect
Oughterside
Torpenhow
Allerby
Crosscanonby
Crosby
Plumbland
Bothel
Ireby
Gilcrux
Aughertree
Uldale
High Ireby
Dearham
Sunderland
BINSEY
Tallentire
Blindcrake
Bridekirk
Trotters World of Animals
Flimby
Broughton Moor
Standingstone
Dovenby
Bassenthwaite
Great Broughton
Papcastle
Camerton
Seaton
Great Clifton
Brigham
Greysouthen
Stainburn
Little Clifton
Eaglesfield
Armaside
Bassenthwaite Lake
Mirehouse
Mossbay
Westfield
Salterbeck
Moss Bay
Deanscales
Dean
Low Lorton
LORDS SEAT
Thornthwaite
CARTHAT HILL
Roman Camp
Merkland Cross
Torduff Point
Hadrian's Wall Path
Sweetheart
Corn Mill
Kirkconnell Flow
Lochar Water
River Annan
R Waver
River Ellen
R Derwent
Fort
A75
A709
A780
A710
A74(M)
B725
B724
B7020
B723
B722
B7076
B5307
B5302
B5300
B5301
A595
A596
B5299
A591
A594
A66
B5291
B5292
155
148
136
137

148
Waterbeck
Solwaybank
Evertown
Rowanburn
Canonbie
Pentonbridge
Milltown
Woodhouselees
Timpanheck
Eaglesfield
Chapelknowe
Merkland Cross
Kirtlebridge
Robgill Tower
Kirkpatrick-Fleming
156
Hollee
Gretna
Springfield
Longtown
Gretna Green
Rigg
Eastriggs
River Lyne
Boltonfellend
Kirkcambeck
Kirklinton
Hethersgill
River Esk
Redkirk Point
Torduff Point
Westlinton
Smithfield
Walton
Hadrian's Wall Path
Burtholme
Scalebyhill
Scaleby
Newtown
Laversdale
Todhills
R Irthing
Crooked Holme
Port Carlisle
R Eden
Oldwall
Brampton
Rockcliffe
Glasson
Irthington
Drumburgh
Burgh by Sands
Beaumont
Low Crosby
High Crosby
Easton
Cargo
Grinsdale
Newby East
Monkhill
Linstock
Kirkandrews upon Eden
Knowlefield
Talkin Tarn
Thurstonfield
Moorhouse
Stanwix
Hayton
Whitrigglees
Finglandrigg Woods
CARLISLE
Warwick
How Mill
Studholme
Kirkbampton
Belle Vue
Laythes
Little Bampton
Little Orton
Scotby
Fenton
Heads Nook
Morton
Harraby
Castle Carrock
Great Orton
Newby West
Wetheral
Great Corby
Aikton
Wiggonby
Cummersdale
Upperby
Wetheral Priory Gatehouse
Biglands
Blackwell
Cumwhinton
Cumwhitton
Drumleaning
Thursby
Cotehill
Dalston
Buckabank
Wigton
West Curthwaite
Wreay
Gaitsgill
Chalk Beck
Aiketgate
Low Hesket
Ainstable
Rosley
Southwaite
Armathwaite
Westward
Welton
High Hesket
R Petteril
R Ive
Ivegill
Staffield
Boltongate
Sebergham
Kirkoswald
343 FAULDS BROW
Calthwaite
Caldbeck
Roe Beck
Ireby
Hesket Newmarket
Hutton End
247 LAZONBY FELL
Aughertree
Uldale
Salkeld Dykes
Branthwaite
Plumpton
Lamonby
Hutton-in-the-Forest
Ellonby
Skelton
Hutton Roof
663 CARROCK FELL
Little Blencow
Catterlen
Langwathby
710 KNOTT
Johnby
Bassenthwaite
137
Great Blencow
138
690 GREAT CALVA
River Caldew
BOWSCALE FELL
Mungrisdale
357 BERRIER HILL
Greystoke
Newbiggin
Penrith
Berrier
Motherby
931 DAW
Mirehouse
Penruddock
Stainton
Brougham
Eamont Bridge
868
Scales
Dalemain
Rheged Discovery Centre
Yanwath
Threlkeld
Dacre
Tirril
Clifton
Countess Pillar
0 1 2 3 4 miles
0 1 2 3 4 5 kilometres

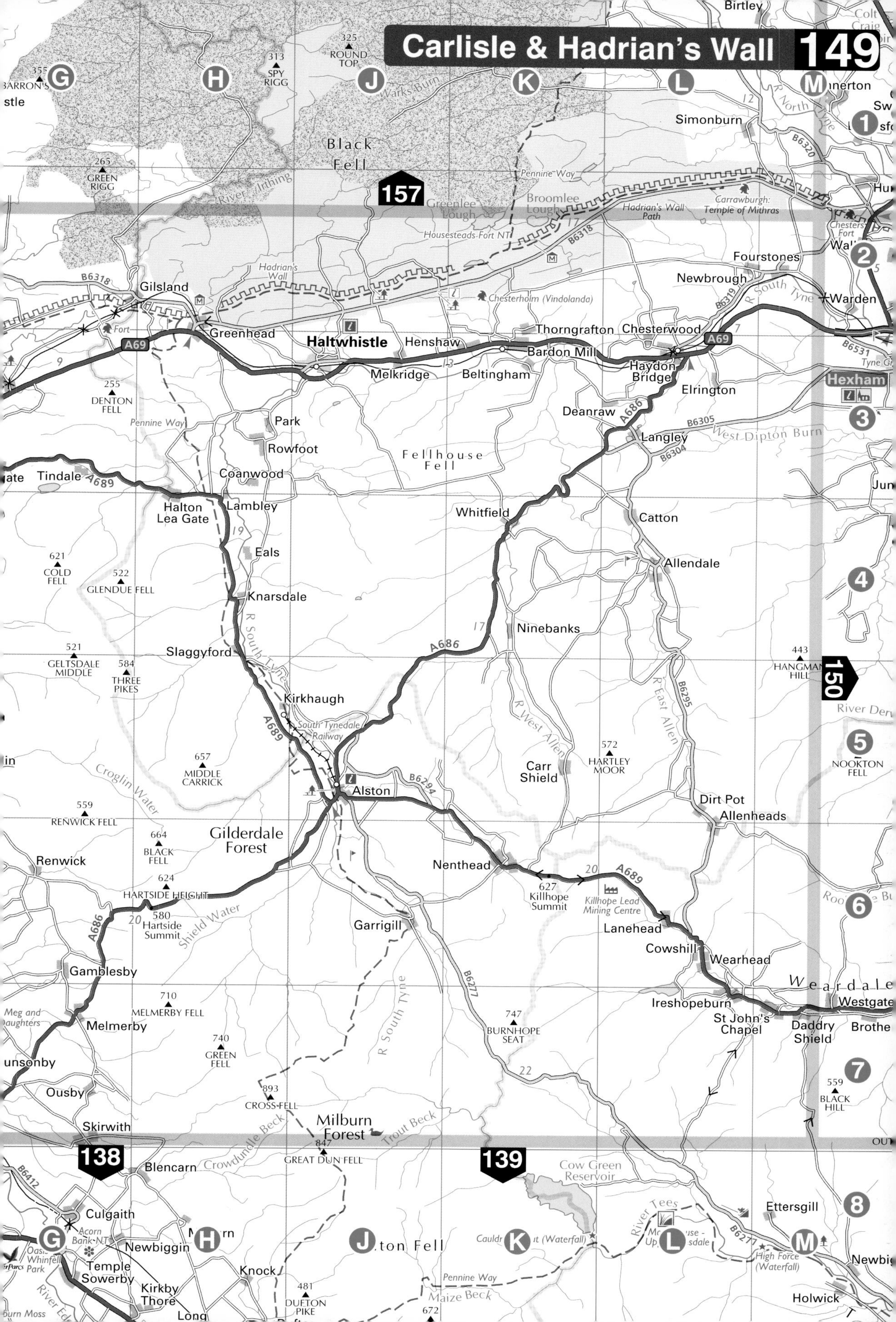
Black Fell
157
Pennine Way
Broomlee Lough
Greenlee Lough
Hadrian's Wall Path
Carrawburgh: Temple of Mithras
Housesteads Fort NT
Hadrian's Wall
Chesterholm (Vindolanda)
Simonburn
Fourstones
Newbrough
Warden
Gilsland
Greenhead
Haltwhistle
Henshaw
Thorngrafton
Chesterwood
Bardon Mill
Haydon Bridge
Melkridge
Beltingham
Elrington
Hexham
Deanraw
Langley
West Dipton Burn
Park
Rowfoot
Fellhouse Fell
Coanwood
Tindale
Halton Lea Gate
Lambley
Whitfield
Catton
Allendale
Eals
Knarsdale
Ninebanks
Slaggyford
Kirkhaugh
South Tynedale Railway
150
Carr Shield
Hartley Moor
Alston
Dirt Pot
Allenheads
Gilderdale Forest
Renwick
Nenthead
Killhope Summit
Killhope Lead Mining Centre
Lanehead
Cowshill
Wearhead
Garrigill
Gamblesby
Weardale
Westgate
Ireshopeburn
St John's Chapel
Daddry Shield
Melmerby
Burnhope Seat
Ousby
Cross Fell
Skirwith
Milburn Forest
138
139
Blencarn
Great Dun Fell
Cow Green Reservoir
Culgaith
Ettersgill
Newbiggin
Knock
Temple Sowerby
Kirkby Thore
Dufton Pike
Pennine Way
Maize Beck
High Force (Waterfall)
Holwick
A69
A686
A689
B6318
B6319
B6320
B6305
B6304
B6294
B6295
B6277
B6412
Cold Fell
Glendue Fell
Geltsdale Middle
Three Pikes
Middle Carrick
Renwick Fell
Black Fell
Hartside Height
Hartside Summit
Melmerby Fell
Green Fell
Denton Fell
Croglin Water
Shield Water
R South Tyne
R West Allen
R East Allen
Nookton Fell
Hangman Hill
Black Hill
Round Top
Spy Rigg
Green Rigg

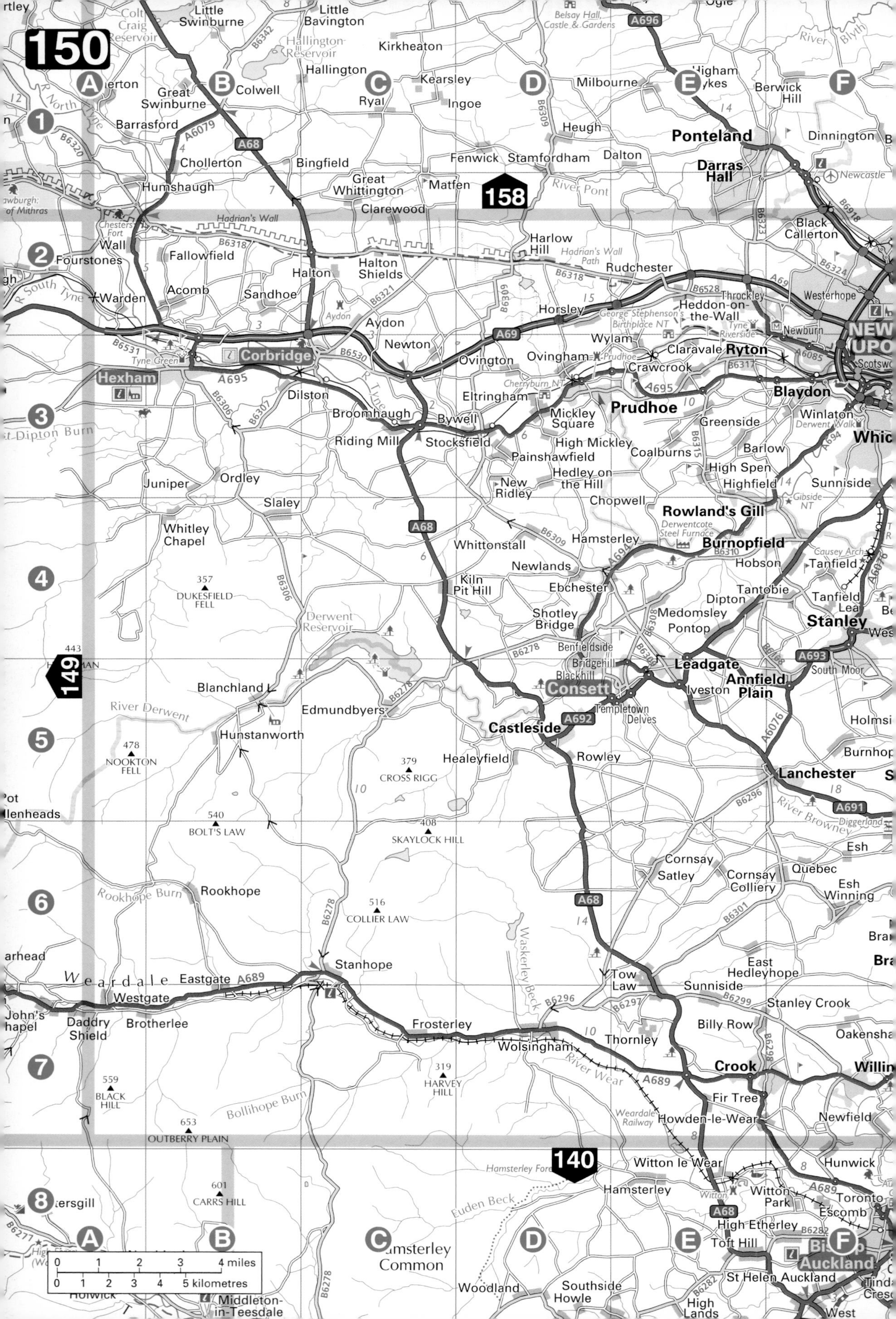

Little Swinburne
Little Bavington
Colt Crag Reservoir
B6342
Hallington Reservoir
Kirkheaton
Belsay Hall, Castle & Gardens
A696
Ogle
River Blyth
A
B
C
D
E
F
Barrasford
Great Swinburne
Colwell
Hallington
Ryal
Kearsley
Ingoe
Milbourne
Higham Dykes
Berwick Hill
R North Tyne
1
B6320
A6079
A68
Chollerton
Bingfield
B6309
Heugh
Ponteland
Dinnington
Fenwick
Stamfordham
Dalton
Darras Hall
Newcastle
Humshaugh
Great Whittington
Matfen
158
River Pont
Clarewood
B6323
B6918
Black Callerton
Hadrian's Wall
Chesters Fort
Wall
2
Fourstones
Fallowfield
B6318
Harlow Hill
Hadrian's Wall Path
Rudchester
B6324
Halton
Halton Shields
Acomb
Sandhoe
R South Tyne
Warden
B6321
Aydon
B6528
Throckley
Westerhope
Heddon-on-the-Wall
Horsley
George Stephenson's Birthplace NT
Tyne Riverside
Newburn
A69
Wylam
Newton
Claravale
Ryton
B6531
Tyne Green
Corbridge
B6530
Ovington
Ovingham
Prudhoe
Crawcrook
B6317
A6085
Scotswood
Hexham
A695
Dilston
Cherryburn NT
Eltringham
Blaydon
B6306
B6307
R Tyne
Broomhaugh
Bywell
Mickley Square
Prudhoe
Greenside
Winlaton
Derwent Walk
3
Dipton Burn
Riding Mill
Stockfield
High Mickley
Coalburns
B6315
A694
Painshawfield
Barlow
Whickham
Ordley
Juniper
New Ridley
Hedley on the Hill
High Spen
Highfield
Sunniside
Gibside NT
Slaley
Chopwell
Rowland's Gill
Whitley Chapel
B6309
Derwentcote Steel Furnace
Hamsterley
Burnopfield
Whittonstall
B6310
Causey Arch
Newlands
Hobson
Tanfield
A6076
4
357
DUKESFIELD FELL
B6306
Kiln Pit Hill
Ebchester
Tantobie
Dipton
Tanfield Lea
Medomsley
Shotley Bridge
Stanley
Derwent Reservoir
Pontop
B6308
443
149
Benfieldside
B6278
Bridgehill
Blackhill
Leadgate
A693
South Moor
Consett
Annfield Plain
Iveston
Blanchland
B6278
Templetown
Delves
River Derwent
Edmundbyers
Castleside
A692
Holmside
5
Hunstanworth
478
NOOKTON FELL
379
CROSS RIGG
Healeyfield
Rowley
A6076
Burnhope
Lanchester
A691
B6296
River Browney
Diggerland
Allenheads
540
BOLT'S LAW
408
SKAYLOCK HILL
Esh
Cornsay
Satley
Cornsay Colliery
Quebec
Esh Winning
Rookhope Burn
Rookhope
6
516
COLLIER LAW
A68
B6301
B6278
Waskerley Beck
Stanhope
East Hedleyhope
Weardale
Eastgate
A689
Tow Law
Sunniside
Westgate
B6299
Stanley Crook
B6296
B6297
St John's Chapel
Daddry Shield
Brotherlee
Frosterley
Thornley
Billy Row
Oakenshaw
Wolsingham
B6298
River Wear
7
559
BLACK HILL
319
HARVEY HILL
A689
Crook
Willington
Fir Tree
Bollihope Burn
Weardale Railway
Howden-le-Wear
Newfield
653
OUTBERRY PLAIN
140
Hamsterley Forest
Witton le Wear
Hunwick
Witton Park
Toronto
8
Ireshopeburn
601
CARRS HILL
Euden Beck
Hamsterley
Escomb
High Etherley
B6282
B6277
Hamsterley Common
Toft Hill
Bishop Auckland
0 1 2 3 4 miles
0 1 2 3 4 5 kilometres
Holwick
Middleton-in-Teesdale
Woodland
Southside
Howle
B6282
St Helen Auckland
High Lands
West

Cramlington
New Hartley
Seaton Sluice
Seaton
Seaton Delaval
St Mary's Lighthouse
Dudley
Wide Open
Earsdon
Whitley Bay
Monkseaton
Killingworth
Shiremoor
Cullercoats
Tynemouth
159
Forest Hall
Rising Sun
North Shields
Longbenton
South Gosforth
Willington Quay
Wallsend
Jesmond
Heaton
Int. Ferry Terminal
Jarrow
Tyne Tunnel
SOUTH SHIELDS
Westoe
Harton
Marsden Bay
Marsden
Souter Lighthouse NT
Bergen
Göteborg
Haugesund
IJmuiden
Kristiansand
Stavanger
Walker
Byker
Hebburn
Monkton
Felling
Wardley
GATESHEAD
West Boldon
Cleadon
Souter Point
Whitburn
Whitburn Bay
East Boldon
Seaburn
Team Valley
Low Fell
Wrekenton
Bowes Railway & Museum
Hylton
Southwick
Roker
Monkwearmouth
Castletown
Springwell
Usworth
Wildfowl & Wetlands Trust
Birtley
South Hylton
SUNDERLAND
WASHINGTON
Washington
Grindon
Hendon
Ouston
Penshaw
Penshaw Monument NT
High Newport
Grangetown
Fatfield
New Silksworth
Tunstall
Pelton
Herrington
Silksworth
Ryhope
River Wear
Shiney Row
Chester-le-Street
Burnmoor
Houghton le Spring
Seaham
Chester Moor
Great Lumley
Hetton-le-Hole
Parkside
Dalton-le-Dale
Plawsworth
West Rainton
East Rainton
Finchale
Kimblesworth
Murton
Low Moorsley
Pity Me
South Hetton
Hawthorn
Pittington
Framwellgate Moor
Easington Colliery
Bearpark
Hallgarth
Crook Hall
Carrville
Easington
Littletown
Haswell
Gilesgate Moor
Haswell Plough
Little Thorpe
Durham
Sherburn
Shotton Colliery
Peterlee
Broom
Sherburn Hill
Ludworth
Shadforth
Horden
Shincliffe
Thornley
Shotton
Blackhall Colliery
Durham Coast
Blackhall Rocks
Cassop Colliery
Wheatley Hill
Castle Eden
Bowburn
Hesleden
Sunderland Bridge
Quarrington Hill
Wingate
Croxdale
Hett
Kelloe
Hutton Henry
Sheraton
Tudhoe
Coxhoe
Trimdon Grange
Hart
Trimdon Colliery
South Wingate
Cornforth
The Headland
Historic Quay
Trimdon
Elwick
HARTLEPOOL
Thrislington
Ferryhill
141
142
Hartlepool Bay
Kirk Merrington
Mainsforth
Bishop Middleham
Dalton Piercy
Leasingthorne
Hardwick Hall
Seaton Carew
Coundon
Chilton
Sedgefield
Shildon
Bradbury
Greatham
Newton Bewley
Mordon
Hartlepool Power Station Visitor Centre
Billingham
River Skerne
Tees

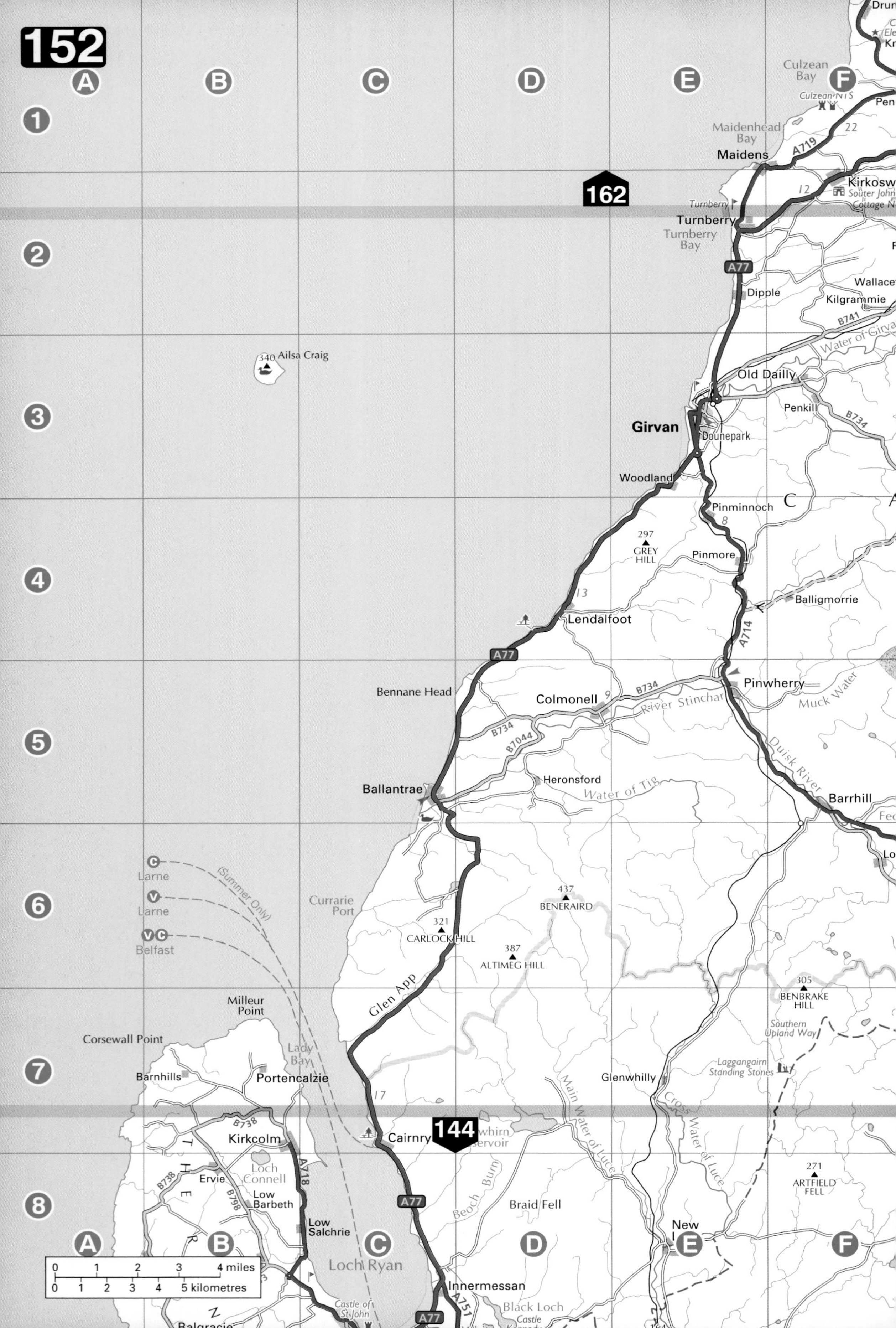

162
Culzean Bay
Culzean NTS
Maidenhead Bay
Maidens
A719
Kirkoswald
Souter Johnnie's Cottage
Turnberry
Turnberry Bay
A77
Dipple
Wallacetown
Kilgrammie
B741
Water of Girvan
Ailsa Craig
340
Old Dailly
Penkill
B734
Girvan
Dounepark
Woodland
Pinminnoch
297
GREY HILL
Pinmore
Balligmorrie
Lendalfoot
A714
Bennane Head
Colmonell
River Stinchar
Pinwherry
Muck Water
B7044
Heronsford
Water of Tig
Ballantrae
Duisk River
Barrhill
Larne
(Summer Only)
Currarie Port
437
BENERAIRD
321
CARLOCK HILL
387
ALTIMEG HILL
Belfast
305
BENBRAKE HILL
Milleur Point
Glen App
Corsewall Point
Lady Bay
Southern Upland Way
Barnhills
Portencalzie
Glenwhilly
Laggangairn Standing Stones
B738
Kirkcolm
Cairnryan
144
Main Water of Luce
Cross Water of Luce
Loch Connell
A718
Ervie
271
ARTFIELD FELL
B798
Low Barbeth
Beoch Burn
Braid Fell
Low Salchrie
New Luce
Loch Ryan
A751
Innermessan
Black Loch
Castle Kennedy
Castle of St John
Balgracie
0 1 2 3 4 miles
0 1 2 3 4 5 kilometres

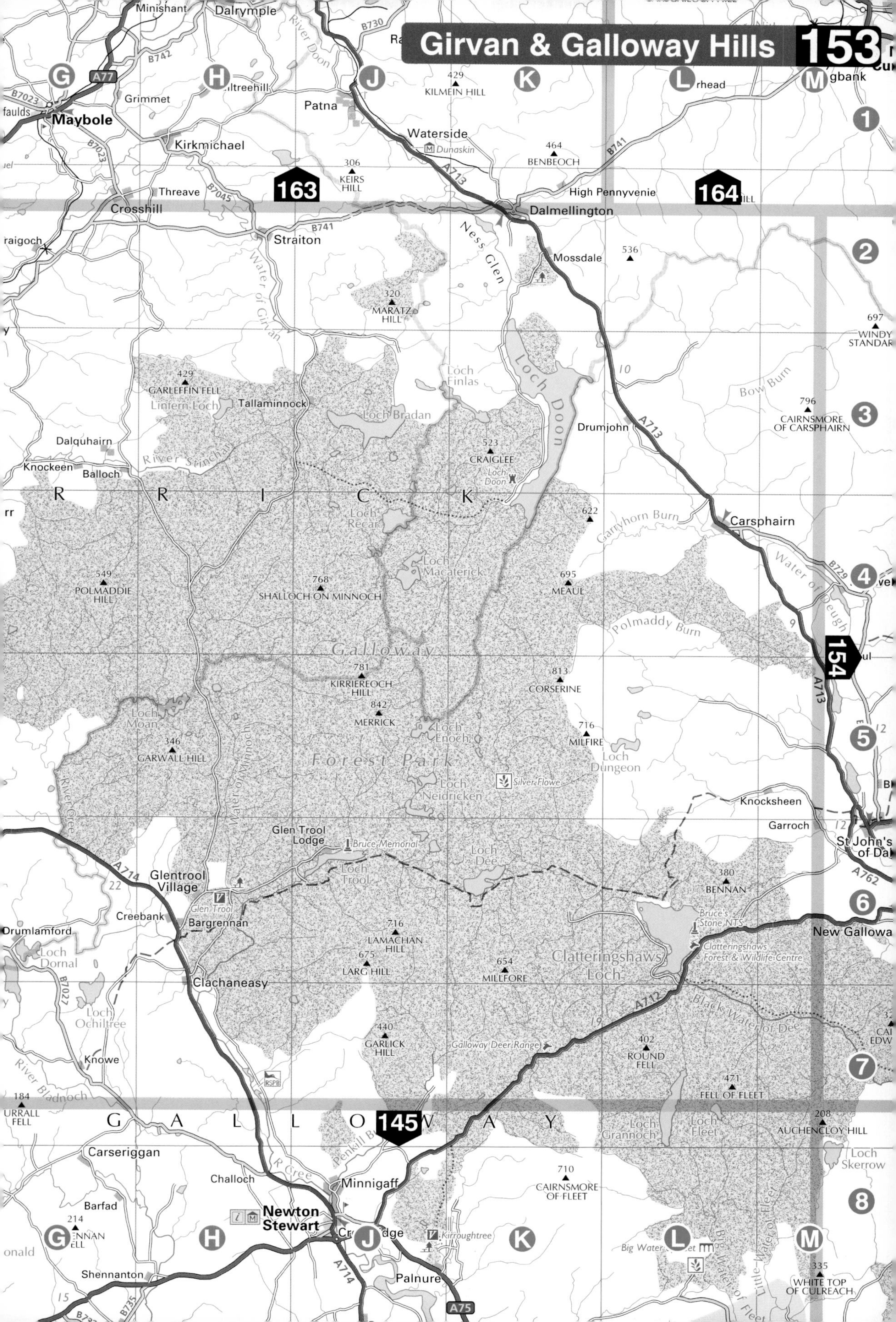
Minishant
Dalrymple
Maybole
Grimmet
Kirkmichael
Patna
Waterside
Dunaskin
Crosshill
Threave
Straiton
Dalmellington
High Pennyvenie
Mossdale
KILMEIN HILL
BENBEOCH
KEIRS HILL
MARATZ HILL
Ness Glen
Water of Girvan
Loch Doon
Loch Finlas
Loch Bradan
GARLEFFIN FELL
Linfern Loch
Tallaminnock
Dalquhairn
River Stinchar
Knockeen
Balloch
CRAIGLEE
Loch Doon
Drumjohn
CAIRNSMORE OF CARSPHAIRN
WINDY STANDARD
Bow Burn
R R I C K
Loch Recar
Garryhorn Burn
Carsphairn
Loch Macaterick
POLMADDIE HILL
SHALLOCH ON MINNOCH
MEAUL
Polmaddy Burn
Water of Deugh
Galloway
KIRRIEREOCH HILL
MERRICK
CORSERINE
Loch Moan
GARWALL HILL
Loch Enoch
MILFIRE
Loch Dungeon
Forest Park
Loch Neldricken
Silver Flowe
Knocksheen
Garroch
St John's of Dalry
River Cree
Water of Minnoch
Glen Trool Lodge
Bruce Memorial
Loch Trool
Loch Dee
Glentrool Village
Glen Trool
BENNAN
Creebank
Bargrennan
Bruce's Stone NTS
New Galloway
Drumlamford
Loch Dornal
LAMACHAN HILL
LARG HILL
MILLFORE
Clatteringshaws Loch
Clatteringshaws Forest & Wildlife Centre
Clachaneasy
Loch Ochiltree
Blacks Water of Dee
GARLICK HILL
Galloway Deer Range
ROUND FELL
Knowe
RSPB
River Bladnoch
FELL OF FLEET
URRALL FELL
G A L L O W A Y
AUCHENCLOY HILL
Loch Grannoch
Loch Fleet
Loch Skerrow
Carseriggan
Penkill Burn
R Cree
Challoch
Minnigaff
CAIRNSMORE OF FLEET
Barfad
Newton Stewart
Creebridge
Kirroughtree
Big Water of Fleet
Little Water of Fleet
Shennanton
Palnure
WHITE TOP OF CULREACH
Big Water
A77
B7023
B742
B730
A713
B741
B7045
B729
A714
A712
A762
B7027
A75
B735
163
164
154
145
G
H
J
K
L
M
1
2
3
4
5
6
7
8

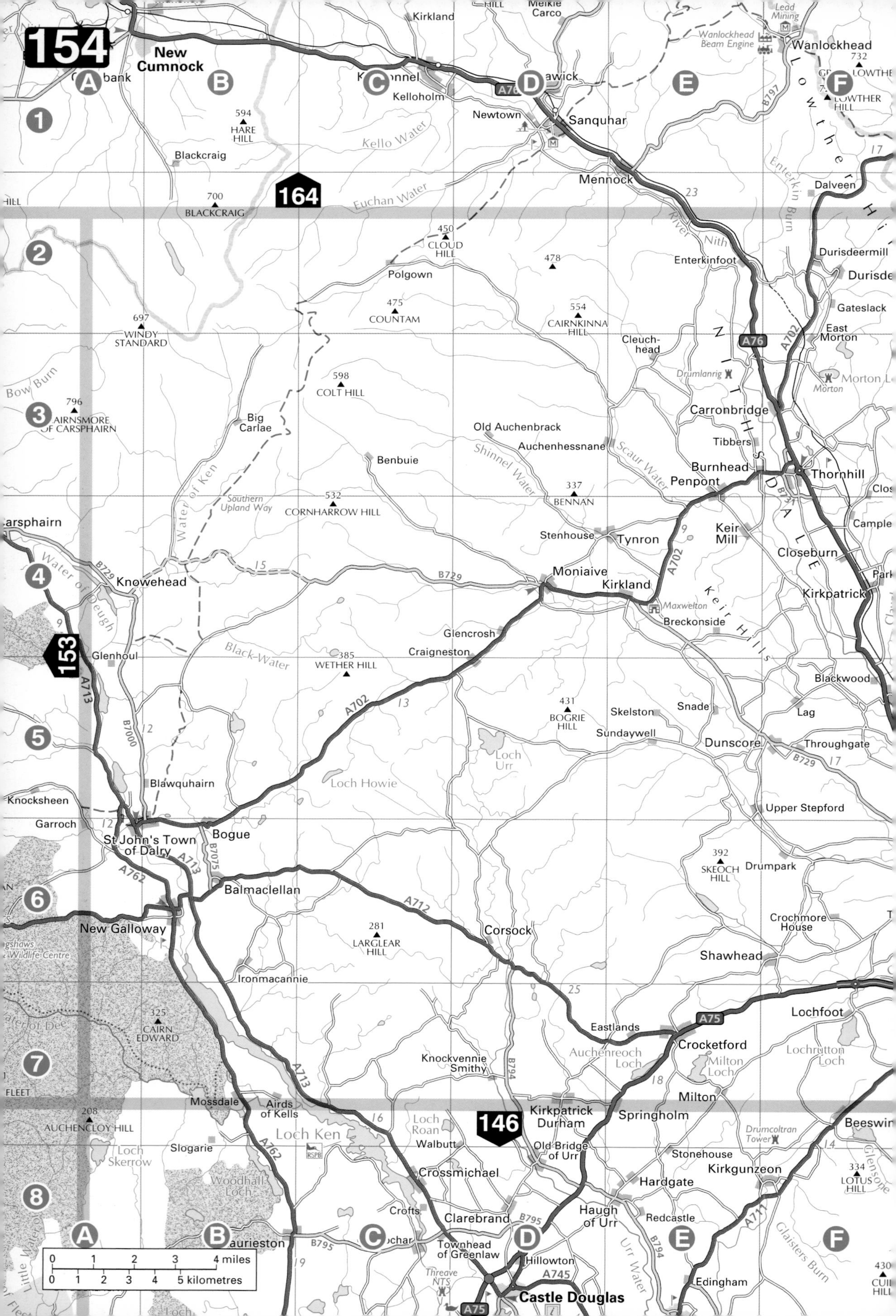
154
New Cumnock
B
Kirkland
Kelloholm
Sanquhar
Newtown
Kello Water
594 HARE HILL
Blackcraig
Wanlockhead
Wanlockhead Beam Engine
Lead Mining
732 LOWTHER HILL
Lowther Hills
Mennock
Dalveen
Enterkin Burn
164
700 BLACKCRAIG
Euchan Water
450 CLOUD HILL
River Nith
Enterkinfoot
Durisdeermill
478
Polgown
475 COUNTAM
554 CAIRNKINNA HILL
Gateslack
East Morton
697 WINDY STANDARD
Cleuch-head
Drumlanrig
Morton
Bow Burn
796 CAIRNSMORE OF CARSPHAIRN
598 COLT HILL
Big Carlae
Old Auchenbrack
Auchenhessnane
Carronbridge
Tibbers
NITHSDALE
Benbuie
Shinnel Water
Scaur Water
Burnhead
Penpont
Thornhill
Water of Ken
Southern Upland Way
532 CORNHARROW HILL
337 BENNAN
Carsphairn
Stenhouse
Tynron
Keir Mill
Cample
Closeburn
Water of Deugh
B729
Knowehead
Moniaive
Kirkland
Kirkpatrick
Maxwelton
Breckonside
Keir Hills
153
Glenhoul
Glencrosh
Craigneston
Black Water
385 WETHER HILL
Blackwood
A713
A702
431 BOGIE HILL
Skelston
Snade
Lag
Sundaywell
Dunscore
Throughgate
B7000
Loch Urr
Loch Howie
Blawquhairn
Knocksheen
Garroch
Upper Stepford
St John's Town of Dalry
Bogue
B7075
392 SKEOCH HILL
Drumpark
A762
Balmaclellan
A712
New Galloway
Corsock
Crochmore House
281 LARGLEAR HILL
Shawhead
Ironmacannie
Wildlife Centre
325 CAIRN EDWARD
Lochfoot
Eastlands
A75
Crocketford
Auchenreoch Loch
Milton Loch
Lochrutton Loch
Knockvennie Smithy
B794
FLEET
Mossdale
Airds of Kells
Milton
146
Kirkpatrick Durham
Springholm
Beeswing
208 AUCHENCLOY HILL
Loch Ken
Loch Roan
Walbutt
Drumcoltran Tower
Loch Skerrow
Slogarie
RSPB
Old Bridge of Urr
Stonehouse
Crossmichael
Kirkgunzeon
334 LOTUS HILL
Woodhall Loch
Hardgate
Crofts
Clarebrand
Haugh of Urr
Redcastle
A711
Laurieston
B795
Townhead of Greenlaw
Urr Water
Glaisters Burn
Threave NTS
Hillowton
A745
Castle Douglas
Edingham
0 1 2 3 4 miles
0 1 2 3 4 5 kilometres

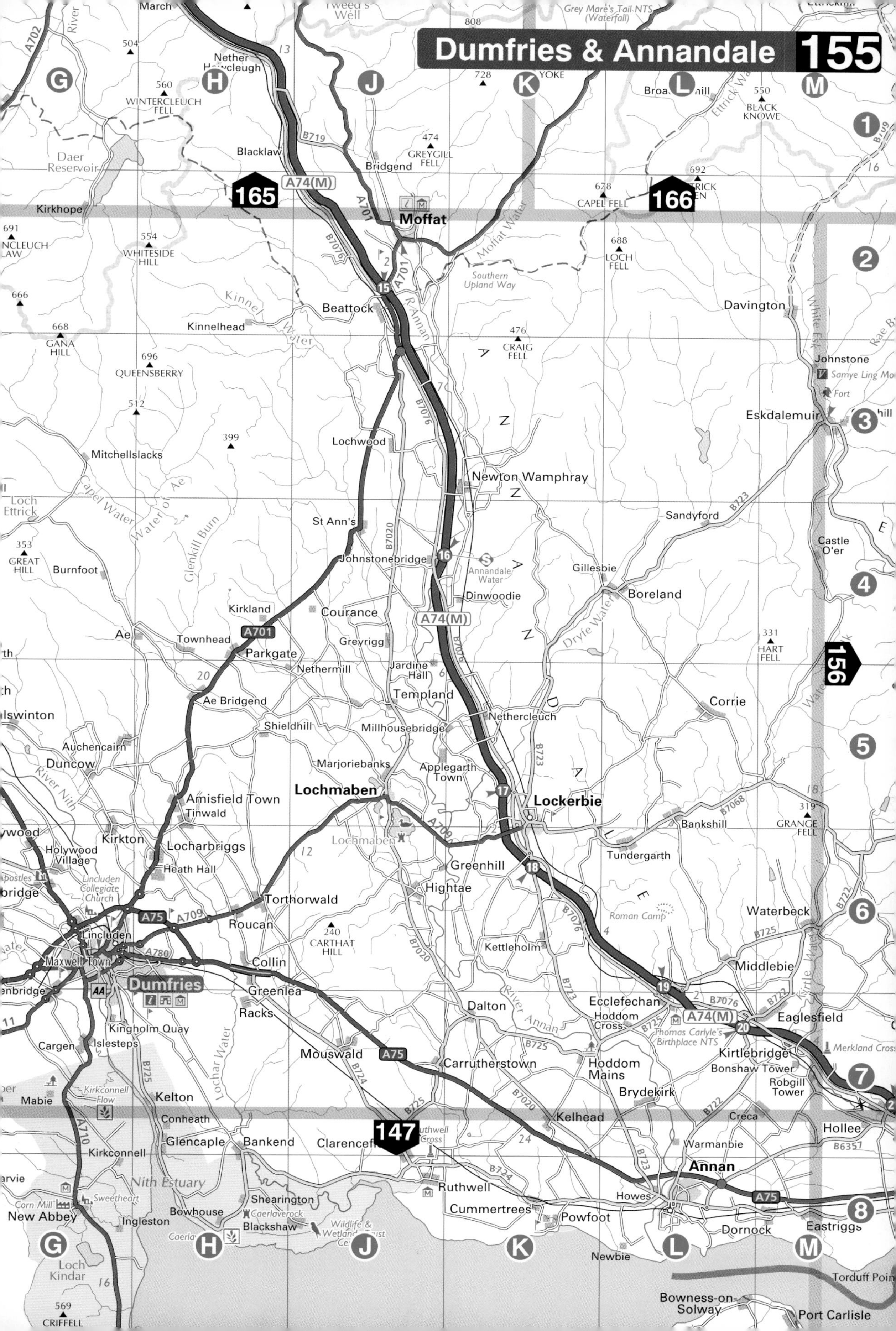

Dumfries & Annandale
155
165
166
156
147
Moffat
Beattock
Kinnelhead
Kirkhope
Daer Reservoir
Blacklaw
Bridgend
Nether Hawcleugh
WINTERCLEUCH FELL
GREYGILL FELL
CAPEL FELL
LOCH FELL
YOKE
BLACK KNOWE
WHITESIDE HILL
GANA HILL
QUEENSBERRY
CRAIG FELL
Southern Upland Way
Grey Mare's Tail NTS (Waterfall)
Davington
Johnstone
Samye Ling Mo
Fort
Eskdalemuir
Castle O'er
Lochwood
Mitchellslacks
Newton Wamphray
Sandyford
St Ann's
Johnstonebridge
Annandale Water
Dinwoodie
Gillesbie
Boreland
GREAT HILL
Burnfoot
Kirkland
Courance
Ae
Townhead
Parkgate
Greyrigg
Nethermill
Jardine Hall
Templand
Ae Bridgend
Shieldhill
Millhousebridge
Nethercleuch
Corrie
HART FELL
Auchencairn
Duncow
Marjoriebanks
Applegarth Town
Lochmaben
Lockerbie
Amisfield Town
Tinwald
Kirkton
Locharbriggs
Holywood Village
Heath Hall
Lincluden Collegiate Church
Greenhill
Hightae
Bankshill
GRANGE FELL
Tundergarth
Roman Camp
Torthorwald
Roucan
CARTHAT HILL
Collin
Kettleholm
Waterbeck
Middlebie
Lincluden
Maxwell Town
Dumfries
Greenlea
Racks
Dalton
Ecclefechan
Hoddom Cross
Thomas Carlyle's Birthplace NTS
Eaglesfield
Kirtlebridge
Merkland Cross
Bonshaw Tower
Robgill Tower
Kingholm Quay
Cargen
Islesteps
Mouswald
Carruthertown
Hoddom Mains
Brydekirk
Mabie
Kirkconnell Flow
Kelton
Conheath
Glencaple
Bankend
Clarencefield
Ruthwell Cross
Kelhead
Creca
Hollee
Warmanbie
Annan
Kirkconnell
Nith Estuary
Ruthwell
Shearington
Bowhouse
Caerlaverock
Blackshaw
Wildlife & Wetland Trust
Cummertrees
Powfoot
Howes
Dornock
Eastriggs
Corn Mill
Sweetheart
New Abbey
Ingleston
Newbie
Loch Kindar
CRIFFELL
Torduff Point
Bowness-on-Solway
Port Carlisle
A74(M)
A701
A75
A709
A780
A710
B7076
B7020
B723
B725
B724
B722
B7068
B6357
B719

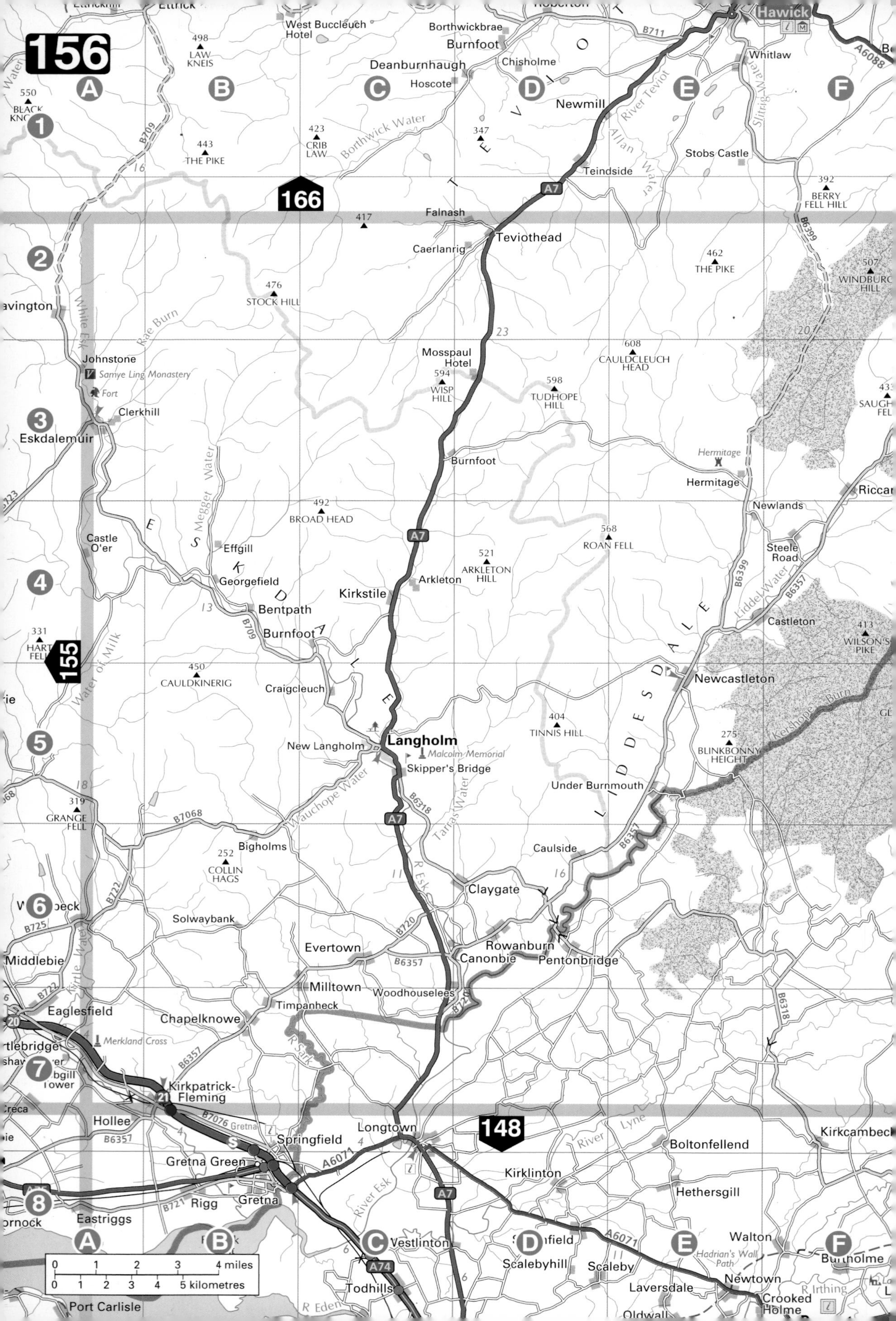

Ettrick
West Buccleuch Hotel
Borthwickbrae
Hawick
Burnfoot
Whitlaw
498 LAW KNEIS
Deanburnhaugh
Chisholme
Hoscote
Newmill
River Teviot
550 BLACK KNO
B709
443 THE PIKE
423 CRIB LAW
Borthwick Water
347
Allan Water
Slitrig Water
Stobs Castle
Teindside
166
A7
392 BERRY FELL HILL
417
Falnash
Teviothead
Caerlanrig
B6399
462 THE PIKE
507 WINDBURGH HILL
476 STOCK HILL
White Esk
Rae Burn
23
608 CAULDCLEUCH HEAD
Mosspaul Hotel
594 WISP HILL
598 TUDHOPE HILL
Johnstone
Samye Ling Monastery
Fort
Clerkhill
Eskdalemuir
Burnfoot
Hermitage
Hermitage
Riccar
Newlands
Megget Water
492 BROAD HEAD
568 ROAN FELL
Castle O'er
Effgill
521 ARKLETON HILL
Arkleton
Steele Road
Georgefield
Kirkstile
Bentpath
Liddel Water
B6357
Castleton
413 WILSON'S PIKE
331 HART FELL
155
Burnfoot
450 CAULDKINERIG
Craigcleuch
Newcastleton
Water of Milk
404 TINNIS HILL
Kershope Burn
275 BLINKBONNY HEIGHT
Langholm
New Langholm
Malcolm Memorial
Skipper's Bridge
Wauchope Water
Under Burnmouth
B6318
Tarras Water
319 GRANGE FELL
B7068
Bigholms
252 COLLIN HAGS
Caulside
B722
R Esk
Claygate
Solwaybank
B725
Kirtle Water
B720
Rowanburn
Evertown
Canonbie
Pentonbridge
Middlebie
B6357
Milltown
Woodhouselees
Eaglesfield
Timpanheck
Chapelknowe
Merkland Cross
R Sark
B6357
B6318
Kirkpatrick-Fleming
Hollee
B7076 Gretna
148
Longtown
Springfield
River Lyne
Kirkcambeck
Boltonfellend
Gretna Green
A6071
Kirklinton
Hethersgill
River Esk
B721
Rigg
Gretna
Eastriggs
Vestlinton
Walton
A6071
Hadrian's Wall Path
Scalebyhill
Scaleby
Newtown
Laversdale
R Irthing
Crooked Holme
A74
Todhills
R Eden
Oldwall
Port Carlisle
0 1 2 3 4 miles
0 1 2 3 4 5 kilometres

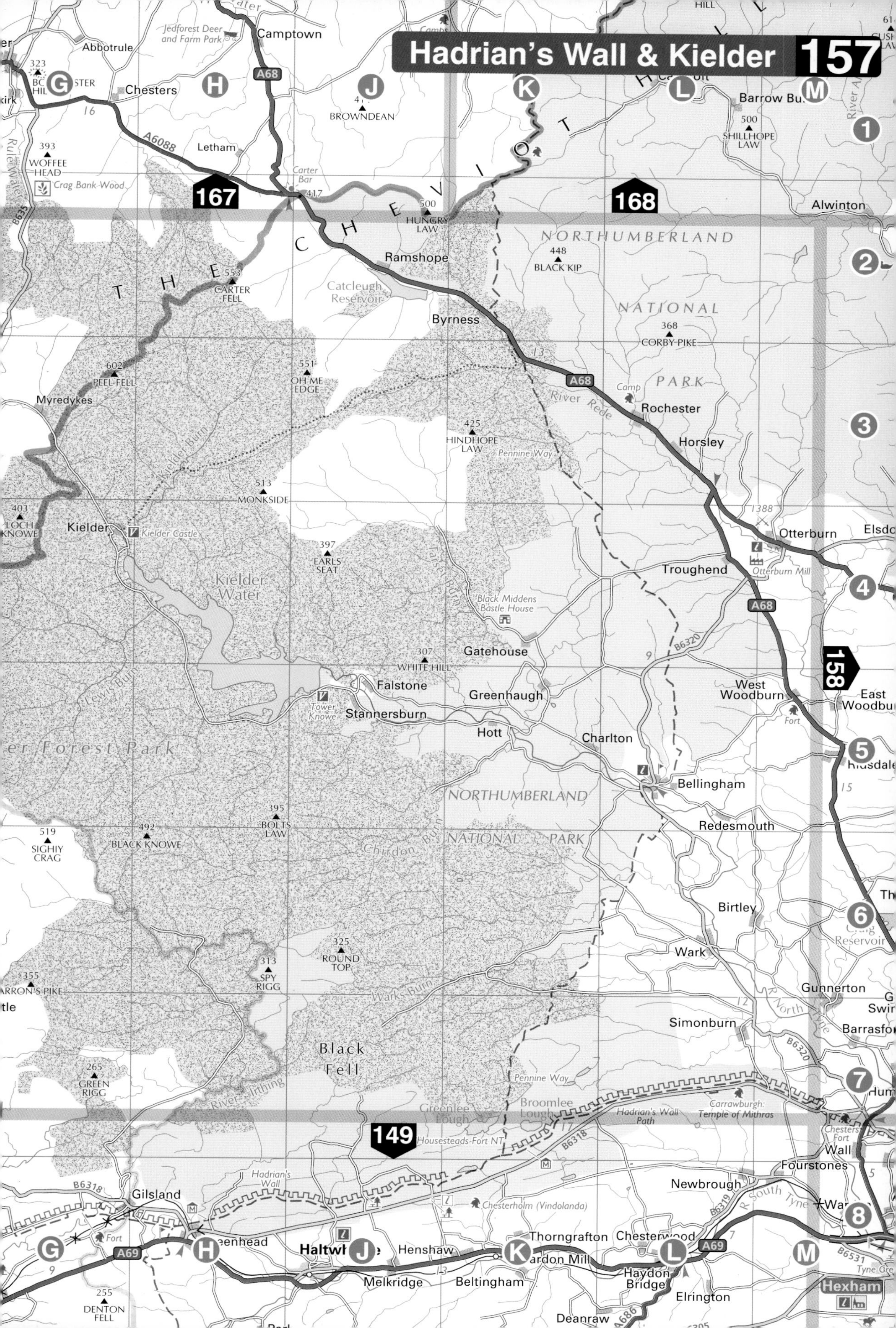
Camptown
Jedforest Deer and Farm Park
Abbotrule
Chesters
A68
A6088
Letham
WOFFEE HEAD
Crag Bank Wood
BROWNDEAN
Carter Bar
HUNGRY LAW
THE CHEVIOT HILLS
Barrow Burn
SHILLHOPE LAW
Alwinton
NORTHUMBERLAND NATIONAL PARK
BLACK KIP
CORBY PIKE
Ramshope
Catcleugh Reservoir
Byrness
CARTER FELL
PEEL FELL
OH ME EDGE
Myredykes
Kielder Burn
Rochester
Horsley
River Rede
HINDHOPE LAW
Pennine Way
MONKSIDE
LOCH KNOWE
Kielder
Kielder Castle
Otterburn
Elsdon
Troughend
Otterburn Mill
EARLS SEAT
Kielder Water
Tarset Burn
Black Middens Bastle House
B6320
Gatehouse
WHITE HILL
Falstone
Greenhaugh
West Woodburn
East Woodburn
Tower Knowe
Stannersburn
Hott
Charlton
Fort
Risdale
Lewis Burn
Kielder Forest Park
Bellingham
NORTHUMBERLAND NATIONAL PARK
Redesmouth
SIGHTY CRAG
BLACK KNOWE
BOLTS LAW
Chirdon Burn
Birtley
Crag Reservoir
ROUND TOP
SPY RIGG
Wark
Warks Burn
Gunnerton
CARRON'S PIKE
R North Tyne
Simonburn
Barrasford
Black Fell
B6320
GREEN RIGG
River Irthing
Greenlee Lough
Broomlee Lough
Hadrian's Wall Path
Carrawburgh: Temple of Mithras
Chesters Fort
Wall
Housesteads Fort NT
B6318
Fourstones
Newbrough
Hadrian's Wall
Gilsland
Chesterholm (Vindolanda)
R South Tyne
B6319
Haltwhistle
Greenhead
Henshaw
Thorngrafton
Chesterwood
A69
Bardon Mill
Melkridge
Beltingham
Haydon Bridge
Elrington
B6531
Hexham
Tyne Green
DENTON FELL
Deanraw
A686
167
168
158
149

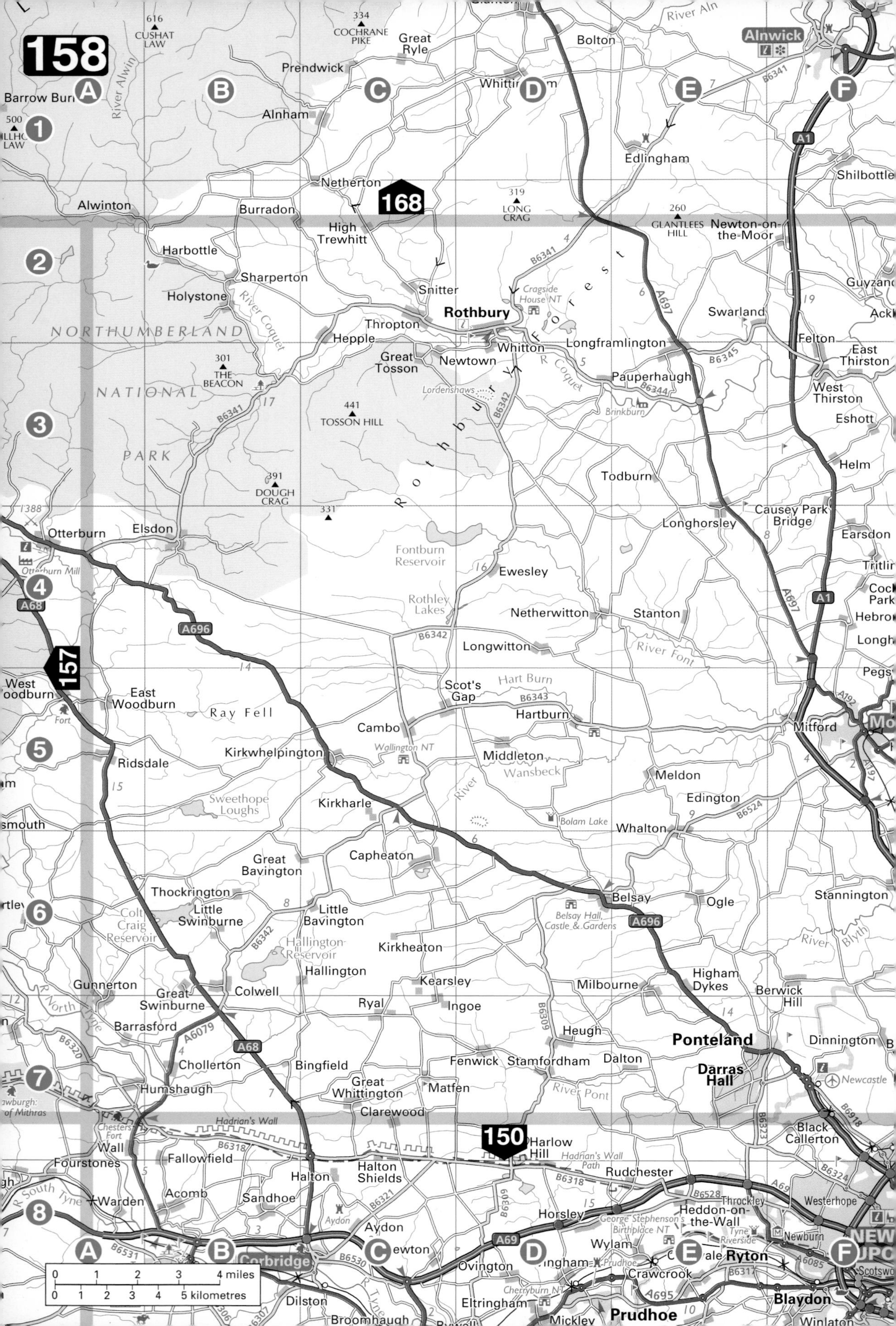

158
Barrow Burn
Alnwick
Bolton
Great Ryle
Prendwick
Alnham
Edlingham
Shilbottle
Netherton
168
Alwinton
Burradon
High Trewhitt
Newton-on-the-Moor
Harbottle
Sharperton
Holystone
Snitter
Rothbury
Thropton
Hepple
Great Tosson
Newtown
Whitton
Longframlington
Swarland
Felton
East Thirston
West Thirston
Pauperhaugh
Eshott
NORTHUMBERLAND
NATIONAL
PARK
Rothbury Forest
Todburn
Helm
Longhorsley
Causey Park Bridge
Otterburn
Elsdon
Fontburn Reservoir
Ewesley
Rothley Lakes
Netherwitton
Stanton
Longwitton
157
West Woodburn
East Woodburn
Ray Fell
Scot's Gap
Cambo
Hartburn
Mitford
Ridsdale
Kirkwhelpington
Middleton
Meldon
Edington
Kirkharle
Whalton
Great Bavington
Capheaton
Thockrington
Little Swinburne
Little Bavington
Belsay
Ogle
Stannington
Kirkheaton
Hallington
Higham Dykes
Gunnerton
Great Swinburne
Colwell
Kearsley
Milbourne
Berwick Hill
Barrasford
Ryal
Ingoe
Heugh
Ponteland
Dinnington
Chollerton
Bingfield
Fenwick
Stamfordham
Dalton
Darras Hall
Humshaugh
Great Whittington
Matfen
Clarewood
Black Callerton
Hadrian's Wall
150
Harlow Hill
Wall
Fourstones
Fallowfield
Halton
Halton Shields
Rudchester
Warden
Acomb
Sandhoe
Horsley
Heddon-on-the-Wall
Throckley
Westerhope
Aydon
Wylam
Newburn
Corbridge
Ovington
Crawcrook
Ryton
Dilston
Eltringham
Prudhoe
Blaydon
Broomhaugh
Mickley
A1
A68
A69
A696
A697
A6079
B6341
B6342
B6343
B6344
B6345
B6309
B6318
B6321
B6323
B6524
B6530
B6531
0 1 2 3 4 miles
0 1 2 3 4 5 kilometres

Boulmer
Seaton Point
Lesbury
Alnmouth
Alnmouth Bay
A1068
169
Warkworth
Amble
Coquet Island
Hauxley
Radcliffe
Broomhill
Druridge Bay
Druridge Bay
Widdrington
North Northumberland Heritage Coast
Widdrington Station
Cresswell
Ulgham
Ellington
A189
Beacon Point
Woodhorn
Ashington
A197
Hirst
Newbiggin-by-the-Sea
Bothal
Wansbeck Riverside
Stakeford
Guide Post
A196
Bedlington
A193
Cowpen
Blyth
B1331
Newsham
A192
A1061
New Hartley
Seaton Sluice
Cramlington
Seaton
B1326
A190
Seaton Delaval
St Mary's Lighthouse
Dudley
Wide Open
Earsdon
Whitley Bay
Monkseaton
Cullercoats
A1056
Killingworth
Shiremoor
Tynemouth
Forest Hall
151
Rising Sun
North Shields
South Gosforth
Longbenton
Willington Quay
Bergen
Göteborg
Haugesund
IJmuiden
Kristiansand
Stavanger
SOUTH SHIELDS
Jesmond
Heaton
Wallsend
Int. Ferry Terminal
Toll
Tyne Tunnel
Jarrow
Westoe
Marsden Bay
Walker
Byker
Hebburn
Marsden
Souter Lighthouse NT
River Tyne
Monkton
Felling
Cleadon
Souter Point
Wardley
West Boldon
Whitburn

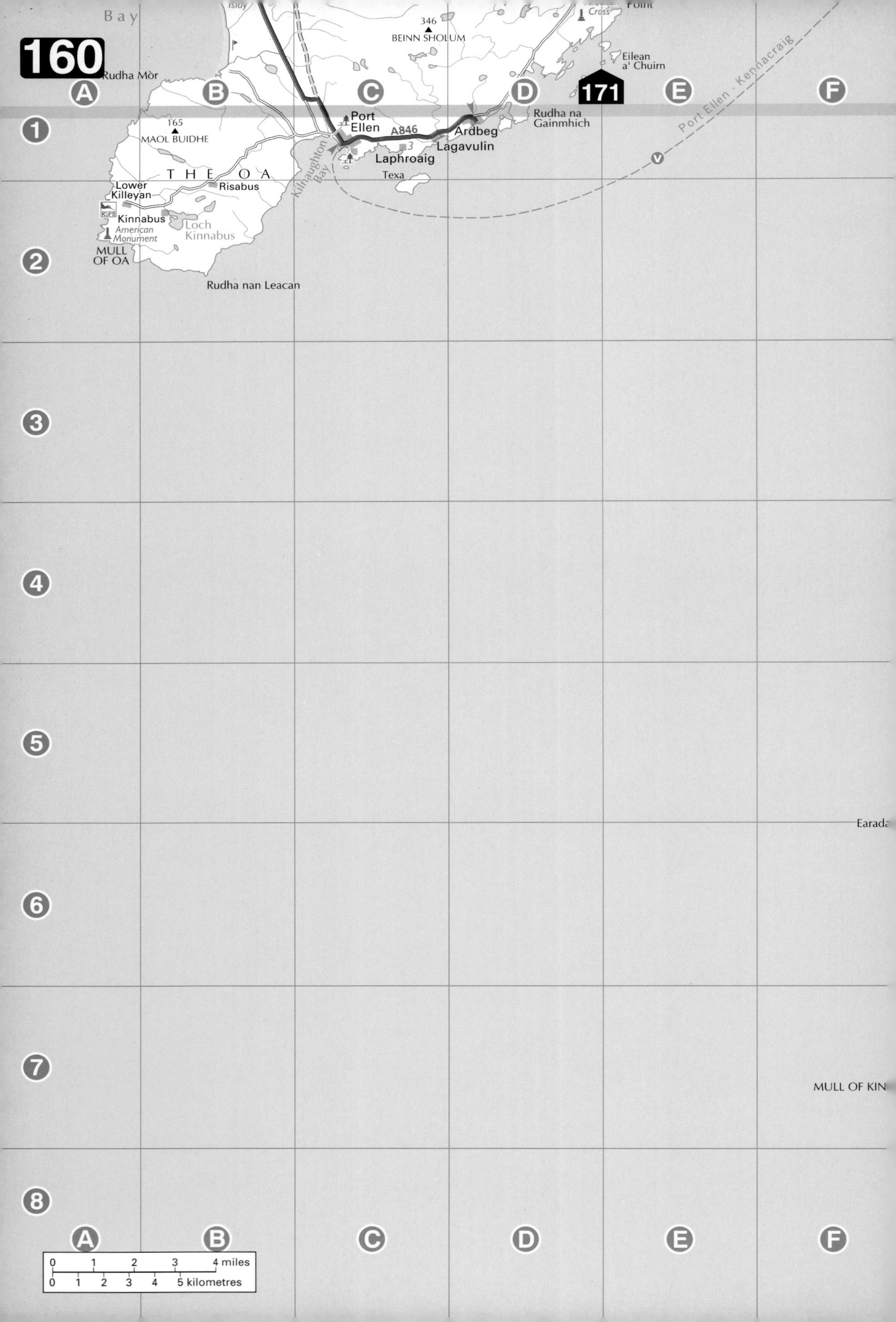

Bay
Islay
346
BEINN SHOLUM
Cross
Point
Eilean
a' Chuirn
171
Port Ellen - Kennacraig
Rudha Mòr
165
MAOL BUIDHE
Port
Ellen
A846
Ardbeg
Rudha na
Gainmhich
Lagavulin
Laphroaig
Texa
THE OA
Kilnaughton
Bay
Lower
Killeyan
Risabus
RSPB
Kinnabus
American
Monument
Loch
Kinnabus
MULL
OF OA
Rudha nan Leacan
Earada
MULL OF KIN
A B C D E F
1 2 3 4 5 6 7 8
0 1 2 3 4 miles
0 1 2 3 4 5 kilometres

GIGHA
Ardminish
Achamore
Rhunahaorine Point
Rhunahaorine
CRUACH MHIC GOUGAIN
264
CNOC-A
SAMHLA
Cour
172
Lochranza
Tayinloan
Sound of Gigha
Cara
Grogport
Barmollack
Pirnmill
Penrioch
North
Loch Tanna
354
CRUACH NAN GABHAR
Whitefarland
A841
715
BEINN BHARRAIN
A83
Muasdale
Carradale Water
B842
Imachar
Balliekine
Carradale
Glenacardoch Point
Belloch
Barr Water
B879
Dippen
Carradale House
Iorsa Water
Glenbarr
MacAlister Clan
454
BEINN AN TUIRC
Carradale Bay
Carradale Point
162
319
408
BORD MOR
Auchagallon Stone Circle
Machrie Bay
Machrie
Cleongart
Machrie Moor Stone Circles
Tormore
Saddell
Bellochantuy Bay
Bellochantuy
Moss Farm Road Stone Circle
Balmich
Saddell Bay
Balmicha
396
SGREADAN HILL
Ugadale
Torbeg
Shiskine
Tangy Loch
Blackwaterfoot
Drumadoon Bay
Kilpatrick
Kilpatrick Dun
Glen Lussa
Brown Head
Kilkenzie
Peninver
Ardnacross Bay
Corriecrav
A83
Kilmichael
Torr a' Chaisteal Fort
Machrihanish Bay
Campbeltown
Campbeltown
Machrihanish
B842
Campbeltown Loch
Island Davarr
Drumlemble
B843
Kilkerran
Kildalloig
352
BEINN GHUILEAN
Achinhoan
385
THE STATE
446
CNOC MOY
Conie Glen
Ru Stafnish
Dalsmeran
Glen Kerran
Glen Breakevie
B842
Strone Glen
Cattadale
Polliwilline Bay
Southend
Macharioch
NN NA LICE
428
Carskey
Dunaverty
Carskey Bay
Sanda Sound
Sheep Island
Borgadalemore Point
Sanda Island
KINTYRE
KILBRANNAN SOUND
G
H
J
K
L
M
1
2
3
4
5
6
7
8

162
173
161
152
Lochranza
Catacol
Glen Catacol
Glen Chalmadale
Cumbrae Island
Portencross
Farland Head
B7048
Seamill
Sannox
North Arran
834
CAISTEAL ABHAIL
Loch Tanna
Penrioch
Pirnmill
A841
715
BEINN BHARRAIN
Glen Iorsa
Corrie
874
GOATFELL
792
BEINN NUIS
Glen Rosa
Merkland Point
Brodick NTS
Iorsa Water
Brodick Bay
ARRAN
Brodick
Strathwhillan
Corriegills
FIRTH OF CLYDE
Auchagallon Stone Circle
Machrie
Machrie Bay
512
A'CHRUACH
Tormore
Machrie Moor Stone Circles
B880
Clauchlands Point
Moss Farm Road Stone Circle
Balmichael
503
BEINN BHREAC
Lamlash
Margnaheglish
Lamlash Bay
Holy Island
Cordon
Torbeg
Shiskine
Blackwaterfoot
Drumadoon Bay
Kilpatrick
Kilpatrick Dun
Brown Head
Auchencairn
Kingscross
Knockenkelly
Glen Scorrodale
Carn Ban
Whiting Bay
Glen Ashdale
Largymore
Corriecravie
Kilmory Water
Torr a' Chaisteal Fort
Sliddery
Largybeg
Dippen Head
Dippen
Kilmory
Lagg
Torrylin Cairn
Bennan
Kildonan
Bennan Head
Pladda
Turnberry
Turnberry Bay
340
Ailsa Craig
0 1 2 3 4 miles
0 1 2 3 4 5 kilometres

174
164
153
Dalry
Highfield
Burnhouse
Gabroc Hill
Crosbie
West Kilbride
Munnoch
Blackshaw
Auchentiber
Dalgarven
High Cross
Stewarton
Crossgates
Kilwinning
Fergushill
Torranyard
Annick Water
Fenwick
Waterside
Laigh Fenwick
Montgreenan
Eglinton
Stevenston
Saltcoats
Ardeer
Cunninghamhead
Kilmaurs
Girdle Toll
Perceton
Moscow
Polbaith Burn
Irvine
Maritime
Springside
Knockentiber
Knockinlaw
Dean Castle
Crosshouse
Dreghorn
Fullarton
The Big Idea
KILMARNOCK
Loudoun Castle
Newmilns
Greenholm
Crookedholm
Hurlford
Galston
R Irvine
Gatehead
Irvine Bay
Drybridge
Earlston
Riccarton
Gailes
Kinfold
Dundonald
Barassie
Middleyard
(Summer only)
Larne
Belfast
Loans
Symington
Craigie
Carnell
Crosshands
Troon
Royal Troon
Helenton
Millburn
Auchmillan
Montgarswood
Monkton
Tarbolton
Bachelors' Club NTS
Mauchline
Failford
Prestwick
Mossblown
Haugh
Catrine
New Prestwick
St Quivox
Stair
Ayr Bay
Whitletts
Annbank
Lugar Water
Wallacetown
Gadgirth
Trabboch
Trabbochburn
Ayr
River Ayr
Ochiltree
Auchinleck
Doonfoot
Belmont
Joppa
Coylton
Palmerston
Heads of Ayr
Burns Cottage
Drongan
Garrallan
Alloway
Burns Monument
Fisherton
Doonholm
Barbieston
Skares
Martnaham Loch
Sinclairston
Dunure
Hollybush
Culroy
Drumshang
Minishant
Dalrymple
Croy Brae (Electric Brae)
Knoweside
River Doon
Rankinston
Dalgig
Culzean Bay
KILMEIN HILL
Culzean NTS
Pennyglen
Guiltreehill
Grimmet
Waterhead
Whitefaulds
Patna
Maybole
Waterside
Dunaskin
Kirkmichael
Crossraguel
KEIRS HILL
BENBEOCH
Kirkoswald
Souter Johnnie's Cottage NTS
Threave
High Pennyvenie
Crosshill
Dalmellington
Straiton
Roan of Craigoch
Ness Glen
Mossdale
Wallacetown
MARATZ HILL
Kilgrammie
Water of Girvan
Dailly
Loch Finlas
GARLEFFIN FELL
Linfern Loch
Tallaminnock
Penkill

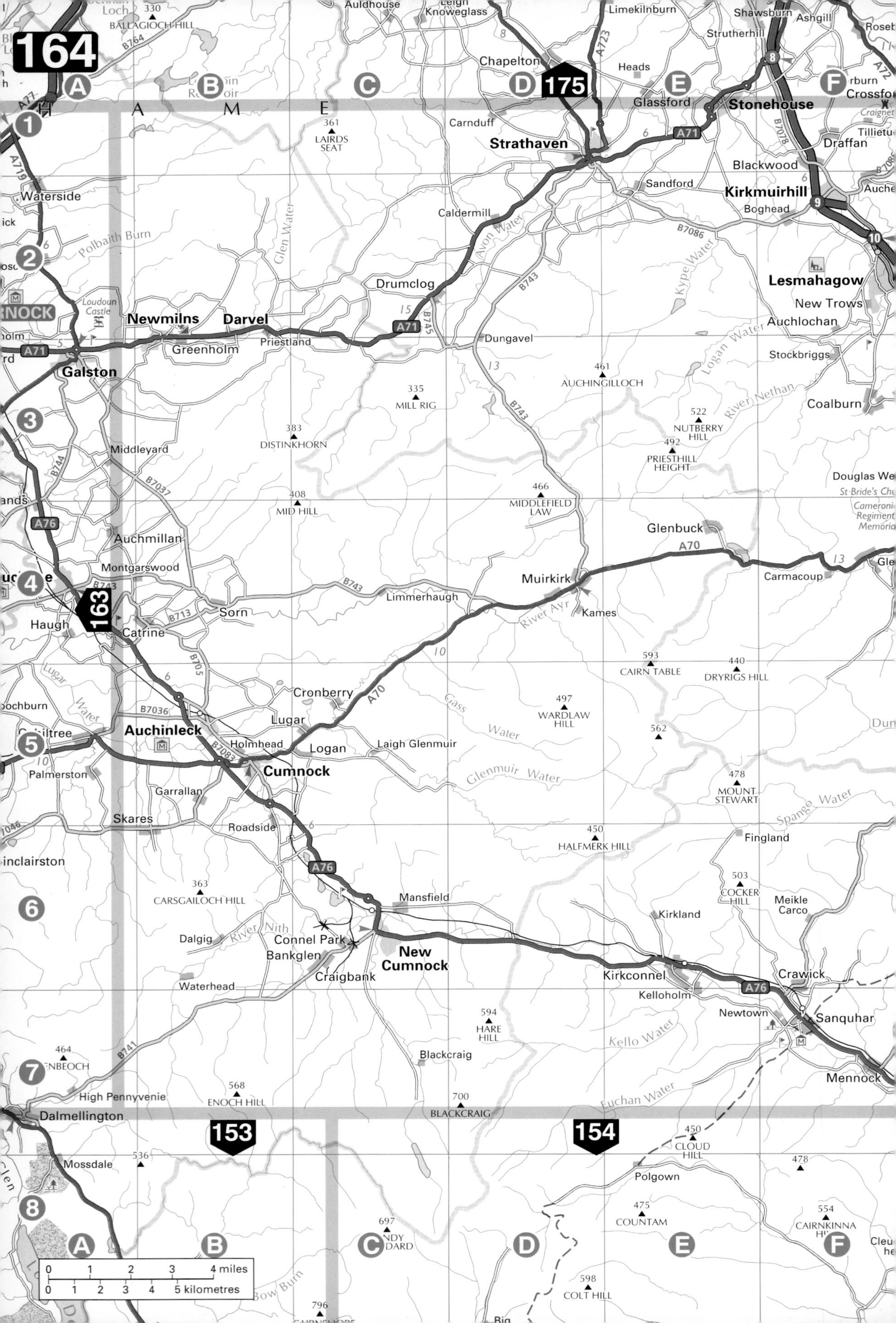
164
175
163
153
154
A
B
C
D
E
F
1
2
3
4
5
6
7
8
Stonehouse
Strathaven
Kirkmuirhill
Lesmahagow
Newmilns
Darvel
Galston
Auchinleck
Cumnock
New Cumnock
Muirkirk
Glassford
Chapelton
Carnduff
Blackwood
Sandford
Boghead
Caldermill
Drumclog
Priestland
Greenholm
Dungavel
Waterside
Auldhouse
Knoweglass
Limekilnburn
Shawsburn
Ashgill
Strutherhill
Heads
Crossford
Draffan
New Trows
Auchlochan
Stockbriggs
Coalburn
Glenbuck
Carmacoup
Kames
Limmerhaugh
Sorn
Catrine
Haugh
Middleyard
Auchmillan
Montgarswood
Cronberry
Lugar
Holmhead
Logan
Laigh Glenmuir
Palmerston
Garrallan
Skares
Roadside
Mansfield
Dalgig
Connel Park
Bankglen
Craigbank
Waterhead
Kirkland
Kirkconnel
Kelloholm
Fingland
Meikle Carco
Crawick
Newtown
Sanquhar
Mennock
Blackcraig
High Pennyvenie
Dalmellington
Mossdale
Polgown
Loudoun Castle
Douglas West
St Bride's Chu
Cameroni Regiment Memoria
361 LAIRDS SEAT
335 MILL RIG
383 DISTINKHORN
408 MID HILL
461 AUCHINGILLOCH
522 NUTBERRY HILL
492 PRIESTHILL HEIGHT
466 MIDDLEFIELD LAW
593 CAIRN TABLE
440 DRYRIGS HILL
497 WARDLAW HILL
562
478 MOUNT STEWART
450 HALFMERK HILL
503 COCKER HILL
363 CARSGAILOCH HILL
594 HARE HILL
464
568 ENOCH HILL
700 BLACKCRAIG
450 CLOUD HILL
478
475 COUNTAM
554 CAIRNKINNA
536
697
598 COLT HILL
796
330 BALLAGIOCH HILL
A71
A76
A70
A77
A719
A723
A72
B7078
B7086
B743
B7086
B745
B744
B7037
B743
B713
B705
B7036
B7083
B741
B764
Polbaith Burn
Glen Water
Avon Water
Kype Water
Logan Water
River Nethan
River Ayr
Gass Water
Glenmuir Water
Spango Water
Lugar Water
River Nith
Kello Water
Euchan Water
Bow Burn
0 1 2 3 4 miles
0 1 2 3 4 5 kilometres

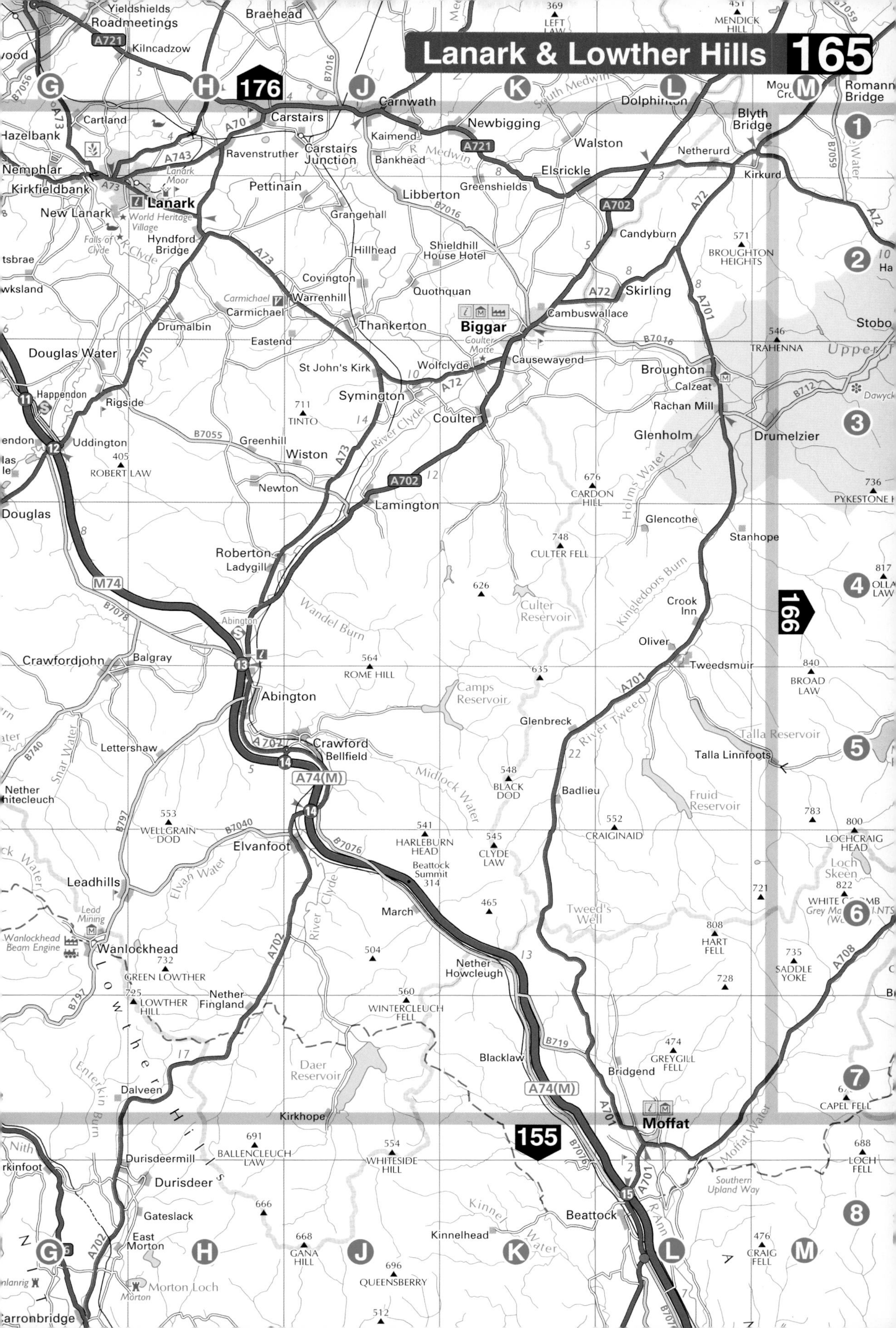
Yieldshields
Roadmeetings
Braehead
Kilncadzow
176
Carnwath
Carstairs
Cartland
Hazelbank
Nemphlar
Kirkfieldbank
Lanark
New Lanark
Ravenstruther
Carstairs Junction
Kaimend
Bankhead
Newbigging
Walston
Dolphinton
Blyth Bridge
Netherurd
Kirkurd
Elsrickle
Greenshields
Libberton
Pettinain
Grangehall
Hyndford Bridge
World Heritage Village
Falls of Clyde
Hillhead
Shieldhill House Hotel
Candyburn
Broughton Heights
Covington
Quothquan
Skirling
Carmichael
Warrenhill
Cambuswallace
Drumalbin
Thankerton
Biggar
Coulter Motte
Eastend
Stobo
Trahenna
Douglas Water
St John's Kirk
Wolfclyde
Causewayend
Broughton
Calzeat
Rachan Mill
Happendon
Rigside
Tinto
Symington
Coulter
Glenholm
Drumelzier
Uddington
Robert Law
Greenhill
Wiston
Newton
Lamington
Cardon Hill
Pykestone Hill
Douglas
Glencothe
Stanhope
Roberton
Ladygill
Culter Fell
Wandel Burn
Culter Reservoir
Kingledoors Burn
Crook Inn
166
Abington
Crawfordjohn
Balgray
Rome Hill
Camps Reservoir
Oliver
Tweedsmuir
Broad Law
Glenbreck
River Tweed
Talla Reservoir
Talla Linnfoots
Lettershaw
Crawford
Bellfield
Midlock Water
Black Dod
Badlieu
Fruid Reservoir
Wellgrain Dod
Elvanfoot
Harleburn Head
Beattock Summit
Clyde Law
Craiginaid
Lochcraig Head
Loch Skeen
Leadhills
Lead Mining
March
Tweed's Well
Wanlockhead Beam Engine
Wanlockhead
Green Lowther
Lowther Hill
Nether Fingland
Nether Howcleugh
Wintercleuch Fell
Hart Fell
Saddle Yoke
Lowther Hills
Daer Reservoir
Blacklaw
Greygill Fell
Bridgend
Dalveen
Enterkin Burn
Kirkhope
Moffat
155
Capel Fell
Ballencleuch Law
Whiteside Hill
Durisdeermill
Durisdeer
Gateslack
East Morton
Kinnel Water
Kinnelhead
Beattock
Southern Upland Way
Loch Fell
Gana Hill
Queensberry
Craig Fell
Morton Loch
Morton
Carronbridge
River Clyde
Elvan Water
Snar Water
Holms Water
Moffat Water
Upper Tweed

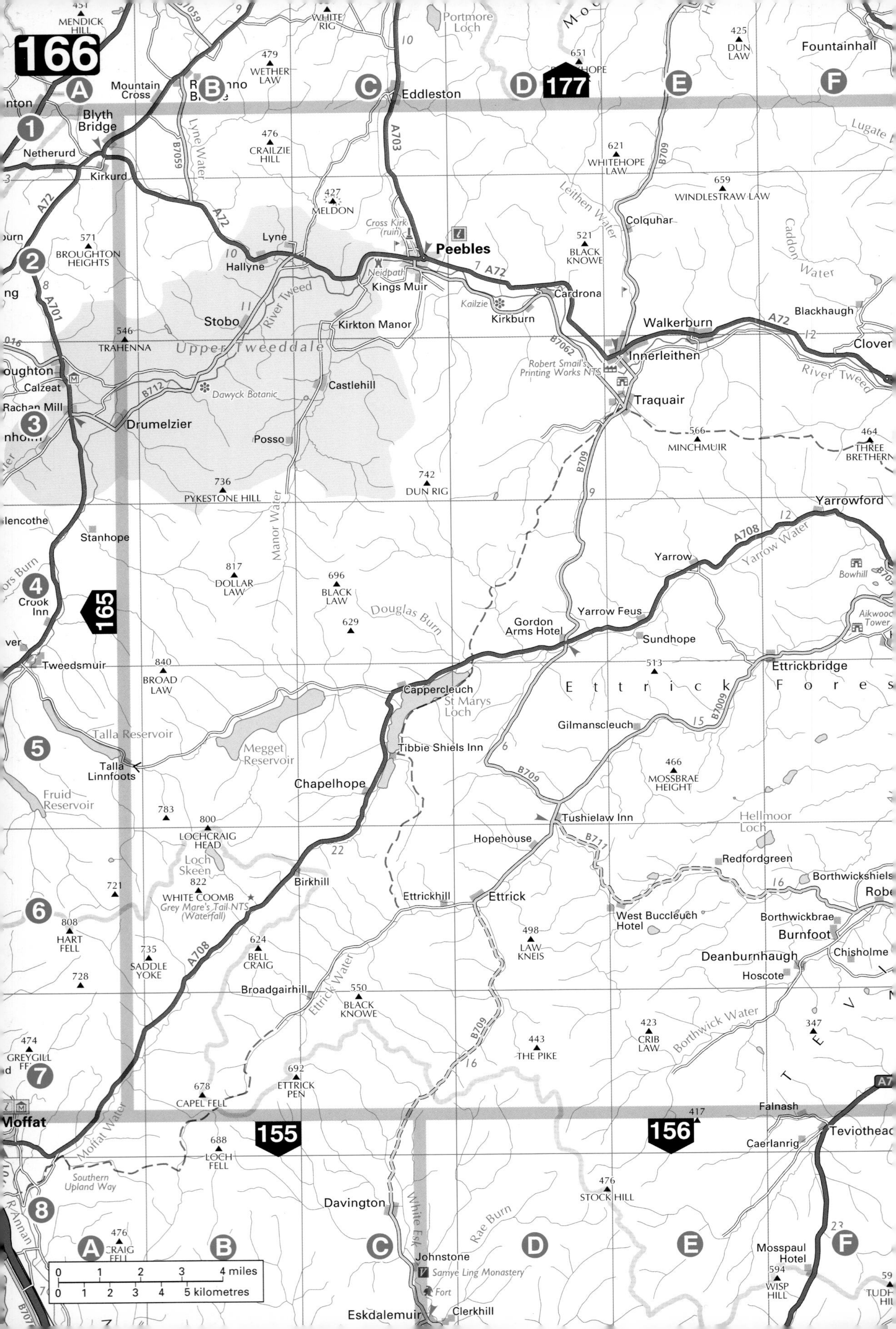
166
177
165
155
156
Mountain Cross
Blyth Bridge
Netherurd
Kirkurd
Eddleston
Portmore Loch
WETHER LAW
WHITE RIG
MENDICK HILL
DUN LAW
Fountainhall
CRAILZIE HILL
WHITEHOPE LAW
WINDLESTRAW LAW
MELDON
Cross Kirk (ruin)
Peebles
Lyne
Hallyne
Neidpath
Kings Muir
Colquhar
BLACK KNOWE
Leithen Water
Caddon Water
BROUGHTON HEIGHTS
Cardrona
Kailzie
Kirkburn
Stobo
River Tweed
Kirkton Manor
Walkerburn
Blackhaugh
Clover
TRAHENNA
Upper Tweeddale
Innerleithen
Robert Smail's Printing Works NTS
Dawyck Botanic
Castlehill
Traquair
Calzeat
Rachan Mill
Drumelzier
Posso
MINCHMUIR
THREE BRETHERN
PYKESTONE HILL
DUN RIG
Yarrowford
Stanhope
DOLLAR LAW
BLACK LAW
Manor Water
Yarrow
Yarrow Water
Bowhill
Crook Inn
Douglas Burn
Gordon Arms Hotel
Yarrow Feus
Sundhope
Aikwood Tower
Tweedsmuir
BROAD LAW
Ettrickbridge
Cappercleuch
St Marys Loch
Ettrick Forest
Gilmanscleuch
Talla Reservoir
Megget Reservoir
Tibbie Shiels Inn
Talla Linnfoots
Chapelhope
MOSSBRAE HEIGHT
Fruid Reservoir
LOCHCRAIG HEAD
Tushielaw Inn
Hellmoor Loch
Hopehouse
Redfordgreen
Loch Skeen
Birkhill
Borthwickshiels
WHITE COOMB
Grey Mare's Tail NTS (Waterfall)
Ettrickhill
Ettrick
West Buccleuch Hotel
HART FELL
Borthwickbrae
Burnfoot
SADDLE YOKE
BELL CRAIG
LAW KNEIS
Deanburnhaugh
Chisholme
Hoscote
Broadgairhill
Ettrick Water
BLACK KNOWE
CRIB LAW
Borthwick Water
THE PIKE
GREYGILL
ETTRICK PEN
CAPEL FELL
Falnash
Moffat
Moffat Water
Teviothead
LOCH FELL
Caerlanrig
Southern Upland Way
STOCK HILL
Davington
White Esk
Rae Burn
Mosspaul Hotel
WISP HILL
CRAIG FELL
R Annan
Johnstone
Samye Ling Monastery
Fort
Eskdalemuir
Clerkhill
0 1 2 3 4 miles
0 1 2 3 4 5 kilometres

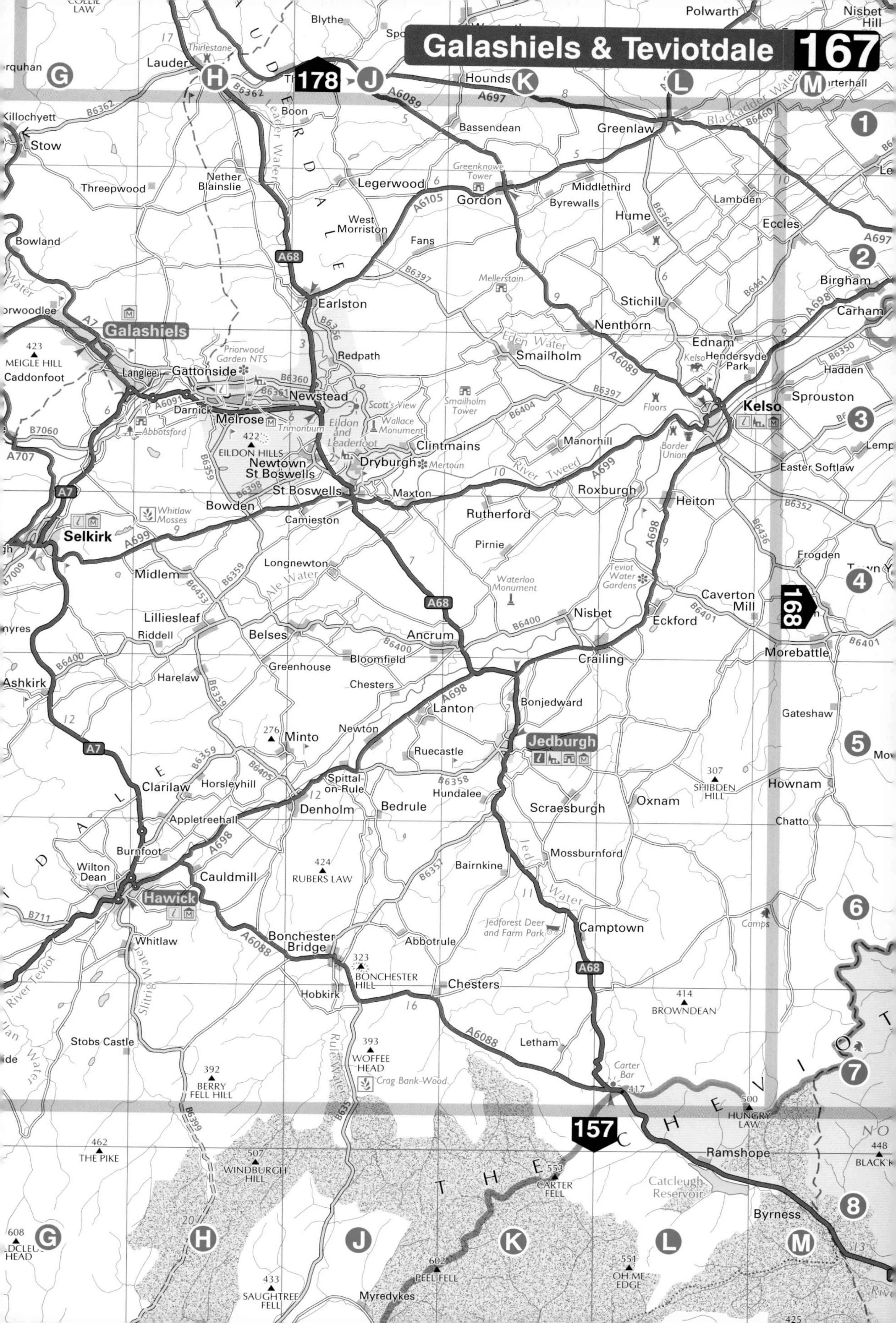
Galashiels & Teviotdale
167
178
168
157
Lauder
Thirlestane
Blythe
Polwarth
Nisbet Hill
Hounds
Greenlaw
Boon
Bassendean
Stow
Threepwood
Nether Blainslie
Legerwood
Gordon
Greenknowe Tower
Middlethird
Byrewalls
Hume
Lambden
Eccles
Bowland
West Morriston
Fans
Earlston
Mellerstain
Stichill
Nenthorn
Birgham
Carham
Galashiels
423
MEIGLE HILL
Caddonfoot
Langlee
Gattonside
Priorwood Garden NTS
Redpath
Smailholm
Eden Water
Ednam
Kelso
Hendersyde Park
Hadden
Sprouston
Newstead
Darnick
Melrose
Abbotsford
Trimontium
Scott's View
Eildon and Leaderfoot
Wallace Monument
Smailholm Tower
Floors
Manorhill
Clintmains
Border Union
422
EILDON HILLS
Newtown St Boswells
Dryburgh
Mertoun
River Tweed
Easter Softlaw
St Boswells
Maxton
Roxburgh
Heiton
Bowden
Whitlaw Mosses
Camieston
Rutherford
Selkirk
Pirnie
Frogden
Midlem
Longnewton
Ale Water
Waterloo Monument
Teviot Water Gardens
Caverton Mill
Lilliesleaf
Riddell
Belses
Ancrum
Nisbet
Eckford
Morebattle
Crailing
Ashkirk
Harelaw
Greenhouse
Bloomfield
Chesters
Bonjedward
Lanton
Gateshaw
276
Minto
Newton
Jedburgh
Ruecastle
Clarilaw
Horsleyhill
Spittal-on-Rule
Hundalee
307
SHIBDEN HILL
Hownam
Appletreehall
Denholm
Bedrule
Scraesburgh
Oxnam
Chatto
Burnfoot
Wilton Dean
424
RUBERS LAW
Bairnkine
Mossburnford
Cauldmill
Hawick
Jed Water
Camps
Whitlaw
Jedforest Deer and Farm Park
Camptown
Bonchester Bridge
Abbotrule
323
BONCHESTER HILL
Hobkirk
Chesters
414
BROWNDEAN
River Teviot
Slitrig Water
Stobs Castle
393
WOFFEE HEAD
Letham
Rule Water
392
BERRY FELL HILL
Crag Bank Wood
Carter Bar
417
500
HUNGRY LAW
THE CHEVIOT
462
THE PIKE
507
WINDBURGH HILL
553
CARTER FELL
Ramshope
448
Catcleugh Reservoir
Byrness
608
602
PEEL FELL
551
OH ME EDGE
433
SAUGHTREE FELL
Myredykes
425
A68
A7
A697
A6089
A6105
A698
A699
A6088
A6091
A707
B6362
B6397
B6356
B6360
B6361
B6359
B6398
B6404
B6364
B6461
B6460
B6350
B6352
B6436
B6400
B6401
B6453
B6358
B6405
B6357
B6399
B7060
B711
B7009

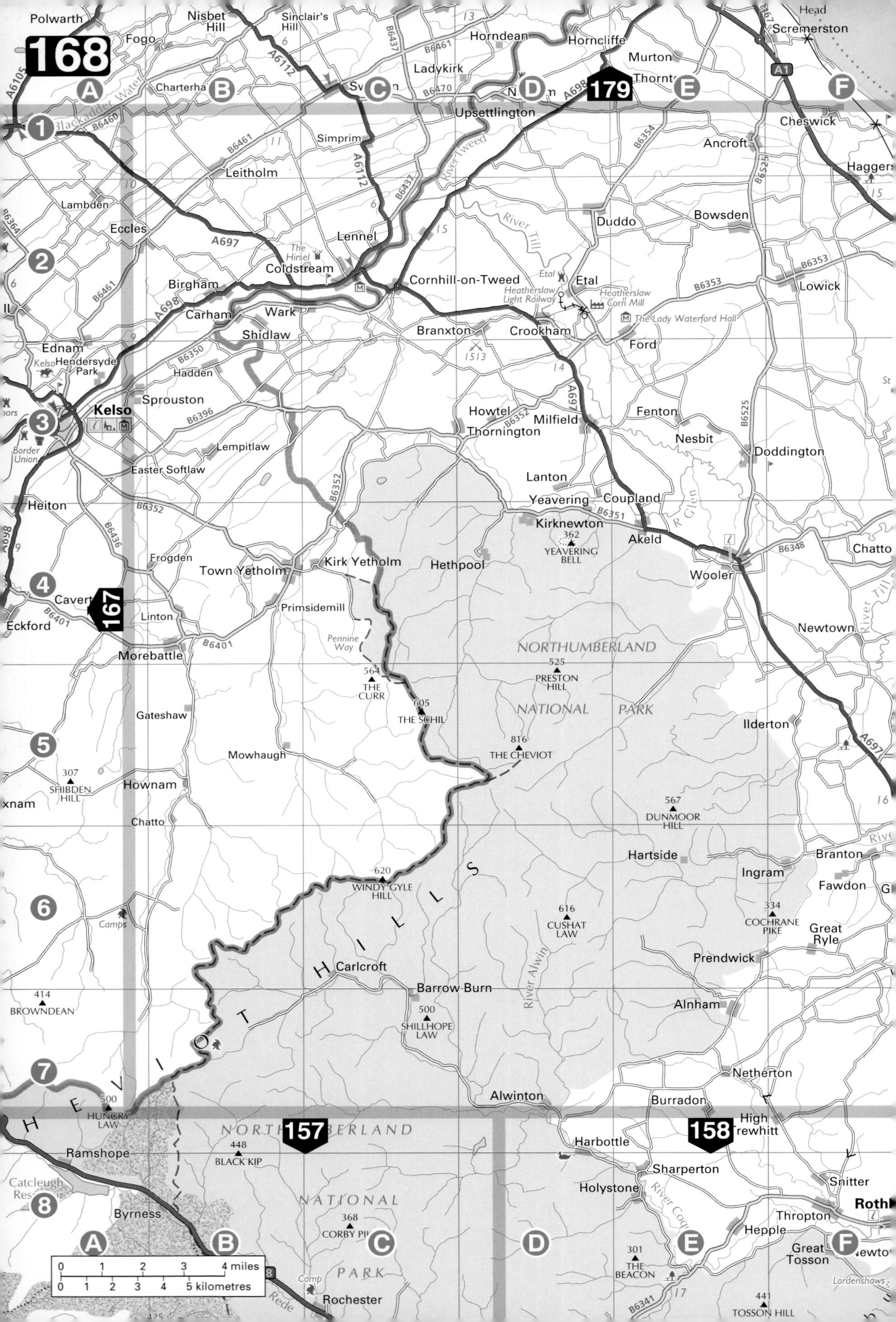
168
179
167
157
158
Polwarth
Fogo
Nisbet Hill
Sinclair's Hill
Horndean
Horncliffe
Murton
Scremerston
Ladykirk
Charterhall
Upsettlington
Cheswick
Simprim
Ancroft
Haggerston
Leitholm
Lambden
Eccles
Duddo
Bowsden
Lennel
The Hirsel
Coldstream
Birgham
Cornhill-on-Tweed
Etal
Heatherslaw Light Railway
Heatherslaw Corn Mill
The Lady Waterford Hall
Lowick
Carham
Wark
Shidlaw
Branxton
Crookham
Ford
Ednam
Kelso
Hendersyde Park
Hadden
Sprouston
Border Union
Lempitlaw
Easter Softlaw
Howtel
Thornington
Milfield
Fenton
Nesbit
Doddington
Lanton
Yeavering
Coupland
Kirknewton
Akeld
Heiton
362 YEAVERING BELL
Wooler
Chatton
Frogden
Town Yetholm
Kirk Yetholm
Hethpool
Caverton
Eckford
Linton
Primsidemill
Pennine Way
Newtown
Morebattle
NORTHUMBERLAND
564 THE CURR
525 PRESTON HILL
Gateshaw
605 THE SCHIL
NATIONAL PARK
Ilderton
Mowhaugh
816 THE CHEVIOT
307 SHIBDEN HILL
Hownam
567 DUNMOOR HILL
Chatto
Hartside
Branton
Ingram
Fawdon
620 WINDY GYLE HILL
CHEVIOT HILLS
Camps
616 CUSHAT LAW
334 COCHRANE PIKE
Great Ryle
Carlcroft
Prendwick
Barrow Burn
River Alwin
414 BROWNDEAN
Alnham
500 SHILLHOPE LAW
Netherton
Alwinton
Burradon
500 HUNGRY LAW
High Trewhitt
Ramshope
448 BLACK KIP
Harbottle
Sharperton
Snitter
Catcleugh Reservoir
Holystone
River Coquet
Byrness
368 CORBY PIKE
Thropton
Hepple
Great Tosson
301 THE BEACON
Rochester
441 TOSSON HILL
Lordenshaws
Rede
Camp
River Tweed
River Till
R Glen
Blackadder Water
1513
0 1 2 3 4 miles
0 1 2 3 4 5 kilometres

CAUSEWAY FLOODED AT HIGH TIDE
HOLY ISLAND
Holy Island
Lindisfarne NT
Lindisfarne Priory
Castle Point
Guile Point
Longstone Lighthouse
NT
FARNE ISLANDS
Staple Sound
Inner Sound
North Northumberland Heritage Coast
Budle Bay
Bamburgh
B1342
Bamburgh
B1340
Belford
B6349
Seahouses
North Sunderland
B1341
Lucker
B6348
Beadnell
Warenford
Swinhoe
A1
Beadnell Bay
Chathill
Newstead
Tughall
B1340
Ellingham
Preston
Newton-by-the-Sea
Preston Pele Tower
Brunton
267
CATERAN HILL
Christon Bank
Embleton
Embleton Bay
North Charlton
Falloden
Dunstanburgh NT
B6347
B1339
South Charlton
Ditchburn
Dunstan
Craster
B6346
Eglingham
Rock
B6341
Rennington
Stamford
Howick Hall
Howick
Beanley
B6341
B1340
Cullernose Point
B6346
Longhoughton
Denwick
Boulmer
River Aln
Alnwick
Bolton
Seaton Point
Lesbury
B6341
Alnmouth
Alnmouth Bay
A1
Edlingham
A1068
Shilbottle
260
GLANTLEES HILL
Newton-on-the-Moor
Warkworth Castle & Hermitage
Warkworth
Amble
Coquet Island
159
Gloster Hill
Hauxley
Guyzance
Togston
A697
Swarland
Acklington
Radcliffe
Felton
East Thirston
Broomhill
B1330
Pauperhaugh
B6344
South Broomhill
Brinkburn
West Thirston
Red Row
Druridge Bay
Eshott
G
H
J
K
L
M
1
2
3
4
5
6
7
8

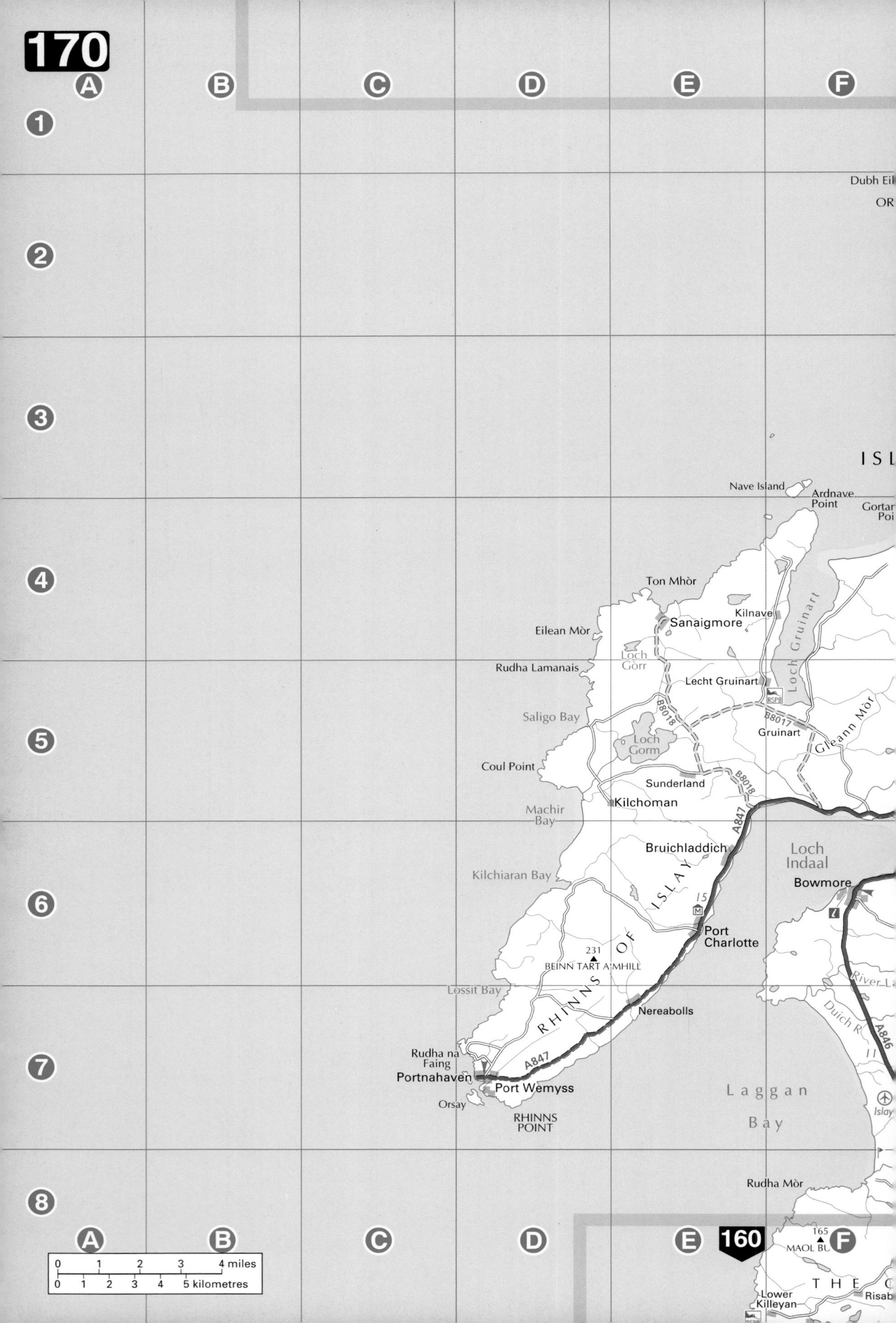

A
B
C
D
E
F
1
2
3
4
5
6
7
8
Dubh Eil
OR
ISL
Nave Island
Ardnave Point
Gortar Poi
Ton Mhòr
Kilnave
Sanaigmore
Loch Gruinart
Eilean Mòr
Loch Gorr
Rudha Lamanais
Lecht Gruinart
RSPB
Saligo Bay
B8018
B8017
Gruinart
Gleann Mòr
Loch Gorm
Coul Point
Sunderland
B8018
Kilchoman
Machir Bay
A847
Bruichladdich
Loch Indaal
Kilchiaran Bay
Bowmore
RHINNS OF ISLAY
15
Port Charlotte
231
BEINN TART A'MHILL
River La
Lossit Bay
Nereabolls
Duich R
A846
Rudha na Faing
A847
Portnahaven
Port Wemyss
Laggan Bay
Orsay
Islay
RHINNS POINT
Rudha Mòr
160
165
MAOL BU
THE
Lower Killeyan
Risab
0 1 2 3 4 miles
0 1 2 3 4 5 kilometres

180 181 172 160

Ardlussa
Lussa Point
Glen Grundale
A846
SOUND OF JURA
Loch Crinan
Crinan
Kilmahumaig
Bellano
Moine Mhor
Kilmichael Glassary Inscribed Stone
A816
Dunadd Fort
Kilmichael
Crinan Canal
B841
Cairnbaan
Bàrnluasgan
Carsaig Bay
Tayvallich
Knapdale
Taynish
Achnamara
Kilmichael of Inverlussa
Càm Loch
Lochgilphead
Kilmory Woodland Park
Loch Gilp
Ardrishaig
Shirvan
Carrick
A83
331 BEINN BHEAG
466 CRUACH LUSACH
Brenfield
Loch Sween
B8025
Keills Chapel
Loch na Cille
Kilbride
Sween
Danna Island
B8024
Lochead
Achahoish
St Cormacs Chapel
Kilmory Knap Chapel
Kilmory
Ellary
Kilmory Bay
Loch Caolisport
Point of Knap
Ormsary
Druimdrishaig
Erines
561 SLIABH GAOIL
Stonefield Castle Hotel
480 DUBH CHREAG
Loch nan Torran
An Tairbeart
Glenralloch
Tarbert
West Tarbert
Cretshengan
Coulaghailtro
Kilberry Sculptured Stones
Kilberry
Kilberry Head
Keppoch Point
213 CRUACH AIRDE
Tiretigan
343 CRUACH-AN T SORCHAIN
Torinturk
West Loch Tarbert
422 CNOC A' BHAILE-SHOIS
Kennacraig
Whitehouse
Kilchamaig
Loch Stornoway
Ardpatrick
B8001
Skipness
Chapel
Skipness Point
Portachoillan
Clachan
Claonaig
Ronachan Point
Ronachan
Kennacraig
(Winter Only)
(Summer Only)
Loch Ciàran
Loch Garasdale
Kinerarach
Tarbert
GIGHA
Sound of Gigha
B842
Crossaig
Lochranza
Catacol
247 CRUACH MHIC GOUGAIN
264 CNOC-AN T-SAMHLAIDH
Rhunahaorine Point
Rhunahaorine
Cour Bay
Cour
Ardminish
Achamore
Tayinloan
Grogport
Barmollack
Pirnmill
Penrioch
Loch Tanna
Ballimore
Fearnoch
Kilfinan Bay
Middle Kame
0 1 2 3 4 miles
0 1 2 3 4 5 kilometres
181
182
171
161

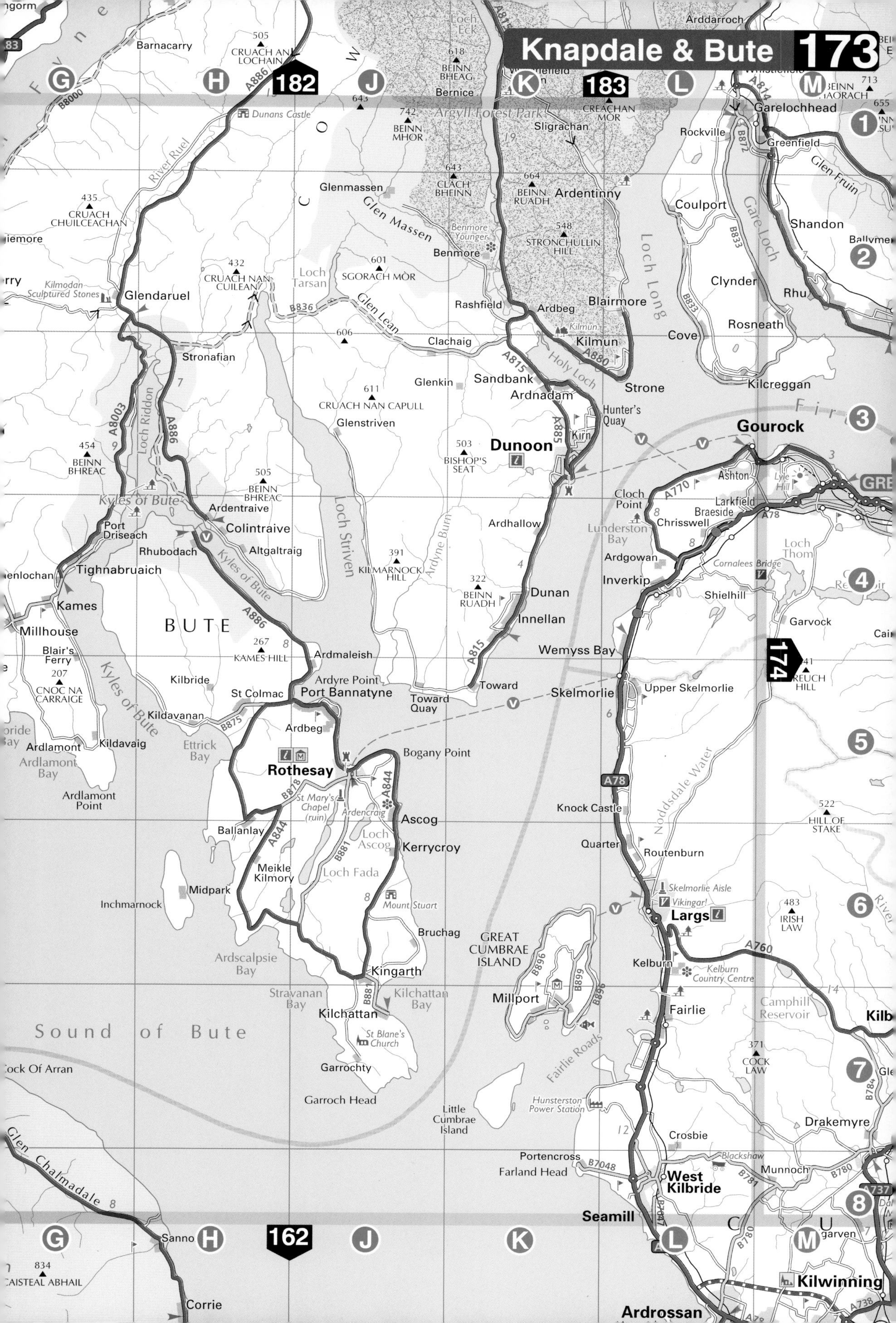
Knapdale & Bute
173
182
183
174
162
Barnacarry
CRUACH AN LOCHAIN
Dunans Castle
BEINN BHEAG
Bernice
BEINN MHOR
Argyll Forest Park
CREACHAN MOR
Sligrachan
Arddarroch
Garelochhead
Rockville
Greenfield
Glen Fruin
Shandon
Coulport
Gare Loch
Clynder
Rhu
Rosneath
Cove
Kilcreggan
Glenmassen
Glen Massen
CLACH BHEINN
BEINN RUADH
Ardentinny
STRONCHULLIN HILL
Loch Long
Benmore Younger
Benmore
CRUACH CHUILCEACHAN
Kilmodan Sculptured Stones
Glendaruel
CRUACH NAN CUILEAN
Loch Tarsan
SGORACH MÒR
Glen Lean
Rashfield
Ardbeg
Blairmore
Kilmun
Strone
Holy Loch
Clachaig
Stronafian
River Ruel
Glenkin
Sandbank
Ardnadam
CRUACH NAN CAPULL
Glenstriven
Hunter's Quay
Kirn
Dunoon
BISHOP'S SEAT
Gourock
Ashton
Lyle Hill
Larkfield
Braeside
Chrisswell
Cloch Point
Lunderston Bay
Ardgowan
Inverkip
Cornalees Bridge
Loch Thom
Shielhill
Garvock
Loch Riddon
BEINN BHREAC
Kyles of Bute
Ardentraive
Colintraive
Port Driseach
Rhubodach
Altgaltraig
Loch Striven
Ardyne Burn
Ardhallow
Tighnabruaich
Kames
Millhouse
KILMARNOCK HILL
BEINN RUADH
Dunan
Innellan
BUTE
Blair's Ferry
CNOC NA CARRAIGE
KAMES HILL
Ardmaleish
Wemyss Bay
Kilbride
St Colmac
Ardyre Point
Port Bannatyne
Toward Quay
Toward
Skelmorlie
Upper Skelmorlie
REUCH HILL
Kildavanan
Ardlamont
Kildavaig
Ardlamont Bay
Ardlamont Point
Ettrick Bay
Ardbeg
Rothesay
Bogany Point
St Mary's Chapel (ruin)
Ardencraig
Ascog
Loch Ascog
Kerrycroy
Ballanlay
Meikle Kilmory
Loch Fada
Midpark
Inchmarnock
Mount Stuart
Bruchag
Noddsdale Water
Knock Castle
Quarter
Routenburn
HILL OF STAKE
Skelmorlie Aisle
Vikingar!
Largs
IRISH LAW
GREAT CUMBRAE ISLAND
Kelburn
Kelburn Country Centre
Millport
Fairlie
Camphill Reservoir
Ardscalpsie Bay
Kingarth
Stravanan Bay
Kilchattan Bay
Kilchattan
St Blane's Church
Sound of Bute
Fairlie Roads
COCK LAW
Garrochty
Garroch Head
Cock Of Arran
Hunsterston Power Station
Little Cumbrae Island
Crosbie
Drakemyre
Portencross
Farland Head
Blackshaw
Munnoch
West Kilbride
Glen Chalmadale
Seamill
Sanno
CAISTEAL ABHAIL
Kilwinning
Corrie
Ardrossan

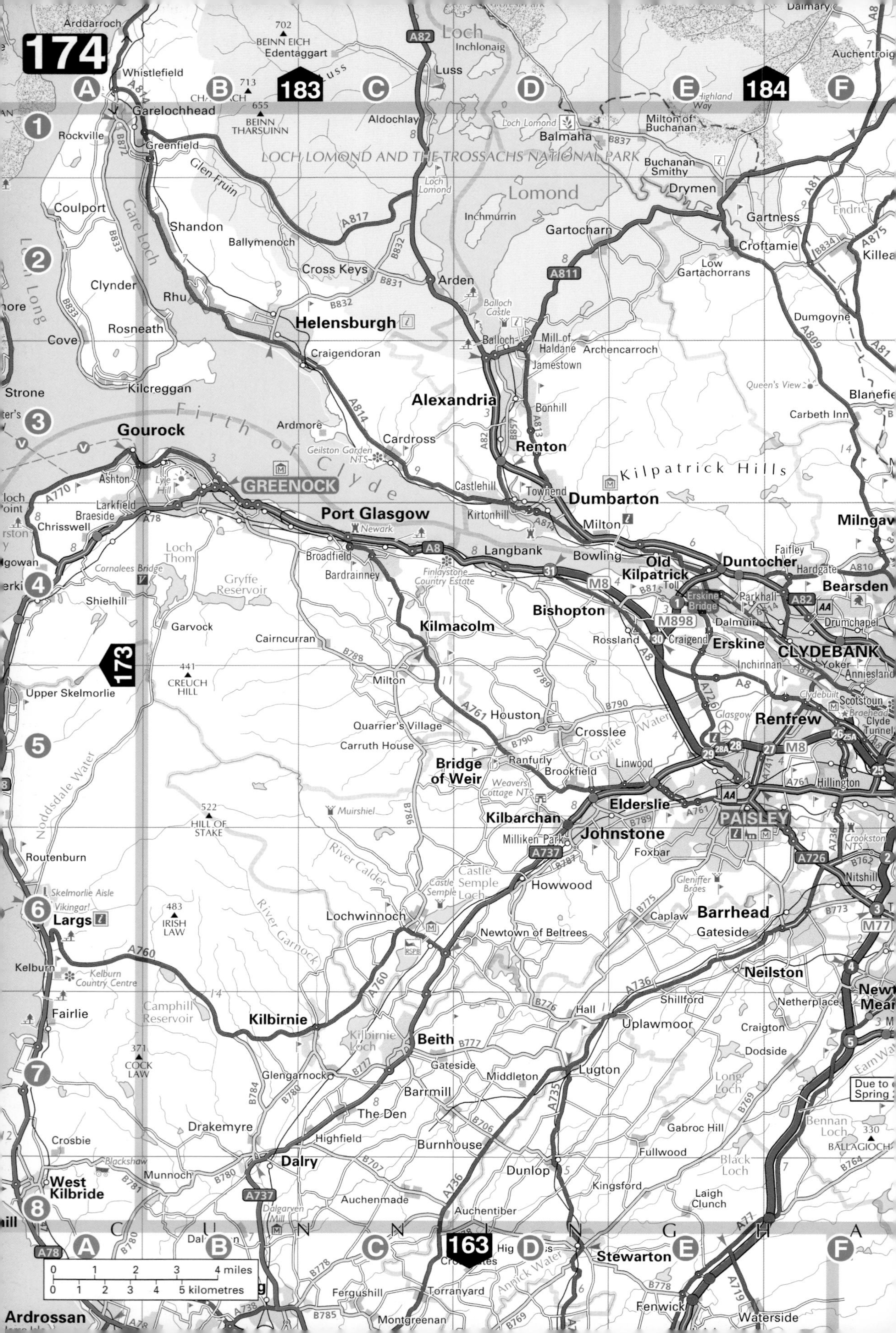

174
Arddarroch
702
BEINN EICH
Edentaggart
Loch
Inchlonaig
Luss
Dalmary
Auchentroig
Whistlefield
713
183
184
A
B
C
D
E
F
655
BEINN THARSUINN
Garelochhead
Aldochlay
Loch Lomond
Balmaha
Milton of Buchanan
Highland Way
1
Rockville
Greenfield
LOCH LOMOND AND THE TROSSACHS NATIONAL PARK
Buchanan Smithy
Drymen
Glen Fruin
Loch Lomond
Lomond
Coulport
Gare Loch
Shandon
Inchmurrin
Gartness
Endrick
Ballymenoch
Gartocharn
Croftamie
Killea
2
Loch Long
Clynder
Cross Keys
Arden
Low Gartachorrans
Rhu
Balloch Castle
Helensburgh
Dumgoyne
Cove
Rosneath
Balloch
Mill of Haldane
Archencarroch
Craigendoran
Jamestown
Queen's View
Strone
Kilcreggan
Alexandria
Blanefie
Bonhill
Carbeth Inn
3
Firth of Clyde
Gourock
Ardmore
Cardross
Renton
Geilston Garden NTS
Ashton
Lyle Hill
GREENOCK
Kilpatrick Hills
Castlehill
Townend
Dumbarton
Larkfield
Braeside
Port Glasgow
Kirtonhill
Milton
Milngav
Chrisswell
Newark
Loch Thom
Broadfield
Langbank
Bowling
Old Kilpatrick
Duntocher
Faifley
Hardgate
Cornalees Bridge
Gryffe Reservoir
Bardrainney
Finlaystone Country Estate
Bearsden
4
Shielhill
Toll
Erskine Bridge
Parkhill
Bishopton
Dalmuir
Drumchapel
Garvock
Kilmacolm
Cairncurran
Rossland
Craigend
Erskine
CLYDEBANK
173
441
CREUCH HILL
Milton
Inchinnan
Yoker
Anniesland
Upper Skelmorlie
Clydebuilt
Scotstoun
Braehead
Houston
Renfrew
Clyde Tunnel
Quarrier's Village
Crosslee
Gryffe Water
Glasgow
5
Carruth House
Linwood
Bridge of Weir
Ranfurly
Brookfield
Noddsdale Water
Weavers Cottage NTS
Hillington
Elderslie
522
HILL OF STAKE
Muirshiel
Kilbarchan
PAISLEY
Johnstone
Milliken Park
Routenburn
River Calder
Foxbar
Crookston NTS
Castle Semple Loch
Howwood
Nitshill
Skelmorlie Aisle
Vikingar!
Gleniffer Braes
6
Largs
483
IRISH LAW
River Garnock
Lochwinnoch
Caplaw
Barrhead
Newtown of Beltrees
Gateside
Kelburn
Kelburn Country Centre
RSPB
Neilston
Fairlie
Camphill Reservoir
Hall
Shillford
Netherplace
Newt Mear
Kilbirnie
Uplawmoor
Kilbirnie Loch
Beith
Craigton
371
COCK LAW
Dodside
7
Glengarnock
Gateside
Middleton
Lugton
Long Loch
Earn Wat
Due to Spring
Barrmill
The Den
Drakemyre
Bennan Loch
Gabroc Hill
330
BALLAGIOCH
Crosbie
Highfield
Burnhouse
Fullwood
Blackshaw
Dalry
Black Loch
West Kilbride
Munnoch
Dunlop
Kingsford
Laigh Clunch
8
Auchenmade
Dalgarven Mill
Auchentiber
163
Stewarton
Fergushill
Torranyard
Fenwick
Ardrossan
Montgreenan
Waterside
Annick Water
A814
B872
B833
A817
B832
B831
A82
A811
B837
A81
A875
B834
A809
A813
B857
A770
A78
A8
M8
B815
M898
A810
B788
B789
A761
B790
A726
A737
A736
B786
B787
A760
B775
B773
M77
B776
B777
B780
B784
B706
B707
B769
B764
A735
A77
A719
B781
B778
B785
B762
A741
0 1 2 3 4 miles
0 1 2 3 4 5 kilometres

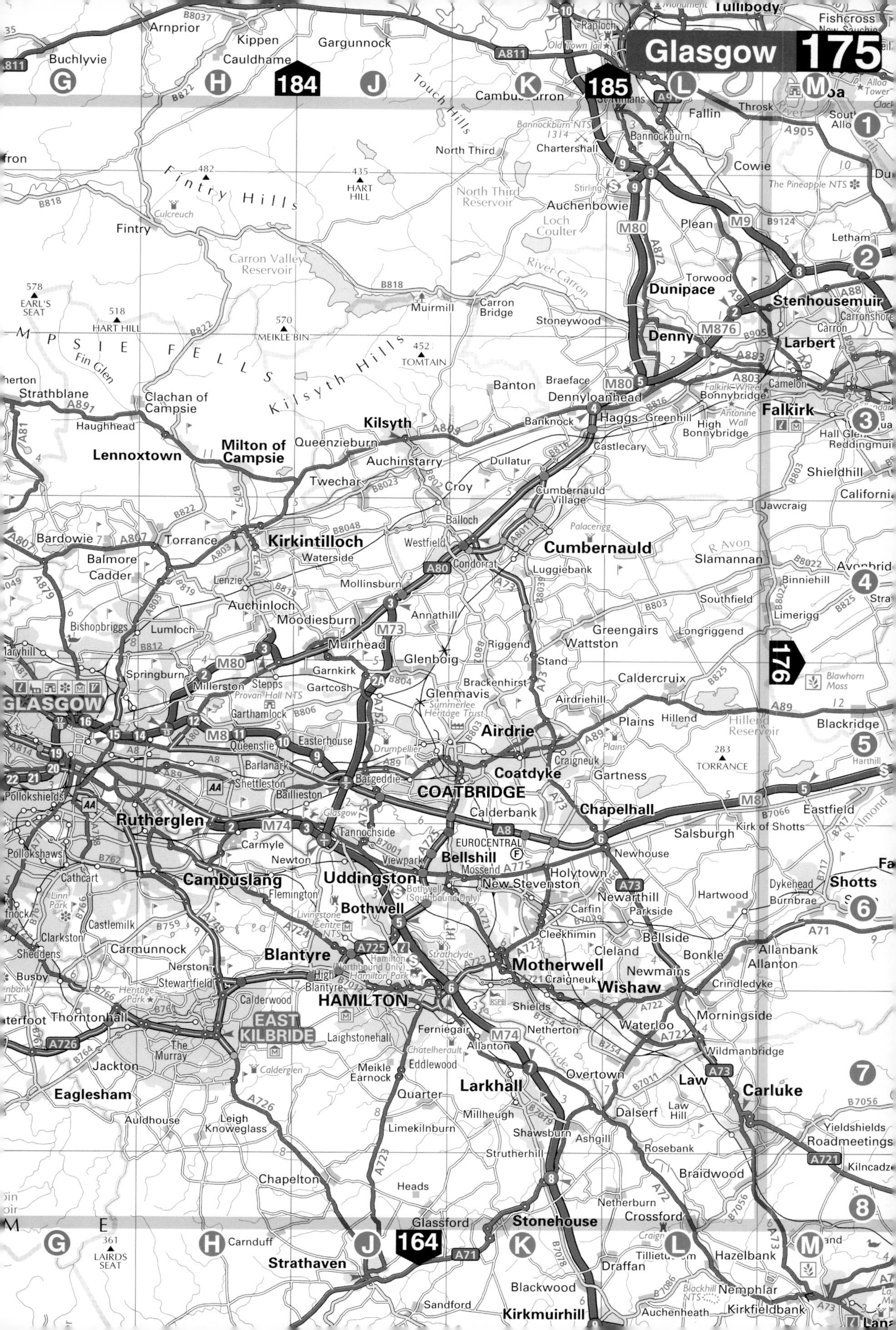
Arnprior
Kippen
Gargunnock
Tullibody
Fishcross
Buchlyvie
Cauldhame
Raploch
Old Town Jail
A811
B8037
184
185
G
H
J
K
L
M
Touch Hills
Cambusbarron
St Ninians
Fallin
Throsk
Bannockburn NTS 1314
Chartershall
Bannockburn
North Third
Cowie
Fintry Hills
482
435
HART HILL
Culcreuch
Fintry
B818
B822
North Third Reservoir
Stirling
Auchenbowie
Loch Coulter
Plean
M9
M80
B9124
Letham
The Pineapple NTS
A905
Carron Valley Reservoir
River Carron
Torwood
Dunipace
Stenhousemuir
Carronshore
578
EARL'S SEAT
518
HART HILL
570
MEIKLE BIN
Muirmill
Carron Bridge
Stoneywood
Denny
M876
B905
Larbert
Carron
452
TOMTAIN
CAMPSIE FELLS
Fin Glen
Kilsyth Hills
Strathblane
A891
Clachan of Campsie
Haughhead
Banton
Braeface
Dennyloanhead
Falkirk Wheel
Bonnybridge
Camelon
Falkirk
A803
A883
A88
Haggs
Greenhill
High Bonnybridge
Antonine Wall
Banknock
Kilsyth
A803
Lennoxtown
Milton of Campsie
Queenzieburn
Castlecary
Hall Glen
Reddingmuir
Auchinstarry
Dullatur
Shieldhill
Twechar
Croy
B8023
B802
Cumbernauld Village
California
B757
B822
Balloch
Jawcraig
Bardowie
A807
Torrance
Kirkintilloch
B8048
Westfield
Palacerigg
Cumbernauld
R Avon
Slamannan
Avonbridge
Balmore
Cadder
Waterside
A80
Condorrat
Luggiebank
B8022
Binniehill
Lenzie
B819
Mollinsburn
A73
B8039
A879
A803
Auchinloch
Moodiesburn
M73
Annathill
B803
Southfield
B825
Limerigg
Bishopbriggs
Lumloch
Muirhead
Riggend
Greengairs
Wattston
Longriggend
B812
Glenboig
B8088
Stand
176
Springburn
M80
Millerston
Stepps
Garnkirk
Gartcosh
Brackenhirst
Caldercruix
Blawhorn Moss
Provan Hall NTS
Glenmavis
Summerlee Heritage Trust
Airdriehill
GLASGOW
Garthamlock
B806
B804
A752
Plains
Hillend
Hillend Reservoir
A89
Blackridge
M8
Queenslie
Easterhouse
Drumpellier
Airdrie
283
TORRANCE
A814
A8
Barlanark
Craigneuk
Gartness
Shettleston
Bargeddie
Coatdyke
Harthill
Pollokshields
Baillieston
COATBRIDGE
Glasgow
Calderbank
Chapelhall
Eastfield
Rutherglen
M74
Tannochside
B7066
Kirk of Shotts
R Almond
Carmyle
B7001
EUROCENTRAL
Salsburgh
Pollokshaws
B762
Newton
Viewpark
A725
Bellshill
Newhouse
Cathcart
Cambuslang
Uddingston
Mossend
A775
Holytown
Shotts
Dykehead
Flemington
Bothwell (Southbound Only)
New Stevenston
A73
Linn Park
Bothwell
Livingstone Centre NTS
Newarthill
Hartwood
Burnbrae
B766
Carfin
Parkside
Castlemilk
B759
A749
A724
B7029
Clarkston
Cleekhimin
Bellside
A71
Sheddens
Carmunnock
Blantyre
A725
Hamilton (Northbound Only)
Strathclyde
Cleland
Bonkle
Allanbank
Allanton
Busby
Nerston
Hamilton Park
A723
Motherwell
Newmains
Stewartfield
High Blantyre
B7012
Craigneuk
Wishaw
Crindledyke
Heritage Park
B766
Calderwood
HAMILTON
RSPB
Shields
A721
A722
Morningside
Thorntonhall
EAST KILBRIDE
B754
Waterloo
Laighstonehall
Ferniegair
Netherton
A721
A726
Chatelherault
Allanton
R Clyde
Wildmanbridge
B764
The Murray
Eddlewood
Calderglen
Jackton
Meikle Earnock
Overtown
Law
A73
Eaglesham
Larkhall
Carluke
B7011
Quarter
B7056
Dalserf
Law Hill
Auldhouse
Leigh Knoweglass
Millheugh
B7078
A726
Limekilnburn
Shawsburn
Ashgill
Yieldshields
Roadmeetings
Struther hill
Rosebank
A721
Kilncadzow
A723
Chapelton
Braidwood
Heads
A72
B7056
Netherburn
Crossford
Glassford
Stonehouse
Craignethan
361
LAIRDS SEAT
Carnduff
164
A71
Strathaven
Tillietudlem
Hazelbank
Draffan
B7078
Blackwood
Blackhill NTS
Nemphlar
B7086
Sandford
Kirkmuirhill
Auchenheath
Kirkfieldbank
A73

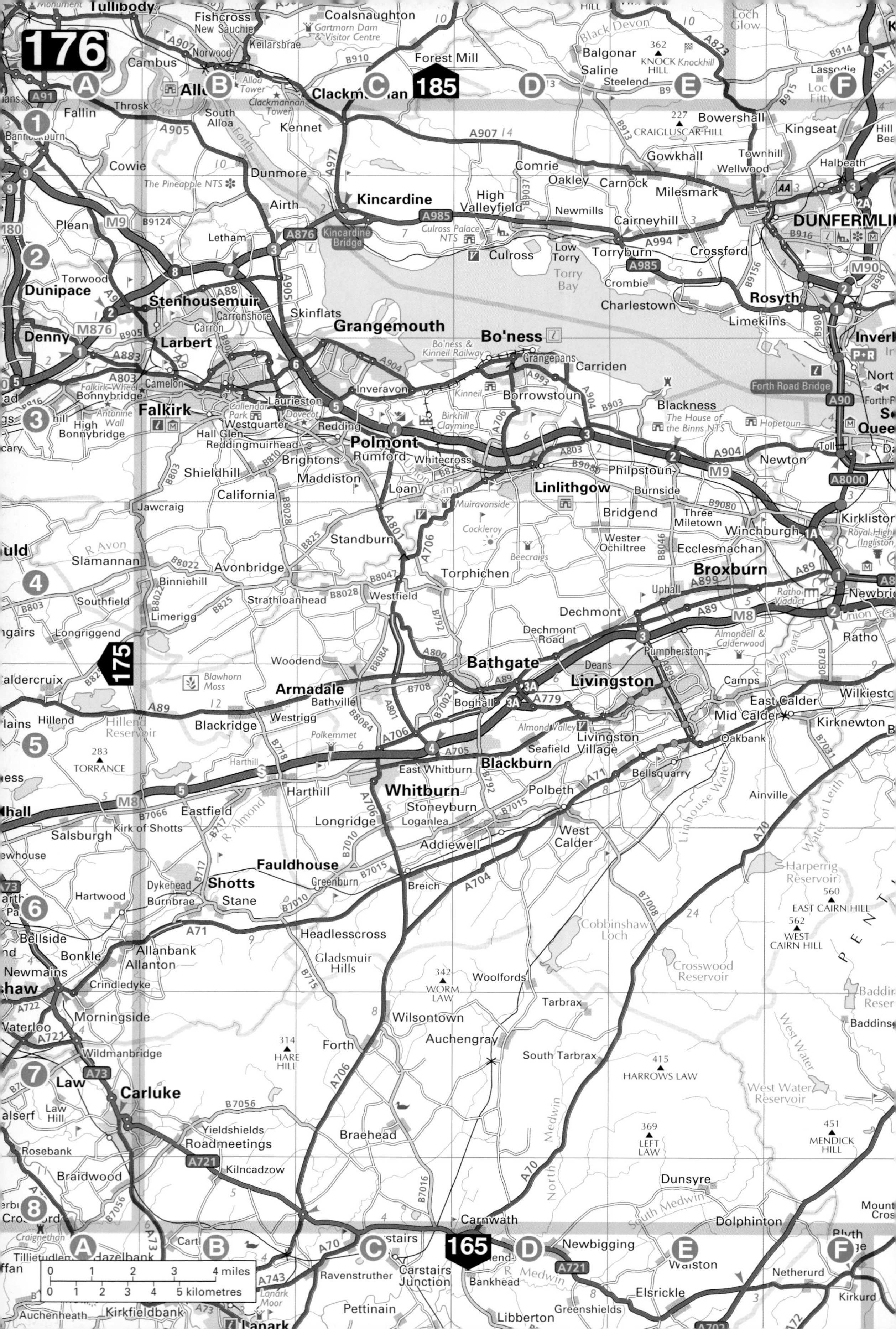
176
185
175
165
Tullibody
Alloa
Clackmannan
Kincardine
Grangemouth
Bo'ness
Falkirk
Stenhousemuir
Larbert
Denny
Dunipace
Polmont
Linlithgow
DUNFERMLINE
Rosyth
Broxburn
Bathgate
Livingston
Armadale
Whitburn
Blackburn
Shotts
Fauldhouse
Carluke
Law
Carnwath
Forth Road Bridge
Kincardine Bridge
Culross
Torry Bay
Blackness
Winchburgh
Uphall
West Calder
Mid Calder
East Calder
Kirknewton
Carstairs
Lanark
Cobbinshaw Loch
Harperrig Reservoir
West Water Reservoir
Crosswood Reservoir
0 1 2 3 4 miles
0 1 2 3 4 5 kilometres

Edinburgh & Firth of Forth
177
186
178
166
G
H
J
K
L
M
1
2
3
4
5
6
7
8
Cluny
Coaltown of Wemyss
Cardenden
Gallatown
Chapel
Kirkcaldy
Linktown
Cowdenbeath
Auchtertool
Donibristle
Balmule
Kinghorn
Aberdour
Pettycur Bay
Pettycur
Burntisland
St Bridget's Kirk
Silversands Bay
Inchcolm Abbey
Dalgety Bay
Inchkeith
Zeebrugge
FIRTH OF FORTH
Cramond Island
Eyebroughy
Dirleton Castle
Dirleton
Gullane Bay
Gullane Point
Muirfield
Gullane
Aberlady Bay
Craigelaw Point
Aberlady
Luffness
Drem
Gosford Bay
Ballencrieff
Spittal
Dalmeny
Eagle Rock
Cramond
Granton
Newhaven
Britannia
Lauriston Castle
Leith
Davidson's Mains
Barnton
Warriston
St Triduana's Chapel
EDINBURGH
Blackhall
Portobello
Musselburgh
Cockenzie and Port Seton
Market Cross
Collegiate Church
Prestonpans
Heritage Museum
Seton Mains
Longniddry
Huntington
Elvingston
Dovecot
Arthur's Seat
251
Duddingston
Joppa
Newcraighall
Craigmillar
Fisherrow
Inveresk Lodge NTS
Inveresk
Wallyford
Tranent
Macmerry
Meadowmill
Gladsmuir
New Winton
Samuelston
Corstorphine
South Gyle
Craiglockhart
Water of Leith
Morningside
Royal Observatory
Blackford Hill
Craigmillar
Hilltown
Newton
Elphinstone
Whitecraig
Crossgatehall
Ormiston
Boggs Holdings
Hermiston
Juniper Green
Colinton
Liberton
Gilmerton
Danderhall
Millerhill
Dalkeith Park
Pencaitland
Currie
Bonaly
Butterfly Farm
Dalkeith
Cousland
East Saltoun
West Saltoun
Malleny NTS
Kinleith
493
Allermuir Hill
Hillend
Straiton
Eskbank
Newbattle
Mayfield
Malleny Mills
Boghall
Loanhead
Bilston
Lasswade
Bonnyrigg
Chesterhill
Dewarton
Pathhead
Gilchriston
Woodhouselee
Castlelaw
Polton
Newtongrange
Mining Museum
Vogrie
Easter Howgate
Roslin
Newtonloan
Newlandrig
Humbie
Milton Bridge
Pentland Hills
Rosewell
Arniston
Fala Dam
448
576
579
Carnethy Hill
Scald Law
Auchendinny
Crichton
Blegbie
Fala
Silverburn
Penicuik
Gorebridge
Carrington
Soutra Summit 363
Pomathorn
R North Esk
Howgate
North Middleton
Temple
394
Dun Law
Mount Lothian
Gilston
380
Turf Law
Carlops
Leadburn
Rosebery Reservoir
Falahill
Craigburn
Heriot
Oxton
Gladhouse Reservoir
Moorfoot Hills
Lamancha
Carfrae
Linton
Heriot Water
Waterheads
324
White Rig
383
Collie Law
Portmore Loch
425
Dun Law
Fountainhall
479
Wether Law
651
Blackhope Scar
Romanno Bridge
Torquhan
Eddleston
Killochyett
476
Crailzie Hill
621
Whitehope Law
Stow
659
Windlestraw Law
Threepwood
427
Meldon
A92
A910
A921
A909
A901
A902
A90
A8
A71
A70
A720
A702
A703
A701
A1
A199
A198
A6137
A6093
A6094
A6124
A68
A7
A766
B981
B925
B9157
B923
B900
B701
B1348
B6414
B6371
B6363
B6355
B6367
B6372
B6368
B6458
B7006
B7003
B7026
B704
B7007
B709
B6362
B6471
B1345
M8

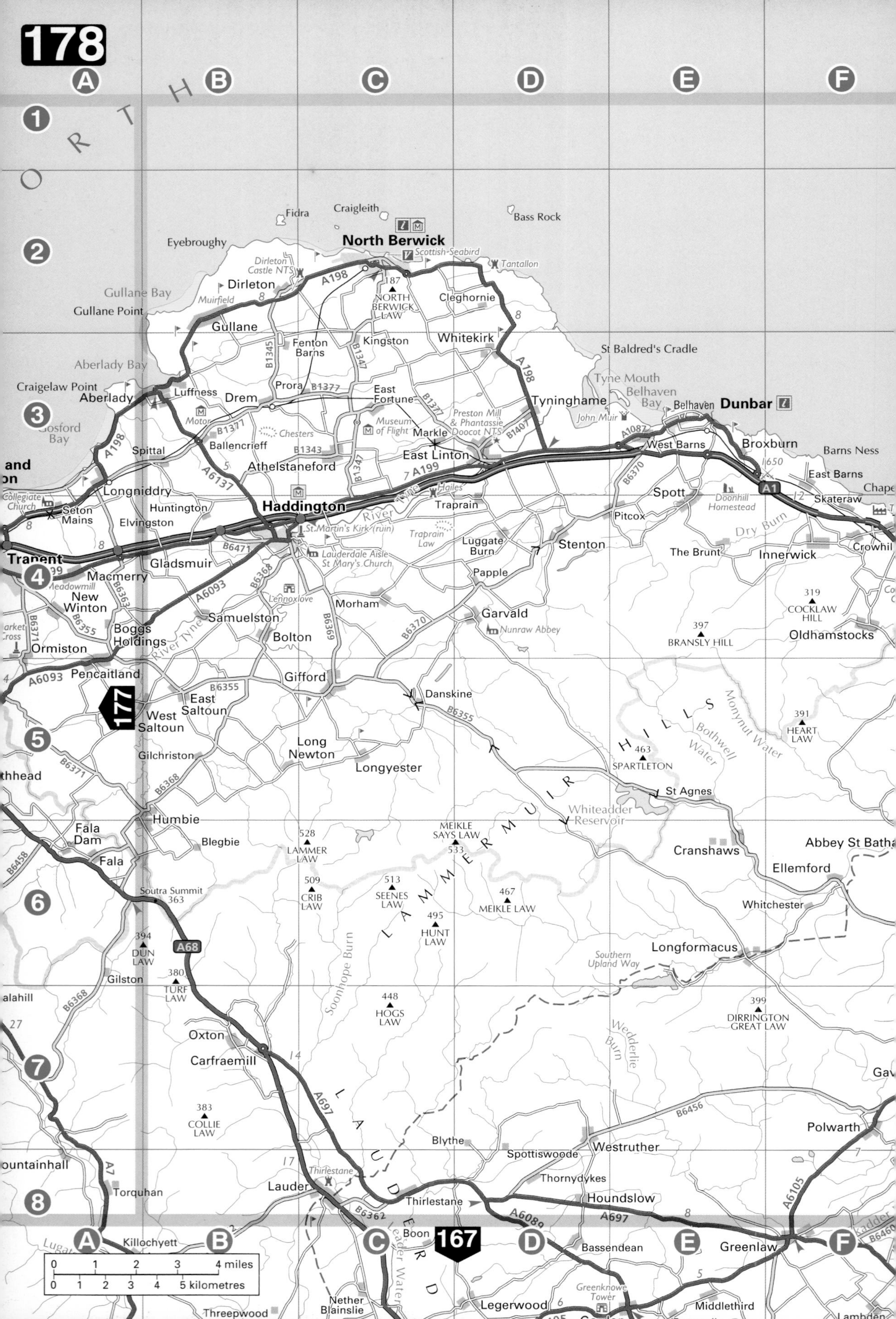

177
167

0 1 2 3 4 miles
0 1 2 3 4 5 kilometres

Reed Point
Cove
Pease Bay
Siccar Point
Fast Castle Head
Cockburnspath
A1107
196
BROWN RIG
Coldingham Loch
ST ABB'S HEAD
St Abbs
Coldingham Bay
Grantshouse
Southern Upland Way
Butterdean
Coldingham
Houndwood
Heugh Head
Cairncross
Eyemouth
262
HORSELEY HILL
A1
Reston
Ayton
Burnmouth
B6438
Auchencrow
Marygold
Lintlaw
Lamberton
A6112
Preston
Chirnside
B6355
Marshall Meadows Bay
Cumledge
Foulden
Edrom
Chirnsidebridge
Manderston
Broadhaugh
Edington
Whiteadder Water
Tithe Barn
1333
North Northumberland Heritage Coast
Allanton
Hutton
A6105
Berwick-upon-Tweed
Duns
Paxton
Town Ramparts
Barracks
Crumstane
Blackadder
B6460
B6461
Tweedmouth
Whitsome
Hilton
Spittal
Huds Head
Nisbet Hill
Sinclair's Hill
B6437
Horndean
Horncliffe
Scremerston
Murton
Ladykirk
A1167
Thornton
Swinton
Norham
A698
Cheswick
Upsettlington
168
CAUSEWAY FLOODED AT HIGH TIDE
Simprim
River Tweed
B6354
Ancroft
Leitholm
B6525
Haggerston
Beal

Bac Mòr or Dutchmans Cap
ULVA
189
Little Colonsay
Staffa
Fingal's Cave
Loch na Keal,
Isle of Mull
Inch Kenneth
Inchkenneth Chapel
(ruin)
491
CREACH BHEINN
Fossil Tree
IONA
Abbey
Baile Mór
Macleans Cross
Sound of Iona
Rudha nan Cearc
Kintra
Fionnphort
Aridhglas
St Columba
Exhibition
Centre
Loch na Lathaich
A849
Bunessan
Loch Assapol
ROSS OF MULL
Soa Island
Erraid
Uisken
Ardchiavaig
Rudha
Ardalanish
Torran Rocks
Eilean
Dubh
Balnahard
Kiloran Bay
COLONSAY
Kiloran
Kilchattan
B8087
Scalasaig
B8086
Machrins
B8085
Garvard
171
Rudha
Bàn
Oronsay
Dubh Eilean
0 1 2 3 4 miles
0 1 2 3 4 5 kilometres

Gruline
Macquarie Mausoleum
BEINN NAN LUS
Rudha an Ridire
Eorsa
ISLE OF MULL
190
BEINN MHEADHC
Craignure
Mull & West Highland Narrow Gauge Railway
766 DUN DA GHAOITHE
Torosay Castle
Duart Bay
Duart Point
Lochdonhead
Lochdon
966 BEN MORE
704 CRUACHAN DEARG
A849
Gorten
Loch Don
Grass Point
Strathcoil
Glen More
Aird of Kinloch
247 CARN BAN
698 BEN CREACH
717 BEN BUIE
Loch Fuaran
Loch Spelve
Croggan
Pennycross
Pennyghael
503 BEINN NA CROISE
Lochbuie
Loch Uisg
Leidle Water
Rudha Seanach
337 MAOL BAN
Loch Buie
377 DRUIM FADA
376 BEINN CHREAGACH
Carsaig
Rudha Dubh
Barrnacarry Bay
FIRTH OF LORNE
Malcolm's Point
Insh Island
Clachan
Clachan-Seil
SEIL
Ellanbeich
Easdale
Balvicar
B844
B8003
Colonsay - Oban
Cuan Ferry Village
Seil Sound
182
Cullipool House
Torsay Island
Degnish
Garbh Eileach
Eilean Dubh Mòr
LUING
GARVELLACHS
Monastery & Beehive Cells
Eileach an Naoimh
LUNGA
Toberonochy
Sound of Luing
Shuna Sound
SHUNA
Arduaine Garden NTS
Scarba, Lunga and the Garvellachs
Craobh Haven
Shuna Point
SCARBA
448 CRUACH SCARBA
B8002
Gulf of Corryvreckan
Aird
Loch Craignish
Craignish Point
Island Macaskin
295 CRUACH NA SEILCHEIG
Glengarrisdale Bay
Glendebadel Bay
364 BEN GARRISDALE
JURA
Loch Crinan
Crinan
Kilmahumaig
Bellanoch
B8025
Lealt Burn
Corpach Bay
Lussa River
Glen Grundale
171
172
Barnluasgan
Carsaig Bay

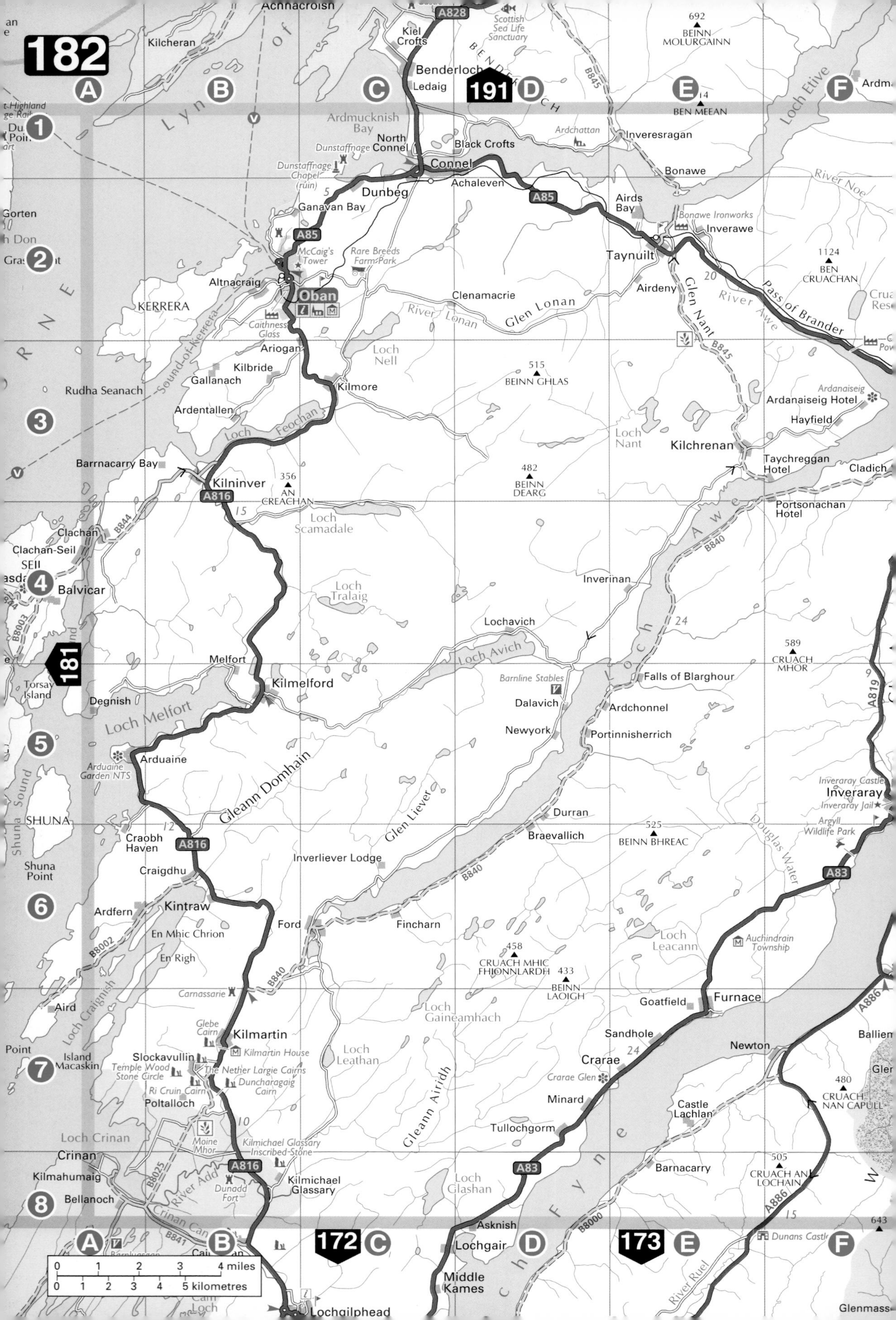

182
Achnacroish
Kilcheran
Kiel Crofts
Scottish Sea Life Sanctuary
692 BEINN MOLURGAINN
Benderloch
Ledaig
191
Ardmucknish Bay
North Connel
Dunstaffnage
Dunstaffnage Chapel (ruin)
Black Crofts
Ardchattan
Inveresragan
Connel
Achaleven
Bonawe
14 BEN MEEAN
Loch Etive
Ardm
River Noe
Dunbeg
Ganavan Bay
Airds Bay
Bonawe Ironworks
Inverawe
Taynuilt
1124 BEN CRUACHAN
Gorten
McCaig's Tower
Rare Breeds Farm Park
Altnacraig
Oban
KERRERA
Caithness Glass
Clenamacrie
River Lonan
Glen Lonan
Airdeny
Glen Nant
River Awe
Pass of Brander
Sound of Kerrera
Ariogan
Loch Nell
Kilbride
Gallanach
Kilmore
515 BEINN GHLAS
Rudha Seanach
Ardentallen
Loch Feochan
Loch Nant
Ardanaiseig
Ardanaiseig Hotel
Hayfield
Kilchrenan
Barnacarry Bay
Kilninver
356 AN CREACHAN
482 BEINN DEARG
Taychreggan Hotel
Cladich
Portsonachan Hotel
Loch Scamadale
Clachan
Clachan-Seil
SEIL
Balvicar
Loch Tralaig
Inverinan
Loch Awe
Lochavich
Loch Avich
589 CRUACH MHOR
181
Melfort
Kilmelford
Torsay Island
Degnish
Barnline Stables
Dalavich
Falls of Blarghour
Ardchonnel
Loch Melfort
Newyork
Portinnisherrich
Arduaine
Arduaine Garden NTS
Gleann Domhain
Glen Liever
Inveraray Castle
Inveraray
Inveraray Jail
Shuna Sound
SHUNA
Durran
525 BEINN BHREAC
Argyll Wildlife Park
Craobh Haven
Braevallich
Douglas Water
Shuna Point
Craigdhu
Inverliever Lodge
Ardfern
Kintraw
Ford
Fincharn
En Mhic Chrion
En Righ
Loch Leacann
Auchindrain Township
458 CRUACH MHIC FHIONNLARDH
433 BEINN LAOIGH
Carnassarie
Loch Craignish
Aird
Loch Gaineamhach
Goatfield
Furnace
Glebe Cairn
Kilmartin
Kilmartin House
Sandhole
Newton
Ballien
Island Macaskin
Slockavullin
Temple Wood Stone Circle
The Nether Largie Cairns
Dunchar aigaig Cairn
Loch Leathan
Crarae
Crarae Glen
480 CRUACH NAN CAPULL
Ri Cruin Cairn
Poltalloch
Gleann Airidh
Minard
Castle Lachlan
Tullochgorm
Loch Crinan
Moine Mhor
Kilmichael Glassary Inscribed Stone
Loch Fyne
Crinan
Kilmahumaig
River Add
Dunadd Fort
Kilmichael Glassary
Loch Glashan
Barnacarry
505 CRUACH AN LOCHAIN
Bellanoch
Crinan Canal
Asknish
172
173
643
Dunans Castle
Lochgair
Middle Kames
River Ruel
Lochgilphead
Glenmasse
0 1 2 3 4 miles
0 1 2 3 4 5 kilometres
A828
A85
A816
B844
B8003
B8002
B840
B845
B8025
B841
B8000
A83
A819
A886

192
184
173
174
Tyndrum
Crianlarich
Stronmilchan
Inverlochy
Upper Kinchrackine
Dalmally
Kilchurn
Glen Kinglass
Glen Strae
Glen Orchy
River Orchy
Glen Lochy
River Lochy
Glen Lochay
Strath Fillan
Glen Falloch
Inverherive Hotel
Ben Lui
LOCH LOMOND AND THE TROSSACHS NATIONAL PARK
West Highland Way
Falls of Falloch
Inverarnan
Ardlui
Loch Sloy
Inveruglas
Stronachlachar
Loch Katrine
Inversnaid Hotel
Loch Arklet
Lochan Shira
Glen Shira
Glenfyne Lodge
Glen Fyne
Cairndow
Ardkinglas Woodland Garden
Glen Kinglas
Loch Fyne
Ardno
St Catherines
Rest and be thankful
Glen Croe
Succoth
Arrochar
Tarbet
Ardgartan
Argyll Forest Park
Loch Lomond
Queen Elizabeth Forest Park
Loch Chon
Kinlochard
Lochgoilhead
Corrow
Douglas Pier
Loch Goil
River Goil
Invernoaden
Loch Eck
Carrick Castle
Whistlefield Inn
Bernice
Portincaple
Arddarroch
Whistlefield
Garelochhead
Rockville
Greenfield
Glen Fruin
Loch Long
Glen Douglas
Inverbeg
Rowardennan Lodge
Rowardennan Hotel
Edentaggart
Glen Luss
Luss
Inchlonaig
Aldoch
Balmaha
Milton of Buchanan
Buchanan Smithy
Ardentinny
Slig
Bridge of Orchy
Hotel
A85
A82
A83
A819
A814
A815
B8074
B8077
B828
B839
B829
B872
B837
BEINN NAN AIGHENAN
BEINN AN DOTHAIDH
BEINN MHANACH
794
988 BEINN EUNAICH
648 BEINN DONACHAN
771 BEINN UDLAIDH
818 BEINN CHAORACH
937 BEINN CHEATHAICH
1130 BEN LUI
1028 BEN OSS
977 BEINN DUBHCHRAIG
1171 BEN MORE
1164 STOBINIAN
636
739
947 BEINN BHUIDHE
946 BEINN A' CHROIN
658 CLACHAN HILL
645 MAOL BREAC
865 STOB A' CHOIN
747 MEALL MÒR
942 BEN VORLICH
1011 BEN IME
912 BEINN AN LOCHAIN
925 BEINN NARNAIN
881 THE COBBLER
416 CRUACH TAIRBEIRT
565 CRUACH NAN CAPULL
845 BEN DONICH
633 CRUINN A' BHEINN
973 BEN LOMOND
700 BEINN BHREA
661 BEN REACH
779 BEINN BHEULA
734 DOUNE HILL
596 BEINN UIRD
586 BEN VRACKIE
702 BEINN EICH
618 BEINN BHEAG
657 CREACHAN
713 BEINN CHAORACH
655 BEINN THARSUINN
643 CLACH BHEINN
664 BEINN RUADH
RSPB
G H J K L M
1 2 3 4 5 6 7 8

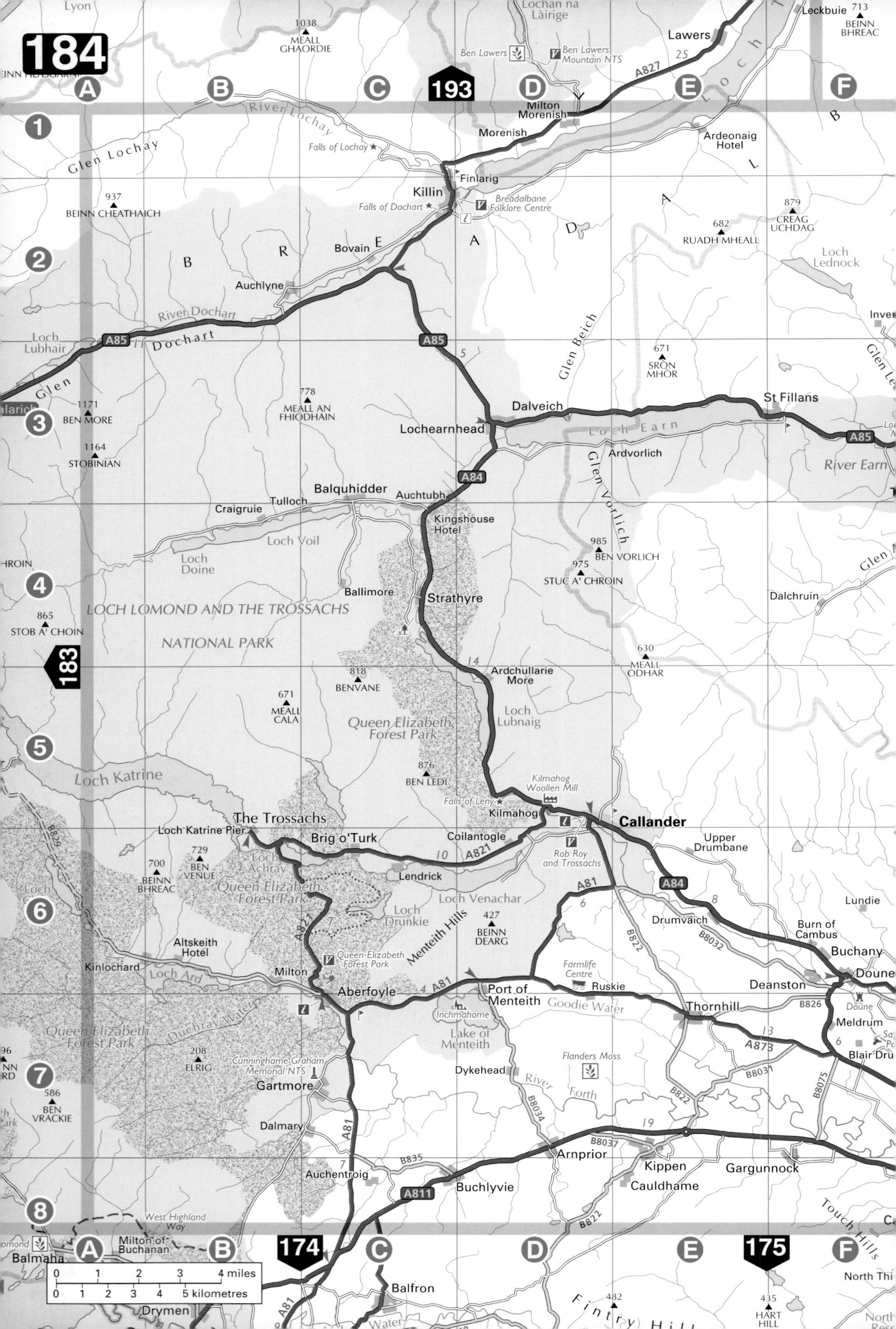

Killin
Finlarig
Falls of Dochart
Breadalbane Folklore Centre
Falls of Lochay
Milton Morenish
Morenish
Lawers
Ardeonaig Hotel
Ben Lawers
Ben Lawers Mountain NTS
Loch Tay
Glen Lochay
River Lochay
BEINN CHEATHAICH
MEALL GHAORDIE
Bovain
Auchlyne
River Dochart
Glen Dochart
Loch Lubhair
BREADALBANE
Lochearnhead
Dalveich
Loch Earn
St Fillans
Ardvorlich
River Earn
Glen Beich
Glen Vorlich
BEN VORLICH
STUC A' CHROIN
SRON MHOR
CREAG UCHDAG
RUADH MHEALL
Loch Lednock
BEN MORE
STOBINIAN
MEALL AN FHIODHAIN
Balquhidder
Auchtubh
Tulloch
Craigruie
Kingshouse Hotel
Loch Voil
Loch Doine
Ballimore
Strathyre
LOCH LOMOND AND THE TROSSACHS NATIONAL PARK
STOB A' CHOIN
BENVANE
MEALL CALA
Ardchullarie More
Loch Lubnaig
Queen Elizabeth Forest Park
BEN LEDI
MEALL ODHAR
Dalchruin
Loch Katrine
The Trossachs
Loch Katrine Pier
Brig o'Turk
Coilantogle
Kilmahog
Kilmahog Woollen Mill
Falls of Leny
Callander
Rob Roy and Trossachs
Upper Drumbane
Lendrick
Loch Venachar
Loch Achray
Loch Drunkie
BEN VENUE
BEINN BHREAC
BEINN DEARG
Menteith Hills
Drumvaich
Burn of Cambus
Lundie
Buchany
Doune
Deanston
Altskeith Hotel
Kinlochard
Loch Ard
Milton
Aberfoyle
Port of Menteith
Inchmahome
Lake of Menteith
Goodie Water
Farmlife Centre
Ruskie
Thornhill
Meldrum
Blair Drummond
Duchray Water
ELRIG
Cunninghame Graham Memorial NTS
Gartmore
Dykehead
Flanders Moss
River Forth
BEN VRACKIE
Dalmary
Auchentroig
Buchlyvie
Arnprior
Kippen
Cauldhame
Gargunnock
Touch Hills
West Highland Way
Milton of Buchanan
Balmaha
Drymen
Balfron
Fintry Hills
HART HILL
North Third
Leckbuie
BEINN BHREAC
0 1 2 3 4 miles
0 1 2 3 4 5 kilometres
193
183
174
175

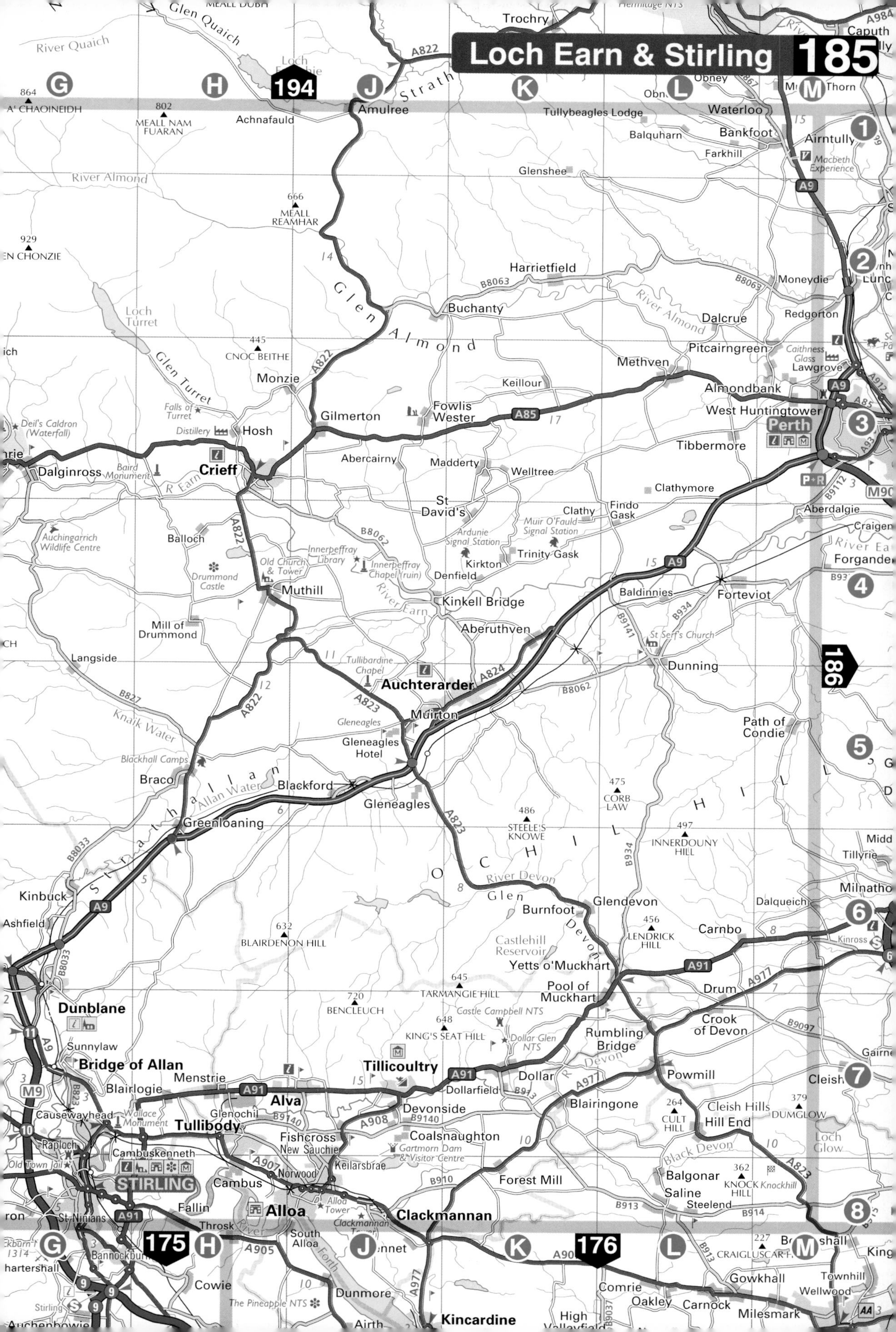
Loch Earn & Stirling
185
194
186
175
176
Amulree
Crieff
Gilmerton
Hosh
Monzie
Harrietfield
Buchanty
Methven
Almondbank
West Huntingtower
Perth
Tibbermore
Fowlis Wester
Abercairny
Madderty
St David's
Muthill
Kinkell Bridge
Aberuthven
Auchterarder
Muirton
Gleneagles Hotel
Blackford
Gleneagles
Braco
Greenloaning
Kinbuck
Dunblane
Bridge of Allan
Menstrie
Alva
Tillicoultry
Dollar
Tullibody
STIRLING
Alloa
Clackmannan
Kincardine
Glendevon
Yetts o'Muckhart
Pool of Muckhart
Rumbling Bridge
Powmill
Dunning
Forteviot
Path of Condie
Carnbo
Drum
Crook of Devon
Blairingone
Saline
Forest Mill
Dunmore
Oakley
Comrie
Carnock

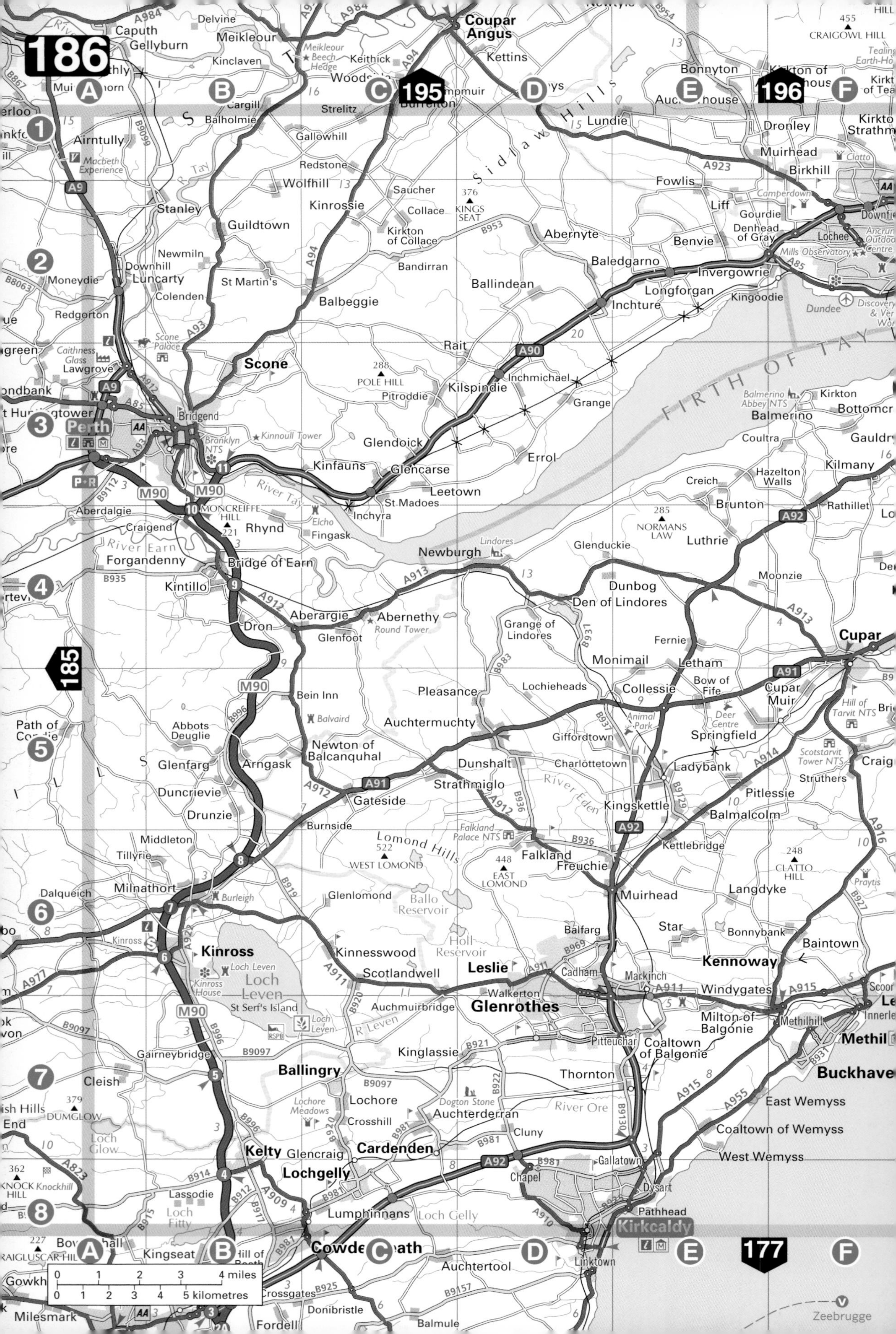
186
195
196
185
177
Coupar Angus
Perth
Scone
Dundee
Cupar
Kinross
Glenrothes
Kirkcaldy
Cowdenbeath
Lochgelly
Kelty
Cardenden
Ballingry
Leslie
Kennoway
Methil
Buckhaven
Newburgh
Auchtermuchty
Falkland
Freuchie
Ladybank
Sidlaw Hills
Lomond Hills
FIRTH OF TAY
Loch Leven
River Tay
River Earn
River Eden
Bridge of Earn
Milnathort
Invergowrie
Longforgan
Inchture
Errol
Glencarse
Balbeggie
Stanley
Luncarty
Abernethy
Strathmiglo
Kingskettle
Markinch
Thornton
Auchterderran
Lumphinnans
Auchtertool
Linktown
Dysart
Gallatown
Windygates
Leven
East Wemyss
West Wemyss
Coaltown of Wemyss
Zeebrugge
0 1 2 3 4 miles
0 1 2 3 4 5 kilometres

Arbroath
Arbirlot
Bonnington
Petterden
Todhills
Monikie
Kirkton of Monikie
196
Wellbank
Newbigging
Kellas
Murroes
Carlungie Earth-House
Upper Victoria
Barry Mill NTS
East Haven
Panbride
West Haven
Carnoustie
Barry
Ardestie Earth-House
Burnside of Duntrune
Douglas and Angus
Baldovie
Buddon
Monifieth
Barnhill
Broughty Ferry
DUNDEE
BUDDON NESS
Tay Bridge
Tayport
Tentsmuir Point
Newport-on-Tay
Scottish National Golf Centre
Leuchars
RAF Leuchars
ST ANDREWS BAY
Balmullo
Guardbridge
River Eden
Kincaple
St Andrews
Strathkinness
Kemback
Botanic Gardens
Brownhills
Boarhills
Craigtoun
Denhead
Stravithie
Pitscottie
Cameron Reservoir
Kingsbarns
Baldinnie
Dunino
Peat Inn
Radernie
Balcomie Links
FIFE NESS
Kingsmuir
Scotland's Secret Bunker
Lathones
Woodside
Largoward
Lochty
Crail
Carnbee
Easter Pitkierie
Kellie Castle NTS
Arncroach
Wester Pitkierie
Kilrenny
Cellardyke
Upper Largo
Colinsburgh
Newton of Balcormo
Fisheries Museum
Anstruther
Lower Largo
Kilconquhar
Pittenweem
St Monans
Largo Bay
Earlsferry
Elie
Isle of May

A
B
C
D
E
F
1
2
3
4
5
6
7
8
Arnab
Grishipoll
Clabhach
Hogh Bay
Ballyhaugh
Totronald
Feall Bay
Arileod
Acha
Uig
Friesland Bay
RSPB
Calgary Point
Crossapol Bay
Loch Breachacha
Rudha Fàsachd
Gunna
Rudha Dubh
Caoles
B8069
Ruaig
Rudha Port Bhiosd
Clachan Mor
Balephetrish Bay
Loch Bhasapoll
B8068
Haugh Bay
Ballevullin
Cornoigmore
Kenovay
Gott Bay
Kilkenneth
Tiree
Scarinish
Moss
B8065
Heylipoll
Middleton
Crossapoll
TIREE
Barrapoll
Hynish Bay
B8067
Balemartine
Loch a Phuill
Mannel
Rinn Thorbhais
Hynish
Balephuil Bay
0 1 2 3 4 miles
0 1 2 3 4 5 kilometres

198
190
180
Kildonnan
393
Eilean nan Each
MUCK
Port Mor
Ockle Point
Sanna Point
Sanna Bay
Sanna Bay
Portuairk
Achnaha
Kilmory
Branault
436
MEALL NAN CON
ARDNAM
Ardnamurchan Point
Achosnich
B8007
Loch Mudle
342
BEINN NA SEILG
Kilchoan
Ormsaigmore
Mingary
527
BEN HIANT
Ardslignish
Bagh a Chaisteil (Castlebay)
Loch Baghasdail (Lochboisdale)
Eilean Mòr
Rudha Mòr
Rudha Sgor-innis
Bousd
Sorisdale
B8072
COLL
Coll - Oban
Eilean Ornsay
Ardmore Point
Auliston Point
Sorne Point
Quinish Point
Glengorm Castle
Tobermory
Calve Island
292
'S AIRDE BEINN
Caliach Point
Dervaig
Achnadrish Lodge
Calgary
B8073
A848
Calgary Bay
444
SPEINNE MÒR
Loch Frisa
Treshnish Point
Ensay
342
CÀRN MÒR
Rudh' a' Chaoil
Burg
Glen Aros
390
Fanmore
CNOC AN DÀ CHINN
Glenaros House
Fladda
Ballygown
Loch Tuath
Lunga
Eas Fors (Waterfall)
333
BEINN NAN CÀRN
Killiechronan
B8035
TRESHNISH ISLES
Gometra
ULVA
Oskamull
B8073
Gruline
Macquarie Mausoleum
Bac Mòr or Dutchmans Cap
Loch na Keal, Isle of Mull
Eorsa
Bac Beag
Little Colonsay
Loch na Keal
591
BEINN A' GH
Staffa
Fingal's Cave
Balnahard
966
G
H
J
K
L
M
1
2
3
4
5
6
7
8

Kildonnan
Rudh' Arisaig
Cruach Doire
199
Druimindarroch
Arisaig House
Prince Charlie's Cairn
Kinlochnanuagh
Loch nan Uamh
200
Lochailort
Inverailort
Sound of Arisaig
Rudha Choalais
Ardnish
Peanmeanach
Loch Ailort
A861
877
ROIS-BHEINN
Smearisary
Glenuig
712
664
BEINN GAIRE
Eilean Shona
Rudha Aird Druimnich
Kinlochmoidart
Glen Forsian
Loch Moidart
Tioram
Ockle Point
Morar, Moidart and Ardnamurchan
239
BEINN BHREAC
Ardmolich
Glen Moidart
MOIDART
Kilmory
Ockle
Ardtoe
Shielfoot
Dalnabreck
Branault
356
BEINN BHREAC
B8044
Kentra
Blain
Mingarrypark
Arevegaig
436
MEALL NAN CON
ARDNAMURCHAN
Polloch
Acharacle
Loch Mudle
437
Claish Moss
846
BEINN RESIPOL
B8007
Kilchoan
Salen
Resipole
Ormsaigmore
Mingary
527
BEN HIANT
Loch Sunart
Glenbeg
512
BEN LAGA
Glencripesdale
Woodend
Ardslignish
Glenborrodale
RSPB
Laga
339
GEÀRR CHREAG
Camasine
Camasachoire
189
Oronsay
Carna
Liddesdale
Auliston Point
A884
Tobermory
Calve Island
Loch Teacuis
571
BEINN LADAIN
522
MEALL A' CHOISE
Lochuisge
292
'S AIRDE BEINN
Drimnin
Glen Dubh
437
BEINN BHUIDHE
Achnadrish Lodge
A848
B849
550
SÌTHEAN NA RAPLAICH
Loch Arienas
738
BEINN MHEADHON
444
SPEINNE MÒR
Loch Frisa
Sound of Mull
Acharn
Gleann Geal
Claggan
Larachbeg
339
MEALL DAMH
Rannoch River
Achranich
Fuinary
Loch Tearnait
Loch Aline
Glen Aros
Aros
Lochaline
Glenaros House
464
GLAIS BHEINN
514
AN SLEAGHOCH
Salen
Fishnish Point
Fishnish Pier
A849
333
BEINN NAN CÀRN
Killiechronan
B8035
Oskamull
B8073
Gruline
Glen Forsa
408
BEINN NAN LUS
Macquarie Mausoleum
Scallastle Bay
Rudha an Ridire
Eorsa
Loch na Keal
Loch Bà
ISLE OF
Altcreich
636
BEINN MHEADHON
Bernera Island
591
BEINN A' GHRÀIG
Craignure
Mull & West Highland Narrow Gauge Railway
181
766
Torosay C.
Duart Bay
Duart Point
Balnahard
B8035
Lochdonhead
Lochdon
704
CRUACHAN
966
0 1 2 3 4 miles
0 1 2 3 4 5 kilometres

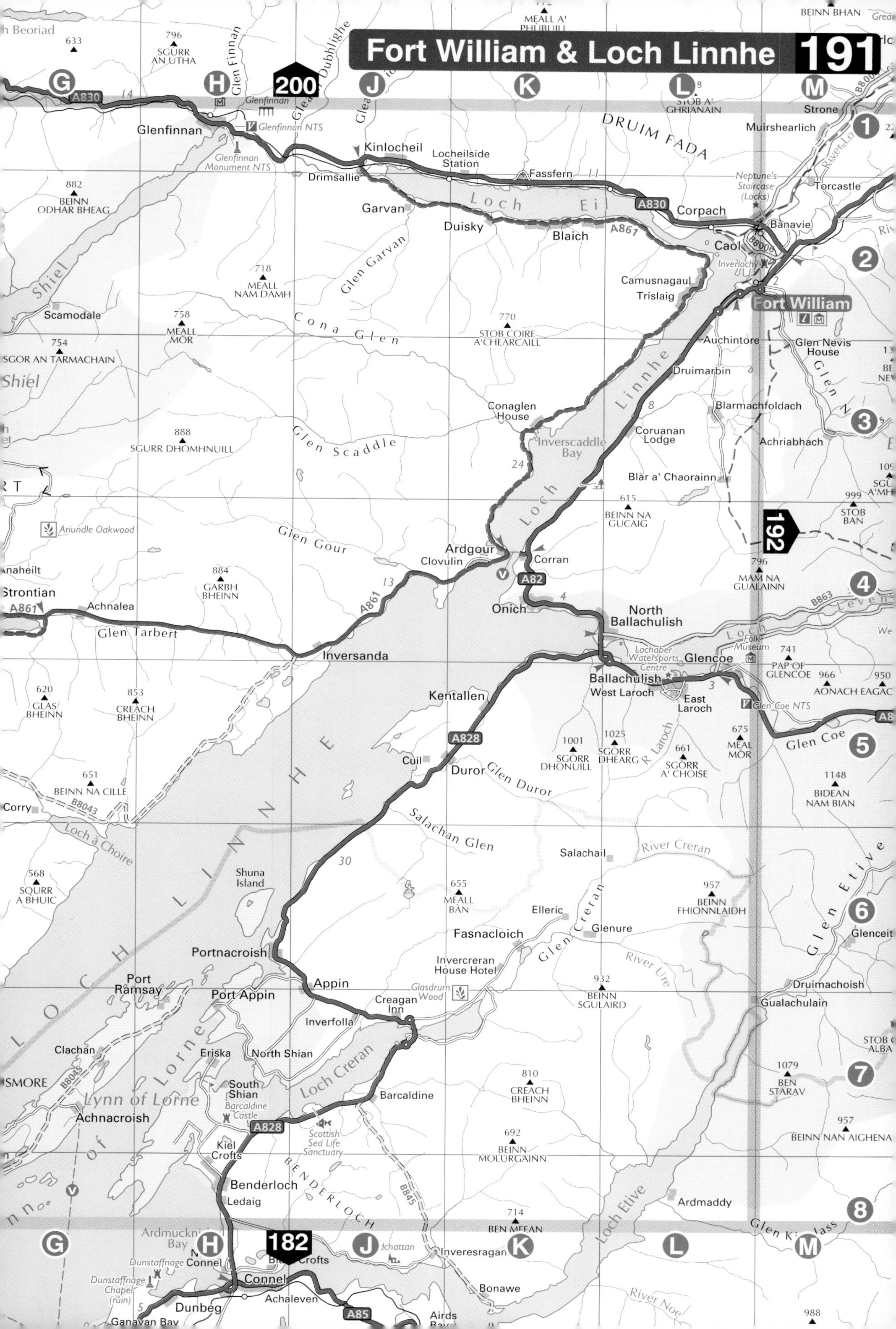

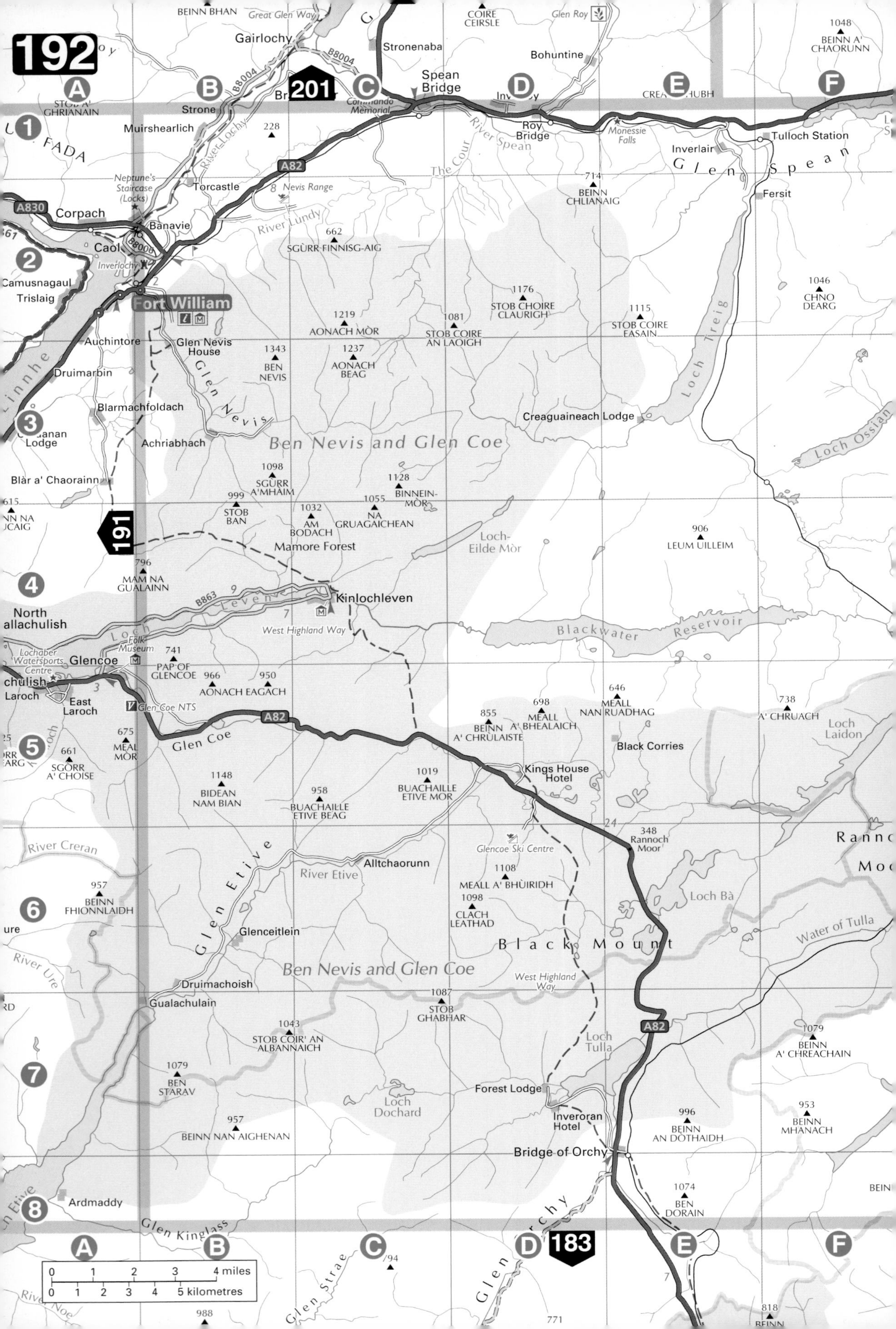
BEINN BHAN
Great Glen Way
Gairlochy
B8004
201
Stronenaba
COIRE CEIRSLE
Glen Roy
Bohuntine
1048
BEINN A' CHAORUNN
A
B
C
D
E
F
STOB A' GHRIANAIN
Strone
Commando Memorial
Spean Bridge
Roy Bridge
Monessie Falls
Tulloch Station
1
Muirshearlich
228
River Lochy
River Spean
Inverlair
Glen Spean
A82
The Cour
Neptune's Staircase (Locks)
Torcastle
Nevis Range
714
BEINN CHLIANAIG
Fersit
A830
Corpach
Banavie
River Lundy
662
SGÙRR FINNISG-AIG
Caol
B8006
2
Inverlochy
Camusnagaul
Trislaig
Fort William
1176
STOB CHOIRE CLAURIGH
1115
STOB COIRE EASAIN
1046
CHNO DEARG
1219
AONACH MÒR
1081
STOB COIRE AN LAOIGH
Auchintore
Glen Nevis House
1343
BEN NEVIS
1237
AONACH BEAG
Loch Treig
Druimarbin
Glen Nevis
Blarmachfoldach
3
Creaguaineach Lodge
Achriabhach
Ben Nevis and Glen Coe
Loch Ossian
Blàr a' Chaorainn
1098
SGÙRR A'MHAIM
1128
BINNEIN MÒR
999
STOB BAN
1032
AM BODACH
1055
NA GRUAGAICHEAN
191
Mamore Forest
Loch Eilde Mòr
906
LEUM UILLEIM
796
MAM NA GUALAINN
4
B863
Loch Leven
Kinlochleven
North Ballachulish
West Highland Way
Blackwater Reservoir
Lochaber Watersports Centre
Glencoe
Folk Museum
741
PAP OF GLENCOE
966
950
AONACH EAGACH
Laroch
East Laroch
Glen Coe NTS
A82
855
BEINN A' CHRULAISTE
698
MEALL A' BHEALAICH
646
MEALL NAN RUADHAG
738
A' CHRUACH
Loch Laidon
5
675
MEALL MÒR
661
SGÒRR A' CHOISE
Glen Coe
Black Corries
1148
BIDEAN NAM BIAN
958
BUACHAILLE ETIVE BEAG
1019
BUACHAILLE ETIVE MOR
Kings House Hotel
River Creran
348
Rannoch Moor
Glencoe Ski Centre
Alltchaorunn
River Etive
1108
MEALL A' BHÙIRIDH
1098
CLACH LEATHAD
957
BEINN FHIONNLAIDH
6
Glen Etive
Loch Bà
Water of Tulla
Glenceitlein
Black Mount
River Ure
Ben Nevis and Glen Coe
West Highland Way
Druimachoish
1087
STOB GHABHAR
Gualachulain
A82
1043
STOB COIR' AN ALBANNAICH
Loch Tulla
1079
BEINN A' CHREACHAIN
7
1079
BEN STARAV
Loch Dochard
Forest Lodge
Inveroran Hotel
957
BEINN NAN AIGHENAN
996
BEINN AN DOTHAIDH
953
BEINN MHANACH
Bridge of Orchy
1074
BEN DORAIN
8
Ardmaddy
Glen Orchy
Glen Kinglass
183
A
B
C
D
E
F
0 1 2 3 4 miles
0 1 2 3 4 5 kilometres
Glen Strae
988
771
818

202
Moy
GEAL CHÀRN
MEALL CRUAIDH
CREAGAN MOR
CÀRN NA CAIM
Loch an Dù
Loch Pattack
BEINN A' CHLACHAIR
CÀRN DEARG
A' MHARCONAICH
Drumochter Summit
GLAS MHEALL MÒR
Loch Ericht
BEINN EIBHINN
BEINN UDLAMAIN
SCAIRNEACH MHOR
Dalnaspidal
BEN ALDER
Loch Garry
Dalnacardoch
Glen Garry
MEALL A'BHEALAICH
SGÒR GAIBHRE
Loch Con
SRON A CHLAONAIDH
BEINN MHOLACH
Loch Errochty
BEINN PHARIAGAIN
Trinafour
Glen Errochty
TORR DUBH
BEINN A' CHUALLAICH
R Ericht
194
Tay Forest Park
Rannoch Station
Dunan
Bridge of Ericht
Killichonan
Loch Rannoch
Kinloch Rannoch
Drumchastle
Dunalastair
R Tummel
Tummel Bridge
B846
B847
Finnart
Inverhadden
Tempar
Dunalastair Water
Loch Eigheach
Bridge of Gaur
Camghouran
Carie
SCHIEHALLION
Loch Rannoch and Glen Lyon
Glengoulandie Deer Park
CÀRN MAIRG
MEALL A' MHUIC
MEALL BUIDHE
BEINN DEARG
CÀRN GORM
CAM CHREAG
Loch an Daimh
Glen Lyon
Bridge of Balgie
River Lyon
Fortingall
Kenmore
Fearnan
Acharn
MEALL LUAIDHE
MEALL A' CHOIRE LEITH
MEALL GARBH
MEALL GREIGH
BEINN NAN OIGHREAG
BEN LAWERS
Lochan na Làirige
Leckbuie
BEINN BHREAC
MEALL GHAORDIE
Ben Lawers
Ben Lawers Mountain NTS
Lawers
A827
Loch Tay
River Lochay
Milton Morenish
184
Glen Lochay
Falls of Lochay
Ardeonaig Hotel
Finlarig
Killin
Falls of Dochart
Breadalbane Folklore Centre
SRÒN A'

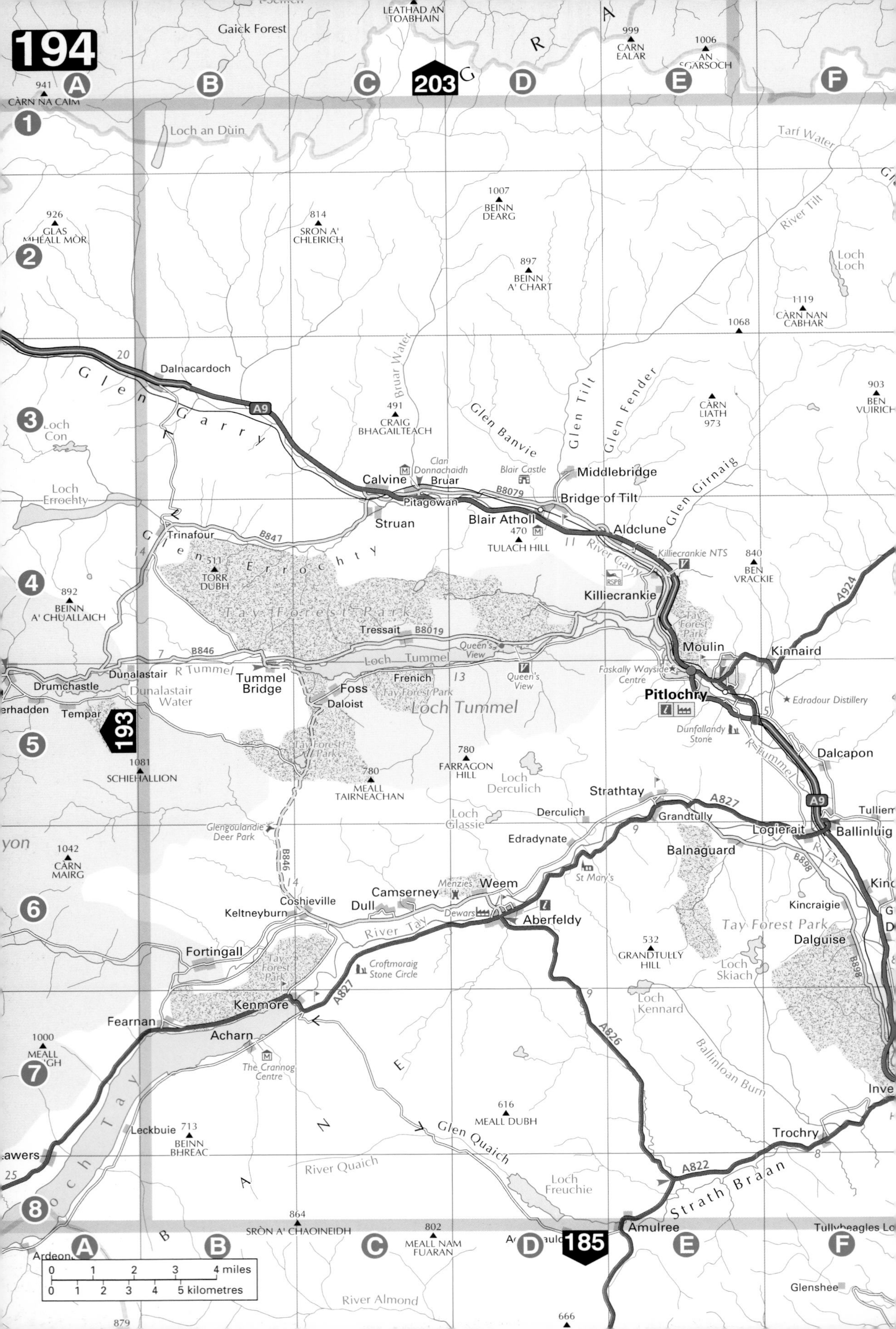
194
203
193
185
Gaick Forest
Loch an Dùin
LEATHAD AN TOABHAIN
999 CÀRN EALAR
1006 AN SGARSOCH
941 CÀRN NA CAIM
Tarf Water
926 GLAS MHEALL MÒR
814 SRON A' CHLEIRICH
1007 BEINN DEARG
897 BEINN A' CHART
River Tilt
Loch Loch
1119 CÀRN NAN CABHAR
1068
Dalnacardoch
Glen Garry
A9
Bruar Water
491 CRAIG BHAGAILTEACH
Glen Banvie
Glen Tilt
Glen Fender
CÀRN LIATH 973
903 BEN VUIRICH
Loch Con
Loch Errochty
Calvine
Clan Donnachaidh
Bruar
Blair Castle
Middlebridge
Bridge of Tilt
Glen Girnaig
B8079
Pitagowan
Struan
Blair Atholl
470 TULACH HILL
Aldclune
Trinafour
B847
Glen Errochty
River Garry
Killiecrankie NTS
840 BEN VRACKIE
511 TORR DUBH
892 BEINN A' CHUALLAICH
Tay Forest Park
RSPB
Killiecrankie
A924
Tressait
B8019
Moulin
Kinnaird
B846
Queen's View
Dunalastair
R Tummel
Loch Tummel
Tummel Bridge
Frenich
Faskally Wayside Centre
Drumchastle
Dunalastair Water
Foss
Daloist
Pitlochry
Edradour Distillery
Tempar
Dunfallandy Stone
R Tummel
Dalcapon
1081 SCHIEHALLION
780 FARRAGON HILL
780 MEALL TAIRNEACHAN
Loch Derculich
Strathtay
A827
Tulliem
Glengoulandie Deer Park
Loch Glassie
Derculich
Grandtully
Logierait
Ballinluig
Edradynate
Balnaguard
1042 CÀRN MAIRG
B898
R Tay
St Mary's
Menzies
Weem
Camserney
Coshieville
Dull
Keltneyburn
Dewars
Aberfeldy
Kincraigie
River Tay
Tay Forest Park
Dalguise
Fortingall
532 GRANDTULLY HILL
Loch Skiach
Croftmoraig Stone Circle
Kenmore
Loch Kennard
Fearnan
Acharn
A826
1000 MEALL
The Crannog Centre
Ballinloan Burn
Loch Tay
616 MEALL DUBH
Leckbuie
713 BEINN BHREAC
Glen Quaich
Trochry
River Quaich
A822
Strath Braan
Loch Freuchie
864 SRÒN A' CHAOINEIDH
802 MEALL NAM FUARAN
Amulree
Tullybeagles Lo
Ardeon
River Almond
Glenshee
879
666
0 1 2 3 4 miles
0 1 2 3 4 5 kilometres

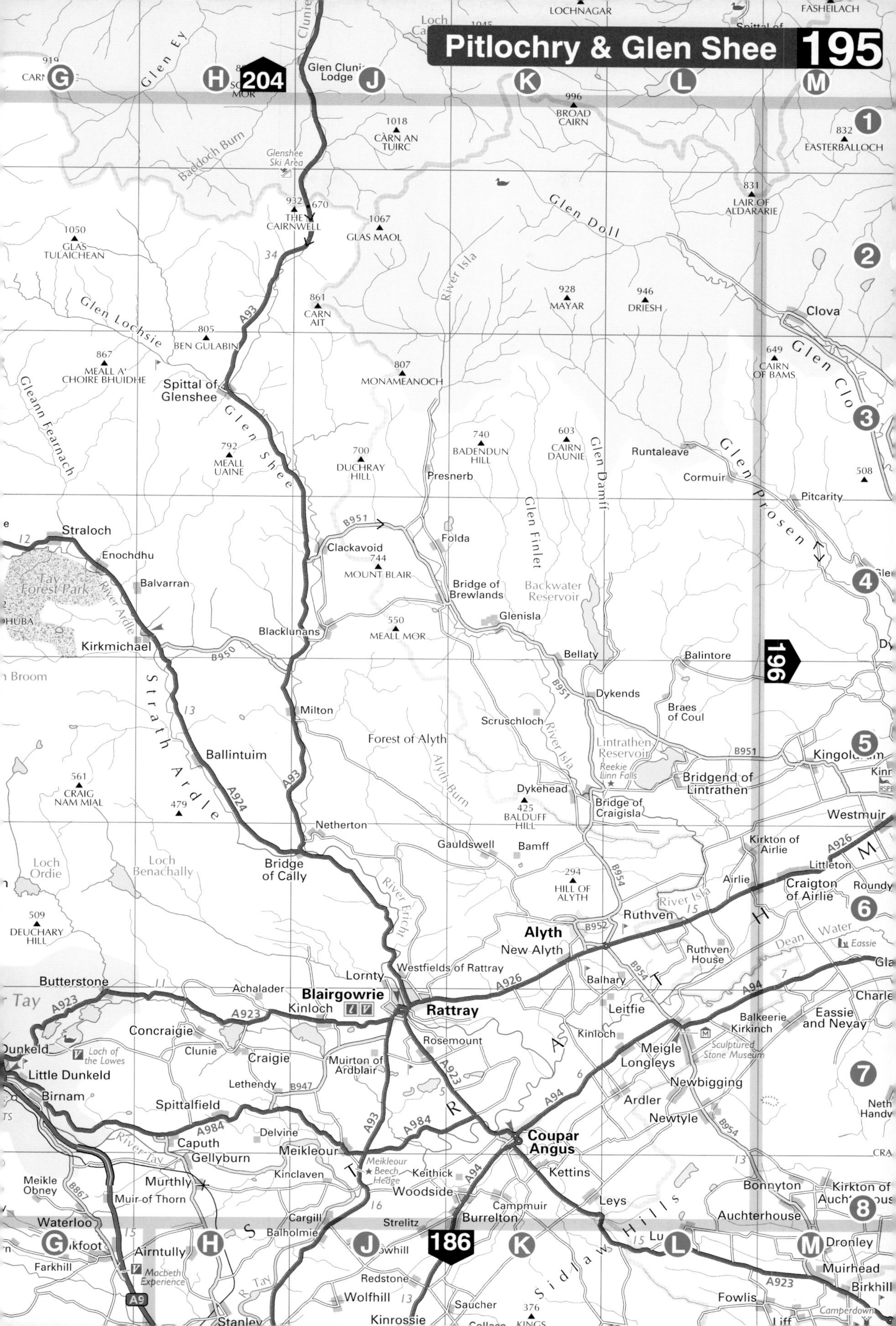
204
196
186
Lochnagar
Fasheilach
Glen Ey
Glen Clunie Lodge
Broad Cairn
Càrn an Tuirc
Easterballoch
Glenshee Ski Area
Baddoch Burn
The Cairnwell
Glas Maol
Lair of Aldararie
Glen Doll
Glas Tulaichean
River Isla
Mayar
Driesh
Clova
Glen Lochsie
Carn Ait
Ben Gulabin
Meall a' Choire Bhuidhe
Spittal of Glenshee
Monameanoch
Cairn of Bams
Glen Clova
Gleann Fearnach
Glen Shee
Meall Uaine
Duchray Hill
Badendun Hill
Cairn Daunie
Glen Damff
Runtaleave
Cormuir
Presnerb
Glen Prosen
Pitcarity
Straloch
Enochdhu
Clackavoid
Mount Blair
Folda
Glen Finlet
Tay Forest Park
Balvarran
River Ardle
Bridge of Brewlands
Backwater Reservoir
Glenisla
Meall Mor
Blacklunans
Kirkmichael
Bellaty
Balintore
Broom
Strath Ardle
Dykends
Milton
Braes of Coul
Scruschloch
Forest of Alyth
Lintrathen Reservoir
Reekie Linn Falls
Kingoldrum
Ballintuim
Alyth Burn
Bridgend of Lintrathen
Craig Nam Mial
Dykehead
Balduff Hill
Bridge of Craigisla
Westmuir
Netherton
Gauldswell
Bamff
Kirkton of Airlie
Loch Ordie
Loch Benachally
Bridge of Cally
Littleton
Airlie
Roundy
Hill of Alyth
Craigton of Airlie
River Isla
Ruthven
River Ericht
Deuchary Hill
Alyth
New Alyth
Ruthven House
Dean Water
Eassie
Lornty
Westfields of Rattray
Butterstone
Achalader
Blairgowrie
Balhary
Tay
Kinloch
Rattray
Leitfie
Charleston
Eassie and Nevay
Balkeerie
Kirkinch
Concraigie
Kinloch
Rosemount
Dunkeld
Loch of the Lowes
Clunie
Craigie
Muirton of Ardblair
Meigle
Sculptured Stone Museum
Longleys
Little Dunkeld
Lethendy
Newbigging
Birnam
Spittalfield
Ardler
Newtyle
Delvine
Coupar Angus
Caputh
River Tay
Gellyburn
Meikleour
Meikle Obney
Murthly
Kinclaven
Meikleour Beech Hedge
Keithick
Kettins
Bonnyton
Woodside
Muir of Thorn
Leys
Campmuir
Auchterhouse
Waterloo
Cargill
Strelitz
Burrelton
Sidlaw Hills
Balholmie
Airntully
Dronley
Farkhill
Macbeth Experience
Redstone
Muirhead
Wolfhill
Fowlis
Birkhill
Saucher
Stanley
Kinrossie
Camperdown

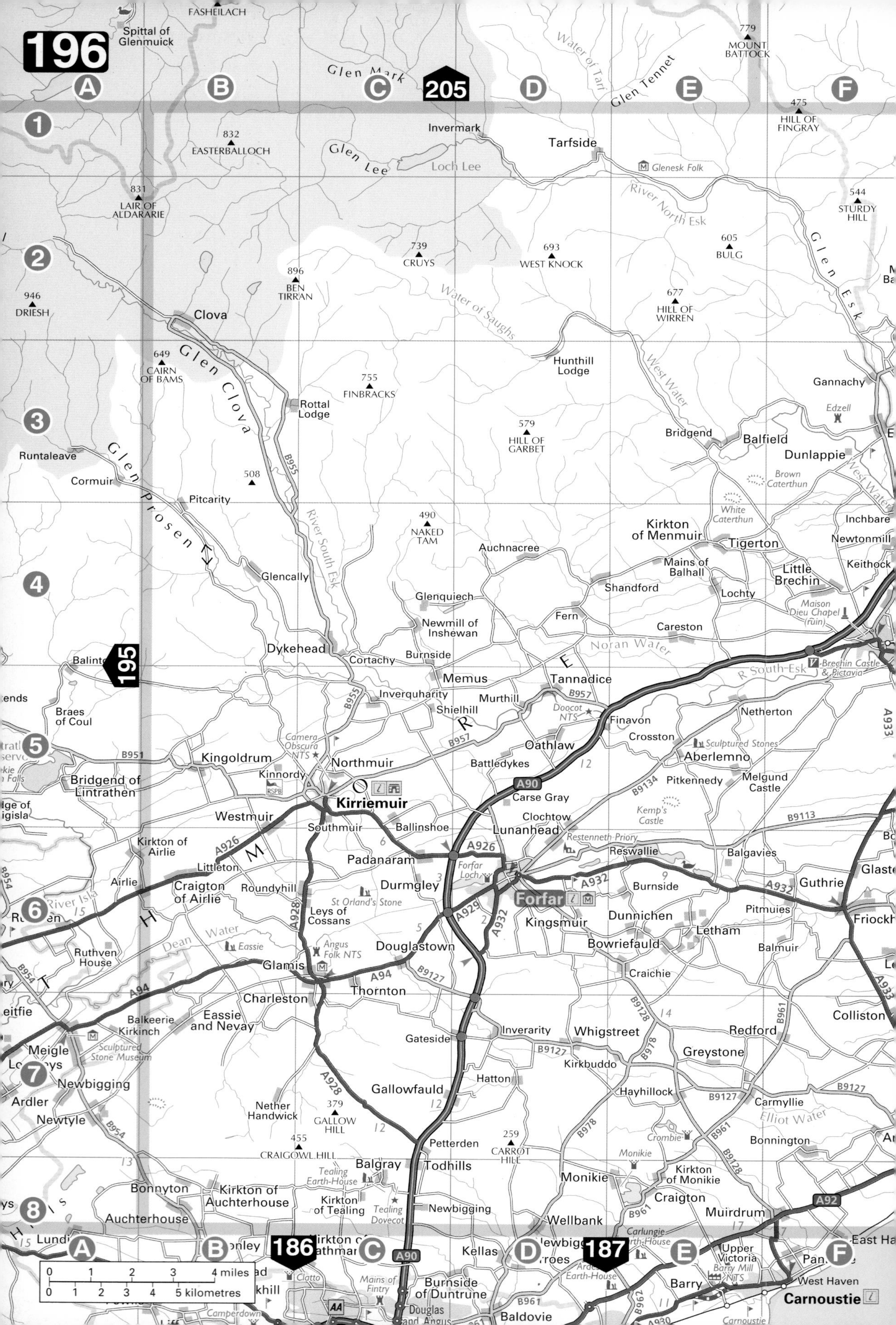

196
FASHEILACH
Spittal of Glenmuick
A
B
C
D
E
F
205
Glen Mark
Water of Tarf
Glen Tennet
779 MOUNT BATTOCK
475 HILL OF FINGRAY
1
832 EASTERBALLOCH
Invermark
Glen Lee
Loch Lee
Tarfside
Glenesk Folk
River North Esk
831 LAIR OF ALDARARIE
544 STURDY HILL
2
739 CRUYS
693 WEST KNOCK
605 BULG
896 BEN TIRRAN
946 DRIESH
Water of Saughs
677 HILL OF WIRREN
Glen Esk
Clova
649 CAIRN OF BAMS
Glen Clova
755 FINBRACKS
Hunthill Lodge
West Water
Gannachy
3
Rottal Lodge
Edzell
579 HILL OF GARBET
Bridgend
Balfield
Runtaleave
Dunlappie
508
B955
Glen Prosen
Cormuir
Brown Caterthun
Pitcarity
White Caterthun
River South Esk
490 NAKED TAM
Kirkton of Menmuir
Inchbare
Tigerton
Newtonmill
Auchnacree
Mains of Balhall
Keithock
Little Brechin
4
Glencally
Shandford
Lochty
Glenquiech
Maison Dieu Chapel (ruin)
Fern
Newmill of Inshewan
Careston
Noran Water
Dykehead
Cortachy
Burnside
Balintore
195
Memus
Tannadice
Brechin Castle & Pictavia
R South Esk
Inverquharity
Murthill
B957
Shielhill
Doocot NTS
Finavon
Netherton
Braes of Coul
Crosston
A933
5
Camera Obscura NTS
B957
Oathlaw
Sculptured Stones
B951
Kingoldrum
Aberlemno
Northmuir
Battledykes
Kinnordy
RSPB
12
Bridgend of Lintrathen
Pitkennedy
Melgund Castle
A90
B9134
Kirriemuir
Carse Gray
Clochtow
Kemp's Castle
Westmuir
B9113
Southmuir
Ballinshoe
Lunanhead
Kirkton of Airlie
A926
Restenneth Priory
A926
Reswallie
Balgavies
Littleton
Padanaram
Forfar Loch
Airlie
Guthrie
Craigton of Airlie
Roundyhill
Durmgley
A932
Burnside
A932
River Isla
Forfar
St Orland's Stone
Pitmuies
6
Leys of Cossans
A929
Dunnichen
A928
Kingsmuir
Dean Water
A932
Eassie
Angus Folk NTS
Letham
Ruthven House
Douglastown
Bowriefauld
Balmuir
B954
Glamis
A94
B9127
Craichie
A94
Charleston
Thornton
Balkeerie
Eassie and Nevay
B9128
Kirkinch
A933
Colliston
Sculptured Stone Museum
Inverarity
Whigstreet
Redford
Meigle
Gateside
B9127
B978
B961
Greystone
7
Kirkbuddo
Newbigging
A928
Hatton
Ardler
Gallowfauld
Hayhillock
B9127
Carmyllie
B9127
Newtyle
Nether Handwick
379 GALLOW HILL
Elliot Water
B954
B978
455 CRAIGOWL HILL
Petterden
259 CARROT HILL
Crombie
B961
Bonnington
Balgray
Todhills
Monikie
Tealing Earth-House
B9128
Bonnyton
Kirkton of Auchterhouse
Monikie
Kirkton of Monikie
Kirkton of Tealing
Tealing Dovecot
Newbigging
Craigton
8
Auchterhouse
B961
Muirdrum
A92
Wellbank
Carlungie Earth-House
186
187
East Haven
Kellas
Upper Victoria
A90
Barry Mill NTS
West Haven
Clatto
Mains of Fintry
Burnside of Duntrune
Barry
Carnoustie
B961
B962
Baldovie
A930
Camperdown
0 1 2 3 4 miles
0 1 2 3 4 5 kilometres

206
Forfar & Angus Coast
Tannachie
Elfhill
LEACHIE HILL
Goosecruives
Drumlithie
Glenbervie
Mondynes
Temple of Fiddes
Crawton
Trelong Bay
Catterline
Kinneff
Todhead Point
Auchenblae
FINELLA HILL
GOYLE HILL
Cairn O'Mount
Fasque
Fordoun
Pittarrow
Redmyre
Arbuthnott
Mains of Haulkerton
Laurencekirk
Inverbervie
Bervie Bay
Gourdon
Redford
Benholm
Bogmuir
Sauchieburn
Luthermuir
Dykelands
Johnshaven
Marykirk
Craigo
Logie Pert
Lochside
Bush
Milton Ness
St Cyrus
Logie
Morphie
Hillside
Dun
House of Dun NTS
Montrose
Montrose Basin
Scurdie Ness
Barnhead
Maryton
Ferryden
Craig
Usan
Westerton
Braehead
Boddin Point
Lunan
Lunan Bay
Inverkeilor
Red Head
Chapelton
Cauldcots
Marywell
Auchmithie
Carlingheugh Bay
The Deil's Head
Arbroath

A
B
C
D
208
E
F
1
2
3
4
5
6
7
8
Talisker Bay
Talisker
Glen Eynort
447
BEINN BHREAC
Loch Eynort
434
AN CRUACHIN
Glenbrittle House
Bualintur
Loch Brittle
Rudh' an Dùnain
CANNA
210
CÀRN A' GHAILL
Garrisdale Point
A'Chill
Canna Harbour
Sanday
Sound of Canna
Rudha Shamhnan Insir
302
MULLACH MÒR
A Bhrideanach
570
ORVAL
Oigh-sgeir
RÙM
810
ASKIVAL
763
SGÙRR NAN GILLEAN
The Small Isles
Rudha nam Meirleach
Eilean nan Each
189
MU
0 1 2 3 4 miles
0 1 2 3 4 5 kilometres

Sligachan
Dunan
Broadford
Torrin
Kirkibost
Elgol
Glasnakille
Broadford Bay
Corry
Waterloo
Lower Breakish
Upper Breakish
Harrapool
Skulamus
Kyle of Lochalsh
Skye Bridge
Kyleakin
Pabay
The Cuillin Hills
Cuillin Hills
Loch Coruisk
Loch na Crèitheach
Loch Slapin
Loch Scavaig
Loch Eishort
Loch Ainort
SGURR NAN GILLEAN
GLAS BHEIN MHÒRN
BEINN NA CAILLICH
BEINN DEORG MHÒR
BLAVEN
SGÙRR ALASDAIR
GARS BHEINN
SGÙRR GHEADAIDH
BEN MEABOST
BEINN NAN CÀRN
Heast
Suisnish
Rudha Suisnish
Drumfearn
BEINN NA SEAMRAIG
SGURR NA COINNICH
BEN ASLAK
Otter Haven
Mol-chlach
SOAY
Rudh' Aonghais
BEINN BHREAC
Strathaird Point
Tokavaig
Ord River
SGORACH BREAC
Duisdalemore
Isleornsay
Ornsay
Loch na Dal
Sandaig Island
Rudha Buidhe
Tarskavaig
Tarskavaig Bay
Achnacloich
Loch nam Uamph
Teangue
Knock
Knock Bay
Ferrindonald
Kilmore
Kilbeg
SOUND OF SLEAT
Rudh' Ard Slisneach
Inverguseran
Glen Guseran
Airor
Clan Donald
Ardvasar
Armadale
Calligarry
DRUIM NA CLUAIN-AIRIDHE
Sandaig
Sandaig Bay
Aird of Sleat
Ard Thurinish
Point of Sleat
Rudha Raonuill
Inverie Bay
na Roinne
SOUND
Courteachan
Mallaig
Mallaigvaig
Marine World
CÀRN A'GHOBHAIR
Glasnacardoch Bay
Loch an Nostaire
SGÙRR BHUIDHE
Stoul
Loch Nevis
Beoraidbeg
Morar
Bracora
Bracorina
Swordland
Glenancross
Loch Morar
Lettermorar
Bunacaimb
CÀRN A' MHÀDAIDH-RUAIDH
Eilean Ighe
Back of Keppoch
Arisaig
Loch nan Ceall
Luinga Mhòr
SIDHEAN MOR
Prince Charlie's Cairn
Rudh' Arisaig
CRUACH DOIRE
Druimindarroch
Arisaig House
Kinlochnanuagh
Loch nan Uamh
Polnish
Inverailort
Ardnish
Rudha Chaolais
Peanmeanach
Loch Ailort
Bay of Laig
Cleadale
Laig
AN CRUACHAN
EIGG
Kildonnan
AN SGÙRR
Sandavore
Eilean Chathastail
Luib Folk
A87
A851
A830
A861
B8083
B8008
209
200
190
G H J K L M
1 2 3 4 5 6 7 8

Badicaul
Balmacara
Auchtertyre
Conchra
Killilan
SGÙMAN COINNTICH
Loch Long
Camas Luinie
Glen Elchaig
Loch na Leitreach
River Elchaig
Falls
Pabay
A
Kyle of Lochalsh
B
C
D
210
E
F
Skye Bridge
Lochalsh Woodland NTS
Kirkton
Nostie
Ardelve
Carndu
Dornie
Eilean Donan
1
A87
Kyleakin
Loch Alsh
Keppoch
Upper Breakish
Letterfearn
Loch Duich
732
SGURR NA COINNICH
603
BEINN A'CHUIRN
840
SGÙRR AN AIRGID
Inverinate
916
A'GHLAS-BHEINN
Kyle Rhea
Bernera
Galltair
Morvich
Carn-gorm
2
Kylerhea
Otter Haven
(Summer Only)
Glenelg Bay
Ratagan
Ault a' chruinn
Invershiel
Shiel Bridge
605
BEN ASLAK
Glenelg
408
BEINN A' CHAOINICH
Moye
350
Mam Ratagan
1031
BEN ATTOW
Eilanreach
Kintail
FIVE SISTERS
561
BEINN NA SEAMRAIG
Glenelg Brochs
Glean Beag
Balvraid
1068
SGÙRR FHUARAN
Glen Shiel
Loch na Dal
Sandaig Island
1719
33
3
Ornsay
974
BEINN SGRITHEAL
773
BEINN NAN CAORACH
1011
THE SADDLE
Rudha Buidhe
945
SGURR NA-SGINE
SOUND OF SLEAT
Arnisdale
Loch Hourn
Rudh' Ard Slisneach
Glen Arnisdale
Corran
614
709
DRUM FADA
4
Inverguseran
784
BEINN NA CAILLICH
Kinloch Hourn
1026
SGURR A MHAORAICH
Barrisdale Bay
Airor
199
Glen Guseran
1019
LADHAR BHEINN
518
DRUIM NA CLUAIN-AIRIDHE
Sandaig
Knoydart
KNOYDART
940
LUINNE BHEINN
Loch
5
Sandaig Bay
Inverie
Loch an Dubh-Lochain
919
Inverie Bay
Rudha Raonuill
1003
SGURR MÒR
Mallaigvaig
Marine World
547
CÀRN A'GHOBHAIR
Loch Nevis
854
BEINN BHUIDHE
Carnoch
1039
SGURR NA CICHE
Loch an Nostaire
437
SGÙRR BHUIDHE
879
SGURR MHURLAGAIN
6
Stoul
859
SGURR NAH-AIDE
Glen Dessarry
Morar
Bracora
Bracorina
Kylesmorar
Tarbet
723
SGARR BREAC
Murlaggan
Swordland
Loch Morar
Glen Pean
Lettermorar
503
716
AN STAC
7
Meoble
River Meoble
710
MEITH BHEINN
949
SGURR NAN COIREACHAN
964
SGURR THUILM
983
GULVAIN
960
600
SIDHEAN MOR
10
Prince Charlie's Cairn
Arisaig House
Kinlochnanuagh
Loch Beoriad
633
796
SGURR AN UTHA
Glen Finnan
Gleann Dubhlighe
Gleann Fionnlighe
Loch nan Uamh
8
Polnish
A830
14
Lochailort
Loch Eilt
Glenfinnan
A
B
190
C
D
E
191
F
Rudha
Glenfinnan Monument NTS
Kinlocheil
Lochielside Station
Drimsallie
0 1 2 3 4 miles
0 1 2 3 4 5 kilometres
877
882

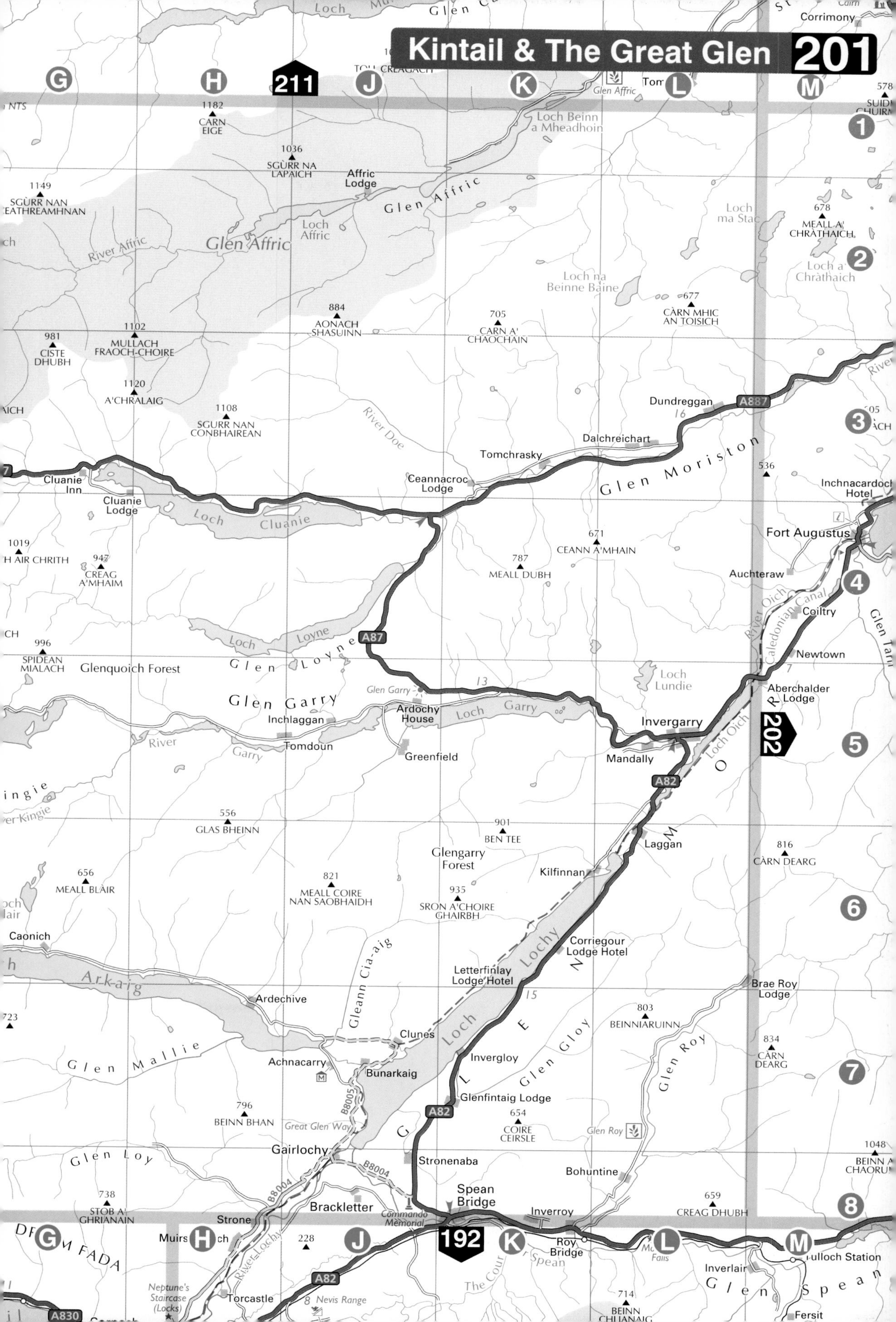
Kintail & The Great Glen
201
Corrimony
G
H
211
J
K
L
M
1
2
3
4
5
6
7
8
1182
CARN EIGE
TOLL CREAGACH
Glen Affric
Tom
Loch Beinn a Mheadhoin
1036
SGÙRR NA LAPAICH
Affric Lodge
1149
SGÙRR NAN CEATHREAMHNAN
Glen Affric
Loch Affric
Glen Affric
River Affric
Loch ma Stac
678
MEALL A' CHRÀTHAICH
Loch a' Chràthaich
Loch na Beinne Baine
677
CÀRN MHIC AN TOISICH
884
AONACH SHASUINN
705
CARN A' CHAOCHAIN
1102
MULLACH FRAOCH-CHOIRE
981
CISTE DHUBH
1120
A'CHRALAIG
1108
SGURR NAN CONBHAIREAN
River Doe
Dundreggan
A887
16
Dalchreichart
Tomchrasky
Glen Moriston
536
Cluanie Inn
Cluanie Lodge
Loch Cluanie
Ceannacroc Lodge
Inchnacardoch Hotel
Fort Augustus
1019
947
CREAG A'MHAIM
671
CEANN A'MHAIN
787
MEALL DUBH
Auchteraw
Loch Loyne
A87
Glen Loyne
996
SPIDEAN MIALACH
Glenquoich Forest
River Oich
Caledonian Canal
Coiltry
Newtown
7
Loch Lundie
Aberchalder Lodge
Glen Garry
Glen Garry
13
Inchlaggan
Ardochy House
Loch Garry
Invergarry
202
River Garry
Tomdoun
Greenfield
Mandally
Loch Oich
A82
556
GLAS BHEINN
901
BEN TEE
Laggan
816
CÀRN DEARG
Glengarry Forest
Kilfinnan
656
MEALL BLÀIR
821
MEALL COIRE NAN SAOBHAIDH
935
SRON A'CHOIRE GHAIRBH
Caonich
Gleann Cia-aig
Loch Lochy
Corriegour Lodge Hotel
Loch Arkaig
Letterfinlay Lodge Hotel
15
Brae Roy Lodge
Ardechive
803
BEINNIARUINN
834
CÀRN DEARG
Clunes
Glen Mallie
Achnacarry
Bunarkaig
Invergloy
Glen Gloy
Glen Roy
Glen Mor
796
BEINN BHAN
B8005
Glenfintaig Lodge
A82
654
COIRE CEIRSLE
Great Glen Way
Glen Roy
1048
Gairlochy
Glen Loy
Stronenaba
B8004
Bohuntine
738
STOB A' GHRIANAIN
Brackletter
Spean Bridge
Commando Memorial
Inverroy
659
CREAG DHUBH
Strone
192
228
Roy Bridge
River Spean
Tulloch Station
Inverlair
Glen Spean
The Cour
Neptune's Staircase (Locks)
Torcastle
A82
Nevis Range
River Lochy
714
A830
Fersit

202
212
201
192
193
Tomich
Corrimony
Balnain
Drumnadrochit
Temple Pier
Lewiston
Urquhart
Falls of Divach
Loch Meiklie
SUIDHE GHUIRMAIN
Lenie
LOCH NESS
Torness
Loch Ruthven
Aberarder
Inverfarigaig
Aultnagoire
Farigaig
Errogie
Dunmaglass
Farraline
Loch ma Stac
MEALL A' CHRÀTHAICH
Loch a' Chràthaich
Loch nan Breac Deorga
Foyers
Gorthleck
BEINN DUBHCHARAIOH
CÀRN MHIC AN TOISICH
Achnaconeran
Glebe
Loch Mhor
Invermoriston
River Moriston
Great Glen Way
Loch Knockie
Whitebridge
Dundreggan
BURACH
CÀRN NA SAOBHAIDHE
Glen Moriston
Inchnacardoch Hotel
Loch Killin
CÀRN NA LARAICHE MAOILE
Glendoe Lodge
Fort Augustus
Monadhl
Glen Doe
Auchteraw
Caledonian Canal
River Oich
Coiltry
Glen Tarff
CÀRN EASGANN BÀNA
SGARAMAN NAM FIADH
Newtown
Loch Lundie
Aberchalder Lodge
CÀRN A' CHUILINN
Invergarry
Loch Oich
CORRIEYAIRACK HILL
MEALL NA-H-AISRE
GEAL CHÀRN
Laggan
CÀRN LEAC
CÀRN DEARG
Glen Markie
River Spey
Blargie
Crathie
Loch Spey
Loch Crunachdan
Glenshera Lodge
BLACK CRAIG
Catlodg
Strathmashie House
Brae Roy Lodge
BEINNIARUINN
CÀRN LIATH
Kinlochlaggan
Gallovie
CÀRN DEARG
Glen Roy
Creag Meagaidh
CREAG MEAGAIDH
Loch Laggan
River Maghie
Roy
Dalwhinni
BEINN A' CHAORUNN
Lochan na h-Earba
River Pattack
BINNEIN SHUAS
Moy
CREAG DHUBH
GEAL CHÀRN
Monessie
Station
CREAGAN MOR
Loch Pattack
Fersit
BEINN
BEINN HUANAIG
0 1 2 3 4 miles
0 1 2 3 4 5 kilometres

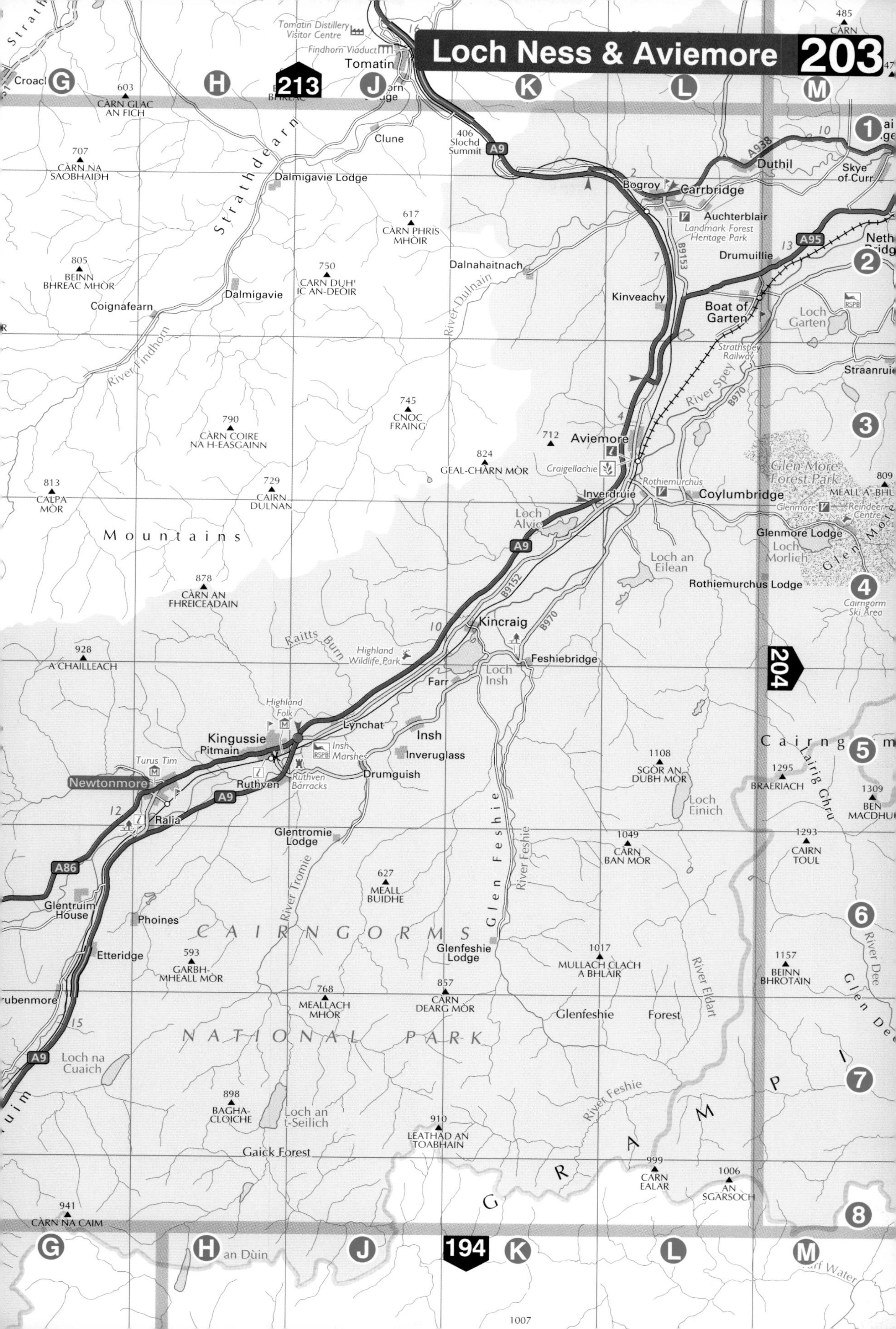

Tomatin Distillery Visitor Centre
Findhorn Viaduct
Tomatin
213
Clune
406 Slochd Summit
A9
Duthil
Skye of Curr
A938
Bogroy
Carrbridge
Auchterblair
Landmark Forest Heritage Park
A95
Drumuillie
B9153
Dalnahaitnach
River Dulnain
Kinveachy
Boat of Garten
Loch Garten
RSPB
Strathspey Railway
Straanruie
River Spey
B970
603 CÀRN GLAC AN FICH
707 CÀRN NA SAOBHAIDH
Strathdearn
Dalmigavie Lodge
617 CÀRN PHRIS MHÒIR
805 BEINN BHREAC MHÒR
750 CARN DUH' IC AN-DEOIR
Dalmigavie
Coignafearn
River Findhorn
745 CNOC FRAING
790 CÀRN COIRE NA H-EASGAINN
712
Aviemore
Craigellachie
824 GEAL-CHÀRN MÒR
Glen More Forest Park
813 CALPA MÒR
729 CAIRN DULNAN
Rothiemurchus
Inverdruie
Coylumbridge
809 MEALL A' BHU
Glenmore
Reindeer Centre
Loch Alvie
Glenmore Lodge
Loch Morlich
Glen More
Mountains
Loch an Eilean
878 CÀRN AN FHREICEADAIN
B9152
Rothiemurchus Lodge
Cairngorm Ski Area
Kincraig
B970
Raitts Burn
Highland Wildlife Park
928 A' CHAILLEACH
Feshiebridge
Loch Insh
Farr
204
Highland Folk
Lynchat
Kingussie
Pitmain
Insh
Insh Marshes
RSPB
Inverglass
1108 SGÒR AN DUBH MÒR
Turus Tim
Newtonmore
Ruthven
Ruthven Barracks
Drumguish
1295 BRAERIACH
Lairig Ghru
1309 BEN MACDHUI
Loch Einich
A9
Ralia
Glen Feshie
River Feshie
Glentromie Lodge
1049 CÀRN BAN MÒR
1293 CAIRN TOUL
A86
River Tromie
627 MEALL BUIDHE
Glentruim House
Phoines
CAIRNGORMS
Glenfeshie Lodge
Etteridge
593 GARBH-MHEALL MÒR
1017 MULLACH CLACH A BHLÀIR
River Eidart
1157 BEINN BHROTAIN
River Dee
Glen Dee
768 MEALLACH MHÒR
857 CÀRN DEARG MÒR
Glenfeshie Forest
NATIONAL PARK
A9
Loch na Cuaich
River Feshie
898 BAGHA-CLOICHE
Loch an t-Seilich
910 LEATHAD AN TOABHAIN
Gaick Forest
GRAMPIAN
999 CÀRN EALAR
1006 AN SGARSOCH
941 CÀRN NA CAIM
194

204
214
203
195
Grantown-on-Spey
Cromdale
Hills of Cromdale
Glenlivet
Glenlivet Distillery
Tomnavoulin
Auchnarrow
Tomintoul
Bridge of Avon
Bridge of Brown
Glen Lochy
Glen Brown
Strath Avon
Speyside Way
Glen Livet
Dulnain Bridge
Craggan
Speybridge
Glenbeg
Duthil
Carrbridge
Skye of Curr
Auchterblair
Landmark Forest Heritage Park
Drumuillie
Nethy Bridge
Dell Wood (Abernethy)
Lettoch
Boat of Garten
Loch Garten
RSPB
Strathspey Railway
River Spey
Straanruie
Dorback Lodge
River Nethy
Blairnamarrow
Lecht Ski Area
Glen More Forest Park
Glenmore
Reindeer Centre
Coylumbridge
Rothiemurchus
Glenmore Lodge
Loch Morlich
Glen More
Loch an Filean
Rothiemurchus Lodge
Cairngorm Ski Area
CAIRNGORMS NATIONAL PARK
Cairngorm Mountains
Glen Avon
River Avon
Loch Builg
River Gairn
Lairig Ghru
Loch Einich
Glen Derry
Glen Lui
Linn of Dee
Quoich Water
River Dee
Glen Dee
River Eidart
Forest
Braemar
Allanaquoich
Keiloch
Inverey
Clunie Water
Loch Callater
Glen Clunie Lodge
Glen Ey
Glenshee Ski Area
Baddoch Burn
GRAMPIAN MOUNTAINS
485 CARN SGRIOB
471
459 CÀRN NA LOINNE
606 CARN TUADHAM
821 GEAL CHÀRN
803 CARN BHEADHAIR
809 MEALL A' BHUACHAILLE
730 MAIM SUIM
792 CARN EALASAID
710 CRAIG VEANN
741 BIG GARVOUN
713 THE BRUACH
829 BROWN COW HILL
1245 CAIRN GORM
1083 BEINN A CHAORRUINN
1171 BEN AVON
1196 NORTH TOP
1295 BRAERIACH
1309 BEN MACDHUI
1084 CARN EAS
900 CULARDOCH
1177 SOUTH TOP
1293 CAIRN TOUL
930 BEINN BHREAC
618 MEALL GORM
1157 BEINN BHROTAIN
813 SGOR MOR
859 MORRONE HILL
816 CARN LIATH
999 CARN EALAR
1006 AN SGARSOCH
919 CARN BHAC
886 SGOR MOR
1045 CAIRN TAGGART
1018 CÀRN AN TUIRC
SGOR AN DUBH MOR
1049
A938
A95
B970
A939
B9136
B9008
B9153
A93
0 1 2 3 4 miles
0 1 2 3 4 5 kilometres

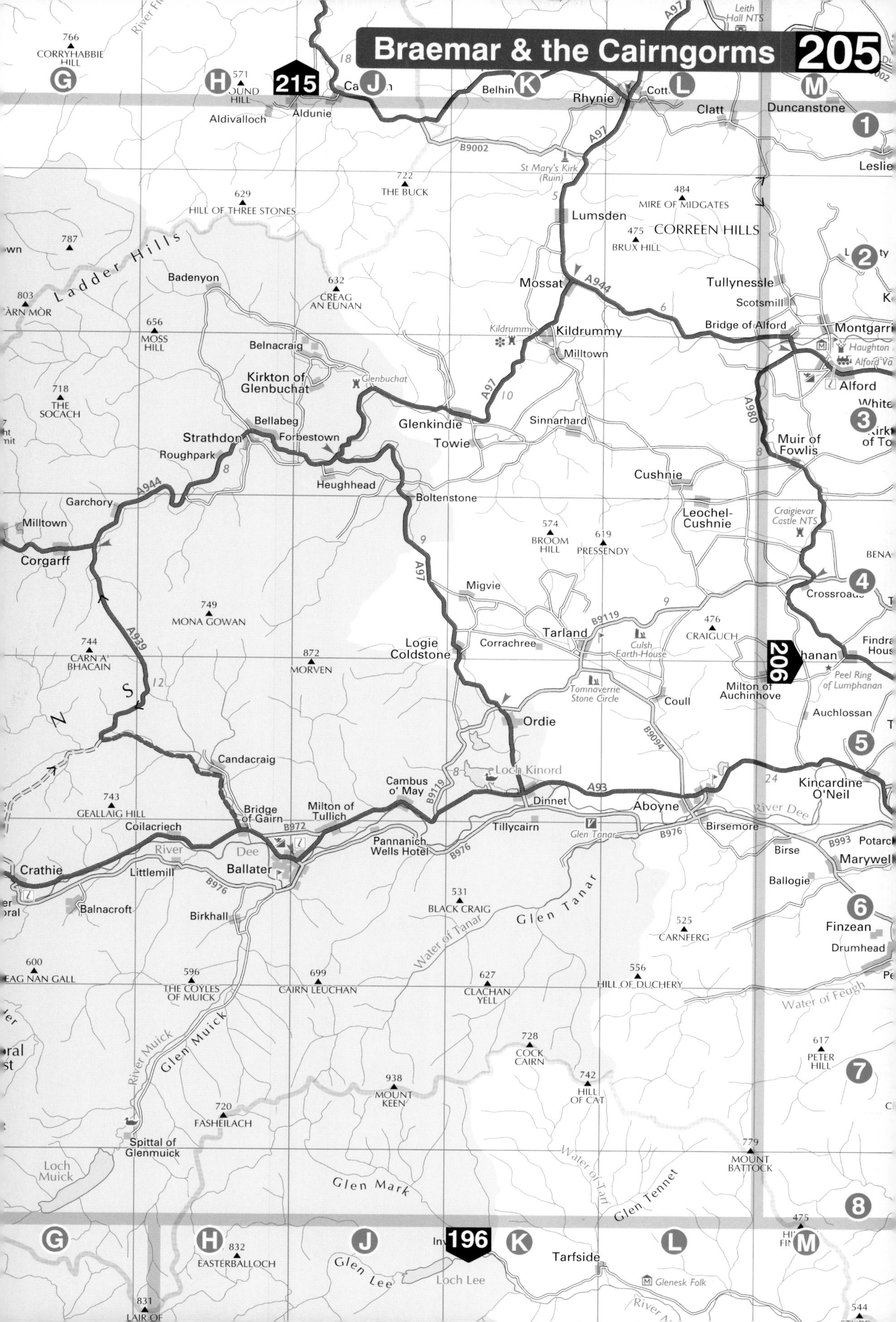
Braemar & the Cairngorms
205
215
206
196
G
H
J
K
L
M
1
2
3
4
5
6
7
8
766
CORRYHABBIE HILL
571
Aldivalloch
Aldunie
Belhin
Rhynie
Clatt
Duncanstone
Leslie
Leith Hall NTS
B9002
A97
St Mary's Kirk (Ruin)
722
THE BUCK
629
HILL OF THREE STONES
484
MIRE OF MIDGATES
Lumsden
475
CORREEN HILLS
BRUX HILL
787
Ladder Hills
Badenyon
632
CREAG AN EUNAN
Mossat
A944
Tullynessle
Scotsmill
803
656
MOSS HILL
Belnacraig
Kildrummy
Milltown
Bridge of Alford
Montgarrie
Haughton
Alford
Kirkton of Glenbuchat
Glenbuchat
718
THE SOCACH
Glenkindie
Towie
Sinnarhard
A980
Bellabeg
Strathdon
Forbestown
Roughpark
Heughhead
Muir of Fowlis
Cushnie
Boltenstone
Garchory
Milltown
Corgarff
Leochel-Cushnie
Craigievar Castle NTS
574
BROOM HILL
619
PRESSENDY
Migvie
Crossroads
749
MONA GOWAN
A939
Tarland
B9119
Culsh Earth-House
476
CRAIGUCH
744
CARN A' BHACAIN
872
MORVEN
Logie Coldstone
Corrachree
Tomnaverrie Stone Circle
Milton of Auchinhove
Peel Ring of Lumphanan
Coull
Auchlossan
Ordie
B9094
Candacraig
Loch Kinord
743
GEALLAIG HILL
Cambus o' May
Dinnet
A93
Aboyne
Kincardine O'Neil
River Dee
Coilacriech
Bridge of Gairn
Milton of Tullich
B972
Tillycairn
Glen Tanar
B976
Birsemore
Pannanich Wells Hotel
Birse
Crathie
Littlemill
Ballater
Marywell
Ballogie
Balnacroft
Birkhall
531
BLACK CRAIG
Glen Tanar
Water of Tanar
525
CARNFERG
Finzean
Drumhead
600
596
THE COYLES OF MUICK
699
CAIRN LEUCHAN
627
CLACHAN YELL
556
HILL OF DUCHERY
Water of Feugh
Glen Muick
River Muick
728
COCK CAIRN
617
PETER HILL
938
MOUNT KEEN
742
HILL OF CAT
720
FASHEILACH
Spittal of Glenmuick
Loch Muick
Water of Tarf
779
MOUNT BATTOCK
Glen Mark
Glen Tennet
475
832
EASTERBALLOCH
Tarfside
Glen Lee
Loch Lee
Glenesk Folk
831
544

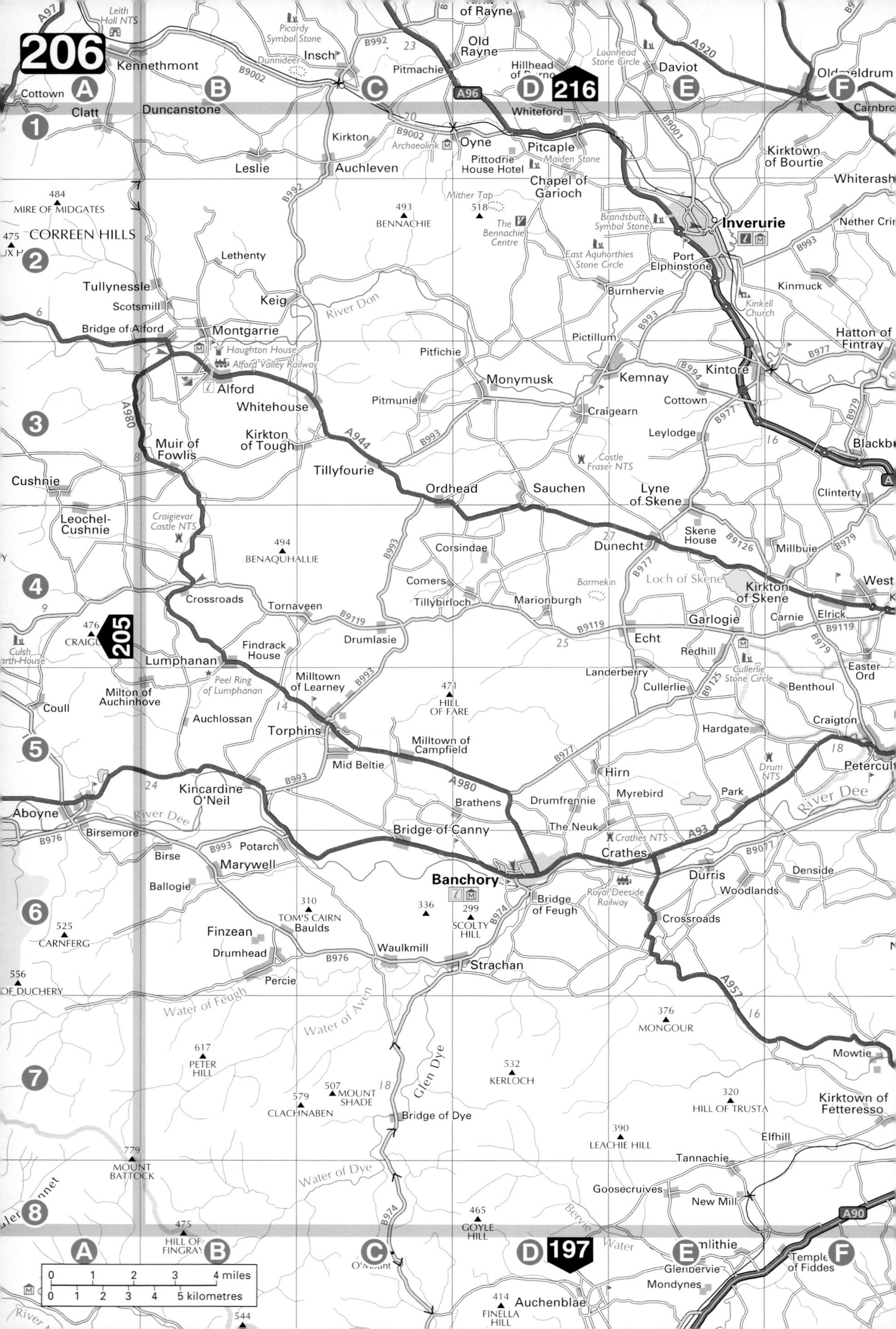
Kennethmont
Clatt
Duncanstone
Insch
Pitmachie
Old Rayne
Daviot
Oldmeldrum
Kirkton
Oyne
Pitcaple
Leslie
Auchleven
Chapel of Garioch
Kirktown of Bourtie
Inverurie
Port Elphinstone
Lethenty
Tullynessle
Keig
Scotsmill
Bridge of Alford
Montgarrie
Alford
Whitehouse
Kirkton of Tough
Muir of Fowlis
Tillyfourie
Monymusk
Kemnay
Kintore
Cushnie
Leochel-Cushnie
Ordhead
Sauchen
Lyne of Skene
Dunecht
Corsindae
Comers
Tillybirloch
Marionburgh
Crossroads
Tornaveen
Drumlasie
Echt
Garlogie
Lumphanan
Milton of Auchinhove
Torphins
Coull
Aboyne
Kincardine O'Neil
Banchory
Crathes
Durris
Finzean
Strachan
Bridge of Dye
Auchenblae
206
205
216
197
4 miles
5 kilometres

Ellon
Ythsie
Esslemont
Tolquhon
Pitmedden Garden
Pitmedden
Logierieve
Kirkton of Logie Buchan
Collieston
217
Forvie
Housieside
Udny Green
Udny Station
Newburgh
Pettymuk
Cultercullen
Foveran
Tillygreig
Delfrigs
Reisque
Newmachar
Causeyend
Whitecairns
Belhelvie
Balmedie
Kinmundy
Cothal
Potterton
Parkhill House
Blackdog
Dyce
Denmore
Bridge of Don
Bankhead
Bucksburn
Kirkwall
Lerwick
Northfield
Old Aberdeen
Kittybrewster
Kingswells
ABERDEEN
Ruthrieston
Torry
Nigg Bay
Mannofield
Kincorth
Cults
Nigg
Bieldside
Banchory-Devenick
Altens Haven
Cove Bay
Charlestown
Kingcausie
Marywell
Hillside
Auchlee
Findon
Portlethen
Cairngrassie
Cammachmore Bay
Downies
Isick House
Cammachmore
Newtonhill
Skateraw
Muchalls
Doonie Point
Garron Point
Stonehaven Bay
Stonehaven
Dunnottar
Crawton
Trelong Bay
Catterline
A90
A920
A975
A956
B999
B9000
B9005
B979
B977
B997
B9119
B9077
A96
G
H
J
K
L
M
1
2
3
4
5
6
7
8

Duntulm
Tairbeart (Tarbert)
Lùb Score
Borneskitaig
Kilmuir
Kilvaxter
Heribusta
Balgown
Loch nam Madadh (Lochmaddy)
218
Waternish Point
Linicro
Totscore
Ascrib Islands
Idrigill
Uig
Uig Bay
Earlish
Geary
283 BEN GEARY
Trumpan
Loch Snizort
Ardmore Point
Gillen
Hallin
A87
DUNVEGAN HEAD
Isay
Mingay
Stein
Lusta
Loch Bay
214 BEN DIUBAIG
Greshornish House Hotel
Loch Greshornish
Kingsburgh
Loch Snizort Beag
Claigan
Bay
Loch Dunvegan
327 BEINN BHREAC
B886
Boreraig
Uig
Treaslane
Flashader
A850
Loch Pooltiel
Upperglen
Feriniquarrie
Totaig
Edinbane
Bernisdale
Oisgill Bay
Milovaig
Glendale
Colbost
Dunvegan
Tote
Waterstein
Lephin
B884
Colbost Croft
Toy
Dunvegan
Skeabost
Skinidin
Giant Angus MacAskill
Kilmuir
Neist Point
Lonmore
265 BEN AKETIL
271 CRUACHAN BEINN A' CHEARCAILL
Moonen Bay
Roskhill
Caroy River
469 HEALAVAL MORE
Roag
Ramasaig
Orbost
Vatten
B885
Hoe Rape
488 HEALAVAL BHEAG
Harlosh
Glen Ose
A863
Ose
ISLE OF
Hoe Point
Loch Caroy
Harlosh Island
Colbost Point
368 BEINN NA BOINEID
Bracadale
Loch Duagrich
Tarner Island
Coillore
Struan
Loch Bracadale
Ullinish Lodge Hotel
Wiay
23
Idrigill Point
Oronsay
Portnalong
Loch Harport
Fiskavaig
B8009
Rudha nan Clach
Fernilea
369 ARNAVAL
Carbost
Drynoch
Merkadale
Talisker Bay
Talisker
Glen Eynort
447 BEINN BHREAC
Grula
198
Loch Eynort
434
0 1 2 3 4 miles
0 1 2 3 4 5 kilometres

Kilmaluag
Flodigarry
Poldorais
Eilean Flodigarry
542
MEAL NA SUIREAMACH
Digg
Staffin Bay
Staffin Island
Brogaig
Stenscholl
Staffin
218
Kilt Rock Waterfall
Ellishader
Trotternish
Marishader
Valtos
611
BEINN EDRA
Garros
Rudha nam Brathairean
Culnaknock
Lealt
Tote
A855
608
CREAG A' LAIN
Old Man of Storr
719
THE STORR
River Romesdal
River Haulton
Loch Leathan
Loch Fada
Borve
Drumuie
Glengrasco
A855
312
Torvaig
Portree
Seafield
417
BEINN NA GREINE
Penifiler
412
BEN TIANAVAIG
Glenmore
Glenvarragill
Mugeary
A87
Camastianavaig
Tianavaig Bay
Ollach
B883
Glen Varragill
The Braes
444
BEN LEE
Peinchorran
Sconser
A863
SKYE
Sligachan
773
GLAMAIG
A87
Loch Ainort
Luib
564
GLAS BHEIN MHÒRN
Luib Folk
965
SGURR NAN GILLEAN
974
The Cuillin Hills
SOUND OF RAASAY
Loch a' Bhràige
RONA
Eilean Tigh
Eilean Fladday
Umachan
Manish Point
Loch Arnish
Torran
Arnish
Brochel
RAASAY
444
DÙN CAAN
Oskaig
Rudha na' Leac
310
BEINN NA LEAC
Clachan
Inverarish
Suisnish Point
Eyre Point
Dunan
Caolas Scalpay
199
SCALPAY
396
MULLACH NA CARN
732
BEINN NA CAILLICH
708
Broadford
Corry
Broadford Bay
Waterloo
Harrapool
Lower Breakish
Upper Breakish
INNER SOUND
67
Longay
27
Pabay
Gairloch
South Erradale
Redpoint
Red Point
Loch Torridon
Rudha na Fearn
Fearnmore
Òb Chuaig
Fearnbeg
Arrina
Kenmore
Cuaig
Callakille
Lonbain
492
AN GARBH-MHEALL
493
CRÒIC-BHEINN
River Applecross
210
Applecross Bay
Applecross
Milton
626
Pass of the Cattle
Camusteel
Camusterrach
Aird Dhubh
Culduie
Bealach-Na-Ba
Toscaig
River Toscaig
Caolas Mòr
Eilean Meadhonach
Eilean Mòr
CROWLIN ISLANDS
Loch Carron
Port-an-Eorna
Drumbuie
Badicaul
Kyle of Lochalsh
Toll
Skye Bridge
Kyleakin
A87

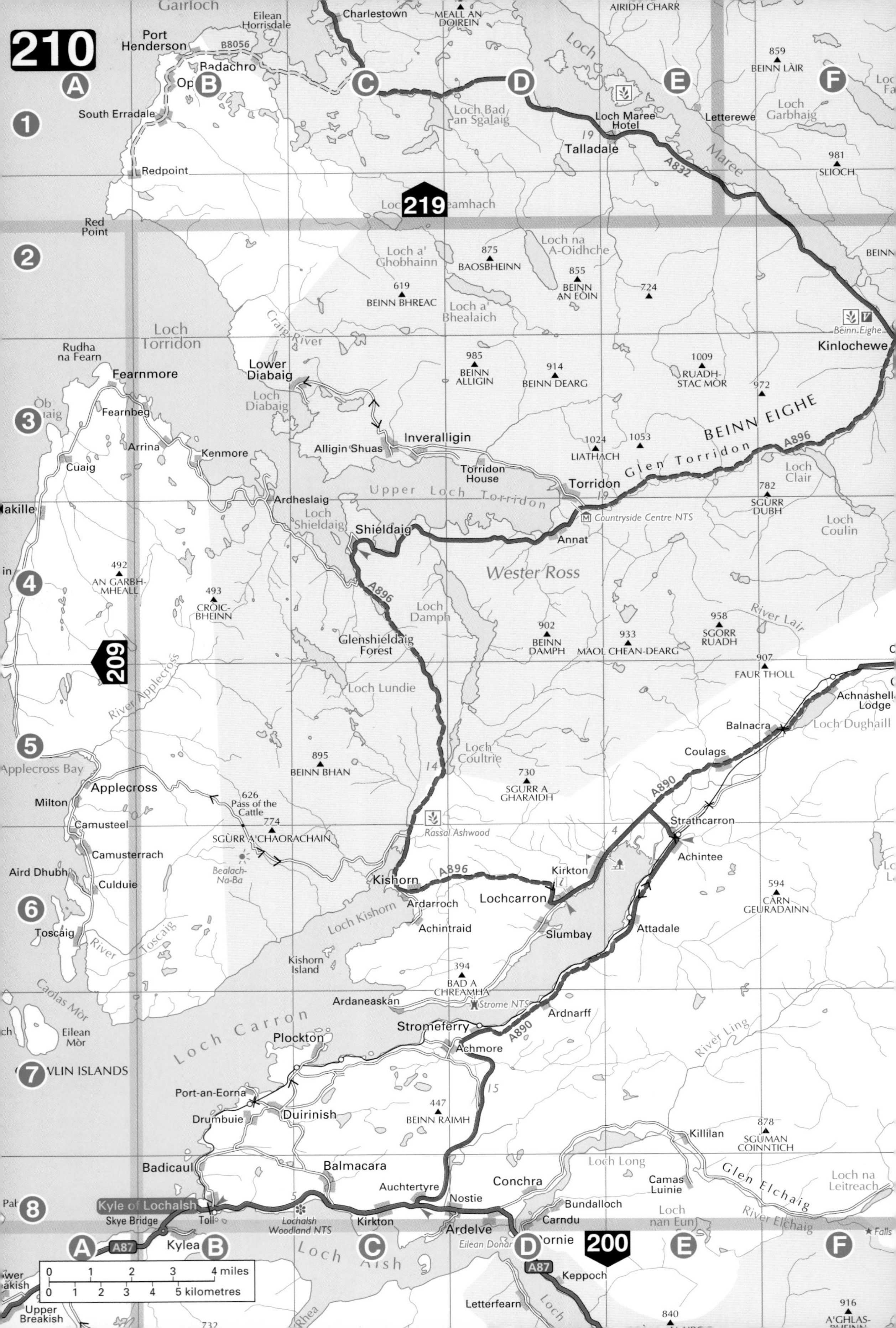

Gairloch
Charlestown
MEALL AN DOIREIN
AIRIDH CHARR
Eilean Horrisdale
Port Henderson
B8056
Badachro
Loch Maree
859 BEINN LÀIR
South Erradale
Loch Bad an Sgalaig
Loch Maree Hotel
Letterewe
Loch Garbhaig
Talladale
A832
981 SLIOCH
Redpoint
219
Red Point
Loch na A-Oidhche
Loch a' Ghobhainn
875 BAOSBHEINN
855 BEINN AN EOIN
724
619 BEINN BHREAC
Loch a' Bhealaich
Beinn Eighe
Loch Torridon
Craig River
Kinlochewe
Rudha na Fearn
Fearnmore
Lower Diabaig
985 BEINN ALLIGIN
914 BEINN DEARG
1009 RUADH-STAC MÒR
972
Loch Diabaig
Fearnbeg
BEINN EIGHE
Arrina
Inveralligin
Alligin Shuas
1024 LIATHACH
1053
A896
Kenmore
Cuaig
Torridon House
Glen Torridon
Loch Clair
Upper Loch Torridon
Torridon
782 SGURR DUBH
Ardheslaig
Loch Shieldaig
Countryside Centre NTS
Loch Coulin
Shieldaig
Annat
492 AN GARBH-MHEALL
Wester Ross
493 CROIC-BHEINN
A896
Loch Damph
River Lair
958 SGORR RUADH
902 BEINN DAMPH
933 MAOL CHEAN-DEARG
Glenshieldaig Forest
209
907 FAUR THOLL
River Applecross
Loch Lundie
Achnashell Lodge
Balnacra
Loch Dughaill
Loch Coultrie
Coulags
Applecross Bay
895 BEINN BHAN
730 SGURR A GHARAIDH
A890
Applecross
626 Pass of the Cattle
Milton
774
Strathcarron
Camusteel
SGÙRR A'CHAORACHAIN
Rassal Ashwood
Achintee
Camusterrach
Bealach-Na-Ba
Kirkton
Aird Dhubh
A896
Kishorn
Culduie
594 CARN GEURADAINN
Lochcarron
Ardarroch
Loch Kishorn
Achintraid
Toscaig
Attadale
Slumbay
River Toscaig
Kishorn Island
394 BAD A CHREAMHA
Caolas Mòr
Ardaneaskan
Strome NTS
Ardnarff
Eilean Mòr
Loch Carron
Stromeferry
River Ling
Plockton
A890
Achmore
VLIN ISLANDS
Port-an-Eorna
447 BEINN RAIMH
Duirinish
Drumbuie
878 SGÙMAN COINNTICH
Killilan
Loch Long
Badicaul
Balmacara
Glen Elchaig
Conchra
Camas Luinie
Loch na Leitreach
Auchtertyre
Kyle of Lochalsh
Nostie
Bundalloch
Loch nan Eun
River Elchaig
Skye Bridge
Toll
Lochalsh Woodland NTS
Kirkton
Carndu
Ardelve
A87
Kylea
Eilean Donan
Dornie
200
Falls
Loch Alsh
A87
Keppoch
0 1 2 3 4 miles
0 1 2 3 4 5 kilometres
Upper Breakish
Letterfearn
840
916 A'GHLAS-

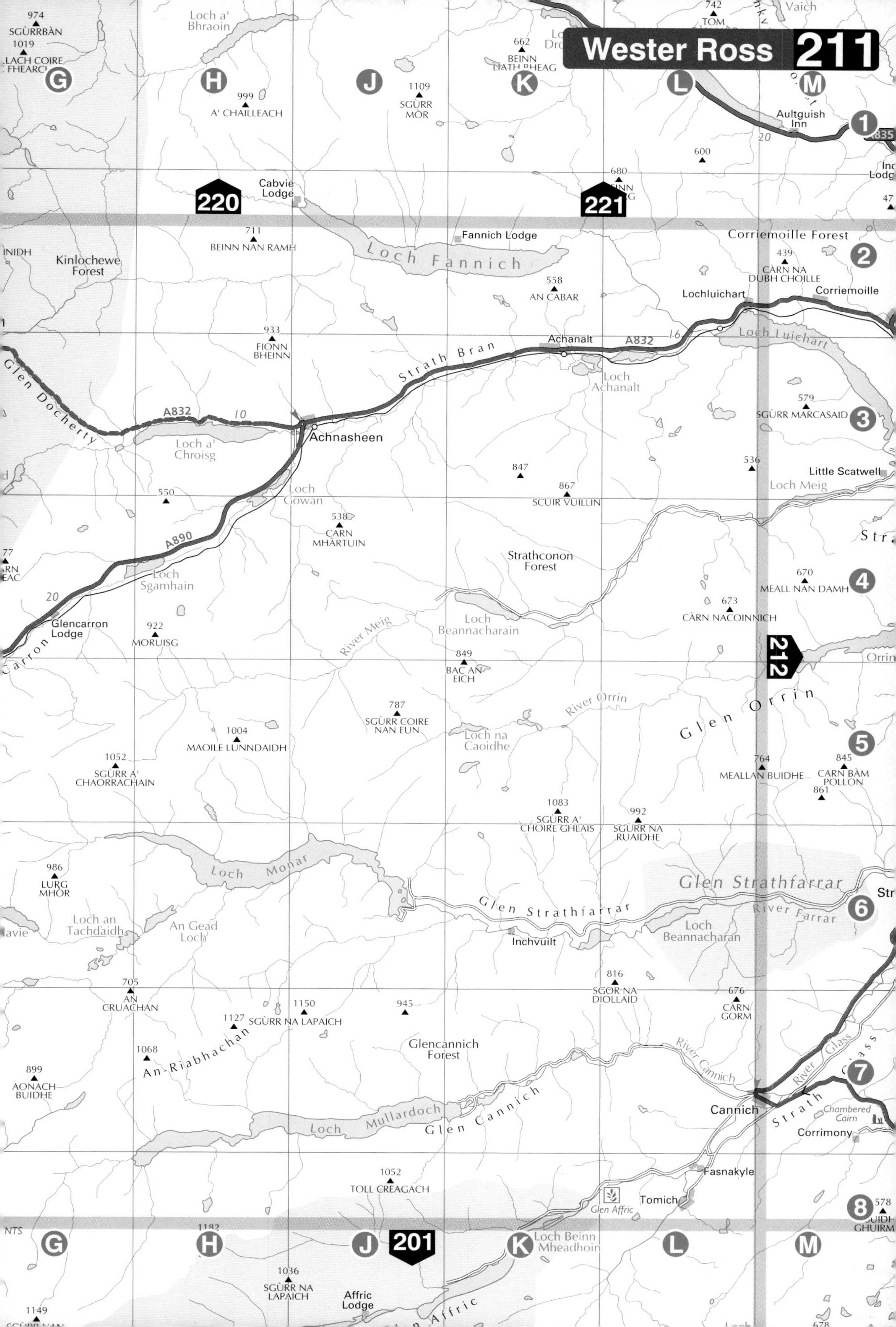

G
H
J
K
L
M
1
2
3
4
5
6
7
8
974
SGÙRRBÀN
1019
Loch a' Bhraoin
999
A' CHAILLEACH
1109
SGÙRR MÒR
662
BEINN LIATH MHEAG
742
TOM
Vaich
Aultguish Inn
A835
20
600
680
220
221
Cabvie Lodge
711
BEINN NAN RAMH
Fannich Lodge
Loch Fannich
Corriemoille Forest
439
CÀRN NA DUBH CHOILLE
Kinlochewe Forest
558
AN CABAR
Lochluichart
Corriemoille
933
FIONN BHEINN
Achanalt
A832
16
Loch Luichart
Strath Bran
Loch Achanalt
Glen Docherty
A832
10
Achnasheen
Loch a' Chroisg
579
SGÙRR MARCASAID
536
Little Scatwell
Loch Meig
847
867
SCUIR VUILLIN
550
Loch Gowan
538
CARN MHÀRTUIN
A890
Strathconon Forest
Loch Sgamhain
670
MEALL NAN DAMH
20
673
CÀRN NACOINNICH
Glencarron Lodge
922
MORUISG
Loch Beannacharain
River Meig
Carron
212
849
BAC AN EICH
Orrin
787
SGÙRR COIRE NAN EUN
River Orrin
Glen Orrin
1004
MAOILE LUNNDAIDH
Loch na Caoidhe
1052
SGÙRR A' CHAORRACHAIN
764
MEALLAN BUIDHE
845
CARN BÀM POLLON
861
1083
SGÙRR A' CHOIRE GHLAIS
992
SGÙRR NA RUAIDHE
Loch Monar
986
LURG MHOR
Glen Strathfarrar
River Farrar
Loch an Tachdaidh
An Gead Loch
Inchvuilt
Loch Beannacharan
705
AN CRUACHAN
816
SGOR NA DIOLLAID
676
CÀRN GORM
1150
1127
SGÙRR NA LAPAICH
945
1068
An-Riabhachan
Glencannich Forest
River Cannich
River Glass
899
AONACH BUIDHE
Cannich
Strath Glass
Chambered Cairn
Corrimony
Loch Mullardoch
Glen Cannich
1052
TOLL CREAGACH
Fasnakyle
Tomich
Glen Affric
578
NTS
1182
201
Loch Beinn Mheadhoin
1036
SGÙRR NA LAPAICH
Affric Lodge
1149
Affric

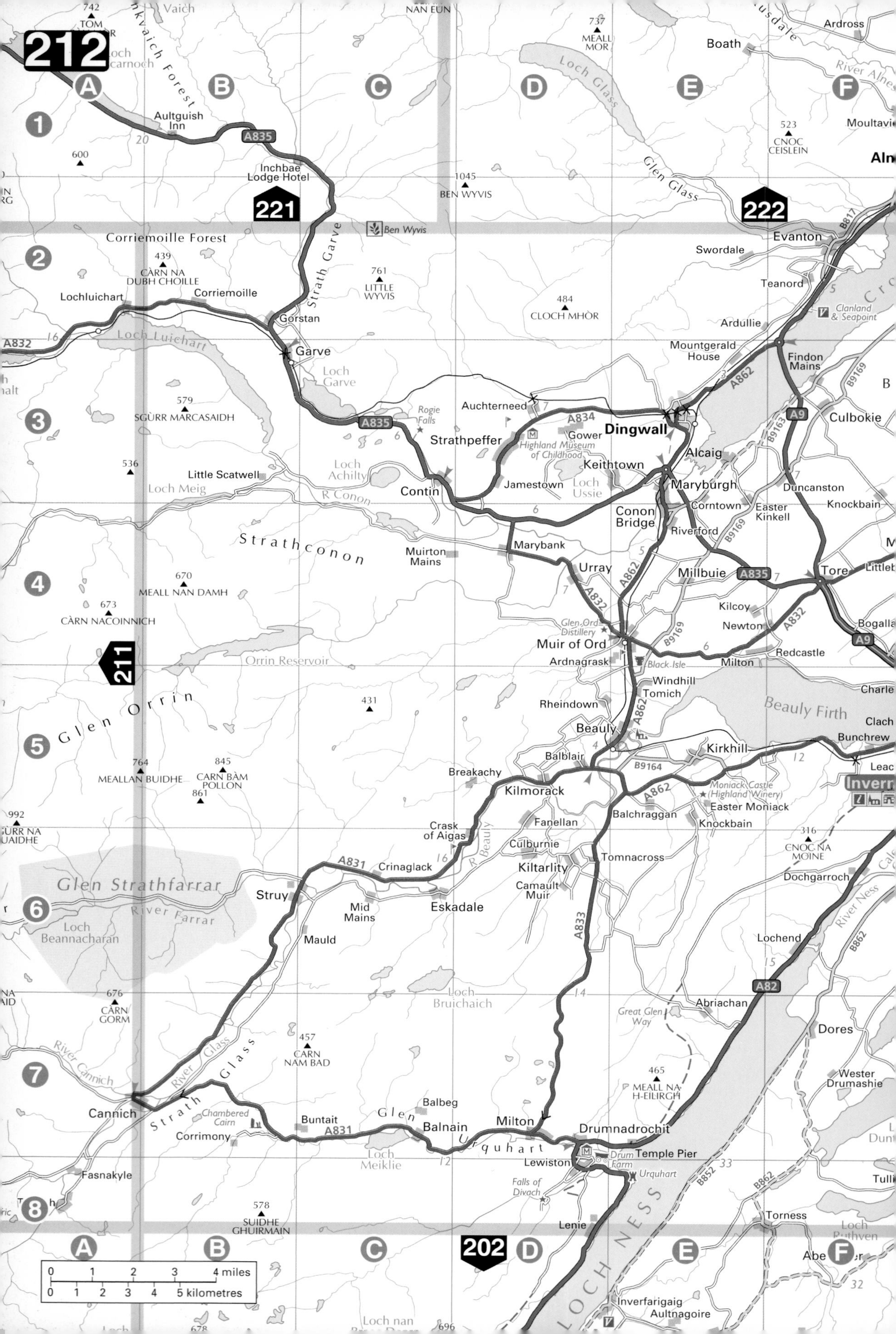
212
221
222
211
202
A
B
C
D
E
F
1
2
3
4
5
6
7
8
Aultguish Inn
A835
Inchbae Lodge Hotel
BEN WYVIS
Ben Wyvis
Loch Glass
Glen Glass
Boath
Ardross
River Alness
MEALL MOR
CNOC CEISLEIN
Moultavie
Evanton
Swordale
Teanord
Clanland & Seaport
Corriemoille Forest
CÀRN NA DUBH CHOILLE
Corriemoille
Lochluichart
Gorstan
Strath Garve
LITTLE WYVIS
CLOCH MHÒR
Ardullie
A832
Loch Luichart
Garve
Loch Garve
Mountgerald House
Findon Mains
SGÙRR MARCASAIDH
Auchterneed
Rogie Falls
Strathpeffer
A834
Dingwall
Gower
Highland Museum of Childhood
Culbokie
A862
A9
B9163
B9169
B817
Alcaig
Keithtown
Little Scatwell
Loch Meig
Loch Achilty
R Conon
Contin
Jamestown
Loch Ussie
Maryburgh
Duncanston
Conon Bridge
Corntown
Easter Kinkell
Knockbain
Riverford
Strathconon
Muirton Mains
Marybank
Urray
Millbuie
Tore
MEALL NAN DAMH
CÀRN NACOINNICH
Kilcoy
Newton
Glen Ord Distillery
Muir of Ord
Ardnagrask
Black Isle
Milton
Redcastle
Orrin Reservoir
Windhill
Tomich
Rheindown
Beauly Firth
Glen Orrin
Beauly
Balblair
Kirkhill
Bunchrew
B9164
MEALLAN BUIDHE
CARN BÀM POLLON
Breakachy
Kilmorack
Moniack Castle (Highland Winery)
Easter Moniack
Balchraggan
Knockbain
Fanellan
Crask of Aigas
R Beauly
Culburnie
Tomnacross
CNOC NA MOINE
A831
Crinaglack
Kiltarlity
Camault Muir
Dochgarroch
Glen Strathfarrar
River Farrar
Loch Beannacharan
Struy
Mid Mains
Eskadale
River Ness
Mauld
A833
Lochend
B862
CARN GORM
Loch Bruichaich
Abriachan
A82
Great Glen Way
River Cannich
River Glass
Strath Glass
CARN NAM BAD
Dores
Wester Drumashie
MEALL NA H-EILIRGH
Balbeg
Cannich
Chambered Cairn
Buntait
Glen Urquhart
Balnain
Milton
Drumnadrochit
Corrimony
Loch Meiklie
Lewiston
Drum Farm
Temple Pier
Urquhart
B852
Fasnakyle
Falls of Divach
SUIDHE GHUIRMAIN
Lenie
LOCH NESS
Torness
Loch Ruthven
0 1 2 3 4 miles
0 1 2 3 4 5 kilometres
Inverfarigaig
Aultnagoire
Loch nan

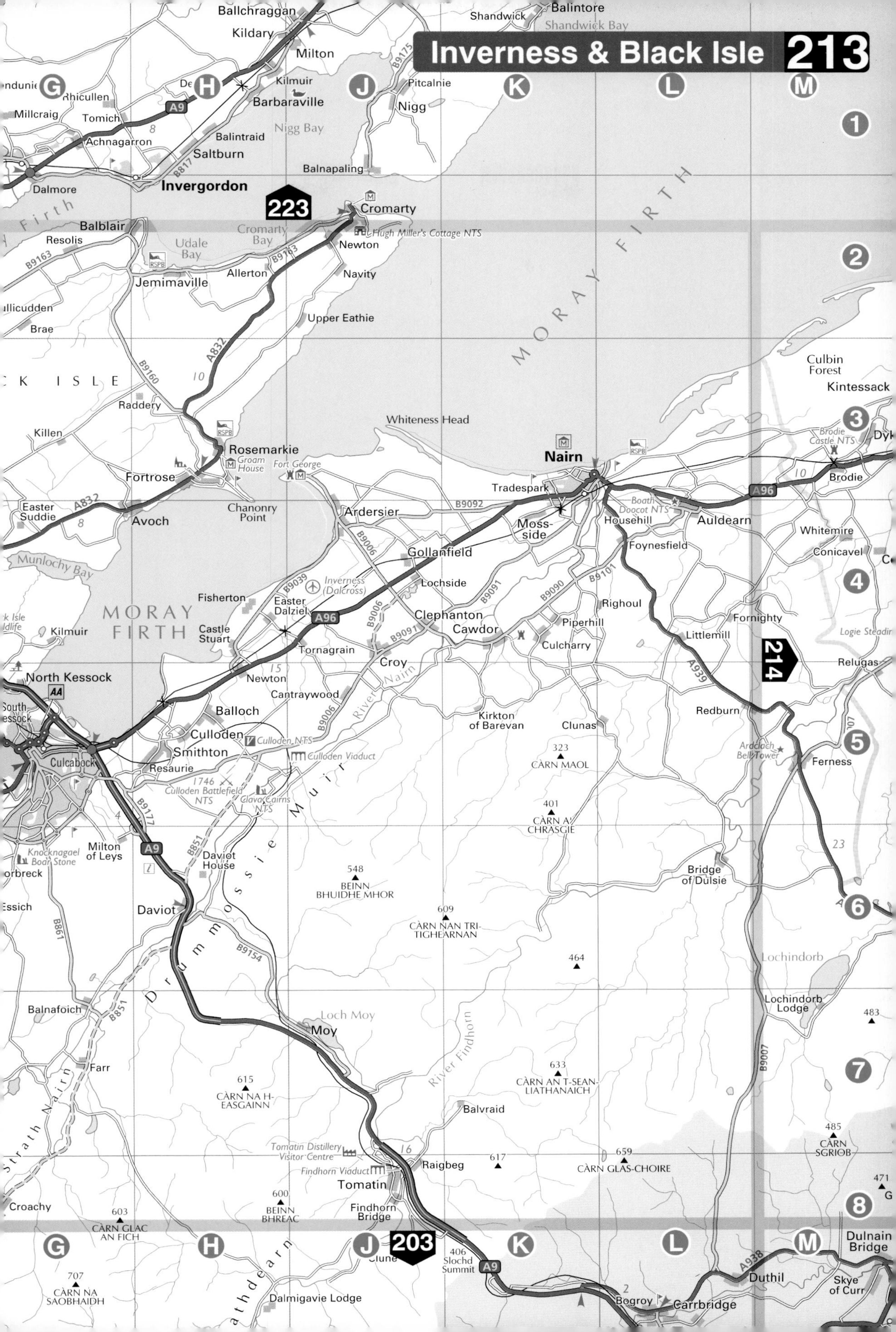

Ballchraggan
Kildary
Milton
Shandwick
Balintore
Shandwick Bay
Rhicullen
Millcraig
Tomich
Achnagarron
Kilmuir
Barbaraville
Pitcalnie
Nigg
Nigg Bay
Balintraid
Saltburn
Balnapaling
Dalmore
Invergordon
223
Cromarty
Balblair
Resolis
Udale Bay
Cromarty Bay
Hugh Miller's Cottage NTS
Newton
Jemimaville
Allerton
Navity
Upper Eathie
Brae
MORAY FIRTH
Culbin Forest
Kintessack
Raddery
Killen
Whiteness Head
Rosemarkie
Groam House
Fort George
Nairn
Brodie Castle NTS
Brodie
Fortrose
Tradespark
Easter Suddie
Avoch
Chanonry Point
Ardersier
Moss-side
Boath Doocot NTS
Househill
Auldearn
Whitemire
Munlochy Bay
Gollanfield
Foynesfield
Conicavel
Inverness (Dalcross)
Lochside
Fisherton
Easter Dalziel
Righoul
Kilmuir
Castle Stuart
Clephanton
Cawdor
Piperhill
Fornighty
Littlemill
Logie Steadir
Tornagrain
Croy
Culcharry
214
Relugas
North Kessock
Newton
River Nairn
Cantraywood
Balloch
Redburn
Kirkton of Barevan
Clunas
Culloden
Culloden NTS
Smithton
Culloden Viaduct
Ardclach Bell Tower
Ferness
Culcabock
Resaurie
323 CÀRN MAOL
1746 Culloden Battlefield NTS
Clava Cairns NTS
Drummossie Muir
401 CÀRN A' CHRASGIE
Knocknagael Boar Stone
Milton of Leys
Daviot House
Bridge of Dulsie
548 BEINN BHUIDHE MHOR
Daviot
609 CÀRN NAN TRI-TIGHEARNAN
464
Lochindorb
Lochindorb Lodge
Balnafoich
Loch Moy
Moy
483
Farr
River Findhorn
633 CÀRN AN T-SEAN-LIATHANAICH
615 CÀRN NA H-EASGAINN
Balvraid
Strath Nairn
485 CÀRN SGRIOB
Tomatin Distillery Visitor Centre
Findhorn Viaduct
Raigbeg
617
659 CÀRN GLAS-CHOIRE
471
Tomatin
600 BEINN BHREAC
Croachy
603 CÀRN GLAC AN FICH
Findhorn Bridge
Dulnain Bridge
203
Clune
406 Slochd Summit
Duthil
Skye of Curr
707 CÀRN NA SAOBHAIDH
Dalmigavie Lodge
Strathdearn
Bogroy
Carrbridge
A9
A96
A832
A939
A938
B9175
B817
B9163
B9160
B9092
B9006
B9039
B9091
B9090
B9101
B9177
B851
B861
B9154
B9007
G H J K L M
1 2 3 4 5 6 7 8

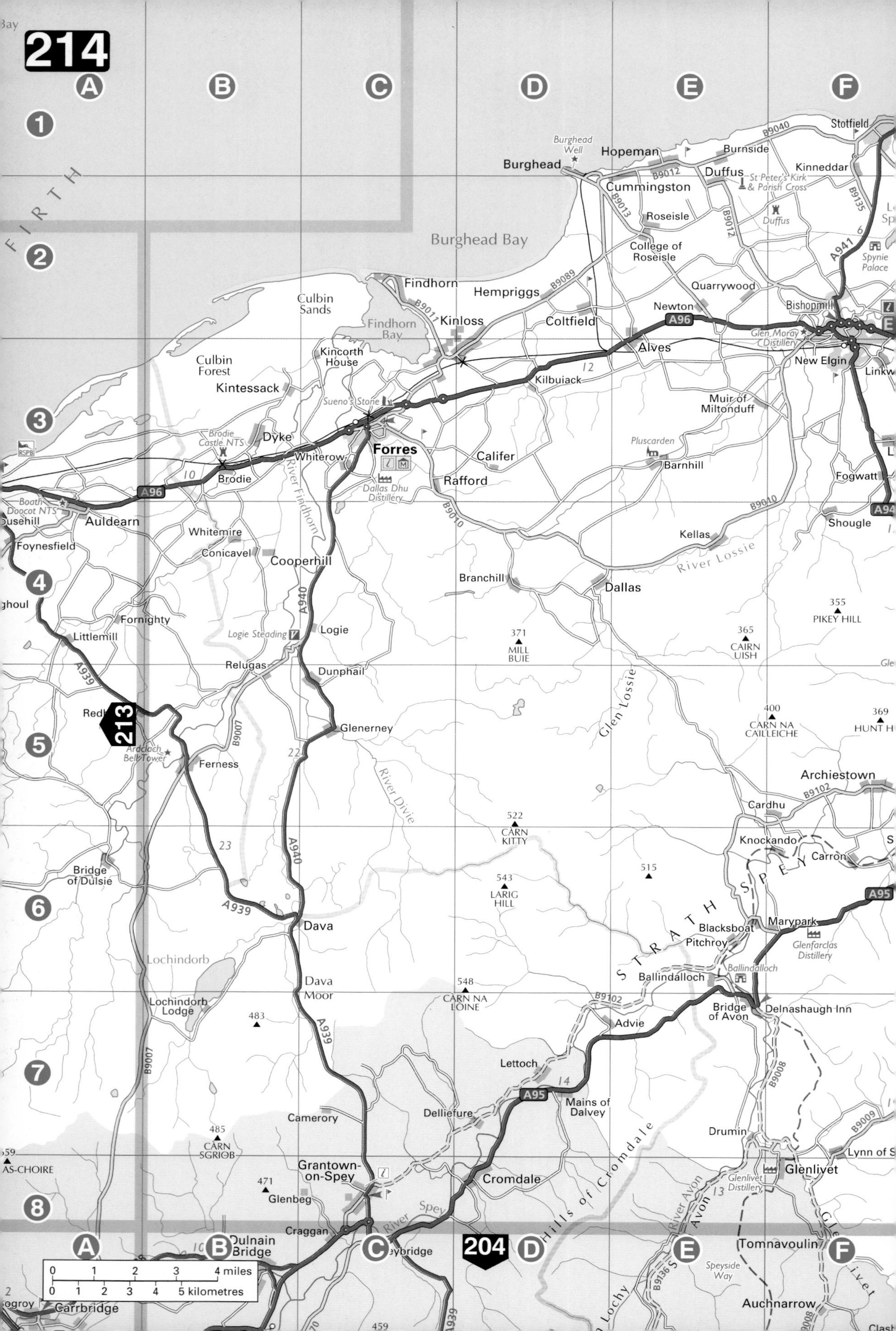
214
A
B
C
D
E
F
1
2
3
4
5
6
7
8
FIRTH
Burghead Bay
Burghead Well
Burghead
Hopeman
Burnside
Stotfield
Kinneddar
Duffus
St Peter's Kirk & Parish Cross
Cummingston
Roseisle
Duffus
College of Roseisle
Spynie Palace
Quarrywood
Findhorn
Hempriggs
Culbin Sands
Findhorn Bay
Kinloss
Coltfield
Newton
Bishopmill
Glen Moray Distillery
Alves
New Elgin
Linkw
Culbin Forest
Kincorth House
Kintessack
Kilbuiack
Muir of Miltonduff
Sueno's Stone
Brodie Castle NTS
Dyke
Forres
Califer
Pluscarden
Barnhill
RSPB
Whiterow
Brodie
Dallas Dhu Distillery
Rafford
Fogwatt
Boath Doocot NTS
Auldearn
Whitemire
Kellas
Shougle
Foynesfield
Conicavel
Cooperhill
River Findhorn
River Lossie
Branchill
Dallas
355
PIKEY HILL
Fornighty
Littlemill
Logie Steading
Logie
371
MILL BUIE
365
CAIRN UISH
Relugas
Dunphail
Glen Lossie
400
CARN NA CAILLEICHE
369
HUNT H
Glenerney
213
Ardclach Bell Tower
Ferness
River Divie
Archiestown
Cardhu
522
CARN KITTY
Knockando
Carron
Bridge of Dulsie
543
LARIG HILL
515
STRATH SPEY
Dava
Marypark
Blacksboat
Pitchroy
Glenfarclas Distillery
Lochindorb
Dava Moor
548
CARN NA LOINE
Ballindalloch
Lochindorb Lodge
483
Bridge of Avon
Delnashaugh Inn
Advie
Lettoch
Mains of Dalvey
Camerory
Delliefure
Drumin
485
CARN SGRIOB
Hills of Cromdale
Lynn of S
Glenlivet
Glenlivet Distillery
Grantown-on-Spey
Cromdale
471
Glenbeg
River Spey
River Avon
Craggan
Dulnain Bridge
204
Tomnavoulin
Speyside Way
Auchnarrow
Carrbridge
0 1 2 3 4 miles
0 1 2 3 4 5 kilometres
459
A96
A940
A939
A95
A941
B9007
B9008
B9009
B9010
B9011
B9012
B9013
B9040
B9089
B9102
B9135
B9136

A
B
C
D
E
F
1
2
3
4
5
6
7
8
Cullen Bay
Cullen
Findlater
Sandend Bay
Sandend
Portsoy
Boyndie Bay
Whitehills
Banff Bay
Banff
Macduff
Gamrie Bay
Gardenstown
Troup Head
Crovie
Tochieneal
Birkenbog
Inver-boyndie
Boyndie
Silverford
Dubford
Protstonhill
Fordyce
Milton
Duff House
Longmanhill
Gamrie
Deskford Church
Berryhillock
Windsole
Ella
Alvah
Clenerty
Minnonie
Netherbrae
Ord
221 BRACKLAMO HILL
Gorrachie
313 LURG HILL
Cornhill
Danshillock
River Deveron
Gordonstown
429 KNOCK HILL
Glenbarry
271 WETHER HILL
Fintry
Muirden
New Byth
Lootcherbrae
Knock
Drumnagorrach
Aberchirder
Garmond
Farmtown
Bridge of Marnoch
Turriff
Cuminestown
River Isla
Clunie
Carnousie
Rothiemay
Muiresk
Inverkeithny
Darra
Howe of Teuchar
Ruthven
215
Auchininna
Maryhill
Bogniebrae
Forgue
Fortrie
Birkenhills
Carlincraig
Glendronach Distillery
Pitglassie
Dykeside
Millbrex
Kirkton
Gourdas
Auchterless
Nordic Ski Centre
Affleck
Balgaveny
Cottown of Gight
Lethenty
Drumblade
Fyvie Castle NTS
R. Ythan
Gordonstown
Fyvie
Woodhead
Haddo
Brideswell
Badenscoth
Strath Bogie
Ythanwells
Rothiebrisbane
Thomastown
Fisherford
Rothienorman
Newtongarry Croft
Kirkstile
Bainshole
Glens of Foudland
St Katherines
Barthol Chapel
Earlsford
Culdrain
419 WICHACH HILL
466 HILL OF FOUDLAND
Culsalmond
Rothmaise
Newseat
Colpy
Tocher
Folla Rule
Cross of Jackston
Gartly
Meikle Wartle
Tulloch
Largie
Kirkton of Rayne
Leith Hall NTS
Picardy Symbol Stone
Old Rayne
Loanhead Stone Circle
Kennethmont
Dunnideer
Insch
Pitmachie
Hillhead of Durno
Daviot
Oldmeldrum
Clatt
Duncanstone
Whiteford
206
Carnbro
Kirkton
Archaeolink
Pitcaple
Maiden Stone
Kirktown of Bourtie
Auchleven
Pittodrie House Hotel
Chapel of Garioch
Whiterash
484 MIRE OF MIDGATES
Mither Tap
493
518
A98
A97
A95
A947
A96
A920
B9139
B9031
B9022
B9025
B9023
B9121
B9105
B9027
B9117
B9024
B9170
B9001
B992
B9002
0 1 2 3 4 miles
0 1 2 3 4 5 kilometres

G H J K L M
1 2 3 4 5 6 7 8
Rosehearty
Pittulie
Sandhaven
Lighthouse
Kinnaird Head
Fraserburgh
Peathill
Craigiefold
Kirktown
Fraserburgh Bay
Cairnbulg
Aberdour Bay
Percyhorner
Maggie's Hoosie
Inverallochy
Whitelinks Bay
B9031
Coburby
Pitblae
Mid Ardlaw
A90
B9033
New Aberdour
Boyndlie
B9032
Memsie
St Combs
A98
Memsie Cairn
Rathen
Crofts of Savoch
A981
Newburgh
Lonmay
Rattray Head
234 WAUGHTON HILL
RSPB Loch of Strathbeg
New Pitsligo
B9093
Strichen
Crimond
Blackhill
A952
New Leeds
B9093
Bonnykelly
Leys
Denhead
Backfolds
Kirktown
St Fergus
Fetterangus
Rora
A950
A981
Deer Abbey
Dunshillock
A90
River Ugie
Maud
B9106
New Deer
B9029
Aden
Mintlaw
Longside
Inverugie
Old Deer
Buchanhaven
Peterhead
Blackhill of Clackriach
A950
Peterhead Bay
A948
B9028
Drymuir
Bulwark
Stuartfield
Inverquhomery
A982
Millbreck
Nether Kinmundy
Hillhead of Cocklaw
Burnhaven
Nethermuir
Little Dens
Knaven
Clola
Buchan Ness
B9030
Kinnadie
Blackhill
Stirling
Boddam
Auchnagatt
Lendrum Terrace
Cairnorrie
Kinknockie
Brownhill
Blackhill
Longhaven
Inkhorn
Coldwells
A90
Bullers of Buchan
A948
A952
Hatton
Auchiries
North Haven
Arthrath
Muirtack
Slains
Cruden Bay
R Ythan
Bogbrae
Chapel Hill
Bay of Cruden
B9005
Ythanbank
A975
Birness
Whinnyfold
The Skares
Auchedly
Altar Tomb of William Forbes
Artrochie
Kinharrachie
Ythsie
Ellon
P+R
Esslemont
B9005
Kirkton of Logie Buchan
Kirktown of Slains
A920
Collieston
B999
Pitmedden
Logierieve
32
Forvie
Housieside
207
B9000
Udny Station
A90
Newburgh
Pettymuk
Cultercullen
Foveran
A975

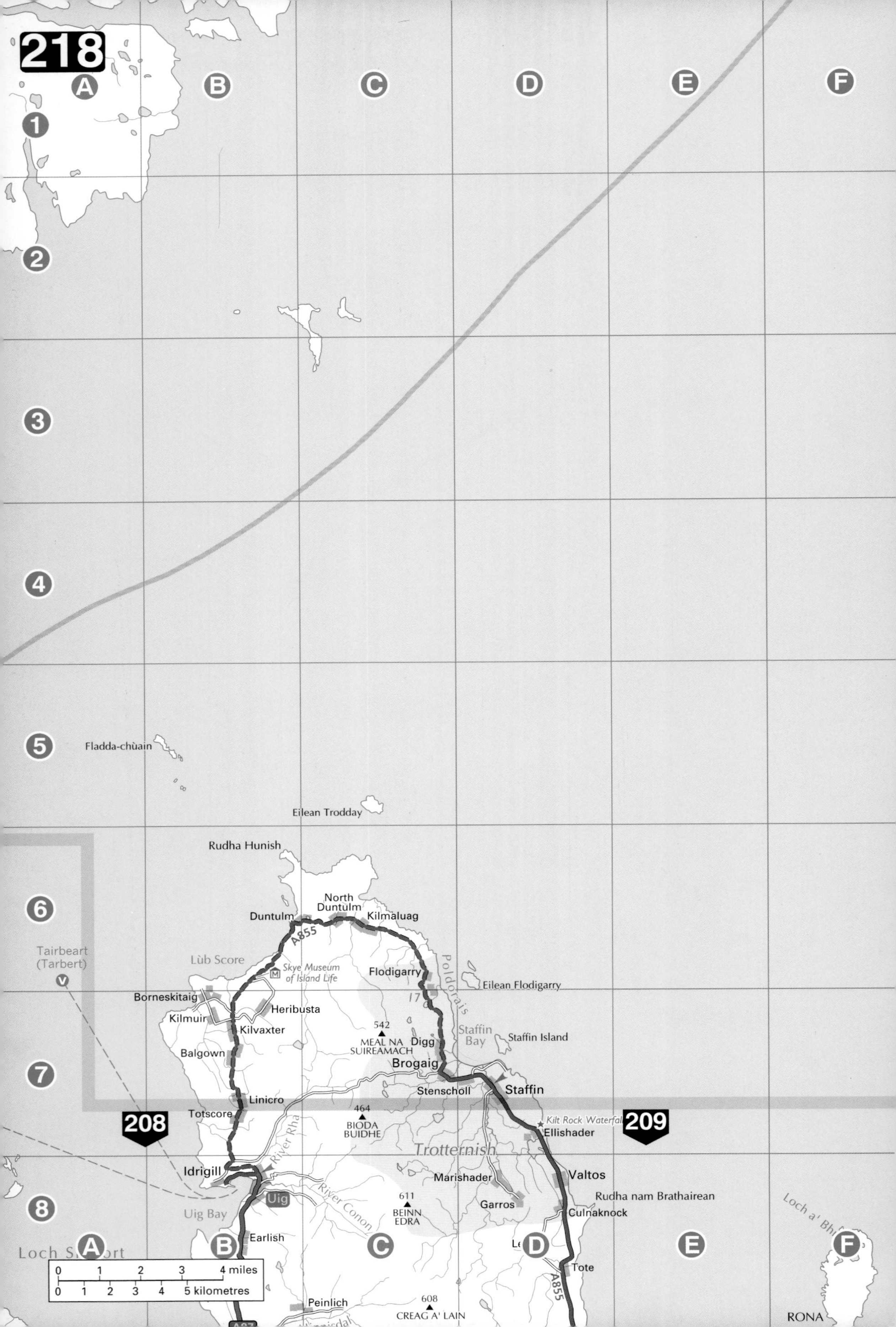
A
B
C
D
E
F
1
2
3
4
5
6
7
8
Fladda-chùain
Eilean Trodday
Rudha Hunish
North Duntulm
Duntulm
Kilmaluag
A855
Tairbeart (Tarbert)
Lùb Score
Skye Museum of Island Life
Flodigarry
Poldorais
Eilean Flodigarry
Borneskitaig
Heribusta
Kilmuir
Kilvaxter
542
MEAL NA SUIREAMACH
Digg
Staffin Bay
Staffin Island
Balgown
Brogaig
Stenscholl
Staffin
Linicro
Totscore
464
BIODA BUIDHE
Kilt Rock Waterfall
208
209
Ellishader
Trotternish
River Rha
Idrigill
Marishader
Valtos
River Conon
Uig
611
BEINN EDRA
Garros
Rudha nam Brathairean
Culnaknock
Uig Bay
Earlish
Loch Snizort
Tote
608
CREAG A' LAIN
Peinlich
RONA
0 1 2 3 4 miles
0 1 2 3 4 5 kilometres

G
H
J
K
L
M
Isle Ristol
Tanera Beg
Tanera Mòr
Steornabhagh (Stornoway)
Glas-leac Beag
Eilean Dubh
Priest Island
Greenstone Point
Cailleach Head
Rudha Beag
Stattic Point
Mellon Udrigle
GRUINARD ISLAND
Badluachrach
A832
Foura
Rudha Reidh
Cove
Laide
Gruinard Bay
Mellon Charles
Ormiscaig
Aultbea
Gruinard
Little Gruinard River
Gruinard River
296 AN CUAIDH
B8057
ISLE OF EWE
Melvaig
Aultgrishin
Loch Ewe
Loch Fada
347 CREAG-MHEAL BEAG
Inverasdale
220
293 CNOC BREAC
Naast
Inverewe Garden NTS
B8021
681 BEINN A' CHAISGEIN BEAG
250 MEALL NA MEINE
North Erradale
Londubh
Poolewe
Fionn
Wester Ross
Big Sand
Strath
A832
Smithstown
Lonemore
Auchtercairn
Heritage Museum
Longa Island
Loch Gairloch
Gairloch
Dubh Loch
791 BEINN AIRIDH CHARR
Eilean Horrisdale
Charlestown
421 MEALL AN DOIREIN
Port Henderson
B8056
Badachro
Opinan
Loch
859 BEINN LAIR
South Erradale
Loch Bad an Sgalaig
Loch Maree Hotel
Letterewe
Loch Garbhaig
Talladale
A832
Maree
Redpoint
981 SLIOCH
Loch Ghaineamhach
Red Point
210
875 BAOSBHEINN
Loch na h-Oidhche
855 BEINN AN EOIN
619 BEINN BHREAC
724
Loch a' Bhealaich
Loch Torridon
Craig River
Rudha na Fearn
Fearnmore
Lower Diabaig
1009 RUADH-STAC MÒR
914 BEINN DEARG
ALLIGIN
Òb Chuaig
Fearnbeg
Loch Diabaig
972
Inveralligin
BEINN EIGHE
Kinloch

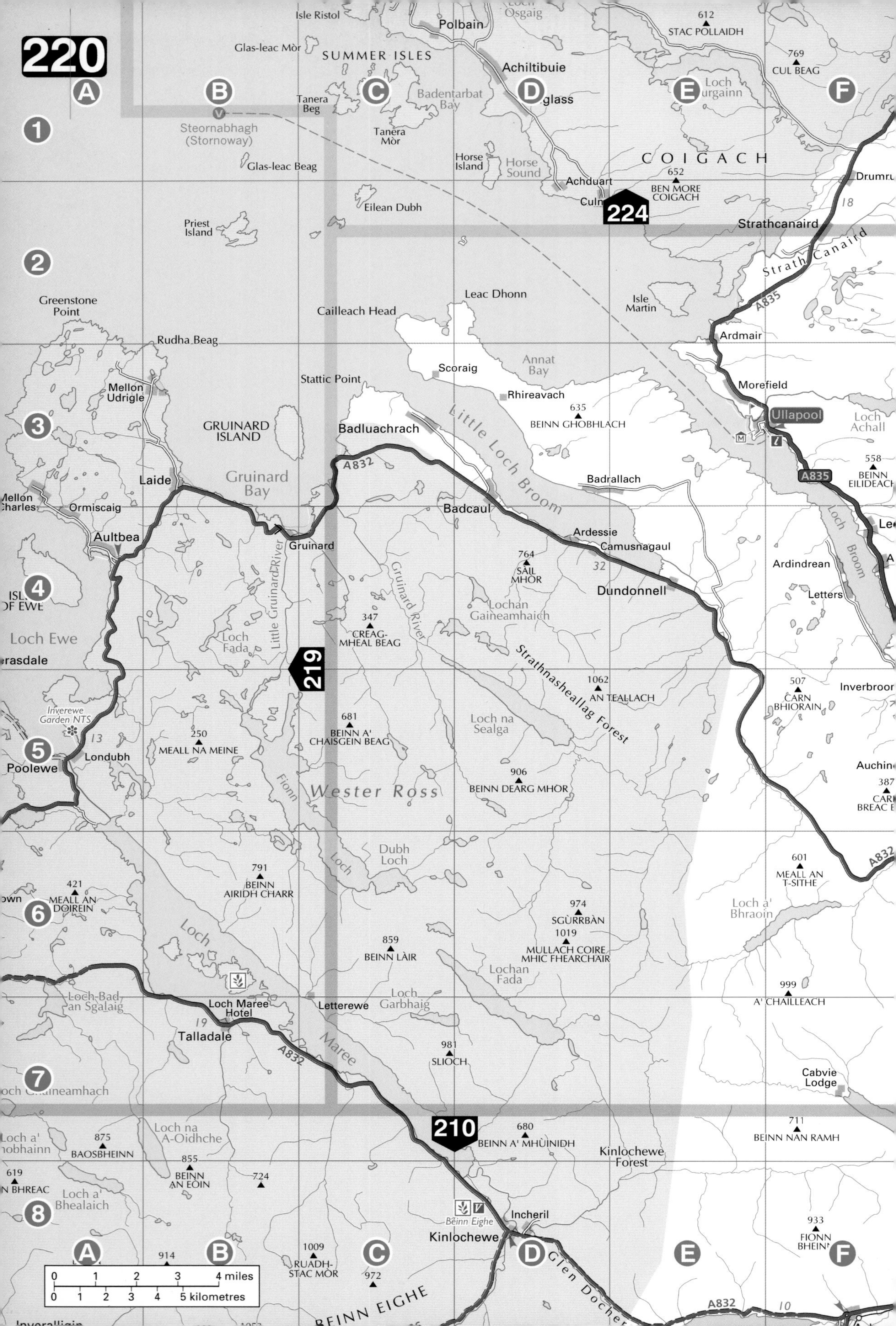

220
A
B
C
D
E
F
1
2
3
4
5
6
7
8
Isle Ristol
Polbain
Loch Osgaig
612
STAC POLLAIDH
Glas-leac Mòr
SUMMER ISLES
Achiltibuie
769
CUL BEAG
Loch Lurgainn
Tanera Beg
Badentarbat Bay
glass
Steornabhagh (Stornoway)
Tanera Mòr
Horse Island
Horse Sound
COIGACH
Glas-leac Beag
Achduart
652
BEN MORE COIGACH
Drumrunie
Culn
224
Eilean Dubh
18
Priest Island
Strathcanaird
Strath Canaird
A835
Greenstone Point
Cailleach Head
Leac Dhonn
Isle Martin
Ardmair
Rudha Beag
Scoraig
Annat Bay
Stattic Point
Morefield
Mellon Udrigle
Rhireavach
635
BEINN GHOBHLACH
Ullapool
Loch Achall
GRUINARD ISLAND
Badluachrach
Little Loch Broom
A832
558
BEINN EILIDEACH
Laide
Gruinard Bay
Badrallach
A835
Mellon Charles
Ormiscaig
Badcaul
Loch Broom
Aultbea
Gruinard
Ardessie
Camusnagaul
764
SAIL MHOR
32
Ardindrean
ISLE OF EWE
Little Gruinard River
Gruinard River
Dundonnell
Letters
Loch Ewe
347
CREAG-MHEAL BEAG
Lochan Gaineamhaich
Loch Fada
219
Strathnasheallag Forest
erasdale
1062
AN TEALLACH
507
CARN BHIORAIN
Inverbroom
Inverewe Garden NTS
681
BEINN A' CHAISGEIN BEAG
Loch na Sealga
13
250
MEALL NA MEINE
Poolewe
Londubh
906
BEINN DEARG MHOR
Auchindrean
387
CARN BREAC
Fionn
Wester Ross
Dubh Loch
Loch
601
MEALL AN T-SITHE
A832
791
BEINN AIRIDH CHARR
421
MEALL AN DOIREIN
974
SGÙRRBÀN
Loch a' Bhraoin
Loch
1019
MULLACH COIRE MHIC FHEARCHAIR
859
BEINN LÀIR
Lochan Fada
999
A' CHAILLEACH
Loch Bad an Sgalaig
Loch Maree Hotel
Letterewe
Loch Garbhaig
19
Talladale
Maree
A832
981
SLIOCH
Cabvie Lodge
210
680
BEINN A' MHÙINIDH
711
BEINN NAN RAMH
875
BAOSBHEINN
Loch na h-Oidhche
Kinlochewe Forest
855
BEINN AN EOIN
724
619
Loch a' Bhealaich
Beinn Eighe
Incheril
933
FIONN BHEINN
Kinlochewe
1009
RUADH-STAC MÒR
914
972
Glen Docherty
0 1 2 3 4 miles
0 1 2 3 4 5 kilometres
BEINN EIGHE
A832
10

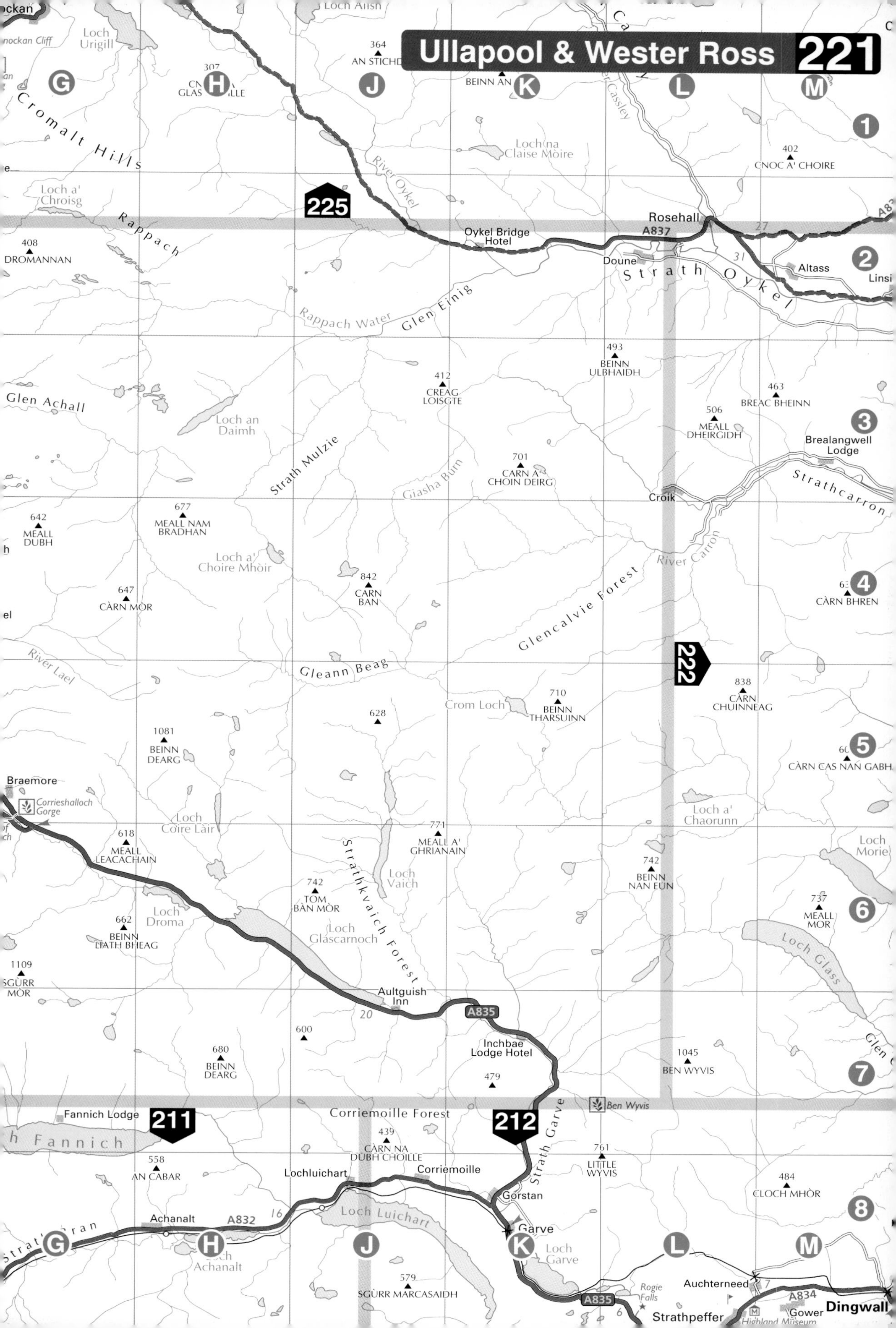
Ullapool & Wester Ross
221
Loch Urigill
Cromalt Hills
Loch a' Chroisg
Rappach
408
DROMANNAN
364
AN STICHD
BEINN AN
Loch na Claise Mòire
River Cassley
402
CNOC A' CHOIRE
River Oykel
225
Rosehall
A837
Oykel Bridge Hotel
Doune
Strath Oykel
Altass
Rappach Water
Glen Einig
493
BEINN ULBHAIDH
412
CREAG LOISGTE
463
BREAC BHEINN
506
MEALL DHEIRGIDH
Glen Achall
Loch an Daimh
Strath Mulzie
Giasha Burn
701
CARN A' CHOIN DEIRG
Brealangwell Lodge
Strathcarron
Croik
677
MEALL NAM BRADHAN
642
MEALL DUBH
Loch a' Choire Mhòir
842
CARN BAN
River Carron
Glencalvie Forest
647
CÀRN MOR
CÀRN BHREN
River Lael
Gleann Beag
222
838
CARN CHUINNEAG
Crom Loch
710
BEINN THARSUINN
628
1081
BEINN DEARG
CÀRN CAS NAN GABH
Braemore
Corrieshalloch Gorge
Loch Coire Lair
Loch a' Chaorunn
618
MEALL LEACACHAIN
771
MEALL A' GHRIANAIN
Loch Morie
Strathkvaich Forest
Loch Vaich
742
BEINN NAN EUN
742
TOM BAN MÒR
Loch Droma
737
MEALL MOR
662
BEINN LIATH BHEAG
Loch Glascarnoch
Loch Glass
1109
SGÙRR MÒR
Aultguish Inn
A835
20
600
Inchbae Lodge Hotel
680
BEINN DEARG
1045
BEN WYVIS
479
Ben Wyvis
Fannich Lodge
211
Loch Fannich
Corriemoille Forest
212
439
CÀRN NA DÙBH CHOILLE
Strath Garve
558
AN CABAR
761
LITTLE WYVIS
Lochluichart
Corriemoille
484
CLOCH MHÒR
Gorstan
Achanalt
A832
16
Loch Luichart
Garve
Strath Bran
Loch Achanalt
Loch Garve
579
SGÙRR MARCASAIDH
Rogie Falls
Auchterneed
A835
Strathpeffer
Highland Museum
A834
Gower
Dingwall

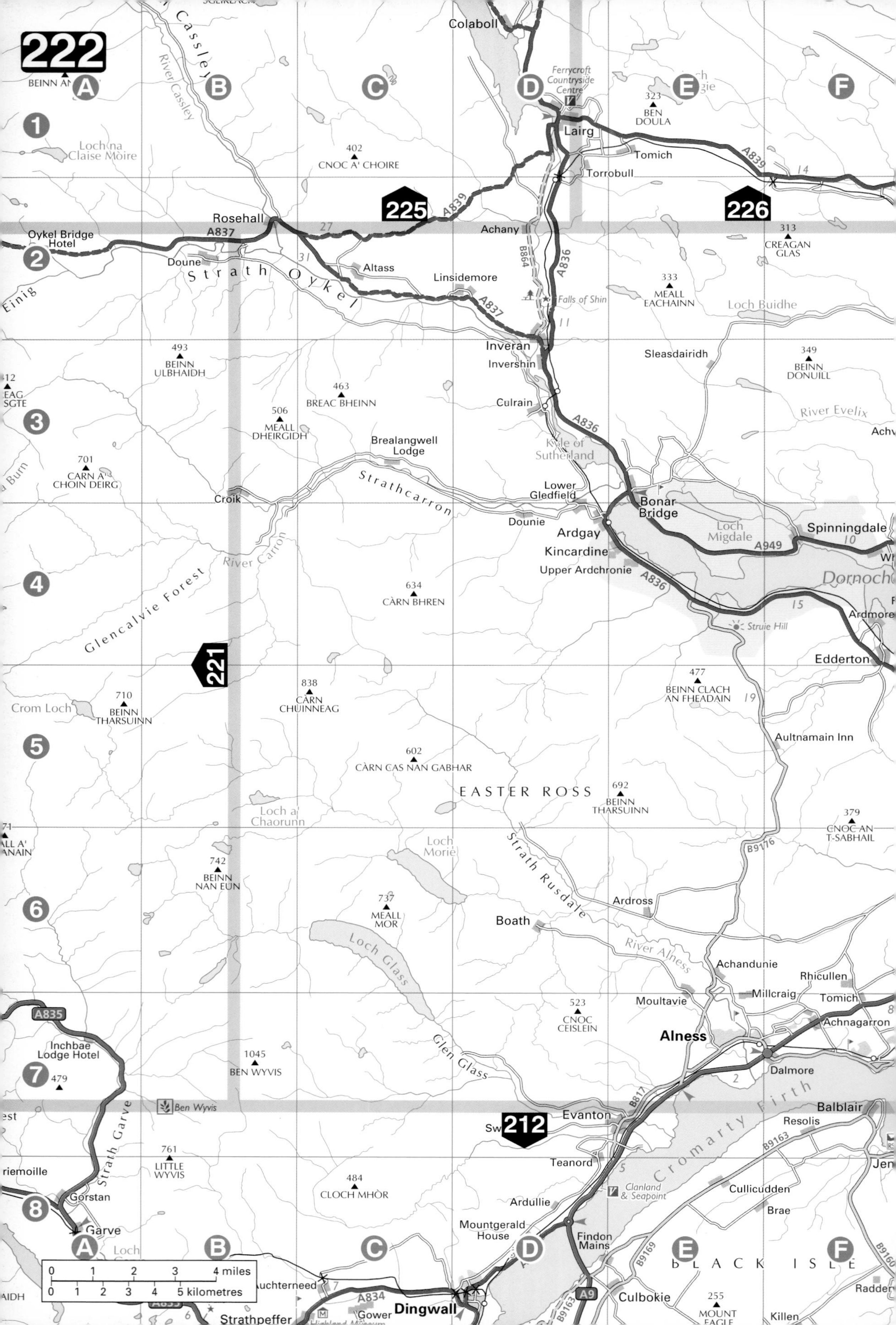
222
225
226
221
212
Colaboll
Ferrycroft Countryside Centre
Lairg
Tomich
Torrobull
323 BEN DOULA
402 CNOC A' CHOIRE
Loch na Claise Mòire
River Cassley
Rosehall
Oykel Bridge Hotel
A837
A839
A836
A949
A9
B864
Achany
313 CREAGAN GLAS
Doune
Strath Oykel
Altass
Linsidemore
Falls of Shin
333 MEALL EACHAINN
Loch Buidhe
Inveran
Invershin
Sleasdairidh
349 BEINN DONUILL
493 BEINN ULBHAIDH
463 BREAC BHEINN
506 MEALL DHEIRGIDH
Culrain
River Evelix
Brealangwell Lodge
Kyle of Sutherland
701 CARN A' CHOIN DEIRG
Strathcarron
Lower Gledfield
Croik
Bonar Bridge
Dounie
Ardgay
Loch Migdale
Spinningdale
Kincardine
Upper Ardchronie
Dornoch
River Carron
Glencalvie Forest
634 CÀRN BHREN
Ardmore
Struie Hill
Edderton
838 CÀRN CHUINNEAG
477 BEINN CLACH AN FHEADAIN
710 BEINN THARSUINN
Crom Loch
Aultnamain Inn
602 CÀRN CAS NAN GABHAR
EASTER ROSS
692 BEINN THARSUINN
Loch a' Chaorunn
379 CNOC AN T-SABHAIL
B9176
Loch Morie
Strath Rusdale
742 BEINN NAN EUN
737 MEALL MOR
Ardross
Boath
Loch Glass
River Alness
Achandunie
Rhicullen
Millcraig
Moultavie
Tomich
523 CNOC CEISLEIN
A835
Inchbae Lodge Hotel
Alness
Achnagarron
Glen Glass
1045 BEN WYVIS
Dalmore
479
Cromarty Firth
Ben Wyvis
Balblair
Evanton
B817
Strath Garve
Resolis
B9163
761 LITTLE WYVIS
Teanord
484 CLOCH MHÒR
Clanland & Seapoint
Cullicudden
Gorstan
Ardullie
Brae
Garve
Mountgerald House
Findon Mains
B9169
BLACK ISLE
B9160
0 1 2 3 4 miles
0 1 2 3 4 5 kilometres
Auchterneed
A834
Culbokie
255 MOUNT EAGLE
Dingwall
Gower
Strathpeffer
Killen

LEAMHNACHD
Strath Brora
River Brora
Dalreavoch Lodge
COL-BHEINN
Lothbeg
Loch Horn
520 BEN HORN
Dalchalm
Brora
378 CAGAR FEOSAIG
Golspie Burn
Doll
227
446 BEN LUNDIE
Backies
A9
383 BEN BHRAGGIE
Rhives
Carn Liath
Dunrobin Castle
Golspie
Torboll
Cambusavie Platform
Loch Fleet
Badninish
Skelbo
Skelbo Street
Fourpenny
Embo
Birichin
B9168
Embo Street
Pitgrudy
Evelix
A949
Camore
Dornoch
A9
Cuthill
Dornoch Firth
Tarbat Ness
Wilkhaven
Brucefield
Innis Mhor
Ferry Point
Portmahomack
Glenmorangie Distillery
Morangie
Inver
Rockfield
B9165
Arboll
284
Tain
Toulvaddie
Loch Eye
Rhynie
Fearn
Balmuchy
B9165
Hill of Fearn
Hilton of Cadboll Chapel (ruin)
Newfield
Tullich
B9166
Hilton
Arabella
Balintore
Ballchraggan
Shandwick
Shandwick Bay
Kildary
Ankerville
Milton
B9175
Kilmuir
Pitcalnie
Barbaraville
Nigg
Nigg Bay
Balintraid
Balnapaling
Cromarty
Cromarty Bay
Hugh Miller's Cott NTS
213
214
Newton
B9163
Allerton
Navity
MORAY FIRTH
Burghead
Findhorn
Culbin Sands
B9011
Findhorn Bay
Upper Eathie
A832
Kincorth House
Culbin Forest
Kintessack
Sueno's Stone
Whiteness Head
Brodie Castle NTS
Dyke
Forres
RSPB

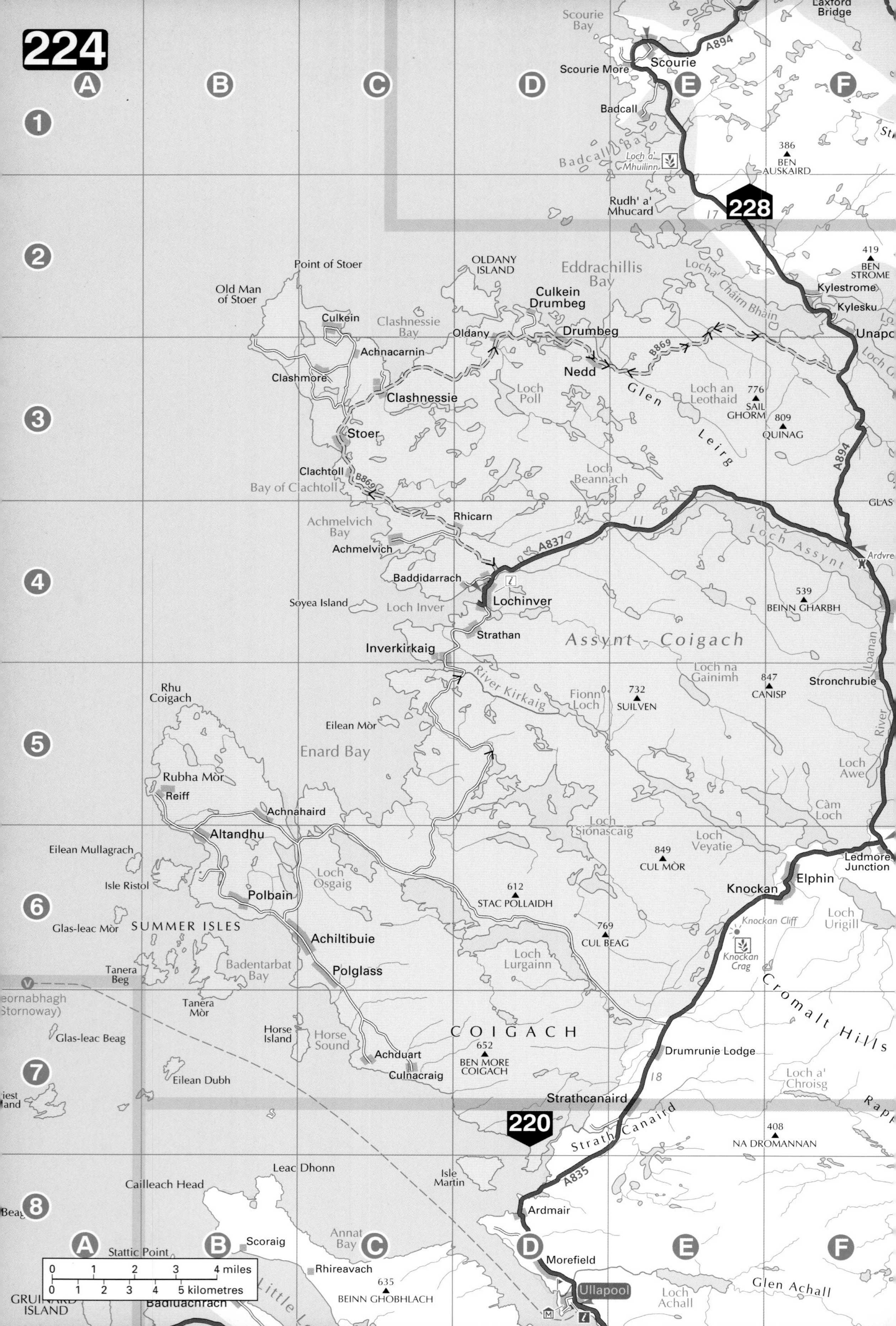

Scourie Bay
Scourie
Scourie More
Laxford Bridge
A894
Badcall
Badcall Bay
Loch a' Mhuilinn
386 BEN AUSKAIRD
228
Rudh' a' Mhucard
419 BEN STROME
Kylestrome
Kylesku
Loch a' Chàirn Bhàin
Eddrachillis Bay
OLDANY ISLAND
Point of Stoer
Old Man of Stoer
Culkein
Clashnessie Bay
Culkein Drumbeg
Drumbeg
Oldany
Achnacarnin
Clashmore
Clashnessie
Nedd
B869
Glen Leirg
Loch Poll
Loch an Leothaid
776 SAIL GHORM
809 QUINAG
Stoer
Clachtoll
Bay of Clachtoll
Loch Beannach
A894
Rhicarn
Achmelvich Bay
Achmelvich
A837
Loch Assynt
Ardvreck
Baddidarrach
Lochinver
Soyea Island
Loch Inver
539 BEINN GHARBH
Strathan
Inverkirkaig
Assynt - Coigach
Loch na Gainimh
847 CANISP
Stronchrubie
River Kirkaig
Fionn Loch
732 SUILVEN
Rhu Coigach
Eilean Mòr
Enard Bay
Rubha Mòr
Reiff
Achnahaird
Loch Awe
Càm Loch
Altandhu
Loch Sionascaig
Loch Veyatie
849 CUL MÒR
Eilean Mullagrach
Isle Ristol
Polbain
Loch Osgaig
612 STAC POLLAIDH
Knockan
Elphin
Ledmore Junction
Glas-leac Mòr
SUMMER ISLES
Achiltibuie
769 CUL BEAG
Knockan Cliff
Knockan Crag
Loch Urigill
Tanera Beg
Badentarbat Bay
Polglass
Loch Lurgainn
Cromalt Hills
Steornabhagh (Stornoway)
Tanera Mòr
Glas-leac Beag
Horse Island
Horse Sound
COIGACH
Achduart
Culnacraig
652 BEN MORE COIGACH
Drumrunie Lodge
Loch a' Chroisg
Eilean Dubh
Strathcanaird
220
Strath Canaird
408 NA DROMANNAN
A835
Leac Dhonn
Isle Martin
Cailleach Head
Ardmair
Static Point
Scoraig
Annat Bay
Morefield
Rhireavach
635 BEINN GHOBHLACH
Ullapool
Loch Achall
Glen Achall
Gruinard Island
Badluachrach
0 1 2 3 4 miles
0 1 2 3 4 5 kilometres
A B C D E F
1 2 3 4 5 6 7 8

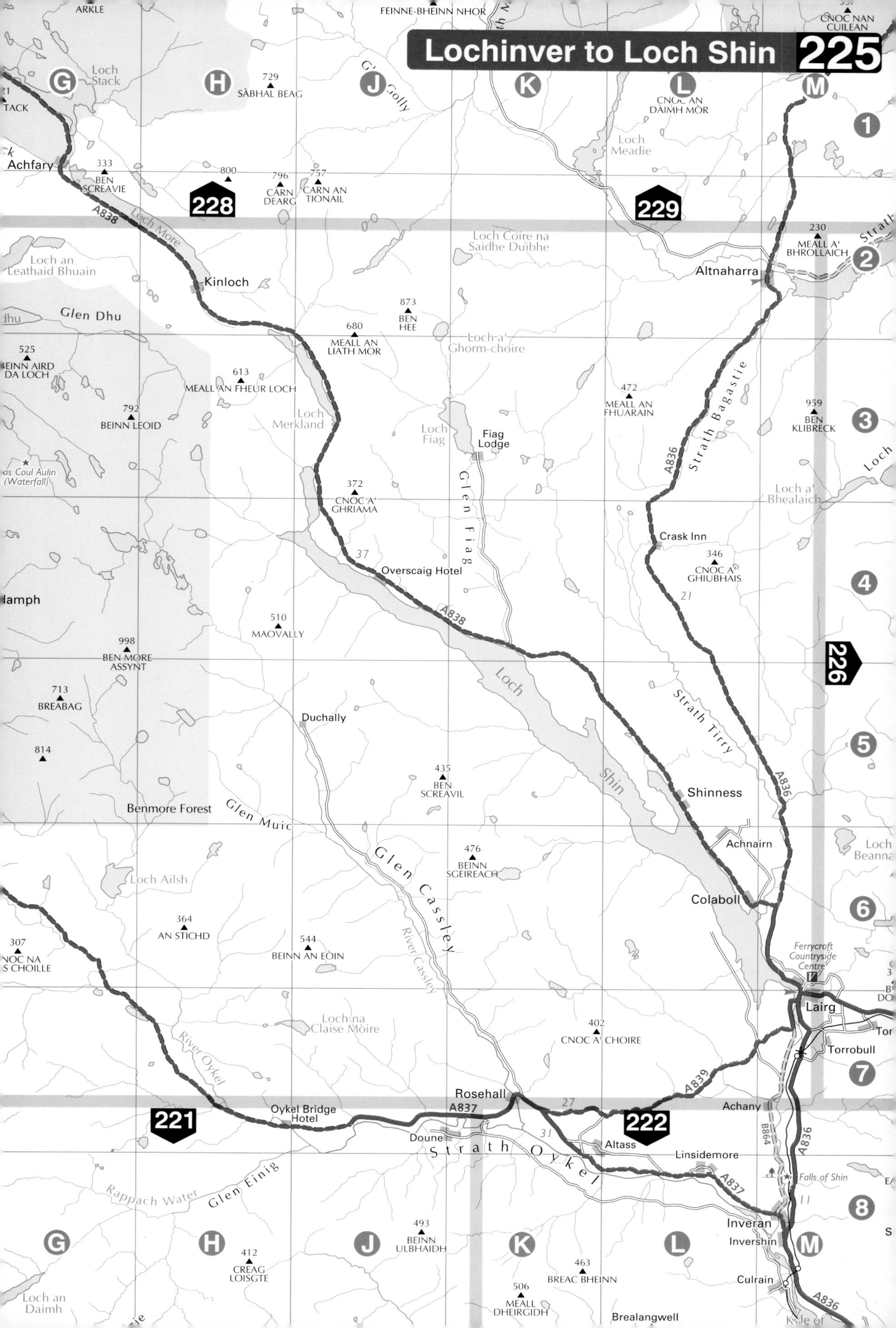
ARKLE
FEINNE-BHEINN NHOR
CNOC NAN CUILEAN
Loch Stack
729 SÀBHAL BEAG
CNOC AN DÀIMH MÒR
Loch Meadie
Achfary
333 BEN SCREAVIE
800
796 CARN DEARG
757 CARN AN TIONAIL
228
229
A838
Loch More
Loch Coire na Saidhe Duibhe
230 MEALL A' BHROLLAICH
Loch an Leathaid Bhuain
Kinloch
Altnaharra
Glen Dhu
873 BEN HEE
680 MEALL AN LIATH MOR
Loch a' Ghorm-choire
525 BEINN AIRD DA LOCH
613 MEALL AN FHEUR LOCH
472 MEALL AN FHUARAIN
Strath Bagastie
959 BEN KLIBRECK
792 BEINN LEOID
Loch Merkland
Loch Fiag
Fiag Lodge
A836
Glen Fiag
Loch a' Bhealaich
372 CNOC A' GHRIAMA
Crask Inn
37
Overscaig Hotel
346 CNOC A' GHIUBHAIS
21
510 MAOVALLY
A838
998 BEN-MORE ASSYNT
226
Loch Shin
713 BREABAG
Duchally
Strath Tirry
814
435 BEN SCREAVIL
A836
Shinness
Benmore Forest
Glen Muic
Achnairn
476 BEINN SGEIREACH
Loch Ailsh
Glen Cassley
Colaboll
364 AN STICHD
307
544 BEINN AN EÒIN
River Cassley
Ferrycroft Countryside Centre
Lairg
Loch na Claise Mòire
402 CNOC A' CHOIRE
River Oykel
Torrobull
A839
Rosehall
27
Achany
221
Oykel Bridge Hotel
A837
222
Doune
31
Altass
Strath Oykel
Linsidemore
B864
A836
Falls of Shin
Rappach Water
Glen Einig
A837
11
493 BEINN ULBHAIDH
Inveran
Invershin
412 CREAG LOISGTE
463 BREAC BHEINN
Culrain
A836
506 MEALL DHEIRGIDH
Loch an Daimh
Brealangwell
G H J K L M
1 2 3 4 5 6 7 8

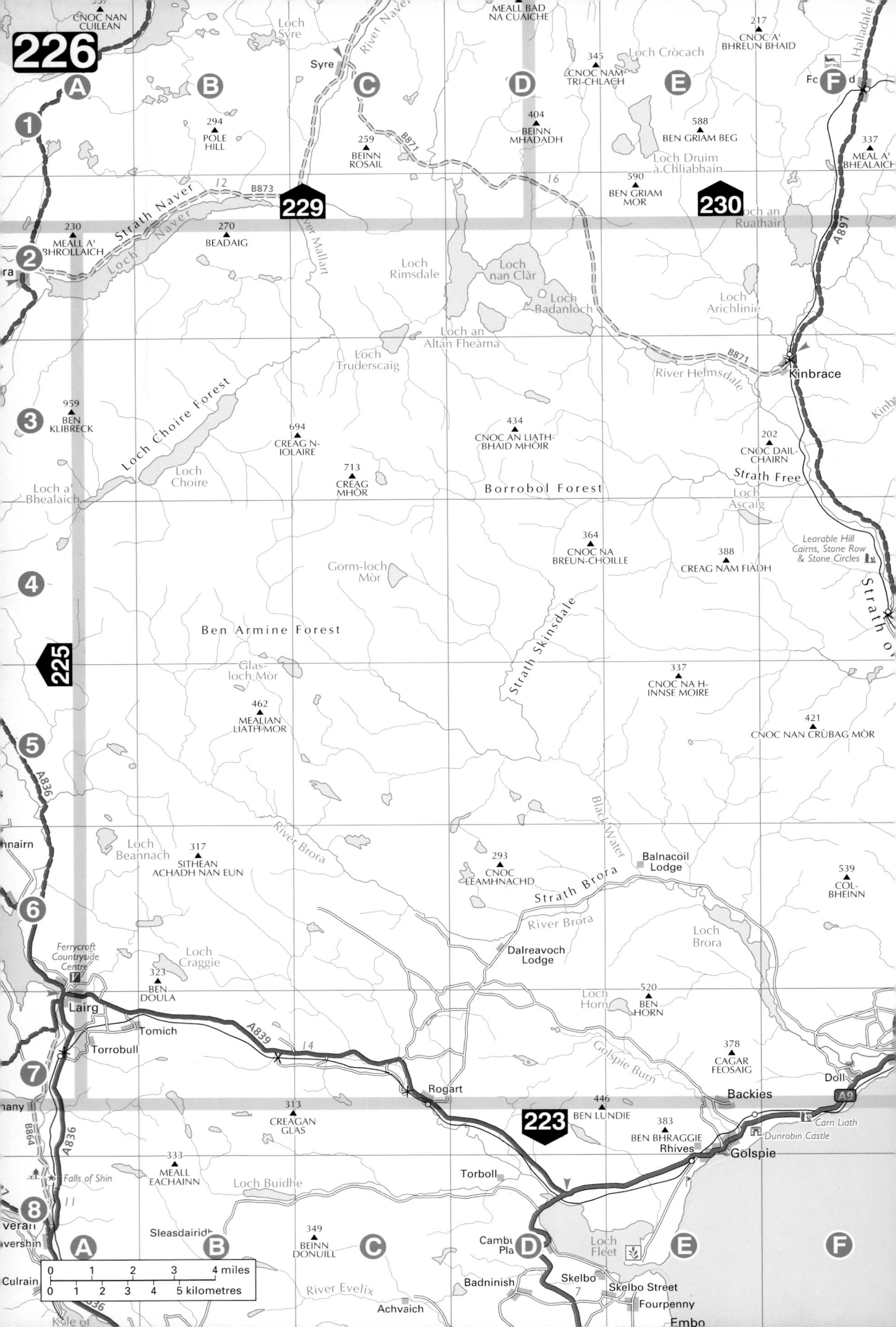
226
229
230
225
223
CNOC NAN CUILEAN
Loch Syre
Syre
River Naver
MEALL BAD NA CUAICHE
345 CNOC NAM TRI-CHLACH
Loch Cròcach
217 CNOC A' BHREUN BHAID
Halladale
294 POLE HILL
259 BEINN ROSAIL
B871
404 BEINN MHADADH
588 BEN GRIAM BEG
337 MEAL A' BHEALAICH
Loch Druim a' Chliabhain
590 BEN GRIAM MOR
B873
Strath Naver
Loch Naver
230 MEALL A' BHROLLAICH
270 BEADAIG
River Mallart
Loch Rimsdale
Loch nan Clàr
Loch Badanloch
Loch an Ruathair
A897
Loch Arichlinie
Loch an Altan Fheàrna
Loch Truderscaig
River Helmsdale
Kinbrace
959 BEN KLIBRECK
Loch Choire Forest
694 CREAG N-IOLAIRE
713 CREAG MHÒR
434 CNOC AN LIATH-BHAID MHÒIR
202 CNOC DAIL-CHAIRN
Strath Free
Loch Choire
Loch a' Bhealaich
Borrobol Forest
Loch Ascaig
364 CNOC NA BREUN-CHOILLE
388 CREAG NAM FIADH
Learable Hill Cairns, Stone Row & Stone Circles
Gorm-loch Mòr
Ben Armine Forest
Strath Skinsdale
Glas-loch Mòr
337 CNOC NA H-INNSE MOIRE
462 MEALIAN LIATH MOR
421 CNOC NAN CRÙBAG MÒR
A836
Black Water
River Brora
Loch Beannach
317 SITHEAN ACHADH NAN EUN
293 CNOC LEAMHNACHD
Balnacoil Lodge
539 COL-BHEINN
Strath Brora
River Brora
Loch Brora
Ferrycroft Countryside Centre
Loch Craggie
Dalreavoch Lodge
323 BEN DOULA
Lairg
Tomich
Torrobull
Loch Horn
520 BEN HORN
A839
Golspie Burn
378 CAGAR FEOSAIG
Rogart
Doll
Backies
A9
313 CREAGAN GLAS
446 BEN LUNDIE
383 BEN BHRAGGIE
Rhives
Carn Liath
Dunrobin Castle
Golspie
B864
A836
Falls of Shin
333 MEALL EACHAINN
Loch Buidhe
Torboll
Sleasdairidh
349 BEINN DONUILL
Loch Fleet
Culrain
River Evelix
Badninish
Skelbo
Skelbo Street
Fourpenny
Achvaich
Embo
0 1 2 3 4 miles
0 1 2 3 4 5 kilometres

SLETILL HILL
Altnabreac Station
CNOC NAN GALL
Rumsdale Water
Strathmore
Dalnawillan Lodge
Loch an Thulachan
Loch Sand
Achavanich
Loch Stemster
248
STEMSTER HILL
Loch Rangag
226
COIRE NA BEINN
Glutt Water
230
348
BEN ALISKY
231
287
BEN-A-CHIELT
Upper Lybster
Glutt Lodge
264
CNOCAN CONACHREAG
Forse House
Swiney
Lybster
Inversho re
Lybster Bay
Forse
440
KNOCKFIN HEIGHTS
Houstry
Land-hallow
Smerral
Latheron
Dunbeath Water
317
CNOC LOCH MHADADH
Latheronwheel
Janetstown
Berriedale Water
A9
Laidhay Croft Museum
437
Braemore
Dunbeath
484
MAIDEN PAP
705
MORVEN
Knockally
518
CNOC AN EIREANNAICH
Ramscraigs
626
SCARABEN
Borgue
Langwell Forest
Newport
554
CREAG SCALABSDALE
Langwell House
Berriedale
Lodge
416
BEINN DUBHAIN
401
CNOC NA MAOILE
A897
404
CREAG THORARAIDH
Torrish
River Helmsdale
Ord of Caithness
Navidale House Hotel
Timespan
East Helmsdale
West Helmsdale
624
591
BEINN NA MEILICH
Helmsdale
Gartymore
Portgower
Glen Loth
Lothmore
Lothbeg
G
H
J
K
L
M
1
2
3
4
5
6
7
8

CAPE WRATH
Cléit Dhubh
371 SGRIBHIS-BHEINN
Faraid Head
297 CNOC A GHIUBHAIS
300 MAOVALLY
Balnakeil Bay
Balnakeil
Sango Bay
THE PARPH
Durness
457 FASHVEN
Sangomore
Smoo
Sandwood Bay
Loch Airigh na Beinne
Keoldale
Sangobeg
Kyle of Durness
Loch Meadaidh
Sandwood Loch
485 CREAG RIABACH
468 BEINN DEARG MHÒR
464 MEALL NA MOINE
423 MEALL MEADHONACH
Rudh' an Fhir Leithe
Strath Shinary
331 GHLAS-BHEINN
A838
Sheigra
Balchreick
Blairmore
Laid
489 MEALL NA CRÀ
Oldshoremore
521 FARVEALL
355 AN SOCACH
773 BEINN SPIONNAIDH
Kinlochbervie
Loch Clash
Badcall
B801
801 CRANSTACKIE
Loch Inchard
Achriesgill
Strath Dionard
River Dionard
Strath Beag
A838
520 AN LEAN-CHA
Rhiconich
Loch na Claise Càrnaich
Rudha Ruadh
908 FOINAVEN
Skerricha
Fanagmore
Tarbet
Loch Laxford
Foindle
HANDA ISLAND
North-west Sutherland
Loch na Tuadh
Laxford Bridge
River Laxford
786 ARKLE
Scourie Bay
FEINNE
A894
Scourie
Scourie More
Loch Stack
729 SÀBHAL BEAG
Glen Golly
Badcall
721 BEN STACK
Strath Stack
Badcall Bay
Loch a' Mhuilinn
386 BEN AUSKAIRD
Achfary
333 BEN SCREAVIE
800
796 CARN DEARG
757 CARN AN TIONAIL
Rudh' a' Mhucard
A838
Loch More

224
225

OLDANY ISLAND
Eddrachillis Bay
419 BEN STROME
Loch an Leathaid-Bhuain
Kinloch
Loch a' Chàirn Bhàin
Kylestrome
Culkein Drumbeg
Kylesku
Loch Glendhu
Glen Dhu
Drumbeg
Unapool
680 MEALL AN LIATH MOR
B869
525 BEINN A' DA LOCH
Nedd
Loch Glencoul
613 MEALL AN FHEUR LOCH
776 SAIL GHORM
809 QUINAG
792 BEINN LEOID
Loch Merkland
0 1 2 3 4 miles
0 1 2 3 4 5 kilometres

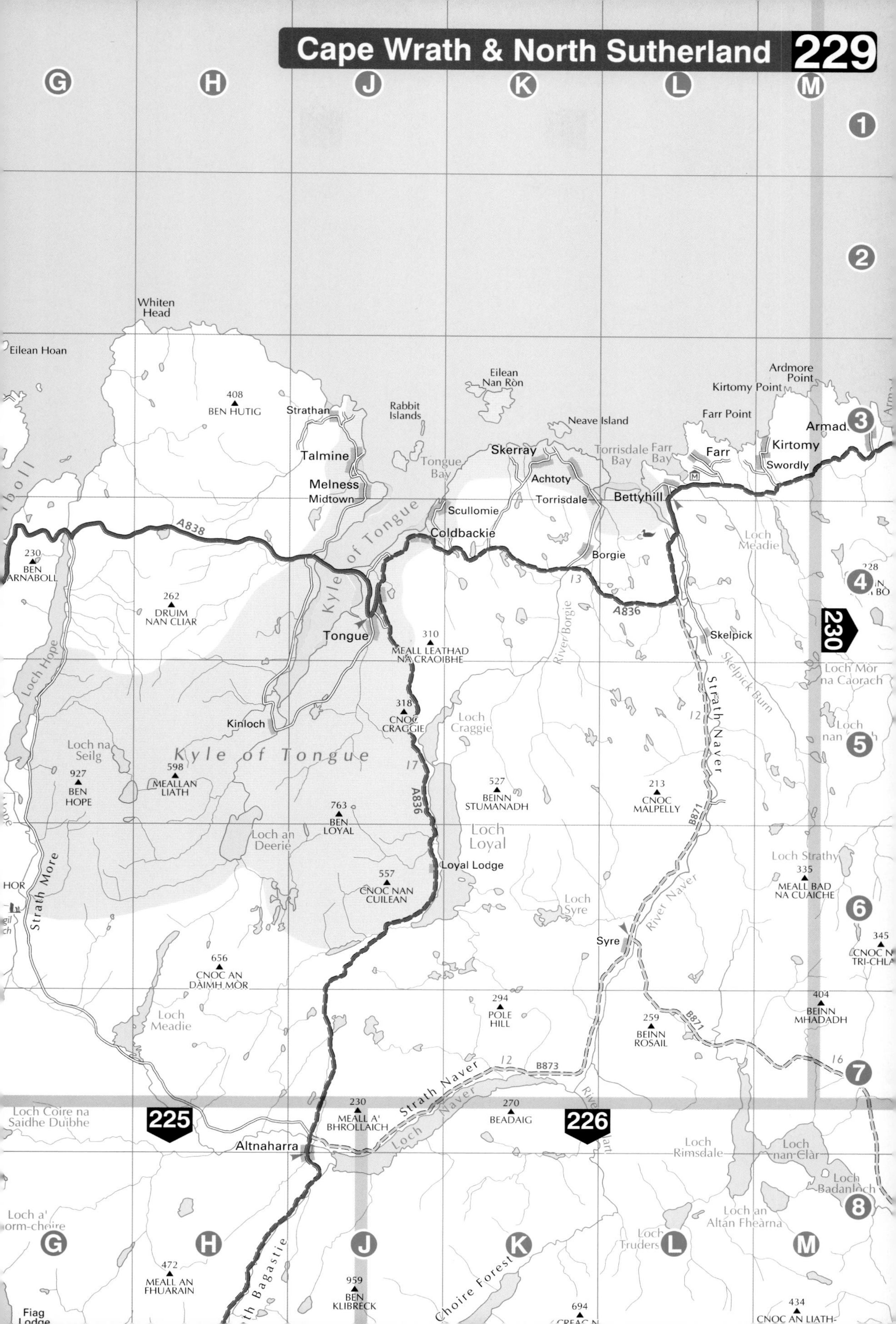
Whiten Head
Eilean Hoan
408 BEN HUTIG
Strathan
Rabbit Islands
Eilean Nan Ròn
Neave Island
Ardmore Point
Kirtomy Point
Farr Point
Armadale
Kirtomy
Swordly
Farr
Farr Bay
Torrisdale Bay
Skerray
Achtoty
Torrisdale
Bettyhill
Talmine
Melness
Midtown
Tongue Bay
Scullomie
Coldbackie
Kyle of Tongue
A838
230 BEN ARNABOLL
262 DRUIM NAN CLIAR
Tongue
310 MEALL LEATHAD NA CRAOIBHE
Borgie
A836
River Borgie
Skelpick
Skelpick Burn
Loch Meadie
Strath Naver
Loch Mòr na Caorach
Loch Hope
Kinloch
318 CNOC CRAGGIE
Loch Craggie
Loch na Seilg
927 BEN HOPE
598 MEALLAN LIATH
763 BEN LOYAL
527 BEINN STUMANADH
213 CNOC MALPELLY
B871
Loch an Deerie
Loch Loyal
Loyal Lodge
557 CNOC NAN CUILEAN
Loch Strathy
335 MEALL BAD NA CUAICHE
Strath More
Loch Syre
River Naver
Syre
345
656 CNOC AN DÀIMH MÒR
294 POLE HILL
259 BEINN ROSAIL
404 BEINN MHADADH
Loch Meadie
Strath Naver
B873
230 MEALL A' BHROLLAICH
270 BEADAIG
Loch Naver
Loch Coire na Saidhe Duibhe
225
226
Altnaharra
Loch Rimsdale
Loch nan Clàr
Loch Badanloch
Loch an Altan Fheàrna
Loch Truders
472 MEALL AN FHUARAIN
959 BEN KLIBRECK
Strath Bagastie
Choire Forest
694
434 CNOC AN LIATH-
Fiag Lodge
230

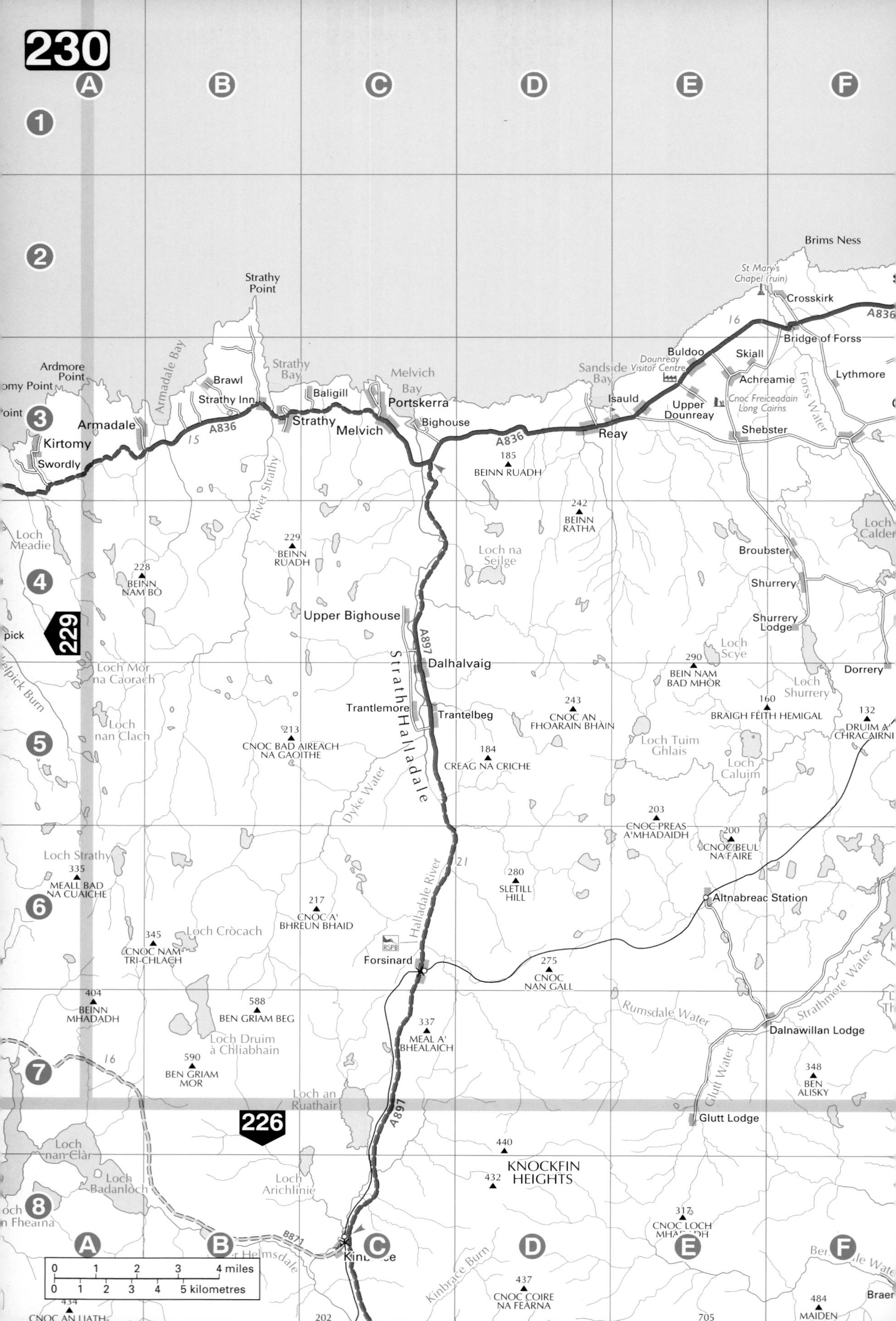

A
B
C
D
E
F
1
2
3
4
5
6
7
8
Brims Ness
St Mary's Chapel (ruin)
Crosskirk
A836
16
Bridge of Forss
Strathy Point
Ardmore Point
Armadale Bay
Strathy Bay
Melvich Bay
Sandside Bay
Dounreay Visitor Centre
Buldoo
Skiall
Achreamie
Lythmore
Forss Water
Brawl
Strathy Inn
Baligill
Portskerra
Isauld
Upper Dounreay
Cnoc Freiceadain Long Cairns
Armadale
Kirtomy
Swordly
A836
15
Strathy
Melvich
Bighouse
Reay
Shebster
185 BEINN RUADH
242 BEINN RATHA
River Strathy
Loch Meadie
229 BEINN RUADH
Loch na Seilge
Loch Calder
Broubster
228 BEINN NAM BO
Shurrery
Upper Bighouse
Shurrery Lodge
229
A897
Loch Scye
Loch Mòr na Caorach
Strath Halladale
Dalhalvaig
290 BEIN NAM BAD MHÒR
Dorrery
Loch Shurrery
Trantlemore
Trantelbeg
243 CNOC AN FHOARAIN BHÀIN
160 BRAIGH FÉITH HEMIGAL
132 DRUIM A' CHRACAIRNI
Loch nan Clach
213 CNOC BAD AIREACH NA GAOITHE
Loch Tuim Ghlais
184 CREAG NA CRICHE
Loch Caluim
Dyke Water
203 CNOC PREAS A'MHADAIDH
200 CNOC BEUL NA FAIRE
Loch Strathy
335 MEALL BAD NA CUAICHE
Halladale River
21
280 SLETILL HILL
Altnabreac Station
217 CNOC A' BHREUN BHAID
345 CNOC NAM TRI-CHLACH
Loch Cròcach
RSPB
Forsinard
275 CNOC NAN GALL
404 BEINN MHADADH
588 BEN GRIAM BEG
337 MEAL A' BHEALAICH
Rumsdale Water
Strathmore Water
Dalnawillan Lodge
Loch Druim à Chliabhain
590 BEN GRIAM MOR
16
Glutt Water
348 BEN ALISKY
Loch an Ruathair
226
A897
Glutt Lodge
Loch nan Clàr
440
KNOCKFIN HEIGHTS
Loch Badanloch
Loch Arichlinie
432
317 CNOC LOCH MHADAIDH
B871
Kinbrace
Kinbrace Burn
0 1 2 3 4 miles
0 1 2 3 4 5 kilometres
434 CNOC AN LIATH-
202
437 CNOC COIRE NA FEARNA
705
484 MAIDEN
Braer

PENTLAND FIRTH
ISLAND OF STROMA
Nethertown
Uppertown
Mell Head
DUNNET HEAD
127
Briga Head
Stromness
St John's Point
Inner Sound
St Margaret's Hope
Scarfskerry
Loch Mey
Gills Bay
DUNCANSBY HEAD
Huna
Kirkstyle
Muckle Stack
John o' Groats
121
DUNNET HILL
Brough
St John's Loch
Rattar
Gills
Mey
Canisbay
Stacks of Duncansby
Holborn Head
West Dunnet
Barrock
Dunnet
Dunnet Bay
A99
A836
B855
Thurso Bay
Thurso
Castlehill
Inkstack
Loch Heilen
Brabstermire
Skirza
Murkle
Castletown
Greenland
Gill Burn
Freswick
Freswick Bay
Ness Head
B874
Olrig House
Slickly
Tain
Auckengill
Weydale
A9
B876
Kirk Burn
Hilliclay
Bowermadden
Nybster
Sortat
Bower
Lyth
17
Sordale
Brough Head
Howe
Burn of Lyth
Knockdee
Roadside
16
Keiss
Halcro
Clayock
Kirk
Gillock
Halkirk
Loch Scarmclate
Loch of Wester
B870
Sinclair Bay
21
Scotscalder Station
Loch Watten
176
SPITTAL HILL
Harpsdale
Castle Girnigoe & Sinclair
Noss Head
Reiss
Winless
River Thurso
Spittal
Watten
A882
Wick River
Backlass
Sibster
Ackergill
Bilbster
Staxigoe
Mybster
Loch of Toftingall
Wick
Papigoe
Milton
Westerdale
Haster
Wick
23
Janets-town
Wick Bay
Achairn Burn
Old Wick
Strath Beg
Newton Row
South Head
Castle of Old Wick
Badlipster
Whiterow
Loch Hempriggs
136
BEINN CHÀITEAG
Tannach
Thrumster
145
BALLHARN HILL
Loch Ruard
Grey Cairns of Camster
Loch of Yarrows
212
HILL OF YARROWS
Sarclet
Achavanich
Loch Stemster
248
STEMSTER HILL
Loch Sand
Loch Rangag
Cairn o'Get
Ulbster
Whaligoe
226
COIRE NA BEINN
Whaligoe Steps
Roster
Bruan
Hill o'Many Stanes
287
BEN-A-CHIELT
Upper Lybster
Mid Clyth
Halberry Head
264
CNOCAN CONACHREAG
227
Forse House
Swiney
Clyth Ness
Occumster
Houstry
Invershore
Lybster
Lybster Bay
Land-hallow
Forse
Smerral
Dunbeath Water
Latheron
Latheronwheel
Janetstown
Laidhay Croft Museum
Dunbeath
Knockally
234

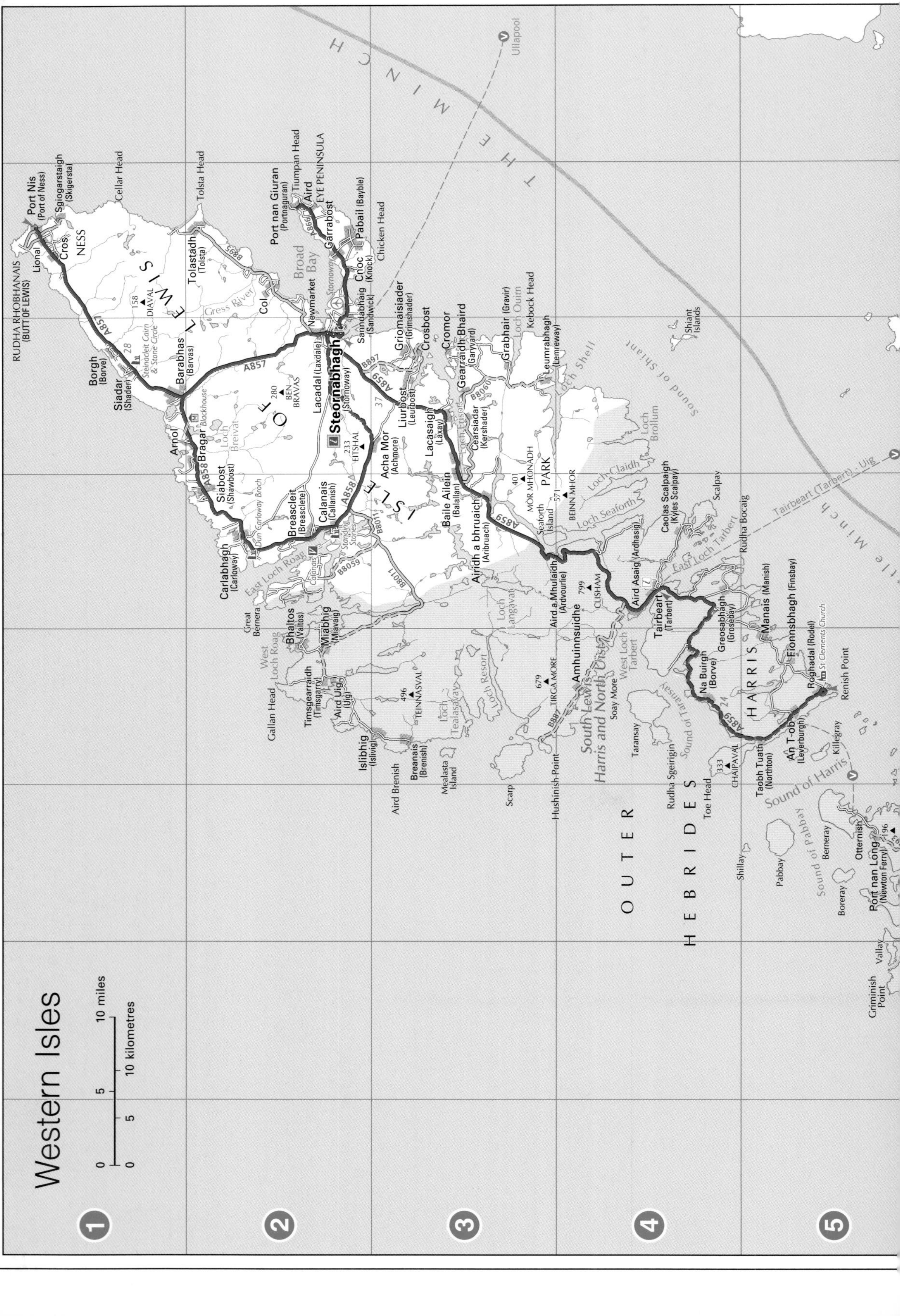

Western Isles

0 5 10 miles
0 5 10 kilometres

1
2
3
4
5

RUDHA RHOBHANAIS (BUTT OF LEWIS)
Lional
Port Nis (Port of Ness)
Cros
Sgiogarstaigh (Skigersta)
NESS
Borgh (Borve)
A857
Cellar Head
Siadar (Shader)
28
Steinacleit Cairn & Stone Circle
158 DIAVAL
LEWIS
Arnol
Barabhas (Barvas)
Tolastadh (Tolsta)
Tolsta Head
Bragar
Blackhouse
A858
Carlabhagh (Carloway)
Siabost (Shawbost)
Loch Breivat
Gress River
B895
Dun Carloway Broch
Great Bernera
West Loch Roag
East Loch Roag
Gallan Head
A857
Col
OF
280 BEN BRAVAS
Port nan Giuran (Portnaguran)
Tiumpan Head
Breascleit (Breasclete)
Broad Bay
Aird
EYE PENINSULA
Bhaltos (Valtos)
Timsgearraidh (Timsgarry)
Lacadal (Laxdale)
Newmarket
A866
Calanais
Calanais (Callanish)
Steornabhagh
Stornoway
Garrabost
Aird Uig (Uig)
Miabhig (Miavaig)
B8059
Standing Stones
233 EITSHAL
(Stornoway)
Islibhig (Islivig)
Sanndabhaig (Sandwick)
Cnoc (Knock)
Pabail (Bayble)
A858
B8011
Chicken Head
B8011
ISLE
Acha Mor (Achmore)
37
A859
B897
Aird Brenish
496 TEINNASVAL
Liurbost (Leurbost)
Griomaisiader (Grimshader)
Breanais (Brenish)
Lacasaigh (Laxay)
Crosbost
THE MINCH
Mealasta Island
Loch Tealasavay
Baile Ailein (Balallan)
Cromor
Loch Erisort
Gearraidh Bhaird (Garyvard)
Loch Resort
Airidh a bhruaich (Aribruach)
Cearsiadar (Kershader)
B8060
Scarp
Loch Langavat
A859
Grabhair (Gravir)
Loch Ouirn
Ullapool
401 MOR MHONADH
Kebock Head
679
Seaforth Island
PARK
Leumrabhagh (Lemreway)
Hushinish Point
B887
TIRGA MORE
Aird a Mhulaidh (Ardvourlie)
571 BEINN MHOR
Amhuinnsuidhe
799 CLISHAM
Loch Shell
South Lewis Harris and North Uist
Soay More
Loch Seaforth
Loch Claidh
OUTER
Taransay
West Loch Tarbert
Aird Asaig (Ardhasig)
Loch Brollum
Sound of Shiant
Tairbeart (Tarbert)
Rudha Sgeirigin
Caolas Scalpaigh (Kyles Scalpay)
Shiant Islands
HEBRIDES
Sound of Taransay
East Loch Tarbert
Toe Head
Na Buirgh (Borve)
Scalpay
333 CHAIPAVAL
A859
24
Greosabhagh (Grosebay)
Shillay
Rudha Bocaig
HARRIS
Taobh Tuath (Northton)
Manais (Manish)
Pabbay
Tairbeart (Tarbert) - Uig
An T-ob (Leverburgh)
Fionnsbhagh (Finsbay)
Sound of Pabbay
Sound of Harris
Roghadal (Rodel)
St Clements Church
Berneray
Boreray
Killegray
Renish Point
Otternish
Little Minch
Griminish Point
Valley
Port nan Long (Newton Ferry)
196

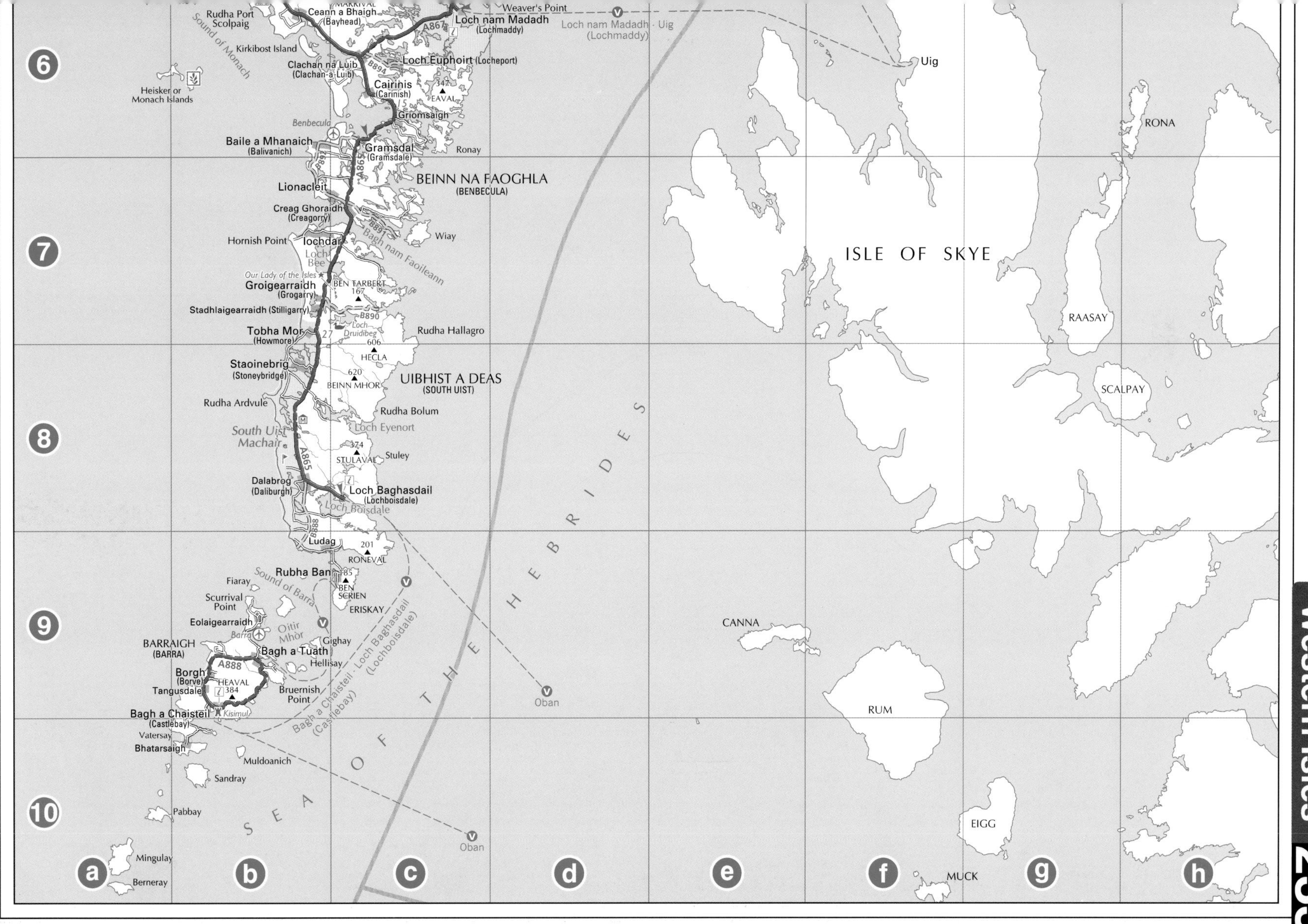

Rudha Port Scolpaig
Sound of Monach
Ceann a Bhaigh
(Bayhead)
Weaver's Point
Loch nam Madadh
(Lochmaddy)
Loch nam Madadh - Uig
(Lochmaddy)
Uig
Kirkibost Island
Clachan na Luib
(Clachan-a-Luib)
Loch Euphoirt (Locheport)
A867
B894
Cairinis
(Carinish)
347
EAVAL
Heisker or
Monach Islands
Griomsaigh
RONA
Benbecula
Baile a Mhanaich
(Balivanich)
Gramsdal
(Gramsdale)
Ronay
A865
BEINN NA FAOGHLA
(BENBECULA)
Lionacleit
Creag Ghoraidh
(Creagorry)
B891
Wiay
Hornish Point
Iochdar
Loch Bee
Bagh nam Faoileann
ISLE OF SKYE
Our Lady of the Isles
Groigearraidh
(Grogarry)
BEN TARBERT
167
Stadhlaigearraidh (Stilligarry)
B890
Loch Druidibeg
RAASAY
Tobha Mor
(Howmore)
Rudha Hallagro
606
HECLA
Staoinebrig
(Stoneybridge)
620
BEINN MHOR
UIBHIST A DEAS
(SOUTH UIST)
SCALPAY
Rudha Ardvule
Rudha Bolum
South Uist Machair
Loch Eyenort
374
STULAVAL
Stuley
Dalabrog
(Daliburgh)
Loch Baghasdail
(Lochboisdale)
Loch Boisdale
B888
Ludag
201
RONEVAL
Rubha Ban
185
BEN SCRIEN
ERISKAY
Fiaray
Sound of Barra
Scurrival Point
Eolaigearraidh
Barra
Oitir Mhor
Gighay
BARRAIGH
(BARRA)
Bagh a Tuath
Hellisay
CANNA
Borgh
(Borve)
A888
HEAVAL
384
Tangusdale
Bruernish Point
Bagh a Chaisteil - Loch Baghasdail
(Castlebay) (Lochboisdale)
Oban
RUM
Bagh a Chaisteil
(Castlebay)
Kisimul
Vatersay
Bhatarsaigh
Muldoanich
Sandray
Pabbay
Mingulay
Berneray
SEA OF THE HEBRIDES
Oban
EIGG
MUCK

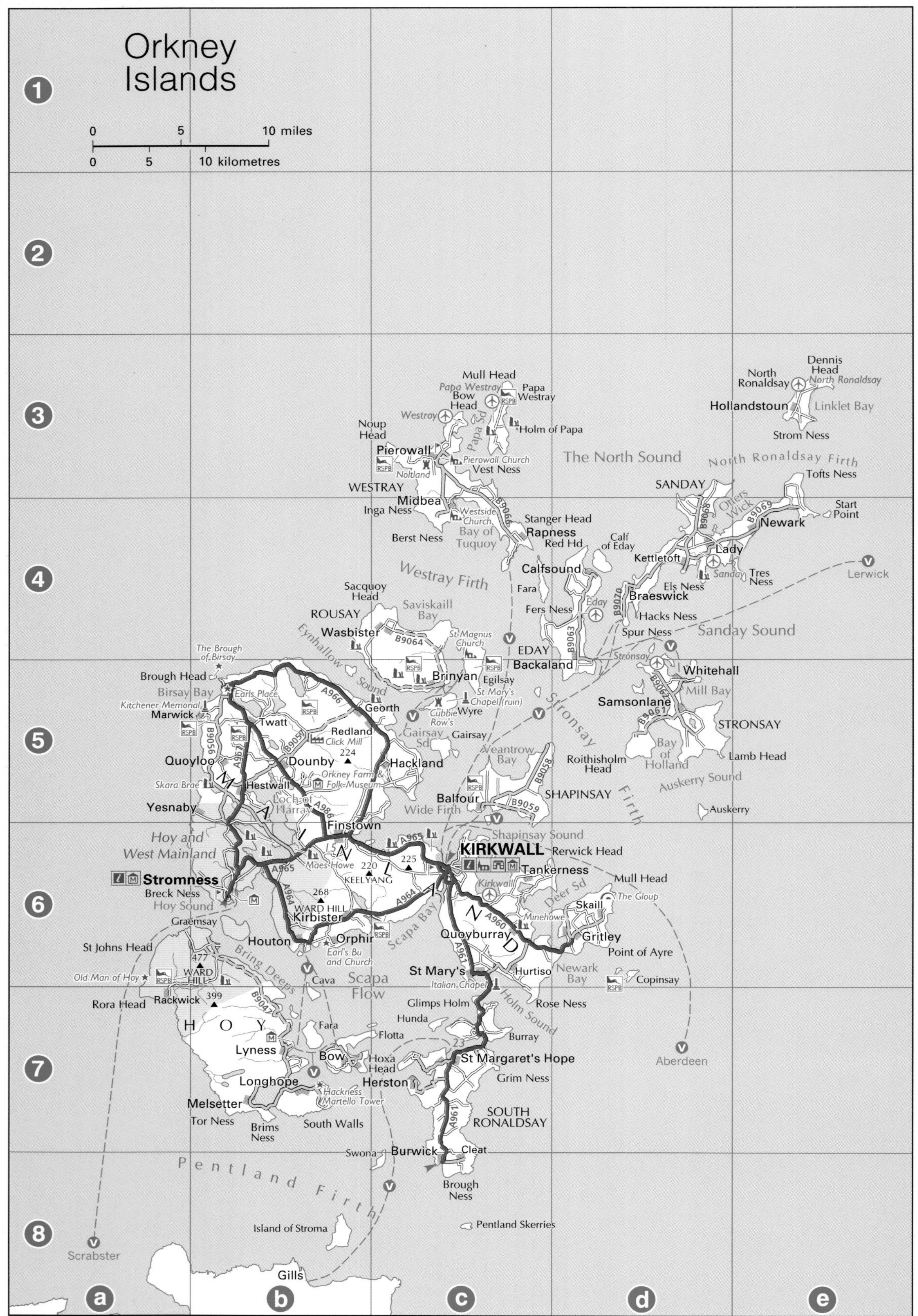
Orkney Islands
0 5 10 miles
0 5 10 kilometres
Mull Head
Papa Westray
Papa Westray
Bow Head
Westray
Noup Head
Holm of Papa
Pierowall
Pierowall Church
Vest Ness
Noltland
WESTRAY
Midbea
Inga Ness
Westside Church
Bay of Tuquoy
Stanger Head
Rapness
Red Hd
Berst Ness
The North Sound
Dennis Head
North Ronaldsay
North Ronaldsay
Hollandstoun
Linklet Bay
Strom Ness
North Ronaldsay Firth
Tofts Ness
SANDAY
Otters Wick
Start Point
Newark
Lady
Kettletoft
Calf of Eday
Calfsound
Tres Ness
Sanday
Lerwick
Westray Firth
Fara
Els Ness
Braeswick
Sacquoy Head
ROUSAY
Saviskaill Bay
Fers Ness
Eday
Hacks Ness
Wasbister
Spur Ness
Sanday Sound
St Magnus Church
EDAY
Stronsay
The Brough of Birsay
Eynhallow Sound
Backaland
Whitehall
Brough Head
Birsay Bay
Earls Place
Brinyan
Egilsay
Mill Bay
Kitchener Memorial
Marwick
St Mary's Chapel (ruin)
Samsonlane
Twatt
Georth
Cubbie Row's
Wyre
Stronsay
STRONSAY
Redland
Click Mill
Gairsay Sd
Gairsay
Veantrow Bay
Bay of Holland
224
Quoyloo
Dounby
Hackland
Roithisholm Head
Lamb Head
Orkney Farm & Folk Museum
Skara Brae
Hestwall
Auskerry Sound
Loch of Harray
SHAPINSAY
Yesnaby
Balfour
Wide Firth
Firth
Auskerry
Finstown
Shapinsay Sound
Hoy and West Mainland
KIRKWALL
Rerwick Head
Maes Howe
225
220
Tankerness
Stromness
KEELYANG
Mull Head
Breck Ness
Kirkwall
The Gloup
Hoy Sound
268
Deer Sd
Skaill
WARD HILL
Graemsay
Kirbister
Minehowe
Scapa Bay
Quoyburray
Gritley
Houton
Orphir
St Johns Head
Earl's Bu and Church
Point of Ayre
Bring Deeps
477
WARD HILL
Cava
Scapa Flow
St Mary's
Hurtiso
Newark Bay
Copinsay
Old Man of Hoy
Italian Chapel
Rackwick
399
Rora Head
Glimps Holm
Rose Ness
Holm Sound
Hunda
HOY
Fara
Flotta
Burray
Lyness
23
Aberdeen
Bow
Hoxa Head
St Margaret's Hope
Longhope
Herston
Grim Ness
Hackness Martello Tower
Melsetter
SOUTH RONALDSAY
Tor Ness
Brims Ness
South Walls
Swona
Burwick
Cleat
Pentland Firth
Brough Ness
Island of Stroma
Pentland Skerries
Scrabster
Gills
MAINLAND
A966
A986
A965
A964
A960
A961
A967
B9056
B9057
B9064
B9066
B9068
B9069
B9070
B9063
B9062
B9061
B9058
B9059
B9047
RSPB
1 2 3 4 5 6 7 8
a b c d e

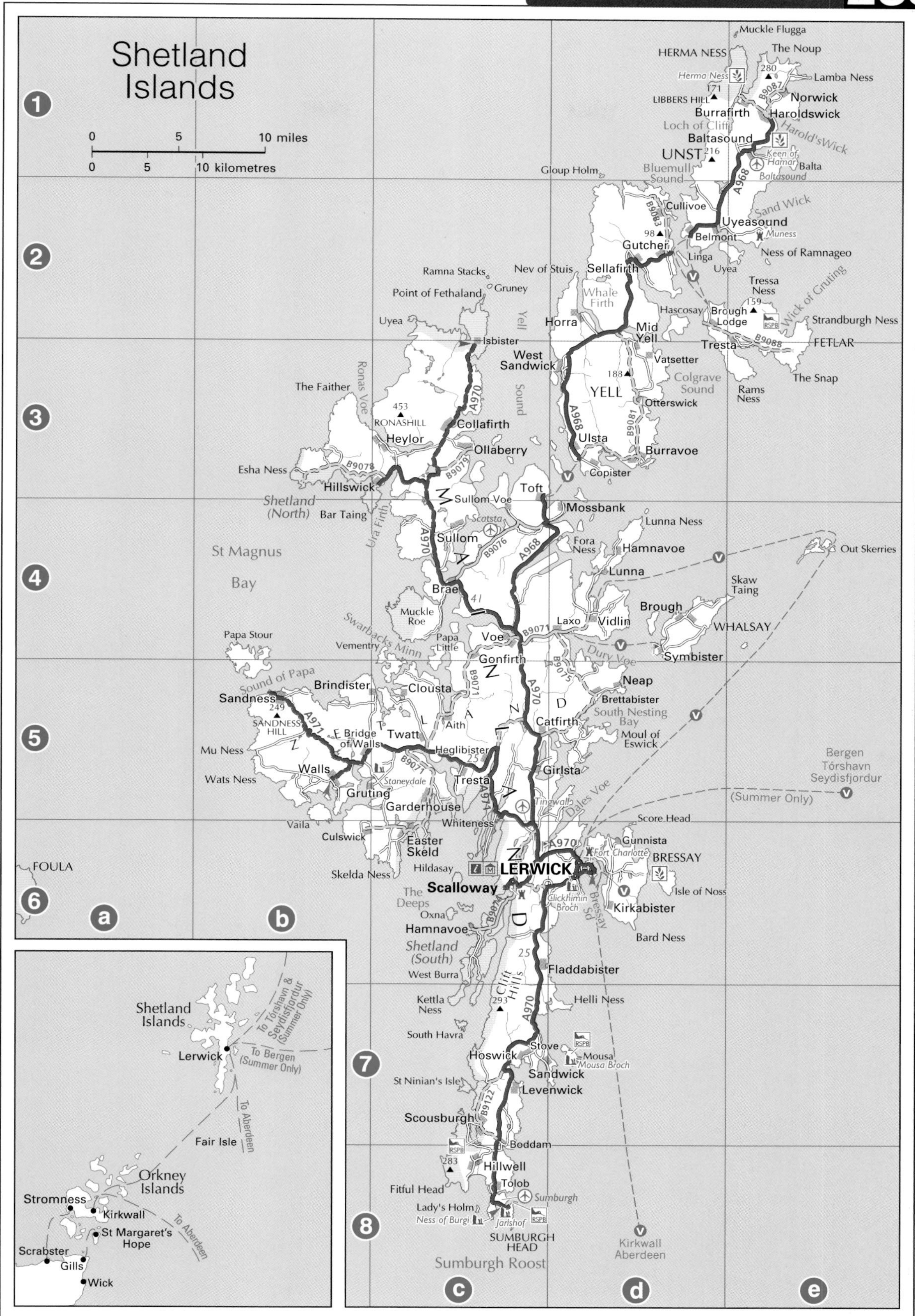
Shetland Islands
0 5 10 miles
0 5 10 kilometres
Muckle Flugga
HERMA NESS
The Noup
Lamba Ness
Norwick
Haroldswick
Burrafirth
Baltasound
UNST
Balta
Uyeasound
Belmont
Cullivoe
Gutcher
Sellafirth
Mid Yell
YELL
Ulsta
Burravoe
Tresta
FETLAR
Ronas Voe
RONASHILL
Heylor
Collafirth
Ollaberry
Hillswick
Esha Ness
Shetland (North)
Toft
Mossbank
Sullom Voe
Sullom
Brae
St Magnus Bay
Lunna Ness
Hamnavoe
Lunna
Out Skerries
Vidlin
Brough
WHALSAY
Symbister
Voe
Papa Stour
Sandness
SANDNESS HILL
Walls
Bridge of Walls
Twatt
Aith
Clousta
Brindister
Gruting
Tresta
Garderhouse
Whiteness
Catfirth
Girlsta
Neap
South Nesting Bay
Bergen Tórshavn Seydisfjordur (Summer Only)
FOULA
LERWICK
Scalloway
BRESSAY
Gunnista
Kirkabister
Hamnavoe
Shetland (South)
Fladdabister
Stove
Hoswick
Sandwick
Levenwick
Mousa
Scousburgh
Boddam
Hillwell
Fitful Head
Sumburgh
SUMBURGH HEAD
Sumburgh Roost
Kirkwall Aberdeen
Lerwick
To Tórshavn & Seydisfjordur (Summer Only)
To Bergen (Summer Only)
To Aberdeen
Fair Isle
Orkney Islands
Stromness
Kirkwall
St Margaret's Hope
Scrabster
Gills
Wick

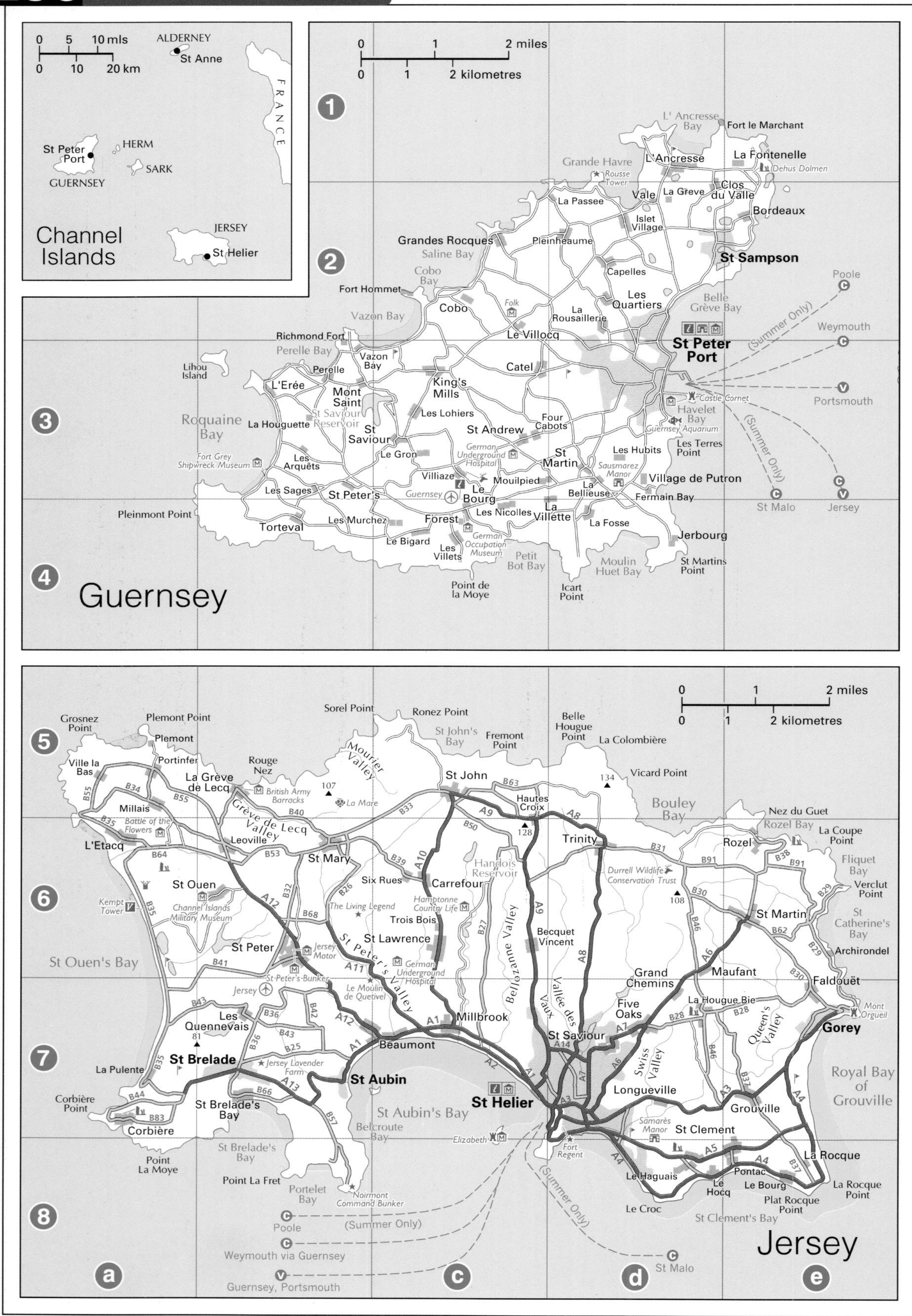
Channel Islands
ALDERNEY
St Anne
HERM
SARK
GUERNSEY
St Peter Port
JERSEY
St Helier
FRANCE
Guernsey
St Peter Port
St Sampson
L'Ancresse
La Fontenelle
Vale
Bordeaux
Cobo
Le Villocq
Catel
King's Mills
St Saviour
St Andrew
St Martin
St Peter's
Torteval
Forest
Le Bourg
Jerbourg
Lihou Island
Rocquaine Bay
Vazon Bay
Pleinmont Point
Icart Point
Poole
Weymouth
Portsmouth
St Malo
Jersey
(Summer Only)
St Helier
St Aubin
St Brelade
St Ouen
St Mary
St John
Trinity
St Martin
Gorey
Grouville
St Clement
St Lawrence
St Peter
St Saviour
Rozel
La Rocque
Corbière
L'Etacq
St Ouen's Bay
St Aubin's Bay
St Brelade's Bay
Bouley Bay
Royal Bay of Grouville
St Clement's Bay
Weymouth via Guernsey
Guernsey, Portsmouth
0 1 2 miles
0 1 2 kilometres

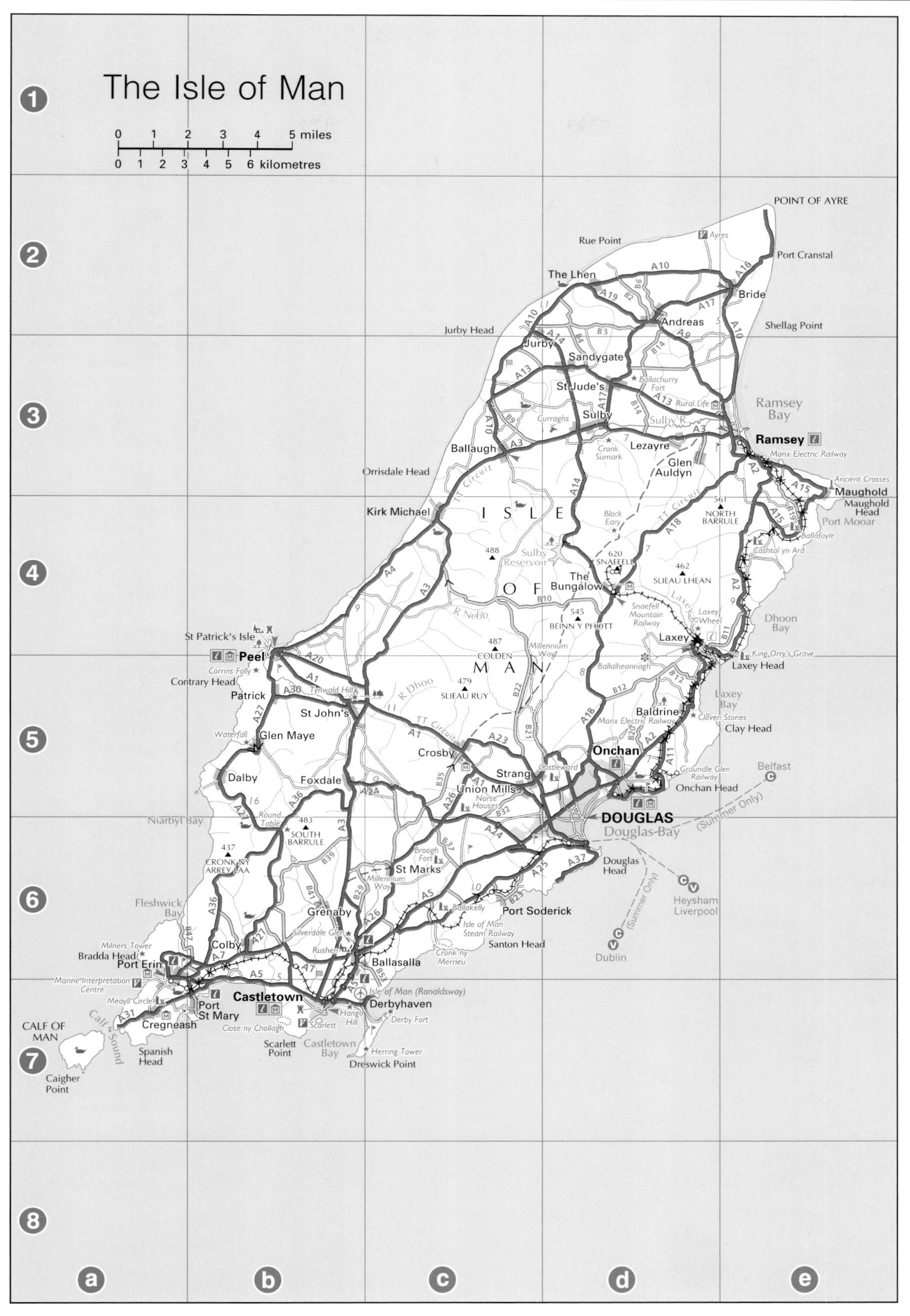
The Isle of Man
0 1 2 3 4 5 miles
0 1 2 3 4 5 6 kilometres
POINT OF AYRE
Rue Point
Port Cranstal
The Lhen
Bride
Andreas
Shellag Point
Jurby Head
Jurby
Sandygate
St Jude's
Ramsey Bay
Sulby
Ballaugh
Lezayre
Ramsey
Glen Auldyn
Orrisdale Head
Maughold
Maughold Head
Port Mooar
Kirk Michael
ISLE OF MAN
NORTH BARRULE
SNAEFELL
The Bungalow
SLIEAU LHEAN
BEINN Y PHOTT
Laxey
Dhoon Bay
St Patrick's Isle
Peel
Laxey Head
Contrary Head
Patrick
COLDEN
SLIEAU RUY
St John's
Baldrine
Laxey Bay
Glen Maye
Clay Head
Crosby
Onchan
Dalby
Foxdale
Strang
Union Mills
Onchan Head
Belfast
Niarbyl Bay
SOUTH BARRULE
DOUGLAS
Douglas Bay
(Summer Only)
CRONK NY ARREY LAA
St Marks
Douglas Head
Fleshwick Bay
Heysham
Liverpool
Grenaby
Port Soderick
Santon Head
Colby
Dublin
Bradda Head
Port Erin
Ballasalla
Castletown
Derbyhaven
Port St Mary
CALF OF MAN
Cregneash
Calf Sound
Scarlett Point
Castletown Bay
Spanish Head
Dreswick Point
Caigher Point
a b c d e

Index to place names

This index lists places appearing in the main-map section of the atlas in alphabetical order. The reference before each name gives the atlas page number and grid reference of the square in which the place appears. The map shows counties, and administrative areas, together with a list of the abbreviated name forms used in the index. The top 100 places of tourist interest are indexed in red, airports in blue.

England

BaNES **Bath & N E Somerset (18)**
Barns **Barnsley (19)**
Beds **Bedfordshire**
Birm **Birmingham**
Bl w D **Blackburn with Darwen (20)**
Bmouth **Bournemouth**
Bolton **Bolton (21)**
Bpool **Blackpool**
Brad **Bradford (22)**
Br & H **Brighton and Hove (23)**
Br For **Bracknell Forest (24)**
Bristl **City of Bristol**
Bucks **Buckinghamshire**
Bury **Bury (25)**
C Derb **City of Derby**
C KuH **City of Kingston upon Hull**
C Leic **City of Leicester**
C Nott **City of Nottingham**
C Pete **City of Peterborough**
C Plym **City of Plymouth**
C Port **City of Portsmouth**
C Sotn **City of Southampton**
C Stke **City of Stoke**
Calder **Calderdale (26)**
Cambs **Cambridgeshire**
Ches **Cheshire**
Cnwll **Cornwall**
Covtry **Coventry**
Cumb **Cumbria**
Darltn **Darlington (27)**
Derbys **Derbyshire**
Devon **Devon**
Donc **Doncaster (28)**
Dorset **Dorset**
Dudley **Dudley (29)**
Dur **Durham**
E R Yk **East Riding of Yorkshire**
E Susx **East Sussex**
Essex **Essex**
Gatesd **Gateshead (30)**
Gloucs **Gloucestershire**
Gt Lon **Greater London**
Halton **Halton (31)**
Hants **Hampshire**
Hartpl **Hartlepool (32)**
Herefs **Herefordshire**
Herts **Hertfordshire**
IoS **Isles of Scilly**
IoW **Isle of Wight**
Kent **Kent**
Kirk **Kirklees (33)**
Knows **Knowsley (34)**
Lancs **Lancashire**
Leeds **Leeds**
Leics **Leicestershire**
Lincs **Lincolnshire**
Lpool **Liverpool**
Luton **Luton**
M Keyn **Milton Keynes**
Manch **Manchester**
Medway **Medway**
Middsb **Middlesbrough**
NE Lin **North East Lincolnshire**
N Linc **North Lincolnshire**
N Som **North Somerset (35)**
N Tyne **North Tyneside (36)**
N u Ty **Newcastle upon Tyne**
N York **North Yorkshire**
Nhants **Northamptonshire**
Norfk **Norfolk**
Notts **Nottinghamshire**
Nthumb **Northumberland**
Oldham **Oldham (37)**
Oxon **Oxfordshire**
Poole **Poole**
R & Cl **Redcar and Cleveland**
Readg **Reading**
Rochdl **Rochdale (38)**
Rothm **Rotherham (39)**
Rutlnd **Rutland**
S Glos **South Gloucestershire (40)**
S on T **Stockton-on-Tees (41)**
S Tyne **South Tyneside (42)**
Salfd **Salford (43)**
Sandw **Sandwell (44)**
Sefton **Sefton (45)**
Sheff **Sheffield**
Shrops **Shropshire**
Slough **Slough (46)**
Solhll **Solihull (47)**
Somset **Somerset**
St Hel **St Helens (48)**
Staffs **Staffordshire**
Sthend **Southend-on-Sea**
Stockp **Stockport (49)**
Suffk **Suffolk**
Sundld **Sunderland**
Surrey **Surrey**
Swindn **Swindon**
Tamesd **Tameside (50)**
Thurr **Thurrock (51)**
Torbay **Torbay**
Traffd **Trafford (52)**
W & M **Windsor & Maidenhead (53)**
W Berk **West Berkshire**
W Susx **West Sussex**
Wakefd **Wakefield (54)**
Warrtn **Warrington (55)**
Warwks **Warwickshire**
Wigan **Wigan (56)**
Wilts **Wiltshire**
Wirral **Wirral (57)**
Wokham **Wokingham (58)**
Wolves **Wolverhampton (59)**
Worcs **Worcestershire**
Wrekin **Telford and Wrekin (60)**
Wsall **Walsall (61)**
York **York**

Scotland

Abers **Aberdeenshire**
Ag & B **Argyll & Bute**
Angus **Angus**
Border **Borders**
C Aber **City of Aberdeen**
C Dund **City of Dundee**
C Edin **City of Edinburgh**
C Glas **City of Glasgow**
Clacks **Clackmannanshire (1)**
D & G **Dumfries & Galloway**
E Ayrs **East Ayrshire**
E Duns **East Dunbartonshire (2)**
E Loth **East Lothian**
E Rens **East Renfrewshire (3)**
Falk **Falkirk**
Fife **Fife**
Highld **Highland**
Inver **Inverclyde (4)**
Mdloth **Midlothian (5)**
Moray **Moray**
N Ayrs **North Ayrshire**
N Lans **North Lanarkshire (6)**
Ork **Orkney Islands**
P & K **Perth & Kinross**
Rens **Renfrewshire (7)**
S Ayrs **South Ayrshire**
Shet **Shetland Islands**
S Lans **South Lanarkshire**
Stirlg **Stirling**
W Duns **West Dunbartonshire (8)**
W Isls **Western Isles**
W Loth **West Lothian**

Wales

Blae G **Blaenau Gwent (9)**
Brdgnd **Bridgend (10)**
Caerph **Caerphilly (11)**
Cardif **Cardiff**
Carmth **Carmarthenshire**
Cerdgn **Ceredigion**
Conwy **Conwy**
Denbgs **Denbighshire**
Flints **Flintshire**
Gwynd **Gwynedd**
IoA **Isle of Anglesey**
Mons **Monmouthshire**
Myr Td **Merthyr Tydfil (12)**
Neath **Neath Port Talbot (13)**
Newpt **Newport (14)**
Pembks **Pembrokeshire**
Powys **Powys**
Rhondd **Rhondda Cynon Taff (15)**
Swans **Swansea**
Torfn **Torfaen (16)**
V Glam **Vale of Glamorgan (17)**
Wrexhm **Wrexham**

Channel Islands & Isle of Man

Guern **Guernsey**
Jersey **Jersey**
IoM **Isle of Man**

ORKNEY ISLANDS
SHETLAND ISLANDS
WESTERN ISLES
HIGHLAND
MORAY
SCOTLAND
Aberdeen
ABERDEENSHIRE
ANGUS
PERTH & KINROSS
Dundee
ARGYLL & BUTE
STIRLING
FIFE
FALK
Edinburgh
E LOTH
W LOTH
Glasgow
NORTH AYRSHIRE
S LANS
BORDERS
E AYRS
S AYRS
DUMFRIES & GALLOWAY
NORTHUMBERLAND
Newcastle upon Tyne
Sunderland
CUMBRIA
DURHAM
R & CL
Middlesbrough
IoM
NORTH YORKSHIRE
York
EAST RIDING OF YORKSHIRE
Blackpool
LANCASHIRE
Leeds
Kingston upon Hull
N LINCS
N E LINCS
Liverpool
Manchester
Sheffield
IoA
CONWY
FLINTS
DENBGS
WREXHAM
CHESHIRE
DERBYS
NOTTS
LINCOLNSHIRE
Stoke-on-Trent
Nottingham
Derby
GWYNEDD
STAFFS
LEICS
RUTLAND
Leicester
Peterborough
NORFOLK
SHROPSHIRE
Birmingham
Coventry
CAMBS
POWYS
WORCS
WARWKS
NHANTS
SUFFOLK
CERDGN
HEREFS
Milton Keynes
BEDS
WALES
ENGLAND
PEMBKS
CARMTH
Luton
MONS
GLOUCS
OXON
HERTS
ESSEX
Swansea
Cardiff
Bristol
Swindon
BUCKS
Southend-on-Sea
Reading
GREATER LONDON
W BERKS
MEDWAY
WILTSHIRE
SURREY
KENT
SOMERSET
HAMPSHIRE
W SUSX
E SUSX
DEVON
DORSET
Southampton
Portsmouth
Bournemouth
Poole
IoW
CHANNEL ISLANDS
Guernsey
Jersey
CORNWALL
Plymouth
Torbay
IoS

A

198 D4 **A'Chill** Highld
102 B7 **Ab Kettleby** Leics
27 G6 **Abbas Combe** Somset
70 D2 **Abberley** Worcs
70 D2 **Abberley Common** Worcs
62 B4 **Abberton** Essex
71 H4 **Abberton** Worcs
60 F5 **Abbess Roding** Essex
54 B3 **Abbey Dore** Herefs
99 L2 **Abbey Green** Staffs
178 F6 **Abbey St Bathans** Border
147 L5 **Abbey Town** Cumb
121 J6 **Abbey Village** Lancs
45 J4 **Abbey Wood** Gt Lon
114 F5 **Abbeydale** Sheff
130 B8 **Abbeystead** Lancs
71 J4 **Abbot's Salford** Warwks
167 J6 **Abbotrule** Border
9 K3 **Abbots Bickington** Devon
100 B7 **Abbots Bromley** Staffs
186 B5 **Abbots Deuglie** P & K
59 H7 **Abbots Langley** Herts
38 D5 **Abbots Leigh** N Som
71 H4 **Abbots Morton** Worcs
89 J7 **Abbots Ripton** Cambs
29 J5 **Abbots Worthy** Hants
14 B5 **Abbotsbury** Dorset
22 F6 **Abbotsham** Devon
7 K3 **Abbotskerswell** Devon
75 J3 **Abbotsley** Cambs
15 J3 **Abbott Street** Dorset
29 G3 **Abbotts Ann** Hants
83 L6 **Abdon** Shrops
52 F7 **Aber-nant** Rhondd
66 B3 **Aberaeron** Cerdgn
52 F7 **Aberaman** Rhondd
81 J2 **Aberangell** Gwynd
202 F1 **Aberarder** Highld
186 B4 **Aberargie** P & K
66 B2 **Aberarth** Cerdgn
51 L7 **Aberavon** Neath
185 J3 **Abercairny** P & K
53 G7 **Abercanaid** Myr Td
37 K2 **Abercarn** Caerph
64 B7 **Abercastle** Pembks
81 H3 **Abercegir** Powys
202 B5 **Aberchalder Lodge** Highld
216 C4 **Aberchirder** Abers
52 C5 **Abercraf** Powys
36 D2 **Abercregan** Neath
52 F7 **Abercwmboi** Rhondd
65 H6 **Abercych** Pembks
37 G2 **Abercynon** Rhondd
185 M4 **Aberdalgie** P & K
52 F7 **Aberdare** Rhondd
94 C7 **Aberdaron** Gwynd
207 H4 **Aberdeen** C Aber
207 G3 **Aberdeen Airport** C Aber
177 G2 **Aberdour** Fife
52 B7 **Aberdulais** Neath
80 E4 **Aberdyfi** Gwynd
68 C5 **Aberedw** Powys
48 D2 **Abereiddy** Pembks
95 G5 **Abererch** Gwynd
53 G7 **Aberfan** Myr Td
194 D6 **Aberfeldy** P & K
108 D7 **Aberffraw** IOA
124 C3 **Aberford** Leeds
184 C7 **Aberfoyle** Stirlg
53 L5 **Abergavenny** Mons
110 C6 **Abergele** Conwy
66 D7 **Abergorlech** Carmth
67 J4 **Abergwesyn** Powys
50 F2 **Abergwili** Carmth
36 D2 **Abergwynfi** Neath
109 J6 **Abergwyngregyn** Gwynd
80 F3 **Abergynolwyn** Gwynd
36 D4 **Aberkenfig** Brdgnd
178 B3 **Aberlady** E Loth
196 E5 **Aberlemno** Angus
81 G2 **Aberllefenni** Powys
68 D6 **Aberllynfi** Powys
215 G5 **Aberlour** Moray
82 D5 **Abermule** Powys
50 D2 **Abernant** Carmth
186 C4 **Abernethy** P & K
186 D2 **Abernyte** P & K
65 J4 **Aberporth** Cerdgn
94 E6 **Abersoch** Gwynd
53 K7 **Abersychan** Torfn
36 F5 **Aberthin** V Glam
53 K7 **Abertillery** Blae G
37 H3 **Abertridwr** Caerph
97 G8 **Abertridwr** Powys
185 K4 **Aberuthven** P & K
80 D6 **Aberystwyth** Cerdgn
41 J2 **Abingdon** Oxon
31 J3 **Abinger** Surrey
31 H2 **Abinger Hammer** Surrey
73 L3 **Abington** Nhants
165 H5 **Abington** S Lans
75 K5 **Abington Pigotts** Cambs
56 C6 **Ablington** Gloucs
114 D5 **Abney** Derbys
205 L5 **Aboyne** Abers
112 E2 **Abram** Wigan
212 E7 **Abriachan** Highld
45 J2 **Abridge** Essex
39 G5 **Abson** S Glos
73 J5 **Abthorpe** Nhants
118 F5 **Aby** Lincs
124 E2 **Acaster Malbis** York
124 E3 **Acaster Selby** N York
121 L5 **Accrington** Lancs
188 F5 **Acha** Ag & B
232 f3 **Acha Mor** W Isls
172 D3 **Achahoish** Ag & B
195 H7 **Achalader** P & K
182 D1 **Achaleven** Ag & B
211 K3 **Achanalt** Highld
222 E6 **Achandunie** Highld
222 D2 **Achany** Highld
190 D3 **Acharacle** Highld
190 E6 **Acharn** Highld
194 B7 **Acharn** P & K
231 H6 **Achavanich** Highld
224 C7 **Achduart** Highld
228 D7 **Achfary** Highld
224 C6 **Achiltibuie** Highld
161 J6 **Achinhoan** Ag & B
210 E6 **Achintee** Highld
210 C6 **Achintraid** Highld
224 C4 **Achmelvich** Highld
210 D7 **Achmore** Highld
232 f3 **Achmore** W Isls
224 C3 **Achnacarnin** Highld
201 J7 **Achnacarry** Highld
199 J4 **Achnacloich** Highld
202 C2 **Achnaconeran** Highld
191 G7 **Achnacroish** Ag & B
189 L6 **Achnadrish Lodge** Ag & B
185 J1 **Achnafauld** P & K
222 F7 **Achnagarron** Highld
189 L3 **Achnaha** Highld
224 B5 **Achnahaird** Highld
225 L6 **Achnairn** Highld
191 G4 **Achnalea** Highld
172 D2 **Achnamara** Ag & B
211 J3 **Achnasheen** Highld
210 F5 **Achnashellach Lodge** Highld
215 G7 **Achnastank** Moray
189 K3 **Achosnich** Highld
190 E6 **Achranich** Highld
230 E3 **Achreamie** Highld
192 B3 **Achriabhach** Highld
228 C5 **Achriesgill** Highld
229 K3 **Achtoty** Highld
88 E6 **Achurch** Nhants
222 F3 **Achvaich** Highld
231 L5 **Ackergill** Highld
141 L4 **Acklam** Middsb
134 B7 **Acklam** N York
84 D4 **Ackleton** Shrops
159 G2 **Acklington** Nthumb
124 C6 **Ackton** Wakefd
124 C7 **Ackworth Moor Top** Wakefd
93 J2 **Acle** Norfk
85 K6 **Acock's Green** Birm
35 J2 **Acol** Kent
150 B2 **Acomb** Nthumb
124 E1 **Acomb** York
54 D2 **Aconbury** Herefs
98 F2 **Acton** Ches
44 D4 **Acton** Gt Lon
99 J4 **Acton** Staffs
77 K5 **Acton** Suffk
70 E2 **Acton** Worcs
70 C4 **Acton Beauchamp** Herefs
112 E6 **Acton Bridge** Ches
83 K3 **Acton Burnell** Shrops
70 C4 **Acton Green** Herefs
97 M3 **Acton Park** Wrexhm
84 B4 **Acton Round** Shrops
83 J5 **Acton Scott** Shrops
99 L8 **Acton Trussell** Staffs
39 J4 **Acton Turville** S Glos
99 H6 **Adbaston** Staffs
26 E7 **Adber** Dorset
101 L5 **Adbolton** Notts
72 F7 **Adderbury** Oxon
98 F4 **Adderley** Shrops
176 D5 **Addiewell** W Loth
123 G1 **Addingham** Brad
58 C3 **Addington** Bucks
45 G7 **Addington** Gt Lon
33 H2 **Addington** Kent
45 G6 **Addiscombe** Gt Lon
43 H7 **Addlestone** Surrey
119 H7 **Addlethorpe** Lincs
59 H6 **Adeyfield** Herts
82 B4 **Adfa** Powys
69 H1 **Adforton** Herefs
35 G4 **Adisham** Kent
56 E3 **Adlestrop** Gloucs
125 K6 **Adlingfleet** E R Yk
121 J7 **Adlington** Lancs
100 B7 **Admaston** Staffs
84 B2 **Admaston** Wrekin
71 L5 **Admington** Warwks
65 J6 **Adpar** Cerdgn
25 L5 **Adsborough** Somset
25 J4 **Adscombe** Somset
58 C3 **Adstock** Bucks
31 H6 **Adversane** W Susx
214 D7 **Advie** Highld
124 E8 **Adwick Le Street** Donc
115 J2 **Adwick upon Dearne** Donc
155 H4 **Ae** D & G
155 H5 **Ae Bridgend** D & G
36 D2 **Afan Forest Park** Neath
216 B6 **Affleck** Abers
14 F4 **Affpuddle** Dorset
201 J2 **Affric Lodge** Highld
110 F6 **Afon-wen** Flints
16 D5 **Afton** IOW
131 K3 **Agglethorpe** N York
111 L4 **Aigburth** Lpool
126 C2 **Aike** E R Yk
148 E5 **Aiketgate** Cumb
148 B4 **Aikton** Cumb
89 G4 **Ailsworth** C Pete
132 E4 **Ainderby Quernhow** N York
132 E2 **Ainderby Steeple** N York
62 D4 **Aingers Green** Essex
120 D7 **Ainsdale** Sefton
148 F5 **Ainstable** Cumb
142 E5 **Ainthorpe** N York
176 F5 **Ainville** W Loth
181 M7 **Aird** Ag & B
144 D3 **Aird** D & G
232 g2 **Aird** W Isls
232 e3 **Aird a Mhulaidh** W Isls
232 e4 **Aird Asaig** W Isls
209 L6 **Aird Dhubh** Highld
181 H2 **Aird of Kinloch** Ag & B
199 J5 **Aird of Sleat** Highld
232 d2 **Aird Uig** W Isls
182 E2 **Airdeny** Ag & B
175 K5 **Airdrie** N Lans
175 K5 **Airdriehill** N Lans
182 E2 **Airds Bay** Ag & B
154 B7 **Airds of Kells** D & G
232 e3 **Airidh a bhruaich** W Isls
146 D4 **Airieland** D & G
195 L6 **Airlie** Angus
125 H5 **Airmyn** E R Yk
186 A1 **Airntully** P & K
199 L4 **Airor** Highld
176 B2 **Airth** Falk
131 G7 **Airton** N York
116 E3 **Aisby** Lincs
103 G5 **Aisby** Lincs
7 G4 **Aish** Devon
7 J4 **Aish** Devon
25 J4 **Aisholt** Somset
132 D2 **Aiskew** N York
143 H5 **Aislaby** N York
134 B3 **Aislaby** N York
141 J5 **Aislaby** S on T
116 F5 **Aisthorpe** Lincs
235 c5 **Aith** Shet
168 E4 **Akeld** Nthumb
73 K6 **Akeley** Bucks
78 D5 **Akenham** Suffk
6 B2 **Albaston** Cnwll
83 G1 **Alberbury** Shrops
19 H3 **Albourne** W Susx
98 C8 **Albrighton** Shrops
84 E3 **Albrighton** Shrops
92 F6 **Alburgh** Norfk
60 C3 **Albury** Herts
31 H2 **Albury** Surrey
31 H3 **Albury Heath** Surrey
212 E3 **Alcaig** Highld
83 J6 **Alcaston** Shrops
71 K3 **Alcester** Warwks
20 B5 **Alciston** E Susx
89 H7 **Alconbury** Cambs
89 H7 **Alconbury Weston** Cambs
132 F6 **Aldborough** N York
106 E5 **Aldborough** Norfk
40 E5 **Aldbourne** Wilts
127 G3 **Aldbrough** E R Yk
140 F5 **Aldbrough St John** N York
58 F5 **Aldbury** Herts

129 K7 **Aldcliffe** Lancs
194 E4 **Aldclune** P & K
79 K3 **Aldeburgh** Suffk
93 J5 **Aldeby** Norfk
43 J2 **Aldenham** Herts
28 D6 **Alderbury** Wilts
106 D8 **Alderford** Norfk
28 C8 **Alderholt** Dorset
39 H3 **Alderley** Gloucs
113 J5 **Alderley Edge** Ches
41 L7 **Aldermaston** W Berk
72 B5 **Alderminster** Warwks
30 E2 **Aldershot** Hants
55 M2 **Alderton** Gloucs
73 K5 **Alderton** Nhants
79 H6 **Alderton** Suffk
39 J4 **Alderton** Wilts
100 F2 **Alderwasley** Derbys
132 D5 **Aldfield** N York
98 B1 **Aldford** Ches
88 E3 **Aldgate** Rutlnd
61 L3 **Aldham** Essex
78 C5 **Aldham** Suffk
18 C5 **Aldingbourne** W Susx
129 G5 **Aldingham** Cumb
34 E7 **Aldington** Kent
71 J5 **Aldington** Worcs
34 E7 **Aldington Corner** Kent
205 H1 **Aldivalloch** Moray
174 C1 **Aldochlay** Ag & B
90 C8 **Aldreth** Cambs
85 J4 **Aldridge** Wsall
79 J3 **Aldringham** Suffk
56 D6 **Aldsworth** Gloucs
215 H8 **Aldunie** Moray
100 E2 **Aldwark** Derbys
133 G6 **Aldwark** N York
18 C6 **Aldwick** W Susx
88 E6 **Aldwincle** Nhants
41 K4 **Aldworth** W Berk
174 D3 **Alexandria** W Duns
25 J4 **Aley** Somset
12 E3 **Alfington** Devon
31 H5 **Alfold** Surrey
31 H4 **Alfold Crossways** Surrey
206 B3 **Alford** Abers
118 F6 **Alford** Lincs
26 E5 **Alford** Somset
101 H2 **Alfreton** Derbys
70 D4 **Alfrick** Worcs
70 D4 **Alfrick Pound** Worcs
20 B5 **Alfriston** E Susx
103 M5 **Algarkirk** Lincs
26 F4 **Alhampton** Somset
125 K6 **Alkborough** N Linc
35 H6 **Alkham** Kent
100 D5 **Alkmonton** Derbys
40 B7 **All Cannings** Wilts
93 H6 **All Saints South Elmham** Suffk
83 J4 **All Stretton** Shrops
7 J5 **Allaleigh** Devon
204 D6 **Allanaquoich** Abers
175 L6 **Allanbank** N Lans
179 H7 **Allanton** Border
175 L6 **Allanton** N Lans
175 K7 **Allanton** S Lans
54 F6 **Allaston** Gloucs
29 J7 **Allbrook** Hants
85 L4 **Allen End** Warwks
60 D5 **Allen's Green** Herts
149 L4 **Allendale** Nthumb
149 L6 **Allenheads** Nthumb
69 J7 **Allensmore** Herefs
101 G6 **Allenton** C Derb
24 B6 **Aller** Devon
26 B5 **Aller** Somset
147 J6 **Allerby** Cumb
12 D4 **Allercombe** Devon
24 D3 **Allerford** Somset
134 D3 **Allerston** N York
125 J2 **Allerthorpe** E R Yk
123 G4 **Allerton** Brad
213 H2 **Allerton** Highld
111 L4 **Allerton** Lpool
124 C5 **Allerton Bywater** Leeds
132 F7 **Allerton Mauleverer** N York
86 C7 **Allesley** Covtry
101 G5 **Allestree** C Derb
88 B4 **Allexton** Leics
113 L7 **Allgreave** Ches
46 D4 **Allhallows** Medway
210 C3 **Alligin Shuas** Highld
13 L4 **Allington** Dorset
102 E4 **Allington** Lincs
39 K5 **Allington** Wilts
40 B7 **Allington** Wilts
28 D4 **Allington** Wilts
129 J4 **Allithwaite** Cumb
185 J8 **Alloa** Clacks
147 J6 **Allonby** Cumb
163 J5 **Alloway** S Ayrs
26 B8 **Allowenshay** Somset
192 C6 **Alltchaorunn** Highld
66 B7 **Alltwalis** Carmth
51 K5 **Alltwen** Neath
66 C5 **Alltyblaca** Cerdgn
26 F8 **Allweston** Dorset
69 G4 **Almeley** Herefs
124 E8 **Almholme** Donc
99 G5 **Almington** Staffs
185 M3 **Almondbank** P & K
123 H7 **Almondbury** Kirk
38 E4 **Almondsbury** S Glos
133 G6 **Alne** N York
222 E7 **Alness** Highld
168 E7 **Alnham** Nthumb
169 J7 **Alnmouth** Nthumb
169 J6 **Alnwick** Nthumb
44 D4 **Alperton** Gt Lon
77 K7 **Alphamstone** Essex
77 K4 **Alpheton** Suffk
11 L6 **Alphington** Devon
114 E8 **Alport** Derbys
98 E1 **Alpraham** Ches
62 C4 **Alresford** Essex
85 L1 **Alrewas** Staffs
99 H2 **Alsager** Ches
100 D2 **Alsop en le Dale** Derbys
149 J5 **Alston** Cumb
13 H2 **Alston** Devon
26 B2 **Alston Sutton** Somset
55 M2 **Alstone** Gloucs
100 C2 **Alstonefield** Staffs
23 L6 **Alswear** Devon
224 B6 **Altandhu** Highld
9 G8 **Altarnun** Cnwll
222 C2 **Altass** Highld
190 D8 **Altcreich** Ag & B
173 H4 **Altgaltraig** Ag & B
61 L7 **Althorne** Essex
125 K8 **Althorpe** N Linc
230 E6 **Altnabreac Station** Highld
182 B2 **Altnacraig** Ag & B
225 M2 **Altnaharra** Highld
115 G8 **Alton** Derbys
30 B4 **Alton** Hants
100 B4 **Alton** Staffs
40 C7 **Alton Barnes** Wilts
14 D3 **Alton Pancras** Dorset
40 C7 **Alton Priors** Wilts
100 B4 **Alton Towers** Staffs
113 H4 **Altrincham** Traffd
184 B6 **Altskeith Hotel** Stirlg
185 J7 **Alva** Clacks
216 D3 **Alvah** Abers
112 D6 **Alvanley** Ches
101 H5 **Alvaston** C Derb
85 J8 **Alvechurch** Worcs
86 B3 **Alvecote** Warwks
27 L6 **Alvediston** Wilts
84 D6 **Alveley** Shrops
23 H6 **Alverdiscott** Devon
17 H3 **Alverstoke** Hants
17 H5 **Alverstone** IOW
123 L6 **Alverthorpe** Wakefd
102 C4 **Alverton** Notts
214 E3 **Alves** Moray
56 F6 **Alvescot** Oxon
38 F3 **Alveston** S Glos
72 B3 **Alveston** Warwks
118 E4 **Alvingham** Lincs
54 E7 **Alvington** Gloucs
89 G4 **Alwalton** Cambs
168 D7 **Alwinton** Nthumb
123 K3 **Alwoodley** Leeds
195 K6 **Alyth** P & K
101 G3 **Ambergate** Derbys
55 J7 **Amberley** Gloucs
18 D3 **Amberley** W Susx
159 G2 **Amble** Nthumb
84 F6 **Amblecote** Dudley
123 G5 **Ambler Thorn** Brad
137 K6 **Ambleside** Cumb
49 G3 **Ambleston** Pembks
57 L4 **Ambrosden** Oxon
125 K7 **Amcotts** N Linc
42 F2 **Amersham** Bucks
28 D3 **Amesbury** Wilts
232 d4 **Amhuinnsuidhe** W Isls
86 B3 **Amington** Staffs
155 H5 **Amisfield Town** D & G
108 F3 **Amlwch** IOA
51 J3 **Ammanford** Carmth
134 B5 **Amotherby** N York
29 H6 **Ampfield** Hants
133 J4 **Ampleforth** N York
56 B7 **Ampney Crucis** Gloucs
56 C7 **Ampney St Mary** Gloucs
56 B7 **Ampney St Peter** Gloucs
28 F3 **Amport** Hants
74 F6 **Ampthill** Beds
77 J1 **Ampton** Suffk
49 K6 **Amroth** Pembks
185 J1 **Amulree** P & K
59 K5 **Amwell** Herts
232 d5 **An t-Ob** W Isls
191 G4 **Anaheilt** Highld
103 G4 **Ancaster** Lincs
168 E1 **Ancroft** Nthumb
167 K4 **Ancrum** Border
119 G6 **Anderby** Lincs
29 G3 **Andover** Hants
56 A4 **Andoversford** Gloucs
237 d2 **Andreas** IOM
45 G6 **Anerley** Gt Lon
111 K3 **Anfield** Lpool
3 G4 **Angarrack** Cnwll
83 L7 **Angelbank** Shrops
48 E6 **Angle** Pembks
108 E5 **Anglesey** IOA
18 E5 **Angmering** W Susx
124 D2 **Angram** N York
223 H6 **Ankerville** Highld
126 C5 **Anlaby** E R Yk
105 H6 **Anmer** Norfk
17 J1 **Anmore** Hants
29 G3 **Anna Valley** Hants
147 L2 **Annan** D & G
210 D4 **Annat** Highld
175 J4 **Annathill** N Lans
163 K5 **Annbank** S Ayrs
71 L4 **Anne Hathaway's Cottage** Warwks
101 J2 **Annesley** Notts
101 J2 **Annesley Woodhouse** Notts
150 F5 **Annfield Plain** Dur
174 F5 **Anniesland** C Glas
120 D5 **Ansdell** Lancs
26 F5 **Ansford** Somset
86 C5 **Ansley** Warwks
100 E7 **Anslow** Staffs
100 D7 **Anslow Gate** Staffs
60 C2 **Anstey** Herts
87 G2 **Anstey** Leics
187 J6 **Anstruther** Fife
19 J2 **Ansty** W Susx
86 E6 **Ansty** Warwks
27 L6 **Ansty** Wilts
147 L4 **Anthorn** Cumb
106 F5 **Antingham** Norfk
103 M3 **Anton's Gowt** Lincs
6 B5 **Antony** Cnwll
112 F5 **Antrobus** Ches
103 J3 **Anwick** Lincs
145 M4 **Anwoth** D & G
32 D2 **Aperfield** Gt Lon
88 E4 **Apethorpe** Nhants
117 J6 **Apley** Lincs
115 G5 **Apperknowle** Derbys
55 K3 **Apperley** Gloucs
191 J6 **Appin** Ag & B
126 B7 **Appleby** N Linc
86 C2 **Appleby Magna** Leics
86 C2 **Appleby Parva** Leics
139 G3 **Appleby-in-Westmorland** Cumb
209 L5 **Applecross** Highld
23 G5 **Appledore** Devon
25 G8 **Appledore** Devon
34 C8 **Appledore** Kent
41 K2 **Appleford** Oxon
155 J5 **Applegarth Town** D & G
28 F2 **Appleshaw** Hants
112 D4 **Appleton** Halton
57 H7 **Appleton** Oxon
112 F5 **Appleton** Warrtn
124 E3 **Appleton Roebuck** N York
112 F5 **Appleton Thorn** Warrtn
141 J6 **Appleton Wiske** N York
133 L3 **Appleton-le-Moors** N York
134 B5 **Appleton-le-Street** N York
167 H6 **Appletreehall** Border
131 K7 **Appletreewick** N York
25 G6 **Appley** Somset
121 G8 **Appley Bridge** Lancs
17 G5 **Apse Heath** IOW
59 J2 **Apsley End** Beds
18 A5 **Apuldram** W Susx
223 H6 **Arabella** Highld
196 F7 **Arbirlot** Angus
223 J5 **Arboll** Highld
42 C6 **Arborfield** Wokham
42 C6 **Arborfield Cross** Wokham
197 G7 **Arbroath** Angus
197 K2 **Arbuthnott** Abers
50 F5 **Archddu** Carmth
141 G4 **Archdeacon Newton** Darltn
174 D3 **Archencarroch** W Duns
214 F5 **Archiestown** Moray
236 e6 **Archirondel** Jersey
99 H1 **Arclid Green** Ches
182 F3 **Ardanaiseig Hotel** Ag & B
210 C7 **Ardaneaskan** Highld
210 C6 **Ardarroch** Highld

160 D1 **Ardbeg** Ag & B
173 J5 **Ardbeg** Ag & B
173 K2 **Ardbeg** Ag & B
220 F4 **Ardcharnich** Highld
180 E4 **Ardchiavaig** Ag & B
182 D5 **Ardchonnel** Ag & B
184 D5 **Ardchullarie More** Stirlg
183 J7 **Arddarroch** Ag & B
201 H7 **Ardechive** Highld
163 H2 **Ardeer** N Ayrs
60 A3 **Ardeley** Herts
210 D8 **Ardelve** Highld
174 C2 **Arden** Ag & B
71 K4 **Ardens Grafton** Warwks
182 B3 **Ardentallen** Ag & B
173 L2 **Ardentinny** Ag & B
173 H4 **Ardentraive** Ag & B
184 E1 **Ardeonaig Hotel** Stirlg
213 J4 **Ardersier** Highld
220 D4 **Ardessie** Highld
182 A6 **Ardfern** Ag & B
222 D4 **Ardgay** Highld
191 K4 **Ardgour** Highld
173 L4 **Ardgowan** Inver
173 K4 **Ardhallow** Ag & B
232 e4 **Ardhasig** W Isls
210 B3 **Ardheslaig** Highld
220 F4 **Ardindrean** Highld
32 C7 **Ardingly** W Susx
41 H3 **Ardington** Oxon
173 G5 **Ardlamont** Ag & B
62 C3 **Ardleigh** Essex
62 C2 **Ardleigh Heath** Essex
195 L7 **Ardler** P & K
57 K3 **Ardley** Oxon
183 K4 **Ardlui** Ag & B
172 B2 **Ardlussa** Ag & B
191 L8 **Ardmaddy** Ag & B
220 E2 **Ardmair** Highld
173 J5 **Ardmaleish** Ag & B
172 B8 **Ardminish** Ag & B
190 E3 **Ardmolich** Highld
174 C3 **Ardmore** Ag & B
222 F4 **Ardmore** Highld
173 K3 **Ardnadam** Ag & B
212 E4 **Ardnagrask** Highld
210 D7 **Ardnarff** Highld
190 F4 **Ardnastang** Highld
183 G5 **Ardno** Ag & B
201 J5 **Ardochy House** Highld
172 C6 **Ardpatrick** Ag & B
172 E2 **Ardrishaig** Ag & B
222 E6 **Ardross** Highld
163 G2 **Ardrossan** N Ayrs
123 K5 **Ardsley East** Leeds
190 B4 **Ardslignish** Highld
171 J7 **Ardtalla** Ag & B
190 C3 **Ardtoe** Highld
182 A5 **Arduaine** Ag & B
212 E2 **Ardullie** Highld
199 K5 **Ardvasar** Highld
184 D3 **Ardvorlich** P & K
232 e3 **Ardvourlie** W Isls
144 D5 **Ardwell** D & G
113 J3 **Ardwick** Manch
70 E1 **Areley Kings** Worcs
190 D3 **Arevegaig** Highld
30 D4 **Arford** Hants
53 J7 **Argoed** Caerph
183 J6 **Argyll Forest Park** Ag & B
232 e3 **Aribruach** W Isls
180 D3 **Aridhglas** Ag & B
188 F5 **Arileod** Ag & B
189 G5 **Arinagour** Ag & B
182 C3 **Ariogan** Ag & B
199 K7 **Arisaig** Highld
199 L7 **Arisaig House** Highld
132 F7 **Arkendale** N York
76 C7 **Arkesden** Essex
130 B5 **Arkholme** Lancs
156 C4 **Arkleton** D & G
44 E2 **Arkley** Gt Lon
115 L1 **Arksey** Donc
115 H7 **Arkwright Town** Derbys
55 L4 **Arle** Gloucs
136 E4 **Arlecdon** Cumb
75 H7 **Arlesey** Beds
84 B2 **Arleston** Wrekin
112 F5 **Arley** Ches
86 C5 **Arley** Warwks
55 G6 **Arlingham** Gloucs
23 K4 **Arlington** Devon
20 B4 **Arlington** E Susx
230 A3 **Armadale** Highld
199 K5 **Armadale** Highld
176 C5 **Armadale** W Loth
137 G2 **Armaside** Cumb
148 E5 **Armathwaite** Cumb
92 F3 **Arminghall** Norfk
85 J1 **Armitage** Staffs
123 K4 **Armley** Leeds
88 F6 **Armston** Nhants
115 L1 **Armthorpe** Donc
188 F4 **Arnabost** Ag & B
131 H5 **Arncliffe** N York
187 H6 **Arncroach** Fife
215 G5 **Arndilly House** Moray
15 H5 **Arne** Dorset
87 H5 **Arnesby** Leics
186 B5 **Arngask** P & K
200 C3 **Arnisdale** Highld
209 J5 **Arnish** Highld
177 K6 **Arniston** Mdloth
232 f1 **Arnol** W Isls
126 E3 **Arnold** E R Yk
101 L4 **Arnold** Notts
184 D7 **Arnprior** Stirlg
129 K4 **Arnside** Cumb
190 B7 **Aros** Ag & B
129 G4 **Arrad Foot** Cumb
126 C2 **Arram** E R Yk
162 B3 **Arran** N Ayrs
132 C2 **Arrathorne** N York
17 G5 **Arreton** IOW
210 B3 **Arrina** Highld
75 K4 **Arrington** Cambs
183 K6 **Arrochar** Ag & B
71 J3 **Arrow** Warwks
83 J2 **Arscott** Shrops
212 F4 **Artafallie** Highld
123 K2 **Arthington** Leeds
87 L7 **Arthingworth** Nhants
217 H6 **Arthrath** Abers
217 J7 **Artrochie** Abers
18 D4 **Arundel** W Susx
136 E3 **Asby** Cumb
173 J5 **Ascog** Ag & B
42 F6 **Ascot** W & M
56 F4 **Ascott-under-Wychwood** Oxon
132 F4 **Asenby** N York
102 B8 **Asfordby** Leics
102 B8 **Asfordby Hill** Leics
103 J4 **Asgarby** Lincs
118 D7 **Asgarby** Lincs
45 L6 **Ash** Kent
35 H3 **Ash** Kent
26 C7 **Ash** Somset
30 E2 **Ash** Surrey
30 E2 **Ash Green** Surrey
86 D6 **Ash Green** Warwks
98 E4 **Ash Magna** Shrops
24 C6 **Ash Mill** Devon
98 E5 **Ash Parva** Shrops
25 J5 **Ash Priors** Somset
78 B5 **Ash Street** Suffk
12 C1 **Ash Thomas** Devon
30 E2 **Ash Vale** Surrey
41 K5 **Ashampstead** W Berk
78 E4 **Ashbocking** Suffk
78 E4 **Ashbocking Green** Suffk
100 D3 **Ashbourne** Derbys
25 G6 **Ashbrittle** Somset
7 H2 **Ashburton** Devon
10 D5 **Ashbury** Devon
40 E4 **Ashbury** Oxon
125 L8 **Ashby** N Linc
118 F7 **Ashby by Partney** Lincs
118 C2 **Ashby cum Fenby** NE Lin
103 H2 **Ashby de la Launde** Lincs
87 K2 **Ashby Folville** Leics
87 H5 **Ashby Magna** Leics
87 G5 **Ashby Parva** Leics
118 D7 **Ashby Puerorum** Lincs
73 H2 **Ashby St Ledgers** Nhants
93 G3 **Ashby St Mary** Norfk
86 D1 **Ashby-de-la-Zouch** Leics
55 L2 **Ashchurch** Gloucs
11 L8 **Ashcombe** Devon
37 M7 **Ashcombe** N Som
26 C4 **Ashcott** Somset
76 E6 **Ashdon** Essex
29 K2 **Ashe** Hants
62 A7 **Asheldham** Essex
77 H6 **Ashen** Essex
58 B5 **Ashendon** Bucks
58 F6 **Asheridge** Bucks
185 G6 **Ashfield** Stirlg
78 E3 **Ashfield** Suffk
92 F8 **Ashfield Green** Suffk
23 H4 **Ashford** Devon
7 G6 **Ashford** Devon
34 D6 **Ashford** Kent
43 H6 **Ashford** Surrey
69 K1 **Ashford Bowdler** Shrops
69 K1 **Ashford Carbonel** Shrops
41 K7 **Ashford Hill** Hants
114 D7 **Ashford in the Water** Derbys
175 K7 **Ashgill** S Lans
12 E1 **Ashill** Devon
91 K3 **Ashill** Norfk
25 L7 **Ashill** Somset
46 E2 **Ashingdon** Essex
159 G5 **Ashington** Nthumb
26 E6 **Ashington** Somset
18 F3 **Ashington** W Susx
167 G5 **Ashkirk** Border
55 J3 **Ashleworth** Gloucs
55 J3 **Ashleworth Quay** Gloucs
77 G3 **Ashley** Cambs
113 H5 **Ashley** Ches
10 F3 **Ashley** Devon
39 L2 **Ashley** Gloucs
29 G5 **Ashley** Hants
16 B4 **Ashley** Hants
35 J5 **Ashley** Kent
87 L5 **Ashley** Nhants
99 H5 **Ashley** Staffs
39 J6 **Ashley** Wilts
58 F6 **Ashley Green** Bucks
41 H8 **Ashmansworth** Hants
22 E7 **Ashmansworthy** Devon
27 K7 **Ashmore** Dorset
41 J6 **Ashmore Green** W Berk
72 C3 **Ashorne** Warwks
115 G8 **Ashover** Derbys
72 C1 **Ashow** Warwks
70 B6 **Ashperton** Herefs
7 J4 **Ashprington** Devon
10 F3 **Ashreigney** Devon
44 D8 **Ashtead** Surrey
112 D7 **Ashton** Ches
3 G5 **Ashton** Cnwll
11 K7 **Ashton** Devon
69 K2 **Ashton** Herefs
173 L3 **Ashton** Inver
73 L5 **Ashton** Nhants
88 F5 **Ashton** Nhants
39 K8 **Ashton Common** Wilts
40 B2 **Ashton Keynes** Wilts
71 H6 **Ashton under Hill** Worcs
112 E2 **Ashton-in-Makerfield** Wigan
113 L2 **Ashton-under-Lyne** Tamesd
16 D1 **Ashurst** Hants
32 F5 **Ashurst** Kent
19 G3 **Ashurst** W Susx
32 D5 **Ashurstwood** W Susx
9 K5 **Ashwater** Devon
75 J6 **Ashwell** Herts
88 C2 **Ashwell** Rutlnd
75 J6 **Ashwell End** Herts
92 D4 **Ashwellthorpe** Norfk
26 F2 **Ashwick** Somset
105 H8 **Ashwicken** Norfk
128 F4 **Askam in Furness** Cumb
124 E7 **Askern** Donc
14 A4 **Askerswell** Dorset
58 D6 **Askett** Bucks
138 D3 **Askham** Cumb
116 C6 **Askham** Notts
124 E2 **Askham Bryan** York
124 E2 **Askham Richard** York
172 F1 **Asknish** Ag & B
131 H2 **Askrigg** N York
123 H2 **Askwith** N York
103 H6 **Aslackby** Lincs
92 D5 **Aslacton** Norfk
102 C4 **Aslockton** Notts
147 K6 **Aspatria** Cumb
60 B3 **Aspenden** Herts
74 D7 **Aspley Guise** Beds
74 D7 **Aspley Heath** Beds
121 J8 **Aspull** Wigan
125 H5 **Asselby** E R Yk
77 L6 **Assington** Suffk
77 H4 **Assington Green** Suffk
99 J1 **Astbury** Ches
73 J4 **Astcote** Nhants
118 C5 **Asterby** Lincs
83 H3 **Asterley** Shrops
83 H5 **Asterton** Shrops
56 F5 **Asthall** Oxon
56 F5 **Asthall Leigh** Oxon
223 G3 **Astle** Highld
98 D8 **Astley** Shrops
86 C5 **Astley** Warwks
113 G2 **Astley** Wigan
70 D2 **Astley** Worcs
84 C4 **Astley Abbots** Shrops
121 K7 **Astley Bridge** Bolton
70 E1 **Astley Cross** Worcs
112 E5 **Aston** Ches
98 E3 **Aston** Ches
114 D5 **Aston** Derbys
111 J7 **Aston** Flints
69 J1 **Aston** Herefs
59 L4 **Aston** Herts
57 G7 **Aston** Oxon
115 J4 **Aston** Rothm
98 D6 **Aston** Shrops
84 E5 **Aston** Shrops
99 H4 **Aston** Staffs
99 K7 **Aston** Staffs

99 K6 **Aston** Staffs
42 C4 **Aston** Wokham
84 B2 **Aston** Wrekin
58 D4 **Aston Abbotts** Bucks
84 B6 **Aston Botterell** Shrops
71 K3 **Aston Cantlow** Warwks
58 E5 **Aston Clinton** Bucks
54 F4 **Aston Crews** Herefs
59 L3 **Aston End** Herts
71 G1 **Aston Fields** Worcs
86 F5 **Aston Flamville** Leics
55 G4 **Aston Ingham** Herefs
72 F4 **Aston le Walls** Nhants
71 L7 **Aston Magna** Gloucs
83 K6 **Aston Munslow** Shrops
83 H6 **Aston on Clun** Shrops
83 G3 **Aston Pigott** Shrops
83 G3 **Aston Rogers** Shrops
58 B7 **Aston Rowant** Oxon
71 J6 **Aston Somerville** Worcs
71 K6 **Aston Subedge** Gloucs
41 K3 **Aston Tirrold** Oxon
41 K3 **Aston Upthorpe** Oxon
84 B5 **Aston-Eyre** Shrops
101 H6 **Aston-upon-Trent** Derbys
75 J6 **Astwick** Beds
74 D5 **Astwood** M Keyn
71 G2 **Astwood** Worcs
71 J3 **Astwood Bank** Worcs
103 H4 **Aswarby** Lincs
118 E7 **Aswardby** Lincs
83 K2 **Atcham** Shrops
14 E4 **Athelhampton** Dorset
78 E1 **Athelington** Suffk
25 M5 **Athelney** Somset
178 C3 **Athelstaneford** E Loth
23 J6 **Atherington** Devon
86 C4 **Atherstone** Warwks
72 B4 **Atherstone on Stour** Warwks
113 G2 **Atherton** Wigan
100 E3 **Atlow** Derbys
210 E6 **Attadale** Highld
117 G3 **Atterby** Lincs
115 G4 **Attercliffe** Sheff
86 D4 **Atterton** Leics
92 C4 **Attleborough** Norfk
86 D5 **Attleborough** Warwks
92 D1 **Attlebridge** Norfk
77 G4 **Attleton Green** Suffk
126 F1 **Atwick** E R Yk
39 J7 **Atworth** Wilts
116 F8 **Aubourn** Lincs
217 G7 **Auchedly** Abers
197 H1 **Auchenblae** Abers
175 L2 **Auchenbowie** Stirlg
146 D5 **Auchencairn** D & G
155 G5 **Auchencairn** D & G
162 D4 **Auchencairn** N Ayrs
179 H6 **Auchencrow** Border
177 H6 **Auchendinny** Mdloth
176 D7 **Auchengray** S Lans
215 J3 **Auchenhalrig** Moray
164 F2 **Auchenheath** S Lans
154 E3 **Auchenhessnane** D & G
173 G4 **Auchenlochan** Ag & B
174 C8 **Auchenmade** N Ayrs
144 F4 **Auchenmalg** D & G
174 C8 **Auchentiber** N Ayrs
184 C8 **Auchentroig** Stirlg
221 G5 **Auchindrean** Highld
216 C5 **Auchininna** Abers
164 B5 **Auchinleck** E Ayrs
175 H4 **Auchinloch** N Lans
175 J3 **Auchinstarry** N Lans
191 L2 **Auchintore** Highld
217 K6 **Auchiries** Abers
207 G6 **Auchlee** Abers
206 C1 **Auchleven** Abers
164 F2 **Auchlochan** S Lans
206 B5 **Auchlossan** Abers
184 B2 **Auchlyne** Stirlg
164 A4 **Auchmillan** E Ayrs
197 G7 **Auchmithie** Angus
186 C6 **Auchmuirbridge** Fife
196 D4 **Auchnacree** Angus
217 H6 **Auchnagatt** Abers
204 F2 **Auchnarrow** Moray
144 B3 **Auchnotteroch** D & G
215 H4 **Auchroisk** Moray
185 K5 **Auchterarder** P & K
202 B4 **Auchteraw** Highld
203 L2 **Auchterblair** Highld
219 J6 **Auchtercairn** Highld
186 C7 **Auchterderran** Fife
196 B8 **Auchterhouse** Angus
216 D6 **Auchterless** Abers
186 D5 **Auchtermuchty** Fife
212 D3 **Auchterneed** Highld
177 H1 **Auchtertool** Fife
210 C8 **Auchtertyre** Highld
184 C4 **Auchtubh** Stirlg
231 L3 **Auckengill** Highld
115 M2 **Auckley** Donc
113 K3 **Audenshaw** Tamesd
98 F4 **Audlem** Ches
99 J3 **Audley** Staffs
76 D6 **Audley End** Essex
76 D6 **Audley End** Essex
77 J4 **Audley End** Suffk
148 A7 **Aughertree** Cumb
125 G3 **Aughton** E R Yk
111 L1 **Aughton** Lancs
129 L6 **Aughton** Lancs
115 J4 **Aughton** Rothm
28 E1 **Aughton** Wilts
112 B1 **Aughton Park** Lancs
213 L4 **Auldearn** Highld
69 J4 **Aulden** Herefs
154 F5 **Auldgirth** D & G
175 H7 **Auldhouse** S Lans
200 E2 **Ault a' chruinn** Highld
115 J7 **Ault Hucknall** Derbys
219 K4 **Aultbea** Highld
219 H4 **Aultgrishin** Highld
221 J7 **Aultguish Inn** Highld
215 J4 **Aultmore** Moray
202 E2 **Aultnagoire** Highld
222 F5 **Aultnamain Inn** Highld
103 H5 **Aunsby** Lincs
38 E3 **Aust** S Glos
116 A3 **Austerfield** Donc
86 C3 **Austrey** Warwks
130 E5 **Austwick** N York
118 E5 **Authorpe** Lincs
40 C6 **Avebury** Wilts
45 L4 **Aveley** Thurr
39 K2 **Avening** Gloucs
102 C2 **Averham** Notts
7 G6 **Aveton Gifford** Devon
203 L3 **Aviemore** Highld
41 G6 **Avington** W Berk
213 G4 **Avoch** Highld
15 L3 **Avon** Dorset
72 E4 **Avon Dassett** Warwks
176 B4 **Avonbridge** Falk
38 D5 **Avonmouth** Bristl
7 G4 **Avonwick** Devon
28 F6 **Awbridge** Hants
12 E3 **Awliscombe** Devon
55 G6 **Awre** Gloucs
101 J4 **Awsworth** Notts
26 B1 **Axbridge** Somset
29 L3 **Axford** Hants
40 E6 **Axford** Wilts
13 H3 **Axminster** Devon
13 G4 **Axmouth** Devon
141 G3 **Aycliffe** Dur
150 C2 **Aydon** Nthumb
54 E7 **Aylburton** Gloucs
12 D4 **Aylesbeare** Devon
58 D5 **Aylesbury** Bucks
126 F8 **Aylesby** NE Lin
33 J2 **Aylesford** Kent
35 H4 **Aylesham** Kent
87 H4 **Aylestone** C Leic
106 E4 **Aylmerton** Norfk
106 E6 **Aylsham** Norfk
70 B6 **Aylton** Gloucs
56 C4 **Aylworth** Gloucs
69 H2 **Aymestrey** Herefs
57 K2 **Aynho** Nhants
59 K5 **Ayot St Lawrence** Herts
163 J5 **Ayr** S Ayrs
131 J2 **Aysgarth** N York
25 G7 **Ayshford** Devon
129 J3 **Ayside** Cumb
88 C4 **Ayston** Rutlnd
60 F5 **Aythorpe Roding** Essex
179 J6 **Ayton** Border
132 C5 **Azerley** N York

B

7 L3 **Babbacombe** Torbay
60 C5 **Babbs Green** Herts
26 E5 **Babcary** Somset
27 G2 **Babington** Somset
76 D4 **Babraham** Cambs
116 B5 **Babworth** Notts
199 K7 **Back of Keppoch** Highld
234 d4 **Backaland** Ork
217 J4 **Backfolds** Abers
111 L6 **Backford** Ches
223 H2 **Backies** Highld
231 H5 **Backlass** Highld
38 C6 **Backwell** N Som
106 D5 **Baconsthorpe** Norfk
54 A2 **Bacton** Herefs
107 H5 **Bacton** Norfk
78 C2 **Bacton** Suffk
122 C6 **Bacup** Lancs
219 J6 **Badachro** Highld
40 D4 **Badbury** Swindn
73 H3 **Badby** Nhants
228 B7 **Badcall** Highld
228 C4 **Badcall** Highld
220 D3 **Badcaul** Highld
86 B8 **Baddesley Clinton** Warwks
86 C4 **Baddesley Ensor** Warwks
224 D4 **Baddidarrach** Highld
176 F7 **Baddinsgill** Border
216 D6 **Badenscoth** Abers
205 H2 **Badenyon** Abers
84 D4 **Badger** Shrops
55 K4 **Badgeworth** Gloucs
26 B2 **Badgworth** Somset
210 B8 **Badicaul** Highld
79 G2 **Badingham** Suffk
34 D4 **Badlesmere** Kent
165 K5 **Badlieu** Border
231 J5 **Badlipster** Highld
220 C3 **Badluachrach** Highld
223 G3 **Badninish** Highld
220 D3 **Badrallach** Highld
71 J5 **Badsey** Worcs
30 E2 **Badshot Lea** Surrey
124 C7 **Badsworth** Wakefd
78 B2 **Badwell Ash** Suffk
118 E6 **Bag Enderby** Lincs
27 H8 **Bagber** Dorset
133 G4 **Bagby** N York
233 b9 **Bagh a Chaisteil** W Isls
233 b9 **Bagh a Tuath** W Isls
111 H6 **Bagillt** Flints
86 D8 **Baginton** Warwks
51 L6 **Baglan** Neath
98 B6 **Bagley** Shrops
26 C3 **Bagley** Somset
30 A3 **Bagmore** Hants
99 L3 **Bagnall** Staffs
83 L8 **Bagot** Shrops
42 E7 **Bagshot** Surrey
39 G3 **Bagstone** S Glos
86 F2 **Bagworth** Leics
54 C3 **Bagwy Llydiart** Herefs
123 H3 **Baildon** Brad
123 H3 **Baildon Green** Brad
233 b6 **Baile a Mhanaich** W Isls
232 f3 **Baile Ailein** W Isls
180 D3 **Baile Mor** Ag & B
175 J5 **Baillieston** C Glas
131 H2 **Bainbridge** N York
216 B7 **Bainshole** Abers
89 G3 **Bainton** C Pete
126 B1 **Bainton** E R Yk
186 F6 **Baintown** Fife
167 K6 **Bairnkine** Border
114 E7 **Bakewell** Derbys
96 E5 **Bala** Gwynd
232 f3 **Balallan** W Isls
212 C7 **Balbeg** Highld
186 C2 **Balbeggie** P & K
212 D5 **Balblair** Highld
213 G2 **Balblair** Highld
115 K2 **Balby** Donc
146 E5 **Balcary** D & G
212 E5 **Balchraggan** Highld
228 B4 **Balchreick** Highld
32 B6 **Balcombe** W Susx
187 K5 **Balcomie Links** Fife
132 E4 **Baldersby** N York
132 E4 **Baldersby St James** N York
121 J4 **Balderstone** Lancs
102 D3 **Balderton** Notts
187 G5 **Baldinnie** Fife
185 L4 **Baldinnies** P & K
75 J7 **Baldock** Herts
187 G2 **Baldovie** C Dund
237 d5 **Baldrine** IOM
20 F3 **Baldslow** E Susx
106 B5 **Bale** Norfk
186 D2 **Baledgarno** P & K
188 C7 **Balemartine** Ag & B
177 G5 **Balerno** C Edin
186 D6 **Balfarg** Fife
196 E3 **Balfield** Angus
234 c5 **Balfour** Ork
174 F1 **Balfron** Stirlg
216 C6 **Balgaveny** Abers
196 E6 **Balgavies** Angus
185 L8 **Balgonar** Fife
144 D6 **Balgowan** D & G
202 F6 **Balgowan** Highld
218 B7 **Balgown** Highld
144 B3 **Balgracie** D & G
196 C8 **Balgray** Angus
165 H5 **Balgray** S Lans
44 F5 **Balham** Gt Lon
195 L6 **Balhary** P & K
186 B1 **Balholmie** P & K
230 C3 **Baligill** Highld
195 L5 **Balintore** Angus
223 J6 **Balintore** Highld
223 G7 **Balintraid** Highld
233 b6 **Balivanich** W Isls
133 G4 **Balk** N York

196 B7 Balkeerie Angus
125 J5 Balkholme E R Yk
191 L5 Ballachulish Highld
173 H6 Ballanlay Ag & B
152 C5 Ballantrae S Ayrs
237 b6 Ballasalla IOM
205 J6 Ballater Abers
237 c3 Ballaugh IOM
223 G6 Ballchraggan Highld
178 B3 Ballencrieff E Loth
188 B6 Ballevullin Ag & B
100 D2 Ballidon Derbys
161 L2 Balliekine N Ayrs
182 F7 Balliemore Ag & B
152 F4 Balligmorrie S Ayrs
172 F2 Ballimore Ag & B
184 C4 Ballimore Stirlg
214 E6 Ballindalloch Moray
186 D2 Ballindean P & K
58 E7 Ballinger Common Bucks
54 E2 Ballingham Herefs
186 C7 Ballingry Fife
194 F6 Ballinluig P & K
196 C5 Ballinshoe Angus
195 H5 Ballintuim P & K
213 H5 Balloch Highld
175 K4 Balloch N Lans
185 H4 Balloch P & K
153 G3 Balloch S Ayrs
174 D3 Balloch W Duns
206 B6 Ballogie Abers
31 G6 Balls Cross W Susx
32 E6 Balls Green E Susx
189 K7 Ballygown Ag & B
171 G5 Ballygrant Ag & B
188 F5 Ballyhaugh Ag & B
174 B2 Ballymenoch Ag & B
210 C8 Balmacara Highld
154 B6 Balmaclellan D & G
146 C6 Balmae D & G
174 D1 Balmaha Stirlg
186 E5 Balmalcolm Fife
146 B5 Balmangan D & G
207 H2 Balmedie Abers
186 F3 Balmerino Fife
162 B3 Balmichael N Ayrs
205 G6 Balmoral Castle Grounds Abers
175 G4 Balmore E Duns
223 J5 Balmuchy Highld
196 F6 Balmuir Angus
177 G2 Balmule Fife
187 G4 Balmullo Fife
226 E6 Balnacoil Lodge Highld
210 F5 Balnacra Highld
205 G6 Balnacroft Abers
213 G7 Balnafoich Highld
194 E6 Balnaguard P & K
180 F1 Balnahard Ag & B
180 F7 Balnahard Ag & B
212 C7 Balnain Highld
228 F2 Balnakeil Highld
223 H7 Balnapaling Highld
124 F6 Balne N York
185 L1 Balquharn P & K
184 C3 Balquhidder Stirlg
86 B7 Balsall Common Solhll
85 J6 Balsall Heath Birm
72 E6 Balscote Oxon
76 E4 Balsham Cambs
235 e1 Baltasound Shet
235 e1 Baltasound Airport Shet
145 J3 Baltersan D & G
26 D4 Baltonsborough Somset
195 G4 Balvarran P & K
181 M4 Balvicar Ag & B
200 C3 Balvraid Highld
213 K7 Balvraid Highld
121 H5 Bamber Bridge Lancs
60 F4 Bamber's Green Essex
169 H3 Bamburgh Nthumb
169 H3 Bamburgh Castle Nthumb
195 K6 Bamff P & K
114 E5 Bamford Derbys
138 D4 Bampton Cumb
24 E6 Bampton Devon
56 F7 Bampton Oxon
138 D4 Bampton Grange Cumb
191 L2 Banavie Highld
72 F6 Banbury Oxon
50 F3 Bancffosfelen Carmth
206 D6 Banchory Abers
207 G5 Banchory-Devenick Abers
50 E3 Bancycapel Carmth
50 D2 Bancyfelin Carmth
186 C2 Bandirran P & K
216 D2 Banff Abers
109 H6 Bangor Gwynd
98 B4 Bangor-is-y-coed Wrexhm
9 G5 Bangors Cnwll
92 C6 Banham Norfk
16 C2 Bank Hants
147 H2 Bankend D & G
185 M1 Bankfoot P & K
164 C6 Bankglen E Ayrs
207 G4 Bankhead C Aber
165 J1 Bankhead S Lans
175 K3 Banknock Falk
120 E6 Banks Lancs
155 L5 Bankshill D & G
106 F6 Banningham Norfk
61 H4 Bannister Green Essex
175 L1 Bannockburn Stirlg
44 E7 Banstead Surrey
6 F6 Bantham Devon
175 K3 Banton N Lans
38 B8 Banwell N Som
34 C3 Bapchild Kent
27 M4 Bapton Wilts
75 L2 Bar Hill Cambs
232 f1 Barabhas W Isls
163 J3 Barassie S Ayrs
223 G6 Barbaraville Highld
163 K5 Barbieston S Ayrs
130 C3 Barbon Cumb
23 L2 Barbrook Devon
73 G1 Barby Nhants
191 J7 Barcaldine Ag & B
72 C6 Barcheston Warwks
19 L3 Barcombe E Susx
19 L3 Barcombe Cross E Susx
131 L2 Barden N York
33 G4 Barden Park Kent
61 G2 Bardfield End Green Essex
61 G3 Bardfield Saling Essex
117 J7 Bardney Lincs
86 F2 Bardon Leics
149 K3 Bardon Mill Nthumb
175 G4 Bardowie E Duns
174 C4 Bardrainney Inver
129 G5 Bardsea Cumb
124 B2 Bardsey Leeds
91 L8 Bardwell Suffk
129 K6 Bare Lancs
69 H4 Barewood Herefs
145 G2 Barfad D & G
92 D3 Barford Norfk
72 C3 Barford Warwks
57 H2 Barford St John Oxon
28 B5 Barford St Martin Wilts
57 H2 Barford St Michael Oxon
35 H5 Barfrestone Kent
175 J5 Bargeddie N Lans
53 J7 Bargoed Caerph
153 H6 Bargrennan D & G
89 G7 Barham Cambs
35 G5 Barham Kent
78 D4 Barham Suffk
88 F2 Barholm Lincs
87 J2 Barkby Leics
87 J2 Barkby Thorpe Leics
102 C5 Barkestone-le-Vale Leics
42 C6 Barkham Wokham
45 H3 Barking Gt Lon
78 C4 Barking Suffk
78 C4 Barking Tye Suffk
45 H3 Barkingside Gt Lon
122 F6 Barkisland Calder
3 J2 Barkla Shop Cnwll
102 F4 Barkston Lincs
124 D4 Barkston Ash N York
75 L7 Barkway Herts
175 H5 Barlanark C Glas
99 K5 Barlaston Staffs
18 C3 Barlavington W Susx
115 J6 Barlborough Derbys
124 F4 Barlby N York
86 E3 Barlestone Leics
76 B6 Barley Herts
122 B3 Barley Lancs
88 B2 Barleythorpe Rutlnd
46 F3 Barling Essex
117 H6 Barlings Lincs
146 E4 Barlochan D & G
115 G6 Barlow Derbys
150 E3 Barlow Gatesd
124 F5 Barlow N York
125 J2 Barmby Moor E R Yk
125 G5 Barmby on the Marsh E R Yk
161 K1 Barmollack Ag & B
80 E1 Barmouth Gwynd
141 H4 Barmpton Darltn
135 J7 Barmston E R Yk
182 E8 Barnacarry Ag & B
88 F3 Barnack C Pete
140 D4 Barnard Castle Dur
57 H6 Barnard Gate Oxon
77 G5 Barnardiston Suffk
146 E4 Barnbarroch D & G
115 J2 Barnburgh Donc
93 K5 Barnby Suffk
124 F8 Barnby Dun Donc
102 E3 Barnby in the Willows Notts
116 A5 Barnby Moor Notts
144 D7 Barncorkrie D & G
44 E5 Barnes Gt Lon
33 H4 Barnes Street Kent
44 E2 Barnet Gt Lon
126 C8 Barnetby le Wold N Linc
106 B6 Barney Norfk
91 K7 Barnham Suffk
18 C5 Barnham W Susx
92 C3 Barnham Broom Norfk
197 G5 Barnhead Angus
187 H2 Barnhill C Dund
214 E3 Barnhill Moray
152 B7 Barnhills D & G
140 D5 Barningham Dur
91 L7 Barningham Suffk
118 C2 Barnoldby le Beck NE Lin
122 C2 Barnoldswick Lancs
31 J6 Barns Green W Susx
115 G1 Barnsley Barns
56 B6 Barnsley Gloucs
23 J5 Barnstaple Devon
61 G4 Barnston Essex
111 J5 Barnston Wirral
102 B5 Barnstone Notts
85 H8 Barnt Green Worcs
177 G4 Barnton C Edin
112 F6 Barnton Ches
88 F6 Barnwell All Saints Nhants
88 F6 Barnwell St Andrew Nhants
55 K4 Barnwood Gloucs
153 G4 Barr S Ayrs
233 b9 Barra Airport W Isls
145 H5 Barrachan D & G
188 B7 Barrapoll Ag & B
158 A7 Barrasford Nthumb
174 F6 Barrhead E Rens
152 F5 Barrhill S Ayrs
76 B5 Barrington Cambs
26 B7 Barrington Somset
3 H4 Barripper Cnwll
174 C7 Barrmill N Ayrs
182 B3 Barrnacarry Bay Ag & B
231 J2 Barrock Highld
55 K3 Barrow Gloucs
121 L3 Barrow Lancs
88 C1 Barrow Rutlnd
27 G5 Barrow Somset
77 H2 Barrow Suffk
168 C7 Barrow Burn Nthumb
38 D6 Barrow Gurney N Som
126 D6 Barrow Haven N Linc
128 E5 Barrow Island Cumb
101 L8 Barrow upon Soar Leics
101 G6 Barrow upon Trent Derbys
128 E5 Barrow-in-Furness Cumb
126 D6 Barrow-upon-Humber N Linc
102 E5 Barrowby Lincs
88 D4 Barrowden Rutlnd
122 C3 Barrowford Lancs
187 J1 Barry Angus
37 H6 Barry V Glam
87 K2 Barsby Leics
93 H5 Barsham Suffk
86 B7 Barston Solhll
69 L6 Bartestree Herefs
216 F7 Barthol Chapel Abers
61 H4 Bartholomew Green Essex
99 H3 Barthomley Ches
28 F8 Bartley Hants
85 H6 Bartley Green Birm
76 E5 Bartlow Cambs
76 B4 Barton Cambs
98 C2 Barton Ches
56 C3 Barton Gloucs
120 E8 Barton Lancs
121 G3 Barton Lancs
141 G5 Barton N York
57 K6 Barton Oxon
7 K3 Barton Torbay
91 G3 Barton Bendish Norfk
39 J2 Barton End Gloucs
57 M2 Barton Hartshorn Bucks
101 K6 Barton in Fabis Notts
86 E3 Barton in the Beans Leics
91 G8 Barton Mills Suffk
88 C7 Barton Seagrave Nhants

26 D5 **Barton St David** Somset
29 H3 **Barton Stacey** Hants
23 L4 **Barton Town** Devon
107 H7 **Barton Turf** Norfk
126 C6 **Barton Waterside** N Linc
59 H2 **Barton-le-Clay** Beds
133 L5 **Barton-le-Street** N York
133 L6 **Barton-le-Willows** N York
16 B4 **Barton-on-Sea** Hants
56 E2 **Barton-on-the-Heath** Warwks
100 D8 **Barton-under-Needwood** Staffs
126 C6 **Barton-upon-Humber** N Linc
232 f1 **Barvas** W Isls
90 D7 **Barway** Cambs
86 F4 **Barwell** Leics
10 E4 **Barwick** Devon
26 E8 **Barwick** Somset
124 B3 **Barwick in Elmet** Leeds
98 B7 **Baschurch** Shrops
72 E2 **Bascote** Warwks
121 K2 **Bashall Eaves** Lancs
46 B3 **Basildon** Essex
29 M2 **Basingstoke** Hants
114 E6 **Baslow** Derbys
25 M3 **Bason Bridge** Somset
37 L3 **Bassaleg** Newpt
167 K1 **Bassendean** Border
137 H2 **Bassenthwaite** Cumb
29 H7 **Bassett** C Sotn
75 K5 **Bassingbourn** Cambs
102 E1 **Bassingham** Lincs
102 F6 **Bassingthorpe** Lincs
60 A3 **Bassus Green** Herts
89 G2 **Baston** Lincs
107 J8 **Bastwick** Norfk
43 H2 **Batchworth** Herts
14 C2 **Batcombe** Dorset
27 G4 **Batcombe** Somset
59 J5 **Batford** Herts
39 H7 **Bath** BaNES
62 F2 **Bath Side** Essex
39 H6 **Bathampton** BaNES
25 G6 **Bathealton** Somset
39 H6 **Batheaston** BaNES
39 H6 **Bathford** BaNES
176 D5 **Bathgate** W Loth
102 C2 **Bathley** Notts
5 L2 **Bathpool** Cnwll
25 K6 **Bathpool** Somset
176 C5 **Bathville** W Loth
26 E2 **Bathway** Somset
123 J5 **Batley** Kirk
71 L7 **Batsford** Gloucs
142 D5 **Battersby** N York
44 F5 **Battersea** Gt Lon
78 B4 **Battisford Tye** Suffk
20 F3 **Battle** E Susx
52 F2 **Battle** Powys
103 L2 **Battle of Britain Memorial Flight** Lincs
196 D5 **Battledykes** Angus
46 C2 **Battlesbridge** Essex
24 E6 **Battleton** Somset
70 F6 **Baughton** Worcs
41 L7 **Baughurst** Hants
206 B6 **Baulds** Abers
40 F3 **Baulking** Oxon
117 L6 **Baumber** Lincs
56 A6 **Baunton** Gloucs
28 B5 **Baverstock** Wilts
92 D2 **Bawburgh** Norfk
106 C7 **Bawdeswell** Norfk
25 M4 **Bawdrip** Somset
79 H6 **Bawdsey** Suffk
115 M3 **Bawtry** Donc
122 B5 **Baxenden** Lancs
86 C4 **Baxterley** Warwks
208 D4 **Bay** Highld
232 g2 **Bayble** W Isls
29 K6 **Baybridge** Hants
129 G5 **Baycliff** Cumb
40 F5 **Baydon** Wilts
60 A6 **Bayford** Herts
27 G5 **Bayford** Somset
233 b6 **Bayhead** W Isls
78 D4 **Baylham** Suffk
54 E3 **Baysham** Herefs
83 J2 **Bayston Hill** Shrops
77 G6 **Baythorne End** Essex
84 C8 **Bayton** Worcs
57 J7 **Bayworth** Oxon
73 L6 **Beachampton** Bucks
91 H3 **Beachamwell** Norfk
20 C6 **Beachy Head** E Susx
12 F2 **Beacon** Devon
62 A3 **Beacon End** Essex
42 C2 **Beacon's Bottom** Bucks
42 F3 **Beaconsfield** Bucks
133 K3 **Beadlam** N York
75 G6 **Beadlow** Beds
169 J4 **Beadnell** Nthumb
10 E2 **Beaford** Devon
124 E5 **Beal** N York
169 G2 **Beal** Nthumb
6 A1 **Bealsmill** Cnwll
13 L3 **Beaminster** Dorset
150 F4 **Beamish** Dur
131 K8 **Beamsley** N York
39 K7 **Beanacre** Wilts
169 G5 **Beanley** Nthumb
10 D7 **Beardon** Devon
12 C3 **Beare** Devon
31 K3 **Beare Green** Surrey
71 L3 **Bearley** Warwks
151 G6 **Bearpark** Dur
174 F4 **Bearsden** E Duns
33 K3 **Bearsted** Kent
99 G5 **Bearstone** Shrops
85 H6 **Bearwood** Birm
15 K3 **Bearwood** Poole
155 J2 **Beattock** D & G
60 F6 **Beauchamp Roding** Essex
53 J5 **Beaufort** Blae G
16 E3 **Beaulieu** Hants
16 E2 **Beaulieu House** Hants
212 E5 **Beauly** Highld
109 H6 **Beaumaris** IOA
148 C3 **Beaumont** Cumb
62 E3 **Beaumont** Essex
236 c7 **Beaumont** Jersey
72 B1 **Beausale** Warwks
29 L6 **Beauworth** Hants
34 D6 **Beaver Green** Kent
10 C5 **Beaworthy** Devon
61 H3 **Beazley End** Essex
111 K5 **Bebington** Wirral
93 J5 **Beccles** Suffk
120 F6 **Becconsall** Lancs
91 G7 **Beck Row** Suffk
128 F3 **Beck Side** Cumb
84 D3 **Beckbury** Shrops
45 G6 **Beckenham** Gt Lon
117 J5 **Beckering** Lincs
136 E6 **Beckermet** Cumb
147 J5 **Beckfoot** Cumb
71 H7 **Beckford** Worcs
40 C6 **Beckhampton** Wilts
102 E2 **Beckingham** Lincs
116 C4 **Beckingham** Notts
27 J2 **Beckington** Somset
83 H7 **Beckjay** Shrops
21 G2 **Beckley** E Susx
57 K5 **Beckley** Oxon
45 H4 **Beckton** Gt Lon
132 D8 **Beckwithshaw** N York
45 J3 **Becontree** Gt Lon
236 c6 **Becquet Vincent** Jersey
132 D2 **Bedale** N York
27 J7 **Bedchester** Dorset
37 G4 **Beddau** Rhondd
95 K3 **Beddgelert** Gwynd
19 L4 **Beddingham** E Susx
44 F6 **Beddington** Gt Lon
44 F6 **Beddington Corner** Gt Lon
78 F2 **Bedfield** Suffk
74 F5 **Bedford** Beds
17 K2 **Bedhampton** Hants
78 E2 **Bedingfield** Suffk
78 E2 **Bedingfield Street** Suffk
132 D7 **Bedlam** N York
34 B5 **Bedlam Lane** Kent
159 G5 **Bedlington** Nthumb
53 H7 **Bedlinog** Myr Td
38 E6 **Bedminster** Bristl
38 E6 **Bedminster Down** Bristl
59 J7 **Bedmond** Herts
99 L8 **Bednall** Staffs
167 J5 **Bedrule** Border
83 G7 **Bedstone** Shrops
37 J3 **Bedwas** Caerph
53 J7 **Bedwellty** Caerph
86 D6 **Bedworth** Warwks
87 J2 **Beeby** Leics
30 B4 **Beech** Hants
99 J5 **Beech** Staffs
42 B7 **Beech Hill** W Berk
40 C8 **Beechingstoke** Wilts
41 J5 **Beedon** W Berk
41 J5 **Beedon Hill** W Berk
135 H8 **Beeford** E R Yk
114 E7 **Beeley** Derbys
117 K2 **Beelsby** NE Lin
41 L6 **Beenham** W Berk
13 G5 **Beer** Devon
26 B5 **Beer** Somset
14 B1 **Beer Hackett** Dorset
25 L7 **Beercrocombe** Somset
7 J7 **Beesands** Devon
118 F5 **Beesby** Lincs
7 J7 **Beeson** Devon
75 H5 **Beeston** Beds
98 D2 **Beeston** Ches
123 K4 **Beeston** Leeds
91 K1 **Beeston** Norfk
101 K5 **Beeston** Notts
106 E4 **Beeston Regis** Norfk
146 F2 **Beeswing** D & G
129 K4 **Beetham** Cumb
25 L8 **Beetham** Somset
106 A8 **Beetley** Norfk
57 J5 **Begbroke** Oxon
49 J6 **Begelly** Pembks
82 D7 **Beguildy** Powys
93 H2 **Beighton** Norfk
115 H5 **Beighton** Sheff
100 F3 **Beighton Hill** Derbys
186 B5 **Bein Inn** P & K
174 C7 **Beith** N Ayrs
35 G4 **Bekesbourne** Kent
107 G8 **Belaugh** Norfk
85 G7 **Belbroughton** Worcs
14 E1 **Belchalwell** Dorset
14 F1 **Belchalwell Street** Dorset
77 J6 **Belchamp Otten** Essex
77 H6 **Belchamp St Paul** Essex
77 J6 **Belchamp Walter** Essex
118 D6 **Belchford** Lincs
169 G3 **Belford** Nthumb
87 H3 **Belgrave** C Leic
178 E3 **Belhaven** E Loth
207 H2 **Belhelvie** Abers
215 K8 **Belhinnie** Abers
131 G7 **Bell Busk** N York
85 G7 **Bell End** Worcs
98 D4 **Bell o' th' Hill** Ches
205 H3 **Bellabeg** Abers
182 A8 **Bellanoch** Ag & B
195 K4 **Bellaty** Angus
148 C4 **Belle Vue** Cumb
123 L6 **Belle Vue** Wakefd
118 E5 **Belleau** Lincs
131 L2 **Bellerby** N York
164 F3 **Bellfield** S Lans
165 J5 **Bellfield** S Lans
58 F6 **Bellingdon** Bucks
157 L5 **Bellingham** Nthumb
161 H2 **Belloch** Ag & B
161 H3 **Bellochantuy** Ag & B
33 G6 **Bells Yew Green** E Susx
175 J6 **Bellshill** N Lans
175 L6 **Bellside** N Lans
176 E5 **Bellsquarry** W Loth
38 E7 **Belluton** BaNES
121 K7 **Belmont** Bl w D
44 E7 **Belmont** Gt Lon
163 J5 **Belmont** S Ayrs
235 d2 **Belmont** Shet
205 J3 **Belnacraig** Abers
101 G3 **Belper** Derbys
101 G3 **Belper Lane End** Derbys
158 D6 **Belsay** Nthumb
167 J4 **Belses** Border
7 H4 **Belsford** Devon
59 G7 **Belsize** Herts
78 D6 **Belstead** Suffk
10 F6 **Belstone** Devon
121 L5 **Belthorn** Lancs
47 K6 **Beltinge** Kent
149 K3 **Beltingham** Nthumb
116 D1 **Beltoft** N Linc
101 H7 **Belton** Leics
102 F4 **Belton** Lincs
116 C1 **Belton** N Linc
93 K3 **Belton** Norfk
88 B3 **Belton** Rutlnd
45 J4 **Belvedere** Gt Lon
102 D5 **Belvoir** Leics
102 D5 **Belvoir Castle** Leics
17 J5 **Bembridge** IOW
28 C5 **Bemerton** Wilts
135 J5 **Bempton** E R Yk
192 B3 **Ben Nevis** Highld
123 H2 **Ben Rhydding** Brad
93 K6 **Benacre** Suffk
233 c6 **Benbecula Airport** W Isls
154 C3 **Benbuie** D & G
191 H8 **Benderloch** Ag & B
33 K6 **Benenden** Kent
150 D4 **Benfieldside** Dur
60 A5 **Bengeo** Herts
71 J5 **Bengeworth** Worcs
79 H3 **Benhall Green** Suffk
79 H3 **Benhall Street** Suffk
197 K3 **Benholm** Abers
133 H7 **Beningbrough** N York
59 M4 **Benington** Herts
104 C3 **Benington** Lincs
109 G5 **Benllech** IOA
173 K2 **Benmore** Ag & B
9 H6 **Bennacott** Cnwll
162 C5 **Bennan** N Ayrs
117 K5 **Benniworth** Lincs
33 J4 **Benover** Kent

41 L3 **Benson** Oxon
206 F5 **Benthoul** C Aber
115 K1 **Bentley** Donc
126 C4 **Bentley** E R Yk
30 C3 **Bentley** Hants
78 D6 **Bentley** Suffk
86 C4 **Bentley** Warwks
23 K4 **Benton** Devon
156 B4 **Bentpath** D & G
24 B5 **Bentwichen** Devon
30 A4 **Bentworth** Hants
186 E2 **Benvie** Angus
14 A2 **Benville** Dorset
89 L5 **Benwick** Cambs
71 J1 **Beoley** Worcs
199 L6 **Beoraidbeg** Highld
18 B3 **Bepton** W Susx
60 D3 **Berden** Essex
6 C3 **Bere Alston** Devon
6 C3 **Bere Ferrers** Devon
14 F4 **Bere Regis** Dorset
48 D2 **Berea** Pembks
93 G4 **Bergh Apton** Norfk
41 L2 **Berinsfield** Oxon
55 G7 **Berkeley** Gloucs
59 G6 **Berkhamsted** Herts
27 J2 **Berkley** Somset
86 B7 **Berkswell** Solhll
45 G4 **Bermondsey** Gt Lon
200 C2 **Bernera** Highld
183 G8 **Bernice** Ag & B
208 F4 **Bernisdale** Highld
41 L2 **Berrick Prior** Oxon
41 L2 **Berrick Salome** Oxon
227 K4 **Berriedale** Highld
137 L2 **Berrier** Cumb
82 D4 **Berriew** Powys
83 K3 **Berrington** Shrops
69 L2 **Berrington** Worcs
69 L2 **Berrington Green** Worcs
25 L2 **Berrow** Somset
70 D3 **Berrow Green** Worcs
7 J4 **Berry Pomeroy** Devon
215 L4 **Berryhillock** Moray
215 L3 **Berryhillock** Moray
23 J3 **Berrynarbor** Devon
97 L3 **Bersham** Wrexhm
20 B5 **Berwick** E Susx
40 C5 **Berwick Bassett** Wilts
158 F6 **Berwick Hill** Nthumb
28 B4 **Berwick St James** Wilts
27 L6 **Berwick St John** Wilts
27 L5 **Berwick St Leonard** Wilts
179 K7 **Berwick-upon-Tweed** Nthumb
102 D7 **Bescaby** Leics
120 E7 **Bescar** Lancs
71 G5 **Besford** Worcs
115 L2 **Bessacarr** Donc
57 J7 **Bessels Leigh** Oxon
135 J6 **Bessingby** E R Yk
106 E5 **Bessingham** Norfk
92 C4 **Besthorpe** Norfk
116 D8 **Besthorpe** Notts
101 K3 **Bestwood Village** Notts
126 C2 **Beswick** E R Yk
31 K2 **Betchworth** Surrey
62 C3 **Beth Chatto Garden** Essex
109 G7 **Bethel** Gwynd
108 E7 **Bethel** IOA
34 C6 **Bethersden** Kent
109 J7 **Bethesda** Gwynd
49 J4 **Bethesda** Pembks
51 K1 **Bethlehem** Carmth
45 G4 **Bethnal Green** Gt Lon
99 H3 **Betley** Staffs
45 L5 **Betsham** Kent
35 J4 **Betteshanger** Kent
13 K3 **Bettiscombe** Dorset
98 C5 **Bettisfield** Wrexhm
37 L3 **Bettws** Newpt
66 D4 **Bettws Bledrws** Cerdgn
82 C4 **Bettws Cedewain** Powys
65 J5 **Bettws Evan** Cerdgn
54 A6 **Bettws-Newydd** Mons
229 L3 **Bettyhill** Highld
36 D3 **Betws** Brdgnd
97 G3 **Betws Gwerfil Goch** Denbgs
96 C2 **Betws-y-Coed** Conwy
110 C6 **Betws-yn-Rhos** Conwy
65 J5 **Beulah** Cerdgn
67 K4 **Beulah** Powys
116 B6 **Bevercotes** Notts
126 C3 **Beverley** E R Yk
39 K2 **Beverstone** Gloucs
156 F7 **Bewcastle** Cumb
84 D7 **Bewdley** Worcs
132 B6 **Bewerley** N York
126 E1 **Bewholme** E R Yk
20 E4 **Bexhill** E Susx
45 J5 **Bexley** Gt Lon
45 J5 **Bexleyheath** Gt Lon
90 F3 **Bexwell** Norfk
77 L2 **Beyton** Suffk
77 L2 **Beyton Green** Suffk
232 d2 **Bhaltos** W Isls
233 b10 **Bhatarsaigh** W Isls
56 C6 **Bibury** Gloucs
57 L4 **Bicester** Oxon
85 L6 **Bickenhill** Solhll
103 L5 **Bicker** Lincs
112 C2 **Bickerstaffe** Lancs
124 C1 **Bickerton** N York
84 F2 **Bickford** Staffs
23 H5 **Bickington** Devon
7 J2 **Bickington** Devon
12 B2 **Bickleigh** Devon
6 D4 **Bickleigh** Devon
45 H6 **Bickley** Gt Lon
134 E2 **Bickley** N York
98 D3 **Bickley Moss** Ches
61 J7 **Bicknacre** Essex
25 H4 **Bicknoller** Somset
33 L2 **Bicknor** Kent
83 J1 **Bicton** Shrops
82 F6 **Bicton** Shrops
32 F5 **Bidborough** Kent
33 L5 **Biddenden** Kent
74 E4 **Biddenham** Beds
39 K5 **Biddestone** Wilts
26 B2 **Biddisham** Somset
73 J6 **Biddlesden** Bucks
99 K2 **Biddulph** Staffs
99 K2 **Biddulph Moor** Staffs
23 G6 **Bideford** Devon
71 K4 **Bidford-on-Avon** Warwks
125 J2 **Bielby** E R Yk
207 G5 **Bieldside** C Aber
17 G6 **Bierley** IOW
58 D5 **Bierton** Bucks
145 H6 **Big Balcraig** D & G
154 B3 **Big Carlae** D & G
53 K6 **Big Pit Blaenavon** Torfn
219 H5 **Big Sand** Highld
6 F6 **Bigbury** Devon
6 F6 **Bigbury-on-Sea** Devon
117 H1 **Bigby** Lincs
165 K2 **Biggar** S Lans
100 E3 **Biggin** Derbys
100 D2 **Biggin** Derbys
124 E4 **Biggin** N York
32 D2 **Biggin Hill** Gt Lon
45 H7 **Biggin Hill Airport** Gt Lon
75 H5 **Biggleswade** Beds
156 B6 **Bigholms** D & G
230 C3 **Bighouse** Highld
29 L4 **Bighton** Hants
148 A4 **Biglands** Cumb
18 D3 **Bignor** W Susx
136 D5 **Bigrigg** Cumb
101 K4 **Bilborough** C Nott
25 G3 **Bilbrook** Somset
124 E2 **Bilbrough** N York
231 K5 **Bilbster** Highld
140 F3 **Bildershaw** Dur
78 B5 **Bildeston** Suffk
46 B2 **Billericay** Essex
87 K3 **Billesdon** Leics
71 K3 **Billesley** Warwks
103 J5 **Billingborough** Lincs
112 D2 **Billinge** St Hel
106 B7 **Billingford** Norfk
92 E7 **Billingford** Norfk
141 K3 **Billingham** S on T
103 J2 **Billinghay** Lincs
115 H1 **Billingley** Barns
31 H6 **Billingshurst** W Susx
84 C6 **Billingsley** Shrops
58 F4 **Billington** Beds
121 L4 **Billington** Lancs
93 J2 **Billockby** Norfk
150 E7 **Billy Row** Dur
121 G3 **Bilsborrow** Lancs
119 G6 **Bilsby** Lincs
18 D5 **Bilsham** W Susx
34 D7 **Bilsington** Kent
101 M1 **Bilsthorpe** Notts
177 H5 **Bilston** Mdloth
85 G4 **Bilston** Wolves
86 D3 **Bilstone** Leics
126 E4 **Bilton** E R Yk
124 D1 **Bilton** N York
132 D7 **Bilton** N York
86 F8 **Bilton** Warwks
117 K3 **Binbrook** Lincs
14 D5 **Bincombe** Dorset
26 E2 **Binegar** Somset
42 D6 **Binfield** Br For
42 C5 **Binfield Heath** Oxon
158 B7 **Bingfield** Nthumb
102 B4 **Bingham** Notts
14 E3 **Bingham's Melcombe** Dorset
123 G3 **Bingley** Brad
106 B5 **Binham** Norfk
86 E7 **Binley** Covtry
29 H2 **Binley** Hants
15 G5 **Binnegar** Dorset
176 B4 **Binniehill** Falk
215 H2 **Binns Farm** Moray
30 F3 **Binscombe** Surrey
17 H4 **Binstead** IOW
30 C3 **Binsted** Hants
18 D4 **Binsted** W Susx
71 K4 **Binton** Warwks
106 B7 **Bintree** Norfk
61 M4 **Birch** Essex
100 C6 **Birch Cross** Staffs
61 M4 **Birch Green** Essex
114 A4 **Birch Vale** Derbys
25 K8 **Birch Wood** Somset
105 J5 **Bircham Newton** Norfk
105 J6 **Bircham Tofts** Norfk
60 E4 **Birchanger** Essex
69 J2 **Bircher** Herefs
37 J4 **Birchgrove** Cardif
32 D7 **Birchgrove** E Susx
51 K5 **Birchgrove** Swans
35 J2 **Birchington** Kent
86 C5 **Birchley Heath** Warwks
100 E1 **Birchover** Derbys
112 F4 **Birchwood** Warrtn
115 M3 **Bircotes** Notts
77 G6 **Birdbrook** Essex
133 G4 **Birdforth** N York
17 M3 **Birdham** W Susx
72 E2 **Birdingbury** Warwks
55 L5 **Birdlip** Gloucs
123 J8 **Birds Edge** Kirk
60 F6 **Birds Green** Essex
134 C6 **Birdsall** N York
84 D6 **Birdsgreen** Shrops
13 K3 **Birdsmoorgate** Dorset
115 G2 **Birdwell** Barns
168 B2 **Birgham** Border
223 G3 **Birichin** Highld
141 H6 **Birkby** N York
120 D7 **Birkdale** Sefton
215 L2 **Birkenbog** Abers
111 K4 **Birkenhead** Wirral
216 E5 **Birkenhills** Abers
123 J5 **Birkenshaw** Kirk
205 H6 **Birkhall** Abers
186 F1 **Birkhill** Angus
166 B6 **Birkhill** D & G
124 E5 **Birkin** N York
69 J4 **Birley** Herefs
115 G3 **Birley Carr** Sheff
46 B7 **Birling** Kent
71 G5 **Birlingham** Worcs
85 J6 **Birmingham** Birm
85 L6 **Birmingham Airport** Solhll
195 G7 **Birnam** P & K
217 J7 **Birness** Abers
206 B6 **Birse** Abers
205 L5 **Birsemore** Abers
123 J5 **Birstall** Kirk
87 H2 **Birstall** Leics
132 C7 **Birstwith** N York
151 G4 **Birtley** Gatesd
69 G2 **Birtley** Herefs
157 L6 **Birtley** Nthumb
70 D7 **Birts Street** Worcs
88 C4 **Bisbrooke** Rutlnd
118 C5 **Biscathorpe** Lincs
24 B6 **Bish Mill** Devon
42 D4 **Bisham** W & M
71 H4 **Bishampton** Worcs
140 F2 **Bishop Auckland** Dur
126 B3 **Bishop Burton** E R Yk
141 H2 **Bishop Middleham** Dur
132 E6 **Bishop Monkton** N York
117 G3 **Bishop Norton** Lincs
38 E7 **Bishop Sutton** BaNES
132 D6 **Bishop Thornton** N York
134 C7 **Bishop Wilton** E R Yk
83 G5 **Bishop's Castle** Shrops
27 G8 **Bishop's Caundle** Dorset
55 L3 **Bishop's Cleeve** Gloucs
70 B5 **Bishop's Frome** Herefs
61 G4 **Bishop's Green** Essex
72 E3 **Bishop's Itchington** Warwks
55 J3 **Bishop's Norton** Gloucs
24 B6 **Bishop's Nympton** Devon
99 H6 **Bishop's Offley** Staffs
60 D4 **Bishop's Stortford** Herts

29 L5 **Bishop's Sutton** Hants
72 C3 **Bishop's Tachbrook** Warwks
23 J5 **Bishop's Tawton** Devon
29 K7 **Bishop's Waltham** Hants
84 E2 **Bishop's Wood** Staffs
117 G4 **Bishopbridge** Lincs
175 G4 **Bishopbriggs** E Duns
214 F2 **Bishopmill** Moray
40 B7 **Bishops Cannings** Wilts
25 J6 **Bishops Hull** Somset
25 J5 **Bishops Lydeard** Somset
35 G4 **Bishopsbourne** Kent
7 K2 **Bishopsteignton** Devon
29 J7 **Bishopstoke** Hants
51 H7 **Bishopston** Swans
58 D6 **Bishopstone** Bucks
19 M5 **Bishopstone** E Susx
69 H5 **Bishopstone** Herefs
47 K6 **Bishopstone** Kent
40 E4 **Bishopstone** Swindn
28 B6 **Bishopstone** Wilts
27 K3 **Bishopstrow** Wilts
25 K8 **Bishopswood** Somset
38 E6 **Bishopsworth** Bristl
124 F2 **Bishopthorpe** York
141 J3 **Bishopton** Darltn
174 E4 **Bishopton** Rens
38 B3 **Bishton** Newpt
100 A7 **Bishton** Staffs
55 K6 **Bisley** Gloucs
42 F8 **Bisley** Surrey
3 K3 **Bissoe** Cnwll
15 L3 **Bisterne** Hants
103 G6 **Bitchfield** Lincs
23 J3 **Bittadon** Devon
6 F4 **Bittaford** Devon
83 L7 **Bitterley** Shrops
29 J8 **Bitterne** C Sotn
87 G6 **Bitteswell** Leics
39 G6 **Bitton** S Glos
42 B4 **Bix** Oxon
87 H4 **Blaby** Leics
56 F6 **Black Bourton** Oxon
150 F2 **Black Callerton** N u Ty
192 E5 **Black Corries** Highld
182 D1 **Black Crofts** Ag & B
11 J3 **Black Dog** Devon
61 J4 **Black Notley** Essex
51 J7 **Black Pill** Swans
93 K6 **Black Street** Suffk
10 C4 **Black Torrington** Devon
179 H7 **Blackadder** Border
7 J5 **Blackawton** Devon
12 E1 **Blackborough** Devon
90 F1 **Blackborough End** Norfk
20 B2 **Blackboys** E Susx
101 G3 **Blackbrook** Derbys
99 H5 **Blackbrook** Staffs
206 F3 **Blackburn** Abers
121 K5 **Blackburn** Bl w D
176 D5 **Blackburn** W Loth
164 C7 **Blackcraig** E Ayrs
207 H3 **Blackdog** Abers
13 K2 **Blackdown** Dorset
115 G2 **Blacker Hill** Barns
45 J5 **Blackfen** Gt Lon
16 E3 **Blackfield** Hants
185 J5 **Blackford** P & K
26 B2 **Blackford** Somset
26 F6 **Blackford** Somset
101 G8 **Blackfordby** Leics
177 G4 **Blackhall** C Edin
151 K6 **Blackhall Colliery** Dur
166 F2 **Blackhaugh** Border
45 G5 **Blackheath** Gt Lon
85 H6 **Blackheath** Sandw
93 J8 **Blackheath** Suffk
31 G3 **Blackheath** Surrey
217 J6 **Blackhill** Abers
217 K3 **Blackhill** Abers
217 K5 **Blackhill** Abers
150 D5 **Blackhill** Dur
217 H5 **Blackhill of Clackriach** Abers
12 C4 **Blackhorse** Devon
165 K7 **Blacklaw** D & G
113 J2 **Blackley** Manch
195 J4 **Blacklunans** P & K
69 K6 **Blackmarstone** Herefs
36 E3 **Blackmill** Brdgnd
30 C5 **Blackmoor** Hants
38 C7 **Blackmoor** N Som
123 G7 **Blackmoorfoot** Kirk
60 F7 **Blackmore** Essex
61 H2 **Blackmore End** Essex
176 E3 **Blackness** Falk
30 D3 **Blacknest** Hants
122 C3 **Blacko** Lancs
120 D4 **Blackpool** Bpool
7 K6 **Blackpool** Devon
120 D4 **Blackpool Airport** Lancs
176 B5 **Blackridge** W Loth
121 J7 **Blackrod** Bolton
214 E6 **Blacksboat** Moray
147 J2 **Blackshaw** D & G
122 E5 **Blackshaw Head** Calder
121 K6 **Blacksnape** Bl w D
19 H3 **Blackstone** W Susx
57 L4 **Blackthorn** Oxon
77 K2 **Blackthorpe** Suffk
125 J5 **Blacktoft** E R Yk
207 G4 **Blacktop** C Aber
100 E3 **Blackwall** Derbys
3 J3 **Blackwater** Cnwll
42 D7 **Blackwater** Hants
17 G5 **Blackwater** IOW
25 K7 **Blackwater** Somset
162 A4 **Blackwaterfoot** N Ayrs
148 D4 **Blackwell** Cumb
114 C6 **Blackwell** Derbys
101 H2 **Blackwell** Derbys
72 B5 **Blackwell** Warwks
71 H1 **Blackwell** Worcs
37 J2 **Blackwood** Caerph
154 F5 **Blackwood** D & G
164 F1 **Blackwood** S Lans
111 L7 **Blacon** Ches
145 J4 **Bladnoch** D & G
57 J5 **Bladon** Oxon
50 D1 **Blaen-y-Coed** Carmth
52 E7 **Blaen-y-cwm** Rhondd
65 H5 **Blaenannerch** Cerdgn
96 A4 **Blaenau Ffestiniog** Gwynd
53 K6 **Blaenavon** Torfn
65 H6 **Blaenffos** Pembks
36 D2 **Blaengarw** Brdgnd
52 D6 **Blaengwrach** Neath
36 D2 **Blaengwynfi** Neath
66 E2 **Blaenpennal** Cerdgn
80 D7 **Blaenplwyf** Cerdgn
65 J5 **Blaenporth** Cerdgn
52 E7 **Blaenrhondda** Rhondd
50 B1 **Blaenwaun** Carmth
38 D8 **Blagdon** N Som
25 K7 **Blagdon** Somset
7 K4 **Blagdon** Torbay
25 K7 **Blagdon Hill** Somset
191 K2 **Blaich** Highld
190 D3 **Blain** Highld
53 J6 **Blaina** Blae G
194 D4 **Blair Atholl** P & K
184 F7 **Blair Drummond** Stirlg
173 G4 **Blair's Ferry** Ag & B
195 J7 **Blairgowrie** P & K
185 K7 **Blairingone** P & K
185 H7 **Blairlogie** Stirlg
173 L2 **Blairmore** Ag & B
228 C4 **Blairmore** Highld
204 F3 **Blairnamarrow** Moray
55 G5 **Blaisdon** Gloucs
61 H4 **Blake End** Essex
84 E7 **Blakebrook** Worcs
84 F7 **Blakedown** Worcs
112 D7 **Blakemere** Ches
69 G6 **Blakemere** Herefs
85 H3 **Blakenall Heath** Wsall
54 F6 **Blakeney** Gloucs
106 B4 **Blakeney** Norfk
99 G3 **Blakenhall** Ches
85 G4 **Blakenhall** Wolves
73 J4 **Blakesley** Nhants
150 B5 **Blanchland** Nthumb
132 C8 **Bland Hill** N York
15 G2 **Blandford Forum** Dorset
15 G2 **Blandford St Mary** Dorset
174 F3 **Blanefield** Stirlg
103 H1 **Blankney** Lincs
175 J6 **Blantyre** S Lans
191 L3 **Blar a' Chaorainn** Highld
202 F6 **Blargie** Highld
191 L3 **Blarmachfoldach** Highld
88 B4 **Blaston** Leics
88 D4 **Blatherwycke** Nhants
129 G2 **Blawith** Cumb
154 B5 **Blawquhairn** D & G
79 H3 **Blaxhall** Suffk
116 A2 **Blaxton** Donc
150 F3 **Blaydon** Gatesd
26 C3 **Bleadney** Somset
37 M8 **Bleadon** N Som
34 F3 **Blean** Kent
102 B3 **Bleasby** Notts
121 H2 **Bleasdale** Lancs
187 G4 **Blebocraigs** Fife
68 E2 **Bleddfa** Powys
56 E4 **Bledington** Gloucs
58 C7 **Bledlow** Bucks
42 D2 **Bledlow Ridge** Bucks
178 B6 **Blegbie** E Loth
138 F2 **Blencarn** Cumb
147 L5 **Blencogo** Cumb
30 B8 **Blendworth** Hants
147 L6 **Blennerhasset** Cumb
57 J4 **Bletchingdon** Oxon
32 B3 **Bletchingley** Surrey
58 E2 **Bletchley** M Keyn
98 F5 **Bletchley** Shrops
49 H4 **Bletherston** Pembks
74 E3 **Bletsoe** Beds
41 K4 **Blewbury** Oxon
106 E6 **Blickling** Norfk
101 L2 **Blidworth** Notts
101 L2 **Blidworth Bottoms** Notts
147 K7 **Blindcrake** Cumb
32 C4 **Blindley Heath** Surrey
5 H2 **Blisland** Cnwll
84 D8 **Bliss Gate** Worcs
28 D8 **Blissford** Hants
73 K4 **Blisworth** Nhants
100 B8 **Blithbury** Staffs
92 B7 **Blo Norton** Norfk
71 L7 **Blockley** Gloucs
93 G2 **Blofield** Norfk
167 J4 **Bloomfield** Border
99 G5 **Blore** Staffs
100 C3 **Blore** Staffs
72 E7 **Bloxham** Oxon
103 H2 **Bloxholm** Lincs
85 H3 **Bloxwich** Wsall
15 G4 **Bloxworth** Dorset
132 B7 **Blubberhouses** N York
24 F3 **Blue Anchor** Somset
46 C7 **Blue Bell Hill** Kent
114 C5 **Blue John Cavern** Derbys
111 J2 **Blundellsands** Sefton
93 L4 **Blundeston** Suffk
75 H4 **Blunham** Beds
40 C3 **Blunsdon St Andrew** Swindn
84 F8 **Bluntington** Worcs
89 L8 **Bluntisham** Cambs
116 F3 **Blyborough** Lincs
93 J7 **Blyford** Suffk
84 E2 **Blymhill** Staffs
115 L4 **Blyth** Notts
159 H5 **Blyth** Nthumb
165 M1 **Blyth Bridge** Border
93 J7 **Blythburgh** Suffk
178 D7 **Blythe** Border
116 D3 **Blyton** Lincs
176 D3 **Bo'ness** Falk
187 J5 **Boarhills** Fife
17 H2 **Boarhunt** Hants
57 L5 **Boarstall** Bucks
203 L2 **Boat of Garten** Highld
222 D6 **Boath** Highld
46 E6 **Bobbing** Kent
84 E5 **Bobbington** Staffs
61 J4 **Bocking** Essex
61 J3 **Bocking Churchstreet** Essex
217 L6 **Boddam** Abers
235 c7 **Boddam** Shet
55 K3 **Boddington** Gloucs
108 D5 **Bodedern** IOA
110 D6 **Bodelwyddan** Denbgs
69 K4 **Bodenham** Herefs
28 D6 **Bodenham** Wilts
69 K4 **Bodenham Moor** Herefs
108 E4 **Bodewryd** IOA
110 F7 **Bodfari** Denbgs
108 F6 **Bodffordd** IOA
94 F5 **Bodfuan** Gwynd
106 D4 **Bodham** Norfk
33 K7 **Bodiam** E Susx
33 K7 **Bodiam Castle** E Susx
72 F6 **Bodicote** Oxon
5 H5 **Bodinnick** Cnwll
20 D3 **Bodle Street Green** E Susx
5 G3 **Bodmin** Cnwll
5 J1 **Bodmin Moor** Cnwll
109 M6 **Bodnant Garden** Conwy
34 E5 **Bodsham Green** Kent
5 G4 **Bodwen** Cnwll
212 F4 **Bogallan** Highld
217 J7 **Bogbrae** Abers
177 L4 **Boggs Holdings** E Loth
177 H5 **Boghall** Mdloth
176 D5 **Boghall** W Loth
164 F2 **Boghead** S Lans
215 H3 **Boghead Farm** Moray
215 H2 **Bogmoor** Moray
197 G3 **Bogmuir** Abers
216 B5 **Bogniebrae** Abers
18 C6 **Bognor Regis** W Susx
203 L2 **Bogroy** Highld
154 B6 **Bogue** D & G

3 L5 **Bohortha** Cnwll
201 L8 **Bohuntine** Highld
140 F3 **Bolam** Dur
7 G7 **Bolberry** Devon
85 K5 **Boldmere** Birm
16 C3 **Boldre** Hants
140 C4 **Boldron** Dur
116 C4 **Bole** Notts
100 F2 **Bolehill** Derbys
24 E7 **Bolham** Devon
25 J8 **Bolham Water** Devon
3 K1 **Bolingey** Cnwll
113 L6 **Bollington** Ches
31 L6 **Bolney** W Susx
74 F3 **Bolnhurst** Beds
197 G6 **Bolshan** Angus
115 J7 **Bolsover** Derbys
114 F3 **Bolsterstone** Sheff
133 G3 **Boltby** N York
205 J3 **Boltenstone** Abers
121 L8 **Bolton** Bolton
138 F3 **Bolton** Cumb
178 B4 **Bolton** E Loth
125 J1 **Bolton** E R Yk
169 G6 **Bolton** Nthumb
131 K8 **Bolton Abbey** N York
122 B1 **Bolton by Bowland** Lancs
129 K6 **Bolton le Sands** Lancs
147 M6 **Bolton Low Houses** Cumb
124 E3 **Bolton Percy** N York
115 J2 **Bolton Upon Dearne** Barns
141 G7 **Bolton-on-Swale** N York
148 E2 **Boltonfellend** Cumb
147 M6 **Boltongate** Cumb
5 J1 **Bolventor** Cnwll
98 C8 **Bomere Heath** Shrops
222 E3 **Bonar Bridge** Highld
182 E2 **Bonawe** Ag & B
126 C7 **Bonby** N Linc
65 H6 **Boncath** Pembks
167 J6 **Bonchester Bridge** Border
10 F4 **Bondleigh** Devon
121 G2 **Bonds** Lancs
85 J2 **Boney Hay** Staffs
174 D3 **Bonhill** W Duns
84 E3 **Boningale** Shrops
167 K5 **Bonjedward** Border
175 L6 **Bonkle** N Lans
196 F7 **Bonnington** Angus
34 E7 **Bonnington** Kent
186 F6 **Bonnybank** Fife
175 L3 **Bonnybridge** Falk
217 G4 **Bonnykelly** Abers
177 J5 **Bonnyrigg** Mdloth
196 B8 **Bonnyton** Angus
100 F2 **Bonsall** Derbys
155 M7 **Bonshaw Tower** D & G
81 J4 **Bont-Dolgadfan** Powys
66 E2 **Bontnewydd** Cerdgn
95 H1 **Bontnewydd** Gwynd
97 G2 **Bontuchel** Denbgs
37 G5 **Bonvilston** V Glam
23 H4 **Boode** Devon
7 K5 **Boohay** Devon
42 D3 **Booker** Bucks
98 E7 **Booley** Shrops
167 J1 **Boon** Border
142 E4 **Boosbeck** R & Cl
61 K2 **Boose's Green** Essex
137 G6 **Boot** Cumb
122 F5 **Booth** Calder
125 H5 **Booth** E R Yk
103 G2 **Boothby Graffoe** Lincs
102 F6 **Boothby Pagnell** Lincs
113 G2 **Boothstown** Salfd
128 D2 **Bootle** Cumb
111 K3 **Bootle** Sefton
70 B1 **Boraston** Shrops
236 e2 **Bordeaux** Guern
34 B3 **Borden** Kent
157 G5 **Border Forest Park**
30 D4 **Bordon** Hants
61 J6 **Boreham** Essex
27 K3 **Boreham** Wilts
20 D4 **Boreham Street** E Susx
44 D2 **Borehamwood** Herts
155 L4 **Boreland** D & G
208 C4 **Boreraig** Highld
232 f1 **Borgh** W Isls
233 b9 **Borgh** W Isls
229 K4 **Borgie** Highld
146 B5 **Borgue** D & G
227 K4 **Borgue** Highld
77 J6 **Borley** Essex
218 B7 **Borneskitaig** Highld
146 A5 **Borness** D & G
33 G2 **Borough Green** Kent
132 F6 **Boroughbridge** N York
101 H5 **Borrowash** Derbys
132 F2 **Borrowby** N York
176 D3 **Borrowstoun** Falk
46 B6 **Borstal** Medway
80 E5 **Borth** Cerdgn
95 K5 **Borth-y-Gest** Gwynd
166 F6 **Borthwickbrae** Border
166 F6 **Borthwickshiels** Border
209 G5 **Borve** Highld
232 f1 **Borve** W Isls
233 b9 **Borve** W Isls
232 d4 **Borve** W Isls
129 L5 **Borwick** Lancs
70 C5 **Bosbury** Herefs
8 E6 **Boscastle** Cnwll
15 L4 **Boscombe** Bmouth
28 D4 **Boscombe** Wilts
17 L2 **Bosham** W Susx
49 G8 **Bosherston** Pembks
113 K7 **Bosley** Ches
4 D4 **Bosoughan** Cnwll
133 L7 **Bossall** N York
8 E6 **Bossiney** Cnwll
34 F5 **Bossingham** Kent
24 D2 **Bossington** Somset
112 F7 **Bostock Green** Ches
104 B4 **Boston** Lincs
124 C2 **Boston Spa** Leeds
4 F7 **Boswinger** Cnwll
2 C5 **Botallack** Cnwll
187 H4 **Botanic Gardens** Fife
59 M7 **Botany Bay** Gt Lon
92 C7 **Botesdale** Suffk
159 G5 **Bothal** Nthumb
41 J5 **Bothampstead** W Berk
116 A6 **Bothamsall** Notts
147 L6 **Bothel** Cumb
13 L4 **Bothenhampton** Dorset
175 J6 **Bothwell** S Lans
59 G7 **Botley** Bucks
29 K8 **Botley** Hants
57 J6 **Botley** Oxon
58 B3 **Botolph Claydon** Bucks
19 G4 **Botolphs** W Susx
102 D5 **Bottesford** Leics
116 E1 **Bottesford** N Linc
76 D3 **Bottisham** Cambs
186 F3 **Bottomcraig** Fife
122 D6 **Bottoms** Calder
6 B4 **Botusfleming** Cnwll
94 E6 **Botwnnog** Gwynd
32 E4 **Bough Beech** Kent
68 C6 **Boughrood** Powys
73 L2 **Boughton** Nhants
91 G3 **Boughton** Norfk
116 B7 **Boughton** Notts
34 D5 **Boughton Aluph** Kent
33 K3 **Boughton Green** Kent
34 B5 **Boughton Malherbe** Kent
33 K3 **Boughton Monchelsea** Kent
34 E3 **Boughton Street** Kent
83 K6 **Bouldon** Shrops
169 K6 **Boulmer** Nthumb
116 F7 **Boultham** Lincs
75 K3 **Bourn** Cambs
103 H7 **Bourne** Lincs
74 D5 **Bourne End** Beds
42 E3 **Bourne End** Bucks
59 G6 **Bourne End** Herts
45 J2 **Bournebridge** Essex
85 J6 **Bournebrook** Birm
15 K4 **Bournemouth** Bmouth
15 L3 **Bournemouth Airport** Dorset
46 E3 **Bournes Green** Sthend
85 G8 **Bournheath** Worcs
85 J7 **Bournville** Birm
27 H5 **Bourton** Dorset
40 E3 **Bourton** Oxon
83 L4 **Bourton** Shrops
40 B7 **Bourton** Wilts
72 E1 **Bourton on Dunsmore** Warwks
56 D2 **Bourton-on-the-Hill** Gloucs
56 D4 **Bourton-on-the-Water** Gloucs
189 G4 **Bousd** Ag & B
129 H3 **Bouth** Cumb
131 L5 **Bouthwaite** N York
184 C2 **Bovain** Stirlg
28 B7 **Boveridge** Dorset
7 J1 **Bovey Tracey** Devon
59 G7 **Bovingdon** Herts
14 F5 **Bovington Tank Museum** Dorset
11 G4 **Bow** Devon
45 G4 **Bow** Gt Lon
234 b7 **Bow** Ork
74 C7 **Bow Brickhill** M Keyn
186 E5 **Bow of Fife** Fife
80 E6 **Bow Street** Cerdgn
55 J6 **Bowbridge** Gloucs
151 H7 **Bowburn** Dur
16 F5 **Bowcombe** IOW
12 E4 **Bowd** Devon
167 H4 **Bowden** Border
39 L6 **Bowden Hill** Wilts
113 H4 **Bowdon** Traffd
231 J3 **Bower** Highld
124 B5 **Bower's Row** Leeds
28 A6 **Bowerchalke** Wilts
231 J3 **Bowermadden** Highld
99 J5 **Bowers** Staffs
46 C3 **Bowers Gifford** Essex
176 F1 **Bowershall** Fife
140 C4 **Bowes** Dur
121 G2 **Bowgreave** Lancs
147 H2 **Bowhouse** D & G
167 G2 **Bowland** Border
69 K4 **Bowley** Herefs
30 E4 **Bowlhead Green** Surrey
123 H4 **Bowling** Brad
174 E4 **Bowling** W Duns
137 J7 **Bowmanstead** Cumb
170 F6 **Bowmore** Ag & B
147 L3 **Bowness-on-Solway** Cumb
137 L7 **Bowness-on-Windermere** Cumb
196 E6 **Bowriefauld** Angus
168 E2 **Bowsden** Nthumb
55 K7 **Box** Gloucs
39 J6 **Box** Wilts
77 L6 **Boxford** Suffk
41 H6 **Boxford** W Berk
18 B4 **Boxgrove** W Susx
33 K2 **Boxley** Kent
59 H6 **Boxmoor** Herts
62 B2 **Boxted** Essex
77 J4 **Boxted** Suffk
62 B2 **Boxted Cross** Essex
62 B2 **Boxted Heath** Essex
75 L2 **Boxworth** Cambs
47 L6 **Boyden Gate** Kent
100 D5 **Boylestone** Derbys
216 C2 **Boyndie** Abers
217 G2 **Boyndlie** Abers
135 H6 **Boynton** E R Yk
197 G6 **Boysack** Angus
9 J6 **Boyton** Cnwll
79 H5 **Boyton** Suffk
27 L4 **Boyton** Wilts
61 G6 **Boyton Cross** Essex
77 G5 **Boyton End** Suffk
74 C3 **Bozeat** Nhants
34 E6 **Brabourne** Kent
34 E6 **Brabourne Lees** Kent
231 K2 **Brabstermire** Highld
208 E6 **Bracadale** Highld
88 F2 **Braceborough** Lincs
117 G7 **Bracebridge Heath** Lincs
116 F7 **Bracebridge Low Fields** Lincs
103 G5 **Braceby** Lincs
122 C2 **Bracewell** Lancs
101 G2 **Brackenfield** Derbys
175 K5 **Brackenhirst** N Lans
201 J8 **Brackletter** Highld
73 H6 **Brackley** Nhants
42 E6 **Bracknell** Br For
185 H5 **Braco** P & K
215 L4 **Bracobrae** Moray
92 E4 **Bracon Ash** Norfk
199 L6 **Bracora** Highld
199 L6 **Bracorina** Highld
100 D3 **Bradbourne** Derbys
141 H2 **Bradbury** Dur
73 J5 **Bradden** Nhants
42 D2 **Bradenham** Bucks
39 M4 **Bradenstoke** Wilts
12 D1 **Bradfield** Devon
62 D2 **Bradfield** Essex
106 F5 **Bradfield** Norfk
114 F3 **Bradfield** Sheff
41 L6 **Bradfield** W Berk
77 K3 **Bradfield Combust** Suffk
99 G2 **Bradfield Green** Ches
62 D3 **Bradfield Heath** Essex
77 K3 **Bradfield St Clare** Suffk
77 K3 **Bradfield St George** Suffk
123 H4 **Bradford** Brad
9 L4 **Bradford** Devon
26 E8 **Bradford Abbas** Dorset
39 J7 **Bradford Leigh** Wilts
14 C4 **Bradford Peverell** Dorset

39 J7 Bradford-on-Avon Wilts
25 J6 Bradford-on-Tone Somset
23 J4 Bradiford Devon
17 H5 Brading IOW
100 E4 Bradley Derbys
29 M3 Bradley Hants
118 C1 Bradley NE Lin
99 K8 Bradley Staffs
85 G4 Bradley Wolves
71 H3 Bradley Worcs
71 H3 Bradley Green Worcs
100 B4 Bradley in the Moors Staffs
38 E4 Bradley Stoke S Glos
101 L6 Bradmore Notts
12 C2 Bradninch Devon
100 A2 Bradnop Staffs
13 L4 Bradpole Dorset
123 G4 Bradshaw Calder
9 K8 Bradstone Devon
113 H8 Bradwall Green Ches
114 D5 Bradwell Derbys
61 K4 Bradwell Essex
74 B6 Bradwell M Keyn
93 K3 Bradwell Norfk
62 B6 Bradwell Waterside Essex
62 B6 Bradwell-on-Sea Essex
9 J3 Bradworthy Devon
213 G2 Brae Highld
235 c4 Brae Shet
201 L6 Brae Roy Lodge Highld
175 K3 Braeface Falk
197 H5 Braehead Angus
145 J4 Braehead D & G
176 C7 Braehead S Lans
204 E6 Braemar Abers
227 J3 Braemore Highld
221 G5 Braemore Highld
195 L5 Braes of Coul Angus
215 J3 Braes of Enzie Moray
173 L4 Braeside Inver
234 d4 Braeswick Ork
182 D6 Braevallich Ag & B
141 H3 Brafferton Darltn
132 F5 Brafferton N York
74 B3 Brafield-on-the-Green Nhants
232 f2 Bragar W Isls
59 L4 Bragbury End Herts
175 L8 Braidwood S Lans
100 E4 Brailsford Derbys
61 J4 Braintree Essex
78 D1 Braiseworth Suffk
29 G6 Braishfield Hants
137 H3 Braithwaite Cumb
115 K3 Braithwell Donc
19 G4 Bramber W Susx
86 E5 Bramcote Warwks
29 L5 Bramdean Hants
93 G3 Bramerton Norfk
59 M5 Bramfield Herts
93 H8 Bramfield Suffk
78 D5 Bramford Suffk
113 K5 Bramhall Stockp
124 C2 Bramham Leeds
123 K2 Bramhope Leeds
41 M8 Bramley Hants
123 K4 Bramley Leeds
115 J3 Bramley Rothm
31 G3 Bramley Surrey
41 M8 Bramley Corner Hants
35 G4 Bramling Kent
11 L5 Brampford Speke Devon
75 J1 Brampton Cambs
148 F3 Brampton Cumb
138 F3 Brampton Cumb
116 D5 Brampton Lincs
106 F7 Brampton Norfk
115 H2 Brampton Rothm
93 J6 Brampton Suffk
54 E3 Brampton Abbotts Herefs
87 L6 Brampton Ash Nhants
83 G8 Brampton Bryan Herefs
115 J4 Brampton-en-le-Morthen Rothm
100 B6 Bramshall Staffs
28 F7 Bramshaw Hants
30 D5 Bramshott Hants
26 B5 Bramwell Somset
61 G3 Bran End Essex
190 B3 Branault Highld
105 J4 Brancaster Norfk
105 J4 Brancaster Staithe Norfk
150 F7 Brancepeth Dur
214 D4 Branchill Moray
214 F1 Branderburgh Moray
126 E2 Brandesburton E R Yk
78 F3 Brandeston Suffk
106 D7 Brandiston Norfk
151 G6 Brandon Dur
102 E3 Brandon Lincs
91 H6 Brandon Suffk
86 E7 Brandon Warwks
92 C2 Brandon Parva Norfk
133 J5 Brandsby N York
117 G3 Brandy Wharf Lincs
15 K4 Branksome Poole
15 K4 Branksome Park Poole
29 H3 Bransbury Hants
116 E5 Bransby Lincs
12 F5 Branscombe Devon
70 E4 Bransford Worcs
16 A3 Bransgore Hants
126 D4 Bransholme C KuH
84 B7 Bransley Shrops
102 D6 Branston Leics
117 G7 Branston Lincs
100 E7 Branston Staffs
117 H7 Branston Booths Lincs
17 G5 Branstone IOW
102 E2 Brant Broughton Lincs
78 D7 Brantham Suffk
136 E3 Branthwaite Cumb
148 B7 Branthwaite Cumb
125 L5 Brantingham E R Yk
115 M2 Branton Donc
168 F6 Branton Nthumb
132 F6 Branton Green N York
168 D2 Branxton Nthumb
100 E2 Brassington Derbys
32 E3 Brasted Kent
32 E3 Brasted Chart Kent
206 D5 Brathens Abers
119 G8 Bratoft Lincs
116 F5 Brattleby Lincs
27 K2 Bratton Wilts
10 C6 Bratton Clovelly Devon
23 K4 Bratton Fleming Devon
26 G5 Bratton Seymour Somset
60 C3 Braughing Herts
73 G2 Braunston Nhants
88 B3 Braunston Rutlnd
87 G3 Braunstone Leics
23 H4 Braunton Devon
134 B4 Brawby N York
230 B3 Brawl Highld
42 E4 Bray W & M
5 M2 Bray Shop Cnwll
87 L6 Braybrooke Nhants
23 L4 Brayford Devon
123 K2 Braythorn N York
124 F4 Brayton N York
42 E4 Braywick W & M
59 J4 Breachwood Green Herts
101 G5 Breadsall Derbys
55 G7 Breadstone Gloucs
3 G5 Breage Cnwll
212 D5 Breakachy Highld
222 C3 Brealangwell Lodge Highld
54 E6 Bream Gloucs
28 D7 Breamore Hants
25 L1 Brean Somset
232 d3 Breanais W Isls
132 E7 Brearton N York
232 e2 Breascleit W Isls
232 e2 Breasclete W Isls
101 J5 Breaston Derbys
66 C7 Brechfa Carmth
196 F4 Brechin Angus
91 L5 Breckles Norfk
154 E4 Breckonside D & G
53 G3 Brecon Powys
52 F3 Brecon Beacons National Park
113 L3 Bredbury Stockp
21 G3 Brede E Susx
69 L3 Bredenbury Herefs
78 F4 Bredfield Suffk
34 B3 Bredgar Kent
46 D7 Bredhurst Kent
71 G6 Bredon Worcs
71 G7 Bredon's Hardwick Worcs
71 G6 Bredon's Norton Worcs
69 G5 Bredwardine Herefs
101 H7 Breedon on the Hill Leics
176 C6 Breich W Loth
121 L8 Breightmet Bolton
125 G4 Breighton E R Yk
69 J6 Breinton Herefs
39 L5 Bremhill Wilts
33 H5 Brenchley Kent
24 B2 Brendon Devon
172 E2 Brenfield Ag & B
232 d3 Brenish W Isls
77 L5 Brent Eleigh Suffk
25 M2 Brent Knoll Somset
7 G4 Brent Mill Devon
60 C2 Brent Pelham Herts
44 D5 Brentford Gt Lon
102 C8 Brentingby Leics
45 L2 Brentwood Essex
21 K1 Brenzett Kent
34 D8 Brenzett Green Kent
85 J1 Brereton Staffs
113 H8 Brereton Green Ches
92 C7 Bressingham Norfk
100 F7 Bretby Derbys
86 E7 Bretford Warwks
71 K5 Bretforton Worcs
121 G6 Bretherton Lancs
235 d5 Brettabister Shet
91 L6 Brettenham Norfk
77 L4 Brettenham Suffk
111 K8 Bretton Flints
84 F2 Brewood Staffs
14 F4 Briantspuddle Dorset
114 F5 Brick Houses Sheff
60 A6 Brickendon Herts
59 J7 Bricket Wood Herts
71 H6 Bricklehampton Worcs
237 e2 Bride IOM
147 K7 Bridekirk Cumb
10 D6 Bridestowe Devon
216 B6 Brideswell Abers
11 J7 Bridford Devon
3 H3 Bridge Cnwll
35 G4 Bridge Kent
132 E5 Bridge Hewick N York
206 B2 Bridge of Alford Abers
185 G7 Bridge of Allan Stirlg
214 E7 Bridge of Avon Moray
204 E2 Bridge of Avon Moray
193 J6 Bridge of Balgie P & K
195 J4 Bridge of Brewlands Angus
204 D2 Bridge of Brown Highld
195 J6 Bridge of Cally P & K
206 C6 Bridge of Canny Abers
195 K5 Bridge of Craigisla Angus
146 C3 Bridge of Dee D & G
207 H4 Bridge of Don C Aber
213 L6 Bridge of Dulsie Highld
206 C7 Bridge of Dye Abers
186 B4 Bridge of Earn P & K
193 H5 Bridge of Ericht P & K
206 D6 Bridge of Feugh Abers
230 F2 Bridge of Forss Highld
205 H6 Bridge of Gairn Abers
193 H5 Bridge of Gaur P & K
216 B4 Bridge of Marnoch Abers
192 E7 Bridge of Orchy Ag & B
194 D4 Bridge of Tilt P & K
215 J3 Bridge of Tynet Moray
235 b5 Bridge of Walls Shet
174 D5 Bridge of Weir Rens
69 H6 Bridge Sollers Herefs
77 K5 Bridge Street Suffk
112 C7 Bridge Trafford Ches
26 E6 Bridgehampton Somset
150 D5 Bridgehill Dur
17 H2 Bridgemary Hants
215 L7 Bridgend Abers
171 G6 Bridgend Ag & B
196 E3 Bridgend Angus
36 E4 Bridgend Brdgnd
165 L7 Bridgend D & G
6 E6 Bridgend Devon
186 F5 Bridgend Fife
215 J7 Bridgend Moray
186 B3 Bridgend P & K
176 E3 Bridgend W Loth
195 L5 Bridgend of Lintrathen Angus
9 H4 Bridgerule Devon
24 E5 Bridgetown Somset
91 L6 Bridgham Norfk
84 C5 Bridgnorth Shrops
85 H2 Bridgtown Staffs
25 L4 Bridgwater Somset
135 J6 Bridlington E R Yk
13 L4 Bridport Dorset
54 E3 Bridstow Herefs
122 C3 Brierfield Lancs
124 C7 Brierley Barns
54 F5 Brierley Gloucs
85 G6 Brierley Hill Dudley
184 C6 Brig o'Turk Stirlg
117 G1 Brigg N Linc
107 G6 Briggate Norfk
143 H5 Briggswath N York

136 F2 Brigham Cumb
135 G8 Brigham E R Yk
123 H6 Brighouse Calder
16 E5 Brighstone IOW
57 G7 Brighthampton Oxon
10 E5 Brightley Devon
20 D2 Brightling E Susx
62 C4 Brightlingsea Essex
19 J5 Brighton Br & H
111 J2 Brighton le Sands Sefton
176 C3 Brightons Falk
41 H5 Brightwalton W Berk
78 F5 Brightwell Suffk
42 A2 Brightwell Baldwin Oxon
42 A2 Brightwell Upperton Oxon
41 L3 Brightwell-cum-Sotwell Oxon
140 D5 Brignall Dur
118 C2 Brigsley NE Lin
129 K2 Brigsteer Cumb
88 D6 Brigstock Nhants
58 A5 Brill Bucks
3 J5 Brill Cnwll
68 F5 Brilley Herefs
69 K2 Brimfield Herefs
69 K2 Brimfield Cross Herefs
115 H6 Brimington Derbys
7 J1 Brimley Devon
55 L5 Brimpsfield Gloucs
41 K7 Brimpton W Berk
55 K7 Brimscombe Gloucs
111 J5 Brimstage Wirral
114 G4 Brincliffe Sheff
125 H4 Brind E R Yk
235 c5 Brindister Shet
121 J5 Brindle Lancs
84 E2 Brineton Staffs
88 B5 Bringhurst Leics
88 F7 Brington Cambs
106 C5 Brininghan Norfk
118 E6 Brinkhill Lincs
76 F4 Brinkley Cambs
86 E7 Brinklow Warwks
40 A4 Brinkworth Wilts
121 J6 Brinscall Lancs
101 J3 Brinsley Notts
115 H4 Brinsworth Rothm
106 C5 Brinton Norfk
234 c5 Brinyan Ork
105 M7 Brisley Norfk
38 F6 Brislington Bristl
34 C6 Brissenden Green Kent
38 E5 Bristol Bristl
38 D7 Bristol Airport N Som
38 E5 Bristol Zoo Bristl
106 C6 Briston Norfk
28 D5 Britford Wilts
53 J7 Brithdir Caerph
96 B8 Brithdir Gwynd
33 J2 British Legion Village Kent
51 L6 Briton Ferry Neath
42 A2 Britwell Salome Oxon
7 L5 Brixham Torbay
6 E5 Brixton Devon
44 F5 Brixton Gt Lon
27 K4 Brixton Deverill Wilts
73 L1 Brixworth Nhants
56 F6 Brize Norton Oxon
56 F6 Brize Norton Airport Oxon
70 F2 Broad Alley Worcs
40 D3 Broad Blunsdon Swindn
71 L6 Broad Campden Gloucs
123 G6 Broad Carr Calder
28 B6 Broad Chalke Wilts
61 L4 Broad Green Essex
70 D4 Broad Green Worcs
48 E5 Broad Haven Pembks
40 C5 Broad Hinton Wilts
41 H7 Broad Laying Hants
71 K5 Broad Marston Worcs
21 G2 Broad Oak E Susx
20 C2 Broad Oak E Susx
54 C4 Broad Oak Herefs
35 G3 Broad Oak Kent
112 D3 Broad Oak St Hel
21 H3 Broad Street E Susx
33 L2 Broad Street Kent
40 C5 Broad Town Wilts
61 H5 Broad's Green Essex
113 M3 Broadbottom Tamesd
17 M2 Broadbridge W Susx
31 J5 Broadbridge Heath W Susx
12 C3 Broadclyst Devon
174 C4 Broadfield Inver
199 K2 Broadford Highld
31 H6 Broadford Bridge W Susx
166 C7 Broadgairhill Border
179 H7 Broadhaugh Border
113 H4 Broadheath Traffd
12 E2 Broadhembury Devon
7 J3 Broadhempston Devon
21 G2 Broadland Row E Susx
215 J3 Broadley Moray
14 D5 Broadmayne Dorset
49 J6 Broadmoor Pembks
13 K3 Broadoak Dorset
35 K2 Broadstairs Kent
15 J4 Broadstone Poole
83 K5 Broadstone Shrops
70 D4 Broadwas Worcs
59 L4 Broadwater Herts
18 F5 Broadwater W Susx
84 E7 Broadwaters Worcs
48 E5 Broadway Pembks
25 L7 Broadway Somset
71 K6 Broadway Worcs
56 D3 Broadwell Gloucs
56 E6 Broadwell Oxon
72 F2 Broadwell Warwks
13 K2 Broadwindsor Dorset
10 F4 Broadwood Kelly Devon
9 K6 Broadwoodwidger Devon
209 J5 Brochel Highld
70 D4 Brockamin Worcs
29 L7 Brockbridge Hants
92 E7 Brockdish Norfk
16 C3 Brockenhurst Hants
164 F2 Brocketsbrae S Lans
78 D2 Brockford Street Suffk
73 J2 Brockhall Nhants
31 K2 Brockham Surrey
56 B4 Brockhampton Gloucs
17 K2 Brockhampton Hants
54 E2 Brockhampton Herefs
123 H7 Brockholes Kirk
126 E7 Brocklesby Lincs
38 C6 Brockley N Som
77 J1 Brockley Suffk
77 G5 Brockley Green Suffk
77 J4 Brockley Green Suffk
83 G3 Brockton Shrops
83 G6 Brockton Shrops
83 L5 Brockton Shrops
99 J6 Brockton Staffs
54 D7 Brockweir Gloucs
55 K5 Brockworth Gloucs
99 L8 Brocton Staffs
162 C3 Brodick N Ayrs
214 B3 Brodie Moray
115 J1 Brodsworth Donc
218 C7 Brogaig Highld
113 K6 Broken Cross Ches
39 K3 Brokenborough Wilts
27 J2 Brokerswood Wilts
111 K5 Bromborough Wirral
92 D7 Brome Suffk
92 D7 Brome Street Suffk
79 G4 Bromeswell Suffk
147 L5 Bromfield Cumb
83 J7 Bromfield Shrops
74 E4 Bromham Beds
39 L7 Bromham Wilts
45 H6 Bromley Gt Lon
84 D4 Bromley Shrops
46 C6 Brompton Medway
141 J7 Brompton N York
134 E3 Brompton N York
25 G5 Brompton Ralph Somset
24 E5 Brompton Regis Somset
140 F7 Brompton-on-Swale N York
70 D7 Bromsberrow Gloucs
55 G2 Bromsberrow Heath Gloucs
71 G1 Bromsgrove Worcs
70 B4 Bromyard Herefs
66 E2 Bronant Cerdgn
65 K5 Brongest Cerdgn
98 C4 Bronington Wrexhm
68 D7 Bronllys Powys
50 E2 Bronwydd Carmth
97 K5 Bronygarth Shrops
28 F8 Brook Hants
16 E5 Brook IOW
34 E6 Brook Kent
30 F4 Brook Surrey
28 F8 Brook Hill Hants
45 L2 Brook Street Essex
34 C7 Brook Street Kent
77 J5 Brook Street Suffk
93 G4 Brooke Norfk
88 B3 Brooke Rutlnd
117 K3 Brookenby Lincs
174 D5 Brookfield Rens
26 F5 Brookhampton Somset
129 L6 Brookhouse Lancs
115 K4 Brookhouse Rothm
99 J1 Brookhouse Green Ches
114 B4 Brookhouses Derbys
21 K1 Brookland Kent
113 H4 Brooklands Traffd
59 L7 Brookmans Park Herts
55 J5 Brookthorpe Gloucs
42 F8 Brookwood Surrey
75 H6 Broom Beds
151 G6 Broom Dur
115 H3 Broom Rothm
71 K4 Broom Warwks
115 H2 Broom Hill Barns
101 K3 Broom Hill Notts
34 D3 Broom Street Kent
93 H5 Broome Norfk
83 H7 Broome Shrops
84 F7 Broome Worcs
113 G4 Broomedge Warrtn
61 H5 Broomfield Essex
33 L3 Broomfield Kent
47 K6 Broomfield Kent
25 K5 Broomfield Somset
125 K5 Broomfleet E R Yk
150 C3 Broomhaugh Nthumb
159 G2 Broomhill Nthumb
226 F7 Brora Highld
84 C3 Broseley Shrops
150 A7 Brotherlee Dur
124 D5 Brotherton N York
142 E4 Brotton R & Cl
230 F4 Broubster Highld
139 H4 Brough Cumb
125 L5 Brough E R Yk
231 J2 Brough Highld
102 D2 Brough Notts
235 d4 Brough Shet
235 d2 Brough Lodge Shet
139 H5 Brough Sowerby Cumb
98 E4 Broughall Shrops
165 L3 Broughton Border
89 K7 Broughton Cambs
111 K8 Broughton Flints
28 F5 Broughton Hants
121 G4 Broughton Lancs
74 C6 Broughton M Keyn
126 B8 Broughton N Linc
122 D1 Broughton N York
134 B5 Broughton N York
88 B7 Broughton Nhants
72 E6 Broughton Oxon
113 J2 Broughton Salfd
99 H5 Broughton Staffs
36 E6 Broughton V Glam
87 G5 Broughton Astley Leics
39 K7 Broughton Gifford Wilts
71 G3 Broughton Green Worcs
71 G4 Broughton Hackett Worcs
145 J6 Broughton Mains D & G
128 F2 Broughton Mills Cumb
147 J7 Broughton Moor Cumb
56 E7 Broughton Poggs Oxon
128 F3 Broughton-in-Furness Cumb
187 H2 Broughty Ferry C Dund
29 L4 Brown Candover Hants
99 K2 Brown Edge Staffs
217 G6 Brownhill Abers
187 H4 Brownhills Fife
85 J3 Brownhills Wsall
41 L7 Browninghill Green Hants
55 K7 Browns Hill Gloucs
7 G5 Brownston Devon
134 E2 Broxa N York
60 B6 Broxbourne Herts
178 E3 Broxburn E Loth
176 E4 Broxburn W Loth
60 F3 Broxted Essex
69 G4 Broxwood Herefs
231 K7 Bruan Highld
194 C3 Bruar P & K
223 K4 Brucefield Highld
173 J6 Bruchag Ag & B
170 E6 Bruichladdich Ag & B
79 G2 Bruisyard Suffk
79 G2 Bruisyard Street Suffk
125 K8 Brumby N Linc
100 C1 Brund Staffs
93 G2 Brundall Norfk
78 F1 Brundish Suffk
78 F1 Brundish Street Suffk

159 G7 **Brunswick Village** N u Ty
122 F2 **Brunthwaite** Brad
87 H5 **Bruntingthorpe** Leics
186 E3 **Brunton** Fife
169 J4 **Brunton** Nthumb
28 E1 **Brunton** Wilts
24 E6 **Brushford** Somset
11 G4 **Brushford Barton** Devon
27 G4 **Bruton** Somset
70 F2 **Bryan's Green** Worcs
15 G2 **Bryanston** Dorset
155 L7 **Brydekirk** D & G
26 D7 **Brympton** Somset
36 C3 **Bryn** Neath
112 E2 **Bryn Gates** Wigan
97 G3 **Bryn Saith Marchog** Denbgs
51 L5 **Bryn-coch** Neath
64 E6 **Bryn-Henllan** Pembks
94 D5 **Bryn-mawr** Gwynd
110 B6 **Bryn-y-Maen** Conwy
51 K3 **Brynaman** Carmth
64 F7 **Brynberian** Pembks
95 H4 **Bryncir** Gwynd
94 D6 **Bryncroes** Gwynd
80 E3 **Bryncrug** Gwynd
97 H3 **Bryneglwys** Denbgs
111 G6 **Brynford** Flints
108 D6 **Bryngwran** IOA
54 B6 **Bryngwyn** Mons
68 D5 **Bryngwyn** Powys
65 K4 **Brynhoffnant** Cerdgn
53 J5 **Brynmawr** Blae G
36 D4 **Brynmenyn** Brdgnd
51 J6 **Brynmill** Swans
36 F4 **Brynna** Rhondd
109 H8 **Brynrefail** Gwynd
37 G4 **Brynsadler** Rhondd
108 F7 **Brynsiencyn** IOA
198 F2 **Bualintur** Highld
86 D8 **Bubbenhall** Warwks
125 H4 **Bubwith** E R Yk
174 E1 **Buchanan Smithy** Stirlg
217 L5 **Buchanhaven** Abers
185 J2 **Buchanty** P & K
184 F6 **Buchany** Stirlg
184 C8 **Buchlyvie** Stirlg
22 E6 **Buck's Cross** Devon
22 E6 **Buck's Mills** Devon
148 C5 **Buckabank** Cumb
75 H2 **Buckden** Cambs
131 H4 **Buckden** N York
93 H3 **Buckenham** Norfk
12 E3 **Buckerell** Devon
7 H3 **Buckfast** Devon
7 H3 **Buckfastleigh** Devon
186 F7 **Buckhaven** Fife
54 D5 **Buckholt** Mons
27 H6 **Buckhorn Weston** Dorset
45 H2 **Buckhurst Hill** Essex
215 J2 **Buckie** Moray
73 K7 **Buckingham** Bucks
58 E5 **Buckland** Bucks
7 G6 **Buckland** Devon
71 J7 **Buckland** Gloucs
75 L7 **Buckland** Herts
35 J6 **Buckland** Kent
41 G2 **Buckland** Oxon
31 K2 **Buckland** Surrey
22 F7 **Buckland Brewer** Devon
58 F6 **Buckland Common** Bucks
27 H2 **Buckland Dinham** Somset
10 C3 **Buckland Filleigh** Devon
7 G2 **Buckland in the Moor** Devon
6 D3 **Buckland Monachorum** Devon
14 D2 **Buckland Newton** Dorset
14 C6 **Buckland Ripers** Dorset
25 L8 **Buckland St Mary** Somset
7 H6 **Buckland-Tout-Saints** Devon
41 K6 **Bucklebury** W Berk
16 E3 **Bucklers Hard** Hants
78 F6 **Bucklesham** Suffk
111 J8 **Buckley** Flints
113 G5 **Bucklow Hill** Ches
102 E7 **Buckminster** Leics
99 K3 **Bucknall** C Stke
117 K7 **Bucknall** Lincs
57 K3 **Bucknell** Oxon
83 G8 **Bucknell** Shrops
215 J2 **Buckpool** Moray
31 H5 **Bucks Green** W Susx
30 D3 **Bucks Horn Oak** Hants
207 G4 **Bucksburn** C Aber
135 J5 **Buckton** E R Yk
169 G2 **Buckton** Nthumb
89 G7 **Buckworth** Cambs
115 L7 **Budby** Notts
9 H5 **Budd's Titson** Cnwll
187 H2 **Buddon** Angus
9 G4 **Bude** Cnwll
5 M4 **Budge's Shop** Cnwll
12 D6 **Budleigh Salterton** Devon
3 K5 **Budock Water** Cnwll
99 G4 **Buerton** Ches
73 J3 **Bugbrooke** Nhants
4 F4 **Bugle** Cnwll
27 H6 **Bugley** Dorset
134 B7 **Bugthorpe** E R Yk
84 B3 **Buildwas** Shrops
68 B4 **Builth Wells** Powys
28 C5 **Bulbridge** Wilts
230 E3 **Buldoo** Highld
28 D3 **Bulford** Wilts
98 D2 **Bulkeley** Ches
86 E6 **Bulkington** Warwks
39 L8 **Bulkington** Wilts
9 K3 **Bulkworthy** Devon
42 E6 **Bullbrook** Br For
29 J3 **Bullington** Hants
117 H6 **Bullington** Lincs
77 J6 **Bulmer** Essex
133 L6 **Bulmer** N York
77 J6 **Bulmer Tye** Essex
45 M3 **Bulphan** Thurr
217 H5 **Bulwark** Abers
101 K4 **Bulwell** C Nott
88 D5 **Bulwick** Nhants
60 C6 **Bumble's Green** Essex
199 K7 **Bunacaimb** Highld
201 J7 **Bunarkaig** Highld
98 E2 **Bunbury** Ches
212 F5 **Bunchrew** Highld
210 D8 **Bundalloch** Highld
180 E3 **Bunessan** Ag & B
93 G5 **Bungay** Suffk
171 H4 **Bunnahabhain** Ag & B
101 L6 **Bunny** Notts
212 C7 **Buntait** Highld
60 B3 **Buntingford** Herts
92 D5 **Bunwell** Norfk
92 D5 **Bunwell Street** Norfk
86 F5 **Burbage** Leics
40 E7 **Burbage** Wilts
42 D4 **Burchett's Green** W & M
28 B5 **Burcombe** Wilts
58 E4 **Burcott** Bucks
77 K7 **Bures** Essex
56 E5 **Burford** Oxon
69 L2 **Burford** Shrops
189 J7 **Burg** Ag & B
30 C5 **Burgates** Hants
19 J2 **Burgess Hill** W Susx
78 F4 **Burgh** Suffk
148 B3 **Burgh by Sands** Cumb
93 K3 **Burgh Castle** Norfk
44 E7 **Burgh Heath** Surrey
119 G7 **Burgh le Marsh** Lincs
106 F7 **Burgh next Aylsham** Norfk
117 L4 **Burgh on Bain** Lincs
93 J2 **Burgh St Margaret** Norfk
93 K5 **Burgh St Peter** Norfk
41 J7 **Burghclere** Hants
214 D1 **Burghead** Moray
42 A6 **Burghfield** W Berk
42 A6 **Burghfield Common** W Berk
69 J5 **Burghill** Herefs
124 E7 **Burghwallis** Donc
46 B7 **Burham** Kent
30 C7 **Buriton** Hants
98 E2 **Burland** Ches
4 F2 **Burlawn** Cnwll
55 K7 **Burleigh** Gloucs
25 G7 **Burlescombe** Devon
14 E4 **Burleston** Dorset
16 B2 **Burley** Hants
88 C2 **Burley** Rutlnd
69 L5 **Burley Gate** Herefs
123 H2 **Burley in Wharfedale** Brad
16 B2 **Burley Street** Hants
123 H2 **Burley Wood Head** Brad
98 E4 **Burleydam** Ches
93 H2 **Burlingham Green** Norfk
98 C7 **Burlton** Shrops
34 E7 **Burmarsh** Kent
72 C6 **Burmington** Warwks
124 F5 **Burn** N York
184 F6 **Burn of Cambus** Stirlg
113 K3 **Burnage** Manch
100 F6 **Burnaston** Derbys
176 B6 **Burnbrae** N Lans
125 K2 **Burnby** E R Yk
138 D7 **Burneside** Cumb
132 D3 **Burneston** N York
38 F7 **Burnett** BaNES
166 F6 **Burnfoot** Border
167 H6 **Burnfoot** Border
155 G4 **Burnfoot** D & G
156 C4 **Burnfoot** D & G
156 C3 **Burnfoot** D & G
185 K6 **Burnfoot** P & K
42 F4 **Burnham** Bucks
105 J4 **Burnham Deepdale** Norfk
59 L5 **Burnham Green** Herts
105 K4 **Burnham Market** Norfk
105 K4 **Burnham Norton** Norfk
105 K4 **Burnham Overy** Norfk
105 K4 **Burnham Overy Staithe** Norfk
105 K4 **Burnham Thorpe** Norfk
46 F2 **Burnham-on-Crouch** Essex
25 L2 **Burnham-on-Sea** Somset
217 L5 **Burnhaven** Abers
154 E3 **Burnhead** D & G
206 D2 **Burnhervie** Abers
84 E4 **Burnhill Green** Staffs
150 F5 **Burnhope** Dur
174 D7 **Burnhouse** N Ayrs
134 F2 **Burniston** N York
122 C4 **Burnley** Lancs
151 H5 **Burnmoor** Dur
179 K6 **Burnmouth** Border
150 F4 **Burnopfield** Dur
131 J7 **Burnsall** N York
196 E6 **Burnside** Angus
196 C4 **Burnside** Angus
186 B5 **Burnside** Fife
214 E1 **Burnside** Moray
176 E3 **Burnside** W Loth
187 G1 **Burnside of Duntrune** Angus
132 C7 **Burnt Yates** N York
177 H2 **Burntisland** Fife
85 J2 **Burntwood** Staffs
85 J2 **Burntwood Green** Staffs
25 J7 **Burnworthy** Somset
31 G2 **Burpham** Surrey
18 E4 **Burpham** W Susx
168 E7 **Burradon** Nthumb
235 e1 **Burrafirth** Shet
235 d3 **Burravoe** Shet
138 F4 **Burrells** Cumb
195 K8 **Burrelton** P & K
13 H2 **Burridge** Devon
17 G1 **Burridge** Hants
132 C3 **Burrill** N York
125 K8 **Burringham** N Linc
10 F2 **Burrington** Devon
69 J1 **Burrington** Herefs
38 C8 **Burrington** N Som
76 F4 **Burrough Green** Cambs
87 L2 **Burrough on the Hill** Leics
130 C4 **Burrow** Lancs
24 E3 **Burrow** Somset
26 A5 **Burrow Bridge** Somset
42 F7 **Burrowhill** Surrey
50 F7 **Burry Green** Swans
50 F5 **Burry Port** Carmth
120 F7 **Burscough** Lancs
120 F7 **Burscough Bridge** Lancs
125 J4 **Bursea** E R Yk
16 F1 **Bursledon** Hants
99 K3 **Burslem** C Stke
78 D5 **Burstall** Suffk
13 K2 **Burstock** Dorset
92 D6 **Burston** Norfk
32 B5 **Burstow** Surrey
126 F5 **Burstwick** E R Yk
131 G2 **Burtersett** N York
148 F3 **Burtholme** Cumb
77 H2 **Burthorpe Green** Suffk
103 L5 **Burtoft** Lincs
111 K6 **Burton** Ches
112 D8 **Burton** Ches
15 M4 **Burton** Dorset
116 F6 **Burton** Lincs
49 G6 **Burton** Pembks
25 J3 **Burton** Somset
39 J4 **Burton** Wilts
135 H6 **Burton Agnes** E R Yk
13 L4 **Burton Bradstock** Dorset
103 G7 **Burton Coggles** Lincs
126 F4 **Burton Constable Hall** E R Yk
60 E4 **Burton End** Essex

135 G5 Burton Fleming E R Yk
86 E5 Burton Hastings Warwks
130 C5 Burton in Lonsdale N York
101 M4 Burton Joyce Notts
88 C8 Burton Latimer Nhants
87 L1 Burton Lazars Leics
132 E6 Burton Leonard N York
101 L7 Burton on the Wolds Leics
87 J4 Burton Overy Leics
103 J4 Burton Pedwardine Lincs
127 G4 Burton Pidsea E R Yk
124 D5 Burton Salmon N York
125 K6 Burton upon Stather N Linc
100 E7 Burton upon Trent Staffs
61 K3 Burton's Green Essex
129 L4 Burton-in-Kendal Cumb
112 E3 Burtonwood Warrtn
98 D2 Burwardsley Ches
84 B6 Burwarton Shrops
33 H7 Burwash E Susx
20 D2 Burwash Common E Susx
20 D2 Burwash Weald E Susx
76 E2 Burwell Cambs
118 E5 Burwell Lincs
108 E3 Burwen IOA
234 c8 Burwick Ork
122 B7 Bury Bury
89 K6 Bury Cambs
24 E6 Bury Somset
18 D3 Bury W Susx
60 D4 Bury Green Herts
77 J2 Bury St Edmunds Suffk
134 C6 Burythorpe N York
175 G6 Busby E Rens
40 E2 Buscot Wilts
197 J4 Bush Abers
69 J4 Bush Bank Herefs
45 G2 Bush Hill Park Gt Lon
85 G3 Bushbury Wolves
43 J2 Bushey Herts
43 J2 Bushey Heath Herts
70 F7 Bushley Worcs
40 B5 Bushton Wilts
26 A4 Bussex Somset
38 D7 Butcombe N Som
26 D5 Butleigh Somset
26 D4 Butleigh Wootton Somset
72 D4 Butlers Marston Warwks
79 H4 Butley Suffk
133 L7 Buttercrambe N York
179 G5 Butterdean Border
140 E3 Butterknowle Dur
12 C2 Butterleigh Devon
137 G4 Buttermere Cumb
123 H5 Buttershaw Brad
195 G7 Butterstone P & K
99 J4 Butterton Staffs
100 B2 Butterton Staffs
104 C4 Butterwick Lincs
133 L4 Butterwick N York
134 F5 Butterwick N York
82 E2 Buttington Powys
84 D7 Buttonoak Shrops
78 B3 Buxhall Suffk
20 A2 Buxted E Susx
114 B6 Buxton Derbys
106 F7 Buxton Norfk
106 E7 Buxton Heath Norfk
53 J4 Bwlch Powys
97 J8 Bwlch-y-cibau Powys
82 B4 Bwlch-y-ffridd Powys
65 H7 Bwlch-y-groes Pembks
82 B8 Bwlch-y-sarnau Powys
97 K2 Bwlchgwyn Wrexhm
66 D3 Bwlchllan Cerdgn
94 E7 Bwlchtocyn Gwynd
150 F7 Byers Green Dur
73 G4 Byfield Nhants
43 H7 Byfleet Surrey
69 H6 Byford Herefs
151 G3 Byker N u Ty
110 D8 Bylchau Conwy
113 G7 Byley Ches
167 K2 Byrewalls Border
157 K2 Byrness Nthumb
12 D5 Bystock Devon
88 F7 Bythorn Cambs
69 G2 Byton Herefs
150 D3 Bywell Nthumb
31 G7 Byworth W Susx

C

117 J2 Cabourne Lincs
171 J5 Cabrach Ag & B
215 J8 Cabrach Moray
121 G2 Cabus Lancs
220 F7 Cabvie Lodge Highld
11 L4 Cadbury Devon
175 G3 Cadder E Duns
59 H4 Caddington Beds
167 G3 Caddonfoot Border
20 C2 Cade Street E Susx
115 K2 Cadeby Donc
86 E3 Cadeby Leics
11 L4 Cadeleigh Devon
3 J7 Cadgwith Cnwll
186 D6 Cadham Fife
113 G3 Cadishead Salfd
51 J6 Cadle Swans
121 G4 Cadley Lancs
40 E6 Cadley Wilts
28 E2 Cadley Wilts
42 C3 Cadmore End Bucks
28 F8 Cadnam Hants
117 G2 Cadney N Linc
37 H6 Cadoxton V Glam
51 L5 Cadoxton Juxta-Neath Neath
95 J1 Caeathro Gwynd
117 G4 Caenby Lincs
66 F6 Caeo Carmth
48 D3 Caer Farchell Pembks
36 D2 Caerau Brdgnd
37 H5 Caerau Cardif
108 D5 Caergeiliog IOA
97 L2 Caergwrle Flints
156 D2 Caerlanrig Border
37 M3 Caerleon Newpt
108 F8 Caernarfon Gwynd
108 F8 Caernarfon Castle Gwynd
37 J3 Caerphilly Caerph
82 B5 Caersws Powys
65 L4 Caerwedros Cerdgn
38 C3 Caerwent Mons
110 F6 Caerwys Flints
233 c6 Cairinis W Isls
172 E1 Cairnbaan Ag & B
217 J2 Cairnbulg Abers
179 J5 Cairncross Border
174 C4 Cairncurran Inver
183 H5 Cairndow Ag & B
176 E2 Cairneyhill Fife
215 J3 Cairnfield House Moray
144 C5 Cairngarroch D & G
204 B5 Cairngorm Mountains
207 G6 Cairngrassie Abers
215 K5 Cairnie Abers
217 G6 Cairnorrie Abers
144 C2 Cairnryan D & G
215 H4 Cairnty Moray
93 L2 Caister-on-Sea Norfk
117 J2 Caistor Lincs
92 F3 Caistor St Edmund Norfk
232 e2 Calanais W Isls
16 E5 Calbourne IOW
111 G6 Calcot Flints
56 C6 Calcot Gloucs
42 A6 Calcot Row W Berk
215 G2 Calcots Moray
148 B6 Caldbeck Cumb
89 G5 Caldecote Cambs
75 L3 Caldecote Cambs
75 J6 Caldecote Herts
75 L3 Caldecote Highfields Cambs
74 E2 Caldecott Nhants
41 J2 Caldecott Oxon
88 C5 Caldecott Rutlnd
136 E6 Calder Bridge Cumb
123 L6 Calder Grove Wakefd
121 G2 Calder Vale Lancs
175 K5 Calderbank N Lans
175 L5 Caldercruix N Lans
164 D2 Caldermill S Lans
175 H7 Calderwood S Lans
38 C3 Caldicot Mons
85 H4 Caldmore W Mids
140 E5 Caldwell N York
234 d4 Calfsound Ork
189 J6 Calgary Ag & B
214 D3 Califer Moray
176 B3 California Falk
93 K1 California Norfk
101 G7 Calke Derbys
209 L4 Callakille Highld
184 D5 Callander Stirlg
232 e2 Callanish W Isls
3 K2 Callestick Cnwll
199 K5 Calligarry Highld
6 A3 Callington Cnwll
69 J7 Callow Herefs
70 E4 Callow End Worcs
40 B4 Callow Hill Wilts
29 G7 Calmore Hants
56 B6 Calmsden Gloucs
39 M6 Calne Wilts
16 F3 Calshot Hants
6 C3 Calstock Cnwll
40 B6 Calstone Wellington Wilts
106 E6 Calthorpe Norfk
107 J7 Calthorpe Street Norfk
148 E6 Calthwaite Cumb
131 G7 Calton N York
100 C3 Calton Staffs
98 E2 Calveley Ches
114 E6 Calver Derbys
98 E5 Calverhall Shrops
11 L3 Calverleigh Devon
73 L6 Calverton M Keyn
101 L3 Calverton Notts
194 C3 Calvine P & K
147 K4 Calvo Cumb
165 L3 Calzeat Border
55 H7 Cam Gloucs
210 E8 Camas Luinie Highld
190 F4 Camasachoirce Highld
190 F4 Camasine Highld
209 H6 Camastianavaig Highld
212 D6 Camault Muir Highld
21 J2 Camber E Susx
42 E7 Camberley Surrey
44 F5 Camberwell Gt Lon
124 F5 Camblesforth N York
158 C5 Cambo Nthumb
3 H4 Camborne Cnwll
75 K3 Cambourne Cambs
76 C3 Cambridge Cambs
55 H7 Cambridge Gloucs
76 C3 Cambridge Airport Cambs
3 H3 Cambrose Cnwll
185 H8 Cambus Clacks
205 J5 Cambus o' May Abers
223 G3 Cambusavie Platform Highld
185 G8 Cambusbarron Stirlg
185 G8 Cambuskenneth Stirlg
175 H6 Cambuslang S Lans
165 K2 Cambuswallace S Lans
44 F4 Camden Town Gt Lon
38 E8 Cameley BaNES
8 E7 Camelford Cnwll
176 B3 Camelon Falk
70 D7 Camer's Green Worcs
214 C7 Camerory Highld
39 G8 Camerton BaNES
136 E2 Camerton Cumb
193 J5 Camghouran P & K
167 J4 Camieston Border
207 G6 Cammachmore Abers
116 F5 Cammeringham Lincs
223 G4 Camore Highld
161 J5 Campbeltown Ag & B
161 H5 Campbeltown Airport Ag & B
154 F4 Cample D & G
195 K8 Campmuir Angus
176 E5 Camps W Loth
124 E7 Campsall Donc
79 G4 Campsea Ash Suffk
75 G6 Campton Beds
167 K6 Camptown Border
48 F4 Camrose Pembks
194 C6 Camserney P & K
220 D4 Camusnagaul Highld
191 L2 Camusnagaul Highld
209 L6 Camusteel Highld
209 L6 Camusterrach Highld
28 F7 Canada Hants
205 H5 Candacraig Abers
118 F7 Candlesby Lincs
165 L2 Candyburn Border
42 B4 Cane End Oxon
46 E2 Canewdon Essex
15 K5 Canford Cliffs Poole
15 J4 Canford Heath Poole
15 J3 Canford Magna Poole
231 L2 Canisbay Highld
86 C7 Canley Covtry
27 K7 Cann Dorset
211 L7 Cannich Highld
45 H4 Canning Town Gt Lon
25 K4 Cannington Somset
85 H2 Cannock Staffs
99 M8 Cannock Chase Staffs
69 H6 Cannon Bridge Herefs
70 B5 Canon Frome Herefs
69 J5 Canon Pyon Herefs
156 C6 Canonbie D & G
73 H4 Canons Ashby Nhants
2 F4 Canonstown Cnwll
34 F3 Canterbury Kent

34 F3 Canterbury Cathedral Kent
93 H3 Cantley Norfk
37 J5 Canton Cardif
213 J5 Cantraywood Highld
130 C5 Cantsfield Lancs
46 D4 Canvey Island Essex
117 G7 Canwick Lincs
9 G6 Canworthy Water Cnwll
191 L2 Caol Highld
232 e4 Caolas Scalpaigh W Isls
188 D6 Caoles Ag & B
201 G6 Caonich Highld
33 H4 Capel Kent
31 K4 Capel Surrey
80 E7 Capel Bangor Cerdgn
108 F5 Capel Coch IOA
96 A2 Capel Curig Conwy
50 F2 Capel Dewi Carmth
66 B6 Capel Dewi Cerdgn
96 C2 Capel Garmon Conwy
51 H4 Capel Hendre Carmth
65 J7 Capel Iwan Carmth
35 H6 Capel le Ferne Kent
108 E6 Capel Mawr IOA
80 E7 Capel Seion Cerdgn
79 H5 Capel St Andrew Suffk
78 C6 Capel St Mary Suffk
80 E6 Capel-Dewi Cerdgn
236 d2 Capelles Guern
109 L6 Capelulo Conwy
111 K6 Capenhurst Ches
158 C6 Capheaton Nthumb
174 E6 Caplaw E Rens
166 C5 Cappercleuch Border
7 J5 Capton Devon
195 H7 Caputh P & K
102 B4 Car Colston Notts
174 F3 Carbeth Inn Stirlg
2 F4 Carbis Bay Cnwll
208 F7 Carbost Highld
208 F5 Carbost Highld
115 G4 Carbrook Sheff
91 L3 Carbrooke Norfk
124 E8 Carcroft Donc
186 C7 Cardenden Fife
214 F5 Cardhu Moray
37 J5 Cardiff Cardif
37 G6 Cardiff Airport V Glam
65 G5 Cardigan Cerdgn
74 F5 Cardington Beds
83 K4 Cardington Shrops
5 H3 Cardinham Cnwll
144 D8 Cardrain D & G
166 D2 Cardrona Border
174 C3 Cardross Ag & B
144 D7 Cardryne D & G
147 L3 Cardurnock Cumb
88 E1 Careby Lincs
196 E4 Careston Angus
49 H6 Carew Pembks
49 H6 Carew Cheriton Pembks
49 H6 Carew Newton Pembks
54 E2 Carey Herefs
175 K6 Carfin N Lans
178 B7 Carfraemill Border
93 H2 Cargate Green Norfk
155 G7 Cargen D & G
155 G6 Cargenbridge D & G
195 J8 Cargill P & K
148 C3 Cargo Cumb
6 C4 Cargreen Cnwll
168 B2 Carham Nthumb
24 F3 Carhampton Somset
3 J3 Carharrack Cnwll
193 K5 Carie P & K
233 c6 Carinish W Isls
16 F5 Carisbrooke IOW
129 H4 Cark Cumb
6 B4 Carkeel Cnwll
232 e2 Carlabhagh W Isls
140 F4 Carlbury Darltn
88 F2 Carlby Lincs
168 C6 Carlcroft Nthumb
3 G5 Carleen Cnwll
122 E1 Carleton N York
92 C3 Carleton Forehoe Norfk
92 D5 Carleton Rode Norfk
93 H3 Carleton St Peter Norfk
216 D5 Carlincraig Abers
39 G8 Carlingcott BaNES
148 D4 Carlisle Cumb
148 E3 Carlisle Airport Cumb
177 G6 Carlops Border
232 e2 Carloway W Isls
124 B7 Carlton Barns
74 D4 Carlton Beds
76 F4 Carlton Cambs
123 L5 Carlton Leeds
86 E3 Carlton Leics
131 K3 Carlton N York
133 J3 Carlton N York
124 F5 Carlton N York
101 L4 Carlton Notts
141 J3 Carlton S on T
79 H2 Carlton Suffk
93 K5 Carlton Colville Suffk
87 K4 Carlton Curlieu Leics
76 F4 Carlton Green Cambs
133 G4 Carlton Husthwaite N York
115 L5 Carlton in Lindrick Notts
132 F4 Carlton Miniott N York
102 F4 Carlton Scroop Lincs
142 B6 Carlton-in-Cleveland N York
102 E2 Carlton-le-Moorland Lincs
116 D8 Carlton-on-Trent Notts
175 L7 Carluke S Lans
164 F4 Carmacoup S Lans
50 E2 Carmarthen Carmth
51 H3 Carmel Carmth
111 G6 Carmel Flints
95 H2 Carmel Gwynd
165 H2 Carmichael S Lans
175 G6 Carmunnock C Glas
175 H6 Carmyle C Glas
196 E7 Carmyllie Angus
3 H3 Carn Brea Cnwll
200 E2 Carn-gorm Highld
135 H6 Carnaby E R Yk
187 J6 Carnbee Fife
185 L6 Carnbo P & K
216 F8 Carnbrogie Abers
210 D8 Carndu Highld
164 D1 Carnduff S Lans
163 L3 Carnell E Ayrs
129 K5 Carnforth Lancs
3 G4 Carnhell Green Cnwll
206 F4 Carnie Abers
3 J4 Carnkie Cnwll
3 H4 Carnkie Cnwll
81 K4 Carno Powys
200 D6 Carnoch Highld
176 E1 Carnock Fife
4 C7 Carnon Downs Cnwll
216 C4 Carnousie Abers
187 J1 Carnoustie Angus
165 J1 Carnwath S Lans
86 C7 Carol Green Solhll
131 J2 Carperby N York
123 L5 Carr Gate Wakefd
149 K5 Carr Shield Nthumb
161 K2 Carradale Ag & B
203 L2 Carrbridge Highld
236 c6 Carrefour Jersey
108 E4 Carreglefn IOA
116 C1 Carrhouse N Linc
172 F2 Carrick Ag & B
183 H8 Carrick Castle Ag & B
176 D3 Carriden Falk
177 J6 Carrington Mdloth
113 H3 Carrington Traffd
97 H4 Carrog Denbgs
176 B2 Carron Falk
214 F6 Carron Moray
175 K2 Carron Bridge Stirlg
154 F3 Carronbridge D & G
176 B2 Carronshore Falk
174 C5 Carruth House Inver
155 J7 Carrutherstown D & G
151 H6 Carrville Dur
181 H3 Carsaig Ag & B
196 D5 Carse Gray Angus
145 G2 Carseriggan D & G
147 H3 Carsethorn D & G
44 F6 Carshalton Gt Lon
100 E2 Carsington Derbys
161 H7 Carskey Ag & B
145 K4 Carsluith D & G
153 L4 Carsphairn D & G
165 H1 Carstairs S Lans
165 J1 Carstairs Junction S Lans
56 F6 Carterton Oxon
4 F5 Carthew Cnwll
132 D3 Carthorpe N York
165 G1 Cartland S Lans
129 H4 Cartmel Cumb
50 F4 Carway Carmth
55 J6 Cashe's Green Gloucs
57 J5 Cassington Oxon
151 J7 Cassop Colliery Dur
130 C4 Casterton Lancs
91 J1 Castle Acre Norfk
74 C3 Castle Ashby Nhants
131 J2 Castle Bolton N York
85 K5 Castle Bromwich Solhll
103 G8 Castle Bytham Lincs
82 D3 Castle Caereinion Powys
76 F6 Castle Camps Cambs
148 F4 Castle Carrock Cumb
26 F5 Castle Cary Somset
39 J5 Castle Combe Wilts
101 H6 Castle Donington Leics
146 D3 Castle Douglas D & G
40 C2 Castle Eaton Swindn
151 K7 Castle Eden Dur
70 C5 Castle Frome Herefs
100 F8 Castle Gresley Derbys
77 H7 Castle Hedingham Essex
78 D5 Castle Hill Suffk
144 D3 Castle Kennedy D & G
182 E7 Castle Lachlan Ag & B
156 A4 Castle O'er D & G
83 H3 Castle Pulverbatch Shrops
105 G7 Castle Rising Norfk
213 H4 Castle Stuart Highld
233 b9 Castlebay W Isls
49 H2 Castlebythe Pembks
175 K3 Castlecary Falk
124 C5 Castleford Wakefd
166 C3 Castlehill Border
231 H2 Castlehill Highld
174 D3 Castlehill W Duns
48 F7 Castlemartin Pembks
175 G6 Castlemilk C Glas
70 E6 Castlemorton Worcs
137 J3 Castlerigg Cumb
150 D5 Castleside Dur
74 B5 Castlethorpe M Keyn
156 E4 Castleton Border
114 D5 Castleton Derbys
142 E5 Castleton N York
37 K4 Castleton Newpt
122 D7 Castleton Rochdl
231 H3 Castletown Highld
237 b7 Castletown IOM
151 J4 Castletown Sundld
123 K2 Castley N York
91 L4 Caston Norfk
89 G4 Castor C Pete
172 F7 Catacol N Ayrs
115 H4 Catcliffe Rothm
40 A5 Catcomb Wilts
26 B4 Catcott Somset
26 B3 Catcott Burtle Somset
236 c3 Catel Guern
32 C3 Caterham Surrey
107 H7 Catfield Norfk
235 c5 Catfirth Shet
45 G5 Catford Gt Lon
121 G4 Catforth Lancs
175 G6 Cathcart C Glas
53 H3 Cathedine Powys
30 B8 Catherington Hants
13 J4 Catherston Leweston Dorset
17 G2 Catisfield Hants
202 F6 Catlodge Highld
76 C6 Catmere End Essex
41 J4 Catmore W Berk
129 L6 Caton Lancs
129 L6 Caton Green Lancs
164 B4 Catrine E Ayrs
20 E3 Catsfield E Susx
26 D6 Catsgore Somset
85 G8 Catshill Worcs
161 H7 Cattadale Ag & B
133 G8 Cattal N York
62 D2 Cattawade Suffk
121 G3 Catterall Lancs
141 G7 Catterick N York
141 G7 Catterick Bridge N York
148 E7 Catterlen Cumb
197 L2 Catterline Abers
124 D2 Catterton N York
31 G3 Catteshall Surrey
87 G7 Catthorpe Leics
14 B3 Cattistock Dorset
149 L4 Catton Cumb
132 E4 Catton N York
92 F2 Catton Norfk
126 E2 Catwick E R Yk
88 F8 Catworth Cambs
55 L6 Caudle Green Gloucs
57 K3 Caulcott Oxon
197 G6 Cauldcots Angus
184 E8 Cauldhame Stirlg
167 H6 Cauldmill Border
100 B3 Cauldon Staffs
86 B1 Cauldwell Derbys
147 G4 Caulkerbush D & G
156 D6 Caulside D & G
27 G8 Caundle Marsh Dorset
102 C1 Caunton Notts
145 J3 Causeway End D & G
61 G4 Causeway End Essex
165 K3 Causewayend S Lans
185 G7 Causewayhead Stirlg
158 F3 Causey Park Bridge Nthumb
207 H2 Causeyend Abers
77 J5 Cavendish Suffk
77 H1 Cavenham Suffk
57 L3 Caversfield Oxon

42 B5 **Caversham** Readg
99 L4 **Caverswall** Staffs
167 L4 **Caverton Mill** Border
213 K4 **Cawdor** Highld
124 E3 **Cawood** N York
6 C5 **Cawsand** Cnwll
106 D7 **Cawston** Norfk
123 K8 **Cawthorne** Barns
75 K3 **Caxton** Cambs
83 K8 **Caynham** Shrops
102 F3 **Caythorpe** Lincs
102 B4 **Caythorpe** Notts
135 G3 **Cayton** N York
233 b6 **Ceann a Bhaigh** W Isls
201 K3 **Ceannacroc Lodge** Highld
232 f3 **Cearsiadar** W Isls
37 L3 **Cefn** Newpt
36 D4 **Cefn Cribwr** Brdgnd
96 E3 **Cefn-brith** Conwy
97 L4 **Cefn-mawr** Wrexhm
49 K3 **Cefn-y-pant** Carmth
67 J5 **Cefngorwydd** Powys
187 J6 **Cellardyke** Fife
99 L3 **Cellarhead** Staffs
108 E3 **Cemaes** IOA
81 H3 **Cemmaes** Powys
81 H3 **Cemmaes Road** Powys
65 J6 **Cenarth** Cerdgn
186 F5 **Ceres** Fife
14 C3 **Cerne Abbas** Dorset
40 B2 **Cerney Wick** Gloucs
108 E6 **Cerrigceinwen** IOA
96 E3 **Cerrigydrudion** Conwy
95 J1 **Ceunant** Gwynd
55 J2 **Chaceley** Gloucs
3 K3 **Chacewater** Cnwll
73 K7 **Chackmore** Bucks
72 F5 **Chacombe** Nhants
71 H5 **Chadbury** Worcs
113 K1 **Chadderton** Oldham
101 G5 **Chaddesden** C Derb
84 F8 **Chaddesley Corbett** Worcs
6 C1 **Chaddlehanger** Devon
41 H5 **Chaddleworth** W Berk
57 G4 **Chadlington** Oxon
72 D4 **Chadshunt** Warwks
102 C7 **Chadwell** Leics
45 J3 **Chadwell Heath** Gt Lon
45 M4 **Chadwell St Mary** Thurr
70 E2 **Chadwick** Worcs
86 B8 **Chadwick End** Solhll
13 J1 **Chaffcombe** Somset
11 G7 **Chagford** Devon
19 K2 **Chailey** E Susx
33 J4 **Chainhurst** Kent
32 B3 **Chaldon** Surrey
16 F6 **Chale** IOW
16 F6 **Chale Green** IOW
43 G3 **Chalfont Common** Bucks
43 G2 **Chalfont St Giles** Bucks
43 G3 **Chalfont St Peter** Bucks
55 K7 **Chalford** Gloucs
27 K2 **Chalford** Wilts
41 M2 **Chalgrove** Oxon
46 A5 **Chalk** Kent
34 B2 **Chalkwell** Kent
23 L3 **Challacombe** Devon
145 H2 **Challoch** D & G
34 D5 **Challock** Kent
59 G3 **Chalton** Beds
30 B7 **Chalton** Hants
42 F4 **Chalvey** Slough
20 B4 **Chalvington** E Susx
43 H2 **Chandler's Cross** Herts
29 H7 **Chandler's Ford** Hants
27 G3 **Chantry** Somset
78 D5 **Chantry** Suffk
186 D8 **Chapel** Fife
123 L3 **Chapel Allerton** Leeds
26 B2 **Chapel Allerton** Somset
4 F2 **Chapel Amble** Cnwll
73 K2 **Chapel Brampton** Nhants
99 J5 **Chapel Chorlton** Staffs
72 F3 **Chapel Green** Warwks
124 E5 **Chapel Haddlesey** N York
217 K7 **Chapel Hill** Abers
103 K2 **Chapel Hill** Lincs
54 D7 **Chapel Hill** Mons
123 L2 **Chapel Hill** N York
82 F7 **Chapel Lawn** Shrops
130 E4 **Chapel le Dale** N York
25 H5 **Chapel Leigh** Somset
206 D1 **Chapel of Garioch** Abers
144 D6 **Chapel Rossan** D & G
41 L6 **Chapel Row** W Berk
119 H6 **Chapel St Leonards** Lincs
137 K6 **Chapel Stile** Cumb
114 B5 **Chapel-en-le-Frith** Derbys
77 G6 **Chapelend Way** Essex
175 K5 **Chapelhall** N Lans
166 C5 **Chapelhope** Border
156 B7 **Chapelknowe** D & G
197 G6 **Chapelton** Angus
23 J6 **Chapelton** Devon
175 J8 **Chapelton** S Lans
121 L7 **Chapeltown** Bl w D
204 F2 **Chapeltown** Moray
115 G3 **Chapeltown** Sheff
9 J6 **Chapmans Well** Devon
27 J2 **Chapmanslade** Wilts
60 B5 **Chapmore End** Herts
61 L3 **Chappel** Essex
13 H2 **Chard** Somset
13 J2 **Chard Junction** Somset
13 H1 **Chardleigh Green** Somset
13 H2 **Chardstock** Devon
39 G3 **Charfield** S Glos
34 C5 **Charing** Kent
71 L6 **Charingworth** Gloucs
57 G4 **Charlbury** Oxon
39 H6 **Charlcombe** BaNES
39 M5 **Charlcutt** Wilts
72 C3 **Charlecote** Warwks
85 H5 **Charlemont** W Mids
23 L5 **Charles** Devon
78 B4 **Charles Tye** Suffk
196 C7 **Charleston** Angus
123 H3 **Charlestown** Brad
207 H5 **Charlestown** C Aber
122 E5 **Charlestown** Calder
5 G5 **Charlestown** Cnwll
176 E2 **Charlestown** Fife
219 J6 **Charlestown** Highld
213 G5 **Charlestown** Highld
113 J2 **Charlestown** Salfd
114 A3 **Charlesworth** Derbys
25 K4 **Charlinch** Somset
186 E5 **Charlottetown** Fife
45 H4 **Charlton** Gt Lon
73 G7 **Charlton** Nhants
157 K5 **Charlton** Nthumb
41 H3 **Charlton** Oxon
25 L6 **Charlton** Somset
27 G2 **Charlton** Somset
18 B3 **Charlton** W Susx
27 K6 **Charlton** Wilts
39 L3 **Charlton** Wilts
28 C1 **Charlton** Wilts
71 H5 **Charlton** Worcs
83 L2 **Charlton** Wrekin
56 B3 **Charlton Abbots** Gloucs
26 D5 **Charlton Adam** Somset
26 F6 **Charlton Horethorne** Somset
55 L4 **Charlton Kings** Gloucs
26 D5 **Charlton Mackrell** Somset
15 G2 **Charlton Marshall** Dorset
27 G5 **Charlton Musgrove** Somset
15 G2 **Charlton on the Hill** Dorset
28 D6 **Charlton-all-Saints** Wilts
57 K5 **Charlton-on-Otmoor** Oxon
30 A5 **Charlwood** Hants
31 L3 **Charlwood** Surrey
14 D4 **Charminster** Dorset
13 J4 **Charmouth** Dorset
58 A3 **Charndon** Bucks
41 G2 **Charney Bassett** Oxon
121 H7 **Charnock Richard** Lancs
78 F3 **Charsfield** Suffk
33 K4 **Chart Sutton** Kent
41 L8 **Charter Alley** Hants
179 G8 **Charterhall** Border
26 D1 **Charterhouse** Somset
175 K1 **Chartershall** Stirlg
34 E4 **Chartham** Kent
34 E4 **Chartham Hatch** Kent
58 F7 **Chartridge** Bucks
42 C5 **Charvil** Wokham
73 G4 **Charwelton** Nhants
85 J2 **Chase Terrace** Staffs
85 J2 **Chasetown** Staffs
56 E3 **Chastleton** Oxon
9 J4 **Chasty** Devon
122 B2 **Chatburn** Lancs
99 H5 **Chatcull** Staffs
46 C6 **Chatham** Medway
61 H5 **Chatham Green** Essex
169 J4 **Chathill** Nthumb
114 E7 **Chatsworth House** Derbys
46 C5 **Chattenden** Medway
90 B6 **Chatteris** Cambs
122 B6 **Chatterton** Lancs
78 C6 **Chattisham** Suffk
168 B5 **Chatto** Border
168 F4 **Chatton** Nthumb
11 G3 **Chawleigh** Devon
30 B4 **Chawton** Hants
100 A4 **Cheadle** Staffs
113 K4 **Cheadle** Stockp
113 K4 **Cheadle Hulme** Stockp
44 E7 **Cheam** Gt Lon
58 B6 **Chearsley** Bucks
99 J6 **Chebsey** Staffs
42 A4 **Checkendon** Oxon
99 G4 **Checkley** Ches
100 B5 **Checkley** Staffs
77 H3 **Chedburgh** Suffk
26 C2 **Cheddar** Somset
58 F4 **Cheddington** Bucks
99 L3 **Cheddleton** Staffs
25 K6 **Cheddon Fitzpaine** Somset
93 H4 **Chedgrave** Norfk
13 L2 **Chedington** Dorset
93 H7 **Chediston** Suffk
56 B5 **Chedworth** Gloucs
25 M4 **Chedzoy** Somset
113 J2 **Cheetham Hill** Manch
11 H3 **Cheldon** Devon
113 J6 **Chelford** Ches
101 G6 **Chellaston** C Derb
74 D4 **Chellington** Beds
84 C5 **Chelmarsh** Shrops
78 E6 **Chelmondiston** Suffk
114 C7 **Chelmorton** Derbys
61 H6 **Chelmsford** Essex
85 L6 **Chelmsley Wood** Solhll
44 F4 **Chelsea** Gt Lon
45 J7 **Chelsfield** Gt Lon
77 L5 **Chelsworth** Suffk
55 L4 **Cheltenham** Gloucs
74 E1 **Chelveston** Nhants
38 C6 **Chelvey** N Som
38 F7 **Chelwood** BaNES
32 D6 **Chelwood Gate** E Susx
40 C2 **Chelworth Lower Green** Wilts
40 B2 **Chelworth Upper Green** Wilts
83 H6 **Cheney Longville** Shrops
43 G2 **Chenies** Bucks
38 D2 **Chepstow** Mons
40 B6 **Cherhill** Wilts
55 K7 **Cherington** Gloucs
72 C6 **Cherington** Warwks
29 L5 **Cheriton** Hants
35 G7 **Cheriton** Kent
50 F6 **Cheriton** Swans
11 H6 **Cheriton Bishop** Devon
11 K4 **Cheriton Fitzpaine** Devon
49 G7 **Cheriton or Stackpole Elidor** Pembks
98 F8 **Cherrington** Wrekin
126 B3 **Cherry Burton** E R Yk
76 C3 **Cherry Hinton** Cambs
70 F4 **Cherry Orchard** Worcs
117 G6 **Cherry Willingham** Lincs
43 H6 **Chertsey** Surrey
14 E3 **Cheselbourne** Dorset
58 F7 **Chesham** Bucks
122 B7 **Chesham** Bury
58 F7 **Chesham Bois** Bucks
60 B7 **Cheshunt** Herts
14 B6 **Chesil Beach** Dorset
85 H3 **Cheslyn Hay** Staffs
85 L8 **Chessetts Wood** Warwks
44 D7 **Chessington** Surrey
44 D7 **Chessington World of Adventures** Gt Lon
112 B7 **Chester** Ches
112 B7 **Chester Cathedral** Ches
151 G5 **Chester Moor** Dur
112 B7 **Chester Zoo** Ches
151 G5 **Chester-le-Street** Dur
26 F3 **Chesterblade** Somset
115 G7 **Chesterfield** Derbys
177 K5 **Chesterhill** Mdloth
167 J5 **Chesters** Border
167 K7 **Chesters** Border

89 G4 **Chesterton** Cambs
76 C3 **Chesterton** Cambs
56 A7 **Chesterton** Gloucs
57 K4 **Chesterton** Oxon
84 D4 **Chesterton** Shrops
72 D3 **Chesterton Green** Warwks
149 L3 **Chesterwood** Nthumb
47 J6 **Chestfield** Kent
7 G4 **Cheston** Devon
99 G6 **Cheswardine** Shrops
168 F1 **Cheswick** Nthumb
14 B2 **Chetnole** Dorset
90 D6 **Chettisham** Cambs
27 L8 **Chettle** Dorset
84 B5 **Chetton** Shrops
99 G7 **Chetwynd** Wrekin
99 H8 **Chetwynd Aston** Wrekin
76 F3 **Cheveley** Cambs
32 E2 **Chevening** Kent
77 H3 **Chevington** Suffk
168 A7 **Cheviot Hills**
24 F7 **Chevithorne** Devon
38 E7 **Chew Magna** BaNES
38 E7 **Chew Stoke** BaNES
38 F6 **Chewton Keynsham** BaNES
26 E2 **Chewton Mendip** Somset
74 C5 **Chicheley** M Keyn
18 B5 **Chichester** W Susx
14 C6 **Chickerell** Dorset
27 K4 **Chicklade** Wilts
30 A7 **Chidden** Hants
30 F4 **Chiddingfold** Surrey
20 B3 **Chiddingly** E Susx
32 E4 **Chiddingstone** Kent
32 F4 **Chiddingstone Causeway** Kent
13 K4 **Chideock** Dorset
17 L2 **Chidham** W Susx
123 K6 **Chidswell** Kirk
41 J5 **Chieveley** W Berk
61 G5 **Chignall Smealy** Essex
61 G6 **Chignall St James** Essex
45 H2 **Chigwell** Essex
45 J2 **Chigwell Row** Essex
29 H4 **Chilbolton** Hants
29 J5 **Chilcomb** Hants
13 M4 **Chilcombe** Dorset
26 F2 **Chilcompton** Somset
86 C2 **Chilcote** Leics
27 J8 **Child Okeford** Dorset
98 F7 **Child's Ercall** Shrops
111 K6 **Childer Thornton** Ches
41 G3 **Childrey** Oxon
71 J6 **Childswickham** Worcs
112 B4 **Childwall** Lpool
14 B3 **Chilfrome** Dorset
18 A3 **Chilgrove** W Susx
34 E4 **Chilham** Kent
10 C8 **Chillaton** Devon
35 H4 **Chillenden** Kent
16 F5 **Chillerton** IOW
79 H4 **Chillesford** Suffk
168 F4 **Chillingham** Nthumb
7 J7 **Chillington** Devon
13 K1 **Chillington** Somset
27 L5 **Chilmark** Wilts
34 C6 **Chilmington Green** Kent
56 F4 **Chilson** Oxon
6 B2 **Chilsworthy** Cnwll
9 J4 **Chilsworthy** Devon
42 C2 **Chiltern Hills**
26 D7 **Chilthorne Domer** Somset
58 B5 **Chilton** Bucks
141 H2 **Chilton** Dur
41 J4 **Chilton** Oxon
29 L4 **Chilton Candover** Hants
26 E6 **Chilton Cantelo** Somset
40 F6 **Chilton Foliat** Wilts
26 B4 **Chilton Polden** Somset
77 H5 **Chilton Street** Suffk
25 L4 **Chilton Trinity** Somset
101 K5 **Chilwell** Notts
29 H7 **Chilworth** Hants
31 G3 **Chilworth** Surrey
57 G7 **Chimney** Oxon
30 A1 **Chineham** Hants
45 G2 **Chingford** Gt Lon
114 B5 **Chinley** Derbys
58 C7 **Chinnor** Oxon
99 G6 **Chipnall** Shrops
76 F1 **Chippenham** Cambs
39 L5 **Chippenham** Wilts
59 H7 **Chipperfield** Herts
60 B2 **Chipping** Herts
121 J2 **Chipping** Lancs
71 L6 **Chipping Campden** Gloucs
56 F3 **Chipping Norton** Oxon
60 E7 **Chipping Ongar** Essex
39 G4 **Chipping Sodbury** S Glos
72 F5 **Chipping Warden** Nhants
25 G6 **Chipstable** Somset
32 E3 **Chipstead** Kent
32 B2 **Chipstead** Surrey
82 F4 **Chirbury** Shrops
97 L5 **Chirk** Wrexhm
179 H6 **Chirnside** Border
179 H7 **Chirnsidebridge** Border
40 B8 **Chirton** Wilts
40 F6 **Chisbury** Wilts
26 C8 **Chiselborough** Somset
40 D4 **Chiseldon** Swindn
57 L7 **Chiselhampton** Oxon
166 F6 **Chisholme** Border
45 H6 **Chislehurst** Gt Lon
47 L6 **Chislet** Kent
122 F5 **Chisley** Calder
59 J6 **Chiswell Green** Herts
44 E4 **Chiswick** Gt Lon
113 M3 **Chisworth** Derbys
30 D6 **Chithurst** W Susx
76 C1 **Chittering** Cambs
27 M3 **Chitterne** Wilts
23 K7 **Chittlehamholt** Devon
23 K6 **Chittlehampton** Devon
10 F3 **Chittlehampton** Devon
39 L6 **Chittoe** Wilts
7 H7 **Chivelstone** Devon
23 H4 **Chivenor** Devon
144 D3 **Chlenry** D & G
42 F7 **Chobham** Surrey
28 E3 **Cholderton** Wilts
58 F6 **Cholesbury** Bucks
158 B7 **Chollerton** Nthumb
41 L3 **Cholsey** Oxon
69 J3 **Cholstrey** Herefs
142 C7 **Chop Gate** N York
159 G5 **Choppington** Nthumb
150 E4 **Chopwell** Gatesd
98 E3 **Chorley** Ches
121 H6 **Chorley** Lancs
84 C6 **Chorley** Shrops
43 H2 **Chorleywood** Herts
43 G2 **Chorleywood West** Herts
99 G3 **Chorlton** Ches
98 C3 **Chorlton Lane** Ches
113 J3 **Chorlton-cum-Hardy** Manch
83 H5 **Choulton** Shrops
76 C6 **Chrishall** Essex
173 L4 **Chrisswell** Inver
90 C4 **Christchurch** Cambs
15 M4 **Christchurch** Dorset
37 M3 **Christchurch** Mons
39 L5 **Christian Malford** Wilts
112 C7 **Christleton** Ches
38 B8 **Christon** N Som
169 J5 **Christon Bank** Nthumb
11 J7 **Christow** Devon
11 K8 **Chudleigh** Devon
7 J1 **Chudleigh Knighton** Devon
11 G3 **Chulmleigh** Devon
121 L5 **Church** Lancs
99 H8 **Church Aston** Wrekin
73 K2 **Church Brampton** Nhants
100 D5 **Church Broughton** Derbys
30 D2 **Church Crookham** Hants
99 J8 **Church Eaton** Staffs
75 H6 **Church End** Beds
61 H3 **Church End** Essex
44 E3 **Church End** Gt Lon
30 A1 **Church End** Hants
57 G3 **Church Enstone** Oxon
124 D3 **Church Fenton** N York
12 F3 **Church Green** Devon
57 H5 **Church Hanborough** Oxon
112 F7 **Church Hill** Ches
142 E7 **Church Houses** N York
15 H6 **Church Knowle** Dorset
87 K5 **Church Langton** Leics
86 F7 **Church Lawford** Warwks
99 J2 **Church Lawton** Ches
100 A5 **Church Leigh** Staffs
71 H4 **Church Lench** Worcs
100 D4 **Church Mayfield** Staffs
98 F1 **Church Minshull** Ches
18 B6 **Church Norton** W Susx
83 K4 **Church Preen** Shrops
83 H3 **Church Pulverbatch** Shrops
73 J3 **Church Stowe** Nhants
46 B5 **Church Street** Kent
83 J5 **Church Stretton** Shrops
37 G3 **Church Village** Rhondd
115 K7 **Church Warsop** Notts
55 H4 **Churcham** Gloucs
55 K4 **Churchdown** Gloucs
47 G2 **Churchend** Essex
85 H5 **Churchfield** Birm
13 H3 **Churchill** Devon
38 C7 **Churchill** N Som
56 F3 **Churchill** Oxon
84 F7 **Churchill** Worcs
71 G4 **Churchill** Worcs
25 K8 **Churchinford** Somset
87 G7 **Churchover** Warwks
25 J8 **Churchstanton** Somset
82 F5 **Churchstoke** Powys
7 G6 **Churchstow** Devon
5 H1 **Churchtown** Cnwll
114 E8 **Churchtown** Derbys
121 G2 **Churchtown** Lancs
7 K5 **Churston Ferrers** Torbay
30 D4 **Churt** Surrey
98 B2 **Churton** Ches
123 K5 **Churwell** Leeds
95 G5 **Chwilog** Gwynd
2 E5 **Chyandour** Cnwll
2 E4 **Chysauster** Cnwll
111 G7 **Cilcain** Flints
66 C3 **Cilcennin** Cerdgn
52 B7 **Cilfrew** Neath
37 G3 **Cilfynydd** Rhondd
65 H6 **Cilgerran** Pembks
51 L4 **Cilmaengwyn** Neath
67 L4 **Cilmery** Powys
51 H2 **Cilsan** Carmth
96 D4 **Ciltalgarth** Gwynd
51 L5 **Cilybebyll** Neath
67 G6 **Cilycwm** Carmth
36 B2 **Cimla** Neath
54 F5 **Cinderford** Gloucs
42 F4 **Cippenham** Slough
56 A7 **Cirencester** Gloucs
45 G4 **City** Gt Lon
45 H4 **City Airport** Gt Lon
188 F5 **Clabhach** Ag & B
173 J3 **Clachaig** Ag & B
182 A4 **Clachan** Ag & B
191 G7 **Clachan** Ag & B
172 C6 **Clachan** Ag & B
209 H6 **Clachan** Highld
188 C6 **Clachan Mor** Ag & B
233 c6 **Clachan na Luib** W Isls
175 G3 **Clachan of Campsie** E Duns
233 c6 **Clachan-a-Luib** W Isls
181 M4 **Clachan-Seil** Ag & B
153 H6 **Clachaneasy** D & G
213 G5 **Clachnaharry** Highld
224 C3 **Clachtoll** Highld
195 J4 **Clackavoid** P & K
185 J8 **Clackmannan** Clacks
214 F3 **Clackmarras** Moray
62 E5 **Clacton-on-Sea** Essex
182 F3 **Cladich** Ag & B
71 J3 **Cladswell** Worcs
190 E6 **Claggan** Highld
208 C4 **Claigan** Highld
30 B7 **Clanfield** Hants
56 F7 **Clanfield** Oxon
28 F2 **Clanville** Hants
26 F5 **Clanville** Somset
172 E6 **Claonaig** Ag & B
60 C3 **Clapgate** Herts
74 F4 **Clapham** Beds
44 F5 **Clapham** Gt Lon
130 E5 **Clapham** N York
18 F4 **Clapham** W Susx
13 K2 **Clapton** Somset
26 F2 **Clapton** Somset
38 C5 **Clapton-in-Gordano** N Som
56 D4 **Clapton-on-the-Hill** Gloucs
150 E3 **Claravale** Gatesd
49 H3 **Clarbeston** Pembks
49 H4 **Clarbeston Road** Pembks
116 B5 **Clarborough** Notts
77 H5 **Clare** Suffk
146 D2 **Clarebrand** D & G
147 J2 **Clarencefield** D & G

150 C2 **Clarewood** Nthumb
167 H5 **Clarilaw** Border
175 G6 **Clarkston** E Rens
224 C3 **Clashmore** Highld
223 G4 **Clashmore** Highld
224 C3 **Clashnessie** Highld
204 F2 **Clashnoir** Moray
185 K4 **Clathy** P & K
185 L3 **Clathymore** P & K
205 L1 **Clatt** Abers
81 L5 **Clatter** Powys
25 G5 **Clatworthy** Somset
121 G3 **Claughton** Lancs
130 B6 **Claughton** Lancs
111 J4 **Claughton** Wirral
71 L2 **Claverdon** Warwks
38 C6 **Claverham** N Som
60 D2 **Clavering** Essex
84 E5 **Claverley** Shrops
39 H7 **Claverton** BaNES
37 G5 **Clawdd-coch** V Glam
97 G3 **Clawdd-newydd** Denbgs
9 J5 **Clawton** Devon
117 J3 **Claxby** Lincs
133 L7 **Claxton** N York
93 H3 **Claxton** Norfk
87 H7 **Clay Coton** Nhants
115 H8 **Clay Cross** Derbys
86 F5 **Claybrooke Magna** Leics
72 F4 **Claydon** Oxon
78 D5 **Claydon** Suffk
156 D6 **Claygate** D & G
33 J4 **Claygate** Kent
44 D7 **Claygate** Surrey
45 H3 **Clayhall** Gt Lon
24 F6 **Clayhanger** Devon
25 J7 **Clayhidon** Devon
21 G2 **Clayhill** E Susx
231 H4 **Clayock** Highld
55 H6 **Claypits** Gloucs
102 D3 **Claypole** Lincs
123 G4 **Clayton** Brad
124 C8 **Clayton** Donc
19 J3 **Clayton** W Susx
123 K7 **Clayton West** Kirk
121 L4 **Clayton-le-Moors** Lancs
121 H6 **Clayton-le-Woods** Lancs
116 B4 **Clayworth** Notts
199 G7 **Cleadale** Highld
151 J3 **Cleadon** S Tyne
6 D3 **Clearbrook** Devon
54 E6 **Clearwell** Gloucs
141 G5 **Cleasby** N York
234 c8 **Cleat** Ork
140 E4 **Cleatlam** Dur
136 D4 **Cleator** Cumb
136 E4 **Cleator Moor** Cumb
123 J5 **Cleckheaton** Kirk
83 L6 **Clee St Margaret** Shrops
83 L7 **Cleehill** Shrops
175 K6 **Cleekhimin** N Lans
127 H8 **Cleethorpes** NE Lin
84 B7 **Cleeton St Mary** Shrops
38 C7 **Cleeve** N Som
41 L4 **Cleeve** Oxon
55 M3 **Cleeve Hill** Gloucs
71 J5 **Cleeve Prior** Worcs
178 D2 **Cleghornie** E Loth
69 J6 **Clehonger** Herefs
186 A7 **Cleish** P & K
175 L6 **Cleland** N Lans
182 C2 **Clenamacrie** Ag & B
104 F7 **Clenchwarton** Norfk
216 E3 **Clenerty** Abers
85 G7 **Clent** Worcs
84 C7 **Cleobury Mortimer** Shrops
84 B6 **Cleobury North** Shrops
161 H3 **Cleongart** Ag & B
213 J4 **Clephanton** Highld
156 A3 **Clerkhill** D & G
154 E3 **Cleuch-head** D & G
40 B5 **Clevancy** Wilts
38 B6 **Clevedon** N Som
120 D2 **Cleveleys** Lancs
39 L4 **Cleverton** Wilts
26 C2 **Clewer** Somset
106 C4 **Cley next the Sea** Norfk
138 E3 **Cliburn** Cumb
29 M2 **Cliddesden** Hants
21 H3 **Cliff End** E Susx
46 C5 **Cliffe** Medway
140 F4 **Cliffe** N York
125 G4 **Cliffe** N York
46 C5 **Cliffe Woods** Medway
68 E5 **Clifford** Herefs
124 C2 **Clifford** Leeds
71 L4 **Clifford Chambers** Warwks
55 G4 **Clifford's Mesne** Gloucs
75 H6 **Clifton** Beds
38 E5 **Clifton** Bristl
101 K5 **Clifton** C Nott
123 H6 **Clifton** Calder
138 D2 **Clifton** Cumb
100 D4 **Clifton** Derbys
115 K3 **Clifton** Donc
120 F4 **Clifton** Lancs
123 J2 **Clifton** N York
57 J2 **Clifton** Oxon
70 F5 **Clifton** Worcs
133 J8 **Clifton** York
86 B2 **Clifton Campville** Staffs
41 K2 **Clifton Hampden** Oxon
74 C4 **Clifton Reynes** M Keyn
87 G7 **Clifton upon Dunsmore** Warwks
70 C3 **Clifton upon Teme** Worcs
35 K1 **Cliftonville** Kent
18 D5 **Climping** W Susx
27 H2 **Clink** Somset
132 D7 **Clint** N York
92 B2 **Clint Green** Norfk
206 F3 **Clinterty** C Aber
167 J3 **Clintmains** Border
93 J2 **Clippesby** Norfk
88 D1 **Clipsham** Rutlnd
87 K7 **Clipston** Nhants
101 M5 **Clipston** Notts
58 F3 **Clipstone** Beds
115 L8 **Clipstone** Notts
121 L3 **Clitheroe** Lancs
98 D7 **Clive** Shrops
117 J2 **Clixby** Lincs
39 M3 **Cloatley** Wilts
97 G2 **Clocaenog** Denbgs
215 J3 **Clochan** Moray
196 D5 **Clochtow** Angus
53 L3 **Clodock** Herefs
217 J5 **Clola** Abers
74 F6 **Clophill** Beds
88 F7 **Clopton** Nhants
78 F4 **Clopton** Suffk
78 F4 **Clopton Corner** Suffk
236 d2 **Clos du Valle** Guern
154 F4 **Closeburn** D & G
154 F3 **Closeburnmill** D & G
14 B1 **Closworth** Somset
59 L2 **Clothall** Herts
112 D8 **Clotton** Ches
122 D5 **Clough Foot** Calder
123 G6 **Clough Head** Calder
143 K7 **Cloughton** N York
235 c5 **Clousta** Shet
196 B2 **Clova** Angus
22 E6 **Clovelly** Devon
167 G3 **Clovenfords** Border
191 K4 **Clovulin** Highld
122 C5 **Clow Bridge** Lancs
115 J6 **Clowne** Derbys
70 C1 **Clows Top** Worcs
201 G3 **Cluanie Inn** Highld
201 G3 **Cluanie Lodge** Highld
145 H4 **Clugston** D & G
82 F7 **Clun** Shrops
213 K5 **Clunas** Highld
83 G7 **Clunbury** Shrops
203 J1 **Clune** Highld
201 J7 **Clunes** Highld
83 H7 **Clungunford** Shrops
216 C4 **Clunie** Abers
195 H7 **Clunie** P & K
83 G7 **Clunton** Shrops
186 D7 **Cluny** Fife
38 F8 **Clutton** BaNES
98 C2 **Clutton** Ches
38 F8 **Clutton Hill** BaNES
53 K5 **Clydach** Mons
51 K5 **Clydach** Swans
36 F2 **Clydach Vale** Rhondd
174 F4 **Clydebank** W Duns
40 B5 **Clyffe Pypard** Wilts
174 A2 **Clynder** Ag & B
49 J4 **Clynderwen** Carmth
52 C7 **Clyne** Neath
95 G3 **Clynnog-fawr** Gwynd
68 E5 **Clyro** Powys
12 C4 **Clyst Honiton** Devon
12 D3 **Clyst Hydon** Devon
12 C5 **Clyst St George** Devon
12 D3 **Clyst St Lawrence** Devon
12 C4 **Clyst St Mary** Devon
232 g2 **Cnoc** W Isls
80 F8 **Cnwch Coch** Cerdgn
5 L1 **Coad's Green** Cnwll
164 F3 **Coalburn** S Lans
150 E3 **Coalburns** Gatesd
55 H7 **Coaley** Gloucs
61 J7 **Coalhill** Essex
38 F4 **Coalpit Heath** S Glos
84 C3 **Coalport** Wrekin
185 J7 **Coalsnaughton** Clacks
186 E7 **Coaltown of Balgonie** Fife
186 E7 **Coaltown of Wemyss** Fife
86 E2 **Coalville** Leics
149 H3 **Coanwood** Nthumb
26 C7 **Coat** Somset
175 J5 **Coatbridge** N Lans
175 K5 **Coatdyke** N Lans
40 D4 **Coate** Swindn
40 B7 **Coate** Wilts
89 K4 **Coates** Cambs
55 L7 **Coates** Gloucs
116 E5 **Coates** Lincs
18 D3 **Coates** W Susx
23 K6 **Cobbaton** Devon
55 L5 **Coberley** Gloucs
46 A6 **Cobham** Kent
43 J7 **Cobham** Surrey
69 J3 **Cobnash** Herefs
236 c2 **Cobo** Guern
217 H2 **Coburby** Abers
205 G4 **Cock Bridge** Abers
61 K7 **Cock Clarks** Essex
61 H4 **Cock Green** Essex
21 H2 **Cock Marling** E Susx
75 J5 **Cockayne Hatley** Beds
179 G4 **Cockburnspath** Border
177 L4 **Cockenzie and Port Seton** E Loth
120 F1 **Cockerham** Lancs
136 F2 **Cockermouth** Cumb
59 J4 **Cockernhoe Green** Herts
51 J6 **Cockett** Swans
140 E3 **Cockfield** Dur
77 K4 **Cockfield** Suffk
44 F2 **Cockfosters** Gt Lon
18 B3 **Cocking** W Susx
18 B2 **Cocking Causeway** W Susx
7 K3 **Cockington** Torbay
26 C2 **Cocklake** Somset
158 F4 **Cockle Park** Nthumb
91 H3 **Cockley Cley** Norfk
42 D4 **Cockpole Green** Wokham
98 B6 **Cockshutt** Shrops
106 B4 **Cockthorpe** Norfk
12 C6 **Cockwood** Devon
114 B5 **Cockyard** Derbys
78 D4 **Coddenham** Suffk
70 C6 **Coddington** Herefs
102 D2 **Coddington** Notts
27 L4 **Codford St Mary** Wilts
27 L4 **Codford St Peter** Wilts
59 K4 **Codicote** Herts
31 H7 **Codmore Hill** W Susx
101 H3 **Codnor** Derbys
39 G5 **Codrington** S Glos
84 F3 **Codsall** Staffs
84 F3 **Codsall Wood** Staffs
97 L2 **Coed Talon** Flints
53 M7 **Coed-y-paen** Mons
108 F5 **Coedana** IOA
97 L3 **Coedpoeth** Wrexhm
7 K3 **Coffinswell** Devon
12 C6 **Cofton** Devon
85 H7 **Cofton Hackett** Worcs
37 J6 **Cogan** V Glam
74 B3 **Cogenhoe** Nhants
61 K4 **Coggeshall** Essex
203 H2 **Coignafearn** Highld
205 H6 **Coilacriech** Abers
184 D6 **Coilantogle** Stirlg
208 E6 **Coillore** Highld
202 B4 **Coiltry** Highld
36 E4 **Coity** Brdgnd
232 g2 **Col** W Isls
225 L6 **Colaboll** Highld
4 D4 **Colan** Cnwll
12 D5 **Colaton Raleigh** Devon
208 C5 **Colbost** Highld
140 F7 **Colburn** N York
138 F3 **Colby** Cumb
237 b6 **Colby** IOM
106 F6 **Colby** Norfk
62 B3 **Colchester** Essex
41 K6 **Cold Ash** W Berk
87 J7 **Cold Ashby** Nhants
39 H6 **Cold Ashton** S Glos
56 C4 **Cold Aston** Gloucs
74 D4 **Cold Brayfield** M Keyn
117 G5 **Cold Hanworth** Lincs
73 J4 **Cold Higham** Nhants
133 H3 **Cold Kirby** N York
61 K7 **Cold Norton** Essex
88 B2 **Cold Overton** Leics
229 J4 **Coldbackie** Highld
19 J4 **Coldean** Br & H
7 J2 **Coldeast** Devon

122 E5 **Colden** Calder
29 J6 **Colden Common** Hants
79 J3 **Coldfair Green** Suffk
31 J3 **Coldharbour** Surrey
179 J5 **Coldingham** Border
99 J6 **Coldmeece** Staffs
35 H5 **Coldred** Kent
11 G4 **Coldridge** Devon
168 C2 **Coldstream** Border
18 D3 **Coldwaltham** W Susx
69 H7 **Coldwell** Herefs
217 H6 **Coldwells** Abers
26 F5 **Cole** Somset
83 G6 **Colebatch** Shrops
12 C2 **Colebrook** Devon
11 H5 **Colebrooke** Devon
102 F1 **Coleby** Lincs
125 L6 **Coleby** N Linc
11 H5 **Coleford** Devon
54 E6 **Coleford** Gloucs
27 G2 **Coleford** Somset
25 H5 **Coleford Water** Somset
92 E6 **Colegate End** Norfk
15 J3 **Colehill** Dorset
32 D6 **Coleman's Hatch** E Susx
98 B6 **Colemere** Shrops
30 B5 **Colemore** Hants
186 B2 **Colenden** P & K
39 J6 **Colerne** Wilts
56 A5 **Colesbourne** Gloucs
42 F2 **Coleshill** Bucks
40 E2 **Coleshill** Oxon
85 L5 **Coleshill** Warwks
26 E1 **Coley** BaNES
31 L5 **Colgate** W Susx
187 H6 **Colinsburgh** Fife
177 H5 **Colinton** C Edin
173 H4 **Colintraive** Ag & B
105 L7 **Colkirk** Norfk
186 C2 **Collace** P & K
235 c3 **Collafirth** Shet
7 G7 **Collaton** Devon
7 K4 **Collaton St Mary** Torbay
214 E2 **College of Roseisle** Moray
42 D7 **College Town** Br For
186 E5 **Collessie** Fife
45 J2 **Collier Row** Gt Lon
33 J4 **Collier Street** Kent
60 B4 **Collier's End** Herts
217 K8 **Collieston** Abers
155 H6 **Collin** D & G
28 E2 **Collingbourne Ducis** Wilts
28 E1 **Collingbourne Kingston** Wilts
124 B2 **Collingham** Leeds
102 D1 **Collingham** Notts
70 B3 **Collington** Herefs
73 L4 **Collingtree** Nhants
112 E3 **Collins Green** Warrtn
196 F7 **Colliston** Angus
12 E2 **Colliton** Devon
88 E3 **Collyweston** Nhants
152 D5 **Colmonell** S Ayrs
75 G3 **Colmworth** Beds
56 B6 **Coln Rogers** Gloucs
56 C6 **Coln St Aldwyns** Gloucs
56 B5 **Coln St Dennis** Gloucs
43 G5 **Colnbrook** Slough
89 L7 **Colne** Cambs
122 D3 **Colne** Lancs
61 K3 **Colne Engaine** Essex
92 E3 **Colney** Norfk
59 K6 **Colney Heath** Herts
216 C7 **Colpy** Abers
166 E2 **Colquhar** Border
102 F7 **Colsterworth** Lincs
102 B5 **Colston Bassett** Notts
33 H4 **Colt's Hill** Kent
214 D2 **Coltfield** Moray
106 F8 **Coltishall** Norfk
129 G3 **Colton** Cumb
124 B4 **Colton** Leeds
124 E2 **Colton** N York
92 D2 **Colton** Norfk
100 B7 **Colton** Staffs
146 F4 **Colvend** D & G
70 D6 **Colwall** Herefs
158 B6 **Colwell** Nthumb
100 A7 **Colwich** Staffs
36 E5 **Colwinston** V Glam
18 C5 **Colworth** W Susx
110 B5 **Colwyn Bay** Conwy
13 G4 **Colyford** Devon
13 G4 **Colyton** Devon
57 H5 **Combe** Oxon
41 G7 **Combe** W Berk
39 H7 **Combe Down** BaNES
7 J3 **Combe Fishacre** Devon
25 J5 **Combe Florey** Somset
39 G7 **Combe Hay** BaNES
23 J3 **Combe Martin** Devon
12 F3 **Combe Raleigh** Devon
13 H1 **Combe St Nicholas** Somset
7 K2 **Combeinteignhead** Devon
112 F6 **Comberbach** Ches
85 L3 **Comberford** Staffs
75 L4 **Comberton** Cambs
69 K2 **Comberton** Herefs
72 C4 **Combrook** Warwks
114 B6 **Combs** Derbys
78 C3 **Combs** Suffk
78 C3 **Combs Ford** Suffk
25 K3 **Combwich** Somset
206 D4 **Comers** Abers
70 E2 **Comhampton** Worcs
49 K4 **Commercial** Pembks
81 J3 **Commins Coch** Powys
5 K2 **Common Moor** Cnwll
142 E5 **Commondale** N York
113 L4 **Compstall** Stockp
146 B4 **Compstonend** D & G
7 K3 **Compton** Devon
29 J6 **Compton** Hants
84 E6 **Compton** Staffs
30 F3 **Compton** Surrey
41 K4 **Compton** W Berk
30 C7 **Compton** W Susx
28 C2 **Compton** Wilts
27 K7 **Compton Abbas** Dorset
56 B5 **Compton Abdale** Gloucs
40 B6 **Compton Bassett** Wilts
40 F3 **Compton Beauchamp** Oxon
26 B1 **Compton Bishop** Somset
28 B5 **Compton Chamberlayne** Wilts
38 F7 **Compton Dando** BaNES
26 C5 **Compton Dundon** Somset
26 B7 **Compton Durville** Somset
38 E4 **Compton Greenfield** S Glos
38 D8 **Compton Martin** BaNES
26 F6 **Compton Pauncefoot** Somset
14 B4 **Compton Valence** Dorset
176 D1 **Comrie** Fife
185 G3 **Comrie** P & K
191 K3 **Conaglen House** Highld
210 D8 **Conchra** Highld
195 H7 **Concraigie** P & K
71 G6 **Conderton** Worcs
56 D3 **Condicote** Gloucs
175 K4 **Condorrat** N Lans
83 J3 **Condover** Shrops
55 J4 **Coney Hill** Gloucs
91 L7 **Coney Weston** Suffk
31 J6 **Coneyhurst Common** W Susx
133 L5 **Coneysthorpe** N York
5 L1 **Congdon's Shop** Cnwll
86 D3 **Congerstone** Leics
105 H7 **Congham** Norfk
113 J8 **Congleton** Ches
38 C7 **Congresbury** N Som
147 H2 **Conheath** D & G
214 B4 **Conicavel** Moray
103 L2 **Coningsby** Lincs
89 H6 **Conington** Cambs
75 K2 **Conington** Cambs
115 K2 **Conisbrough** Donc
118 E3 **Conisholme** Lincs
137 J7 **Coniston** Cumb
126 E4 **Coniston** E R Yk
131 G8 **Coniston Cold** N York
131 J6 **Conistone** N York
111 J7 **Connah's Quay** Flints
182 C1 **Connel** Ag & B
164 C6 **Connel Park** E Ayrs
3 G4 **Connor Downs** Cnwll
212 E4 **Conon Bridge** Highld
122 E2 **Cononley** N York
99 M3 **Consall** Staffs
150 E5 **Consett** Dur
132 B2 **Constable Burton** N York
3 J5 **Constantine** Cnwll
4 D2 **Constantine Bay** Cnwll
212 C3 **Contin** Highld
109 L6 **Conwy** Conwy
77 K2 **Conyer's Green** Suffk
20 E4 **Cooden** E Susx
62 E4 **Cook's Green** Essex
9 K4 **Cookbury** Devon
42 E4 **Cookham** W & M
42 E4 **Cookham Dean** W & M
42 E4 **Cookham Rise** W & M
71 J3 **Cookhill** Warwks
93 H7 **Cookley** Suffk
84 E7 **Cookley** Worcs
42 B3 **Cookley Green** Oxon
207 G6 **Cookney** Abers
77 L4 **Cooks Green** Suffk
61 G6 **Cooksmill Green** Essex
31 J6 **Coolham** W Susx
46 C5 **Cooling** Medway
7 L2 **Coombe** Devon
12 E4 **Coombe** Devon
39 H2 **Coombe** Gloucs
30 A7 **Coombe** Hants
28 C6 **Coombe Bissett** Wilts
7 K2 **Coombe Cellars** Devon
25 G5 **Coombe End** Somset
55 K3 **Coombe Hill** Gloucs
14 F5 **Coombe Keynes** Dorset
7 L3 **Coombe Pafford** Torbay
19 G4 **Coombes** W Susx
69 G2 **Coombes-Moor** Herefs
214 B4 **Cooperhill** Moray
60 D7 **Coopersale Common** Essex
35 J3 **Cop Street** Kent
78 D6 **Copdock** Suffk
61 L4 **Copford Green** Essex
132 E6 **Copgrove** N York
235 d3 **Copister** Shet
75 G5 **Cople** Beds
140 D3 **Copley** Dur
124 E2 **Copmanthorpe** York
99 J6 **Copmere End** Staffs
120 F3 **Copp** Lancs
9 G5 **Coppathorne** Cnwll
99 K8 **Coppenhall** Staffs
2 F4 **Copperhouse** Cnwll
89 H7 **Coppingford** Cambs
11 H4 **Copplestone** Devon
121 H7 **Coppull** Lancs
31 K6 **Copsale** W Susx
121 K4 **Copster Green** Lancs
86 F5 **Copston Magna** Warwks
132 E5 **Copt Hewick** N York
86 F2 **Copt Oak** Leics
32 B5 **Copthorne** W Susx
28 F8 **Copythorne** Hants
45 K3 **Corbets Tey** Gt Lon
236 a7 **Corbiere** Jersey
150 C3 **Corbridge** Nthumb
88 C5 **Corby** Nhants
103 G7 **Corby Glen** Lincs
162 D4 **Cordon** N Ayrs
84 B8 **Coreley** Shrops
25 K7 **Corfe** Somset
15 H6 **Corfe Castle** Dorset
15 J3 **Corfe Mullen** Dorset
83 J6 **Corfton** Shrops
205 G4 **Corgarff** Abers
29 L7 **Corhampton** Hants
86 C6 **Corley** Warwks
86 C6 **Corley Ash** Warwks
195 L3 **Cormuir** Angus
77 K6 **Cornard Tye** Suffk
151 H7 **Cornforth** Dur
216 B3 **Cornhill** Abers
168 C2 **Cornhill-on-Tweed** Nthumb
122 D5 **Cornholme** Calder
188 C6 **Cornoigmore** Ag & B
150 E6 **Cornsay** Dur
150 F6 **Cornsay Colliery** Dur
212 E3 **Corntown** Highld
36 E5 **Corntown** V Glam
56 F3 **Cornwell** Oxon
6 E4 **Cornwood** Devon
7 J5 **Cornworthy** Devon
191 L2 **Corpach** Highld
106 D6 **Corpusty** Norfk
205 K4 **Corrachree** Abers
200 C4 **Corran** Highld
191 K4 **Corran** Highld
155 L5 **Corrie** D & G
162 C2 **Corrie** N Ayrs
162 B5 **Corriecravie** N Ayrs
162 D3 **Corriegills** N Ayrs
201 K6 **Corriegour Lodge Hotel** Highld
212 B2 **Corriemoille** Highld
212 B7 **Corrimony** Highld
116 E4 **Corringham** Lincs
46 B4 **Corringham** Thurr
81 G2 **Corris** Gwynd
81 G2 **Corris Uchaf** Gwynd
183 H7 **Corrow** Ag & B
199 K1 **Corry** Highld
10 F5 **Corscombe** Devon
13 M2 **Corscombe** Dorset
55 J2 **Corse Lawn** Gloucs

39 K6 **Corsham** Wilts
206 D4 **Corsindae** Abers
27 J3 **Corsley** Wilts
27 J3 **Corsley Heath** Wilts
154 D6 **Corsock** D & G
39 G7 **Corston** BaNES
39 L4 **Corston** Wilts
177 G4 **Corstorphine** C Edin
196 C4 **Cortachy** Angus
93 L4 **Corton** Suffk
27 L4 **Corton** Wilts
26 F6 **Corton Denham** Somset
191 L3 **Coruanan Lodge** Highld
97 G4 **Corwen** Denbgs
10 C7 **Coryton** Devon
46 C4 **Coryton** Thurr
87 G4 **Cosby** Leics
85 G5 **Coseley** Dudley
73 L6 **Cosgrove** Nhants
17 J2 **Cosham** C Port
49 G6 **Cosheston** Pembks
194 C6 **Coshieville** P & K
101 J4 **Cossall** Notts
87 H2 **Cossington** Leics
26 A4 **Cossington** Somset
92 E2 **Costessey** Norfk
101 L7 **Costock** Notts
102 D7 **Coston** Leics
92 C3 **Coston** Norfk
57 G7 **Cote** Oxon
112 E7 **Cotebrook** Ches
148 E5 **Cotehill** Cumb
101 K7 **Cotes** Leics
87 G6 **Cotesbach** Leics
101 M5 **Cotgrave** Notts
207 G3 **Cothal** Abers
102 C3 **Cotham** Notts
140 C4 **Cotherstone** Dur
57 J7 **Cothill** Oxon
13 G3 **Cotleigh** Devon
101 J4 **Cotmanhay** Derbys
76 B3 **Coton** Cambs
73 J1 **Coton** Nhants
99 J7 **Coton** Staffs
99 K7 **Coton Clanford** Staffs
83 J2 **Coton Hill** Shrops
86 B1 **Coton in the Elms** Derbys
55 M6 **Cotswolds**
7 H4 **Cott** Devon
121 G4 **Cottam** Lancs
116 D5 **Cottam** Notts
76 C2 **Cottenham** Cambs
60 A3 **Cottered** Herts
88 F5 **Cotterstock** Nhants
87 K8 **Cottesbrooke** Nhants
88 C2 **Cottesmore** Rutlnd
126 C4 **Cottingham** E R Yk
88 B5 **Cottingham** Nhants
123 G3 **Cottingley** Brad
57 L2 **Cottisford** Oxon
78 C2 **Cotton** Suffk
215 L8 **Cottown** Abers
206 E3 **Cottown** Abers
216 F6 **Cottown of Gight** Abers
6 C3 **Cotts** Devon
71 J3 **Coughton** Warwks
172 C5 **Coulaghailtro** Ag & B
210 E5 **Coulags** Highld
205 L5 **Coull** Abers
173 L2 **Coulport** Ag & B
32 B2 **Coulsdon** Gt Lon
27 L2 **Coulston** Wilts
165 K3 **Coulter** S Lans
133 K5 **Coulton** N York
186 F3 **Coultra** Fife
83 L3 **Cound** Shrops
141 G2 **Coundon** Dur
131 H2 **Countersett** N York
12 B4 **Countess Wear** Devon
87 H4 **Countesthorpe** Leics
24 B2 **Countisbury** Devon
195 K7 **Coupar Angus** P & K
168 D3 **Coupland** Nthumb
172 D8 **Cour** Ag & B
155 J4 **Courance** D & G
51 H2 **Court Henry** Carmth
199 L6 **Courteachan** Highld
73 L4 **Courteenhall** Nhants
47 G2 **Courtsend** Essex
25 J5 **Courtway** Somset
177 K5 **Cousland** Mdloth
33 H6 **Cousley Wood** E Susx
173 L2 **Cove** Ag & B
179 G4 **Cove** Border
24 E7 **Cove** Devon
30 E1 **Cove** Hants
219 J3 **Cove** Highld
207 H5 **Cove Bay** C Aber
93 L6 **Covehithe** Suffk
85 G3 **Coven** Staffs
90 C6 **Coveney** Cambs
118 D3 **Covenham St Bartholomew** Lincs
118 D3 **Covenham St Mary** Lincs
86 D7 **Coventry** Covtry
86 D8 **Coventry Airport** Warwks
3 K7 **Coverack** Cnwll
3 H5 **Coverack Bridges** Cnwll
131 L3 **Coverham** N York
74 F1 **Covington** Cambs
165 J2 **Covington** S Lans
71 K5 **Cow Honeybourne** Worcs
130 C4 **Cowan Bridge** Lancs
20 C3 **Cowbeech** E Susx
103 L8 **Cowbit** Lincs
36 F5 **Cowbridge** V Glam
32 E5 **Cowden** Kent
177 G1 **Cowdenbeath** Fife
100 F3 **Cowers Lane** Derbys
16 F3 **Cowes** IOW
133 G2 **Cowesby** N York
31 K6 **Cowfold** W Susx
38 E3 **Cowhill** S Glos
175 L1 **Cowie** Stirlg
11 K5 **Cowley** Devon
55 L5 **Cowley** Gloucs
43 H4 **Cowley** Gt Lon
57 K7 **Cowley** Oxon
121 H6 **Cowling** Lancs
122 E2 **Cowling** N York
132 C3 **Cowling** N York
77 G4 **Cowlinge** Suffk
159 H5 **Cowpen** Nthumb
17 K1 **Cowplain** Hants
149 L6 **Cowshill** Dur
38 C7 **Cowslip Green** N Som
132 F8 **Cowthorpe** N York
98 F4 **Coxbank** Ches
101 G4 **Coxbench** Derbys
8 F5 **Coxford** Cnwll
105 K6 **Coxford** Norfk
33 J3 **Coxheath** Kent
151 H7 **Coxhoe** Dur
26 D3 **Coxley** Somset
26 D3 **Coxley Wick** Somset
45 K2 **Coxtie Green** Essex
133 H4 **Coxwold** N York
36 E4 **Coychurch** Brdgnd
163 K5 **Coylton** S Ayrs
203 L3 **Coylumbridge** Highld
36 D4 **Coytrahen** Brdgnd
71 J2 **Crabbs Cross** Worcs
31 K6 **Crabtree** W Susx
138 F3 **Crackenthorpe** Cumb
8 F5 **Crackington Haven** Cnwll
84 D2 **Crackleybank** Shrops
131 J7 **Cracoe** N York
25 G8 **Craddock** Devon
85 G6 **Cradley** Dudley
70 D5 **Cradley** Herefs
85 G6 **Cradley Heath** Sandw
52 F2 **Cradoc** Powys
6 B5 **Crafthole** Cnwll
58 E4 **Crafton** Bucks
122 E5 **Cragg Vale** Calder
204 C1 **Craggan** Highld
150 F5 **Craghead** Dur
52 D3 **Crai** Powys
215 L3 **Craibstone** Moray
196 E6 **Craichie** Angus
197 H5 **Craig** Angus
211 G4 **Craig** Highld
51 K4 **Craig Llangiwg** Neath
164 C6 **Craigbank** E Ayrs
177 H7 **Craigburn** Border
156 C5 **Craigcleuch** D & G
216 F7 **Craigdam** Abers
182 B6 **Craigdhu** Ag & B
206 D3 **Craigearn** Abers
215 G5 **Craigellachie** Moray
186 B4 **Craigend** P & K
174 E4 **Craigend** Rens
174 C3 **Craigendoran** Ag & B
145 G3 **Craighlaw** D & G
171 K5 **Craighouse** Ag & B
195 H7 **Craigie** P & K
163 K3 **Craigie** S Ayrs
217 H2 **Craigiefold** Abers
146 D4 **Craigley** D & G
177 H4 **Craiglockhart** C Edin
215 H4 **Craiglug** Moray
177 J4 **Craigmillar** C Edin
154 D5 **Craigneston** D & G
175 K5 **Craigneuk** N Lans
175 K6 **Craigneuk** N Lans
190 E8 **Craignure** Ag & B
197 H4 **Craigo** Angus
186 F5 **Craigrothie** Fife
184 B4 **Craigruie** Stirlg
196 E8 **Craigton** Angus
206 F5 **Craigton** C Aber
174 F7 **Craigton** E Rens
196 B6 **Craigton of Airlie** Angus
187 K5 **Crail** Fife
167 L4 **Crailing** Border
116 C2 **Craiselound** N Linc
132 C2 **Crakehall** N York
133 L6 **Crambe** N York
159 G6 **Cramlington** Nthumb
177 G3 **Cramond** C Edin
177 G4 **Cramond Bridge** C Edin
113 H7 **Cranage** Ches
99 J5 **Cranberry** Staffs
28 B8 **Cranborne** Dorset
33 K6 **Cranbrook** Kent
74 D6 **Cranfield** Beds
43 J5 **Cranford** Gt Lon
88 D7 **Cranford St Andrew** Nhants
88 D7 **Cranford St John** Nhants
55 K5 **Cranham** Gloucs
112 D2 **Crank** St Hel
31 H4 **Cranleigh** Surrey
26 F3 **Cranmore** Somset
87 L4 **Cranoe** Leics
79 G2 **Cransford** Suffk
178 E6 **Cranshaws** Border
4 C4 **Crantock** Cnwll
103 G3 **Cranwell** Lincs
91 H4 **Cranwich** Norfk
92 B3 **Cranworth** Norfk
182 A6 **Craobh Haven** Ag & B
182 E7 **Crarae** Ag & B
225 L4 **Crask Inn** Highld
212 D6 **Crask of Aigas** Highld
169 K5 **Craster** Nthumb
93 G7 **Cratfield** Suffk
206 E6 **Crathes** Abers
206 D6 **Crathes Castle** Abers
205 G6 **Crathie** Abers
202 E6 **Crathie** Highld
141 K5 **Crathorne** N York
83 H6 **Craven Arms** Shrops
150 E3 **Crawcrook** Gatesd
165 J5 **Crawford** S Lans
165 G5 **Crawfordjohn** S Lans
164 F6 **Crawick** D & G
29 H4 **Crawley** Hants
57 G5 **Crawley** Oxon
31 L4 **Crawley** W Susx
32 C5 **Crawley Down** W Susx
122 B5 **Crawshawbooth** Lancs
197 L1 **Crawton** Abers
131 H4 **Cray** N York
45 K5 **Crayford** Gt Lon
133 H5 **Crayke** N York
46 B2 **Crays Hill** Essex
24 F8 **Craze Lowman** Devon
24 C7 **Creacombe** Devon
233 c7 **Creag Ghoraidh** W Isls
191 J7 **Creagan Inn** Ag & B
233 c7 **Creagorry** W Isls
192 E3 **Creaguaineach Lodge** Highld
73 K1 **Creaton** Nhants
155 M7 **Creca** D & G
69 J5 **Credenhill** Herefs
11 J5 **Crediton** Devon
153 H6 **Creebank** D & G
145 J2 **Creebridge** D & G
25 L6 **Creech Heathfield** Somset
25 L6 **Creech St Michael** Somset
4 E6 **Creed** Cnwll
45 J4 **Creekmouth** Gt Lon
78 D3 **Creeting St Mary** Suffk
103 G8 **Creeton** Lincs
145 K3 **Creetown** D & G
237 a7 **Cregneash** IOM
186 E3 **Creich** Fife
37 G4 **Creigiau** Cardif
6 C5 **Cremyll** Cnwll
83 L3 **Cressage** Shrops
114 D6 **Cressbrook** Derbys
49 H6 **Cresselly** Pembks
42 D3 **Cressex** Bucks
61 J4 **Cressing** Essex
159 H4 **Cresswell** Nthumb
49 H6 **Cresswell** Pembks
99 L5 **Cresswell** Staffs
115 K6 **Creswell** Derbys
78 F3 **Cretingham** Suffk
172 C5 **Cretshengan** Ag & B
83 G1 **Crew Green** Powys
98 B2 **Crewe** Ches
99 G2 **Crewe** Ches
99 G2 **Crewe Green** Ches
13 K1 **Crewkerne** Somset
101 G5 **Crewton** C Derb
183 L3 **Crianlarich** Stirlg
66 C4 **Cribyn** Cerdgn
95 J5 **Criccieth** Gwynd
101 G2 **Crich** Derbys
177 K6 **Crichton** Mdloth
87 H8 **Crick** Nhants
68 C6 **Crickadarn** Powys
13 J2 **Cricket St Thomas** Somset

53 K4 **Crickhowell** Powys
40 C2 **Cricklade** Wilts
44 E3 **Cricklewood** Gt Lon
124 D6 **Cridling Stubbs** N York
185 H3 **Crieff** P & K
82 F1 **Criggion** Powys
123 L7 **Crigglestone** Wakefd
217 K3 **Crimond** Abers
90 F3 **Crimplesham** Norfk
72 B5 **Crimscote** Warwks
212 C6 **Crinaglack** Highld
182 A8 **Crinan** Ag & B
175 L6 **Crindledyke** N Lans
92 E3 **Cringleford** Norfk
49 J5 **Crinow** Pembks
213 G8 **Croachy** Highld
154 F6 **Crochmore House** D & G
45 J6 **Crockenhill** Kent
42 B3 **Crocker End** Oxon
11 H6 **Crockernwell** Devon
27 K3 **Crockerton** Wilts
154 E7 **Crocketford** D & G
32 D3 **Crockham Hill** Kent
48 D2 **Croes-goch** Pembks
65 L5 **Croes-lan** Cerdgn
36 D2 **Croeserw** Neath
95 L4 **Croesor** Gwynd
50 E3 **Croesyceiliog** Carmth
37 L2 **Croesyceiliog** Torfn
87 G4 **Croft** Leics
104 E1 **Croft** Lincs
112 F3 **Croft** Warrtn
141 H5 **Croft-on-Tees** N York
174 E2 **Croftamie** Stirlg
124 B6 **Crofton** Wakefd
146 C2 **Crofts** D & G
215 G4 **Crofts** Moray
215 H3 **Crofts of Dipple** Moray
217 K3 **Crofts of Savoch** Abers
51 G6 **Crofty** Swans
181 L3 **Croggan** Ag & B
148 F5 **Croglin** Cumb
222 B3 **Croik** Highld
223 H7 **Cromarty** Highld
176 E2 **Crombie** Fife
214 D8 **Cromdale** Highld
59 M3 **Cromer** Herts
106 F4 **Cromer** Norfk
100 F2 **Cromford** Derbys
39 G3 **Cromhall** S Glos
232 f3 **Cromor** W Isls
102 D1 **Cromwell** Notts
164 C5 **Cronberry** E Ayrs
30 C2 **Crondall** Hants
112 C4 **Cronton** Knows
138 C7 **Crook** Cumb
150 E7 **Crook** Dur
165 L4 **Crook Inn** Border
185 L7 **Crook of Devon** P & K
148 E3 **Crooked Holme** Cumb
163 L3 **Crookedholm** E Ayrs
114 F4 **Crookes** Sheff
168 D2 **Crookham** Nthumb
41 K7 **Crookham** W Berk
30 C2 **Crookham Village** Hants
129 L3 **Crooklands** Cumb
72 F5 **Cropredy** Oxon
87 G2 **Cropston** Leics
71 H5 **Cropthorne** Worcs
134 B3 **Cropton** N York
102 B5 **Cropwell Bishop** Notts
102 B5 **Cropwell Butler** Notts
232 g1 **Cros** W Isls
173 L7 **Crosbie** N Ayrs
232 f3 **Crosbost** W Isls
147 J7 **Crosby** Cumb
237 c5 **Crosby** IOM
125 K7 **Crosby** N Linc
111 J2 **Crosby** Sefton
139 G5 **Crosby Garret** Cumb
138 F4 **Crosby Ravensworth** Cumb
26 E3 **Croscombe** Somset
26 B1 **Cross** Somset
54 B4 **Cross Ash** Mons
123 G3 **Cross Flatts** Brad
124 B4 **Cross Gates** Leeds
123 L4 **Cross Green** Leeds
77 J4 **Cross Green** Suffk
77 K4 **Cross Green** Suffk
78 B4 **Cross Green** Suffk
51 H3 **Cross Hands** Carmth
83 K3 **Cross Houses** Shrops
20 B2 **Cross in Hand** E Susx
65 L3 **Cross Inn** Cerdgn
174 C2 **Cross Keys** Ag & B
17 G4 **Cross Lane** IOW
84 C4 **Cross Lane Head** Shrops
100 F4 **Cross o' th' hands** Derbys
216 E7 **Cross of Jackston** Abers
92 E7 **Cross Street** Suffk
113 H5 **Cross Town** Ches
33 K4 **Cross-at-Hand** Kent
172 E7 **Crossaig** Ag & B
188 C7 **Crossapoll** Ag & B
147 J6 **Crosscanonby** Cumb
106 F5 **Crossdale Street** Norfk
176 E2 **Crossford** Fife
175 L8 **Crossford** S Lans
177 K5 **Crossgatehall** E Loth
163 J1 **Crossgates** E Ayrs
176 F1 **Crossgates** Fife
134 F3 **Crossgates** N York
129 L6 **Crossgill** Lancs
163 L4 **Crosshands** E Ayrs
186 C7 **Crosshill** Fife
163 J7 **Crosshill** S Ayrs
163 K2 **Crosshouse** E Ayrs
37 K3 **Crosskeys** Caerph
230 F2 **Crosskirk** Highld
129 H2 **Crosslands** Cumb
174 D5 **Crosslee** Rens
146 C2 **Crossmichael** D & G
206 B4 **Crossroads** Abers
206 E6 **Crossroads** Abers
196 E5 **Crosston** Angus
70 E2 **Crossway Green** Worcs
14 E5 **Crossways** Dorset
64 F6 **Crosswell** Pembks
129 J2 **Crosthwaite** Cumb
121 G6 **Croston** Lancs
92 F1 **Crostwick** Norfk
44 F3 **Crouch End** Gt Lon
14 D1 **Crouch Hill** Dorset
28 B6 **Croucheston** Wilts
73 G7 **Croughton** Nhants
216 F2 **Crovie** Abers
114 D2 **Crow Edge** Barns
54 F3 **Crow Hill** Herefs
3 H4 **Crowan** Cnwll
32 F6 **Crowborough** E Susx
25 H4 **Crowcombe** Somset
114 C7 **Crowdecote** Derbys
58 C7 **Crowell** Oxon
78 D3 **Crowfield** Suffk
178 F4 **Crowhill** E Loth
20 F3 **Crowhurst** E Susx
32 D4 **Crowhurst** Surrey
89 J2 **Crowland** Lincs
78 B1 **Crowland** Suffk
2 F5 **Crowlas** Cnwll
125 J7 **Crowle** N Linc
71 G4 **Crowle** Worcs
71 G3 **Crowle Green** Worcs
41 L3 **Crowmarsh Gifford** Oxon
78 F1 **Crown Corner** Suffk
6 C4 **Crownhill** C Plym
92 C3 **Crownthorpe** Norfk
3 H5 **Crowntown** Cnwll
2 D5 **Crows-an-Wra** Cnwll
42 D7 **Crowthorne** Wokham
112 E6 **Crowton** Ches
151 G7 **Croxdale** Dur
100 B5 **Croxden** Staffs
43 H2 **Croxley Green** Herts
75 J3 **Croxton** Cambs
126 D7 **Croxton** N Linc
106 B6 **Croxton** Norfk
91 K6 **Croxton** Norfk
99 H6 **Croxton** Staffs
102 D6 **Croxton Kerrial** Leics
213 J4 **Croy** Highld
175 J3 **Croy** N Lans
23 G4 **Croyde** Devon
75 K5 **Croydon** Cambs
44 F6 **Croydon** Gt Lon
203 G7 **Crubenmore** Highld
83 H2 **Cruckmeole** Shrops
83 H2 **Cruckton** Shrops
217 K6 **Cruden Bay** Abers
98 F8 **Crudgington** Wrekin
39 L2 **Crudwell** Wilts
37 K2 **Crumlin** Caerph
5 K5 **Crumplehorn** Cnwll
113 J2 **Crumpsall** Manch
34 E5 **Crundale** Kent
49 K5 **Crunwear** Pembks
29 H1 **Crux Easton** Hants
50 F3 **Crwbin** Carmth
42 E2 **Cryers Hill** Bucks
65 G7 **Crymmych** Pembks
52 C6 **Crynant** Neath
45 G5 **Crystal Palace** Gt Lon
209 L3 **Cuaig** Highld
181 L4 **Cuan Ferry Village** Ag & B
72 D2 **Cubbington** Warwks
4 C4 **Cubert** Cnwll
58 D4 **Cublington** Bucks
69 H6 **Cublington** Herefs
32 B7 **Cuckfield** W Susx
27 H6 **Cucklington** Somset
115 K7 **Cuckney** Notts
57 L7 **Cuddesdon** Oxon
58 C5 **Cuddington** Bucks
112 E7 **Cuddington** Ches
98 C3 **Cuddington Heath** Ches
32 D2 **Cudham** Gt Lon
10 D8 **Cudliptown** Devon
15 K3 **Cudnell** Bmouth
124 B8 **Cudworth** Barns
13 J1 **Cudworth** Somset
59 M7 **Cuffley** Herts
191 J5 **Cuil** Highld
199 G2 **Cuillin Hills** Highld
212 F3 **Culbokie** Highld
212 D6 **Culburnie** Highld
213 G5 **Culcabock** Highld
213 K4 **Culcharry** Highld
112 F3 **Culcheth** Warrtn
215 L7 **Culdrain** Abers
209 L6 **Culduie** Highld
77 J1 **Culford** Suffk
138 E2 **Culgaith** Cumb
41 J2 **Culham** Oxon
224 C2 **Culkein** Highld
224 D2 **Culkein Drumbeg** Highld
39 L2 **Culkerton** Gloucs
215 L2 **Cullen** Moray
159 J7 **Cullercoats** N Tyne
206 E5 **Cullerlie** Abers
213 G2 **Cullicudden** Highld
123 G3 **Cullingworth** Brad
181 L5 **Cullipool House** Ag & B
235 d2 **Cullivoe** Shet
213 H5 **Culloden** Highld
12 C2 **Cullompton** Devon
25 H7 **Culm Davy** Devon
83 J6 **Culmington** Shrops
25 H8 **Culmstock** Devon
224 C7 **Culnacraig** Highld
146 D5 **Culnaightrie** D & G
209 H2 **Culnaknock** Highld
222 D3 **Culrain** Highld
176 D2 **Culross** Fife
163 H6 **Culroy** S Ayrs
216 C7 **Culsalmond** Abers
145 K5 **Culscadden** D & G
145 G5 **Culshabbin** D & G
235 b6 **Culswick** Shet
207 H1 **Cultercullen** Abers
207 G5 **Cults** C Aber
45 M7 **Culverstone Green** Kent
103 G4 **Culverthorpe** Lincs
73 G5 **Culworth** Nhants
163 G7 **Culzean Castle** S Ayrs
175 K4 **Cumbernauld** N Lans
175 K3 **Cumbernauld Village** N Lans
119 G6 **Cumberworth** Lincs
216 F4 **Cuminestown** Abers
179 G6 **Cumledge** Border
148 D4 **Cummersdale** Cumb
147 K2 **Cummertrees** D & G
214 E1 **Cummingston** Moray
164 B5 **Cumnock** E Ayrs
57 J7 **Cumnor** Oxon
148 F5 **Cumrew** Cumb
155 J5 **Cumrue** D & G
148 D4 **Cumwhinton** Cumb
148 E4 **Cumwhitton** Cumb
132 F5 **Cundall** N York
163 J2 **Cunninghamhead** N Ayrs
186 F4 **Cupar** Fife
186 F5 **Cupar Muir** Fife
114 E6 **Curbar** Derbys
17 G1 **Curbridge** Hants
57 G6 **Curbridge** Oxon
29 K8 **Curdridge** Hants
85 L5 **Curdworth** Warwks
25 L7 **Curland** Somset
41 J6 **Curridge** W Berk
177 G5 **Currie** C Edin
25 L6 **Curry Mallet** Somset
26 B6 **Curry Rivel** Somset
33 J5 **Curtisden Green** Kent
7 H5 **Curtisknowle** Devon
3 H6 **Cury** Cnwll
205 L3 **Cushnie** Abers
145 J7 **Cutcloy** D & G
24 E4 **Cutcombe** Somset
223 G4 **Cuthill** Highld
70 F2 **Cutnall Green** Worcs
56 C3 **Cutsdean** Gloucs
115 G6 **Cutthorpe** Derbys
42 A2 **Cuxham** Oxon
46 B6 **Cuxton** Medway
117 K2 **Cuxwold** Lincs
110 E6 **Cwm** Denbgs
53 H4 **Cwm Crawnon** Powys
81 J2 **Cwm Llinau** Powys
65 J6 **Cwm-cou** Cerdgn
51 H3 **Cwm-y-glo** Carmth
109 H8 **Cwm-y-glo** Gwynd
36 B3 **Cwmafan** Neath
52 F7 **Cwmaman** Rhondd
50 B1 **Cwmbach** Carmth
68 D6 **Cwmbach** Powys
52 F7 **Cwmbach** Rhondd

68 B4 **Cwmbach Llechrhyd** Powys
37 L2 **Cwmbran** Torfn
37 K2 **Cwmcarn** Caerph
54 C6 **Cwmcarvan** Mons
52 F7 **Cwmdare** Rhondd
53 J4 **Cwmdu** Powys
51 J6 **Cwmdu** Swans
65 L7 **Cwmduad** Carmth
36 D3 **Cwmfelin** Brdgnd
53 H7 **Cwmfelin** Myr Td
49 K4 **Cwmfelin Boeth** Carmth
37 J3 **Cwmfelinfach** Caerph
50 E3 **Cwmffrwd** Carmth
52 C5 **Cwmgiedd** Powys
51 K4 **Cwmgors** Carmth
51 H4 **Cwmgwili** Carmth
65 K6 **Cwmhiraeth** Carmth
51 L3 **Cwmllynfell** Neath
51 G3 **Cwmmawr** Carmth
36 E2 **Cwmparc** Rhondd
65 K6 **Cwmpengraig** Carmth
66 B5 **Cwmsychbant** Cerdgn
53 K6 **Cwmtillery** Blae G
81 H8 **Cwmystwyth** Cerdgn
66 C5 **Cwrt-newydd** Cerdgn
36 D2 **Cymer** Neath
36 G3 **Cymmer** Rhondd
67 H6 **Cynghordy** Carmth
36 C2 **Cynonville** Neath
97 G4 **Cynwyd** Denbgs
65 L8 **Cynwyl Elfed** Carmth

D

7 K3 **Daccombe** Devon
138 C2 **Dacre** Cumb
132 B7 **Dacre** N York
132 B6 **Dacre Banks** N York
149 M7 **Daddry Shield** Dur
73 J6 **Dadford** Bucks
86 E4 **Dadlington** Leics
45 J3 **Dagenham** Gt Lon
55 M6 **Daglingworth** Gloucs
59 G5 **Dagnall** Bucks
152 F2 **Dailly** S Ayrs
187 G4 **Dairsie** Fife
233 b8 **Dalabrog** W Isls
182 D5 **Dalavich** Ag & B
146 E3 **Dalbeattie** D & G
237 b5 **Dalby** IOM
133 K5 **Dalby** N York
194 F5 **Dalcapon** P & K
226 F7 **Dalchalm** Highld
201 L3 **Dalchreichart** Highld
184 F4 **Dalchruin** P & K
185 L2 **Dalcrue** P & K
12 D5 **Dalditch** Devon
101 H5 **Dale** Derbys
48 D6 **Dale** Pembks
163 H1 **Dalgarven** N Ayrs
177 G2 **Dalgety Bay** Fife
164 B6 **Dalgig** E Ayrs
185 G3 **Dalginross** P & K
194 F6 **Dalguise** P & K
230 C5 **Dalhalvaig** Highld
77 G3 **Dalham** Suffk
233 b8 **Daliburgh** W Isls
177 K5 **Dalkeith** Mdloth
214 D4 **Dallas** Moray
78 F4 **Dallinghoo** Suffk
20 D2 **Dallington** E Susx
73 K3 **Dallington** Nhants
183 H3 **Dalmally** Ag & B
184 C7 **Dalmary** Stirlg
153 K2 **Dalmellington** E Ayrs
176 F3 **Dalmeny** C Edin
203 H2 **Dalmigavie** Highld
203 H2 **Dalmigavie Lodge** Highld
222 F7 **Dalmore** Highld
174 E4 **Dalmuir** W Duns
190 E3 **Dalnabreck** Highld
194 B3 **Dalnacardoch** P & K
203 K2 **Dalnahaitnach** Highld
193 K2 **Dalnaspidal** P & K
230 F7 **Dalnawillan Lodge** Highld
194 C5 **Daloist** P & K
186 A6 **Dalqueich** P & K
153 G3 **Dalquhairn** S Ayrs
226 D6 **Dalreavoch Lodge** Highld
174 B7 **Dalry** N Ayrs
163 J6 **Dalrymple** E Ayrs
175 L7 **Dalserf** S Lans
161 G6 **Dalsmeran** Ag & B
148 C5 **Dalston** Cumb
45 G3 **Dalston** Gt Lon
155 G5 **Dalswinton** D & G
155 K7 **Dalton** D & G
140 E5 **Dalton** N York
132 F4 **Dalton** N York
158 E7 **Dalton** Nthumb
141 L2 **Dalton Piercy** Hartpl
128 F5 **Dalton-in-Furness** Cumb
151 K5 **Dalton-le-Dale** Dur
141 H5 **Dalton-on-Tees** N York
165 G7 **Dalveen** D & G
184 D3 **Dalveich** Stirlg
202 F7 **Dalwhinnie** Highld
13 G3 **Dalwood** Devon
28 C7 **Damerham** Hants
93 J2 **Damgate** Norfk
61 J6 **Danbury** Essex
142 F5 **Danby** N York
141 H7 **Danby Wiske** N York
215 G5 **Dandaleith** Moray
177 J5 **Danderhall** Mdloth
60 B4 **Dane End** Herts
87 H3 **Dane Hills** C Leic
34 E4 **Dane Street** Kent
113 L7 **Danebridge** Ches
32 D7 **Danehill** E Susx
216 D3 **Danshillock** Abers
178 C5 **Danskine** E Loth
45 K5 **Darenth** Kent
112 E5 **Daresbury** Halton
115 H1 **Darfield** Barns
34 E3 **Dargate** Kent
5 K3 **Darite** Cnwll
85 H4 **Darlaston** Wsall
85 H4 **Darlaston Green** Wsall
132 C7 **Darley** N York
101 G5 **Darley Abbey** C Derb
100 E1 **Darley Bridge** Derbys
114 F8 **Darley Dale** Derbys
85 L8 **Darley Green** Solhll
132 B7 **Darley Head** N York
59 J4 **Darleyhall** Herts
72 B6 **Darlingscott** Warwks
141 H4 **Darlington** Darltn
116 C6 **Darlton** Notts
167 H3 **Darnick** Border
81 H3 **Darowen** Powys
216 E5 **Darra** Abers
9 G2 **Darracott** Devon
23 G4 **Darracott** Devon
158 E7 **Darras Hall** Nthumb
124 D6 **Darrington** Wakefd
79 J1 **Darsham** Suffk
26 E3 **Darshill** Somset
45 K5 **Dartford** Kent
7 H4 **Dartington** Devon
11 G8 **Dartmoor National Park** Devon
7 K5 **Dartmouth** Devon
123 L7 **Darton** Barns
164 B2 **Darvel** E Ayrs
121 K6 **Darwen** Bl w D
43 G5 **Datchet** W & M
59 L4 **Datchworth** Herts
121 K8 **Daubhill** Bolton
39 M4 **Dauntsey** Wilts
214 C6 **Dava** Highld
112 F7 **Davenham** Ches
73 H3 **Daventry** Nhants
177 G4 **Davidson's Mains** C Edin
8 F7 **Davidstow** Cnwll
155 M2 **Davington** D & G
34 D3 **Davington Hill** Kent
216 E8 **Daviot** Abers
213 H6 **Daviot** Highld
213 H6 **Daviot House** Highld
215 K4 **Davoch of Grange** Moray
31 K3 **Dawesgreen** Surrey
84 C2 **Dawley** Wrekin
12 B6 **Dawlish** Devon
12 C6 **Dawlish Warren** Devon
110 B6 **Dawn** Conwy
101 L4 **Daybrook** Notts
56 E3 **Daylesford** Gloucs
35 K4 **Deal** Kent
136 E3 **Dean** Cumb
23 L2 **Dean** Devon
7 H3 **Dean** Devon
29 H5 **Dean** Hants
29 K7 **Dean** Hants
57 G4 **Dean** Oxon
26 F3 **Dean** Somset
45 L6 **Dean Bottom** Kent
57 J6 **Dean Court** Oxon
7 H3 **Dean Prior** Devon
166 F6 **Deanburnhaugh** Border
7 G3 **Deancombe** Devon
121 K8 **Deane** Bolton
29 K2 **Deane** Hants
122 F7 **Deanhead** Kirk
27 M7 **Deanland** Dorset
149 L3 **Deanraw** Nthumb
176 D5 **Deans** W Loth
136 F2 **Deanscales** Cumb
73 L6 **Deanshanger** Nhants
215 H4 **Deanshaugh** Moray
184 F6 **Deanston** Stirlg
147 J7 **Dearham** Cumb
78 F4 **Debach** Suffk
60 E2 **Debden** Essex
45 H2 **Debden** Essex
78 E2 **Debenham** Suffk
70 E5 **Deblin's Green** Worcs
176 E4 **Dechmont** W Loth
176 D4 **Dechmont Road** W Loth
57 J2 **Deddington** Oxon
62 C2 **Dedham** Essex
42 F5 **Dedworth** W & M
88 D5 **Deene** Nhants
88 D5 **Deenethorpe** Nhants
114 F3 **Deepcar** Sheff
89 G2 **Deeping Gate** C Pete
89 H2 **Deeping St James** Lincs
89 J1 **Deeping St Nicholas** Lincs
55 K3 **Deerhurst** Gloucs
71 G5 **Defford** Worcs
52 E3 **Defynnog** Powys
109 L5 **Deganwy** Conwy
182 A5 **Degnish** Ag & B
141 J6 **Deighton** N York
124 F2 **Deighton** York
109 H8 **Deiniolen** Gwynd
8 E7 **Delabole** Cnwll
112 E7 **Delamere** Ches
207 H2 **Delfrigs** Abers
18 A5 **Dell Quay** W Susx
214 D7 **Dellefure** Highld
214 E7 **Delnashaugh Inn** Moray
223 G6 **Delny** Highld
150 E5 **Delves** Dur
195 H7 **Delvine** P & K
103 H5 **Dembleby** Lincs
186 D4 **Den of Lindores** Fife
115 J2 **Denaby** Donc
110 E7 **Denbigh** Denbgs
186 F4 **Denbrae** Fife
7 J3 **Denbury** Devon
101 H4 **Denby** Derbys
123 J8 **Denby Dale** Kirk
41 G3 **Denchworth** Oxon
128 F5 **Dendron** Cumb
185 K4 **Denfield** P & K
88 E7 **Denford** Nhants
62 B7 **Dengie** Essex
43 H3 **Denham** Bucks
77 H3 **Denham** Suffk
92 E8 **Denham** Suffk
43 H3 **Denham Green** Bucks
217 J4 **Denhead** Abers
187 G5 **Denhead** Fife
186 F2 **Denhead of Gray** C Dund
167 J5 **Denholm** Border
123 G4 **Denholme** Brad
30 A8 **Denmead** Hants
207 H3 **Denmore** C Aber
79 G2 **Dennington** Suffk
175 L2 **Denny** Falk
175 L3 **Dennyloanhead** Falk
122 E7 **Denshaw** Oldham
206 F6 **Denside** Abers
35 G6 **Densole** Kent
77 H4 **Denston** Suffk
100 C4 **Denstone** Staffs
34 E3 **Denstroude** Kent
130 D3 **Dent** Cumb
89 G6 **Denton** Cambs
140 F4 **Denton** Darltn
19 L5 **Denton** E Susx
35 G5 **Denton** Kent
102 E6 **Denton** Lincs
123 H2 **Denton** N York
74 B3 **Denton** Nhants
93 G5 **Denton** Norfk
113 L3 **Denton** Tamesd
90 E3 **Denver** Norfk
169 J6 **Denwick** Nthumb
92 C4 **Deopham** Norfk
92 C4 **Deopham Green** Norfk
77 H3 **Depden** Suffk
45 G4 **Deptford** Gt Lon
28 A4 **Deptford** Wilts
101 G5 **Derby** C Derb
23 J5 **Derby** Devon
237 b7 **Derbyhaven** IOM
194 D5 **Derculich** P & K
92 B2 **Dereham** Norfk
53 H7 **Deri** Caerph
35 G5 **Derringstone** Kent
99 K7 **Derrington** Staffs
39 L6 **Derry Hill** Wilts
125 J8 **Derrythorpe** N Linc
105 H6 **Dersingham** Norfk
189 K6 **Dervaig** Ag & B
97 G3 **Derwen** Denbgs
80 F4 **Derwenlas** Powys
137 J3 **Derwent Water** Cumb
88 B6 **Desborough** Nhants
86 F3 **Desford** Leics
215 L3 **Deskford** Moray
33 K2 **Detling** Kent
54 C7 **Devauden** Mons

81 G7 **Devil's Bridge** Cerdgn
40 A7 **Devizes** Wilts
6 C5 **Devonport** C Plym
185 J7 **Devonside** Clacks
4 C7 **Devoran** Cnwll
177 K5 **Dewarton** Mdloth
14 E3 **Dewlish** Dorset
123 K6 **Dewsbury** Kirk
97 K8 **Deytheur** Powys
121 L4 **Dial Hall** Lancs
18 F2 **Dial Post** W Susx
16 E2 **Dibden** Hants
16 E2 **Dibden Purlieu** Hants
92 E6 **Dickleburgh** Norfk
56 B2 **Didbrook** Gloucs
41 K3 **Didcot** Oxon
41 K3 **Didcot Railway Centre** Oxon
75 H2 **Diddington** Cambs
83 K6 **Diddlebury** Shrops
18 A3 **Didling** W Susx
39 J3 **Didmarton** Gloucs
113 J3 **Didsbury** Manch
103 H2 **Digby** Lincs
218 C7 **Digg** Highld
122 F8 **Diggle** Oldham
112 C1 **Digmoor** Lancs
66 C4 **Dihewyd** Cerdgn
107 G7 **Dilham** Norfk
99 L4 **Dilhorne** Staffs
75 G2 **Dillington** Cambs
150 B3 **Dilston** Nthumb
27 K2 **Dilton** Wilts
27 J2 **Dilton Marsh** Wilts
69 H4 **Dilwyn** Herefs
94 E5 **Dinas** Gwynd
64 E6 **Dinas** Pembks
37 J6 **Dinas Powys** V Glam
81 J1 **Dinas-Mawddwy** Gwynd
26 E3 **Dinder** Somset
69 K6 **Dinedor** Herefs
54 C6 **Dingestow** Mons
111 K4 **Dingle** Lpool
87 L6 **Dingley** Nhants
212 E3 **Dingwall** Highld
205 K5 **Dinnet** Abers
158 F7 **Dinnington** N u Ty
115 K4 **Dinnington** Rothm
26 B8 **Dinnington** Somset
95 K1 **Dinorwic** Gwynd
58 C5 **Dinton** Bucks
28 A5 **Dinton** Wilts
155 K4 **Dinwoodie** D & G
9 J2 **Dinworthy** Devon
25 J6 **Dipford** Somset
161 K2 **Dippen** Ag & B
162 D5 **Dippen** N Ayrs
10 C7 **Dippertown** Devon
215 H3 **Dipple** Moray
152 E2 **Dipple** S Ayrs
7 G4 **Diptford** Devon
150 E4 **Dipton** Dur
178 B2 **Dirleton** E Loth
149 L5 **Dirt Pot** Nthumb
101 J7 **Diseworth** Leics
132 F5 **Dishforth** N York
113 L5 **Disley** Ches
92 D7 **Diss** Norfk
136 D3 **Distington** Cumb
28 C5 **Ditchampton** Wilts
169 H5 **Ditchburn** Nthumb
26 F4 **Ditcheat** Somset
93 G5 **Ditchingham** Norfk
19 J3 **Ditchling** E Susx
83 K2 **Ditherington** Shrops
39 J6 **Ditteridge** Wilts
7 K5 **Dittisham** Devon
112 D4 **Ditton** Halton
33 J2 **Ditton** Kent
76 F3 **Ditton Green** Cambs
83 L5 **Ditton Priors** Shrops
55 M2 **Dixton** Gloucs
54 D5 **Dixton** Mons
113 M1 **Dobcross** Oldham
5 K3 **Dobwalls** Cnwll
11 H7 **Doccombe** Devon
212 F6 **Dochgarroch** Highld
130 B5 **Docker** Lancs
105 J5 **Docking** Norfk
69 L3 **Docklow** Herefs
137 L3 **Dockray** Cumb
100 A5 **Dod's Leigh** Staffs
98 E4 **Dodd's Green** Ches
60 F7 **Doddinghurst** Essex
90 B5 **Doddington** Cambs
34 C4 **Doddington** Kent
116 E7 **Doddington** Lincs
168 E3 **Doddington** Nthumb
84 B7 **Doddington** Shrops
11 K7 **Doddiscombsleigh** Devon
73 H3 **Dodford** Nhants
85 G8 **Dodford** Worcs
39 H4 **Dodington** S Glos
25 J4 **Dodington** Somset
98 A1 **Dodleston** Ches
174 F7 **Dodside** E Rens
114 F1 **Dodworth** Barns
103 K2 **Dogdyke** Lincs
30 C2 **Dogmersfield** Hants
82 B2 **Dolanog** Powys
95 J4 **Dolbenmaen** Gwynd
81 K3 **Dolfach** Powys
82 C6 **Dolfor** Powys
109 L7 **Dolgarrog** Conwy
96 B8 **Dolgellau** Gwynd
226 F7 **Doll** Highld
185 K7 **Dollar** Clacks
185 K7 **Dollarfield** Clacks
111 H6 **Dolphin** Flints
129 L8 **Dolphinholme** Lancs
176 F8 **Dolphinton** S Lans
10 E3 **Dolton** Devon
110 B6 **Dolwen** Conwy
96 B3 **Dolwyddelan** Conwy
97 L8 **Domgay** Powys
115 L2 **Doncaster** Donc
27 K6 **Donhead St Andrew** Wilts
27 K6 **Donhead St Mary** Wilts
177 G2 **Donibristle** Fife
25 G3 **Doniford** Somset
103 K5 **Donington** Lincs
118 C5 **Donington on Bain** Lincs
86 C2 **Donisthorpe** Leics
56 D3 **Donnington** Gloucs
83 L2 **Donnington** Shrops
41 J6 **Donnington** W Berk
18 B5 **Donnington** W Susx
84 C2 **Donnington** Wrekin
25 M8 **Donyatt** Somset
163 H5 **Doonfoot** S Ayrs
163 J6 **Doonholm** S Ayrs
204 D3 **Dorback Lodge** Highld
14 D4 **Dorchester** Dorset
41 L2 **Dorchester** Oxon
86 C4 **Dordon** Warwks
114 F5 **Dore** Sheff
212 F7 **Dores** Highld
31 K2 **Dorking** Surrey
32 D5 **Dormans Land** Surrey
69 L6 **Dormington** Herefs
71 H3 **Dormston** Worcs
42 F5 **Dorney** Bucks
200 D1 **Dornie** Highld
223 H4 **Dornoch** Highld
147 M2 **Dornock** D & G
230 F5 **Dorrery** Highld
85 L8 **Dorridge** Solhll
103 H2 **Dorrington** Lincs
83 J3 **Dorrington** Shrops
99 G4 **Dorrington** Shrops
71 K4 **Dorsington** Warwks
69 G6 **Dorstone** Herefs
58 B5 **Dorton** Bucks
237 d6 **Douglas** IOM
165 G4 **Douglas** S Lans
187 G2 **Douglas and Angus** C Dund
165 G3 **Douglas Castle** S Lans
183 H7 **Douglas Pier** Ag & B
165 G3 **Douglas Water** S Lans
164 F3 **Douglas West** S Lans
196 C6 **Douglastown** Angus
26 F3 **Doulting** Somset
234 b5 **Dounby** Ork
221 L2 **Doune** Highld
184 F6 **Doune** Stirlg
152 E3 **Dounepark** S Ayrs
222 D4 **Dounie** Highld
6 D3 **Dousland** Devon
114 B6 **Dove Holes** Derbys
147 J7 **Dovenby** Cumb
35 J6 **Dover** Kent
35 J6 **Dover Castle** Kent
62 F2 **Dovercourt** Essex
70 F2 **Doverdale** Worcs
100 C5 **Doveridge** Derbys
31 L2 **Doversgreen** Surrey
194 F6 **Dowally** P & K
55 M4 **Dowdeswell** Gloucs
53 G6 **Dowlais** Myr Td
10 E3 **Dowland** Devon
26 A8 **Dowlish Wake** Somset
40 C2 **Down Ampney** Gloucs
55 K4 **Down Hatherley** Gloucs
11 H4 **Down St Mary** Devon
6 D5 **Down Thomas** Devon
5 L5 **Downderry** Cnwll
45 H7 **Downe** Gt Lon
39 J2 **Downend** Gloucs
38 F5 **Downend** S Glos
186 F2 **Downfield** C Dund
5 L2 **Downgate** Cnwll
6 A2 **Downgate** Cnwll
46 B2 **Downham** Essex
45 H5 **Downham** Gt Lon
122 B2 **Downham** Lancs
90 E3 **Downham Market** Norfk
26 E6 **Downhead** Somset
27 G3 **Downhead** Somset
186 A2 **Downhill** P & K
140 E7 **Downholme** N York
207 H6 **Downies** Abers
42 D2 **Downley** Bucks
43 J8 **Downside** Surrey
16 C4 **Downton** Hants
28 D6 **Downton** Wilts
83 H8 **Downton on the Rock** Herefs
103 J6 **Dowsby** Lincs
39 G5 **Doynton** S Glos
37 K3 **Draethen** Caerph
164 F1 **Draffan** S Lans
116 B4 **Drakeholes** Notts
174 B7 **Drakemyre** N Ayrs
71 G5 **Drakes Broughton** Worcs
131 K8 **Draughton** N York
87 L7 **Draughton** Nhants
125 G5 **Drax** N York
72 F1 **Draycote** Warwks
101 H6 **Draycott** Derbys
71 L7 **Draycott** Gloucs
26 C2 **Draycott** Somset
100 D6 **Draycott in the Clay** Staffs
99 M4 **Draycott in the Moors** Staffs
17 J2 **Drayton** C Port
88 B5 **Drayton** Leics
92 E2 **Drayton** Norfk
72 E6 **Drayton** Oxon
41 J2 **Drayton** Oxon
26 B6 **Drayton** Somset
85 G7 **Drayton** Worcs
85 L4 **Drayton Bassett** Staffs
58 E5 **Drayton Beauchamp** Bucks
85 L4 **Drayton Manor Park** Staffs
58 D3 **Drayton Parslow** Bucks
41 L2 **Drayton St Leonard** Oxon
48 F5 **Dreen Hill** Pembks
65 K6 **Drefach** Carmth
51 G3 **Drefach** Carmth
66 C5 **Drefach** Cerdgn
163 J2 **Dreghorn** N Ayrs
35 H6 **Drellingore** Kent
178 B3 **Drem** E Loth
11 H6 **Drewsteignton** Devon
118 E6 **Driby** Lincs
134 F7 **Driffield** E R Yk
56 B7 **Driffield** Gloucs
2 D5 **Drift** Cnwll
136 E7 **Drigg** Cumb
123 J5 **Drighlington** Leeds
190 B5 **Drimnin** Highld
13 K2 **Drimpton** Dorset
191 J1 **Drimsallie** Highld
124 E2 **Dringhouses** York
77 L3 **Drinkstone** Suffk
77 L3 **Drinkstone Green** Suffk
100 A6 **Drointon** Staffs
70 F2 **Droitwich** Worcs
186 B4 **Dron** P & K
115 G5 **Dronfield** Derbys
163 K5 **Drongan** E Ayrs
186 E1 **Dronley** Angus
14 E2 **Droop** Dorset
29 L7 **Droxford** Hants
113 K2 **Droylsden** Tamesd
97 G4 **Druid** Denbgs
48 E4 **Druidston** Pembks
192 B6 **Druimachoish** Highld
191 L3 **Druimarbin** Highld
172 C4 **Druimdrishaig** Ag & B
199 L7 **Druimindarroch** Highld
172 F3 **Drum** Ag & B
185 L7 **Drum** P & K
165 H2 **Drumalbin** S Lans
224 D3 **Drumbeg** Highld
216 B6 **Drumblade** Abers
144 C6 **Drumbreddon** D & G
210 B7 **Drumbuie** Highld
148 A3 **Drumburgh** Cumb
146 F4 **Drumburn** D & G
174 F4 **Drumchapel** C Glas
193 L5 **Drumchastle** P & K
164 C2 **Drumclog** S Lans
187 G6 **Drumeldrie** Fife
165 M3 **Drumelzier** Border
199 L3 **Drumfearn** Highld
206 D5 **Drumfrennie** Abers
203 J5 **Drumguish** Highld
206 B6 **Drumhead** Abers
214 E7 **Drumin** Moray
153 L3 **Drumjohn** D & G
153 G6 **Drumlamford** S Ayrs
206 C4 **Drumlasie** Abers
148 A5 **Drumleaning** Cumb
161 H5 **Drumlemble** Ag & B
197 J1 **Drumlithie** Abers

145 H6 **Drummoddie** D & G
144 D7 **Drummore** D & G
215 J5 **Drummuir** Moray
212 D7 **Drumnadrochit** Highld
215 L4 **Drumnagorrach** Moray
154 F6 **Drumpark** D & G
224 E7 **Drumrunie Lodge** Highld
163 G6 **Drumshang** S Ayrs
209 G5 **Drumuie** Highld
204 B2 **Drumuillie** Highld
184 E6 **Drumvaich** Stirlg
186 B5 **Drunzie** P & K
102 D3 **Dry Doddington** Lincs
75 L3 **Dry Drayton** Cambs
138 F4 **Drybeck** Cumb
215 K2 **Drybridge** Moray
163 J3 **Drybridge** N Ayrs
54 F4 **Drybrook** Gloucs
167 J3 **Dryburgh** Border
3 G5 **Drym** Cnwll
174 E2 **Drymen** Stirlg
217 G5 **Drymuir** Abers
208 F7 **Drynoch** Highld
216 F2 **Dubford** Abers
225 J5 **Duchally** Highld
57 G6 **Ducklington** Oxon
76 C7 **Duddenhoe End** Essex
177 J4 **Duddingston** C Edin
88 E4 **Duddington** Nhants
25 K7 **Duddlestone** Somset
84 B6 **Duddlewick** Shrops
168 D2 **Duddo** Nthumb
112 D8 **Duddon** Ches
97 M5 **Dudleston** Shrops
85 G5 **Dudley** Dudley
159 G7 **Dudley** N Tyne
85 G5 **Dudley Port** Sandw
15 K3 **Dudsbury** Dorset
101 G4 **Duffield** Derbys
36 C2 **Duffryn** Neath
215 H6 **Dufftown** Moray
214 E2 **Duffus** Moray
139 G3 **Dufton** Cumb
134 D6 **Duggleby** N York
210 B7 **Duirinish** Highld
199 L3 **Duisdalemore** Highld
191 K2 **Duisky** Highld
78 C6 **Duke Street** Suffk
113 L2 **Dukinfield** Tamesd
26 E3 **Dulcote** Somset
12 D2 **Dulford** Devon
194 C6 **Dull** P & K
175 K3 **Dullatur** N Lans
76 F3 **Dullingham** Cambs
76 F3 **Dullingham Ley** Cambs
204 B1 **Dulnain Bridge** Highld
75 H3 **Duloe** Beds
5 K4 **Duloe** Cnwll
24 E5 **Dulverton** Somset
45 G5 **Dulwich** Gt Lon
174 D4 **Dumbarton** W Duns
71 H7 **Dumbleton** Gloucs
155 G6 **Dumfries** D & G
174 F2 **Dumgoyne** Stirlg
29 L3 **Dummer** Hants
35 K2 **Dumpton** Kent
197 G4 **Dun** Angus
193 L5 **Dunalastair** P & K
173 K4 **Dunan** Ag & B
209 J8 **Dunan** Highld
193 G5 **Dunan** P & K
161 H7 **Dunaverty** Ag & B
25 L3 **Dunball** Somset
178 E3 **Dunbar** E Loth
227 L3 **Dunbeath** Highld
182 C2 **Dunbeg** Ag & B
185 G6 **Dunblane** Stirlg
186 E4 **Dunbog** Fife
212 F3 **Duncanston** Highld
216 B8 **Duncanstone** Abers
11 K7 **Dunchideock** Devon
72 F1 **Dunchurch** Warwks
155 G5 **Duncow** D & G
186 B5 **Duncrievie** P & K
18 C3 **Duncton** W Susx
186 F2 **Dundee** C Dund
186 F2 **Dundee Airport** C Dund
26 C5 **Dundon** Somset
163 J3 **Dundonald** S Ayrs
220 E4 **Dundonnell** Highld
147 L5 **Dundraw** Cumb
201 L3 **Dundreggan** Highld
146 D5 **Dundrennan** D & G
38 E6 **Dundry** N Som
206 E4 **Dunecht** Abers
176 F2 **Dunfermline** Fife
40 C2 **Dunfield** Gloucs
164 D3 **Dungavel** S Lans
21 L3 **Dungeness** Kent
116 D6 **Dunham** Notts
113 H4 **Dunham Town** Traffd
113 G4 **Dunham Woodhouses** Traffd
112 C6 **Dunham-on-the-Hill** Ches
70 F2 **Dunhampton** Worcs
117 G5 **Dunholme** Lincs
187 J5 **Dunino** Fife
175 L2 **Dunipace** Falk
33 G3 **Dunk's Green** Kent
195 G7 **Dunkeld** P & K
39 G8 **Dunkerton** BaNES
12 E2 **Dunkeswell** Devon
123 L2 **Dunkeswick** N York
34 E3 **Dunkirk** Kent
39 H4 **Dunkirk** S Glos
196 F3 **Dunlappie** Angus
70 E2 **Dunley** Worcs
174 D8 **Dunlop** E Ayrs
202 F2 **Dunmaglass** Highld
176 B1 **Dunmore** Falk
231 J2 **Dunnet** Highld
196 E6 **Dunnichen** Angus
185 L4 **Dunning** P & K
126 E1 **Dunnington** E R Yk
71 J4 **Dunnington** Warwks
133 K8 **Dunnington** York
122 B5 **Dunnockshaw** Lancs
173 K3 **Dunoon** Ag & B
214 C5 **Dunphail** Moray
144 E4 **Dunragit** D & G
179 G7 **Duns** Border
57 J3 **Duns Tew** Oxon
103 J6 **Dunsby** Lincs
154 F5 **Dunscore** D & G
124 F8 **Dunscroft** Donc
142 D4 **Dunsdale** R & Cl
42 C5 **Dunsden Green** Oxon
9 J3 **Dunsdon** Devon
31 G4 **Dunsfold** Surrey
11 J6 **Dunsford** Devon
186 D5 **Dunshalt** Fife
217 J5 **Dunshillock** Abers
101 J1 **Dunsill** Notts
143 H5 **Dunsley** N York
84 F6 **Dunsley** Staffs
58 E6 **Dunsmore** Bucks
121 K1 **Dunsop Bridge** Lancs
59 G4 **Dunstable** Beds
100 D7 **Dunstall** Staffs
169 K5 **Dunstan** Nthumb
24 F3 **Dunster** Somset
151 G3 **Dunston** Gatesd
117 H8 **Dunston** Lincs
92 F3 **Dunston** Norfk
99 L8 **Dunston** Staffs
6 E5 **Dunstone** Devon
7 G2 **Dunstone** Devon
126 D4 **Dunswell** E R Yk
176 E8 **Dunsyre** S Lans
6 B1 **Dunterton** Devon
55 L6 **Duntisbourne Abbots** Gloucs
55 M6 **Duntisbourne Rouse** Gloucs
14 D2 **Duntish** Dorset
174 E4 **Duntocher** W Duns
75 J5 **Dunton** Beds
58 D3 **Dunton** Bucks
105 L6 **Dunton** Norfk
87 G5 **Dunton Bassett** Leics
32 F2 **Dunton Green** Kent
218 C6 **Duntulm** Highld
163 G6 **Dunure** S Ayrs
51 H6 **Dunvant** Swans
208 D5 **Dunvegan** Highld
79 K1 **Dunwich** Suffk
3 K5 **Durgan** Cnwll
151 G6 **Durham** Dur
151 G6 **Durham Cathedral** Dur
154 F2 **Durisdeer** D & G
154 F2 **Durisdeermill** D & G
25 L4 **Durleigh** Somset
29 K7 **Durley** Hants
40 E7 **Durley** Wilts
29 K7 **Durley Street** Hants
35 H3 **Durlock** Kent
35 J2 **Durlock** Kent
196 C6 **Durmgley** Angus
228 F3 **Durness** Highld
191 K5 **Duror** Highld
182 D5 **Durran** Ag & B
18 F5 **Durrington** W Susx
28 D3 **Durrington** Wilts
206 E6 **Durris** Abers
39 H2 **Dursley** Gloucs
55 G4 **Dursley Cross** Gloucs
25 L5 **Durston** Somset
15 G2 **Durweston** Dorset
73 K3 **Duston** Nhants
203 L1 **Duthil** Highld
112 E5 **Dutton** Ches
76 C5 **Duxford** Cambs
57 G7 **Duxford** Oxon
76 C5 **Duxford Aircraft Museum** Cambs
109 L6 **Dwygyfylchi** Conwy
108 F7 **Dwyran** IOA
207 G3 **Dyce** C Aber
95 K7 **Dyffryn Ardudwy** Gwynd
52 D6 **Dyffryn Cellwen** Neath
103 J7 **Dyke** Lincs
214 B3 **Dyke** Moray
195 K5 **Dykehead** Angus
196 C4 **Dykehead** Angus
176 B6 **Dykehead** N Lans
184 D7 **Dykehead** Stirlg
197 H3 **Dykelands** Abers
195 K5 **Dykends** Angus
216 D5 **Dykeside** Abers
34 E8 **Dymchurch** Kent
55 G2 **Dymock** Gloucs
39 H5 **Dyrham** S Glos
186 E8 **Dysart** Fife
110 E5 **Dyserth** Denbgs

E

120 F2 **Eagland Hill** Lancs
116 E7 **Eagle** Lincs
141 K4 **Eaglescliffe** S on T
136 F2 **Eaglesfield** Cumb
155 M7 **Eaglesfield** D & G
175 G7 **Eaglesham** E Rens
121 L7 **Eagley** Bolton
102 A1 **Eakring** Notts
125 J7 **Ealand** N Linc
44 D4 **Ealing** Gt Lon
149 H4 **Eals** Nthumb
138 D2 **Eamont Bridge** Cumb
122 D2 **Earby** Lancs
84 C5 **Eardington** Shrops
69 H3 **Eardisland** Herefs
68 F5 **Eardisley** Herefs
98 A7 **Eardiston** Shrops
70 C2 **Eardiston** Worcs
89 L8 **Earith** Cambs
86 F4 **Earl Shilton** Leics
78 F2 **Earl Soham** Suffk
114 C7 **Earl Sterndale** Derbys
70 F6 **Earl's Croome** Worcs
112 E3 **Earlestown** St Hel
42 C6 **Earley** Wokham
208 F3 **Earlish** Highld
74 C2 **Earls Barton** Nhants
61 K3 **Earls Colne** Essex
71 G3 **Earls Common** Worcs
86 D7 **Earlsdon** Covtry
187 H7 **Earlsferry** Fife
44 E5 **Earlsfield** Gt Lon
216 F7 **Earlsford** Abers
123 K6 **Earlsheaton** Kirk
167 J2 **Earlston** Border
163 K3 **Earlston** E Ayrs
32 B4 **Earlswood** Surrey
85 K8 **Earlswood** Warwks
17 M3 **Earnley** W Susx
159 H7 **Earsdon** N Tyne
158 F4 **Earsdon** Nthumb
93 G5 **Earsham** Norfk
18 C4 **Eartham** W Susx
142 C5 **Easby** N York
181 L4 **Easdale** Ag & B
30 E6 **Easebourne** W Susx
86 F7 **Easenhall** Warwks
30 F3 **Eashing** Surrey
58 B6 **Easington** Bucks
151 K6 **Easington** Dur
127 J6 **Easington** E R Yk
142 F4 **Easington** R & Cl
151 K6 **Easington Colliery** Dur
133 H5 **Easingwold** N York
196 B7 **Eassie and Nevay** Angus
37 G6 **East Aberthaw** V Glam
7 H6 **East Allington** Devon
24 D6 **East Anstey** Devon
17 H5 **East Ashey** IOW
17 M2 **East Ashling** W Susx
134 F3 **East Ayton** N York
117 K5 **East Barkwith** Lincs
33 J3 **East Barming** Kent
143 G5 **East Barnby** N York
44 F2 **East Barnet** Gt Lon
178 F3 **East Barns** E Loth
105 L5 **East Barsham** Norfk
106 E4 **East Beckham** Norfk
43 H5 **East Bedfont** Gt Lon
78 C7 **East Bergholt** Suffk
106 A8 **East Bilney** Norfk
20 A5 **East Blatchington** E Susx
151 J3 **East Boldon** S Tyne
16 D3 **East Boldre** Hants
91 L2 **East Bradenham** Norfk
25 M2 **East Brent** Somset
102 B4 **East Bridgford** Notts
23 L5 **East Buckland** Devon
12 D5 **East Budleigh** Devon
116 D1 **East Butterwick** N Linc
176 E5 **East Calder** W Loth
92 E3 **East Carleton** Norfk

123 J2 **East Carlton** Leeds
88 B5 **East Carlton** Nhants
14 E5 **East Chaldon (Chaldon Herring)** Dorset
41 G3 **East Challow** Oxon
7 H7 **East Charleton** Devon
14 A2 **East Chelborough** Dorset
19 K3 **East Chiltington** E Susx
26 C8 **East Chinnock** Somset
28 C2 **East Chisenbury** Wilts
31 H2 **East Clandon** Surrey
58 C3 **East Claydon** Bucks
26 D8 **East Coker** Somset
25 J5 **East Combe** Somset
26 E3 **East Compton** Somset
7 J5 **East Cornworthy** Devon
125 G3 **East Cottingwith** E R Yk
16 F4 **East Cowes** IOW
125 G6 **East Cowick** E R Yk
141 H6 **East Cowton** N York
27 G3 **East Cranmore** Somset
15 H6 **East Creech** Dorset
20 B6 **East Dean** E Susx
54 F4 **East Dean** Gloucs
28 F6 **East Dean** Hants
18 B3 **East Dean** W Susx
23 J3 **East Down** Devon
116 C6 **East Drayton** Notts
45 G5 **East Dulwich** Gt Lon
38 E7 **East Dundry** N Som
126 C5 **East Ella** C KuH
41 H7 **East End** Hants
16 D3 **East End** Hants
33 L6 **East End** Kent
57 H5 **East End** Oxon
26 F3 **East End** Somset
28 D2 **East Everleigh** Wilts
33 J3 **East Farleigh** Kent
87 K6 **East Farndon** Nhants
116 D2 **East Ferry** Lincs
178 C3 **East Fortune** E Loth
41 G5 **East Garston** W Berk
87 J2 **East Goscote** Leics
40 E7 **East Grafton** Wilts
28 E5 **East Grimstead** Wilts
32 D5 **East Grinstead** W Susx
21 J2 **East Guldeford** E Susx
73 J2 **East Haddon** Nhants
41 K3 **East Hagbourne** Oxon
126 E6 **East Halton** N Linc
45 H4 **East Ham** Gt Lon
41 H2 **East Hanney** Oxon
61 J7 **East Hanningfield** Essex
124 C6 **East Hardwick** Wakefd
92 B6 **East Harling** Norfk
141 K7 **East Harlsey** N York
28 C5 **East Harnham** Wilts
26 E1 **East Harptree** BaNES
141 K4 **East Hartburn** S on T
30 D7 **East Harting** W Susx
27 L5 **East Hatch** Wilts
75 K4 **East Hatley** Cambs
132 B2 **East Hauxwell** N York
187 J1 **East Haven** Angus
103 K4 **East Heckington** Lincs
150 E6 **East Hedleyhope** Dur
227 H5 **East Helmsdale** Highld
41 J3 **East Hendred** Oxon
134 E4 **East Heslerton** N York
20 B3 **East Hoathly** E Susx
15 G5 **East Holme** Dorset
26 E3 **East Horrington** Somset
31 H2 **East Horsley** Surrey
15 K4 **East Howe** Bmouth
25 M3 **East Huntspill** Somset
41 J4 **East Ilsley** W Berk
118 E8 **East Keal** Lincs
40 C6 **East Kennett** Wilts
124 B2 **East Keswick** Leeds
175 H7 **East Kilbride** S Lans
118 D8 **East Kirkby** Lincs
14 F5 **East Knighton** Dorset
27 K5 **East Knoyle** Wilts
26 B7 **East Lambrook** Somset
35 J5 **East Langdon** Kent
87 K5 **East Langton** Leics
191 L5 **East Laroch** Highld
18 B4 **East Lavant** W Susx
18 C3 **East Lavington** W Susx
140 E5 **East Layton** N York
101 K7 **East Leake** Notts
11 G4 **East Leigh** Devon
7 H4 **East Leigh** Devon
105 K8 **East Lexham** Norfk
178 D3 **East Linton** E Loth
41 H3 **East Lockinge** Oxon
116 C2 **East Lound** N Linc
15 G6 **East Lulworth** Dorset
134 E5 **East Lutton** N York
26 E5 **East Lydford** Somset
33 J2 **East Malling** Kent
30 D8 **East Marden** W Susx
116 C6 **East Markham** Notts
28 B7 **East Martin** Hants
122 D1 **East Marton** N York
30 B6 **East Meon** Hants
62 C5 **East Mersea** Essex
43 J6 **East Molesey** Surrey
15 G4 **East Morden** Dorset
123 G3 **East Morton** Brad
154 F3 **East Morton** D & G
133 L4 **East Ness** N York
87 L4 **East Norton** Leics
7 J2 **East Ogwell** Devon
27 J7 **East Orchard** Dorset
33 H4 **East Peckham** Kent
49 G6 **East Pennar** Pembks
26 E4 **East Pennard** Somset
75 G2 **East Perry** Cambs
7 H7 **East Portlemouth** Devon
7 H8 **East Prawle** Devon
18 E5 **East Preston** W Susx
14 D1 **East Pulham** Dorset
9 K2 **East Putford** Devon
25 H3 **East Quantoxhead** Somset
151 H5 **East Rainton** Sundld
118 C2 **East Ravendale** NE Lin
105 L7 **East Raynham** Norfk
124 B2 **East Rigton** Leeds
141 K6 **East Rounton** N York
105 K6 **East Rudham** Norfk
106 E4 **East Runton** Norfk
107 H6 **East Ruston** Norfk
178 B5 **East Saltoun** E Loth
44 D5 **East Sheen** Gt Lon
41 H5 **East Shefford** W Berk
116 C3 **East Stockwith** Lincs
15 G5 **East Stoke** Dorset
102 C3 **East Stoke** Notts
27 J6 **East Stour** Dorset
35 H3 **East Stourmouth** Kent
23 K6 **East Stowford** Devon
29 K4 **East Stratton** Hants
35 J5 **East Studdal** Kent
5 J3 **East Taphouse** Cnwll
158 F3 **East Thirston** Nthumb
46 B5 **East Tilbury** Thurr
30 B5 **East Tisted** Hants
117 J5 **East Torrington** Lincs
92 C2 **East Tuddenham** Norfk
28 F5 **East Tytherley** Hants
39 L5 **East Tytherton** Wilts
11 J4 **East Village** Devon
83 K5 **East Wall** Shrops
91 G1 **East Walton** Norfk
26 D2 **East Water** Somset
10 F6 **East Week** Devon
28 F7 **East Wellow** Hants
186 E7 **East Wemyss** Fife
176 C5 **East Whitburn** W Loth
45 J5 **East Wickham** Gt Lon
49 J6 **East Williamston** Pembks
91 G1 **East Winch** Norfk
28 E5 **East Winterslow** Wilts
17 L3 **East Wittering** W Susx
131 L3 **East Witton** N York
158 A5 **East Woodburn** Nthumb
41 H7 **East Woodhay** Hants
30 C4 **East Worldham** Hants
91 K5 **East Wretham** Norfk
9 H2 **East Youlstone** Devon
23 G6 **East-the-Water** Devon
141 H4 **Eastbourne** Darltn
20 C5 **Eastbourne** E Susx
79 J2 **Eastbridge** Suffk
122 F2 **Eastburn** Brad
43 J2 **Eastbury** Herts
41 G5 **Eastbury** W Berk
131 J8 **Eastby** N York
47 G5 **Eastchurch** Kent
55 K6 **Eastcombe** Gloucs
43 J3 **Eastcote** Gt Lon
73 K4 **Eastcote** Nhants
85 L7 **Eastcote** Solhll
28 A1 **Eastcott** Wilts
39 L2 **Eastcourt** Wilts
40 E7 **Eastcourt** Wilts
46 F2 **Eastend** Essex
165 J2 **Eastend** S Lans
205 G6 **Easter Balmoral** Abers
38 E4 **Easter Compton** S Glos
213 H4 **Easter Dalziel** Highld
177 H5 **Easter Howgate** Mdloth
212 E4 **Easter Kinkell** Highld
212 E5 **Easter Moniack** Highld
206 F4 **Easter Ord** Abers
187 J6 **Easter Pitkierie** Fife
235 c6 **Easter Skeld** Shet
168 A3 **Easter Softlaw** Border
213 G4 **Easter Suddie** Highld
18 C5 **Eastergate** W Susx
175 J5 **Easterhouse** C Glas
86 C7 **Eastern Green** Covtry
28 A1 **Easterton** Wilts
176 B5 **Eastfield** N Lans
135 G3 **Eastfield** N York
150 B7 **Eastgate** Dur
106 D7 **Eastgate** Norfk
42 E6 **Easthampstead** Br For
69 H2 **Easthampton** Herefs
83 L4 **Easthope** Shrops
61 L4 **Easthorpe** Essex
11 H3 **Eastington** Devon
56 C5 **Eastington** Gloucs
55 H6 **Eastington** Gloucs
154 E7 **Eastlands** D & G
56 D6 **Eastleach Martin** Gloucs
56 D6 **Eastleach Turville** Gloucs
23 H5 **Eastleigh** Devon
29 J7 **Eastleigh** Hants
34 C4 **Eastling** Kent
17 J3 **Eastney** C Port
70 D6 **Eastnor** Herefs
125 J7 **Eastoft** N Linc
75 G1 **Easton** Cambs
148 B3 **Easton** Cumb
11 G6 **Easton** Devon
14 D7 **Easton** Dorset
29 K5 **Easton** Hants
102 F6 **Easton** Lincs
92 D2 **Easton** Norfk
26 D3 **Easton** Somset
79 G3 **Easton** Suffk
39 K6 **Easton** Wilts
39 K3 **Easton Grey** Wilts
74 C3 **Easton Maudit** Nhants
88 E3 **Easton on the Hill** Nhants
40 D7 **Easton Royal** Wilts
38 D5 **Easton-in-Gordano** N Som
89 K4 **Eastrea** Cambs
147 M2 **Eastriggs** D & G
125 J4 **Eastrington** E R Yk
40 D2 **Eastrop** Swindn
35 J4 **Eastry** Kent
38 E5 **Eastville** Bristl
104 C2 **Eastville** Lincs
102 C6 **Eastwell** Leics
60 C5 **Eastwick** Herts
122 E5 **Eastwood** Calder
101 J3 **Eastwood** Notts
46 D3 **Eastwood** Sthend
72 E2 **Eathorpe** Warwks
112 E8 **Eaton** Ches
113 K7 **Eaton** Ches
102 D6 **Eaton** Leics
92 E3 **Eaton** Norfk
116 B6 **Eaton** Notts
57 H7 **Eaton** Oxon
83 K5 **Eaton** Shrops
58 F4 **Eaton Bray** Beds
83 L3 **Eaton Constantine** Shrops
58 F4 **Eaton Green** Beds
56 E7 **Eaton Hastings** Oxon
83 K3 **Eaton Mascott** Shrops
75 H3 **Eaton Socon** Cambs
98 F7 **Eaton upon Tern** Shrops
134 D3 **Ebberston** N York
27 M6 **Ebbesborne Wake** Wilts
53 J6 **Ebbw Vale** Blae G
150 D4 **Ebchester** Dur
12 C5 **Ebford** Devon
55 J6 **Ebley** Gloucs
98 C3 **Ebnal** Ches
71 L6 **Ebrington** Gloucs
41 J8 **Ecchinswell** Hants
178 F5 **Ecclaw** Border
155 L7 **Ecclefechan** D & G
168 A2 **Eccles** Border
46 B7 **Eccles** Kent

Eccles - Eskdale Green

113 H2 **Eccles** Salfd
92 B5 **Eccles Road** Norfk
114 F5 **Ecclesall** Sheff
115 G3 **Ecclesfield** Sheff
99 J6 **Eccleshall** Staffs
123 H4 **Eccleshill** Brad
176 E4 **Ecclesmachan** W Loth
112 B8 **Eccleston** Ches
121 G6 **Eccleston** Lancs
112 C3 **Eccleston** St Hel
206 E4 **Echt** Abers
167 L4 **Eckford** Border
115 H5 **Eckington** Derbys
71 G6 **Eckington** Worcs
74 B2 **Ecton** Nhants
114 C4 **Edale** Derbys
234 d4 **Eday Airport** Ork
19 H4 **Edburton** W Susx
222 F4 **Edderton** Highld
177 H8 **Eddleston** Border
175 J7 **Eddlewood** S Lans
45 G6 **Eden Park** Gt Lon
32 D4 **Edenbridge** Kent
122 B6 **Edenfield** Lancs
138 E2 **Edenhall** Cumb
103 H7 **Edenham** Lincs
114 E7 **Edensor** Derbys
183 K8 **Edentaggart** Ag & B
115 L1 **Edenthorpe** Donc
94 E5 **Edern** Gwynd
85 J6 **Edgbaston** Birm
58 B4 **Edgcott** Bucks
24 D4 **Edgcott** Somset
55 J6 **Edge** Gloucs
83 H2 **Edge** Shrops
106 C5 **Edgefield** Norfk
106 D5 **Edgefield Green** Norfk
123 H6 **Edgerton** Kirk
55 L6 **Edgeworth** Gloucs
99 G8 **Edgmond** Wrekin
83 H6 **Edgton** Shrops
44 D2 **Edgware** Gt Lon
121 L6 **Edgworth** Bl w D
208 E4 **Edinbane** Highld
177 H4 **Edinburgh** C Edin
176 F4 **Edinburgh Airport** C Edin
177 H4 **Edinburgh Castle** C Edin
177 G4 **Edinburgh Zoo** C Edin
86 B2 **Edingale** Staffs
146 E3 **Edingham** D & G
102 A2 **Edingley** Notts
107 G6 **Edingthorpe** Norfk
107 G6 **Edingthorpe Green** Norfk
179 J7 **Edington** Border
158 E5 **Edington** Nthumb
26 B4 **Edington** Somset
27 L2 **Edington** Wilts
26 B3 **Edington Burtle** Somset
26 A2 **Edingworth** Somset
88 D3 **Edith Weston** Rutlnd
25 M2 **Edithmead** Somset
58 F4 **Edlesborough** Bucks
169 G7 **Edlingham** Nthumb
118 C7 **Edlington** Lincs
15 K1 **Edmondsham** Dorset
151 G5 **Edmondsley** Dur
102 E8 **Edmondthorpe** Leics
45 G2 **Edmonton** Gt Lon
150 C5 **Edmundbyers** Dur
167 L2 **Ednam** Border
194 D6 **Edradynate** P & K
179 H7 **Edrom** Border
98 D6 **Edstaston** Shrops
71 L3 **Edstone** Warwks
101 L5 **Edwalton** Notts
115 L7 **Edwinstowe** Notts
75 J6 **Edworth** Beds
70 B3 **Edwyn Ralph** Herefs
196 F3 **Edzell** Angus
197 G3 **Edzell Woods** Angus
37 G4 **Efail Isaf** Rhondd
36 B2 **Efail-fach** Neath
94 F5 **Efailnewydd** Gwynd
49 K3 **Efailwen** Carmth
97 H2 **Efenechtyd** Denbgs
156 B4 **Effgill** D & G
31 J2 **Effingham** Surrey
11 K5 **Efford** Devon
121 K7 **Egerton** Bolton
34 B5 **Egerton** Kent
6 D4 **Eggbuckland** C Plym
11 G3 **Eggesford** Devon
58 F3 **Eggington** Beds
100 E6 **Egginton** Derbys
141 K4 **Egglescliffe** S on T
140 C3 **Eggleston** Dur
43 G6 **Egham** Surrey
88 C3 **Egleton** Rutlnd
169 G5 **Eglingham** Nthumb
4 F2 **Egloshayle** Cnwll
9 H7 **Egloskerry** Cnwll
98 C4 **Eglwys Cross** Wrexhm
109 M7 **Eglwysbach** Conwy
65 G6 **Eglwyswrw** Pembks
116 B7 **Egmanton** Notts
136 D5 **Egremont** Cumb
111 K3 **Egremont** Wirral
143 G6 **Egton** N York
143 G6 **Egton Bridge** N York
61 M3 **Eight Ash Green** Essex
200 C2 **Eilanreach** Highld
67 K2 **Elan Village** Powys
38 E3 **Elberton** S Glos
6 D5 **Elburton** C Plym
40 C4 **Elcombe** Swindn
55 H2 **Eldersfield** Worcs
174 E5 **Elderslie** Rens
141 G2 **Eldon** Dur
206 F7 **Elfhill** Abers
85 L2 **Elford** Staffs
214 F2 **Elgin** Moray
199 H3 **Elgol** Highld
35 G6 **Elham** Kent
187 H7 **Elie** Fife
108 D4 **Elim** IOA
29 G8 **Eling** Hants
116 B6 **Elkesley** Notts
55 L5 **Elkstone** Gloucs
216 C3 **Ella** Abers
7 L3 **Ellacombe** Torbay
181 L4 **Ellanbeich** Ag & B
123 G6 **Elland** Calder
172 C3 **Ellary** Ag & B
100 C4 **Ellastone** Staffs
129 K7 **Ellel** Lancs
178 F6 **Ellemford** Border
31 H4 **Ellen's Green** Surrey
99 J7 **Ellenhall** Staffs
141 K7 **Ellerbeck** N York
143 G4 **Ellerby** N York
98 F7 **Ellerdine Heath** Wrekin
191 K6 **Elleric** Ag & B
125 L5 **Ellerker** E R Yk
125 G3 **Ellerton** E R Yk
141 G7 **Ellerton** N York
58 D6 **Ellesborough** Bucks
98 B5 **Ellesmere** Shrops
111 L6 **Ellesmere Port** Ches
93 H5 **Ellingham** Norfk
169 H4 **Ellingham** Nthumb
132 B3 **Ellingstring** N York
75 H1 **Ellington** Cambs
159 G4 **Ellington** Nthumb
27 J3 **Elliots Green** Somset
29 M3 **Ellisfield** Hants
209 H2 **Ellishader** Highld
86 E2 **Ellistown** Leics
217 H7 **Ellon** Abers
148 D7 **Ellonby** Cumb
126 B5 **Elloughton** E R Yk
54 E6 **Ellwood** Gloucs
90 C3 **Elm** Cambs
45 K3 **Elm Park** Gt Lon
70 F2 **Elmbridge** Worcs
76 C6 **Elmdon** Essex
85 L6 **Elmdon** Solhll
45 G6 **Elmers End** Gt Lon
86 F4 **Elmesthorpe** Leics
85 K2 **Elmhurst** Staffs
71 H6 **Elmley Castle** Worcs
70 F1 **Elmley Lovett** Worcs
55 H5 **Elmore** Gloucs
55 H5 **Elmore Back** Gloucs
78 C5 **Elmsett** Suffk
62 C3 **Elmstead Market** Essex
34 F5 **Elmsted Court** Kent
35 H3 **Elmstone** Kent
55 K3 **Elmstone Hardwicke** Gloucs
134 F7 **Elmswell** E R Yk
78 B2 **Elmswell** Suffk
115 J6 **Elmton** Derbys
224 F6 **Elphin** Highld
177 K4 **Elphinstone** E Loth
206 F4 **Elrick** Abers
145 G5 **Elrig** D & G
149 L3 **Elrington** Nthumb
158 B4 **Elsdon** Nthumb
60 E3 **Elsenham** Essex
57 K6 **Elsfield** Oxon
126 C7 **Elsham** N Linc
207 G6 **Elsick House** Abers
92 C1 **Elsing** Norfk
122 D2 **Elslack** N York
17 H3 **Elson** Hants
165 K2 **Elsrickle** S Lans
30 E3 **Elstead** Surrey
30 D7 **Elsted** W Susx
103 H7 **Elsthorpe** Lincs
102 C3 **Elston** Notts
11 G2 **Elstone** Devon
74 F5 **Elstow** Beds
44 D2 **Elstree** Herts
126 F4 **Elstronwick** E R Yk
120 F3 **Elswick** Lancs
151 G3 **Elswick** N u Ty
75 K2 **Elsworth** Cambs
137 K6 **Elterwater** Cumb
45 H5 **Eltham** Gt Lon
75 J3 **Eltisley** Cambs
88 F5 **Elton** Cambs
112 C6 **Elton** Ches
100 E1 **Elton** Derbys
69 J1 **Elton** Herefs
102 C5 **Elton** Notts
141 J4 **Elton** S on T
150 D3 **Eltringham** Nthumb
165 J6 **Elvanfoot** S Lans
101 H6 **Elvaston** Derbys
91 J7 **Elveden** Suffk
30 D1 **Elvetham Heath** Hants
178 A4 **Elvingston** E Loth
35 H5 **Elvington** Kent
125 G2 **Elvington** York
141 K2 **Elwick** Hartpl
99 H1 **Elworth** Ches
25 G4 **Elworthy** Somset
90 D7 **Ely** Cambs
37 H5 **Ely** Cardif
74 C5 **Emberton** M Keyn
169 J5 **Embleton** Nthumb
223 H3 **Embo** Highld
223 H3 **Embo Street** Highld
26 E2 **Emborough** Somset
131 J8 **Embsay** N York
16 C2 **Emery Down** Hants
123 K7 **Emley** Kirk
58 C7 **Emmington** Oxon
90 C3 **Emneth** Cambs
90 D3 **Emneth Hungate** Norfk
88 D2 **Empingham** Rutlnd
30 C5 **Empshott** Hants
17 L2 **Emsworth** Hants
41 H7 **Enborne** W Berk
41 H7 **Enborne Row** W Berk
87 G4 **Enderby** Leics
129 L3 **Endmoor** Cumb
99 L2 **Endon** Staffs
99 L2 **Endon Bank** Staffs
60 B7 **Enfield** Gt Lon
60 B7 **Enfield Lock** Gt Lon
60 B7 **Enfield Wash** Gt Lon
28 C2 **Enford** Wilts
39 G4 **Engine Common** S Glos
41 L6 **Englefield** W Berk
43 G6 **Englefield Green** Surrey
54 E5 **English Bicknor** Gloucs
98 C6 **English Frankton** Shrops
39 G7 **Englishcombe** BaNES
29 G2 **Enham-Alamein** Hants
25 K4 **Enmore** Somset
27 J6 **Enmore Green** Dorset
136 E4 **Ennerdale Bridge** Cumb
195 G4 **Enochdhu** P & K
189 J6 **Ensay** Ag & B
15 K3 **Ensbury** Bmouth
83 H1 **Ensdon** Shrops
23 J6 **Ensis** Devon
57 G3 **Enstone** Oxon
154 E2 **Enterkinfoot** D & G
84 E6 **Enville** Staffs
233 b9 **Eolaigearraidh** W Isls
55 H5 **Epney** Gloucs
101 M3 **Epperstone** Notts
60 D7 **Epping** Essex
60 C6 **Epping Green** Essex
60 C6 **Epping Upland** Essex
140 F5 **Eppleby** N York
44 E7 **Epsom** Surrey
72 D6 **Epwell** Oxon
116 C2 **Epworth** N Linc
97 M4 **Erbistock** Wrexhm
85 K5 **Erdington** Birm
32 F6 **Eridge Green** E Susx
172 E4 **Erines** Ag & B
191 H7 **Eriska** Ag & B
91 G7 **Eriswell** Suffk
45 K4 **Erith** Gt Lon
27 L2 **Erlestoke** Wilts
6 F5 **Ermington** Devon
106 E6 **Erpingham** Norfk
202 E2 **Errogie** Highld
186 D3 **Errol** P & K
174 E4 **Erskine** Rens
144 B2 **Ervie** D & G
78 F7 **Erwarton** Suffk
68 C6 **Erwood** Powys
141 H5 **Eryholme** N York
97 J2 **Eryrys** Denbgs
140 F2 **Escomb** Dur
124 F2 **Escrick** York
81 G3 **Esgairgeiliog** Powys
150 F6 **Esh** Dur
150 F6 **Esh Winning** Dur
43 J7 **Esher** Surrey
158 F3 **Eshott** Nthumb
212 C6 **Eskadale** Highld
177 J5 **Eskbank** Mdloth
137 G6 **Eskdale Green** Cumb

156 A3 **Eskdalemuir** D & G
120 E3 **Esprick** Lancs
88 F2 **Essendine** Rutlnd
59 L6 **Essendon** Herts
213 G6 **Essich** Highld
85 G3 **Essington** Staffs
217 H7 **Esslemont** Abers
142 C4 **Eston** R & Cl
168 D2 **Etal** Nthumb
40 B7 **Etchilhampton** Wilts
33 J7 **Etchingham** E Susx
34 F6 **Etchinghill** Kent
100 B8 **Etchinghill** Staffs
42 F5 **Eton** W & M
42 F5 **Eton Wick** W & M
99 K3 **Etruria** C Stke
203 G6 **Etteridge** Highld
139 K2 **Ettersgill** Dur
99 G1 **Ettiley Heath** Ches
85 G4 **Ettingshall** Wolves
72 C5 **Ettington** Warwks
89 G3 **Etton** C Pete
126 B2 **Etton** E R Yk
166 D6 **Ettrick** Border
166 F4 **Ettrickbridge** Border
166 C6 **Ettrickhill** Border
100 F6 **Etwall** Derbys
91 K7 **Euston** Suffk
121 H6 **Euxton** Lancs
212 F2 **Evanton** Highld
103 H3 **Evedon** Lincs
223 G4 **Evelix** Highld
68 F3 **Evenjobb** Powys
73 H7 **Evenley** Oxon
56 E3 **Evenlode** Gloucs
140 E3 **Evenwood** Dur
26 F4 **Evercreech** Somset
125 J3 **Everingham** E R Yk
28 D2 **Everleigh** Wilts
59 G2 **Eversholt** Beds
14 B2 **Evershot** Dorset
42 C7 **Eversley** Hants
42 C7 **Eversley Cross** Hants
125 L4 **Everthorpe** E R Yk
75 H4 **Everton** Beds
16 C4 **Everton** Hants
111 K3 **Everton** Lpool
116 B4 **Everton** Notts
156 C6 **Evertown** D & G
70 C5 **Evesbatch** Herefs
71 J5 **Evesham** Worcs
87 J3 **Evington** C Leic
114 F3 **Ewden Village** Sheff
44 E7 **Ewell** Surrey
35 H6 **Ewell Minnis** Kent
41 M3 **Ewelme** Oxon
40 A2 **Ewen** Gloucs
36 D5 **Ewenny** V Glam
103 J3 **Ewerby** Lincs
158 D4 **Ewesley** Nthumb
31 H4 **Ewhurst** Surrey
20 F2 **Ewhurst Green** E Susx
31 H4 **Ewhurst Green** Surrey
111 J7 **Ewloe** Flints
10 C6 **Eworthy** Devon
30 D2 **Ewshot** Hants
54 B3 **Ewyas Harold** Herefs
10 E4 **Exbourne** Devon
16 E3 **Exbury** Hants
24 E6 **Exebridge** Somset
132 D3 **Exelby** N York
11 L6 **Exeter** Devon
12 C4 **Exeter Airport** Devon
24 D4 **Exford** Somset
83 J3 **Exfordsgreen** Shrops
71 K4 **Exhall** Warwks
86 D6 **Exhall** Warwks
42 A4 **Exlade Street** Oxon
12 B5 **Exminster** Devon
24 D4 **Exmoor National Park**
12 C6 **Exmouth** Devon
76 E2 **Exning** Suffk
35 G5 **Exted** Kent
12 C5 **Exton** Devon
29 L7 **Exton** Hants
88 D2 **Exton** Rutlnd
24 E5 **Exton** Somset
11 K6 **Exwick** Devon
114 E6 **Eyam** Derbys
73 G4 **Eydon** Nhants
89 J3 **Eye** C Pete
69 J2 **Eye** Herefs
92 D8 **Eye** Suffk
179 K5 **Eyemouth** Border
75 J5 **Eyeworth** Beds
33 L3 **Eyhorne Street** Kent
79 G4 **Eyke** Suffk
75 H3 **Eynesbury** Cambs
45 K6 **Eynsford** Kent
57 H6 **Eynsham** Oxon
13 L4 **Eype** Dorset
208 F4 **Eyre** Highld
35 H5 **Eythorne** Kent
69 J3 **Eyton** Herefs
98 C7 **Eyton** Shrops
83 G6 **Eyton** Shrops
83 L3 **Eyton on Severn** Shrops
84 B1 **Eyton upon the Weald Moors** Wrekin

F

41 H8 **Faccombe** Hants
141 L6 **Faceby** N York
82 B1 **Fachwen** Powys
98 E3 **Faddiley** Ches
133 K2 **Fadmoor** N York
51 K5 **Faerdre** Swans
174 F4 **Faifley** W Duns
38 D6 **Failand** N Som
163 L4 **Failford** S Ayrs
113 K2 **Failsworth** Oldham
29 J7 **Fair Oak** Hants
42 A7 **Fair Oak Green** Hants
80 E2 **Fairbourne** Gwynd
124 D5 **Fairburn** N York
114 B6 **Fairfield** Derbys
85 G7 **Fairfield** Worcs
56 D7 **Fairford** Gloucs
146 F4 **Fairgirth** D & G
120 D5 **Fairhaven** Lancs
173 L7 **Fairlie** N Ayrs
21 G4 **Fairlight** E Susx
12 E3 **Fairmile** Devon
43 J7 **Fairmile** Surrey
167 G3 **Fairnilee** Border
99 H6 **Fairoak** Staffs
45 L7 **Fairseat** Kent
61 J5 **Fairstead** Essex
32 E7 **Fairwarp** E Susx
37 H5 **Fairwater** Cardif
22 F6 **Fairy Cross** Devon
105 L6 **Fakenham** Norfk
91 K7 **Fakenham Magna** Suffk
177 L6 **Fala** Mdloth
177 L6 **Fala Dam** Mdloth
177 L7 **Falahill** Border
117 H5 **Faldingworth** Lincs
236 e7 **Faldouet** Jersey
39 G2 **Falfield** S Glos
79 G6 **Falkenham** Suffk
176 B3 **Falkirk** Falk
186 D6 **Falkland** Fife
185 H8 **Fallin** Stirlg
169 J5 **Falloden** Nthumb
113 J3 **Fallowfield** Manch
150 B2 **Fallowfield** Nthumb
182 E5 **Falls of Blarghour** Ag & B
19 K4 **Falmer** E Susx
3 K5 **Falmouth** Cnwll
156 D2 **Falnash** Border
134 F2 **Falsgrave** N York
157 J5 **Falstone** Nthumb
228 B5 **Fanagmore** Highld
59 G3 **Fancott** Beds
212 D5 **Fanellan** Highld
142 C7 **Fangdale Beck** N York
134 B8 **Fangfoss** E R Yk
189 K7 **Fanmore** Ag & B
211 K2 **Fannich Lodge** Highld
167 J2 **Fans** Border
74 C7 **Far Bletchley** M Keyn
73 L3 **Far Cotton** Nhants
137 J7 **Far End** Cumb
55 H7 **Far Green** Gloucs
112 D2 **Far Moor** Wigan
55 L7 **Far Oakridge** Gloucs
137 K7 **Far Sawrey** Cumb
118 C6 **Far Thorpe** Lincs
89 H5 **Farcet** Cambs
17 H2 **Fareham** Hants
85 J2 **Farewell** Staffs
40 F2 **Faringdon** Oxon
121 H5 **Farington** Lancs
185 L1 **Farkhill** P & K
148 F3 **Farlam** Cumb
38 D6 **Farleigh** N Som
32 C2 **Farleigh** Surrey
39 J8 **Farleigh Hungerford** Somset
29 L3 **Farleigh Wallop** Hants
119 G6 **Farlesthorpe** Lincs
129 L4 **Farleton** Cumb
130 B6 **Farleton** Lancs
100 B4 **Farley** Staffs
28 E5 **Farley** Wilts
77 G4 **Farley Green** Suffk
31 H3 **Farley Green** Surrey
42 C7 **Farley Hill** Wokham
55 H5 **Farleys End** Gloucs
17 J2 **Farlington** C Port
133 J6 **Farlington** N York
84 B7 **Farlow** Shrops
38 F7 **Farmborough** BaNES
56 B3 **Farmcote** Gloucs
66 E5 **Farmers** Carmth
56 C5 **Farmington** Gloucs
57 J6 **Farmoor** Oxon
215 L4 **Farmtown** Moray
215 J3 **Farnachty** Moray
45 H7 **Farnborough** Gt Lon
30 E2 **Farnborough** Hants
41 H4 **Farnborough** W Berk
72 E5 **Farnborough** Warwks
30 E1 **Farnborough Park** Hants
30 E1 **Farnborough Street** Hants
31 G3 **Farncombe** Surrey
74 D2 **Farndish** Beds
98 B2 **Farndon** Ches
102 C3 **Farndon** Notts
169 K2 **Farne Islands** Nthumb
197 G5 **Farnell** Angus
27 L7 **Farnham** Dorset
60 D3 **Farnham** Essex
132 E7 **Farnham** N York
79 H3 **Farnham** Suffk
30 D3 **Farnham** Surrey
42 F4 **Farnham Common** Bucks
42 F4 **Farnham Royal** Bucks
45 K6 **Farningham** Kent
123 J2 **Farnley** Leeds
123 K4 **Farnley** Leeds
123 H7 **Farnley Tyas** Kirk
101 M2 **Farnsfield** Notts
113 G1 **Farnworth** Bolton
112 D4 **Farnworth** Halton
229 L3 **Farr** Highld
213 G7 **Farr** Highld
203 K5 **Farr** Highld
202 E2 **Farraline** Highld
12 C4 **Farringdon** Devon
26 F1 **Farrington Gurney** BaNES
73 G6 **Farthinghoe** Nhants
73 H4 **Farthingstone** Nhants
123 H6 **Fartown** Kirk
123 J4 **Fartown** Leeds
12 F4 **Farway Street** Devon
191 K6 **Fasnacloich** Ag & B
211 L8 **Fasnakyle** Highld
191 K2 **Fassfern** Highld
151 H4 **Fatfield** Sundld
176 C6 **Fauldhouse** W Loth
61 J5 **Faulkbourne** Essex
27 H1 **Faulkland** Somset
98 E6 **Fauls** Shrops
34 D3 **Faversham** Kent
132 F5 **Fawdington** N York
151 G2 **Fawdon** N u Ty
168 F6 **Fawdon** Nthumb
45 L6 **Fawkham Green** Kent
57 G4 **Fawler** Oxon
42 C3 **Fawley** Bucks
16 F2 **Fawley** Hants
41 H4 **Fawley** W Berk
125 K5 **Faxfleet** E R Yk
31 K5 **Faygate** W Susx
111 K3 **Fazakerley** Lpool
85 L3 **Fazeley** Staffs
132 B4 **Fearby** N York
223 H5 **Fearn** Highld
194 B7 **Fearnan** P & K
210 B3 **Fearnbeg** Highld
209 L3 **Fearnmore** Highld
172 F3 **Fearnoch** Ag & B
85 G3 **Featherstone** Staffs
124 C6 **Featherstone** Wakefd
71 H3 **Feckenham** Worcs
61 L4 **Feering** Essex
140 C7 **Feetham** N York
32 C5 **Felbridge** Surrey
106 E5 **Felbrigg** Norfk
32 C5 **Felcourt** Surrey
51 G2 **Felin gwm Isaf** Carmth
51 G1 **Felin gwm Uchaf** Carmth
51 G2 **Felindre** Carmth
65 K6 **Felindre** Carmth
82 D7 **Felindre** Powys
51 J5 **Felindre** Swans
64 F6 **Felindre Farchog** Pembks
133 G3 **Felixkirk** N York
79 G7 **Felixstowe** Suffk
151 G3 **Felling** Gatesd
74 E3 **Felmersham** Beds
106 F6 **Felmingham** Norfk
18 C5 **Felpham** W Susx
77 L3 **Felsham** Suffk
61 G4 **Felsted** Essex
43 J5 **Feltham** Gt Lon
43 H6 **Felthamhill** Gt Lon
106 E8 **Felthorpe** Norfk
69 L5 **Felton** Herefs
38 D7 **Felton** N Som
158 F3 **Felton** Nthumb
98 B8 **Felton Butler** Shrops
91 G5 **Feltwell** Norfk
76 C3 **Fen Ditton** Cambs

75 L2 **Fen Drayton** Cambs
92 B4 **Fen Street** Norfk
122 C3 **Fence** Lancs
115 H4 **Fence** Rothm
132 D2 **Fencote** N York
57 L5 **Fencott** Oxon
104 D1 **Fendike Corner** Lincs
121 J5 **Feniscowles** Bl w D
12 E3 **Feniton** Devon
84 D6 **Fenn Green** Shrops
46 D5 **Fenn Street** Medway
100 D3 **Fenny Bentley** Derbys
12 E3 **Fenny Bridges** Devon
72 E4 **Fenny Compton** Warwks
86 D4 **Fenny Drayton** Leics
75 K2 **Fenstanton** Cambs
99 K4 **Fenton** C Stke
89 K7 **Fenton** Cambs
148 E4 **Fenton** Cumb
116 D6 **Fenton** Lincs
102 E3 **Fenton** Lincs
116 C5 **Fenton** Notts
168 E3 **Fenton** Nthumb
178 B3 **Fenton Barns** E Loth
124 F7 **Fenwick** Donc
163 L2 **Fenwick** E Ayrs
169 G2 **Fenwick** Nthumb
158 D7 **Fenwick** Nthumb
4 C7 **Feock** Cnwll
171 H4 **Feolin Ferry** Ag & B
163 J2 **Fergushill** N Ayrs
208 B4 **Feriniquarrie** Highld
236 d3 **Fermain Bay** Guern
196 D4 **Fern** Angus
36 F2 **Ferndale** Rhondd
15 K3 **Ferndown** Dorset
214 B5 **Ferness** Moray
40 F3 **Fernham** Oxon
70 F3 **Fernhill Heath** Worcs
30 E5 **Fernhurst** W Susx
186 E4 **Fernie** Fife
175 K7 **Ferniegair** S Lans
208 F7 **Fernilea** Highld
114 A5 **Fernilee** Derbys
132 E7 **Ferrensby** N York
199 K4 **Ferrindonald** Highld
18 F5 **Ferring** W Susx
223 G4 **Ferry Point** Highld
197 H5 **Ferryden** Angus
141 H2 **Ferryhill** Dur
50 D4 **Ferryside** Carmth
223 G4 **Ferrytown** Highld
92 C6 **Fersfield** Norfk
192 F2 **Fersit** Highld
203 K4 **Feshiebridge** Highld
31 J1 **Fetcham** Surrey
217 J4 **Fetterangus** Abers
197 G2 **Fettercairn** Abers
132 B8 **Fewston** N York
67 G2 **Ffair Rhos** Cerdgn
51 J2 **Ffairfach** Carmth
96 A4 **Ffestiniog** Gwynd
95 L4 **Ffestiniog Railway** Gwynd
51 H5 **Fforest** Carmth
51 J6 **Fforest Fach** Swans
65 L5 **Ffostrasol** Cerdgn
97 L2 **Ffrith** Flints
111 G5 **Ffynnongroyw** Flints
225 K3 **Fiag Lodge** Highld
32 C2 **Fickleshole** Surrey
55 L2 **Fiddington** Gloucs
25 K4 **Fiddington** Somset
27 J8 **Fiddleford** Dorset
4 C5 **Fiddlers Green** Cnwll
100 A5 **Field** Staffs
129 J3 **Field Broughton** Cumb
106 B5 **Field Dalling** Norfk
86 F2 **Field Head** Leics
215 J4 **Fife Keith** Moray
27 H6 **Fifehead Magdalen** Dorset
14 E1 **Fifehead Neville** Dorset
14 E1 **Fifehead St Quintin** Dorset
56 E4 **Fifield** Oxon
42 E5 **Fifield** W & M
28 D3 **Figheldean** Wilts
93 K2 **Filby** Norfk
135 H4 **Filey** N York
74 C5 **Filgrave** M Keyn
56 E6 **Filkins** Oxon
23 L5 **Filleigh** Devon
11 H3 **Filleigh** Devon
116 F4 **Fillingham** Lincs
86 C6 **Fillongley** Warwks
38 E5 **Filton** S Glos
134 D7 **Fimber** E R Yk
196 D5 **Finavon** Angus
91 G3 **Fincham** Norfk
42 D7 **Finchampstead** Wokham
182 C6 **Fincharn** Ag & B
30 C8 **Finchdean** Hants
61 G2 **Finchingfield** Essex
44 F2 **Finchley** Gt Lon
100 F6 **Findern** Derbys
214 C2 **Findhorn** Moray
213 J8 **Findhorn Bridge** Highld
185 L4 **Findo Gask** P & K
215 K2 **Findochty** Moray
207 H6 **Findon** Abers
18 F4 **Findon** W Susx
212 F3 **Findon Mains** Highld
206 B4 **Findrack House** Abers
74 D1 **Finedon** Nhants
78 F1 **Fingal Street** Suffk
186 C4 **Fingask** P & K
42 C3 **Fingest** Bucks
132 B2 **Finghall** N York
164 E6 **Fingland** D & G
35 J4 **Finglesham** Kent
62 B4 **Fingringhoe** Essex
184 C1 **Finlarig** Stirlg
57 M2 **Finmere** Oxon
193 H5 **Finnart** P & K
78 C1 **Finningham** Suffk
116 A2 **Finningley** Donc
232 d5 **Finsbay** W Isls
71 H1 **Finstall** Worcs
129 H2 **Finsthwaite** Cumb
57 G5 **Finstock** Oxon
234 b6 **Finstown** Ork
216 E4 **Fintry** Abers
175 H2 **Fintry** Stirlg
206 B6 **Finzean** Abers
180 D3 **Fionnphort** Ag & B
232 d5 **Fionnsbhagh** W Isls
150 E7 **Fir Tree** Dur
130 C2 **Firbank** Cumb
115 K4 **Firbeck** Rothm
132 D3 **Firby** N York
134 B6 **Firby** N York
118 F8 **Firsby** Lincs
17 G4 **Fishbourne** IOW
18 A5 **Fishbourne** W Susx
18 A5 **Fishbourne Roman Palace** W Susx
141 J2 **Fishburn** Dur
185 J7 **Fishcross** Clacks
29 J7 **Fisher's Pond** Hants
216 C7 **Fisherford** Abers
177 K4 **Fisherrow** E Loth
213 H4 **Fisherton** Highld
163 H6 **Fisherton** S Ayrs
27 M4 **Fisherton de la Mere** Wilts
64 D6 **Fishguard** Pembks
125 G7 **Fishlake** Donc
190 D7 **Fishnish Pier** Ag & B
38 F5 **Fishponds** Bristl
104 B4 **Fishtoft** Lincs
104 A3 **Fishtoft Drove** Lincs
208 E7 **Fiskavaig** Highld
117 H6 **Fiskerton** Lincs
102 C3 **Fiskerton** Notts
28 D2 **Fittleton** Wilts
18 D2 **Fittleworth** W Susx
98 C8 **Fitz** Shrops
25 H5 **Fitzhead** Somset
124 C7 **Fitzwilliam** Wakefd
19 M2 **Five Ash Down** E Susx
32 F7 **Five Ashes** E Susx
33 H4 **Five Oak Green** Kent
236 d7 **Five Oaks** Jersey
31 H5 **Five Oaks** W Susx
26 A6 **Fivehead** Somset
9 G8 **Fivelanes** Cnwll
42 E3 **Flackwell Heath** Bucks
71 H5 **Fladbury** Worcs
235 c6 **Fladdabister** Shet
114 C7 **Flagg** Derbys
135 K5 **Flamborough** E R Yk
135 K5 **Flamborough Head** E R Yk
134 B4 **Flamingo Land Theme Park** N York
59 H5 **Flamstead** Herts
18 C5 **Flansham** W Susx
123 L6 **Flanshaw** Wakefd
131 H7 **Flasby** N York
114 A7 **Flash** Staffs
208 E4 **Flashader** Highld
59 G7 **Flaunden** Herts
102 C4 **Flawborough** Notts
133 G6 **Flawith** N York
38 D6 **Flax Bourton** N Som
132 F7 **Flaxby** N York
55 G5 **Flaxley** Gloucs
25 H4 **Flaxpool** Somset
133 K6 **Flaxton** N York
87 J5 **Fleckney** Leics
73 G2 **Flecknoe** Warwks
116 D6 **Fledborough** Notts
14 C6 **Fleet** Dorset
30 D2 **Fleet** Hants
104 C7 **Fleet** Lincs
104 C7 **Fleet Hargate** Lincs
120 D2 **Fleetwood** Lancs
36 F6 **Flemingston** V Glam
175 H6 **Flemington** S Lans
77 J1 **Flempton** Suffk
147 L6 **Fletchertown** Cumb
19 L2 **Fletching** E Susx
9 G4 **Flexbury** Cnwll
30 F2 **Flexford** Surrey
147 H7 **Flimby** Cumb
33 J6 **Flimwell** E Susx
111 H6 **Flint** Flints
102 C4 **Flintham** Notts
126 F4 **Flinton** E R Yk
105 H6 **Flitcham** Norfk
74 F7 **Flitton** Beds
74 F7 **Flitwick** Beds
125 K7 **Flixborough** N Linc
125 K7 **Flixborough Stather** N Linc
135 G4 **Flixton** N York
93 G6 **Flixton** Suffk
113 H3 **Flixton** Traffd
123 J7 **Flockton** Kirk
123 K7 **Flockton Green** Kirk
218 C6 **Flodigarry** Highld
129 H4 **Flookburgh** Cumb
92 E4 **Flordon** Norfk
73 J3 **Flore** Nhants
78 C5 **Flowton** Suffk
3 L4 **Flushing** Cnwll
12 E4 **Fluxton** Devon
71 H4 **Flyford Flavell** Worcs
46 B4 **Fobbing** Thurr
215 H3 **Fochabers** Moray
125 K6 **Fockerby** N Linc
26 E5 **Foddington** Somset
81 L2 **Foel** Powys
125 H3 **Foggathorpe** E R Yk
179 G8 **Fogo** Border
214 F3 **Fogwatt** Moray
228 B5 **Foindle** Highld
195 J4 **Folda** Angus
100 B5 **Fole** Staffs
86 D6 **Foleshill** Covtry
26 F8 **Folke** Dorset
35 H7 **Folkestone** Kent
103 H5 **Folkingham** Lincs
20 B5 **Folkington** E Susx
89 G5 **Folksworth** Cambs
135 G4 **Folkton** N York
216 D7 **Folla Rule** Abers
132 E8 **Follifoot** N York
10 E5 **Folly Gate** Devon
27 L5 **Fonthill Bishop** Wilts
27 L5 **Fonthill Gifford** Wilts
27 K7 **Fontmell Magna** Dorset
27 J8 **Fontmell Parva** Dorset
18 C4 **Fontwell** W Susx
114 D6 **Foolow** Derbys
205 H3 **Forbestown** Abers
140 F5 **Forcett** N York
182 C6 **Ford** Ag & B
58 C6 **Ford** Bucks
115 H5 **Ford** Derbys
22 F6 **Ford** Devon
7 J7 **Ford** Devon
56 C3 **Ford** Gloucs
168 E2 **Ford** Nthumb
25 H5 **Ford** Somset
100 B2 **Ford** Staffs
18 D5 **Ford** W Susx
39 J5 **Ford** Wilts
61 G5 **Ford End** Essex
25 J7 **Ford Street** Somset
32 F5 **Fordcombe** Kent
177 G2 **Fordell** Fife
82 E4 **Forden** Powys
7 H3 **Forder Green** Devon
76 F1 **Fordham** Cambs
61 L3 **Fordham** Essex
90 E4 **Fordham** Norfk
28 D8 **Fordingbridge** Hants
135 G4 **Fordon** E R Yk
197 J2 **Fordoun** Abers
61 L3 **Fordstreet** Essex
35 G3 **Fordwich** Kent
216 B2 **Fordyce** Abers
99 L7 **Forebridge** Staffs
101 G7 **Foremark** Derbys
236 c4 **Forest** Guern
122 B1 **Forest Becks** Lancs
113 L6 **Forest Chapel** Ches
54 F5 **Forest of Dean** Gloucs
45 H3 **Forest Gate** Gt Lon
31 J3 **Forest Green** Surrey
151 G2 **Forest Hall** N Tyne
45 G5 **Forest Hill** Gt Lon
57 L6 **Forest Hill** Oxon
132 E7 **Forest Lane Head** N York
192 D7 **Forest Lodge** Ag & B
185 K8 **Forest Mill** Clacks
32 D6 **Forest Row** E Susx
30 C8 **Forestside** W Susx
196 D6 **Forfar** Angus
186 A4 **Forgandenny** P & K
37 L2 **Forge Hammer** Torfn
215 J4 **Forgie** Moray
215 J4 **Forgieside** Moray

216 B5 **Forgue** Abers
111 J1 **Formby** Sefton
92 D5 **Forncett End** Norfk
92 E5 **Forncett St Mary** Norfk
92 E5 **Forncett St Peter** Norfk
77 J2 **Fornham All Saints** Suffk
77 J2 **Fornham St Martin** Suffk
213 L4 **Fornighty** Highld
214 C3 **Forres** Moray
99 L4 **Forsbrook** Staffs
227 M2 **Forse** Highld
227 M2 **Forse House** Highld
230 C6 **Forsinard** Highld
202 B4 **Fort Augustus** Highld
236 c2 **Fort Hommet** Guern
236 d1 **Fort le Marchant** Guern
191 L2 **Fort William** Highld
185 L4 **Forteviot** P & K
176 C7 **Forth** S Lans
55 K2 **Forthampton** Gloucs
194 B6 **Fortingall** P & K
29 H3 **Forton** Hants
121 G1 **Forton** Lancs
83 H1 **Forton** Shrops
13 J2 **Forton** Somset
99 H7 **Forton** Staffs
216 C5 **Fortrie** Abers
213 H3 **Fortrose** Highld
14 D7 **Fortuneswell** Dorset
60 B7 **Forty Hill** Gt Lon
40 F8 **Fosbury** Wilts
56 E4 **Foscot** Oxon
104 A5 **Fosdyke** Lincs
194 C5 **Foss** P & K
56 B5 **Fossebridge** Gloucs
60 D6 **Foster Street** Essex
100 D6 **Foston** Derbys
87 H4 **Foston** Leics
102 E4 **Foston** Lincs
133 L6 **Foston** N York
135 H7 **Foston on the Wolds** E R Yk
118 D3 **Fotherby** Lincs
88 F5 **Fotheringhay** Nhants
86 B4 **Foul End** Warwks
179 J7 **Foulden** Border
91 H4 **Foulden** Norfk
122 D3 **Foulridge** Lancs
106 B7 **Foulsham** Norfk
177 L8 **Fountainhall** Border
78 B1 **Four Ashes** Suffk
236 c3 **Four Cabots** Guern
97 K8 **Four Crosses** Powys
32 E4 **Four Elms** Kent
25 K4 **Four Forks** Somset
90 C1 **Four Gotes** Cambs
3 J4 **Four Lanes** Cnwll
30 A4 **Four Marks** Hants
108 C5 **Four Mile Bridge** IOA
86 B7 **Four Oaks** Solhll
50 F4 **Four Roads** Carmth
33 K7 **Four Throws** Kent
223 H3 **Fourpenny** Highld
149 M2 **Fourstones** Nthumb
28 A5 **Fovant** Wilts
207 H2 **Foveran** Abers
5 H5 **Fowey** Cnwll
33 J4 **Fowlhall** Kent
186 E2 **Fowlis** Angus
185 J3 **Fowlis Wester** P & K
76 B5 **Fowlmere** Cambs
69 L7 **Fownhope** Herefs
174 E6 **Foxbar** Rens
27 G1 **Foxcote** Somset
237 b5 **Foxdale** IOM
77 J5 **Foxearth** Essex
128 F3 **Foxfield** Cumb
4 F5 **Foxhole** Cnwll
134 F5 **Foxholes** N York
106 C7 **Foxley** Norfk
100 B3 **Foxt** Staffs
76 B5 **Foxton** Cambs
87 K5 **Foxton** Leics
141 K7 **Foxton** N York
84 B7 **Foxwood** Shrops
54 E3 **Foy** Herefs
202 D2 **Foyers** Highld
213 L4 **Foynesfield** Highld
4 E4 **Fraddon** Cnwll
85 L2 **Fradley** Staffs
99 M6 **Fradswell** Staffs
135 J7 **Fraisthorpe** E R Yk
20 A2 **Framfield** E Susx
92 F3 **Framingham Earl** Norfk
92 F3 **Framingham Pigot** Norfk
79 G2 **Framlingham** Suffk
14 C4 **Frampton** Dorset
104 B5 **Frampton** Lincs
38 F4 **Frampton Cotterell** S Glos
55 L7 **Frampton Mansell** Gloucs
55 H6 **Frampton on Severn** Gloucs
78 E3 **Framsden** Suffk
151 G6 **Framwellgate Moor** Dur
121 J3 **Frances Green** Lancs
84 E7 **Franche** Worcs
111 H4 **Frankby** Wirral
85 H7 **Frankley** Worcs
72 E1 **Frankton** Warwks
33 G6 **Frant** E Susx
217 J2 **Fraserburgh** Abers
62 C4 **Frating** Essex
62 C4 **Frating Green** Essex
17 J3 **Fratton** C Port
6 B5 **Freathy** Cnwll
76 F1 **Freckenham** Suffk
120 F5 **Freckleton** Lancs
102 D7 **Freeby** Leics
29 J2 **Freefolk** Hants
57 H5 **Freeland** Oxon
93 J3 **Freethorpe** Norfk
93 J3 **Freethorpe Common** Norfk
104 B4 **Freiston** Lincs
23 H5 **Fremington** Devon
140 D7 **Fremington** N York
38 F5 **Frenchay** S Glos
194 C5 **Frenich** P & K
30 D3 **Frensham** Surrey
120 C8 **Freshfield** Sefton
39 H7 **Freshford** Wilts
16 D5 **Freshwater** IOW
92 F7 **Fressingfield** Suffk
78 E6 **Freston** Suffk
231 L3 **Freswick** Highld
55 G6 **Fretherne** Gloucs
106 F8 **Frettenham** Norfk
186 E6 **Freuchie** Fife
49 G5 **Freystrop** Pembks
85 H4 **Friar Park** W Mids
90 C3 **Friday Bridge** Cambs
79 H3 **Friday Street** Suffk
134 D7 **Fridaythorpe** E R Yk
44 F2 **Friern Barnet** Gt Lon
188 F5 **Friesland Bay** Ag & B
117 H5 **Friesthorpe** Lincs
102 F3 **Frieston** Lincs
42 D3 **Frieth** Bucks
41 H2 **Frilford** Oxon
41 K5 **Frilsham** W Berk
42 E8 **Frimley** Surrey
46 C6 **Frindsbury** Medway
105 H5 **Fring** Norfk
57 L3 **Fringford** Oxon
34 B4 **Frinsted** Kent
62 F4 **Frinton-on-Sea** Essex
196 F6 **Friockheim** Angus
102 B8 **Frisby on the Wreake** Leics
104 D2 **Friskney** Lincs
20 B6 **Friston** E Susx
79 J3 **Friston** Suffk
101 G3 **Fritchley** Derbys
28 E8 **Fritham** Hants
23 G7 **Frithelstock** Devon
23 G7 **Frithelstock Stone** Devon
104 A3 **Frithville** Lincs
33 K5 **Frittenden** Kent
7 J6 **Frittiscombe** Devon
93 K4 **Fritton** Norfk
92 F5 **Fritton** Norfk
57 K3 **Fritwell** Oxon
123 H4 **Frizinghall** Brad
136 E4 **Frizington** Cumb
55 H7 **Frocester** Gloucs
83 K3 **Frodesley** Shrops
112 D6 **Frodsham** Ches
76 B5 **Frog End** Cambs
70 E2 **Frog Pool** Worcs
168 B4 **Frogden** Border
114 E6 **Froggatt** Derbys
100 A3 **Froghall** Staffs
7 H7 **Frogmore** Devon
89 H2 **Frognall** Lincs
6 A3 **Frogwell** Cnwll
87 G5 **Frolesworth** Leics
27 H2 **Frome** Somset
14 B2 **Frome St Quintin** Dorset
70 C5 **Fromes Hill** Herefs
97 L4 **Fron Isaf** Wrexhm
96 D5 **Fron-goch** Gwynd
97 K4 **Froncysyllte** Denbgs
150 C7 **Frosterley** Dur
40 F6 **Froxfield** Wilts
30 B6 **Froxfield Green** Hants
29 H7 **Fryern Hill** Hants
61 G7 **Fryerning** Essex
190 C6 **Fuinary** Highld
102 F3 **Fulbeck** Lincs
76 D4 **Fulbourn** Cambs
56 E5 **Fulbrook** Oxon
29 J5 **Fulflood** Hants
25 K5 **Fulford** Somset
99 L5 **Fulford** Staffs
124 F2 **Fulford** York
44 E5 **Fulham** Gt Lon
19 H4 **Fulking** W Susx
134 B7 **Full Sutton** E R Yk
163 H2 **Fullarton** N Ayrs
61 H5 **Fuller Street** Essex
29 G4 **Fullerton** Hants
118 D6 **Fulletby** Lincs
72 C5 **Fullready** Warwks
174 E7 **Fullwood** E Ayrs
43 G4 **Fulmer** Bucks
106 B6 **Fulmodeston** Norfk
117 H5 **Fulnetby** Lincs
103 L7 **Fulney** Lincs
118 D3 **Fulstow** Lincs
57 G4 **Fulwell** Oxon
151 J3 **Fulwell** Sundld
121 H4 **Fulwood** Lancs
114 F4 **Fulwood** Sheff
92 D4 **Fundenhall** Norfk
17 L2 **Funtington** W Susx
184 F3 **Funtullich** P & K
13 H2 **Furley** Devon
182 E7 **Furnace** Ag & B
51 G5 **Furnace** Carmth
114 A5 **Furness Vale** Derbys
60 C3 **Furneux Pelham** Herts
28 F7 **Furzley** Hants
60 F6 **Fyfield** Essex
28 F3 **Fyfield** Hants
57 H7 **Fyfield** Oxon
40 C6 **Fyfield** Wilts
40 D7 **Fyfield** Wilts
143 J6 **Fylingthorpe** N York
30 D6 **Fyning** W Susx
216 E6 **Fyvie** Abers

G

174 E7 **Gabroc Hill** E Ayrs
87 K2 **Gaddesby** Leics
59 H5 **Gaddesden Row** Herts
163 K5 **Gadgirth** S Ayrs
38 C2 **Gaer-llwyd** Mons
108 F7 **Gaerwen** IOA
163 H3 **Gailes** N Ayrs
85 G2 **Gailey** Staffs
140 F4 **Gainford** Dur
116 D4 **Gainsborough** Lincs
77 G7 **Gainsford End** Essex
219 J6 **Gairloch** Highld
201 J8 **Gairlochy** Highld
186 B7 **Gairneybridge** P & K
123 H3 **Gaisby** Brad
148 C5 **Gaitsgill** Cumb
167 G3 **Galashiels** Border
129 K7 **Galgate** Lancs
26 F5 **Galhampton** Somset
182 B3 **Gallanach** Ag & B
186 E8 **Gallatown** Fife
61 H7 **Galleywood** Essex
202 E7 **Gallovie** Highld
153 J5 **Galloway Forest Park**
196 D7 **Gallowfauld** Angus
186 B1 **Gallowhill** P & K
200 C2 **Galltair** Highld
7 G7 **Galmpton** Devon
7 K5 **Galmpton** Torbay
132 C5 **Galphay** N York
163 L3 **Galston** E Ayrs
14 E5 **Galton** Dorset
149 G6 **Gamblesby** Cumb
75 J4 **Gamlingay** Cambs
75 J4 **Gamlingay Great Heath** Beds
216 F2 **Gamrie** Abers
116 B6 **Gamston** Notts
101 L5 **Gamston** Notts
182 B2 **Ganavan Bay** Ag & B
96 B7 **Ganllwyd** Gwynd
196 F3 **Gannachy** Angus
126 E4 **Ganstead** E R Yk
133 L5 **Ganthorpe** N York
134 F4 **Ganton** N York
215 H4 **Garbity** Moray
92 B7 **Garboldisham** Norfk
205 G4 **Garchory** Abers
114 E2 **Garden Village** Sheff
42 D6 **Gardeners Green** Wokham
216 F2 **Gardenstown** Abers
235 c5 **Garderhouse** Shet
27 H4 **Gare Hill** Somset
173 L1 **Garelochhead** Ag & B
41 H2 **Garford** Oxon
124 B4 **Garforth** Leeds
131 H8 **Gargrave** N York
184 F8 **Gargunnock** Stirlg
92 E6 **Garlic Street** Norfk
145 K5 **Garlieston** D & G
35 J2 **Garlinge** Kent
34 F4 **Garlinge Green** Kent
206 E4 **Garlogie** Abers
216 F4 **Garmond** Abers
215 H2 **Garmouth** Moray
83 L3 **Garmston** Shrops

95 J4 **Garn-Dolbenmaen** Gwynd
175 J5 **Garnkirk** N Lans
232 g2 **Garrabost** W Isls
164 B5 **Garrallan** E Ayrs
3 J6 **Garras** Cnwll
95 K4 **Garreg** Gwynd
149 J6 **Garrigill** Cumb
153 M6 **Garroch** D & G
144 D7 **Garrochtrie** D & G
173 J7 **Garrochty** Ag & B
209 H2 **Garros** Highld
130 E2 **Garsdale Head** Cumb
39 L3 **Garsdon** Wilts
99 L5 **Garshall Green** Staffs
57 L7 **Garsington** Oxon
121 G2 **Garstang** Lancs
59 J7 **Garston** Herts
112 B5 **Garston** Lpool
171 G6 **Gartachossan** Ag & B
175 J5 **Gartcosh** N Lans
97 K4 **Garth** Denbgs
67 K5 **Garth** Powys
80 E6 **Garth Penrhyncoch** Cerdgn
138 D7 **Garth Row** Cumb
175 H5 **Garthamlock** C Glas
82 E4 **Garthmyl** Powys
102 D7 **Garthorpe** Leics
125 K6 **Garthorpe** N Linc
215 L7 **Gartly** Abers
184 C7 **Gartmore** Stirlg
175 K5 **Gartness** N Lans
174 F2 **Gartness** Stirlg
174 D2 **Gartocharn** W Duns
127 G4 **Garton** E R Yk
134 F7 **Garton-on-the-Wolds** E R Yk
227 H5 **Gartymore** Highld
178 D4 **Garvald** E Loth
191 J2 **Garvan** Highld
171 G1 **Garvard** Ag & B
212 B3 **Garve** Highld
92 B3 **Garvestone** Norfk
174 B4 **Garvock** Inver
54 C4 **Garway** Herefs
54 C4 **Garway Common** Herefs
232 f3 **Garyvard** W Isls
27 H5 **Gasper** Wilts
39 K6 **Gastard** Wilts
91 L7 **Gasthorpe** Norfk
60 D5 **Gaston Green** Essex
16 F5 **Gatcombe** IOW
116 D5 **Gate Burton** Lincs
133 L7 **Gate Helmsley** N York
124 E5 **Gateforth** N York
163 K3 **Gatehead** E Ayrs
157 K4 **Gatehouse** Nthumb
145 M4 **Gatehouse of Fleet** D & G
106 A7 **Gateley** Norfk
132 E3 **Gatenby** N York
168 B5 **Gateshaw** Border
151 G3 **Gateshead** Gatesd
196 D7 **Gateside** Angus
174 E6 **Gateside** E Rens
186 C5 **Gateside** Fife
174 C7 **Gateside** N Ayrs
154 F2 **Gateslack** D & G
113 J4 **Gatley** Stockp
167 H3 **Gattonside** Border
32 B5 **Gatwick Airport** W Susx
87 K4 **Gaulby** Leics
186 F3 **Gauldry** Fife
195 K6 **Gauldswell** P & K
117 K6 **Gautby** Lincs
179 G7 **Gavinton** Border
58 B2 **Gawcott** Bucks
113 K7 **Gawsworth** Ches
130 D3 **Gawthrop** Cumb
129 G3 **Gawthwaite** Cumb
72 D4 **Gaydon** Warwks
74 B5 **Gayhurst** M Keyn
131 G2 **Gayle** N York
140 E5 **Gayles** N York
73 K4 **Gayton** Nhants
105 H8 **Gayton** Norfk
99 M6 **Gayton** Staffs
118 F5 **Gayton le Marsh** Lincs
105 H8 **Gayton Thorpe** Norfk
105 G7 **Gaywood** Norfk
77 G2 **Gazeley** Suffk
232 f3 **Gearraidh Bhaird** W Isls
208 D3 **Geary** Highld
77 L3 **Gedding** Suffk
35 H5 **Geddinge** Kent
88 C6 **Geddington** Nhants
101 L4 **Gedling** Notts
104 C7 **Gedney** Lincs
104 C7 **Gedney Broadgate** Lincs
104 D6 **Gedney Drove End** Lincs
104 C7 **Gedney Dyke** Lincs
89 L2 **Gedney Hill** Lincs
88 E3 **Geeston** Rutlnd
93 H5 **Geldeston** Norfk
110 F8 **Gellifor** Denbgs
37 H2 **Gelligaer** Caerph
95 M4 **Gellilydan** Gwynd
51 K5 **Gellinudd** Neath
195 H8 **Gellyburn** P & K
50 C2 **Gellywen** Carmth
146 D3 **Gelston** D & G
102 E4 **Gelston** Lincs
135 H7 **Gembling** E R Yk
85 J2 **Gentleshaw** Staffs
43 G4 **George Green** Bucks
23 L6 **George Nympton** Devon
156 B4 **Georgefield** D & G
23 G4 **Georgeham** Devon
234 b5 **Georth** Ork
10 C6 **Germansweek** Devon
4 D8 **Gerrans** Cnwll
43 G3 **Gerrards Cross** Bucks
142 E5 **Gerrick** R & Cl
77 J6 **Gestingthorpe** Essex
82 E2 **Geuffordd** Powys
45 K3 **Gidea Park** Gt Lon
175 G6 **Giffnock** E Rens
178 C5 **Gifford** E Loth
186 E5 **Giffordtown** Fife
130 F6 **Giggleswick** N York
125 K5 **Gilberdyke** E R Yk
178 B5 **Gilchriston** E Loth
147 K7 **Gilcrux** Cumb
123 K5 **Gildersome** Leeds
115 K4 **Gildingwells** Rothm
151 H6 **Gilesgate Moor** Dur
36 F6 **Gileston** V Glam
53 J7 **Gilfach** Caerph
36 F3 **Gilfach Goch** Brdgnd
65 L3 **Gilfachrheda** Cerdgn
136 E3 **Gilgarran** Cumb
133 K2 **Gillamoor** N York
208 D3 **Gillen** Highld
155 L4 **Gillesbie** D & G
133 J4 **Gilling East** N York
140 F6 **Gilling West** N York
27 J6 **Gillingham** Dorset
46 C6 **Gillingham** Medway
93 J5 **Gillingham** Norfk
231 J4 **Gillock** Highld
231 K2 **Gills** Highld
166 E5 **Gilmanscleuch** Border
177 J5 **Gilmerton** C Edin
185 J3 **Gilmerton** P & K
140 C5 **Gilmonby** Dur
87 H6 **Gilmorton** Leics
149 G2 **Gilsland** Nthumb
60 D5 **Gilston** Herts
177 L6 **Gilston** Mdloth
53 K5 **Gilwern** Mons
107 G5 **Gimingham** Norfk
78 C2 **Gipping** Suffk
103 M3 **Gipsey Bridge** Lincs
163 J2 **Girdle Toll** N Ayrs
235 c5 **Girlsta** Shet
141 J5 **Girsby** N York
146 A4 **Girthon** D & G
76 B3 **Girton** Cambs
116 D7 **Girton** Notts
152 E3 **Girvan** S Ayrs
122 C2 **Gisburn** Lancs
93 K5 **Gisleham** Suffk
78 C1 **Gislingham** Suffk
92 D6 **Gissing** Norfk
12 E3 **Gittisham** Devon
68 E4 **Gladestry** Powys
177 M4 **Gladsmuir** E Loth
51 K5 **Glais** Swans
143 G6 **Glaisdale** N York
196 C6 **Glamis** Angus
111 G5 **Glan-y-don** Flints
51 J3 **Glanaman** Carmth
106 C4 **Glandford** Norfk
49 K2 **Glandwr** Pembks
80 F4 **Glandyfi** Cerdgn
36 D3 **Glanllynfi** Brdgnd
169 G6 **Glanton** Nthumb
14 D2 **Glanvilles Wootton** Dorset
88 E5 **Glapthorn** Nhants
115 J7 **Glapwell** Derbys
68 D6 **Glasbury** Powys
86 B3 **Glascote** Staffs
68 D4 **Glascwm** Powys
96 E3 **Glasfryn** Conwy
175 G5 **Glasgow** C Glas
174 E5 **Glasgow Airport** Rens
175 G5 **Glasgow Science Centre** C Glas
109 H7 **Glasinfryn** Gwynd
199 L6 **Glasnacardoch Bay** Highld
199 H3 **Glasnakille** Highld
145 J7 **Glasserton** D & G
175 J8 **Glassford** S Lans
55 G4 **Glasshouse** Gloucs
132 B6 **Glasshouses** N York
148 A3 **Glasson** Cumb
129 K7 **Glasson** Lancs
149 G7 **Glassonby** Cumb
196 F6 **Glasterlaw** Angus
88 C4 **Glaston** Rutlnd
26 D4 **Glastonbury** Somset
89 H6 **Glatton** Cambs
113 G3 **Glazebrook** Warrtn
112 F3 **Glazebury** Warrtn
84 C5 **Glazeley** Shrops
128 F5 **Gleaston** Cumb
202 D2 **Glebe** Highld
123 L3 **Gledhow** Leeds
146 B5 **Gledpark** D & G
97 L5 **Gledrid** Shrops
77 J5 **Glemsford** Suffk
237 d3 **Glen Auldyn** IOM
204 E8 **Glen Clunie Lodge** Abers
237 b5 **Glen Maye** IOM
192 B3 **Glen Nevis House** Highld
87 H4 **Glen Parva** Leics
153 J6 **Glen Trool Lodge** D & G
215 G6 **Glenallachie** Highld
199 K6 **Glenancross** Highld
190 B7 **Glenaros House** Ag & B
161 H3 **Glenbarr** Ag & B
216 B4 **Glenbarry** Abers
190 C4 **Glenbeg** Highld
214 C8 **Glenbeg** Highld
197 J1 **Glenbervie** Abers
175 J5 **Glenboig** N Lans
190 C4 **Glenborrodale** Highld
183 G7 **Glenbranter** Ag & B
165 K5 **Glenbreck** Border
198 F2 **Glenbrittle House** Highld
164 E4 **Glenbuck** E Ayrs
196 B4 **Glencally** Angus
147 H2 **Glencaple** D & G
211 G4 **Glencarron Lodge** Highld
186 C3 **Glencarse** P & K
192 B6 **Glenceitlein** Highld
191 L5 **Glencoe** Highld
165 L4 **Glencothe** Border
186 C7 **Glencraig** Fife
154 D4 **Glencrosh** D & G
208 B4 **Glendale** Highld
173 G2 **Glendaruel** Ag & B
185 K6 **Glendevon** P & K
202 C4 **Glendoe Lodge** Highld
186 C3 **Glendoick** P & K
186 D4 **Glenduckie** Fife
185 J5 **Gleneagles** P & K
185 J5 **Gleneagles Hotel** P & K
170 F7 **Glenegedale** Ag & B
200 C2 **Glenelg** Highld
214 C5 **Glenerney** Moray
186 B5 **Glenfarg** P & K
203 K6 **Glenfeshie Lodge** Highld
87 G3 **Glenfield** Leics
191 H1 **Glenfinnan** Highld
201 K7 **Glenfintaig Lodge** Highld
186 C4 **Glenfoot** P & K
183 H4 **Glenfyne Lodge** Ag & B
174 C7 **Glengarnock** N Ayrs
231 G3 **Glengolly** Highld
189 K5 **Glengorm Castle** Ag & B
209 G5 **Glengrasco** Highld
165 L3 **Glenholm** Border
154 A5 **Glenhoul** D & G
195 K4 **Glenisla** Angus
173 K3 **Glenkin** Ag & B
205 K3 **Glenkindie** Abers
214 F8 **Glenlivet** Moray
146 C3 **Glenlochar** D & G
186 C6 **Glenlomond** P & K
144 E4 **Glenluce** D & G
173 J2 **Glenmassen** Ag & B
175 K5 **Glenmavis** N Lans
209 G6 **Glenmore** Highld
204 B4 **Glenmore Lodge** Highld
196 C4 **Glenquiech** Angus
172 E5 **Glenralloch** Ag & B
137 L4 **Glenridding** Cumb
186 D7 **Glenrothes** Fife
185 K1 **Glenshee** P & K
202 E6 **Glenshera Lodge** Highld
173 J3 **Glenstriven** Ag & B
117 G4 **Glentham** Lincs
203 J6 **Glentromie Lodge** Highld
153 H6 **Glentrool Village** D & G
203 G6 **Glentruim House** Highld
116 F4 **Glentworth** Lincs
190 D2 **Glenuig** Highld
191 K6 **Glenure** Ag & B

209 G6 **Glenvarragill** Highld
152 E7 **Glenwhilly** D & G
164 F4 **Glespin** S Lans
54 E4 **Glewstone** Herefs
89 H3 **Glinton** C Pete
87 L4 **Glooston** Leics
114 B3 **Glossop** Derbys
159 G2 **Gloster Hill** Nthumb
55 J4 **Gloucester** Glouc
55 K4 **Gloucestershire Airport** Gloucs
122 F2 **Glusburn** N York
227 H2 **Glutt Lodge** Highld
4 E3 **Gluvian** Cnwll
57 H4 **Glympton** Oxon
97 J5 **Glyn Ceiriog** Wrexhm
52 D6 **Glyn-Neath** Neath
65 K5 **Glynarthen** Cerdgn
52 D7 **Glyncorrwg** Neath
19 L4 **Glynde** E Susx
97 J4 **Glyndyfrdwy** Denbgs
52 D5 **Glyntawe** Powys
65 K6 **Glynteg** Carmth
99 J7 **Gnosall** Staffs
99 J7 **Gnosall Heath** Staffs
87 L4 **Goadby** Leics
102 C7 **Goadby Marwood** Leics
40 A5 **Goatacre** Wilts
182 E7 **Goatfield** Ag & B
26 F7 **Goathill** Dorset
143 H6 **Goathland** N York
25 K5 **Goathurst** Somset
97 L5 **Gobowen** Shrops
30 F3 **Godalming** Surrey
33 L6 **Goddard's Green** Kent
75 J1 **Godmanchester** Cambs
14 C3 **Godmanstone** Dorset
34 E5 **Godmersham** Kent
26 C3 **Godney** Somset
3 G5 **Godolphin Cross** Cnwll
51 L4 **Godre'r-graig** Neath
17 G6 **Godshill** IOW
32 C3 **Godstone** Surrey
53 L6 **Goetre** Mons
60 B7 **Goff's Oak** Herts
53 K5 **Gofilon** Mons
177 G4 **Gogar** C Edin
80 F7 **Goginan** Cerdgn
95 J4 **Golan** Gwynd
5 H5 **Golant** Cnwll
5 M2 **Golberdon** Cnwll
112 E3 **Golborne** Wigan
123 G7 **Golcar** Kirk
38 A4 **Goldcliff** Newpt
33 H4 **Golden Green** Kent
30 B3 **Golden Pot** Hants
44 E3 **Golders Green** Gt Lon
61 L6 **Goldhanger** Essex
74 F4 **Goldington** Beds
143 H4 **Goldsborough** N York
132 F7 **Goldsborough** N York
2 F5 **Goldsithney** Cnwll
43 G8 **Goldsworth Park** Surrey
115 J2 **Goldthorpe** Barns
22 F6 **Goldworthy** Devon
213 J4 **Gollanfield** Highld
223 H2 **Golspie** Highld
28 D4 **Gomeldon** Wilts
31 H2 **Gomshall** Surrey
102 B3 **Gonalston** Notts
235 c4 **Gonfirth** Shet
60 F5 **Good Easter** Essex
91 H3 **Gooderstone** Norfk
23 J5 **Goodleigh** Devon
125 K2 **Goodmanham** E R Yk
45 J3 **Goodmayes** Gt Lon
34 D3 **Goodnestone** Kent
35 H4 **Goodnestone** Kent
54 E4 **Goodrich** Herefs
54 E4 **Goodrich Castle** Herefs
7 K4 **Goodrington** Torbay
122 B5 **Goodshaw Fold** Lancs
64 C6 **Goodwick** Pembks
29 G3 **Goodworth Clatford** Hants
125 H5 **Goole** E R Yk
71 H4 **Goom's Hill** Worcs
3 J2 **Goonbell** Cnwll
3 K1 **Goonhavern** Cnwll
3 J2 **Goonvrea** Cnwll
62 D3 **Goose Green** Essex
62 D3 **Goose Green** Essex
38 F5 **Goose Green** S Glos
206 E8 **Goosecruives** Abers
11 G6 **Gooseford** Devon
41 G3 **Goosey** Oxon
121 H3 **Goosnargh** Lancs
113 H7 **Goostrey** Ches
167 K2 **Gordon** Border
166 D4 **Gordon Arms Hotel** Border
216 B3 **Gordonstown** Abers
216 D6 **Gordonstown** Abers
177 K6 **Gorebridge** Mdloth
90 B2 **Gorefield** Cambs
40 C8 **Gores** Wilts
236 e7 **Gorey** Jersey
41 L4 **Goring** Oxon
18 F5 **Goring-by-Sea** W Susx
93 L3 **Gorleston on Sea** Norfk
216 E3 **Gorrachie** Abers
4 F7 **Gorran** Cnwll
4 F7 **Gorran Haven** Cnwll
40 D3 **Gorse Hill** Swindn
111 G6 **Gorsedd** Flints
51 H5 **Gorseinon** Swans
66 C4 **Gorsgoch** Cerdgn
51 H3 **Gorslas** Carmth
55 G3 **Gorsley** Gloucs
54 F3 **Gorsley Common** Herefs
212 B2 **Gorstan** Highld
98 A1 **Gorstello** Ches
100 C6 **Gorsty Hill** Staffs
181 L2 **Gorten** Ag & B
202 E2 **Gorthleck** Highld
113 K3 **Gorton** Manch
78 D4 **Gosbeck** Suffk
103 L6 **Gosberton** Lincs
61 J3 **Gosfield** Essex
136 E6 **Gosforth** Cumb
151 G2 **Gosforth** N u Ty
84 F5 **Gospel End** Staffs
17 H3 **Gosport** Hants
55 H7 **Gossington** Gloucs
101 K6 **Gotham** Notts
55 L3 **Gotherington** Gloucs
25 K5 **Gotton** Somset
33 J5 **Goudhurst** Kent
118 C5 **Goulceby** Lincs
216 E6 **Gourdas** Abers
186 F2 **Gourdie** Angus
197 K3 **Gourdon** Abers
173 L3 **Gourock** Inver
174 F5 **Govan** C Glas
7 H6 **Goveton** Devon
124 F6 **Gowdall** E R Yk
212 D3 **Gower** Highld
51 G7 **Gower** Swans
51 H6 **Gowerton** Swans
176 E1 **Gowkhall** Fife
126 F2 **Goxhill** E R Yk
126 D6 **Goxhill** N Linc
232 f3 **Grabhair** W Isls
18 C3 **Graffham** W Susx
75 H2 **Grafham** Cambs
31 G3 **Grafham** Surrey
132 F6 **Grafton** N York
56 F7 **Grafton** Oxon
98 B8 **Grafton** Shrops
71 H6 **Grafton** Worcs
71 G4 **Grafton Flyford** Worcs
73 L5 **Grafton Regis** Nhants
88 D7 **Grafton Underwood** Nhants
34 B5 **Grafty Green** Kent
109 M6 **Graig** Conwy
97 J2 **Graig-fechan** Denbgs
46 E5 **Grain** Medway
118 C2 **Grainsby** Lincs
118 E3 **Grainthorpe** Lincs
4 E6 **Grampound** Cnwll
4 E5 **Grampound Road** Cnwll
233 c6 **Gramsdal** W Isls
233 c6 **Gramsdale** W Isls
58 C3 **Granborough** Bucks
102 C5 **Granby** Notts
236 d7 **Grand Chemins** Jersey
101 H7 **Grand Prix Collection Donington** Leics
72 F2 **Grandborough** Warwks
236 c2 **Grandes Rocques** Guern
194 E5 **Grandtully** P & K
137 H4 **Grange** Cumb
46 D6 **Grange** Medway
186 D3 **Grange** P & K
215 K4 **Grange Crossroads** Moray
214 C3 **Grange Hall** Moray
45 H2 **Grange Hill** Gt Lon
123 J7 **Grange Moor** Kirk
186 D4 **Grange of Lindores** Fife
151 G4 **Grange Villa** Dur
129 J4 **Grange-over-Sands** Cumb
165 J2 **Grangehall** S Lans
100 E2 **Grangemill** Derbys
176 C3 **Grangemouth** Falk
176 D3 **Grangepans** Falk
142 C3 **Grangetown** R & Cl
151 K4 **Grangetown** Sundld
135 H7 **Gransmoor** E R Yk
64 C7 **Granston** Pembks
76 B4 **Grantchester** Cambs
102 E5 **Grantham** Lincs
177 H3 **Granton** C Edin
214 C8 **Grantown-on-Spey** Highld
179 G5 **Grantshouse** Border
117 H1 **Grasby** Lincs
137 K5 **Grasmere** Cumb
113 L1 **Grasscroft** Oldham
111 L4 **Grassendale** Lpool
131 J6 **Grassington** N York
115 H7 **Grassmoor** Derbys
116 C7 **Grassthorpe** Notts
28 F3 **Grateley** Hants
75 J2 **Graveley** Cambs
59 L3 **Graveley** Herts
34 E3 **Graveney** Kent
46 A5 **Gravesend** Kent
232 f3 **Gravir** W Isls
116 F3 **Grayingham** Lincs
138 E7 **Grayrigg** Cumb
45 L4 **Grays** Thurr
30 E4 **Grayshott** Hants
30 F4 **Grayswood** Surrey
115 H3 **Greasbrough** Rothm
111 H4 **Greasby** Wirral
101 J3 **Greasley** Notts
76 D5 **Great Abington** Cambs
88 D7 **Great Addington** Nhants
71 K3 **Great Alne** Warwks
111 K1 **Great Altcar** Lancs
60 B5 **Great Amwell** Herts
138 F5 **Great Asby** Cumb
78 B2 **Great Ashfield** Suffk
142 C5 **Great Ayton** N York
61 H6 **Great Baddow** Essex
39 J4 **Great Badminton** S Glos
61 G2 **Great Bardfield** Essex
75 G4 **Great Barford** Beds
85 J4 **Great Barr** Sandw
56 E5 **Great Barrington** Gloucs
112 C7 **Great Barrow** Ches
77 K2 **Great Barton** Suffk
134 B4 **Great Barugh** N York
158 C6 **Great Bavington** Nthumb
78 F5 **Great Bealings** Suffk
40 F7 **Great Bedwyn** Wilts
62 D4 **Great Bentley** Essex
74 B3 **Great Billing** Nhants
105 J6 **Great Bircham** Norfk
78 D4 **Great Blakenham** Suffk
138 C2 **Great Blencow** Cumb
98 F7 **Great Bolas** Wrekin
31 J1 **Great Bookham** Surrey
2 D4 **Great Bosullow** Cnwll
72 F5 **Great Bourton** Oxon
87 L5 **Great Bowden** Leics
76 F4 **Great Bradley** Suffk
61 K5 **Great Braxted** Essex
78 C4 **Great Bricett** Suffk
58 E3 **Great Brickhill** Bucks
99 K6 **Great Bridgeford** Staffs
73 J2 **Great Brington** Nhants
62 C3 **Great Bromley** Essex
136 E2 **Great Broughton** Cumb
142 C6 **Great Broughton** N York
112 F6 **Great Budworth** Ches
141 H4 **Great Burdon** Darltn
46 B2 **Great Burstead** Essex
142 B6 **Great Busby** N York
118 E4 **Great Carlton** Lincs
88 E2 **Great Casterton** Rutlnd
39 K7 **Great Chalfield** Wilts
34 C6 **Great Chart** Kent
84 E1 **Great Chatwell** Staffs
76 D6 **Great Chesterford** Essex
27 M1 **Great Cheverell** Wilts
76 B6 **Great Chishill** Cambs
62 E5 **Great Clacton** Essex
136 E2 **Great Clifton** Cumb
126 F8 **Great Coates** NE Lin
71 G6 **Great Comberton** Worcs
148 E4 **Great Corby** Cumb
77 K6 **Great Cornard** Suffk
126 F3 **Great Cowden** E R Yk
40 F2 **Great Coxwell** Oxon
88 B7 **Great Cransley** Nhants
91 J3 **Great Cressingham** Norfk
137 J3 **Great Crosthwaite** Cumb
100 D5 **Great Cubley** Derbys
87 L2 **Great Dalby** Leics
74 C2 **Great Doddington** Nhants

91 K1 **Great Dunham** Norfk
61 G4 **Great Dunmow** Essex
28 C4 **Great Durnford** Wilts
60 F3 **Great Easton** Essex
88 B5 **Great Easton** Leics
120 F3 **Great Eccleston** Lancs
92 B4 **Great Ellingham** Norfk
27 H2 **Great Elm** Somset
7 H4 **Great Englebourne** Devon
73 H3 **Great Everdon** Nhants
75 L4 **Great Eversden** Cambs
78 B3 **Great Finborough** Suffk
91 K2 **Great Fransham** Norfk
59 G5 **Great Gaddesden** Herts
89 G6 **Great Gidding** Cambs
134 C8 **Great Givendale** E R Yk
79 H3 **Great Glemham** Suffk
87 J4 **Great Glen** Leics
102 E5 **Great Gonerby** Lincs
75 J4 **Great Gransden** Cambs
75 K5 **Great Green** Cambs
77 K4 **Great Green** Suffk
134 B4 **Great Habton** N York
103 J4 **Great Hale** Lincs
60 E4 **Great Hallingbury** Essex
58 D7 **Great Hampden** Bucks
74 C1 **Great Harrowden** Nhants
121 L4 **Great Harwood** Lancs
57 M7 **Great Haseley** Oxon
126 F3 **Great Hatfield** E R Yk
99 M7 **Great Haywood** Staffs
124 F6 **Great Heck** N York
77 K6 **Great Henny** Essex
39 K8 **Great Hinton** Wilts
91 L5 **Great Hockham** Norfk
62 E4 **Great Holland** Essex
62 B2 **Great Horkesley** Essex
60 C3 **Great Hormead** Herts
123 H4 **Great Horton** Brad
58 C2 **Great Horwood** Bucks
115 H1 **Great Houghton** Barns
73 L3 **Great Houghton** Nhants
114 D6 **Great Hucklow** Derbys
135 H7 **Great Kelk** E R Yk
58 D6 **Great Kimble** Bucks
42 E2 **Great Kingshill** Bucks
137 J6 **Great Langdale** Cumb
141 H7 **Great Langton** N York
61 H4 **Great Leighs** Essex
126 E8 **Great Limber** Lincs
74 C6 **Great Linford** M Keyn
77 K1 **Great Livermere** Suffk
114 D6 **Great Longstone** Derbys
151 H5 **Great Lumley** Dur
70 D5 **Great Malvern** Worcs
77 J7 **Great Maplestead** Essex
120 D4 **Great Marton** Bpool
105 J7 **Great Massingham** Norfk
57 L7 **Great Milton** Oxon
58 E7 **Great Missenden** Bucks
121 K3 **Great Mitton** Lancs
35 K4 **Great Mongeham** Kent
92 E5 **Great Moulton** Norfk
139 H4 **Great Musgrave** Cumb
98 B8 **Great Ness** Shrops
54 B6 **Great Oak** Mons
62 E3 **Great Oakley** Essex
88 C6 **Great Oakley** Nhants
59 J3 **Great Offley** Herts
139 G4 **Great Ormside** Cumb
148 B4 **Great Orton** Cumb
133 G6 **Great Ouseburn** N York
87 K6 **Great Oxendon** Nhants
61 G6 **Great Oxney Green** Essex
75 H2 **Great Paxton** Cambs
120 E4 **Great Plumpton** Lancs
93 G2 **Great Plumstead** Norfk
102 F6 **Great Ponton** Lincs
124 B5 **Great Preston** Leeds
89 J7 **Great Raveley** Cambs
56 D5 **Great Rissington** Gloucs
56 F2 **Great Rollright** Oxon
106 A6 **Great Ryburgh** Norfk
168 F6 **Great Ryle** Nthumb
83 J3 **Great Ryton** Shrops
61 H3 **Great Saling** Essex
148 F7 **Great Salkeld** Cumb
76 F7 **Great Sampford** Essex
111 K7 **Great Saughall** Ches
41 G5 **Great Shefford** W Berk
76 C4 **Great Shelford** Cambs
141 H6 **Great Smeaton** N York
105 M5 **Great Snoring** Norfk
39 L4 **Great Somerford** Wilts
99 G6 **Great Soudley** Shrops
141 H3 **Great Stainton** Darltn
46 E2 **Great Stambridge** Essex
75 G2 **Great Staughton** Cambs
118 F8 **Great Steeping** Lincs
38 F4 **Great Stoke** S Glos
138 D3 **Great Strickland** Cumb
89 J8 **Great Stukeley** Cambs
117 K6 **Great Sturton** Lincs
158 B6 **Great Swinburne** Nthumb
57 H3 **Great Tew** Oxon
61 L3 **Great Tey** Essex
23 H7 **Great Torrington** Devon
158 C3 **Great Tosson** Nthumb
61 K5 **Great Totham** Essex
61 L5 **Great Totham** Essex
129 G5 **Great Urswick** Cumb
46 F3 **Great Wakering** Essex
77 K5 **Great Waldingfield** Suffk
105 M5 **Great Walsingham** Norfk
61 H5 **Great Waltham** Essex
45 L2 **Great Warley** Essex
71 H7 **Great Washbourne** Gloucs
11 G7 **Great Weeke** Devon
88 D5 **Great Weldon** Nhants
78 C6 **Great Wenham** Suffk
158 C7 **Great Whittington** Nthumb
62 A5 **Great Wigborough** Essex
76 D3 **Great Wilbraham** Cambs
28 B4 **Great Wishford** Wilts
55 K5 **Great Witcombe** Gloucs
70 D2 **Great Witley** Worcs
72 B7 **Great Wolford** Warwks
77 G5 **Great Wratting** Essex
59 K3 **Great Wymondley** Herts
85 H3 **Great Wyrley** Staffs
93 L3 **Great Yarmouth** Norfk
77 H6 **Great Yeldham** Essex
88 F2 **Greatford** Lincs
100 B4 **Greatgate** Staffs
30 C5 **Greatham** Hants
141 L2 **Greatham** Hartpl
18 E3 **Greatham** W Susx
21 L2 **Greatstone-on-Sea** Kent
73 G6 **Greatworth** Nhants
60 B4 **Green End** Herts
60 B2 **Green End** Herts
133 G7 **Green Hammerton** N York
85 H2 **Green Heath** Staffs
26 E2 **Green Ore** Somset
138 C6 **Green Quarter** Cumb
60 D4 **Green Street** Herts
59 K7 **Green Street** Herts
45 L6 **Green Street Green** Kent
60 C4 **Green Tye** Herts
176 C6 **Greenburn** W Loth
173 M1 **Greenfield** Ag & B
74 F7 **Greenfield** Beds
111 H6 **Greenfield** Flints
201 J5 **Greenfield** Highld
113 M2 **Greenfield** Oldham
43 J4 **Greenford** Gt Lon
175 K4 **Greengairs** N Lans
123 J3 **Greengates** Brad
120 E4 **Greenhalgh** Lancs
25 G7 **Greenham** Somset
157 K5 **Greenhaugh** Nthumb
149 H3 **Greenhead** Nthumb
155 J6 **Greenhill** D & G
175 L3 **Greenhill** Falk
47 K6 **Greenhill** Kent
165 H3 **Greenhill** S Lans
45 L5 **Greenhithe** Kent
164 B3 **Greenholm** E Ayrs
167 H5 **Greenhouse** Border
131 L6 **Greenhow Hill** N York
231 J3 **Greenland** Highld
115 H4 **Greenland** Sheff
167 L1 **Greenlaw** Border
155 H6 **Greenlea** D & G
185 H6 **Greenloaning** P & K
122 B7 **Greenmount** Bury
174 B3 **Greenock** Inver
129 G3 **Greenodd** Cumb
73 J4 **Greens Norton** Nhants
165 K2 **Greenshields** S Lans
150 E3 **Greenside** Gatesd
123 H7 **Greenside** Kirk
62 B3 **Greenstead** Essex
61 K3 **Greenstead Green** Essex
25 L6 **Greenway** Somset
45 G4 **Greenwich** Gt Lon
56 B3 **Greet** Gloucs
69 L1 **Greete** Shrops
118 D7 **Greetham** Lincs
88 D2 **Greetham** RutInd
123 G6 **Greetland** Calder
26 B4 **Greinton** Somset
237 b6 **Grenaby** IOM
74 C3 **Grendon** Nhants
86 C4 **Grendon** Warwks
58 B4 **Grendon Underwood** Bucks
115 G3 **Grenoside** Sheff
232 e4 **Greosabhagh** W Isls
97 M2 **Gresford** Wrexhm
106 E5 **Gresham** Norfk
208 E4 **Greshornish House Hotel** Highld
91 L1 **Gressenhall** Norfk
91 L1 **Gressenhall Green** Norfk
130 B5 **Gressingham** Lancs
140 D5 **Greta Bridge** Dur
148 B2 **Gretna** D & G
148 B2 **Gretna Green** D & G
56 A2 **Gretton** Gloucs
88 C5 **Gretton** Nhants
83 K4 **Gretton** Shrops
132 C4 **Grewelthorpe** N York
155 J4 **Greyrigg** D & G
42 B4 **Greys Green** Oxon
136 E2 **Greysouthen** Cumb
138 B2 **Greystoke** Cumb
196 E7 **Greystone** Angus
30 B2 **Greywell** Hants
86 D5 **Griff** Warwks
53 L7 **Griffithstown** Torfn
121 J7 **Grimeford Village** Lancs
115 G4 **Grimesthorpe** Sheff
124 C8 **Grimethorpe** Barns
70 E3 **Grimley** Worcs
163 H7 **Grimmet** S Ayrs
118 E4 **Grimoldby** Lincs
98 A7 **Grimpo** Shrops
121 H4 **Grimsargh** Lancs
127 G7 **Grimsby** NE Lin
73 J4 **Grimscote** Nhants
9 H4 **Grimscott** Cnwll
232 f3 **Grimshader** W Isls
103 H7 **Grimsthorpe** Lincs
102 B7 **Grimston** Leics
105 H7 **Grimston** Norfk
14 C4 **Grimstone** Dorset
77 L2 **Grimstone End** Suffk
135 H5 **Grindale** E R Yk
114 E6 **Grindleford** Derbys
121 L2 **Grindleton** Lancs
98 D4 **Grindley Brook** Shrops
114 D6 **Grindlow** Derbys
100 B2 **Grindon** Staffs
151 J4 **Grindon** Sundld
116 C4 **Gringley on the Hill** Notts
148 C4 **Grinsdale** Cumb
98 D7 **Grinshill** Shrops
140 D7 **Grinton** N York
232 f3 **Griomaisiader** W Isls
233 c6 **Griomsaigh** W Isls
188 F4 **Grishipoll** Ag & B
135 H3 **Gristhorpe** N York
91 L4 **Griston** Norfk
234 d6 **Gritley** Ork
40 B4 **Grittenham** Wilts
39 K4 **Grittleton** Wilts
128 F3 **Grizebeck** Cumb
137 K7 **Grizedale** Cumb
87 G3 **Groby** Leics
110 D8 **Groes** Conwy
37 G4 **Groes-faen** Rhondd
37 H3 **Groes-Wen** Caerph

233 b7 **Grogarry** W Isls
161 K1 **Grogport** Ag & B
233 b7 **Groigearraidh** W Isls
110 F5 **Gronant** Flints
32 F5 **Groombridge** E Susx
232 e4 **Grosebay** W Isls
54 B3 **Grosmont** Mons
143 H6 **Grosmont** N York
77 L6 **Groton** Suffk
236 e7 **Grouville** Jersey
116 C5 **Grove** Notts
41 H3 **Grove** Oxon
33 K3 **Grove Green** Kent
45 H5 **Grove Park** Gt Lon
51 H5 **Grovesend** Swans
219 L4 **Gruinard** Highld
170 F5 **Gruinart** Ag & B
208 F8 **Grula** Highld
190 B7 **Gruline** Ag & B
78 F4 **Grundisburgh** Suffk
235 c5 **Gruting** Shet
192 B7 **Gualachulain** Highld
187 G4 **Guardbridge** Fife
70 E5 **Guarlford** Worcs
194 F6 **Guay** P & K
236 c3 **Guernsey Airport** Guern
21 G3 **Guestling Green** E Susx
21 G3 **Guestling Thorn** E Susx
106 C6 **Guestwick** Norfk
121 K5 **Guide** Bl w D
159 G5 **Guide Post** Nthumb
75 K5 **Guilden Morden** Cambs
112 C7 **Guilden Sutton** Ches
31 G2 **Guildford** Surrey
186 B2 **Guildtown** P & K
87 J8 **Guilsborough** Nhants
82 E2 **Guilsfield** Powys
163 J7 **Guiltreehill** S Ayrs
23 J4 **Guineaford** Devon
142 D4 **Guisborough** R & Cl
123 J3 **Guiseley** Leeds
106 B7 **Guist** Norfk
56 C3 **Guiting Power** Gloucs
178 B2 **Gullane** E Loth
2 E5 **Gulval** Cnwll
6 C2 **Gulworthy** Devon
49 J7 **Gumfreston** Pembks
87 K5 **Gumley** Leics
20 C3 **Gun Hill** E Susx
102 E7 **Gunby** Lincs
118 F7 **Gunby** Lincs
29 L5 **Gundleton** Hants
23 K5 **Gunn** Devon
139 L7 **Gunnerside** N York
158 A7 **Gunnerton** Nthumb
125 K7 **Gunness** N Linc
6 C2 **Gunnislake** Cnwll
235 d6 **Gunnista** Shet
116 D3 **Gunthorpe** N Linc
106 B5 **Gunthorpe** Norfk
102 B4 **Gunthorpe** Notts
3 H6 **Gunwalloe** Cnwll
16 F4 **Gurnard** IoW
26 F2 **Gurney Slade** Somset
52 B6 **Gurnos** Powys
15 J1 **Gussage All Saints** Dorset
27 L8 **Gussage St Andrew** Dorset
15 J1 **Gussage St Michael** Dorset
35 J5 **Guston** Kent
235 d2 **Gutcher** Shet
196 F6 **Guthrie** Angus
90 B3 **Guyhirn** Cambs
158 F2 **Guyzance** Nthumb
110 F5 **Gwaenysgor** Flints
108 E6 **Gwalchmai** IoA
51 K3 **Gwaun-Cae-Gurwen** Carmth
3 J6 **Gweek** Cnwll
68 B6 **Gwenddwr** Powys
3 J4 **Gwennap** Cnwll
111 H7 **Gwernaffield** Flints
54 B7 **Gwernesney** Mons
66 C7 **Gwernogle** Carmth
111 H8 **Gwernymynydd** Flints
110 F5 **Gwespyr** Flints
3 G4 **Gwinear** Cnwll
3 G3 **Gwithian** Cnwll
97 G3 **Gwyddelwern** Denbgs
66 B7 **Gwyddgrug** Carmth
96 D1 **Gwytherin** Conwy

H

83 H3 **Habberley** Shrops
84 E7 **Habberley** Worcs
122 B4 **Habergham** Lancs
119 G7 **Habertoft** Lincs
126 E7 **Habrough** NE Lin
103 J7 **Hacconby** Lincs
103 G5 **Haceby** Lincs
79 G3 **Hacheston** Suffk
44 F6 **Hackbridge** Gt Lon
115 H5 **Hackenthorpe** Sheff
92 C3 **Hackford** Norfk
132 C2 **Hackforth** N York
234 c5 **Hackland** Ork
74 B4 **Hackleton** Nhants
35 J4 **Hacklinge** Kent
134 F2 **Hackness** N York
45 G3 **Hackney** Gt Lon
117 G5 **Hackthorn** Lincs
138 D3 **Hackthorpe** Cumb
168 B3 **Hadden** Border
58 C6 **Haddenham** Bucks
90 C7 **Haddenham** Cambs
178 B4 **Haddington** E Loth
116 E8 **Haddington** Lincs
93 J4 **Haddiscoe** Norfk
216 F6 **Haddo** Abers
89 G5 **Haddon** Cambs
114 A3 **Hadfield** Derbys
60 C4 **Hadham Ford** Herts
46 D3 **Hadleigh** Essex
78 B6 **Hadleigh** Suffk
70 F2 **Hadley** Worcs
100 C7 **Hadley End** Staffs
44 E1 **Hadley Wood** Gt Lon
33 H3 **Hadlow** Kent
20 B2 **Hadlow Down** E Susx
98 D7 **Hadnall** Shrops
76 D5 **Hadstock** Essex
71 G3 **Hadzor** Worcs
168 F2 **Haggerston** Nthumb
175 K3 **Haggs** Falk
69 L6 **Hagley** Herefs
85 G7 **Hagley** Worcs
118 D7 **Hagworthingham** Lincs
75 H3 **Hail Weston** Cambs
136 E5 **Haile** Cumb
57 G5 **Hailey** Oxon
20 C4 **Hailsham** E Susx
45 J2 **Hainault** Gt Lon
106 F8 **Hainford** Norfk
117 K5 **Hainton** Lincs
135 H6 **Haisthorpe** E R Yk
48 F6 **Hakin** Pembks
102 B2 **Halam** Notts
176 F1 **Halbeath** Fife
24 F8 **Halberton** Devon
231 J4 **Halcro** Highld
129 K4 **Hale** Cumb
112 C5 **Hale** Halton
28 D7 **Hale** Hants
30 D2 **Hale** Surrey
113 H4 **Hale** Traffd
20 B3 **Hale Green** E Susx
33 H4 **Hale Street** Kent
93 H4 **Hales** Norfk
99 G5 **Hales** Staffs
34 F3 **Hales Place** Kent
85 G6 **Halesowen** Dudley
93 H7 **Halesworth** Suffk
112 C4 **Halewood** Knows
7 J2 **Halford** Devon
72 C5 **Halford** Warwks
84 E5 **Halfpenny Green** Staffs
83 G2 **Halfway House** Shrops
46 F5 **Halfway Houses** Kent
123 G5 **Halifax** Calder
231 G4 **Halkirk** Highld
111 H7 **Halkyn** Flints
174 D7 **Hall** E Rens
137 H7 **Hall Dunnerdale** Cumb
176 B3 **Hall Glen** Falk
85 K7 **Hall Green** Birm
59 L3 **Hall's Green** Herts
20 A3 **Halland** E Susx
87 L4 **Hallaton** Leics
38 F8 **Hallatrow** BaNES
149 G3 **Hallbankgate** Cumb
38 D4 **Hallen** S Glos
151 H6 **Hallgarth** Dur
208 D3 **Hallin** Highld
46 B7 **Halling** Medway
118 D4 **Hallington** Lincs
158 C6 **Hallington** Nthumb
121 K7 **Halliwell** Bolton
102 B3 **Halloughton** Notts
70 E3 **Hallow** Worcs
7 J7 **Hallsands** Devon
166 B2 **Hallyne** Border
55 G7 **Halmore** Gloucs
18 B4 **Halnaker** W Susx
120 E7 **Halsall** Lancs
73 H6 **Halse** Nhants
25 H5 **Halse** Somset
2 E4 **Halsetown** Cnwll
127 G5 **Halsham** E R Yk
61 K2 **Halstead** Essex
45 J7 **Halstead** Kent
87 L3 **Halstead** Leics
14 A2 **Halstock** Dorset
25 H4 **Halsway** Somset
118 C8 **Haltham** Lincs
58 E6 **Halton** Bucks
129 K6 **Halton** Lancs
123 L4 **Halton** Leeds
150 C2 **Halton** Nthumb
97 L4 **Halton** Wrexhm
131 K8 **Halton East** N York
131 G4 **Halton Gill** N York
118 F7 **Halton Holegate** Lincs
149 H4 **Halton Lea Gate** Nthumb
150 C2 **Halton Shields** Nthumb
130 F8 **Halton West** N York
149 J3 **Haltwhistle** Nthumb
93 J3 **Halvergate** Norfk
7 H5 **Halwell** Devon
10 C5 **Halwill** Devon
10 C5 **Halwill Junction** Devon
13 G3 **Ham** Devon
55 G7 **Ham** Gloucs
44 D5 **Ham** Gt Lon
35 J4 **Ham** Kent
25 L6 **Ham** Somset
41 G7 **Ham** Wilts
71 H2 **Ham Green** Worcs
26 D4 **Ham Street** Somset
16 F2 **Hamble-le-Rice** Hants
42 C3 **Hambleden** Bucks
29 M7 **Hambledon** Hants
30 F4 **Hambledon** Surrey
120 E3 **Hambleton** Lancs
124 E4 **Hambleton** N York
26 B6 **Hambridge** Somset
17 L2 **Hambrook** W Susx
118 D7 **Hameringham** Lincs
89 G7 **Hamerton** Cambs
175 J7 **Hamilton** S Lans
14 B2 **Hamlet** Dorset
44 E4 **Hammersmith** Gt Lon
85 J3 **Hammerwich** Staffs
27 J8 **Hammoon** Dorset
235 c6 **Hamnavoe** Shet
235 d4 **Hamnavoe** Shet
20 C5 **Hampden Park** E Susx
56 C5 **Hampnett** Gloucs
124 D7 **Hampole** Donc
15 K3 **Hampreston** Dorset
44 E3 **Hampstead** Gt Lon
41 K5 **Hampstead Norrey's** W Berk
132 C7 **Hampsthwaite** N York
89 H5 **Hampton** Cambs
43 J6 **Hampton** Gt Lon
47 K6 **Hampton** Kent
84 D6 **Hampton** Shrops
40 D3 **Hampton** Swindn
71 H5 **Hampton** Worcs
69 L6 **Hampton Bishop** Herefs
44 D6 **Hampton Court Palace & Gardens** Gt Lon
98 D3 **Hampton Heath** Ches
86 B7 **Hampton in Arden** Solhll
70 F2 **Hampton Lovett** Worcs
72 B3 **Hampton Lucy** Warwks
72 C2 **Hampton Magna** Warwks
57 J5 **Hampton Poyle** Oxon
44 D6 **Hampton Wick** Gt Lon
28 E7 **Hamptworth** Wilts
19 L3 **Hamsey** E Susx
100 C8 **Hamstall Ridware** Staffs
41 H7 **Hamstead Marshall** W Berk
150 E4 **Hamsterley** Dur
140 E2 **Hamsterley** Dur
34 D7 **Hamstreet** Kent
15 J4 **Hamworthy** Poole
100 D6 **Hanbury** Staffs
71 G2 **Hanbury** Worcs
99 J4 **Hanchurch** Staffs
12 D4 **Hand and Pen** Devon
112 B7 **Handbridge** Ches
31 L5 **Handcross** W Susx
113 J5 **Handforth** Ches
98 C2 **Handley** Ches
101 G1 **Handley** Derbys
85 J5 **Handsworth** Birm
115 H4 **Handsworth** Sheff
87 L8 **Hanging Houghton** Nhants
28 B4 **Hanging Langford** Wilts
19 H4 **Hangleton** Br & H
38 F6 **Hanham** S Glos
98 F4 **Hankelow** Ches
39 L3 **Hankerton** Wilts
99 K3 **Hanley** C Stke

70 E6 **Hanley Castle** Worcs
70 B2 **Hanley Child** Worcs
70 E6 **Hanley Swan** Worcs
70 C2 **Hanley William** Worcs
131 G7 **Hanlith** N York
98 C4 **Hanmer** Wrexhm
23 J5 **Hannaford** Devon
29 K1 **Hannington** Hants
74 B1 **Hannington** Nhants
40 D2 **Hannington** Swindn
40 D2 **Hannington Wick** Swindn
74 B5 **Hanslope** M Keyn
103 H7 **Hanthorpe** Lincs
44 D4 **Hanwell** Gt Lon
72 E5 **Hanwell** Oxon
83 J2 **Hanwood** Shrops
43 J6 **Hanworth** Gt Lon
106 E5 **Hanworth** Norfk
165 G3 **Happendon** S Lans
107 H6 **Happisburgh** Norfk
107 H6 **Happisburgh Common** Norfk
112 C6 **Hapsford** Ches
122 B4 **Hapton** Lancs
92 E4 **Hapton** Norfk
7 H4 **Harberton** Devon
7 H5 **Harbertonford** Devon
34 F3 **Harbledown** Kent
85 H6 **Harborne** Birm
86 F7 **Harborough Magna** Warwks
158 B2 **Harbottle** Nthumb
7 G4 **Harbourneford** Devon
72 D3 **Harbury** Warwks
102 C6 **Harby** Leics
116 E7 **Harby** Notts
11 K8 **Harcombe** Devon
12 F4 **Harcombe** Devon
13 J4 **Harcombe Bottom** Devon
123 G3 **Harden** Brad
85 H4 **Harden** Wsall
206 E5 **Hardgate** Abers
146 E2 **Hardgate** D & G
174 F4 **Hardgate** W Duns
18 E3 **Hardham** W Susx
92 C3 **Hardingham** Norfk
73 L3 **Hardingstone** Nhants
27 H2 **Hardington** Somset
13 M1 **Hardington Mandeville** Somset
13 M1 **Hardington Marsh** Somset
26 D8 **Hardington Moor** Somset
22 C7 **Hardisworthy** Devon
16 E2 **Hardley** Hants
93 H4 **Hardley Street** Norfk
131 G2 **Hardraw** N York
115 H8 **Hardstoft** Derbys
17 H3 **Hardway** Hants
27 G5 **Hardway** Somset
58 D4 **Hardwick** Bucks
75 L3 **Hardwick** Cambs
74 B1 **Hardwick** Nhants
92 F5 **Hardwick** Norfk
57 G6 **Hardwick** Oxon
57 L3 **Hardwick** Oxon
55 H5 **Hardwicke** Gloucs
55 K3 **Hardwicke** Gloucs
61 M4 **Hardy's Green** Essex
123 G4 **Hare Croft** Brad
62 D3 **Hare Green** Essex
42 D5 **Hare Hatch** Wokham
60 C6 **Hare Street** Essex
60 C3 **Hare Street** Herts
118 D7 **Hareby** Lincs
43 H3 **Harefield** Gt Lon
100 D5 **Harehill** Derbys
123 L4 **Harehills** Leeds
167 H5 **Harelaw** Border
156 D6 **Harelaw** D & G
55 J6 **Harescombe** Gloucs
55 J6 **Haresfield** Gloucs
29 J5 **Harestock** Hants
123 L2 **Harewood** Leeds
54 D3 **Harewood End** Herefs
6 F4 **Harford** Devon
98 C1 **Hargrave** Ches
74 F1 **Hargrave** Nhants
77 H3 **Hargrave Green** Suffk
78 E7 **Harkstead** Suffk
86 B2 **Harlaston** Staffs
102 E6 **Harlaxton** Lincs
122 C4 **Harle Syke** Lancs
95 K6 **Harlech** Gwynd
83 K1 **Harlescott** Shrops
44 E4 **Harlesden** Gt Lon
115 J6 **Harlesthorpe** Derbys
7 J6 **Harleston** Devon
92 F6 **Harleston** Norfk
78 B3 **Harleston** Suffk
73 K2 **Harlestone** Nhants
115 G2 **Harley** Rothm
83 L3 **Harley** Shrops
59 G2 **Harlington** Beds
115 J2 **Harlington** Donc
43 H5 **Harlington** Gt Lon
208 D6 **Harlosh** Highld
60 D6 **Harlow** Essex
150 D2 **Harlow Hill** Nthumb
125 H3 **Harlthorpe** E R Yk
76 B4 **Harlton** Cambs
4 D2 **Harlyn** Cnwll
15 J6 **Harman's Cross** Dorset
131 L2 **Harmby** N York
59 L5 **Harmer Green** Herts
98 C7 **Harmer Hill** Shrops
116 F8 **Harmston** Lincs
83 L3 **Harnage** Shrops
56 B7 **Harnhill** Gloucs
45 K2 **Harold Hill** Gt Lon
45 K3 **Harold Wood** Gt Lon
48 E4 **Haroldston West** Pembks
235 e1 **Haroldswick** Shet
133 K3 **Harome** N York
59 J5 **Harpenden** Herts
12 E4 **Harpford** Devon
135 H7 **Harpham** E R Yk
105 J7 **Harpley** Norfk
70 C3 **Harpley** Worcs
73 K3 **Harpole** Nhants
231 G4 **Harpsdale** Highld
116 F4 **Harpswell** Lincs
113 K2 **Harpurhey** Manch
148 D4 **Harraby** Cumb
23 J6 **Harracott** Devon
199 K2 **Harrapool** Highld
185 K2 **Harrietfield** P & K
33 L3 **Harrietsham** Kent
44 F3 **Harringay** Gt Lon
136 D3 **Harrington** Cumb
118 E6 **Harrington** Lincs
87 L7 **Harrington** Nhants
88 D4 **Harringworth** Nhants
132 D8 **Harrogate** N York
74 D3 **Harrold** Beds
44 D3 **Harrow** Gt Lon
77 J4 **Harrow Green** Suffk
44 D3 **Harrow on the Hill** Gt Lon
44 D2 **Harrow Weald** Gt Lon
6 B2 **Harrowbarrow** Cnwll
76 B4 **Harston** Cambs
102 D6 **Harston** Leics
125 J3 **Harswell** E R Yk
151 L7 **Hart** Hartpl
158 D5 **Hartburn** Nthumb
77 J4 **Hartest** Suffk
32 E6 **Hartfield** E Susx
89 J8 **Hartford** Cambs
112 F6 **Hartford** Ches
61 G4 **Hartford End** Essex
42 C8 **Hartfordbridge** Hants
140 F6 **Hartforth** N York
27 J7 **Hartgrove** Dorset
98 D2 **Harthill** Ches
176 B5 **Harthill** N Lans
115 J5 **Harthill** Rothm
100 C1 **Hartington** Derbys
22 D6 **Hartland** Devon
22 C6 **Hartland Quay** Devon
70 E1 **Hartlebury** Worcs
151 L7 **Hartlepool** Hartpl
139 H5 **Hartley** Cumb
45 L6 **Hartley** Kent
33 K6 **Hartley** Kent
42 B8 **Hartley Wespall** Hants
30 C1 **Hartley Wintney** Hants
46 D7 **Hartlip** Kent
133 L6 **Harton** N York
151 J2 **Harton** S Tyne
55 J3 **Hartpury** Gloucs
123 J6 **Hartshead** Kirk
99 J4 **Hartshill** C Stke
86 D5 **Hartshill** Warwks
100 F7 **Hartshorne** Derbys
168 E6 **Hartside** Nthumb
73 L4 **Hartwell** Nhants
132 C6 **Hartwith** N York
175 L6 **Hartwood** N Lans
166 F4 **Hartwoodmyres** Border
46 A7 **Harvel** Kent
84 F8 **Harvington** Worcs
71 J5 **Harvington** Worcs
116 B3 **Harwell** Notts
41 J3 **Harwell** Oxon
62 F2 **Harwich** Essex
143 K7 **Harwood Dale** N York
115 L3 **Harworth** Notts
85 G6 **Hasbury** Dudley
31 G4 **Hascombe** Surrey
87 K7 **Haselbech** Nhants
13 L1 **Haselbury Plucknett** Somset
72 B2 **Haseley** Warwks
71 K3 **Haselor** Warwks
55 J3 **Hasfield** Gloucs
120 E8 **Haskayne** Lancs
78 F4 **Hasketon** Suffk
30 E5 **Haslemere** Surrey
122 B6 **Haslingden** Lancs
76 B4 **Haslingfield** Cambs
99 G2 **Haslington** Ches
93 H3 **Hassingham** Norfk
19 J3 **Hassocks** W Susx
114 E6 **Hassop** Derbys
231 K5 **Haster** Highld
34 E5 **Hastingleigh** Kent
21 G4 **Hastings** E Susx
60 D6 **Hastingwood** Essex
58 F6 **Hastoe** Herts
151 J6 **Haswell** Dur
151 J6 **Haswell Plough** Dur
25 L7 **Hatch Beauchamp** Somset
43 J3 **Hatch End** Gt Lon
112 D6 **Hatchmere** Ches
117 K2 **Hatcliffe** NE Lin
125 G8 **Hatfield** Donc
69 L3 **Hatfield** Herefs
59 L6 **Hatfield** Herts
60 E5 **Hatfield Broad Oak** Essex
60 E5 **Hatfield Heath** Essex
61 J5 **Hatfield Peverel** Essex
125 G8 **Hatfield Woodhouse** Donc
41 G2 **Hatford** Oxon
29 G2 **Hatherden** Hants
10 D4 **Hatherleigh** Devon
101 J7 **Hathern** Leics
56 D6 **Hatherop** Gloucs
114 E5 **Hathersage** Derbys
114 E5 **Hathersage Booths** Derbys
99 G3 **Hatherton** Ches
85 G2 **Hatherton** Staffs
75 K4 **Hatley St George** Cambs
6 B4 **Hatt** Cnwll
113 M3 **Hattersley** Tamesd
217 K6 **Hatton** Abers
196 D7 **Hatton** Angus
100 E6 **Hatton** Derbys
43 J5 **Hatton** Gt Lon
117 K6 **Hatton** Lincs
83 J5 **Hatton** Shrops
112 E5 **Hatton** Warrtn
72 B2 **Hatton** Warwks
206 F3 **Hatton of Fintray** Abers
163 L4 **Haugh** E Ayrs
215 J6 **Haugh of Glass** Moray
146 E2 **Haugh of Urr** D & G
118 D5 **Haugham** Lincs
175 G3 **Haughhead** E Duns
78 B3 **Haughley** Suffk
78 B2 **Haughley Green** Suffk
98 B6 **Haughton** Shrops
84 D2 **Haughton** Shrops
99 K7 **Haughton** Staffs
141 H4 **Haughton le Skerne** Darltn
98 E2 **Haughton Moss** Ches
60 B4 **Haultwick** Herts
86 B2 **Haunton** Staffs
236 c6 **Hautes Croix** Jersey
159 G2 **Hauxley** Nthumb
76 B4 **Hauxton** Cambs
17 K2 **Havant** Hants
17 G4 **Havenstreet** IOW
124 B7 **Havercroft** Wakefd
48 F4 **Haverfordwest** Pembks
76 F5 **Haverhill** Suffk
128 E4 **Haverigg** Cumb
45 K2 **Havering-atte-Bower** Essex
74 B6 **Haversham** M Keyn
129 H3 **Haverthwaite** Cumb
38 C7 **Havyat** N Som
111 J7 **Hawarden** Flints
61 J4 **Hawbush Green** Essex
92 F4 **Hawe's Green** Norfk
65 K5 **Hawen** Cerdgn
131 G2 **Hawes** N York
70 E3 **Hawford** Worcs
167 G6 **Hawick** Border
13 J3 **Hawkchurch** Devon
77 H4 **Hawkedon** Suffk
27 K2 **Hawkeridge** Wilts
39 H3 **Hawkesbury** S Glos
39 H3 **Hawkesbury Upton** S Glos
33 K6 **Hawkhurst** Kent
35 G6 **Hawkinge** Kent
30 C5 **Hawkley** Hants
24 D5 **Hawkridge** Somset
137 K7 **Hawkshead** Cumb
137 K7 **Hawkshead Hill** Cumb
165 G2 **Hawksland** S Lans
61 G2 **Hawkspur Green** Essex
98 E6 **Hawkstone** Shrops

131 H5 **Hawkswick** N York
123 H3 **Hawksworth** Leeds
102 C4 **Hawksworth** Notts
46 E2 **Hawkwell** Essex
42 E8 **Hawley** Hants
56 B4 **Hawling** Gloucs
133 H2 **Hawnby** N York
122 F3 **Haworth** Brad
77 J3 **Hawstead** Suffk
151 K5 **Hawthorn** Dur
103 K2 **Hawthorn Hill** Lincs
102 C3 **Hawton** Notts
133 J7 **Haxby** York
116 C2 **Haxey** N Linc
60 C3 **Hay Street** Herts
68 E6 **Hay-on-Wye** Powys
112 E3 **Haydock** St Hel
149 L3 **Haydon Bridge** Nthumb
40 C3 **Haydon Wick** Swindn
43 J4 **Hayes** Gt Lon
45 H6 **Hayes** Gt Lon
43 H4 **Hayes End** Gt Lon
182 F3 **Hayfield** Ag & B
114 B4 **Hayfield** Derbys
196 E7 **Hayhillock** Angus
2 F4 **Hayle** Cnwll
85 G6 **Hayley Green** Dudley
17 K3 **Hayling Island** Hants
24 E7 **Hayne** Devon
11 H7 **Hayne** Devon
74 F6 **Haynes (Church End)** Beds
75 G6 **Haynes (Northwood End)** Beds
75 G6 **Haynes (Silver End)** Beds
74 F6 **Haynes (West End)** Beds
48 F3 **Hayscastle** Pembks
48 F3 **Hayscastle Cross** Pembks
147 K6 **Hayton** Cumb
148 E4 **Hayton** Cumb
125 J2 **Hayton** E R Yk
116 B5 **Hayton** Notts
7 H1 **Haytor Vale** Devon
9 K3 **Haytown** Devon
19 J2 **Haywards Heath** W Susx
124 E7 **Haywood** Donc
113 L4 **Hazel Grove** Stockp
165 G1 **Hazelbank** S Lans
14 E2 **Hazelbury Bryan** Dorset
61 K7 **Hazeleigh** Essex
186 E3 **Hazelton Walls** Fife
101 G4 **Hazelwood** Derbys
42 E2 **Hazlemere** Bucks
159 G7 **Hazlerigg** N u Ty
56 B4 **Hazleton** Gloucs
105 G5 **Heacham** Norfk
29 J5 **Headbourne Worthy** Hants
33 L4 **Headcorn** Kent
123 K4 **Headingley** Leeds
57 K6 **Headington** Oxon
140 F4 **Headlam** Dur
176 B6 **Headlesscross** N Lans
41 K7 **Headley** Hants
30 D4 **Headley** Hants
31 K1 **Headley** Surrey
116 C6 **Headon** Notts
175 J8 **Heads** S Lans
148 E4 **Heads Nook** Cumb
101 G3 **Heage** Derbys
140 C7 **Healaugh** N York
124 D2 **Healaugh** N York
113 J4 **Heald Green** Stockp
25 K7 **Heale** Somset
26 B6 **Heale** Somset
132 B4 **Healey** N York
150 D5 **Healeyfield** Dur
126 F7 **Healing** NE Lin
2 E5 **Heamoor** Cnwll
101 H3 **Heanor** Derbys
23 H4 **Heanton Punchardon** Devon
116 E4 **Heapham** Lincs
24 B5 **Heasley Mill** Devon
199 K2 **Heast** Highld
115 J7 **Heath** Derbys
123 L6 **Heath** Wakefd
58 F3 **Heath and Reach** Beds
30 D2 **Heath End** Surrey
71 J1 **Heath Green** Worcs
155 H6 **Heath Hall** D & G
85 H2 **Heath Hayes & Wimblebury** Staffs
84 D2 **Heath Hill** Shrops
85 G4 **Heath Town** Wolves
100 D1 **Heathcote** Derbys
86 E2 **Heather** Leics
20 C2 **Heathfield** E Susx
25 J6 **Heathfield** Somset
43 H5 **Heathrow Airport** Gt Lon
84 E5 **Heathton** Shrops
100 B6 **Heatley** Staffs
113 G4 **Heatley** Warrtn
123 H4 **Heaton** Brad
151 G2 **Heaton** N u Ty
113 L8 **Heaton** Staffs
120 E7 **Heaton's Bridge** Lancs
33 G2 **Heaverham** Kent
12 B4 **Heavitree** Devon
151 H3 **Hebburn** S Tyne
131 J6 **Hebden** N York
122 E5 **Hebden Bridge** Calder
60 A4 **Hebing End** Herts
49 K3 **Hebron** Carmth
158 F4 **Hebron** Nthumb
42 B7 **Heckfield** Hants
92 E7 **Heckfield Green** Suffk
61 M4 **Heckfordbridge** Essex
103 J4 **Heckington** Lincs
123 J5 **Heckmondwike** Kirk
39 M6 **Heddington** Wilts
150 E2 **Heddon-on-the-Wall** Nthumb
93 G5 **Hedenham** Norfk
29 J8 **Hedge End** Hants
42 F3 **Hedgerley** Bucks
25 L5 **Hedging** Somset
150 D3 **Hedley on the Hill** Nthumb
85 H2 **Hednesford** Staffs
126 F5 **Hedon** E R Yk
42 E3 **Hedsor** Bucks
235 c5 **Heglibister** Shet
141 G3 **Heighington** Darltn
117 G7 **Heighington** Lincs
70 D1 **Heightington** Worcs
167 L4 **Heiton** Border
23 H3 **Hele** Devon
12 C2 **Hele** Devon
25 J6 **Hele** Somset
174 B2 **Helensburgh** Ag & B
163 J4 **Helenton** S Ayrs
3 K6 **Helford** Cnwll
3 K5 **Helford Passage** Cnwll
105 K7 **Helhoughton** Norfk
76 F6 **Helions Bumpstead** Essex
5 G2 **Helland** Cnwll
9 H6 **Hellescott** Cnwll
92 E2 **Hellesdon** Norfk
73 G3 **Hellidon** Nhants
131 G7 **Hellifield** N York
20 C4 **Hellingly** E Susx
158 F3 **Helm** Nthumb
73 H5 **Helmdon** Nhants
123 G7 **Helme** Kirk
78 E3 **Helmingham** Suffk
227 H5 **Helmsdale** Highld
122 B6 **Helmshore** Lancs
133 J3 **Helmsley** N York
133 G5 **Helperby** N York
134 E5 **Helperthorpe** N York
103 J4 **Helpringham** Lincs
89 G3 **Helpston** C Pete
112 C6 **Helsby** Ches
3 H5 **Helston** Cnwll
8 E8 **Helstone** Cnwll
138 D3 **Helton** Cumb
93 H2 **Hemblington** Norfk
59 H6 **Hemel Hempstead** Herts
6 E4 **Hemerdon** Devon
125 G4 **Hemingbrough** N York
118 C6 **Hemingby** Lincs
75 K1 **Hemingford Abbots** Cambs
75 K1 **Hemingford Grey** Cambs
78 D4 **Hemingstone** Suffk
101 J6 **Hemington** Leics
88 F6 **Hemington** Nhants
27 G2 **Hemington** Somset
79 G6 **Hemley** Suffk
142 B4 **Hemlington** Middsb
92 F5 **Hempnall** Norfk
92 F5 **Hempnall Green** Norfk
214 D2 **Hempriggs** Moray
76 F6 **Hempstead** Essex
106 D5 **Hempstead** Norfk
107 J6 **Hempstead** Norfk
105 L6 **Hempton** Norfk
57 H2 **Hempton** Oxon
107 K8 **Hemsby** Norfk
116 F4 **Hemswell** Lincs
116 F4 **Hemswell Cliff** Lincs
124 C7 **Hemsworth** Wakefd
25 H8 **Hemyock** Devon
167 L3 **Hendersyde Park** Border
44 E3 **Hendon** Gt Lon
151 K4 **Hendon** Sundld
51 H5 **Hendy** Carmth
19 G3 **Henfield** W Susx
37 J2 **Hengoed** Caerph
68 E4 **Hengoed** Powys
77 J2 **Hengrave** Suffk
60 E3 **Henham** Essex
82 C2 **Heniarth** Powys
25 L6 **Henlade** Somset
14 D2 **Henley** Dorset
26 B5 **Henley** Somset
78 E4 **Henley** Suffk
30 E6 **Henley** W Susx
20 E3 **Henley's Down** E Susx
71 L2 **Henley-in-Arden** Warwks
42 C4 **Henley-on-Thames** Oxon
65 K6 **Henllan** Cerdgn
110 E7 **Henllan** Denbgs
37 K3 **Henllys** Torfn
75 H6 **Henlow** Beds
11 J8 **Hennock** Devon
77 K6 **Henny Street** Essex
49 H3 **Henry's Moat (Castell Hendre)** Pembks
109 L6 **Henryd** Conwy
124 F5 **Hensall** N York
149 K3 **Henshaw** Nthumb
136 D4 **Hensingham** Cumb
93 K6 **Henstead** Suffk
29 J6 **Hensting** Hants
27 G7 **Henstridge** Somset
27 G7 **Henstridge Ash** Somset
58 C7 **Henton** Oxon
26 C3 **Henton** Somset
70 E4 **Henwick** Worcs
5 L2 **Henwood** Cnwll
36 E4 **Heol-y-Cyw** Brdgnd
158 C2 **Hepple** Nthumb
158 F5 **Hepscott** Nthumb
122 E5 **Heptonstall** Calder
114 D1 **Hepworth** Kirk
92 B8 **Hepworth** Suffk
48 E6 **Herbrandston** Pembks
69 K6 **Hereford** Herefs
35 K2 **Hereson** Kent
218 B7 **Heribusta** Highld
177 L7 **Heriot** Border
177 G4 **Hermiston** C Edin
156 E3 **Hermitage** Border
14 C2 **Hermitage** Dorset
41 J5 **Hermitage** W Berk
49 L2 **Hermon** Pembks
47 K6 **Herne** Kent
47 K6 **Herne Bay** Kent
44 F5 **Herne Hill** Gt Lon
33 H3 **Herne Pound** Kent
23 J6 **Herner** Devon
34 E3 **Hernhill** Kent
5 K4 **Herodsfoot** Cnwll
152 D5 **Heronsford** S Ayrs
30 A3 **Herriard** Hants
93 K4 **Herringfleet** Suffk
77 G1 **Herringswell** Suffk
115 J3 **Herringthorpe** Rothm
151 H4 **Herrington** Sundld
35 G3 **Hersden** Kent
43 J7 **Hersham** Surrey
20 D3 **Herstmonceux** E Susx
234 c7 **Herston** Ork
60 B5 **Hertford** Herts
60 B5 **Hertford Heath** Herts
60 A5 **Hertingfordbury** Herts
148 C7 **Hesket Newmarket** Cumb
120 F5 **Hesketh Bank** Lancs
121 J3 **Hesketh Lane** Lancs
151 K7 **Hesleden** Dur
124 F1 **Heslington** York
133 H8 **Hessay** York
5 L4 **Hessenford** Cnwll
77 L3 **Hessett** Suffk
126 C5 **Hessle** E R Yk
124 C6 **Hessle** Wakefd
43 J5 **Heston** Gt Lon
234 b5 **Hestwall** Ork
111 J5 **Heswall** Wirral
57 L3 **Hethe** Oxon
92 D3 **Hethersett** Norfk
148 E2 **Hethersgill** Cumb
168 D4 **Hethpool** Nthumb
151 G7 **Hett** Dur
131 H7 **Hetton** N York
151 J5 **Hetton-le-Hole** Sundld
158 D7 **Heugh** Nthumb
179 H6 **Heugh Head** Border
205 J3 **Heughhead** Abers
93 G8 **Heveningham** Suffk
32 E4 **Hever** Kent
129 K3 **Heversham** Cumb
106 E7 **Hevingham** Norfk
4 F6 **Hewas Water** Cnwll
54 E7 **Hewelsfield** Gloucs
13 K2 **Hewish** Somset
13 J2 **Hewood** Dorset

150 B3 **Hexham** Nthumb
45 K6 **Hextable** Kent
115 K2 **Hexthorpe** Donc
59 J2 **Hexton** Herts
9 K8 **Hexworthy** Cnwll
6 F2 **Hexworthy** Devon
61 K6 **Heybridge** Essex
61 G7 **Heybridge** Essex
6 D6 **Heybrook Bay** Devon
76 B6 **Heydon** Cambs
106 D6 **Heydon** Norfk
103 G5 **Heydour** Lincs
188 C7 **Heylipoll** Ag & B
235 c3 **Heylor** Shet
129 J7 **Heysham** Lancs
18 B3 **Heyshott** W Susx
27 L3 **Heytesbury** Wilts
57 G3 **Heythrop** Oxon
122 C7 **Heywood** Rochdl
27 K2 **Heywood** Wilts
116 F2 **Hibaldstow** N Linc
115 J1 **Hickleton** Donc
107 J7 **Hickling** Norfk
102 B6 **Hickling** Notts
107 J7 **Hickling Green** Norfk
31 L7 **Hickstead** W Susx
71 L6 **Hidcote Bartrim** Gloucs
71 L6 **Hidcote Boyce** Gloucs
124 C6 **High Ackworth** Wakefd
144 C6 **High Ardwell** D & G
154 F5 **High Auldgirth** D & G
148 F6 **High Bankhill** Cumb
60 C7 **High Beach** Essex
130 C5 **High Bentham** N York
23 J7 **High Bickington** Devon
130 B4 **High Biggins** Cumb
175 J6 **High Blantyre** S Lans
175 L3 **High Bonnybridge** Falk
23 L5 **High Bray** Devon
33 G5 **High Brooms** Kent
130 C4 **High Casterton** Cumb
133 L8 **High Catton** E R Yk
141 G4 **High Coniscliffe** Darltn
148 E3 **High Crosby** Cumb
163 K1 **High Cross** E Ayrs
30 B6 **High Cross** Hants
60 B4 **High Cross** Herts
71 L2 **High Cross** Warwks
144 D7 **High Drummore** D & G
60 F5 **High Easter** Essex
132 B3 **High Ellington** N York
98 E8 **High Ercall** Wrekin
140 F2 **High Etherley** Dur
61 J3 **High Garrett** Essex
132 C5 **High Grantley** N York
92 D3 **High Green** Norfk
92 E5 **High Green** Norfk
115 G3 **High Green** Sheff
70 F5 **High Green** Worcs
34 B7 **High Halden** Kent
46 C5 **High Halstow** Medway
26 B5 **High Ham** Somset
132 D7 **High Harrogate** N York
98 E7 **High Hatton** Shrops
143 J5 **High Hawsker** N York
148 E6 **High Hesket** Cumb
123 K8 **High Hoyland** Barns
32 E7 **High Hurstwood** E Susx
134 B5 **High Hutton** N York
147 M7 **High Ireby** Cumb
133 H4 **High Kilburn** N York
140 E3 **High Lands** Dur
113 L4 **High Lane** Stockp
3 G4 **High Lanes** Cnwll
113 G5 **High Legh** Ches
141 K5 **High Leven** S on T
38 F8 **High Littleton** BaNES
137 G3 **High Lorton** Cumb
116 D7 **High Marnham** Notts
115 K2 **High Melton** Donc
150 D3 **High Mickley** Nthumb
151 J4 **High Newport** Sundld
129 J3 **High Newton** Cumb
129 G2 **High Nibthwaite** Cumb
99 H7 **High Offley** Staffs
60 E7 **High Ongar** Essex
84 E1 **High Onn** Staffs
62 C4 **High Park Corner** Essex
163 L7 **High Pennyvenie** E Ayrs
60 F4 **High Roding** Essex
18 F4 **High Salvington** W Susx
150 E3 **High Spen** Gatesd
4 F5 **High Street** Cnwll
79 J4 **High Street** Suffk
118 C7 **High Toynton** Lincs
158 C2 **High Trewhitt** Nthumb
151 G4 **High Urpeth** Dur
176 D2 **High Valleyfield** Fife
137 K7 **High Wray** Cumb
60 D5 **High Wych** Herts
42 E2 **High Wycombe** Bucks
114 F1 **Higham** Barns
101 H2 **Higham** Derbys
33 G4 **Higham** Kent
46 B5 **Higham** Kent
122 B3 **Higham** Lancs
77 H2 **Higham** Suffk
78 B7 **Higham** Suffk
158 E6 **Higham Dykes** Nthumb
74 D2 **Higham Ferrers** Nhants
59 J2 **Higham Gobion** Beds
45 G3 **Higham Hill** Gt Lon
86 E4 **Higham on the Hill** Leics
10 C4 **Highampton** Devon
45 H2 **Highams Park** Gt Lon
25 L3 **Highbridge** Somset
32 C7 **Highbrook** W Susx
123 J7 **Highburton** Kirk
44 F3 **Highbury** Gt Lon
27 G2 **Highbury** Somset
41 H8 **Highclere** Hants
16 B4 **Highcliffe** Dorset
14 E2 **Higher Ansty** Dorset
121 G4 **Higher Bartle** Lancs
14 D4 **Higher Bockhampton** Dorset
7 L5 **Higher Brixham** Torbay
13 K1 **Higher Chillington** Somset
113 G2 **Higher Folds** Wigan
7 L3 **Higher Gabwell** Devon
129 J7 **Higher Heysham** Lancs
113 G3 **Higher Irlam** Salfd
97 L1 **Higher Kinnerton** Flints
23 J4 **Higher Muddiford** Devon
121 G5 **Higher Penwortham** Lancs
4 C6 **Higher Town** Cnwll
4 F4 **Higher Town** Cnwll
2 b1 **Higher Town** IOS
121 H5 **Higher Walton** Lancs
112 E4 **Higher Walton** Warrtn
13 H2 **Higher Wambrook** Somset
14 D4 **Higher Waterston** Dorset
121 J6 **Higher Wheelton** Lancs
112 F5 **Higher Whitley** Ches
14 B3 **Higher Wraxhall** Dorset
98 C4 **Higher Wych** Ches
150 E3 **Highfield** Gatesd
174 C7 **Highfield** N Ayrs
44 F3 **Highgate** Gt Lon
203 J4 **Highland Wildlife Park** Highld
115 H5 **Highlane** Derbys
55 H4 **Highleadon** Gloucs
18 A6 **Highleigh** W Susx
84 D6 **Highley** Shrops
42 B4 **Highmoor** Oxon
42 B4 **Highmoor Cross** Oxon
55 H4 **Highnam** Gloucs
34 B3 **Highsted** Kent
34 E3 **Highstreet** Kent
77 H7 **Highstreet Green** Essex
31 G4 **Highstreet Green** Surrey
155 J6 **Hightae** D & G
111 J2 **Hightown** Sefton
77 L4 **Hightown Green** Suffk
7 J2 **Highweek** Devon
44 E2 **Highwood Hill** Gt Lon
40 D2 **Highworth** Swindn
91 J4 **Hilborough** Norfk
33 G4 **Hilden Park** Kent
32 F4 **Hildenborough** Kent
76 D5 **Hildersham** Cambs
99 L5 **Hilderstone** Staffs
135 J6 **Hilderthorpe** E R Yk
14 C2 **Hilfield** Dorset
90 E4 **Hilgay** Norfk
38 F2 **Hill** S Glos
72 F2 **Hill** Warwks
30 C6 **Hill Brow** Hants
99 H5 **Hill Chorlton** Staffs
25 H6 **Hill Common** Somset
104 B3 **Hill Dyke** Lincs
185 L7 **Hill End** Fife
70 F6 **Hill End** Gloucs
46 D7 **Hill Green** Kent
17 G2 **Hill Head** Hants
176 F1 **Hill of Beath** Fife
223 H5 **Hill of Fearn** Highld
100 B8 **Hill Ridware** Staffs
123 H6 **Hill Side** Kirk
186 F5 **Hill of Tarvit Mansion House** Fife
123 L7 **Hill Top** Wakefd
124 D5 **Hillam** N York
15 J3 **Hillbutts** Dorset
100 F3 **Hillcliffiane** Derbys
40 C8 **Hillcott** Wilts
176 F2 **Hillend** Fife
177 H5 **Hillend** Mdloth
175 L5 **Hillend** N Lans
58 B3 **Hillesden** Bucks
39 H3 **Hillesley** Gloucs
25 J6 **Hillfarrance** Somset
165 J2 **Hillhead** S Lans
217 K5 **Hillhead of Cocklaw** Abers
216 D8 **Hillhead of Durno** Abers
231 H3 **Hilliclay** Highld
43 H4 **Hillingdon** Gt Lon
174 F5 **Hillington** C Glas
105 H7 **Hillington** Norfk
87 G8 **Hillmorton** Warwks
146 D3 **Hillowton** D & G
115 J7 **Hills Town** Derbys
207 H5 **Hillside** Abers
197 H4 **Hillside** Angus
29 G7 **Hillstreet** Hants
235 c3 **Hillswick** Shet
10 D8 **Hilltown** Devon
177 J4 **Hilltown** E Loth
235 c8 **Hillwell** Shet
40 A5 **Hilmarton** Wilts
39 K8 **Hilperton** Wilts
17 J2 **Hilsea** C Port
127 G4 **Hilston** E R Yk
179 H7 **Hilton** Border
75 K2 **Hilton** Cambs
139 G3 **Hilton** Cumb
100 E6 **Hilton** Derbys
14 E2 **Hilton** Dorset
140 F3 **Hilton** Dur
223 J6 **Hilton** Highld
141 K5 **Hilton** S on T
84 D4 **Hilton** Shrops
71 G3 **Himbleton** Worcs
84 F5 **Himley** Staffs
129 L3 **Hincaster** Cumb
44 D6 **Hinchley Wood** Surrey
86 E5 **Hinckley** Leics
92 B7 **Hinderclay** Suffk
143 G4 **Hinderwell** N York
30 E4 **Hindhead** Surrey
112 F1 **Hindley** Wigan
70 F3 **Hindlip** Worcs
106 C6 **Hindolveston** Norfk
27 K5 **Hindon** Wilts
106 B5 **Hindringham** Norfk
92 B3 **Hingham** Norfk
99 G7 **Hinstock** Shrops
78 C5 **Hintlesham** Suffk
69 G6 **Hinton** Herefs
39 G5 **Hinton** S Glos
83 H2 **Hinton** Shrops
29 L6 **Hinton Ampner** Hants
26 E1 **Hinton Blewett** BaNES
39 H8 **Hinton Charterhouse** BaNES
15 J2 **Hinton Martell** Dorset
71 H6 **Hinton on the Green** Worcs
40 E4 **Hinton Parva** Swindn
26 B8 **Hinton St George** Somset
27 H7 **Hinton St Mary** Dorset
57 G7 **Hinton Waldrist** Oxon
73 H6 **Hinton-in-the-Hedges** Nhants
85 L3 **Hints** Staffs
74 D3 **Hinwick** Beds
34 D6 **Hinxhill** Kent
76 C5 **Hinxton** Cambs
75 J6 **Hinxworth** Herts
123 H5 **Hipperholme** Calder
140 F7 **Hipswell** N York
206 D5 **Hirn** Abers
97 G7 **Hirnant** Powys
159 G5 **Hirst** Nthumb
124 F5 **Hirst Courtney** N York
52 E6 **Hirwaun** Rhondd
23 J6 **Hiscott** Devon
76 B2 **Histon** Cambs
78 B4 **Hitcham** Suffk
78 B4 **Hitcham Causeway** Suffk
78 B4 **Hitcham Street** Suffk
59 K3 **Hitchin** Herts
45 H5 **Hither Green** Gt Lon
11 H5 **Hittisleigh** Devon
125 J4 **Hive** E R Yk
100 A7 **Hixon** Staffs
35 H3 **Hoaden** Kent

100 C7 **Hoar Cross** Staffs
54 D3 **Hoarwithy** Herefs
47 K7 **Hoath** Kent
82 F7 **Hobarris** Shrops
167 J7 **Hobkirk** Border
150 F4 **Hobson** Dur
102 A8 **Hoby** Leics
92 C2 **Hockering** Norfk
102 B2 **Hockerton** Notts
46 D2 **Hockley** Essex
85 L8 **Hockley Heath** Solhll
58 F3 **Hockliffe** Beds
91 G6 **Hockwold cum Wilton** Norfk
25 G7 **Hockworthy** Devon
60 B6 **Hoddesdon** Herts
121 L6 **Hoddlesden** Bl w D
155 L7 **Hoddom Cross** D & G
155 K7 **Hoddom Mains** D & G
49 H7 **Hodgeston** Pembks
98 E6 **Hodnet** Shrops
45 L7 **Hodsall Street** Kent
115 L4 **Hodsock** Notts
40 D4 **Hodson** Swindn
115 K6 **Hodthorpe** Derbys
92 B1 **Hoe** Norfk
34 D4 **Hogben's Hill** Kent
58 D3 **Hoggeston** Bucks
86 B5 **Hoggrill's End** Warwks
121 J5 **Hoghton** Lancs
100 E3 **Hognaston** Derbys
119 H6 **Hogsthorpe** Lincs
104 B7 **Holbeach** Lincs
89 K2 **Holbeach Drove** Lincs
104 C6 **Holbeach Hurn** Lincs
104 B8 **Holbeach St Johns** Lincs
104 B6 **Holbeach St Mark's** Lincs
104 C6 **Holbeach St Matthew** Lincs
115 K6 **Holbeck** Notts
71 H3 **Holberrow Green** Worcs
6 F5 **Holbeton** Devon
44 F4 **Holborn** Gt Lon
101 G4 **Holbrook** Derbys
78 E6 **Holbrook** Suffk
16 E2 **Holbury** Hants
12 B7 **Holcombe** Devon
26 F2 **Holcombe** Somset
25 G7 **Holcombe Rogus** Devon
73 L1 **Holcot** Nhants
122 B1 **Holden** Lancs
73 K2 **Holdenby** Nhants
61 G3 **Holder's Green** Essex
83 L5 **Holdgate** Shrops
103 H3 **Holdingham** Lincs
13 J2 **Holditch** Dorset
10 B4 **Hole** Devon
25 J3 **Holford** Somset
124 E1 **Holgate** York
129 H4 **Holker** Cumb
105 L4 **Holkham** Norfk
105 L4 **Holkham Hall** Norfk
9 K4 **Hollacombe** Devon
103 L3 **Holland Fen** Lincs
62 E5 **Holland-on-Sea** Essex
234 e3 **Hollandstoun** Ork
148 A2 **Hollee** D & G
79 H5 **Hollesley** Suffk
7 K4 **Hollicombe** Torbay
33 L3 **Hollingbourne** Kent
19 J4 **Hollingbury** Br & H
58 E3 **Hollingdon** Bucks
100 E5 **Hollington** Derbys
100 B5 **Hollington** Staffs
114 A3 **Hollingworth** Tamesd
115 G5 **Hollins End** Sheff
113 G4 **Hollins Green** Warrtn
114 B7 **Hollinsclough** Staffs
10 F3 **Hollocombe** Devon
100 F2 **Holloway** Derbys
44 F3 **Holloway** Gt Lon
73 K1 **Hollowell** Nhants
112 C7 **Hollowmoor Heath** Ches
156 C6 **Hollows** D & G
70 F6 **Holly Green** Worcs
53 J7 **Hollybush** Caerph
163 K6 **Hollybush** E Ayrs
70 D6 **Hollybush** Herefs
127 H5 **Hollym** E R Yk
114 C1 **Holmbridge** Kirk
31 J3 **Holmbury St Mary** Surrey
5 G5 **Holmbush** Cnwll
99 K7 **Holmcroft** Staffs
89 H6 **Holme** Cambs
129 L4 **Holme** Cumb
114 C1 **Holme** Kirk
132 E3 **Holme** N York
102 D2 **Holme** Notts
122 C5 **Holme Chapel** Lancs
124 E3 **Holme Green** N York
91 K3 **Holme Hale** Norfk
69 L7 **Holme Lacy** Herefs
69 G4 **Holme Marsh** Herefs
105 H4 **Holme next the Sea** Norfk
126 B2 **Holme on the Wolds** E R Yk
101 L5 **Holme Pierrepont** Notts
147 J5 **Holme St Cuthbert** Cumb
125 J3 **Holme upon Spalding Moor** E R Yk
69 K6 **Holmer** Herefs
42 E2 **Holmer Green** Bucks
113 H7 **Holmes Chapel** Ches
114 F6 **Holmesfield** Derbys
120 F6 **Holmeswood** Lancs
32 B3 **Holmethorpe** Surrey
115 H7 **Holmewood** Derbys
123 H8 **Holmfirth** Kirk
164 B5 **Holmhead** E Ayrs
127 J5 **Holmpton** E R Yk
136 E7 **Holmrook** Cumb
150 F5 **Holmside** Dur
7 G3 **Holne** Devon
14 C1 **Holnest** Dorset
24 E3 **Holnicote** Somset
9 J4 **Holsworthy** Devon
9 K3 **Holsworthy Beacon** Devon
15 J2 **Holt** Dorset
106 C5 **Holt** Norfk
39 K7 **Holt** Wilts
70 E3 **Holt** Worcs
98 B2 **Holt** Wrexhm
71 J1 **Holt End** Worcs
70 E2 **Holt Heath** Worcs
133 K8 **Holtby** York
57 L6 **Holton** Oxon
27 G6 **Holton** Somset
93 J7 **Holton** Suffk
117 J5 **Holton cum Beckering** Lincs
118 C2 **Holton le Clay** Lincs
117 H3 **Holton le Moor** Lincs
78 C6 **Holton St Mary** Suffk
14 D1 **Holwell** Dorset
59 K2 **Holwell** Herts
102 B7 **Holwell** Leics
56 E6 **Holwell** Oxon
139 K2 **Holwick** Dur
169 H2 **Holy Island** Nthumb
108 C5 **Holy Island** IOA
30 B4 **Holybourne** Hants
108 C5 **Holyhead** IOA
115 G7 **Holymoorside** Derbys
42 E5 **Holyport** W & M
158 B2 **Holystone** Nthumb
175 K6 **Holytown** N Lans
75 L1 **Holywell** Cambs
4 B4 **Holywell** Cnwll
14 B2 **Holywell** Dorset
111 G6 **Holywell** Flints
123 G6 **Holywell Green** Calder
25 H7 **Holywell Lake** Somset
91 G7 **Holywell Row** Suffk
155 G6 **Holywood** D & G
155 G6 **Holywood Village** D & G
84 B3 **Homer** Shrops
111 K2 **Homer Green** Sefton
93 G6 **Homersfield** Suffk
28 C6 **Homington** Wilts
77 L7 **Honey Tye** Suffk
71 K5 **Honeybourne** Worcs
10 F4 **Honeychurch** Devon
40 C7 **Honeystreet** Wilts
86 B8 **Honiley** Warwks
107 G6 **Honing** Norfk
92 D2 **Honingham** Norfk
102 F4 **Honington** Lincs
91 K8 **Honington** Suffk
72 C6 **Honington** Warwks
12 F3 **Honiton** Devon
123 H7 **Honley** Kirk
113 G5 **Hoo Green** Ches
46 C5 **Hoo St Werburgh** Medway
6 D5 **Hooe** C Plym
20 E4 **Hooe** E Susx
120 D3 **Hoohill** Bpool
125 H5 **Hook** E R Yk
30 B1 **Hook** Hants
49 G5 **Hook** Pembks
44 D7 **Hook** Surrey
40 B4 **Hook** Wilts
45 L6 **Hook Green** Kent
33 H6 **Hook Green** Kent
57 G2 **Hook Norton** Oxon
14 A3 **Hooke** Dorset
11 K5 **Hookway** Devon
115 K3 **Hooton Levitt** Rothm
124 D8 **Hooton Pagnell** Donc
115 J3 **Hooton Roberts** Rothm
114 D5 **Hope** Derbys
7 G7 **Hope** Devon
97 L2 **Hope** Flints
83 L8 **Hope** Shrops
100 C2 **Hope** Staffs
83 J5 **Hope Bowdler** Shrops
54 F4 **Hope Mansell** Herefs
69 K4 **Hope under Dinmore** Herefs
166 D6 **Hopehouse** Border
214 E1 **Hopeman** Moray
83 H6 **Hopesay** Shrops
133 K8 **Hopgrove** York
132 F7 **Hopperton** N York
84 D5 **Hopstone** Shrops
100 E2 **Hopton** Derbys
99 L7 **Hopton** Staffs
92 B7 **Hopton** Suffk
83 K7 **Hopton Cangeford** Shrops
83 G7 **Hopton Castle** Shrops
93 L4 **Hopton on Sea** Norfk
84 B7 **Hopton Wafers** Shrops
83 H7 **Hoptonheath** Shrops
85 L3 **Hopwas** Staffs
85 J7 **Hopwood** Worcs
20 C3 **Horam** E Susx
103 J5 **Horbling** Lincs
123 K6 **Horbury** Wakefd
151 K6 **Horden** Dur
16 C4 **Hordle** Hants
98 B6 **Hordley** Shrops
38 E5 **Horfield** Bristl
92 E8 **Horham** Suffk
62 B3 **Horkesley Heath** Essex
126 B6 **Horkstow** N Linc
72 E5 **Horley** Oxon
32 B5 **Horley** Surrey
26 E5 **Hornblotton Green** Somset
130 B5 **Hornby** Lancs
141 J6 **Hornby** N York
132 C2 **Hornby** N York
118 C7 **Horncastle** Lincs
45 K3 **Hornchurch** Gt Lon
179 J7 **Horncliffe** Nthumb
179 J8 **Horndean** Border
30 B8 **Horndean** Hants
10 D8 **Horndon** Devon
46 A4 **Horndon on the Hill** Thurr
32 C4 **Horne** Surrey
24 D3 **Horner** Somset
107 H8 **Horning** Norfk
88 B4 **Horninghold** Leics
100 E7 **Horninglow** Staffs
76 C3 **Horningsea** Cambs
27 J3 **Horningsham** Wilts
105 M7 **Horningtoft** Norfk
22 F6 **Horns Cross** Devon
126 F2 **Hornsea** E R Yk
44 F3 **Hornsey** Gt Lon
72 E5 **Hornton** Oxon
235 d2 **Horra** Shet
6 D2 **Horrabridge** Devon
7 H2 **Horridge** Devon
77 J3 **Horringer** Suffk
121 L2 **Horrocksford** Lancs
6 B2 **Horsebridge** Devon
20 C4 **Horsebridge** E Susx
29 G5 **Horsebridge** Hants
83 G3 **Horsebridge** Shrops
76 E5 **Horseheath** Cambs
131 K4 **Horsehouse** N York
43 G8 **Horsell** Surrey
98 C4 **Horseman's Green** Wrexhm
107 K7 **Horsey** Norfk
25 L4 **Horsey** Somset
92 E1 **Horsford** Norfk
123 J3 **Horsforth** Leeds
31 K5 **Horsham** W Susx
70 D3 **Horsham** Worcs
92 E1 **Horsham St Faith** Norfk
117 K7 **Horsington** Lincs
27 G6 **Horsington** Somset
101 G4 **Horsley** Derbys
39 J2 **Horsley** Gloucs
157 L3 **Horsley** Nthumb
150 D2 **Horsley** Nthumb
101 H4 **Horsley Woodhouse** Derbys
62 D3 **Horsleycross Street** Essex
167 H5 **Horsleyhill** Border
33 J5 **Horsmonden** Kent
57 L6 **Horspath** Oxon
106 F8 **Horstead** Norfk
32 C7 **Horsted Keynes** W Susx
58 F4 **Horton** Bucks
15 J2 **Horton** Dorset
122 C1 **Horton** Lancs
74 B4 **Horton** Nhants
39 H4 **Horton** S Glos
25 L7 **Horton** Somset
99 L2 **Horton** Staffs
50 F7 **Horton** Swans
43 G5 **Horton** W & M
40 B7 **Horton** Wilts

84 C1 **Horton** Wrekin
98 C3 **Horton Green** Ches
130 F5 **Horton in Ribblesdale** N York
45 K6 **Horton Kirby** Kent
57 L5 **Horton-cum-Studley** Oxon
121 J7 **Horwich** Bolton
23 H6 **Horwood** Devon
166 F6 **Hoscote** Border
102 B6 **Hose** Leics
185 H3 **Hosh** P & K
235 c7 **Hoswick** Shet
125 L4 **Hotham** E R Yk
34 C5 **Hothfield** Kent
101 L7 **Hoton** Leics
157 K5 **Hott** Nthumb
99 G3 **Hough** Ches
112 C4 **Hough Green** Halton
102 F3 **Hough-on-the-Hill** Lincs
102 E4 **Hougham** Lincs
75 K1 **Houghton** Cambs
29 G5 **Houghton** Hants
49 G6 **Houghton** Pembks
18 D4 **Houghton** W Susx
74 F6 **Houghton Conquest** Beds
21 H2 **Houghton Green** E Susx
151 H5 **Houghton le Spring** Sundld
87 J3 **Houghton on the Hill** Leics
59 G4 **Houghton Regis** Beds
105 L5 **Houghton St Giles** Norfk
42 B8 **Hound Green** Hants
178 D8 **Houndslow** Border
179 H5 **Houndwood** Border
43 J5 **Hounslow** Gt Lon
61 G4 **Hounslow Green** Essex
213 L4 **Househill** Highld
123 J6 **Houses Hill** Kirk
149 K2 **Housesteads Roman Fort** Nthumb
207 G1 **Housieside** Abers
174 D5 **Houston** Rens
227 K2 **Houstry** Highld
234 b6 **Houton** Ork
19 J5 **Hove** Br & H
102 B3 **Hoveringham** Notts
107 G8 **Hoveton** Norfk
133 K4 **Hovingham** N York
54 E3 **How Caple** Herefs
148 E4 **How Mill** Cumb
125 H5 **Howden** E R Yk
150 E7 **Howden-le-Wear** Dur
231 K3 **Howe** Highld
132 E4 **Howe** N York
92 F4 **Howe** Norfk
61 J7 **Howe Green** Essex
216 E5 **Howe of Teuchar** Abers
61 H5 **Howe Street** Essex
77 G7 **Howe Street** Essex
61 K7 **Howegreen** Essex
103 J4 **Howell** Lincs
147 L2 **Howes** D & G
68 B3 **Howey** Powys
177 H6 **Howgate** Mdloth
169 K5 **Howick** Nthumb
140 D3 **Howle** Dur
99 G7 **Howle** Wrekin
54 E4 **Howle Hill** Herefs
76 E7 **Howlett End** Essex
13 H1 **Howley** Somset
233 b7 **Howmore** W Isls
168 B5 **Hownam** Border
117 H2 **Howsham** N Linc
133 L6 **Howsham** N York
168 D3 **Howtel** Nthumb
174 D6 **Howwood** Rens
92 E7 **Hoxne** Suffk
111 H4 **Hoylake** Wirral
115 G2 **Hoyland Nether** Barns
114 E1 **Hoyland Swaine** Barns
48 E6 **Hubberston** Pembks
123 K2 **Huby** N York
133 J6 **Huby** N York
55 K4 **Hucclecote** Gloucs
33 L2 **Hucking** Kent
101 K3 **Hucknall** Notts
123 H7 **Huddersfield** Kirk
71 G3 **Huddington** Worcs
140 E7 **Hudswell** N York
134 D7 **Huggate** E R Yk
2 b2 **Hugh Town** IOS
42 E2 **Hughenden Valley** Bucks
83 L4 **Hughley** Shrops
10 D3 **Huish** Devon
40 C7 **Huish** Wilts
25 G5 **Huish Champflower** Somset
26 B6 **Huish Episcopi** Somset
58 D5 **Hulcott** Bucks
12 C5 **Hulham** Devon
100 E3 **Hulland** Derbys
100 E3 **Hulland Ward** Derbys
39 K4 **Hullavington** Wilts
46 D2 **Hullbridge** Essex
113 J3 **Hulme** Manch
99 L4 **Hulme** Staffs
112 E4 **Hulme** Warrtn
100 C2 **Hulme End** Staffs
113 J7 **Hulme Walfield** Ches
93 K6 **Hulver Street** Suffk
16 E5 **Hulverstone** IOW
126 D7 **Humberside Airport** N Linc
118 D1 **Humberston** NE Lin
87 J3 **Humberstone** C Leic
178 B5 **Humbie** E Loth
126 F4 **Humbleton** E R Yk
103 G6 **Humby** Lincs
167 L2 **Hume** Border
158 A7 **Humshaugh** Nthumb
231 L2 **Huna** Highld
87 G4 **Huncote** Leics
167 K5 **Hundalee** Border
140 C3 **Hunderthwaite** Dur
118 E7 **Hundleby** Lincs
49 G7 **Hundleton** Pembks
77 G5 **Hundon** Suffk
120 F6 **Hundred End** Lancs
68 C4 **Hundred House** Powys
87 K3 **Hungarton** Leics
25 G4 **Hungerford** Somset
41 G6 **Hungerford** W Berk
41 G6 **Hungerford Newtown** W Berk
69 J7 **Hungerstone** Herefs
135 H4 **Hunmanby** N York
72 D2 **Hunningham** Warwks
73 K3 **Hunsbury Hill** Nhants
60 C5 **Hunsdon** Herts
132 F8 **Hunsingore** N York
123 L4 **Hunslet** Leeds
149 G7 **Hunsonby** Cumb
105 G4 **Hunstanton** Norfk
150 B5 **Hunstanworth** Dur
99 G4 **Hunsterson** Ches
77 L2 **Hunston** Suffk
18 B5 **Hunston** W Susx
38 F7 **Hunstrete** BaNES
123 J5 **Hunsworth** Kirk
173 K3 **Hunter's Quay** Ag & B
25 M6 **Huntham** Somset
196 D3 **Hunthill Lodge** Angus
75 J1 **Huntingdon** Cambs
93 G8 **Huntingfield** Suffk
112 B8 **Huntington** Ches
178 B4 **Huntington** E Loth
68 E4 **Huntington** Herefs
85 H2 **Huntington** Staffs
133 J7 **Huntington** York
55 G4 **Huntley** Gloucs
215 L6 **Huntly** Abers
29 J4 **Hunton** Hants
33 J4 **Hunton** Kent
132 B2 **Hunton** N York
24 E3 **Huntscott** Somset
24 F7 **Huntsham** Devon
23 H6 **Huntshaw** Devon
25 L3 **Huntspill** Somset
25 K5 **Huntstile** Somset
25 L4 **Huntworth** Somset
140 F2 **Hunwick** Dur
106 C5 **Hunworth** Norfk
28 D5 **Hurdcott** Wilts
113 L6 **Hurdsfield** Ches
42 D4 **Hurley** W & M
86 B4 **Hurley** Warwks
86 B4 **Hurley Common** Warwks
163 L3 **Hurlford** E Ayrs
15 L3 **Hurn** Dorset
29 H6 **Hursley** Hants
140 D6 **Hurst** N York
42 C5 **Hurst** Wokham
33 J7 **Hurst Green** E Susx
62 C5 **Hurst Green** Essex
121 K3 **Hurst Green** Lancs
32 D3 **Hurst Green** Surrey
29 H3 **Hurstbourne Priors** Hants
29 G2 **Hurstbourne Tarrant** Hants
19 J3 **Hurstpierpoint** W Susx
122 C4 **Hurstwood** Lancs
234 c6 **Hurtiso** Ork
141 H5 **Hurworth Place** Darltn
141 H5 **Hurworth-on-Tees** Darltn
87 J6 **Husbands Bosworth** Leics
74 D7 **Husborne Crawley** Beds
133 H4 **Husthwaite** N York
101 J2 **Huthwaite** Notts
119 G6 **Huttoft** Lincs
179 J7 **Hutton** Border
134 F8 **Hutton** E R Yk
45 M2 **Hutton** Essex
121 G5 **Hutton** Lancs
37 M8 **Hutton** N Som
141 H7 **Hutton Bonville** N York
134 F3 **Hutton Buscel** N York
132 E5 **Hutton Conyers** N York
126 C1 **Hutton Cranswick** E R Yk
148 D7 **Hutton End** Cumb
151 K7 **Hutton Henry** Dur
142 D4 **Hutton Lowcross** R & Cl
140 E5 **Hutton Magna** Dur
148 C7 **Hutton Roof** Cumb
130 B4 **Hutton Roof** Cumb
141 K6 **Hutton Rudby** N York
133 G4 **Hutton Sessay** N York
124 D1 **Hutton Wandesley** N York
133 L2 **Hutton-le-Hole** N York
12 B3 **Huxham** Devon
98 D1 **Huxley** Ches
112 C4 **Huyton** Knows
128 D2 **Hycemoor** Cumb
113 L3 **Hyde** Tamesd
58 F7 **Hyde Heath** Bucks
99 K8 **Hyde Lea** Staffs
165 H2 **Hyndford Bridge** S Lans
188 C8 **Hynish** Ag & B
82 F5 **Hyssington** Powys
16 E2 **Hythe** Hants
34 F7 **Hythe** Kent
43 G6 **Hythe End** W & M

I

14 E2 **Ibberton** Dorset
100 E2 **Ible** Derbys
15 L1 **Ibsley** Hants
86 E2 **Ibstock** Leics
42 C2 **Ibstone** Bucks
29 G2 **Ibthorpe** Hants
143 H5 **Iburndale** N York
29 K1 **Ibworth** Hants
91 J4 **Ickburgh** Norfk
43 H3 **Ickenham** Gt Lon
57 M6 **Ickford** Bucks
35 G3 **Ickham** Kent
59 K2 **Ickleford** Herts
21 H3 **Icklesham** E Susx
76 C5 **Ickleton** Cambs
91 H8 **Icklingham** Suffk
122 E2 **Ickornshaw** N York
75 G5 **Ickwell Green** Beds
77 J3 **Ickworth** Suffolk
56 E4 **Icomb** Gloucs
56 E4 **Idbury** Oxon
10 E3 **Iddesleigh** Devon
11 K6 **Ide** Devon
32 E3 **Ide Hill** Kent
7 K1 **Ideford** Devon
21 H2 **Iden** E Susx
33 J5 **Iden Green** Kent
33 K6 **Iden Green** Kent
123 H3 **Idle** Brad
4 C6 **Idless** Cnwll
72 C5 **Idlicote** Warwks
28 D4 **Idmiston** Wilts
100 F3 **Idridgehay** Derbys
208 F2 **Idrigill** Highld
40 E4 **Idstone** Oxon
57 K7 **Iffley** Oxon
31 L4 **Ifield** W Susx
15 L4 **Iford** Bmouth
19 L4 **Iford** E Susx
38 C3 **Ifton** Mons
98 E5 **Ightfield** Shrops
33 G2 **Ightham** Kent
79 J4 **Iken** Suffk
100 C3 **Ilam** Staffs
26 D6 **Ilchester** Somset
168 F5 **Ilderton** Nthumb
45 H3 **Ilford** Gt Lon
26 A7 **Ilford** Somset
23 H2 **Ilfracombe** Devon
101 J4 **Ilkeston** Derbys
93 H6 **Ilketshall St Andrew** Suffk
93 H6 **Ilketshall St Margaret** Suffk
123 G2 **Ilkley** Brad
5 L1 **Illand** Cnwll
85 H7 **Illey** Dudley
3 H3 **Illogan** Cnwll
87 K4 **Illston on the Hill** Leics
58 C6 **Ilmer** Bucks
72 B5 **Ilmington** Warwks
26 A8 **Ilminster** Somset
7 H2 **Ilsington** Devon

51 H7 **Ilston** Swans
132 B4 **Ilton** N York
25 M7 **Ilton** Somset
161 L2 **Imachar** N Ayrs
126 F7 **Immingham** NE Lin
126 F7 **Immingham Dock** NE Lin
76 C2 **Impington** Cambs
112 C6 **Ince** Ches
111 K2 **Ince Blundell** Sefton
112 E1 **Ince-in-Makerfield** Wigan
221 K7 **Inchbae Lodge Hotel** Highld
196 F4 **Inchbare** Angus
215 G4 **Inchberry** Moray
211 G3 **Incheril** Highld
174 E5 **Inchinnan** Rens
201 J5 **Inchlaggan** Highld
186 D3 **Inchmichael** P & K
202 B3 **Inchnacardoch Hotel** Highld
224 F4 **Inchnadamph** Highld
186 D2 **Inchture** P & K
211 K6 **Inchvuilt** Highld
186 C4 **Inchyra** P & K
4 E4 **Indian Queens** Cnwll
61 G7 **Ingatestone** Essex
114 E1 **Ingbirchworth** Barns
99 L7 **Ingestre** Staffs
116 F5 **Ingham** Lincs
107 H7 **Ingham** Norfk
77 J1 **Ingham** Suffk
107 H6 **Ingham Corner** Norfk
101 G6 **Ingleby** Derbys
141 K6 **Ingleby Arncliffe** N York
141 K4 **Ingleby Barwick** S on T
142 C6 **Ingleby Greenhow** N York
10 E4 **Ingleigh Green** Devon
39 G7 **Inglesbatch** BaNES
56 D7 **Inglesham** Swindn
147 G2 **Ingleston** D & G
140 F3 **Ingleton** Dur
130 D5 **Ingleton** N York
121 H3 **Inglewhite** Lancs
158 C7 **Ingoe** Nthumb
121 G4 **Ingol** Lancs
105 G6 **Ingoldisthorpe** Norfk
119 H7 **Ingoldmells** Lincs
103 G6 **Ingoldsby** Lincs
168 F6 **Ingram** Nthumb
45 M2 **Ingrave** Essex
122 F3 **Ingrow** Brad
38 E3 **Ingst** S Glos
88 E2 **Ingthorpe** Rutlnd
106 E6 **Ingworth** Norfk
71 H3 **Inkberrow** Worcs
217 H6 **Inkhorn** Abers
41 G7 **Inkpen** W Berk
231 J2 **Inkstack** Highld
173 K4 **Innellan** Ag & B
166 E3 **Innerleithen** Border
186 F7 **Innerleven** Fife
144 C3 **Innermessan** D & G
178 F4 **Innerwick** E Loth
215 G2 **Innesmill** Moray
216 C8 **Insch** Abers
203 J5 **Insh** Highld
120 F3 **Inskip** Lancs
23 G5 **Instow** Devon
115 H5 **Intake** Sheff
204 F6 **Inver** Abers
223 J5 **Inver** Highld
194 F7 **Inver** P & K
216 C2 **Inver-boyndie** Abers
190 F1 **Inverailort** Highld
210 C3 **Inveralligin** Highld
217 K2 **Inverallochy** Abers
222 D2 **Inveran** Highld
182 F5 **Inveraray** Ag & B
209 J7 **Inverarish** Highld
196 D7 **Inverarity** Angus
183 K4 **Inverarnan** Stirlg
219 J4 **Inverasdale** Highld
176 C3 **Inveravon** Falk
182 E2 **Inverawe** Ag & B
183 K7 **Inverbeg** Ag & B
197 K2 **Inverbervie** Abers
220 F5 **Inverbroom** Highld
191 K6 **Invercreran House Hotel** Ag & B
203 L3 **Inverdruie** Highld
177 K4 **Inveresk** E Loth
182 E1 **Inveresragan** Ag & B
219 K5 **Inverewe Garden** Highld
204 D7 **Inverey** Abers
202 D2 **Inverfarigaig** Highld
191 J7 **Inverfolla** Ag & B
201 L5 **Invergarry** Highld
184 F2 **Invergeldie** P & K
201 K7 **Invergloy** Highld
222 F7 **Invergordon** Highld
186 F2 **Invergowrie** P & K
200 B4 **Inverguseran** Highld
193 L5 **Inverhadden** P & K
183 L3 **Inverherive Hotel** Stirlg
200 B5 **Inverie** Highld
182 E4 **Inverinan** Ag & B
200 E2 **Inverinate** Highld
197 G6 **Inverkeilor** Angus
176 F2 **Inverkeithing** Fife
216 C5 **Inverkeithny** Abers
173 L4 **Inverkip** Inver
224 C4 **Inverkirkaig** Highld
220 F4 **Inverlael** Highld
192 E1 **Inverlair** Highld
182 C6 **Inverliever Lodge** Ag & B
183 H2 **Inverlochy** Ag & B
196 D1 **Invermark** Angus
215 J6 **Invermarkie** Abers
202 C3 **Invermoriston** Highld
213 G5 **Inverness** Highld
213 J4 **Inverness Dalcross Airport** Highld
183 G7 **Invernoaden** Ag & B
192 D7 **Inveroran Hotel** Ag & B
196 C5 **Inverquharity** Angus
217 J5 **Inverquhomery** Abers
201 K8 **Inverroy** Highld
191 J4 **Inversanda** Highld
200 E2 **Invershiel** Highld
222 D3 **Invershin** Highld
231 J8 **Invershore** Highld
183 K5 **Inversnaid Hotel** Stirlg
217 L5 **Inverugie** Abers
183 K5 **Inveruglas** Ag & B
203 J5 **Inveruglass** Highld
206 E2 **Inverurie** Abers
10 E5 **Inwardleigh** Devon
61 L4 **Inworth** Essex
233 b7 **Iochdar** W Isls
180 C3 **Iona** Ag & B
30 D6 **Iping** W Susx
7 J3 **Ipplepen** Devon
41 M4 **Ipsden** Oxon
100 A3 **Ipstones** Staffs
78 E5 **Ipswich** Suffk
111 J5 **Irby** Wirral
118 F8 **Irby in the Marsh** Lincs
117 K1 **Irby upon Humber** NE Lin
74 D2 **Irchester** Nhants
147 M7 **Ireby** Cumb
130 C4 **Ireby** Lancs
128 F4 **Ireleth** Cumb
149 L7 **Ireshopeburn** Dur
100 F3 **Ireton Wood** Derbys
113 G3 **Irlam** Salfd
103 G7 **Irnham** Lincs
39 G4 **Iron Acton** S Glos
84 C3 **Iron Bridge Museum** Wrekin
84 C3 **Ironbridge** Wrekin
154 B6 **Ironmacannie** D & G
101 H3 **Ironville** Derbys
107 H7 **Irstead** Norfk
148 E3 **Irthington** Cumb
74 D1 **Irthlingborough** Nhants
134 F3 **Irton** N York
163 H2 **Irvine** N Ayrs
230 E3 **Isauld** Highld
235 c2 **Isbister** Shet
19 L3 **Isfield** E Susx
88 C8 **Isham** Nhants
30 C3 **Isington** Hants
170 F7 **Islay Airport** Ag & B
26 A7 **Isle Abbotts** Somset
26 A7 **Isle Brewers** Somset
45 G4 **Isle of Dogs** Gt Lon
237 b7 **Isle of Man Ronaldsway Airport** IOM
15 J5 **Isle of Purbeck** Dorest
46 F6 **Isle of Sheppey** Kent
145 K7 **Isle of Whithorn** D & G
17 G5 **Isle of Wight** IOW
90 F8 **Isleham** Cambs
199 L3 **Isleornsay** Highld
2 b2 **Isles of Scilly St Mary's Airport** IOS
155 G7 **Islesteps** D & G
236 d2 **Islet Village** Guern
44 D5 **Isleworth** Gt Lon
101 H7 **Isley Walton** Leics
232 d3 **Islibhig** W Isls
44 F3 **Islington** Gt Lon
88 E7 **Islip** Nhants
57 K5 **Islip** Oxon
232 d3 **Islivig** W Isls
83 L2 **Isombridge** Wrekin
45 M6 **Istead Rise** Kent
29 K5 **Itchen Abbas** Hants
29 K5 **Itchen Stoke** Hants
31 J5 **Itchingfield** W Susx
106 D6 **Itteringham** Norfk
11 G5 **Itton** Devon
38 C2 **Itton** Mons
148 D6 **Ivegill** Cumb
43 G4 **Iver** Bucks
43 G4 **Iver Heath** Bucks
150 E5 **Iveston** Dur
58 F5 **Ivinghoe** Bucks
58 F4 **Ivinghoe Aston** Bucks
69 J3 **Ivington** Herefs
69 J4 **Ivington Green** Herefs
33 G3 **Ivy Hatch** Kent
6 F5 **Ivybridge** Devon
21 K1 **Ivychurch** Kent
46 E6 **Iwade** Kent
27 K8 **Iwerne Courtney or Shroton** Dorset
27 K8 **Iwerne Minster** Dorset
77 L1 **Ixworth** Suffk
91 K8 **Ixworth Thorpe** Suffk

J

12 C4 **Jack-in-the-Green** Devon
175 G7 **Jackton** S Lans
9 G5 **Jacobstow** Cnwll
10 E4 **Jacobstowe** Devon
49 H7 **Jameston** Pembks
212 D3 **Jamestown** Highld
174 D3 **Jamestown** W Duns
231 L5 **Janets-town** Highld
227 L3 **Janetstown** Highld
155 J5 **Jardine Hall** D & G
151 H3 **Jarrow** S Tyne
61 H3 **Jasper's Green** Essex
175 L4 **Jawcraig** Falk
62 D5 **Jaywick** Essex
167 K5 **Jedburgh** Border
49 J6 **Jeffreyston** Pembks
213 H2 **Jemimaville** Highld
236 d4 **Jerbourg** Guern
236 b7 **Jersey Airport** Jersey
151 G2 **Jesmond** N u Ty
20 B5 **Jevington** E Susx
59 H5 **Jockey End** Herts
112 B5 **John Lennon Airport** Lpool
231 L2 **John o'Groats** Highld
148 D7 **Johnby** Cumb
197 J3 **Johnshaven** Abers
48 F5 **Johnston** Pembks
155 M3 **Johnstone** D & G
174 D5 **Johnstone** Rens
155 J4 **Johnstonebridge** D & G
50 E2 **Johnstown** Carmth
97 L4 **Johnstown** Wrexhm
177 J4 **Joppa** C Edin
66 D2 **Joppa** Cerdgn
163 K5 **Joppa** S Ayrs
64 C7 **Jordanston** Pembks
45 K5 **Joyden's Wood** Kent
150 B3 **Juniper** Nthumb
177 G5 **Juniper Green** C Edin
237 c2 **Jurby** IOM

K

139 H5 **Kaber** Cumb
165 J1 **Kaimend** S Lans
173 G4 **Kames** Ag & B
164 D4 **Kames** E Ayrs
4 C7 **Kea** Cnwll
125 K7 **Keadby** N Linc
104 B1 **Keal Cotes** Lincs
113 H1 **Kearsley** Bolton
158 C6 **Kearsley** Nthumb
35 H6 **Kearsney** Kent
130 B4 **Kearstwick** Cumb
77 G5 **Kedington** Suffk
100 F4 **Kedleston** Derbys
126 E8 **Keelby** Lincs
99 J4 **Keele** Staffs
123 G4 **Keelham** Brad
48 F4 **Keeston** Pembks
39 L8 **Keevil** Wilts
101 J7 **Kegworth** Leics
3 G3 **Kehelland** Cnwll
206 B2 **Keig** Abers
122 F3 **Keighley** Brad
185 J8 **Keilarsbrae** Clacks
185 K3 **Keillour** P & K
204 E6 **Keiloch** Abers
171 K5 **Keils** Ag & B
26 D5 **Keinton Mandeville** Somset
154 E4 **Keir Mill** D & G
139 G3 **Keisley** Cumb
231 L4 **Keiss** Highld

215 J4 **Keith** Moray
195 K8 **Keithick** P & K
196 F4 **Keithock** Angus
212 E3 **Keithtown** Highld
122 D2 **Kelbrook** Lancs
173 L6 **Kelburn** N Ayrs
103 G4 **Kelby** Lincs
139 K6 **Keld** N York
124 F3 **Kelfield** N York
102 C2 **Kelham** Notts
147 K2 **Kelhead** D & G
120 E5 **Kellamergh** Lancs
187 G1 **Kellas** Angus
214 E4 **Kellas** Moray
7 J7 **Kellaton** Devon
106 C4 **Kelling** Norfk
124 E5 **Kellington** N York
151 J7 **Kelloe** Dur
164 E6 **Kelloholm** D & G
9 K8 **Kelly** Devon
87 K7 **Kelmarsh** Nhants
56 E7 **Kelmscot** Oxon
79 H2 **Kelsale** Suffk
112 D7 **Kelsall** Ches
75 K7 **Kelshall** Herts
147 L5 **Kelsick** Cumb
167 L3 **Kelso** Border
115 G8 **Kelstedge** Derbys
118 C4 **Kelstern** Lincs
39 G6 **Kelston** BaNES
194 B6 **Keltneyburn** P & K
155 H7 **Kelton** D & G
186 B8 **Kelty** Fife
61 K4 **Kelvedon** Essex
60 F7 **Kelvedon Hatch** Essex
2 C5 **Kelynack** Cnwll
187 G4 **Kemback** Fife
84 D3 **Kemberton** Shrops
39 M2 **Kemble** Gloucs
71 G6 **Kemerton** Worcs
53 M6 **Kemeys Commander** Mons
206 E3 **Kemnay** Abers
19 J5 **Kemp Town** Br & H
54 F3 **Kempley** Gloucs
55 G3 **Kempley Green** Gloucs
70 F5 **Kempsey** Worcs
40 D2 **Kempsford** Gloucs
29 L2 **Kempshott** Hants
74 F5 **Kempston** Beds
83 G6 **Kempton** Shrops
32 F2 **Kemsing** Kent
34 C7 **Kenardington** Kent
69 J6 **Kenchester** Herefs
56 E6 **Kencot** Oxon
129 L2 **Kendal** Cumb
36 C4 **Kenfig** Brdgnd
72 C1 **Kenilworth** Warwks
32 B2 **Kenley** Gt Lon
83 L4 **Kenley** Shrops
210 B3 **Kenmore** Highld
194 B7 **Kenmore** P & K
11 L7 **Kenn** Devon
38 B6 **Kenn** N Som
172 D5 **Kennacraig** Ag & B
11 J4 **Kennerleigh** Devon
111 L2 **Kennessee Green** Sefton
176 C1 **Kennet** Clacks
215 L8 **Kennethmont** Abers
77 G2 **Kennett** Cambs
11 L7 **Kennford** Devon
92 C6 **Kenninghall** Norfk
34 D5 **Kennington** Kent
57 K7 **Kennington** Oxon
186 F6 **Kennoway** Fife
25 L7 **Kenny** Somset
90 F7 **Kennyhill** Suffk
134 C6 **Kennythorpe** N York
188 C6 **Kenovay** Ag & B
208 F4 **Kensaleyre** Highld
44 E4 **Kensington** Gt Lon
59 G4 **Kensworth** Beds
59 G4 **Kensworth Common** Beds
55 H4 **Kent's Green** Gloucs
28 F6 **Kent's Oak** Hants
191 K5 **Kentallen** Highld
54 B3 **Kentchurch** Herefs
77 G2 **Kentford** Suffk
12 D2 **Kentisbeare** Devon
23 K3 **Kentisbury** Devon
44 F3 **Kentish Town** Gt Lon
138 C6 **Kentmere** Cumb
12 B5 **Kenton** Devon
44 D3 **Kenton** Gt Lon
150 F2 **Kenton** N u Ty
78 E2 **Kenton** Suffk
190 D3 **Kentra** Highld
4 C6 **Kenwyn** Cnwll
228 F3 **Keoldale** Highld
200 D1 **Keppoch** Highld
133 G2 **Kepwick** N York
86 D6 **Keresley** Covtry
2 D5 **Kerris** Cnwll
82 D5 **Kerry** Powys
173 J6 **Kerrycroy** Ag & B
116 B8 **Kersall** Notts
12 D5 **Kersbrook** Devon
78 B5 **Kersey** Suffk
232 f3 **Kershader** W Isls
12 D2 **Kerswell** Devon
70 F5 **Kerswell Green** Worcs
78 F5 **Kesgrave** Suffk
93 L6 **Kessingland** Suffk
4 F6 **Kestle** Cnwll
4 D4 **Kestle Mill** Cnwll
45 H7 **Keston** Gt Lon
137 J3 **Keswick** Cumb
92 E3 **Keswick** Norfk
118 E6 **Ketsby** Lincs
88 C7 **Kettering** Nhants
92 E3 **Ketteringham** Norfk
195 K8 **Kettins** Angus
77 L4 **Kettlebaston** Suffk
186 E6 **Kettlebridge** Fife
86 B3 **Kettlebrook** Staffs
78 F3 **Kettleburgh** Suffk
155 K6 **Kettleholm** D & G
113 M5 **Kettleshulme** Ches
132 C7 **Kettlesing** N York
132 C7 **Kettlesing Bottom** N York
106 A6 **Kettlestone** Norfk
116 D6 **Kettlethorpe** Lincs
234 d4 **Kettletoft** Ork
131 H5 **Kettlewell** N York
88 E3 **Ketton** Rutlnd
44 D5 **Kew** Gt Lon
44 D5 **Kew Gardens** Gt Lon
37 M7 **Kewstoke** N Som
116 E4 **Kexby** Lincs
125 G1 **Kexby** York
113 K8 **Key Green** Ches
87 J3 **Keyham** Leics
16 C4 **Keyhaven** Hants
127 G5 **Keyingham** E R Yk
19 J3 **Keymer** W Susx
38 F6 **Keynsham** BaNES
74 F3 **Keysoe** Beds
74 F3 **Keysoe Row** Beds
88 F7 **Keyston** Cambs
101 L6 **Keyworth** Notts
151 G4 **Kibblesworth** Gatesd
87 K5 **Kibworth Beauchamp** Leics
87 K5 **Kibworth Harcourt** Leics
45 H5 **Kidbrooke** Gt Lon
84 E7 **Kidderminster** Worcs
57 J5 **Kidlington** Oxon
42 B5 **Kidmore End** Oxon
145 J7 **Kidsdale** D & G
99 J2 **Kidsgrove** Staffs
50 E4 **Kidwelly** Carmth
191 H8 **Kiel Crofts** Ag & B
157 G4 **Kielder** Nthumb
171 H5 **Kiells** Ag & B
174 D5 **Kilbarchan** Rens
199 K4 **Kilbeg** Highld
172 C5 **Kilberry** Ag & B
174 C7 **Kilbirnie** N Ayrs
182 B3 **Kilbride** Ag & B
172 C3 **Kilbride** Ag & B
173 H5 **Kilbride** Ag & B
214 D3 **Kilbuiack** Moray
101 G4 **Kilburn** Derbys
44 E4 **Kilburn** Gt Lon
133 H4 **Kilburn** N York
87 J4 **Kilby** Leics
172 D6 **Kilchamaig** Ag & B
180 E7 **Kilchattan** Ag & B
173 J7 **Kilchattan** Ag & B
191 G8 **Kilcheran** Ag & B
189 L4 **Kilchoan** Highld
170 D5 **Kilchoman** Ag & B
182 E3 **Kilchrenan** Ag & B
187 H6 **Kilconquhar** Fife
55 G3 **Kilcot** Gloucs
212 E4 **Kilcoy** Highld
173 L3 **Kilcreggan** Ag & B
142 D5 **Kildale** N York
161 J5 **Kildalloig** Ag & B
223 G6 **Kildary** Highld
173 G5 **Kildavaig** Ag & B
173 H5 **Kildavanan** Ag & B
227 G4 **Kildonan** Highld
162 D5 **Kildonan** N Ayrs
226 F4 **Kildonan Lodge** Highld
199 G7 **Kildonnan** Highld
144 C4 **Kildrochet House** D & G
205 K2 **Kildrummy** Abers
122 F2 **Kildwick** N York
172 F3 **Kilfinan** Ag & B
201 K6 **Kilfinnan** Highld
49 J6 **Kilgetty** Pembks
152 F2 **Kilgrammie** S Ayrs
38 C2 **Kilgwrrwg Common** Mons
135 G6 **Kilham** E R Yk
188 B7 **Kilkenneth** Ag & B
161 H4 **Kilkenzie** Ag & B
161 J5 **Kilkerran** Ag & B
9 H3 **Kilkhampton** Cnwll
115 J5 **Killamarsh** Derbys
51 H6 **Killay** Swans
174 F2 **Killearn** Stirlg
213 G3 **Killen** Highld
140 F3 **Killerby** Darltn
12 C3 **Killerton** Devon
193 J5 **Killichonan** P & K
190 B7 **Killiechronan** Ag & B
194 E4 **Killiecrankie** P & K
210 E7 **Killilan** Highld
184 C2 **Killin** Stirlg
132 D7 **Killinghall** N York
130 C2 **Killington** Cumb
159 G7 **Killingworth** N Tyne
167 G1 **Killochyett** Border
174 C4 **Kilmacolm** Inver
184 D5 **Kilmahog** Stirlg
182 A8 **Kilmahumaig** Ag & B
218 C6 **Kilmaluag** Highld
186 F3 **Kilmany** Fife
163 K2 **Kilmarnock** E Ayrs
182 B7 **Kilmartin** Ag & B
163 K2 **Kilmaurs** E Ayrs
182 B5 **Kilmelford** Ag & B
27 G2 **Kilmersdon** Somset
29 L6 **Kilmeston** Hants
161 H5 **Kilmichael** Ag & B
182 B8 **Kilmichael Glassary** Ag & B
172 D2 **Kilmichael of Inverlussa** Ag & B
13 H3 **Kilmington** Devon
27 H4 **Kilmington** Wilts
27 H4 **Kilmington Common** Wilts
27 H4 **Kilmington Street** Wilts
212 D5 **Kilmorack** Highld
182 C3 **Kilmore** Ag & B
199 K4 **Kilmore** Highld
172 C4 **Kilmory** Ag & B
190 B3 **Kilmory** Highld
162 B5 **Kilmory** N Ayrs
208 D5 **Kilmuir** Highld
218 B7 **Kilmuir** Highld
213 G4 **Kilmuir** Highld
223 G6 **Kilmuir** Highld
173 K3 **Kilmun** Ag & B
150 C4 **Kiln Pit Hill** Nthumb
170 F4 **Kilnave** Ag & B
176 B8 **Kilncadzow** S Lans
33 J6 **Kilndown** Kent
182 B3 **Kilninver** Ag & B
127 J7 **Kilnsea** E R Yk
131 H6 **Kilnsey** N York
126 C1 **Kilnwick** E R Yk
180 E7 **Kiloran** Ag & B
162 A4 **Kilpatrick** N Ayrs
54 C3 **Kilpeck** Herefs
125 J5 **Kilpin** E R Yk
187 J6 **Kilrenny** Fife
73 H1 **Kilsby** Nhants
186 C3 **Kilspindie** P & K
144 D7 **Kilstay** D & G
175 J3 **Kilsyth** N Lans
212 D6 **Kiltarlity** Highld
142 E4 **Kilton** R & Cl
142 E4 **Kilton Thorpe** R & Cl
218 B7 **Kilvaxter** Highld
25 H3 **Kilve** Somset
102 D4 **Kilvington** Notts
163 H2 **Kilwinning** N Ayrs
92 C3 **Kimberley** Norfk
101 J4 **Kimberley** Notts
115 H3 **Kimberworth** Rothm
151 G5 **Kimblesworth** Dur
75 G2 **Kimbolton** Cambs
69 K3 **Kimbolton** Herefs
87 H6 **Kimcote** Leics
15 H6 **Kimmeridge** Dorset
28 F3 **Kimpton** Hants
59 K4 **Kimpton** Herts
226 F3 **Kinbrace** Highld
185 G6 **Kinbuck** Stirlg
187 G4 **Kincaple** Fife
176 C2 **Kincardine** Fife
222 E4 **Kincardine** Highld
206 B5 **Kincardine O'Neil** Abers
195 J8 **Kinclaven** P & K
207 H5 **Kincorth** C Aber
214 C3 **Kincorth House** Moray
203 K4 **Kincraig** Highld
194 F6 **Kincraigie** P & K
194 F6 **Kindallachan** P & K
172 B7 **Kinerarach** Ag & B
56 C3 **Kineton** Gloucs
72 D4 **Kineton** Warwks
186 C3 **Kinfauns** P & K
163 J3 **Kinfold** S Ayrs
81 G3 **King Arthur's Labyrinth** Gwynd
85 K1 **King's Bromley** Staffs
88 E4 **King's Cliffe** Nhants
71 J3 **King's Coughton** Warwks
85 J7 **King's Heath** Birm
85 H4 **King's Hill** Wsall

104 F8 **King's Lynn** Norfk
236 c3 **King's Mills** Guern
85 J7 **King's Norton** Birm
87 K4 **King's Norton** Leics
23 L7 **King's Nympton** Devon
69 J4 **King's Pyon** Herefs
29 G5 **King's Somborne** Hants
14 D1 **King's Stag** Dorset
55 J7 **King's Stanley** Gloucs
72 G7 **King's Sutton** Oxon
59 K4 **King's Walden** Herts
173 J6 **Kingarth** Ag & B
207 G5 **Kingcausie** Abers
54 B6 **Kingcoed** Mons
117 H3 **Kingerby** Lincs
9 H4 **Kingford** Devon
56 E3 **Kingham** Oxon
155 G7 **Kingholm Quay** D & G
177 H2 **Kinghorn** Fife
186 D7 **Kinglassie** Fife
196 B5 **Kingoldrum** Angus
186 E2 **Kingoodie** P & K
54 E3 **Kings Caple** Herefs
33 H3 **Kings Hill** Kent
192 D5 **Kings House Hotel** Highld
59 H7 **Kings Langley** Herts
138 E3 **Kings Meaburn** Cumb
166 C2 **Kings Muir** Border
86 F7 **Kings Newnham** Warwks
89 J7 **Kings Ripton** Cambs
38 D5 **Kings Weston** Bristl
29 J5 **Kings Worthy** Hants
6 C5 **Kingsand** Cnwll
187 K5 **Kingsbarns** Fife
7 H6 **Kingsbridge** Devon
24 F4 **Kingsbridge** Somset
208 F4 **Kingsburgh** Highld
44 D3 **Kingsbury** Gt Lon
86 B4 **Kingsbury** Warwks
26 B7 **Kingsbury Episcopi** Somset
41 K8 **Kingsclere** Hants
39 J2 **Kingscote** Gloucs
23 H7 **Kingscott** Devon
162 D4 **Kingscross** N Ayrs
26 D6 **Kingsdon** Somset
35 K5 **Kingsdown** Kent
40 D3 **Kingsdown** Swindn
39 J6 **Kingsdown** Wilts
176 F1 **Kingseat** Fife
58 C6 **Kingsey** Bucks
31 K4 **Kingsfold** W Susx
206 F4 **Kingsford** C Aber
174 E8 **Kingsford** E Ayrs
35 K1 **Kingsgate** Kent
77 K3 **Kingshall Street** Suffk
23 J4 **Kingsheanton** Devon
184 C4 **Kingshouse Hotel** Stirlg
7 K3 **Kingskerswell** Devon
186 E5 **Kingskettle** Fife
69 J3 **Kingsland** Herefs
108 C5 **Kingsland** IOA
112 D6 **Kingsley** Ches
30 C4 **Kingsley** Hants
100 A3 **Kingsley** Staffs
30 E5 **Kingsley Green** W Susx
73 L3 **Kingsley Park** Nhants
196 D6 **Kingsmuir** Angus
187 J5 **Kingsmuir** Fife
34 D6 **Kingsnorth** Kent
85 J4 **Kingstanding** Birm
7 K2 **Kingsteignton** Devon
54 D2 **Kingsthorne** Herefs
73 L2 **Kingsthorpe** Nhants
75 L4 **Kingston** Cambs
6 A2 **Kingston** Cnwll
6 F6 **Kingston** Devon
14 E1 **Kingston** Dorset
15 H6 **Kingston** Dorset
178 C3 **Kingston** E Loth
16 F6 **Kingston** IOW
35 G4 **Kingston** Kent
57 H7 **Kingston Bagpuize** Oxon
58 C7 **Kingston Blount** Oxon
27 J4 **Kingston Deverill** Wilts
40 F3 **Kingston Lisle** Oxon
19 K4 **Kingston near Lewes** E Susx
101 J6 **Kingston on Soar** Notts
215 H2 **Kingston on Spey** Moray
14 B4 **Kingston Russell** Dorset
38 B6 **Kingston Seymour** N Som
25 K5 **Kingston St Mary** Somset
126 D5 **Kingston upon Hull** C KuH
44 D6 **Kingston upon Thames** Gt Lon
69 H7 **Kingstone** Herefs
26 B8 **Kingstone** Somset
100 B6 **Kingstone** Staffs
7 K5 **Kingswear** Devon
207 G4 **Kingswells** C Aber
84 F5 **Kingswinford** Dudley
58 B4 **Kingswood** Bucks
39 H3 **Kingswood** Gloucs
38 F5 **Kingswood** S Glos
25 H4 **Kingswood** Somset
31 L1 **Kingswood** Surrey
71 L1 **Kingswood** Warwks
84 E3 **Kingswood Common** Staffs
117 J6 **Kingthorpe** Lincs
68 F3 **Kington** Herefs
38 F3 **Kington** S Glos
71 H4 **Kington** Worcs
39 L5 **Kington Langley** Wilts
27 H6 **Kington Magna** Dorset
39 K5 **Kington St Michael** Wilts
203 H5 **Kingussie** Highld
26 D5 **Kingweston** Somset
217 H7 **Kinharrachie** Abers
147 G2 **Kinharvie** D & G
185 J4 **Kinkell Bridge** P & K
217 J6 **Kinknockie** Abers
177 G5 **Kinleith** C Edin
84 C7 **Kinlet** Shrops
225 H2 **Kinloch** Highld
229 H5 **Kinloch** Highld
198 F5 **Kinloch** Highld
195 J7 **Kinloch** P & K
195 L7 **Kinloch** P & K
200 E4 **Kinloch Hourn** Highld
193 L5 **Kinloch Rannoch** P & K
184 B6 **Kinlochard** Stirlg
228 C4 **Kinlochbervie** Highld
191 J1 **Kinlocheil** Highld
210 F3 **Kinlochewe** Highld
202 E7 **Kinlochlaggan** Highld
192 C4 **Kinlochleven** Highld
190 E2 **Kinlochmoidart** Highld
200 B8 **Kinlochnanuagh** Highld
214 C3 **Kinloss** Moray
110 D5 **Kinmel Bay** Conwy
206 F2 **Kinmuck** Abers
207 G2 **Kinmundy** Abers
160 B2 **Kinnabus** Ag & B
217 H5 **Kinnadie** Abers
194 F5 **Kinnaird** P & K
197 G5 **Kinnaird Castle** Angus
214 F1 **Kinneddar** Moray
197 K2 **Kinneff** Abers
155 H2 **Kinnelhead** D & G
196 F6 **Kinnell** Angus
97 M7 **Kinnerley** Shrops
69 G5 **Kinnersley** Herefs
70 F5 **Kinnersley** Worcs
68 E2 **Kinnerton** Powys
186 C6 **Kinnesswood** P & K
140 D3 **Kinninvie** Dur
196 B5 **Kinnordy** Angus
102 B6 **Kinoulton** Notts
186 B6 **Kinross** P & K
186 C2 **Kinrossie** P & K
69 G2 **Kinsham** Herefs
71 G7 **Kinsham** Worcs
124 C7 **Kinsley** Wakefd
15 K3 **Kinson** Bmouth
41 G6 **Kintbury** W Berk
214 B3 **Kintessack** Moray
200 F2 **Kintail** Highld
186 B4 **Kintillo** P & K
83 H8 **Kinton** Herefs
98 A8 **Kinton** Shrops
206 E3 **Kintore** Abers
171 H7 **Kintour** Ag & B
180 D3 **Kintra** Ag & B
182 B6 **Kintraw** Ag & B
161 J2 **Kintyre** Ag & B
203 L2 **Kinveachy** Highld
84 E6 **Kinver** Staffs
124 C4 **Kippax** Leeds
184 E7 **Kippen** Stirlg
146 E4 **Kippford or Scaur** D & G
33 H5 **Kipping's Cross** Kent
234 b6 **Kirbister** Ork
165 M1 **Kirburd** Border
93 G3 **Kirby Bedon** Norfk
102 B8 **Kirby Bellars** Leics
93 H5 **Kirby Cane** Norfk
62 E4 **Kirby Cross** Essex
87 G3 **Kirby Fields** Leics
134 D6 **Kirby Grindalythe** N York
140 E6 **Kirby Hill** N York
132 F5 **Kirby Hill** N York
133 G3 **Kirby Knowle** N York
62 F4 **Kirby le Soken** Essex
134 B4 **Kirby Misperton** N York
87 G3 **Kirby Muxloe** Leics
93 H5 **Kirby Row** Norfk
141 K7 **Kirby Sigston** N York
134 C7 **Kirby Underdale** E R Yk
132 E3 **Kirby Wiske** N York
31 G6 **Kirdford** W Susx
231 K4 **Kirk** Highld
124 F7 **Kirk Bramwith** Donc
124 B1 **Kirk Deighton** N York
126 C5 **Kirk Ella** E R Yk
101 J4 **Kirk Hallam** Derbys
133 G7 **Kirk Hammerton** N York
100 E3 **Kirk Ireton** Derbys
100 F5 **Kirk Langley** Derbys
141 G2 **Kirk Merrington** Dur
237 c4 **Kirk Michael** IOM
175 L5 **Kirk of Shotts** N Lans
124 F8 **Kirk Sandall** Donc
124 D7 **Kirk Smeaton** N York
168 C4 **Kirk Yetholm** Border
235 d6 **Kirkabister** Shet
146 A5 **Kirkandrews** D & G
148 C4 **Kirkandrews upon Eden** Cumb
148 B4 **Kirkbampton** Cumb
147 G3 **Kirkbean** D & G
147 M4 **Kirkbride** Cumb
196 E7 **Kirkbuddo** Angus
166 D2 **Kirkburn** Border
134 F7 **Kirkburn** E R Yk
123 J7 **Kirkburton** Kirk
111 L2 **Kirkby** Knows
117 H3 **Kirkby** Lincs
142 C6 **Kirkby** N York
141 G7 **Kirkby Fleetham** N York
103 H2 **Kirkby Green** Lincs
101 J2 **Kirkby in Ashfield** Notts
103 J4 **Kirkby la Thorpe** Lincs
130 B4 **Kirkby Lonsdale** Cumb
131 G7 **Kirkby Malham** N York
86 F4 **Kirkby Mallory** Leics
132 C5 **Kirkby Malzeard** N York
118 C8 **Kirkby on Bain** Lincs
123 L2 **Kirkby Overblow** N York
139 H5 **Kirkby Stephen** Cumb
138 F3 **Kirkby Thore** Cumb
103 H6 **Kirkby Underwood** Lincs
124 D3 **Kirkby Wharf** N York
128 F3 **Kirkby-in-Furness** Cumb
133 L3 **Kirkbymoorside** N York
186 D8 **Kirkcaldy** Fife
148 F2 **Kirkcambeck** Cumb
146 B5 **Kirkchrist** D & G
144 B2 **Kirkcolm** D & G
164 E6 **Kirkconnel** D & G
147 G2 **Kirkconnell** D & G
146 B3 **Kirkconnell** D & G
145 G3 **Kirkcowan** D & G
146 B5 **Kirkcudbright** D & G
111 K3 **Kirkdale** Lpool
165 G2 **Kirkfieldbank** S Lans
146 F2 **Kirkgunzeon** D & G
120 F4 **Kirkham** Lancs
134 B6 **Kirkham** N York
123 K6 **Kirkhamgate** Wakefd
158 C5 **Kirkharle** Nthumb
149 H5 **Kirkhaugh** Nthumb
123 H6 **Kirkheaton** Kirk
158 C6 **Kirkheaton** Nthumb
212 E5 **Kirkhill** Highld
165 J7 **Kirkhope** S Lans
199 H2 **Kirkibost** Highld
195 L7 **Kirkinch** P & K
145 J5 **Kirkinner** D & G
175 H4 **Kirkintilloch** E Duns
136 E4 **Kirkland** Cumb
164 E6 **Kirkland** D & G
154 E4 **Kirkland** D & G
155 H4 **Kirkland** D & G
142 D3 **Kirkleatham** R & Cl
141 K5 **Kirklevington** S on T
93 L5 **Kirkley** Suffk
132 D4 **Kirklington** N York
102 B2 **Kirklington** Notts
148 D2 **Kirklinton** Cumb
176 F4 **Kirkliston** C Edin
145 K4 **Kirkmabreck** D & G
144 D7 **Kirkmaiden** D & G
195 H4 **Kirkmichael** P & K
163 J7 **Kirkmichael** S Ayrs
164 F2 **Kirkmuirhill** S Lans
168 D4 **Kirknewton** Nthumb
176 F5 **Kirknewton** W Loth
215 L7 **Kirkney** Abers
148 F6 **Kirkoswald** Cumb

163 G7 **Kirkoswald** S Ayrs
154 F4 **Kirkpatrick** D & G
154 D7 **Kirkpatrick Durham** D & G
156 B7 **Kirkpatrick-Fleming** D & G
128 D4 **Kirksanton** Cumb
123 K4 **Kirkstall** Leeds
103 K1 **Kirkstead** Lincs
215 L7 **Kirkstile** Abers
156 C4 **Kirkstile** D & G
231 L2 **Kirkstyle** Highld
124 B6 **Kirkthorpe** Wakefd
206 C1 **Kirkton** Abers
216 F5 **Kirkton** Abers
155 G6 **Kirkton** D & G
186 F3 **Kirkton** Fife
210 C8 **Kirkton** Highld
210 D6 **Kirkton** Highld
185 K4 **Kirkton** P & K
166 C2 **Kirkton Manor** Border
195 L6 **Kirkton of Airlie** Angus
196 B8 **Kirkton of Auchterhouse** Angus
213 K5 **Kirkton of Barevan** Highld
186 C2 **Kirkton of Collace** P & K
205 J3 **Kirkton of Glenbuchat** Abers
217 J7 **Kirkton of Logie Buchan** Abers
196 E4 **Kirkton of Menmuir** Angus
196 E8 **Kirkton of Monikie** Angus
216 D7 **Kirkton of Rayne** Abers
206 F4 **Kirkton of Skene** Abers
186 F1 **Kirkton of Strathmartine** Angus
196 C8 **Kirkton of Tealing** Angus
206 C3 **Kirkton of Tough** Abers
217 J2 **Kirktown** Abers
217 K4 **Kirktown** Abers
206 F1 **Kirktown of Bourtie** Abers
206 F7 **Kirktown of Fetteresso** Abers
215 H6 **Kirktown of Mortlach** Moray
217 K8 **Kirktown of Slains** Abers
165 M1 **Kirkurd** Border
234 c6 **Kirkwall** Ork
234 c6 **Kirkwall Airport** Ork
158 C5 **Kirkwhelpington** Nthumb
126 D7 **Kirmington** N Linc
117 K3 **Kirmond le Mire** Lincs
173 K3 **Kirn** Ag & B
196 C5 **Kirriemuir** Angus
93 G4 **Kirstead Green** Norfk
155 M7 **Kirtlebridge** D & G
77 G3 **Kirtling** Cambs
76 F4 **Kirtling Green** Suffk
57 J4 **Kirtlington** Oxon
229 M3 **Kirtomy** Highld
104 A5 **Kirton** Lincs
116 B7 **Kirton** Notts
78 F6 **Kirton** Suffk
116 F2 **Kirton in Lindsey** N Linc
174 D4 **Kirtonhill** W Duns
145 J4 **Kirwaugh** D & G
210 C6 **Kishorn** Highld
73 K3 **Kislingbury** Nhants
25 G6 **Kittisford** Somset
207 H4 **Kittybrewster** C Aber
54 C2 **Kivernoll** Herefs
116 D5 **Knaith** Lincs
27 J6 **Knap Corner** Dorset
42 F8 **Knaphill** Surrey
25 L6 **Knapp** Somset
134 D4 **Knapton** N York
107 G5 **Knapton** Norfk
124 E1 **Knapton** York
75 K2 **Knapwell** Cambs
132 E7 **Knaresborough** N York
149 H4 **Knarsdale** Nthumb
217 G5 **Knaven** Abers
132 F2 **Knayton** N York
59 L4 **Knebworth** Herts
125 H5 **Knedlington** E R Yk
116 B8 **Kneesall** Notts
75 L5 **Kneesworth** Cambs
102 B4 **Kneeton** Notts
50 F7 **Knelston** Swans
99 L5 **Knenhall** Staffs
72 E4 **Knightcote** Warwks
99 J7 **Knightley** Staffs
87 H4 **Knighton** C Leic
14 C1 **Knighton** Dorset
82 F8 **Knighton** Powys
25 J3 **Knighton** Somset
99 G4 **Knighton** Staffs
99 H6 **Knighton** Staffs
70 B1 **Knighton on Teme** Worcs
70 D4 **Knightwick** Worcs
68 F3 **Knill** Herefs
102 D6 **Knipton** Leics
100 E3 **Kniveton** Derbys
138 F2 **Knock** Cumb
199 K4 **Knock** Highld
215 L4 **Knock** Moray
232 g2 **Knock** W Isls
173 L5 **Knock Castle** N Ayrs
227 K3 **Knockally** Highld
224 F6 **Knockan** Highld
214 F6 **Knockando** Moray
212 E5 **Knockbain** Highld
212 F3 **Knockbain** Highld
231 H4 **Knockdee** Highld
39 J3 **Knockdown** Wilts
153 G3 **Knockeen** S Ayrs
162 D4 **Knockenkelly** N Ayrs
163 K2 **Knockentiber** E Ayrs
32 E2 **Knockholt** Kent
32 E2 **Knockholt Pound** Kent
97 M7 **Knockin** Shrops
163 K2 **Knockinlaw** E Ayrs
144 B3 **Knocknain** D & G
153 M5 **Knocksheen** D & G
154 D7 **Knockvennie Smithy** D & G
79 J3 **Knodishall** Suffk
26 C6 **Knole** Somset
113 J5 **Knolls Green** Ches
98 B5 **Knolton** Wrexhm
27 L3 **Knook** Wilts
88 B2 **Knossington** Leics
120 E2 **Knott End-on-Sea** Lancs
74 E2 **Knotting** Beds
74 E3 **Knotting Green** Beds
124 D5 **Knottingley** Wakefd
112 B3 **Knotty Ash** Lpool
83 L7 **Knowbury** Shrops
153 G7 **Knowe** D & G
154 A4 **Knowehead** D & G
163 G6 **Knoweside** S Ayrs
42 D4 **Knowl Hill** W & M
38 E6 **Knowle** Bristl
23 H4 **Knowle** Devon
11 H5 **Knowle** Devon
12 C2 **Knowle** Devon
12 D6 **Knowle** Devon
83 L8 **Knowle** Shrops
85 L7 **Knowle** Solhll
24 E3 **Knowle** Somset
121 J3 **Knowle Green** Lancs
13 J1 **Knowle St Giles** Somset
148 D4 **Knowlefield** Cumb
112 C3 **Knowsley** Knows
112 C3 **Knowsley Safari Park** Knows
24 C6 **Knowstone** Devon
33 K5 **Knox Bridge** Kent
82 F8 **Knucklas** Powys
74 D2 **Knuston** Nhants
113 H5 **Knutsford** Ches
122 F6 **Krumlin** Calder
3 J7 **Kuggar** Cnwll
210 B8 **Kyle of Lochalsh** Highld
200 B1 **Kyleakin** Highld
200 B2 **Kylerhea** Highld
232 e4 **Kyles Scalpay** W Isls
224 F2 **Kylesku** Highld
200 C6 **Kylesmorar** Highld
224 F2 **Kylestrome** Highld
84 C1 **Kynnersley** Wrekin
69 L2 **Kyrewood** Worcs

L

236 d1 **L'Ancresse** Guern
236 b3 **L'Eree** Guern
236 a6 **L'Etacq** Jersey
236 d3 **La Bellieuse** Guern
236 e1 **La Fontenelle** Guern
236 d4 **La Fosse** Guern
236 d2 **La Greve** Guern
236 b5 **La Greve de Lecq** Jersey
236 d7 **La Hougue Bie** Jersey
236 b3 **La Houguette** Guern
236 d2 **La Passee** Guern
236 a7 **La Pulente** Jersey
236 e8 **La Rocque** Jersey
236 d2 **La Rousaillerie** Guern
236 d4 **La Villette** Guern
232 f2 **Lacadal** W Isls
232 f3 **Lacasaigh** W Isls
117 K1 **Laceby** NE Lin
58 D7 **Lacey Green** Bucks
113 G6 **Lach Dennis** Ches
77 H1 **Lackford** Suffk
77 H1 **Lackford Green** Suffk
39 K6 **Lacock** Wilts
72 E3 **Ladbroke** Warwks
33 J4 **Laddingford** Kent
4 D5 **Ladock** Cnwll
234 d4 **Lady** Ork
128 E3 **Lady Hall** Cumb
186 E5 **Ladybank** Fife
165 H4 **Ladygill** S Lans
179 J8 **Ladykirk** Border
85 J6 **Ladywood** Birm
70 F3 **Ladywood** Worcs
154 F5 **Lag** D & G
190 D4 **Laga** Highld
160 C1 **Lagavulin** Ag & B
162 B5 **Lagg** N Ayrs
201 L6 **Laggan** Highld
202 F6 **Laggan** Highld
228 F4 **Laid** Highld
219 L3 **Laide** Highld
199 G7 **Laig** Highld
174 E8 **Laigh Clunch** E Ayrs
163 L2 **Laigh Fenwick** E Ayrs
164 C5 **Laigh Glenmuir** E Ayrs
175 J7 **Laighstonehall** S Lans
46 B3 **Laindon** Essex
225 M7 **Lairg** Highld
123 J4 **Laisterdyke** Brad
17 H5 **Lake** IOW
15 J4 **Lake** Poole
28 C4 **Lake** Wilts
137 H5 **Lake District National Park** Cumb
91 G6 **Lakenheath** Suffk
90 D4 **Lakesend** Norfk
36 D4 **Laleston** Brdgnd
177 G7 **Lamancha** Border
77 K7 **Lamarsh** Essex
106 F7 **Lamas** Norfk
167 L2 **Lambden** Border
33 H6 **Lamberhurst** Kent
33 H6 **Lamberhurst Down** Kent
179 K6 **Lamberton** Border
44 F4 **Lambeth** Gt Lon
77 G4 **Lambfair Green** Suffk
101 M4 **Lambley** Notts
149 H4 **Lambley** Nthumb
40 F5 **Lambourn** W Berk
45 J2 **Lambourne End** Essex
31 L4 **Lambs Green** W Susx
5 K3 **Lamellion** Cnwll
6 C1 **Lamerton** Devon
151 G4 **Lamesley** Gatesd
165 J3 **Lamington** S Lans
162 C3 **Lamlash** N Ayrs
148 D7 **Lamonby** Cumb
2 E6 **Lamorna** Cnwll
4 D7 **Lamorran** Cnwll
66 D5 **Lampeter** Cerdgn
49 K5 **Lampeter Velfrey** Pembks
49 H7 **Lamphey** Pembks
136 F3 **Lamplugh** Cumb
87 L8 **Lamport** Nhants
26 F4 **Lamyatt** Somset
165 G2 **Lanark** S Lans
129 K7 **Lancaster** Lancs
150 F5 **Lanchester** Dur
19 G5 **Lancing** W Susx
2 C6 **Land's End** Cnwll
2 C5 **Land's End Airport** Cnwll
227 L2 **Land-hallow** Highld
76 C2 **Landbeach** Cambs
23 G6 **Landcross** Devon
206 E4 **Landerberry** Abers
28 E7 **Landford** Wilts
50 F6 **Landimore** Swans
23 J5 **Landkey** Devon
23 J5 **Landkey Town** Devon
51 J6 **Landore** Swans
6 B4 **Landrake** Cnwll
7 H3 **Landscove** Devon
6 C4 **Landulph** Cnwll
4 C4 **Lane** Cnwll
42 D3 **Lane End** Bucks
27 J3 **Lane End** Wilts
128 D2 **Lane End Waberthwaite** Cumb
100 E5 **Lane Ends** Derbys
140 E5 **Lane Head** Dur
9 G7 **Laneast** Cnwll
116 D6 **Laneham** Notts
149 L6 **Lanehead** Dur
25 K6 **Langaller** Somset
102 B5 **Langar** Notts
174 D4 **Langbank** Rens
123 G1 **Langbar** N York
130 F6 **Langcliffe** N York
134 E2 **Langdale End** N York
16 E2 **Langdown** Hants
186 E6 **Langdyke** Fife
62 B4 **Langenhoe** Essex
75 H6 **Langford** Beds
12 D2 **Langford** Devon
61 K6 **Langford** Essex
102 D2 **Langford** Notts

56 E7 **Langford** Oxon
25 H6 **Langford Budville** Somset
78 B7 **Langham** Essex
106 B4 **Langham** Norfk
88 B2 **Langham** Rutlnd
77 L1 **Langham** Suffk
121 K4 **Langho** Lancs
156 C5 **Langholm** D & G
167 H3 **Langlee** Border
16 F3 **Langley** Hants
59 K4 **Langley** Herts
33 K3 **Langley** Kent
149 L3 **Langley** Nthumb
43 G5 **Langley** Slough
25 G5 **Langley** Somset
30 D5 **Langley** W Susx
71 L3 **Langley** Warwks
39 L5 **Langley Burrell** Wilts
61 L4 **Langley Green** Essex
25 G5 **Langley Marsh** Somset
150 F6 **Langley Park** Dur
93 H3 **Langley Street** Norfk
76 C7 **Langley Upper Green** Essex
20 D5 **Langney** E Susx
115 L4 **Langold** Notts
9 J7 **Langore** Cnwll
26 B6 **Langport** Somset
103 L3 **Langrick** Lincs
39 H6 **Langridge** BaNES
147 K5 **Langrigg** Cumb
30 B6 **Langrish** Hants
114 E2 **Langsett** Barns
185 G5 **Langside** P & K
132 C2 **Langthorne** N York
132 F6 **Langthorpe** N York
140 C6 **Langthwaite** N York
134 F6 **Langtoft** E R Yk
89 G2 **Langtoft** Lincs
140 F4 **Langton** Dur
118 C7 **Langton** Lincs
118 E7 **Langton** Lincs
134 C6 **Langton** N York
117 J6 **Langton by Wragby** Lincs
32 F5 **Langton Green** Kent
14 C6 **Langton Herring** Dorset
15 J6 **Langton Matravers** Dorset
10 C2 **Langtree** Devon
148 F7 **Langwathby** Cumb
227 K4 **Langwell House** Highld
117 H6 **Langworth** Lincs
5 H3 **Lanhydrock House & Gardens** Cnwll
5 G3 **Lanivet** Cnwll
5 H2 **Lank** Cnwll
5 G4 **Lanlivery** Cnwll
3 J4 **Lanner** Cnwll
5 J4 **Lanreath** Cnwll
5 J5 **Lansallos** Cnwll
8 E7 **Lanteglos** Cnwll
5 J5 **Lanteglos Highway** Cnwll
167 J5 **Lanton** Border
168 D3 **Lanton** Nthumb
11 H3 **Lapford** Devon
160 C1 **Laphroaig** Ag & B
84 F2 **Lapley** Staffs
71 L1 **Lapworth** Warwks
190 E6 **Larachbeg** Highld
176 B3 **Larbert** Falk
216 B7 **Largie** Abers
172 F2 **Largiemore** Ag & B
187 H5 **Largoward** Fife
173 L6 **Largs** N Ayrs
162 D5 **Largybeg** N Ayrs
162 D4 **Largymore** N Ayrs
173 L4 **Larkfield** Inver
33 J2 **Larkfield** Kent
175 K7 **Larkhall** S Lans
28 C3 **Larkhill** Wilts
92 B5 **Larling** Norfk
140 C4 **Lartington** Dur
30 A3 **Lasham** Hants
99 K2 **Lask Edge** Staffs
186 B8 **Lassodie** Fife
177 J5 **Lasswade** Mdloth
133 L2 **Lastingham** N York
61 L7 **Latchingdon** Essex
6 B2 **Latchley** Cnwll
74 C5 **Lathbury** M Keyn
227 L2 **Latheron** Highld
227 L3 **Latheronwheel** Highld
187 H5 **Lathones** Fife
59 G7 **Latimer** Bucks
38 F4 **Latteridge** S Glos
27 G6 **Lattiford** Somset
40 C2 **Latton** Wilts
178 C8 **Lauder** Border
50 C4 **Laugharne** Carmth
116 D6 **Laughterton** Lincs
20 A3 **Laughton** E Susx
87 J5 **Laughton** Leics
116 D3 **Laughton** Lincs
103 H6 **Laughton** Lincs
115 K4 **Laughton-en-le-Morthen** Rothm
9 H4 **Launcells** Cnwll
9 J7 **Launceston** Cnwll
57 L4 **Launton** Oxon
197 H3 **Laurencekirk** Abers
146 B3 **Laurieston** D & G
176 B3 **Laurieston** Falk
74 D4 **Lavendon** M Keyn
77 K5 **Lavenham** Suffk
37 J6 **Lavernock** V Glam
148 E3 **Laversdale** Cumb
28 D5 **Laverstock** Wilts
29 J2 **Laverstoke** Hants
71 J7 **Laverton** Gloucs
132 C5 **Laverton** N York
27 H2 **Laverton** Somset
98 A2 **Lavister** Wrexhm
175 L7 **Law** S Lans
175 L7 **Law Hill** S Lans
193 L7 **Lawers** P & K
62 C2 **Lawford** Essex
25 H4 **Lawford** Somset
186 A3 **Lawgrove** P & K
9 J7 **Lawhitton** Cnwll
130 E6 **Lawkland** N York
49 H6 **Lawrenny** Pembks
77 K4 **Lawshall** Suffk
232 f3 **Laxay** W Isls
232 f2 **Laxdale** W Isls
237 d4 **Laxey** IOM
93 G8 **Laxfield** Suffk
228 C6 **Laxford Bridge** Highld
235 d4 **Laxo** Shet
125 J5 **Laxton** E R Yk
88 D4 **Laxton** Nhants
116 B7 **Laxton** Notts
122 F3 **Laycock** Brad
61 M4 **Layer Breton** Essex
61 L4 **Layer Marney** Essex
62 A4 **Layer-de-la-Haye** Essex
78 B6 **Layham** Suffk
13 K2 **Laymore** Dorset
125 H3 **Laytham** E R Yk
147 M4 **Laythes** Cumb
148 F6 **Lazonby** Cumb
236 c4 **Le Bigard** Guern
236 c4 **Le Bourg** Guern
236 e8 **Le Bourg** Jersey
236 c3 **Le Gron** Guern
236 d8 **Le Haguais** Jersey
236 d8 **Le Hocq** Jersey
236 c2 **Le Villocq** Guern
101 G2 **Lea** Derbys
54 F4 **Lea** Herefs
116 D4 **Lea** Lincs
83 G5 **Lea** Shrops
39 L3 **Lea** Wilts
86 B5 **Lea Marston** Warwks
212 F5 **Leachkin** Highld
177 H7 **Leadburn** Mdloth
60 F5 **Leaden Roding** Essex
102 F3 **Leadenham** Lincs
150 E5 **Leadgate** Dur
165 G6 **Leadhills** S Lans
56 F5 **Leafield** Oxon
59 H4 **Leagrave** Luton
104 C3 **Leake Common Side** Lincs
142 F5 **Lealholm** N York
209 H3 **Lealt** Highld
72 F2 **Leamington Hastings** Warwks
72 D2 **Leamington Spa** Warwks
20 C4 **Leap Cross** E Susx
129 K3 **Leasgill** Cumb
103 H3 **Leasingham** Lincs
141 G2 **Leasingthorne** Dur
31 K1 **Leatherhead** Surrey
123 J2 **Leathley** N York
98 C8 **Leaton** Shrops
34 D4 **Leaveland** Kent
77 L6 **Leavenheath** Suffk
134 C6 **Leavening** N York
45 H7 **Leaves Green** Gt Lon
135 G3 **Lebberston** N York
56 E7 **Lechlade on Thames** Gloucs
170 E5 **Lecht Gruinart** Ag & B
130 C4 **Leck** Lancs
193 L7 **Leckbuie** P & K
29 G4 **Leckford** Hants
73 K6 **Leckhampstead** Bucks
41 H5 **Leckhampstead** W Berk
41 H5 **Leckhampstead Thicket** W Berk
55 L4 **Leckhampton** Gloucs
220 F4 **Leckmelm** Highld
126 C2 **Leconfield** E R Yk
191 H8 **Ledaig** Ag & B
58 E4 **Ledburn** Bucks
70 C6 **Ledbury** Herefs
69 H4 **Ledgemoor** Herefs
224 F6 **Ledmore Junction** Highld
124 C4 **Ledsham** Leeds
124 C5 **Ledston** Leeds
57 H3 **Ledwell** Oxon
23 H3 **Lee** Devon
45 H5 **Lee** Gt Lon
98 D6 **Lee Brockhurst** Shrops
46 B3 **Lee Chapel** Essex
58 E6 **Lee Clump** Bucks
6 E5 **Lee Mill** Devon
17 G3 **Lee-on-the-Solent** Hants
83 J4 **Leebotwood** Shrops
128 F5 **Leece** Cumb
33 L3 **Leeds** Kent
123 K4 **Leeds** Leeds
123 J3 **Leeds Bradford Airport** Leeds
33 L3 **Leeds Castle** Kent
3 G4 **Leedstown** Cnwll
99 M2 **Leek** Staffs
72 C2 **Leek Wootton** Warwks
132 D2 **Leeming** N York
132 D2 **Leeming Bar** N York
100 E5 **Lees** Derbys
113 L2 **Lees** Oldham
100 E5 **Lees Green** Derbys
87 L2 **Leesthorpe** Leics
97 K1 **Leeswood** Flints
186 C3 **Leetown** P & K
112 F6 **Leftwich** Ches
118 E5 **Legbourne** Lincs
167 J2 **Legerwood** Border
42 F5 **Legoland** W & M
117 J4 **Legsby** Lincs
87 H3 **Leicester** C Leic
87 G3 **Leicester Forest East** Leics
14 C2 **Leigh** Dorset
55 K3 **Leigh** Gloucs
32 F4 **Leigh** Kent
31 L3 **Leigh** Surrey
112 F2 **Leigh** Wigan
40 B3 **Leigh** Wilts
70 D4 **Leigh** Worcs
46 D4 **Leigh Beck** Essex
39 K5 **Leigh Delamere** Wilts
34 B7 **Leigh Green** Kent
175 H7 **Leigh Knoweglass** S Lans
15 J3 **Leigh Park** Dorset
70 D4 **Leigh Sinton** Worcs
27 G3 **Leigh upon Mendip** Somset
38 E6 **Leigh Woods** N Som
46 D3 **Leigh-on-Sea** Sthend
85 J3 **Leighswood** W Mids
39 J3 **Leighterton** Gloucs
82 E3 **Leighton** Powys
84 B3 **Leighton** Shrops
89 G7 **Leighton Bromswold** Cambs
58 F3 **Leighton Buzzard** Beds
69 J2 **Leinthall Earls** Herefs
69 J1 **Leinthall Starkes** Herefs
83 H8 **Leintwardine** Herefs
87 G5 **Leire** Leics
79 J3 **Leiston** Suffk
195 L7 **Leitfie** P & K
177 H3 **Leith** C Edin
168 B1 **Leitholm** Border
2 F4 **Lelant** Cnwll
126 F4 **Lelley** E R Yk
168 B3 **Lempitlaw** Border
232 f3 **Lemreway** W Isls
59 L5 **Lemsford** Herts
71 J5 **Lenchwick** Worcs
152 D4 **Lendalfoot** S Ayrs
184 C6 **Lendrick** Stirlg
217 L6 **Lendrum Terrace** Abers
34 B4 **Lenham** Kent
34 B5 **Lenham Heath** Kent
202 D1 **Lenie** Highld
168 C2 **Lennel** Border
146 A5 **Lennox Plunton** D & G
175 H3 **Lennoxtown** E Duns
101 K5 **Lenton** C Nott
103 G6 **Lenton** Lincs
106 D8 **Lenwade** Norfk
175 H4 **Lenzie** E Duns
205 L4 **Leochel-Cushnie** Abers
69 K3 **Leominster** Herefs
55 J7 **Leonard Stanley** Gloucs
236 b6 **Leoville** Jersey
208 B4 **Lephin** Highld
134 B7 **Leppington** N York
123 J7 **Lepton** Kirk
5 J4 **Lerryn** Cnwll
235 d6 **Lerwick** Shet

236 b3 **Les Arquets** Guern
236 d3 **Les Hubits** Guern
236 c3 **Les Lohiers** Guern
236 c4 **Les Murchez** Guern
236 c4 **Les Nicolles** Guern
236 d2 **Les Quartiers** Guern
236 b7 **Les Quennevais** Jersey
236 b3 **Les Sages** Guern
236 c4 **Les Villets** Guern
169 J6 **Lesbury** Nthumb
206 B1 **Leslie** Abers
186 D6 **Leslie** Fife
164 F2 **Lesmahagow** S Lans
8 F6 **Lesnewth** Cnwll
107 H6 **Lessingham** Norfk
147 L5 **Lessonhall** Cumb
144 B3 **Leswalt** D & G
43 J2 **Letchmore Heath** Herts
59 L2 **Letchworth Garden City** Herts
41 G4 **Letcombe Bassett** Oxon
41 G3 **Letcombe Regis** Oxon
196 E6 **Letham** Angus
167 K7 **Letham** Border
176 B2 **Letham** Falk
186 E4 **Letham** Fife
197 G7 **Letham Grange** Angus
195 H7 **Lethendy** P & K
206 B2 **Lethenty** Abers
216 F6 **Lethenty** Abers
78 F3 **Letheringham** Suffk
106 C5 **Letheringsett** Norfk
219 L6 **Letterewe** Highld
200 D2 **Letterfearn** Highld
201 K6 **Letterfinlay Lodge Hotel** Highld
199 M7 **Lettermorar** Highld
220 F4 **Letters** Highld
165 H5 **Lettershaw** S Lans
48 F2 **Letterston** Pembks
204 C2 **Lettoch** Highld
214 D7 **Lettoch** Highld
69 G5 **Letton** Herefs
59 M5 **Letty Green** Herts
115 K4 **Letwell** Rothm
187 G3 **Leuchars** Fife
232 f3 **Leumrabhagh** W Isls
232 f3 **Leurbost** W Isls
84 F1 **Levedale** Staffs
60 D3 **Level's Green** Essex
126 D2 **Leven** E R Yk
186 F7 **Leven** Fife
129 K3 **Levens** Cumb
60 B4 **Levens Green** Herts
113 K3 **Levenshulme** Manch
235 c7 **Levenwick** Shet
232 d5 **Leverburgh** W Isls
90 C2 **Leverington** Cambs
59 H6 **Leverstock Green** Herts
104 C3 **Leverton** Lincs
78 F6 **Levington** Suffk
134 C2 **Levisham** N York
56 F6 **Lew** Oxon
9 H8 **Lewannick** Cnwll
10 C7 **Lewdown** Devon
19 L4 **Lewes** E Susx
48 F3 **Leweston** Pembks
45 G5 **Lewisham** Gt Lon
212 D8 **Lewiston** Highld
42 B2 **Lewknor** Oxon
34 C3 **Lewson Street** Kent
10 C7 **Lewtrenchard** Devon
62 A3 **Lexden** Essex
25 K4 **Lexworthy** Somset
59 G7 **Ley Hill** Bucks
33 H2 **Leybourne** Kent
131 L2 **Leyburn** N York
59 K3 **Leygreen** Herts
121 H6 **Leyland** Lancs
206 E3 **Leylodge** Abers
217 J4 **Leys** Abers
195 K8 **Leys** Angus
196 C6 **Leys of Cossans** Angus
47 G6 **Leysdown-on-Sea** Kent
196 F6 **Leysmill** Angus
69 L2 **Leysters** Herefs
45 G3 **Leyton** Gt Lon
45 H3 **Leytonstone** Gt Lon
5 M1 **Lezant** Cnwll
237 d3 **Lezayre** IOM
215 G3 **Lhanbryde** Moray
52 F3 **Libanus** Powys
165 J2 **Libberton** S Lans
177 J4 **Liberton** C Edin
85 K2 **Lichfield** Staffs
85 H7 **Lickey** Worcs
85 H8 **Lickey End** Worcs
30 F6 **Lickfold** W Susx
190 F4 **Liddesdale** Highld
40 E4 **Liddington** Swindn
77 G3 **Lidgate** Suffk
74 E6 **Lidlington** Beds
186 E2 **Liff** Angus
85 J7 **Lifford** Birm
9 K7 **Lifton** Devon
9 K7 **Liftondown** Devon
72 D4 **Lighthorne** Warwks
72 D4 **Lighthorne Heath** Warwks
42 F7 **Lightwater** Surrey
87 H7 **Lilbourne** Nhants
84 D1 **Lilleshall** Wrekin
59 J3 **Lilley** Herts
167 H4 **Lilliesleaf** Border
73 K6 **Lillingstone Dayrell** Bucks
73 K6 **Lillingstone Lovell** Bucks
26 F8 **Lillington** Dorset
15 K4 **Lilliput** Poole
25 J3 **Lilstock** Somset
59 H3 **Limbury** Luton
55 J2 **Lime Street** Worcs
175 J7 **Limekilnburn** S Lans
176 E2 **Limekilns** Fife
176 B4 **Limerigg** Falk
16 E6 **Limerstone** IOW
26 D6 **Limington** Somset
164 C4 **Limmerhaugh** E Ayrs
93 H3 **Limpenhoe** Norfk
39 H7 **Limpley Stoke** Wilts
32 D3 **Limpsfield** Surrey
32 D3 **Limpsfield Chart** Surrey
101 K3 **Linby** Notts
30 E5 **Linchmere** W Susx
155 G6 **Lincluden** D & G
116 F7 **Lincoln** Lincs
70 E2 **Lincomb** Worcs
128 F4 **Lindal in Furness** Cumb
129 J4 **Lindale** Cumb
32 C7 **Lindfield** W Susx
30 D4 **Lindford** Hants
123 G6 **Lindley** Kirk
123 J2 **Lindley Green** N York
70 C2 **Lindridge** Worcs
61 G3 **Lindsell** Essex
77 L5 **Lindsey** Suffk
78 B5 **Lindsey Tye** Suffk
142 E4 **Lingdale** R & Cl
69 G2 **Lingen** Herefs
32 C4 **Lingfield** Surrey
93 H2 **Lingwood** Norfk
218 B7 **Linicro** Highld
55 J2 **Linkend** Worcs
41 G8 **Linkenholt** Hants
5 L2 **Linkinhorne** Cnwll
177 J1 **Linktown** Fife
214 F3 **Linkwood** Moray
83 G5 **Linley** Shrops
70 C4 **Linley Green** Herefs
84 C4 **Linleygreen** Shrops
176 D3 **Linlithgow** W Loth
222 D2 **Linsidemore** Highld
58 E3 **Linslade** Beds
93 G7 **Linstead Parva** Suffk
148 D4 **Linstock** Cumb
85 H8 **Linthurst** Worcs
123 G7 **Linthwaite** Kirk
179 H6 **Lintlaw** Border
215 L2 **Lintmill** Moray
168 B4 **Linton** Border
76 E5 **Linton** Cambs
86 C1 **Linton** Derbys
54 F3 **Linton** Herefs
33 K3 **Linton** Kent
124 B2 **Linton** Leeds
131 J6 **Linton** N York
54 F3 **Linton Hill** Gloucs
133 G7 **Linton-on-Ouse** N York
117 J4 **Linwood** Lincs
174 E5 **Linwood** Rens
233 b7 **Lionacleit** W Isls
232 g1 **Lional** W Isls
30 D5 **Liphook** Hants
111 J3 **Liscard** Wirral
24 D5 **Liscombe** Somset
5 K3 **Liskeard** Cnwll
30 C5 **Liss** Hants
135 H7 **Lissett** E R Yk
117 J5 **Lissington** Lincs
37 J4 **Lisvane** Cardif
37 M3 **Liswerry** Newpt
105 L8 **Litcham** Norfk
73 J4 **Litchborough** Nhants
29 J2 **Litchfield** Hants
111 K2 **Litherland** Sefton
75 K6 **Litlington** Cambs
20 B5 **Litlington** E Susx
76 D5 **Little Abington** Cambs
88 D8 **Little Addington** Nhants
145 J5 **Little Airies** D & G
71 K3 **Little Alne** Warwks
111 J1 **Little Altcar** Sefton
60 B5 **Little Amwell** Herts
139 G5 **Little Asby** Cumb
85 K4 **Little Aston** Staffs
142 C5 **Little Ayton** N York
61 J6 **Little Baddow** Essex
39 J4 **Little Badminton** S Glos
148 A4 **Little Bampton** Cumb
61 G2 **Little Bardfield** Essex
75 H3 **Little Barford** Beds
106 D5 **Little Barningham** Norfk
56 D5 **Little Barrington** Gloucs
112 C7 **Little Barrow** Ches
158 C6 **Little Bavington** Nthumb
40 F7 **Little Bedwyn** Wilts
62 D3 **Little Bentley** Essex
59 M6 **Little Berkhamsted** Herts
74 B3 **Little Billing** Nhants
58 F4 **Little Billington** Beds
54 D2 **Little Birch** Herefs
78 D5 **Little Blakenham** Suffk
148 E7 **Little Blencow** Cumb
31 G7 **Little Bognor** W Susx
100 F2 **Little Bolehill** Derbys
113 G4 **Little Bollington** Ches
31 J1 **Little Bookham** Surrey
72 F5 **Little Bourton** Oxon
77 G4 **Little Bradley** Suffk
61 K5 **Little Braxted** Essex
196 F4 **Little Brechin** Angus
58 E2 **Little Brickhill** M Keyn
73 J2 **Little Brington** Nhants
62 C3 **Little Bromley** Essex
112 E7 **Little Budworth** Ches
46 A2 **Little Burstead** Essex
103 G8 **Little Bytham** Lincs
118 E4 **Little Carlton** Lincs
88 E2 **Little Casterton** Rutlnd
118 E5 **Little Cawthorpe** Lincs
43 G2 **Little Chalfont** Bucks
34 C5 **Little Chart** Kent
76 D6 **Little Chesterford** Essex
27 M2 **Little Cheverell** Wilts
76 B6 **Little Chishill** Cambs
62 E4 **Little Clacton** Essex
136 E2 **Little Clifton** Cumb
71 G5 **Little Comberton** Worcs
20 E4 **Little Common** E Susx
56 E3 **Little Compton** Warwks
77 K6 **Little Cornard** Suffk
69 L4 **Little Cowarne** Herefs
40 F2 **Little Coxwell** Oxon
132 C2 **Little Crakehall** N York
91 K4 **Little Cressingham** Norfk
111 K2 **Little Crosby** Sefton
100 D5 **Little Cubley** Derbys
87 L2 **Little Dalby** Leics
217 K5 **Little Dens** Abers
54 D2 **Little Dewchurch** Herefs
76 F3 **Little Ditton** Cambs
90 D6 **Little Downham** Cambs
134 F7 **Little Driffield** E R Yk
91 K2 **Little Dunham** Norfk
195 G7 **Little Dunkeld** P & K
61 G4 **Little Dunmow** Essex
28 C5 **Little Durnford** Wilts
60 F3 **Little Easton** Essex
101 G4 **Little Eaton** Derbys
92 B4 **Little Ellingham** Norfk
73 H3 **Little Everdon** Nhants
75 L4 **Little Eversden** Cambs
56 E7 **Little Faringdon** Oxon
132 D2 **Little Fencote** N York
124 D4 **Little Fenton** N York
91 K2 **Little Fransham** Norfk
59 G5 **Little Gaddesden** Herts
79 H3 **Little Glemham** Suffk
55 G3 **Little Gorsley** Herefs
75 J4 **Little Gransden** Cambs
27 G2 **Little Green** Somset
118 D3 **Little Grimsby** Lincs
60 C4 **Little Hadham** Herts
103 J4 **Little Hale** Lincs
101 J4 **Little Hallam** Derbys
60 D4 **Little Hallingbury** Essex
74 C1 **Little Harrowden** Nhants
57 M7 **Little Haseley** Oxon
126 E2 **Little Hatfield** E R Yk

48 E5 **Little Haven** Pembks
85 K3 **Little Hay** Staffs
100 A7 **Little Haywood** Staffs
86 D6 **Little Heath** Covtry
69 K2 **Little Hereford** Herefs
62 A2 **Little Horkesley** Essex
60 C3 **Little Hormead** Herts
19 M3 **Little Horsted** E Susx
123 H4 **Little Horton** Brad
58 C2 **Little Horwood** Bucks
115 H1 **Little Houghton** Barns
74 B3 **Little Houghton** Nhants
114 D5 **Little Hucklow** Derbys
133 G4 **Little Hutton** N York
74 C2 **Little Irchester** Nhants
27 H3 **Little Keyford** Somset
58 D6 **Little Kimble** Bucks
72 D4 **Little Kineton** Warwks
58 E7 **Little Kingshill** Bucks
146 E3 **Little Knox** D & G
137 J6 **Little Langdale** Cumb
28 B4 **Little Langford** Wilts
9 K4 **Little Lashbrook** Devon
112 F6 **Little Leigh** Ches
61 H5 **Little Leighs** Essex
121 L8 **Little Lever** Bolton
74 B5 **Little Linford** M Keyn
26 C6 **Little Load** Somset
20 C2 **Little London** E Susx
60 D3 **Little London** Essex
29 G2 **Little London** Hants
41 L8 **Little London** Hants
114 D6 **Little Longstone** Derbys
70 D6 **Little Malvern** Worcs
77 J7 **Little Maplestead** Essex
70 C7 **Little Marcle** Herefs
42 E3 **Little Marlow** Bucks
105 J7 **Little Massingham** Norfk
92 E3 **Little Melton** Norfk
53 L7 **Little Mill** Mons
57 L7 **Little Milton** Oxon
58 F7 **Little Missenden** Bucks
139 H5 **Little Musgrave** Cumb
98 B8 **Little Ness** Shrops
49 G2 **Little Newcastle** Pembks
140 E4 **Little Newsham** Dur
26 C7 **Little Norton** Somset
62 F3 **Little Oakley** Essex
88 C6 **Little Oakley** Nhants
84 E1 **Little Onn** Staffs
148 C4 **Little Orton** Cumb
86 B6 **Little Packington** Warwks
75 H3 **Little Paxton** Cambs
4 E2 **Little Petherick** Cnwll
93 G2 **Little Plumstead** Norfk
102 F6 **Little Ponton** Lincs
73 H4 **Little Preston** Nhants
89 J7 **Little Raveley** Cambs
125 J6 **Little Reedness** E R Yk
132 F8 **Little Ribston** N York
56 D4 **Little Rissington** Gloucs
56 F3 **Little Rollright** Oxon
106 A6 **Little Ryburgh** Norfk
148 F7 **Little Salkeld** Cumb
76 F7 **Little Sampford** Essex
111 K7 **Little Saughall** Ches
77 H2 **Little Saxham** Suffk
212 B3 **Little Scatwell** Highld
133 G5 **Little Sessay** N York
76 C4 **Little Shelford** Cambs
11 K5 **Little Silver** Devon
120 E3 **Little Singleton** Lancs
125 G3 **Little Skipwith** N York
124 D6 **Little Smeaton** N York
106 A6 **Little Snoring** Norfk
39 H4 **Little Sodbury** S Glos
29 G5 **Little Somborne** Hants
39 L4 **Little Somerford** Wilts
99 G6 **Little Soudley** Shrops
141 J3 **Little Stainton** Darltn
112 B6 **Little Stanney** Ches
75 G3 **Little Staughton** Beds
118 F8 **Little Steeping** Lincs
78 D3 **Little Stonham** Suffk
87 J4 **Little Stretton** Leics
83 J5 **Little Stretton** Shrops
138 E4 **Little Strickland** Cumb
89 H7 **Little Stukeley** Cambs
99 J6 **Little Sugnall** Staffs
158 B6 **Little Swinburne** Nthumb
146 C4 **Little Sypland** D & G
57 G3 **Little Tew** Oxon
61 L4 **Little Tey** Essex
90 D7 **Little Thetford** Cambs
151 K6 **Little Thorpe** Dur
77 G4 **Little Thurlow Green** Suffk
45 L4 **Little Thurrock** Thurr
10 D2 **Little Torrington** Devon
121 K4 **Little Town** Lancs
128 F5 **Little Urswick** Cumb
46 F3 **Little Wakering** Essex
76 D6 **Little Walden** Essex
77 K5 **Little Waldingfield** Suffk
105 M5 **Little Walsingham** Norfk
61 H5 **Little Waltham** Essex
55 M2 **Little Washbourne** Gloucs
126 B4 **Little Weighton** E R Yk
88 D5 **Little Weldon** Nhants
78 C6 **Little Wenham** Suffk
84 B3 **Little Wenlock** Wrekin
26 F6 **Little Weston** Somset
17 H4 **Little Whitefield** IOW
76 D3 **Little Wilbraham** Cambs
55 K5 **Little Witcombe** Gloucs
70 D2 **Little Witley** Worcs
41 K2 **Little Wittenham** Oxon
72 C7 **Little Wolford** Warwks
44 F7 **Little Woodcote** Surrey
77 G5 **Little Wratting** Suffk
74 D2 **Little Wymington** Beds
59 K3 **Little Wymondley** Herts
85 H3 **Little Wyrley** Staffs
77 H6 **Little Yeldham** Essex
116 D5 **Littleborough** Notts
122 D7 **Littleborough** Rochdl
35 G3 **Littlebourne** Kent
14 B5 **Littlebredy** Dorset
212 F4 **Littleburn** Highld
76 D6 **Littlebury** Essex
76 C6 **Littlebury Green** Essex
54 F5 **Littledean** Gloucs
23 G6 **Littleham** Devon
12 D6 **Littleham** Devon
18 D5 **Littlehampton** W Susx
31 K5 **Littlehaven** W Susx
7 J4 **Littlehempston** Devon
205 H6 **Littlemill** Abers
213 L4 **Littlemill** Highld
57 K7 **Littlemore** Oxon
101 G5 **Littleover** C Derb
90 E6 **Littleport** Cambs
21 L2 **Littlestone-on-Sea** Kent
87 G4 **Littlethorpe** Leics
132 E5 **Littlethorpe** N York
196 B6 **Littleton** Angus
112 C7 **Littleton** Ches
146 B4 **Littleton** D & G
29 J5 **Littleton** Hants
26 C5 **Littleton** Somset
43 H6 **Littleton** Surrey
39 J4 **Littleton Drew** Wilts
27 M2 **Littleton Pannell** Wilts
38 E3 **Littleton-on-Severn** S Glos
151 H6 **Littletown** Dur
42 D4 **Littlewick Green** W & M
40 F2 **Littleworth** Oxon
99 L7 **Littleworth** Staffs
70 F4 **Littleworth** Worcs
61 H4 **Littley Green** Essex
26 E1 **Litton** BaNES
114 D6 **Litton** Derbys
131 G5 **Litton** N York
14 A4 **Litton Cheney** Dorset
232 f3 **Liurbost** W Isls
111 K4 **Liverpool** Lpool
123 J5 **Liversedge** Kirk
7 J2 **Liverton** Devon
142 F4 **Liverton** R & Cl
176 E5 **Livingston** W Loth
176 E5 **Livingston Village** W Loth
7 G5 **Lixton** Devon
111 G7 **Lixwm** Flints
3 J8 **Lizard** Cnwll
95 G4 **Llanaelhaearn** Gwynd
66 F1 **Llanafan** Cerdgn
109 G4 **Llanallgo** IOA
97 J6 **Llanarmon Dyffryn Ceiriog** Wrexhm
97 J2 **Llanarmon-yn-Ial** Denbgs
65 L3 **Llanarth** Cerdgn
54 B5 **Llanarth** Mons
51 G2 **Llanarthne** Carmth
110 F5 **Llanasa** Flints
80 E7 **Llanbadarn Fawr** Cerdgn
82 C7 **Llanbadarn Fynydd** Powys
54 B7 **Llanbadoc** Mons
38 B3 **Llanbeder** Newpt
95 K6 **Llanbedr** Gwynd
53 K4 **Llanbedr** Powys
97 H1 **Llanbedr-Dyffryn-Clwyd** Denbgs
109 L7 **Llanbedr-y-Cennin** Conwy
109 G5 **Llanbedrgoch** IOA
94 F6 **Llanbedrog** Gwynd
95 K1 **Llanberis** Gwynd
37 G6 **Llanbethery** V Glam
82 C8 **Llanbister** Powys
36 F5 **Llanblethian** V Glam
49 L3 **Llanboidy** Carmth
37 J3 **Llanbradach** Caerph
81 J3 **Llanbrynmair** Powys
37 G6 **Llancadle** V Glam
37 G6 **Llancarfan** V Glam
54 D4 **Llancloudy** Herefs
37 J5 **Llandaff** Cardif
95 K6 **Llandanwg** Gwynd
109 G7 **Llanddanielfab** IOA
51 G3 **Llanddarog** Carmth
66 D1 **Llanddeiniol** Cerdgn
109 H7 **Llanddeiniolen** Gwynd
96 F5 **Llandderfel** Gwynd
108 D4 **Llanddeusant** IOA
53 G2 **Llanddew** Powys
50 F7 **Llanddewi** Swans
66 F4 **Llanddewi Brefi** Cerdgn
53 M5 **Llanddewi Rhydderch** Mons
49 K4 **Llanddewi Velfrey** Pembks
68 C2 **Llanddewi Ystradenni** Powys
109 M8 **Llanddoget** Conwy
109 H5 **Llanddona** IOA
50 B3 **Llanddowror** Carmth
110 C6 **Llanddulas** Conwy
95 K7 **Llanddwywe** Gwynd
109 G5 **Llanddyfnan** IOA
53 H3 **Llandefaelog-Trer-Graig** Powys
68 C7 **Llandefalle** Powys
109 H6 **Llandegfan** IOA
97 J3 **Llandegla** Denbgs
68 D2 **Llandegley** Powys
37 M2 **Llandegveth** Mons
51 J2 **Llandeilo** Carmth
68 C5 **Llandeilo Graban** Powys
48 E3 **Llandeloy** Pembks
54 B7 **Llandenny** Mons
38 B3 **Llandevaud** Newpt
38 B3 **Llandevenny** Mons
82 B5 **Llandinam** Powys
49 J3 **Llandissilio** Pembks
54 D7 **Llandogo** Mons
36 F6 **Llandough** V Glam
37 J5 **Llandough** V Glam
67 G7 **Llandovery** Carmth
36 E5 **Llandow** V Glam
66 F6 **Llandre** Carmth
80 E6 **Llandre** Cerdgn
49 J2 **Llandre Isaf** Pembks
97 G5 **Llandrillo** Denbgs
110 B5 **Llandrillo-yn-Rhos** Conwy
68 B3 **Llandrindod Wells** Powys
97 L8 **Llandrinio** Powys
109 L5 **Llandudno** Conwy
109 M6 **Llandudno Junction** Conwy
94 E5 **Llandudwen** Gwynd
67 J6 **Llandulas** Powys
95 H2 **Llandwrog** Gwynd
51 J3 **Llandybie** Carmth
50 E3 **Llandyfaelog** Carmth
65 K6 **Llandyfriog** Cerdgn
109 H7 **Llandygai** Gwynd
65 H5 **Llandygwydd** Cerdgn
110 F8 **Llandyrnog** Denbgs
82 E4 **Llandyssil** Powys
65 L6 **Llandysul** Cerdgn
37 K4 **Llanedeyrn** Cardif
68 B6 **Llaneglwys** Powys
80 D3 **Llanegryn** Gwynd
51 G2 **Llanegwad** Carmth
108 F3 **Llaneilian** IOA
110 B6 **Llanelian-yn-Rhos** Conwy
97 H3 **Llanelidan** Denbgs

68 D7 **Llanelieu** Powys
53 L5 **Llanellen** Mons
51 G5 **Llanelli** Carmth
96 A8 **Llanelltyd** Gwynd
68 B4 **Llanelwedd** Powys
95 K7 **Llanenddwyn** Gwynd
94 E6 **Llanengan** Gwynd
108 E5 **Llanerchymedd** IOA
82 B2 **Llanerfyl** Powys
108 D5 **Llanfachraeth** IOA
96 B7 **Llanfachreth** Gwynd
108 D6 **Llanfaelog** IOA
94 D6 **Llanfaelrhys** Gwynd
108 D4 **Llanfaethlu** IOA
95 K6 **Llanfair** Gwynd
82 C3 **Llanfair Caereinion** Powys
66 E4 **Llanfair Clydogau** Cerdgn
97 H2 **Llanfair Dyffryn Clwyd** Denbgs
109 G6 **Llanfair P G** IOA
110 C7 **Llanfair Talhaiarn** Conwy
82 E7 **Llanfair Waterdine** Shrops
109 G7 **Llanfair-is-gaer** Gwynd
108 F7 **Llanfair-y-Cwmwd** IOA
108 C6 **Llanfair-yn-Neubwll** IOA
109 K6 **Llanfairfechan** Conwy
108 D4 **Llanfairynghornwy** IOA
49 K4 **Llanfallteg** Carmth
49 K4 **Llanfallteg West** Carmth
80 D7 **Llanfarian** Cerdgn
97 J7 **Llanfechain** Powys
108 E3 **Llanfechell** IOA
97 J1 **Llanferres** Denbgs
96 F3 **Llanfihangel Glyn Myfyr** Conwy
67 K7 **Llanfihangel Nant Bran** Powys
68 D2 **Llanfihangel Rhydithon** Powys
38 C3 **Llanfihangel Rogiet** Mons
108 D6 **Llanfihangel yn Nhowyn** IOA
66 B6 **Llanfihangel-ar-Arth** Carmth
80 F7 **Llanfihangel-y-Creuddyn** Cerdgn
95 K5 **Llanfihangel-y-traethau** Gwynd
82 C1 **Llanfihangel-yng-Ngwynfa** Powys
53 H2 **Llanfilo** Powys
53 L5 **Llanfoist** Mons
96 E5 **Llanfor** Gwynd
37 L2 **Llanfrechfa** Torfn
53 G3 **Llanfrynach** Powys
97 H2 **Llanfwrog** Denbgs
108 C5 **Llanfwrog** IOA
97 H8 **Llanfyllin** Powys
66 D8 **Llanfynydd** Carmth
97 L2 **Llanfynydd** Flints
49 L2 **Llanfyrnach** Pembks
81 L2 **Llangadfan** Powys
66 F8 **Llangadog** Carmth
108 E7 **Llangadwaladr** IOA
108 F7 **Llangaffo** IOA
67 K5 **Llangammarch Wells** Powys
36 E5 **Llangan** V Glam
54 D4 **Llangarron** Herefs
51 H2 **Llangathen** Carmth
53 K4 **Llangattock** Powys
54 A4 **Llangattock Lingoed** Mons
97 J7 **Llangedwyn** Powys
108 F6 **Llangefni** IOA
36 E3 **Llangeinor** Brdgnd
108 F7 **Llangeinwen** IOA
66 E3 **Llangeitho** Cerdgn
65 L6 **Llangeler** Carmth
80 D3 **Llangelynin** Gwynd
50 F3 **Llangendeirne** Carmth
51 H5 **Llangennech** Carmth
50 E7 **Llangennith** Swans
110 B7 **Llangernyw** Conwy
94 E6 **Llangian** Gwynd
64 C7 **Llangloffan** Pembks
49 K3 **Llanglydwen** Carmth
109 J5 **Llangoed** IOA
97 K4 **Llangollen** Denbgs
49 J3 **Llangolman** Pembks
53 H3 **Llangors** Powys
96 D6 **Llangower** Gwynd
65 K4 **Llangranog** Cerdgn
108 F6 **Llangristiolus** IOA
54 D4 **Llangrove** Herefs
68 E1 **Llangunllo** Powys
50 E2 **Llangunnor** Carmth
81 K7 **Llangurig** Powys
96 F4 **Llangwm** Conwy
54 B7 **Llangwm** Mons
49 G5 **Llangwm** Pembks
54 B7 **Llangwm-isaf** Mons
94 D6 **Llangwnnadl** Gwynd
66 D1 **Llangwyryfon** Cerdgn
66 E4 **Llangybi** Cerdgn
95 G4 **Llangybi** Gwynd
38 A2 **Llangybi** Mons
110 F8 **Llangynhafal** Denbgs
53 J4 **Llangynidr** Powys
50 B2 **Llangynin** Carmth
50 D3 **Llangynog** Carmth
97 G7 **Llangynog** Powys
36 D3 **Llangynwyd** Brdgnd
53 H3 **Llanhamlach** Powys
36 F4 **Llanharan** Rhondd
36 F4 **Llanharry** Rhondd
38 A2 **Llanhennock** Mons
53 K7 **Llanhilleth** Blae G
81 K6 **Llanidloes** Powys
94 E5 **Llaniestyn** Gwynd
68 E6 **Llanigon** Powys
80 E8 **Llanilar** Cerdgn
36 F4 **Llanilid** Rhondd
65 L3 **Llanina** Cerdgn
37 J4 **Llanishen** Cardif
54 C7 **Llanishen** Mons
109 J7 **Llanllechid** Gwynd
54 B7 **Llanllowell** Mons
82 B3 **Llanllugan** Powys
50 E2 **Llanllwch** Carmth
82 C5 **Llanllwchaiarn** Powys
66 C6 **Llanllwni** Carmth
95 H3 **Llanllyfni** Gwynd
50 F6 **Llanmadoc** Swans
36 F6 **Llanmaes** V Glam
38 B3 **Llanmartin** Newpt
50 B4 **Llanmiloe** Carmth
110 D7 **Llannefydd** Conwy
51 G4 **Llannon** Carmth
94 F5 **Llannor** Gwynd
66 C2 **Llanon** Cerdgn
53 L6 **Llanover** Mons
65 L8 **Llanpumsaint** Carmth
97 H7 **Llanrhaeadr-ym-Mochnant** Powys
48 D2 **Llanrhian** Pembks
50 F6 **Llanrhidian** Swans
96 B1 **Llanrhychwyn** Conwy
108 D4 **Llanrhyddlad** IOA
66 C1 **Llanrhystud** Cerdgn
54 C4 **Llanrothal** Herefs
109 G8 **Llanrug** Gwynd
37 K4 **Llanrumney** Cardif
96 C1 **Llanrwst** Conwy
50 C4 **Llansadurnen** Carmth
66 F7 **Llansadwrn** Carmth
109 H6 **Llansadwrn** IOA
50 E4 **Llansaint** Carmth
51 K6 **Llansamlet** Swans
109 M6 **Llansanffraid Glan Conwy** Conwy
110 C7 **Llansannan** Conwy
53 H4 **Llansantffraed** Powys
67 L2 **Llansantffraed-Cwmdeuddwr** Powys
68 C4 **Llansantffraed-in-Elvel** Powys
66 C2 **Llansantffraid** Cerdgn
97 K7 **Llansantffraid-ym-Mechain** Powys
66 E7 **Llansawel** Carmth
97 K6 **Llansilin** Powys
54 C7 **Llansoy** Mons
52 F3 **Llanspyddid** Powys
48 F6 **Llanstadwell** Pembks
50 D4 **Llansteffan** Carmth
37 L2 **Llantarnam** Torfn
49 K5 **Llanteg** Pembks
53 M5 **Llanthewy Skirrid** Mons
53 L3 **Llanthony** Mons
53 L5 **Llantilio Pertholey** Mons
54 B5 **Llantilio-Crossenny** Mons
38 B2 **Llantrisant** Mons
37 G4 **Llantrisant** Rhondd
37 G6 **Llantrithyd** V Glam
37 G3 **Llantwit Fardre** Rhondd
36 F6 **Llantwit Major** V Glam
96 D6 **Llanuwchllyn** Gwynd
38 B3 **Llanvaches** Newpt
38 C3 **Llanvair Discoed** Mons
54 A5 **Llanvapley** Mons
54 A5 **Llanvetherine** Mons
53 L4 **Llanvihangel Crucorney** Mons
96 F8 **Llanwddyn** Powys
66 C5 **Llanwenog** Cerdgn
38 A3 **Llanwern** Newpt
50 C1 **Llanwinio** Carmth
95 H2 **Llanwnda** Gwynd
64 C6 **Llanwnda** Pembks
66 C5 **Llanwnnen** Cerdgn
82 B5 **Llanwnog** Powys
66 F7 **Llanwrda** Carmth
81 H3 **Llanwrin** Powys
67 L2 **Llanwrthwl** Powys
67 J5 **Llanwrtyd Wells** Powys
82 C4 **Llanwyddelan** Powys
97 K7 **Llanyblodwel** Shrops
50 D3 **Llanybri** Carmth
66 C5 **Llanybydder** Carmth
49 J3 **Llanycefn** Pembks
64 D7 **Llanychaer Bridge** Pembks
96 D8 **Llanymawddwy** Gwynd
97 K7 **Llanymynech** Powys
108 D5 **Llanynghenedl** IOA
110 F8 **Llanynys** Denbgs
68 B3 **Llanyre** Powys
95 H5 **Llanystumdwy** Gwynd
53 H3 **Llanywern** Powys
49 H4 **Llawhaden** Pembks
81 K5 **Llawryglyn** Powys
97 M2 **Llay** Wrexhm
53 H6 **Llechrhyd** Caerph
65 H5 **Llechryd** Cerdgn
66 E1 **Lledrod** Cerdgn
94 E5 **Lleyn Peninsula** Gwynd
94 F4 **Llithfaen** Gwynd
111 G6 **Lloc** Flints
68 D6 **Llowes** Powys
52 F6 **Llwydcoed** Rhondd
82 B1 **Llwydiarth** Powys
66 B3 **Llwyncelyn** Cerdgn
65 L4 **Llwyndafydd** Cerdgn
80 D2 **Llwyngwril** Gwynd
97 K5 **Llwynmawr** Wrexhm
36 F2 **Llwynypia** Rhondd
97 L7 **Llynclys** Shrops
108 E5 **Llynfaes** IOA
49 H3 **Llys-y-fran** Pembks
110 B6 **Llysfaen** Conwy
68 C6 **Llyswen** Powys
36 E5 **Llysworney** V Glam
52 D3 **Llywel** Powys
176 C3 **Loan** Falk
177 J5 **Loanhead** Mdloth
147 G4 **Loaningfoot** D & G
163 J3 **Loans** S Ayrs
10 C7 **Lobhillcross** Devon
233 c8 **Loch Baghasdail** W Isls
233 c6 **Loch Euphoirt** W Isls
184 B6 **Loch Katrine Pier** Stirlg
183 L8 **Loch Lomond**
219 L7 **Loch Maree Hotel** Highld
233 c6 **Loch nam Madadh** W Isls
202 E1 **Loch Ness** Highld
200 B8 **Lochailort** Highld
190 D7 **Lochaline** Highld
144 C4 **Lochans** D & G
155 H6 **Locharbriggs** D & G
182 D4 **Lochavich** Ag & B
183 G2 **Lochawe** Ag & B
233 c8 **Lochboisdale** W Isls
181 J3 **Lochbuie** Ag & B
210 D6 **Lochcarron** Highld
181 L2 **Lochdon** Ag & B
181 L2 **Lochdonhead** Ag & B
172 D3 **Lochead** Ag & B
184 D3 **Lochearnhead** Stirlg
186 F2 **Lochee** C Dund
191 K2 **Locheilside Station** Highld
212 F6 **Lochend** Highld
233 c6 **Locheport** W Isls
154 F7 **Lochfoot** D & G
172 F1 **Lochgair** Ag & B
186 C8 **Lochgelly** Fife
172 E2 **Lochgilphead** Ag & B
183 H6 **Lochgoilhead** Ag & B
186 D5 **Lochieheads** Fife
215 G2 **Lochill** Moray
214 B7 **Lochindorb Lodge** Highld
224 D4 **Lochinver** Highld
211 L2 **Lochluichart** Highld
155 J5 **Lochmaben** D & G
233 c6 **Lochmaddy** W Isls
186 C7 **Lochore** Fife
172 F7 **Lochranza** N Ayrs
197 H4 **Lochside** Abers
155 G6 **Lochside** D & G
213 J4 **Lochside** Highld
152 F6 **Lochton** S Ayrs
196 E4 **Lochty** Angus
187 H5 **Lochty** Fife
190 F5 **Lochuisge** Highld
174 C6 **Lochwinnoch** Rens
155 J3 **Lochwood** D & G
5 G4 **Lockengate** Cnwll
155 K5 **Lockerbie** D & G

40 C6 **Lockeridge** Wilts
28 F6 **Lockerley** Hants
38 A8 **Locking** N Som
112 F3 **Locking Stumps** Warrtn
126 B2 **Lockington** E R Yk
99 G6 **Lockleywood** Shrops
17 G2 **Locks Heath** Hants
45 H6 **Locksbottom** Gt Lon
134 C2 **Lockton** N York
87 L3 **Loddington** Leics
88 B7 **Loddington** Nhants
7 G6 **Loddiswell** Devon
93 H4 **Loddon** Norfk
76 D3 **Lode** Cambs
85 L7 **Lode Heath** Solhll
13 L4 **Loders** Dorset
30 F6 **Lodsworth** W Susx
123 L5 **Lofthouse** Leeds
131 L5 **Lofthouse** N York
123 L5 **Lofthouse Gate** Wakefd
142 F4 **Loftus** R & Cl
164 C5 **Logan** E Ayrs
176 C6 **Loganlea** W Loth
99 G5 **Loggerheads** Staffs
197 H4 **Logie** Angus
186 F4 **Logie** Fife
214 C4 **Logie** Moray
205 K4 **Logie Coldstone** Abers
197 G4 **Logie Pert** Angus
194 F6 **Logierait** P & K
217 H8 **Logierieve** Abers
49 K3 **Login** Carmth
75 L2 **Lolworth** Cambs
209 L4 **Lonbain** Highld
125 K2 **Londesborough** E R Yk
44 F4 **London** Gt Lon
4 F6 **London Apprentice** Cnwll
59 K7 **London Colney** Herts
132 D3 **Londonderry** N York
102 F5 **Londonthorpe** Lincs
219 K5 **Londubh** Highld
219 J6 **Lonemore** Highld
38 D6 **Long Ashton** N Som
84 D8 **Long Bank** Worcs
102 D4 **Long Bennington** Lincs
14 B4 **Long Bredy** Dorset
73 J2 **Long Buckby** Nhants
102 B6 **Long Clawson** Leics
99 J7 **Long Compton** Staffs
56 F2 **Long Compton** Warwks
58 B6 **Long Crendon** Bucks
15 J1 **Long Crichel** Dorset
44 D6 **Long Ditton** Surrey
115 H7 **Long Duckmanton** Derbys
101 J5 **Long Eaton** Derbys
112 C7 **Long Green** Ches
55 J2 **Long Green** Worcs
57 H5 **Long Hanborough** Oxon
72 E2 **Long Itchington** Warwks
86 F7 **Long Lawford** Warwks
26 C6 **Long Load** Somset
58 E5 **Long Marston** Herts
124 D1 **Long Marston** N York
71 L5 **Long Marston** Warwks
138 F3 **Long Marton** Cumb
77 J5 **Long Melford** Suffk
39 K3 **Long Newnton** Gloucs
178 B5 **Long Newton** E Loth
130 F7 **Long Preston** N York
126 E3 **Long Riston** E R Yk
92 E5 **Long Stratton** Norfk
74 B5 **Long Street** M Keyn
30 C3 **Long Sutton** Hants
104 C7 **Long Sutton** Lincs
26 C6 **Long Sutton** Somset
78 B2 **Long Thurlow** Suffk
84 B1 **Long Waste** Wrekin
101 J7 **Long Whatton** Leics
41 K2 **Long Wittenham** Oxon
151 G2 **Longbenton** N Tyne
56 D3 **Longborough** Gloucs
85 H7 **Longbridge** Birm
27 K4 **Longbridge Deverill** Wilts
26 F8 **Longburton** Dorset
100 E2 **Longcliffe** Derbys
7 J4 **Longcombe** Devon
40 F3 **Longcot** Oxon
83 J3 **Longden** Shrops
85 J2 **Longdon** Staffs
70 E7 **Longdon** Worcs
85 J2 **Longdon Green** Staffs
84 B1 **Longdon upon Tern** Wrekin
11 K6 **Longdown** Devon
3 J4 **Longdowns** Cnwll
45 L6 **Longfield** Kent
100 E5 **Longford** Derbys
55 J4 **Longford** Gloucs
98 F5 **Longford** Shrops
99 G8 **Longford** Wrekin
186 E2 **Longforgan** P & K
178 E6 **Longformacus** Border
158 E3 **Longframlington** Nthumb
15 K3 **Longham** Dorset
91 L1 **Longham** Norfk
217 L6 **Longhaven** Abers
158 F4 **Longhirst** Nthumb
55 G4 **Longhope** Gloucs
234 b7 **Longhope** Ork
158 E4 **Longhorsley** Nthumb
169 J6 **Longhoughton** Nthumb
100 E5 **Longlane** Derbys
27 J3 **Longleat Safari Park** Wilts
55 J4 **Longlevens** Gloucs
122 F6 **Longley** Calder
195 L7 **Longleys** P & K
216 E2 **Longmanhill** Abers
30 C5 **Longmoor Camp** Hants
214 F3 **Longmorn** Moray
113 K6 **Longmoss** Ches
167 J4 **Longnewton** Border
141 J4 **Longnewton** S on T
55 H5 **Longney** Gloucs
177 L3 **Longniddry** E Loth
83 J4 **Longnor** Shrops
114 C8 **Longnor** Staffs
29 H3 **Longparish** Hants
121 J3 **Longridge** Lancs
176 C5 **Longridge** W Loth
175 L4 **Longriggend** N Lans
2 E5 **Longrock** Cnwll
99 L2 **Longsdon** Staffs
217 K5 **Longside** Abers
76 B2 **Longstanton** Cambs
29 G4 **Longstock** Hants
75 K4 **Longstowe** Cambs
28 C2 **Longstreet** Wilts
89 H4 **Longthorpe** C Pete
138 B3 **Longthwaite** Cumb
99 K4 **Longton** C Stke
121 G5 **Longton** Lancs
148 C2 **Longtown** Cumb
53 L3 **Longtown** Herefs
236 d7 **Longueville** Jersey
83 K5 **Longville in the Dale** Shrops
58 C6 **Longwick** Bucks
158 D4 **Longwitton** Nthumb
146 C3 **Longwood** D & G
57 G7 **Longworth** Oxon
178 C5 **Longyester** E Loth
217 J3 **Lonmay** Abers
208 D5 **Lonmore** Highld
5 K5 **Looe** Cnwll
33 K3 **Loose** Kent
58 D7 **Loosley Row** Bucks
216 B4 **Lootcherbrae** Abers
26 B8 **Lopen** Somset
98 C6 **Loppington** Shrops
46 C7 **Lords Wood** Medway
195 J6 **Lornty** P & K
101 H3 **Loscoe** Derbys
214 F1 **Lossiemouth** Moray
4 F6 **Lost Gardens of Heligan** Cnwll
113 G6 **Lostock Gralam** Ches
113 G6 **Lostock Green** Ches
121 H5 **Lostock Hall** Lancs
5 H4 **Lostwithiel** Cnwll
227 G6 **Lothbeg** Highld
122 E2 **Lothersdale** N York
227 G6 **Lothmore** Highld
101 K8 **Loughborough** Leics
51 H6 **Loughor** Swans
45 H2 **Loughton** Essex
74 B6 **Loughton** M Keyn
84 B6 **Loughton** Shrops
103 H8 **Lound** Lincs
116 B4 **Lound** Notts
93 K4 **Lound** Suffk
101 G8 **Lount** Leics
118 D4 **Louth** Lincs
122 B5 **Love Clough** Lancs
30 B8 **Lovedean** Hants
28 E7 **Lover** Wilts
115 L2 **Loversall** Donc
61 G6 **Loves Green** Essex
49 J5 **Loveston** Pembks
26 E5 **Lovington** Somset
124 C6 **Low Ackworth** Wakefd
144 B2 **Low Barbeth** D & G
130 C5 **Low Bentham** N York
130 B4 **Low Biggins** Cumb
138 E6 **Low Borrowbridge** Cumb
114 E3 **Low Bradfield** Sheff
122 F2 **Low Bradley** N York
116 C2 **Low Burnham** N Linc
133 L8 **Low Catton** E R Yk
148 D3 **Low Crosby** Cumb
141 J5 **Low Dinsdale** Darltn
124 E5 **Low Eggborough** N York
132 C3 **Low Ellington** N York
151 G3 **Low Fell** Gatesd
174 E2 **Low Gartachorrans** Stirlg
132 C5 **Low Grantley** N York
26 B5 **Low Ham** Somset
132 D7 **Low Harrogate** N York
148 E5 **Low Hesket** Cumb
134 B6 **Low Hutton** N York
137 G3 **Low Lorton** Cumb
116 D7 **Low Marnham** Notts
142 E7 **Low Mill** N York
151 H5 **Low Moorsley** Sundld
134 D6 **Low Mowthorpe** N York
129 J3 **Low Newton** Cumb
149 G3 **Low Row** Cumb
140 B7 **Low Row** N York
144 B2 **Low Salchrie** D & G
125 L7 **Low Santon** N Linc
92 E4 **Low Tharston** Norfk
176 D2 **Low Torry** Fife
141 J5 **Low Worsall** N York
137 K6 **Low Wray** Cumb
102 A3 **Lowdham** Notts
25 J4 **Lower Aisholt** Somset
14 E2 **Lower Ansty** Dorset
55 J3 **Lower Apperley** Gloucs
11 J7 **Lower Ashton** Devon
42 C4 **Lower Assendon** Oxon
121 G4 **Lower Bartle** Lancs
41 L5 **Lower Basildon** W Berk
31 L6 **Lower Beeding** W Susx
88 E5 **Lower Benefield** Nhants
71 H2 **Lower Bentley** Worcs
72 F4 **Lower Boddington** Nhants
30 D3 **Lower Bourne** Surrey
72 C6 **Lower Brailes** Warwks
199 L2 **Lower Breakish** Highld
70 E3 **Lower Broadheath** Worcs
70 C4 **Lower Brockhampton Manor** Herefs
69 K6 **Lower Bullingham** Herefs
28 D7 **Lower Burgate** Hants
75 H5 **Lower Caldecote** Beds
55 H7 **Lower Cam** Gloucs
68 B7 **Lower Chapel** Powys
27 L5 **Lower Chicksgrove** Wilts
28 F2 **Lower Chute** Wilts
45 G3 **Lower Clapton** Gt Lon
85 G7 **Lower Clent** Worcs
123 J8 **Lower Cumberworth** Kirk
74 F2 **Lower Dean** Beds
210 C3 **Lower Diabaig** Highld
20 B4 **Lower Dicker** E Susx
83 G6 **Lower Down** Shrops
133 G6 **Lower Dunsforth** N York
70 B5 **Lower Egleton** Herefs
74 D6 **Lower End** M Keyn
35 H5 **Lower Eythorne** Kent
38 D5 **Lower Failand** N Som
30 B4 **Lower Farringdon** Hants
43 H6 **Lower Feltham** Gt Lon
30 C3 **Lower Froyle** Hants
7 L2 **Lower Gabwell** Devon
222 D4 **Lower Gledfield** Highld
26 C3 **Lower Godney** Somset
75 G7 **Lower Gravenhurst** Beds
32 F5 **Lower Green** Kent
33 G5 **Lower Green** Kent
43 H6 **Lower Halliford** Surrey
46 E6 **Lower Halstow** Kent
15 J4 **Lower Hamworthy** Poole
34 F4 **Lower Hardres** Kent
58 C5 **Lower Hartwell** Bucks
68 F4 **Lower Hergest** Herefs
57 J3 **Lower Heyford** Oxon
123 H7 **Lower Houses** Kirk
113 G3 **Lower Irlam** Salfd

160 A2 **Lower Killeyan** Ag & B
97 M1 **Lower Kinnerton** Ches
38 C7 **Lower Langford** N Som
187 G6 **Lower Largo** Fife
100 A5 **Lower Leigh** Staffs
23 K4 **Lower Loxhore** Devon
54 E5 **Lower Lydbrook** Gloucs
69 H2 **Lower Lye** Herefs
37 K3 **Lower Machen** Newpt
25 J4 **Lower Merridge** Somset
73 G6 **Lower Middleton Cheney** Nhants
71 H5 **Lower Moor** Worcs
38 F3 **Lower Morton** S Glos
60 C6 **Lower Nazeing** Essex
37 J6 **Lower Penarth** V Glam
84 F4 **Lower Penn** Staffs
113 H6 **Lower Peover** Ches
71 L5 **Lower Quinton** Warwks
78 C6 **Lower Raydon** Suffk
25 G4 **Lower Roadwater** Somset
39 L4 **Lower Seagry** Wilts
74 E6 **Lower Shelton** Beds
42 C4 **Lower Shiplake** Oxon
72 F3 **Lower Shuckburgh** Warwks
56 D4 **Lower Slaughter** Gloucs
35 H6 **Lower Standen** Kent
39 L4 **Lower Stanton St Quintin** Wilts
46 D5 **Lower Stoke** Medway
38 F2 **Lower Stone** Gloucs
91 L5 **Lower Stow Bedon** Norfk
106 F5 **Lower Street** Norfk
78 D4 **Lower Street** Suffk
59 H3 **Lower Sundon** Beds
16 F1 **Lower Swanwick** Hants
56 D3 **Lower Swell** Gloucs
100 A5 **Lower Tean** Staffs
7 G2 **Lower Town** Devon
64 D6 **Lower Town** Pembks
72 D5 **Lower Tysoe** Warwks
11 K8 **Lower Upcott** Devon
29 K7 **Lower Upham** Hants
25 H4 **Lower Vexford** Somset
26 B2 **Lower Weare** Somset
71 G6 **Lower Westmancote** Worcs
27 H3 **Lower Whatley** Somset
112 E5 **Lower Whitley** Ches
29 M4 **Lower Wield** Hants
20 C5 **Lower Willingdon** E Susx
113 J7 **Lower Withington** Ches
28 C4 **Lower Woodford** Wilts
14 B3 **Lower Wraxhall** Dorset
87 K3 **Lowesby** Leics
93 L5 **Lowestoft** Suffk
137 G3 **Loweswater** Cumb
31 L4 **Lowfield Heath** W Susx
88 E7 **Lowick** Nhants
168 F2 **Lowick** Nthumb
129 G3 **Lowick Green** Cumb
71 L2 **Lowsonford** Warwks
138 D3 **Lowther** Cumb
135 G7 **Lowthorpe** E R Yk
25 J7 **Lowton** Somset
11 L2 **Loxbeare** Devon
31 G4 **Loxhill** Surrey
23 K4 **Loxhore** Devon
72 C4 **Loxley** Warwks
26 A1 **Loxton** N Som
31 H5 **Loxwood** W Susx
229 J6 **Loyal Lodge** Highld
87 K6 **Lubenham** Leics
24 E3 **Luccombe** Somset
17 H6 **Luccombe Village** IOW
169 H4 **Lucker** Nthumb
6 B2 **Luckett** Cnwll
77 J7 **Lucking Street** Essex
39 J4 **Luckington** Wilts
24 E4 **Luckwell Bridge** Somset
69 J2 **Lucton** Herefs
233 b9 **Ludag** W Isls
118 D3 **Ludborough** Lincs
6 F5 **Ludbrook** Devon
49 K5 **Ludchurch** Pembks
122 F5 **Luddenden** Calder
122 F5 **Luddenden Foot** Calder
46 A6 **Luddesdown** Kent
125 J7 **Luddington** N Linc
71 L4 **Luddington** Warwks
89 G6 **Luddington in the Brook** Nhants
117 K4 **Ludford** Lincs
83 K8 **Ludford** Shrops
58 A4 **Ludgershall** Bucks
28 E2 **Ludgershall** Wilts
2 E5 **Ludgvan** Cnwll
107 H8 **Ludham** Norfk
83 K7 **Ludlow** Shrops
26 B8 **Ludney** Somset
27 K6 **Ludwell** Wilts
151 J6 **Ludworth** Dur
9 J6 **Luffincott** Devon
178 B3 **Luffness** E Loth
164 C5 **Lugar** E Ayrs
178 D4 **Luggate Burn** E Loth
175 K4 **Luggiebank** N Lans
174 D7 **Lugton** E Ayrs
69 K6 **Lugwardine** Herefs
209 J8 **Luib** Highld
69 H6 **Lulham** Herefs
86 B2 **Lullington** Derbys
27 H2 **Lullington** Somset
38 D7 **Lulsgate Bottom** N Som
70 D4 **Lulsley** Worcs
122 F6 **Lumb** Calder
122 C5 **Lumb** Lancs
124 D4 **Lumby** N York
175 H4 **Lumloch** E Duns
206 B4 **Lumphanan** Abers
186 C8 **Lumphinnans** Fife
205 K2 **Lumsden** Abers
197 H6 **Lunan** Angus
196 D6 **Lunanhead** Angus
186 A2 **Luncarty** P & K
126 B2 **Lund** E R Yk
125 G4 **Lund** N York
186 E1 **Lundie** Angus
184 F6 **Lundie** Stirlg
187 G6 **Lundin Links** Fife
187 G6 **Lundin Mill** Fife
235 d4 **Lunna** Shet
33 J2 **Lunsford** Kent
20 E4 **Lunsford's Cross** E Susx
111 K2 **Lunt** Sefton
12 F2 **Luppitt** Devon
7 G5 **Lupridge** Devon
123 L6 **Lupset** Wakefd
129 L4 **Lupton** Cumb
30 F6 **Lurgashall** W Susx
11 L2 **Lurley** Devon
7 J4 **Luscombe** Devon
183 L8 **Luss** Ag & B
208 D3 **Lusta** Highld
11 H8 **Lustleigh** Devon
69 J2 **Luston** Herefs
197 G3 **Luthermuir** Abers
186 E4 **Luthrie** Fife
12 D2 **Luton** Devon
7 K1 **Luton** Devon
59 H4 **Luton** Luton
46 C6 **Luton** Medway
59 J4 **Luton Airport** Luton
87 G6 **Lutterworth** Leics
6 E4 **Lutton** Devon
7 G4 **Lutton** Devon
104 C7 **Lutton** Lincs
89 G6 **Lutton** Nhants
24 F4 **Luxborough** Somset
5 G4 **Luxulyan** Cnwll
231 J7 **Lybster** Highld
83 G6 **Lydbury North** Shrops
21 K2 **Lydd** Kent
21 L2 **Lydd Airport** Kent
35 H5 **Lydden** Kent
35 K2 **Lydden** Kent
88 C4 **Lyddington** Rutlnd
25 H5 **Lydeard St Lawrence** Somset
10 D7 **Lydford** Devon
26 E5 **Lydford on Fosse** Somset
122 D5 **Lydgate** Calder
83 G5 **Lydham** Shrops
40 C3 **Lydiard Millicent** Wilts
40 C4 **Lydiard Tregoze** Swindn
111 K2 **Lydiate** Sefton
85 H7 **Lydiate Ash** Worcs
27 H8 **Lydlinch** Dorset
54 F7 **Lydney** Gloucs
49 J7 **Lydstep** Pembks
85 G6 **Lye** Dudley
32 F6 **Lye Green** E Susx
71 L2 **Lye Green** Warwks
27 J3 **Lye's Green** Wilts
41 H2 **Lyford** Oxon
34 F6 **Lymbridge Green** Kent
13 J4 **Lyme Regis** Dorset
34 F6 **Lyminge** Kent
16 C4 **Lymington** Hants
18 D5 **Lyminster** W Susx
113 G4 **Lymm** Warrtn
34 F7 **Lympne** Kent
25 M1 **Lympsham** Somset
12 C5 **Lympstone** Devon
92 D3 **Lynch Green** Norfk
203 J5 **Lynchat** Highld
16 C2 **Lyndhurst** Hants
88 C3 **Lyndon** Rutlnd
166 B2 **Lyne** Border
43 G7 **Lyne** Surrey
206 E4 **Lyne of Skene** Abers
98 C6 **Lyneal** Shrops
56 F4 **Lyneham** Oxon
40 A5 **Lyneham** Wilts
40 A5 **Lyneham Airport** Wilts
234 b7 **Lyness** Ork
106 C8 **Lyng** Norfk
25 M5 **Lyng** Somset
23 L2 **Lynmouth** Devon
214 F7 **Lynn of Shenval** Moray
34 C3 **Lynsted** Kent
23 L2 **Lynton** Devon
14 C2 **Lyon's Gate** Dorset
69 G4 **Lyonshall** Herefs
15 H4 **Lytchett Matravers** Dorset
15 H4 **Lytchett Minster** Dorset
231 K3 **Lyth** Highld
120 E5 **Lytham** Lancs
120 D5 **Lytham St Anne's** Lancs
143 H5 **Lythe** N York
230 F3 **Lythmore** Highld

M

3 K4 **Mabe Burnthouse** Cnwll
155 G7 **Mabie** D & G
119 G4 **Mablethorpe** Lincs
113 K6 **Macclesfield** Ches
216 D2 **Macduff** Abers
161 J7 **Macharioch** Ag & B
37 K3 **Machen** Caerph
162 A3 **Machrie** N Ayrs
161 G5 **Machrihanish** Ag & B
180 E8 **Machrins** Ag & B
81 G4 **Machynlleth** Powys
51 G5 **Machynys** Carmth
100 F5 **Mackworth** Derbys
177 L4 **Macmerry** E Loth
10 D6 **Maddaford** Devon
185 K3 **Madderty** P & K
176 C3 **Maddiston** Falk
99 H4 **Madeley** Staffs
76 B3 **Madingley** Cambs
69 H6 **Madley** Herefs
70 E5 **Madresfield** Worcs
2 E5 **Madron** Cnwll
65 L3 **Maen-y-groes** Cerdgn
49 J3 **Maenclochog** Pembks
36 F5 **Maendy** V Glam
95 L4 **Maentwrog** Gwynd
99 H5 **Maer** Staffs
36 F2 **Maerdy** Rhondd
97 L7 **Maesbrook** Shrops
97 L7 **Maesbury** Shrops
97 L7 **Maesbury Marsh** Shrops
65 K5 **Maesllyn** Cerdgn
36 D3 **Maesteg** Brdgnd
51 H3 **Maesybont** Carmth
37 J2 **Maesycwmmer** Caerph
215 H5 **Maggieknockater** Moray
60 D3 **Maggots End** Essex
20 C4 **Magham Down** E Susx
111 K2 **Maghull** Sefton
38 B3 **Magor** Mons
27 J4 **Maiden Bradley** Wilts
38 E6 **Maiden Head** N Som
14 B3 **Maiden Newton** Dorset
49 G7 **Maiden Wells** Pembks
32 B6 **Maidenbower** W Susx
7 L3 **Maidencombe** Torbay
13 H4 **Maidenhayne** Devon
42 E4 **Maidenhead** W & M
163 G7 **Maidens** S Ayrs
118 D5 **Maidenwell** Lincs
73 H4 **Maidford** Nhants
73 K7 **Maids Moreton** Bucks
33 K3 **Maidstone** Kent
87 L7 **Maidwell** Nhants
37 L3 **Maindee** Newpt
196 E4 **Mains of Balhall** Angus
197 G2 **Mains of Balnakettle** Abers

214 D7 **Mains of Dalvey** Highld
197 H2 **Mains of Haulkerton** Abers
141 H2 **Mainsforth** Dur
147 G4 **Mainsriddle** D & G
82 F6 **Mainstone** Shrops
55 J4 **Maisemore** Gloucs
101 G4 **Makeney** Derbys
7 G7 **Malborough** Devon
44 E6 **Malden** Surrey
61 K6 **Maldon** Essex
131 G6 **Malham** N York
199 L6 **Mallaig** Highld
199 L5 **Mallaigvaig** Highld
177 G5 **Malleny Mills** C Edin
108 E7 **Malltraeth** IOA
81 J2 **Mallwyd** Gwynd
39 L3 **Malmesbury** Wilts
24 C2 **Malmsmead** Somset
98 C3 **Malpas** Ches
4 D7 **Malpas** Cnwll
37 L3 **Malpas** Newpt
115 K3 **Maltby** Rothm
141 L5 **Maltby** S on T
118 F5 **Maltby le Marsh** Lincs
62 B4 **Malting Green** Essex
34 B6 **Maltman's Hill** Kent
134 C5 **Malton** N York
70 D5 **Malvern Hills**
70 E5 **Malvern Link** Worcs
70 D6 **Malvern Wells** Worcs
145 H4 **Malzie** D & G
70 C1 **Mamble** Worcs
53 L7 **Mamhilad** Mons
3 K6 **Manaccan** Cnwll
82 C3 **Manafon** Powys
232 d5 **Manais** W Isls
11 H8 **Manaton** Devon
118 E4 **Manby** Lincs
86 D4 **Mancetter** Warwks
113 J3 **Manchester** Manch
113 J5 **Manchester Airport** Manch
111 K7 **Mancot** Flints
201 L5 **Mandally** Highld
179 G7 **Manderston House** Border
90 C5 **Manea** Cambs
85 K4 **Maney** Birm
140 F4 **Manfield** N York
38 F5 **Mangotsfield** S Glos
232 d5 **Manish** W Isls
112 D6 **Manley** Ches
53 J7 **Manmoel** Caerph
188 C7 **Mannel** Ag & B
31 K5 **Manning's Heath** W Susx
40 C8 **Manningford Bohune** Wilts
40 C8 **Manningford Bruce** Wilts
123 H4 **Manningham** Brad
15 K2 **Mannington** Dorset
62 D2 **Manningtree** Essex
207 H4 **Mannofield** C Aber
45 H3 **Manor Park** Gt Lon
49 H7 **Manorbier** Pembks
49 H7 **Manorbier Newton** Pembks
167 K3 **Manorhill** Border
64 C7 **Manorowen** Pembks
69 H5 **Mansell Gamage** Herefs
69 H5 **Mansell Lacy** Herefs
164 C6 **Mansfield** E Ayrs
101 K1 **Mansfield** Notts
115 K8 **Mansfield Woodhouse** Notts
27 J7 **Manston** Dorset
124 B4 **Manston** Leeds
35 J2 **Manston Airport** Kent
15 J2 **Manswood** Dorset
88 F1 **Manthorpe** Lincs
116 F2 **Manton** N Linc
88 C3 **Manton** Rutlnd
40 D6 **Manton** Wilts
60 D3 **Manuden** Essex
26 F6 **Maperton** Somset
102 B1 **Maplebeck** Notts
42 A5 **Mapledurham** Oxon
30 B2 **Mapledurwell** Hants
31 K6 **Maplehurst** W Susx
45 K7 **Maplescombe** Kent
100 D3 **Mapleton** Derbys
101 H4 **Mapperley** Derbys
101 L4 **Mapperley Park** C Nott
13 L3 **Mapperton** Dorset
71 J2 **Mappleborough Green** Warwks
126 F2 **Mappleton** E R Yk
123 L7 **Mapplewell** Barns
14 E2 **Mappowder** Dorset
4 C5 **Marazanvose** Cnwll
2 F5 **Marazion** Cnwll
98 E4 **Marbury** Ches
90 B4 **March** Cambs
165 J6 **March** S Lans
41 J2 **Marcham** Oxon
98 E6 **Marchamley** Shrops
100 C6 **Marchington** Staffs
98 A3 **Marchwiel** Wrexhm
16 D1 **Marchwood** Hants
36 E6 **Marcross** V Glam
69 K5 **Marden** Herefs
33 J4 **Marden** Kent
40 C8 **Marden** Wilts
33 K5 **Marden Thorn** Kent
53 L5 **Mardy** Mons
103 L1 **Mareham le Fen** Lincs
118 C7 **Mareham on the Hill** Lincs
18 E3 **Marehill** W Susx
19 M2 **Maresfield** E Susx
126 E5 **Marfleet** C KuH
98 A2 **Marford** Wrexhm
36 B3 **Margam** Neath
27 J7 **Margaret Marsh** Dorset
61 G7 **Margaretting** Essex
61 G7 **Margaretting Tye** Essex
35 K1 **Margate** Kent
162 D3 **Margnaheglish** N Ayrs
145 M5 **Margrie** D & G
142 E4 **Margrove Park** R & Cl
91 G2 **Marham** Norfk
9 G4 **Marhamchurch** Cnwll
89 G3 **Marholm** C Pete
24 B6 **Mariansleigh** Devon
46 F5 **Marine Town** Kent
206 D4 **Marionburgh** Abers
209 H2 **Marishader** Highld
6 C3 **Maristow** Devon
163 H2 **Maritime Centre** N Ayrs
155 J5 **Marjoriebanks** D & G
26 B2 **Mark** Somset
33 G6 **Mark Cross** E Susx
32 E5 **Markbeech** Kent
119 G5 **Markby** Lincs
86 E3 **Market Bosworth** Leics
89 G2 **Market Deeping** Lincs
98 F5 **Market Drayton** Shrops
87 K6 **Market Harborough** Leics
28 A1 **Market Lavington** Wilts
88 C1 **Market Overton** Rutlnd
117 J4 **Market Rasen** Lincs
118 C5 **Market Stainton** Lincs
125 K3 **Market Weighton** E R Yk
92 B7 **Market Weston** Suffk
86 F2 **Markfield** Leics
53 J7 **Markham** Caerph
116 B6 **Markham Moor** Notts
186 E6 **Markinch** Fife
132 D6 **Markington** N York
178 C3 **Markle** E Loth
61 L4 **Marks Tey** Essex
38 F7 **Marksbury** BaNES
59 H5 **Markyate** Herts
40 D6 **Marlborough** Wilts
71 K4 **Marlcliff** Warwks
7 K3 **Marldon** Devon
79 G3 **Marlesford** Suffk
92 D2 **Marlingford** Norfk
48 D5 **Marloes** Pembks
42 D3 **Marlow** Bucks
42 D3 **Marlow Bottom** Bucks
32 D4 **Marlpit Hill** Kent
27 H7 **Marnhull** Dorset
113 L4 **Marple** Stockp
115 K1 **Marr** Donc
140 D7 **Marrick** N York
122 F7 **Marsden** Kirk
151 J3 **Marsden** S Tyne
57 K7 **Marsh Baldon** Oxon
118 E2 **Marsh Chapel** Lincs
57 M4 **Marsh Gibbon** Bucks
12 D4 **Marsh Green** Devon
32 D4 **Marsh Green** Kent
115 H5 **Marsh Lane** Derbys
24 F3 **Marsh Street** Somset
59 K6 **Marshalswick** Herts
106 E7 **Marsham** Norfk
35 J3 **Marshborough** Kent
83 J5 **Marshbrook** Shrops
37 K4 **Marshfield** Newpt
39 H5 **Marshfield** S Glos
8 F6 **Marshgate** Cnwll
90 D2 **Marshland St James** Norfk
13 J3 **Marshwood** Dorset
140 D6 **Marske** N York
142 D3 **Marske-by-the-Sea** R & Cl
69 G3 **Marston** Herefs
102 E4 **Marston** Lincs
57 K6 **Marston** Oxon
99 L6 **Marston** Staffs
27 L1 **Marston** Wilts
85 L6 **Marston Green** Solhll
26 E6 **Marston Magna** Somset
40 C2 **Marston Meysey** Wilts
100 C5 **Marston Montgomery** Derbys
74 E6 **Marston Moretaine** Beds
100 E6 **Marston on Dove** Derbys
73 G6 **Marston St Lawrence** Nhants
87 K6 **Marston Trussell** Nhants
54 D4 **Marstow** Herefs
58 F5 **Marsworth** Bucks
40 F7 **Marten** Wilts
113 J6 **Marthall** Ches
107 J8 **Martham** Norfk
28 B7 **Martin** Hants
35 J5 **Martin** Kent
103 J1 **Martin** Lincs
118 C7 **Martin** Lincs
70 F3 **Martin Hussingtree** Worcs
23 L2 **Martinhoe** Devon
14 C5 **Martinstown** Dorset
78 F5 **Martlesham** Suffk
78 F5 **Martlesham Heath** Suffk
49 H5 **Martletwy** Pembks
70 D3 **Martley** Worcs
26 C7 **Martock** Somset
113 J7 **Marton** Ches
126 F3 **Marton** E R Yk
116 D5 **Marton** Lincs
142 B4 **Marton** Middsb
132 F6 **Marton** N York
134 B3 **Marton** N York
82 F3 **Marton** Shrops
72 E2 **Marton** Warwks
132 E5 **Marton-le-Moor** N York
29 K5 **Martyr Worthy** Hants
234 b5 **Marwick** Ork
23 H4 **Marwood** Devon
6 D1 **Mary Tavy** Devon
212 D4 **Marybank** Highld
212 E3 **Maryburgh** Highld
207 G5 **Maryculter** Abers
179 G6 **Marygold** Border
216 F5 **Maryhill** Abers
175 G4 **Maryhill** C Glas
197 H3 **Marykirk** Abers
44 F4 **Marylebone** Gt Lon
121 H8 **Marylebone** Wigan
214 F6 **Marypark** Moray
147 H7 **Maryport** Cumb
144 D7 **Maryport** D & G
10 C7 **Marystow** Devon
197 H5 **Maryton** Angus
206 B6 **Marywell** Abers
207 H5 **Marywell** Abers
197 G7 **Marywell** Angus
132 C4 **Masham** N York
130 C4 **Masongill** N York
115 J6 **Mastin Moor** Derbys
60 E5 **Matching Green** Essex
60 E5 **Matching Tye** Essex
158 C7 **Matfen** Nthumb
33 H5 **Matfield** Kent
38 D3 **Mathern** Mons
70 D5 **Mathon** Herefs
48 E2 **Mathry** Pembks
106 D5 **Matlask** Norfk
100 F1 **Matlock** Derbys
100 F2 **Matlock Bath** Derbys
55 J5 **Matson** Gloucs
116 B4 **Mattersey** Notts
42 B8 **Mattingley** Hants
92 C2 **Mattishall** Norfk
92 C2 **Mattishall Burgh** Norfk
163 L4 **Mauchline** E Ayrs
217 H5 **Maud** Abers
236 d6 **Maufant** Jersey
56 D3 **Maugersbury** Gloucs
237 e3 **Maughold** IOM
212 C6 **Mauld** Highld
74 F6 **Maulden** Beds
138 F4 **Maulds Meaburn** Cumb
132 E3 **Maunby** N York
69 L4 **Maund Bryan** Herefs
25 G5 **Maundown** Somset
93 K2 **Mautby** Norfk
85 J1 **Mavesyn Ridware** Staffs
118 E7 **Mavis Enderby** Lincs
147 J5 **Mawbray** Cumb
121 G7 **Mawdesley** Lancs
36 C4 **Mawdlam** Brdgnd
3 J6 **Mawgan** Cnwll
4 D3 **Mawgan Porth** Cnwll

3 J3 **Mawla** Cnwll
3 K5 **Mawnan** Cnwll
3 K5 **Mawnan Smith** Cnwll
89 G2 **Maxey** C Pete
86 B6 **Maxstoke** Warwks
34 F5 **Maxted Street** Kent
167 J4 **Maxton** Border
35 J6 **Maxton** Kent
155 G6 **Maxwell Town** D & G
9 H6 **Maxworthy** Cnwll
99 J3 **May Bank** Staffs
163 H7 **Maybole** S Ayrs
43 G8 **Maybury** Surrey
33 G7 **Mayfield** E Susx
177 K5 **Mayfield** Mdloth
100 D4 **Mayfield** Staffs
31 G1 **Mayford** Surrey
20 C3 **Maynard's Green** E Susx
93 J4 **Maypole Green** Norfk
77 K3 **Maypole Green** Suffk
39 G8 **Meadgate** BaNES
58 D6 **Meadle** Bucks
151 G6 **Meadowfield** Dur
9 K8 **Meadwell** Devon
147 K5 **Mealrigg** Cumb
123 K3 **Meanwood** Leeds
26 C3 **Meare** Somset
25 M6 **Meare Green** Somset
25 L6 **Meare Green** Somset
174 F7 **Mearns** E Rens
74 B2 **Mears Ashby** Nhants
86 D2 **Measham** Leics
129 J4 **Meathop** Cumb
6 D3 **Meavy** Devon
88 B5 **Medbourne** Leics
115 L7 **Meden Vale** Notts
42 D4 **Medmenham** Bucks
150 E4 **Medomsley** Dur
30 A4 **Medstead** Hants
99 M1 **Meerbrook** Staffs
60 C2 **Meesden** Herts
10 E3 **Meeth** Devon
107 G6 **Meeting House Hill** Norfk
50 C2 **Meidrim** Carmth
82 D2 **Meifod** Powys
195 L7 **Meigle** P & K
164 F6 **Meikle Carco** D & G
175 J7 **Meikle Earnock** S Lans
173 H6 **Meikle Kilmory** Ag & B
195 G8 **Meikle Obney** P & K
216 D7 **Meikle Wartle** Abers
195 J7 **Meikleour** P & K
50 F4 **Meinciau** Carmth
99 L4 **Meir** C Stke
75 L5 **Melbourn** Cambs
101 G7 **Melbourne** Derbys
125 H2 **Melbourne** E R Yk
27 K7 **Melbury Abbas** Dorset
14 B2 **Melbury Bubb** Dorset
14 B2 **Melbury Osmond** Dorset
74 E2 **Melchbourne** Beds
14 E2 **Melcombe Bingham** Dorset
10 E6 **Meldon** Devon
158 E5 **Meldon** Nthumb
75 L5 **Meldreth** Cambs
184 F7 **Meldrum** Stirlg
182 B5 **Melfort** Ag & B
196 E5 **Melgund Castle** Angus
110 E5 **Meliden** Denbgs
97 G3 **Melin-y-wig** Denbgs
138 D3 **Melkinthorpe** Cumb
149 J3 **Melkridge** Nthumb
39 K7 **Melksham** Wilts
130 B5 **Melling** Lancs
111 L2 **Melling** Sefton
92 C8 **Mellis** Suffk
219 K3 **Mellon Charles** Highld
219 K3 **Mellon Udrigle** Highld
121 J4 **Mellor** Lancs
113 M4 **Mellor** Stockp
121 J4 **Mellor Brook** Lancs
27 G2 **Mells** Somset
149 G7 **Melmerby** Cumb
131 K3 **Melmerby** N York
132 E4 **Melmerby** N York
229 J3 **Melness** Highld
13 L3 **Melplash** Dorset
167 H3 **Melrose** Border
234 b7 **Melsetter** Ork
140 F5 **Melsonby** N York
123 G7 **Meltham** Kirk
126 B5 **Melton** E R Yk
79 G4 **Melton** Suffk
106 C6 **Melton Constable** Norfk
102 C8 **Melton Mowbray** Leics
126 D7 **Melton Ross** N Linc
219 H4 **Melvaig** Highld
83 G1 **Melverley** Shrops
230 C3 **Melvich** Highld
13 H2 **Membury** Devon
217 H2 **Memsie** Abers
196 C5 **Memus** Angus
109 H6 **Menai Bridge** IOA
92 F6 **Mendham** Suffk
26 D2 **Mendip Hills**
78 D2 **Mendlesham** Suffk
78 D2 **Mendlesham Green** Suffk
5 L4 **Menheniot** Cnwll
164 F7 **Mennock** D & G
123 H2 **Menston** Brad
185 H7 **Menstrie** Clacks
58 E4 **Mentmore** Bucks
200 C7 **Meoble** Highld
83 J2 **Meole Brace** Shrops
29 L7 **Meonstoke** Hants
45 M6 **Meopham** Kent
90 B7 **Mepal** Cambs
75 G7 **Meppershall** Beds
113 G5 **Mere** Ches
27 J5 **Mere** Wilts
120 F6 **Mere Brow** Lancs
122 C4 **Mereclough** Lancs
33 H3 **Mereworth** Kent
86 B6 **Meriden** Solhll
208 F7 **Merkadale** Highld
48 F7 **Merrion** Pembks
26 C8 **Merriott** Somset
31 G2 **Merrow** Surrey
43 J2 **Merry Hill** Herts
84 F4 **Merryhill** Wolves
5 L3 **Merrymeet** Cnwll
34 E6 **Mersham** Kent
32 B3 **Merstham** Surrey
18 B5 **Merston** W Susx
17 G5 **Merstone** IOW
4 D6 **Merther** Cnwll
67 L6 **Merthyr Cynog** Powys
36 D5 **Merthyr Mawr** Brdgnd
53 G6 **Merthyr Tydfil** Myr Td
53 G7 **Merthyr Vale** Myr Td
10 D3 **Merton** Devon
44 E6 **Merton** Gt Lon
91 K4 **Merton** Norfk
57 L4 **Merton** Oxon
24 B7 **Meshaw** Devon
61 L4 **Messing** Essex
116 E2 **Messingham** N Linc
93 G7 **Metfield** Suffk
6 B3 **Metherell** Cnwll
103 H1 **Metheringham** Lincs
186 F7 **Methil** Fife
186 F7 **Methilhill** Fife
124 B5 **Methley** Leeds
217 G6 **Methlick** Abers
185 L3 **Methven** P & K
91 G4 **Methwold** Norfk
91 G4 **Methwold Hythe** Norfk
93 H5 **Mettingham** Suffk
106 E5 **Metton** Norfk
4 F6 **Mevagissey** Cnwll
115 J2 **Mexborough** Donc
231 K2 **Mey** Highld
94 D6 **Meyllteyrn** Gwynd
56 C7 **Meysey Hampton** Gloucs
232 d2 **Miabhig** W Isls
232 d2 **Miavaig** W Isls
54 D3 **Michaelchurch** Herefs
69 G7 **Michaelchurch Escley** Herefs
37 J5 **Michaelston-le-Pit** V Glam
37 K4 **Michaelstone-y-Fedw** Newpt
5 G1 **Michaelstow** Cnwll
29 K4 **Micheldever** Hants
29 K3 **Micheldever Station** Hants
29 G6 **Michelmersh** Hants
78 D3 **Mickfield** Suffk
112 C7 **Mickle Trafford** Ches
115 K3 **Micklebring** Donc
143 G5 **Mickleby** N York
124 C4 **Micklefield** Leeds
31 K2 **Mickleham** Surrey
100 F5 **Mickleover** C Derb
140 B3 **Mickleton** Dur
71 L5 **Mickleton** Gloucs
124 B5 **Mickletown** Leeds
132 C4 **Mickley** N York
77 J3 **Mickley Green** Suffk
150 D3 **Mickley Square** Nthumb
217 H2 **Mid Ardlaw** Abers
206 C5 **Mid Beltie** Abers
176 E5 **Mid Calder** W Loth
231 K7 **Mid Clyth** Highld
18 B4 **Mid Lavant** W Susx
212 C6 **Mid Mains** Highld
235 d3 **Mid Yell** Shet
234 c4 **Midbea** Ork
57 J3 **Middle Aston** Oxon
57 H3 **Middle Barton** Oxon
26 C8 **Middle Chinnock** Somset
58 B3 **Middle Claydon** Bucks
55 M6 **Middle Duntisbourne** Gloucs
115 H6 **Middle Handley** Derbys
172 F1 **Middle Kames** Ag & B
71 J5 **Middle Littleton** Worcs
100 C4 **Middle Mayfield** Staffs
117 H4 **Middle Rasen** Lincs
7 K2 **Middle Rocombe** Devon
46 D5 **Middle Stoke** Medway
2 a2 **Middle Town** IOS
72 D5 **Middle Tysoe** Warwks
28 F4 **Middle Wallop** Hants
28 E5 **Middle Winterslow** Wilts
28 C4 **Middle Woodford** Wilts
155 L6 **Middlebie** D & G
194 D3 **Middlebridge** P & K
131 L3 **Middleham** N York
39 J6 **Middlehill** Wilts
83 K5 **Middlehope** Shrops
14 C2 **Middlemarsh** Dorset
141 L4 **Middlesbrough** Middsb
129 L2 **Middleshaw** Cumb
131 K5 **Middlesmoor** N York
141 G2 **Middlestone** Dur
123 K6 **Middlestown** Wakefd
167 K2 **Middlethird** Border
188 B7 **Middleton** Ag & B
114 D8 **Middleton** Derbys
100 F2 **Middleton** Derbys
77 K6 **Middleton** Essex
29 H3 **Middleton** Hants
69 K1 **Middleton** Herefs
123 L5 **Middleton** Leeds
174 D7 **Middleton** N Ayrs
123 G2 **Middleton** N York
134 B3 **Middleton** N York
88 B5 **Middleton** Nhants
90 F1 **Middleton** Norfk
158 D5 **Middleton** Nthumb
186 B6 **Middleton** P & K
113 K1 **Middleton** Rochdl
83 K7 **Middleton** Shrops
79 J2 **Middleton** Suffk
50 E7 **Middleton** Swans
85 L4 **Middleton** Warwks
73 G6 **Middleton Cheney** Nhants
79 J2 **Middleton Moor** Suffk
69 K2 **Middleton on the Hill** Herefs
125 L2 **Middleton on the Wolds** E R Yk
141 J5 **Middleton One Row** Darltn
132 E4 **Middleton Quernhow** N York
84 C6 **Middleton Scriven** Shrops
141 J5 **Middleton St George** Darltn
57 K4 **Middleton Stoney** Oxon
141 G6 **Middleton Tyas** N York
139 L3 **Middleton-in-Teesdale** Dur
18 C5 **Middleton-on-Sea** W Susx
82 F2 **Middletown** Powys
113 G7 **Middlewich** Ches
5 L2 **Middlewood** Cnwll
78 D3 **Middlewood Green** Suffk
163 M3 **Middleyard** E Ayrs
26 B5 **Middlezoy** Somset
39 H7 **Midford** BaNES
41 K6 **Midgham** W Berk
122 F5 **Midgley** Calder
123 K7 **Midgley** Wakefd
114 E2 **Midhopestones** Sheff
30 E6 **Midhurst** W Susx
167 H4 **Midlem** Border
173 H6 **Midpark** Ag & B
26 F1 **Midsomer Norton** BaNES
229 J4 **Midtown** Highld
205 K4 **Migvie** Abers
26 F7 **Milborne Port** Somset
14 F3 **Milborne St Andrew** Dorset
26 F7 **Milborne Wick** Somset
158 E6 **Milbourne** Nthumb
39 L3 **Milbourne** Wilts
138 F2 **Milburn** Cumb
38 F3 **Milbury Heath** S Glos
132 F6 **Milby** N York
72 E7 **Milcombe** Oxon

77 L5 **Milden** Suffk
91 G8 **Mildenhall** Suffk
40 E6 **Mildenhall** Wilts
19 H4 **Mile Oak** Br & H
46 F5 **Mile Town** Kent
105 L8 **Mileham** Norfk
113 J2 **Miles Platting** Manch
176 E2 **Milesmark** Fife
168 D3 **Milfield** Nthumb
101 G4 **Milford** Derbys
99 L7 **Milford** Staffs
30 F3 **Milford** Surrey
48 F6 **Milford Haven** Pembks
16 C4 **Milford on Sea** Hants
54 E6 **Milkwall** Gloucs
122 F6 **Mill Bank** Calder
113 L4 **Mill Brow** Stockp
42 C4 **Mill End** Bucks
60 B2 **Mill End** Herts
76 F5 **Mill Green** Cambs
61 G7 **Mill Green** Essex
103 L7 **Mill Green** Lincs
77 L6 **Mill Green** Suffk
78 B3 **Mill Green** Suffk
78 D3 **Mill Green** Suffk
44 E2 **Mill Hill** Gt Lon
99 J5 **Mill Meece** Staffs
185 H4 **Mill of Drummond** P & K
174 D2 **Mill of Haldane** W Duns
78 C1 **Mill Street** Suffk
236 a5 **Millais** Jersey
30 D5 **Milland** W Susx
217 J5 **Millbreck** Abers
216 F5 **Millbrex** Abers
30 D3 **Millbridge** Surrey
74 E6 **Millbrook** Beds
29 G8 **Millbrook** C Sotn
6 B5 **Millbrook** Cnwll
236 c7 **Millbrook** Jersey
206 F4 **Millbuie** Abers
212 E4 **Millbuie** Highld
163 K4 **Millburn** S Ayrs
21 G2 **Millcorner** E Susx
222 E7 **Millcraig** Highld
100 C2 **Milldale** Staffs
114 C6 **Miller's Dale** Derbys
177 J4 **Millerhill** Mdloth
175 H5 **Millerston** N Lans
68 F5 **Millhalf** Herefs
175 K7 **Millheugh** S Lans
173 G4 **Millhouse** Ag & B
114 E2 **Millhouse Green** Barns
155 K5 **Millhousebridge** D & G
115 G5 **Millhouses** Sheff
174 D6 **Milliken Park** Rens
125 J1 **Millington** E R Yk
128 E4 **Millom** Cumb
173 K7 **Millport** N Ayrs
130 C2 **Millthrop** Cumb
207 G5 **Milltimber** C Aber
205 G4 **Milltown** Abers
205 K3 **Milltown** Abers
156 C6 **Milltown** D & G
23 J4 **Milltown** Devon
206 C5 **Milltown of Campfield** Abers
215 G6 **Milltown of Edinvillie** Moray
206 C5 **Milltown of Learney** Abers
186 B6 **Milnathort** P & K
175 G4 **Milngavie** W Duns
122 D7 **Milnrow** Rochdl
129 K3 **Milnthorpe** Cumb
208 B4 **Milovaig** Highld
84 B8 **Milson** Shrops
34 B3 **Milstead** Kent
28 D3 **Milston** Wilts
73 H5 **Milthorpe** Nhants
76 C2 **Milton** Cambs
148 F3 **Milton** Cumb
144 F4 **Milton** D & G
154 E7 **Milton** D & G
100 F7 **Milton** Derbys
231 L5 **Milton** Highld
209 L5 **Milton** Highld
212 D7 **Milton** Highld
212 E4 **Milton** Highld
223 G6 **Milton** Highld
174 C5 **Milton** Inver
46 A5 **Milton** Kent
215 L2 **Milton** Moray
37 M7 **Milton** N Som
116 B6 **Milton** Notts
72 F7 **Milton** Oxon
41 J3 **Milton** Oxon
195 H5 **Milton** P & K
49 H6 **Milton** Pembks
26 C6 **Milton** Somset
184 B6 **Milton** Stirlg
174 D4 **Milton** W Duns
14 F3 **Milton Abbas** Dorset
9 K8 **Milton Abbot** Devon
177 H5 **Milton Bridge** Mdloth
58 F3 **Milton Bryan** Beds
26 F4 **Milton Clevedon** Somset
6 D3 **Milton Combe** Devon
9 K3 **Milton Damerel** Devon
74 E4 **Milton Ernest** Beds
98 C2 **Milton Green** Ches
41 J3 **Milton Hill** Oxon
74 C6 **Milton Keynes** M Keyn
40 D7 **Milton Lilbourne** Wilts
73 K4 **Milton Malsor** Nhants
184 D1 **Milton Morenish** P & K
206 B5 **Milton of Auchinhove** Abers
186 E7 **Milton of Balgonie** Fife
174 E1 **Milton of Buchanan** Stirlg
175 H3 **Milton of Campsie** E Duns
213 G6 **Milton of Leys** Highld
205 J6 **Milton of Tullich** Abers
27 J5 **Milton on Stour** Dorset
46 E6 **Milton Regis** Kent
56 E4 **Milton-under-Wychwood** Oxon
25 H6 **Milverton** Somset
72 C2 **Milverton** Warwks
99 L6 **Milwich** Staffs
182 D7 **Minard** Ag & B
55 K7 **Minchinhampton** Gloucs
24 F3 **Minehead** Somset
97 L3 **Minera** Wrexhm
40 A3 **Minety** Wilts
95 K5 **Minffordd** Gwynd
190 D3 **Mingarrypark** Highld
118 D8 **Miningsby** Lincs
5 L2 **Minions** Cnwll
163 J6 **Minishant** S Ayrs
81 J2 **Minllyn** Gwynd
145 J2 **Minnigaff** D & G
216 E3 **Minnonie** Abers
132 F6 **Minskip** N York
16 C1 **Minstead** Hants
30 D7 **Minsted** W Susx
46 F5 **Minster** Kent
35 J2 **Minster** Kent
56 F5 **Minster Lovell** Oxon
83 G3 **Minsterley** Shrops
55 H5 **Minsterworth** Gloucs
14 C2 **Minterne Magna** Dorset
117 K6 **Minting** Lincs
217 J5 **Mintlaw** Abers
167 H5 **Minto** Border
83 H5 **Minton** Shrops
136 D4 **Mirehouse** Cumb
123 J6 **Mirfield** Kirk
55 L6 **Miserden** Gloucs
37 G4 **Miskin** Rhondd
116 B3 **Misson** Notts
87 G6 **Misterton** Leics
116 C3 **Misterton** Notts
13 L2 **Misterton** Somset
62 D2 **Mistley** Essex
44 F6 **Mitcham** Gt Lon
54 C6 **Mitchel Troy** Mons
54 F4 **Mitcheldean** Gloucs
4 D5 **Mitchell** Cnwll
155 G3 **Mitchellslacks** D & G
158 F5 **Mitford** Nthumb
3 J2 **Mithian** Cnwll
73 H7 **Mixbury** Oxon
113 H5 **Mobberley** Ches
100 A4 **Mobberley** Staffs
82 B5 **Mochdre** Powys
145 H5 **Mochrum** D & G
33 J4 **Mockbeggar** Kent
136 F3 **Mockerkin** Cumb
6 F5 **Modbury** Devon
99 L5 **Moddershall** Staffs
109 G4 **Moelfre** IOA
97 J6 **Moelfre** Powys
155 J2 **Moffat** D & G
75 G5 **Mogerhanger** Beds
86 C1 **Moira** Leics
199 G3 **Mol-chlach** Highld
34 D4 **Molash** Kent
111 H8 **Mold** Flints
123 H7 **Moldgreen** Kirk
60 E3 **Molehill Green** Essex
126 C3 **Molescroft** E R Yk
88 F7 **Molesworth** Cambs
24 C5 **Molland** Devon
111 L7 **Mollington** Ches
72 F5 **Mollington** Oxon
175 J4 **Mollinsburn** N Lans
197 J1 **Mondynes** Abers
78 F3 **Monewden** Suffk
185 M2 **Moneydie** P & K
154 D4 **Moniaive** D & G
187 H2 **Monifieth** Angus
196 E8 **Monikie** Angus
186 E5 **Monimail** Fife
124 D5 **Monk Fryston** N York
29 L1 **Monk Sherborne** Hants
78 E2 **Monk Soham** Suffk
60 F3 **Monk Street** Essex
31 K6 **Monk's Gate** W Susx
44 E1 **Monken Hadley** Gt Lon
70 B5 **Monkhide** Herefs
148 C3 **Monkhill** Cumb
84 B5 **Monkhopton** Shrops
69 J3 **Monkland** Herefs
23 G7 **Monkleigh** Devon
36 E6 **Monknash** V Glam
10 E4 **Monkokehampton** Devon
77 L5 **Monks Eleigh** Suffk
113 J6 **Monks Heath** Ches
34 F6 **Monks Horton** Kent
86 F6 **Monks Kirby** Warwks
159 H7 **Monkseaton** N Tyne
25 G4 **Monksilver** Somset
118 F7 **Monksthorpe** Lincs
53 M7 **Monkswood** Mons
12 F2 **Monkton** Devon
47 M6 **Monkton** Kent
163 J4 **Monkton** S Ayrs
151 H3 **Monkton** S Tyne
39 H7 **Monkton Combe** BaNES
27 J4 **Monkton Deverill** Wilts
39 J7 **Monkton Farleigh** Wilts
25 K6 **Monkton Heathfield** Somset
13 J3 **Monkton Wyld** Dorset
151 J4 **Monkwearmouth** Sundld
30 A5 **Monkwood** Hants
85 G4 **Monmore Green** Wolves
54 D5 **Monmouth** Mons
69 G5 **Monnington on Wye** Herefs
145 H6 **Monreith** D & G
236 b3 **Mont Saint** Guern
26 D7 **Montacute** Somset
83 H1 **Montford** Shrops
83 H1 **Montford Bridge** Shrops
206 B2 **Montgarrie** Abers
164 A4 **Montgarswood** E Ayrs
82 E4 **Montgomery** Powys
163 J2 **Montgreenan** N Ayrs
197 H5 **Montrose** Angus
28 F3 **Monxton** Hants
114 D7 **Monyash** Derbys
206 D3 **Monymusk** Abers
185 H3 **Monzie** P & K
175 J4 **Moodiesburn** N Lans
186 E4 **Moonzie** Fife
123 L3 **Moor Allerton** Leeds
15 J2 **Moor Crichel** Dorset
122 F5 **Moor End** Calder
133 H7 **Moor Monkton** N York
118 D8 **Moorby** Lincs
15 K4 **Moordown** Bmouth
112 E5 **Moore** Halton
125 G7 **Moorends** Donc
101 J3 **Moorgreen** Notts
123 H3 **Moorhead** Brad
148 B4 **Moorhouse** Cumb
116 C7 **Moorhouse** Notts
32 D3 **Moorhouse Bank** Surrey
26 B4 **Moorlinch** Somset
142 E4 **Moorsholm** R & Cl
27 H7 **Moorside** Dorset
5 K3 **Moorswater** Cnwll
124 C7 **Moorthorpe** Wakefd
123 K3 **Moortown** Leeds
117 H2 **Moortown** Lincs
223 G5 **Morangie** Highld
199 L6 **Morar** Highld
89 G5 **Morborne** Cambs
11 H4 **Morchard Bishop** Devon
13 K4 **Morcombelake** Dorset
88 D4 **Morcott** Rutlnd
97 L6 **Morda** Shrops
15 H4 **Morden** Dorset
44 E6 **Morden** Gt Lon
69 L6 **Mordiford** Herefs
141 H2 **Mordon** Dur
83 G5 **More** Shrops
24 E6 **Morebath** Devon
168 B4 **Morebattle** Border
129 J6 **Morecambe** Lancs
40 C3 **Moredon** Swindn
220 E3 **Morefield** Highld
35 G7 **Morehall** Kent
7 H5 **Moreleigh** Devon
184 D1 **Morenish** P & K
136 D3 **Moresby** Cumb

29 K6 **Morestead** Hants
14 F4 **Moreton** Dorset
60 E6 **Moreton** Essex
69 K2 **Moreton** Herefs
58 B6 **Moreton** Oxon
111 J4 **Moreton** Wirral
98 E7 **Moreton Corbet** Shrops
69 L5 **Moreton Jeffries** Herefs
72 C4 **Moreton Morrell** Warwks
69 K5 **Moreton on Lugg** Herefs
73 H5 **Moreton Pinkney** Nhants
98 F5 **Moreton Say** Shrops
55 H6 **Moreton Valence** Gloucs
56 D2 **Moreton-in-Marsh** Gloucs
11 H7 **Moretonhampstead** Devon
94 E4 **Morfa Nefyn** Gwynd
178 C4 **Morham** E Loth
138 E3 **Morland** Cumb
113 J5 **Morley** Ches
101 H4 **Morley** Derbys
123 K5 **Morley** Leeds
113 J5 **Morley Green** Ches
92 C4 **Morley St Botolph** Norfk
177 H4 **Morningside** C Edin
175 L7 **Morningside** N Lans
92 F5 **Morningthorpe** Norfk
158 F5 **Morpeth** Nthumb
197 H4 **Morphie** Abers
100 C8 **Morrey** Staffs
51 J6 **Morriston** Swans
106 B4 **Morston** Norfk
23 G3 **Mortehoe** Devon
115 J4 **Morthen** Rothm
41 M7 **Mortimer** W Berk
41 M7 **Mortimer West End** Hants
44 E5 **Mortlake** Gt Lon
148 C4 **Morton** Cumb
101 H1 **Morton** Derbys
116 D3 **Morton** Lincs
103 H7 **Morton** Lincs
102 B3 **Morton** Notts
97 L7 **Morton** Shrops
92 D1 **Morton on the Hill** Norfk
132 E2 **Morton-on-Swale** N York
2 D4 **Morvah** Cnwll
5 K4 **Morval** Cnwll
200 E2 **Morvich** Highld
84 C5 **Morville** Shrops
6 C2 **Morwellham Quay** Devon
9 G2 **Morwenstow** Cnwll
115 H5 **Mosborough** Sheff
163 L2 **Moscow** E Ayrs
85 J6 **Moseley** Birm
85 G4 **Moseley** Wolves
70 E3 **Moseley** Worcs
188 B7 **Moss** Ag & B
124 F7 **Moss** Donc
112 D3 **Moss Bank** St Hel
120 F2 **Moss Edge** Lancs
213 K4 **Moss-side** Highld
205 K2 **Mossat** Abers
235 d4 **Mossbank** Shet
136 D2 **Mossbay** Cumb
163 K4 **Mossblown** S Ayrs
167 K6 **Mossburnford** Border
154 B7 **Mossdale** D & G
153 K2 **Mossdale** E Ayrs
175 K6 **Mossend** N Lans
113 L2 **Mossley** Tamesd
156 D3 **Mosspaul Hotel** Border
215 H3 **Mosstodloch** Moray
121 H7 **Mossy Lea** Lancs
145 L5 **Mossyard** D & G
13 L2 **Mosterton** Dorset
113 K2 **Moston** Manch
111 G5 **Mostyn** Flints
27 J6 **Motcombe** Dorset
6 F6 **Mothecombe** Devon
138 B2 **Motherby** Cumb
175 K6 **Motherwell** N Lans
44 E6 **Motspur Park** Gt Lon
45 H5 **Mottingham** Gt Lon
28 F6 **Mottisfont** Hants
16 E5 **Mottistone** IOW
113 M3 **Mottram in Longdendale** Tamesd
113 K5 **Mottram St Andrew** Ches
236 c3 **Mouilpied** Guern
112 D7 **Mouldsworth** Ches
194 E4 **Moulin** P & K
19 J4 **Moulsecoomb** Br & H
41 L4 **Moulsford** Oxon
74 C6 **Moulsoe** M Keyn
222 E7 **Moultavie** Highld
112 F7 **Moulton** Ches
104 A7 **Moulton** Lincs
141 G6 **Moulton** N York
73 L2 **Moulton** Nhants
77 G2 **Moulton** Suffk
37 G6 **Moulton** V Glam
103 M8 **Moulton Chapel** Lincs
104 A6 **Moulton Seas End** Lincs
93 H3 **Moulton St Mary** Norfk
5 J3 **Mount** Cnwll
3 J3 **Mount Ambrose** Cnwll
61 L2 **Mount Bures** Essex
3 J2 **Mount Hawke** Cnwll
177 H6 **Mount Lothian** Mdloth
101 G3 **Mount Pleasant** Derbys
77 G5 **Mount Pleasant** Suffk
122 F5 **Mount Tabor** Calder
123 G4 **Mountain** Brad
53 G7 **Mountain Ash** Rhondd
176 F8 **Mountain Cross** Border
20 E2 **Mountfield** E Susx
212 E3 **Mountgerald House** Highld
4 D4 **Mountjoy** Cnwll
60 F8 **Mountnessing** Essex
38 D2 **Mounton** Mons
87 H2 **Mountsorrel** Leics
30 F3 **Mousehill** Surrey
2 E6 **Mousehole** Cnwll
155 J7 **Mouswald** D & G
168 B5 **Mowhaugh** Border
87 J5 **Mowsley** Leics
206 F7 **Mowtie** Abers
213 J7 **Moy** Highld
202 C8 **Moy** Highld
200 D2 **Moye** Highld
64 F5 **Moylgrove** Pembks
161 H2 **Muasdale** Ag & B
54 D3 **Much Birch** Herefs
70 B5 **Much Cowarne** Herefs
54 C2 **Much Dewchurch** Herefs
60 C4 **Much Hadham** Herts
120 F6 **Much Hoole** Lancs
54 F2 **Much Marcle** Herefs
84 B4 **Much Wenlock** Shrops
207 G6 **Muchalls** Abers
26 B6 **Muchelney** Somset
26 C6 **Muchelney Ham** Somset
5 K4 **Muchlarnick** Cnwll
106 D4 **Muckleburgh Collection** Norfk
99 G5 **Mucklestone** Staffs
118 E5 **Muckton** Lincs
23 J4 **Muddiford** Devon
20 B3 **Muddles Green** E Susx
16 A4 **Mudeford** Dorset
26 E7 **Mudford** Somset
26 E7 **Mudford Sock** Somset
175 G3 **Mugdock** Stirlg
209 G6 **Mugeary** Highld
100 F4 **Mugginton** Derbys
206 B3 **Muir of Fowlis** Abers
214 E3 **Muir of Miltonduff** Moray
212 E4 **Muir of Ord** Highld
195 G8 **Muir of Thorn** P & K
216 D4 **Muirden** Abers
196 F8 **Muirdrum** Angus
216 D5 **Muiresk** Abers
186 E1 **Muirhead** Angus
186 E6 **Muirhead** Fife
175 J4 **Muirhead** N Lans
164 D4 **Muirkirk** E Ayrs
175 J2 **Muirmill** Stirlg
192 B1 **Muirshearlich** Highld
217 J6 **Muirtack** Abers
185 J5 **Muirton** P & K
212 C4 **Muirton Mains** Highld
195 J7 **Muirton of Ardblair** P & K
139 K7 **Muker** N York
92 E4 **Mulbarton** Norfk
215 H4 **Mulben** Moray
181 J1 **Mull** Ag & B
3 H7 **Mullion** Cnwll
3 H7 **Mullion Cove** Cnwll
119 G6 **Mumby** Lincs
70 B4 **Munderfield Row** Herefs
70 B4 **Munderfield Stocks** Herefs
107 G5 **Mundesley** Norfk
91 H5 **Mundford** Norfk
93 G4 **Mundham** Norfk
61 K7 **Mundon Hill** Essex
137 K2 **Mungrisdale** Cumb
213 G4 **Munlochy** Highld
174 B8 **Munnoch** N Ayrs
70 B6 **Munsley** Herefs
83 K6 **Munslow** Shrops
11 G7 **Murchington** Devon
57 L5 **Murcott** Oxon
231 H2 **Murkle** Highld
200 F6 **Murlaggan** Highld
187 G1 **Murroes** Angus
89 L3 **Murrow** Cambs
58 D3 **Mursley** Bucks
196 D5 **Murthill** Angus
195 H8 **Murthly** P & K
139 G3 **Murton** Cumb
151 J5 **Murton** Dur
179 K8 **Murton** Nthumb
133 K8 **Murton** York
13 H4 **Musbury** Devon
177 K4 **Musselburgh** E Loth
102 D5 **Muston** Leics
135 H4 **Muston** N York
44 F3 **Muswell Hill** Gt Lon
146 C5 **Mutehill** D & G
93 K6 **Mutford** Suffk
185 H4 **Muthill** P & K
231 H5 **Mybster** Highld
52 B3 **Myddfai** Carmth
98 C7 **Myddle** Shrops
66 B4 **Mydroilyn** Cerdgn
4 C8 **Mylor** Cnwll
4 C8 **Mylor Bridge** Cnwll
49 K2 **Mynachlog ddu** Pembks
83 H5 **Myndtown** Shrops
38 C2 **Mynydd-bach** Mons
51 J6 **Mynydd-Bach** Swans
206 E5 **Myrebird** Abers
157 G3 **Myredykes** Border
30 E1 **Mytchett** Surrey
122 E5 **Mytholm** Calder
122 F5 **Mytholmroyd** Calder
132 F6 **Myton-on-Swale** N York

N

232 d4 **Na Buirgh** W Isls
219 J5 **Naast** Highld
124 F2 **Naburn** York
34 F4 **Nackington** Kent
78 F6 **Nacton** Suffk
135 G7 **Nafferton** E R Yk
25 K5 **Nailsbourne** Somset
38 C6 **Nailsea** N Som
86 E3 **Nailstone** Leics
55 J7 **Nailsworth** Gloucs
213 K3 **Nairn** Highld
111 G7 **Nannerch** Flints
87 G1 **Nanpantan** Leics
4 F5 **Nanpean** Cnwll
5 G3 **Nanstallon** Cnwll
95 K2 **Nant Peris** Gwynd
36 E2 **Nant-y-moel** Brdgnd
65 L3 **Nanternis** Cerdgn
50 F2 **Nantgaredig** Carmth
96 F1 **Nantglyn** Denbgs
68 B2 **Nantmel** Powys
95 K4 **Nantmor** Gwynd
98 F3 **Nantwich** Ches
53 J6 **Nantyglo** Blae G
42 D2 **Naphill** Bucks
72 F3 **Napton on the Hill** Warwks
49 J4 **Narberth** Pembks
87 G4 **Narborough** Leics
91 H2 **Narborough** Norfk
95 H3 **Nasareth** Gwynd
87 K7 **Naseby** Nhants
73 L7 **Nash** Bucks
37 M4 **Nash** Newpt
69 L1 **Nash** Shrops
30 A3 **Nash's Green** Hants
88 F4 **Nassington** Nhants
139 H6 **Nateby** Cumb
120 F2 **Nateby** Lancs
87 H3 **National Space Science Centre** C Leic
129 L2 **Natland** Cumb
78 B5 **Naughton** Suffk
56 C4 **Naunton** Gloucs
70 F6 **Naunton** Worcs
71 G4 **Naunton Beauchamp** Worcs
103 G2 **Navenby** Lincs
45 K1 **Navestock** Essex
60 E8 **Navestock Side** Essex
227 J5 **Navidale House Hotel** Highld
213 J2 **Navity** Highld
133 K3 **Nawton** N York
77 L7 **Nayland** Suffk
60 C6 **Nazeing** Essex
235 d5 **Neap** Shet
100 B4 **Near Cotton** Staffs
137 K7 **Near Sawrey** Cumb
44 E3 **Neasden** Gt Lon

141 H5 **Neasham** Darltn
51 L6 **Neath** Neath
30 C4 **Neatham** Hants
107 H7 **Neatishead** Norfk
66 D2 **Nebo** Cerdgn
96 C2 **Nebo** Conwy
95 H3 **Nebo** Gwynd
108 F4 **Nebo** IOA
91 K2 **Necton** Norfk
224 D3 **Nedd** Highld
78 B5 **Nedging** Suffk
78 B4 **Nedging Tye** Suffk
92 F6 **Needham** Norfk
78 C4 **Needham Market** Suffk
75 L1 **Needingworth** Cambs
84 C7 **Neen Savage** Shrops
84 B8 **Neen Sollars** Shrops
84 B6 **Neenton** Shrops
94 E4 **Nefyn** Gwynd
174 E6 **Neilston** E Rens
37 H2 **Nelson** Caerph
122 C3 **Nelson** Lancs
165 G1 **Nemphlar** S Lans
38 D7 **Nempnett Thrubwell** BaNES
149 K6 **Nenthead** Cumb
167 K2 **Nenthorn** Border
97 K1 **Nercwys** Flints
170 E7 **Nereabolls** Ag & B
175 H6 **Nerston** S Lans
168 E3 **Nesbit** Nthumb
123 G1 **Nesfield** N York
111 J6 **Ness Botanic Gardens** Ches
98 B8 **Nesscliffe** Shrops
111 J6 **Neston** Ches
39 K6 **Neston** Wilts
84 B5 **Netchwood** Shrops
113 J6 **Nether Alderley** Ches
167 H2 **Nether Blainslie** Border
102 B7 **Nether Broughton** Notts
14 C3 **Nether Cerne** Dorset
26 E7 **Nether Compton** Dorset
206 F2 **Nether Crimond** Abers
215 H2 **Nether Dallachy** Moray
11 L5 **Nether Exe** Devon
165 H7 **Nether Fingland** S Lans
196 B7 **Nether Handwick** Angus
115 H3 **Nether Haugh** Rothm
116 C6 **Nether Headon** Notts
101 G3 **Nether Heage** Derbys
73 J3 **Nether Heyford** Nhants
165 K6 **Nether Howcleugh** S Lans
129 K6 **Nether Kellet** Lancs
217 K5 **Nether Kinmundy** Abers
115 K7 **Nether Langwith** Notts
115 G7 **Nether Moor** Derbys
114 E6 **Nether Padley** Derbys
133 J8 **Nether Poppleton** York
133 G2 **Nether Silton** N York
25 J4 **Nether Stowey** Somset
28 F4 **Nether Wallop** Hants
136 F6 **Nether Wasdale** Cumb
56 E4 **Nether Westcote** Gloucs
86 B5 **Nether Whitacre** Warwks
165 G5 **Nether Whitecleuch** S Lans
58 B5 **Nether Winchendon** Bucks
28 D2 **Netheravon** Wilts
216 F3 **Netherbrae** Abers
175 L8 **Netherburn** S Lans
13 L3 **Netherbury** Dorset
123 L2 **Netherby** N York
155 K5 **Nethercleuch** D & G
54 E7 **Netherend** Gloucs
20 E2 **Netherfield** E Susx
20 E3 **Netherfield Road** E Susx
28 C5 **Netherhampton** Wilts
13 K2 **Netherhay** Dorset
146 C6 **Netherlaw** D & G
207 G6 **Netherley** Abers
155 H5 **Nethermill** D & G
217 G5 **Nethermuir** Abers
123 H6 **Netheroyd Hill** Kirk
174 F7 **Netherplace** E Rens
86 C2 **Netherseal** Derbys
123 H8 **Netherthong** Kirk
196 E5 **Netherton** Angus
7 K2 **Netherton** Devon
85 G6 **Netherton** Dudley
175 K7 **Netherton** N Lans
168 E7 **Netherton** Nthumb
195 J6 **Netherton** P & K
84 D6 **Netherton** Shrops
175 G3 **Netherton** Stirlg
123 K6 **Netherton** Wakefd
136 D5 **Nethertown** Cumb
231 L1 **Nethertown** Highld
100 C8 **Nethertown** Staffs
165 L1 **Netherurd** Border
158 D4 **Netherwitton** Nthumb
204 B2 **Nethy Bridge** Highld
16 F2 **Netley** Hants
29 G8 **Netley Marsh** Hants
42 B3 **Nettlebed** Oxon
26 F2 **Nettlebridge** Somset
13 M4 **Nettlecombe** Dorset
59 G6 **Nettleden** Herts
117 G6 **Nettleham** Lincs
33 H3 **Nettlestead** Kent
33 H3 **Nettlestead Green** Kent
17 H4 **Nettlestone** IOW
151 G5 **Nettlesworth** Dur
117 J2 **Nettleton** Lincs
39 J5 **Nettleton** Wilts
28 C4 **Netton** Wilts
64 F6 **Nevern** Pembks
88 B5 **Nevill Holt** Leics
147 G2 **New Abbey** D & G
217 G2 **New Aberdour** Abers
45 G7 **New Addington** Gt Lon
29 L5 **New Alresford** Hants
195 K6 **New Alyth** P & K
45 L6 **New Ash Green** Kent
102 D3 **New Balderton** Notts
45 L6 **New Barn** Kent
44 F2 **New Barnet** Gt Lon
169 G5 **New Bewick** Nthumb
86 F7 **New Bilton** Warwks
104 A2 **New Bolingbroke** Lincs
116 F7 **New Boultham** Lincs
74 B6 **New Bradwell** M Keyn
115 G7 **New Brampton** Derbys
151 G6 **New Brancepeth** Dur
111 J3 **New Brighton** Wirral
92 C5 **New Buckenham** Norfk
216 F4 **New Byth** Abers
92 E2 **New Costessey** Norfk
124 B6 **New Crofton** Wakefd
45 G5 **New Cross** Gt Lon
26 B7 **New Cross** Somset
164 C6 **New Cumnock** E Ayrs
217 G5 **New Deer** Abers
43 H4 **New Denham** Bucks
73 K3 **New Duston** Nhants
133 J7 **New Earswick** York
115 K2 **New Edlington** Donc
214 F3 **New Elgin** Moray
126 E3 **New Ellerby** E R Yk
45 H5 **New Eltham** Gt Lon
71 J3 **New End** Worcs
89 H4 **New England** C Pete
89 H4 **New Fletton** C Pete
16 C2 **New Forest** Hants
154 B6 **New Galloway** D & G
187 G5 **New Gilston** Fife
2 a1 **New Grimsby** IOS
159 H6 **New Hartley** Nthumb
43 H7 **New Haw** Surrey
105 L4 **New Holkham** Norfk
126 D5 **New Holland** N Linc
115 J7 **New Houghton** Derbys
105 J6 **New Houghton** Norfk
130 B2 **New Hutton** Cumb
66 B6 **New Inn** Carmth
53 L7 **New Inn** Torfn
82 F7 **New Invention** Shrops
165 G2 **New Lanark** S Lans
156 C5 **New Langholm** D & G
104 C2 **New Leake** Lincs
217 J4 **New Leeds** Abers
123 L8 **New Lodge** Barns
121 G5 **New Longton** Lancs
144 E3 **New Luce** D & G
44 E6 **New Malden** Gt Lon
142 D3 **New Marske** R & Cl
57 K6 **New Marston** Oxon
206 E8 **New Mill** Abers
2 E4 **New Mill** Cnwll
123 H8 **New Mill** Kirk
4 D5 **New Mills** Cnwll
113 M4 **New Mills** Derbys
82 C4 **New Mills** Powys
16 B4 **New Milton** Hants
62 D2 **New Mistley** Essex
49 H3 **New Moat** Pembks
116 A7 **New Ollerton** Notts
217 G3 **New Pitsligo** Abers
163 J4 **New Prestwick** S Ayrs
65 L3 **New Quay** Cerdgn
93 G2 **New Rackheath** Norfk
68 E3 **New Radnor** Powys
150 D3 **New Ridley** Nthumb
21 L2 **New Romney** Kent
115 L2 **New Rossington** Donc
185 J7 **New Sauchie** Clacks
124 B6 **New Sharlston** Wakefd
151 J4 **New Silksworth** Sundld
102 F5 **New Somerby** Lincs
175 K6 **New Stevenston** N Lans
75 H5 **New Town** Beds
27 L7 **New Town** Dorset
27 M7 **New Town** Dorset
19 M2 **New Town** E Susx
53 H7 **New Tredegar** Caerph
164 F2 **New Trows** S Lans
90 C2 **New Walsoken** Cambs
118 C1 **New Waltham** NE Lin
177 L4 **New Winton** E Loth
103 L2 **New York** Lincs
123 J2 **Newall** Leeds
234 e4 **Newark** Ork
102 D2 **Newark-on-Trent** Notts
175 K6 **Newarthill** N Lans
177 J5 **Newbattle** Mdloth
147 L3 **Newbie** D & G
138 C2 **Newbiggin** Cumb
148 F5 **Newbiggin** Cumb
138 F2 **Newbiggin** Cumb
139 K2 **Newbiggin** Dur
131 J3 **Newbiggin** N York
159 H5 **Newbiggin-by-the-Sea** Nthumb
139 G6 **Newbiggin-on-Lune** Cumb
195 L7 **Newbigging** Angus
196 C8 **Newbigging** Angus
187 H1 **Newbigging** Angus
165 K1 **Newbigging** S Lans
115 G6 **Newbold** Derbys
86 F7 **Newbold on Avon** Warwks
72 B5 **Newbold on Stour** Warwks
72 C3 **Newbold Pacey** Warwks
86 F3 **Newbold Verdon** Leics
89 H3 **Newborough** C Pete
108 E7 **Newborough** IOA
100 C7 **Newborough** Staffs
78 F6 **Newbourne** Suffk
176 F4 **Newbridge** C Edin
37 K2 **Newbridge** Caerph
2 D5 **Newbridge** Cnwll
155 G6 **Newbridge** D & G
28 F7 **Newbridge** Hants
16 E5 **Newbridge** IOW
70 E6 **Newbridge Green** Worcs
67 L3 **Newbridge on Wye** Powys
149 L2 **Newbrough** Nthumb
11 J4 **Newbuildings** Devon
217 H3 **Newburgh** Abers
207 J1 **Newburgh** Abers
186 D4 **Newburgh** Fife
121 G7 **Newburgh** Lancs
133 H4 **Newburgh Priory** N York
150 F2 **Newburn** N u Ty
27 G2 **Newbury** Somset
41 J6 **Newbury** W Berk
45 J3 **Newbury Park** Gt Lon
138 E3 **Newby** Cumb
122 B2 **Newby** Lancs
142 B5 **Newby** N York
130 D5 **Newby** N York
129 H3 **Newby Bridge** Cumb
148 E4 **Newby East** Cumb
148 C4 **Newby West** Cumb
132 E3 **Newby Wiske** N York
54 C5 **Newcastle** Mons
82 E6 **Newcastle** Shrops
158 F7 **Newcastle Airport** Nthumb
65 J6 **Newcastle Emlyn** Carmth
151 G3 **Newcastle upon Tyne** N u Ty
99 J4 **Newcastle-under-Lyme** Staffs
156 E5 **Newcastleton** Border
65 H6 **Newchapel** Pembks
32 C5 **Newchapel** Surrey
17 G5 **Newchurch** IOW
34 E7 **Newchurch** Kent
38 C2 **Newchurch** Mons
68 E4 **Newchurch** Powys
100 D7 **Newchurch** Staffs
177 J4 **Newcraighall** C Edin
31 K3 **Newdigate** Surrey

42 E6 **Newell Green** Br For
33 L7 **Newenden** Kent
55 G3 **Newent** Gloucs
150 F7 **Newfield** Dur
223 H6 **Newfield** Highld
48 E3 **Newgale** Pembks
59 M6 **Newgate Street** Herts
98 E4 **Newhall** Ches
177 H3 **Newhaven** C Edin
19 L5 **Newhaven** E Susx
143 H5 **Newholm** N York
175 L6 **Newhouse** N Lans
19 L2 **Newick** E Susx
46 E6 **Newington** Kent
35 G7 **Newington** Kent
41 L2 **Newington** Oxon
126 D4 **Newland** C KuH
54 D6 **Newland** Gloucs
125 G5 **Newland** N York
24 C4 **Newland** Somset
70 E5 **Newland** Worcs
177 K6 **Newlandrig** Mdloth
156 E4 **Newlands** Border
150 D4 **Newlands** Nthumb
215 G4 **Newlands of Dundurcas** Moray
2 E5 **Newlyn** Cnwll
4 C5 **Newlyn East** Cnwll
207 G2 **Newmachar** Abers
175 L6 **Newmains** N Lans
77 K5 **Newman's Green** Suffk
76 F2 **Newmarket** Suffk
232 f2 **Newmarket** W Isls
167 G7 **Newmill** Border
215 K4 **Newmill** Moray
196 C4 **Newmill of Inshewan** Angus
123 L7 **Newmillerdam** Wakefd
177 G5 **Newmills** C Edin
176 D2 **Newmills** Fife
54 D6 **Newmills** Mons
186 B2 **Newmiln** P & K
164 B2 **Newmilns** E Ayrs
61 G6 **Newney Green** Essex
55 G5 **Newnham** Gloucs
30 B2 **Newnham** Hants
75 J6 **Newnham** Herts
34 C3 **Newnham** Kent
73 H3 **Newnham** Nhants
70 B2 **Newnham** Worcs
9 J7 **Newport** Cnwll
23 J5 **Newport** Devon
125 K4 **Newport** E R Yk
76 D7 **Newport** Essex
39 G2 **Newport** Gloucs
227 K4 **Newport** Highld
16 F5 **Newport** IOW
37 L3 **Newport** Newpt
64 E6 **Newport** Pembks
99 H8 **Newport** Wrekin
74 C5 **Newport Pagnell** M Keyn
187 G2 **Newport-on-Tay** Fife
4 C4 **Newquay** Cnwll
4 D3 **Newquay Airport** Cnwll
216 D7 **Newseat** Abers
121 G4 **Newsham** Lancs
140 E5 **Newsham** N York
132 E3 **Newsham** N York
159 H6 **Newsham** Nthumb
125 H5 **Newsholme** E R Yk
123 H7 **Newsome** Kirk
167 H3 **Newstead** Border
101 K3 **Newstead** Notts
169 H4 **Newstead** Nthumb
215 K5 **Newtack** Moray
124 C4 **Newthorpe** N York
101 J4 **Newthorpe** Notts
182 F7 **Newton** Ag & B
75 J5 **Newton** Beds
167 J5 **Newton** Border
36 C5 **Newton** Brdgnd
90 B1 **Newton** Cambs
76 B5 **Newton** Cambs
112 B7 **Newton** Ches
98 D1 **Newton** Ches
128 F5 **Newton** Cumb
101 H2 **Newton** Derbys
53 M2 **Newton** Herefs
69 K4 **Newton** Herefs
212 F4 **Newton** Highld
213 H5 **Newton** Highld
213 J2 **Newton** Highld
121 K1 **Newton** Lancs
103 H5 **Newton** Lincs
177 J4 **Newton** Mdloth
214 E2 **Newton** Moray
215 H2 **Newton** Moray
88 C6 **Newton** Nhants
91 J1 **Newton** Norfk
102 B4 **Newton** Notts
150 C3 **Newton** Nthumb
175 H6 **Newton** S Lans
165 H3 **Newton** S Lans
25 H4 **Newton** Somset
100 B7 **Newton** Staffs
77 K6 **Newton** Suffk
176 E3 **Newton** W Loth
87 G7 **Newton** Warwks
7 K2 **Newton Abbot** Devon
147 L4 **Newton Arlosh** Cumb
141 G3 **Newton Aycliffe** Dur
141 K2 **Newton Bewley** Hartpl
74 D4 **Newton Blossomville** M Keyn
74 E2 **Newton Bromswold** Beds
86 D2 **Newton Burgoland** Leics
117 H4 **Newton by Toft** Lincs
6 A3 **Newton Ferrers** Cnwll
6 E6 **Newton Ferrers** Devon
232 c5 **Newton Ferry** W Isls
92 E4 **Newton Flotman** Norfk
87 J4 **Newton Harcourt** Leics
113 K2 **Newton Heath** Manch
124 C2 **Newton Kyme** N York
58 D2 **Newton Longville** Bucks
174 F7 **Newton Mearns** E Rens
141 G5 **Newton Morrell** N York
186 B5 **Newton of Balcanquhal** P & K
187 H6 **Newton of Balcormo** Fife
133 H7 **Newton on Ouse** N York
116 D6 **Newton on Trent** Lincs
12 E4 **Newton Poppleford** Devon
57 L3 **Newton Purcell** Oxon
86 C3 **Newton Regis** Warwks
138 C2 **Newton Reigny** Cumb
231 L5 **Newton Row** Highld
100 F7 **Newton Solney** Derbys
11 K5 **Newton St Cyres** Devon
92 F1 **Newton St Faith** Norfk
39 G7 **Newton St Loe** BaNES
9 K3 **Newton St Petrock** Devon
29 H4 **Newton Stacey** Hants
145 J3 **Newton Stewart** D & G
28 E4 **Newton Tony** Wilts
23 H6 **Newton Tracey** Devon
142 C5 **Newton under Roseberry** R & Cl
125 H2 **Newton upon Derwent** E R Yk
30 B5 **Newton Valence** Hants
155 K3 **Newton Wamphray** D & G
120 F4 **Newton with Scales** Lancs
169 J4 **Newton-by-the-Sea** Nthumb
132 C2 **Newton-le-Willows** N York
112 E3 **Newton-le-Willows** St Hel
134 C2 **Newton-on-Rawcliffe** N York
158 F2 **Newton-on-the-Moor** Nthumb
216 B7 **Newtongarry Croft** Abers
177 J5 **Newtongrange** Mdloth
207 G6 **Newtonhill** Abers
177 J5 **Newtonloan** Mdloth
196 F4 **Newtonmill** Angus
203 H5 **Newtonmore** Highld
98 F3 **Newtown** Ches
99 K1 **Newtown** Ches
147 J5 **Newtown** Cumb
148 E3 **Newtown** Cumb
164 F7 **Newtown** D & G
12 D3 **Newtown** Devon
24 B6 **Newtown** Devon
54 F7 **Newtown** Gloucs
29 L8 **Newtown** Hants
70 B5 **Newtown** Herefs
70 C6 **Newtown** Herefs
202 B4 **Newtown** Highld
16 E4 **Newtown** IOW
158 C3 **Newtown** Nthumb
168 F4 **Newtown** Nthumb
15 K4 **Newtown** Poole
82 C5 **Newtown** Powys
98 B7 **Newtown** Shrops
98 C6 **Newtown** Shrops
25 L8 **Newtown** Somset
112 E1 **Newtown** Wigan
70 F4 **Newtown** Worcs
87 G2 **Newtown Linford** Leics
174 D6 **Newtown of Beltrees** Rens
167 J3 **Newtown St Boswells** Border
195 L7 **Newtyle** Angus
182 D5 **Newyork** Ag & B
49 G6 **Neyland** Pembks
25 H7 **Nicholashayne** Devon
51 G7 **Nicholaston** Swans
132 D7 **Nidd** N York
207 H5 **Nigg** C Aber
223 H6 **Nigg** Highld
24 D6 **Nightcott** Somset
40 C4 **Nine Elms** Swindn
149 K4 **Ninebanks** Nthumb
70 B2 **Nineveh** Worcs
20 E3 **Ninfield** E Susx
16 E5 **Ningwood** IOW
167 K4 **Nisbet** Border
179 G7 **Nisbet Hill** Border
16 G6 **Niton** IOW
174 F6 **Nitshill** C Glas
98 D3 **No Man's Heath** Ches
86 C2 **No Man's Heath** Warwks
117 H8 **Nocton** Lincs
57 K5 **Noke** Oxon
48 E4 **Nolton** Pembks
48 E4 **Nolton Haven** Pembks
11 J3 **Nomansland** Devon
28 E7 **Nomansland** Wilts
98 C6 **Noneley** Shrops
35 H4 **Nonington** Kent
129 L3 **Nook** Cumb
44 D6 **Norbiton** Gt Lon
98 E3 **Norbury** Ches
100 C4 **Norbury** Derbys
44 F6 **Norbury** Gt Lon
83 G5 **Norbury** Shrops
99 H7 **Norbury** Staffs
70 F2 **Norchard** Worcs
90 D4 **Nordelph** Norfk
84 C4 **Nordley** Shrops
93 K2 **Norfolk Broads** Norfk
179 J8 **Norham** Nthumb
123 G6 **Norland Town** Calder
112 E6 **Norley** Ches
16 D3 **Norleywood** Hants
12 D2 **Norman's Green** Devon
117 G4 **Normanby** Lincs
125 K7 **Normanby** N Linc
134 B3 **Normanby** N York
142 C4 **Normanby** R & Cl
117 J3 **Normanby le Wold** Lincs
30 F2 **Normandy** Surrey
101 G5 **Normanton** C Derb
102 D4 **Normanton** Leics
102 F4 **Normanton** Lincs
102 B2 **Normanton** Notts
124 B6 **Normanton** Wakefd
86 D2 **Normanton le Heath** Leics
101 K7 **Normanton on Soar** Notts
101 L6 **Normanton on the Wolds** Notts
116 C7 **Normanton on Trent** Notts
115 K5 **North Anston** Rothm
42 E6 **North Ascot** Br For
57 J3 **North Aston** Oxon
29 H7 **North Baddesley** Hants
191 L4 **North Ballachulish** Highld
26 E5 **North Barrow** Somset
105 L5 **North Barsham** Norfk
46 C3 **North Benfleet** Essex
18 C5 **North Bersted** W Susx
178 C2 **North Berwick** E Loth
17 H1 **North Boarhunt** Hants
11 H7 **North Bovey** Devon
27 J1 **North Bradley** Wilts
10 C8 **North Brentor** Devon
27 G4 **North Brewham** Somset
23 G4 **North Buckland** Devon
93 H2 **North Burlingham** Norfk
26 F6 **North Cadbury** Somset
116 F6 **North Carlton** Lincs
115 L4 **North Carlton** Notts
125 K4 **North Cave** E R Yk
56 A6 **North Cerney** Gloucs

19 K2 **North Chailey** E Susx
28 D7 **North Charford** Hants
169 H5 **North Charlton** Nthumb
44 E6 **North Cheam** Gt Lon
27 G6 **North Cheriton** Somset
13 K4 **North Chideock** Dorset
125 K3 **North Cliffe** E R Yk
116 D6 **North Clifton** Notts
118 E4 **North Cockerington** Lincs
182 C1 **North Connel** Ag & B
36 C4 **North Cornelly** Brdgnd
191 G5 **North Corry** Highld
118 E2 **North Cotes** Lincs
93 K5 **North Cove** Suffk
141 G6 **North Cowton** N York
74 D5 **North Crawley** M Keyn
105 K5 **North Creake** Norfk
25 L6 **North Curry** Somset
125 L1 **North Dalton** E R Yk
124 B1 **North Deighton** N York
34 B4 **North Downs**
125 G3 **North Duffield** N York
218 C6 **North Duntulm** Highld
35 G5 **North Elham** Kent
106 B7 **North Elmham** Norfk
124 D7 **North Elmsall** Wakefd
17 J3 **North End** C Port
61 G4 **North End** Essex
28 C7 **North End** Hants
74 D2 **North End** Nhants
18 D5 **North End** W Susx
219 H5 **North Erradale** Highld
87 J3 **North Evington** C Leic
61 K7 **North Fambridge** Essex
126 B5 **North Ferriby** E R Yk
135 H8 **North Frodingham** E R Yk
15 M1 **North Gorley** Hants
79 G3 **North Green** Suffk
134 C6 **North Grimston** N York
17 K2 **North Hayling** Hants
5 L1 **North Hill** Cnwll
43 H4 **North Hillingdon** Gt Lon
57 J6 **North Hinksey** Oxon
31 K3 **North Holmwood** Surrey
7 G5 **North Huish** Devon
116 F7 **North Hykeham** Lincs
117 H2 **North Kelsey** Lincs
213 G5 **North Kessock** Highld
126 E6 **North Killingholme** N Linc
132 F3 **North Kilvington** N York
87 H6 **North Kilworth** Leics
103 J3 **North Kyme** Lincs
135 K5 **North Landing** E R Yk
58 D6 **North Lee** Bucks
57 H5 **North Leigh** Oxon
116 C5 **North Leverton with Habblesthorpe** Notts
71 J5 **North Littleton** Worcs
92 C6 **North Lopham** Norfk
88 D3 **North Luffenham** Rutlnd
30 D7 **North Marden** W Susx
58 C4 **North Marston** Bucks
177 K6 **North Middleton** Mdloth
144 C4 **North Milmain** D & G
24 B5 **North Molton** Devon
41 K3 **North Moreton** Oxon
18 B5 **North Mundham** W Susx
102 D2 **North Muskham** Notts
125 L3 **North Newbald** E R Yk
72 E6 **North Newington** Oxon
40 C8 **North Newnton** Wilts
25 L5 **North Newton** Somset
39 H2 **North Nibley** Gloucs
142 B4 **North Ormesby** Middsb
118 C3 **North Ormsby** Lincs
132 E2 **North Otterington** N York
117 H3 **North Owersby** Lincs
13 L1 **North Perrott** Somset
25 L5 **North Petherton** Somset
9 H6 **North Petherwin** Cnwll
91 J3 **North Pickenham** Norfk
71 G4 **North Piddle** Worcs
7 H7 **North Pool** Devon
13 M3 **North Poorton** Dorset
176 F3 **North Queensferry** C Edin
24 B5 **North Radworthy** Devon
103 G3 **North Rauceby** Lincs
118 E5 **North Reston** Lincs
123 K1 **North Rigton** N York
113 K7 **North Rode** Ches
234 e3 **North Ronaldsay Airport** Ork
90 F1 **North Runcton** Norfk
116 D7 **North Scarle** Lincs
191 H7 **North Shian** Ag & B
151 J2 **North Shields** N Tyne
46 F3 **North Shoebury** Sthend
120 D3 **North Shore** Bpool
89 K4 **North Side** C Pete
118 F3 **North Somercotes** Lincs
132 D4 **North Stainley** N York
45 L4 **North Stifford** Thurr
39 G6 **North Stoke** BaNES
41 L3 **North Stoke** Oxon
18 D4 **North Stoke** W Susx
34 D3 **North Street** Kent
41 M6 **North Street** W Berk
169 J3 **North Sunderland** Nthumb
9 J5 **North Tamerton** Cnwll
10 F4 **North Tawton** Devon
175 K1 **North Third** Stirlg
118 D2 **North Thoresby** Lincs
28 E2 **North Tidworth** Wilts
10 D3 **North Town** Devon
26 E3 **North Town** Somset
42 E4 **North Town** W & M
92 C2 **North Tuddenham** Norfk
107 G6 **North Walsham** Norfk
29 K3 **North Waltham** Hants
30 B2 **North Warnborough** Hants
60 D7 **North Weald Bassett** Essex
116 C4 **North Wheatley** Notts
38 E8 **North Widcombe** BaNES
117 K4 **North Willingham** Lincs
115 H8 **North Wingfield** Derbys
102 F7 **North Witham** Lincs
26 F8 **North Wootton** Dorset
105 G7 **North Wootton** Norfk
26 E3 **North Wootton** Somset
39 J5 **North Wraxall** Wilts
142 F6 **North York Moors National Park**
58 F4 **Northall** Bucks
141 J7 **Northallerton** N York
29 H8 **Northam** C Sotn
23 G5 **Northam** Devon
73 L3 **Northampton** Nhants
70 E2 **Northampton** Worcs
59 L7 **Northaw** Herts
13 H1 **Northay** Somset
89 H3 **Northborough** C Pete
35 J4 **Northbourne** Kent
29 K4 **Northbrook** Hants
30 F5 **Northchapel** W Susx
58 F6 **Northchurch** Herts
9 J6 **Northcott** Devon
57 J7 **Northcourt** Oxon
35 K2 **Northdown** Kent
72 E4 **Northend** Warwks
113 J4 **Northenden** Manch
85 H7 **Northfield** Birm
207 G4 **Northfield** C Aber
126 C5 **Northfield** E R Yk
88 E2 **Northfields** Lincs
45 M5 **Northfleet** Kent
21 G2 **Northiam** E Susx
75 G5 **Northill** Beds
29 K4 **Northington** Hants
104 B2 **Northlands** Lincs
56 C5 **Northleach** Gloucs
12 F3 **Northleigh** Devon
10 D5 **Northlew** Devon
57 H7 **Northmoor** Oxon
196 C5 **Northmuir** Angus
17 K2 **Northney** Hants
43 J4 **Northolt** Gt Lon
111 H7 **Northop** Flints
111 J7 **Northop Hall** Flints
116 E3 **Northorpe** Lincs
103 K5 **Northorpe** Lincs
123 G5 **Northowram** Calder
15 H5 **Northport** Dorset
106 F5 **Northrepps** Norfk
232 d5 **Northton** W Isls
157 L2 **Northumberland National Park** Nthumb
25 H5 **Northway** Somset
112 F6 **Northwich** Ches
70 E3 **Northwick** Worcs
91 H4 **Northwold** Norfk
43 H3 **Northwood** Gt Lon
16 F4 **Northwood** IOW
98 C6 **Northwood** Shrops
55 G5 **Northwood Green** Gloucs
124 E7 **Norton** Donc
19 M5 **Norton** E Susx
55 J3 **Norton** Gloucs
134 C5 **Norton** N York
73 H2 **Norton** Nhants
115 L6 **Norton** Notts
68 F2 **Norton** Powys
141 K3 **Norton** S on T
84 D4 **Norton** Shrops
77 L2 **Norton** Suffk
18 C4 **Norton** W Susx
39 K4 **Norton** Wilts
70 F4 **Norton** Worcs
71 J5 **Norton** Worcs
27 K3 **Norton Bavant** Wilts
99 K6 **Norton Bridge** Staffs
85 H2 **Norton Canes** Staffs
69 H5 **Norton Canon** Herefs
102 E2 **Norton Disney** Lincs
25 J6 **Norton Fitzwarren** Somset
16 D5 **Norton Green** IOW
38 E7 **Norton Hawkfield** BaNES
60 F6 **Norton Heath** Essex
99 G5 **Norton in Hales** Shrops
72 B2 **Norton Lindsey** Warwks
77 L2 **Norton Little Green** Suffk
38 E7 **Norton Malreward** BaNES
27 H1 **Norton St Philip** Somset
26 C7 **Norton sub Hamdon** Somset
93 J4 **Norton Subcourse** Norfk
69 G5 **Norton Wood** Herefs
86 D3 **Norton-Juxta-Twycross** Leics
132 F5 **Norton-le-Clay** N York
102 C1 **Norwell** Notts
116 B8 **Norwell Woodhouse** Notts
92 F2 **Norwich** Norfk
92 E2 **Norwich Airport** Norfk
92 F2 **Norwich Cathedral** Norfk
235 e1 **Norwick** Shet
185 J8 **Norwood** Clacks
43 J5 **Norwood Green** Gt Lon
31 L3 **Norwood Hill** Surrey
6 E6 **Noss Mayo** Devon
132 D4 **Nosterfield** N York
210 D8 **Nostie** Highld
56 C4 **Notgrove** Gloucs
36 C5 **Nottage** Brdgnd
6 B4 **Notter** Cnwll
101 L5 **Nottingham** C Nott
101 J7 **Nottingham East Midlands Airport** Leics
123 L7 **Notton** Wakefd
39 K6 **Notton** Wilts
70 E2 **Noutard's Green** Worcs
83 H2 **Nox** Shrops
42 A3 **Nuffield** Oxon
133 H7 **Nun Monkton** N York
125 K2 **Nunburnholme** E R Yk
86 D5 **Nuneaton** Warwks
57 K7 **Nuneham Courtenay** Oxon
45 G5 **Nunhead** Gt Lon
126 E1 **Nunkeeling** E R Yk
27 G3 **Nunney** Somset
133 K4 **Nunnington** N York
127 G8 **Nunsthorpe** NE Lin
142 C4 **Nunthorpe** Middsb
124 F1 **Nunthorpe** York
142 C5 **Nunthorpe Village** Middsb
28 D6 **Nunton** Wilts
132 E5 **Nunwick** N York
29 G7 **Nursling** Hants
17 L2 **Nutbourne** W Susx
18 E3 **Nutbourne** W Susx
32 B3 **Nutfield** Surrey
101 K4 **Nuthall** Notts
76 B7 **Nuthampstead** Herts

31 K6 **Nuthurst** W Susx
32 D7 **Nutley** E Susx
231 L3 **Nybster** Highld
18 B6 **Nyetimber** W Susx
30 D6 **Nyewood** W Susx
11 G4 **Nymet Rowland** Devon
11 G5 **Nymet Tracey** Devon
55 J7 **Nympsfield** Gloucs
18 C5 **Nyton** W Susx

O

34 B3 **Oad Street** Kent
87 J4 **Oadby** Leics
10 D5 **Oak Cross** Devon
100 B4 **Oakamoor** Staffs
176 E5 **Oakbank** W Loth
37 J2 **Oakdale** Caerph
25 J6 **Oake** Somset
84 F3 **Oaken** Staffs
121 H2 **Oakenclough** Lancs
84 C2 **Oakengates** Wrekin
150 F7 **Oakenshaw** Dur
123 H5 **Oakenshaw** Kirk
100 F1 **Oaker Side** Derbys
66 B3 **Oakford** Cerdgn
24 E6 **Oakford** Devon
88 C2 **Oakham** Rutlnd
30 C4 **Oakhanger** Hants
26 F3 **Oakhill** Somset
76 B2 **Oakington** Cambs
55 H4 **Oakle Street** Gloucs
74 E4 **Oakley** Beds
57 M5 **Oakley** Bucks
176 D1 **Oakley** Fife
29 K2 **Oakley** Hants
92 E7 **Oakley** Suffk
55 K7 **Oakridge** Gloucs
39 M2 **Oaksey** Wilts
86 D2 **Oakthorpe** Leics
101 G5 **Oakwood** C Derb
31 J4 **Oakwoodhill** Surrey
122 F3 **Oakworth** Brad
34 D3 **Oare** Kent
24 C3 **Oare** Somset
40 D7 **Oare** Wilts
103 G5 **Oasby** Lincs
26 B6 **Oath** Somset
196 D5 **Oathlaw** Angus
43 H7 **Oatlands Park** Surrey
182 B2 **Oban** Ag & B
83 G7 **Obley** Shrops
195 G8 **Obney** P & K
26 F7 **Oborne** Dorset
78 D1 **Occold** Suffk
231 J7 **Occumster** Highld
163 L5 **Ochiltree** E Ayrs
101 H5 **Ockbrook** Derbys
31 H1 **Ockham** Surrey
190 B3 **Ockle** Highld
31 J4 **Ockley** Surrey
69 L5 **Ocle Pychard** Herefs
26 D7 **Odcombe** Somset
39 H7 **Odd Down** BaNES
71 G3 **Oddingley** Worcs
56 E3 **Oddington** Gloucs
57 K5 **Oddington** Oxon
74 D3 **Odell** Beds
30 C2 **Odiham** Hants
123 H4 **Odsal** Brad
75 K6 **Odsey** Herts
28 D6 **Odstock** Wilts
86 E3 **Odstone** Leics
72 D2 **Offchurch** Warwks
71 J5 **Offenham** Worcs
113 K4 **Offerton** Gt Man
19 L3 **Offham** E Susx
33 H2 **Offham** Kent
18 D4 **Offham** W Susx
75 J2 **Offord Cluny** Cambs
75 J2 **Offord Darcy** Cambs
78 C5 **Offton** Suffk
12 F3 **Offwell** Devon
40 D6 **Ogbourne Maizey** Wilts
40 D6 **Ogbourne St Andrew** Wilts
40 D5 **Ogbourne St George** Wilts
158 E6 **Ogle** Nthumb
112 C5 **Oglet** Lpool
36 D5 **Ogmore** V Glam
36 E3 **Ogmore Vale** Brdgnd
36 D5 **Ogmore-by-Sea** V Glam
14 F1 **Okeford Fitzpaine** Dorset
10 E5 **Okehampton** Devon
87 L8 **Old** Nhants
207 H4 **Old Aberdeen** C Aber
29 L5 **Old Alresford** Hants
154 D3 **Old Auchenbrack** D & G
101 K4 **Old Basford** C Nott
30 A2 **Old Basing** Hants
169 G5 **Old Bewick** Nthumb
118 E8 **Old Bolingbroke** Lincs
123 J2 **Old Bramhope** Leeds
115 G6 **Old Brampton** Derbys
146 D2 **Old Bridge of Urr** D & G
92 C5 **Old Buckenham** Norfk
41 J8 **Old Burghclere** Hants
133 H3 **Old Byland** N York
115 L2 **Old Cantley** Donc
127 G8 **Old Clee** NE Lin
25 G3 **Old Cleeve** Somset
115 L8 **Old Clipstone** Notts
152 F3 **Old Dailly** S Ayrs
102 A7 **Old Dalby** Leics
217 J5 **Old Deer** Abers
115 K3 **Old Edlington** Donc
126 E3 **Old Ellerby** E R Yk
79 G7 **Old Felixstowe** Suffk
89 H4 **Old Fletton** C Pete
54 E4 **Old Forge** Herefs
2 a1 **Old Grimsby** IOS
60 B4 **Old Hall Green** Herts
60 D5 **Old Harlow** Essex
105 G4 **Old Hunstanton** Norfk
89 K7 **Old Hurst** Cambs
130 B2 **Old Hutton** Cumb
4 D7 **Old Kea** Cnwll
174 E4 **Old Kilpatrick** W Duns
59 L4 **Old Knebworth** Herts
121 K4 **Old Langho** Lancs
104 C3 **Old Leake** Lincs
134 C5 **Old Malton** N York
124 C4 **Old Micklefield** Leeds
72 C2 **Old Milverton** Warwks
78 C3 **Old Newton** Suffk
68 E3 **Old Radnor** Powys
216 D8 **Old Rayne** Abers
21 K2 **Old Romney** Kent
19 G4 **Old Shoreham** W Susx
39 H4 **Old Sodbury** S Glos
102 F5 **Old Somerby** Lincs
73 L6 **Old Stratford** Nhants
84 F6 **Old Swinford** Dudley
132 F3 **Old Thirsk** N York
130 B3 **Old Town** Cumb
20 C5 **Old Town** E Susx
2 b2 **Old Town** IOS
113 J3 **Old Trafford** Traffd
75 G5 **Old Warden** Beds
89 G7 **Old Weston** Cambs
231 L5 **Old Wick** Highld
43 G5 **Old Windsor** W & M
34 E4 **Old Wives Lees** Kent
43 G8 **Old Woking** Surrey
224 D2 **Oldany** Highld
71 K2 **Oldberrow** Warwks
85 H5 **Oldbury** Sandw
84 C5 **Oldbury** Shrops
86 C5 **Oldbury** Warwks
39 J3 **Oldbury on the Hill** Gloucs
38 E2 **Oldbury-on-Severn** S Glos
53 L3 **Oldcastle** Mons
115 L4 **Oldcotes** Notts
70 E2 **Oldfield** Worcs
27 H2 **Oldford** Somset
113 L1 **Oldham** Oldham
178 F4 **Oldhamstocks** E Loth
38 F6 **Oldland** S Glos
216 F8 **Oldmeldrum** Abers
6 B2 **Oldmill** Cnwll
37 M8 **Oldmixon** N Som
228 C4 **Oldshoremore** Highld
133 H4 **Oldstead** N York
148 E3 **Oldwall** Cumb
50 F6 **Oldwalls** Swans
100 C8 **Olive Green** Staffs
165 L4 **Oliver** Border
29 J6 **Oliver's Battery** Hants
235 c3 **Ollaberry** Shet
209 H6 **Ollach** Highld
113 H6 **Ollerton** Ches
116 A7 **Ollerton** Notts
98 F7 **Ollerton** Shrops
74 C4 **Olney** M Keyn
231 H3 **Olrig House** Highld
85 K6 **Olton** Solhll
38 E3 **Olveston** S Glos
70 E2 **Ombersley** Worcs
116 B7 **Ompton** Notts
237 d5 **Onchan** IOM
100 B2 **Onecote** Staffs
83 J7 **Onibury** Shrops
191 K4 **Onich** Highld
52 C6 **Onllwyn** Neath
99 H4 **Onneley** Staffs
31 G2 **Onslow Village** Surrey
112 E6 **Onston** Ches
219 H6 **Opinan** Highld
215 G3 **Orbliston** Moray
208 D5 **Orbost** Highld
119 G7 **Orby** Lincs
25 K6 **Orchard Portman** Somset
28 B3 **Orcheston** Wilts
54 C3 **Orcop** Herefs
54 C3 **Orcop Hill** Herefs
216 C3 **Ord** Abers
206 C3 **Ordhead** Abers
205 K5 **Ordie** Abers
215 H3 **Ordiequish** Moray
150 B3 **Ordley** Nthumb
116 B5 **Ordsall** Notts
21 G4 **Ore** E Susx
79 J4 **Orford** Suffk
112 E4 **Orford** Warrtn
15 H4 **Organford** Dorset
34 D7 **Orlestone** Kent
69 J2 **Orleton** Herefs
70 C2 **Orleton** Worcs
74 C1 **Orlingbury** Nhants
142 C4 **Ormesby** R & Cl
93 K1 **Ormesby St Margaret** Norfk
93 K1 **Ormesby St Michael** Norfk
219 K4 **Ormiscaig** Highld
177 L4 **Ormiston** E Loth
189 L4 **Ormsaigmore** Highld
172 C4 **Ormsary** Ag & B
120 F8 **Ormskirk** Lancs
171 G2 **Oronsay** Ag & B
234 b6 **Orphir** Ork
45 J6 **Orpington** Gt Lon
111 K3 **Orrell** Sefton
112 D2 **Orrell** Wigan
146 D5 **Orroland** D & G
45 M4 **Orsett** Thurr
84 E1 **Orslow** Staffs
102 C4 **Orston** Notts
138 F5 **Orton** Cumb
88 B7 **Orton** Nhants
84 F4 **Orton** Staffs
89 H4 **Orton Longueville** C Pete
89 H4 **Orton Waterville** C Pete
86 C3 **Orton-on-the-Hill** Leics
75 L4 **Orwell** Cambs
121 J4 **Osbaldeston** Lancs
124 F1 **Osbaldwick** York
86 E3 **Osbaston** Leics
97 L7 **Osbaston** Shrops
17 G4 **Osborne House** IOW
103 H5 **Osbournby** Lincs
112 D7 **Oscroft** Ches
208 E6 **Ose** Highld
101 H8 **Osgathorpe** Leics
117 H3 **Osgodby** Lincs
124 F4 **Osgodby** N York
135 G3 **Osgodby** N York
209 H6 **Oskaig** Highld
189 L7 **Oskamull** Ag & B
100 D4 **Osmaston** Derbys
14 D5 **Osmington** Dorset
14 E6 **Osmington Mills** Dorset
123 L4 **Osmondthorpe** Leeds
141 K7 **Osmotherley** N York
57 J6 **Osney** Oxon
34 D3 **Ospringe** Kent
123 K6 **Ossett** Wakefd
116 C8 **Ossington** Notts
44 D5 **Osterley** Gt Lon
133 K4 **Oswaldkirk** N York
121 L5 **Oswaldtwistle** Lancs
97 L6 **Oswestry** Shrops
32 F2 **Otford** Kent
33 K3 **Otham** Kent
26 B5 **Othery** Somset
123 J2 **Otley** Leeds
78 E4 **Otley** Suffk
172 F2 **Otter Ferry** Ag & B
29 J6 **Otterbourne** Hants
131 G7 **Otterburn** N York
157 M4 **Otterburn** Nthumb
8 F6 **Otterham** Cnwll
25 K3 **Otterhampton** Somset
232 c5 **Otternish** W Isls
43 G7 **Ottershaw** Surrey
235 d3 **Otterswick** Shet
12 E5 **Otterton** Devon
6 C2 **Ottery** Devon
12 E4 **Ottery St Mary** Devon
34 F6 **Ottinge** Kent
127 G5 **Ottringham** E R Yk
147 K6 **Oughterside** Cumb
114 F3 **Oughtibridge** Sheff
113 G4 **Oughtrington** Warrtn
133 H5 **Oulston** N York
147 M5 **Oulton** Cumb
106 D6 **Oulton** Norfk
99 K5 **Oulton** Staffs
93 L5 **Oulton** Suffk
93 L5 **Oulton Broad** Suffk
106 D6 **Oulton Street** Norfk
88 F6 **Oundle** Nhants
84 F5 **Ounsdale** Staffs
149 G7 **Ousby** Cumb
77 G3 **Ousden** Suffk
125 K6 **Ousefleet** E R Yk
151 G4 **Ouston** Dur
120 E3 **Out Rawcliffe** Lancs

137 K7 **Outgate** Cumb
139 H6 **Outhgill** Cumb
71 K2 **Outhill** Warwks
123 G6 **Outlane** Kirk
90 D3 **Outwell** Norfk
32 B4 **Outwood** Surrey
99 H8 **Outwoods** Staffs
123 L5 **Ouzlewell Green** Leeds
75 L1 **Over** Cambs
26 E7 **Over Compton** Dorset
114 D7 **Over Haddon** Derbys
129 L5 **Over Kellet** Lancs
57 H4 **Over Kiddington** Oxon
56 F3 **Over Norton** Oxon
113 H6 **Over Peover** Ches
133 G2 **Over Silton** N York
25 J4 **Over Stowey** Somset
26 B7 **Over Stratton** Somset
28 F4 **Over Wallop** Hants
86 B5 **Over Whitacre** Warwks
57 H3 **Over Worton** Oxon
71 G6 **Overbury** Worcs
14 D6 **Overcombe** Dorset
26 C4 **Overleigh** Somset
111 L6 **Overpool** Ches
225 J4 **Overscaig Hotel** Highld
86 C1 **Overseal** Derbys
34 E3 **Oversland** Kent
74 B2 **Overstone** Nhants
106 F4 **Overstrand** Norfk
72 F6 **Overthorpe** Nhants
207 G3 **Overton** C Aber
29 K2 **Overton** Hants
129 J7 **Overton** Lancs
133 H7 **Overton** N York
69 K1 **Overton** Shrops
50 F7 **Overton** Swans
123 K7 **Overton** Wakefd
98 A4 **Overton** Wrexhm
130 C4 **Overtown** Lancs
175 L7 **Overtown** N Lans
58 C4 **Oving** Bucks
18 B5 **Oving** W Susx
19 K5 **Ovingdean** Br & H
150 D3 **Ovingham** Nthumb
140 E4 **Ovington** Dur
77 H6 **Ovington** Essex
29 K5 **Ovington** Hants
91 K3 **Ovington** Norfk
150 D3 **Ovington** Nthumb
28 F7 **Ower** Hants
14 E5 **Owermoigne** Dorset
115 G4 **Owlerton** Sheff
42 D7 **Owlsmoor** Br For
58 C6 **Owlswick** Bucks
117 H1 **Owmby** Lincs
117 G4 **Owmby** Lincs
29 K6 **Owslebury** Hants
124 E7 **Owston** Donc
87 L3 **Owston** Leics
116 D2 **Owston Ferry** N Linc
127 G4 **Owstwick** E R Yk
127 H5 **Owthorne** E R Yk
102 A5 **Owthorpe** Notts
91 G3 **Oxborough** Norfk
13 L3 **Oxbridge** Dorset
118 D6 **Oxcombe** Lincs
61 G3 **Oxen End** Essex
129 G3 **Oxen Park** Cumb
129 L2 **Oxenholme** Cumb
122 F4 **Oxenhope** Brad
26 C3 **Oxenpill** Somset
55 L2 **Oxenton** Gloucs
40 F8 **Oxenwood** Wilts
57 K6 **Oxford** Oxon
43 J2 **Oxhey** Herts
72 C5 **Oxhill** Warwks
84 F3 **Oxley** Wolves
61 L5 **Oxley Green** Essex
90 C6 **Oxlode** Cambs
167 L5 **Oxnam** Border
106 F7 **Oxnead** Norfk
43 J7 **Oxshott** Surrey
114 F2 **Oxspring** Barns
32 C3 **Oxted** Surrey
178 B7 **Oxton** Border
124 D2 **Oxton** N York
101 M3 **Oxton** Notts
51 G7 **Oxwich** Swans
50 F7 **Oxwich Green** Swans
221 K2 **Oykel Bridge Hotel** Highld
206 D1 **Oyne** Abers
51 H7 **Oystermouth** Swans

P

232 g2 **Pabail** W Isls
86 D1 **Packington** Leics
196 C6 **Padanaram** Angus
58 B2 **Padbury** Bucks
44 F4 **Paddington** Gt Lon
46 B7 **Paddlesworth** Kent
35 G6 **Paddlesworth** Kent
33 H4 **Paddock Wood** Kent
122 B4 **Padiham** Lancs
132 B7 **Padside** N York
4 E2 **Padstow** Cnwll
41 L7 **Padworth** W Berk
18 B6 **Pagham** W Susx
46 F2 **Paglesham** Essex
7 K4 **Paignton** Torbay
86 F6 **Pailton** Warwks
68 D5 **Painscastle** Powys
150 D3 **Painshawfield** Nthumb
134 C7 **Painsthorpe** E R Yk
55 K6 **Painswick** Gloucs
34 D3 **Painter's Forstal** Kent
174 E5 **Paisley** Rens
93 L5 **Pakefield** Suffk
77 L2 **Pakenham** Suffk
42 E5 **Paley Street** W & M
85 H4 **Palfrey** Wsall
92 D7 **Palgrave** Suffk
14 E4 **Pallington** Dorset
163 L5 **Palmerston** E Ayrs
146 E4 **Palnackie** D & G
145 J3 **Palnure** D & G
115 J7 **Palterton** Derbys
41 L8 **Pamber End** Hants
41 L8 **Pamber Green** Hants
41 L7 **Pamber Heath** Hants
55 L2 **Pamington** Gloucs
15 J3 **Pamphill** Dorset
76 C5 **Pampisford** Cambs
187 J1 **Panbride** Angus
9 H4 **Pancrasweek** Devon
53 M4 **Pandy** Mons
110 B8 **Pandy Tudur** Conwy
61 H3 **Panfield** Essex
41 M5 **Pangbourne** W Berk
19 J4 **Pangdean** W Susx
123 L1 **Pannal** N York
132 D8 **Pannal Ash** N York
205 J6 **Pannanich Wells Hotel** Abers
97 L7 **Pant** Shrops
95 H3 **Pant Glas** Gwynd
36 E4 **Pant-ffrwyth** Brdgnd
81 L8 **Pant-y-dwr** Powys
111 H8 **Pant-y-mwyn** Flints
111 G6 **Pantasaph** Flints
81 G4 **Pantglas** Powys
117 K5 **Panton** Lincs
93 H2 **Panxworth** Norfk
234 c3 **Papa Westray Airport** Ork
136 F2 **Papcastle** Cumb
231 L5 **Papigoe** Highld
178 D4 **Papple** E Loth
101 K3 **Papplewick** Notts
75 K3 **Papworth Everard** Cambs
75 J2 **Papworth St Agnes** Cambs
5 G5 **Par** Cnwll
121 G7 **Parbold** Lancs
26 E4 **Parbrook** Somset
96 D5 **Parc** Gwynd
38 B3 **Parc Seymour** Newpt
136 F3 **Pardshaw** Cumb
79 G3 **Parham** Suffk
206 E5 **Park** Abers
154 F4 **Park** D & G
149 H3 **Park** Nthumb
42 B3 **Park Corner** Oxon
34 D6 **Park Farm** Kent
17 G2 **Park Gate** Hants
123 J3 **Park Gate** Leeds
44 D4 **Park Royal** Gt Lon
59 J6 **Park Street** Herts
54 E6 **Parkend** Gloucs
33 G4 **Parkers Green** Kent
111 J6 **Parkgate** Ches
155 H4 **Parkgate** D & G
31 K3 **Parkgate** Surrey
174 E4 **Parkhall** W Duns
22 F6 **Parkham** Devon
207 G3 **Parkhill House** Abers
51 G7 **Parkmill** Swans
151 K5 **Parkside** Dur
175 L6 **Parkside** N Lans
15 J4 **Parkstone** Poole
60 C6 **Parndon** Essex
23 L3 **Parracombe** Devon
89 L2 **Parson Drove** Cambs
62 B3 **Parson's Heath** Essex
174 F5 **Partick** C Glas
113 G3 **Partington** Traffd
118 F7 **Partney** Lincs
136 D3 **Parton** Cumb
19 G2 **Partridge Green** W Susx
100 D2 **Parwich** Derbys
73 L6 **Passenham** Nhants
30 D4 **Passfield** Hants
107 G5 **Paston** Norfk
19 J4 **Patcham** Br & H
18 E4 **Patching** W Susx
38 E4 **Patchway** S Glos
132 B6 **Pateley Bridge** N York
185 M5 **Path of Condie** P & K
186 E8 **Pathhead** Fife
177 K5 **Pathhead** Mdloth
163 K7 **Patna** E Ayrs
40 B8 **Patney** Wilts
237 b5 **Patrick** IOM
132 C2 **Patrick Brompton** N York
113 H2 **Patricroft** Salfd
127 H6 **Patrington** E R Yk
127 H6 **Patrington Haven** E R Yk
35 G4 **Patrixbourne** Kent
137 L4 **Patterdale** Cumb
84 E4 **Pattingham** Staffs
73 J4 **Pattishall** Nhants
61 K3 **Pattiswick Green** Essex
2 E5 **Paul** Cnwll
28 C5 **Paul's Dene** Wilts
73 K5 **Paulerspury** Bucks
126 E5 **Paull** E R Yk
26 F1 **Paulton** BaNES
158 D3 **Pauperhaugh** Nthumb
74 E4 **Pavenham** Beds
25 L3 **Pawlett** Somset
71 L6 **Paxford** Gloucs
179 J7 **Paxton** Border
12 E3 **Payhembury** Devon
122 C1 **Paythorne** Lancs
19 L5 **Peacehaven** E Susx
114 D3 **Peak District National Park**
114 C5 **Peak Forest** Derbys
89 H3 **Peakirk** C Pete
190 E1 **Peanmeanach** Highld
31 L5 **Pease Pottage** W Susx
39 G8 **Peasedown St John** BaNES
41 J5 **Peasemore** W Berk
79 H2 **Peasenhall** Suffk
31 H3 **Peaslake** Surrey
112 D3 **Peasley Cross** St Hel
21 H2 **Peasmarsh** E Susx
187 G5 **Peat Inn** Fife
217 H2 **Peathill** Abers
87 H5 **Peatling Magna** Leics
87 H5 **Peatling Parva** Leics
77 J7 **Pebmarsh** Essex
71 K5 **Pebworth** Worcs
122 E5 **Pecket Well** Calder
98 D2 **Peckforton** Ches
45 G5 **Peckham** Gt Lon
86 F4 **Peckleton** Leics
34 F7 **Pedlinge** Kent
85 G6 **Pedmore** Dudley
26 B4 **Pedwell** Somset
166 C2 **Peebles** Border
237 b4 **Peel** IOM
35 G6 **Peene** Kent
59 J2 **Pegsdon** Beds
159 G5 **Pegswood** Nthumb
35 K2 **Pegwell** Kent
209 H7 **Peinchorran** Highld
208 F3 **Peinlich** Highld
62 B5 **Peldon** Essex
85 H3 **Pelsall** Wsall
151 G4 **Pelton** Dur
5 K5 **Pelynt** Cnwll
51 G5 **Pemberton** Carmth
112 D2 **Pemberton** Wigan
50 E5 **Pembrey** Carmth
69 H3 **Pembridge** Herefs
49 G7 **Pembroke** Pembks
49 G6 **Pembroke Dock** Pembks
48 E4 **Pembrokeshire Coast National Park** Pembks
33 G5 **Pembury** Kent
51 L4 **Pen Rhiwfawr** Neath
80 F6 **Pen-bont Rhydybeddau** Cerdgn
49 J3 **Pen-ffordd** Pembks
65 H6 **Pen-rhiw** Pembks
54 D6 **Pen-twyn** Mons
97 K7 **Pen-y-bont** Powys
97 G7 **Pen-y-bont-fawr** Powys
65 G6 **Pen-y-bryn** Pembks
54 C6 **Pen-y-clawdd** Mons
37 G3 **Pen-y-coedcae** Rhondd
48 E3 **Pen-y-cwn** Pembks
111 G7 **Pen-y-felin** Flints
97 H7 **Pen-y-Garnedd** Powys
94 D5 **Pen-y-graig** Gwynd
97 J3 **Pen-y-stryt** Denbgs
54 D6 **Penallt** Mons
49 J7 **Penally** Pembks
54 E3 **Penalt** Herefs
37 J6 **Penarth** V Glam
65 J4 **Penbryn** Cerdgn

66 B7 **Pencader** Carmth
177 L5 **Pencaitland** E Loth
108 D6 **Pencarnisiog** IOA
66 C5 **Pencarreg** Carmth
53 H3 **Pencelli** Powys
51 G6 **Penclawdd** Swans
36 E4 **Pencoed** Brdgnd
69 L4 **Pencombe** Herefs
54 E4 **Pencraig** Herefs
97 G6 **Pencraig** Powys
2 C4 **Pendeen** Cnwll
52 E6 **Penderyn** Rhondd
50 B4 **Pendine** Carmth
113 H2 **Pendlebury** Salfd
121 L3 **Pendleton** Lancs
55 H2 **Pendock** Worcs
8 D8 **Pendoggett** Cnwll
13 M1 **Pendomer** Somset
37 G5 **Pendoylan** V Glam
81 G4 **Penegoes** Powys
37 J2 **Pengam** Caerph
37 K5 **Pengam** Cardif
45 G6 **Penge** Gt Lon
8 E7 **Pengelly** Cnwll
4 F6 **Pengrugla** Cnwll
3 K2 **Penhallow** Cnwll
3 J4 **Penhalvean** Cnwll
40 D3 **Penhill** Swindn
38 B3 **Penhow** Newpt
177 H6 **Penicuik** Mdloth
209 G6 **Penifiler** Highld
161 J4 **Peninver** Ag & B
114 E2 **Penistone** Barns
152 F3 **Penkill** S Ayrs
85 G2 **Penkridge** Staffs
9 G5 **Penlean** Cnwll
98 B4 **Penley** Wrexhm
36 F5 **Penllyn** V Glam
96 C3 **Penmachno** Conwy
37 J2 **Penmaen** Caerph
51 G7 **Penmaen** Swans
109 K6 **Penmaenmawr** Conwy
95 M8 **Penmaenpool** Gwynd
37 G6 **Penmark** V Glam
95 J4 **Penmorfa** Gwynd
109 G6 **Penmynydd** IOA
42 F2 **Penn** Bucks
42 F2 **Penn Street** Bucks
80 F4 **Pennal** Gwynd
216 F2 **Pennan** Abers
81 J4 **Pennant** Powys
83 G4 **Pennerley** Shrops
122 E4 **Pennines**
128 F4 **Pennington** Cumb
53 H3 **Pennorth** Powys
129 G3 **Penny Bridge** Cumb
104 B6 **Penny Hill** Lincs
181 G3 **Pennycross** Ag & B
181 H3 **Pennyghael** Ag & B
163 H7 **Pennyglen** S Ayrs
11 K3 **Pennymoor** Devon
65 H5 **Penparc** Cerdgn
53 L6 **Penperlleni** Mons
5 J5 **Penpoll** Cnwll
3 H4 **Penponds** Cnwll
154 E4 **Penpont** D & G
65 K5 **Penrhiw-pal** Cerdgn
37 G2 **Penrhiwceiber** Rhondd
65 K6 **Penrhiwllan** Cerdgn
94 F5 **Penrhos** Gwynd
54 B5 **Penrhos** Mons
110 A5 **Penrhyn Bay** Conwy
109 H6 Penrhyn Castle Gwynd
95 K5 **Penrhyndeudraeth** Gwynd
50 F7 **Penrice** Swans
161 L1 **Penrioch** N Ayrs
138 D2 **Penrith** Cumb
4 D2 **Penrose** Cnwll
138 B2 **Penruddock** Cumb
3 K4 **Penryn** Cnwll
50 E2 **Pensarn** Carmth
110 C5 **Pensarn** Conwy
70 C2 **Pensax** Worcs
27 H5 **Penselwood** Somset
38 F7 **Pensford** BaNES
71 G5 **Pensham** Worcs
151 H4 **Penshaw** Sundld
32 F4 **Penshurst** Kent
5 L2 **Pensilva** Cnwll
4 F6 **Pentewan** Cnwll
109 H7 **Pentir** Gwynd
4 C4 **Pentire** Cnwll
77 J5 **Pentlow** Essex
91 G2 **Pentney** Norfk
29 G3 **Penton Mewsey** Hants
156 D6 **Pentonbridge** Cumb
109 G5 **Pentraeth** IOA
36 F2 **Pentre** Rhondd
98 A8 **Pentre** Shrops
108 F6 **Pentre Berw** IOA
83 G7 **Pentre Hodrey** Shrops
110 F8 **Pentre Llanrhaeadr** Denbgs
36 E5 **Pentre Meyrick** V Glam
52 E2 **Pentre-bach** Powys
97 J2 **Pentre-celyn** Denbgs
81 J3 **Pentre-celyn** Powys
51 J6 **Pentre-chwyth** Swans
65 L6 **Pentre-cwrt** Carmth
51 H3 **Pentre-Gwenlais** Carmth
96 C1 **Pentre-tafarn-y-fedw** Conwy
53 G7 **Pentrebach** Myr Td
97 J3 **Pentredwr** Denbgs
95 J5 **Pentrefelin** Gwynd
96 D3 **Pentrefoelas** Conwy
65 K4 **Pentregat** Cerdgn
101 G3 **Pentrich** Derbys
28 B7 **Pentridge Hill** Dorset
37 J2 **Pentwynmaur** Caerph
37 H4 **Pentyrch** Cardif
5 G5 **Penwithick** Cnwll
51 H2 **Penybanc** Carmth
68 C2 **Penybont** Powys
97 L4 **Penycae** Wrexhm
97 L1 **Penyffordd** Flints
36 F3 **Penygraig** Rhondd
51 H3 **Penygroes** Carmth
95 H2 **Penygroes** Gwynd
108 F4 **Penysarn** IOA
52 F6 **Penywaun** Rhondd
2 E5 **Penzance** Cnwll
2 E5 Penzance Heliport Cnwll
71 G4 **Peopleton** Worcs
98 F7 **Peplow** Shrops
163 J2 **Perceton** N Ayrs
206 B6 **Percie** Abers
217 H2 **Percyhorner** Abers
236 b3 **Perelle** Guern
24 E3 **Periton** Somset
44 D4 **Perivale** Gt Lon
12 D4 **Perkins Village** Devon
115 M7 **Perlethorpe** Notts
3 K4 **Perranarworthal** Cnwll
3 K1 **Perranporth** Cnwll
2 F5 **Perranuthnoe** Cnwll
3 K4 **Perranwell** Cnwll
3 K2 **Perranzabuloe** Cnwll
85 J5 **Perry Barr** Birm
39 L3 **Perry Green** Wilts
99 J6 **Pershall** Staffs
71 G5 **Pershore** Worcs
74 F2 **Pertenhall** Beds
186 B3 **Perth** P & K
98 A5 **Perthy** Shrops
69 L6 **Perton** Herefs
84 F4 **Perton** Staffs
6 D1 **Peter Tavy** Devon
59 J4 **Peter's Green** Herts
89 H4 **Peterborough** C Pete
69 G6 **Peterchurch** Herefs
206 F5 **Peterculter** C Aber
217 L5 **Peterhead** Abers
151 K6 **Peterlee** Dur
10 C3 **Peters Marland** Devon
30 C6 **Petersfield** Hants
44 D5 **Petersham** Gt Lon
37 G5 **Peterston-super-Ely** V Glam
37 K4 **Peterstone Wentlooge** Newpt
54 E3 **Peterstow** Herefs
34 F4 **Petham** Kent
9 H6 **Petherwin Gate** Cnwll
10 D3 **Petrockstow** Devon
21 H3 **Pett** E Susx
78 E3 **Pettaugh** Suffk
196 C7 **Petterden** Angus
165 J2 **Pettinain** S Lans
79 G4 **Pettistree** Suffk
24 F6 **Petton** Devon
45 J6 **Petts Wood** Gt Lon
177 H2 **Pettycur** Fife
207 G1 **Pettymuk** Abers
31 G6 **Petworth** W Susx
20 D5 **Pevensey** E Susx
40 D7 **Pewsey** Wilts
71 G3 **Phepson** Worcs
22 D6 **Philham** Devon
166 F4 **Philiphaugh** Border
2 F4 **Phillack** Cnwll
4 D7 **Philleigh** Cnwll
176 E3 **Philpstoun** W Loth
30 C1 **Phoenix Green** Hants
203 G6 **Phoines** Highld
26 C6 **Pibsbury** Somset
136 E3 **Pica** Cumb
115 K1 **Pickburn** Donc
134 C3 **Pickering** N York
86 C6 **Pickford** Covtry
132 E3 **Pickhill** N York
83 J4 **Picklescott** Shrops
113 G6 **Pickmere** Ches
25 J5 **Pickney** Somset
121 K6 **Pickup Bank** Bl w D
87 L2 **Pickwell** Leics
88 E2 **Pickworth** Lincs
103 H5 **Pickworth** Lincs
206 E3 **Pictillum** Abers
112 B7 **Picton** Ches
141 K5 **Picton** N York
19 L5 **Piddinghoe** E Susx
74 B4 **Piddington** M Keyn
57 M5 **Piddington** Oxon
14 D3 **Piddlehinton** Dorset
14 D3 **Piddletrenthide** Dorset
89 K7 **Pidley** Cambs
140 F4 **Piercebridge** Darltn
234 c3 **Pierowall** Ork
45 L2 **Pilgrims Hatch** Essex
116 E3 **Pilham** Lincs
6 A3 **Pillaton** Cnwll
72 C5 **Pillerton Hersey** Warwks
72 C5 **Pillerton Priors** Warwks
115 G2 **Pilley** Barns
16 D3 **Pilley** Hants
120 E2 **Pilling** Lancs
38 D4 **Pilning** S Glos
114 C8 **Pilsbury** Derbys
13 K3 **Pilsdon** Dorset
114 E7 **Pilsley** Derbys
101 H1 **Pilsley** Derbys
93 H2 **Pilson Green** Norfk
19 L2 **Piltdown** E Susx
23 J5 **Pilton** Devon
88 E6 **Pilton** Nhants
88 D3 **Pilton** Rutlnd
26 E3 **Pilton** Somset
15 G1 **Pimperne** Dorset
59 L3 **Pin Green** Herts
103 L7 **Pinchbeck** Lincs
12 C4 **Pinhoe** Devon
72 B2 **Pinley Green** Warwks
152 E4 **Pinminnoch** S Ayrs
152 E4 **Pinmore** S Ayrs
12 E5 **Pinn** Devon
43 J3 **Pinner** Gt Lon
43 J3 **Pinner Green** Gt Lon
71 G5 **Pinvin** Worcs
152 E5 **Pinwherry** S Ayrs
101 J2 **Pinxton** Derbys
69 K5 **Pipe and Lyde** Herefs
99 G4 **Pipe Gate** Shrops
213 K4 **Piperhill** Highld
88 B6 **Pipewell** Nhants
30 F1 **Pirbright** Surrey
167 K4 **Pirnie** Border
161 L1 **Pirnmill** N Ayrs
59 J2 **Pirton** Herts
70 F5 **Pirton** Worcs
42 B3 **Pishill** Oxon
94 F4 **Pistyll** Gwynd
194 C3 **Pitagowan** P & K
217 J2 **Pitblae** Abers
185 M3 **Pitcairngreen** P & K
223 H6 **Pitcalnie** Highld
206 D1 **Pitcaple** Abers
196 B4 **Pitcarity** Angus
58 C7 **Pitch Green** Bucks
30 E4 **Pitch Place** Surrey
55 J6 **Pitchcombe** Gloucs
58 C4 **Pitchcott** Bucks
83 K3 **Pitchford** Shrops
214 E6 **Pitchroy** Moray
26 F5 **Pitcombe** Somset
178 E4 **Pitcox** E Loth
206 D3 **Pitfichie** Abers
216 D5 **Pitglassie** Abers
223 H3 **Pitgrudy** Highld
196 E5 **Pitkennedy** Angus
186 E5 **Pitlessie** Fife
194 E5 **Pitlochry** P & K
216 C8 **Pitmachie** Abers
203 H5 **Pitmain** Highld
217 G8 **Pitmedden** Abers
217 G8 Pitmedden Garden Abers
25 K7 **Pitminster** Somset
196 F6 **Pitmuies** Angus
206 C3 **Pitmunie** Abers
26 C5 **Pitney** Somset
186 C3 **Pitroddie** P & K
187 G5 **Pitscottie** Fife
46 C3 **Pitsea** Essex
73 L2 **Pitsford** Nhants
58 F5 **Pitstone** Bucks
25 G7 **Pitt** Devon
197 H2 **Pittarrow** Abers
187 J6 **Pittenweem** Fife
186 D7 **Pitteuchar** Fife
151 H6 **Pittington** Dur
206 D1 **Pittodrie House Hotel** Abers
28 E5 **Pitton** Wilts
217 H2 **Pittulie** Abers
151 G5 **Pity Me** Dur
31 K2 **Pixham** Surrey
175 L5 **Plains** N Lans
83 K4 **Plaish** Shrops
101 G2 **Plaistow** Derbys

45 H4 **Plaistow** Gt Lon
31 G5 **Plaistow** W Susx
28 F7 **Plaitford** Hants
108 C6 **Plas Cymyran** IOA
33 G2 **Platt** Kent
151 G5 **Plawsworth** Dur
33 G3 **Plaxtol** Kent
42 C5 **Play Hatch** Oxon
21 H2 **Playden** E Susx
78 F5 **Playford** Suffk
55 H2 **Playley Green** Gloucs
83 H3 **Plealey** Shrops
175 L2 **Plean** Stirlg
186 D5 **Pleasance** Fife
121 J5 **Pleasington** Bl w D
115 J8 **Pleasley** Derbys
236 d2 **Pleinheaume** Guern
236 a5 **Plemont** Jersey
112 C7 **Plemstall** Ches
61 G5 **Pleshey** Essex
210 C7 **Plockton** Highld
83 H6 **Plowden** Shrops
83 G3 **Plox Green** Shrops
34 B5 **Pluckley** Kent
34 B5 **Pluckley Thorne** Kent
147 K6 **Plumbland** Cumb
113 G6 **Plumley** Ches
148 E7 **Plumpton** Cumb
19 K3 **Plumpton** E Susx
73 H5 **Plumpton** Nhants
19 K3 **Plumpton Green** E Susx
45 J4 **Plumstead** Gt Lon
106 D5 **Plumstead** Norfk
101 L6 **Plumtree** Notts
102 C5 **Plungar** Leics
34 C7 **Plurenden** Kent
14 D3 **Plush** Dorset
65 K4 **Plwmp** Cerdgn
6 C5 **Plymouth** C Plym
6 D4 **Plymouth Airport** C Plym
6 D5 **Plympton** C Plym
6 D5 **Plymstock** C Plym
12 D2 **Plymtree** Devon
133 K3 **Pockley** N York
125 J2 **Pocklington** E R Yk
26 D6 **Podimore** Somset
74 D3 **Podington** Beds
99 H5 **Podmore** Staffs
103 J6 **Pointon** Lincs
15 L4 **Pokesdown** Bmouth
224 B6 **Polbain** Highld
6 A4 **Polbathic** Cnwll
176 D5 **Polbeth** W Loth
3 H5 **Poldark Mine** Cnwll
88 F6 **Polebrook** Nhants
20 C5 **Polegate** E Susx
86 C3 **Polesworth** Warwks
224 C6 **Polglass** Highld
4 F5 **Polgooth** Cnwll
154 C2 **Polgown** D & G
18 E5 **Poling** W Susx
18 E4 **Poling Corner** W Susx
5 H5 **Polkerris** Cnwll
124 F6 **Pollington** E R Yk
190 F3 **Polloch** Highld
175 G6 **Pollokshaws** C Glas
175 G5 **Pollokshields** C Glas
4 F6 **Polmassick** Cnwll
176 C3 **Polmont** Falk
200 B8 **Polnish** Highld
5 K5 **Polperro** Cnwll
5 H5 **Polruan** Cnwll
78 B6 **Polstead** Suffk
182 B7 **Poltalloch** Ag & B
12 C3 **Poltimore** Devon
177 J5 **Polton** Mdloth
178 F7 **Polwarth** Border
9 H7 **Polyphant** Cnwll
4 E1 **Polzeath** Cnwll
177 H6 **Pomathorn** Mdloth
45 G2 **Ponders End** Gt Lon
89 J5 **Pondersbridge** Cambs
3 K4 **Ponsanooth** Cnwll
7 G2 **Ponsworthy** Devon
82 C2 **Pont Robert** Powys
51 G2 **Pont-ar-gothi** Carmth
67 L7 **Pont-faen** Powys
52 D6 **Pont-Nedd-Fechan** Neath
36 C2 **Pont-rhyd-y-fen** Neath
96 B2 **Pont-y-pant** Conwy
236 e8 **Pontac** Jersey
50 F3 **Pontantwn** Carmth
51 K5 **Pontardawe** Neath
51 H5 **Pontarddulais** Swans
66 B8 **Pontarsais** Carmth
97 L1 **Pontblyddyn** Flints
124 C6 **Pontefract** Wakefd
158 F7 **Ponteland** Nthumb
81 G7 **Ponterwyd** Cerdgn
83 H3 **Pontesbury** Shrops
83 H3 **Pontesford** Shrops
97 K5 **Pontfadog** Wrexhm
64 E7 **Pontfaen** Pembks
65 K4 **Pontgarreg** Cerdgn
50 F4 **Ponthenry** Carmth
37 M2 **Ponthir** Torfn
65 J5 **Ponthirwaun** Cerdgn
37 J2 **Pontllanfraith** Caerph
51 H5 **Pontlliw** Swans
95 G3 **Pontlyfni** Gwynd
37 L2 **Pontnewydd** Torfn
150 E4 **Pontop** Dur
67 G2 **Pontrhydfendigaid** Cerdgn
81 G8 **Pontrhydygroes** Cerdgn
54 B3 **Pontrilas** Herefs
20 D3 **Ponts Green** E Susx
66 B5 **Pontshaen** Cerdgn
54 F4 **Pontshill** Herefs
53 G5 **Pontsticill** Powys
65 L6 **Pontwelly** Carmth
50 F4 **Pontyates** Carmth
51 G4 **Pontyberem** Carmth
97 L2 **Pontybodkin** Flints
37 G4 **Pontyclun** Rhondd
36 D3 **Pontycymer** Brdgnd
53 L7 **Pontypool** Torfn
37 G3 **Pontypridd** Rhondd
37 K2 **Pontywaun** Caerph
3 H3 **Pool** Cnwll
123 J2 **Pool** Leeds
185 L7 **Pool of Muckhart** Clacks
77 H6 **Pool Street** Essex
15 J4 **Poole** Poole
39 M2 **Poole Keynes** Gloucs
219 K5 **Poolewe** Highld
138 C3 **Pooley Bridge** Cumb
99 K1 **Poolfold** Staffs
55 G3 **Poolhill** Gloucs
45 G4 **Poplar** Gt Lon
16 F4 **Porchfield** IOW
92 F3 **Poringland** Norfk
3 J5 **Porkellis** Cnwll
24 D3 **Porlock** Somset
24 D2 **Porlock Weir** Somset
191 H7 **Port Appin** Ag & B
171 H5 **Port Askaig** Ag & B
173 J5 **Port Bannatyne** Ag & B
147 M3 **Port Carlisle** Cumb
170 E6 **Port Charlotte** Ag & B
173 G4 **Port Driseach** Ag & B
50 F7 **Port Einon** Swans
160 C1 **Port Ellen** Ag & B
206 E2 **Port Elphinstone** Abers
237 a6 **Port Erin** IOM
8 D8 **Port Gaverne** Cnwll
174 C4 **Port Glasgow** Inver
219 H6 **Port Henderson** Highld
8 D8 **Port Isaac** Cnwll
144 D6 **Port Logan** D & G
189 K1 **Port Mor** Highld
232 g2 **Port nan Giuran** W Isls
232 c5 **Port nan Long** W Isls
232 g1 **Port Nis** W Isls
184 D6 **Port of Menteith** Stirlg
232 g1 **Port of Ness** W Isls
8 C8 **Port Quin** Cnwll
191 H7 **Port Ramsay** Ag & B
237 c6 **Port Soderick** IOM
237 b7 **Port St Mary** IOM
111 K5 **Port Sunlight** Wirral
36 B3 **Port Talbot** Neath
170 D7 **Port Wemyss** Ag & B
145 H6 **Port William** D & G
210 B7 **Port-an-Eorna** Highld
172 C6 **Portachoillan** Ag & B
172 F4 **Portavadie** Ag & B
38 D5 **Portbury** N Som
17 H2 **Portchester** Hants
152 B7 **Portencalzie** D & G
173 K8 **Portencross** N Ayrs
14 B5 **Portesham** Dorset
215 K2 **Portessie** Moray
48 F4 **Portfield Gate** Pembks
10 B7 **Portgate** Devon
215 J2 **Portgordon** Moray
227 H5 **Portgower** Highld
4 C4 **Porth** Cnwll
36 F3 **Porth** Rhondd
3 K5 **Porth Navas** Cnwll
3 K6 **Porthallow** Cnwll
5 K5 **Porthallow** Cnwll
36 C5 **Porthcawl** Brdgnd
4 D2 **Porthcothan** Cnwll
2 C6 **Porthcurno** Cnwll
64 A7 **Porthgain** Pembks
2 C6 **Porthgwarra** Cnwll
37 G6 **Porthkerry** V Glam
3 H6 **Porthleven** Cnwll
95 K5 **Porthmadog** Gwynd
3 K6 **Porthoustock** Cnwll
5 G5 **Porthpean** Cnwll
3 J2 **Porthtowan** Cnwll
51 G3 **Porthyrhyd** Carmth
183 J8 **Portincaple** Ag & B
236 a5 **Portinfer** Jersey
125 J4 **Portington** E R Yk
182 D5 **Portinnisherrich** Ag & B
137 H3 **Portinscale** Cumb
38 C5 **Portishead** N Som
215 K2 **Portknockie** Moray
14 D7 **Portland** Dorset
207 H6 **Portlethen** Abers
146 F4 **Portling** D & G
4 E7 **Portloe** Cnwll
223 K4 **Portmahomack** Highld
95 K5 **Portmeirion** Gwynd
4 F6 **Portmellon** Cnwll
191 H6 **Portnacroish** Ag & B
232 g2 **Portnaguran** W Isls
170 D7 **Portnahaven** Ag & B
208 E7 **Portnalong** Highld
177 J4 **Portobello** C Edin
85 G4 **Portobello** Wolves
28 D4 **Porton** Wilts
144 B4 **Portpatrick** D & G
3 H3 **Portreath** Cnwll
209 G5 **Portree** Highld
4 D8 **Portscatho** Cnwll
17 J3 **Portsea** C Port
230 C3 **Portskerra** Highld
38 D3 **Portskewett** Mons
19 H4 **Portslade** Br & H
19 H5 **Portslade-by-Sea** Br & H
144 B3 **Portslogan** D & G
17 J3 **Portsmouth** C Port
122 D5 **Portsmouth** Calder
182 F3 **Portsonachan Hotel** Ag & B
216 B2 **Portsoy** Abers
29 H8 **Portswood** C Sotn
189 K3 **Portuairk** Highld
85 J8 **Portway** Worcs
6 A5 **Portwrinkle** Cnwll
145 K7 **Portyerrock** D & G
77 H5 **Poslingford** Suffk
166 B3 **Posso** Border
10 F8 **Postbridge** Devon
58 B7 **Postcombe** Oxon
34 F6 **Postling** Kent
93 G2 **Postwick** Norfk
206 B6 **Potarch** Abers
58 F3 **Potsgrove** Beds
113 L5 **Pott Shrigley** Ches
59 G6 **Potten End** Herts
134 F4 **Potter Brompton** N York
107 J8 **Potter Heigham** Norfk
117 H7 **Potterhanworth** Lincs
117 H7 **Potterhanworth Booths** Lincs
39 M8 **Potterne** Wilts
39 M8 **Potterne Wick** Wilts
59 L7 **Potters Bar** Herts
59 J6 **Potters Crouch** Herts
87 G4 **Potters Marston** Leics
73 L6 **Potterspury** Nhants
207 H3 **Potterton** Abers
141 L6 **Potto** N York
75 J5 **Potton** Beds
9 G4 **Poughill** Cnwll
11 K3 **Poughill** Devon
15 M2 **Poulner** Hants
39 L7 **Poulshot** Wilts
56 C7 **Poulton** Gloucs
120 D3 **Poulton-le-Fylde** Lancs
20 B2 **Pound Green** E Susx
77 G4 **Pound Green** Suffk
32 B5 **Pound Hill** W Susx
51 H6 **Poundffald** Swans
57 M3 **Poundon** Bucks
7 G2 **Poundsgate** Devon
9 G5 **Poundstock** Cnwll
145 K5 **Pouton** D & G
31 L3 **Povey Cross** Surrey
168 F6 **Powburn** Nthumb
12 C5 **Powderham** Devon
13 M3 **Powerstock** Dorset
147 K2 **Powfoot** D & G
147 M4 **Powhill** Cumb
70 E4 **Powick** Worcs
185 L7 **Powmill** P & K
14 E5 **Poxwell** Dorset
43 G5 **Poyle** Slough
19 H4 **Poynings** W Susx
26 F7 **Poyntington** Dorset
113 L5 **Poynton** Ches
98 E8 **Poynton Green** Wrekin
3 G5 **Praa Sands** Cnwll
45 J7 **Pratt's Bottom** Gt Lon
3 H4 **Praze-an-Beeble** Cnwll
98 D5 **Prees** Shrops

98 E6 **Prees Green** Shrops
120 E2 **Preesall** Lancs
65 L5 **Pren-gwyn** Cerdgn
168 E6 **Prendwick** Nthumb
95 K4 **Prenteg** Gwynd
112 C3 **Prescot** Knows
25 H8 **Prescott** Devon
195 J3 **Presnerb** Angus
110 E5 **Prestatyn** Denbgs
113 K6 **Prestbury** Ches
55 L4 **Prestbury** Gloucs
69 G2 **Presteigne** Powys
26 F4 **Prestleigh** Somset
179 G6 **Preston** Border
19 J4 **Preston** Br & H
7 K2 **Preston** Devon
14 D5 **Preston** Dorset
178 D3 **Preston** E Loth
126 F4 **Preston** E R Yk
56 B7 **Preston** Gloucs
59 K3 **Preston** Herts
34 D3 **Preston** Kent
35 H3 **Preston** Kent
121 H4 **Preston** Lancs
169 H4 **Preston** Nthumb
88 C3 **Preston** Rutlnd
25 H4 **Preston** Somset
77 L4 **Preston** Suffk
7 K4 **Preston** Torbay
40 B5 **Preston** Wilts
71 L2 **Preston Bagot** Warwks
58 A3 **Preston Bissett** Bucks
25 H6 **Preston Bowyer** Somset
98 D7 **Preston Brockhurst** Shrops
112 E5 **Preston Brook** Halton
29 L3 **Preston Candover** Hants
73 H4 **Preston Capes** Nhants
71 L2 **Preston Green** Warwks
98 C8 **Preston Gubbals** Shrops
72 B4 **Preston on Stour** Warwks
112 E5 **Preston on the Hill** Halton
69 H6 **Preston on Wye** Herefs
129 L3 **Preston Patrick** Cumb
26 D7 **Preston Plucknett** Somset
84 C1 **Preston upon the Weald Moors** Wrekin
69 L5 **Preston Wynne** Herefs
131 K2 **Preston-under-Scar** N York
177 K4 **Prestonpans** E Loth
113 J1 **Prestwich** Bury
163 J4 **Prestwick** S Ayrs
163 J4 **Prestwick Airport** S Ayrs
58 E7 **Prestwood** Bucks
90 E6 **Prickwillow** Cambs
26 D2 **Priddy** Somset
129 L5 **Priest Hutton** Lancs
164 B2 **Priestland** E Ayrs
82 F4 **Priestweston** Shrops
179 G6 **Primrosehill** Border
168 B4 **Primsidemill** Border
58 D7 **Princes Risborough** Bucks
72 E1 **Princethorpe** Warwks
6 E2 **Princetown** Devon
72 F4 **Priors Hardwick** Warwks
72 F3 **Priors Marston** Warwks
55 K3 **Priors Norton** Gloucs
40 C3 **Priory Vale** Swindn
39 G7 **Priston** BaNES
46 E3 **Prittlewell** Sthend
30 B6 **Privett** Hants
4 E6 **Probus** Cnwll
178 C3 **Prora** E Loth
147 K6 **Prospect** Cumb
3 H5 **Prospidnick** Cnwll
216 F2 **Protstonhill** Abers
150 D3 **Prudhoe** Nthumb
38 F7 **Publow** BaNES
60 C4 **Puckeridge** Herts
26 B7 **Puckington** Somset
39 G5 **Pucklechurch** S Glos
111 K6 **Puddington** Ches
11 J3 **Puddington** Devon
14 E4 **Puddletown** Dorset
123 J4 **Pudsey** Leeds
18 E3 **Pulborough** W Susx
98 A2 **Pulford** Ches
14 D2 **Pulham** Dorset
92 E6 **Pulham Market** Norfk
92 E6 **Pulham St Mary** Norfk
74 F7 **Pulloxhill** Beds
176 E4 **Pumpherston** W Loth
66 E6 **Pumsaint** Carmth
49 G2 **Puncheston** Pembks
14 A5 **Puncknowle** Dorset
20 C2 **Punnett's Town** E Susx
17 J2 **Purbrook** Hants
45 K4 **Purfleet** Thurr
25 L3 **Puriton** Somset
61 K7 **Purleigh** Essex
44 F7 **Purley** Gt Lon
42 A5 **Purley** W Berk
27 G7 **Purse Caundle** Dorset
13 K2 **Purtington** Somset
55 G7 **Purton** Gloucs
54 F6 **Purton** Gloucs
40 C3 **Purton** Wilts
40 C3 **Purton Stoke** Wilts
73 K5 **Pury End** Nhants
41 G2 **Pusey** Oxon
70 B6 **Putley** Herefs
70 B6 **Putley Green** Herefs
55 H6 **Putloe** Gloucs
44 E5 **Putney** Gt Lon
236 d3 **Putron Village** Guern
30 F2 **Puttenham** Surrey
73 L6 **Puxley** Nhants
38 B7 **Puxton** N Som
50 F5 **Pwll** Carmth
50 C3 **Pwll Trap** Carmth
97 H2 **Pwll-glas** Denbgs
36 C2 **Pwll-y-glaw** Neath
68 B7 **Pwllgloyw** Powys
94 F5 **Pwllheli** Gwynd
38 D2 **Pwllmeyric** Mons
101 H3 **Pye Bridge** Derbys
19 J3 **Pyecombe** W Susx
36 C4 **Pyle** Brdgnd
25 H5 **Pyleigh** Somset
26 E4 **Pylle** Somset
90 C6 **Pymoor** Cambs
13 L4 **Pymore** Dorset
43 H8 **Pyrford** Surrey
42 B2 **Pyrton** Oxon
88 C8 **Pytchley** Nhants
9 J4 **Pyworthy** Devon

Q

103 L6 **Quadring** Lincs
58 C4 **Quainton** Bucks
25 J4 **Quantock Hills** Somset
28 F3 **Quarley** Hants
101 G4 **Quarndon** Derbys
174 C5 **Quarrier's Village** Inver
103 H4 **Quarrington** Lincs
151 H7 **Quarrington Hill** Dur
85 G6 **Quarry Bank** Dudley
214 E2 **Quarrywood** Moray
173 L6 **Quarter** N Ayrs
175 J7 **Quarter** S Lans
84 D5 **Quatford** Shrops
84 D6 **Quatt** Shrops
150 F6 **Quebec** Dur
55 J5 **Quedgeley** Gloucs
90 E7 **Queen Adelaide** Cambs
26 E6 **Queen Camel** Somset
38 F6 **Queen Charlton** BaNES
184 B6 **Queen Elizabeth Forest Park** Stirlg
27 H5 **Queen Oak** Dorset
33 H4 **Queen Street** Kent
17 H5 **Queen's Bower** IOW
46 E5 **Queenborough** Kent
70 F6 **Queenhill** Worcs
123 G4 **Queensbury** Brad
111 K7 **Queensferry** Flints
175 H5 **Queenslie** C Glas
175 J3 **Queenzieburn** N Lans
60 E3 **Quendon** Essex
87 J2 **Queniborough** Leics
56 C7 **Quenington** Gloucs
85 J4 **Queslett** Birm
5 L3 **Quethiock** Cnwll
92 B6 **Quidenham** Norfk
28 C5 **Quidhampton** Wilts
73 L4 **Quinton** Nhants
4 D4 **Quintrell Downs** Cnwll
10 C8 **Quither** Devon
179 G5 **Quixwood** Border
9 K5 **Quoditch** Devon
87 H1 **Quorn** Leics
165 J2 **Quothquan** S Lans
234 c6 **Quoyburray** Ork
234 b5 **Quoyloo** Ork

R

165 L3 **Rachan Mill** Border
109 J7 **Rachub** Gwynd
24 D7 **Rackenford** Devon
18 E3 **Rackham** W Susx
93 G1 **Rackheath** Norfk
155 H7 **Racks** D & G
234 a7 **Rackwick** Ork
100 F5 **Radbourne** Derbys
113 H1 **Radcliffe** Bury
159 G2 **Radcliffe** Nthumb
101 M5 **Radcliffe on Trent** Notts
73 J7 **Radclive** Bucks
213 H3 **Raddery** Highld
187 G5 **Radernie** Fife
72 D2 **Radford Semele** Warwks
59 K7 **Radlett** Herts
57 K7 **Radley** Oxon
60 F6 **Radley Green** Essex
42 C2 **Radnage** Bucks
27 G1 **Radstock** BaNES
73 H6 **Radstone** Nhants
72 D5 **Radway** Warwks
74 E3 **Radwell** Beds
75 J7 **Radwell** Herts
76 E6 **Radwinter** Essex
37 H4 **Radyr** Cardif
214 C3 **Rafford** Moray
102 A8 **Ragdale** Leics
54 B6 **Raglan** Mons
116 D6 **Ragnall** Notts
213 J8 **Raigbeg** Highld
70 F4 **Rainbow Hill** Worcs
112 C2 **Rainford** St Hel
45 K4 **Rainham** Gt Lon
46 D6 **Rainham** Medway
112 C4 **Rainhill** St Hel
112 D4 **Rainhill Stoops** St Hel
113 L6 **Rainow** Ches
132 E4 **Rainton** N York
101 L2 **Rainworth** Notts
134 D7 **Raisthorpe** N York
186 D3 **Rait** P & K
118 D5 **Raithby** Lincs
118 E7 **Raithby** Lincs
30 D5 **Rake** W Susx
203 H5 **Ralia** Highld
208 B5 **Ramasaig** Highld
3 J4 **Rame** Cnwll
6 B6 **Rame** Cnwll
14 B3 **Rampisham** Dorset
128 F6 **Rampside** Cumb
76 B2 **Rampton** Cambs
116 D5 **Rampton** Notts
122 B6 **Ramsbottom** Bury
40 F6 **Ramsbury** Wilts
227 K3 **Ramscraigs** Highld
30 B6 **Ramsdean** Hants
41 L8 **Ramsdell** Hants
57 G5 **Ramsden** Oxon
46 B2 **Ramsden Bellhouse** Essex
89 K6 **Ramsey** Cambs
62 E2 **Ramsey** Essex
237 e3 **Ramsey** IOM
89 K6 **Ramsey Forty Foot** Cambs
89 J6 **Ramsey Heights** Cambs
61 M6 **Ramsey Island** Essex
89 K5 **Ramsey Mereside** Cambs
89 J6 **Ramsey St Mary's** Cambs
35 K2 **Ramsgate** Kent
131 L5 **Ramsgill** N York
157 J2 **Ramshope** Nthumb
100 B4 **Ramshorn** Staffs
30 F5 **Ramsnest Common** Surrey
118 B5 **Ranby** Lincs
116 A5 **Ranby** Notts
117 J5 **Rand** Lincs
55 J6 **Randwick** Gloucs
174 D5 **Ranfurly** Rens
100 D7 **Rangemore** Staffs
39 G3 **Rangeworthy** S Glos
163 L6 **Rankinston** E Ayrs
121 K5 **Rann** Bl w D
193 G5 **Rannoch Station** P & K
24 E3 **Ranscombe** Somset
116 A4 **Ranskill** Notts
99 J7 **Ranton** Staffs
99 J7 **Ranton Green** Staffs
93 H1 **Ranworth** Norfk
185 G7 **Raploch** Stirlg
234 c4 **Rapness** Ork
146 D5 **Rascarrel** D & G
173 K2 **Rashfield** Ag & B
71 G2 **Rashwood** Worcs
133 G5 **Raskelf** N York
123 H6 **Rastrick** Calder
200 E2 **Ratagan** Highld

87 G3 **Ratby** Leics
86 D4 **Ratcliffe Culey** Leics
101 J6 **Ratcliffe on Soar** Notts
87 J1 **Ratcliffe on the Wreake** Leics
217 J3 **Rathen** Abers
186 F3 **Rathillet** Fife
130 F7 **Rathmell** N York
176 F4 **Ratho** C Edin
215 K2 **Rathven** Moray
72 E5 **Ratley** Warwks
35 H4 **Ratling** Kent
83 H4 **Ratlinghope** Shrops
231 J2 **Rattar** Highld
7 H4 **Rattery** Devon
77 L3 **Rattlesden** Suffk
20 C5 **Ratton Village** E Susx
195 J7 **Rattray** P & K
88 E8 **Raunds** Nhants
115 J3 **Ravenfield** Rothm
136 F7 **Ravenglass** Cumb
93 H4 **Raveningham** Norfk
143 K6 **Ravenscar** N York
74 F4 **Ravensden** Beds
101 K2 **Ravenshead** Notts
123 J6 **Ravensthorpe** Kirk
73 J1 **Ravensthorpe** Nhants
86 E2 **Ravenstone** Leics
74 B4 **Ravenstone** M Keyn
139 G6 **Ravenstonedale** Cumb
165 H1 **Ravenstruther** S Lans
140 E5 **Ravensworth** N York
125 G6 **Rawcliffe** E R Yk
133 J8 **Rawcliffe** York
123 J3 **Rawdon** Leeds
34 B3 **Rawling Street** Kent
115 H3 **Rawmarsh** Rothm
46 C2 **Rawreth** Essex
12 F2 **Rawridge** Devon
122 B6 **Rawtenstall** Lancs
78 C6 **Raydon** Suffk
46 D2 **Rayleigh** Essex
61 H4 **Rayne** Essex
44 E6 **Raynes Park** Gt Lon
76 E2 **Reach** Cambs
122 B4 **Read** Lancs
42 B5 **Reading** Readg
34 B8 **Reading Street** Kent
35 K2 **Reading Street** Kent
138 E4 **Reagill** Cumb
223 G3 **Rearquhar** Highld
87 J2 **Rearsby** Leics
230 D3 **Reay** Highld
47 L6 **Reculver** Kent
25 H7 **Red Ball** Somset
15 K4 **Red Hill** Bmouth
71 K4 **Red Hill** Warwks
77 G1 **Red Lodge** Suffk
49 L5 **Red Roses** Carmth
159 G3 **Red Row** Nthumb
109 G5 **Red Wharf Bay** IOA
49 J6 **Redberth** Pembks
59 J5 **Redbourn** Herts
116 F2 **Redbourne** N Linc
54 D6 **Redbrook** Gloucs
98 D4 **Redbrook** Wrexhm
34 C7 **Redbrook Street** Kent
213 L5 **Redburn** Highld
142 D3 **Redcar** R & Cl
146 E2 **Redcastle** D & G
212 E4 **Redcastle** Highld
176 C3 **Redding** Falk
176 C3 **Reddingmuirhead** Falk
71 J2 **Redditch** Worcs
77 J4 **Rede** Suffk
92 F6 **Redenhall** Norfk
157 L5 **Redesmouth** Nthumb
197 J3 **Redford** Abers
196 F7 **Redford** Angus
30 E6 **Redford** W Susx
166 E6 **Redfordgreen** Border
186 A2 **Redgorton** P & K
92 C7 **Redgrave** Suffk
206 E4 **Redhill** Abers
59 M2 **Redhill** Herts
38 D7 **Redhill** N Som
32 B3 **Redhill** Surrey
93 J6 **Redisham** Suffk
38 E5 **Redland** Bristl
234 b5 **Redland** Ork
78 E1 **Redlingfield** Suffk
78 E1 **Redlingfield Green** Suffk
27 G5 **Redlynch** Somset
28 D7 **Redlynch** Wilts
70 D2 **Redmarley** Worcs
55 H2 **Redmarley D'Abitot** Gloucs
141 J3 **Redmarshall** S on T
102 D5 **Redmile** Leics
131 K2 **Redmire** N York
197 J2 **Redmyre** Abers
98 A6 **Rednal** Shrops
167 J3 **Redpath** Border
219 H7 **Redpoint** Highld
3 J3 **Redruth** Cnwll
186 C1 **Redstone** P & K
38 B4 **Redwick** Newpt
38 D3 **Redwick** S Glos
141 G3 **Redworth** Darltn
75 L7 **Reed** Herts
93 J3 **Reedham** Norfk
125 J6 **Reedness** E R Yk
117 H6 **Reepham** Lincs
106 D7 **Reepham** Norfk
140 C7 **Reeth** N York
86 C7 **Reeves Green** Solhll
224 B5 **Reiff** Highld
31 L2 **Reigate** Surrey
135 H4 **Reighton** N York
207 G2 **Reisque** Abers
231 L5 **Reiss** Highld
2 F5 **Relubbus** Cnwll
214 B5 **Relugas** Moray
42 C4 **Remenham** Wokham
42 C4 **Remenham Hill** Wokham
101 L7 **Rempstone** Notts
56 A6 **Rendcomb** Gloucs
79 H2 **Rendham** Suffk
174 F5 **Renfrew** Rens
74 F4 **Renhold** Beds
115 J6 **Renishaw** Derbys
169 J5 **Rennington** Nthumb
174 D3 **Renton** W Duns
149 G6 **Renwick** Cumb
93 J1 **Repps** Norfk
100 F6 **Repton** Derbys
213 H5 **Resaurie** Highld
4 F7 **Rescassa** Cnwll
190 E4 **Resipole** Highld
3 H3 **Reskadinnick** Cnwll
213 G2 **Resolis** Highld
52 C7 **Resolven** Neath
183 J6 **Rest and be thankful** Ag & B
179 H6 **Reston** Border
196 E6 **Reswallie** Angus
116 B5 **Retford** Notts
61 J7 **Rettendon** Essex
103 M1 **Revesby** Lincs
16 F4 **Rew Street** IOW
12 B3 **Rewe** Devon
93 K7 **Reydon** Suffk
92 B3 **Reymerston** Norfk
49 J5 **Reynalton** Pembks
50 F7 **Reynoldston** Swans
6 A1 **Rezare** Cnwll
67 H5 **Rhandirmwyn** Carmth
67 L2 **Rhayader** Powys
212 D5 **Rheindown** Highld
111 G7 **Rhes-y-cae** Flints
97 H1 **Rhewl** Denbgs
97 J4 **Rhewl** Denbgs
224 D4 **Rhicarn** Highld
228 C5 **Rhiconich** Highld
222 F6 **Rhicullen** Highld
52 E6 **Rhigos** Rhondd
220 D3 **Rhireavach** Highld
223 H2 **Rhives** Highld
37 J4 **Rhiwbina** Cardif
37 K3 **Rhiwderyn** Newpt
109 H7 **Rhiwlas** Gwynd
33 H4 **Rhoden Green** Kent
34 F6 **Rhodes Minnis** Kent
48 C3 **Rhodiad-y-brenin** Pembks
146 C3 **Rhonehouse** D & G
37 G6 **Rhoose** V Glam
65 L7 **Rhos** Carmth
51 L5 **Rhos** Neath
110 B5 **Rhos-on-Sea** Conwy
96 E5 **Rhos-y-gwaliau** Gwynd
108 E3 **Rhosbeirio** IOA
108 C6 **Rhoscolyn** IOA
48 F6 **Rhoscrowther** Pembks
111 H7 **Rhosesmor** Flints
68 D5 **Rhosgoch** Powys
65 H6 **Rhoshill** Pembks
94 D6 **Rhoshirwaun** Gwynd
80 D3 **Rhoslefain** Gwynd
97 L3 **Rhosllanerchrugog** Wrexhm
108 F6 **Rhosmeirch** IOA
108 D6 **Rhosneigr** IOA
50 E7 **Rhossili** Swans
95 H2 **Rhostryfan** Gwynd
97 L3 **Rhostyllen** Wrexhm
108 F4 **Rhosybol** IOA
97 L4 **Rhosymedre** Wrexhm
174 B2 **Rhu** Ag & B
110 F6 **Rhuallt** Denbgs
173 H4 **Rhubodach** Ag & B
110 E6 **Rhuddlan** Denbgs
172 C8 **Rhunahaorine** Ag & B
95 L4 **Rhyd** Gwynd
95 K3 **Rhyd-Ddu** Gwynd
96 D5 **Rhyd-uchaf** Gwynd
80 E6 **Rhyd-y pennau** Cerdgn
94 F5 **Rhyd-y-clafdy** Gwynd
110 C6 **Rhyd-y-foel** Conwy
109 H7 **Rhyd-y-groes** Gwynd
50 F1 **Rhydargaeau** Carmth
66 D6 **Rhydcymerau** Carmth
65 K5 **Rhydlewis** Cerdgn
66 B5 **Rhydowen** Cerdgn
51 K4 **Rhydyfro** Neath
110 D5 **Rhyl** Denbgs
53 H6 **Rhymney** Caerph
186 B4 **Rhynd** P & K
215 L8 **Rhynie** Abers
223 J5 **Rhynie** Highld
84 D8 **Ribbesford** Worcs
121 H4 **Ribbleton** Lancs
121 J4 **Ribchester** Lancs
126 F8 **Riby** Lincs
124 F3 **Riccall** N York
156 F3 **Riccarton** Border
163 K3 **Riccarton** E Ayrs
69 J1 **Richards Castle** Herefs
44 D5 **Richmond** Gt Lon
140 F6 **Richmond** N York
115 H4 **Richmond** Sheff
236 b3 **Richmond Fort** Guern
99 L7 **Rickerscote** Staffs
38 C8 **Rickford** N Som
7 H7 **Rickham** Devon
92 C7 **Rickinghall** Suffk
60 D2 **Rickling** Essex
60 E3 **Rickling Green** Essex
43 H2 **Rickmansworth** Herts
167 H4 **Riddell** Border
10 F3 **Riddlecombe** Devon
123 G3 **Riddlesden** Brad
15 H5 **Ridge** Dorset
59 K7 **Ridge** Herts
27 L5 **Ridge** Wilts
86 C4 **Ridge Lane** Warwks
38 D7 **Ridgehill** N Som
115 H5 **Ridgeway** Derbys
77 G6 **Ridgewell** Essex
19 M2 **Ridgewood** E Susx
74 E7 **Ridgmont** Beds
150 C3 **Riding Mill** Nthumb
107 H6 **Ridlington** Norfk
88 B3 **Ridlington** Rutlnd
158 A5 **Ridsdale** Nthumb
133 J3 **Rievaulx** N York
133 J3 **Rievaulx Abbey** N York
148 B2 **Rigg** D & G
175 K4 **Riggend** N Lans
213 K4 **Righoul** Highld
118 F6 **Rigsby** Lincs
165 G3 **Rigside** S Lans
121 J5 **Riley Green** Lancs
5 L2 **Rilla Mill** Cnwll
134 D5 **Rillington** N York
122 B2 **Rimington** Lancs
26 E6 **Rimpton** Somset
127 H5 **Rimswell** E R Yk
49 G3 **Rinaston** Pembks
84 D4 **Rindleford** Shrops
146 C4 **Ringford** D & G
92 D2 **Ringland** Norfk
19 L3 **Ringmer** E Susx
6 F6 **Ringmore** Devon
7 L2 **Ringmore** Devon
215 G5 **Ringorm** Moray
93 J5 **Ringsfield** Suffk
93 J6 **Ringsfield Corner** Suffk
59 G5 **Ringshall** Bucks
78 C4 **Ringshall** Suffk
78 C4 **Ringshall Stocks** Suffk
88 E7 **Ringstead** Nhants
105 H4 **Ringstead** Norfk
15 L2 **Ringwood** Hants
35 K5 **Ringwould** Kent
20 B4 **Ripe** E Susx
101 H3 **Ripley** Derbys
15 M3 **Ripley** Hants
132 D7 **Ripley** N York
31 H1 **Ripley** Surrey
30 A6 **Riplington** Hants
132 D5 **Ripon** N York
103 H6 **Rippingale** Lincs
35 J5 **Ripple** Kent
70 F6 **Ripple** Worcs
122 F6 **Ripponden** Calder
160 B2 **Risabus** Ag & B
69 K4 **Risbury** Herefs
77 H2 **Risby** Suffk
37 K3 **Risca** Caerph
126 E3 **Rise** E R Yk
103 K6 **Risegate** Lincs
74 F3 **Riseley** Beds
42 B7 **Riseley** Wokham
78 E2 **Rishangles** Suffk
121 L4 **Rishton** Lancs
122 F6 **Rishworth** Calder
101 J5 **Risley** Derbys
112 F3 **Risley** Warrtn
132 C5 **Risplith** N York
35 J6 **River** Kent
30 F6 **River** W Susx

212 E4 **Riverford** Highld
32 F3 **Riverhead** Kent
121 J7 **Rivington** Lancs
73 L4 **Roade** Nhants
176 B7 **Roadmeetings** S Lans
164 B5 **Roadside** E Ayrs
231 H4 **Roadside** Highld
25 G4 **Roadwater** Somset
208 D5 **Roag** Highld
153 G2 **Roan of Craigoch** S Ayrs
60 D2 **Roast Green** Essex
37 J5 **Roath** Cardif
166 F6 **Roberton** Border
165 H4 **Roberton** S Lans
20 E2 **Robertsbridge** E Susx
123 J6 **Roberttown** Kirk
49 J4 **Robeston Wathen** Pembks
155 M7 **Robgill Tower** D & G
143 K6 **Robin Hood's Bay** N York
10 E2 **Roborough** Devon
6 D4 **Roborough** Devon
112 B4 **Roby** Knows
100 C5 **Rocester** Staffs
48 E3 **Roch** Pembks
122 D7 **Rochdale** Rochdl
4 F4 **Roche** Cnwll
46 C6 **Rochester** Medway
157 L3 **Rochester** Nthumb
46 E3 **Rochford** Essex
70 B2 **Rochford** Worcs
4 E2 **Rock** Cnwll
169 J5 **Rock** Nthumb
70 D1 **Rock** Worcs
111 K4 **Rock Ferry** Wirral
12 C4 **Rockbeare** Devon
28 C7 **Rockbourne** Hants
148 C3 **Rockcliffe** Cumb
146 E4 **Rockcliffe** D & G
7 L4 **Rockend** Torbay
223 K5 **Rockfield** Highld
54 C5 **Rockfield** Mons
24 B2 **Rockford** Devon
38 F2 **Rockhampton** S Glos
82 F7 **Rockhill** Shrops
88 C5 **Rockingham** Nhants
92 B4 **Rockland All Saints** Norfk
93 G3 **Rockland St Mary** Norfk
92 B4 **Rockland St Peter** Norfk
116 B6 **Rockley** Notts
40 D6 **Rockley** Wilts
173 L1 **Rockville** Ag & B
42 D3 **Rockwell End** Bucks
55 J6 **Rodborough** Gloucs
40 C4 **Rodbourne** Swindn
39 L4 **Rodbourne** Wilts
14 B5 **Rodden** Dorset
27 J2 **Rode** Somset
99 J2 **Rode Heath** Ches
232 d5 **Rodel** W Isls
83 L1 **Roden** Wrekin
24 F4 **Rodhuish** Somset
83 L1 **Rodington** Wrekin
83 L1 **Rodington Heath** Wrekin
55 H5 **Rodley** Gloucs
39 L2 **Rodmarton** Gloucs
19 L4 **Rodmell** E Susx
34 B3 **Rodmersham** Kent
34 B3 **Rodmersham Green** Kent
26 C2 **Rodney Stoke** Somset
100 D4 **Rodsley** Derbys
59 K6 **Roe Green** Herts
75 K7 **Roe Green** Herts
132 E6 **Roecliffe** N York
44 E5 **Roehampton** Gt Lon
31 K5 **Roffey** W Susx
226 C7 **Rogart** Highld
30 D6 **Rogate** W Susx
37 L3 **Rogerstone** Newpt
232 d5 **Roghadal** W Isls
38 C3 **Rogiet** Mons
41 L2 **Roke** Oxon
151 J3 **Roker** Sundld
93 J1 **Rollesby** Norfk
87 K4 **Rolleston** Leics
102 C3 **Rolleston** Notts
100 E6 **Rolleston** Staffs
126 F2 **Rolston** E R Yk
33 L6 **Rolvenden** Kent
33 L6 **Rolvenden Layne** Kent
140 C3 **Romaldkirk** Dur
37 M3 **Roman Amphitheatre Caerleon** Newpt
39 H7 **Roman Baths & Pump Room** BaNES
132 E2 **Romanby** N York
177 G8 **Romanno Bridge** Border
24 B7 **Romansleigh** Devon
208 F4 **Romesdal** Highld
15 K1 **Romford** Dorset
45 K3 **Romford** Gt Lon
113 L4 **Romiley** Stockp
29 G6 **Romsey** Hants
84 D6 **Romsley** Shrops
85 G7 **Romsley** Worcs
172 C7 **Ronachan** Ag & B
150 B6 **Rookhope** Dur
17 G5 **Rookley** IOW
26 A2 **Rooks Bridge** Somset
25 H5 **Rooks Nest** Somset
132 C3 **Rookwith** N York
127 G4 **Roos** E R Yk
75 G3 **Roothams Green** Beds
29 M5 **Ropley** Hants
29 L5 **Ropley Dean** Hants
103 G5 **Ropsley** Lincs
217 K4 **Rora** Abers
82 F4 **Rorrington** Shrops
215 J4 **Rosarie** Moray
3 K1 **Rose** Cnwll
24 C6 **Rose Ash** Devon
61 L3 **Rose Green** Essex
77 L6 **Rose Green** Suffk
77 L5 **Rose Green** Suffk
18 B5 **Rose Green** W Susx
122 C4 **Rose Hill** Lancs
175 L7 **Rosebank** S Lans
49 J2 **Rosebush** Pembks
142 F7 **Rosedale Abbey** N York
225 K7 **Rosehall** Highld
217 H2 **Rosehearty** Abers
214 E2 **Roseisle** Moray
20 C5 **Roselands** E Susx
49 G5 **Rosemarket** Pembks
213 H3 **Rosemarkie** Highld
25 J7 **Rosemary Lane** Devon
195 J7 **Rosemount** P & K
4 E3 **Rosenannon** Cnwll
177 J6 **Rosewell** Mdloth
141 K3 **Roseworth** S on T
138 D4 **Rosgill** Cumb
208 D5 **Roskhill** Highld
148 B6 **Rosley** Cumb
177 H5 **Roslin** Mdloth
86 B1 **Rosliston** Derbys
174 B2 **Rosneath** Ag & B
146 B6 **Ross** D & G
54 E4 **Ross-on-Wye** Herefs
98 A2 **Rossett** Wrexhm
132 D8 **Rossett Green** N York
115 L2 **Rossington** Donc
174 E4 **Rossland** Rens
231 J7 **Roster** Highld
113 H5 **Rostherne** Ches
137 H4 **Rosthwaite** Cumb
100 C4 **Roston** Derbys
176 F2 **Rosyth** Fife
158 D2 **Rothbury** Nthumb
87 J1 **Rotherby** Leics
32 F7 **Rotherfield** E Susx
42 B4 **Rotherfield Greys** Oxon
42 B4 **Rotherfield Peppard** Oxon
115 H3 **Rotherham** Rothm
73 K3 **Rothersthorpe** Nhants
30 B1 **Rotherwick** Hants
215 G4 **Rothes** Moray
173 J5 **Rothesay** Ag & B
216 E6 **Rothiebrisbane** Abers
215 M5 **Rothiemay** Moray
204 B4 **Rothiemurchus Lodge** Highld
216 D7 **Rothienorman** Abers
87 H2 **Rothley** Leics
216 D7 **Rothmaise** Abers
123 L5 **Rothwell** Leeds
117 J2 **Rothwell** Lincs
88 B7 **Rothwell** Nhants
196 B3 **Rottal Lodge** Angus
19 K5 **Rottingdean** Br & H
136 D5 **Rottington** Cumb
155 H6 **Roucan** D & G
34 F3 **Rough Common** Kent
105 K7 **Rougham** Norfk
77 K3 **Rougham Green** Suffk
205 H3 **Roughpark** Abers
118 C8 **Roughton** Lincs
106 F5 **Roughton** Norfk
84 D5 **Roughton** Shrops
60 F5 **Roundbush Green** Essex
13 K1 **Roundham** Somset
123 L3 **Roundhay** Leeds
40 A7 **Roundway** Wilts
196 C6 **Roundyhill** Angus
71 H4 **Rous Lench** Worcs
13 H4 **Rousdon** Devon
57 J3 **Rousham** Oxon
173 L6 **Routenburn** N Ayrs
126 D3 **Routh** E R Yk
129 K2 **Row** Cumb
61 J4 **Row Green** Essex
156 D6 **Rowanburn** D & G
183 L7 **Rowardennan Hotel** Stirlg
183 L7 **Rowardennan Lodge** Stirlg
114 A4 **Rowarth** Derbys
38 C8 **Rowberrow** Somset
39 L7 **Rowde** Wilts
109 L6 **Rowen** Conwy
149 H3 **Rowfoot** Nthumb
62 B4 **Rowhedge** Essex
72 B2 **Rowington** Warwks
114 E6 **Rowland** Derbys
17 K1 **Rowland's Castle** Hants
150 E4 **Rowland's Gill** Gatesd
30 D3 **Rowledge** Surrey
150 D5 **Rowley** Dur
126 B4 **Rowley** E R Yk
86 D6 **Rowley Green** Covtry
85 H6 **Rowley Regis** Sandw
54 A3 **Rowlstone** Herefs
31 H4 **Rowly** Surrey
17 H3 **Rowner** Hants
71 J1 **Rowney Green** Worcs
29 G7 **Rownhams** Hants
136 E4 **Rowrah** Cumb
58 D4 **Rowsham** Bucks
114 E7 **Rowsley** Derbys
103 H2 **Rowston** Lincs
112 C8 **Rowton** Ches
98 E8 **Rowton** Wrekin
167 L4 **Roxburgh** Border
125 L6 **Roxby** N Linc
75 G4 **Roxton** Beds
61 G6 **Roxwell** Essex
192 D1 **Roy Bridge** Highld
177 H4 **Royal Botanic Gardens** C Edin
60 C6 **Roydon** Essex
105 H7 **Roydon** Norfk
92 D7 **Roydon** Norfk
60 C6 **Roydon Hamlet** Essex
124 B7 **Royston** Barns
75 L6 **Royston** Herts
122 D8 **Royton** Oldham
236 e6 **Rozel** Jersey
97 L4 **Ruabon** Wrexhm
188 D6 **Ruaig** Ag & B
4 D7 **Ruan Lanihorne** Cnwll
3 J7 **Ruan Major** Cnwll
3 J7 **Ruan Minor** Cnwll
54 F4 **Ruardean** Gloucs
54 F5 **Ruardean Hill** Gloucs
54 F5 **Ruardean Woodside** Gloucs
85 H7 **Rubery** Birm
233 c9 **Rubha Ban** W Isls
69 J6 **Ruckhall** Herefs
34 D7 **Ruckinge** Kent
83 K4 **Ruckley** Shrops
141 L6 **Rudby** N York
150 E2 **Rudchester** Nthumb
101 L6 **Ruddington** Notts
27 J2 **Rudge** Somset
38 F3 **Rudgeway** S Glos
31 H5 **Rudgwick** W Susx
61 K7 **Rudley Green** Essex
39 J6 **Rudloe** Wilts
37 J3 **Rudry** Caerph
135 H6 **Rudston** E R Yk
99 L2 **Rudyard** Staffs
167 J5 **Ruecastle** Border
120 F7 **Rufford** Lancs
124 D1 **Rufforth** York
87 G7 **Rugby** Warwks
100 B8 **Rugeley** Staffs
25 K6 **Ruishton** Somset
43 H3 **Ruislip** Gt Lon
215 J4 **Rumbach** Moray
185 L7 **Rumbling Bridge** P & K
93 H7 **Rumburgh** Suffk
4 D2 **Rumford** Cnwll
176 C3 **Rumford** Falk
37 K5 **Rumney** Cardif
112 D5 **Runcorn** Halton
18 B5 **Runcton** W Susx
90 E2 **Runcton Holme** Norfk
30 E3 **Runfold** Surrey
92 C3 **Runhall** Norfk
93 K2 **Runham** Norfk
25 H6 **Runnington** Somset
143 G4 **Runswick** N York
195 L3 **Runtaleave** Angus
46 C2 **Runwell** Essex
42 D5 **Ruscombe** Wokham
62 E5 **Rush Green** Essex
45 K3 **Rush Green** Gt Lon
70 B7 **Rushall** Herefs
92 E6 **Rushall** Norfk
28 C1 **Rushall** Wilts
77 K3 **Rushbrooke** Suffk
83 K5 **Rushbury** Shrops
60 A2 **Rushden** Herts
74 D2 **Rushden** Nhants

91 K7 **Rushford** Norfk
20 D3 **Rushlake Green** E Susx
93 K6 **Rushmere** Suffk
30 E4 **Rushmoor** Surrey
70 F1 **Rushock** Worcs
113 J3 **Rusholme** Manch
112 E8 **Rushton** Ches
88 B6 **Rushton** Nhants
113 L8 **Rushton Spencer** Staffs
70 E4 **Rushwick** Worcs
141 G2 **Rushyford** Dur
184 D7 **Ruskie** Stirlg
103 H3 **Ruskington** Lincs
129 H2 **Rusland** Cumb
31 K4 **Rusper** W Susx
54 F5 **Ruspidge** Gloucs
31 L4 **Russ Hill** Surrey
42 B3 **Russell's Water** Oxon
32 F5 **Rusthall** Kent
18 E5 **Rustington** W Susx
134 E3 **Ruston** N York
135 G6 **Ruston Parva** E R Yk
143 H5 **Ruswarp** N York
167 K4 **Rutherford** Border
175 H6 **Rutherglen** S Lans
4 F3 **Ruthernbridge** Cnwll
97 H2 **Ruthin** Denbgs
207 H4 **Ruthrieston** C Aber
215 L5 **Ruthven** Abers
195 L6 **Ruthven** Angus
203 H5 **Ruthven** Highld
195 L6 **Ruthven House** Angus
4 E4 **Ruthvoes** Cnwll
147 J2 **Ruthwell** D & G
98 B7 **Ruyton-XI-Towns** Shrops
158 C7 **Ryal** Nthumb
13 K4 **Ryall** Dorset
70 F6 **Ryall** Worcs
33 H2 **Ryarsh** Kent
137 K6 **Rydal** Cumb
17 H4 **Ryde** IOW
21 H2 **Rye** E Susx
21 H2 **Rye Foreign** E Susx
70 D7 **Rye Street** Worcs
88 F2 **Ryhall** Rutlnd
124 B7 **Ryhill** Wakefd
151 K4 **Ryhope** Sundld
117 G5 **Ryland** Lincs
101 K5 **Rylands** Notts
131 H7 **Rylstone** N York
14 B1 **Ryme Intrinseca** Dorset
124 E3 **Ryther** N York
150 E3 **Ryton** Gatesd
84 D3 **Ryton** Shrops
86 E8 **Ryton-on-Dunsmore** Warwks

S

122 B3 **Sabden** Lancs
60 B4 **Sacombe** Herts
151 G5 **Sacriston** Dur
141 H4 **Sadberge** Darltn
161 K3 **Saddell** Ag & B
87 J5 **Saddington** Leics
90 E1 **Saddle Bow** Norfk
19 H4 **Saddlescombe** W Susx
76 D6 **Saffron Walden** Essex
49 H6 **Sageston** Pembks
91 K3 **Saham Hills** Norfk
91 K3 **Saham Toney** Norfk
98 C1 **Saighton** Ches
179 J5 **St Abbs** Border
178 E5 **St Agnes** Border
3 J2 **St Agnes** Cnwll
59 J6 **St Albans** Herts
4 C5 **St Allen** Cnwll
236 c3 **St Andrew** Guern
37 H6 **St Andrew's Major** V Glam
187 H4 **St Andrews** Fife
13 L4 **St Andrews Well** Dorset
155 J4 **St Ann's** D & G
6 B2 **St Ann's Chapel** Cnwll
6 F6 **St Ann's Chapel** Devon
120 D5 **St Anne's** Lancs
3 K6 **St Anthony** Cnwll
20 D5 **St Anthony's Hill** E Susx
38 D2 **St Arvans** Mons
110 E6 **St Asaph** Denbgs
36 F6 **St Athan** V Glam
236 b7 **St Aubin** Jersey
4 F5 **St Austell** Cnwll
136 D5 **St Bees** Cumb
5 G5 **St Blazey** Cnwll
167 J3 **St Boswells** Border
236 b7 **St Brelade** Jersey
236 b7 **St Brelade's Bay** Jersey
4 F2 **St Breock** Cnwll
5 H1 **St Breward** Cnwll
54 E6 **St Briavels** Gloucs
36 D5 **St Bride's Major** V Glam
37 H5 **St Brides super-Ely** V Glam
37 L4 **St Brides Wentlooge** Newpt
6 C4 **St Budeaux** C Plym
2 D6 **St Buryan** Cnwll
183 G6 **St Catherines** Ag & B
55 J7 **St Chloe** Gloucs
50 C3 **St Clears** Carmth
5 K3 **St Cleer** Cnwll
4 D6 **St Clement** Cnwll
236 e8 **St Clement** Jersey
9 G7 **St Clether** Cnwll
173 H5 **St Colmac** Ag & B
4 E3 **St Columb Major** Cnwll
4 D4 **St Columb Minor** Cnwll
4 E4 **St Columb Road** Cnwll
217 K2 **St Combs** Abers
93 G6 **St Cross South Elmham** Suffk
197 J4 **St Cyrus** Abers
185 K4 **St David's** P & K
48 C3 **St David's** Pembks
3 J3 **St Day** Cnwll
4 E4 **St Dennis** Cnwll
65 G5 **St Dogmaels** Cerdgn
6 B3 **St Dominick** Cnwll
36 E6 **St Donats** V Glam
4 F1 **St Endellion** Cnwll
4 D4 **St Enoder** Cnwll
4 D6 **St Erme** Cnwll
6 B4 **St Erney** Cnwll
2 F4 **St Erth** Cnwll
3 G4 **St Erth Praze** Cnwll
4 D2 **St Ervan** Cnwll
4 F6 **St Ewe** Cnwll
37 H5 **St Fagans** Cardif
37 H5 **St Fagans Welsh Life Museum** Cardif
217 K4 **St Fergus** Abers
184 F3 **St Fillans** P & K
49 J7 **St Florence** Pembks
8 F5 **St Gennys** Cnwll
110 D6 **St George** Conwy
37 H5 **St George's** V Glam
38 B7 **St Georges** N Som
6 A4 **St Germans** Cnwll
23 H7 **St Giles in the Wood** Devon
9 K6 **St Giles-on-the-Heath** Cnwll
81 L8 **St Harmon** Powys
140 F2 **St Helen Auckland** Dur
92 E1 **St Helena** Norfk
17 J5 **St Helens** IOW
112 D3 **St Helens** St Hel
44 E6 **St Helier** Gt Lon
236 d7 **St Helier** Jersey
2 F5 **St Hilary** Cnwll
36 F5 **St Hilary** V Glam
59 K3 **St Ippollitts** Herts
48 E6 **St Ishmael's** Pembks
4 E2 **St Issey** Cnwll
5 L3 **St Ive** Cnwll
75 K1 **St Ives** Cambs
2 F3 **St Ives** Cnwll
93 G7 **St James South Elmham** Suffk
73 L3 **St James's End** Nhants
6 B5 **St John** Cnwll
236 c5 **St John** Jersey
237 b5 **St John's** IOM
23 H5 **St John's Chapel** Devon
149 M7 **St John's Chapel** Dur
90 D2 **St John's Fen End** Norfk
165 J3 **St John's Kirk** S Lans
154 B6 **St John's Town of Dalry** D & G
44 F4 **St John's Wood** Gt Lon
32 F3 **St Johns** Kent
43 G8 **St Johns** Surrey
70 E4 **St Johns** Worcs
237 d3 **St Jude's** IOM
2 C5 **St Just** Cnwll
4 D8 **St Just-in-Roseland** Cnwll
216 E7 **St Katherines** Abers
3 K6 **St Keverne** Cnwll
5 G1 **St Kew** Cnwll
5 G2 **St Kew Highway** Cnwll
5 K4 **St Keyne** Cnwll
62 A6 **St Lawrence** Essex
17 G6 **St Lawrence** IOW
236 c6 **St Lawrence** Jersey
35 K2 **St Lawrence** Kent
58 E6 **St Leonards** Bucks
15 L2 **St Leonards** Dorset
20 F4 **St Leonards** E Susx
2 C6 **St Levan** Cnwll
37 H6 **St Lythans** V Glam
5 G2 **St Mabyn** Cnwll
186 C3 **St Madoes** P & K
93 G6 **St Margaret South Elmham** Suffk
35 K5 **St Margaret's at Cliffe** Kent
234 c7 **St Margaret's Hope** Ork
69 G7 **St Margarets** Herefs
60 B5 **St Margarets** Herts
237 c6 **St Marks** IOM
5 K5 **St Martin** Cnwll
236 d3 **St Martin** Guern
236 e6 **St Martin** Jersey
186 B2 **St Martin's** P & K
97 L5 **St Martins** Shrops
236 b6 **St Mary** Jersey
29 H2 **St Mary Bourne** Hants
36 F6 **St Mary Church** V Glam
45 J6 **St Mary Cray** Gt Lon
21 L1 **St Mary in the Marsh** Kent
234 c6 **St Mary's** Ork
21 L1 **St Mary's Bay** Kent
46 D5 **St Mary's Hoo** Medway
7 L3 **St Marychurch** Torbay
54 C5 **St Maughans Green** Mons
3 L5 **St Mawes** Cnwll
4 D3 **St Mawgan** Cnwll
6 B3 **St Mellion** Cnwll
37 K4 **St Mellons** Cardif
4 D2 **St Merryn** Cnwll
4 F5 **St Mewan** Cnwll
4 F7 **St Michael Caerhays** Cnwll
25 L5 **St Michael Church** Somset
4 D7 **St Michael Penkevil** Cnwll
93 H6 **St Michael South Elmham** Suffk
120 F3 **St Michael's on Wyre** Lancs
34 B7 **St Michaels** Kent
69 L2 **St Michaels** Worcs
4 F1 **St Minver** Cnwll
187 H6 **St Monans** Fife
5 J3 **St Neot** Cnwll
75 H3 **St Neots** Cambs
64 C7 **St Nicholas** Pembks
37 H5 **St Nicholas** V Glam
47 L6 **St Nicholas at Wade** Kent
185 G8 **St Ninians** Stirlg
93 J4 **St Olaves** Norfk
62 D5 **St Osyth** Essex
236 b6 **St Ouen** Jersey
54 D3 **St Owens Cross** Herefs
59 K4 **St Paul's Walden** Herts
45 J6 **St Pauls Cray** Gt Lon
236 b6 **St Peter** Jersey
236 d3 **St Peter Port** Guern
236 b3 **St Peter's** Guern
35 K2 **St Peter's** Kent
5 J3 **St Pinnock** Cnwll
163 J5 **St Quivox** S Ayrs
236 d2 **St Sampson** Guern
236 c3 **St Saviour** Guern
236 d7 **St Saviour** Jersey
4 E5 **St Stephen** Cnwll
4 E5 **St Stephen's Coombe** Cnwll
9 J7 **St Stephens** Cnwll
6 B4 **St Stephens** Cnwll
8 E8 **St Teath** Cnwll
5 G1 **St Tudy** Cnwll
48 F7 **St Twynnells** Pembks
5 J5 **St Veep** Cnwll
197 G7 **St Vigeans** Angus
4 F3 **St Wenn** Cnwll
54 D3 **St Weonards** Herefs
71 K6 **Saintbury** Gloucs
191 L6 **Salachail** Ag & B
7 H7 **Salcombe** Devon
12 F5 **Salcombe Regis** Devon
61 M5 **Salcott** Essex
113 H3 **Sale** Traffd
71 G3 **Sale Green** Worcs
118 F5 **Saleby** Lincs
20 F2 **Salehurst** E Susx
80 F6 **Salem** Cerdgn
95 J2 **Salem** Gwynd
190 C7 **Salen** Ag & B
190 D4 **Salen** Highld
74 D6 **Salford** Beds
56 F3 **Salford** Oxon
113 J2 **Salford** Salfd

71 J4 **Salford Priors** Warwks
32 B4 **Salfords** Surrey
93 G1 **Salhouse** Norfk
185 L8 **Saline** Fife
28 C5 **Salisbury** Wilts
28 C5 Salisbury Cathedral Wilts
28 B3 **Salisbury Plain** Wilts
148 F7 **Salkeld Dykes** Cumb
106 D7 **Salle** Norfk
118 D6 **Salmonby** Lincs
56 B4 **Salperton** Gloucs
175 L5 **Salsburgh** N Lans
99 L6 **Salt** Staffs
123 H3 **Saltaire** Brad
6 B4 **Saltash** Cnwll
223 G7 **Saltburn** Highld
142 E3 **Saltburn-by-the-Sea** R & Cl
102 D7 **Saltby** Leics
163 G2 **Saltcoats** N Ayrs
19 K5 **Saltdean** Br & H
136 D3 **Salterbeck** Cumb
122 D2 **Salterforth** Lancs
28 C4 **Salterton** Wilts
118 F3 **Saltfleet** Lincs
118 F4 **Saltfleetby All Saints** Lincs
118 F3 **Saltfleetby St Clement** Lincs
118 F4 **Saltfleetby St Peter** Lincs
39 G6 **Saltford** BaNES
106 C4 **Salthouse** Norfk
125 J5 **Saltmarshe** E R Yk
111 L8 **Saltney** Flints
133 L4 **Salton** N York
23 G6 **Saltrens** Devon
34 F7 **Saltwood** Kent
18 F5 **Salvington** W Susx
70 F3 **Salwarpe** Worcs
13 L3 **Salwayash** Dorset
71 J3 **Sambourne** Warwks
99 G7 **Sambrook** Wrekin
121 H4 **Samlesbury** Lancs
25 H7 **Sampford Arundel** Somset
25 G3 **Sampford Brett** Somset
10 F5 **Sampford Courtenay** Devon
25 H7 **Sampford Moor** Somset
25 G8 **Sampford Peverell** Devon
6 D2 **Sampford Spiney** Devon
234 d5 **Samsonlane** Ork
178 B4 **Samuelston** E Loth
170 E4 **Sanaigmore** Ag & B
2 D5 **Sancreed** Cnwll
125 L3 **Sancton** E R Yk
124 B3 **Sand Hills** Leeds
125 J3 **Sand Hole** E R Yk
133 L7 **Sand Hutton** N York
199 L5 **Sandaig** Highld
123 L6 **Sandal Magna** Wakefd
199 G7 **Sandavore** Highld
234 d4 Sanday Airport Ork
99 H1 **Sandbach** Ches
173 K3 **Sandbank** Ag & B
15 K5 **Sandbanks** Poole
216 B2 **Sandend** Abers
45 G7 **Sanderstead** Gt Lon
139 G4 **Sandford** Cumb
11 J4 **Sandford** Devon
15 H5 **Sandford** Dorset
15 M3 **Sandford** Hants
17 G6 **Sandford** IOW
38 B8 **Sandford** N Som
164 E2 **Sandford** S Lans
26 F7 **Sandford Orcas** Dorset
57 H3 **Sandford St Martin** Oxon
57 K7 **Sandford-on-Thames** Oxon
35 G7 **Sandgate** Kent
217 H2 **Sandhaven** Abers
144 D5 **Sandhead** D & G
57 K6 **Sandhills** Oxon
30 F4 **Sandhills** Surrey
150 B2 **Sandhoe** Nthumb
182 E7 **Sandhole** Ag & B
125 J4 **Sandholme** E R Yk
42 D7 **Sandhurst** Br For
55 J4 **Sandhurst** Gloucs
33 K7 **Sandhurst** Kent
132 F3 **Sandhutton** N York
101 J5 **Sandiacre** Derbys
119 G5 **Sandilands** Lincs
28 C7 **Sandleheath** Hants
57 J7 **Sandleigh** Oxon
27 H6 **Sandley** Dorset
235 b5 **Sandness** Shet
61 H6 **Sandon** Essex
75 K7 **Sandon** Herts
99 L6 **Sandon** Staffs
99 L6 **Sandon Bank** Staffs
17 H5 **Sandown** IOW
5 K4 **Sandplace** Cnwll
59 K6 **Sandridge** Herts
105 H6 **Sandringham** Norfk
143 H5 **Sandsend** N York
125 H8 **Sandtoft** N Linc
34 B5 **Sandway** Kent
35 J3 **Sandwich** Kent
235 c7 **Sandwick** Shet
232 g2 **Sandwick** W Isls
136 D4 **Sandwith** Cumb
75 H5 **Sandy** Beds
39 L6 **Sandy Lane** Wilts
11 G6 **Sandy Park** Devon
155 L4 **Sandyford** D & G
7 K2 **Sandygate** Devon
237 d3 **Sandygate** IOM
146 F4 **Sandyhills** D & G
129 J6 **Sandylands** Lancs
228 F3 **Sangobeg** Highld
228 F3 **Sangomore** Highld
70 E2 **Sankyn's Green** Worcs
189 K3 **Sanna Bay** Highld
232 g2 **Sanndabhaig** W Isls
162 C1 **Sannox** N Ayrs
164 F7 **Sanquhar** D & G
136 F6 **Santon Bridge** Cumb
91 J6 **Santon Downham** Suffk
86 F5 **Sapcote** Leics
70 C2 **Sapey Common** Herefs
91 K7 **Sapiston** Suffk
55 L7 **Sapperton** Gloucs
103 G5 **Sapperton** Lincs
104 B6 **Saracen's Head** Lincs
231 L6 **Sarclet** Highld
17 G2 **Sarisbury** Hants
94 D6 **Sarn** Gwynd
81 K4 **Sarn** Powys
82 E5 **Sarn** Powys
65 K4 **Sarnau** Cerdgn
82 E1 **Sarnau** Powys
69 H4 **Sarnesfield** Herefs
51 H3 **Saron** Carmth
109 G7 **Saron** Gwynd
59 H7 **Sarratt** Herts
47 L6 **Sarre** Kent
56 F4 **Sarsden** Oxon
150 E6 **Satley** Dur
23 L6 **Satterleigh** Devon
129 H2 **Satterthwaite** Cumb
206 D3 **Sauchen** Abers
186 C2 **Saucher** P & K
197 G3 **Sauchieburn** Abers
55 H6 **Saul** Gloucs
116 C4 **Saundby** Notts
49 K6 **Saundersfoot** Pembks
58 C7 **Saunderton** Bucks
23 G4 **Saunton** Devon
118 E7 **Sausthorpe** Lincs
123 K6 **Savile Town** Kirk
73 G2 **Sawbridge** Warwks
60 D5 **Sawbridgeworth** Herts
134 E3 **Sawdon** N York
122 B2 **Sawley** Lancs
132 C6 **Sawley** N York
76 C5 **Sawston** Cambs
89 H6 **Sawtry** Cambs
102 D8 **Saxby** Leics
117 G4 **Saxby** Lincs
126 B6 **Saxby All Saints** N Linc
102 B7 **Saxelbye** Leics
78 C3 **Saxham Street** Suffk
116 E6 **Saxilby** Lincs
106 B5 **Saxlingham** Norfk
92 F4 **Saxlingham Green** Norfk
92 F4 **Saxlingham Nethergate** Norfk
92 E4 **Saxlingham Thorpe** Norfk
79 H2 **Saxmundham** Suffk
76 F3 **Saxon Street** Cambs
102 B4 **Saxondale** Notts
78 F2 **Saxtead** Suffk
78 F2 **Saxtead Green** Suffk
78 F2 **Saxtead Little Green** Suffk
106 D6 **Saxthorpe** Norfk
124 D3 **Saxton** N York
19 H3 **Sayers Common** W Susx
133 K5 **Scackleton** N York
137 H5 **Scafell Pike** Cumb
116 A3 **Scaftworth** Notts
134 C5 **Scagglethorpe** N York
180 E8 **Scalasaig** Ag & B
125 K5 **Scalby** E R Yk
134 F2 **Scalby** N York
73 L1 **Scaldwell** Nhants
148 D3 **Scaleby** Cumb
148 D3 **Scalebyhill** Cumb
137 K2 **Scales** Cumb
129 G5 **Scales** Cumb
102 C7 **Scalford** Leics
142 F4 **Scaling** N York
235 c6 **Scalloway** Shet
118 C5 **Scamblesby** Lincs
191 G2 **Scamodale** Highld
134 D4 **Scampston** N York
116 F5 **Scampton** Lincs
212 F6 **Scaniport** Highld
123 G7 **Scapegoat Hill** Kirk
135 G2 **Scarborough** N York
4 E5 **Scarcewater** Cnwll
115 J7 **Scarcliffe** Derbys
124 B3 **Scarcroft** Leeds
231 J2 **Scarfskerry** Highld
140 D5 **Scargill** Dur
188 D7 **Scarinish** Ag & B
120 E7 **Scarisbrick** Lancs
91 L2 **Scarning** Norfk
102 B4 **Scarrington** Notts
118 C1 **Scartho** Lincs
235 c4 Scatsta Airport Shet
116 F1 **Scawby** N Linc
115 K1 **Scawsby** Donc
115 K1 **Scawthorpe** Donc
133 H3 **Scawton** N York
19 K2 **Scayne's Hill** W Susx
53 H3 **Scethrog** Powys
123 H8 **Scholes** Kirk
124 B3 **Scholes** Leeds
115 H3 **Scholes** Rothm
112 E1 **Scholes** Wigan
123 K7 **Scissett** Kirk
64 C7 **Scleddau** Pembks
115 L5 **Scofton** Notts
92 D7 **Scole** Norfk
186 B3 **Scone** P & K
209 H7 **Sconser** Highld
186 F6 **Scoonie** Fife
103 H2 **Scopwick** Lincs
220 C3 **Scoraig** Highld
126 C2 **Scorborough** E R Yk
3 J3 **Scorrier** Cnwll
121 G2 **Scorton** Lancs
141 G7 **Scorton** N York
158 C5 **Scot's Gap** Nthumb
148 D4 **Scotby** Cumb
140 F6 **Scotch Corner** N York
129 K7 **Scotforth** Lancs
117 G6 **Scothern** Lincs
186 C6 **Scotlandwell** P & K
231 G4 **Scotscalder Station** Highld
206 B2 **Scotsmill** Abers
174 F5 **Scotstoun** C Glas
150 F3 **Scotswood** N u Ty
116 E2 **Scotter** Lincs
116 E2 **Scotterthorpe** Lincs
116 E2 **Scotton** Lincs
140 F7 **Scotton** N York
132 E7 **Scotton** N York
92 B4 **Scoulton** Norfk
228 B6 **Scourie** Highld
228 B6 **Scourie More** Highld
235 c7 **Scousburgh** Shet
231 G2 **Scrabster** Highld
167 K5 **Scraesburgh** Border
104 C4 **Scrane End** Lincs
87 J3 **Scraptoft** Leics
93 K1 **Scratby** Norfk
133 L7 **Scrayingham** N York
103 H4 **Scredington** Lincs
118 F7 **Scremby** Lincs
179 L8 **Scremerston** Nthumb
102 B4 **Screveton** Notts
132 E7 **Scriven** N York
115 M4 **Scrooby** Notts
100 D6 **Scropton** Derbys
103 L2 **Scrub Hill** Lincs
195 K5 **Scruschloch** Angus
132 D2 **Scruton** N York
229 J4 **Scullomie** Highld
105 L6 **Sculthorpe** Norfk
125 K7 **Scunthorpe** N Linc
107 J6 **Sea Palling** Norfk
13 K2 **Seaborough** Dorset
35 G7 **Seabrook** Kent
151 J3 **Seaburn** Sundld
124 B4 **Seacroft** Leeds
209 G5 **Seafield** Highld
176 D5 **Seafield** W Loth
20 A6 **Seaford** E Susx
111 K3 **Seaforth** Sefton
101 L8 **Seagrave** Leics
151 K5 **Seaham** Dur
169 J3 **Seahouses** Nthumb
32 F2 **Seal** Kent
30 E2 **Seale** Surrey
142 B5 **Seamer** N York
134 F3 **Seamer** N York
173 L8 **Seamill** N Ayrs
117 H1 **Searby** Lincs
47 H6 **Seasalter** Kent
136 E6 **Seascale** Cumb
137 H7 **Seathwaite** Cumb
137 H4 **Seatoller** Cumb
5 L5 **Seaton** Cnwll
136 E2 **Seaton** Cumb

13 G4 **Seaton** Devon
126 E2 **Seaton** E R Yk
35 G3 **Seaton** Kent
159 H6 **Seaton** Nthumb
88 C4 **Seaton** Rutlnd
142 B2 **Seaton Carew** Hartpl
159 H6 **Seaton Delaval** Nthumb
125 J3 **Seaton Ross** E R Yk
159 H6 **Seaton Sluice** Nthumb
13 K4 **Seatown** Dorset
142 C7 **Seave Green** N York
17 J4 **Seaview** IOW
147 K4 **Seaville** Cumb
26 B7 **Seavington St Mary** Somset
26 B7 **Seavington St Michael** Somset
148 C6 **Sebergham** Cumb
86 C3 **Seckington** Warwks
130 C2 **Sedbergh** Cumb
38 D2 **Sedbury** Gloucs
131 G2 **Sedbusk** N York
71 H6 **Sedgeberrow** Worcs
102 D5 **Sedgebrook** Lincs
141 J2 **Sedgefield** Dur
105 H5 **Sedgeford** Norfk
27 K5 **Sedgehill** Wilts
85 G5 **Sedgley** Dudley
129 L3 **Sedgwick** Cumb
20 F3 **Sedlescombe** E Susx
58 D5 **Sedrup** Bucks
39 L7 **Seend** Wilts
39 L7 **Seend Cleeve** Wilts
42 F3 **Seer Green** Bucks
93 G4 **Seething** Norfk
111 K2 **Sefton** Sefton
99 K7 **Seighford** Staffs
109 H7 **Seion** Gwynd
84 E4 **Seisdon** Staffs
97 K5 **Selattyn** Shrops
30 C5 **Selborne** Hants
124 F4 **Selby** N York
30 F7 **Selham** W Susx
45 G6 **Selhurst** Gt Lon
167 G4 **Selkirk** Border
54 E3 **Sellack** Herefs
235 d2 **Sellafirth** Shet
34 E6 **Sellindge** Kent
34 D4 **Selling** Kent
39 L7 **Sells Green** Wilts
85 J6 **Selly Oak** Birm
20 B4 **Selmeston** E Susx
45 G7 **Selsdon** Gt Lon
18 B6 **Selsey** W Susx
130 E4 **Selside** N York
55 J7 **Selsley** Gloucs
35 G5 **Selsted** Kent
101 J2 **Selston** Notts
24 E3 **Selworthy** Somset
78 B5 **Semer** Suffk
39 K7 **Semington** Wilts
27 K6 **Semley** Wilts
31 G1 **Send** Surrey
37 H3 **Senghenydd** Caerph
2 C6 **Sennen** Cnwll
2 C6 **Sennen Cove** Cnwll
52 E3 **Sennybridge** Powys
133 G4 **Sessay** N York
90 F2 **Setchey** Norfk
177 L4 **Seton Mains** E Loth
130 F6 **Settle** N York
134 C5 **Settrington** N York
25 J5 **Seven Ash** Somset
45 J3 **Seven Kings** Gt Lon
52 C6 **Seven Sisters** Neath
61 M3 **Seven Star Green** Essex
71 K7 **Seven Wells** Gloucs
56 B4 **Sevenhampton** Gloucs
40 E3 **Sevenhampton** Swindn
32 F3 **Sevenoaks** Kent
32 F3 **Sevenoaks Weald** Kent
38 D4 **Severn Beach** S Glos
70 F5 **Severn Stoke** Worcs
34 D6 **Sevington** Kent
76 E6 **Sewards End** Essex
59 G4 **Sewell** Beds
135 J5 **Sewerby** E R Yk
3 J5 **Seworgan** Cnwll
102 E7 **Sewstern** Leics
232 g1 **Sgiogarstaigh** W Isls
58 A6 **Shabbington** Bucks
86 D3 **Shackerstone** Leics
30 F3 **Shackleford** Surrey
232 f1 **Shader** W Isls
151 H6 **Shadforth** Dur
93 J6 **Shadingfield** Suffk
34 C7 **Shadoxhurst** Kent
91 L6 **Shadwell** Norfk
76 B6 **Shaftenhoe End** Herts
27 K6 **Shaftesbury** Dorset
124 B7 **Shafton** Barns
113 G2 **Shakerley** Wigan
40 F7 **Shalbourne** Wilts
30 B3 **Shalden** Hants
7 L2 **Shaldon** Devon
16 E5 **Shalfleet** IOW
61 H3 **Shalford** Essex
31 G3 **Shalford** Surrey
61 H3 **Shalford Green** Essex
34 E4 **Shalmsford Street** Kent
73 J7 **Shalstone** Bucks
31 G3 **Shamley Green** Surrey
196 D4 **Shandford** Angus
174 B2 **Shandon** Ag & B
223 J6 **Shandwick** Highld
87 K4 **Shangton** Leics
17 H6 **Shanklin** IOW
138 E4 **Shap** Cumb
15 H3 **Shapwick** Dorset
26 B4 **Shapwick** Somset
101 H6 **Shardlow** Derbys
85 G3 **Shareshill** Staffs
124 B6 **Sharlston** Wakefd
74 E3 **Sharnbrook** Beds
86 F5 **Sharnford** Leics
121 G4 **Sharoe Green** Lancs
132 E5 **Sharow** N York
59 H2 **Sharpenhoe** Beds
158 B2 **Sharperton** Nthumb
54 F7 **Sharpness** Gloucs
106 C5 **Sharrington** Norfk
84 E7 **Shatterford** Worcs
6 D3 **Shaugh Prior** Devon
99 G3 **Shavington** Ches
122 D8 **Shaw** Oldham
41 J6 **Shaw** W Berk
39 K7 **Shaw** Wilts
132 C6 **Shaw Mills** N York
232 e2 **Shawbost** W Isls
98 E7 **Shawbury** Shrops
87 G7 **Shawell** Leics
29 J6 **Shawford** Hants
154 F6 **Shawhead** D & G
175 K7 **Shawsburn** S Lans
147 H2 **Shearington** D & G
87 J5 **Shearsby** Leics
25 L5 **Shearston** Somset
10 C3 **Shebbear** Devon
99 H7 **Shebdon** Staffs
230 E3 **Shebster** Highld
175 G6 **Sheddens** E Rens
29 K8 **Shedfield** Hants
100 C1 **Sheen** Derbys
123 H6 **Sheepridge** Kirk
123 L4 **Sheepscar** Leeds
55 K6 **Sheepscombe** Gloucs
6 E3 **Sheepstor** Devon
10 C4 **Sheepwash** Devon
86 D3 **Sheepy Magna** Leics
86 D3 **Sheepy Parva** Leics
60 E5 **Sheering** Essex
46 F5 **Sheerness** Kent
43 H7 **Sheerwater** Surrey
30 C6 **Sheet** Hants
115 G4 **Sheffield** Sheff
115 H4 **Sheffield City Airport** Sheff
75 G6 **Shefford** Beds
228 B4 **Sheigra** Highld
83 L3 **Sheinton** Shrops
83 H7 **Shelderton** Shrops
85 L6 **Sheldon** Birm
114 D7 **Sheldon** Derbys
12 E2 **Sheldon** Devon
34 D4 **Sheldwich** Kent
92 D6 **Shelfanger** Norfk
102 A4 **Shelford** Notts
168 D2 **Shellacres** Border
123 J7 **Shelley** Kirk
78 B6 **Shelley** Suffk
40 F2 **Shellingford** Oxon
60 F6 **Shellow Bowells** Essex
70 D2 **Shelsley Beauchamp** Worcs
70 C2 **Shelsley Walsh** Worcs
74 F2 **Shelton** Beds
92 F5 **Shelton** Norfk
102 C4 **Shelton** Notts
99 J5 **Shelton Under Harley** Staffs
83 G4 **Shelve** Shrops
69 K6 **Shelwick** Herefs
45 L2 **Shenfield** Essex
72 D6 **Shenington** Oxon
59 K7 **Shenley** Herts
74 B7 **Shenley Brook End** M Keyn
74 B7 **Shenley Church End** M Keyn
69 H6 **Shenmore** Herefs
145 H3 **Shennanton** D & G
85 K3 **Shenstone** Staffs
84 F8 **Shenstone** Worcs
86 E4 **Shenton** Leics
59 L4 **Shephall** Herts
44 E4 **Shepherd's Bush** Gt Lon
35 H5 **Shepherdswell** Kent
123 J8 **Shepley** Kirk
43 H6 **Shepperton** Surrey
76 B5 **Shepreth** Cambs
101 J8 **Shepshed** Leics
26 B7 **Shepton Beauchamp** Somset
26 F3 **Shepton Mallet** Somset
27 G5 **Shepton Montague** Somset
33 K3 **Shepway** Kent
151 K7 **Sheraton** Dur
26 F7 **Sherborne** Dorset
56 D5 **Sherborne** Gloucs
26 E1 **Sherborne** Somset
29 L1 **Sherborne St John** Hants
72 C3 **Sherbourne** Warwks
151 H6 **Sherburn** Dur
134 E4 **Sherburn** N York
151 H6 **Sherburn Hill** Dur
124 D4 **Sherburn in Elmet** N York
31 H2 **Shere** Surrey
105 L6 **Shereford** Norfk
28 F6 **Sherfield English** Hants
42 B8 **Sherfield on Loddon** Hants
7 H6 **Sherford** Devon
133 K6 **Sheriff Hutton** N York
84 D2 **Sheriffhales** Shrops
106 E4 **Sheringham** Norfk
74 C5 **Sherington** M Keyn
105 H6 **Shernborne** Norfk
27 L4 **Sherrington** Wilts
39 J3 **Sherston** Wilts
101 K4 **Sherwood** C Nott
101 L2 **Sherwood Forest** Notts
175 H5 **Shettleston** C Glas
121 H8 **Shevington** Wigan
6 B5 **Sheviock** Cnwll
123 G5 **Shibden Head** Brad
16 F5 **Shide** IOW
168 B2 **Shidlaw** Nthumb
200 E2 **Shiel Bridge** Highld
210 C4 **Shieldaig** Highld
155 H5 **Shieldhill** D & G
176 B3 **Shieldhill** Falk
165 J2 **Shieldhill House Hotel** S Lans
175 K7 **Shields** N Lans
190 D3 **Shielfoot** Highld
196 C5 **Shielhill** Angus
173 L4 **Shielhill** Inver
84 D2 **Shifnal** Shrops
169 J7 **Shilbottle** Nthumb
141 G3 **Shildon** Dur
174 E6 **Shillford** E Rens
24 F6 **Shillingford** Devon
41 L2 **Shillingford** Oxon
11 K6 **Shillingford Abbot** Devon
11 K7 **Shillingford St George** Devon
14 F1 **Shillingstone** Dorset
75 G7 **Shillington** Beds
56 E6 **Shilton** Oxon
86 E6 **Shilton** Warwks
92 D6 **Shimpling** Norfk
77 J4 **Shimpling** Suffk
77 K4 **Shimpling Street** Suffk
151 H6 **Shincliffe** Dur
151 H4 **Shiney Row** Sundld
42 B6 **Shinfield** Wokham
225 L5 **Shinness** Highld
33 G3 **Shipbourne** Kent
91 L3 **Shipdham** Norfk
38 C8 **Shipham** Somset
7 K3 **Shiphay** Torbay
42 C5 **Shiplake** Oxon
123 H3 **Shipley** Brad
31 J6 **Shipley** W Susx
32 B5 **Shipley Bridge** Surrey
93 H5 **Shipmeadow** Suffk
41 J2 **Shippon** Oxon
72 B6 **Shipston on Stour** Warwks
56 B4 **Shipton** Gloucs
133 H7 **Shipton** N York
83 L5 **Shipton** Shrops
28 E3 **Shipton Bellinger** Hants
13 L4 **Shipton Gorge** Dorset
17 L3 **Shipton Green** W Susx
39 K3 **Shipton Moyne** Gloucs
57 J5 **Shipton-on-Cherwell** Oxon
56 F4 **Shipton-under-Wychwood** Oxon
125 K2 **Shiptonthorpe** E R Yk
42 B2 **Shirburn** Oxon
120 E7 **Shirdley Hill** Lancs
115 K7 **Shirebrook** Derbys
115 G3 **Shiregreen** Sheff

38 D5 **Shirehampton** Bristl
159 H7 **Shiremoor** N Tyne
38 C2 **Shirenewton** Mons
115 K5 **Shireoaks** Notts
101 H2 **Shirland** Derbys
29 H8 **Shirley** C Sotn
100 E4 **Shirley** Derbys
45 G6 **Shirley** Gt Lon
85 K7 **Shirley** Solhll
29 L8 **Shirrell Heath** Hants
172 E2 **Shirvan** Ag & B
23 J4 **Shirwell** Devon
162 B4 **Shiskine** N Ayrs
69 H3 **Shobdon** Herefs
11 K5 **Shobrooke** Devon
102 B7 **Shoby** Leics
98 C3 **Shocklach** Ches
46 F3 **Shoeburyness** Sthend
35 K4 **Sholden** Kent
16 F1 **Sholing** C Sotn
9 G2 **Shop** Cnwll
78 F2 **Shop Street** Suffk
45 G4 **Shoreditch** Gt Lon
25 K6 **Shoreditch** Somset
45 K7 **Shoreham** Kent
19 G5 **Shoreham Airport** W Susx
19 H5 **Shoreham-by-Sea** W Susx
29 L6 **Shorley** Hants
46 B5 **Shorne** Kent
20 A3 **Shortgate** E Susx
4 C6 **Shortlanesend** Cnwll
74 F5 **Shortstown** Beds
16 F5 **Shorwell** IOW
27 G1 **Shoscombe** BaNES
92 F4 **Shotesham** Norfk
46 C2 **Shotgate** Essex
78 F7 **Shotley** Suffk
150 D4 **Shotley Bridge** Dur
78 F7 **Shotley Gate** Suffk
78 F7 **Shotley Street** Suffk
34 D4 **Shottenden** Kent
71 L4 **Shottery** Warwks
72 E5 **Shotteswell** Warwks
79 G5 **Shottisham** Suffk
100 F3 **Shottle** Derbys
100 F3 **Shottlegate** Derbys
151 K6 **Shotton** Dur
111 J7 **Shotton** Flints
151 J6 **Shotton Colliery** Dur
176 B6 **Shotts** N Lans
111 K6 **Shotwick** Ches
214 F4 **Shougle** Moray
90 F2 **Shouldham** Norfk
90 F2 **Shouldham Thorpe** Norfk
70 E3 **Shoulton** Worcs
83 H1 **Shrawardine** Shrops
70 E2 **Shrawley** Worcs
72 B2 **Shrewley** Warwks
83 J2 **Shrewsbury** Shrops
28 B3 **Shrewton** Wilts
18 C5 **Shripney** W Susx
40 E3 **Shrivenham** Oxon
92 B5 **Shropham** Norfk
69 L6 **Shucknall** Herefs
76 E5 **Shudy Camps** Cambs
55 L4 **Shurdington** Gloucs
42 D5 **Shurlock Row** W & M
230 F4 **Shurrery** Highld
230 F4 **Shurrery Lodge** Highld
25 J3 **Shurton** Somset
86 B5 **Shustoke** Warwks
99 K7 **Shut Heath** Staffs
13 G3 **Shute** Devon
72 E6 **Shutford** Oxon
70 F7 **Shuthonger** Gloucs
73 K4 **Shutlanger** Nhants
86 B3 **Shuttington** Warwks
115 J6 **Shuttlewood** Derbys
122 B6 **Shuttleworth** Bury
232 e2 **Siabost** W Isls
232 f1 **Siadar** W Isls
87 K6 **Sibbertoft** Nhants
72 D6 **Sibford Ferris** Oxon
72 D6 **Sibford Gower** Oxon
77 H7 **Sible Hedingham** Essex
60 F3 **Sibley's Green** Essex
104 B3 **Sibsey** Lincs
89 G4 **Sibson** Cambs
86 D4 **Sibson** Leics
231 K5 **Sibster** Highld
116 B6 **Sibthorpe** Notts
102 C4 **Sibthorpe** Notts
79 H1 **Sibton** Suffk
77 K3 **Sicklesmere** Suffk
124 B2 **Sicklinghall** N York
12 E4 **Sidbury** Devon
84 C6 **Sidbury** Shrops
38 B8 **Sidcot** N Som
45 J5 **Sidcup** Gt Lon
113 J7 **Siddington** Ches
56 B7 **Siddington** Gloucs
106 F4 **Sidestrand** Norfk
12 E4 **Sidford** Devon
18 B6 **Sidlesham** W Susx
20 E4 **Sidley** E Susx
12 E5 **Sidmouth** Devon
126 E2 **Sigglesthorne** E R Yk
36 F6 **Sigingstone** V Glam
41 L7 **Silchester** Hants
87 H1 **Sileby** Leics
128 D3 **Silecroft** Cumb
92 D4 **Silfield** Norfk
103 H4 **Silk Willoughby** Lincs
114 F1 **Silkstone** Barns
114 F1 **Silkstone Common** Barns
151 J4 **Silksworth** Sundld
147 K4 **Silloth** Cumb
134 E2 **Silpho** N York
122 F2 **Silsden** Brad
74 F7 **Silsoe** Beds
27 H5 **Silton** Dorset
61 K4 **Silver End** Essex
177 G6 **Silverburn** Mdloth
129 K4 **Silverdale** Lancs
99 J3 **Silverdale** Staffs
216 E2 **Silverford** Abers
73 J5 **Silverstone** Nhants
12 B2 **Silverton** Devon
84 B7 **Silvington** Shrops
157 L7 **Simonburn** Nthumb
25 H7 **Simons Burrow** Devon
24 B4 **Simonsbath** Somset
122 B4 **Simonstone** Lancs
168 C1 **Simprim** Border
74 C7 **Simpson** M Keyn
48 F4 **Simpson Cross** Pembks
179 G7 **Sinclair's Hill** Border
163 L6 **Sinclairston** E Ayrs
132 E3 **Sinderby** N York
113 G4 **Sinderland Green** Traffd
42 C6 **Sindlesham** Wokham
101 G6 **Sinfin** C Derb
120 E3 **Singleton** Lancs
18 B3 **Singleton** W Susx
46 A6 **Singlewell** Kent
205 K3 **Sinnarhard** Abers
134 B3 **Sinnington** N York
70 E3 **Sinton** Worcs
70 E3 **Sinton Green** Worcs
33 K5 **Sissinghurst** Kent
39 G5 **Siston** S Glos
3 H5 **Sithney** Cnwll
34 B3 **Sittingbourne** Kent
84 E5 **Six Ashes** Staffs
76 E3 **Six Mile Bottom** Cambs
236 c6 **Six Rues** Jersey
117 K4 **Sixhills** Lincs
34 F5 **Sixmile Cottages** Kent
27 M7 **Sixpenny Handley** Dorset
129 K3 **Sizergh Castle** Cumb
234 d6 **Skaill** Ork
164 B6 **Skares** E Ayrs
207 G6 **Skateraw** Abers
178 F4 **Skateraw** E Loth
208 F5 **Skeabost** Highld
140 F6 **Skeeby** N York
87 L3 **Skeffington** Leics
127 J6 **Skeffling** E R Yk
101 J1 **Skegby** Notts
116 C7 **Skegby** Notts
119 H8 **Skegness** Lincs
223 H3 **Skelbo** Highld
223 H3 **Skelbo Street** Highld
124 D7 **Skelbrooke** Donc
104 B5 **Skeldyke** Lincs
116 F6 **Skellingthorpe** Lincs
124 E7 **Skellow** Donc
123 J7 **Skelmanthorpe** Kirk
112 C1 **Skelmersdale** Lancs
173 L5 **Skelmorlie** N Ayrs
229 L4 **Skelpick** Highld
154 E5 **Skelston** D & G
148 D7 **Skelton** Cumb
125 H5 **Skelton** E R Yk
132 E5 **Skelton** N York
142 E4 **Skelton** R & Cl
133 J7 **Skelton** York
137 K6 **Skelwith Bridge** Cumb
118 F7 **Skendleby** Lincs
206 E4 **Skene House** Abers
54 C4 **Skenfrith** Mons
135 G7 **Skerne** E R Yk
229 K3 **Skerray** Highld
228 C5 **Skerricha** Highld
129 K6 **Skerton** Lancs
86 E5 **Sketchley** Leics
51 J6 **Sketty** Swans
51 K6 **Skewen** Neath
133 K5 **Skewsby** N York
230 E3 **Skiall** Highld
126 C4 **Skidby** E R Yk
232 g1 **Skigersta** W Isls
24 F6 **Skilgate** Somset
102 E7 **Skillington** Lincs
147 K4 **Skinburness** Cumb
176 B2 **Skinflats** Falk
208 C5 **Skinidin** Highld
172 F6 **Skipness** Ag & B
135 J8 **Skipsea** E R Yk
122 E1 **Skipton** N York
132 E4 **Skipton-on-Swale** N York
125 G3 **Skipwith** N York
126 E3 **Skirlaugh** E R Yk
165 L2 **Skirling** Border
42 C3 **Skirmett** Bucks
134 B7 **Skirpenbeck** E R Yk
149 G7 **Skirwith** Cumb
231 L2 **Skirza** Highld
199 K2 **Skulamus** Highld
208 F6 **Skye** Highld
61 L4 **Skye Green** Essex
204 B1 **Skye of Curr** Highld
122 E5 **Slack** Calder
216 F5 **Slacks of Cairnbanno** Abers
55 K6 **Slad** Gloucs
23 H3 **Slade** Devon
24 C6 **Slade** Somset
45 K5 **Slade Green** Kent
115 K4 **Slade Hooton** Rothm
149 H4 **Slaggyford** Nthumb
130 D8 **Slaidburn** Lancs
123 G7 **Slaithwaite** Kirk
150 B4 **Slaley** Nthumb
176 B4 **Slamannan** Falk
58 F4 **Slapton** Bucks
7 J6 **Slapton** Devon
73 J5 **Slapton** Nhants
31 L5 **Slaugham** W Susx
39 J5 **Slaughterford** Wilts
87 L5 **Slawston** Leics
30 D4 **Sleaford** Hants
103 H4 **Sleaford** Lincs
138 E4 **Sleagill** Cumb
84 B1 **Sleapford** Wrekin
222 E3 **Sleasdairidh** Highld
134 E6 **Sledmere** E R Yk
140 B5 **Sleightholme** Dur
143 H5 **Sleights** N York
231 K3 **Slickly** Highld
162 B5 **Sliddery** N Ayrs
209 G7 **Sligachan** Highld
173 K1 **Sligrachan** Ag & B
55 H7 **Slimbridge** Gloucs
99 J6 **Slindon** Staffs
18 C4 **Slindon** W Susx
31 J5 **Slinfold** W Susx
133 L4 **Slingsby** N York
59 H4 **Slip End** Beds
75 K6 **Slip End** Herts
88 D7 **Slipton** Nhants
100 B8 **Slitting Mill** Staffs
182 B7 **Slockavullin** Ag & B
146 B2 **Slogarie** D & G
11 H7 **Sloncombe** Devon
119 G7 **Sloothby** Lincs
43 G4 **Slough** Slough
25 L7 **Slough Green** Somset
210 D6 **Slumbay** Highld
129 K6 **Slyne** Lancs
167 K3 **Smailholm** Border
19 G3 **Small Dole** W Susx
85 K6 **Small Heath** Birm
34 B8 **Small Hythe** Kent
107 G7 **Smallburgh** Norfk
101 H4 **Smalley** Derbys
32 B5 **Smallfield** Surrey
13 H3 **Smallridge** Devon
92 B7 **Smallworth** Norfk
29 G2 **Smannell** Hants
34 B6 **Smarden** Kent
34 B6 **Smarden Bell** Kent
32 F5 **Smart's Hill** Kent
190 D2 **Smearisary** Highld
12 F1 **Smeatharpe** Devon
34 E6 **Smeeth** Kent
87 K5 **Smeeton Westerby** Leics
227 L2 **Smerral** Highld
84 F5 **Smestow** Staffs
85 H6 **Smethwick** Sandw
101 G8 **Smisby** Derbys
76 F6 **Smith's Green** Essex
148 D2 **Smithfield** Cumb
219 J6 **Smithstown** Highld
213 H5 **Smithton** Highld
228 F3 **Smoo** Highld
61 L4 **Smythe's Green** Essex
154 E5 **Snade** D & G
83 G3 **Snailbeach** Shrops
76 F2 **Snailwell** Cambs
134 E3 **Snainton** N York
124 F6 **Snaith** E R Yk
132 D3 **Snape** N York
79 H3 **Snape** Suffk
79 H3 **Snape Street** Suffk
45 H3 **Snaresbrook** Gt Lon
86 D2 **Snarestone** Leics
117 H5 **Snarford** Lincs
34 D8 **Snargate** Kent
34 D8 **Snave** Kent
143 J5 **Sneaton** N York

117 H5 **Snelland** Lincs
100 D4 **Snelston** Derbys
92 B5 **Snetterton** Norfk
105 G5 **Snettisham** Norfk
158 C2 **Snitter** Nthumb
117 G3 **Snitterby** Lincs
72 B3 **Snitterfield** Warwks
83 L7 **Snitton** Shrops
46 B7 **Snodland** Kent
60 C2 **Snow End** Herts
95 K2 **Snowdon** Gwynd
96 C6 **Snowdonia National Park**
71 K7 **Snowshill** Gloucs
17 J1 **Soake** Hants
29 L7 **Soberton** Hants
29 L8 **Soberton Heath** Hants
141 J5 **Sockburn** Darltn
90 E8 **Soham** Cambs
232 c5 **Solas** W Isls
29 M4 **Soldridge** Hants
46 A6 **Sole Street** Kent
34 E5 **Sole Street** Kent
85 L7 **Solihull** Solhll
69 H4 **Sollers Dilwyn** Herefs
54 E2 **Sollers Hope** Herefs
48 D3 **Solva** Pembks
156 B6 **Solwaybank** D & G
87 L2 **Somerby** Leics
117 H1 **Somerby** Lincs
101 H2 **Somercotes** Derbys
15 M4 **Somerford** Dorset
40 A2 **Somerford Keynes** Gloucs
17 M3 **Somerley** W Susx
93 K4 **Somerleyton** Suffk
100 C5 **Somersal Herbert** Derbys
118 D6 **Somersby** Lincs
89 L7 **Somersham** Cambs
78 C5 **Somersham** Suffk
57 J3 **Somerton** Oxon
26 C5 **Somerton** Somset
77 J4 **Somerton** Suffk
19 G5 **Sompting** W Susx
42 C5 **Sonning** Wokham
42 B4 **Sonning Common** Oxon
15 M3 **Sopley** Hants
39 J3 **Sopworth** Wilts
145 J5 **Sorbie** D & G
231 G3 **Sordale** Highld
189 H4 **Sorisdale** Ag & B
164 B4 **Sorn** E Ayrs
231 K3 **Sortat** Highld
136 F3 **Sosgill** Cumb
117 K5 **Sotby** Lincs
117 J8 **Sots Hole** Lincs
93 J6 **Sotterley** Suffk
111 H7 **Soughton** Flints
58 E3 **Soulbury** Bucks
139 H5 **Soulby** Cumb
57 K2 **Souldern** Oxon
74 E3 **Souldrop** Beds
215 H4 **Sound Muir** Moray
38 F5 **Soundwell** S Glos
10 D6 **Sourton** Devon
128 F3 **Soutergate** Cumb
91 J2 **South Acre** Norfk
35 H6 **South Alkham** Kent
7 J7 **South Allington** Devon
185 J8 **South Alloa** Falk
30 E7 **South Ambersham** W Susx
115 K5 **South Anston** Rothm
34 D6 **South Ashford** Kent
16 D3 **South Baddesley** Hants
124 F1 **South Bank** York
26 E5 **South Barrow** Somset
44 F7 **South Beddington** Gt Lon
46 C3 **South Benfleet** Essex
18 C5 **South Bersted** W Susx
124 F7 **South Bramwith** Donc
7 G4 **South Brent** Devon
27 G4 **South Brewham** Somset
159 G3 **South Broomhill** Nthumb
93 H3 **South Burlingham** Norfk
26 F6 **South Cadbury** Somset
116 F6 **South Carlton** Lincs
115 L5 **South Carlton** Notts
125 L4 **South Cave** E R Yk
40 B2 **South Cerney** Gloucs
19 K3 **South Chailey** E Susx
169 H5 **South Charlton** Nthumb
27 G6 **South Cheriton** Somset
140 F2 **South Church** Dur
125 K4 **South Cliffe** E R Yk
116 D7 **South Clifton** Notts
118 E4 **South Cockerington** Lincs
36 C4 **South Cornelly** Brdgnd
93 K7 **South Cove** Suffk
105 K5 **South Creake** Norfk
87 K2 **South Croxton** Leics
126 B2 **South Dalton** E R Yk
19 K4 **South Downs**
125 G4 **South Duffield** N York
118 D4 **South Elkington** Lincs
124 D7 **South Elmsall** Wakefd
219 H7 **South Erradale** Highld
46 E2 **South Fambridge** Essex
126 B6 **South Ferriby** N Linc
126 C5 **South Field** E R Yk
15 M1 **South Gorley** Hants
151 G2 **South Gosforth** N u Ty
46 B2 **South Green** Essex
33 L2 **South Green** Kent
92 C2 **South Green** Norfk
177 G4 **South Gyle** C Edin
61 H8 **South Hanningfield** Essex
30 C7 **South Harting** W Susx
17 K3 **South Hayling** Hants
58 E7 **South Heath** Bucks
151 J6 **South Hetton** Dur
124 B7 **South Hiendley** Wakefd
5 M2 **South Hill** Cnwll
57 K7 **South Hinksey** Oxon
31 K3 **South Holmwood** Surrey
45 K4 **South Hornchurch** Gt Lon
7 G7 **South Huish** Devon
116 F8 **South Hykeham** Lincs
151 J4 **South Hylton** Sundld
117 H2 **South Kelsey** Lincs
213 G5 **South Kessock** Highld
126 E7 **South Killingholme** N Linc
132 F3 **South Kilvington** N York
87 H6 **South Kilworth** Nhants
124 C7 **South Kirkby** Wakefd
103 K3 **South Kyme** Lincs
56 F5 **South Lawn** Oxon
57 H6 **South Leigh** Oxon
116 C5 **South Leverton** Notts
71 J5 **South Littleton** Worcs
92 C7 **South Lopham** Norfk
88 D3 **South Luffenham** Rutlnd
19 L4 **South Malling** E Susx
40 D3 **South Marston** Swindn
32 B3 **South Merstham** Surrey
124 D4 **South Milford** N York
7 G7 **South Milton** Devon
59 L7 **South Mimms** Herts
23 L6 **South Molton** Devon
150 F5 **South Moor** Dur
41 K3 **South Moreton** Oxon
18 B5 **South Mundham** W Susx
125 L4 **South Newbald** E R Yk
57 H2 **South Newington** Oxon
28 C4 **South Newton** Wilts
101 H2 **South Normanton** Derbys
45 G6 **South Norwood** Gt Lon
45 L4 **South Ockendon** Thurr
118 E6 **South Ormsby** Lincs
132 E3 **South Otterington** N York
117 H3 **South Owersby** Lincs
31 L2 **South Park** Surrey
13 L2 **South Perrott** Dorset
26 B7 **South Petherton** Somset
9 J8 **South Petherwin** Cnwll
91 J3 **South Pickenham** Norfk
6 B4 **South Pill** Cnwll
7 H7 **South Pool** Devon
13 M3 **South Poorton** Dorset
176 F3 **South Queensferry** C Edin
24 B5 **South Radworthy** Devon
103 G4 **South Rauceby** Lincs
105 L7 **South Raynham** Norfk
118 E5 **South Reston** Lincs
90 F2 **South Runcton** Norfk
116 D8 **South Scarle** Notts
191 H7 **South Shian** Ag & B
151 J2 **South Shields** S Tyne
120 D4 **South Shore** Bpool
132 D6 **South Stainley** N York
39 H7 **South Stoke** BaNES
41 L4 **South Stoke** Oxon
18 D4 **South Stoke** W Susx
34 E3 **South Street** Kent
47 J6 **South Street** Kent
176 D7 **South Tarbrax** S Lans
10 F6 **South Tawton** Devon
118 E6 **South Thoresby** Lincs
93 H2 **South Walsham** Norfk
30 B3 **South Warnborough** Hants
45 L2 **South Weald** Essex
42 B2 **South Weston** Oxon
9 H6 **South Wheatley** Cnwll
38 E8 **South Widcombe** BaNES
87 H4 **South Wigston** Leics
34 D6 **South Willesborough** Kent
117 K5 **South Willingham** Lincs
151 K7 **South Wingate** Dur
101 G2 **South Wingfield** Derbys
102 F8 **South Witham** Lincs
61 J7 **South Woodham Ferrers** Essex
105 G7 **South Wootton** Norfk
39 J7 **South Wraxall** Wilts
10 F6 **South Zeal** Devon
43 J4 **Southall** Gt Lon
55 L3 **Southam** Gloucs
72 E3 **Southam** Warwks
29 H8 **Southampton** C Sotn
29 J7 **Southampton Airport** Hants
45 H6 **Southborough** Gt Lon
33 G5 **Southborough** Kent
15 L4 **Southbourne** Bmouth
17 L2 **Southbourne** W Susx
92 B3 **Southburgh** Norfk
134 F8 **Southburn** E R Yk
46 E3 **Southchurch** Sthend
9 G5 **Southcott** Cnwll
10 E5 **Southcott** Devon
11 H8 **Southcott** Devon
58 D5 **Southcourt** Bucks
19 L5 **Southease** E Susx
161 H7 **Southend** Ag & B
46 E3 **Southend Airport** Essex
46 E3 **Southend-on-Sea** Sthend
36 D5 **Southerndown** V Glam
147 G4 **Southerness** D & G
12 D4 **Southerton** Devon
90 E5 **Southery** Norfk
175 L4 **Southfield** Falk
45 L5 **Southfleet** Kent
44 F2 **Southgate** Gt Lon
51 G7 **Southgate** Swans
75 H6 **Southill** Beds
29 J2 **Southington** Hants
12 F4 **Southleigh** Devon
62 A7 **Southminster** Essex
41 H2 **Southmoor** Oxon
196 C5 **Southmuir** Angus
75 H2 **Southoe** Cambs
78 E2 **Southolt** Suffk
88 F3 **Southorpe** C Pete
14 C4 **Southover** Dorset
123 G5 **Southowram** Calder
120 D6 **Southport** Sefton
106 F5 **Southrepps** Norfk
117 J7 **Southrey** Lincs
56 D7 **Southrop** Gloucs
30 A3 **Southrope** Hants
17 J3 **Southsea** C Port
140 E2 **Southside** Dur
93 L3 **Southtown** Norfk
148 D6 **Southwaite** Cumb
44 F4 **Southwark** Gt Lon
31 J6 **Southwater** W Susx
102 B2 **Southwell** Notts
17 J2 **Southwick** Hants
88 E5 **Southwick** Nhants
151 J4 **Southwick** Sundld
19 H5 **Southwick** W Susx
27 J1 **Southwick** Wilts
93 K7 **Southwold** Suffk
122 F6 **Sowerby** Kirk
132 F4 **Sowerby** N York
122 F5 **Sowerby Bridge** Calder
123 G6 **Sowood** Calder
6 D3 **Sowton** Devon
12 C4 **Sowton** Devon
122 F6 **Soyland Town** Calder
76 F6 **Spain's End** Essex

103 L7 **Spalding** Lincs
125 H4 **Spaldington** E R Yk
89 G8 **Spaldwick** Cambs
116 D7 **Spalford** Notts
103 H5 **Spanby** Lincs
106 C8 **Sparham** Norfk
129 G3 **Spark Bridge** Cumb
26 E6 **Sparkford** Somset
85 K6 **Sparkhill** Birm
6 E4 **Sparkwell** Devon
114 C5 **Sparrowpit** Derbys
33 H6 **Sparrows Green** E Susx
29 H5 **Sparsholt** Hants
41 G3 **Sparsholt** Oxon
133 L2 **Spaunton** N York
25 K4 **Spaxton** Somset
201 K8 **Spean Bridge** Highld
28 F6 **Spearywell** Hants
58 D7 **Speen** Bucks
41 J6 **Speen** W Berk
135 J4 **Speeton** N York
112 C5 **Speke** Lpool
32 F5 **Speldhurst** Kent
60 D4 **Spellbrook** Herts
99 J1 **Spen Green** Ches
42 B6 **Spencers Wood** Wokham
131 L2 **Spennithorne** N York
151 G7 **Spennymoor** Dur
70 F4 **Spetchley** Worcs
15 G3 **Spetisbury** Dorset
93 H7 **Spexhall** Suffk
215 H2 **Spey Bay** Moray
204 C1 **Speybridge** Highld
215 G6 **Speyview** Moray
118 E7 **Spilsby** Lincs
115 J5 **Spinkhill** Derbys
222 F4 **Spinningdale** Highld
115 L3 **Spital Hill** Donc
178 B3 **Spittal** E Loth
231 H5 **Spittal** Highld
179 L7 **Spittal** Nthumb
49 G3 **Spittal** Pembks
205 G7 **Spittal of Glenmuick** Abers
195 H3 **Spittal of Glenshee** P & K
167 J5 **Spittal-on-Rule** Border
195 H7 **Spittalfield** P & K
92 F1 **Spixworth** Norfk
10 E4 **Splatt** Devon
19 L2 **Splayne's Green** E Susx
37 K5 **Splottlands** Cardif
124 B1 **Spofforth** N York
101 H5 **Spondon** C Derb
92 D4 **Spooner Row** Norfk
91 J2 **Sporle** Norfk
178 E4 **Spott** E Loth
178 D7 **Spottiswoode** Border
73 K1 **Spratton** Nhants
30 D3 **Spreakley** Surrey
11 G5 **Spreyton** Devon
6 D5 **Spriddlestone** Devon
117 G5 **Spridlington** Lincs
175 G5 **Springburn** C Glas
148 B2 **Springfield** D & G
61 H6 **Springfield** Essex
186 E5 **Springfield** Fife
154 E7 **Springholm** D & G
163 J2 **Springside** N Ayrs
116 E4 **Springthorpe** Lincs
151 H4 **Springwell** Sundld
126 F4 **Sproatley** E R Yk
113 G7 **Sproston Green** Ches
115 K2 **Sprotbrough** Donc
78 D5 **Sproughton** Suffk
168 A3 **Sprouston** Border
92 F2 **Sprowston** Norfk
102 D7 **Sproxton** Leics
133 J3 **Sproxton** N York
98 D2 **Spurstow** Ches
14 A4 **Spyway** Dorset
84 D4 **Stableford** Shrops
114 F4 **Stacey Bank** Sheff
130 F6 **Stackhouse** N York
49 G7 **Stackpole** Pembks
6 D5 **Staddiscombe** C Plym
57 L7 **Stadhampton** Oxon
233 b7 **Stadhlaigearraidh** W Isls
148 F6 **Staffield** Cumb
218 D7 **Staffin** Highld
99 L7 **Stafford** Staffs
74 E5 **Stagsden** Beds
136 E2 **Stainburn** Cumb
123 K2 **Stainburn** N York
102 E7 **Stainby** Lincs
123 L7 **Staincross** Barns
140 E3 **Staindrop** Dur
43 G6 **Staines** Surrey
124 F7 **Stainforth** Donc
130 F6 **Stainforth** N York
120 D4 **Staining** Lancs
123 G6 **Stainland** Calder
143 J5 **Stainsacre** N York
138 C2 **Stainton** Cumb
129 L3 **Stainton** Cumb
115 K3 **Stainton** Donc
140 D4 **Stainton** Dur
141 L4 **Stainton** Middsb
117 H6 **Stainton by Langworth** Lincs
117 K3 **Stainton le Vale** Lincs
128 F5 **Stainton with Adgarley** Cumb
143 K7 **Staintondale** N York
163 K5 **Stair** E Ayrs
144 E4 **Stairhaven** D & G
143 G4 **Staithes** N York
159 G5 **Stakeford** Nthumb
17 K2 **Stakes** Hants
27 G7 **Stalbridge** Dorset
27 G7 **Stalbridge Weston** Dorset
107 H7 **Stalham** Norfk
34 C4 **Stalisfield Green** Kent
26 E7 **Stallen** Dorset
126 F7 **Stallingborough** NE Lin
120 E2 **Stalmine** Lancs
113 L2 **Stalybridge** Tamesd
77 G6 **Stambourne** Essex
77 G6 **Stambourne Green** Essex
88 E3 **Stamford** Lincs
169 J5 **Stamford** Nthumb
112 C7 **Stamford Bridge** Ches
133 L7 **Stamford Bridge** E R Yk
45 G3 **Stamford Hill** Gt Lon
158 D7 **Stamfordham** Nthumb
58 F3 **Stanbridge** Beds
122 F3 **Stanbury** Brad
175 K5 **Stand** N Lans
176 C4 **Standburn** Falk
85 G3 **Standeford** Staffs
33 L5 **Standen** Kent
27 J2 **Standerwick** Somset
30 D4 **Standford** Hants
147 J7 **Standingstone** Cumb
121 H7 **Standish** Wigan
57 H7 **Standlake** Oxon
29 H6 **Standon** Hants
60 C4 **Standon** Herts
99 J5 **Standon** Staffs
176 B6 **Stane** N Lans
105 M7 **Stanfield** Norfk
75 H6 **Stanford** Beds
34 F6 **Stanford** Kent
70 C4 **Stanford Bishop** Herefs
70 C2 **Stanford Bridge** Worcs
41 L6 **Stanford Dingley** W Berk
41 G2 **Stanford in the Vale** Oxon
46 B4 **Stanford le Hope** Thurr
87 H7 **Stanford on Avon** Nhants
101 K7 **Stanford on Soar** Notts
70 C2 **Stanford on Teme** Worcs
115 J6 **Stanfree** Derbys
142 E4 **Stanghow** R & Cl
89 H4 **Stanground** C Pete
105 J5 **Stanhoe** Norfk
165 L4 **Stanhope** Border
150 C6 **Stanhope** Dur
88 D6 **Stanion** Nhants
101 H4 **Stanley** Derbys
150 F4 **Stanley** Dur
186 B2 **Stanley** P & K
99 L3 **Stanley** Staffs
150 E7 **Stanley Crook** Dur
55 M3 **Stanley Pontlarge** Gloucs
19 K4 **Stanmer** Br & H
44 D2 **Stanmore** Gt Lon
29 J5 **Stanmore** Hants
157 J5 **Stannersburn** Nthumb
77 K3 **Stanningfield** Suffk
158 F6 **Stannington** Nthumb
114 F4 **Stannington** Sheff
158 F5 **Stannington Station** Nthumb
69 G3 **Stansbatch** Herefs
77 H4 **Stansfield** Suffk
77 J5 **Stanstead** Suffk
60 E4 **Stansted Airport** Essex
60 C5 **Stanstead Abbotts** Herts
77 J5 **Stanstead Street** Suffk
45 L7 **Stansted** Kent
60 E3 **Stansted Mountfitchet** Essex
71 J7 **Stanton** Gloucs
158 E4 **Stanton** Nthumb
100 C4 **Stanton** Staffs
91 L8 **Stanton** Suffk
101 G6 **Stanton by Bridge** Derbys
101 J5 **Stanton by Dale** Derbys
38 E7 **Stanton Drew** BaNES
40 D3 **Stanton Fitzwarren** Swindn
57 H6 **Stanton Harcourt** Oxon
114 E8 **Stanton in Peak** Derbys
83 K7 **Stanton Lacy** Shrops
114 E8 **Stanton Lees** Derbys
83 L5 **Stanton Long** Shrops
101 M6 **Stanton on the Wolds** Notts
39 G7 **Stanton Prior** BaNES
40 C7 **Stanton St Bernard** Wilts
57 L6 **Stanton St John** Oxon
39 K4 **Stanton St Quintin** Wilts
77 L2 **Stanton Street** Suffk
86 F2 **Stanton under Bardon** Leics
98 E7 **Stanton upon Hine Heath** Shrops
38 E7 **Stanton Wick** BaNES
61 M3 **Stanway** Essex
56 B2 **Stanway** Gloucs
43 H5 **Stanwell** Surrey
74 E1 **Stanwick** Nhants
148 D4 **Stanwix** Cumb
233 b8 **Staoinebrig** W Isls
143 G7 **Stape** N York
99 G3 **Stapeley** Ches
100 E7 **Stapenhill** Staffs
35 H4 **Staple** Kent
25 H3 **Staple** Somset
25 G7 **Staple Cross** Devon
20 F2 **Staple Cross** E Susx
25 K7 **Staple Fitzpaine** Somset
32 B7 **Staplefield** W Susx
76 C4 **Stapleford** Cambs
60 A5 **Stapleford** Herts
102 D8 **Stapleford** Leics
102 E2 **Stapleford** Lincs
101 J5 **Stapleford** Notts
28 B4 **Stapleford** Wilts
45 K2 **Stapleford Abbotts** Essex
25 K6 **Staplegrove** Somset
25 K6 **Staplehay** Somset
33 K5 **Staplehurst** Kent
34 E3 **Staplestreet** Kent
69 G2 **Stapleton** Herefs
86 E4 **Stapleton** Leics
141 G5 **Stapleton** N York
83 J3 **Stapleton** Shrops
26 C7 **Stapleton** Somset
25 J8 **Stapley** Somset
75 G3 **Staploe** Beds
70 C6 **Staplow** Herefs
186 E6 **Star** Fife
65 H7 **Star** Pembks
38 C8 **Star** Somset
132 E7 **Starbeck** N York
131 H5 **Starbotton** N York
12 C6 **Starcross** Devon
72 D1 **Stareton** Warwks
60 D2 **Starlings Green** Essex
92 F6 **Starston** Norfk
140 D4 **Startforth** Dur
39 L4 **Startley** Wilts
35 J4 **Statenborough** Kent
26 A5 **Stathe** Somset
102 C6 **Stathern** Leics
75 G2 **Staughton Green** Cambs
54 D5 **Staunton** Gloucs
55 H3 **Staunton** Gloucs
69 G3 **Staunton Green** Herefs
69 G3 **Staunton on Arrow** Herefs
69 G5 **Staunton on Wye** Herefs
129 H3 **Staveley** Cumb
138 C7 **Staveley** Cumb
115 H6 **Staveley** Derbys
132 E6 **Staveley** N York
7 J3 **Staverton** Devon
55 K4 **Staverton** Gloucs
73 G3 **Staverton** Nhants
39 J7 **Staverton** Wilts
26 A4 **Stawell** Somset
25 G6 **Stawley** Somset
231 L5 **Staxigoe** Highld
134 F4 **Staxton** N York
120 E2 **Staynall** Lancs
131 K5 **Stean** N York
73 G6 **Steane** Nhants
133 J5 **Stearsby** N York
25 L3 **Steart** Somset
61 G3 **Stebbing** Essex
61 H4 **Stebbing Green** Essex

61 G3 **Stebbing Park** Essex
30 E6 **Stedham** W Susx
156 F4 **Steele Road** Border
185 L8 **Steelend** Fife
69 K3 **Steen's Bridge** Herefs
30 C6 **Steep** Hants
122 F5 **Steep Lane** Calder
61 M7 **Steeple** Essex
27 K1 **Steeple Ashton** Wilts
57 J3 **Steeple Aston** Oxon
76 F6 **Steeple Bumpstead** Essex
58 B3 **Steeple Claydon** Bucks
89 G7 **Steeple Gidding** Cambs
28 B4 **Steeple Langford** Wilts
75 K6 **Steeple Morden** Cambs
122 F2 **Steeton** Brad
208 D3 **Stein** Highld
34 F5 **Stelling Minnis** Kent
26 B7 **Stembridge** Somset
4 F4 **Stenalees** Cnwll
154 D4 **Stenhouse** D & G
176 B2 **Stenhousemuir** Falk
218 D7 **Stenscholl** Highld
178 D4 **Stenton** E Loth
232 f2 **Steornabhagh** W Isls
49 K6 **Stepaside** Pembks
45 G4 **Stepney** Gt Lon
74 E7 **Steppingley** Beds
175 H5 **Stepps** N Lans
79 H3 **Sternfield** Suffk
40 B8 **Stert** Wilts
76 F3 **Stetchworth** Cambs
59 L3 **Stevenage** Herts
163 H2 **Stevenston** N Ayrs
29 K2 **Steventon** Hants
41 J3 **Steventon** Oxon
76 E6 **Steventon End** Essex
74 E4 **Stevington** Beds
74 E6 **Stewartby** Beds
175 H7 **Stewartfield** S Lans
163 K1 **Stewarton** E Ayrs
58 D3 **Stewkley** Bucks
25 L7 **Stewley** Somset
19 G4 **Steyning** W Susx
48 F6 **Steynton** Pembks
9 G3 **Stibb** Cnwll
10 C2 **Stibb Cross** Devon
40 E7 **Stibb Green** Wilts
106 B6 **Stibbard** Norfk
88 F4 **Stibbington** Cambs
167 L2 **Stichill** Border
4 F5 **Sticker** Cnwll
104 B1 **Stickford** Lincs
10 F6 **Sticklepath** Devon
60 D2 **Stickling Green** Essex
104 B2 **Stickney** Lincs
106 A4 **Stiffkey** Norfk
233 b7 **Stilligarry** W Isls
124 F3 **Stillingfleet** N York
133 J6 **Stillington** N York
141 J3 **Stillington** S on T
89 H5 **Stilton** Cambs
55 G7 **Stinchcombe** Gloucs
14 D4 **Stinsford** Dorset
83 G4 **Stiperstones** Shrops
217 L6 **Stirling** Abers
185 G8 **Stirling** Stirlg
75 H2 **Stirtloe** Cambs
131 H8 **Stirton** N York
61 J3 **Stisted** Essex
3 J4 **Stithians** Cnwll
86 D7 **Stivichall** Covtry
117 K7 **Stixwould** Lincs
112 B6 **Stoak** Ches
166 B2 **Stobo** Border
15 H5 **Stoborough** Dorset
167 G7 **Stobs Castle** Border
158 F3 **Stobswood** Nthumb
61 H7 **Stock** Essex
38 C7 **Stock** N Som
71 H3 **Stock Green** Worcs
71 H3 **Stock Wood** Worcs
29 G4 **Stockbridge** Hants
164 F3 **Stockbriggs** S Lans
46 D7 **Stockbury** Kent
41 H6 **Stockcross** W Berk
88 B4 **Stockerston** Leics
54 F2 **Stocking** Herefs
60 D3 **Stocking Pelham** Herts
86 D5 **Stockingford** Warwks
13 G2 **Stockland** Devon
25 K3 **Stockland Bristol** Somset
11 K4 **Stockleigh English** Devon
11 K4 **Stockleigh Pomeroy** Devon
39 M6 **Stockley** Wilts
26 B7 **Stocklinch** Somset
113 K4 **Stockport** Stockp
114 E2 **Stocksbridge** Sheff
150 D3 **Stocksfield** Nthumb
69 K3 **Stockton** Herefs
93 H5 **Stockton** Norfk
84 C4 **Stockton** Shrops
72 E2 **Stockton** Warwks
27 M4 **Stockton** Wilts
84 D1 **Stockton** Wrekin
112 E4 **Stockton Heath** Warrtn
70 C2 **Stockton on Teme** Worcs
133 K7 **Stockton on the Forest** York
141 K4 **Stockton-on-Tees** S on T
38 F6 **Stockwood** Bristl
14 B2 **Stockwood** Dorset
35 G3 **Stodmarsh** Kent
106 C5 **Stody** Norfk
224 C3 **Stoer** Highld
26 E8 **Stoford** Somset
28 B4 **Stoford** Wilts
25 H4 **Stogumber** Somset
25 J3 **Stogursey** Somset
86 D7 **Stoke** Covtry
22 C6 **Stoke** Devon
29 H2 **Stoke** Hants
17 K3 **Stoke** Hants
46 D5 **Stoke** Medway
13 L3 **Stoke Abbott** Dorset
88 B5 **Stoke Albany** Nhants
78 D1 **Stoke Ash** Suffk
101 M4 **Stoke Bardolph** Notts
70 B2 **Stoke Bliss** Worcs
73 L4 **Stoke Bruerne** Nhants
77 G5 **Stoke by Clare** Suffk
12 B3 **Stoke Canon** Devon
29 J4 **Stoke Charity** Hants
6 A2 **Stoke Climsland** Cnwll
70 B4 **Stoke Cross** Herefs
43 J8 **Stoke D'Abernon** Surrey
88 E6 **Stoke Doyle** Nhants
88 C4 **Stoke Dry** Rutlnd
69 L6 **Stoke Edith** Herefs
28 B6 **Stoke Farthing** Wilts
91 G4 **Stoke Ferry** Norfk
7 K6 **Stoke Fleming** Devon
7 J4 **Stoke Gabriel** Devon
38 F4 **Stoke Gifford** S Glos
86 E4 **Stoke Golding** Leics
74 B5 **Stoke Goldington** M Keyn
58 E3 **Stoke Hammond** Bucks
92 F3 **Stoke Holy Cross** Norfk
70 B5 **Stoke Lacy** Herefs
57 K3 **Stoke Lyne** Oxon
58 D6 **Stoke Mandeville** Bucks
45 G3 **Stoke Newington** Gt Lon
55 K3 **Stoke Orchard** Gloucs
42 F4 **Stoke Poges** Bucks
69 K3 **Stoke Prior** Herefs
71 G2 **Stoke Prior** Worcs
23 K4 **Stoke Rivers** Devon
102 F6 **Stoke Rochford** Lincs
42 B4 **Stoke Row** Oxon
25 M6 **Stoke St Gregory** Somset
25 K6 **Stoke St Mary** Somset
26 F3 **Stoke St Michael** Somset
83 L6 **Stoke St Milborough** Shrops
26 C7 **Stoke sub Hamdon** Somset
58 B7 **Stoke Talmage** Oxon
27 H5 **Stoke Trister** Somset
98 F6 **Stoke upon Tern** Shrops
14 E2 **Stoke Wake** Dorset
78 B7 **Stoke-by-Nayland** Suffk
99 K3 **Stoke-on-Trent** C Stke
99 K4 **Stoke-upon-Trent** C Stke
15 G5 **Stokeford** Dorset
116 C6 **Stokeham** Notts
7 L2 **Stokeinteignhead** Devon
42 C2 **Stokenchurch** Bucks
7 J7 **Stokenham** Devon
83 H6 **Stokesay Castle** Shrops
93 J2 **Stokesby** Norfk
142 B5 **Stokesley** N York
25 K3 **Stolford** Somset
26 F2 **Ston Easton** Somset
60 F7 **Stondon Massey** Essex
58 C5 **Stone** Bucks
39 G2 **Stone** Gloucs
21 J1 **Stone** Kent
115 K4 **Stone** Rothm
99 K5 **Stone** Staffs
84 F7 **Stone** Worcs
26 B2 **Stone Allerton** Somset
35 J4 **Stone Cross** Kent
33 G3 **Stone Street** Kent
93 H6 **Stone Street** Suffk
38 B7 **Stonebridge** N Som
86 B6 **Stonebridge** Solhll
101 H2 **Stonebroom** Derbys
33 J6 **Stonecrouch** Kent
126 D4 **Stoneferry** C KuH
172 E4 **Stonefield Castle Hotel** Ag & B
33 H7 **Stonegate** E Susx
133 K4 **Stonegrave** N York
207 G7 **Stonehaven** Abers
28 C3 **Stonehenge** Wilts
6 C5 **Stonehouse** C Plym
112 D7 **Stonehouse** Ches
146 E2 **Stonehouse** D & G
55 J6 **Stonehouse** Gloucs
175 K8 **Stonehouse** S Lans
86 D8 **Stoneleigh** Warwks
62 E3 **Stones Green** Essex
102 D7 **Stonesby** Leics
57 H4 **Stonesfield** Oxon
215 G2 **Stonewells** Moray
114 E6 **Stoney Middleton** Derbys
86 F4 **Stoney Stanton** Leics
27 G5 **Stoney Stoke** Somset
26 F4 **Stoney Stratton** Somset
83 H2 **Stoney Stretton** Shrops
233 b8 **Stoneybridge** W Isls
176 D5 **Stoneyburn** W Loth
87 H3 **Stoneygate** C Leic
144 C4 **Stoneykirk** D & G
207 G3 **Stoneywood** C Aber
175 L2 **Stoneywood** Falk
78 D3 **Stonham Aspal** Suffk
85 J3 **Stonnall** Staffs
42 B3 **Stonor** Oxon
87 K4 **Stonton Wyville** Leics
115 J7 **Stony Houghton** Derbys
73 L6 **Stony Stratford** M Keyn
23 K5 **Stoodleigh** Devon
24 E7 **Stoodleigh** Devon
18 D2 **Stopham** W Susx
59 J3 **Stopsley** Luton
232 f2 **Stornoway** W Isls
232 g2 **Stornoway Airport** W Isls
18 E3 **Storrington** W Susx
125 H2 **Storwood** E R Yk
214 F1 **Stotfield** Moray
75 J7 **Stotfold** Beds
84 C6 **Stottesdon** Shrops
87 J3 **Stoughton** Leics
31 G2 **Stoughton** Surrey
17 L1 **Stoughton** W Susx
200 B6 **Stoul** Highld
70 F4 **Stoulton** Worcs
27 H6 **Stour Provost** Dorset
27 J6 **Stour Row** Dorset
84 F6 **Stourbridge** Dudley
15 G1 **Stourpaine** Dorset
70 E1 **Stourport-on-Severn** Worcs
84 F6 **Stourton** Staffs
72 C6 **Stourton** Warwks
27 H5 **Stourton** Wilts
27 G7 **Stourton Caundle** Dorset
235 c7 **Stove** Shet
93 J6 **Stoven** Suffk
167 G1 **Stow** Border
116 E5 **Stow** Lincs
90 F3 **Stow Bardolph** Norfk
91 L4 **Stow Bedon** Norfk
75 G1 **Stow Longa** Cambs
61 K7 **Stow Maries** Essex
76 D3 **Stow-cum-Quy** Cambs
56 D3 **Stow-on-the-Wold** Gloucs
90 E3 **Stowbridge** Norfk
82 F8 **Stowe** Shrops
100 A6 **Stowe by Chartley** Staffs
27 G6 **Stowell** Somset
38 E7 **Stowey** BaNES
10 C5 **Stowford** Devon
23 K3 **Stowford** Devon
10 C7 **Stowford** Devon
77 L2 **Stowlangtoft** Suffk
78 C3 **Stowmarket** Suffk
34 F6 **Stowting** Kent
34 F6 **Stowting Common** Kent
78 C3 **Stowupland** Suffk
204 B3 **Straanruie** Moray
206 D6 **Strachan** Abers
182 F6 **Strachur** Ag & B

197 G4 **Strachthro Hospital** Angus
92 F8 **Stradbroke** Suffk
77 H4 **Stradishall** Suffk
90 F3 **Stradsett** Norfk
102 E3 **Stragglethorpe** Lincs
177 H5 **Straiton** Mdloth
153 H2 **Straiton** S Ayrs
207 G2 **Straloch** Abers
195 G4 **Straloch** P & K
100 B5 **Stramshall** Staffs
237 c5 **Strang** IOM
113 J2 **Strangeways** Salfd
54 E3 **Strangford** Herefs
144 C3 **Stranraer** D & G
42 A7 **Stratfield Mortimer** W Berk
42 B7 **Stratfield Saye** Hants
42 B7 **Stratfield Turgis** Hants
45 H3 **Stratford** Gt Lon
79 H3 **Stratford St Andrew** Suffk
78 C7 **Stratford St Mary** Suffk
28 C6 **Stratford Tony** Wilts
72 B4 **Stratford-upon-Avon** Warwks
219 J5 **Strath** Highld
224 D4 **Strathan** Highld
229 J3 **Strathan** Highld
164 D1 **Strathaven** S Lans
175 G3 **Strathblane** Stirlg
220 F2 **Strathcanaird** Highld
210 E6 **Strathcarron** Highld
181 K2 **Strathcoil** Ag & B
205 H3 **Strathdon** Abers
187 G4 **Strathkinness** Fife
176 C4 **Strathloanhead** W Loth
202 F6 **Strathmashie House** Highld
186 C5 **Strathmiglo** Fife
212 D3 **Strathpeffer** Highld
194 E5 **Strathtay** P & K
162 D3 **Strathwhillan** N Ayrs
230 B3 **Strathy** Highld
230 B3 **Strathy Inn** Highld
184 C4 **Strathyre** Stirlg
9 G4 **Stratton** Cnwll
14 C4 **Stratton** Dorset
56 A7 **Stratton** Gloucs
57 L3 **Stratton Audley** Oxon
40 D3 **Stratton St Margaret** Swindn
92 E5 **Stratton St Michael** Norfk
106 F7 **Stratton Strawless** Norfk
26 F2 **Stratton-on-the-Fosse** Somset
187 J5 **Stravithie** Fife
19 K3 **Streat** E Susx
44 F5 **Streatham** Gt Lon
59 H3 **Streatley** Beds
41 L4 **Streatley** W Berk
12 F5 **Street** Devon
26 C4 **Street** Somset
86 F6 **Street Ashton** Warwks
97 M5 **Street Dinas** Shrops
34 F4 **Street End** Kent
18 A5 **Street End** W Susx
26 F4 **Street on the Fosse** Somset
85 K2 **Streethay** Staffs
141 H7 **Streetlam** N York
76 E5 **Streetly End** Cambs
186 C1 **Strelitz** P & K
101 K4 **Strelley** Notts
133 K7 **Strensall** York
25 L3 **Stretcholt** Somset
7 J6 **Strete** Devon
113 H3 **Stretford** Traffd
76 C6 **Strethall** Essex
90 D8 **Stretham** Cambs
18 B4 **Strettington** W Susx
101 H1 **Stretton** Derbys
88 D1 **Stretton** Rutlnd
84 F2 **Stretton** Staffs
100 E7 **Stretton** Staffs
112 F5 **Stretton** Warrtn
70 B5 **Stretton Grandison** Herefs
72 B6 **Stretton on Fosse** Warwks
69 J6 **Stretton Sugwas** Herefs
86 F7 **Stretton under Fosse** Warwks
83 L4 **Stretton Westwood** Shrops
86 E8 **Stretton-on-Dunsmore** Warwks
217 H4 **Strichen** Abers
25 J3 **Stringston** Somset
74 C3 **Strixton** Nhants
38 E2 **Stroat** Gloucs
210 D7 **Stromeferry** Highld
234 b6 **Stromness** Ork
183 L5 **Stronachlachar** Stirlg
173 H3 **Stronafian** Ag & B
224 F5 **Stronchrubie** Highld
173 L3 **Strone** Ag & B
192 B1 **Strone** Highld
201 J8 **Stronenaba** Highld
183 G2 **Stronmilchan** Ag & B
234 d5 **Stronsay Airport** Ork
191 G4 **Strontian** Highld
46 B6 **Strood** Medway
55 J6 **Stroud** Gloucs
30 B6 **Stroud** Hants
55 J6 **Stroud Green** Gloucs
102 E6 **Stroxton** Lincs
208 E6 **Struan** Highld
194 C4 **Struan** P & K
93 H3 **Strumpshaw** Norfk
175 K7 **Strutherhill** S Lans
186 F5 **Struthers** Fife
212 B6 **Struy** Highld
217 H5 **Stuartfield** Abers
17 G2 **Stubbington** Hants
122 B6 **Stubbins** N York
102 E3 **Stubton** Lincs
28 D8 **Stuckton** Hants
59 G5 **Studham** Beds
148 A4 **Studholme** Cumb
15 J6 **Studland** Dorset
71 J2 **Studley** Warwks
39 L6 **Studley** Wilts
132 D5 **Studley Roger** N York
132 D5 **Studley Royal** N York
90 D7 **Stuntney** Cambs
77 G5 **Sturmer** Essex
27 H8 **Sturminster Common** Dorset
15 H3 **Sturminster Marshall** Dorset
27 H8 **Sturminster Newton** Dorset
35 G3 **Sturry** Kent
116 F2 **Sturton** N Linc
116 E5 **Sturton by Stow** Lincs
116 C5 **Sturton le Steeple** Notts
92 D7 **Stuston** Suffk
124 D3 **Stutton** N York
78 D7 **Stutton** Suffk
113 J5 **Styal** Ches
215 H3 **Stynie** Moray
115 L4 **Styrrup** Notts
183 K6 **Succoth** Ag & B
70 C4 **Suckley** Worcs
88 D6 **Sudborough** Nhants
79 J4 **Sudbourne** Suffk
102 F4 **Sudbrook** Lincs
38 D3 **Sudbrook** Mons
117 G6 **Sudbrooke** Lincs
100 D6 **Sudbury** Derbys
44 D3 **Sudbury** Gt Lon
77 K6 **Sudbury** Suffk
70 F2 **Suddington** Worcs
134 F2 **Suffield** N York
106 F6 **Suffield** Norfk
99 H6 **Sugnall** Staffs
69 J6 **Sugwas Pool** Herefs
199 J3 **Suisnish** Highld
237 d3 **Sulby** IOM
73 G5 **Sulgrave** Nhants
73 H5 **Sulgrave Manor** Nhants
41 M5 **Sulham** W Berk
41 M6 **Sulhamstead** W Berk
235 c4 **Sullom** Shet
235 c4 **Sullom Voe** Shet
37 J6 **Sully** V Glam
235 c8 **Sumburgh Airport** Shet
132 C6 **Summerbridge** N York
4 D5 **Summercourt** Cnwll
105 J5 **Summerfield** Norfk
140 F4 **Summerhouse** Darltn
18 B4 **Summersdale** W Susx
122 B7 **Summerseat** Bury
57 K6 **Summertown** Oxon
43 J6 **Sunbury** Surrey
154 E5 **Sundaywell** D & G
170 E5 **Sunderland** Ag & B
147 L7 **Sunderland** Cumb
129 J7 **Sunderland** Lancs
151 J4 **Sunderland** Sundld
151 G7 **Sunderland Bridge** Dur
166 E4 **Sundhope** Border
32 E3 **Sundridge** Kent
42 F6 **Sunningdale** W & M
42 F6 **Sunninghill** W & M
57 J7 **Sunningwell** Oxon
150 E7 **Sunniside** Dur
150 F3 **Sunniside** Gatesd
101 G6 **Sunnyhill** C Derb
121 K6 **Sunnyhurst** Bl w D
185 G7 **Sunnylaw** Stirlg
57 J6 **Sunnymead** Oxon
44 D6 **Surbiton** Gt Lon
103 L6 **Surfleet** Lincs
93 G3 **Surlingham** Norfk
61 L4 **Surrex** Essex
106 E5 **Sustead** Norfk
116 D2 **Susworth** Lincs
9 J3 **Sutcombe** Devon
9 J3 **Sutcombemill** Devon
118 E6 **Sutterby** Lincs
103 M5 **Sutterton** Lincs
75 J5 **Sutton** Beds
89 G4 **Sutton** C Pete
90 C7 **Sutton** Cambs
7 G7 **Sutton** Devon
20 A5 **Sutton** E Susx
44 E7 **Sutton** Gt Lon
35 J5 **Sutton** Kent
124 D5 **Sutton** N York
107 H7 **Sutton** Norfk
102 C5 **Sutton** Notts
84 D6 **Sutton** Shrops
99 H7 **Sutton** Staffs
79 G5 **Sutton** Suffk
18 D3 **Sutton** W Susx
45 K6 **Sutton at Hone** Kent
87 L5 **Sutton Bassett** Nhants
39 L5 **Sutton Benger** Wilts
101 K7 **Sutton Bonington** Notts
104 D7 **Sutton Bridge** Lincs
86 E4 **Sutton Cheney** Leics
85 K4 **Sutton Coldfield** Birm
41 J2 **Sutton Courtenay** Oxon
116 B5 **Sutton cum Lound** Notts
132 D5 **Sutton Grange** N York
31 G1 **Sutton Green** Surrey
132 D4 **Sutton Howgrave** N York
101 J2 **Sutton in Ashfield** Notts
84 C3 **Sutton Maddock** Shrops
26 A4 **Sutton Mallet** Somset
27 M5 **Sutton Mandeville** Wilts
26 F6 **Sutton Montis** Somset
119 G5 **Sutton on Sea** Lincs
100 E5 **Sutton on the Hill** Derbys
116 D7 **Sutton on Trent** Notts
29 J4 **Sutton Scotney** Hants
89 L2 **Sutton St Edmund** Lincs
104 C8 **Sutton St James** Lincs
69 K5 **Sutton St Nicholas** Herefs
125 G2 **Sutton upon Derwent** E R Yk
33 L4 **Sutton Valence** Kent
27 K3 **Sutton Veny** Wilts
27 K7 **Sutton Waldron** Dorset
112 D5 **Sutton Weaver** Ches
38 E8 **Sutton Wick** BaNES
41 J2 **Sutton Wick** Oxon
122 F2 **Sutton-in-Craven** N York
126 E4 **Sutton-on-Hull** C KuH
133 J6 **Sutton-on-the-Forest** N York
72 C6 **Sutton-under-Brailes** Warwks
133 G3 **Sutton-under-Whitestonecliffe** N York
118 E6 **Swaby** Lincs
100 F8 **Swadlincote** Derbys
91 J2 **Swaffham** Norfk
76 D3 **Swaffham Bulbeck** Cambs
76 E2 **Swaffham Prior** Cambs
107 G6 **Swafield** Norfk
141 L6 **Swainby** N York
92 F4 **Swainsthorpe** Norfk
39 H6 **Swainswick** BaNES
72 E6 **Swalcliffe** Oxon
47 J6 **Swalecliffe** Kent
117 K2 **Swallow** Lincs
116 F7 **Swallow Beck** Lincs
27 L6 **Swallowcliffe** Wilts
42 B7 **Swallowfield** Wokham
113 G6 **Swan Green** Ches
15 J6 **Swanage** Dorset
58 D3 **Swanbourne** Bucks
126 B5 **Swanland** E R Yk
45 K6 **Swanley** Kent
45 K6 **Swanley Village** Kent
29 L7 **Swanmore** Hants
86 E1 **Swannington** Leics
106 D8 **Swannington** Norfk
116 F7 **Swanpool Garden Suburb** Lincs

45 L5 **Swanscombe** Kent
51 J6 **Swansea** Swans
51 H7 **Swansea Airport** Swans
106 F7 **Swanton Abbot** Norfk
92 B1 **Swanton Morley** Norfk
106 B6 **Swanton Novers** Norfk
101 H2 **Swanwick** Derbys
17 G1 **Swanwick** Hants
103 H4 **Swarby** Lincs
92 E3 **Swardeston** Norfk
101 G6 **Swarkestone** Derbys
158 E2 **Swarland** Nthumb
29 K4 **Swarraton** Hants
129 G4 **Swarthmoor** Cumb
103 J5 **Swaton** Lincs
75 L2 **Swavesey** Cambs
16 C3 **Sway** Hants
103 G7 **Swayfield** Lincs
29 H7 **Swaythling** C Sotn
11 K5 **Sweetham** Devon
32 E7 **Sweethaws** E Susx
8 F5 **Sweets** Cnwll
5 H4 **Sweetshouse** Cnwll
79 H2 **Swefling** Suffk
86 D2 **Swepstone** Leics
57 G2 **Swerford** Oxon
113 J7 **Swettenham** Ches
78 E4 **Swilland** Suffk
124 B4 **Swillington** Leeds
23 K5 **Swimbridge** Devon
23 J5 **Swimbridge Newland** Devon
56 F5 **Swinbrook** Oxon
132 C7 **Swincliffe** N York
116 E8 **Swinderby** Lincs
55 L3 **Swindon** Gloucs
84 F5 **Swindon** Staffs
40 D4 **Swindon** Swindn
126 E4 **Swine** E R Yk
125 H6 **Swinefleet** E R Yk
74 F2 **Swineshead** Beds
103 L4 **Swineshead** Lincs
227 M2 **Swiney** Highld
87 H7 **Swinford** Leics
35 G6 **Swingfield Minnis** Kent
35 H6 **Swingfield Street** Kent
77 L5 **Swingleton Green** Suffk
169 J4 **Swinhoe** Nthumb
131 K2 **Swinithwaite** N York
100 C3 **Swinscoe** Staffs
137 H3 **Swinside** Cumb
103 G7 **Swinstead** Lincs
179 H8 **Swinton** Border
132 C4 **Swinton** N York
134 B5 **Swinton** N York
115 J2 **Swinton** Rothm
113 H2 **Swinton** Salfd
87 G2 **Swithland** Leics
212 E2 **Swordale** Highld
200 B6 **Swordland** Highld
229 M3 **Swordly** Highld
99 J5 **Swynnerton** Staffs
13 M5 **Swyre** Dorset
81 L3 **Sychtyn** Powys
55 L5 **Syde** Gloucs
45 G5 **Sydenham** Gt Lon
58 B7 **Sydenham** Oxon
6 B2 **Sydenham Damerel** Devon
105 K6 **Syderstone** Norfk
14 C3 **Sydling St Nicholas** Dorset
41 J8 **Sydmonton** Hants
102 C3 **Syerston** Notts
95 K3 **Sygun Copper Mine** Gwynd
124 F6 **Sykehouse** Donc
235 d4 **Symbister** Shet
163 J3 **Symington** S Ayrs
165 J3 **Symington** S Lans
54 E5 **Symonds Yat** Herefs
13 K4 **Symondsbury** Dorset
229 L6 **Syre** Highld
56 B4 **Syreford** Gloucs
73 J6 **Syresham** Nhants
87 J2 **Syston** Leics
102 F4 **Syston** Lincs
70 E2 **Sytchampton** Worcs
74 B2 **Sywell** Nhants

T

57 J4 **Tackley** Oxon
92 D4 **Tacolneston** Norfk
124 D2 **Tadcaster** N York
114 C7 **Taddington** Derbys
56 C2 **Taddington** Gloucs
41 L7 **Tadley** Hants
75 K5 **Tadlow** Cambs
72 E6 **Tadmarton** Oxon
44 E8 **Tadworth** Surrey
37 H4 **Taff's Well** Cardif
36 B3 **Taibach** Neath
231 J3 **Tain** Highld
223 G5 **Tain** Highld
232 e4 **Tairbeart** W Isls
60 F4 **Takeley** Essex
60 E4 **Takeley Street** Essex
80 E5 **Tal-y-bont** Cerdgn
109 L7 **Tal-y-Bont** Conwy
95 K7 **Tal-y-bont** Gwynd
109 J7 **Tal-y-bont** Gwynd
109 M7 **Tal-y-Cafn** Conwy
54 B5 **Tal-y-coed** Mons
12 D3 **Talaton** Devon
48 E5 **Talbenny** Pembks
12 E3 **Taleford** Devon
81 K4 **Talerddig** Powys
65 L4 **Talgarreg** Cerdgn
68 D7 **Talgarth** Powys
208 E7 **Talisker** Highld
99 J2 **Talke** Staffs
148 F4 **Talkin** Cumb
166 A5 **Talla Linnfoots** Border
219 L7 **Talladale** Highld
153 J3 **Tallaminnock** S Ayrs
98 C4 **Tallarn Green** Wrexhm
147 K7 **Tallentire** Cumb
66 E7 **Talley** Carmth
88 F2 **Tallington** Lincs
229 J3 **Talmine** Highld
50 D1 **Talog** Carmth
66 D4 **Talsarn** Cerdgn
95 K5 **Talsarnau** Gwynd
4 E3 **Talskiddy** Cnwll
109 G6 **Talwrn** IOA
53 H4 **Talybont-on-Usk** Powys
95 H2 **Talysarn** Gwynd
6 C4 **Tamerton Foliot** C Plym
86 B3 **Tamworth** Staffs
65 J5 **Tan-y-groes** Cerdgn
32 C3 **Tandridge** Surrey
150 F4 **Tanfield** Dur
150 F4 **Tanfield Lea** Dur
28 F2 **Tangley** Hants
18 B4 **Tangmere** W Susx
233 b9 **Tangusdale** W Isls
234 c6 **Tankerness** Ork
115 G2 **Tankersley** Barns
47 J6 **Tankerton** Kent
231 K6 **Tannach** Highld
206 E8 **Tannachie** Abers
196 D5 **Tannadice** Angus
85 J8 **Tanner's Green** Worcs
78 F2 **Tannington** Suffk
175 J6 **Tannochside** N Lans
100 F1 **Tansley** Derbys
88 F5 **Tansor** Nhants
150 F4 **Tantobie** Dur
142 B5 **Tanton** N York
71 K1 **Tanworth in Arden** Warwks
232 d5 **Taobh Tuath** W Isls
42 E4 **Taplow** Bucks
172 B7 **Tarbert** Ag & B
172 E5 **Tarbert** Ag & B
232 e4 **Tarbert** W Isls
183 K6 **Tarbet** Ag & B
228 B5 **Tarbet** Highld
200 B6 **Tarbet** Highld
163 K4 **Tarbolton** S Ayrs
176 D7 **Tarbrax** S Lans
71 H2 **Tardebigge** Worcs
196 D1 **Tarfside** Angus
205 K4 **Tarland** Abers
120 F6 **Tarleton** Lancs
55 L7 **Tarlton** Gloucs
26 B2 **Tarnock** Somset
112 D8 **Tarporley** Ches
25 H5 **Tarr** Somset
15 H2 **Tarrant Crawford** Dorset
27 L8 **Tarrant Gunville** Dorset
15 H1 **Tarrant Hinton** Dorset
15 H2 **Tarrant Keyneston** Dorset
15 H1 **Tarrant Launceston** Dorset
15 H2 **Tarrant Monkton** Dorset
15 H2 **Tarrant Rawston** Dorset
15 H2 **Tarrant Rushton** Dorset
19 L5 **Tarring Neville** E Susx
70 B6 **Tarrington** Herefs
199 J4 **Tarskavaig** Highld
217 G7 **Tarves** Abers
194 F4 **Tarvie** P & K
112 C7 **Tarvin** Ches
92 E4 **Tasburgh** Norfk
100 D7 **Tatenhill** Staffs
118 D5 **Tathwell** Lincs
32 D2 **Tatsfield** Surrey
98 C2 **Tattenhall** Ches
105 K6 **Tatterford** Norfk
105 K6 **Tattersett** Norfk
103 K2 **Tattershall** Lincs
103 L1 **Tattershall Thorpe** Lincs
78 D6 **Tattingstone** Suffk
78 D6 **Tattingstone White Horse** Suffk
13 J2 **Tatworth** Somset
215 J4 **Tauchers** Moray
25 K6 **Taunton** Somset
92 E2 **Taverham** Norfk
49 K5 **Tavernspite** Pembks
6 C2 **Tavistock** Devon
10 F5 **Taw Green** Devon
23 J5 **Tawstock** Devon
114 A5 **Taxal** Derbys
194 C4 **Tay Forest Park** P & K
182 F3 **Taychreggan Hotel** Ag & B
161 H1 **Tayinloan** Ag & B
55 G4 **Taynton** Gloucs
56 E5 **Taynton** Oxon
182 E2 **Taynuilt** Ag & B
187 G2 **Tayport** Fife
172 C2 **Tayvallich** Ag & B
117 J4 **Tealby** Lincs
151 G3 **Team Valley** Gatesd
199 K4 **Teangue** Highld
212 F2 **Teanord** Highld
138 E6 **Tebay** Cumb
59 G3 **Tebworth** Beds
11 J6 **Tedburn St Mary** Devon
55 L2 **Teddington** Gloucs
44 D6 **Teddington** Gt Lon
70 C3 **Tedstone Delamere** Herefs
70 C3 **Tedstone Wafer** Herefs
141 J5 **Teesside Airport** S on T
73 K1 **Teeton** Nhants
27 M5 **Teffont Evias** Wilts
27 M5 **Teffont Magna** Wilts
65 H7 **Tegryn** Pembks
88 C1 **Teigh** Rutlnd
7 K2 **Teigngrace** Devon
12 B7 **Teignmouth** Devon
166 F7 **Teindside** Border
84 C2 **Telford** Wrekin
27 J1 **Tellisford** Somset
19 L5 **Telscombe** E Susx
193 L5 **Tempar** P & K
155 J5 **Templand** D & G
5 J2 **Temple** Cnwll
177 J6 **Temple** Mdloth
66 C4 **Temple Bar** Cerdgn
38 F8 **Temple Cloud** BaNES
35 H5 **Temple Ewell** Kent
71 K4 **Temple Grafton** Warwks
56 C3 **Temple Guiting** Gloucs
124 F5 **Temple Hirst** N York
115 H7 **Temple Normanton** Derbys
197 K1 **Temple of Fiddes** Abers
212 E7 **Temple Pier** Highld
138 E2 **Temple Sowerby** Cumb
27 G6 **Templecombe** Somset
11 K3 **Templeton** Devon
49 J5 **Templeton** Pembks
150 E5 **Templetown** Dur
75 H4 **Tempsford** Beds
90 E4 **Ten Mile Bank** Norfk
69 L2 **Tenbury Wells** Worcs
49 J7 **Tenby** Pembks
62 D3 **Tendring** Essex
62 D3 **Tendring Green** Essex
62 D3 **Tendring Heath** Essex
34 B7 **Tenterden** Kent
61 J5 **Terling** Essex
98 F6 **Ternhill** Shrops
155 G6 **Terregles** D & G
133 K5 **Terrington** N York
104 E7 **Terrington St Clement** Norfk
90 D2 **Terrington St John** Norfk
33 J3 **Teston** Kent
29 G8 **Testwood** Hants
39 K2 **Tetbury** Gloucs
98 B6 **Tetchill** Shrops
9 J5 **Tetcott** Devon
118 D6 **Tetford** Lincs
118 D2 **Tetney** Lincs
58 B7 **Tetsworth** Oxon
84 F4 **Tettenhall** Wolves
101 J1 **Teversal** Notts
76 C3 **Teversham** Cambs
156 D2 **Teviothead** Border
59 L5 **Tewin** Herts
55 K2 **Tewkesbury** Gloucs

34 C3 **Teynham** Kent
123 H3 **Thackley** Brad
18 F3 **Thakeham** W Susx
58 B6 **Thame** Oxon
44 D6 **Thames Ditton** Surrey
45 J4 **Thamesmead** Gt Lon
34 F4 **Thanington** Kent
165 J2 **Thankerton** S Lans
92 E5 **Tharston** Norfk
41 K6 **Thatcham** W Berk
60 F2 **Thaxted** Essex
56 B7 **The Beeches** Gloucs
209 H7 **The Braes** Highld
178 E4 **The Brunt** E Loth
237 d4 **The Bungalow** IOM
55 K5 **The Butts** Gloucs
42 C2 **The City** Bucks
28 E5 **The Common** Wilts
83 J6 **The Corner** Shrops
174 C7 **The Den** N Ayrs
5 G5 **The Eden Project** Cnwll
34 B5 **The Forstal** Kent
34 D6 **The Forstal** Kent
128 E3 **The Green** Cumb
61 J4 **The Green** Essex
143 G6 **The Green** N York
151 M7 **The Headland** Hartpl
128 E3 **The Hill** Cumb
58 E6 **The Lee** Bucks
237 d2 **The Lhen** IOM
215 G2 **The Lochs** Moray
33 K7 **The Moor** Kent
51 J7 **The Mumbles** Swans
175 H7 **The Murray** S Lans
206 D5 **The Neuk** Abers
55 K4 **The Reddings** Gloucs
185 G3 **The Ross** P & K
21 H1 **The Stocks** Kent
39 L8 **The Strand** Wilts
132 D3 **Theakston** N York
125 K6 **Thealby** N Linc
26 C3 **Theale** Somset
41 M6 **Theale** W Berk
126 D3 **Thearne** E R Yk
79 J2 **Theberton** Suffk
87 J6 **Theddingworth** Leics
118 F4 **Theddlethorpe All Saints** Lincs
119 G4 **Theddlethorpe St Helen** Lincs
92 B7 **Thelnetham** Suffk
92 E7 **Thelveton** Norfk
112 F4 **Thelwall** Warrtn
106 C7 **Themelthorpe** Norfk
73 G6 **Thenford** Nhants
75 L6 **Therfield** Herts
91 K6 **Thetford** Norfk
91 J5 **Thetford Forest Park**
60 D7 **Theydon Bois** Essex
39 J5 **Thickwood** Wilts
118 C7 **Thimbleby** Lincs
141 K7 **Thimbleby** N York
111 J5 **Thingwall** Wirral
133 G4 **Thirkleby** N York
133 G3 **Thirlby** N York
178 C8 **Thirlestane** Border
137 J4 **Thirlspot** Cumb
132 C3 **Thirn** N York
132 F3 **Thirsk** N York
120 E3 **Thistleton** Lancs
102 E8 **Thistleton** Rutlnd
90 F7 **Thistley Green** Suffk
134 C7 **Thixendale** N York
158 B6 **Thockrington** Nthumb
90 B3 **Tholomas Drove** Cambs
133 G6 **Tholthorpe** N York
216 B6 **Thomastown** Abers
91 K4 **Thompson** Norfk
46 B6 **Thong** Kent
131 J3 **Thoralby** N York
117 K3 **Thoresway** Lincs
117 K3 **Thorganby** Lincs
125 G3 **Thorganby** N York
142 E7 **Thorgill** N York
93 J8 **Thorington** Suffk
78 B7 **Thorington Street** Suffk
131 H8 **Thorlby** N York
60 D4 **Thorley** Herts
16 D5 **Thorley Street** IOW
133 G5 **Thormanby** N York
141 K4 **Thornaby-on-Tees** S on T
106 C5 **Thornage** Norfk
73 L7 **Thornborough** Bucks
132 D4 **Thornborough** N York
123 J4 **Thornbury** Brad
9 K3 **Thornbury** Devon
70 B3 **Thornbury** Herefs
38 F3 **Thornbury** S Glos
87 J7 **Thornby** Nhants
100 A2 **Thorncliff** Staffs
13 J2 **Thorncombe** Dorset
78 D1 **Thorndon** Suffk
10 D6 **Thorndon Cross** Devon
125 G7 **Thorne** Donc
26 D7 **Thorne** Somset
25 H7 **Thorne St Margaret** Somset
124 B3 **Thorner** Leeds
89 K3 **Thorney** C Pete
116 E6 **Thorney** Notts
26 B6 **Thorney** Somset
16 A3 **Thorney Hill** Hants
25 L6 **Thornfalcon** Somset
26 E8 **Thornford** Dorset
149 K2 **Thorngrafton** Nthumb
126 F5 **Thorngumbald** E R Yk
105 H4 **Thornham** Norfk
78 D1 **Thornham Magna** Suffk
92 D8 **Thornham Parva** Suffk
88 F4 **Thornhaugh** C Pete
29 J8 **Thornhill** C Sotn
154 F3 **Thornhill** D & G
114 D5 **Thornhill** Derbys
123 K6 **Thornhill** Kirk
184 E7 **Thornhill** Stirlg
135 H6 **Thornholme** E R Yk
15 G2 **Thornicombe** Dorset
168 D3 **Thornington** Nthumb
150 E7 **Thornley** Dur
151 J6 **Thornley** Dur
174 F6 **Thornliebank** E Rens
77 G4 **Thorns** Suffk
114 A4 **Thornsett** Derbys
137 H3 **Thornthwaite** Cumb
132 B7 **Thornthwaite** N York
196 C6 **Thornton** Angus
123 G4 **Thornton** Brad
73 L7 **Thornton** Bucks
125 H2 **Thornton** E R Yk
186 E7 **Thornton** Fife
120 D3 **Thornton** Lancs
86 F3 **Thornton** Leics
118 C7 **Thornton** Lincs
141 L4 **Thornton** Middsb
179 K8 **Thornton** Nthumb
126 D6 **Thornton Curtis** N Linc
44 F6 **Thornton Heath** Gt Lon
111 J5 **Thornton Hough** Wirral
130 D5 **Thornton in Lonsdale** N York
134 C3 **Thornton le Dale** N York
117 H3 **Thornton le Moor** Lincs
131 H2 **Thornton Rust** N York
132 B3 **Thornton Steward** N York
132 C3 **Thornton Watlass** N York
122 D2 **Thornton-in-Craven** N York
132 F2 **Thornton-le-Beans** N York
133 L6 **Thornton-le-Clay** N York
132 F2 **Thornton-le-Moor** N York
112 C6 **Thornton-le-Moors** Ches
132 F3 **Thornton-le-Street** N York
175 G7 **Thorntonhall** S Lans
178 F4 **Thorntonloch** E Loth
178 D8 **Thornydykes** Border
137 L3 **Thornythwaite** Cumb
102 C4 **Thoroton** Notts
124 C2 **Thorp Arch** Leeds
100 D3 **Thorpe** Derbys
126 B2 **Thorpe** E R Yk
131 J6 **Thorpe** N York
102 C3 **Thorpe** Notts
43 G6 **Thorpe** Surrey
92 E7 **Thorpe Abbotts** Norfk
102 C7 **Thorpe Arnold** Leics
124 D7 **Thorpe Audlin** Donc
134 D5 **Thorpe Bassett** N York
46 E3 **Thorpe Bay** Sthend
88 C4 **Thorpe by Water** Rutlnd
86 C2 **Thorpe Constantine** Staffs
93 G2 **Thorpe End** Norfk
62 E4 **Thorpe Green** Essex
77 L4 **Thorpe Green** Suffk
115 G3 **Thorpe Hesley** Rothm
124 F7 **Thorpe in Balne** Donc
116 E5 **Thorpe in the Fallows** Lincs
87 L5 **Thorpe Langton** Leics
125 K2 **Thorpe le Street** E R Yk
43 G6 **Thorpe Lea** Surrey
88 B7 **Thorpe Malsor** Nhants
73 G5 **Thorpe Mandeville** Nhants
106 F5 **Thorpe Market** Norfk
92 E1 **Thorpe Marriot** Norfk
77 L4 **Thorpe Morieux** Suffk
116 E7 **Thorpe on the Hill** Lincs
43 G6 **Thorpe Park** Surrey
115 K5 **Thorpe Salvin** Rothm
87 K2 **Thorpe Satchville** Leics
92 F2 **Thorpe St Andrew** Norfk
104 D1 **Thorpe St Peter** Lincs
141 J3 **Thorpe Thewles** S on T
103 J2 **Thorpe Tilney** Lincs
133 G7 **Thorpe Underwood** N York
88 E7 **Thorpe Waterville** Nhants
124 E4 **Thorpe Willoughby** N York
62 E4 **Thorpe-le-Soken** Essex
79 K3 **Thorpeness** Suffk
62 C4 **Thorrington** Essex
11 L4 **Thorverton** Devon
92 D7 **Thrandeston** Suffk
88 E7 **Thrapston** Nhants
98 C4 **Threapwood** Ches
100 B4 **Threapwood** Staffs
163 J7 **Threave** S Ayrs
146 C3 **Threave Castle** D & G
32 B5 **Three Bridges** W Susx
33 L5 **Three Chimneys** Kent
68 D6 **Three Cocks** Powys
51 H6 **Three Crosses** Swans
20 D2 **Three Cups Corner** E Susx
33 H6 **Three Leg Cross** E Susx
15 K2 **Three Legged Cross** Dorset
42 B6 **Three Mile Cross** Wokham
176 E3 **Three Miletown** W Loth
21 G3 **Three Oaks** E Susx
103 H5 **Threekingham** Lincs
167 H2 **Threepwood** Border
137 J3 **Threlkeld** Cumb
131 J6 **Threshfield** N York
93 K2 **Thrigby** Norfk
101 H8 **Thringstone** Leics
132 D2 **Thrintoft** N York
76 B5 **Thriplow** Cambs
60 B3 **Throcking** Herts
150 E2 **Throckley** N u Ty
71 H4 **Throckmorton** Worcs
15 L4 **Throop** Bmouth
158 C2 **Thropton** Nthumb
176 B1 **Throsk** Stirlg
154 F5 **Throughgate** D & G
11 G6 **Throwleigh** Devon
34 C4 **Throwley Forstal** Kent
101 J6 **Thrumpton** Notts
231 L6 **Thrumster** Highld
127 H8 **Thrunscoe** NE Lin
55 K7 **Thrupp** Gloucs
60 D6 **Thrushesbush** Essex
87 J1 **Thrussington** Leics
28 F3 **Thruxton** Hants
69 J7 **Thruxton** Herefs
115 J3 **Thrybergh** Rothm
101 H6 **Thulston** Derbys
46 C3 **Thundersley** Essex
87 H2 **Thurcaston** Leics
115 J4 **Thurcroft** Rothm
106 E5 **Thurgarton** Norfk
102 B3 **Thurgarton** Notts
114 F2 **Thurgoland** Barns
87 G4 **Thurlaston** Leics
72 F1 **Thurlaston** Warwks
25 K7 **Thurlbear** Somset
102 E1 **Thurlby** Lincs
89 G1 **Thurlby** Lincs
119 G6 **Thurlby** Lincs
74 F3 **Thurleigh** Beds
7 G7 **Thurlestone** Devon
76 F4 **Thurlow** Suffk
25 L5 **Thurloxton** Somset
114 E2 **Thurlstone** Barns
93 J4 **Thurlton** Norfk
87 H2 **Thurmaston** Leics
87 J3 **Thurnby** Leics
93 J1 **Thurne** Norfk
33 K2 **Thurnham** Kent
88 F6 **Thurning** Nhants
106 C6 **Thurning** Norfk
115 J1 **Thurnscoe** Barns
148 B5 **Thursby** Cumb
106 B5 **Thursford** Norfk
30 E4 **Thursley** Surrey
231 G2 **Thurso** Highld
111 H5 **Thurstaston** Wirral
77 L2 **Thurston** Suffk

148 B4 **Thurstonfield** Cumb
123 H7 **Thurstonland** Kirk
93 G4 **Thurton** Norfk
100 E5 **Thurvaston** Derbys
92 B3 **Thuxton** Norfk
139 K7 **Thwaite** N York
78 D2 **Thwaite** Suffk
129 H2 **Thwaite Head** Cumb
93 G4 **Thwaite St Mary** Norfk
135 G5 **Thwing** E R Yk
185 L3 **Tibbermore** P & K
154 E3 **Tibbers** D & G
55 H4 **Tibberton** Gloucs
70 F3 **Tibberton** Worcs
99 G7 **Tibberton** Wrekin
166 C5 **Tibbie Shiels Inn** Border
92 D5 **Tibenham** Norfk
101 H1 **Tibshelf** Derbys
134 E7 **Tibthorpe** E R Yk
33 H7 **Ticehurst** E Susx
29 L5 **Tichborne** Hants
88 E2 **Tickencote** Rutlnd
38 C6 **Tickenham** N Som
115 L3 **Tickhill** Donc
83 J5 **Ticklerton** Shrops
101 G7 **Ticknall** Derbys
126 D3 **Tickton** E R Yk
40 F8 **Tidcombe** Wilts
57 M6 **Tiddington** Oxon
72 B4 **Tiddington** Warwks
33 G7 **Tidebrook** E Susx
6 A4 **Tideford** Cnwll
38 E2 **Tidenham** Gloucs
114 D6 **Tideswell** Derbys
41 M5 **Tidmarsh** W Berk
72 C6 **Tidmington** Warwks
48 F5 **Tiers Cross** Pembks
73 K4 **Tiffield** Nhants
196 E4 **Tigerton** Angus
233 b6 **Tigh a Ghearraidh** W Isls
233 b6 **Tigharry** W Isls
173 G4 **Tighnabruaich** Ag & B
7 H4 **Tigley** Devon
74 F2 **Tilbrook** Cambs
45 M5 **Tilbury** Thurr
86 C7 **Tile Hill** Covtry
42 A5 **Tilehurst** Readg
30 E3 **Tilford** Surrey
31 L4 **Tilgate** W Susx
26 E4 **Tilham Street** Somset
185 J7 **Tillicoultry** Clacks
164 F1 **Tillietudlem** S Lans
62 B7 **Tillingham** Essex
69 J5 **Tillington** Herefs
30 F6 **Tillington** W Susx
69 J5 **Tillington Common** Herefs
206 D4 **Tillybirloch** Abers
205 K5 **Tillycairn** Abers
206 C3 **Tillyfourie** Abers
207 G2 **Tillygreig** Abers
186 B6 **Tillyrie** P & K
35 J4 **Tilmanstone** Kent
104 F8 **Tilney All Saints** Norfk
104 E8 **Tilney High End** Norfk
90 D2 **Tilney St Lawrence** Norfk
28 B2 **Tilshead** Wilts
98 D5 **Tilstock** Shrops
98 C3 **Tilston** Ches
98 E1 **Tilstone Fearnall** Ches
59 G3 **Tilsworth** Beds
87 L3 **Tilton on the Hill** Leics
39 J2 **Tiltups End** Gloucs
103 J2 **Timberland** Lincs
113 K8 **Timbersbrook** Ches
24 E3 **Timberscombe** Somset
132 B8 **Timble** N York
156 B7 **Timpanheck** D & G
113 H4 **Timperley** Traffd
38 F8 **Timsbury** BaNES
29 G6 **Timsbury** Hants
232 d2 **Timsgarry** W Isls
232 d2 **Timsgearraidh** W Isls
77 J1 **Timworth** Suffk
77 J2 **Timworth Green** Suffk
14 E4 **Tincleton** Dorset
149 G3 **Tindale** Cumb
140 F2 **Tindale Crescent** Dur
58 A2 **Tingewick** Bucks
123 K5 **Tingley** Leeds
59 G2 **Tingrith** Beds
235 c6 **Tingwall Airport** Shet
9 K7 **Tinhay** Devon
115 H4 **Tinsley** Sheff
32 B5 **Tinsley Green** W Susx
8 E6 **Tintagel** Cnwll
8 D6 **Tintagel Castle** Cnwll
54 D7 **Tintern Abbey** Mons
54 D7 **Tintern Parva** Mons
26 D7 **Tintinhull** Somset
114 A3 **Tintwistle** Derbys
155 H5 **Tinwald** D & G
88 E3 **Tinwell** Rutlnd
85 G5 **Tipton** Sandw
12 E4 **Tipton St John** Devon
61 L5 **Tiptree** Essex
61 L5 **Tiptree Heath** Essex
67 J6 **Tirabad** Powys
188 C7 **Tiree Airport** Ag & B
172 C6 **Tiretigan** Ag & B
55 J3 **Tirley** Gloucs
53 H7 **Tirphil** Caerph
138 D2 **Tirril** Cumb
27 L5 **Tisbury** Wilts
100 D3 **Tissington** Derbys
22 C6 **Titchberry** Devon
17 G2 **Titchfield** Hants
88 E7 **Titchmarsh** Nhants
105 J4 **Titchwell** Norfk
102 B5 **Tithby** Notts
69 G3 **Titley** Herefs
32 D3 **Titsey** Surrey
99 K5 **Tittensor** Staffs
105 L7 **Tittleshall** Norfk
70 E1 **Titton** Worcs
98 D1 **Tiverton** Ches
24 E8 **Tiverton** Devon
92 E6 **Tivetshall St Margaret** Norfk
92 E6 **Tivetshall St Mary** Norfk
24 E3 **Tivington** Somset
99 L7 **Tixall** Staffs
88 E4 **Tixover** Rutlnd
189 L5 **Tobermory** Ag & B
181 L5 **Toberonochy** Ag & B
233 b7 **Tobha Mor** W Isls
216 D7 **Tocher** Abers
215 L2 **Tochieneal** Moray
40 B4 **Tockenham** Wilts
121 K6 **Tockholes** Bl w D
38 E3 **Tockington** S Glos
133 G8 **Tockwith** N York
27 J7 **Todber** Dorset
158 E3 **Todburn** Nthumb
59 G3 **Toddington** Beds
56 B2 **Toddington** Gloucs
72 B7 **Todenham** Gloucs
196 C8 **Todhills** Angus
148 C3 **Todhills** Cumb
122 D5 **Todmorden** Calder
115 J5 **Todwick** Rothm
75 L4 **Toft** Cambs
88 F1 **Toft** Lincs
235 c3 **Toft** Shet
140 E2 **Toft Hill** Dur
93 J4 **Toft Monks** Norfk
117 H4 **Toft next Newton** Lincs
105 L6 **Toftrees** Norfk
159 G2 **Togston** Nthumb
199 J3 **Tokavaig** Highld
42 B5 **Tokers Green** Oxon
232 g2 **Tolastadh** W Isls
124 E8 **Toll Bar** Donc
25 H5 **Tolland** Somset
27 L7 **Tollard Royal** Wilts
14 B3 **Toller Fratrum** Dorset
14 B3 **Toller Porcorum** Dorset
13 M3 **Toller Whelme** Dorset
133 H6 **Tollerton** N York
101 L5 **Tollerton** Notts
62 A6 **Tollesbury** Essex
61 L5 **Tolleshunt D'Arcy** Essex
61 L5 **Tolleshunt Knights** Essex
61 L5 **Tolleshunt Major** Essex
235 c8 **Tolob** Shet
14 E4 **Tolpuddle** Dorset
232 g2 **Tolsta** W Isls
44 D6 **Tolworth** Gt Lon
213 J8 **Tomatin** Highld
201 K3 **Tomchrasky** Highld
201 H5 **Tomdoun** Highld
226 A7 **Tomich** Highld
211 L8 **Tomich** Highld
212 E5 **Tomich** Highld
222 F7 **Tomich** Highld
204 E2 **Tomintoul** Moray
212 D6 **Tomnacross** Highld
204 F1 **Tomnavoulin** Moray
33 G4 **Tonbridge** Kent
36 D4 **Tondu** Brdgnd
25 H6 **Tonedale** Somset
123 J4 **Tong** Brad
34 C4 **Tong** Kent
84 E3 **Tong** Shrops
84 E2 **Tong Norton** Shrops
123 J4 **Tong Street** Brad
101 H7 **Tonge** Leics
30 E2 **Tongham** Surrey
146 C4 **Tongland** D & G
229 J4 **Tongue** Highld
37 H4 **Tongwynlais** Cardif
52 B7 **Tonna** Neath
60 B5 **Tonwell** Herts
36 F3 **Tonypandy** Rhondd
36 F3 **Tonyrefail** Rhondd
57 K7 **Toot Baldon** Oxon
60 E7 **Toot Hill** Essex
40 C4 **Toothill** Swindn
44 F5 **Tooting** Gt Lon
44 F5 **Tooting Bec** Gt Lon
132 F4 **Topcliffe** N York
92 F5 **Topcroft** Norfk
92 F5 **Topcroft Street** Norfk
77 G6 **Toppesfield** Essex
92 E4 **Toprow** Norfk
12 C5 **Topsham** Devon
162 A4 **Torbeg** N Ayrs
223 G2 **Torboll** Highld
213 G6 **Torbreck** Highld
7 J3 **Torbryan** Devon
192 B2 **Torcastle** Highld
7 J7 **Torcross** Devon
212 F4 **Tore** Highld
172 D5 **Torinturk** Ag & B
116 D5 **Torksey** Lincs
39 H5 **Tormarton** S Glos
161 M3 **Tormore** N Ayrs
213 J4 **Tornagrain** Highld
206 C4 **Tornaveen** Abers
212 E8 **Torness** Highld
140 F2 **Toronto** Dur
181 L1 **Torosay Castle** Ag & B
147 L6 **Torpenhow** Cumb
176 C4 **Torphichen** W Loth
206 C5 **Torphins** Abers
6 C5 **Torpoint** Cnwll
7 L3 **Torquay** Torbay
177 L8 **Torquhan** Border
209 J5 **Torran** Highld
175 H4 **Torrance** E Duns
163 J1 **Torranyard** N Ayrs
210 D3 **Torridon** Highld
210 D3 **Torridon House** Highld
199 J2 **Torrin** Highld
161 K3 **Torrisdale** Ag & B
229 K3 **Torrisdale** Highld
227 G5 **Torrish** Highld
129 K6 **Torrisholme** Lancs
226 A7 **Torrobull** Highld
207 H4 **Torry** C Aber
176 D2 **Torryburn** Fife
236 b4 **Torteval** Guern
155 H6 **Torthorwald** D & G
84 E8 **Torton** Worcs
39 G2 **Tortworth** S Glos
209 H5 **Torvaig** Highld
137 J7 **Torver** Cumb
175 L2 **Torwood** Falk
167 G2 **Torwoodlee** Border
116 A4 **Torworth** Notts
209 L6 **Toscaig** Highld
75 J3 **Toseland** Cambs
130 E7 **Tosside** N York
77 L2 **Tostock** Suffk
208 C4 **Totaig** Highld
208 F5 **Tote** Highld
209 H3 **Tote** Highld
16 D5 **Totland** IOW
114 F5 **Totley** Sheff
7 J4 **Totnes** Devon
101 J5 **Toton** Notts
188 F5 **Totronald** Ag & B
208 F2 **Totscore** Highld
45 G3 **Tottenham** Gt Lon
90 F2 **Tottenhill** Norfk
44 E2 **Totteridge** Gt Lon
59 G4 **Totternhoe** Beds
122 B7 **Tottington** Bury
29 G8 **Totton** Hants
25 J5 **Toulton** Somset
223 J5 **Toulvaddie** Highld
33 K3 **Tovil** Kent
150 E6 **Tow Law** Dur
173 K5 **Toward** Ag & B
173 J5 **Toward Quay** Ag & B
73 K5 **Towcester** Nhants
2 E4 **Towednack** Cnwll
58 B6 **Towersey** Oxon
205 K3 **Towie** Abers
90 B4 **Town End** Cambs
128 F2 **Town End** Cumb
19 L3 **Town Littleworth** E Susx
91 H6 **Town Street** Suffk
168 B4 **Town Yetholm** Border
174 D3 **Townend** W Duns
114 D2 **Townhead** Barns
155 H4 **Townhead** D & G
146 C3 **Townhead of Greenlaw** D & G
176 F1 **Townhill** Fife
41 K8 **Towns End** Hants
3 G5 **Townshend** Cnwll
133 K7 **Towthorpe** York
124 D3 **Towton** N York
110 D5 **Towyn** Conwy
111 K4 **Toxteth** Lpool
32 E3 **Toy's Hill** Kent
118 E8 **Toynton All Saints** Lincs

163 K5 **Trabboch** E Ayrs
163 L5 **Trabbochburn** E Ayrs
213 K3 **Tradespark** Highld
65 J4 **Traethsaith** Cerdgn
52 E3 **Trallong** Powys
101 G2 **Tramway Museum** Derbys
177 L4 **Tranent** E Loth
111 J4 **Tranmere** Wirral
230 C5 **Trantelbeg** Highld
230 C5 **Trantlemore** Highld
51 J2 **Trapp** Carmth
178 D4 **Traprain** E Loth
166 E3 **Traquair** Border
23 K6 **Traveller's Rest** Devon
122 D3 **Trawden** Lancs
96 A5 **Trawsfynydd** Gwynd
80 E5 **Tre Taliesin** Cerdgn
65 L5 **Tre-groes** Cerdgn
36 F3 **Trealaw** Rhondd
120 F4 **Treales** Lancs
108 C5 **Trearddur Bay** IOA
208 F4 **Treaslane** Highld
8 D7 **Trebarwith** Cnwll
4 E1 **Trebetherick** Cnwll
24 F4 **Treborough** Somset
5 M1 **Trebullett** Cnwll
6 A1 **Treburley** Cnwll
52 D3 **Trecastle** Powys
64 D7 **Trecwn** Pembks
52 F7 **Trecynon** Rhondd
9 G8 **Tredaule** Cnwll
53 H6 **Tredegar** Blae G
55 K3 **Tredington** Gloucs
72 C5 **Tredington** Warwks
38 B2 **Tredunhock** Mons
2 D6 **Treen** Cnwll
115 H4 **Treeton** Rothm
64 C6 **Trefasser** Pembks
53 H2 **Trefecca** Powys
81 L5 **Trefeglwys** Powys
49 G3 **Treffgarne** Pembks
48 E3 **Treffgarne Owen** Pembks
37 G3 **Trefforest** Rhondd
66 D3 **Trefilan** Cerdgn
64 B7 **Trefin** Pembks
110 E7 **Trefnant** Denbgs
97 K6 **Trefonen** Shrops
94 F4 **Trefor** Gwynd
8 E7 **Trefrew** Cnwll
109 L8 **Trefriw** Conwy
9 H7 **Tregadillett** Cnwll
54 B6 **Tregare** Mons
66 F3 **Tregaron** Cerdgn
109 H7 **Tregarth** Gwynd
9 H7 **Tregeare** Cnwll
97 J5 **Tregeiriog** Wrexhm
108 D3 **Tregele** IOA
3 K6 **Tregidden** Cnwll
48 D2 **Treglemais** Pembks
9 G5 **Tregole** Cnwll
4 E3 **Tregonetha** Cnwll
4 E6 **Tregony** Cnwll
68 E6 **Tregoyd** Powys
82 C4 **Tregynon** Powys
37 G3 **Trehafod** Rhondd
6 B4 **Trehan** Cnwll
37 H2 **Treharris** Myr Td
52 E7 **Treherbert** Rhondd
6 A1 **Trekenner** Cnwll
8 D7 **Treknow** Cnwll
110 F5 **Trelawnyd** Flints
65 J7 **Trelech** Carmth
48 C2 **Treleddyd-fawr** Pembks
37 H2 **Trelewis** Myr Td
8 C8 **Trelights** Cnwll
5 G1 **Trelill** Cnwll
4 C7 **Trelissick Garden** Cnwll
54 D6 **Trelleck** Mons
110 F5 **Trelogan** Flints
4 E3 **Trelow** Cnwll
95 K4 **Tremadog** Gwynd
8 F7 **Tremail** Cnwll
65 H5 **Tremain** Cerdgn
9 G6 **Tremaine** Cnwll
5 K3 **Tremar** Cnwll
6 B4 **Trematon** Cnwll
110 F6 **Tremeirchion** Denbgs
4 D3 **Trenance** Cnwll
4 E2 **Trenance** Cnwll
9 G5 **Trencreek** Cnwll
3 H5 **Trenear** Cnwll
9 G7 **Treneglos** Cnwll
26 E7 **Trent** Dorset
23 K2 **Trentishoe** Devon
36 E5 **Treoes** V Glam
36 E2 **Treorchy** Rhondd
5 G1 **Trequite** Cnwll
36 F5 **Trerhyngyll** V Glam
5 M4 **Trerulefoot** Cnwll
2 a1 **Tresco Heliport** IOS
3 G5 **Trescowe** Cnwll
4 C4 **Tresean** Cnwll
39 H3 **Tresham** Gloucs
4 D6 **Tresillian** Cnwll
9 G5 **Treskinnick Cross** Cnwll
9 G7 **Tresmeer** Cnwll
8 F6 **Tresparrett** Cnwll
194 C4 **Tressait** P & K
235 c5 **Tresta** Shet
235 e3 **Tresta** Shet
116 C5 **Treswell** Notts
8 E6 **Trethevey** Cnwll
2 C6 **Trethewey** Cnwll
5 G5 **Trethurgy** Cnwll
54 D4 **Tretire** Herefs
53 J4 **Tretower** Powys
97 K2 **Treuddyn** Flints
9 G8 **Trevague** Cnwll
8 E6 **Trevalga** Cnwll
98 B2 **Trevalyn** Wrexhm
4 D3 **Trevarrian** Cnwll
4 C4 **Treveal** Cnwll
8 E8 **Treveighan** Cnwll
3 J2 **Trevellas Downs** Cnwll
5 K3 **Trevelmond** Cnwll
3 K5 **Treverva** Cnwll
2 C6 **Trevescan** Cnwll
4 E5 **Treviscoe** Cnwll
4 D2 **Trevone** Cnwll
97 L4 **Trevor** Denbgs
8 E7 **Trewalder** Cnwll
9 J8 **Trewarlett** Cnwll
8 E7 **Trewarmett** Cnwll
9 G7 **Treween** Cnwll
9 H7 **Trewen** Cnwll
9 G8 **Trewint** Cnwll
4 D7 **Trewithian** Cnwll
4 F5 **Trewoon** Cnwll
30 D7 **Treyford** W Susx
122 F6 **Triangle** Calder
151 J7 **Trimdon** Dur
151 J7 **Trimdon Colliery** Dur
151 J7 **Trimdon Grange** Dur
107 G5 **Trimingham** Norfk
78 F6 **Trimley** Suffk
50 F5 **Trimsaran** Carmth
23 H3 **Trimstone** Devon
194 B4 **Trinafour** P & K
58 F5 **Tring** Herts
196 F4 **Trinity** Angus
236 d6 **Trinity** Jersey
185 K4 **Trinity Gask** P & K
25 J4 **Triscombe** Somset
191 L2 **Trislaig** Highld
4 D5 **Trispen** Cnwll
158 F4 **Tritlington** Nthumb
194 F7 **Trochry** P & K
65 K5 **Troedyraur** Cerdgn
53 G7 **Troedyrhiw** Myr Td
236 c6 **Trois Bois** Jersey
3 H4 **Troon** Cnwll
163 H3 **Troon** S Ayrs
123 L3 **Tropical World Roundhay Park** Leeds
184 B5 **Trossachs** Stirlg
91 K8 **Troston** Suffk
70 F4 **Trotshill** Worcs
33 H2 **Trottiscliffe** Kent
30 D6 **Trotton** W Susx
157 L4 **Troughend** Nthumb
137 L6 **Troutbeck** Cumb
137 L7 **Troutbeck Bridge** Cumb
115 H5 **Troway** Derbys
39 J8 **Trowbridge** Wilts
101 J4 **Trowell** Notts
92 F3 **Trowse Newton** Norfk
27 H3 **Trudoxhill** Somset
25 K6 **Trull** Somset
208 C3 **Trumpan** Highld
70 B6 **Trumpet** Herefs
76 C4 **Trumpington** Cambs
107 G5 **Trunch** Norfk
4 C6 **Truro** Cnwll
4 C6 **Truro Cathedral** Cnwll
11 K7 **Trusham** Devon
100 E5 **Trusley** Derbys
119 G5 **Trusthorpe** Lincs
84 F5 **Trysull** Staffs
57 H7 **Tubney** Oxon
7 J5 **Tuckenhay** Devon
84 E6 **Tuckhill** Shrops
3 H3 **Tuckingmill** Cnwll
27 L5 **Tuckingmill** Wilts
15 L4 **Tuckton** Bmouth
77 G1 **Tuddenham** Suffk
78 E5 **Tuddenham** Suffk
33 G4 **Tudeley** Kent
151 G7 **Tudhoe** Dur
94 D5 **Tudweiliog** Gwynd
55 J5 **Tuffley** Gloucs
29 J3 **Tufton** Hants
49 H2 **Tufton** Pembks
87 L4 **Tugby** Leics
83 L6 **Tugford** Shrops
169 J4 **Tughall** Nthumb
185 H7 **Tullibody** Clacks
212 F8 **Tullich** Highld
223 J6 **Tullich** Highld
194 F5 **Tulliemet** P & K
216 F7 **Tulloch** Abers
184 C4 **Tulloch** Stirlg
192 F1 **Tulloch Station** Highld
182 D7 **Tullochgorm** Ag & B
185 L1 **Tullybeagles Lodge** P & K
206 B2 **Tullynessle** Abers
44 F5 **Tulse Hill** Gt Lon
51 G3 **Tumble** Carmth
103 L1 **Tumby** Lincs
103 L2 **Tumby Woodside** Lincs
194 B5 **Tummel Bridge** P & K
33 G5 **Tunbridge Wells** Kent
155 L6 **Tundergarth** D & G
39 G8 **Tunley** BaNES
99 K3 **Tunstall** C Stke
127 H4 **Tunstall** E R Yk
34 B3 **Tunstall** Kent
130 B5 **Tunstall** Lancs
140 F7 **Tunstall** N York
93 J2 **Tunstall** Norfk
99 H6 **Tunstall** Staffs
79 H4 **Tunstall** Suffk
151 J4 **Tunstall** Sundld
114 C6 **Tunstead** Derbys
107 G7 **Tunstead** Norfk
114 B5 **Tunstead Milton** Derbys
30 A2 **Tunworth** Hants
87 K5 **Tur Langton** Leics
42 B8 **Turgis Green** Hants
56 C4 **Turkdean** Gloucs
39 J7 **Turleigh** Wilts
69 G7 **Turnastone** Herefs
152 E2 **Turnberry** S Ayrs
100 F3 **Turnditch** Derbys
32 C6 **Turner's Hill** W Susx
14 F4 **Turners Puddle** Dorset
177 G4 **Turnhouse** C Edin
14 F2 **Turnworth** Dorset
216 D4 **Turriff** Abers
121 L7 **Turton Bottoms** Bl w D
89 L4 **Turves** Cambs
74 D4 **Turvey** Beds
42 C3 **Turville** Bucks
73 H6 **Turweston** Bucks
166 D5 **Tushielaw Inn** Border
98 D3 **Tushingham cum Grindley** Ches
100 E6 **Tutbury** Staffs
38 D2 **Tutshill** Gloucs
106 F6 **Tuttington** Norfk
116 C7 **Tuxford** Notts
234 b5 **Twatt** Ork
235 c5 **Twatt** Shet
175 J3 **Twechar** E Duns
179 K7 **Tweedmouth** Nthumb
165 L4 **Tweedsmuir** Border
3 K3 **Twelveheads** Cnwll
113 H7 **Twemlow Green** Ches
103 J7 **Twenty** Lincs
39 G7 **Twerton** BaNES
44 D5 **Twickenham** Gt Lon
55 J4 **Twigworth** Gloucs
19 H2 **Twineham** W Susx
77 J6 **Twinstead** Essex
24 C5 **Twitchen** Devon
114 F8 **Two Dales** Derbys
86 B4 **Two Gates** Staffs
86 D3 **Twycross** Leics
86 C3 **Twycross Zoo** Leics
58 A3 **Twyford** Bucks
29 J6 **Twyford** Hants
87 K2 **Twyford** Leics
106 B7 **Twyford** Norfk
42 C5 **Twyford** Wokham
146 B4 **Twynholm** D & G
70 F7 **Twyning** Gloucs
70 F6 **Twyning Green** Gloucs
51 L2 **Twynllanan** Carmth
88 D7 **Twywell** Nhants
97 K4 **Ty'n-dwr** Denbgs
109 L7 **Ty'n-y-Groes** Conwy
96 F4 **Ty-nant** Conwy
69 H6 **Tyberton** Herefs
51 H4 **Tycroes** Carmth
97 H8 **Tycrwyn** Powys
104 D8 **Tydd Gote** Lincs
90 B1 **Tydd St Giles** Cambs
104 C8 **Tydd St Mary** Lincs
76 E7 **Tye Green** Essex
113 G2 **Tyldesley** Wigan
34 F3 **Tyler Hill** Kent
36 F2 **Tylorstown** Rhondd
37 G4 **Tyn-y-nant** Rhondd
183 K2 **Tyndrum** Stirlg
151 J2 **Tynemouth** N Tyne
178 D3 **Tyninghame** E Loth
154 E4 **Tynron** D & G
38 D6 **Tyntesfield** Somset
66 F1 **Tynygraig** Cerdgn
74 C5 **Tyringham** M Keyn
36 D5 **Tythegston** Brdgnd

113 K6 **Tytherington** Ches
38 F3 **Tytherington** S Glos
27 K3 **Tytherington** Wilts
13 H2 **Tytherleigh** Devon
39 L5 **Tytherton Lucas** Wilts
5 H5 **Tywardreath** Cnwll
80 D4 **Tywyn** Gwynd

U

79 G1 **Ubbeston Green** Suffk
38 D8 **Ubley** BaNES
141 G6 **Uckerby** N York
19 M2 **Uckfield** E Susx
70 F6 **Uckinghall** Worcs
55 K3 **Uckington** Gloucs
83 L2 **Uckington** Shrops
175 J6 **Uddingston** S Lans
165 G3 **Uddington** S Lans
21 H2 **Udimore** E Susx
207 G1 **Udny Green** Abers
207 G1 **Udny Station** Abers
25 G8 **Uffculme** Devon
88 F3 **Uffington** Lincs
40 F3 **Uffington** Oxon
83 K2 **Uffington** Shrops
89 G3 **Ufford** C Pete
79 G4 **Ufford** Suffk
72 E3 **Ufton** Warwks
41 M6 **Ufton Nervet** W Berk
161 K4 **Ugadale** Ag & B
7 G5 **Ugborough** Devon
93 J7 **Uggeshall** Suffk
143 H5 **Ugglebarnby** N York
114 E4 **Ughill** Sheff
60 E3 **Ugley** Essex
60 E3 **Ugley Green** Essex
143 G5 **Ugthorpe** N York
188 F5 **Uig** Ag & B
208 C4 **Uig** Highld
208 F2 **Uig** Highld
232 d2 **Uig** W Isls
209 G5 **Uigshader** Highld
180 E4 **Uisken** Ag & B
231 K7 **Ulbster** Highld
137 L3 **Ulcat Row** Cumb
118 F6 **Ulceby** Lincs
126 D7 **Ulceby** N Linc
126 E7 **Ulceby Skitter** N Linc
33 L4 **Ulcombe** Kent
147 M7 **Uldale** Cumb
55 H7 **Uley** Gloucs
159 G4 **Ulgham** Nthumb
220 E3 **Ullapool** Highld
71 K2 **Ullenhall** Warwks
124 D3 **Ulleskelf** N York
87 G6 **Ullesthorpe** Leics
115 J4 **Ulley** Rothm
69 L4 **Ullingswick** Herefs
208 E6 **Ullinish Lodge Hotel** Highld
136 E3 **Ullock** Cumb
138 B3 **Ullswater** Cumb
128 E2 **Ulpha** Cumb
135 J7 **Ulrome** E R Yk
235 d3 **Ulsta** Shet
129 G4 **Ulverston** Cumb
15 J6 **Ulwell** Dorset
209 J4 **Umachan** Highld
23 J6 **Umberleigh** Devon
224 F2 **Unapool** Highld
156 E5 **Under Burnmouth** Border
32 F3 **Under River** Kent
129 K2 **Underbarrow** Cumb
123 J4 **Undercliffe** Brad
83 K2 **Underdale** Shrops
101 J3 **Underwood** Notts
38 C3 **Undy** Mons
237 c5 **Union Mills** IOM
115 G6 **Unstone** Derbys
14 C2 **Up Cerne** Dorset
12 B2 **Up Exe** Devon
112 D1 **Up Holland** Lancs
30 D8 **Up Marden** W Susx
26 E7 **Up Mudford** Somset
30 B2 **Up Nately** Hants
29 H5 **Up Somborne** Hants
14 C3 **Up Sydling** Dorset
28 C1 **Upavon** Wilts
46 D6 **Upchurch** Kent
24 B5 **Upcott** Devon
24 E6 **Upcott** Somset
106 D8 **Upgate** Norfk
14 B2 **Uphall** Dorset
176 E4 **Uphall** W Loth
11 K3 **Upham** Devon
29 K7 **Upham** Hants
69 H2 **Uphampton** Herefs
70 E2 **Uphampton** Worcs
37 L8 **Uphill** N Som
174 E7 **Uplawmoor** E Rens
55 H3 **Upleadon** Gloucs
142 D4 **Upleatham** R & Cl
13 L4 **Uploders** Dorset
24 F7 **Uplowman** Devon
13 H4 **Uplyme** Devon
45 K3 **Upminster** Gt Lon
12 F2 **Upottery** Devon
75 G7 **Upper & Lower Stondon** Beds
83 J6 **Upper Affcot** Shrops
222 E4 **Upper Ardchronie** Highld
84 D7 **Upper Arley** Worcs
41 L5 **Upper Basildon** W Berk
19 G4 **Upper Beeding** W Susx
88 E5 **Upper Benefield** Nhants
71 H2 **Upper Bentley** Worcs
230 C4 **Upper Bighouse** Highld
72 F4 **Upper Boddington** Nhants
72 C6 **Upper Brailes** Warwks
199 L2 **Upper Breakish** Highld
70 E4 **Upper Broadheath** Worcs
102 B7 **Upper Broughton** Notts
41 K6 **Upper Bucklebury** W Berk
28 D7 **Upper Burgate** Hants
75 H5 **Upper Caldecote** Beds
73 G3 **Upper Catesby** Nhants
67 L6 **Upper Chapel** Powys
27 L5 **Upper Chicksgrove** Wilts
28 F2 **Upper Chute** Wilts
45 G3 **Upper Clapton** Gt Lon
29 G3 **Upper Clatford** Hants
55 M5 **Upper Coberley** Gloucs
83 K3 **Upper Cound** Shrops
123 J8 **Upper Cumberworth** Kirk
215 H2 **Upper Dallachy** Moray
35 K4 **Upper Deal** Kent
74 F2 **Upper Dean** Beds
114 E1 **Upper Denby** Kirk
20 B4 **Upper Dicker** E Susx
230 E3 **Upper Dounreay** Highld
62 F2 **Upper Dovercourt** Essex
184 E6 **Upper Drumbane** Stirlg
133 G6 **Upper Dunsforth** N York
30 F3 **Upper Eashing** Surrey
213 J2 **Upper Eathie** Highld
70 B5 **Upper Egleton** Herefs
100 B2 **Upper Elkstone** Staffs
100 C4 **Upper Ellastone** Staffs
30 B4 **Upper Farringdon** Hants
55 H6 **Upper Framilode** Gloucs
30 C3 **Upper Froyle** Hants
26 C3 **Upper Godney** Somset
75 G7 **Upper Gravenhurst** Beds
76 E7 **Upper Green** Essex
41 G7 **Upper Green** W Berk
30 D2 **Upper Hale** Surrey
43 H6 **Upper Halliford** Surrey
88 C3 **Upper Hambleton** Rutlnd
34 F3 **Upper Harbledown** Kent
32 E6 **Upper Hartfield** E Susx
55 L4 **Upper Hatherley** Gloucs
123 H6 **Upper Heaton** Kirk
133 L7 **Upper Helmsley** N York
68 F4 **Upper Hergest** Herefs
73 J3 **Upper Heyford** Nhants
57 J3 **Upper Heyford** Oxon
69 J4 **Upper Hill** Herefs
123 J6 **Upper Hopton** Kirk
100 A1 **Upper Hulme** Staffs
40 D2 **Upper Inglesham** Swindn
51 H6 **Upper Killay** Swans
183 G2 **Upper Kinchrackine** Ag & B
40 F4 **Upper Lambourn** W Berk
85 H3 **Upper Landywood** Staffs
38 C7 **Upper Langford** N Som
115 K7 **Upper Langwith** Derbys
187 G6 **Upper Largo** Fife
100 A5 **Upper Leigh** Staffs
85 J2 **Upper Longdon** Staffs
231 J7 **Upper Lybster** Highld
54 E5 **Upper Lydbrook** Gloucs
69 H2 **Upper Lye** Herefs
84 E8 **Upper Milton** Worcs
40 A3 **Upper Minety** Wilts
215 H4 **Upper Mulben** Moray
83 L5 **Upper Netchwood** Shrops
100 B5 **Upper Nobut** Staffs
18 C3 **Upper Norwood** W Susx
133 H8 **Upper Poppleton** York
71 L5 **Upper Quinton** Warwks
28 F6 **Upper Ratley** Hants
70 B2 **Upper Rochford** Worcs
145 L3 **Upper Ruscoe** D & G
70 C2 **Upper Sapey** Herefs
39 L4 **Upper Seagry** Wilts
74 E5 **Upper Shelton** Beds
106 D4 **Upper Sheringham** Norfk
173 L5 **Upper Skelmorlie** N Ayrs
56 D4 **Upper Slaughter** Gloucs
54 F6 **Upper Soudley** Gloucs
35 H6 **Upper Standen** Kent
154 E5 **Upper Stepford** D & G
92 F3 **Upper Stoke** Norfk
73 J3 **Upper Stowe** Nhants
28 D7 **Upper Street** Hants
107 G8 **Upper Street** Norfk
93 H1 **Upper Street** Norfk
77 H4 **Upper Street** Suffk
78 D4 **Upper Street** Suffk
59 H3 **Upper Sundon** Beds
56 D3 **Upper Swell** Gloucs
92 E4 **Upper Tasburgh** Norfk
100 A5 **Upper Tean** Staffs
100 E1 **Upper Town** Derbys
69 L5 **Upper Town** Herefs
38 D7 **Upper Town** N Som
77 K2 **Upper Town** Suffk
51 G3 **Upper Tumble** Carmth
72 D5 **Upper Tysoe** Warwks
187 J1 **Upper Victoria** Angus
72 F5 **Upper Wardington** Oxon
19 L3 **Upper Wellingham** E Susx
92 F7 **Upper Weybread** Suffk
29 L4 **Upper Wield** Hants
58 C5 **Upper Winchendon** Bucks
28 C4 **Upper Woodford** Wilts
39 J5 **Upper Wraxall** Wilts
148 D4 **Upperby** Cumb
208 E4 **Upperglen** Highld
113 M1 **Uppermill** Oldham
123 H8 **Upperthong** Kirk
30 F6 **Upperton** W Susx
231 L1 **Uppertown** Highld
88 C4 **Uppingham** Rutlnd
83 L2 **Uppington** Shrops
133 G3 **Upsall** N York
168 C1 **Upsettlington** Border
60 C7 **Upshire** Essex
35 G3 **Upstreet** Kent
58 C5 **Upton** Bucks
89 G4 **Upton** C Pete
89 H7 **Upton** Cambs
112 B7 **Upton** Ches
5 L2 **Upton** Cnwll
12 E2 **Upton** Devon
7 G7 **Upton** Devon
14 E5 **Upton** Dorset
15 J4 **Upton** Dorset
29 G1 **Upton** Hants
29 G7 **Upton** Hants
86 D4 **Upton** Leics
116 E4 **Upton** Lincs
93 H2 **Upton** Norfk
102 B2 **Upton** Notts
116 C6 **Upton** Notts
41 K3 **Upton** Oxon
43 G5 **Upton** Slough
24 F5 **Upton** Somset
26 C6 **Upton** Somset
124 D7 **Upton** Wakefd
27 K5 **Upton** Wilts
111 J4 **Upton** Wirral
54 F3 **Upton Bishop** Herefs
39 G6 **Upton Cheyney** S Glos

84 B5 Upton Cressett Shrops
5 L2 Upton Cross Cnwll
30 B2 Upton Grey Hants
11 J4 Upton Hellions Devon
27 L4 Upton Lovell Wilts
83 K2 Upton Magna Shrops
27 G4 Upton Noble Somset
11 L5 Upton Pyne Devon
27 K2 Upton Scudamore Wilts
71 G4 Upton Snodsbury Worcs
55 K5 Upton St Leonards Gloucs
70 F6 Upton upon Severn Worcs
71 G2 Upton Warren Worcs
18 C3 Upwaltham W Susx
90 C3 Upwell Norfk
60 D3 Upwick Green Herts
89 J6 Upwood Cambs
40 B8 Urchfont Wilts
113 H3 Urmston Traffd
215 G2 Urquhart Moray
142 C6 Urra N York
212 D4 Urray Highld
197 H5 Usan Angus
151 G6 Ushaw Moor Dur
54 B7 Usk Mons
117 H3 Usselby Lincs
151 H4 Usworth Sundld
112 D8 Utkinton Ches
122 F3 Utley Brad
11 J5 Uton Devon
118 D3 Utterby Lincs
100 C5 Uttoxeter Staffs
43 H4 Uxbridge Gt Lon
235 d2 Uyeasound Shet
49 G5 Uzmaston Pembks

V

236 d2 Vale Guern
80 F7 Vale of Rheidol Railway Cerdgn
108 C5 Valley IoA
209 H2 Valtos Highld
232 d2 Valtos W Isls
46 B3 Vange Essex
235 d3 Vatsetter Shet
208 D5 Vatten Highld
53 G6 Vaynor Myr Td
236 b3 Vazon Bay Guern
68 D7 Velindre Powys
12 D4 Venn Ottery Devon
9 K3 Venngreen Devon
17 G6 Ventnor IoW
6 E4 Venton Devon
29 G1 Vernham Dean Hants
41 G8 Vernham Street Hants
15 K2 Verwood Dorset
4 E7 Veryan Cnwll
128 E5 Vickerstown Cumb
4 F4 Victoria Cnwll
235 d4 Vidlin Shet
215 G2 Viewfield Moray
175 J6 Viewpark N Lans
45 M7 Vigo Kent
236 a5 Ville la Bas Jersey
236 c3 Villiaze Guern
20 C3 Vines Cross E Susx
43 G6 Virginia Water Surrey
9 K6 Virginstow Devon
27 G2 Vobster Somset
235 c4 Voe Shet
69 G7 Vowchurch Herefs

W

140 E3 Wackerfield Dur
92 E5 Wacton Norfk
70 F5 Wadborough Worcs
58 C5 Waddesdon Bucks
7 K4 Waddeton Devon
117 G3 Waddingham Lincs
121 L2 Waddington Lancs
116 F8 Waddington Lincs
4 F2 Wadebridge Cnwll
13 H1 Wadeford Somset
88 E6 Wadenhoe Nhants
60 B4 Wadesmill Herts
33 H6 Wadhurst E Susx
114 F7 Wadshelf Derbys
115 K3 Wadworth Donc
104 D2 Wainfleet All Saints Lincs
9 G5 Wainhouse Corner Cnwll
46 C6 Wainscott Medway
122 F5 Wainstalls Calder
139 H5 Waitby Cumb
118 C2 Waithe Lincs
123 L6 Wakefield Wakefd
88 D4 Wakerley Nhants
61 L3 Wakes Colne Essex
93 K8 Walberswick Suffk
18 C4 Walberton W Susx
146 D2 Walbutt D & G
26 D3 Walcombe Somset
103 H5 Walcot Lincs
83 L2 Walcot Shrops
40 D4 Walcot Swindn
92 D7 Walcot Green Norfk
87 H6 Walcote Leics
103 J2 Walcott Lincs
107 H6 Walcott Norfk
124 E6 Walden Stubbs N York
46 C7 Walderslade Medway
17 L1 Walderton W Susx
13 L4 Walditch Dorset
151 G5 Waldridge Dur
79 G5 Waldringfield Suffk
20 B2 Waldron E Susx
115 J5 Wales Rothm
26 E6 Wales Somset
117 J3 Walesby Lincs
116 B7 Walesby Notts
83 H8 Walford Herefs
54 E4 Walford Herefs
98 C8 Walford Heath Shrops
99 G3 Walgherton Ches
74 B1 Walgrave Nhants
122 C5 Walk Mill Lancs
113 G2 Walkden Salfd
151 H3 Walker N u Ty
69 K5 Walker's Green Herefs
166 E3 Walkerburn Border
116 C3 Walkeringham Notts
116 C3 Walkerith Lincs
59 M3 Walkern Herts
186 D6 Walkerton Fife
16 B4 Walkford Dorset
6 D2 Walkhampton Devon
126 B3 Walkington E R Yk
115 G4 Walkley Sheff
71 J2 Walkwood Worcs
150 A2 Wall Nthumb
85 K3 Wall Staffs
153 G2 Wallacetown S Ayrs
163 J5 Wallacetown S Ayrs
19 L4 Wallands Park E Susx
111 J3 Wallasey Wirral
41 L3 Wallingford Oxon
44 F6 Wallington Gt Lon
17 H2 Wallington Hants
75 K7 Wallington Herts
15 K4 Wallisdown Poole
235 b5 Walls Shet
151 H2 Wallsend N Tyne
177 K4 Wallyford E Loth
35 K5 Walmer Kent
121 G5 Walmer Bridge Lancs
85 K5 Walmley Birm
93 H8 Walpole Suffk
104 E8 Walpole Cross Keys Norfk
90 D2 Walpole Highway Norfk
104 D8 Walpole St Andrew Norfk
90 C1 Walpole St Peter Norfk
85 H4 Walsall Wsall
122 D6 Walsden Calder
78 B1 Walsham le Willows Suffk
132 F8 Walshford N York
90 C2 Walsoken Norfk
165 K1 Walston S Lans
59 K3 Walsworth Herts
34 E5 Waltham Kent
118 C2 Waltham NE Lin
60 C7 Waltham Abbey Essex
29 K7 Waltham Chase Hants
60 B7 Waltham Cross Herts
102 D7 Waltham on the Wolds Leics
42 D5 Waltham St Lawrence W & M
148 F3 Walton Cumb
115 G7 Walton Derbys
124 C2 Walton Leeds
87 H6 Walton Leics
74 C7 Walton M Keyn
68 F3 Walton Powys
26 C4 Walton Somset
79 G7 Walton Suffk
17 M2 Walton W Susx
123 L6 Walton Wakefd
98 E8 Walton Wrekin
55 K2 Walton Cardiff Gloucs
49 H3 Walton East Pembks
31 L1 Walton on the Hill Surrey
62 F4 Walton on the Naze Essex
101 L8 Walton on the Wolds Leics
38 B6 Walton Park N Som
48 E5 Walton West Pembks
38 B5 Walton-in-Gordano N Som
121 H5 Walton-le-Dale Lancs
43 J6 Walton-on-Thames Surrey
99 L7 Walton-on-the-Hill Staffs
100 E8 Walton-on-Trent Derbys
141 G4 Walworth Darltn
45 G4 Walworth Gt Lon
48 E5 Walwyn's Castle Pembks
13 H2 Wambrook Somset
30 F2 Wanborough Surrey
40 E4 Wanborough Swindn
44 E5 Wandsworth Gt Lon
93 K7 Wangford Suffk
87 H2 Wanlip Leics
165 G6 Wanlockhead D & G
20 C5 Wannock E Susx
88 F4 Wansford C Pete
135 G7 Wansford E R Yk
33 K4 Wanshurst Green Kent
45 H3 Wanstead Gt Lon
27 G3 Wanstrow Somset
55 G7 Wanswell Gloucs
41 H3 Wantage Oxon
72 E2 Wappenbury Warwks
73 J5 Wappenham Nhants
20 C3 Warbleton E Susx
41 L2 Warborough Oxon
89 K7 Warboys Cambs
120 D3 Warbreck Bpool
9 G6 Warbstow Cnwll
113 G4 Warburton Traffd
139 H4 Warcop Cumb
150 A2 Warden Nthumb
72 F5 Wardington Oxon
98 E2 Wardle Ches
122 D6 Wardle Rochdl
151 H3 Wardley Gatesd
88 B4 Wardley Rutlnd
114 D6 Wardlow Derbys
90 C6 Wardy Hill Cambs
60 B5 Ware Herts
15 H5 Wareham Dorset
34 D7 Warehorne Kent
169 H4 Warenford Nthumb
60 C5 Wareside Herts
75 J4 Waresley Cambs
42 E6 Warfield Br For
7 K6 Warfleet Devon
42 C5 Wargrave Wokham
105 M4 Warham All Saints Norfk
105 M4 Warham St Mary Norfk
168 C2 Wark Nthumb
157 L6 Wark Nthumb
23 K6 Warkleigh Devon
88 C7 Warkton Nhants
72 F6 Warkworth Nhants
159 G2 Warkworth Nthumb
132 E2 Warlaby N York
5 J3 Warleggan Cnwll
122 F5 Warley Town Calder
32 C2 Warlingham Surrey
147 L2 Warmanbie D & G
124 B6 Warmfield Wakefd
99 G1 Warmingham Ches
88 F5 Warmington Nhants
72 E5 Warmington Warwks
27 K3 Warminster Wilts
38 F5 Warmley S Glos
115 K2 Warmsworth Donc
14 E5 Warmwell Dorset
29 L6 Warnford Hants
31 J5 Warnham W Susx
18 D4 Warningcamp W Susx
31 L6 Warninglid W Susx
113 K7 Warren Ches
48 F7 Warren Pembks
42 D4 Warren Row W & M
34 C4 Warren Street Kent
165 J2 Warrenhill S Lans
74 C4 Warrington M Keyn
112 E4 Warrington Warrtn
177 H4 Warriston C Edin
16 F2 Warsash Hants
100 C2 Warslow Staffs
115 K7 Warsop Notts
125 K1 Warter E R Yk
132 C4 Warthermaske N York
133 K7 Warthill N York
20 D4 Wartling E Susx
102 B7 Wartnaby Leics
120 E5 Warton Lancs
129 K5 Warton Lancs
86 C3 Warton Warwks
148 E4 Warwick Cumb
72 C2 Warwick Warwks
72 C2 Warwick Castle Warwks
234 c4 Wasbister Ork

137 G5 **Wasdale Head** Cumb
5 G2 **Washaway** Cnwll
7 J5 **Washbourne** Devon
78 D6 **Washbrook** Suffk
11 L2 **Washfield** Devon
25 G3 **Washford** Somset
11 J3 **Washford Pyne** Devon
117 G7 **Washingborough** Lincs
151 H4 **Washington** Sundld
18 F3 **Washington** W Susx
72 C3 **Wasperton** Warwks
133 H4 **Wass** N York
25 G3 **Watchet** Somset
40 E3 **Watchfield** Oxon
138 D7 **Watchgate** Cumb
11 H8 **Water** Devon
125 J3 **Water End** E R Yk
89 G4 **Water Newton** Cambs
85 L5 **Water Orton** Warwks
73 J7 **Water Stratford** Bucks
76 C2 **Waterbeach** Cambs
18 B4 **Waterbeach** W Susx
155 M6 **Waterbeck** D & G
14 E5 **Watercombe** Dorset
100 B3 **Waterfall** Staffs
175 G7 **Waterfoot** S Lans
60 A5 **Waterford** Herts
8 F8 **Watergate** Cnwll
164 B6 **Waterhead** E Ayrs
177 H7 **Waterheads** Border
100 B3 **Waterhouses** Staffs
33 H3 **Wateringbury** Kent
199 K2 **Waterloo** Highld
175 L7 **Waterloo** N Lans
195 G8 **Waterloo** P & K
49 G6 **Waterloo** Pembks
111 K2 **Waterloo** Sefton
17 J1 **Waterlooville** Hants
138 C3 **Watermillock** Cumb
57 L6 **Waterperry** Oxon
25 G6 **Waterrow** Somset
98 F8 **Waters Upton** Wrekin
18 D3 **Watersfield** W Susx
121 K5 **Waterside** Bl w D
163 K7 **Waterside** E Ayrs
163 L2 **Waterside** E Ayrs
175 J4 **Waterside** E Duns
208 B5 **Waterstein** Highld
57 M6 **Waterstock** Oxon
48 F6 **Waterston** Pembks
43 J2 **Watford** Herts
73 H2 **Watford** Nhants
132 B6 **Wath** N York
132 E4 **Wath** N York
115 H2 **Wath upon Dearne** Rothm
90 E2 **Watlington** Norfk
42 B2 **Watlington** Oxon
231 J5 **Watten** Highld
92 B8 **Wattisfield** Suffk
78 B4 **Wattisham** Suffk
13 L4 **Watton** Dorset
126 C1 **Watton** E R Yk
91 K4 **Watton** Norfk
60 A4 **Watton-at-Stone** Herts
175 K4 **Wattston** N Lans
37 J3 **Wattsville** Caerph
206 C6 **Waulkmill** Abers
51 H6 **Waunarlwydd** Swans
80 E6 **Waunfawr** Cerdgn
95 J2 **Waunfawr** Gwynd
74 C6 **Wavendon** M Keyn
147 L5 **Waverbridge** Cumb
112 C8 **Waverton** Ches
147 L5 **Waverton** Cumb
126 D3 **Wawne** E R Yk
107 J7 **Waxham** Norfk
11 K3 **Way Village** Devon
13 K2 **Wayford** Somset
13 L3 **Waytown** Dorset
25 H4 **Weacombe** Somset
56 F7 **Weald** Oxon
44 D3 **Wealdstone** Gt Lon
123 K2 **Weardley** Leeds
26 B2 **Weare** Somset
23 G6 **Weare Giffard** Devon
149 L6 **Wearhead** Dur
26 B5 **Wearne** Somset
105 K7 **Weasenham All Saints** Norfk
105 K7 **Weasenham St Peter** Norfk
113 J2 **Weaste** Salfd
112 E6 **Weaverham** Ches
134 E5 **Weaverthorpe** N York
71 H2 **Webheath** Worcs
216 F7 **Wedderlairs** Abers
86 D5 **Weddington** Warwks
40 B8 **Wedhampton** Wilts
26 C2 **Wedmore** Somset
85 H4 **Wednesbury** Sandw
85 G4 **Wednesfield** Wolves
58 D4 **Weedon** Bucks
73 J3 **Weedon** Nhants
73 H5 **Weedon Lois** Nhants
85 K3 **Weeford** Staffs
9 H5 **Week St Mary** Cnwll
29 J5 **Weeke** Hants
88 C7 **Weekley** Nhants
126 D3 **Weel** E R Yk
62 D4 **Weeley** Essex
62 D4 **Weeley Heath** Essex
194 D6 **Weem** P & K
71 J4 **Weethley** Warwks
91 H5 **Weeting** Norfk
127 H6 **Weeton** E R Yk
120 E4 **Weeton** Lancs
123 K2 **Weeton** N York
123 K3 **Weetwood** Leeds
122 C5 **Weir** Lancs
6 C3 **Weir Quay** Devon
92 C2 **Welborne** Norfk
102 F2 **Welbourn** Lincs
133 L6 **Welburn** N York
141 J6 **Welbury** N York
102 F5 **Welby** Lincs
22 C7 **Welcombe** Devon
87 J7 **Welford** Nhants
41 H5 **Welford** W Berk
71 K4 **Welford-on-Avon** Warwks
87 L5 **Welham** Leics
116 B5 **Welham** Notts
59 L6 **Welham Green** Herts
30 C3 **Well** Hants
118 F6 **Well** Lincs
132 D3 **Well** N York
59 K3 **Well Head** Herts
70 E6 **Welland** Worcs
196 D8 **Wellbank** Angus
72 C4 **Wellesbourne** Warwks
45 J5 **Welling** Gt Lon
74 C2 **Wellingborough** Nhants
105 L7 **Wellingham** Norfk
103 G2 **Wellingore** Lincs
136 F6 **Wellington** Cumb
69 K5 **Wellington** Herefs
25 H7 **Wellington** Somset
84 B2 **Wellington** Wrekin
70 C6 **Wellington Heath** Herefs
39 H8 **Wellow** BaNES
16 E5 **Wellow** IOW
116 A7 **Wellow** Notts
26 D3 **Wells** Somset
105 L4 **Wells-next-the-sea** Norfk
61 G4 **Wellstye Green** Essex
185 K3 **Welltree** P & K
176 E2 **Wellwood** Fife
90 D5 **Welney** Norfk
98 A6 **Welsh Frankton** Shrops
54 D4 **Welsh Newton** Herefs
36 F5 **Welsh St Donats** V Glam
98 C5 **Welshampton** Shrops
82 E3 **Welshpool** Powys
148 C6 **Welton** Cumb
126 B5 **Welton** E R Yk
117 G5 **Welton** Lincs
73 H2 **Welton** Nhants
119 G7 **Welton le Marsh** Lincs
118 C4 **Welton le Wold** Lincs
127 H6 **Welwick** E R Yk
59 L5 **Welwyn** Herts
59 L5 **Welwyn Garden City** Herts
98 D6 **Wem** Shrops
25 L4 **Wembdon** Somset
44 D3 **Wembley** Gt Lon
6 D6 **Wembury** Devon
10 F3 **Wembworthy** Devon
173 L4 **Wemyss Bay** Inver
76 D7 **Wendens Ambo** Essex
57 K4 **Wendlebury** Oxon
91 L2 **Wendling** Norfk
58 E6 **Wendover** Bucks
3 H5 **Wendron** Cnwll
75 K5 **Wendy** Cambs
93 J7 **Wenhaston** Suffk
89 J7 **Wennington** Cambs
45 K4 **Wennington** Gt Lon
130 C5 **Wennington** Lancs
100 E1 **Wensley** Derbys
131 K2 **Wensley** N York
124 D6 **Wentbridge** Wakefd
83 H5 **Wentnor** Shrops
90 C7 **Wentworth** Cambs
115 G2 **Wentworth** Rothm
37 H6 **Wenvoe** V Glam
69 H4 **Weobley** Herefs
69 H4 **Weobley Marsh** Herefs
18 E4 **Wepham** W Susx
90 F3 **Wereham** Norfk
89 H3 **Werrington** C Pete
9 J7 **Werrington** Cnwll
112 B6 **Wervin** Ches
120 F4 **Wesham** Lancs
101 G2 **Wessington** Derbys
91 H1 **West Acre** Norfk
7 G6 **West Alvington** Devon
24 D6 **West Anstey** Devon
118 C6 **West Ashby** Lincs
17 M2 **West Ashling** W Susx
27 K1 **West Ashton** Wilts
140 F3 **West Auckland** Dur
134 F3 **West Ayton** N York
25 J5 **West Bagborough** Somset
112 D5 **West Bank** Halton
117 K5 **West Barkwith** Lincs
143 G5 **West Barnby** N York
178 E3 **West Barns** E Loth
105 L5 **West Barsham** Norfk
13 L4 **West Bay** Dorset
106 D5 **West Beckham** Norfk
43 H5 **West Bedfont** Surrey
62 A3 **West Bergholt** Essex
14 A5 **West Bexington** Dorset
91 G1 **West Bilney** Norfk
19 J4 **West Blatchington** Br & H
151 J3 **West Boldon** S Tyne
123 H4 **West Bowling** Brad
34 E6 **West Brabourne** Kent
91 K2 **West Bradenham** Norfk
121 L2 **West Bradford** Lancs
26 E4 **West Bradley** Somset
123 K7 **West Bretton** Wakefd
101 L5 **West Bridgford** Notts
85 H5 **West Bromwich** Sandw
166 E6 **West Buccleuch Hotel** Border
23 K5 **West Buckland** Devon
25 J7 **West Buckland** Somset
131 J3 **West Burton** N York
116 D1 **West Butterwick** N Linc
43 H7 **West Byfleet** Surrey
144 D8 **West Cairngaan** D & G
93 K2 **West Caister** Norfk
176 D5 **West Calder** W Loth
26 E6 **West Camel** Somset
14 E5 **West Chaldon** Dorset
41 G3 **West Challow** Oxon
7 H7 **West Charleton** Devon
159 G3 **West Chevington** Nthumb
18 E3 **West Chiltington** W Susx
26 C8 **West Chinnock** Somset
31 H2 **West Clandon** Surrey
35 J5 **West Cliffe** Kent
26 D8 **West Coker** Somset
26 E3 **West Compton** Somset
14 B4 **West Compton Abbas** Dorset
125 G3 **West Cottingwith** N York
124 F6 **West Cowick** E R Yk
51 H7 **West Cross** Swans
148 B5 **West Curthwaite** Cumb
18 B3 **West Dean** W Susx
28 E6 **West Dean** Wilts
89 G2 **West Deeping** Lincs
111 L3 **West Derby** Lpool
90 F4 **West Dereham** Norfk
23 H3 **West Down** Devon
43 H4 **West Drayton** Gt Lon
116 B6 **West Drayton** Notts
231 J2 **West Dunnet** Highld
126 C5 **West Ella** E R Yk
74 E4 **West End** Beds
29 J8 **West End** Hants
38 C6 **West End** N Som
93 K2 **West End** Norfk
42 F7 **West End** Surrey
27 M6 **West End** Wilts
42 A7 **West End Green** Hants
33 J3 **West Farleigh** Kent
73 G4 **West Farndon** Nhants
97 M7 **West Felton** Shrops
19 M4 **West Firle** E Susx
40 E7 **West Grafton** Wilts
30 C1 **West Green** Hants
28 E6 **West Grimstead** Wilts
31 K6 **West Grinstead** W Susx
124 E5 **West Haddlesey** N York
73 J1 **West Haddon** Nhants
41 K3 **West Hagbourne** Oxon
84 F7 **West Hagley** Worcs
101 H4 **West Hallam** Derbys
125 L6 **West Halton** N Linc

45 H4 **West Ham** Gt Lon
115 H6 **West Handley** Derbys
41 H2 **West Hanney** Oxon
61 H7 **West Hanningfield** Essex
28 C5 **West Harnham** Wilts
38 E8 **West Harptree** BaNES
30 C7 **West Harting** W Susx
25 L7 **West Hatch** Somset
27 L5 **West Hatch** Wilts
187 J1 **West Haven** Angus
85 J7 **West Heath** Birm
227 H5 **West Helmsdale** Highld
41 H3 **West Hendred** Oxon
134 E4 **West Heslerton** N York
38 B7 **West Hewish** N Som
12 D4 **West Hill** Devon
32 C6 **West Hoathly** W Susx
15 G5 **West Holme** Dorset
45 M3 **West Horndon** Essex
26 E3 **West Horrington** Somset
31 H2 **West Horsley** Surrey
35 H6 **West Hougham** Kent
15 K4 **West Howe** Bmouth
185 M3 **West Huntingtower** P & K
25 L3 **West Huntspill** Somset
34 F7 **West Hythe** Kent
41 J4 **West Ilsley** W Berk
17 L3 **West Itchenor** W Susx
40 C6 **West Kennett** Wilts
173 L8 **West Kilbride** N Ayrs
45 L7 **West Kingsdown** Kent
39 J5 **West Kington** Wilts
111 H4 **West Kirby** Wirral
134 D4 **West Knapton** N York
14 D5 **West Knighton** Dorset
27 K5 **West Knoyle** Wilts
26 B7 **West Lambrook** Somset
35 J5 **West Langdon** Kent
191 L5 **West Laroch** Highld
30 E7 **West Lavington** W Susx
28 A2 **West Lavington** Wilts
140 E5 **West Layton** N York
101 K7 **West Leake** Notts
11 G4 **West Leigh** Devon
7 H4 **West Leigh** Devon
25 H5 **West Leigh** Somset
91 J1 **West Lexham** Norfk
133 K6 **West Lilling** N York
176 F7 **West Linton** Border
39 H5 **West Littleton** S Glos
41 H3 **West Lockinge** Oxon
14 F6 **West Lulworth** Dorset
134 E5 **West Lutton** N York
26 E5 **West Lydford** Somset
25 L5 **West Lyng** Somset
104 F7 **West Lynn** Norfk
33 H2 **West Malling** Kent
70 D5 **West Malvern** Worcs
30 C8 **West Marden** W Susx
116 B6 **West Markham** Notts
127 G8 **West Marsh** NE Lin
122 D1 **West Marton** N York
27 K7 **West Melbury** Dorset
29 M6 **West Meon** Hants
62 B5 **West Mersea** Essex
84 E7 **West Midlands Safari Park** Worcs
13 L3 **West Milton** Dorset
46 E5 **West Minster** Kent
43 J6 **West Molesey** Surrey
25 K5 **West Monkton** Somset
15 K2 **West Moors** Dorset
15 G4 **West Morden** Dorset
167 J2 **West Morriston** Border
26 E7 **West Mudford** Somset
133 L4 **West Ness** N York
126 F3 **West Newton** E R Yk
105 H6 **West Newton** Norfk
25 L5 **West Newton** Somset
44 F5 **West Norwood** Gt Lon
7 J2 **West Ogwell** Devon
27 J7 **West Orchard** Dorset
40 C6 **West Overton** Wilts
15 K3 **West Parley** Dorset
33 H3 **West Peckham** Kent
151 G4 **West Pelton** Dur
26 D4 **West Pennard** Somset
4 B4 **West Pentire** Cnwll
75 G2 **West Perry** Cambs
24 D3 **West Porlock** Somset
14 D2 **West Pulham** Dorset
9 K2 **West Putford** Devon
25 H3 **West Quantoxhead** Somset
11 K4 **West Raddon** Devon
151 H5 **West Rainton** Dur
117 H4 **West Rasen** Lincs
105 L7 **West Raynham** Norfk
141 K6 **West Rounton** N York
90 F7 **West Row** Suffk
105 K6 **West Rudham** Norfk
106 E4 **West Runton** Norfk
178 B5 **West Saltoun** E Loth
11 J4 **West Sandford** Devon
235 d3 **West Sandwick** Shet
131 K3 **West Scrafton** N York
14 D4 **West Stafford** Dorset
116 C3 **West Stockwith** Notts
17 M2 **West Stoke** W Susx
27 H6 **West Stour** Dorset
35 H3 **West Stourmouth** Kent
77 J1 **West Stow** Suffk
40 C7 **West Stowell** Wilts
78 B1 **West Street** Suffk
132 D4 **West Tanfield** N York
5 J3 **West Taphouse** Cnwll
172 E5 **West Tarbert** Ag & B
18 F5 **West Tarring** W Susx
158 F3 **West Thirston** Nthumb
17 L3 **West Thorney** W Susx
101 L7 **West Thorpe** Notts
45 L4 **West Thurrock** Thurr
46 A4 **West Tilbury** Thurr
29 M5 **West Tisted** Hants
117 J5 **West Torrington** Lincs
17 K3 **West Town** Hants
38 C6 **West Town** N Som
28 F5 **West Tytherley** Hants
90 C2 **West Walton** Norfk
90 C2 **West Walton Highway** Norfk
28 F7 **West Wellow** Hants
6 D6 **West Wembury** Devon
186 E7 **West Wemyss** Fife
76 E5 **West Wickham** Cambs
45 G6 **West Wickham** Gt Lon
49 H6 **West Williamston** Pembks
90 F1 **West Winch** Norfk
28 E5 **West Winterslow** Wilts
17 L3 **West Wittering** W Susx
131 K2 **West Witton** N York
157 M5 **West Woodburn** Nthumb
41 H7 **West Woodhay** W Berk
30 C4 **West Worldham** Hants
18 F5 **West Worthing** W Susx
76 E4 **West Wratting** Essex
9 H2 **West Youlstone** Cnwll
35 G3 **Westbere** Kent
102 D4 **Westborough** Lincs
15 K4 **Westbourne** Bmouth
17 L2 **Westbourne** W Susx
35 J2 **Westbrook** Kent
41 H6 **Westbrook** W Berk
73 J7 **Westbury** Bucks
83 G2 **Westbury** Shrops
27 K2 **Westbury** Wilts
27 K2 **Westbury Leigh** Wilts
55 G5 **Westbury on Severn** Gloucs
38 E5 **Westbury-on-Trym** Bristl
26 D2 **Westbury-sub-Mendip** Somset
120 E4 **Westby** Lancs
46 E3 **Westcliff-on-Sea** Sthend
27 G4 **Westcombe** Somset
56 E4 **Westcote** Gloucs
58 B5 **Westcott** Bucks
12 C2 **Westcott** Devon
31 J2 **Westcott** Surrey
40 E7 **Westcourt** Wilts
20 B5 **Westdean** E Susx
8 E7 **Westdowns** Cnwll
212 F7 **Wester Drumashie** Highld
176 D4 **Wester Ochiltree** W Loth
187 J6 **Wester Pitkierie** Fife
220 C5 **Wester Ross** Highld
231 G5 **Westerdale** Highld
142 E6 **Westerdale** N York
78 E5 **Westerfield** Suffk
18 C5 **Westergate** W Susx
32 D3 **Westerham** Kent
150 F2 **Westerhope** N u Ty
7 K4 **Westerland** Devon
39 G4 **Westerleigh** S Glos
197 G5 **Westerton** Angus
26 F2 **Westfield** BaNES
136 D2 **Westfield** Cumb
21 G3 **Westfield** E Susx
230 F3 **Westfield** Highld
175 J4 **Westfield** N Lans
92 B2 **Westfield** Norfk
176 C4 **Westfield** W Loth
195 J6 **Westfields of Rattray** P & K
150 A7 **Westgate** Dur
125 J8 **Westgate** N Linc
35 J2 **Westgate on Sea** Kent
93 J7 **Westhall** Suffk
14 C6 **Westham** Dorset
20 D5 **Westham** E Susx
26 B3 **Westham** Somset
18 B4 **Westhampnett** W Susx
26 C3 **Westhay** Somset
69 L5 **Westhide** Herefs
206 F4 **Westhill** Abers
69 J4 **Westhope** Herefs
83 J6 **Westhope** Shrops
103 L6 **Westhorpe** Lincs
78 C2 **Westhorpe** Suffk
112 F1 **Westhoughton** Bolton
130 D5 **Westhouse** N York
101 H2 **Westhouses** Derbys
31 K2 **Westhumble** Surrey
6 F5 **Westlake** Devon
23 G5 **Westleigh** Devon
25 G7 **Westleigh** Devon
79 J2 **Westleton** Suffk
77 J2 **Westley** Suffk
76 E3 **Westley Waterless** Cambs
58 C6 **Westlington** Bucks
148 D3 **Westlinton** Cumb
35 H3 **Westmarsh** Kent
19 K3 **Westmeston** E Susx
60 B3 **Westmill** Herts
44 F4 **Westminster** Gt Lon
196 B5 **Westmuir** Angus
147 K6 **Westnewton** Cumb
151 J2 **Westoe** S Tyne
39 G6 **Weston** BaNES
99 G3 **Weston** Ches
12 E3 **Weston** Devon
12 F5 **Weston** Devon
30 B6 **Weston** Hants
59 L3 **Weston** Herts
103 M7 **Weston** Lincs
123 H2 **Weston** N York
73 H5 **Weston** Nhants
116 C7 **Weston** Notts
83 L5 **Weston** Shrops
97 L6 **Weston** Shrops
99 L6 **Weston** Staffs
41 H5 **Weston** W Berk
69 L6 **Weston Beggard** Herefs
87 L5 **Weston by Welland** Nhants
29 J4 **Weston Colley** Hants
76 E4 **Weston Colville** Cambs
30 B3 **Weston Corbett** Hants
99 L4 **Weston Coyney** C Stke
73 L3 **Weston Favell** Nhants
76 F4 **Weston Green** Cambs
84 D2 **Weston Heath** Shrops
99 H7 **Weston Jones** Staffs
92 D1 **Weston Longville** Norfk
98 B7 **Weston Lullingfields** Shrops
30 B3 **Weston Patrick** Hants
97 L5 **Weston Rhyn** Shrops
71 K6 **Weston Subedge** Gloucs
58 D6 **Weston Turville** Bucks
54 F4 **Weston under Penyard** Herefs
72 D1 **Weston under Wetherley** Warwks
100 F4 **Weston Underwood** Derbys
74 C4 **Weston Underwood** M Keyn
38 C5 **Weston-in-Gordano** N Som
57 K4 **Weston-on-the-Green** Oxon
37 L7 **Weston-Super-Mare** N Som
84 E2 **Weston-under-Lizard** Staffs
98 E6 **Weston-under-Redcastle** Shrops
101 H6 **Weston-upon-Trent** Derbys
39 J3 **Westonbirt** Gloucs

59 G2 Westoning Beds
26 A4 Westonzoyland Somset
134 B6 Westow N York
26 B7 Westport Somset
176 B3 Westquarter Falk
234 c3 Westray Airport Ork
41 K4 Westridge Green W Berk
176 B5 Westrigg W Loth
40 D2 Westrop Swindn
178 D7 Westruther Border
90 B4 Westry Cambs
148 B6 Westward Cumb
23 G5 Westward Ho! Devon
34 D5 Westwell Kent
56 E6 Westwell Oxon
34 C5 Westwell Leacon Kent
76 B2 Westwick Cambs
12 C3 Westwood Devon
35 K2 Westwood Kent
39 J8 Westwood Wilts
116 C2 Westwoodside N Linc
148 E4 Wetheral Cumb
124 B2 Wetherby Leeds
78 B3 Wetherden Suffk
78 D2 Wetheringsett Suffk
61 H2 Wethersfield Essex
78 D2 Wetherup Street Suffk
99 L3 Wetley Rocks Staffs
98 F1 Wettenhall Ches
100 C2 Wetton Staffs
134 E7 Wetwang E R Yk
99 H5 Wetwood Staffs
40 F8 Wexcombe Wilts
106 D4 Weybourne Norfk
92 F7 Weybread Suffk
92 F7 Weybread Street Suffk
43 H7 Weybridge Surrey
13 H3 Weycroft Devon
231 H3 Weydale Highld
28 F3 Weyhill Hants
14 D6 Weymouth Dorset
74 B7 Whaddon Bucks
75 L5 Whaddon Cambs
55 J5 Whaddon Gloucs
39 K7 Whaddon Wilts
28 D6 Whaddon Wilts
115 K7 Whaley Derbys
114 A5 Whaley Bridge Derbys
115 K7 Whaley Thorns Derbys
231 K7 Whaligoe Highld
121 L4 Whalley Lancs
158 E6 Whalton Nthumb
104 A7 Whaplode Lincs
89 K2 Whaplode Drove Lincs
72 E4 Wharf Warwks
130 E5 Wharfe N York
120 F4 Wharles Lancs
74 D6 Wharley End Beds
114 F3 Wharncliffe Side Sheff
134 D6 Wharram-le-Street N York
69 K4 Wharton Herefs
140 E6 Whashton N York
129 L4 Whasset Cumb
72 C5 Whatcote Warwks
86 B4 Whateley Warwks
78 B5 Whatfield Suffk
13 J2 Whatley Somset
27 G3 Whatley Somset
20 F3 Whatlington E Susx
34 F5 Whatsole Street Kent
101 G2 Whatstandwell Derbys
102 C5 Whatton Notts
145 J5 Whauphill D & G
93 K5 Wheatacre Norfk
59 K5 Wheathampstead Herts
84 B6 Wheathill Shrops
30 C4 Wheatley Hants
57 L6 Wheatley Oxon
151 J6 Wheatley Hill Dur
115 L1 Wheatley Hills Donc
84 F2 Wheaton Aston Staffs
24 E4 Wheddon Cross Somset
99 H2 Wheelock Ches
121 J6 Wheelton Lancs
125 G2 Wheldrake York
56 D7 Whelford Gloucs
59 G6 Whelpley Hill Bucks
60 A4 Whempstead Herts
133 K5 Whenby N York
77 J3 Whepstead Suffk
78 E6 Wherstead Suffk
29 H3 Wherwell Hants
114 C6 Wheston Derbys
33 H4 Whetsted Kent
87 G4 Whetstone Leics
128 D3 Whicham Cumb
72 C7 Whichford Warwks
150 F3 Whickham Gatesd
11 G6 Whiddon Down Devon
196 D7 Whigstreet Angus
73 J2 Whilton Nhants
12 D3 Whimple Devon
107 H6 Whimpwell Green Norfk
92 B2 Whinburgh Norfk
146 C4 Whinnie Liggate D & G
217 K7 Whinnyfold Abers
17 G4 Whippingham IOW
59 G4 Whipsnade Beds
59 G4 Whipsnade Wild Animal Park Beds
12 B4 Whipton Devon
116 E7 Whisby Lincs
88 B2 Whissendine Rutlnd
105 L7 Whissonsett Norfk
183 J8 Whistlefield Ag & B
183 G8 Whistlefield Inn Ag & B
42 C5 Whistley Green Wokham
112 C3 Whiston Knows
74 B3 Whiston Nhants
115 H4 Whiston Rothm
84 F2 Whiston Staffs
100 B3 Whiston Staffs
128 D3 Whitbeck Cumb
70 D3 Whitbourne Herefs
151 J3 Whitburn S Tyne
176 C5 Whitburn W Loth
143 J5 Whitby N York
178 F6 Whitchester Border
38 F6 Whitchurch BaNES
58 D4 Whitchurch Bucks
37 J4 Whitchurch Cardif
6 D2 Whitchurch Devon
29 J2 Whitchurch Hants
54 D4 Whitchurch Herefs
41 M5 Whitchurch Oxon
48 D3 Whitchurch Pembks
98 D4 Whitchurch Shrops
13 K4 Whitchurch Canonicorum Dorset
41 M5 Whitchurch Hill Oxon
14 D5 Whitcombe Dorset
83 H5 Whitcot Shrops
82 F6 Whitcott Keysett Shrops
25 H7 White Ball Somset
121 H3 White Chapel Lancs
61 L3 White Colne Essex
3 H6 White Cross Cnwll
70 E7 White End Worcs
14 D3 White Lackington Dorset
71 G4 White Ladies Aston Worcs
61 J4 White Notley Essex
118 E6 White Pit Lincs
60 E5 White Roding Essex
69 L6 White Stone Herefs
42 D5 White Waltham W & M
86 B5 Whiteacre Heath Warwks
202 D3 Whitebridge Highld
54 D6 Whitebrook Mons
207 H2 Whitecairns Abers
45 G4 Whitechapel Gt Lon
54 E6 Whitecliffe Gloucs
177 K4 Whitecraig E Loth
144 E4 Whitecrook D & G
176 C3 Whitecross Falk
222 F4 Whiteface Highld
161 L2 Whitefarland N Ayrs
163 H7 Whitefaulds S Ayrs
113 J1 Whitefield Bury
25 G5 Whitefield Somset
206 D1 Whiteford Abers
112 F7 Whitegate Ches
234 d5 Whitehall Ork
136 D4 Whitehaven Cumb
30 C5 Whitehill Hants
216 C2 Whitehills Abers
206 C3 Whitehouse Abers
172 D6 Whitehouse Ag & B
178 D3 Whitekirk E Loth
26 B7 Whitelackington Somset
17 G6 Whiteley Bank IOW
214 B4 Whitemire Moray
101 K4 Whitemoor C Nott
4 F4 Whitemoor Cnwll
235 c6 Whiteness Shet
28 E6 Whiteparish Wilts
206 F2 Whiterashes Abers
231 L5 Whiterow Highld
214 C3 Whiterow Moray
55 J6 Whiteshill Gloucs
20 B3 Whitesmith E Susx
13 H1 Whitestaunton Somset
11 K6 Whitestone Cross Devon
121 K2 Whitewell Lancs
35 J5 Whitfield Kent
73 H6 Whitfield Nhants
149 K4 Whitfield Nthumb
38 F3 Whitfield S Glos
13 G4 Whitford Devon
111 G5 Whitford Flints
125 J6 Whitgift E R Yk
99 K6 Whitgreave Staffs
145 J6 Whithorn D & G
162 D4 Whiting Bay N Ayrs
124 B4 Whitkirk Leeds
49 L4 Whitland Carmth
167 G6 Whitlaw Border
163 J5 Whitletts S Ayrs
124 E6 Whitley N York
42 B6 Whitley Readg
115 G3 Whitley Sheff
39 K6 Whitley Wilts
159 J7 Whitley Bay N Tyne
150 B4 Whitley Chapel Nthumb
123 J6 Whitley Lower Kirk
55 H6 Whitminster Gloucs
99 J4 Whitmore Staffs
25 G7 Whitnage Devon
72 D2 Whitnash Warwks
68 F5 Whitney-on-Wye Herefs
147 M4 Whitrigglees Cumb
28 C7 Whitsbury Hants
179 H7 Whitsome Border
38 B4 Whitson Newpt
47 J6 Whitstable Kent
9 H5 Whitstone Cnwll
168 F6 Whittingham Nthumb
83 H5 Whittingslow Shrops
115 G6 Whittington Derbys
56 A4 Whittington Gloucs
130 B4 Whittington Lancs
91 G4 Whittington Norfk
97 L6 Whittington Shrops
85 L2 Whittington Staffs
84 F6 Whittington Staffs
86 C4 Whittington Warwks
70 F4 Whittington Worcs
121 H6 Whittle-le-Woods Lancs
73 K5 Whittlebury Nhants
89 J4 Whittlesey Cambs
76 C5 Whittlesford Cambs
125 L5 Whitton N Linc
158 D3 Whitton Nthumb
68 F2 Whitton Powys
141 J3 Whitton S on T
83 L8 Whitton Shrops
150 D4 Whittonstall Nthumb
41 J8 Whitway Hants
115 K6 Whitwell Derbys
59 K4 Whitwell Herts
17 G6 Whitwell IOW
141 G7 Whitwell N York
88 D2 Whitwell Rutlnd
106 D7 Whitwell Street Norfk
133 L6 Whitwell-on-the-Hill N York
86 E1 Whitwick Leics
122 D6 Whitworth Lancs
98 D5 Whixall Shrops
133 G7 Whixley N York
140 E4 Whorlton Dur
141 L6 Whorlton N York
69 L3 Whyle Herefs
32 C2 Whyteleafe Surrey
123 H4 Wibsey Brad
86 F6 Wibtoft Warwks
70 D3 Wichenford Worcs
34 B4 Wichling Kent
15 L4 Wick Bmouth
231 L5 Wick Highld
39 G5 Wick S Glos
36 E6 Wick V Glam
18 D5 Wick W Susx
71 G5 Wick Worcs
231 L5 Wick Airport Highld
38 A7 Wick St Lawrence N Som
76 E1 Wicken Cambs
73 L6 Wicken Nhants
60 D2 Wicken Bonhunt Essex
117 H5 Wickenby Lincs
77 L6 Wicker Street Green Suffk
115 J3 Wickersley Rothm
46 C2 Wickford Essex
17 H1 Wickham Hants
41 H6 Wickham W Berk
61 K5 Wickham Bishops Essex
78 D2 Wickham Green Suffk
79 G4 Wickham Market Suffk
78 C2 Wickham Skeith Suffk
77 J7 Wickham St Paul Essex

78 C1 **Wickham Street** Suffk
35 G3 **Wickhambreaux** Kent
77 H4 **Wickhambrook** Suffk
71 J6 **Wickhamford** Worcs
93 J3 **Wickhampton** Norfk
92 C3 **Wicklewood** Norfk
106 E5 **Wickmere** Norfk
39 G3 **Wickwar** S Glos
60 E2 **Widdington** Essex
159 G3 **Widdrington** Nthumb
159 G4 **Widdrington Station** Nthumb
159 G7 **Wide Open** N Tyne
7 G1 **Widecombe in the Moor** Devon
5 L4 **Widegates** Cnwll
9 G4 **Widemouth Bay** Cnwll
61 H6 **Widford** Essex
60 C5 **Widford** Herts
42 E2 **Widmer End** Bucks
101 M6 **Widmerpool** Notts
45 H6 **Widmore** Gt Lon
112 D5 **Widnes** Halton
13 G3 **Widworthy** Devon
112 E1 **Wigan** Wigan
26 C7 **Wigborough** Somset
12 E4 **Wiggaton** Devon
90 E2 **Wiggenhall St Germans** Norfk
90 E2 **Wiggenhall St Mary Magdalen** Norfk
90 E2 **Wiggenhall St Mary the Virgin** Norfk
58 F6 **Wigginton** Herts
57 H2 **Wigginton** Oxon
86 B3 **Wigginton** Staffs
133 J7 **Wigginton** York
130 F7 **Wigglesworth** N York
148 B4 **Wiggonby** Cumb
124 D2 **Wighill** N York
105 M4 **Wighton** Norfk
84 F4 **Wightwick** Wolves
69 H2 **Wigmore** Herefs
46 D6 **Wigmore** Medway
116 E7 **Wigsley** Notts
88 F6 **Wigsthorpe** Nhants
87 H4 **Wigston** Leics
86 F5 **Wigston Parva** Leics
115 L5 **Wigthorpe** Notts
103 L5 **Wigtoft** Lincs
148 A5 **Wigton** Cumb
145 J4 **Wigtown** D & G
123 L3 **Wike** Leeds
88 B5 **Wilbarston** Nhants
125 H1 **Wilberfoss** E R Yk
90 C7 **Wilburton** Cambs
74 C2 **Wilby** Nhants
92 B5 **Wilby** Norfk
78 F1 **Wilby** Suffk
40 C7 **Wilcot** Wilts
98 B8 **Wilcott** Shrops
113 M7 **Wildboarclough** Ches
75 G4 **Wilden** Beds
84 E8 **Wilden** Worcs
175 L7 **Wildmanbridge** S Lans
85 G7 **Wildmoor** Worcs
116 D3 **Wildsworth** Lincs
98 F4 **Wilkesley** Ches
223 K4 **Wilkhaven** Highld
176 F5 **Wilkieston** W Loth
12 D1 **Willand** Devon
111 K6 **Willaston** Ches
99 G3 **Willaston** Ches
74 C6 **Willen** M Keyn
86 D7 **Willenhall** Covtry
85 H4 **Willenhall** Wsall
126 C4 **Willerby** E R Yk
134 F4 **Willerby** N York
71 K6 **Willersey** Gloucs
68 F5 **Willersley** Herefs
34 D6 **Willesborough** Kent
34 D6 **Willesborough Lees** Kent
44 E3 **Willesden** Gt Lon
39 J3 **Willesley** Wilts
25 H5 **Willett** Somset
84 C4 **Willey** Shrops
86 F6 **Willey** Warwks
30 F2 **Willey Green** Surrey
72 F5 **Williamscot** Oxon
59 L2 **Willian** Herts
60 F6 **Willingale** Essex
20 C5 **Willingdon** E Susx
76 B1 **Willingham** Cambs
116 E5 **Willingham by Stow** Lincs
76 F4 **Willingham Green** Cambs
75 G4 **Willington** Beds
100 F6 **Willington** Derbys
150 F7 **Willington** Dur
33 K3 **Willington** Kent
72 C6 **Willington** Warwks
151 H2 **Willington Quay** N Tyne
125 H4 **Willitoft** E R Yk
25 H4 **Williton** Somset
119 G6 **Willoughby** Lincs
73 G2 **Willoughby** Warwks
87 H5 **Willoughby Waterleys** Leics
101 M7 **Willoughby-on-the-Wolds** Notts
116 F3 **Willoughton** Lincs
61 H4 **Willows Green** Essex
26 B6 **Willtown** Somset
71 L3 **Wilmcote** Warwks
13 G3 **Wilmington** Devon
20 B5 **Wilmington** E Susx
45 K5 **Wilmington** Kent
113 J5 **Wilmslow** Ches
121 K4 **Wilpshire** Lancs
123 G3 **Wilsden** Brad
103 G4 **Wilsford** Lincs
40 C8 **Wilsford** Wilts
28 C4 **Wilsford** Wilts
123 G8 **Wilshaw** Kirk
132 B6 **Wilsill** N York
101 H7 **Wilson** Leics
176 C7 **Wilsontown** S Lans
74 F5 **Wilstead** Beds
88 F2 **Wilsthorpe** Lincs
58 E5 **Wilstone** Herts
54 E3 **Wilton** Herefs
134 D3 **Wilton** N York
142 C4 **Wilton** R & Cl
28 C5 **Wilton** Wilts
40 E7 **Wilton** Wilts
167 G6 **Wilton Dean** Border
76 E6 **Wimbish** Essex
76 E7 **Wimbish Green** Essex
44 E6 **Wimbledon** Gt Lon
90 B5 **Wimblington** Cambs
113 G8 **Wimboldsley** Ches
15 J3 **Wimborne Minster** Dorset
28 B8 **Wimborne St Giles** Dorset
90 E3 **Wimbotsham** Norfk
75 L4 **Wimpole** Cambs
72 B5 **Wimpstone** Warwks
27 G5 **Wincanton** Somset
176 E4 **Winchburgh** W Loth
56 A3 **Winchcombe** Gloucs
21 H3 **Winchelsea** E Susx
29 J5 **Winchester** Hants
33 J5 **Winchet Hill** Kent
30 C1 **Winchfield** Hants
42 F2 **Winchmore Hill** Bucks
44 F2 **Winchmore Hill** Gt Lon
113 L7 **Wincle** Ches
115 G3 **Wincobank** Sheff
137 L7 **Windermere** Cumb
72 D6 **Winderton** Warwks
212 E5 **Windhill** Highld
42 F7 **Windlesham** Surrey
4 D2 **Windmill** Cnwll
20 D4 **Windmill Hill** E Susx
25 L7 **Windmill Hill** Somset
56 D5 **Windrush** Gloucs
216 B3 **Windsole** Abers
42 F5 **Windsor** W & M
42 F5 **Windsor Castle** W & M
77 K4 **Windsor Green** Suffk
55 J7 **Windsoredge** Gloucs
72 C1 **Windy Arbour** Warwks
186 E7 **Windygates** Fife
31 L7 **Wineham** W Susx
127 G5 **Winestead** E R Yk
92 D6 **Winfarthing** Norfk
17 G5 **Winford** IoW
38 D7 **Winford** N Som
68 F5 **Winforton** Herefs
14 F5 **Winfrith Newburgh** Dorset
58 E4 **Wing** Bucks
88 C3 **Wing** Rutlnd
151 J7 **Wingate** Dur
115 G7 **Wingerworth** Derbys
59 G3 **Wingfield** Beds
92 F7 **Wingfield** Suffk
27 J1 **Wingfield** Wilts
35 H3 **Wingham** Kent
35 G5 **Wingmore** Kent
58 E4 **Wingrave** Bucks
102 B2 **Winkburn** Notts
42 E6 **Winkfield** Br For
42 E6 **Winkfield Row** Br For
100 B3 **Winkhill** Staffs
10 F4 **Winkleigh** Devon
132 C5 **Winksley** N York
150 F3 **Winlaton** Gatesd
231 K5 **Winless** Highld
120 F2 **Winmarleigh** Lancs
29 J5 **Winnall** Hants
42 C6 **Winnersh** Wokham
112 F6 **Winnington** Ches
38 B8 **Winscombe** N Som
112 F7 **Winsford** Ches
24 E4 **Winsford** Somset
23 H4 **Winsham** Devon
13 J2 **Winsham** Somset
100 F7 **Winshill** Staffs
51 K6 **Winshwen** Swans
149 G7 **Winskill** Cumb
30 A2 **Winslade** Hants
39 J7 **Winsley** Wilts
58 C3 **Winslow** Bucks
56 C6 **Winson** Gloucs
28 F8 **Winsor** Hants
129 J2 **Winster** Cumb
100 E1 **Winster** Derbys
140 E4 **Winston** Dur
78 E3 **Winston** Suffk
55 L6 **Winstone** Gloucs
10 D3 **Winswell** Devon
14 D5 **Winterborne Came** Dorset
14 F2 **Winterborne Clenston** Dorset
14 F2 **Winterborne Houghton** Dorset
15 G3 **Winterborne Kingston** Dorset
14 D5 **Winterborne Monkton** Dorset
14 F2 **Winterborne Stickland** Dorset
14 F3 **Winterborne Whitechurch** Dorset
15 G3 **Winterborne Zelston** Dorset
38 F4 **Winterbourne** S Glos
41 J6 **Winterbourne** W Berk
14 C4 **Winterbourne Abbas** Dorset
40 C5 **Winterbourne Bassett** Wilts
28 D4 **Winterbourne Dauntsey** Wilts
28 D5 **Winterbourne Earls** Wilts
28 D4 **Winterbourne Gunner** Wilts
40 C6 **Winterbourne Monkton** Wilts
14 C4 **Winterbourne Steepleton** Dorset
28 B3 **Winterbourne Stoke** Wilts
131 H7 **Winterburn** N York
125 L6 **Winteringham** N Linc
99 H2 **Winterley** Ches
28 E5 **Winterslow** Wilts
125 L6 **Winterton** N Linc
107 K8 **Winterton-on-Sea** Norfk
102 D2 **Winthorpe** Notts
15 K4 **Winton** Bmouth
139 H5 **Winton** Cumb
134 D5 **Wintringham** N York
89 G7 **Winwick** Cambs
87 J8 **Winwick** Nhants
112 E3 **Winwick** Warrtn
100 F2 **Wirksworth** Derbys
111 J4 **Wirral**
98 D4 **Wirswall** Ches
90 C2 **Wisbech** Cambs
90 B2 **Wisbech St Mary** Cambs
31 H6 **Wisborough Green** W Susx
49 K6 **Wiseman's Bridge** Pembks
116 B4 **Wiseton** Notts
175 L7 **Wishaw** N Lans
85 L5 **Wishaw** Warwks
43 H8 **Wisley Gardens** Surrey
117 K6 **Wispington** Lincs
93 H7 **Wissett** Suffk
62 A2 **Wissington** Suffk
83 H6 **Wistanstow** Shrops
98 F6 **Wistanswick** Shrops
99 G2 **Wistaston** Ches
49 H4 **Wiston** Pembks
165 J3 **Wiston** S Lans
18 F3 **Wiston** W Susx
89 K7 **Wistow** Cambs
124 F4 **Wistow** N York
121 L3 **Wiswell** Lancs
90 C7 **Witcham** Cambs
15 J2 **Witchampton** Dorset
90 C7 **Witchford** Cambs
26 C6 **Witcombe** Somset
61 K5 **Witham** Essex
27 H3 **Witham Friary** Somset
88 F1 **Witham on the Hill** Lincs
118 C5 **Withcall** Lincs
19 J4 **Withdean** Br & H
33 H7 **Witherenden Hill** E Susx
11 J3 **Witheridge** Devon
86 D4 **Witherley** Leics
118 F5 **Withern** Lincs
127 H5 **Withernsea** E R Yk
126 F3 **Withernwick** E R Yk
92 F7 **Withersdale Street** Suffk
76 F5 **Withersfield** Essex

129 J3 **Witherslack** Cumb
129 J3 **Witherslack Hall** Cumb
4 F3 **Withiel** Cnwll
24 F5 **Withiel Florey** Somset
56 B5 **Withington** Gloucs
69 L5 **Withington** Herefs
113 J3 **Withington** Manch
83 L2 **Withington** Shrops
100 B5 **Withington** Staffs
11 K3 **Withleigh** Devon
85 H8 **Withybed Green** Worcs
86 E6 **Withybrook** Warwks
24 F3 **Withycombe** Somset
32 E6 **Withyham** E Susx
24 D4 **Withypool** Somset
38 E6 **Withywood** Bristl
30 F4 **Witley** Surrey
78 E4 **Witnesham** Suffk
57 G6 **Witney** Oxon
88 F3 **Wittering** C Pete
21 H1 **Wittersham** Kent
85 J5 **Witton** Birm
93 G2 **Witton** Norfk
107 H6 **Witton** Norfk
151 G5 **Witton Gilbert** Dur
140 E2 **Witton le Wear** Dur
140 F2 **Witton Park** Dur
25 G5 **Wiveliscombe** Somset
30 A4 **Wivelrod** Hants
19 K2 **Wivelsfield** E Susx
19 K2 **Wivelsfield Green** E Susx
62 C4 **Wivenhoe** Essex
106 C4 **Wiveton** Norfk
62 E3 **Wix** Essex
71 K4 **Wixford** Warwks
77 G6 **Wixoe** Essex
58 F2 **Woburn** Beds
58 F2 **Woburn Abbey** Beds
74 D7 **Woburn Sands** M Keyn
43 G8 **Woking** Surrey
42 D6 **Wokingham** Wokham
135 G5 **Wold Newton** E R Yk
118 C3 **Wold Newton** NE Lin
32 C3 **Woldingham** Surrey
49 G3 **Wolf's Castle** Pembks
165 K3 **Wolfclyde** S Lans
105 G6 **Wolferton** Norfk
186 B2 **Wolfhill** P & K
48 F3 **Wolfsdale** Pembks
84 F6 **Wollaston** Dudley
74 C2 **Wollaston** Nhants
83 G2 **Wollaston** Shrops
101 K4 **Wollaton** C Nott
98 F6 **Wollerton** Shrops
85 G6 **Wollescote** Dudley
100 A7 **Wolseley Bridge** Staffs
150 D7 **Wolsingham** Dur
99 J3 **Wolstanton** Staffs
86 E7 **Wolston** Warwks
57 J6 **Wolvercote** Oxon
85 G4 **Wolverhampton** Wolves
84 E5 **Wolverhampton Business Airport** Staffs
84 E7 **Wolverley** Worcs
41 K6 **Wolverton** Hants
74 B6 **Wolverton** M Keyn
72 B3 **Wolverton** Warwks
27 H5 **Wolverton** Wilts
54 C7 **Wolvesnewton** Mons
86 E6 **Wolvey** Warwks
86 E5 **Wolvey Heath** Warwks
141 K3 **Wolviston** S on T
133 K3 **Wombleton** N York
84 F5 **Wombourne** Staffs
115 H2 **Wombwell** Barns
35 G4 **Womenswold** Kent
124 E6 **Womersley** N York
31 G3 **Wonersh** Surrey
12 B4 **Wonford** Devon
29 J4 **Wonston** Hants
42 E3 **Wooburn** Bucks
42 E3 **Wooburn Green** Bucks
71 J4 **Wood Bevington** Warwks
106 C6 **Wood Dalling** Norfk
43 J4 **Wood End** Gt Lon
60 B3 **Wood End** Herts
71 K1 **Wood End** Warwks
118 C8 **Wood Enderby** Lincs
44 F2 **Wood Green** Gt Lon
85 G3 **Wood Hayes** Wolves
106 B6 **Wood Norton** Norfk
107 H7 **Wood Street** Norfk
30 F2 **Wood Street** Surrey
89 J7 **Wood Walton** Cambs
20 D2 **Wood's Corner** E Susx
33 H6 **Wood's Green** E Susx
115 J5 **Woodall** Rothm
93 G1 **Woodbastwick** Norfk
101 M3 **Woodborough** Notts
40 C7 **Woodborough** Wilts
12 F4 **Woodbridge** Devon
78 F5 **Woodbridge** Suffk
12 C5 **Woodbury** Devon
12 C5 **Woodbury Salterton** Devon
55 J7 **Woodchester** Gloucs
34 C7 **Woodchurch** Kent
24 E3 **Woodcombe** Somset
44 F7 **Woodcote** Gt Lon
41 M4 **Woodcote** Oxon
84 D1 **Woodcote** Wrekin
38 D2 **Woodcroft** Gloucs
76 F3 **Woodditton** Cambs
57 K5 **Woodeaton** Oxon
190 F4 **Woodend** Highld
73 H5 **Woodend** Nhants
176 C4 **Woodend** W Loth
17 M2 **Woodend** W Susx
60 E3 **Woodend Green** Essex
28 D7 **Woodfalls** Wilts
9 G3 **Woodford** Cnwll
39 G2 **Woodford** Gloucs
45 H2 **Woodford** Gt Lon
88 D7 **Woodford** Nhants
113 K5 **Woodford** Stockp
45 H2 **Woodford Bridge** Gt Lon
73 G4 **Woodford Halse** Nhants
45 H2 **Woodford Wells** Gt Lon
85 H6 **Woodgate** Birm
25 H7 **Woodgate** Devon
18 C5 **Woodgate** W Susx
71 H2 **Woodgate** Worcs
28 D7 **Woodgreen** Hants
131 J2 **Woodhall** N York
117 K8 **Woodhall Spa** Lincs
58 B4 **Woodham** Bucks
43 H7 **Woodham** Surrey
61 J7 **Woodham Ferrers** Essex
61 K6 **Woodham Mortimer** Essex
61 K6 **Woodham Walter** Essex
216 E6 **Woodhead** Abers
26 A6 **Woodhill** Somset
159 H4 **Woodhorn** Nthumb
123 K4 **Woodhouse** Leeds
87 G1 **Woodhouse** Leics
115 H4 **Woodhouse** Sheff
124 B6 **Woodhouse** Wakefd
87 G2 **Woodhouse Eaves** Leics
177 H5 **Woodhouselee** Mdloth
156 D6 **Woodhouselees** D & G
100 D8 **Woodhouses** Staffs
89 K7 **Woodhurst** Cambs
19 K5 **Woodingdean** Br & H
123 K5 **Woodkirk** Leeds
207 G2 **Woodland** Abers
7 J3 **Woodland** Devon
6 F5 **Woodland** Devon
140 D2 **Woodland** Dur
34 F6 **Woodland** Kent
152 E3 **Woodland** S Ayrs
206 E6 **Woodlands** Abers
124 E8 **Woodlands** Donc
15 K2 **Woodlands** Dorset
16 C1 **Woodlands** Hants
132 E8 **Woodlands** N York
25 J4 **Woodlands** Somset
42 E5 **Woodlands Park** W & M
7 H6 **Woodleigh** Devon
42 C5 **Woodley** Wokham
55 L3 **Woodmancote** Gloucs
56 A6 **Woodmancote** Gloucs
39 H2 **Woodmancote** Gloucs
17 L2 **Woodmancote** W Susx
19 H3 **Woodmancote** W Susx
29 K3 **Woodmancott** Hants
126 C3 **Woodmansey** E R Yk
30 E6 **Woodmansgreen** W Susx
32 B2 **Woodmansterne** Surrey
12 C5 **Woodmanton** Devon
35 J4 **Woodnesborough** Kent
88 F5 **Woodnewton** Nhants
121 G4 **Woodplumpton** Lancs
92 B3 **Woodrising** Norfk
99 H7 **Woodseaves** Staffs
115 K5 **Woodsetts** Rothm
14 E4 **Woodsford** Dorset
42 F6 **Woodside** Br For
187 G5 **Woodside** Fife
45 G6 **Woodside** Gt Lon
195 K8 **Woodside** P & K
57 H5 **Woodstock** Oxon
89 H4 **Woodston** C Pete
93 G5 **Woodton** Norfk
22 F6 **Woodtown** Devon
69 K2 **Woofferton** Shrops
26 D3 **Wookey** Somset
26 D2 **Wookey Hole** Somset
14 F5 **Wool** Dorset
23 G3 **Woolacombe** Devon
35 H5 **Woolage Green** Kent
54 E7 **Woolaston** Gloucs
54 E7 **Woolaston Common** Gloucs
25 M3 **Woolavington** Somset
30 E6 **Woolbeding** W Susx
12 E5 **Woolbrook** Devon
24 F5 **Woolcotts** Somset
168 E4 **Wooler** Nthumb
22 E7 **Woolfardisworthy** Devon
11 J3 **Woolfardisworthy** Devon
176 D6 **Woolfords** S Lans
41 L6 **Woolhampton** W Berk
69 L7 **Woolhope** Herefs
14 E2 **Woolland** Dorset
39 H6 **Woolley** BaNES
89 G8 **Woolley** Cambs
123 L7 **Woolley** Wakefd
59 L4 **Woolmer Green** Herts
71 G2 **Woolmere Green** Worcs
13 K2 **Woolminstone** Somset
77 L3 **Woolpit** Suffk
83 J4 **Woolstaston** Shrops
102 D5 **Woolsthorpe** Lincs
102 F7 **Woolsthorpe-by-Colsterworth** Lincs
16 E1 **Woolston** C Sotn
97 L7 **Woolston** Shrops
83 H6 **Woolston** Shrops
25 H4 **Woolston** Somset
26 F5 **Woolston** Somset
112 F4 **Woolston** Warrtn
7 H3 **Woolston Green** Devon
55 L3 **Woolstone** Gloucs
74 C6 **Woolstone** M Keyn
40 F3 **Woolstone** Oxon
112 B4 **Woolton** Lpool
41 H7 **Woolton Hill** Hants
78 E6 **Woolverstone** Suffk
27 H2 **Woolverton** Somset
45 H4 **Woolwich** Gt Lon
69 G4 **Woonton** Herefs
99 G4 **Woore** Shrops
92 F8 **Wootten Green** Suffk
74 E5 **Wootton** Beds
35 G5 **Wootton** Kent
126 D7 **Wootton** N Linc
73 L3 **Wootton** Nhants
57 H4 **Wootton** Oxon
57 J7 **Wootton** Oxon
100 C4 **Wootton** Staffs
40 B4 **Wootton Bassett** Wilts
17 G4 **Wootton Bridge** IOW
24 E3 **Wootton Courtenay** Somset
13 J4 **Wootton Fitzpaine** Dorset
40 D7 **Wootton Rivers** Wilts
29 L2 **Wootton St Lawrence** Hants
71 L2 **Wootton Wawen** Warwks
70 F4 **Worcester** Worcs
44 E6 **Worcester Park** Gt Lon
84 F6 **Wordsley** Dudley
84 D4 **Worfield** Shrops
136 D2 **Workington** Cumb
115 L5 **Worksop** Notts
126 C7 **Worlaby** N Linc
41 J5 **World's End** W Berk
29 M8 **Worlds End** Hants
19 J2 **Worlds End** W Susx
38 A7 **Worle** N Som
98 F2 **Worleston** Ches
93 J5 **Worlingham** Suffk
11 H3 **Worlington** Devon
91 G8 **Worlington** Suffk
78 F2 **Worlingworth** Suffk
132 D6 **Wormald Green** N York
54 B2 **Wormbridge** Herefs
90 F2 **Wormegay** Norfk
54 C3 **Wormelow Tump** Herefs
114 C6 **Wormhill** Derbys
61 M2 **Wormingford** Essex
57 M6 **Worminghall** Bucks
71 J7 **Wormington** Gloucs

186 F3 **Wormit** Fife
72 F4 **Wormleighton** Warwks
60 B6 **Wormley** Herts
30 F4 **Wormley** Surrey
34 B3 **Wormshill** Kent
69 H5 **Wormsley** Herefs
30 F2 **Worplesdon** Surrey
114 F3 **Worrall** Sheff
115 G2 **Worsbrough** Barns
115 G2 **Worsbrough Bridge** Barns
115 G2 **Worsbrough Dale** Barns
113 H2 **Worsley** Salfd
107 G7 **Worstead** Norfk
122 C4 **Worsthorne** Lancs
6 E5 **Worston** Devon
122 B3 **Worston** Lancs
35 J4 **Worth** Kent
15 H6 **Worth Matravers** Dorset
92 C7 **Wortham** Suffk
83 G3 **Worthen** Shrops
98 B4 **Worthenbury** Wrexhm
106 B8 **Worthing** Norfk
18 F5 **Worthing** W Susx
101 H7 **Worthington** Leics
114 F2 **Wortley** Barns
123 K4 **Wortley** Leeds
131 H2 **Worton** N York
39 L8 **Worton** Wilts
92 F6 **Wortwell** Norfk
58 B5 **Wotton Underwood** Bucks
39 H2 **Wotton-under-Edge** Gloucs
74 C6 **Woughton on the Green** M Keyn
46 B7 **Wouldham** Kent
84 D5 **Woundale** Shrops
62 E2 **Wrabness** Essex
23 H4 **Wrafton** Devon
117 J6 **Wragby** Lincs
124 C6 **Wragby** Wakefd
7 G4 **Wrangaton** Devon
104 C3 **Wrangle** Lincs
25 H7 **Wrangway** Somset
25 L6 **Wrantage** Somset
126 C8 **Wrawby** N Linc
38 C6 **Wraxall** N Som
26 E4 **Wraxall** Somset
130 B6 **Wray** Lancs
43 G5 **Wraysbury** W & M
130 C5 **Wrayton** Lancs
120 E4 **Wrea Green** Lancs
148 D5 **Wreay** Cumb
30 D3 **Wrecclesham** Surrey
151 G3 **Wrekenton** Gatesd
134 B3 **Wrelton** N York
98 E3 **Wrenbury** Ches
92 E4 **Wreningham** Norfk
93 K6 **Wrentham** Suffk
83 H3 **Wrentnall** Shrops
125 G4 **Wressle** E R Yk
126 B8 **Wressle** N Linc
75 J5 **Wrestlingworth** Beds
91 G4 **Wretton** Norfk
97 M3 **Wrexham** Wrexhm
84 E7 **Wribbenhall** Worcs
99 H3 **Wrinehill** Staffs
38 C7 **Wrington** N Som
27 G1 **Writhlington** BaNES
61 G6 **Writtle** Essex
84 B2 **Wrockwardine** Wrekin
116 B2 **Wroot** N Linc
123 H3 **Wrose** Brad
33 G2 **Wrotham** Kent
40 C4 **Wroughton** Swindn
17 G6 **Wroxall** IOW
72 B1 **Wroxall** Warwks
83 L2 **Wroxeter** Shrops
107 G8 **Wroxham** Norfk
72 E6 **Wroxton** Oxon
100 D4 **Wyaston** Derbys
104 B4 **Wyberton East** Lincs
75 H3 **Wyboston** Beds
99 G3 **Wybunbury** Ches
71 G2 **Wychbold** Worcs
85 L1 **Wychnor** Staffs
30 C4 **Wyck** Hants
56 D4 **Wyck Rissington** Gloucs
140 E4 **Wycliffe** Dur
122 D3 **Wycoller** Lancs
102 C7 **Wycomb** Leics
42 E3 **Wycombe Marsh** Bucks
60 B2 **Wyddial** Herts
34 E5 **Wye** Kent
123 H5 **Wyke** Brad
27 H6 **Wyke** Dorset
26 F4 **Wyke Champflower** Somset
14 C6 **Wyke Regis** Dorset
134 E3 **Wykeham** N York
86 D7 **Wyken** Covtry
84 D4 **Wyken** Shrops
98 B7 **Wykey** Shrops
150 E3 **Wylam** Nthumb
85 K5 **Wylde Green** Birm
28 A4 **Wylye** Wilts
101 L7 **Wymeswold** Leics
74 D2 **Wymington** Beds
102 D8 **Wymondham** Leics
92 D3 **Wymondham** Norfk
14 B3 **Wynford Eagle** Dorset
71 G5 **Wyre Piddle** Worcs
101 L6 **Wysall** Notts
85 J7 **Wythall** Worcs
57 J6 **Wytham** Oxon
113 J4 **Wythenshawe** Manch
89 K8 **Wyton** Cambs
126 E4 **Wyton** E R Yk
78 C2 **Wyverstone** Suffk
78 B2 **Wyverstone Street** Suffk

Y

109 G7 **Y Felinheli** Gwynd
65 G5 **Y Ferwig** Cerdgn
95 G5 **Y Ffor** Gwynd
97 G2 **Y Gyffylliog** Denbgs
96 F4 **Y Maerdy** Conwy
94 D6 **Y Rhiw** Gwynd
116 E1 **Yaddlethorpe** N Linc
141 H7 **Yafforth** N York
7 K4 **Yalberton** Torbay
33 J3 **Yalding** Kent
138 D2 **Yanwath** Cumb
56 B5 **Yanworth** Gloucs
125 J1 **Yapham** E R Yk
18 D5 **Yapton** W Susx
38 B8 **Yarborough** N Som
118 E3 **Yarburgh** Lincs
13 G2 **Yarcombe** Devon
24 B6 **Yard** Devon
85 K6 **Yardley** Birm
73 L5 **Yardley Gobion** Nhants
74 C3 **Yardley Hastings** Nhants
85 K7 **Yardley Wood** Birm
69 L6 **Yarkhill** Herefs
26 D3 **Yarley** Somset
26 F5 **Yarlington** Somset
141 K5 **Yarm** S on T
16 D4 **Yarmouth** IOW
27 K1 **Yarnbrook** Wilts
99 K6 **Yarnfield** Staffs
23 J6 **Yarnscombe** Devon
57 J5 **Yarnton** Oxon
69 J2 **Yarpole** Herefs
166 E4 **Yarrow** Border
166 E4 **Yarrow Feus** Border
166 F4 **Yarrowford** Border
88 F4 **Yarwell** Nhants
39 G4 **Yate** S Glos
42 D7 **Yateley** Hants
40 B6 **Yatesbury** Wilts
41 K5 **Yattendon** W Berk
69 H2 **Yatton** Herefs
54 F3 **Yatton** Herefs
38 B7 **Yatton** N Som
39 K5 **Yatton Keynell** Wilts
17 H5 **Yaverland** IOW
92 B2 **Yaxham** Norfk
89 H5 **Yaxley** Cambs
92 D8 **Yaxley** Suffk
69 H5 **Yazor** Herefs
43 J4 **Yeading** Gt Lon
123 J3 **Yeadon** Leeds
129 K5 **Yealand Conyers** Lancs
129 K4 **Yealand Redmayne** Lancs
6 E5 **Yealmpton** Devon
133 J5 **Yearsley** N York
98 B8 **Yeaton** Shrops
100 D4 **Yeaveley** Derbys
168 D4 **Yeavering** Nthumb
134 D4 **Yedingham** N York
57 G6 **Yelford** Oxon
75 J3 **Yelling** Cambs
87 H7 **Yelvertoft** Nhants
6 D3 **Yelverton** Devon
93 G3 **Yelverton** Norfk
27 G7 **Yenston** Somset
11 H5 **Yeoford** Devon
9 J7 **Yeolmbridge** Cnwll
26 D7 **Yeovil** Somset
26 D7 **Yeovil Marsh** Somset
26 D6 **Yeovilton** Somset
26 D6 **Yeovilton Fleet Air Arm Museum** Somset
234 b5 **Yesnaby** Ork
14 B1 **Yetminster** Dorset
12 D5 **Yettington** Devon
185 L6 **Yetts o' Muckhart** Clacks
85 H4 **Yew Tree** W Mids
74 E2 **Yielden** Beds
176 B7 **Yieldshields** S Lans
43 H4 **Yiewsley** Gt Lon
37 G2 **Ynysboeth** Rhondd
37 J2 **Ynysddu** Caerph
36 F3 **Ynyshir** Rhondd
51 K5 **Ynystawe** Swans
37 G2 **Ynysybwl** Rhondd
83 H2 **Yockleton** Shrops
125 J5 **Yokefleet** E R Yk
174 F5 **Yoker** C Glas
124 F1 **York** York
124 F1 **York Minster** York
42 E7 **York Town** Surrey
34 E3 **Yorkletts** Kent
54 F6 **Yorkley** Gloucs
131 G4 **Yorkshire Dales National Park**
114 E8 **Youlgreave** Derbys
134 B7 **Youlthorpe** E R Yk
133 G6 **Youlton** N York
61 H4 **Young's End** Essex
100 C8 **Yoxall** Staffs
79 H2 **Yoxford** Suffk
96 C3 **Ysbyty Ifan** Conwy
67 G1 **Ysbyty Ystwyth** Cerdgn
111 G7 **Ysceifiog** Flints
52 B6 **Ystalyfera** Powys
36 F2 **Ystrad** Rhondd
66 C4 **Ystrad Aeron** Cerdgn
66 F2 **Ystrad Meurig** Cerdgn
37 H2 **Ystrad Mynach** Caerph
52 E5 **Ystradfellte** Powys
52 C6 **Ystradgynlais** Powys
36 F5 **Ystradowen** V Glam
217 G7 **Ythanbank** Abers
216 C6 **Ythanwells** Abers
217 G7 **Ythsie** Abers

Z

11 G4 **Zeal Monachorum** Devon
27 H5 **Zeals** Wilts
2 E4 **Zennor** Cnwll
101 J7 **Zouch** Notts